Mobil
Travel Guide

Mid-Atlantic 2004

Delaware

Maryland

New Jersey

Pennsylvania

Virginia

Washington D.C.

West Virginia

ExxonMobil
Travel Publications

Maps by

RAND M?NALLY

Acknowledgements

We gratefully acknowledge the help of our representatives for their efficient and perceptive inspections of the lodging and dining establishments listed; the establishments' proprietors for their cooperation in showing their facilities and providing information about them; the many users of previous editions who have taken the time to share their experiences; and for their time and information, the thousands of chambers of commerce, convention and visitors bureaus, city, state, and provincial tourism offices, and government agencies who assisted in our research.

Mobil Travel Guide is also grateful to all the highly talented writers who contributed entries to this book.

Printing Acknowledgement: North American Corporation of Illinois

www.mobiltravelguide.com

Contents

MAP SYMBOLS

Free limited-access highway	Interstate highway	Urbanized area in state maps; in city maps
New — under construction	U.S. highway	Separate cities within metro area
Toll limited-access highway	State or provincial highway	National capital; state capital; cities; towns (size of type indicates relative population)
New — under construction	Other highway	U.S. or Canadian National Park
Other multilane highway	Miles between arrows	State/Provincial Park or Recreation Area
Principal highway	One mile or less not shown	National Forest or Grassland, city park
Other through highway	Interchanges and interchange numbers	Point of interest
Other road		Hospital, medical center
Unpaved road	Time zone boundary	Continental divide
Ferry		

© 2003 Rand McNally & Company

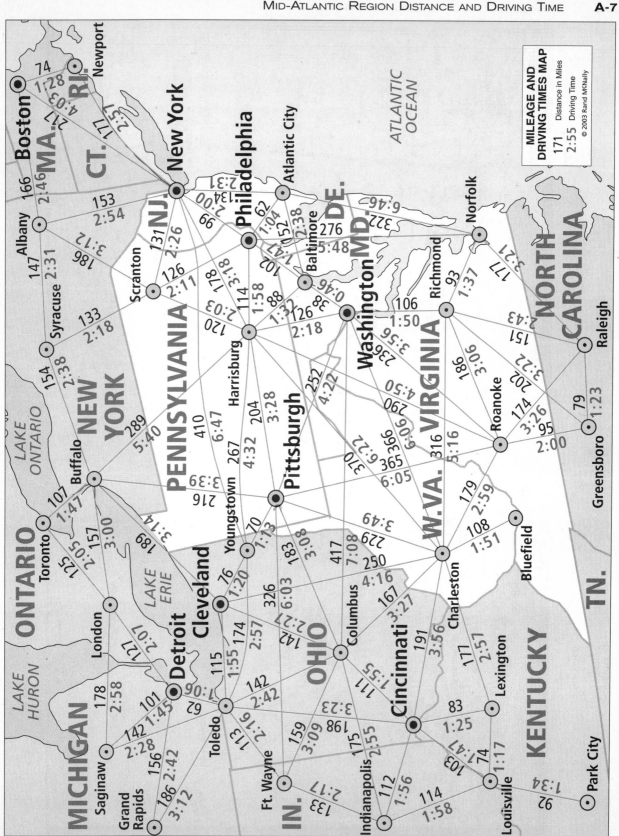

MILEAGE AND
DRIVING TIMES MAP
171   Distance in Miles
2:55   Driving Time
© 2003 Rand McNally

Cities and Towns

© 2003 Rand McNally & Company   03-1

Cities and Towns

Wilmington, DE

© 2003 Rand McNally

Dover, DE

© 2003 Rand McNally

Baltimore, MD

© 2003 Rand McNally

Central Baltimore, MD

Annapolis, MD

Columbia, MD

© 2003 Rand McNally

Hagerstown, MD

© 2003 Rand McNally

Frederick, MD

© 2003 Rand McNally

Newark, NJ & Vicinity

Vineland, NJ

Trenton, NJ

Atlantic City, NJ

Pittsburgh, PA & Vicinity

Philadelphia, PA & Vicinity

Harrisburg, PA

Reading, PA

Altoona, PA

Allentown / Bethlehem, PA

© 2003 Rand McNally

Richmond / Petersburg, VA

© 2003 Rand McNally

© 2003 Rand McNally

Shenandoah National Park, VA (South)

Shenandoah National Park, VA (North)

© 2003 Rand McNally

Central Washington, DC

The following places are identified only by a letter-number key:

© 2003 Rand McNally

	Atlanta, GA	Billings, MT	Boston, MA	Charlotte, NC	Chicago, IL	Cincinnati, OH	Cleveland, OH	Dallas, TX	Denver, CO	Detroit, MI	Houston, TX	Indianapolis, IN	Kansas City, MO	Los Angeles, CA	Memphis, TN	Miami, FL	Milwaukee, WI	Minneapolis, MN	New Orleans, LA	New York, NY	Omaha, NE	Philadelphia, PA	Phoenix, AZ	Pittsburgh, PA	Portland, OR	St. Louis, MO	Salt Lake City, UT	San Francisco, CA	Seattle, WA	Tulsa, OK	Washington, D.C.	Wichita, KS
Albany, NY	1014	2076	166	777	820	727	478	1682	1814	648	1770	791	1287	2833	1230	1407	921	1236	1441	153	1274	238	2544	472	2927	1040	2206	2953	2899	1433	365	1477
Albuquerque, NM	1406	994	2247	1629	1341	1397	1606	644	439	1591	890	1290	783	799	1014	1960	1424	1222	1170	2019	979	1939	463	1649	1385	1041	626	1097	1456	650	1886	593
Amarillo, TX	1121	971	1962	1344	1056	1112	1321	359	424	1306	605	1005	604	1124	1309	1043	885	1734	716	1654	748	1364	1666	756	911	1382	1737	365	1601	417		
Atlanta, GA		1890	1100	243	712	463	715	791	1415	723	797	529	810	2205	393	661	811	1132	468	896	1000	816	1862	686	2604	556	1883	2503	2675	798	635	972
Baltimore, MD	673	1960	407	436	704	523	379	1366	1693	532	1454	592	1088	2681	914	1080	805	1120	1125	203	1158	102	2345	251	2811	841	2090	2837	2783	1234	38	1278
Billings, MT	1890		2242	2055	1247	1547	1598	1429	555	1534	1547	1429	555	1176	1954	2067	896	2017	1206	1716	891	1333	549	1179	821	1238	1961	1064				
Birmingham, AL	148	1839	1185	391	661	467	719	647	1364	727	671	478	759	2058	246	783	760	1081	342	981	949	901	1722	753	2553	505	1832	2356	2624	651	743	825
Bismarck, ND	1558	417	1828	1610	833	1133	1184	1274	709	1120	1521	1019	790	1595	1318	2219	762	429	1709	1631	608	1603	1515	1302	1310	1045	927	1598	1240	1037	1547	802
Boise, ID	2184	621	2673	2349	1702	1959	2029	1704	830	1965	1951	1852	1352	846	1900	2845	1741	1466	2229	2498	1223	2447	995	2147	425	1627	338	646	496	1513	2392	1339
Boston, MA	1100	2242		863	986	893	644	1768	1980	814	1856	957	1453	2999	1396	1556	1087	1402	1527	211	1440	313	2710	586	3093	1206	2372	3119	3065	1599	441	1643
Buffalo, NY	896	1787	461	659	531	438	189	1376	1525	359	1495	502	998	2544	924	1381	632	947	1243	417	985	412	2255	216	2638	751	1917	2664	2610	1144	388	1188
Charleston, SC	321	2196	966	207	911	619	721	1112	1721	850	1113	730	1116	2526	714	580	1010	1325	784	762	1306	661	2183	654	2910	862	2189	2824	2901	1175	525	1306
Charlotte, NC	243	2055	863		770	478	516	1034	1580	645	1040	589	975	2428	617	724	869	1184	711	659	1155	534	2092	449	2769	721	2048	2726	2840	1021	398	1165
Cheyenne, WY	1450	455	1939	1615	968	1225	1295	974	100	1231	1221	1118	638	1102	1166	2111	1007	878	1499	1764	499	1714	906	1413	1155	893	434	1181	1226	783	1658	452
Chicago, IL	712	1247	986	770		293	342	933	1009	278	1089	179	529	2028	536	1373	92	407	927	811	469	761	1804	460	2122	300	1401	2148	2070	693	705	719
Cincinnati, OH	463	1547	893	478	293		252	938	1208	260	1057	112	603	2196	486	1124	392	707	805	660	796	580	1860	290	2379	356	1658	2405	2370	749	524	793
Cleveland, OH	715	1598	644	516	342	252		1190	1336	170	1309	316	812	2355	738	1238	443	758	1057	486	796	436	2069	135	2449	565	1728	2475	2421	958	380	1002
Columbus, OH	574	1606	783	433	352	111	142	1049	1276	204	1168	175	671	2264	597	1155	451	766	916	553	794	473	1928	183	2447	424	1726	2473	2429	817	417	861
Dallas, TX	791	1429	1768	1034	933	938	1190		882	1198	247	882	552	1440	454	1316	1016	991	526	1564	664	1484	1069	1228	2124	633	1403	1741	2195	262	1326	365
Davenport, IA	792	1166	1135	898	175	421	491	915	843	427	1091	316	241	359	941	960	303	910	1609	609	996	266	1235	1982	989	612	854	553				
Denver, CO	1415	555	1980	1580	1009	1208	1336	882		1272	1129	1101	605	1022	1097	2076	1048	919	1407	1805	540	1750	809	1460	1250	858	529	1276	1321	691	1694	517
Des Moines, IA	961	997	1304	1067	333	590	660	746	674	596	926	483	194	1693	623	1622	372	243	1014	1129	134	1079	1440	778	1787	350	1066	1813	1820	443	1023	384
Detroit, MI	723	1534	814	645	278	260	170	1198	1272		1317	310	702	1993	746	1367	379	694	1065	639	732	589	2054	288	2385	550	1664	2411	2357	943	533	955
Duluth, MN	1189	861	1459	1241	464	764	815	1145	1073	751	1325	650	593	2092	965	1850	393	157	1356	1284	533	1234	1839	933	1754	681	1465	2042	1684	842	1178	783
El Paso, TX	1426	1178	2394	1669	1488	1544	1753	633	623	1738	753	1437	930	807	1087	1939	1571	1369	1100	2197	1016	2117	436	1796	1627	1188	868	1188	1698	797	1959	740
Fargo, ND	1369	607	1639	1421	644	944	995	1087	901	931	1334	830	603	1785	1131	2030	573	240	1522	1464	421	1414	1707	1113	1500	858	1117	1788	1430	1048	1358	725
Flagstaff, AZ	1733	1070	2574	1956	1668	1724	1933	971	673	1918	1217	1617	1110	472	1341	2287	1751	1549	1497	2346	1210	2266	136	1976	1279	1368	520	770	1350	977	2213	920
Houston, TX	797	1676	1856	1040	1089	1057	1309	247	1129	1317		1025	732	1560	573	1190	1179	1171	351	1652	911	1572	1189	1347	2371	837	1650	1941	2442	505	1414	612
Indianapolis, IN	529	1433	957	589	179	112	316	882	1101	310	1025		496	2089	472	1190	278	593	816	729	619	649	1753	359	2272	249	1551	2298	2256	642	593	686
Jackson, MS	383	1817	1424	626	747	692	944	408	1225	952	442	683	737	1873	210	907	911	1117	187	1308	819	1231	1677	1089	2747	467	1955	1746	2149	538	534	708
Jacksonville, FL	346	2236	1142	383	1058	796	897	1001	1761	1026	875	875	1156	2431	712	341	1157	1478	546	938	1346	837	2060	830	2950	902	2229	2742	3021	1117	701	1291
Kansas City, MO	810	1078	1453	975	529	603	812	552	605	792	732	496		1626	526	1471	568	439	917	1225	188	1145	1246	855	1792	253	1071	1818	1863	249	1089	190
Knoxville, TN	215	1826	928	229	542	250	502	840	1351	510	928	386	876	2199	384	876	641	956	599	724	1016	646	2540	492	1819	2497	2611	792	486	936		
Las Vegas, NV	1982	966	2726	2205	1755	1956	2082	1220	749	2018	1466	1849	1353	275	1590	2536	1794	1665	1746	2551	1286	2498	292	2208	1021	1606	416	569	1122	1226	2462	1265
Lexington, KY	386	1669	935	401	375	83	335	874	1194	343	993	188	589	2175	422	1047	474	789	741	731	779	645	1839	373	2383	335	1662	2409	2454	728	543	779
Little Rock, AR	531	1513	1453	754	655	623	875	315	966	883	434	591	389	1682	139	1165	745	826	441	1249	577	1169	1346	913	2208	403	1487	1980	2279	275	1011	449
Los Angeles, CA	2205	1239	2999	2428	2028	2196	2355	1440	1022	2291	1560	2069	1813		2746	2687	2067	1938	1907	2824	1559	2738	371	2448	967	1840	689	381	1141	1449	2685	1392
Louisville, KY	415	1595	996	475	297	105	355	835	1120	363	954	114	515	2101	383	1076	396	711	702	763	705	683	1765	393	2309	261	1588	2335	2380	654	617	705
Memphis, TN	393	1606	1316	617	536	486	738	454	1097	746	573	472	526	1813		1027	626	908	392	1112	716	1032	1477	776	2320	284	1599	2111	2391	406	874	580
Miami, FL	661	2551	1483	724	1373	1124	1238	1316	2076	1367	1190	1190	1471	2746	1027		1472	1793	861	1279	1661	1215	2375	1171	3265	1217	2544	3057	3336	1432	1042	1606
Milwaukee, WI	811	1176	1087	869	92	392	443	1016	1048	379	1179	278	568	2067	626	1472		336	1017	912	508	862	1887	561	2069	383	1440	2187	1999	776	806	758
Minneapolis, MN	1132	843	1402	1184	407	707	758	991	919	694	1171	593	439	1938	908	1793	336		1299	1227	379	1177	1685	876	1736	624	1311	2058	1666	688	1121	629
Mobile, AL	329	2003	1429	572	920	726	978	598	1415	986	472	737	923	2028	398	718	1019	1305	143	1225	1113	1145	1667	1009	2657	681	1934	2067	2738	724	964	898
Montréal, QC	1227	1909	324	990	848	829	590	1767	1842	575	1856	873	1539	2861	1315	1632	949	1264	1654	384	1302	463	2632	617	2955	1128	2234	2981	2732	1521	590	1525
Nashville, TN	242	1650	1106	407	472	278	530	663	1175	538	782	289	570	2022	211	903	571	892	527	902	760	822	1686	568	2364	316	1643	2320	2435	615	664	750
New Orleans, LA	468	1954	1527	711	927	805	1057	526	1407	1065	351	816	917	1907	392	861	1017	1299		1323	1107	1243	1536	1095	2649	675	1928	2267	2769	679	1085	890
New York, NY	896	2067	211	659	811	660	486	1564	1805	639	1652	729	1225	2824	1112	1279	912	1227	1323		1265	109	2482	388	2918	978	2197	2944	2890	1371	237	1415
Norfolk, VA	557	2147	577	320	891	601	566	1348	1781	719	1384	713	1176	2729	918	948	992	1307	1055	373	1366	276	2393	438	2970	922	2249	2996	3041	1315	196	1563
Odessa, TX	1147	1204	2122	1390	1244	1292	1509	354	649	1494	546	1193	792	1088	808	1672	1327	1231	882	1918	904	1838	717	1552	1784	944	1025	1469	1855	553	1680	605
Oklahoma City, OK	862	1221	1702	1085	796	852	1061	208	674	1046	455	745	344	1343	470	1496	879	783	753	1474	456	1394	1007	1104	1916	496	1195	1641	1987	105	1342	157
Omaha, NE	1000	896	1440	1165	469	726	796	664	540	732	911	619	188	1559	716	1661	508	379	1107	1265		1215	1346	914	1653	443	932	1679	1724	435	1159	302
Orlando, FL	440	2330	1284	525	1152	903	1039	1091	1855	1163	969	969	1250	2525	806	229	1251	1572	640	1080	1440	979	2154	972	3044	996	2323	2836	3115	1211	843	1385
Philadelphia, PA	816	2017	313	534	761	580	436	1484	1750	589	1572	649	1145	2738	1032	1178	862	1177	1243	109	1215		2402	308	2868	898	2147	2894	2841	1291	136	1335
Phoenix, AZ	1862	1206	2710	2092	1804	1860	2069	1069	809	2054	1371	1477	2375	1887	1685	1516	1842	1889	1587	2482	1346	2402		2112	1338	1504	656	752	1486	1113	2349	1056
Pittsburgh, PA	686	1716	586	449	460	290	135	1228	1460	288	1347	359	855	2448	771	1561	561	876	1095	388	914	308	2112		2567	608	1846	2593	2539	1001	252	1045
Portland, ME	1229	2343	117	964	1087	994	745	1897	2081	915	1985	1058	1554	3100	1445	1584	1188	1503	1656	312	1541	414	2811	687	3194	1307	2473	3220	3166	1700	542	1744
Portland, OR	2604	891	3093	2769	2122	2379	2449	2124	1250	2385	2372	3265	2069	1736	2449	2918	1653	2088	1338	2567		2047	758	636	1704	1933	2812	1759				
Rapid City, SD	1521	373	1904	1686	909	1209	1260	1069	400	1196	1316	1095	709	1312	1237	2182	838	609	1628	1729	527	1679	1206	1378	1266	964	644	1391	1196	878	1632	704
Reno, NV	2406	955	2895	2571	1924	2181	2251	1665	1052	2187	1911	2074	1594	473	2122	3067	1963	1834	2193	2720	1455	2670	735	2369	578	1849	522	224	752	1735	2614	1561
Roanoke, VA	430	1917	678	193	663	370	429	1098	1550	558	1186	482	945	2457	646	915	762	1077	857	474	1135	394	2121	365	2739	691	2018	2765	2810	1050	236	1135
St. Louis, MO	556	1333	1206	721	300	356	565	633	858	550	837	249	253	1840	284	1217	383	624	675	978	443	898	1648	608	2047		1326	2073	2118	393	878	443
Salt Lake City, UT	1883	549	2372	2048	1401	1658	1728	1403	529	1664	1650	1551	1071	689	1599	2544	1440	1311	1928	2197	932	2147	656	1846	758	1326		746	829	1212	2091	1038
San Antonio, TX	992	1483	2051	1235	1210	1215	1467	277	936	1475	199	1159	817	1365	731	1385	1293	1256	546	1847	929	1767	994	1505	2100	910	1341	1746	2171	539	1609	630
San Diego, CA	2154	1299	3064	2397	2088	2214	2423	1361	1082	2351	1463	2127	1998	128	2257	2601	2127	1988	1828	2767	1546	2716	354	2466	1091	1858	749	505	1265	1467	2703	1417
San Francisco, CA	2503	1179	3119	2726	2148	2405	2475	1741	1276	2411	1941	2298	1818	381	2111	3057	2070	2058	2267	2944	1679	2894	752	2593	636	2073	746		810	1747	2838	1785
Sault Ste Marie, ON	1047	1282	943	960	452	584	502	1357	1446	350	1510	537	966	2465	957	1708	404	549	1347	939	906	925	2228	624	2175	724	1838	2585	2105	1117	869	1129
Seattle, WA	2675	821	3065	2840	2070	2370	2421	2195	1321	2357	2442	3336	1999	1666	2720	2892	1724	2840	1486	2539	174	2118	829	810		2004	2784	1830				
Shreveport, LA	605	1614	1646	848	851	819	1071	186	1067	1079	239	787	566	1628	331	1130	941	1005	347	1442	752	1362	1257	1109	2309	599	1588	1927	2380	339	1204	550
Sioux Falls, SD	1177	717	1564	1342	569	876	920	849	654	856	1096	769	365	1673	893	1838	498	269	1284	1389	183	1339	1460	1038	1610	620	989	1736	1540	612	1283	487
Spokane, WA	2431	539	2783	2596	1788	2088	2139	1970	1096	2075	2217	1974	1619	1215	2147	3092	1717	1384	2495	2608	1437	2558	1377	2257	352	1874	720	885	282	1779	2502	1605
Springfield, MO	684	1247	1418	849	512	568	777	423	796	762	663	461	166	1630	283	1345	595	606	674	1190	261	1214	1240	820	1961	212	1240	1928	2032	183	1090	263
Tallahassee, FL	270	2143	1301	470	965	733	985	839	1668	992	713	782	1063	2269	550	478	1064	1385	384	1097	1253	996	1898	917	2857	809	2136	2580	2928	955	860	1129
Tampa, FL	458	2348	1340	581	1170	921	1095	1113	1873	1181	987	987	1268	2543	824	273	1269	1590	658	1136	1458	1035	2172	1028	3062	1014	2341	2854	3133	1229	899	1403
Toronto, ON	961	1773	566	766	517	498	296	1436	1511	244	1555	548	1243	2623	984	1488	618	933	1321	523	2624	797	1903	565	2596	1190	2596	1190	495	1194		
Tulsa, OK	798	1238	1599	1021	693	749	958	262	691	943	505	642	249	1449	406	1432	776	688	679	1371	435	1291	1113	1001	1933	393	1212	1747	2004		1271	174
Washington, D.C.	635	1961	441	398	705	524	380	1326	1694	533	1414	593	1089	2685	874	1042	806	1121	1085	237	1159	136	2349	252	2812	878	2091	2838	2784	1271		1279
Wichita, KS	972	1064	1643	1165	719	793	1002	365	517	955	612	686	190	1392	580	1606	758	629	890	1415	302	1335	1056	1045	1759	443	1038	1785	1830	174	1279	

Mileages © 2003 Rand McNally-TDM, Inc.

Welcome

Dear Traveler,

Since its inception in 1958, Mobil Travel Guide has served as a trusted advisor to auto travelers in search of value in lodging, dining, and destinations. Now in its 46th year, the Mobil Travel Guide is the hallmark of our ExxonMobil family of travel publications, and we're proud to offer an array of products and services from our Mobil, Exxon, and Esso brands in North America to facilitate life on the road.

Whether you're looking for business or pleasure venues, our nationwide network of independent, professional evaluators offers their expertise on thousands of travel options, allowing you to plan a quick family getaway, a full-service business meeting, or an unforgettable Five-Star celebration.

Your feedback is important to us as we strive to improve our product offerings and better meet today's travel needs. Whether you travel once a week or once a year, please take the time to contact us at www.mobiltravelguide.com. We hope to hear from you soon.

Best wishes for safe and enjoyable travels.

Lee R. Raymond
Chairman and CEO
Exxon Mobil Corporation

A Word to Our Readers

Travelers are on the roads in great numbers these days. They're exploring the country on day trips, weekend getaways, business trips, and extended family vacations, visiting major cities and small towns along the way. Because time is precious and the travel industry is ever-changing, having accurate, reliable travel information at your fingertips is critical. Mobil Travel Guide has been providing invaluable insight to travelers for more than 45 years, and we are committed to continuing this service well into the future.

The Mobil Corporation (known as Exxon Mobil Corporation since a 1999 merger) began producing the Mobil Travel Guide books in 1958, following the introduction of the US highway system in 1956. The first edition covered only five southwestern states. Since then, our books have become the premier travel guides in North America, covering the 48 contiguous states and Canada. Now, ExxonMobil presents the latest editions of our annual travel guides, with a fresh new look. We also recently introduced road atlases and specialty publications, a robust new Web site, as well as the first fully integrated, auto-centric travel support program called MobilCompanion, the driving force in travel. (See the inside back cover for more information).

Since its founding, Mobil Travel Guide has served as an advocate for travelers seeking knowledge about hotels, restaurants, and places to visit. Based on an objective process, we make recommendations to our customers that we believe will enhance the quality and value of their travel experiences. Our trusted One- to Five-Star rating system is the oldest and most respected lodging and restaurant inspection and rating program in North America. Most hoteliers, restaurateurs, and industry observers favorably regard the rigor of our inspection program and understand the prestige and benefits that come with receiving a Mobil Travel Guide star rating.

The Mobil Travel Guide process of rating each establishment includes:
- Unannounced facility inspections
- Incognito service evaluations for Mobil Four- and Five-Star properties
- A review of unsolicited comments from the general public
- Senior management oversight

For each property, more than 450 attributes, including cleanliness, physical facilities, employee attitude, and courtesy, are measured and evaluated to produce a mathematically derived score, which is then blended with the other elements to form an overall score. These quantifiable scores allow comparative analysis among properties and form the basis that Mobil Travel Guide uses to assign its Mobil One- to Five-Star ratings.

This process focuses largely on guest expectations, guest experience, and consistency of service, not just physical facilities and amenities. It is fundamentally a relative rating system that rewards those properties that continually strive for and achieve excellence each year. Indeed, the very best properties are consistently raising the bar for those that wish to compete with them. These properties proactively respond to consumers' needs even in today's uncertain times.

Only facilities that meet Mobil Travel Guide's standards earn the privilege of being listed in the guide. Deteriorating, poorly managed establishments are deleted. A Mobil Travel Guide listing constitutes a positive quality recommendation; every listing is an accolade, a recognition of achievement. Our One- to Five-Star rating system highlights its level of service. Extensive in-house research is constantly underway to determine new additions to our lists.

- The Mobil Five-Star Award indicates that a property is one of the very best in the country and consistently provides gracious and courteous service, superlative quality in its facility, and a unique ambience. The lodgings and restaurants at the Five-Star level consistently and proactively respond to consumers' needs and continue their commitment to excellence, doing so with grace and perseverance.

- Also highly regarded is the Mobil Four-Star Award, which honors properties for outstanding achievement in overall facility and for providing very strong service levels in all areas. These award-winners provide a distinctive experience for the ever-demanding and sophisticated consumer.

- The Mobil Three-Star Award recognizes an excellent property that provides full services and amenities. This category ranges from exceptional hotels with limited services to elegant restaurants with a less-formal atmosphere.

- A Mobil Two-Star property is a clean and comfortable establishment that has expanded amenities or a distinctive environment. A Two-Star property is an excellent place to stay or dine.

- A Mobil One-Star property is limited in its amenities and services but focuses on providing a value experience while meeting travelers' expectations. The property can be expected to be clean, comfortable, and convenient.

Allow us to emphasize that we do not charge establishments for inclusion in our guides. We have no relationship with any of the businesses and attractions we list and act only as a consumer advocate. In essence, we do the investigative legwork so that you won't have to.

Keep in mind, too, that the hospitality business is ever-changing. Restaurants and lodgings—particularly small chains and standalone establishments—change management or even go out of business with surprising quickness. Although we make every effort to double-check information during our annual updates, we nevertheless recommend that you call ahead to make sure the place you've selected is still open and offers all the amenities you're looking for. We've provided phone numbers; when available, we also list fax numbers and Web site addresses.

We hope that your travels are enjoyable and relaxing and that our books help you get the most out of every trip you take. If any aspect of your accommodation, dining, or sightseeing experience motivates you to comment, please drop us a line. We depend a great deal on our readers' remarks, so you can be assured that we will read your comments and assimilate them into our research. General comments about our books are also welcome. You can write to us at Mobil Travel Guide, 1460 Renaissance Drive, Suite 401, Park Ridge, IL 60068, or send an e-mail to info@mobiltravelguide.com.

Take your Mobil Travel Guide books along on every trip you take. We're confident that you'll be pleased with their convenience, ease of use, and breadth of dependable coverage.

Happy travels!

How to Use This Book

The Mobil Travel Guide travel planners are designed for ease of use. The book begins with a general introduction that provides a geographical and historical orientation to the state and gives basic statewide tourist information, from climate to popular highways to seatbelt laws. The remainder is devoted to travel destinations within the state—mainly cities and towns, but also national and state parks and tourist areas—which are arranged alphabetically.

The following sections explain the wealth of information you'll find about those travel destinations: information about the area, things to see and do there, and where to stay and eat.

Maps and Map Coordinates

At the front of this book in the full-color section, we have provided state maps as well as maps of selected larger cities to help you find your way around once you leave the highway. You'll find a key to the map symbols on the Contents page at the beginning of the map section.

Next to most cities and towns throughout the book, you'll find a set of map coordinates, such as C-2. These coordinates reference the maps at the front of this book and help you find the location you're looking for quickly and easily.

Destination Information

Because many travel destinations are close to other cities and towns where travelers might find additional attractions, accommodations, and restaurants, we've included cross-references to those cities and towns when it makes sense to do so. We also list addresses and phone numbers for travel information resources—usually the local chamber of commerce or office of tourism—as well as pertinent statistics and, in many cases, a brief introduction to the area.

Information about airports, ground transportation, and suburbs is included for large cities.

Driving and Walking Tours

The driving tours that we include for many states are usually day trips that make for interesting side excursions, although they can be longer. They offer you a way to get off the beaten path and visit an area that

travelers often overlook. These trips frequently cover areas of natural beauty or historical significance.

Each walking tour focuses on a particularly interesting area of a city or town. Again, these tours can provide a break from everyday tourist attractions. The tours often include places to stop for meals or snacks. ◆

What to See and Do

The Mobil Travel Guide offers information about nearly 20,000 museums, art galleries, amusement parks, historic sites, national and state parks, ski areas, and many other types of attractions. A white star on a black background ★ signals that the attraction is a must-see—one of the best in the state. Because municipal parks, public tennis courts, swimming pools, and small educational institutions are common to most towns, they generally are not mentioned.

In an attraction's description, you'll find the months, days, and, in some cases, hours of operation; the address/directions, telephone number, and Web site (if there is one); and the admission price category. The following are the ranges we use for admission fees:

- ✪ **FREE**
- ✪ **$** = Up to $5
- ✪ **$$** = $5.01-$10
- ✪ **$$$** = $10.01-$15
- ✪ **$$$$** = Over $15

Special Events

Special events are either annual events that last only a short time, such as festivals and fairs, or longer, seasonal events such as horseracing, summer theater and concerts, and professional sports. The Mobil Travel Guide Special Events listings also include infrequently occurring occasions that mark certain dates or events, such as a centennial or other commemorative celebration.

Side Trips

We recognize that your travels don't always end where state lines fall, so we've included some side trips that technically fall outside the scope of this book but that travelers frequently visit when they're in this region. Nearby national park, major cities, and other major draws fall into this category. You'll find side trips for a particular area at the end of that state's city listings.

Lodging and Restaurant Listings

Lodgings and restaurants are usually listed under the city or town in which they are located. Make sure to check the related cities and towns that appear right beneath the city heading for additional options, especially if you're traveling to a major metropolitan area that includes many suburbs. In large cities, lodgings located within 5 miles of major commercial airports are listed under a separate "Airport Area" heading that follows the city section.

LODGINGS

Travelers have different wants and needs when it comes to accommodations. To help you pinpoint properties that meet your particular needs, each lodging property is classified by type according to the following characteristics:

- **Motels/Motor Lodges.** These accommodations are in low-rise structures with rooms that are easily accessible to parking, which is usually free. Properties have small, functional lobbies, and guests enter their rooms from the outdoors. Service is often limited, and dining may not be offered in lower-rated motels. Shops and businesses are generally found only in higher-rated properties, as are bell staff, room service, and restaurants serving three meals daily.

- **Hotels.** A hotel is an establishment that provides lodging in a clean, comfortable environment. Guests can expect private bathrooms as well as some measure of guest services, such as luggage assistance, room service, and daily maid service.

- **Resorts.** A resort is an establishment that provides lodging in a facility that is typically located on a larger piece of land. Recreational activities are emphasized and often include golf, spa, and tennis. Guests can expect more than one food and beverage establishment on the property, which aims to provide a variety of food choices at a variety of price points.

- **All Suites.** In an all suites property, guest accommodations consist of two rooms: a bedroom and a living room. Higher-rated properties offer facilities and services comparable to regular hotels.

- **B&Bs/Small Inns.** The hotel alternative for those who prefer the comforts of home and a personal touch. It may be a structure of historic significance and often is located in an interesting setting. Breakfast is usually included and often is treated as a special occasion. Cocktails and refreshments may be served in the late afternoon or evening. Rooms are often individually decorated, but telephones, televisions, and private bathrooms may not be available in every room.

- **Boutique Hotels.** Frequently a small hotel of fewer than 150 guest rooms, a boutique hotel is more about décor than about functionality and service. In many cases, the unique décor is trendsetting and hip, but don't let it fool you…there are, more often than not, inherent weaknesses in the facility with regard to size of the guest rooms, bathrooms, and so on. Services offered usually match those of a larger hotel but are done on a more personal and, often, more interesting manner.

- **Guest Ranches.** Like resorts, guest ranches specialize in stays of three days or more. These lodgings also offer meal plans and extensive outdoor activities. Horseback riding is usually a feature; stables and trails are found on the ranch property, and trail rides and daily instruction are part of the program. Many guest ranches are working ranches, ranging from casual to rustic, and guests are encouraged to participate in ranch life. Eating is often family style and may include cookouts. Western saddles are assumed; phone ahead to inquire about English saddle availability.

- **Extended Stay.** These hotels specialize in stays of three days or more and usually offer weekly room rates. Service is often limited, and dining may not be offered at lower-rated properties.

- **Casino Hotels.** Casino hotels incorporate areas that offer games of chance such as blackjack, poker, and slot machines and are found only in states where gambling is legal. These hotels offer a wide range of services and amenities comparable to regular hotels.

Because most lodgings offer the following features and services, information about them does not appear in the listings unless exceptions exist:

- Year-round operation with a single rate structure
- Major credit cards accepted (note that Exxon or Mobil Corporation credit cards cannot be used to pay for room or other charges)
- Air-conditioning and heat, often with individual room controls
- Bathroom with tub and/or shower in each room
- Cable television
- Cots and cribs available
- Daily maid service
- Elevators
- In-room telephones

Each lodging listing gives the name, address/location (when no street address is available), neighborhood and/or directions from downtown (in major cities), phone number(s), fax number, total number of guest rooms, and seasons open (if not year-round). Also included are details on business, luxury, recreational, and dining facilities on the property or nearby. A key to the symbols at the end of each listing can be found on the inside front cover of this book.

For every property, we also provide pricing information. Because lodging rates change frequently, we often opt to list a pricing category rather than specific prices; however, we provide specific room rates wherever possible. The pricing categories break down as follows:

- ☼ **$** = Up to $150
- ☼ **$$** = $151-$250
- ☼ **$$$** = $251-$350
- ☼ **$$$$** = $351 and up

All prices quoted by the Mobil Travel Guide are in effect at the time of publication; however, prices cannot be guaranteed. In some locations, short-term price variations may exist because of special events or holidays. Whenever possible, these price variations are noted. Certain resorts have complicated rate structures that vary with the time of year; always confirm rates when making your plans.

RESTAURANTS

All dining establishments listed in our books have a full kitchen and offer table service and a complete menu. Parking on or near the premises, in a lot or garage, is assumed. If parking is not available, we note that fact in the listing.

Each listing also gives the cuisine type, address (or directions if no street address is available), neighborhood and/or directions from downtown (in major cities), phone and fax numbers, Web site (if available), meals served, days of operation (if not open daily year-round), reservation policy, and pricing category or, whenever possible, specific à la carte entrée prices. We also indicate if a child's menu is offered. The price categories are defined as follows per diner and assume that you order an appetizer, entrée, and one drink:

- ☼ **$** = $15 and under
- ☼ **$$** = $16-$35
- ☼ **$$$** = $36-$85
- ☼ **$$$$** = $86 and up

QUALITY RATINGS

The Mobil Travel Guide has been rating lodgings and restaurants in the United States since the first edition was published in 1958. For years, the guide was the only source of such ratings, and it remains among the few guidebooks to rate restaurants across the country and in Canada.

All listed establishments have been inspected by experienced field representatives and/or evaluated by a senior staff member. Our ratings are based on detailed inspection reports of the individual properties, on written evaluations of staff members who stay and dine anonymously, and on an extensive review of reader comments. Rating categories reflect both the features a property offers and its quality in relation to similar establishments.

Here are the definitions for the star ratings for lodgings:

- ☼ ★ : A Mobil One-Star lodging is a limited-service hotel, motel, or inn that is considered a clean, comfortable, and reliable establishment.
- ☼ ★★ : A Mobil Two-Star lodging is considered a clean, comfortable, and reliable establishment that has expanded amenities, such as a full-service restaurant on the premises.
- ☼ ★★★ : A Mobil Three-Star lodging is well appointed, with a full-service restaurant and expanded amenities, such as a fitness center, golf course, tennis courts, 24-hour room service, and optional turndown service.
- ☼ ★★★★ : A Mobil Four-Star lodging provides a luxury experience with expanded amenities in a distinctive environment. Services may include, but are not limited to, automatic turndown service, 24-hour room service, and valet parking.
- ☼ ★★★★★ : A Mobil Five-Star lodging provides consistently superlative service in an exceptionally distinctive luxury environment, with expanded services. Attention to detail is evident throughout the hotel, resort, or inn, from bed linens to staff uniforms.

The Mobil Travel Guide star ratings for restaurants are defined as follows:

- ☼ ★ : A Mobil One-Star restaurant provides a distinctive experience through culinary specialty, local flair, or individual atmosphere.
- ☼ ★★ : A Mobil Two-Star restaurant serves fresh food in a clean setting with efficient service. Value is considered in this category, as is family friendliness.
- ☼ ★★★ : A Mobil Three-Star restaurant has good food, warm and skillful service, and enjoyable décor.
- ☼ ★★★★ : A Mobil Four-Star restaurant provides professional service, distinctive presentations, and wonderful food.
- ☼ ★★★★★ : A Mobil Five-Star restaurant offers one of few flawless dining experiences in the country. These establishments consistently provide their guests with exceptional food, superlative service, elegant décor, and exquisite presentations of each detail surrounding a meal.

TERMS AND ABBREVIATIONS IN LISTINGS

The following terms and abbreviations are used throughout the Mobil Travel Guide lodging and restaurant listings to indicate which amenities and services are available at each establishment. We've done our best to provide accurate and up-to-date information, but things do change, so if a particular feature is essential to you, please contact the establishment directly to make sure that it is available.

Complete meal Soup and/or salad, entrée, and dessert, plus a nonalcoholic beverage.

Continental breakfast Usually coffee and a roll or doughnut.

D Followed by a price, indicates the room rate for a double room—two people in one room in one or two beds (the charge may be higher for two double beds).

Each additional The extra charge for each additional person beyond the stated number of persons.

In-room modem link Every guest room has a connection for a modem that's separate from the main phone line.

Kitchen(s) A kitchen or kitchenette that contains a stove or microwave, sink, and refrigerator and is either part of the room or a separate, adjoining room. If the kitchen is not fully equipped, the listing will indicate "no equipt" or "some equipt."

Laundry service Either coin-operated laundry facilities or overnight valet service is available.

Luxury level A special section of a lodging, spanning at least an entire floor, that offers increased luxury accommodations. Management must provide no less than three of these four services: separate check-in and check-out, concierge, private lounge, and private elevator service (with key access). Complimentary breakfast and snacks are commonly offered.

Movies Prerecorded videos are available for rental or check-out.

Prix fixe A full, multicourse meal for a stated price; usually available at finer restaurants.

Valet parking An attendant is available to park and retrieve your car.

VCR VCRs are present in all guest rooms.

VCR available VCRs are available for hookup in guest rooms.

SPECIAL INFORMATION FOR TRAVELERS WITH DISABILITIES

The Mobil Travel Guide [D] symbol indicates establishments that are at least partially accessible to people with mobility problems. Our criteria for accessibility are unique to our publications. Please do not confuse them with the universal symbol for wheelchair accessibility.

When the [D] symbol follows a listing, the establishment is equipped with facilities to accommodate people using wheelchairs or crutches or otherwise needing easy access to doorways and rest rooms. Travelers with severe mobility problems or with hearing or visual impairments may or may not find the facilities they need. Always phone ahead to make sure that an establishment can meet your needs.

All lodgings bearing our [D] symbol have the following facilities:

- ISA-designated parking near access ramps
- Level or ramped entryways to buildings
- Swinging building entryway doors a minimum of 39 inches wide
- Public rest rooms on the main level with space to operate a wheelchair and handrails at commode areas
- Elevator(s) equipped with grab bars and lowered control buttons
- Restaurant(s) with accessible doorway(s), rest rooms with space to operate a wheelchair, and handrails at commode areas
- Guest room entryways that are at least 39 inches wide
- Low-pile carpet in rooms
- Telephones at bedside and in the bathroom
- Beds placed at wheelchair height
- Bathrooms with a minimum doorway width of 3 feet
- Bath with an open sink (no cabinet) and room to operate a wheelchair
- Handrails at commode areas and in the tub
- Wheelchair-accessible peepholes in room entry door
- Wheelchair-accessible closet rods and shelves

All restaurants bearing our [D] symbol offer the following facilities:

- ISA-designated parking beside access ramps
- Level or ramped front entryways to the building
- Tables that accommodate wheelchairs
- Main-floor rest rooms with an entryway that's at least 3 feet wide
- Rest rooms with space to operate a wheelchair and handrails at commode areas

Making the Most of Your Trip

A few hardy souls might look back with fondness on a trip during which the car broke down, leaving them stranded for three days, or a vacation that cost twice what it was supposed to. For most travelers, though, the best trips are those that are safe, smooth, and within budget. To help you make your trip the best it can be, we've assembled a few tips and resources.

Saving Money

ON LODGING

Many hotels and motels offer discounts—for senior citizens, business travelers, families, you name it. It never hurts to ask—politely, that is. Sometimes, especially in the late afternoon, desk clerks are instructed to fill beds, and you might be offered a lower rate or a nicer room to entice you to stay. Simply ask the reservation agent for the best rate available. Also, make sure to try both the toll-free number and the local number. You may be able to get a lower rate from one than the other.

Becoming a member of MobilCompanion will entitle you to discounted rates at many well-known hotels around the country. For more information, call 877/785-6788 or visit www.mobilcompanion.com.

Timing your trip right can cut your lodging costs as well. Look for bargains on stays over multiple nights, in the off-season, and on weekdays or weekends, depending on the location. Many hotels in major metropolitan areas, for example, have special weekend packages that offer considerable savings on rooms; they may include breakfast, cocktails, and dinner discounts.

Another way to save money is to choose accommodations that give you more than just a standard room. Rooms with kitchen facilities enable you to cook some meals yourself, reducing your restaurant costs. A suite might save money for two couples traveling together. Even hotel luxury levels can provide good value, as many include breakfast or cocktails in the price of a room.

State and city taxes, as well as special room taxes, can increase your room rate by as much as 25 percent per day. We are unable to include information about taxes in our listings, but we strongly urge you to ask about taxes when making reservations so that you understand the total cost of your lodgings before you book.

Watch out for telephone-usage charges that hotels frequently impose on long-distance, credit-card, and other calls. Before phoning from your room, read the information given to you at check-in, and then be sure to review your bill carefully when checking out. You won't be expected to pay for charges that the hotel didn't spell out. Consider using your cell phone if you have one; or, if public telephones are available in the hotel lobby, your cost savings may outweigh the inconvenience of using them.

Here are some additional ways to save on lodgings:
- Stay in B&B accommodations; they're generally less expensive than standard hotel rooms, and the complimentary breakfasts cut down on food costs.
- If you're traveling with children, find lodgings at which kids stay free.
- When visiting major cities, stay just outside the city limits; these rooms are usually less expensive than those in downtown locations.
- Consider visiting national parks during the low season, when prices of lodgings near the parks drop 25 percent or more.
- When calling a hotel, ask whether it is running any special promotions or if any discounts are available; many times reservationists are told not to volunteer deals unless specifically asked about them.
- Check for hotel packages; some offer nightly rates that include a rental car or discounts on major attractions.

ON DINING

There are several ways to get a less expensive meal at a more expensive restaurant. Early-bird dinners are popular in many parts of the country and offer considerable savings. If you're interested in sampling a Mobil Four- or Five-Star establishment, consider going at lunchtime. Although the prices are probably still relatively high at midday, they may be half of those at dinner, and you'll experience the same ambience, service, and cuisine.

As a member of MobilCompanion, you can enroll in iDine. This program earns you up to 20 percent cash back at more than 1,900 restaurants on meals purchased with the credit card you register; the rebate appears on your credit card bill. For more information about MobilCompanion and iDine, call 877/785-6788 or go to www.mobilcompanion.com.

ON ENTERTAINMENT

Although many national parks, monuments, seashores, historic sites, and recreation areas may be used free of charge, others charge an entrance fee (ranging from $1 to $6 per person or $5 to $20 per carload) and/or a usage fee for special services and facilities. If you plan to make several visits to national recreation areas, consider one of the following money-saving programs offered by the National Park Service:

✪ National Parks Pass. This annual pass is good for entrance to any national park that charges an entrance fee. If the park charges a per-vehicle fee, the pass holder and any accompanying passengers in a private noncommercial vehicle may enter. If the park charges a per-person fee, the pass applies to the holder's spouse, children, and parents as well as the holder. It is valid for entrance fees only; it does not cover parking, camping, or other fees. You can purchase a National Parks Pass in person at any national park where an entrance fee is charged; by mail from the National Park Foundation, PO Box 34108, Washington, DC 20043-4108; by calling 888/GO-PARKS; or at www.nationalparks.org. The cost is $50.

✪ Golden Eagle. When affixed to a National Parks Pass, this sticker, available to people who are between 17 and 61 years of age, extends coverage to sites managed by the US Fish and Wildlife Service, the US Forest Service, and the Bureau of Land Management. It is good until the National Parks Pass to which it is affixed expires and does not cover usage fees. You can purchase one at National Park Service, Fish and Wildlife Service, and Bureau of Land Management fee stations. The cost is $15.

✪ Golden Age Passport. Available to citizens and permanent US residents 62 and older, this passport is a lifetime entrance permit to fee-charging national recreation areas. The fee exemption extends to those accompanying the permit holder in a private noncommercial vehicle or, in the case of walk-in facilities, to the holder's spouse and children. The passport also entitles the holder to a 50 percent discount on federal usage fees charged in park areas, but not on concessions. Golden Age Passports must be obtained in person and are available at most National Park Service units that charge an entrance fee. The applicant must show proof of age, such as a driver's license or birth certificate (Medicare cards are not acceptable proof). The cost is $10.

✪ Golden Access Passport. Issued to citizens and permanent US residents who are physically disabled or visually impaired, this passport is a free lifetime entrance permit to fee-charging national recreation areas. The fee exemption extends to those accompanying the permit holder in a private noncommercial vehicle or, in the case of walk-in facilities, to the holder's spouse and children. The passport also entitles the holder to a 50 percent discount on usage fees charged in park areas, but not on concessions. Golden Access Passports must be obtained in person and are available at most National Park Service units that charge an entrance fee. Proof of eligibility to receive federal benefits (under programs such as Disability Retirement, Compensation for Military Service-Connected Disability, and the Coal Mine Safety and Health Act) is required, or an affidavit must be signed attesting to eligibility.

A money-saving move in several large cities is to purchase a CityPass. If you plan to visit several museums and other major attractions, CityPass is a terrific option because it gets you into several sites for one substantially reduced price. Currently, CityPass is available in Boston, Chicago, Hollywood, New York, Philadelphia, San Francisco, Seattle, and southern California (which includes Disneyland, Sea World, and the San Diego Zoo). For more information or to buy one, call 888/330-5008 or visit www.citypass.net. You can also buy a CityPass from any participating CityPass attraction.

Here are some additional ways to save on entertainment and shopping:

✪ Check with your hotel's concierge for various coupons and special offers; they often have two-for-one tickets for area attractions and coupons for discounts at area stores and restaurants.

✪ Purchase same-day concert or theater tickets for half-price through the local cheap-tickets outlet, such as TKTS in New York City or Hot Tix in Chicago.

✪ Visit museums on their free or "by donation" days, when you can pay what you wish rather than a specific admission fee.

✪ Save receipts from purchases in Canada; visitors to Canada can get a rebate on federal taxes and some provincial sales taxes.

ON TRANSPORTATION

Transportation is a big part of any vacation budget. Here are some ways to reduce your costs:

✪ If you're renting a car, shop early over the Internet; you can book a car during the low season for less, even if you'll be using it in the high season.

✪ Rental car discounts are often available if you rent for one week or longer and reserve in advance.

- Get the best gas mileage out of your vehicle by making sure that it's properly tuned up and keeping your tires properly inflated. If your tires need to be replaced, you can save money on a new set of Michelins by becoming a member of MobilCompanion.
- Travel at moderate speeds on the open road; higher speeds require more gasoline.
- Fill the tank before you return your rental car; rental companies charge to refill the tank and do so at prices of up to 50 percent more than at local gas stations.
- Make a checklist of travel essentials and purchase them before you leave; don't get stuck buying expensive sunscreen at your hotel or overpriced film at the aiport.

FOR SENIOR CITIZENS

Look for the senior-citizen discount symbol SC in this book's lodging and restaurant listings. Always call ahead to confirm that a discount is being offered, and be sure to carry proof of age. At places not listed in this book, it never hurts to ask if a senior-citizen discount is offered. Additional information for mature travelers is available from the American Association of Retired Persons (AARP), 601 E St NW, Washington, DC 20049; phone 202/434-2277; www.aarp.org.

Tipping

Tips are expressions of appreciation for good service. However, you are never obligated to tip if you receive poor service.

IN HOTELS

- Door attendants usually get $1 for hailing a cab.
- Bell staff expect $2 per bag.
- Concierges are tipped according to the service they perform. Tipping is not mandatory when you've asked for suggestions on sightseeing or restaurants or for help in making dining reservations. However, a tip of $5 is appropriate when a concierge books you a table at a restaurant known to be difficult to get into. For obtaining theater or sporting event tickets, $5 to $10 is expected.
- Maids should be tipped $1 to $2 per day. Hand your tip directly to the maid, or leave it with a note saying that the money has been left expressly for the maid.

IN RESTAURANTS

Before tipping, carefully review your check for any gratuity or service charge that is already included in your bill. If you're in doubt, ask your server.

- Coffee shop and counter service waitstaff usually receive 15 percent of the bill, before sales tax.
- In full-service restaurants, tip 18 percent of the bill, before sales tax.
- In fine restaurants, where gratuities are shared among a larger staff, 18 to 20 percent is appropriate.
- In most cases, the maitre d' is tipped only if the service has been extraordinary, and only on the way out. At upscale properties in major metropolitan areas, $20 is the minimum.
- If there is a wine steward, tip $20 for exemplary service and beyond, or more if the wine was decanted or the bottle was very expensive.
- Tip $1 to $2 per coat at the coat check.

AT AIRPORTS

Curbside luggage handlers expect $1 per bag. Car-rental shuttle drivers who help with your luggage appreciate a $1 or $2 tip.

Staying Safe

The best way to deal with emergencies is to avoid them in the first place. However, unforeseen situations do happen, so you should be prepared for them.

IN YOUR CAR

Before you head out on a road trip, make sure that your car has been serviced and is in good working order. Change the oil, check the battery and belts, make sure that your windshield washer fluid is full and your tires are properly inflated (which can also improve your gas mileage). Other inspections recommended by the vehicle's manufacturer should also be made.

Next, be sure you have the tools and equipment needed to deal with a routine breakdown:

- Jack
- Spare tire
- Lug wrench
- Repair kit
- Emergency tools
- Jumper cables
- Spare fan belt
- Fuses
- Flares and/or reflectors
- Flashlight
- First-aid kit
- In winter, a windshield scraper and snow shovel

Many emergency supplies are sold in special packages that include the essentials you need to stay safe in the event of a breakdown.

Also bring all appropriate and up-to-date documentation—licenses, registration, and insurance cards—and know what your insurance covers. Bring an extra set of keys, too, just in case.

En route, always buckle up! In most states, wearing a seatbelt is required by law.

If your car does break down, do the following:
- Get out of traffic as soon as possible—pull well off the road.
- Raise the hood and turn on your emergency flashers or tie a white cloth to the roadside door handle or antenna.
- Stay in your car.
- Use flares or reflectors to keep your vehicle from being hit.

If you are a member of MobilCompanion, remember that En Route Support is always ready to help when you need it. Just give us a call and we'll locate and dispatch an emergency roadside service to assist you, as well as provide you with significant savings on the service.

IN YOUR HOTEL OR MOTEL

Chances are slim that you will encounter a hotel or motel fire, but you can protect yourself by doing the following:
- Once you've checked in, make sure that the smoke detector in your room is working properly.
- Find the property's fire safety instructions, usually posted on the inside of the room door.
- Locate the fire extinguishers and at least two fire exits.
- Never use an elevator in a fire.

For personal security, use the peephole in your room door and make sure that anyone claiming to be a hotel employee can show proper identification. Call the front desk if you feel threatened at any time.

PROTECTING AGAINST THEFT

To guard against theft wherever you go:
- Don't bring anything of more value than you need.
- If you do bring valuables, leave them at your hotel rather than in your car.
- If you bring something very expensive, lock it in a safe. Many hotels put one in each room; others will store your valuables in the hotel's safe.
- Don't carry more money than you need. Use traveler's checks and credit cards or visit cash machines to withdraw more cash when you run out.

For Travelers with Disabilities

To get the kind of service you need and have a right to expect, don't hesitate when making a reservation to question the management about the availability of accessible rooms, parking, entrances, restaurants, lounges, or any other facilities that are important to you, and confirm what is meant by "accessible."

The Mobil Travel Guide D symbol indicates establishments that are at least partially accessible to people with special mobility needs (people using wheelchairs or crutches or otherwise needing easy access to buildings and rooms). Keep in mind that our criteria for accessibility are unique to our publication and should not be confused with the universal symbol for wheelchair accessibility. Further information about these criteria can be found in the earlier section "How to Use This Book."

A thorough listing of published material for travelers with disabilities is available from the Disability Bookshop, Twin Peaks Press, Box 129, Vancouver, WA 98666; phone 360/694-2462; disabilitybookshop. virtualave.net. Another reliable organization is the Society for Accessible Travel & Hospitality (SATH), 347 Fifth Ave, Suite 610, New York, NY 10016; phone 212/447-7284; www.sath.org.

Traveling to Canada

Citizens of the United States should be aware of these conditions when entering Canada:
- Visas are not required.
- Visitors may tour the provinces for up to three months without paying a fee.
- Proof of citizenship, such as a passport, birth certificate, or voter registration card, is required. A driver's license is not acceptable proof of citizenship.
- Naturalized citizens will need their naturalization certificates or their US passports to reenter the United States.
- Children under 18 traveling on their own should carry a letter from a parent or guardian giving them permission to travel in Canada.
- Drivers are advised to carry their motor vehicle registration cards.
- If the car is not registered in the driver's name, a letter from the registered owner authorizing use of the vehicle should be available.
- If the car is a rental, carry a copy of the rental contract stipulating permission for use in Canada.

- Ask your car insurer for a Canadian Non-Resident Inter-Province Motor Vehicle Liability Insurance Card. This card ensures that your insurance company will meet the minimum insurance requirements in Canada.
- The use of seatbelts by drivers and passengers is compulsory in all provinces.
- Rabies vaccination certificates are required for dogs or cats.
- A permit is required for the use of citizens band (CB) radios.

The Canadian dollar's rate of exchange with the US dollar varies; contact your local bank for the latest figures.

For the most current and detailed listing of Customs regulations and sources, ask for the annually revised brochure *Canada: Travel Information,* available upon request from the Canadian consulate or embassy in your area.

Important Toll-Free Numbers and Online Information

Hotels and Motels

Adams Mark 800/444-2326
www.adamsmark.com

AmericInn 800/634-3444
www.americinn.com

AmeriHost Inn Hotels 800/434-5800
www.amerihostinn.com

Amerisuites 800/833-1516
www.amerisuites.com

Baymont Inns 877/BAYMONT
www.baymontinns.com

Best Inns & Suites 800/237-8466
www.bestinn.com

Best Value Inns 888/315-BEST
www.bestvalueinn.com

Best Western International 800/WESTERN
www.bestwestern.com

Budget Host Inn 800/BUDHOST
www.budgethost.com

Candlewood Suites 888/CANDLEWOOD
www.candlewoodsuites.com

Clarion Hotels 800/252-7466
www.choicehotels.com

Comfort Inns and Suites 800/252-7466
www.choicehotels.com

Country Hearth Inns 800/848-5767
www.countryhearth.com

Country Inns & Suites 800/456-4000
www.countryinns.com

Courtyard by Marriott 888/236-2427
www.courtyard.com

Cross Country Inn 800/621-1429
www.crosscountryinns.com

Crowne Plaza Hotels and Resorts 800/227-6963
www.crowneplaza.com

Days Inn 800/544-8313
www.daysinn.com

Delta Hotels 800/268-1133
www.deltahotels.com

Destination Hotels & Resorts 800/434-7347
www.destinationhotels.com

Doubletree Hotels 800/222-8733
www.doubletree.com

Drury Inns 800/378-7946
www.druryinn.com

Econolodge 800/553-2666
www.econolodge.com

Economy Inns of America 800/826-0778
www.innsofamerica.com

Embassy Suites 800/362-2779
www.embassysuites.com

ExelInns of America 800/FOREXEL
www.exelinns.com

Extended StayAmerica 800/EXTSTAY
www.extstay.com

Fairfield Inn by Marriott 888/236-2427
www.fairfieldinn.com

Fairmont Hotels 800/441-1414
www.fairmont.com

Four Points by Sheraton 888/625-5144
www.starwood.com

Four Seasons 800/545-4000
www.fourseasons.com

Hampton Inn/Hampton Inn and Suites 800/426-7866
www.hamptoninn.com

Hard Rock Hotels, Resorts and Casinos 800/HRDROCK
www.hardrock.com

Harrah's Entertainment 800/HARRAHS
www.harrahs.com

Harvey Hotels 800/922-9222
www.bristolhotels.com

Hawthorn Suites 800/527-1133
www.hawthorn.com

Hilton Hotels and Resorts (US) 800/774-1500
www.hilton.com

Holiday Inn Express 800/HOLIDAY
www.sixcontinentshotel.com

Holiday Inn Hotels and Resorts 800/HOLIDAY
www.holiday-inn.com

Homestead Studio Suites 888/782-9473
www.stayhsd.com

Homewood Suites 800/225-5466
www.homewoodsuites.com

Howard Johnson 800/406-1411
www.hojo.com

Hyatt 800/633-7313
www.hyatt.com

Ian Schrager . . . . Contact individual hotel
www.ianschragerhotels.com

Inter-Continental 888/567-8725
www.intercontinental.com

Joie de Vivre 800/738-7477
www.jdvhospitality.com

Kimpton Hotels 888/546-7866
www.kimptongroup.com

Knights Inn 800/843-5644
www.knightsinn.com

La Quinta 800/531-5900
www.laquinta.com
Le Meridien 800/543-4300
www.lemeridien.com
Leading Hotels of the World 800/223-6800
www.lhw.com
Loews Hotels 800/235-6397
www.loewshotels.com
MainStay Suites 800/660-6246
www.choicehotels.com
Mandarin Oriental 800/526-6566
www.mandarin-oriental.com
Marriott Conference Centers 888/236-2427
www.conferencecenters.com
Marriott Hotels, Resorts, and Suites 888/236-2427
www.marriott.com
Marriott Vacation Club International 800/845-5279
www.marriott.com/vacationclub
Microtel Inns & Suites 800/771-7171
www.microtelinn.com
Millennium & Copthorne Hotels 866/866-8086
www.mill-cop.com
Motel 6 .... 800/4MOTEL6
www.motel6.com
Omni Hotels 800/843-6664
www.omnihotels.com
Pan Pacific Hotels and Resorts 800/327-8585
www.panpac.com
Park Inn & Park Plaza 888/201-1801
www.parkhtls.com
The Peninsula Group .... Contact individual hotel
www.peninsula.com
Preferred Hotels & Resorts Worldwide 800/323-7500
www.preferredhotels.com
Quality Inn 800/228-5151
www.qualityinn.com
Radisson Hotels 800/333-3333
www.radisson.com
Raffles International Hotels and Resorts 800/637-9477
www.raffles.com
Ramada International 888/298-2054
www.ramada.com
Ramada Plazas, Limiteds, and Inns 800/2RAMADA
www.ramadahotels.com
Red Lion Inns 800/733-5466
www.redlion.com
Red Roof Inns 800/733-7663
www.redroof.com
Regal Hotels 800/222-8888
www.regal-hotels.com
Regent International 800/545-4000
www.regenthotels.com
Relais & Chateaux 800/735-2478
www.relaischateaux.com

Renaissance Hotels 888/236-2427
www.renaissancehotels.com
Residence Inns 888/236-2427
www.residenceinn.com
Ritz-Carlton 800/241-3333
www.ritzcarlton.com
Rockresorts 888/FORROCKS
www.rockresorts.com
Rodeway Inns 800/228-2000
www.rodeway.com
Rosewood Hotels & Resorts 888/767-3966
www.rosewood-hotels.com
Scottish Inn 800/251-1962
www.bookroomsnow.com
Select Inn 800/641-1000
www.selectinn.com
Sheraton 888/625-5144
www.sheraton.com
Shilo Inns 800/222-2244
www.shiloinns.com
Shoney's Inns 800/552-4667
www.shoneysinn.com
Signature/Jameson Inns 800/822-5252
www.jamesoninns.com
Sleep Inns 800/453-3746
www.sleepinn.com
Small Luxury Hotels of the World 800/525-4800
www.slh.com
Sofitel 800/763-4835
www.sofitel.com
SpringHill Suites 888/236-2427
www.springhillsuites.com
SRS Worldhotels 800/223-5652
www.srs-worldhotels.com
St. Regis Luxury Collection 888/625-5144
www.stregis.com
Staybridge Suites by Holiday Inn 800/238-8000
www.staybridge.com
Summerfield Suites by Wyndham 800/833-4353
www.summerfieldsuites.com
Summit International 800/457-4000
www.summithotels.com
Super 8 Motels 800/800-8000
www.super8.com
The Sutton Place Hotels 866/378-8866
www.suttonplace.com
Swissotel 800/637-9477
www.swissotel.com
TownePlace Suites 888/236-2427
www.towneplace.com
Travelodge 800/578-7878
www.travelodge.com
Universal 800/23LOEWS
www.loewshotel.com

Vagabond Inns 800/522-1555
www.vagabondinns.com
W Hotels 888/625-5144
www.whotels.com
Wellesley Inn and Suites 800/444-8888
www.wellesleyinnandsuites.com
WestCoast Hotels 800/325-4000
www.westcoasthotels.com
Westin Hotels & Resorts 800/937-8461
www.westin.com
Wingate Inns 800/228-1000
www.wingateinns.com
Woodfin Suite Hotels 800/966-3346
www.woodfinsuitehotels.com
Wyndham Hotels & Resorts 800/996-3426
www.wyndham.com

Airlines

Air Canada 888/247-2262
www.aircanada.ca
Alaska 800/252-7522
www.alaskaair.com
American 800/433-7300
www.aa.com
America West 800/235-9292
www.americawest.com
ATA 800/435-9282
www.ata.com
British Airways 800/247-9297
www.british-airways.com
Continental 800/523-3273
www.flycontinental.com
Delta 800/221-1212
www.delta-air.com
Island Air 800/323-3345
www.islandair.com
Mesa 800/637-2247
www.mesa-air.com
Northwest 800/225-2525
www.nwa.com
Southwest 800/435-9792
www.southwest.com
United 800/241-6522
www.ual.com
US Airways 800/428-4322
www.usairways.com

Car Rentals

Advantage 800/777-5500
www.arac.com
Alamo 800/327-9633
www.goalamo.com
Allstate 800/634-6186
www.bnm.com/as.htm

Avis 800/831-2847
www.avis.com
Budget 800/527-0700
www.budgetrentacar.com
Dollar 800/800-4000
www.dollarcar.com
Enterprise 800/325-8007
www.pickenterprise.com
Hertz 800/654-3131
www.hertz.com
National 800/227-7368
www.nationalcar.com
Payless 800/729-5377
www.800-payless.com
Rent-A-Wreck.com 800/535-1391
www.rent-a-wreck.com
Sears 800/527-0770
www.budget.com
Thrifty 800/847-4389
www.thrifty.com

Four-Star and Five-Star Establishments in the Mid-Atlantic

Delaware
★★★★ Lodgings
Hotel du Pont, *Wilmington*
Inn at Montchanin Village, *Wilmington*

District of Columbia
★★★★ Lodgings
Four Seasons Hotel, *Washington*
The Hay-Adams, *Washington*
Park Hyatt Washington, *Washington*
The Ritz-Carlton, Washington, *Washington*
The St. Regis, Washington, *Washington*

★★★★ Restaurants
Citronelle, *Washington*
Gerard's Place, *Washington*
Kinkead's, *Washington*
Willard Room, *Washington*

Maryland
★★★★ Restaurants
Charleston, *Baltimore*
The Oregon Grille, *Cockeysville*

New Jersey
★★★★ Restaurant
Restaurant Serenade, *Chatham*

Pennsylvania
★★★★★ Restaurant
Le Bec-Fin, *Philadelphia*

★★★★ Lodgings
Four Seasons Hotel Philadelphia, *Philadelphia*
The Hotel Hershey, *Hershey*
Nemacolin Woodlands Resort, *Uniontown*
The Rittenhouse Hotel, *Philadelphia*
The Ritz-Carlton, Philadelphia, *Philadelphia*

★★★★ Restaurants
Brasserie Perrier, *Philadelphia*
Jake's Restaurant, *Philadelphia*
Lacroix at the Rittenhouse, *Philadelphia*

Virginia
★★★★★ Lodgings
The Inn at Little Washington, *Washington*
The Jefferson Hotel, *Richmond*

★★★★★ Restaurant
The Inn at Little Washington, *Washington*

★★★★ Lodgings
Clifton—The Country Inn, *Charlottesville*
Keswick Hall at Monticello, *Keswick*
The Ritz-Carlton, Pentagon City, *Arlington County (Ronald Reagan Washington-National Airport Area)*
The Ritz-Carlton, *Tyson's Corner*
Williamsburg Inn, *Williamsburg*

West Virginia
★★★★ Lodging
The Greenbrier, *White Sulphur Springs*

★★★★ Restaurant
The Tavern Room, *White Sulphur Springs*

Delaware

Delaware "... is like a diamond, diminutive, but having within it inherent value," wrote John Lofland, the eccentric "Bard of Milford," in 1847. The state is 96 miles long and from 9 to 35 miles wide. With more than half of its 1,982 square miles (excluding marshes) used for farming, Delaware produces a flood of agricultural products. Poultry makes up approximately half of the state's total farm income; soybeans, corn, tomatoes, strawberries, asparagus, fruit, and other crops bring in about $170 million each year. Booming industry in northern and central Delaware balances the agricultural sector of the economy. Consistent state corporate policies have persuaded more than 183,000 corporations to make their headquarters in the "corporate capital of the world." Forty major US banks alone have established lending and credit operations in the state.

Compact but diverse, Delaware has rolling, forested hills in the north, stretches of bare sand dunes in the south, and mile upon mile of lonely marsh along the coast. Visitors can tour a modern agricultural or chemical research center in the morning and search for buried pirate treasures in the afternoon. The *deBraak*, which foundered off Lewes in 1798, was raised in 1986 because of the belief that it may have had a fortune in captured Spanish coin or bullion aboard. The coins, which frequently come ashore at Coin Beach below Rehoboth, are believed to come from the *Faithful Steward*, a passenger vessel lost in 1785.

Delaware's history started on a grim note. The first colonists, 28 men under Dutch auspices, landed in the spring of 1631 near what is now Lewes. A year later, after an argument with a Lenni-Lenape chief, the bones of all 28 were found mingled with those of their cattle and strewn over their burned fields. In 1638, a group of Swedes established the first permanent settlement, Fort Christina, at a spot now in Wilmington. This was also the first permanent settlement of Swedes in North America. Dutch, English, Scottish, and Irish colonists soon followed, with German, Italian, and Polish groups coming in the late 19th century.

Population: 783,600

Area: 1,982 square miles

Elevation: 0-447 feet

Peak: Ebright Road (New Castle County)

Entered Union: First state to ratify Constitution (December 7, 1787)

Capital: Dover

Motto: Liberty and independence

Nickname: First State, Small Wonder, The Diamond State, Blue Hen State

Flower: Peach Blossom

Bird: Blue Hen

Tree: American Holly

Fair: July in Harrington (see Dover)

Time Zone: Eastern

Website: www.state.de.us

Fun Facts: Horseshoe crabs may be viewed in large numbers up and down the Delaware shore in May. The crabs endure extremes of temperature and salinity. They can also go for a year without eating and have remained basically the same since the days of the dinosaur.

Henry Hudson, in Dutch service, discovered Delaware Bay in 1609. A year later, Thomas Argall reported it to English navigators, naming it for his superior, Lord de la Warr, Governor of Virginia. Ownership changed rapidly from Swedish to Dutch to English hands. Later, the area was claimed by both Lord Baltimore and the Penn family. The Maryland-Delaware boundary was set by British court order in 1750 and surveyed as part of the Mason-Dixon Line in 1763-1767. The boundary with New Jersey, also long disputed, was confirmed by the Supreme Court in 1935.

The "First State" (first to adopt the Constitution–December 7, 1787) is proud of its history of sturdy independence, both military and political. During the Revolution, the "Delaware line" was a crack regiment of the Continental Army. After heavy casualties in 1780, the unit was reorganized. The men would "fight all day and dance all night," according to a dispatch by General Greene. How well they danced is open to

Calendar Highlights

MAY
Wilmington Garden Day *(Wilmington)*. Tour of famous houses and gardens.

JUNE
Zwaanendael Heritage Garden Tour *(Lewes)*. Phone *302/645-8073*. Tour of the hidden gardens of Lewes. Vendors.

JULY
Delaware State Fair *(Dover)*. *(Harrington)*. Phone *302/398-3269*. Arts and crafts, home and trade show, carnival rides, and entertainment; homemaking, agricultural, and livestock exhibits.

OCTOBER
Sea Witch Halloween and Fiddlers' Festival *(Rehoboth Beach)*. Phone *800/441-1329, ext 11.*

question, but they fought with such gallantry that they were mentioned in nearly all of the General's dispatches.

Delaware statesman John Dickinson, "penman of the Revolution" and one of the state's five delegates to the Constitutional Convention, was instrumental in the decision to write a new document rather than simply patch up the Articles of Confederation. Later he effected the compromise on representation, a problem that had threatened to break up the convention completely.

In addition to Lofland and Dickinson, Delaware has produced many literary figures, including the 19th-century playwright and novelist Robert Montgomery Bird, writer and illustrator Howard Pyle, Henry Seidel Canby (founder of the *Saturday Review*), and novelist John P. Marquand.

A fine highway network tempts motorists to drive through diminutive Delaware without really seeing it. Those who take time to leave the major highways and explore the countryside will find much that is rewarding.

When to Go/Climate

Delaware's climate is generally mild; long Indian summers are not unusual and there's seldom frost until late autumn. Temperatures at the shore can be 10°F higher in winter or lower in summer than inland temperatures.

AVERAGE HIGH/LOW TEMPERATURES (°F)

Wilmington

Jan 39/22	**May** 73/52	**Sept** 78/58
Feb 42/25	**June** 81/62	**Oct** 67/46
Mar 52/33	**July** 86/67	**Nov** 56/37
Apr 63/42	**Aug** 84/66	**Dec** 44/28

Parks and Recreation

Water-related activities, hiking, riding, various other sports, picnicking, and visitor centers are available in many state parks. Delaware state parks are open all year, 8 am-sunset, except Fort Delaware (late Apr-late Sept). Most areas have fishing, boat ramps, and picnicking. There is a vehicle entrance fee from Memorial Day-Labor Day, daily; May and Sept-Oct, weekends and holidays. Camping is available from mid-Mar-mid-Nov at Delaware Seashore; Apr-Oct at Lums Pond, Trap Pond, and Cape Henlopen; year-round at Killens Pond. There is a two-week maximum stay at campgrounds; reservations encouraged; campsites run from $12-$26/night/site. For further information contact Department of Natural Resources and Environmental Control, Division of Parks and Recreation, 89 Kings Highway, Dover 19901; 302/739-4702.

FISHING AND HUNTING

Both fresh and saltwater fishing are excellent. The state owns, leases, or licenses 33,000 acres of game lands and fishing waters. More than 50 well-stocked state and privately owned ponds are scattered throughout the state. Many miles of ocean shoreline between Rehoboth Beach and Indian River Inlet are ideal for surf fishing. Common saltwater fish include trout, bluefish, porgie, sea bass, flounder, and croaker; freshwater fish include bass, bluegill, pickerel, crappie, perch, and trout.

An annual nonresident hunting license is $86; nonresident 3-day small game license $35; nonresident trapping license $25; additional single deer permit $10. An annual resident freshwater fishing license is $8.50; nonresident license $15; 7-day nonresident license $5.20. A license is not required for tidal saltwater fishing. For further information on fishing or hunting, contact the Department of Natural Resources and Environmental Control, Division of Fish and Wildlife, 89 Kings Highway, Dover 19901; 302/739-4431 or 800/523-3336.

ATLANTIC BEACHES

Graced with a beautiful 25-mile stretch of Atlantic beach, Delaware has done more than many Eastern states to preserve much of the land from excessive development. From north to south, three impressive state parks maintain the coast's natural look, and between these parks, several small resort towns retain an old-fashioned, early-20th century flavor. The charm quotient is high and honky-tonk lures are minimal. Though most people think of the beach as a summer destination, you will find this one-day, 25-mile drive rewarding any time of the year. Indeed, many visitors, especially bird watchers and shell collectors, enjoy hiking the beaches in spring and fall when the summer sunbathers are absent. Begin in Lewes, a community that dates its founding to a Dutch whaling colony in 1631. Stroll tree-shaded 2nd Street, the main street, to browse the town's shops and view its rich architectural heritage, then drive east about a mile on Savannah Road, following the signs to 3,785-acre Cape Henlopen State Park. On your left, you will pass the dock for the Cape May-Lewes Ferry, which shuttles across Delaware Bay between Delaware and New Jersey, a 70-minute crossing. The park juts between the bay and the ocean, offering hiking and bicycling trails that meander among pine forests, salt marshes, and grass-topped dunes. Just inside the park, the Seaside Nature Center features a small aquarium displaying examples of local sea life, including the region's famed blue crabs. In mid-May, the park is a resting stop for shore birds migrating north from South America to their summer breeding grounds in the Arctic. The park enjoys a long beach of golden sand. From the parking lot, a high boardwalk crosses the dunes, leaving the cars hidden behind. Only a bath house invades the otherwise unblemished seascape. From Lewes, take US 9 west briefly to State Route 1 south, which parallels the coast for the length of this drive. You will detour from it only once—at Rehoboth Beach, the next stop. One of the Mid-Atlantic's most popular beach resorts, Rehoboth hasn't lost its small-town appeal. The beach is long and inviting, and at sunset, many people promenade on the boardwalk that links one end of the community to the other. In recent years, Rehoboth has blossomed into a sophisticated destination, evidenced by its numerous fine bed-and-breakfast inns; upscale restaurants; and quality shops selling designer beach attire, expensive antiques, and excellent contemporary crafts and home furnishings. But you can also find more typical beach wear and fare—such as burgers and hot dogs—on the boardwalk. There's even a small amusement arcade called Funland. South of Rehoboth on Route 1 is Dewey Beach, a much smaller resort town with a cluster of lively pubs that have a reputation of attracting a young singles crowd. To the south is 2,656-acre Delaware Seashore State Park, another natural preserve offering such traditional beach activities as swimming, surfing, fishing, picnicking, hiking, and boating on Indian River Bay. Further south is the little resort town of Bethany Beach, favored by families renting a vacation home or condominium, and beyond that is 442-acre Fenwick Island State Park, another natural area. End the tour just across the state line in sprawling Ocean City, Maryland, a bustling beach town that is the antithesis of Delaware's quieter beach experience. **(Approximately 25 miles)**

Driving Information

Safety belts are mandatory for all persons in front seat of vehicle. Children under 4 years and 40 pounds in weight must be in approved safety seats anywhere in vehicle; children ages 4-15 must use regulation seat belts anywhere in vehicle. Phone 302/739-5938.

INTERSTATE HIGHWAY SYSTEM

The following alphabetical listing of Delaware towns in this book shows that these cities are within 10 miles of the indicated interstate highway. Check a highway map for the nearest exit.

Highway Number	Cities/Towns within 10 Miles
Interstate 95	Newark, New Castle, Wilmington.

Additional Visitor Information

Delaware Tourism Office, 99 Kings Highway, Dover 19901, will provide tourist information; phone 800/441-8846.

Visitor centers also provide information and brochures on points of interest in the state. Their locations are as follows: Delaware Memorial Bridge Plaza, junction I-295 and the bridge at New Castle; I-95 rest area, Greater Wilmington Convention and Visitors Bureau, Wilmington; Delaware State Information Center, Duke of York & Federal sts, Dover; Smyrna, 1 mile N on US 13; Bethany-Fenwick Area Chamber of Commerce, DE 1, N of Fenwick Island.

BRANDYWINE VALLEY

Cut by slender Brandywine Creek, the Brandywine Valley, just north of Wilmington, is a serene canvas of rolling hills, broad fields of corn and yellow sunflowers, rambling split-rail fences, horse pastures, ancient stone barns, and narrow country roads lined by towering old trees. Scattered within this scenic realm, one of the Mid-Atlantic's loveliest, is a wonderfully diverse collection of fine arts, history, and house museums, most of which were bequeathed by the du Pont family, the wealthy industrialists whose forebear, Pierre Samuel du Pont, arrived from France in 1800. Pierre's son, Eleuthere Irenee (E. I.) du Pont, established a black powder factory, harnessing the Brandywine for power and creating the du Pont fortune. Brandywine Creek flows southeast from Pennsylvania's Chester County through prosperous Wilmington suburbs to the Delaware River. The wealth here has earned the valley the nickname of "Chateau Country" because of its many grand homes, typically set far back from the road. For more than 30 years, an environmental organization called the Brandywine Conservancy has worked to protect the valley's open pastoral look from the threatening sprawl of both Philadelphia and Wilmington. Begin this one day, 50-mile tour into the scenic and artistic riches of the region in Wilmington. Your first stop is the Delaware Art Museum at 2301 Kentmere Parkway, which features a strong collection of American sculpture and painting, including works by Brandywine resident Andrew Wyeth. To reach the museum from downtown Wilmington, take 12th Street north to State Route 52 north. Take a right on North Bancroft to Kentmere. Founded in 1912, the museum also houses a premier collection of the works of Howard Pyle, a famous Wilmington illustrator of that era. Many of his illustrations depict pirates, witches, and other fanciful characters drawn to accompany adventure stories in magazines and books. More realistic is Pyle's 1911 portrait of General Robert E. Lee surrendering his Confederate army at Appomattox, commissioned to illustrate a piece in *Harper's Monthly Magazine.* From the museum, return to Route 52 north. Turn right at Route 141 to the Hagley Museum, which sits on the site of the first du Pont powder works, amid 230 acres of gardens and exhibits. The museum recalls industrial life in mid-19th-century America. A bit further upstream along Brandywine Creek is Eleutherian Mills, the lovely Georgian-style house E. I. du Pont built in 1803. Double back on Route 141 to Route 100 north (Montchanin Road) to the village of Montchanin. Here, 11 varied structures that served as homes for workers at the du Pont mills have been converted into a luxury retreat, the 37-room Inn at Montchanin Village. Even if you aren't a guest, stroll the block-long cobblestone main street, which is named Privy Lane for the comical row of gray concrete privies standing behind the dwellings in military precision. Today the privies, a reminder of an earlier era, store garden equipment. Consider lunch at the inn's whimsically named restaurant, Krazy Kat's, one of Brandywine's best. Continue north on Route 100 to Brandywine State Park for a chance to hike along Brandywine Creek. Stay on Route 100 north to Smiths Bridge Road, where you make a left turn. Continue west via Centerville Road to Route 52, and turn south (left). At the sign, turn left into Winterthur, a nine-story museum of American decorative arts set in the midst of 985 acres of gardens. This was the estate of Henry Francis du Pont, who collected antique furniture, porcelain, silver, rugs, and draperies crafted from 1640 to 1860. These items are organized in period rooms, including a 17th-century Lancaster, Pennsylvania, bedroom and an 18th-century Tidewater, Virginia plantation sitting room. The gardens reflect du Pont's goal of creating a masterpiece of 20th-century American naturalism. Return to Wilmington on Route 52 south. **(Approximately 50 miles)**

Bethany Beach (D-10)

See also Fenwick Island, Lewes, Rehoboth Beach

Founded 1901 **Pop** 903 **Elev** 8 ft **Area code** 302 **Zip** 19930

Information Bethany-Fenwick Area Chamber of Commerce, Coastal Hwy/DE 1, PO Box 1450; 302/539-2100 or 800/962-7873

Web www.bethany-fenwick.org

A quiet beach town on the Atlantic Ocean, Bethany Beach was founded as a site for revival camp meetings; hence the biblical name. Surf fishing and swimming are excellent here.

What to See and Do

Holts Landing State Park. *8 miles NW via DE 26 and DE 346, N of Millville. Phone 302/539-9060 or 302/539-1055 (summer).* A 203-acre park located along the Indian River Bay. Fishing, crabbing, clamming, sailing, boating (launch ramp providing access to bay); picnicking, playground, ball fields. Standard hours, fees.

Special Event

Boardwalk Arts Festival. *The Boardwalk, Garfield Pkwy. Phone 302/539-2100.* Juried, original handmade works; woodcarving, photography, jewelry, batik, watercolor paintings. Early Sept.

Motel/Motor Lodge

★ **BETHANY ARMS.** *99 Hollywood St (19930). Phone 302/539-9603.* 52 units, 2-3 story, 36 kitchen units. No elevator. July-Aug: S, D $105-$160; each additional $10; under 6 free; weekly rates; lower rates mid-Mar-June, Sept-mid-Oct. Closed mid-Oct-mid-Mar. Crib $5. TV; cable. Restaurant adjacent 7 am-9 pm. Check-out 11 am. Many refrigerators. Balconies. On ocean; beach. Cr cds: MC, V.

D ❧

Dover (C-9)

See also Odessa, Smyrna

Founded 1717 **Pop** 32,135 **Elev** 36 ft **Area code** 302 **Zip** 19901

Information Central Delaware Chamber of Commerce, 9 E Loockerman St, Suite 2-A, PO Box 576, 19903; 302/734-7513

Web www.cdcc.net

The capital of Delaware since 1777, Dover was laid out by William Penn around the city's lovely green. For almost 200 years there were coach houses and inns on King's Road between Philadelphia and Lewes. Circling the green north and south on State Street are fine 18th- and 19th-century houses.

Today, because of Delaware's favorable corporation laws, more than 60,000 US firms pay taxes in Dover. At Dover Air Force Base, south off US 113, the Military Airlift Command operates one of the biggest air cargo terminals in the world, utilizing the giant C5-A Galaxy aircraft. Dover is also the home of Delaware State College, Wesley College, and the Terry campus of Delaware Technical and Community College.

What to See and Do

Delaware Agricultural Museum and Village. *866 N Du Pont Hwy (US 13). Phone 302/734-1618.* Museum of farm life from early settlement to 1960. Main exhibition hall and historic structures representing a late-19th-century farming community; includes gristmill, blacksmith-wheelwright shop, farmhouse, outbuildings, one-room schoolhouse, store, and train station. Gift shop. (Apr-Dec, Tues-Sun; rest of year, Mon-Fri) **$$**

Delaware Public Archives. *121 Duke of York St. Phone 302/739-5318.* Delaware's historical public records.(Mon-Sat; closed holidays) **FREE**

Delaware State Museums. *316 S Governors Ave.* Complex of three buildings:

> **Delaware Archeology Museum.** *Bank Ln and Governors Ave. Phone 302/739-4266.* (1790) Housed in an old church, exhibits devoted to archaeology. (Tues-Sat; closed holidays) **FREE**

> **Johnson Victrola Museum.** *Bank Ln and New St. Phone 302/739-4266.* Tribute to Eldridge Reeves Johnson, founder of the Victor Talking Machine Company. Collection of talking machines, Victrolas, early recordings, and equipment. (Tues-Sat; closed holidays) **FREE**

> **Museum of Small Town Life.** *316 S Governors Ave. Phone 302/739-4266.* Turn-of-the-century drugstore, printing press, pharmacy, carpenter shop, general store, post office, shoemaker's shop, printer's shop; Johnson building. (Tues-Sat; closed holidays) **FREE**

Delaware State Visitor Center. *The Green. 406 Federal St. Phone 302/739-4266.* Administered by Delaware State Museums, center offers information on attractions throughout state. Exhibit galleries. (Mon-Sat, Sun afternoons; closed holidays) **FREE**

Dover Heritage Trail. *1071 S Governors Ave. Departs from State Visitor Center. Phone 302/739-4266.* Guided walking tour of historic areas, buildings, and other attractions. (By appointment only) **$$**

John Dickinson Plantation. *340 Kitts Hummrock Rd (19901). 6 miles SE, near junction US 113 and DE 9. Phone 302/739-3277.* (1740) Restored boyhood residence of Dickinson, the "penman of the Revolution." Reconstructed farm complex. (Tues-Sat; also Sun afternoons Mar-Dec) **FREE**

Killens Pond State Park. *5025 Killens Pond Rd. 13 miles S via US 13. Phone 302/284-4526.* A 1,083-acre park with a 66-acre pond. Swimming pool, fishing, boating (rentals); hiking, fitness trails, game fields, picnicking, camping (hookups, dump station). Standard hours, fees.

The Old State House. *The Green. 406 Federal St (19901). Phone 302/739-4266.* (1792) Delaware's seat of government since 1777, the State House, restored in 1976, contains a courtroom, ceremonial governor's office, legislative chambers, and county offices, including Levy Courtroom. A portrait of George Washington in the Senate Chamber was commissioned in 1802 by the legislature as a memorial to the nation's first president. Although Delaware's General Assembly moved to nearby Legislative Hall in 1934, the State House remains the state's symbolic capitol. (Tues-Sun; closed holidays) **FREE**

Trap Pond State Park. *Rte 24 and Trap Pond Rd (19956). Contact RD2 Box 331, Laurel 19956. Phone 302/875-5153.* Boating, canoeing, fishing; hiking, biking, camping. Standard fees.

Special Events

Delaware State Fair. *17 miles S on US 13 in Harrington. Phone 302/398-3269.* Arts and crafts, home and trade show, carnival rides, shows; homemaking, agricultural, and livestock exhibits. Mid-July.

Dover Downs. *1131 N DuPont Hwy (US 13). Phone 302/674-4600.* Racing events include NASCAR Winston Cup auto racing (June, Sept); harness racing (mid-Nov-Apr). Call for fees and schedule.

Harrington Raceway. *17 miles S on US 13, at fairgrounds in Harrington. Phone 302/398-7223.* Harness racing. Betting most nights. Sept-Apr.

Old Dover Days. *Contact Kent County Tourism, 800/233-KENT.* Tours of historic houses and gardens not usually open to the public. Crafts exhibits, many other activities. First weekend in May.

Motels/Motor Lodges

★ **BUDGET INN.** *1426 N DuPont Hwy (19901). Phone 302/734-4433; fax 302/734-4433.* 68 rooms, 2 story. May-Sept: S $42-$50; D $47-$55; each additional $5; lower rates rest of year. Crib free. Complimentary coffee in lobby. Check-out 11 am. TV; cable. Coin laundry. Restaurant opposite 8 am-9 pm. Pool, lifeguard. Sundries. Cr cds: A, C, D, DS, ER, MC, V.

⬛ ⬛ ⬛

★ **COMFORT INN.** *222 S DuPont Hwy (19901). Phone 302/674-3300; toll-free 800/228-5150. www.comfortinn.com.* 94 rooms, 2 story. May-Sept: S $47-$51; D $51-$55; each additional $5; kitchen units $65; family, weekly rates; higher rates NASCAR races; lower rates rest of year. Crib free. TV; cable. Pool; lifeguard. Complimentary continental breakfast. Restaurant adjacent 11 am-10 pm. Check-out noon. Sundries. Some refrigerators. Grill. Cr cds: A, C, D, DS, ER, JCB, MC, V.

⬛ ⬛ **SC**

Hotel

★ ★ ★ **SHERATON DOVER HOTEL.** *1570 N Du Pont Hwy (19901). Phone 302/678-8500; toll-free 800/544-5064; fax 302/678-9073. www.sheratondover.com.* This hotel is conveniently located just minutes from shopping and local attractions in historic Dover. 152 rooms, 7 story. S, D $95; each additional $10; under 18 free. Check-out noon. TV; cable. In-room modem link. Restaurant 6:30 am-10 pm. Bar 4 pm-1 am; entertainment except Mon-Sat. Room service to 10:30 pm. Exercise equipment. Indoor pool, whirlpool. Meeting rooms. Business services. Sundries. Cr cds: A, C, D, DS, ER, MC, V.

D ⬛ ⬛ ⬛ **SC**

Restaurant

★ ★ ★ **BLUE COAT INN.** *800 N State St (19901). Phone 302/674-1776; fax 302/674-1807.* Enjoy casual dining at this quaint restaurant serving a variety of menu delights. Hours: 11:30 am-9 pm; Fri to 10 pm; Sat 11:30 am-3 pm, 4:30-10 pm; Sun noon-9 pm. Closed Dec 25. Lunch $4.95-$11.95, dinner $8.95-$32.95. Bar. Children's menu. Lake setting. Cr cds: A, C, D, DS, MC, V.

Fenwick Island (E-10)

See also Bethany Beach, Lewes, Rehoboth Beach; also see Ocean City, MD

Pop 342 **Elev** 4 ft **Area code** 302 **Zip** 19944

Information Bethany-Fenwick Area Chamber of Commerce, Coastal Hwy/DE 1, PO Box 1450, Bethany Beach 19930; 302/539-2100 or 800/962-7873

Web www.bethany-fenwick.org

Fenwick Island, at the southeast corner of Delaware, was named for Thomas Fenwick, a wealthy Virginia landowner who purchased the land in 1686. For a time, a dispute raged over whether Fenwick Island was part of Maryland or Pennsylvania. It ended in 1751 when the Transpeninsular Line placed Fenwick Island in Delaware. In 1775, James and Jacob Brasure, residents of the island, began extracting salt from the ocean and until 1825, "salt making" was big business. In the latter part of the 19th century, Fenwick Island grew as a religious-oriented summer campground. After World War I, Fenwick Island became fashionable as a summer resort.

What to See and Do

DiscoverSea Shipwreck Museum. *708 Ocean Hwy. Phone 302/539-9366 or 888/743-5524.* Contains changing exhibits of shipwreck artifacts recovered on the Delmarva Peninsula. (Memorial Day-Labor Day, daily; rest of year, Sat- Sun) **FREE**

Fenwick Island Lighthouse. *W of town via DE 54. Phone 302/250-1098.* Historic 87-foot-tall lighthouse; light was first turned on Aug 1, 1859. (June-Aug, two Wed afternoons per month; also by appointment)

Fenwick Island State Park. *1 mile N on DE 1. Phone 302/539-9060; 302/539-1055 (summer).* This 208-acre seashore park is located between the Atlantic Ocean and Little Assawoman Bay. Surfing, swimming, bathhouse, surf fishing, sailing (rentals). Standard hours, fees.

Special Event

Surf Fishing Tournaments. *DE 1, North. Phone 302/539-2100.* Second Sat in May and Columbus Day weekend.

Motel/Motor Lodge

★ **ATLANTIC BUDGET INN.** *Ocean Hwy and DE 54 (19944). Phone 302/539-7673; toll-free 800/432-8038; fax 302/539-7673. www.atlanticbudgetinn.com.* 48 rooms, 1-2 story, 3 kitchen units. Memorial Day, July 4-Labor Day (3-day minimum): S, D $90-$105; each additional $8; kitchen units $105; lower rates mid-Apr-June, after Labor Day-Oct. Closed rest of year. Crib $5. TV; cable. Pool; lifeguard. Complimentary coffee in lobby. Restaurant nearby. Check-out 11 am. Refrigerators, microwaves. Beach 1 block. Cr cds: A, D, DS, MC, V.

Restaurant

★ ★ **TOM & TERRY'S.** *DE 54 at the Bay (19944). Phone 302/436-4161; fax 302/227-7980.* Specializes in fresh local seafood, prime rib. Hours: 11:30 am-10 pm; early-bird dinner 5-6 pm. Closed Dec 25. Lunch $6.95-$10.50, dinner $12.95-$25.95. Bar. Cr cds: DS, MC, V.

D

Fort Delaware State Park (B-9)

See also Newark, New Castle, Odessa, Wilmington

(On Pea Patch Island, opposite Delaware City)

This grim gray fort was built as a coastal defense in 1860. The fort was used as a prisoner of war depot for three years, housing up to 12,500 Confederate prisoners at a time. The damp, low-lying terrain and the poor conditions encouraged epidemics, leading to some 2,400 deaths. The fort was modernized in 1896 and remained in commission until 1943.

Restoration of the site is a continuing process. Available are overlook of heronry, picnicking, and living history programs. Museum has scale model of fort, model Civil War relics, orientation video. Special events throughout summer. Boat trip to island from Delaware City (mid-June-Labor Day, Wed-Sun; last weekend Apr-mid-June and Sept, Sat, Sun, and holidays). No pets. Contact the Park Superintendent, 45 Clinton St, PO Box 170, Delaware City 19706; 302/834-7941. Round trip **$$$**

Lewes (D-10)

See also Bethany Beach, Fenwick Island, Rehoboth Beach

Settled 1631 **Pop** 2,932 **Elev** 10 ft **Area code** 302 **Zip** 19958

Information Chamber of Commerce, Fisher-Martin House, 120 Kings Hwy, PO Box 1; 302/645-8073

Web www.leweschamber.com

Lewes (LOO-is) has been home base to Delaware Bay pilots for 300 years. Weather-beaten, cypress-shingled houses still line the streets where pirates plundered and Captain Kidd bargained away his loot. The treacherous sandbars outside the harbor have claimed their share of ships, and stories of sunken treasures have circulated for centuries. Some buildings show scars from cannonballs that hit their mark when the British bombarded Lewes in the War of 1812. Traces of the original stockade were discovered in 1964.

What to See and Do

Cape Henlopen State Park. *42 Cape Henlopen Dr. 1 mile E of ferry terminal. Phone 302/645-8983.* More than 3,000 acres at the confluence of Delaware Bay and the Atlantic Ocean; site of decommissioned Fort Miles, part of the US coastal defense system during WWII. Supervised

Dutch Heritage in Lewes

As an Atlantic beach destination, historic Lewes (pronounced Loo-is) is an offbeat choice, a place that recommends itself to vacationers for whom sand and sea (about a mile away) are only part of the pleasure. Dating its origins to a Dutch attempt at establishing a whaling station in 1631, it is Delaware's oldest community and enjoys a rich architectural heritage. The neighborhood adjacent to the pleasure boat harbor on the Lewes & Rehoboth Canal is dotted with beautifully restored cottages and mansions from the 18th and 19th centuries, which once housed ship's pilots working Delaware Bay. A 1-mile, one-hour stroll through the Historic District is an engaging journey into the past. Begin at the Zwaanendael Museum, a red-brick curiosity with a delightful stair-stepping gable decorated with carved stonework. Built in 1931, it was adapted from the 17th-century town hall of Hoorn in the Netherlands, from which Lewes' first colonists arrived. As the museum, which details the town's history, explains, all 28 (some sources say 32) were killed in a dispute with local Native Americans. In 1682, the area became part of an English grant to William Penn, the founder of Pennsylvania. Behind the museum, the gambrel-roofed Fisher-Martin House (1730) houses the Visitor Information Center. From the museum, head up 2nd Street, Lewes' "main street," in the shade of a canopy of giant, old trees. Take time out to nibble on an ice cream cone while resting on a park bench. At 218 2nd Street, Lewes' oldest home, the little red and yellow shingled Ryves Holt House, is believed to have been built in about 1665. Once a colonial inn, it also housed the Officer of the Port. A few steps to the right at 118 Front Street, which parallels the canal, a cannonball fired by a British vessel in the War of 1812 still juts from the brick foundation of the Cannonball House Marine Museum (1797). Inside are nautical exhibits. Many of the town's Victorian homes are richly adorned with gingerbread trim, and several are brightly painted. One of the prettiest, just off 2nd Street (double back to get here), is the Ann Eliza Baker House, a dazzler in yellow, gold, purple, and orange. This house is a fine example of Lewes' "folk Victorian" style: note the lovely flower gardens and small fountains in this neighborhood. Head north up 3rd Street to Shipcarpenter Street, where the Lewes Historical Society maintains an outdoor museum of early Delaware architecture. Several are "scooter" houses; that is, they are relocated from elsewhere—a local custom. Conclude this tour just up Shipcarpenter to the west at Shipcarpenter Square, an attractive development of restored 18th- and 19th-century scooter homes, all private residences, set around a nicely landscaped mall.

swimming, fishing; nature center, programs, trails, picnicking, concession, camping (water hookups, dump station). Standard hours, fees.

Lewes-Cape May, NJ, Ferry. *Sandman Blvd and Lincoln Dr (08204).* Phone 302/645-6313 or 800/643-3779 *(reservations).* Sole connection between US 13 (Ocean Hwy) on the Delmarva Peninsula and southern terminus of Garden State Parkway (NJ). Trip across Delaware Bay (16 miles) takes 70 minutes. (Daily; 22 crossings in summer, 10 in winter, 14-18 in spring and fall) **$$$$**

Lewes Historical Society Complex. *110 Shipcarpenter St (19958).* Phone 302/564-7670. The restored buildings located here were moved here to create a feel for Lewes' early days. (June-Labor Day, Tues-Sat) Tickets at Rabbit's Ferry House. Walking tours and varied events take place during summer season. Buildings include

Burton-Ingram House. (circa 1800) Log home made from hand-hewn timbers with cypress shingles. Houses beautiful antiques.

Cannonball House & Marine Museum. *118 Front St.* Built in late 18th century. Originally called the David Rowland Home, it was hit by a cannonball during the War of 1812 and renamed.

Doctor's Office. *Third St* (circa 1850) Medical and Dental museum.

Hiram R. Burton House. *Second and Shipcarpenter sts* (circa 1780) Houses antique furnishings and an 18th-century kitchen. Also includes a reading room with materials dedicated to Delaware history.

Plank House. Swedish log cabin restored to reflect the home of an early settler.

Rabbit's Ferry House. *Third St* (circa 1789) An 18th-century farmhouse with original paneling and period pieces.

Thompson Country Store. *Shipcarpenter and Third sts* (1800) Moved from original location in Tompsonville, DE. Thompson family ran as a store until 1962. **$$**

Restored buildings. *Phone 302/645-7670.* Maintained by the Lewes Historical Society. Cannon Ball House and US Lifesaving Station have marine exhibits and lightship *Overfalls.* Other buildings open are Thompson country store, Plank House, Rabbit's Ferry House, Burton-Ingram House, Ellegood House, Hiram R. Burton House, and old doctor's office. (June-Labor Day, Tues-Sat) Tickets at Rabbit's Ferry House. Walking tours and varied events take place during summer season.

Zwaanendael Museum. *Savannah Rd and Kings Hwy. Phone 302/645-1148.* This adaptation of the Hoorn, Holland, town hall was built in 1931 as a memorial to the original Dutch founders of Lewes (1631). It highlights the town's maritime heritage with colonial, Native American, and Dutch exhibits. (Tues-Sun; closed Mon, holidays)

Special Events

Coast Day. *University of Delaware Marine Studies Complex. 700 Pilottown Rd (19958). Phone 302/645-4346.* Facilities and research vessel open to public; marine exhibits, research demonstrations, nautical films. First Sun in Oct.

Great Delaware Kite Festival. *In Cape Henlopen State Park (see also). 42 Henlopen Dr. Phone 302/645-8983.* Festival heralds the beginning of spring on the Fri before Easter.

Lewes Garden Tour. *120 Kings Hwy. Phone 302/645-8073.* Visit the hidden gardens of Lewes. Vendors. Third Sat in June.

Motels/Motor Lodges

★ **ANGLER'S MOTEL.** *110 Anglers Rd (19958). Phone 302/645-2831.* 25 rooms, 1-2 story, 2 kitchen units. Mid-May-mid-Sept (3-day minimum weekends, holidays): S, D $70-$105; each additional $5; kitchen units $85-$105; lower rates rest of year. Closed Dec-Feb. Crib free. TV; cable. Pool. Restaurant nearby. Check-out 11 am. Refrigerators. Picnic tables, grills. Sun deck. Overlooks canal, marina opposite. Boat docking. Cr cds: A, MC, V.

★ **BEACON.** *514 E Savannah Rd (19958). Phone 302/645-4888; toll-free 800/735-4888; fax 302/645-8138. www.lewestoday.com/beacon.* 66 rooms, 3 story. Aug: S, D $105-$155; each additional $5; under 12 free; holiday rates; lower rates rest of year. Closed mid-Nov-Mar. Crib $5. TV; cable (premium), VCR available (movies). Complimentary coffee in lobby. Restaurant adjacent 6 am-6 pm. Check-out 11 am. Meeting rooms. Business services available. Bellstaff. Pool. Refrigerators. Balconies. Cr cds: A, DS, MC, V.

Hotel

★ ★ ★ **ZWAANENDAEL INN.** *142 2nd St (19958). Phone 302/645-6466; toll-free 800/824-8754; fax 302/645-7196. www.beach-net.com/newdevoninn.* Listed in the National Historic Register, this antique-filled inn pleases guests with its charm and elegance. Guests should enjoy nearby antique shopping and beaches, as there are no televisions or room service in these cozy rooms. 26 rooms, 4 story. Mid-June-mid-Oct: S, D $65-$130; suites $110-$170; package plans; lower rates rest of year. Restaurant 11 am-10 pm. Check-out 11 am. Business services available. Shopping arcade. Built 1926. Cr cds: A, C, D, DS, MC, V.

B&B/Small Inn

★ ★ ★ **INN AT CANAL SQUARE.** *122 Market St (19958). Phone 302/644-3377; toll-free 888/644-1911; fax 302/644-3565. www.theinnatcanalsquare.com.* Adjacent to the beautiful historic district, this charming bed-and-breakfast is the only waterfront inn in Lewes. 26 rooms, 4 story. Pet accepted. Complimentary continental breakfast. Check-out 11 am, check-in 3 pm. TV; cable (premium). In-room modem link. Restaurant. Concierge. On canal. Cr cds: A, MC, V. **$**

Restaurants

★ **ASHBY'S OYSTER HOUSE.** *24 Peddlers Village (19958). Phone 302/945-4070; fax 302/945-4057.* Seafood menu. Closed Thanksgiving, Dec 25. Sun breakfast buffet, breakfast, lunch, dinner. Bar. Children's menu. Casual attire. Cr cds: A, DS, MC, V. **$$**

★ ★ ★ **THE BUTTERY.** *102 Second St (19958). Phone 302/645-7755; fax 302/644-4909. www.buttery restaurant.com.* This charming and delectable restaurant, located in the newly restored Trader Mansion, will tempt every appetite. Guests can choose from a variety of tasty salads or entrees and will not be disappointed. Try the English bangers at Sunday brunch. French menu. Hours: 11 am-2:30 pm, 5-10 pm; Sun 10:30 am-2:30 pm, 5-10 pm. Lunch $7-$18, dinner $22-$35, Brunch $17.95. Entertainment. Reservations accepted. Cr cds: DS, MC, V.

★ **LIGHTHOUSE.** *Savannah Rd at Anglers Rd (19958). Phone 302/645-6271; fax 302/645-1608. www.lighthouselewes.com.* Hours: 6 am-10 pm; Sept-Mar 7 am-9 pm. Closed Thanksgiving, Dec 24, 25. Bar from 11 am. Breakfast $3.75-$6.95, lunch $3.25-$12.95, dinner $12.95-$17.95. Children's menu. Specializes in fresh seafood. Entertainment weekends. Outdoor seating. Overlooks Lewes Harbor. Cr cds: MC, V.

Little Creek

See also Dover

Restaurant

★ ★ **VILLAGE INN.** *DE 9 (19901). Phone 302/734-3245; fax 302/734-3238.* Hours: 11 am-2 pm, 4:30-10 pm; Sat 11 am-10 pm; Sun noon-9 pm. Closed Dec 25. Reservations accepted. Bar. Lunch $4.95-$9.95, dinner $12.95-$19.95. Specialties: stuffed flounder, prime rib. Colonial décor; fireplace, antiques. Cr cds: C, D, DS, ER, MC, V.

Ⓓ

Newark (A-9)

See also New Castle, Wilmington

Settled 1685 **Pop** 28,547 **Elev** 124 ft **Area code** 302

Information Greater Wilmington Convention & Visitors Bureau-Visitors Center, 100 W 10th St, Wilmington 19801; 302/737-4059

Newark grew up at the crossroads of two well-traveled Native American trails. The site of the only Revolutionary War battle on Delaware soil is at nearby Cooch's Bridge, southeast of Newark. According to tradition, Betsy Ross's flag was first raised in battle at Cooch's Bridge on September 3, 1777.

What to See and Do

University of Delaware. *196 S College Ave. Phone 302/831-8123.* (1743) 18,000 students. Founded as a small private academy; stately elm trees, fine lawns, and Georgian-style brick buildings adorn the central campus. Tours from Visitors Center (Mon-Fri, Sat). On campus is

> **University of Delaware Mineral Collection.** *24 E Main St (19716). Phone 302/831-8242.* Also fossil exhibit. Penny Hall, Academy St. (Mon-Fri, by appointment only; closed holidays) **FREE**

White Clay Creek State Park. *425 Wedgewood Rd. 3 miles NW via DE 896. Phone 302/368-6900.* A 1,483-acre day park with farmlands, forest, and streams. Fishing; nature and fitness trails, picnicking. Standard hours, fees.

Motels/Motor Lodges

★ ★ **BEST WESTERN DELAWARE INN & CONFERENCE CENTER.** *260 Chapman Rd (19702). Phone 302/738-3400; toll-free 800/633-3203; fax 302/738-3414. www.bestwestern.com.* 99 rooms, 2 story. S $55-$65; D $60-$75; each additional $5; under 18 free; weekend rates. Crib free. Check-out noon. TV; cable. Restaurant 5-9

pm. Bar 4 pm-1 am. Room service. Pool. Meeting rooms. Business services. Sundries. Cr cds: A, C, D, DS, MC, V.

Ⓓ ⌷ ⌷

★ **COMFORT INN.** *100 McIntosh Plaza (19713). Phone 302/453-9100; toll-free 800/252-7466; fax 302/453-9114. www.comfortinn.com.* 108 rooms. S $41.95; D $46.95; each additional $5. Crib free. TV. Restaurant adjacent open 24 hours. Check-out 11 am. Some refrigerators. Cr cds: A, C, D, DS, JCB, MC, V.

Ⓓ ⌷ SC

★ ★ **HOLIDAY INN.** *1203 Christiana Rd (19713). Phone 302/737-2700; toll-free 800/465-4329; fax 302/737-3214.* 144 rooms, 2 story. S $71-$81; D $77-$87; each additional $6; under 18 free. Crib free. TV; cable. Pool; lifeguard. Restaurant 6:30 am-10 pm. Room service. Bar noon-1 am. Check-out noon. Coin laundry. Meeting rooms. Business services available. In-room modem link. Valet service. Sundries. Cr cds: A, C, D, DS, JCB, MC, V.

Ⓓ ⌷ ⌷ SC

★ **HOWARD JOHNSON.** *1119 S College Ave (19713). Phone 302/368-8521; toll-free 800/654-2000; fax 302/368-9868. www.hojo.com.* 142 rooms, 2 story. S, D $55; each additional $10; under 18 free. Crib free. Pet accepted. TV; cable. Pool. Complimentary continental breakfast. Check-out noon. Meeting rooms. Business services available. In-room modem link. Valet service. Health club privileges. Private patios, balconies. Cr cds: A, C, D, DS, ER, JCB, MC, V.

Ⓓ ⌷ ⌷ ⌷ SC

★ ★ **QUALITY INN.** *1120 S College Ave (19713). Phone 302/368-8715; toll-free 800/228-5150; fax 302/368-6454. www.qualityinn.com.* 102 rooms, 2 story. S $50-$54; D $56-$60; each additional $6; under 18 free. Crib free. Pet accepted. TV; cable, VCR available (movies). Pool; lifeguard. Complimentary continental breakfast. Check-out 11 am. Meeting room. Business services available. In-room modem link. Some refrigerators. Cr cds: A, C, D, DS, JCB, MC, V.

Ⓓ ⌷ ⌷ ⌷ SC

Hotel

★ ★ ★ **HILTON WILMINGTON/CHRISTIANA.** *100 Continental Dr (19713). Phone 302/454-1500; toll-free 800/774-1500; fax 302/454-0233. www.hilton.com.* 266 rooms, 4 story. S, D $99-$199; each additional $10; suites $185-$325; family plans; higher rates university graduation. Crib free. Check-out 11:30 am. TV; cable. In-room modem link. Restaurant 6:30 am-10 pm. Bar 11-1 am. Exercise equipment. Heated pool, whirlpool, poolside service, lifeguard. Golf privileges. Tennis privileges. Meeting rooms. Business center. Concierge. Luxury level. Cr cds: A, C, D, DS, ER, JCB, MC, V.

Restaurant

★ **KLONDIKE KATE'S.** *158 E Main St (19711). Phone 302/737-6100; fax 302/737-6199. www.klondikekates.com.* Hours: 11-1 am; Sun from 10 am. Closed Thanksgiving, Dec 25. Southwestern menu. Bar. Lunch, dinner $4.95-$12.95. Children's menu. Outdoor seating. In former courthouse/jail. Cr cds: A, D, DS, MC, V.

New Castle (A-9)

See also Newark, Wilmington

Settled 1651 **Pop** 4,862 **Elev** 19 ft **Area code** 302 **Zip** 19720

Information Mayor and Council of New Castle, 220 Delaware St; 302/322-9801

Web www.newcastlecity.net

New Castle—meeting place of the Colonial assemblies, first capital of the state, and an early center of culture and communication—was one of Delaware's first settlements. Its fine harbor made it a busy port in the 18th century until its commerce was taken over by Wilmington, which is closer to Philadelphia. Today, New Castle is a historian's and architect's delight—charming, mellow, and relaxed. Three signers of the Declaration of Independence made their homes here: George Read, Thomas McKean, and George Ross, Jr. (considered a Pennsylvanian by some). New Castle lies at the foot of the Delaware Memorial Bridge, which connects with the southern end of the New Jersey Turnpike.

What to See and Do

Amstel House Museum. *2 E 4th St at Delaware St. Phone 302/322-2794.* (1730) Restored brick mansion of seventh governor of Delaware; an earlier structure was incorporated into the service wing. Houses Colonial furnishings and arts; complete Colonial kitchen. (Mar-Dec, Tues-Sun; rest of year, Sat and Sun; closed holidays) Combination ticket available with Old Dutch House. **$**

George Read II House. *42 The Strand. Phone 302/322-8411.* (1804) Federal house with elegant interiors: gilded fanlights; silver door hardware; carved woodwork; relief plasterwork. Furnished with period antiques; garden design dates from 1847. (Mar-Dec, Tues-Sun; rest of year, Sat and Sun) **$$**

The Green. *Delaware and 3rd sts.* Laid out by direction of Peter Stuyvesant, this public square of the old town is surrounded by dozens of historically important buildings.

New Castle Court House Museum. *211 Delaware St, on The Green. Phone 302/323-4453.* (1732) Original Colonial capitol and oldest surviving courthouse in the state; furnishings and exhibits on display; cupola is the center of a 12-mile circle that delineates the Delaware-Pennsylvania border. (Tues-Sun; closed holidays) **FREE**

Old Dutch House. *32 E 3rd St. Phone 302/322-2794.* (late 17th century) Thought to be Delaware's oldest dwelling in its original form; Dutch Colonial furnishings; decorative arts. (Mar-Dec, Tues-Sun; rest of year, Sat and Sun; closed holidays) Combination ticket available with Amstel House Museum. **$**

Old Library Museum. *40 E 3rd St. Phone 302/322-2794.* (1892) Unusual semioctagonal Victorian building houses temporary exhibits relating to area. (Sat-Sun) **FREE**

Special Events

Band concerts. *Battery Park. Phone 302/328-4188.* Wed evenings, June-early Aug.

Separation Day. *Battery Park. Phone 302/322-9802.* Observance of Delaware's declaration of independence from Great Britain. Regatta, shows, bands, concerts, fireworks. June.

Motels/Motor Lodges

★ **RAMADA INN.** *1612 N DuPont Hwy (19720). Phone 302/658-8511; fax 302/658-3071. www.ramada.com.* 120 rooms, 2 story. S $75-$81; D $78-$84; each additional $10; under 18 free. Crib free. Check-out noon. TV; cable. In-room modem link. Valet services. Complimentary continental breakfast. Restaurant 7 am-10 pm. Bar 4:30 pm-midnight. Room service. Pool, poolside service, lifeguard. Meeting rooms. Business services. Sundries. Cr cds: A, D, DS, MC, V.

★ **RODEWAY INN.** *111 S DuPont Hwy (19720). Phone 302/328-6246; toll-free 800/321-6246; fax 302/328-9493. www.rodewayinn.com.* 40 rooms. S $49-$59; D $55-$69; each additional $5; under 18 free. Crib $5. Pet accepted. Complimentary continental breakfast. Check-out noon. TV; cable. Some refrigerators, microwaves. Restaurant adjacent 11 am-10 pm. Business services available. Cr cds: A, C, D, DS, JCB, MC, V.

Restaurants

★ ★ **AIR TRANSPORT COMMAND.** *143 N DuPont Hwy (19720). Phone 302/328-3527; fax 302/328-3832.* Hours: 11 am-4 pm, 5-11 pm; Fri to midnight; Sat 4:30 pm-midnight; Sun 4-10 pm; Sun brunch 10 am-3 pm. Lunch $4.50-$8.95, dinner $9.95-$23.95. Sun brunch $14.95. Bar to 1 am. Children's menu. Reservations accepted, required Sat. Outdoor seating. Replica of WWII-era Scottish farmhouse; war memorabilia. Cr cds: A, D, DS, MC, V.

D

★ ★ **ARSENAL AT NEW CASTLE.** *30 Market St (19720). Phone 302/328-1290; fax 302/328-3106. www.arsenal1812.com.* Hours: 11:30 am-2:30 pm, 5-9 pm; Sun 1-8 pm. Closed Mon. Lunch $4.75-$13.95, dinner $11.95-$28.95. Building constructed in 1809 by the Federal government; originally used as arsenal. Reservations accepted. Cr cds: A, D, DS, MC, V.

★ **SALTY SAM'S PIER 13.** *130 S DuPont Hwy (19720). Phone 302/323-1408; fax 302/323-1232.* Seafood menu. Closed most major holidays. Lunch, dinner. Bar. Children's menu. Casual attire. Outdoor seating. Credit Cards accepted. **$$**

D

Odessa (B-9)

See also New Castle, Smyrna, Wilmington

Settled 1721 **Pop** 286 **Elev** 50 ft **Area code** 302 **Zip** 19730

Once a prosperous grain shipping center, Odessa tried to protect its shipping trade by haughtily telling the Delaware Railroad, in 1855, to lay its tracks elsewhere. To glorify itself that same year, the town changed its name from Cantwell's Bridge to that of the Russian grain port on the Black Sea. But the sloops and schooners that transported grain eventually found less shortsighted ports of call. Odessa was an important station on the Underground Railroad for many years before the Civil War. Now it is a crossroads town at the junction of US 13 and DE 299. The town exhibits numerous fine examples of 18th- and 19th-century domestic architecture.

What to See and Do

Fort Delaware State Park. *(see) Approximately 9 miles NE on Pea Patch Island, opposite Delaware City.*

Corbit-Sharp House. *118 Main St.* (1774) Georgian house built by William Corbit, Odessa's leading citizen, was lived in by his family for 150 years. Restored and furnished with many family pieces, the interior reflects period from 1774-1818. Maintained by Winterthur Museum, Garden, and Library (see WILMINGTON).

Wilson-Warner House. *Main St. Phone 302/378-4069.* (1769) Handsome red brick Georgian house, with L-shape plan typical of early Delaware architecture, is accurately furnished to portray life in early 19th century. Maintained by Winterthur Museum, Garden, and Library (see WILMINGTON).

Historic Houses of Odessa. *109 Main St. Phone 302/378-4069.* For full tour of houses, arrive by 2 pm. (Tues-Sun; closed holidays, Jan-Feb) Individual house tickets available. **$$$**

Brick Hotel Gallery and Manney Collection of Belter Furniture. *Main Street. Phone 302/378-4069.* Federal, 19th-century building was a hotel and tavern for nearly a century. Gallery houses the largest private collection of Belter furniture in existence. Very high-styled Victorian furniture, Belter parlor and bedroom suites, made in New York in the mid-19th century, were famous for craftsmanship, particularly elaborate carvings. **$$**

Lums Pond State Park. *1068 Howell School Rd. Approximately 3 miles W on DE 299 to Middletown, then 8 miles N on US 301 and DE 71. Phone 302/368-6989.* More than 1,800-acre park centered around 200-acre pond. Fishing, boating (rentals); hiking and fitness trails, game courts, picnicking, camping (showers, dump station; Apr-Oct). Standard hours, fees. **$$**

Rehoboth Beach (D-10)

See also Bethany Beach, Fenwick Island, Lewes

Settled 1872 **Pop** 1,495 **Elev** 16 ft **Area code** 302 **Zip** 19971

Information Rehoboth Beach-Dewey Beach Chamber of Commerce, 501 Rehoboth Ave, PO Box 216; 302/227-2233 or 800/441-1329

Web www.beach-fun.com

The "nation's summer capital" got its nickname by being a favorite with Washington diplomats and legislators. A 2 1/2-hour drive from Washington, D.C., the largest summer resort in Delaware began as a spot for camp meetings amid sweet-smelling pine groves. In the 1920s, real estate boomed, triggering Rehoboth Beach's rebirth as a resort town with a variety of accommodations, shopping areas, and eateries. Deep sea and freshwater fishing, sailing, swimming, and biking and strolling along cherry tree-lined Rehoboth Avenue have kept it a favorite retreat from Washington's summer heat.

What to See and Do

Delaware Seashore State Park. *850 Inlet Rd. 6 miles S on DE 1. Phone 302/227-2800.* This 7-mile strip of land separates Rehoboth and Indian River bays from the Atlantic. Bay and ocean swimming, fishing, surfing, boating (marina, launch, rentals); picnicking, concession, primitive and improved campsites (hookups). Standard hours, fees.

Special Events

Bandstand concerts. *Bandstand, 501 Rehoboth Ave. Phone 302/227-6181.* Open-air concerts. Sat and Sun evenings, Memorial Day-Labor Day.

Sea Witch Halloween and Fiddlers' Festival. *501 Rehoboth Ave. Phone 800/441-1329, ext 12.* Late Oct.

Motels/Motor Lodges

★ **ADAMS OCEANFRONT VILLAS.** *4 Read St, Dewey Beach (19971). Phone 302/227-3030; toll-free 800/ 448-8080; fax 302/227-1034. www.adamsoceanfront.com.* 23 rooms, 3 story. No elevator. Late June-Aug: S, D $95-$115; each additional $6; villas (up to 7) $250-$295 (3-day minimum); lower rates mid-Mar-late June, Sept-Oct. Closed rest of year. Complimentary continental breakfast. Check-out 11 am; villas 10 am. TV; cable (premium). Pool. On beachfront. Cr cds: MC, V.

⬤⬤⬤

★ **ADMIRAL.** *2 Baltimore Ave (19971). Phone 302/ 227-2103; toll-free 888/882-4188; fax 302/227-3620. www.admiralrehoboth.com.* 73 rooms, 5 story. June-Labor Day: S, D $110-$199; each additional $10; suites $155-$245; weekend rates; 3-day minimum stay in season; lower rates rest of year. TV; cable. Indoor pool, whirlpool. Cr cds: A, DS, MC, V.

⬤⬤⬤

★ **THE ATLANTIC BUDGET INN.** *154 Rehoboth Ave (19971). Phone 302/227-9446; toll-free 800/245-2112; fax 302/227-9446.* 97 rooms, 1-4 story, 10 kitchens. Mid-July-late Aug, holiday weekends: D $69-$159; each additional $10; kitchens $109-$179; under 11 free; lower rates rest of year. Crib $6. Complimentary coffee. Check-out 11 am. TV; cable, VCR available (movies). Some refrigerators, microwaves. Coin laundry. Pool. Cr cds: A, DS, MC, V.

⬤⬤⬤⬤

★ **ATLANTIC VIEW MOTEL.** *2 Clayton St, North Dewey Beach (19971). Phone 302/227-3878; toll-free 800/777-4162; fax 302/227-5372. www.atlanticview.com.* 35 rooms, 4 story. No elevator. Mid-June-Labor Day (2-4-day minimum): S, D $99-$169; each additional $7; lower rates Apr-mid-June, after Labor Day-mid-Oct. Closed rest of

year. Crib $5. TV; cable (premium). Pool. Complimentary coffee in lobby. Check-out 11 am. Coin laundry. Refrigerators. Balconies. Cr cds: A, DS, MC, V.

⬤⬤⬤⬤

★ **BAY RESORT MOTEL.** *126 Bellevue St, Dewey Beach (19971). Phone 302/227-6400; toll-free 800/922-9240; fax 302/227-5800. www.bayresort.com.* 68 kitchen units, 3 story. July-Labor Day: D $119-$199; each additional $10; under 12 free; weekend, weekly rates; lower rates Apr-June and Sept-Oct. Closed rest of year. Crib $10. TV; cable (premium). Pool. Complimentary continental breakfast. Check-out 11 am. Coin laundry. Some private patios, balconies. Cr cds: DS, MC, V.

⬤⬤⬤

★ **BEACH VIEW MOTEL.** *6 Wilmington Ave (19971). Phone 302/227-2999; toll-free 800/288-5962; fax 302/226-2640. www.beachviewmotel.com.* 38 rooms, 4 story. Mid-June-early Sept: D $80-$155; each additional $7; under 7 free; lower rates Apr-mid-June, early Sept-Nov. Closed rest of year. Complimentary continental breakfast. Check-out 11 am. TV; cable (premium). Laundry services. Pool. Cr cds: A, DS, MC, V.

⬤⬤

★ **BEST WESTERN GOLD LEAF.** *1400 Hwy 1 (19971). Phone 302/226-1100; toll-free 800/528-1234; fax 302/226-9785. www.bestwestern.com.* 75 rooms, 4 story. Mid-June-Aug: S, D $149-$189; each additional $10; under 12 free; lower rates rest of year. Complimentary continental breakfast. Check-out 11 am. TV; cable (premium). Laundry services. Pool. Covered parking. Cr cds: A, C, D, DS, ER, JCB, MC, V.

⬤⬤⬤ SC

★ **BRIGHTON SUITES HOTEL.** *34 Wilmington Ave (19971). Phone 302/227-5780; toll-free 800/227-5788; fax 302/227-6815. www.brightonsuites.com.* 66 suites, 4 story. July-Aug: suites $189-$239; each additional $10; under 16 free; mid-week rates; package plans; lower rates rest of year. Crib $6. TV; cable (premium). Heated pool. Coffee in rooms. Restaurant opposite 11 am-9 pm. Check-out 11 am. Meeting rooms. Business services available. Bellstaff in season. Garage parking. Exercise equipment. Refrigerators, wet bars; microwaves available. Cr cds: A, C, D, DS, MC, V.

⬤⬤⬤ SC

★★ **DINNER BELL INN.** *2 Christian St (19971). Phone 302/227-2561; toll-free 800/425-2355; fax 302/227-0323. www.dinnerbellinn.com.* 28 rooms, 2 story, 4 kitchen units, 1 cottage. Late June-Aug: D $85-$175; each additional $15; kitchen units $150-$210; cottage $250; under 12 free; lower rates Apr-mid-June and late Sept. Closed Jan-Feb. Crib $15. TV; cable (premium). Complimentary continental breakfast. Restaurant 4-10 pm. Bar. Check-out 11 am. Meeting room. Business services available. Individually decorated rooms. Ocean 2 blocks. Cr cds: A, MC, V.

★ **ECONO LODGE.** *4361 DE 1 (19971). Phone 302/227-0500; toll-free 800/645-2690; fax 302/227-2170. www.econolodge.com.* 79 rooms, 3 story. June-Sept: S, D $85-$135; each additional $10; under 16 free; lower rates rest of year. Crib free. TV; cable (premium). Pool; lifeguard. Complimentary coffee in lobby. Check-out 11 am. Coin laundry. Business services available. Some refrigerators. Microwaves available. Lawn games. Balconies. Cr cds: A, C, D, DS, JCB, MC, V.

★ **HARBOR VIEW.** *DE 1 (19930). Phone 302/539-0500; fax 302/539-5170.* 60 rooms, 2 story, 8 kitchen units. July-Aug: S, D $95-$139; each additional $10; kitchen units $100-$139; lower rates rest of year. Crib $10. TV; cable (premium). Pool. Complimentary continental breakfast. Restaurant 5-10 pm; closed Dec-Jan. Check-out 11 am. Meeting room. Refrigerators, microwaves. Balconies. Picnic tables, grills. On bay; swimming. Cr cds: A, D, DS, MC, V.

★ ★ **HENLOPEN HOTEL.** *511 N Boardwalk (19971). Phone 302/227-2551; toll-free 800/441-8450; fax 302/227-8147. www.henlopenhotel.com.* 93 rooms, 8 story. July-Aug (2-day minimum weekends, holidays): S, D $179-$279; each additional $10; under 16 free; varied lower rates Apr-May and Sept-Oct. Closed Jan-Mar 15. Crib free. TV; cable. Coffee in rooms. Restaurant 8-11 am, 5-10 pm. Check-out 11 am. Meeting rooms. Business services available. Some refrigerators. Balconies. On beach; ocean views. Cr cds: A, MC, V.

★ **OCEANUS MOTEL.** *6 Second St (19971). Phone 302/227-8200; toll-free 800/852-5011. www.oceanusmotel.com.* 38 rooms, 3 story. No elevator. July-Aug: D $129-$169; each additional $10; under 12 free; weekly rates; lower rates Apr-June, Sept-Oct. Closed rest of year. Complimentary continental breakfast. Check-out noon. TV; cable (premium). Laundry services. Pool; lifeguard. Cr cds: DS, MC, V.

★ **SANDCASTLE.** *123 Second St (19971). Phone 302/227-0400; toll-free 800/372-2112. www.thesandcastlemotel.com.* 60 rooms, 3 story. July-Labor Day: S, D $100-$130; each additional $10; under 12 free; lower rates Mar-July

and Labor Day-Dec. Closed rest of year. Check-out 11 am. TV; cable. Sauna. Indoor pool. Cr cds: A, DS, MC, V.

★ **SEA ESTA MOTEL III.** *1409 DE 1, Dewey Beach (19971). Phone 302/227-4343; toll-free 800/436-6591; fax 302/227-3049. www.seaesta.com.* 33 kitchen units, 3 story. July-Aug: S, D $100-$150; each additional $10; under 12 free; lower rates rest of year. Pet accepted; $5/day. TV; cable (premium). Complimentary coffee in lobby. Check-out 11 am. Covered parking. Balconies. Ocean 1 block; swimming beach. Cr cds: A, D, DS, MC, V.

Hotel

★ ★ ★ **BOARDWALK PLAZA HOTEL.** *2 Olive Ave (19971). Phone 302/227-7169; toll-free 800/332-3224; fax 302/227-0561. www.boardwalkplaza.com.* The charm and comfort of this Victorian-style hotel on Rehoboth Beach will delight guests. Enjoy the scenic ocean views at Victoria's restaurant. 84 units, 4 story, 45 suites, 6 kitchen units. Memorial Day-Labor Day: S, D $135-$300; each additional $20; suites $245-$395; kitchen units $1,800-$3,000/week (Memorial Day-Labor Day 1-week minimum); under 6 free; lower rates rest of year. Crib free. TV; cable, VCR available (movies). Indoor/outdoor pool; poolside service. Complimentary coffee in rooms. Restaurant 7 am-10 pm. Room service. Check-out 11 am. Meeting rooms. Business services available. In-room modem link. Exercise equipment. Minibars; microwaves available. Some balconies. On beach; ocean swimming. Victorian décor and architectural detail in modern structure; antiques, period furnishings; glass-encased oceanview elevator; rooftop sun deck. Luxury level. Cr cds: A, D, DS, MC, V.

B&B/Small Inn

★ ★ ★ **CHESAPEAKE LANDING.** *101 Chesapeake St (19971). Phone 302/227-2973; fax 302/227-0301. www.chesapeakelanding.com.* Guests will feel like they are in their own home at this cozy bed and breakfast. Enjoy lakeside paddleboating or the nearby beaches and outlet shopping. 4 rooms, 3 story. No elevator, room phones. Children over 16 years only. Complimentary full breakfast. Check-out noon, check-in 2 pm. TV; VCR available (movies). Pool. In-room modem link. Health club privileges. Totally nonsmoking. Cr cds: MC, V. **$$**

Restaurants

★ ★ **BLUE MOON.** *35 Baltimore Ave (19971). Phone 302/227-6515; fax 302/227-3702. www.bluemoonrehoboth. com.* Seafood, vegetarian menu. Closed Jan. Dinner, Sun brunch $6.25-$9.50. Bar. Reservations accepted. Outdoor seating. Cr cds: A, D, DS, MC, V. **$$**

D

★ ★ ★ **CHEZ LA MER.** *210 2nd St (19971). Phone 302/227-6494; fax 302/227-6797.* Decorated French-country style, this restaurant offers a number of different settings with their own charm. Hours: 5:30-10 pm; Fri, Sat to 10: 30 pm. Closed Mon-Wed off season; Thanksgiving; also Dec-Mar. Reservations accepted. Continental menu. Bar to 1 am. Dinner $16-$23. Children's menu. Specializes in fresh seafood, veal. Outdoor seating. Restored house with French provincial décor. Sun porch. Cr cds: A, D, DS, MC, V.

★ ★ **LA LA LAND.** *22 Wilmington Ave (19971). Phone 302/227-3887; fax 302/227-4877. www.lalalandrestaurant. com.* Lunch, dinner. Bar. Reservations accepted. Outdoor seating. Cr cds: A, C, D, DS, MC, V. **$$**

★ ★ **LAMP POST.** *4534 DE 1 (19971). Phone 302/645-9132; fax 302/645-9206.* Seafood, steak menu. Closed Thanksgiving, Dec 25. Lunch, dinner. Bar. Children's menu. Cr cds: A, DS, MC, V. **$**

D

★★**RUSTY RUDDER.** *113 Dickinson St, Dewey Beach (19971). Phone 302/227-3888; fax 302/226-2402. www. dmv.com/rustyrudder.* Specializes in prime rib, seafood. Hours: 11:30 am-9 pm, Fri, Sat to 10 pm; Memorial Day-Labor Day to 11 pm; Sun to 9 pm; Sun brunch 10 am-2 pm. Lunch $5.95-$8.95, dinner $14.95-$25.95. Sun brunch $12.95. Bar to 1 am. Salad bar. Entertainment. Children's menu. Outdoor seating. Cr cds: A, C, D, DS, MC, V.

D SC ⊠

★ ★ **SYDNEY'S SIDE STREET.** *25 Christian St (19971). Phone 302/227-1339; fax 302/227-1332. www. sydneysofrehoboth.com.* Hours: 4 pm-1 am. Closed Thanksgiving, Dec 25; hours vary Nov-Apr. Dinner $9.50-$19.50. Bar. Live music. Restored old schoolhouse. Reservations accepted. Outdoor seating. Cr cds: A, D, DS, MC, V.

D SC

★ **TIJUANA TAXI.** *207 Rehoboth Ave (19971). Phone 302/227-1986; fax 302/645-9427.* Mexican menu. Mexican cantina atmosphere. Specializes in chili, nachos, vegetarian dishes. Hours: 5-11 pm; Fri, Sat noon-midnight; Sun noon-11 pm. Closed Sun; Dec 25. Lunch, dinner. Bar. Cr cds: MC, V. **$**

D

Smyrna (B-9)

See also Dover, Odessa

Founded 1768 **Pop** 5,679 **Elev** 36 ft **Area code** 302 **Zip** 19977

Information Chamber of Commerce, PO Box 576, Dover 19903; 302/653-9291; or visit the Smyrna Visitors Center, 5500 DuPont Hwy; 302/653-8910

Named in 1806 for the chief seaport of Turkish Asia Minor, Smyrna in the 1850s was an active shipping center for produce grown in central Delaware.

What to See and Do

Bombay Hook National Wildlife Refuge. *2591 Whitehall Neck Rd. 5 miles E on DE 6, then 3 miles S on DE 9. Phone 302/653-6872.* Annual fall and spring resting and feeding spot for migratory waterfowl, including a variety of ducks and tens of thousands of snow geese and Canada geese; also home for bald eagles, shorebirds, deer, fox, and muskrat. Auto tour route (12 miles), wildlife foot trails, observation towers; visitor center offering interpretive and environmental education programs. (Spring and fall, daily, summer and winter, Mon-Fri) Golden Eagle, Golden Age, and Golden Access passports accepted (see MAKING THE MOST OF YOUR TRIP). **$$**

Smyrna Museum. *11 S Main St. Phone 302/653-8844.* Furnishings and memorabilia from early Federal to late Victorian periods; changing exhibits. (Sat, limited hours)

Restaurants

★ ★ **THOMAS ENGLAND HOUSE.** *1165 S DuPont Blvd (US 13) (19977). Phone 302/653-1420; fax 302/ 653-1352.* Continental menu. Specializes in fresh seafood, prime rib. Hours: 4-10 pm; weekends to 11 pm. Dinner $9.95-$29.95. Bar. Children's menu. Reservations accepted, required Sat. Colonial building; housed troops during Revolutionary War; was stop on Underground Railroad. Cr cds: A, D, DS, MC, V.

★ **WAYSIDE INN.** *103 N DuPont Hwy (19977). Phone 302/653-8047.* Hours: 11 am-9 pm; Sun to 8 pm. Reservations accepted. Lunch $4.25-$8.50, dinner $10.95-$22.50. Children's menu. Specializes in seafood, prime rib. Cr cds: A, C, D, DS, ER, MC, V.

D

Wilmington (A-9)

In PA, see also Chester, Kennett Square, Philadelphia

Settled 1638 **Pop** 72,664 **Elev** 120 ft **Area code** 302

Information Greater Wilmington Convention & Visitors Bureau, 100 W 10th St, 19801; 302/652-4088

Web www.wilmcvb.org

Wilmington, the "chemical capital of the world," international hub of industry and shipping, is the largest city in Delaware. The Swedish, Dutch, and British have all left their mark on the city. The first settlement was made by Swedes seeking their fortunes; they founded the colony of New Sweden. In 1655, the little colony was taken without bloodshed by Dutch soldiers under Peter Stuyvesant, governor of New Amsterdam. Nine years later, the English became entrenched in the town, which grew, under the influence of wealthy Quakers, as a market and shipping center. Abundant water power in creeks of the Brandywine River Valley plus accessibility to other eastern ports stimulated early industrial growth. When Eleuthère du Pont built his powder mill on Brandywine Creek in 1802, the valley had already known a century of industry. From here come vulcanized fiber, glazed leathers, dyed cotton, rubber hose, autos, and many other products.

What to See and Do

Amtrak Station. *Martin Luther King Blvd and French St.* Victorian railroad station, which continues to function as such, designed by master architect Frank Furness. Restored. (Daily)

Banning Park. *2 miles S on DE 4. Middleboro Rd and Maryland Ave. Phone 302/323-6422.* Fishing; tennis, playing fields, picnicking, pavilions. (Daily) **FREE**

Bellevue State Park. *800 Carr Rd. 4 miles NE via I-95, Marsh Rd exit. Phone 302/577-3390.* Fishing; nature, fitness, and horseback riding trails; bicycling, tennis, game courts, picnicking (pavilions). Standard hours, fees.

Brandywine Creek State Park. *Rtes 92 and 100. Phone 302/577-3534.* A 1,000-acre day-use park. Fishing; nature and fitness trails; cross-country skiing. Picnicking. Nature center. Standard hours, fees. **$$** Per vehicle.

Brandywine Springs Park. *3300 Faulkland Rd. 4 miles W on DE 41. Phone 302/395-5652.* Site of a once-famous resort hotel (1827-1845) for Southern planters and politicos. Here, Lafayette met Washington under the Council Oak before the Battle of Brandywine in 1777. Picnicking, fireplaces, pavilions, baseball fields. Pets on leash only. (Daily) **FREE**

Brandywine Zoo and Park. *1001 N Park Dr. On both sides of Brandywine River, from Augustine to Market St bridges. Phone 302/571-7747.* Designed by Frederick Law Olmsted, the park includes Josephine Garden with fountain and roses; stands of Japanese cherry trees. The zoo, along North Park Dr, features animals from North and South America (daily). Picnicking, playgrounds. **$$**

Delaware Art Museum. *2301 Kentmere Pkwy. Phone 302/571-9590.* Expanded facility features Howard Pyle Collection of American illustrations with works by Pyle, N. C. Wyeth, and Maxfield Parrish; American painting collection, with works by West, Homer, Church, Glackens, and Hopper; Bancroft Collection of English Pre-Raphaelite art, with works by Rossetti and Burne-Jones; and Phelps Collection of Andrew Wyeth works; also changing exhibits, children's participatory gallery; store. (Tues-Sun; closed holidays) Guided tours by appointment. **$$$**

Delaware History Museum. *504 Market St. Phone 302/656-0637.* Changing exhibits on history and decorative arts. (Tues-Sat; closed holidays) **$$**

Delaware Museum of Natural History. *4840 Kennett Pike. 5 miles NW on DE 52 in Greenville. Phone 302/658-9111.* Exhibits of shells, birds, mammals; also largest bird egg and a 500-pound clam. (Daily; closed holidays) **$$**

Fort Christina Monument. *Foot of E 7th St. Phone 302/652-5629.* Monument marks location where Swedes settled in 1638. Presented in 1938 to Wilmington by the people of Sweden, monument consists of black granite plinth surmounted by pioneers' flagship, the *Kalmar Nyckel*, sculpted by Carl Milles. Complex includes nearby log cabin, moved to this location as a reminder of Finnish and Swedish contributions to our nation.

Fort Delaware State Park. *(see)* Approximately 15 miles S on Pea Patch Island, opposite Delaware City.

Grand Opera House. *818 Market St Mall. Phone 302/658-7898; 302/652-5577 (ticket box office).* (1871) Historic landmark built by Masons, this restored Victorian theater now serves as Delaware's Center for the Performing Arts, home of Opera Delaware (Nov-May) and Delaware Symphony (Sept-May). Facade is fine example of style of the Second Empire interpreted in cast iron.

Hagley Museum. *298 Buck Rd. 3 miles NW off DE 141. Phone 302/658-2400.* Old riverside stone mill buildings, one-room schoolhouse, and millwright shop highlight 19th-century explosive manufacturing and community life; 240-acre historic site of E. I. du Pont's original black powder mills, includes exhibit building with working models and dioramas, operating waterwheel, stationary steam engine, and a fully-operable 1875 machine shop. Admission includes bus ride along river for tour of 1803

Wilmington's Public Art

The Brandywine Valley, just outside Wilmington, is noted for its magnificent museums and gardens. What is often overlooked is the wealth of outdoor statuary in public squares and office courtyards in the historic heart of the old city. Much of it is representational, but there are abstract pieces and whimsical work or two. *Indeed,* a picture book describing the collection has been published for several years. On a one-hour, 1-mile walk through the city's commercial center, you can almost imagine you are in a sculpture garden. Begin at Rodney Square outside the elegant Hotel du Pont at 11th and Market streets. Dominating the view is the famous 1923 statue of Caesar Rodney, which shows him astride his horse galloping toward Philadelphia, about 30 miles north, to cast the deciding vote for the Declaration of Independence in 1776. A city hallmark, the Rodney is one of the world's rare equestrian sculptures of a horse in full gallop, its two front legs in the air and the weight of the statue resting on the two rear hooves. The challenge of balancing the statue was solved in part by weighting the horse's tail. Head north on Market Street to 13th Street and two blocks west (left) to Orange Street to the Brandywine Gateway, where you'll see the intriguing kinetic fountain at the foot of the Hercules Building (facing 13th Street) in Hercules Plaza. Three solid granite balls rest on three marble pillars in the middle of a large pool. The spheres are arranged so that water flowing over them suggests they are rotating. Retrace your path to 8th and Market and then turn east (left) to Spencer and Freedom plazas between French and Market streets. In Spencer Plaza, *Father and Son,* a larger-then-life bronze statue, touchingly depicts a black man with a child in his arms. It is the work of Charles Park, a local artist. A plaque notes that this was the one-time site of the Mother African Union Methodist Protestant Church, the first black church in America wholly controlled by descendants of Africans. Just across French Street in Freedom Plaza, in the shadow of a cluster of modern municipal buildings, is an arresting statue, *The Holocaust.* Both abstract and realistic, it shows the tortured bodies of the victims pressed against three unyielding pillars, a symbol of the force of destruction. On a more positive note, end your tour at the plaque honoring abolitionist Harriet Tubman and Thomas Garrett and the Underground Railroad, the road north to freedom for Southern slaves before the Civil War.

Eleutherian Mills, residence with antiques reflecting five generations of du Ponts, a 19th-century garden, and a barn with a collection of antique wagons. Museum store. (Mid-Mar-Dec, daily; rest of year, Sat and Sun, limited hours Mon-Fri; closed holidays) **$$$$**

Holy Trinity (Old Swedes) Church and Hendrickson House. *606 Church St. Phone 302/652-5629.* Founded by Swedish settlers in 1698, the church stands as originally built and still has regular services. The house, a Swedish farmhouse built in 1690, is now a museum containing 17th- and 18th-century artifacts. (Mon-Sat; closed holidays) **DONATION.**

Nemours Mansion and Gardens. *1600 Rockland Rd. Rockland Rd between DE 141 and US 202. Phone 302/651-6912.* Country estate (300 acres) of Alfred I. du Pont. Mansion (1910) is modified Louis XVI, by Carrère and Hastings, with 102 rooms of rare antique furniture, Asian rugs, tapestries, and paintings dating from 12th century. Formal French gardens extend 1/3 of a mile along main vista from house with terraces, statuary, and pools. Tours (May-Nov, Tues-Sun; reservations required) Over 16 years only. **$$$**

Rockwood Museum. *610 Shipley Rd. Phone 302/761-4340.* A 19th-century Gothic Revival estate with gardens in English Romantic style. On grounds are manor house, conservatory, porter's lodge, and other outbuildings. Museum furnished with English, European, and American decorative arts of the 17th-19th centuries. Guided tours (Mar-Dec, Tues-Sun; Jan and Feb, Tues-Sat). (See SPECIAL EVENTS) **$$**

Willingtown Square. *505 N Market St Mall. Phone 302/655-7161.* Historic square surrounded by four 18th-century houses moved to this location between 1973-1976. Serves as office and conference space.

Wilmington & Western Railroad. *1601 Railroad Ave. 4 miles SW, near junction DE 2 and DE 41 at Greenbank Station. Phone 302/998-1930.* Round-trip steam-train ride (9 miles) to and from Mount Cuba picnic grove. (May-Oct, Sun; rest of year, schedule varies) **$$$**

Winterthur Museum, Garden, and Library. *6 miles NW on DE 52. Phone 302/888-4907 or 800/448-3883.* Henry Francis du Pont established this world-class antiques museum, naturalistic garden, and Americana library on a 979-acre grand country estate in the early 1950s. Inspiring period rooms showcase thousands of objects made or used in America between 1640 and 1860, ranging from historic clothing and craftsmen's tools to metalworks, ceramics, and paintings. On the grounds are rolling hills, streams, meadows, and forests and a garden that blooms from late January to November. Cooks will enjoy demonstrations of open-hearth cooking and kitchen gardening. Little ones can ride a garden tram or gently finger growing things in a fairy-tale garden or the Enchanted Woods. Walkers can stroll on gentle paths, and history buffs will enjoy African-American history presentations as well as the thousands of exquisite collectibles. (Tues-Sun; closed Jan, Feb, Easter, July 4, Thanksgiving, Dec 24-25) **$$$**

Special Events

Harvest Moon Festival. *3511 Barley Mill Rd. 3 miles NW via US 41, at Ashland Nature Center in Hockessin. Phone 302/239-2334.* Cider-pressing demonstrations, hay rides, nature walks, farm animals, arts and crafts, musical entertainment, pony rides, games. First weekend in Oct.

Horse racing. Delaware Park. *777 Delaware Park Blvd. 7 miles S on I-95 exit 4 B. Phone 302/994-2521.* Thoroughbred racing. Late-Apr-mid-Nov.

Victorian Ice Cream Festival. *Rockwood Museum. 610 Shipley Rd. Phone 302/761-4340.* Victorian festival featuring high-wheeled bicycles, hot-air balloons, marionettes, old-fashioned medicine show, baby parade, crafts; homemade ice cream. Mid-July.

Wilmington Garden Day. *Phone 302/428-6172.* Tour of famous gardens and houses. First Sat in May.

Winterthur Point-to-Point Races. *Phone 302/888-4600.* May.

Motels/Motor Lodges

★ **BEST WESTERN BRANDYWINE VALLEY INN.** *1807 Concord Pike (19803). Phone 302/656-9436; toll-free 800/537-7772; fax 302/656-8564. www.bestwestern.com.* 95 rooms, 12 kitchen units, 2 story. S $77; D $97; each additional $5; kitchen suites $110; under 18 free. Pet accepted. Check-out noon. TV; cable (premium), VCR available. In-room modem link. Exercise equipment. Pool, children's pool, whirlpool. Cr cds: A, C, D, DS, MC, V.

D 🐾 ⤢ 🏃 🏊

★★ **COURTYARD BY MARRIOTT.** *1102 West St (19801). Phone 302/429-7600; fax 302/429-9167. www.courtyard.com.* 126 rooms, 10 story. S $139-$170; D $149-$180; each additional $10; weekend rates. Crib free. Check-out noon. TV; cable (premium). In-room modem link. Refrigerators; some in-room whirlpools; microwaves available. Coffee in rooms. Guest laundry. Health club privileges. Exercise equipment. Garage $8.50; free Fri, Sat. Airport transportation. Business services available. Cr cds: A, C, D, DS, JCB, MC, V.

D 🏃 🏊

★★ **HOLIDAY INN.** *4000 Concord Pike (19803). Phone 302/478-2222; toll-free 800/465-4329; fax 302/479-0850. www.holiday-inn.com.* 138 rooms, 2 story. S, D $99; each additional $6; under 18 free; weekend rates. Crib free. TV; cable (premium). Pool; lifeguard. Coffee in rooms. Restaurant 7 am-10 pm. Room service. Bar 4 pm-midnight. Check-out noon. Coin laundry. Meeting rooms. Business services available. In-room modem link. Bellstaff. Sundries. Health club privileges. Cr cds: A, C, D, DS, JCB, MC, V.

D ⤢ 🏊 SC

Hotels

★★ **BRANDYWINE SUITES HOTEL.** *707 N King St (19801). Phone 302/656-9300; toll-free 800/756-0070; fax 302/656-2459.* Located in the heart of Wilmington, this small, luxurious European-style hotel offers intimate attention to visitors. Guest suites are comfortable and spacious. 49 suites, 4 story. D $129-$169; under 12 free; weekend rates. Complimentary continental breakfast. Check-out noon, check-in 3 pm. TV; cable (premium), VCR available (movies). In-room modem link. Restaurant 6:30-8:30 am, 11:30 am-2 pm, 5-10 pm; Sat, Sun 8-10 am, 5-10 pm. Bar 2-10 pm. Parking. Free airport transportation. Cr cds: A, C, D, DS, MC, V.

D 🏊 SC

★★ **DOUBLETREE HOTEL.** *4727 Concord Pike (19803). Phone 302/478-6000; toll-free 800/333-3333; fax 302/477-1492. www.doubletree.com.* 154 rooms, 7 story. S, D $129-$189; each additional $10; suites $189-$229; under 18 free. Crib $10. TV; cable (premium), VCR available (movies). Pool. Restaurant 6:30 am-10 pm. Bar 5-11 pm. Check-out noon. Meeting rooms. Business services available. In-room modem link. Exercise equipment. Health club privileges. Some refrigerators. Cr cds: A, C, D, DS, ER, JCB, MC, V.

D ⤢ 🏃 🏊 SC

★★★ **HOLIDAY INN.** *630 Naamans Rd, Claymont (19703). Phone 302/792-2700; fax 302/798-6182. www.holiday-inn.com.* Conveniently located just minutes from the airport, this hotel has large, stylish guest suites in a comfortable setting. 193 rooms, 7 story. S, D $99-$136; each additional $15; suites $150-$275; under 12 free; weekend rates. Pet accepted; $60. TV; cable (premium). Pool. Playground. Coffee in rooms. Restaurant 6:30 am-2 pm, 4:30-11 pm. Bar 3:30 pm-1 am. Check-out noon. Meeting rooms. Business services available. In-room modem link. Valet service. Free airport transportation. Exercise equipment. Some refrigerators; microwaves available. Cr cds: A, C, D, DS, JCB, MC, V.

D 🐾 ⤢ 🏃 🏊 SC

★★★ **HOTEL DU PONT.** *11th and Market sts (19801). Phone 302/594-3100; toll-free 800/441-9019; fax 302/594-3108. www.hoteldupont.com.* The Hotel du

Pont has been a Delaware institution since its opening in 1913. Constructed to rival the grand hotels of Europe, this palatial hotel carries a distinguished air. Located in downtown Wilmington, the hotel enjoys proximity to the city's attractions while remaining in the heart of the scenic Brandywine Valley, where championship golf and estate tours are de rigueur. Luxury is in the details here, from the ornate plasterwork to the gleaming brass. The guest rooms are classically decorated with mahogany furnishings, cream tones, and imported linens. Patrons dine on sublime French cuisine while listening to the gentle strains of a harp at the Green Room. From its coffered ceiling to its oak-paneled walls, its turn-of-the-century décor is the height of elegance. The Brandywine Room offers a delightful change of pace, with its inviting ambience resembling a private club and its contemporary American fare. 217 rooms, 10 story. Pet accepted. Check-out noon, check-in 3 pm. TV; cable (premium), VCR available. In-room modem link. Room service 24 hours. Restaurant. Bar; entertainment. Babysitting services available. In-house fitness room, massage, sauna. Valet parking. Airport transportation. Business center. Concierge. Cr cds: A, C, D, DS, ER, JCB, MC, V. **$$**

★ ★ ★ **SHERATON SUITES WILMINGTON.** *422 Delaware Ave (19801). Phone 302/654-8300; fax 302/654-6036. www.sheraton.com.* 228 suites, 16 story. D $89-$260; each additional $15; under 18 free; weekend rates. Check-out noon, check-in 3 pm. TV; cable (premium), VCR available. In-room modem link. Laundry services. Restaurant 6:30-10 am, 11:30 am-10:30 pm; Sun 7 am-10:30 pm. Bar. Health club privileges. Exercise equipment, sauna. Indoor pool. Airport transportation. Business center. Cr cds: A, C, D, DS, ER, JCB, MC, V.

★ ★ ★ **WYNDHAM WILMINGTON HOTEL.** *700 King St (33140). Phone 302/655-0400; toll-free 800/wyndham; fax 302/655-0430. www.wyndham.com.* 219 rooms, 9 story. S, D $79-$199 under 17 free. Suites $89-$189. Check-out noon, check-in 3 pm. TV; cable (premium). In-room modem link. Restaurant 6:30 am-10 pm. Bar to midnight. Exercise equipment. Pool, whirlpool. Business center. Concierge. Cr cds: A, C, D, DS, ER, JCB, MC, V.

B&B/Small Inns

★ ★ ★ **THE BOULEVARD BED AND BREAKFAST.** *1909 Baynard Blvd (19802). Phone 302/656-9700; fax 302/656-9701.* This red brick inn, built in 1913, provides relaxation and comfort with its guest accommodations. Wake up to a delicious breakfast that might include

lemon pancakes with raspberry syrup, or enjoy mulled apple cider in the afternoon. 6 rooms, 2 share bath, 3 story. S $65-$80; D $70-$85; each additional $10-$15; holiday weekends (2-day minimum). TV; cable (premium), VCR (free movies). Complimentary full breakfast. Check-out 11 am, check-in 2 pm. Business services available. In-room modem link. Antiques. Cr cds: A, MC, V.

★ ★ ★ **DARLEY MANOR INN.** *3701 Philadelphia Pike, Claymont (19703). Phone 302/792-2127; toll-free 800/824-4703; fax 302/798-6143. www.darinn.com.* Visitors will appreciate this beautiful bed-and-breakfast set in the quiet countryside of Wilmington. It offers an intimate setting. 6 rooms, 3 story. No elevator. Children over 6 years only. Complimentary full breakfast. Check-out noon, check-in 4 pm. TV; cable; VCR. Exercise equipment. Totally nonsmoking. Cr cds: A, C, D, DS, MC, V. **$**

★ ★ ★ ★ **INN AT MONTCHANIN VILLAGE.** *Rte 100 and Kirk Rd, Montchanin (19710). Phone 302/888-2133; toll-free 800/269-2473; fax 302/888-0389. www.montchanin.com.* Experience the charm of a 19th-century hamlet while staying at The Inn at Montchanin Village in Delaware's historic Brandywine Valley. Once part of the Winterthur Estate and located on the National Register of Historic Places, the inn endears itself to visitors with its white picket fence, winding walkways, and country sensibilities. This winsome inn is a perfect base for travelers perusing nearby antique stores, enjoying scenic country drives, or admiring the glorious blooms at Longwood Garden. The warm innkeepers pay meticulous attention to detail, incorporating luxurious amenities while maintaining the integrity of this quaint village. Four-poster and canopy beds set a romantic tone, while marble bathrooms add a sophisticated element to the lovely guest rooms. Gourmets cross state lines just for a meal at Krazy Kat's (see also), where refined nouvelle cuisine takes on the tranquil countryside. 28 rooms, 1-3 story. Check-out 11 am, check-in 3 pm. TV; VCR available. In-room modem link. Fireplaces. Restaurant. Room service. Babysitting services available. In-house fitness room, health club privileges. Concierge. Totally nonsmoking. Cr cds: A, C, D, DS, MC, V. **$$**

Restaurants

★ ★ ★ **BACK BURNER.** *425 Hockessin Corner, Hockessin (19707). Phone 302/239-2314; fax 302/234-3212. www.backburner.com.* Enjoy intimate conversation at this darkly lit restaurant converted from an old barn. Hours: 11:15 am-2:15 pm, 5-9 pm; Fri, Sat 11:15 am-2:15 pm, 5:30-9:45 pm. Closed Sun; Jan. 1, Dec 25. Lunch

$6-$12, dinner $13-$25. Bar. Elegeant dining in country atmosphere; renovated barn with arched walls, display kitchen. Reservations required. Cr cds: A, C, D, DS, ER, MC, V.

[D]

★ ★ ★ **BISTRO 1717.** *1717 Delaware Ave (19806). Phone 302/777-0464; fax 302/777-3477. www.blacktrumpet bistro.baweb.com.* A sister operation of chef/owner Karen Boyd's Black Trumpet Bistro, this slightly more casual spot offers creative salads, sandwiches, entrees, and house-made desserts. The Trolley Square location has a relaxed, urban atmosphere and offers take-out for diners on the run. Small French bistro. Hours: 11:30 am-10 pm. Closed Sun. Lunch, dinner $5.50-$21. Entertainment: guitarist Mon-Thurs. Cr cds: A, MC, V.

[D] [⬛]

★ ★ **BRANDYWINE ROOM.** *11th and Market Sts (19801). Phone 302/594-3156; fax 302/594-3070. www.hoteldupont.com.* American menu. Hours: 6-11 pm; Sun 5-10 pm. Closed Fri, Sat. Dinner $21-$31. Bar. Casual attire. Reservations accepted. Cr cds: A, C, D, DS, ER, JCB, MC, V.

[D]

★ ★ ★ **COLUMBUS INN.** *2216 Pennsylvania Ave (19806). Phone 302/571-1492; fax 302/571-1111. www.columbusinn.com.* This charming restaurant attracts an eclectic crowd with cuisine that has a flavorful twist. American menu. Hours: 11 am-11 pm; Fri, Sat to midnight. Closed Memorial Day, Labor Day, Dec 25. Dinner $19.50-$36.95. Bar. Entertainment Fri, Sat. Children's menu. Early American décor in 200-year-old house. Casual attire. Reservations accepted. Valet parking. Outdoor seating. Cr cds: A, C, D, DS, ER, MC, V.

[D]

★ ★ ★ **GREEN ROOM.** *11th and Market sts (19801). Phone 302/594-3154; toll-free 800/441-9019; fax 302/594-3070. www.hoteldupont.com.* As this restaurant is upscale and expensive, patrons are expected to play the part with proper attire. The menu offers a variety of selections with a Continental flare. Also good for its live entertainment. French menu. Breakfast, lunch, dinner, Sun brunch. Bar. Live music. Children's menu. Jacket required (dinner). Valet parking available. Cr cds: A, D, DS, ER, JCB, MC, V. **$$$**

[D]

★ ★ ★ **HARRY'S SAVOY GRILL.** *2020 Naaman's Rd (19810). Phone 302/475-3000; fax 302/475-9990. www.harrys-savoy.com.* The atmosphere is warm and inviting for all. Seafood menu. Hours: 11 am-10:30 pm; Fri to 11:30 pm; Sat 4:30-11:30 pm; Sun 4-10:30 pm; Sun brunch 10:30 am-3 pm; early-bird dinner Mon-Fri to 6 pm. Closed Dec 25. Sun brunch $7.95-$14.95. Bar to

1 am. Children's menu. Reservations accepted. Outdoor seating. Cr cds: A, D, DS, MC, V.

[D] [⬛]

★ ★ **J G COOK'S RIVERVIEW INN.** *60 Main St, Pennsville (08070). Phone 856/678-3700; fax 856/678-2087. www.riverviewinn.net.* Closed Mon; Jan 1, Dec 25. Lunch, dinner. Bar. Children's menu. Outdoor seating. Cr cds: A, D, DS, MC, V. **$$$**

[D] [⬛]

★ **KID SHELLEENS.** *1801 W 14th St (19806). Phone 302/658-4600; fax 302/658-7910. www.kidshelleens.com.* American menu. Hours: 11 am-midnight; Sun brunch 10 am-2 pm. Closed Thanksgiving, Dec 25. Dinner $8.95-$18.95. Bar. Children's menu. Casual atmosphere, attire. Outdoor seating. Cr cds: A, DS, MC, V.

[D]

★ ★ ★ **KRAZY KAT'S.** *Rte 100 and Kirk Rd, Montchanin (19710). Phone 302/888-2133; toll-free 800/269-2473; fax 302/888-0389. www.montchanin.com.* Serving bold yet refined French-Asian cuisine, Krazy Kat's is set in a romantic 19th-century blacksmith's shop neighboring the charming and historic Inn at Montchanin Village (see also INN AT MONTCHANIN VILLAGE). With its wild, whimsical animal-themed décor (the seats are covered in plush zebra and leopard prints), you may not know what to expect. But the food here is phenomenal and far from silly—although it will make you smile because the plates are truly exquisite. The kitchen's inventive menu includes signatures like grilled wild boar tenderloin satay with ginger jus, sesame-roasted fingerling potatoes, and red cabbage daikon slaw—a robust warmer for a cold winter's night. Fresh seafood, seasonal salads, organic chicken, filet mignon, and Muscovy duck are also on the menu, each perfectly prepared in French style and gently accented with Asian flavors. The wine list is extensive and spans the globe, from America's Northwest to Italy, France, Australia, and New Zealand. Breakfast, lunch, dinner. Jacket required. Outdoor seating. Totally nonsmoking. Cr cds: A, D, DS, MC, V. **$$$**

[D] [⬛]

★ ★ ★ **PICCOLO MONDO.** *3604 Silverside Rd (19810). Phone 302/478-9028; fax 302/478-9028.* Hours: 11:30 am-2 pm, 5-10 pm; Sat from 5 pm. Closed Sun; most major holidays. Reservations accepted. Italian menu. Bar. Wine list. A la carte entrées: lunch $6-$9, dinner $10-$18. Specialties: risotto primavera, grilled shrimp on rosemary branch, cannelloni con frutti di mare. Own pastries. Italian décor with open hearth kitchen; wine bottles displayed. Cr cds: A, C, D, DS, ER, MC, V.

[D]

★ ★ ★ **RESTAURANT 821.** *821 Market St (19801). Phone 302/652-8821; fax 302/652-4481. www.restaurant821.com.* Located directly across from Wilmington's historic opera house, this is the perfect spot for taking in dinner before or after a show. The atmosphere is sophisticated and the American menu with international accents has many excellent choices. Specializes in braised short ribs, iron skillet monk fish. Hours: 11:30 am-10 pm; Fri to 10:30 pm; Sat 5-11 pm. Closed Sun. Reservations accepted. Wine, beer. Lunch $9-$16; dinner $20-$32. Entertainment. Cr cds: A, C, D, DS, MC, V.

[D] [⊠]

★ ★ ★ **TOSCANA KITCHEN AND BAR.** *1412 N DuPont St (19806). Phone 302/654-8001; fax 302/655-8090. www.toscanakitchen.com.* This is a favorite for private and intimate parties. Italian menu. Hours: 11:30 am-2 pm, 5:30-10 pm; Sun 5:30-9:30 pm. Closed major holidays. Dinner $12-$24. Bar. Casual attire. Reservations required weekends. Cr cds: A, D, DS, MC, V.

[D]

★ ★ ★ **VINCENTE'S.** *1601 Concord Pike (19803). Phone 302/652-5142; fax 302/652-0514.* With a variety of creative menu items, this upscale but casual restaurant is always superb and diners will leave with a happy palette. French, Italian menu. Hours: 11 am-10 pm; Sat from 4 pm. Closed Sun; most major holidays. Dinner $12.95-$36.95. Bar. Children's menu. Casual attire. Reservations required weekends. Cr cds: A, C, D, DS, ER, MC, V.

[D]

★ ★ ★ **ZANZIBAR BLUE.** *1000 West St (19801). Phone 302/472-7000; fax 302/472-7002. www.zanzibarblue .com.* Eclectic menu. Lunch, dinner, Sun brunch. Bar. Credit cards accepted. **$$$**

[D]

Maryland

Maryland prides itself on its varied terrain and diverse economy. Metropolitan life around the great cities of Baltimore and Washington, D.C. (the land was ceded from Maryland in 1791) is balanced by the rural atmosphere in central and southern Maryland and on the Eastern Shore, across the Chesapeake Bay. Green mountains in the western counties contrast with white Atlantic beaches. A flourishing travel industry, agricultural and dairy wealth in central Maryland, the seafood industry of the Bay and its tidal rivers, manufacturing and commerce in the cities, plus federal government and defense contracts combine to make the state prosperous.

Population: 5,296,486
Area: 9,838 square miles
Elevation: 0-3,360 feet
Peak: Backbone Mountain (Garrett County)
Entered Union: Seventh of original 13 states (April 28, 1788)
Capital: Annapolis
Motto: Manly deeds, womanly words
Nickname: Old Line State, Free State
Flower: Black-Eyed Susan
Bird: Baltimore Oriole
Tree: White Oak
Fair: August-September in Timonium (see Towson)
Time Zone: Eastern
Website: www.mdisfun.org

Maryland's 3 1/2 centuries of history began in March 1634 when Lord Baltimore's brother, Leonard Calvert, solemnly knelt on tiny St. Clements Island, near the wide mouth of the Potomac, and named his new province in honor of Henrietta Maria, wife of Charles I, King of England. Calvert's awkward little ships, the *Ark* and the *Dove*, then carried the 222 passengers, including religious refugees, to a Native American village a few miles away. They purchased the village and named it Saint Maries Citty (now St. Mary's City). Religious tolerance was practiced from the colony's founding and was assured by law in 1649. The land was cleared, tobacco was planted, and over the years, profits built elegant mansions, many of which still stand.

Maryland was one of the 13 original colonies. Its first capital was St. Mary's City. In 1694, the capital was transferred to Annapolis, where it remains today.

Every war waged on US soil has seen major action by Marylanders. In 1755, British General Edward Braddock, assisted by Lieutenant Colonel George Washington, trained his army at Cumberland for the fight against the French and Indians. In the Revolution, General William Howe invaded Maryland at the head of Chesapeake Bay, and a battle was joined at Brandywine Creek in Pennsylvania before the British moved on to capture Philadelphia. Maryland troops in the Battle of Long Island made a heroic bayonet coverage of the retreat. The courageous action of the "Old Line" gave the state one of its nicknames. The War of 1812 saw Fort McHenry at Baltimore withstand attack by land and sea, with the action immortalized in the national anthem by Francis Scott Key, a Frederick lawyer. In the Civil War, Maryland was a major battleground at Antietam; troops moved back and forth through the state for the four bloody years of destruction.

A border state with commercial characteristics of both North and South, Maryland found its original dependence on tobacco relieved by the emerging Industrial Revolution. Modern factories, mills, and ironworks around Baltimore became important to the state's economy. Educational institutions were established and the port of Baltimore, at the mouth of the Patapsco River, flourished. In the mid-19th century, with the Baltimore & Ohio Railroad and the Chesapeake & Ohio Canal carrying freight to the fast-developing western states, Maryland thrived.

Sports enthusiasts have always thought well of Maryland. The state's thousands of miles of tidal shoreline allow plenty of elbow room for aquatic

Calendar Highlights

FEBRUARY

National Outdoor Show *(Cambridge). Phone 800/ 522-TOUR.* Goose and duck calling, log sawing, crab picking, trap setting contests; entertainment.

APRIL

Point-to-Point Steeplechase *(Cockeysville). Phone 410/557-9466.* Three well-known meets on consecutive weekends—My Lady's Manor, Grand National, and Maryland Hunt Cup.

MAY

Maryland Preakness Celebration *(Baltimore). Phone 410/837-3030.* Statewide festival; events include hot-air balloon festival, parade, steeplechase, celebrity golf tournament, block parties, and schooner race.

Mid-Atlantic Maritime Festival *(St. Michaels). Chesapeake Bay Maritime Museum. Phone 410/745-2916.* Nautical celebration with fly-fishing demonstration, skipjack races, boat building contest, boat parade, seafood festival, cooking contest.

AUGUST

Montgomery County Agricultural Fair *(Gaithersburg). Phone 301/926-3100.* One of the East Coast's leading county fairs; emphasis on agriculture, 4-H activities; animal exhibits, home arts; antique farm equipment; tractor pull, horse pull, demolition derby; rodeo; entertainment.

State Fair *(Towson). Timonium Fairgrounds. Phone 410/252-0200.* Ten-day festival of home arts; entertainment, midway; agricultural demonstrations, thoroughbred horse racing, livestock presentations.

SEPTEMBER

New Market Days *(Frederick). In New Market. Phone 301/831-6755.* Nostalgic revival of the atmosphere of a 19th-century village; costumed guides, period crafts, and events held in the "Antiques Capital of Maryland."

OCTOBER

St Mary's County Oyster Festival *(Leonardtown). County Fairgrounds. Phone 301/863-5015.* National oyster shucking contests; oyster cook-off, seafood and crafts.

Autumn Glory Festival *(Oakland). Phone 301/387-4386.* Celebrates fall foliage. Features arts and crafts, 5-string banjo contest, state fiddle contest, western Maryland tournament of bands, parades, antique show.

NOVEMBER

Annapolis by Candlelight *(Annapolis). For information, contact Historic Annapolis Foundation, 800-603-4020.*

---

diversion. Maryland's race tracks include Pimlico (see BALTIMORE), featuring the nationally known Preakness Stakes, and Laurel. The "Maryland Million" is held alternately at Laurel and Pimlico. Deer hunting is allowed in most counties and goose hunting on the Eastern Shore. Historical sites cover the landscape, and more are constantly being opened up to the public by the state and National Park Service. Highways are good; reaching places in the Baltimore-Washington, D.C., area is simplified by direct, high-speed, four-lane highways constructed around, between, and radiating from these cities.

When to Go/Climate

Spring and autumn are popular times to visit Maryland. Winter weather is unpredictable and summers can be hot and humid.

AVERAGE HIGH/LOW TEMPERATURES (°F)

Baltimore

Jan 40/23	**May** 74/53	**Sept** 79/58
Feb 44/26	**June** 83/62	**Oct** 67/46
Mar 54/34	**July** 87/67	**Nov** 57/37
Apr 64/43	**Aug** 85/66	**Dec** 42/28

Parks and Recreation

Water-related activities, hiking, riding, various other sports, picnicking and visitor centers, as well as camping, are available in many state parks. Most state-maintained areas have small charges for parking and special services. Camping: $2-$22/site/night; stays limited to 2 weeks; most areas are open late Mar-early Dec, but season varies from one park to the next; check-out 3 pm; reservations for a stay of 1 week are available at Assateague—they may be obtained by writing directly to the park (see OCEAN CITY). Pets allowed at the following parks (some special restrictions may apply; phone ahead): Green Ridge Forest, Elk Neck, Patapsco (Hollofield), Point Lookout, Rocky Gap, Savage River Forest, Susquehanna, Swallow Falls, Garrett Forest, Potomac Forest, and Pocomoke River (Milburn Landing). Day use: 8 am-sunset; closed Dec 25; fee Mar-Oct. For complete information, including information on cabins, contact the Maryland Department of Natural Resources, State Forest and Park Service, Tawes State Office Building E-3, 580 Taylor Ave, Annapolis 21401; 888/432-2267 or 800/830-3974. It is advisable to call parks before visiting, as some may be closed during the off-season.

FISHING AND HUNTING

Nontidal, nonresident fishing license, $20; 5-day, $7; trout stamp, $5. Chesapeake Bay nonresident fishing license, $12; 5-day, $4.

Nonresident hunting licenses: consolidated, $86-$135, depending on state of residence; 3-day, $35; waterfowl stamp $6; regular deer stamp, $9.50; bow hunting deer stamp, $3.50; black powder deer stamp, $3.50; 2nd deer stamp, $10. For latest information, including *Maryland Sportfishing Guide* or the *Guide to Hunting, Trapping in Maryland,* contact Maryland Department of Natural Resources, Licensing & Registration Service, 580 Taylor Ave B-1, Annapolis 21404-1869. Phone 410/260-8200.

Driving Information

Safety belts are mandatory for driver and passengers in front seat of vehicle. Children 10 years and under must be in approved passenger restraints anywhere in the vehicle. Children under 4 years or weighing 40 pounds or less must be in approved safety seats. Phone 410/486-3101.

INTERSTATE HIGHWAY SYSTEM

The following alphabetical listing of Maryland towns in this book shows that these cities are within 10 miles of the indicated Interstate highways. Check a highway map for the nearest exit.

Highway Number	Cities/Towns within 10 Miles
Interstate 68	Cumberland.
Interstate 70	Baltimore, Columbia, Ellicott City, Frederick, Hagerstown.
Interstate 81	Hagerstown.
Interstate 83	Baltimore, Cockeysville, Towson.
Interstate 95	Aberdeen, Baltimore, College Park, Elkton, Havre de Grace, Laurel, Silver Spring, Towson.

Additional Visitor Information

The Maryland guide to travel, *Destination Maryland*, and a calendar of events can be obtained from the Maryland Office of Tourism Development, 217 E Redwood St, Baltimore 21202. Phone 800/543-1036.

There are several visitor information centers in Maryland; visitors who stop by will find information and brochures helpful in planning stops at points of interest. Their locations are as follows: on I-95 (N and S) near Laurel; on I-70 (E and W) between Hagerstown and Frederick; on US 15 S at Emmitsburg; on I-95 S near North East; on US 48 E near Friendsville; on US 13 N near Maryland-Virginia line; in the State House, Annapolis; Crain memorial, on US 301 N, Newburg; and in Bay Country, on US 301 N/S, Centreville. (Daily; closed holidays)

EASTERN SHORE OF THE CHESAPEAKE BAY

North America's largest estuary, the Chesapeake Bay commands more than 4,500 miles of shoreline, much of it in Maryland. A vast sea known for its rich history and savory shellfish, it is one of the Mid-Atlantic's most popular destinations. Inviting inns, other lodgings, and fine seafood restaurants are plentiful on Maryland's Eastern Shore. A two-day driving tour covering about 250 miles makes a fine introduction to the bay and to the watermen and their families who harvest the seafood that appears on every menu. Begin your drive in Annapolis, Maryland's beautiful old capital, which doubles as the bay's sailing headquarters. In summer, catch the regular Wednesday evening races, when as many as 100 boats may compete. The finish is easily visible from City Dock at the foot of the city's colonial-era streets. From Annapolis, take US 50 east across the soaring Chesapeake Bay Bridge. Just before you reach the bridge, a five-minute detour leads to Sandy Point State Park, the only stop on this drive where you can take a dip in the bay. At the eastern end of the bridge, turn north onto US 301 to State Route 213 north to Chestertown. Founded in 1706, Chestertown is a pretty village with a collection of 18th- and 19th-century homes, several of them situated along the scenic Chester River. After browsing in the shops of High and Cross streets, take Route 20 west to Rock Hall, a sailing and charter fishing port. Retrace your path to Chestertown, and take Route 213 south to US 50 south. In Easton, take Route 33 west to the historic sailing port of St. Michaels, an inviting place to spend the night. One of the Mid-Atlantic's prettiest little towns, its lovely inns, fine restaurants, offbeat shops on Talbot Street, and expansive bay views are irresistible. So, too, are the charming little back streets, lined with lovely homes dating back to the 18th and 19th centuries. Your first stop should be the Chesapeake Bay Maritime Museum, which focuses on the Chesapeake. The museum's 18-acre harbor site features more than a dozen historic structures, including a fully restored 1879 lighthouse complete with flashing light. Stop by Waterman's Wharf, where you can try your skill at crab fishing. The Waterfowling Building displays beautifully carved duck decoys. Boat builders are often at work restoring historic bay work boats for the museum's large collection. The *Patriot*, a cruise ship departing from the museum's dock, takes visitors on a 60-minute tour up the Miles River, a bay tributary. From St. Michaels, follow Route 33 to its end at Tilghman Island, a charter fishing port. Plan on having lunch at one of its waterside seafood houses. On the return trip to St. Michaels, stop about 3 miles east of the city and take the road south (right) to Bellevue. There you can catch the little Bellevue-Oxford Ferry for a ten-minute ride across the Tred Avon River to Oxford, a sleepy pleasure boat port dating back to 1694. To stretch your legs, take a walk along The Strand, a lovely river promenade, or rent a bicycle and pedal among the quiet streets. From Oxford, return to Annapolis via Route 333 and US 50, stopping briefly in Easton to admire its attractive, colonial-looking town center and to investigate its engaging shops and galleries. **(Approximately 250 miles)**

DEEP CREEK LAKE, MARYLAND'S WESTERN PLAYGROUND

Out in Western Maryland's Garrett County, the local folks like to call massive Deep Creek Lake the state's "hidden secret." But the secret is getting out, and the massive lake has become the centerpiece for a wealth of vigorous outdoor adventures: water skiing, whitewater rafting, hiking, bank-road bicycling, kayaking, fly-fishing, canoeing, sailing, and swimming. On a drive around the lake, you can partake in as many activities as you choose—outfitters are on hand to rent all the necessary equipment—or simply enjoy the sublime mountain views. Maryland's largest fresh water lake, Deep Creek, is 12 miles long, but so etched with fingerlike coves that the shoreline stretches for 65 miles. Surrounded by the forested ridges and splashing streams of mountain wilderness, the lake, at an altitude of 2,300 feet, treats summer visitors to a cooling respite from the city. Begin this two-day, 400-mile drive in Baltimore and head west on I-70 and I-68 to exit 14 at Keysers Ridge. Take US 219 south to the Visitor Center, which is on the right just outside the village of McHenry. Plan to spend the night in one of McHenry's inns, hotels, or motels. The trip from Baltimore to McHenry is about 180 miles, a scenic ride that carries you across a series of green mountain ridges. To break up the trip, pull off I-68 at Cumberland, immediately recognizable by the castle-like spires and turrets of its courthouse and churches. George Washington is said to have assumed his first military command at Fort Cumberland, and his one-room log cabin and remnants of the fort can still be seen here. Cumberland is the terminus of the Chesapeake and Ohio Canal, which originates in Washington D.C., and you can rent a bicycle and ride along the tow path for miles. At Deep Creek Lake, follow the signs to Deep Creek Lake State Park, which maintains a nice 700-foot-long sandy swimming beach, a lovely place to relax after the trip from the city. The Discovery Center, an attractive structure of stone, wood, and soaring windows, features displays about the region's natural history and mining heritage. Ranger talks, walks, and canoe trips are offered. On the second day of your trip, take US 219 south from McHenry to the turn-off to Swallow Falls State Park. For any easy hike, follow the 11/2-mile path that scrambles in a loop past four waterfalls. At the trail head, the park has preserved a 37-acre stand of virgin hemlock and white pine estimated to be 300 years old. After 1/4 mile, Muddy Creek Falls—the state's highest at 52 feet—cascades down a staircase of rocks into a large pool. You are welcome to splash in the many pools along this trail. Next, follow signs south to the town of Oakland and then begin your scenic return to Baltimore via Route 135 northeast to US 220 north to I-68 east. Just beyond Bloomington on Route 135, make a detour left on Savage River Road. For about 51/2 miles along this road, the Savage River splashes. So narrow, mean, and harrowing is the course, say local tourism officials, that was picked as the site of the 1989 Whitewater World Championships and the 1992 US Canoe & Kayak Team Olympic Trials. A couple of suspension bridges built for the events still leap the river. While here, imagine yourself trying to negotiate a kayak through the frenzied chaos of water and rocks. Retrace your path to Route 135 northeast. About 10 miles east of Cumberland, take a break at Rocky Gap State Park, two minutes off the interstate, which tempts with a couple of fine sandy beaches in a forested mountain setting. **(Approximately 400 miles)**

Aberdeen (B-8)

Pop 13,842 **Elev** 83 ft **Area code** 410 **Zip** 21001

This is the home of the 75,000-acre Aberdeen Proving Grounds, a federal reservation along Chesapeake Bay. Various types of army materiel, ranging from gunsights to tanks, are tested under simulated combat conditions.

What to See and Do

PECO Energy Company. *4948 Conowingo Rd (21034). 7 miles NE on US 40 or I-95, then 11 miles NW on US 222 to Conowingo. Phone 410/457-5011.* Hydroelectric plant on the Susquehanna River. Limited area of plant is open for guided tours (Apr-Sept, Sat; rest of year, by appointment; closed holidays). Contact the Conowingo Information Center. **FREE** Nearby is

Recreation area. *Phone 410/457-5011.* Fourteen-mile-long man-made lake; swimming pool (fee), boating (ramps, marinas), fishing; fishermen's gallery (over 12 years only); picnicking, hiking. **FREE**

US Army Ordnance Museum. *At Aberdeen Proving Ground, off I-95 exit 85, 3 miles E on MD 22, follow signs. Phone 410/278-3602.* Tanks, artillery, self-propelled artillery, extensive small arms, and ammunition collection. (Daily; closed holidays) **FREE**

Motels/Motor Lodges

★ **DAYS INN.** *783 W Bel Air Ave (21001). Phone 410/272-8500; fax 410/272-5782. www.daysinn.com.* 49 rooms, 2 story. S $43; D $47; each additional $4; under 16 free. Crib free. Pet accepted; $5. Complimentary continental breakfast. Check-out 11 am. TV; cable (premium). Refrigerators available. Pool. Business services. Cr cds: A, C, D, DS, MC, V.

🄳 🛏 🌊 🛶

★ ★ **HOLIDAY INN.** *1007 Beards Hill Rd (21001). Phone 410/272-8100; toll-free 800/465-4329; fax 410/272-1714. www.holiday-inn.com.* 122 rooms, 5 story. S, D $95-$115; each additional $10; suites $150; kitchen units $105-$120; under 18 free; weekend rates. Pet accepted. TV; cable (premium), VCR available. Indoor pool. Restaurant 6 am-2 pm, 5-10 pm; Sat, Sun from 7 am. Bar. Check-out noon. Meeting rooms. Sundries. Exercise equipment. Health club privileges. Some refrigerators. Balconies. Cr cds: A, C, D, DS, JCB, MC, V.

🄳 🛏 🌊 🕴 🛶 🆂🅲

★ ★ **QUALITY INN.** *793 W Bel Air Ave (24382). Phone 410/272-6000; fax 410/272-2287. www.qualityinn.com.* 124 rooms, 2 story. Feb-Oct: S, D $49.95-$59.95; each additional $5; under 19 free; weekly, weekend rates; lower rates rest of year. Crib free. TV; cable (premium), VCR available. Pool; wading pool. Complimentary continental breakfast. Restaurant adjacent 6 am-2 pm, 5-10 pm. Check-out noon. Coin laundry. Meeting rooms. Business services available. Cr cds: A, C, D, DS, JCB, MC, V.

🄳 🌊 🛶 🆂🅲

Annapolis (C-7)

See also Baltimore, Baltimore/ Washington International Airport Area

Founded 1649 **Pop** 35,838 **Elev** 57 ft **Area code** 410 and 443

Information Annapolis and Anne Arundel County Conference and Visitors Bureau, 26 West St, 21401; 410/268-TOUR. Information is also available at the Visitor Information Booth located at the city dock.

Web www.visit-annapolis.org

The capital of Maryland, gracious and dignified in the Colonial tradition, Annapolis has had a rich history for more than 300 years. Planned and laid out as the provincial capital in 1695, it was the first peacetime capital of the United States (Congress met here November 26, 1783 to August 13, 1784). In 1845, the US Naval Academy was established here at the Army's Fort Severn. Town life centers on sport and commercial water-oriented activities, state government, and the academy. Every May, at commencement time, thousands of visitors throng the narrow brick streets.

> ### City Fun Facts—Annapolis
> The United States Naval Academy was founded on October 10, 1845 at Annapolis.

What to See and Do

Boat Trips. *980 Awald Rd # 202. From city dock at foot of Main St. Phone 410/268-7600, 410/269-6776 (Baltimore) or 301/261-2719 (DC).* Forty-minute narrated tours of city harbor, USNA, and Severn River aboard *Harbor Queen* (Memorial Day-Labor Day, daily); 90-minute cruises to locations aboard *Annapolitan II* and *Rebecca,* cruises to St. Michael's aboard the *Annapolitan II* (Memorial Day-Labor Day); 40-minute cruises up Spa Creek, residential areas, city harbor, and USNA aboard the *Miss Anne* and *Miss Anne II* (Memorial Day-Labor Day). Some cruises early spring and late fall, weather permitting. Fees vary.

Chesapeake Bay Bridge. *357 Pier 1 Rd (21666).* The 7 1/4-mile link of US 50 across the Bay. Toll (charged eastbound only) **$$**

History and Government in Annapolis

In the years just prior to the American Revolution, the colonial elite flocked to the bustling seaport of Annapolis, Maryland's capital on the Chesapeake Bay. This was the city's "golden age" and many, George Washington among them, were drawn by its spirited social life and elegant mansions built by wealthy tobacco planters. You can see some of the same sights Washington might have enjoyed on a one-hour, one-mile stroll through the city's well-preserved Historic District. Begin at the Visitor Center, 26 West Street, where tourist parking is available. From the center head east (left) on West Street; detour around St. Anne's Church (1859), noting its Tiffany windows; pause on School Street to view Government House, the Georgian-style Maryland Governor's residence (remodeled 1936); and then climb the stairs, as Washington surely did, to the Maryland State House on State Circle (1772), the oldest state capitol in continuous legislative use. Perched atop the city's highest hill, the State House provides a panoramic view of the bay. Inside, the Old Senate Chamber appears as it did on December 23, 1783, when Washington resigned his commission as the victorious commander of the Continental Army. At 21 State Circle, the John Shaw House (1720s) was the home of the city's premier cabinet maker, whose furniture is displayed in the State House. Continue east from State Circle on Maryland Avenue, lined with antique shops, to the Hammond-Harwood Home (1774) at No. 19. A house museum, this Georgian structure features what is considered by many to be the most beautiful doorway in America. Double back one block on Maryland Avenue, pausing briefly at the Chase-Lloyd House (1769), another elegant Georgian mansion where Francis Scott Key, author of the "Star-Spangled Banner" was married in 1802. Turn toward the harbor (left) onto Prince George Street. The William Paca House (1765) at No. 186 and its two-acre colonial garden, carefully restored for authenticity, are national treasures. Now a house museum, the Paca house was the home of Maryland's Revolutionary War governor and a signer of the Declaration of Independence. Built in the symmetrical five-part structure of the city's finest colonial homes, it is considered one of the best examples of a Georgian home in America. Neighboring Brice House (1767) at 42 East Street is another magnificent Georgian mansion built by a wealthy merchant. To conclude this tour, continue downhill on Prince George Street, and turn west (right) one block onto Randall Street to City Dark for refreshments at Middleton Tavern. Once an "Inn for Seafaring Men" it has been serving Annapolis visitors since 1754.

Chesapeake Sailing School. *7074 Bembe Beach Rd (21403). Phone 410/269-1594; 301/261-2810; toll-free 800/966-0032.* There's nothing like sun, water, and a stiff breeze for shaking off doldrums. This school offers everything from weekend sailing classes for beginners (no experience necessary) to live-aboard five-day cruises on gorgeous Chesapeake Bay, with basic and advanced instruction for individuals, families, and corporate groups. Depending on the class, you might cast off in a zippy 22-foot Tanzer or a state-of-the-art catamaran. You can also rent sailboats and go out on your own. (Apr-Oct)

Government House. *101 School St. Between State and Church cirs. Phone 410/974-3531.* (1868) This Victorian structure was remodeled in 1935 into a Georgian country house; furnishings reflect Maryland's history and culture. Tours by appointment (Jan-mid-Apr, Tues and Thurs; rest of year, Tues-Thurs). **FREE**

Hammond-Harwood House. *19 Maryland Ave, at King George St, 1 block W of US Naval Academy. Phone 410/269-1714.* (1774) Georgian house designed by William Buckland; antique furnishings; garden. Matthias Hammond, a Revolutionary patriot, was its first owner. Guided tours. (Daily; closed Jan 1, Thanksgiving, Dec 25) **$$**

Historic Annapolis Foundation. *Tours leave from museum store, 77 Main St. Phone 410/267-7619 or 410/269-0432.* Self-guided audiocassette walking tours. Includes Historic District, State House, Old Treasury, US Naval Academy, and William Paca House. (Mar-Nov, daily) **$$**

Historic Annapolis Foundation Welcome Center and Museum Store. *77 Main St. Phone 410/268-5576.* This 1815 building stands on the site of a storehouse for Revolutionary War troops that burned in 1790. Audiocassette walking tours. Products reflecting Annapolis history. (Mon-Sat, also Sun afternoons; closed Thanksgiving, Dec 25)

London Town. *839 Londontown Rd. 8 miles SE via MD 2 S, (Mayo Rd) in Edgewater. Phone 410/222-1919.* (circa 1760) Once considered a site for Maryland's capital; the only surviving structure of the Lost Town is the William Brown House, a Georgian mansion on the banks of South River. Has 8 acres of woodland gardens. Museum and garden shop; boat docking. Special events. Guided tours. (Mon-Sat, also Sun afternoon; closed holidays). **$$**

Sailing Tours. *80 Compromise St. Phone 410/263-8619.* Two-hour narrated trips through Chesapeake Bay aboard 74-foot sailing yacht *Woodwind.* (May-Sept, Tues-Sun four trips daily, Mon Sunset Sail only; Apr, Oct, Nov, schedule varies) Departs from Pusser's Landing next to City Dock. **$$$$**

Sandy Point State Park. *1100 E College Pkwy (21401). 7 miles E on US 50, at W end of Chesapeake Bay Bridge. Phone 410/974-2149.* On 786 acres. The park's location on the Atlantic Flyway makes it a fine area for bird-watching; view of Bay Bridge and oceangoing vessels. Swimming in bay at two guarded beaches, two bathhouses, surf fishing, crabbing, boating (rentals, launches); concession. Standard fees. (See SPECIAL EVENTS)

St. John's College. *College Ave. Phone 410/626-2539.* (1784) 475 students. Nonsectarian liberal arts college. This 36-acre campus, one of the oldest in the country, is a National Historic Landmark. The college succeeded King William's School, founded in 1696. George Washington's two nephews and step-grandson studied here; Francis Scott Key was an alumnus. On campus are

> **Charles Carroll, Barrister House.** *107 Duke of Gloucester St (21401). Phone 410/269-1737.* (1722) Birthplace of the author of the Maryland Bill of Rights; moved in 1955 to the campus and restored; now an administration building. Not open to the public.

> **Elizabeth Myers Mitchell Art Gallery.** *60 College Ave (21401). Phone 410/626-2556.* Displays museumquality traveling exhibitions. (Academic year, Tues-Sun) **FREE**

> **McDowell Hall.** *60 College Ave (21401).* (begun 1742, finished 1789) Named for St. John's first president; originally built as the Governor's Mansion. Lafayette was feted here in 1824. Not open to the public.

State House. *91 State Cir (21401). Phone 410/974-3400.* (1772-1779) Oldest state house in continuous legislative use in US, this was the first peacetime capitol of the US. Here in 1784, a few weeks after receiving George Washington's resignation as commander-in-chief, Congress ratified the Treaty of Paris, which officially ended the Revolutionary War. Visitors Information Center. Guide service (closed Jan 1, Thanksgiving). (Daily; closed Dec 25) **FREE**

Three Centuries Tours of Annapolis. *Morning tour leaves from Visitor Center at 26 West St; afternoon tour leaves from Visitor Information Booth on City Dock. Phone 410/263-5401, to confirm departure points and schedule.* Walking tours of US Naval Academy and Historic District conducted by guides in Colonial attire. Tour includes historic Maryland State House, St. John's College, Naval Academy Chapel, crypt of John Paul Jones, Bancroft Hall dormitory, and Armel-Leftwich Visitor Center. (Apr-Oct, daily) **$$$**

United States Naval Academy. *121 Blake Rd (21402). From Baltimore, take I-97 S or Maryland Rte 2 S for 26 miles and get off on Rowe Blvd (exit 24). Take Rowe Blvd 1.6 miles to where it dead-ends at College Ave and turn left. At the first stoplight, which is King George St, turn right. Follow King George St for 2 blocks. Enter Gate 1; visitor parking is on your right. Phone 410/263-6933.* Opened in 1845, the Naval Academy is located in Maryland's picturesque capital, Annapolis, a 30-minute drive from Baltimore. The beautiful campus sits at the edge of the Chesapeake Bay and Severn River, occupying 338 acres. Tours of the campus are available through the academy's Armel-Leftwich Visitor Center, where you can immerse yourself in naval history and life. You will see the tomb of John Paul Jones, the chapel, the midshipmen's living quarters, and the naval museum. The center also shows the orientation film *To Lead and to Serve,* exhibits the original wooden figurehead of the *Tecumseh,* and displays the Freedom 7 space capsule. If you time your visit right, you can witness the Noon Formation. During this impressive daily event, all present midshipmen gather, line up, and march in for the noon meal with military precision. Note: Access to the Academy grounds is limited. Please check the current security restrictions before planning a visit. All visitors over the age of 16 must have a valid picture ID. (Daily; closed major holidays) **$$**

William Paca Garden. *186 Prince George St (21401).* Restored 2-acre pleasure garden originally developed in 1765 by William Paca, a signer of the Declaration of Independence and governor of Maryland during the Revolutionary War. Includes waterways, formal parterres, and a garden wilderness. (Mon-Sat, also Sun afternoons; closed Thanksgiving, Dec 25) Also here is

> **William Paca House.** *186 Prince George St (21401). Phone 410/263-5553.* Paca built this five-part Georgian mansion in 1765. (Mon-Sat, also Sun afternoons; closed Thanksgiving, Dec 25) **$$$**

Special Events

Annapolis by Candlelight. *2614 Ogleton Rd. Phone 410/267-0432.* For information and reservations contact Historic Annapolis Foundation. Usually early Nov.

Chesapeake Appreciation Days. *Sandy Point State Park. 1100 E College Pkwy (21401). Phone 410/974-2149.* Skipjack sailing festival honors state's oystermen. Usually last weekend in Oct.

Christmas in Annapolis. *For free events calendar, phone 410/268-8687.* Features decorated 18th-century mansions, parade of yachts, private home tours, pub crawls, concerts, holiday meals, First Night celebration, caroling by candlelight at the State House and other events. Thanksgiving-Jan 1.

Maryland Renaissance Festival. *1821 Crownsville Rd (21401). Phone 410/266-7303.* Food, crafters, minstrels, dramatic productions. Usually last week in Aug-third weekend in Oct.

Maryland Seafood Festival. *Sandy Point State Park. 1100 E College Pkwy (21401). Phone 410/974-2149.* Food; entertainment. Usually weekend after Labor Day.

US Powerboat Show. *100 Severn Ave. Phone 410/268-8828.* Extensive in-water display of powerboats; exhibits of related marine products. Mid-Oct.

US Sailboat Show. *100 Severn Ave. Phone 410/268-8828.* Features world's largest in-water display of sailboats; exhibits of related marine products. Early-mid-Oct.

Motels/Motor Lodges

★ **BEST WESTERN ANNAPOLIS.** *2520 Riva Rd (21401). Phone 410/224-2800; fax 410/266-5539. www.bestwestern.com.* 152 rooms, 2 story. Mid-Mar-mid-Nov: S, D $59-$119; suites $119-$129; lower rates rest of year. Crib free. Complimentary continental breakfast. Check-out 11 am. TV; cable (premium). Some refrigerators. Coin laundry. Restaurant adjacent 11 am-10 pm. Bar. Health club privileges. Game room. Pool. Meeting rooms. Business services. Cr cds: A, C, D, DS, JCB, MC, V.

[D] [≈] [≝]

★ **COMFORT INN.** *76 Old Mill Bottom Rd (21401). Phone 410/757-8500; fax 410/757-4409. www.comfortinn.com.* 60 rooms, 2 story. Apr-Oct: S $65-$110; D $70-$120; each additional $5; under 18 free; lower rates rest of year. Crib free. TV; cable (premium). Pool; lifeguard. Complimentary continental breakfast. Check-out 11 am. Coin laundry. Business services available. Cr cds: A, C, D, DS, ER, JCB, MC, V.

[D] [≈] [≝] [SC]

★★ **COURTYARD BY MARRIOTT.** *2559 Riva Rd (21401). Phone 410/266-1555; toll-free 800/321-2211; fax 410/266-6376. www.courtyard.com.* 149 units, 3 story. S, D $109-$119; suites $129-$149; under 12 free. Crib free. TV; cable (premium). Indoor pool; whirlpool, lifeguard. Complimentary coffee in rooms. Restaurant 6:30 am-1:30 pm; Sat, Sun from 7 am. Bar 4-10 pm. Check-out noon. Coin laundry. Meeting rooms. Business services available. In-room modem link. Valet service. Sundries. Exercise equipment. Refrigerator in suites. Cr cds: A, C, D, DS, MC, V.

[D] [≈] [大] [≝] [SC]

Hotels

★★★ **LOEWS ANNAPOLIS HOTEL.** *126 West St (21401). Phone 410/263-7777; toll-free 800/526-2593;* *fax 410/263-0084. www.loewsannapolis.com.* Located in the heart of downtown Annapolis, this hotel is within walking distance to many of the city's historical sites. It also has 17,000 square feet of flexible meeting space that business travelers will find convenient and comfortable. 217 rooms, 6 story, 11 suites. S, D $119-$185; each additional $15; suites $185-$350; under 17 free. Crib free. Pet accepted. Check-out noon. TV; cable (premium). In-room modem link. Private patios, balconies. Refrigerators, minibars. Restaurant (See also CORINTHIAN). Bar 11-2 am. Health club privileges. Exercise equipment. Pool privileges. Barber, beauty shop. Valet parking $10. Meeting rooms. Business center. Concierge. Gift shop. Luxury level. Cr cds: A, C, D, DS, MC, V.

[D] [🏊] [≈] [大] [≝] [SC] [🏃]

★★★ **MARRIOTT ANNAPOLIS WATERFRONT.** *80 Compromise St (21401). Phone 410/268-7555; fax 410/269-5864. www.marriott.com.* With guest rooms overlooking Chesapeake Bay, this hotel is conveniently located to nearby shops and restaurants in colonial Annapolis. 150 rooms, 6 story. May-Sept: S, D $159-$269; varied rates rest of year. Crib free. Check-out 11 am. TV; cable (premium), VCR available. In-room modem link. Some balconies, in-room whirlpools; refrigerators, microwaves available. Restaurant 6:30 am-11 pm. Bar 11-2 am. Exercise equipment. Garage $12. Meeting rooms. Business services. On waterfront; 300 foot dockage. Cr cds: A, C, D, DS, ER, JCB, MC, V.

[D] [大] [≝]

★★ **RADISSON HOTEL ANNAPOLIS.** *210 Holiday Ct (21401). Phone 410/224-3150; toll-free 800/333-3333; fax 410/224-3413. www.radisson.com.* 220 rooms, 6 story. S $79-$119; D $89-$129; suites $139; under 18 free. Crib free. Pet accepted. TV; cable (premium). Pool; lifeguard. Restaurant 6:30 am-2 pm, 5-10 pm. Room service. Bar 4 pm-midnight. Check-out noon. Meeting rooms. Business services available. In-room modem link. Bellstaff. Valet service. Sundries. Health club privileges. Microwaves available. Cr cds: A, C, D, DS, ER, JCB, MC, V.

[D] [🏊] [≈] [≝] [SC]

★★★ **SHERATON BARCELO ANNAPOLIS.** *173 Jennifer Rd (21401). Phone 410/266-3131; toll-free 800/625-5144; fax 410/266-6247. www.sheraton.com.* 197 rooms, 6 story. S $89-$139; D $99-$149; each additional $10; suites $109-$209; under 18 free; holiday rates; higher rates special events. Check-out noon. TV; cable. In-room modem link. Restaurant 6:30 am-2:30 pm, 5-10 pm. Bar 4 pm-midnight. Room service 5-10 pm. Health club privileges. Exercise equipment, sauna. Indoor pool, whirlpool. Cr cds: A, C, D, DS, MC, V.

[D] [≈] [大] [≝] [SC]

B&B/Small Inns

★ ★ **CHESAPEAKE BAY LIGHTHOUSE BED AND BREAKFAST.** *1423 Sharps Point Rd (21401). Phone 410/757-0248; fax 410/757-0248.* 5 rooms, 2 story. No room phones. S, D $110-$210; each additional $10. Children over 12 only. TV in sitting room. Complimentary continental breakfast. Check-out 11 am, check-in 3-7 pm. Working lighthouse on Chesapeake Bay. Totally nonsmoking. Cr cds: DS, MC, V.

★ ★ **GIBSON'S LODGINGS.** *110 Prince George St (21401). Phone 410/268-5555; fax 410/268-2775. www.avmcyber.com/gibson.* 20 rooms, 13 share bath in 3 buildings, 3 story. Some room phones. S $58-$110; D $68-$125; each additional $15. TV in some rooms; cable, VCR available. Complimentary continental breakfast; afternoon refreshments. Check-out 11 am, check-in 2 pm. Meeting room. Business services available. Microwaves available. Antiques; library. Totally nonsmoking. Cr cds: A, MC, V.

★ ★ ★ **HISTORIC INNS OF ANNAPOLIS.** *58 State Cir (21401). Phone 410/263-2641; toll-free 800/847-8882; fax 410/268-3813.* Formerly inhabited by two Maryland governors named Calvert, this tastefully restored Colonial and Victorian residence also has a contemporary conference center. 51 rooms, 4 story. S, D $125-$175; each additional $10; suites $185-$285; under 18 free; higher rates special events. Crib free. Check-out noon, check-in 3 pm. TV; cable (premium). In-room modem link. Refrigerators, microwaves available. Health club privileges. Golf privileges. Lighted tennis privileges. Valet parking $12. Meeting rooms. Business services. 18th-century state house with modern addition; colonial gardens, atrium. Cr cds: A, C, D, DS, JCB, MC, V.

★ ★ **MARYLAND INN.** *58 State Cir (21401). Phone 410/263-2641; toll-free 800/847-8882; fax 410/268-3813.* 44 rooms, 4 story. S $105-$135; D $105-$165; each additional $10; suites $145-$260; under 18 free; higher rates special events. Crib free. Check-out noon, check-in 3 pm. TV; cable (premium). In-room modem link. Some refrigerators; microwaves available. Restaurant (See also TREATY OF PARIS). Bar; entertainment. Health club privileges. Lighted tennis, golf privileges. Valet parking $12. Business services. Historic inn built in 1772. View of bay. Cr cds: A, C, D, DS, JCB, MC, V.

★ ★ ★ **PRINCE GEORGE INN.** *232 Prince George St (21401). Phone 410/263-6418; fax 410/626-0009.*

www.princegeorgeinn.com. Step back in time at this quiet, charming bed-and-breakfast originally built in the late 1800s. With a full gourmet breakfast and intimate, antique-filled guest rooms, visitors will feel like they've been to grandma's house. 4 rooms, 2 share bath, 3 story. No room phones. S $90-$100; D $110-$115; under 8 free; weekends (2-day minimum). Parking $4. TV; cable, VCR. Complimentary full breakfast. Check-out noon, check-in 4-6 pm. Refrigerators. Victorian townhouse built in 1884. Totally nonsmoking. Cr cds: DS, MC, V.

★ ★ **ROBERT JOHNSON HOUSE.** *23 State Circle (21401). Phone 410/263-2641; toll-free 800/847-8882; fax 410/268-3613.* 29 rooms, 4 story. S $105-$135; D $105-$165; each additional $10; suites $260; under 18 free; higher rates special events. Crib free. Check-out noon, check-in 3 pm. TV; cable (premium). In-room modem link. Refrigerators, microwaves available. Health club privileges. Golf privileges. Lighted tennis privileges. Valet parking $12. Business services. Consists of 18th-century mansion plus two connecting townhouses of the same period. Cr cds: A, C, D, DS, JCB, MC, V.

★ ★ **WILLIAM PAGE INN.** *8 Martin St (21401). Phone 410/626-1506; toll-free 800/364-4160; fax 410/263-4841. www.williampageinn.com.* 5 rooms, 2 share bath, 3 story. S, D $95-$195; weekly rates. Complimentary full breakfast. Check-out noon, check-in 4-6 pm. Business services available. Former clubhouse (1908). Totally nonsmoking. Cr cds: MC, V.

Restaurants

★ ★ ★ **CAFÉ BRETTON.** *849 Baltimore-Annapolis Blvd, Severna Park (21146). Phone 410/647-8222.* Hours: 5-10 pm; early-bird dinner to 6 pm. Closed Sun, Mon; some major holidays. Reservations required Fri, Sat. French menu. Bar. Wine list. Dinner $10.95-$26.95. Specializes in lamb shank, seafood. Own baking. Country French atmosphere with original artwork. Totally nonsmoking. Cr cds: A, DS, MC, V.

★ ★ **CAFE NORMANDIE.** *185 Main St (21401). Phone 410/263-3382; fax 410/263-3566.* French, seafood menu. Breakfast, lunch, dinner. Bar. Cr cds: A, D, DS, MC, V. **$$**

★★ **CARROL'S CREEK.** *410 Severn Ave, Eastport (21403). Phone 410/263-8102; fax 410/269-7536. www. carrollscreek.com.* Seafood menu. Lunch $4.95-$9.95, dinner $14-$22. Sun brunch $16.95. Bar. Reservations required holidays. Outdoor seating. On water. Cr cds: A, DS, MC, V.
[D]

★★★ **CORINTHIAN.** *126 West St (21401). Phone 410/263-1299; fax 410/263-0084.* Located in the Loews Annapolis Hotel, this restaurant has a creative menu with tempting flavors. Hours: 6:30 am-2 pm, 5-10 pm; Sun brunch from 10 am. Reservations accepted Sat. Bar. Wine list. Breakfast $6.50-$14.95, lunch $6.95-$15.95, dinner $18.95-$28.95. Sun brunch $22. Children's menu. Specializes in fresh seafood, prime beef. Valet parking. Elegant atmosphere. Cr cds: A, D, DS, MC, V.
[D] [SC]

★★ **FRED'S.** *2348 Solomon's Island Rd (21401). Phone 410/224-2386; fax 410/224-2539.* Hours: 11 am-10 pm; Fri, Sat to 11 pm; early-bird dinner Mon-Fri 4-6 pm, Sat, Sun noon-6 pm. Closed Thanksgiving, Dec 25. Reservations accepted. Continental menu. Bar. Lunch $4.50-$8.95, dinner $9.95-$33.95. Children's menu. Specializes in seafood, steak, Italian dishes. Victorian décor; antiques. Family-owned. Cr cds: A, D, MC, V.
[D]

★★ **GRIFFIN'S.** *22 Market Space (21401). Phone 410/268-2576; fax 410/280-0195. www.griffins-citydock.com.* Hours: 11 am-midnight; Fri, Sat to 1 am; Sun brunch 11 am-1 pm. Closed Dec 25. Reservations accepted Mon-Thurs. Bar to 1:30 am. Lunch $6.95-$8.95, dinner $8.95-$12.95. Sun brunch $6.95-$9.95. Children's menu. Specializes in seafood, steak, pasta. Own desserts. Cr cds: A, C, D, DS, ER, MC, V.
[D]

★★★ **HARRY BROWNE'S.** *66 State Cir (21401). Phone 410/263-4332; fax 410/263-8049. www. harrybrownes.com.* Known as one of the best upscale restaurants in town, it overlooks the Maryland State House in downtown Annapolis. The fare is consistently good, the ambiance inviting, and service pleasurable. Continental menu. Hours: 11 am-3 pm, 5:30-10 pm; weekends to 11 pm. Closed Jan 1, Dec 25. Lunch $6.95-$12, dinner $17-$22. Bar. Entertainment Mon, Fri, Sat. Reservations accepted. Valet parking Fri, Sat. Cr cds: A, DS, MC, V.
[D]

★★ **LEWNES' STEAKHOUSE.** *401 4th St (21403). Phone 410/263-1617. www.lewnessteakhouse.com.* Specializes in prime steak, seafood. 1950s steakhouse atmosphere; casual fine dining. Hours: 5-10 pm; Fri, Sat to 10:30 pm. Closed Thanksgiving, Dec 25. A la carte

entrees: dinner $18-$29. Bar. Reservations required. Cr cds: D, MC, V.
[D]

★★ **MIDDLETON TAVERN.** *2 Market Space (21401). Phone 410/263-3323; fax 410/263-3807. www.middletontavern.com.* Specializes in seafood, crab dishes. Hours: 11:30-2 am; Sat, Sun from 10 am. Lunch $5.95-$20, dinner $15.95-$29.95. Bar. Entertainment. Restored building (1750), traditional tavern décor. Outdoor seating. Cr cds: A, DS, MC, V.

★★★ **NORTHWOODS.** *609 Melvin Ave (21401). Phone 410/268-2609; fax 410/268-0930.* This rustic, upscale seafood restaurant has a warm and romantic feel with great views of Annapolis Harbor. With a good wine selection and a variety of fresh local seafood, it is a favorite for both business and intimate dinners. Hours: 5:30-10 pm; Sun 5-9 pm. Closed most major holidays. Reservations accepted. Continental menu. Wine list. Dinner $18.95-$23. Complete meals: dinner $26.95. Specializes in fresh seafood, Italian dishes. Outdoor seating. Casual elegance in romantic setting. Cr cds: A, C, D, DS, MC, V.
[D]

★★ **O'LEARY'S SEAFOOD.** *310 3rd St (21403). Phone 410/263-0884; fax 410/263-5869.* Hours: 5:30-10 pm; Fri, Sat 5-11 pm; Sun 5-10 pm. Closed Thanksgiving, Dec 24, 25. Reservations accepted. Bar. Dinner $10.95-$29.95. Children's menu. Specializes in seafood. Own desserts. Cr cds: A, C, D, DS, ER, MC, V.

★★★ **TREATY OF PARIS.** *58 State Cir (21401). Phone 410/263-2641; fax 410/268-3813. www.annapolisinns.com.* This landmark is praised for its game and seafood selections. With menu items such as warm duck breast salad, beef wellington, or rack of lamb, guests will bask in both the presentation and flavors of the masterful fares. Early American tavern atmosphere; fireplace. Continental menu. Hours: 7 am-2:30 pm, 5:30-10:30 pm; Fri, Sat to 11:30 pm; Sun to 9:30 pm; Sun brunch 10 am-2:30 pm. Closed Jan 1. Salad bar (lunch). Dinner $14-$22, Sun brunch $18.95. Bar 11-2 am; Sun to 1 am. Reservations accepted, required Fri, Sat. Valet parking (dinner). Cr cds: A, D, MC, V.
[SC]

Antietam National Battlefield (B-5)

(11 miles S on MD 65)

On September 17, 1862, the bloodiest day in Civil War annals, more than 23,000 men were killed or wounded as

Union forces blocked the first Confederate invasion of the North. A Union advantage was gained beforehand when a soldier accidentally found Lee's orders wrapped around some cigars. In spite of knowing Lee's tactical game plan, McClellan moved cautiously. The battle, critical because British aid to the Confederacy depended on the outcome, was a tactical draw but a strategic victory for the North. This victory allowed Lincoln to issue the Emancipation Proclamation, which expanded the war from simply reuniting the country to a crusade to end slavery. The rebels withdrew across the Potomac on the night of September 18, but for some reason McClellan, with twice the manpower, delayed his pursuit. Lincoln relieved him of command of the Army of the Potomac seven weeks later. Clara Barton, who was to found the Red Cross 19 years later, tended the wounded at a field hospital on the battlefield.

Approximately 350 iron tablets, monuments, and battlefield maps, located on 8 miles of paved avenues, describe the events of the battle. The Visitor Center houses a museum and offers information, literature, and a 26-minute orientation movie (shown on the hour). Visitor Center (daily; closed January 1, Thanksgiving, December 25); battlefield (daily); ranger-conducted walks, talks, and demonstrations (Memorial Day-Labor Day, daily). Golden Age Passport (see MAKING THE MOST OF YOUR TRIP). For information phone 301/432-5124. Entrance fee per person. **$**

Baltimore (B-7)

See also Major Cities

Settled 1661 **Pop** 654,154 **Elev** 32 ft **Area code** 410 and 443

Information Baltimore Area Convention & Visitors Association, 100 Light St, 12th floor, 21202; 410/659-7300 or 800/343-3468

Web www.baltimore.org

Suburbs Aberdeen, Cockeysville, Columbia, Ellicott City, Pikesville, Towson.

Metropolis of Maryland and one of America's great cities, Baltimore is a city of neighborhoods built on strong ethnic foundations, a city of historic events that helped shape the nation, and a city that has achieved an incredible downtown renaissance in the past 20 years. It is a major East Coast manufacturing center and, almost from its beginning, a world seaport. Several colleges and universities, foremost of which is Johns Hopkins, make their home here.

Lying midway between North and South and enjoying a rich cultural mixture of both, Baltimore is one of the nation's oldest cities. When British troops threatened Philadelphia during the Revolutionary War, the Continental Congress fled to Baltimore, which served as the nation's capital for a little more than two months.

In October 1814, a British fleet attacked the city by land and sea. The defenders of Fort McHenry withstood the naval bombardment for 25 hours until the British gave up. Francis Scott Key saw the huge American flag still flying above the fort and was inspired to pen "The Star-Spangled Banner."

Rapid growth in the early 19th century resulted from the opening of the National Road and then the nation's first railroad, the Baltimore & Ohio.

Politics was a preoccupation in those days, and the city hosted many national party conventions. At least seven presidents and three losing candidates were nominated here. Edgar Allan Poe's mysterious death in the city may have been at the hands of shady electioneers.

Untouched physically by the Civil War, effects came later when Southerners flooded in to rebuild their fortunes and commerce was disrupted by the loss of Southern markets. A disastrous fire in 1904 destroyed 140 acres of the business district but the city recovered rapidly and, during the two World Wars, was a major shipbuilding and naval repair center.

In the 1950s and early 1960s, Baltimore was the victim of the apathy and general decay that struck the industrial Northeast. But the city fought back, replacing hundreds of acres of slums, rotting wharves, and warehouses with gleaming new office plazas, parks, and public buildings. The Inner Harbor was transformed into a huge public area with shops, museums, restaurants, and frequent concerts and festivals. Millions of tourists and proud Baltimoreans flock downtown to enjoy the sights and activities.

Famous residents and native sons and daughters include Babe Ruth; Edgar Allan Poe; H. L. Mencken; Mother Elizabeth Ann Seton; Eubie Blake; Ogden Nash; Thurgood Marshall; Wallis Warfield Simpson, who became the Duchess of Windsor; and more recent sports legends Brooks Robinson, Johnny Unitas, Jim Palmer, and Cal Ripken.

Additional Visitor Information

For additional accommodations, see BALTIMORE/WASHINGTON INTERNATIONAL AIRPORT AREA, which follows BALTIMORE.

Maps, brochures, and calendars of events are available at the Baltimore Area Visitors Center, 301 E Pratt St, Constellation Pier, 21202; phone 410/837-INFO or 800/282-6632.

Transportation

Airport. See BALTIMORE/WASHINGTON INTERNATIONAL AIRPORT AREA.

Car Rental Agencies See IMPORTANT TOLL-FREE NUMBERS.

Public Transportation Bus and subway (Mass Transit Administration), phone 410/539-5000.

Rail Passenger Service Amtrak 800/872-7245; MARC (commuter train serving Baltimore and Washington, D.C.) 800/325-RAIL or 410/291-4267.

What to See and Do

American Visionary Art Museum. *800 Key Hwy (21230). Phone 410/244-1900.* Visitors with a penchant for the off-beat or the just plain bizarre should not miss this singular museum. The Whirligig—a 55-foot-tall, wind-powered, pinwheel-like sculpture made from bicycle wheels, car parts, and cables—stands in Sculpture Plaza as a towering symbol of the museum's mission. The museum defines visionary art as works produced by individuals without formal training whose art stems from an inner vision. Opened in 1995, the museum has more than 4,000 pieces in its collection. The main building holds seven indoor galleries. Separate from this building are the wildflower garden, a wedding chapel and altar built out of tree limbs and flowers, and the tall sculpture barn, which once showcased psychic Uri Geller's art, including a car he covered with 5,000 psychically bent forks and spoons. The museum also plans to add a "Thou Art Creative Center," an interactive area for visitors. (Tues-Sun 10 am-6 pm; closed Mon, Thanksgiving, Dec 25) **$$**

Antique Row. *N Howard and W Read sts (21201).* Antique Row, which has existed in Baltimore for over 100 years, is an antique lover's paradise. With more than 20 dealers and shops that also include restoration services, the area offers enough displayed and hidden treasures to satisfy diehard shoppers and casual browsers alike. The different shops specialize in items such as European furniture, Tiffany lamps, china, and rare books.

The Avenue in Hampden. *36th St (21211).* Although the 4 blocks that make up the Avenue total only a half mile, visitors will be amazed at all there is to see in this eclectic North Baltimore neighborhood. Novelty shops, vintage clothing stores, casual restaurants, and art galleries line Hampden's main drag, and the treasures that guests can find in these shops range from kitschy to sublime. If you're looking for a down-home meal, drop in at Mamie's Café or Café Hon.

B & O Railroad Museum. *901 W Pratt St (21223). Phone 410/752-2490.* This museum, affiliated with the Smithsonian, celebrates the birthplace of railroading in America and depicts the industry's economic and cultural influences. Encompassing 40 acres, the museum's collection of locomotives is the oldest and most comprehensive in the country. Its exhibits are divided among three main buildings. In the Roundhouse, visitors can board and explore more than a dozen of the "iron horses," which include a rail post office car and the Tom Thumb train. The second floor of the Annex building has an impressive display of working miniature-scale trains. The Mount Clair Station, exhibiting the story of the B & O railroad, was built in 1851 to replace the 1829 original, which was the first rail depot in the country. Outside, the museum features more trains, such as the Chessie, the largest steam locomotive. On certain weekends, visitors can take a train ride. In 2003, the museum marked its 175th anniversary. (Daily; closed major holidays) **$$**

Babe Ruth Birthplace and Museum. *216 Emory St (21230). Phone 410/727-1539.* Although Babe Ruth played for the New York Yankees, Baltimore calls him one of its native sons. The house where this legend was born has been transformed into a museum that showcases his life and career. Visitors can see rare family photographs as well as a complete record of his home runs. The museum also features exhibits about the Baltimore Colts and Orioles. Every February 6, the museum commemorates Babe Ruth's birthday by offering free admission to all visitors. (Daily 10 am-5 pm, until 4 pm Nov-Mar; closed Jan 1, Thanksgiving, Dec 25) **$$**

Baltimore Crab. *Throughout the City.* A visit to Charm City wouldn't be complete without a sampling of the local delicacy. Crab is a staple of Maryland's economy and diet. It comes prepared in a variety of forms: deep-fried, soft-shelled, or flaked and served as crab cakes. However, the classic version is steamed hard crabs. Restaurants serve steamed crab without adornment. Don't be put off when your waiter covers the table with plain brown paper and then hands you a wooden mallet, paper napkins, and a plastic bib. When the crabs come to the table, they will be hot, red from the steam, and covered in Old Bay Seasoning. Once you crack open the shell and taste the sweet, white meat, you'll be hooked. Crab is in season from March to October, but peak season is July through September.

Baltimore Maritime Museum. *802 S Caroline St (21231). Inner Harbor area. Phone 410/396-3453.* This museum's featured ships include the USS *Torsk*, a World War II submarine; the Coast Guard cutter *Taney*; and the lightship *Chesapeake*. All the ships have been designated National Historic Landmarks. (Spring, summer, and fall, Sun-Thurs 10 am-5:30 pm, Fri-Sat until 6:30 pm; winter, Fri-Sun 10:30 am-5 pm) **$$**

Baltimore Museum of Art. *10 Art Museum Dr (21218). Near N Charles and 31st sts. Phone 410/396-7100.* Located near Johns Hopkins University, this museum opened in 1923 and was designed by John Russell Pope, the architect of the National Gallery in Washington, D.C. The museum has eight permanent exhibits featuring works from the periods of Impressionism to modern art. It boasts the second largest collection of works by Andy Warhol.

However, its jewel is the Cone collection, which includes more than 3,000 pieces by artists such as Picasso, Van Gogh, Renoir, Cezanne, and Matisse. The Matisse collection is the largest in the Western Hemisphere. Visitors will also want to see the 3-acre sculpture garden, which contains art by Alexander Calder and Henry Moore. (Wed-Fri 11 am-5 pm, Sat-Sun 11 am-6 pm; free admission first Thurs of each month; closed Mon, Tues, major holidays) **$$**

Baltimore Museum of Industry. *1415 Key Hwy, Inner Harbor South (21230). Phone 410/727-4808.* This museum educates visitors about the vital role that industry and manufacturing played in Baltimore's economic and cultural development. Located in a renovated oyster cannery on the west side of the Inner Harbor, the museum opened in 1977. Its exhibits showcase such trades as printing, garment making, canning, and metalworking. Guests will learn about the invention of Noxema, the disposable bottle cap, and even the first umbrella. Or they can explore the SS *Baltimore*, the only operating coal-fired tugboat on the East Coast that is now a National Historic Landmark. Visitors can also see the Mini-Mariner, a restored 1937 working prototype of the World War II boat bomber. The museum also has "Theatre on the Harbor," which presents touring and in-house productions. Past shows have included "Gizmo's Invention Show" and "Right Place, Right Time, Wright Brothers." (Mon-Sat; closed Thanksgiving, Dec 24 and 25) **$$$**

Baltimore Orioles (MLB). *Oriole Park at Camden Yards. 333 W Camden St. Phone 410/685-9800.*

Baltimore Ravens (NFL). *PSINet Stadium. 1101 Russell St. Phone 410/230-8000.*

Baltimore Streetcar Museum. *1901 Falls Rd, under North Ave Bridge. Phone 410/547-0264.* Eleven electric streetcars and two horsecars used in city between 1859-1963; 1 1/4-mile rides (fee). (June-Oct, Sat and Sun afternoons; rest of year, Sun afternoons only; also open Memorial Day, July 4, Labor Day) **$$**

Baltimore Zoo. *1 Druid Hill Park Lake Dr (21217). Phone 410/366-5466; www.baltimorezoo.org.* Located in Druid Hill Park, this third oldest zoo in the United States covers 180 acres and features more than 2,250 animals. Children will be intrigued by the scaly inhabitants of the reptile house. They can also travel to another continent by visiting the giraffes and elephants in the African Safari exhibit, as well as ride the carousel or try out the climbing wall. The zoo also hosts special events during Halloween and Christmas. (Daily; closed Thanksgiving, Dec 25) **$$$$**

Basilica of the National Shrine of the Assumption. *408 N Charles St (21201). Phone 410/727-3565.* Now a co-cathedral, this was the first Roman Catholic cathedral in the US. Bishop John Carroll, head of the diocese of Baltimore from its establishment in 1789, blessed the cornerstone in 1806. The church was dedicated in 1821. Architectural design by B. H. Latrobe. Tours (by appointment). (Daily)

Battle Monument. *3219 Old North Point Rd (21222).* (1815) Memorial to those who fell defending the city in the War of 1812.

Boordy Vineyards. *12820 Long Green Pike, Fork (21051). Phone 410/592-5015.* Guests who live by the maxim *In Vino Veritas* should visit Maryland's oldest family-run winery. Only a 15-minute drive from Baltimore, Boordy sits in the serene countryside. With its rows and rows of delicate plants and 19th-century farm buildings, this winery will surely charm visitors. Daily tours are available, and Boordy hosts special events, such as wine tastings and live musical performances. **FREE**

Charles Center. *Charles and Lombard sts. downtown.* Business area with European-style plazas, part of an overhead walkway system, shops, restaurants, and outdoor activities. Prize-winning office building by Mies van der Rohe borders center plaza. Also here is

> **Baltimore Center for the Performing Arts—Morris A. Mechanic Theatre.** *25 Hopkins Plaza (21201). Phone 410/481-SEAT.* Hosts Broadway productions.

Church Home and Hospital. *Broadway and Fairmount Ave.* Edgar Allan Poe died here in 1849.

City Court House. *St. Paul and Fayette sts, downtown.* (1900) On steps is statue of Cecil Calvert, brother of Leonard and founder of Maryland as the second Lord Baltimore.

City Hall. *100 N Holliday St, downtown. Tours by appointment. Phone 410/396-3100.* Post-Civil War architecture, restored to original detail. **FREE**

City of Baltimore Conservatory. *Druid Hill Park. 2600 Madison Ave (21217). Phone 410/396-0180.* This graceful building (circa 1885) houses a large variety of tropical plants. Special shows during Easter, Nov, and Christmas. (Thurs-Sun) **FREE**

Cockpit in Court Summer Theatre. *7201 Rossville Blvd.* (See SPECIAL EVENTS)

Cylburn Arboretum. *4915 Greenspring Ave. Phone 410/396-0180.* Marked nature trails. Nature museum, ornithological room, horticultural library in restored mansion; shade and formal gardens, All-American Selection Garden, Garden of the Senses. (Daily) **FREE**

Duckpin Bowling. *Throughout the City.* Despite its name, no ducks play a part in this game, which originated in Baltimore in 1900. The object of the game is similar to that of bowling except that the pins and balls are smaller. However, first-time players should not be fooled by the diminutive pieces. They'll soon discover that the smaller pins are, in fact, even harder to knock down! Alleys are open throughout Baltimore, including at Taylor's

Stoneleigh Duckpin Bowling Center, 6703 York Rd. 410/377-8115. **$**

Edgar Allan Poe Grave. *At Westminster Hall and Burying Ground and Catacombs, Fayette and Greene sts, downtown.* Baltimore's oldest cemeteries also contain the graves of many prominent early Marylanders. Tour of catacombs by appointment (Apr-Nov, first and third Fri and Sat). **$$**

Edgar Allan Poe House and Museum. *203 N Amity St (21223). Phone 410/396-7932.* The famed author and father of the macabre lived in this house from 1832 to 1835. The faint of heart should beware, as several psychics have reported ghostly presences here. Haunted or not, the house and museum scare up many Poe artifacts, such as period furniture, a desk and telescope owned by Poe, and Gustave Dore's illustrations of *The Raven.* Around January 19, the museum hosts a birthday celebration that includes readings and theatrical performances of Poe's work. (Apr-Dec) **$**

Enoch Pratt Free Library. *400 Cathedral St, at Franklin St, downtown. Phone 410/396-5430.* City's public library. H. L. Mencken and Edgar Allan Poe collections. (Sept-May, daily; rest of year, Mon-Sat; closed holidays)

Federal Hill. *Charles and Cross sts (21227).* View of city harbor and skyline. Named after a celebration that occurred here in 1788 to mark Maryland's ratification of the Constitution.

Fell's Point. *812 S Ann St (21231). Broadway, S of Fleet St to the harbor.* Shipbuilding and maritime center, this neighborhood dates back to 1730; approximately 350 original residential structures. Working tugboats and tankers can be observed from docks.

First Unitarian Church. *Charles and Franklin sts, in Mt. Vernon Pl area. Phone 410/685-2330.* (1817) William Ellery Channing preached a sermon here that hastened the establishment of the Unitarian denomination. Example of Classic Revival architecture.

Fort McHenry National Monument and Historic Shrine. *End of E Fort Ave (21230). Phone 410/962-4299.* Fort McHenry boasts a stunning view of the harbor, authentic re-created structures, and a wealth of living history that will fascinate both history buffs and casual visitors. In addition to being the site of the battle that inspired Francis Scott Key to pen "The Star-Spangled Banner" in 1814, the fort was a defensive position during the Revolutionary War, a POW camp for Confederate prisoners during the Civil War, and an army hospital during World War I. The fort's exhibits showcase these exciting events. Park rangers are knowledgeable and helpful, and they encourage visitors to participate in the twice-daily flag changes. Summer weekends feature precision drill and music performed by volunteers in Revolutionary War uniforms. (Daily; closed Jan 1, Dec 25) **$$**

Narrated cruises. *Phone 410/962-4299.* The *Baltimore Patriot* departs from Inner Harbor Finger Pier to Fort McHenry and Fell's Point (Memorial Day-Labor Day). Also departures from Fort McHenry and Fell's Point. For other tours, contact Maryland Tours, Inc. **$$$**

Gunpowder Falls State Park. *2813 Jerusalem Rd. Phone 410/592-2897.* Approximately 16,000 acres, located in Gunpowder River Valley. **Hammerman Area,** E on US 40, right onto Ebenezer Rd, 5 miles to park entrance in Chase, is a developed day-use area. Offers swimming beach, windsurfing beach, boating, marina (Dundee Creek); picnicking, playground. Other areas offer hiking/biking trails, canoeing, trout fishing. Standard fees.

Harbor cruises. *301 Light St. Depart from Inner Harbor.*

Baltimore Patriot. *Phone 410/685-4288.* Ninety-minute tours around Baltimore's Inner Harbor. (Apr-Oct, daily)

MV Lady Baltimore. *West Bulkhead, 301 Light St. Phone 410/727-3113 or 800/695-LADY.* Round-trip cruises to Annapolis (June-Aug, Wed); also cruises to the Chesapeake & Delaware Canal (three selected Sun in Oct). *Bay Lady* has lunch and dinner cruises (Apr-Oct, daily; limited schedule rest of year).

Harborplace. *200 E Pratt St (21202). Phone 410/332-4191.* This shopping center is the most recognizable symbol of Baltimore's downtown and harbor renaissance. With its architecture of glass and exposed pipes and beams, Harborplace serves as a model for other cities' revitalization plans. Developed by James W. Rouse, the shopping mecca opened in 1980 and boasts more than 130 stores and restaurants. Visitors who want to take a break can go outside and walk on the brick-paved promenade that runs along the water's edge. Harborplace also has a small outdoor amphitheater, where, in good weather, guests are treated to free performances by jugglers, musicians, singers, and military and concert bands. (Daily)

Holocaust Memorial. *Corner of Water, Gay, and Lombard sts (21202), downtown. Phone 410/752-2630.* Simple stone memorial to the victims of the Holocaust.

Jewish Historical Society of Maryland. *15 Lloyd St, downtown. Phone 410/732-6400.* Buildings include Lloyd St Synagogue (1845), the oldest in Maryland; B'nai Israel Synagogue (1876); Jewish Museum of Maryland. (Tues-Thurs and Sun afternoons; or by appointment; closed Jewish holidays) Research archives (Mon-Fri, by appointment). **$**

Johns Hopkins Medical Institutions. *550 N Broadway (21205). Phone 410/955-7894.* (1889) Widely known as a leading medical school, research center, and teaching hospital. Victorian buildings.

Johns Hopkins University. *3400 N Charles St. Phone 410/516-8000.* Founded in 1876 and located in northern

Baltimore, Johns Hopkins is an impressive institution of scholarship and research. It enrolls 18,000 students and is renowned for the Bloomberg School of Public Health, the Peabody Institute, a music conservatory, and its Applied Physics Laboratory, located 30 minutes outside of Baltimore. *US News & World Report* continuously ranks its affiliated hospital, which has its own separate campus in eastern Baltimore, as one of the top medical facilities in the country. Guests to the campus should visit the Homewood mansion. This elegant, Federal red-bricked building was once owned by Charles Carroll, one of the signers of the Declaration of Independence. It was deeded to the university in 1902 and now serves as a historic home. Guided tours are available. On campus grounds are

Bufano Sculpture Garden. *3400 N Charles St. Dunning Park, behind Mudd Hall.* A wooded retreat with animals sculpted by artist Beniamino Bufano. **FREE**

Evergreen House. *4545 N Charles St, approximately 2 miles N of Homewood campus. Phone 410/516-0341.* On 26 wooded acres; features Classical Revival architecture and formal garden. Library (35,000 volumes). Post-impressionist paintings, Japanese and Chinese collections, and Tiffany glass. Tours (daily). **$$$**

Homewood House Museum. *3400 N Charles St. Phone 410/516-5589.* (1801) Former country home of Charles Carroll, Jr., whose father was a signer of the Declaration of Independence; period furnishings. (Tues-Sat, also Sun afternoons) Guided tours (hourly). **$$$**

Joseph Meyerhoff Symphony Hall. *1212 Cathedral St. Phone 410/783-8000 or 410/783-8100.* Permanent residence of the Baltimore Symphony Orchestra.

Lacrosse Hall of Fame Museum. *113 W University Pkwy. Phone 410/235-6882.* Team trophies, display of lacrosse artifacts and memorabilia, including rare photographs and art, vintage equipment and uniforms. Also historical video documentary. (Feb-May, Tues-Sat; June-Jan, Mon-Fri; closed holidays) **$$**

Lexington Market. *400 W Lexington St (21201). Between Eutaw and Paca sts, downtown. Phone 410/685-6169.* This under-roof market is more than two centuries old. Covering 2 blocks, it has more than 130 stalls offering fresh vegetables, seafood, meats, baked goods, and prepared foods that will whet any appetite. Vendors outside the market sell clothing, jewelry, T-shirts, and other miscellaneous items. Throughout the year, the market hosts several events, such as the Chocolate Festival in October, which boasts free samples and a chocolate-eating contest. But the most anticipated event at the market is Lunch with the Elephants. Every March, Ringling Brothers and Barnum & Bailey Circus elephants parade up Eutaw Street accompanied by fanfare, live music, and clowns. When they finally reach the market, they are served "lunch," which consists of 1,100 oranges, 1,000 apples,

500 heads of lettuce, 700 bananas, 400 pears, and 500 carrots. (Mon-Sat; closed holidays) **FREE**

Lovely Lane Museum. *2200 St. Paul St. Phone 410/889-4458.* Permanent and changing exhibits of items of Methodist church history since 1760. Guided tours (Mon-Fri; also Sun after services and by appointment; closed holidays). **FREE**

Maryland Historical Society. *201 W Monument St (21201). Phone 410/685-3750.* The state's oldest cultural institution includes a library, a museum, and even a small press that promotes scholarship about Maryland's history and material culture. The library has more than 5.4 million works and is a valuable resource for genealogists. The society's collection of historical artifacts includes the original draft of "The Star Spangled Banner" and the world's largest collection of 19th-century American silver. It also sponsors educational programs, such as lectures and living history presentations. (Daily) **$**

Maryland Institute, College of Art. *Main building, 1300 Mt. Royal Ave, at Lanvale St. Phone 410/669-9200.* (1826) 880 students. Institute hosts frequent contemporary art exhibitions. Cafeteria. Campus distinguished by recycled buildings and white marble Italianate main building. (Daily)

Maryland Science Center & Davis Planetarium. *601 Light St (21230). Phone 410/685-5225 (recording).* This interactive center proves that science is anything but boring. Located in the Inner Harbor, the three-story building contains hundreds of exhibits guaranteed to spark young (and older) minds. In the Chesapeake Bay exhibit, you can learn about the delicate ecosystem that exists beneath the water. Or you can explore the mysteries of the human body in BodyLink. The Kids Room, for guests 8 and younger, gives children the chance to operate a fish camera or dress up like turtles. Don't miss the Hubble Space Telescope National Visitor Center, a 4,000-square-foot interactive space gallery, which has more than 20 hands-on activities and 120 high-resolution images that allow guests to see space through the Hubble's eye. Those who can't get enough of outer space should also visit the Davis Planetarium and the Crosby-Ramsey Memorial Observatory, both on site. The center's IMAX theater will thrill guests with its five-stories-tall movie screen and 3-D capability. (Daily) **$$$**

Minnie V Harbor Tours. *Docks near Pier 1, Pratt St, Inner Harbor area. Phone 410/685-9062.* A 45-foot Chesapeake Bay skipjack sloop built in 1906. Ninety-minute harbor tours give 24 passengers the opportunity to help crew the boat (open weekends).

Morgan State University. *1700 E Cold Spring Ln (21251). Phone 443/885-3333.* (1867) 5,100 students. The James E. Lewis Museum of Art has changing exhibits (Mon-Fri; weekends by appointment; closed holidays).

Mother Seton House. *600 N Paca St, downtown. Phone 410/523-3443.* Home of St. Elizabeth Ann Bayley Seton from 1808-1809. Here she established the forerunner of the parochial school system, as well as an order of nuns that eventually became the Daughters & Sisters of Charity in the US and Canada. (Sat and Sun afternoons, also by appointment; closed Jan 1, Easter, Dec 25) **FREE**

Mount Clare Museum House. *In Carroll Park at 1500 Washington Blvd. Phone 410/837-3262.* (1760) Oldest mansion in Baltimore, former home of Charles Carroll, barrister. 18th- and 19th-century furnishings. Guided tours on the hour. (Tues-Sun; closed holidays) **$$$**

Mount Vernon Place United Methodist Church. *10 E Mt. Vernon Place. Phone 410/685-5290.* (circa 1850) Brownstone with balcony and grillwork extending entire width of house; spiral staircase suspended from three floors; library with century-old painting on ceiling; drawing room. (Mon-Fri; closed holidays and Mon after Easter) **FREE**

MPT (Maryland Public Television). *11767 Owings Mills Blvd # 2. Phone 410/356-5600 or 800/223-3MPT (surrounding states).* Tours of state's television network studios. (By appointment) **FREE**

⭐ **National Aquarium.** *501 E Pratt St. Pier 3, Inner Harbor area. Phone 410/576-3800.* This aquarium's glass-and-steel, pyramid-shaped architecture is as unusual and stunning as the more than 15,000 sea creatures it houses. Located in the Inner Harbor, the National Aquarium introduces guests to stingrays, sharks, puffins, seals, and even a giant Pacific octopus. Visitors can explore the danger and mystery of a living South American tropical rain forest complete with poisonous frogs, exotic birds, piranha, and swinging tamirin monkeys. You will delight in the underwater beauty of the replicated Atlantic coral reef. The Children's Cove, a touch pool, provides an interactive experience for kids. In the Marine Mammal Pavilion, a high-tech dolphin show entertains and teaches guests about these intelligent creatures. Visitors particularly enjoy watching trainers feed the animals. Daily feeding schedules are posted in the lobby. (Daily; closed Thanksgiving, Dec 25) **$$$$** Visitors can cross an enclosed skywalk to reach the adjacent

Marine Mammal Pavilion. *Pier 4, 501 E Pratt St.* This unique structure features a 1,300-seat amphitheater surrounding a 1.2-million-gallon pool, which houses Atlantic bottlenose dolphins; underwater viewing areas enable visitors to observe the mammals from below the surface. (Daily) Special video programs about dolphins and whales; educational arcade with computerized video screens and other participatory exhibits around the pavilion's upper deck. Visitor service area located in the atrium. Gift shop. Café. A life-size replica of a humpback whale spans two levels of the atrium. Discovery Room houses a collection of

marine artifacts. Resource Center is an aquatic learning center for school visitors; library boasts extensive collection of marine science material.

Old Otterbein United Methodist Church. *112 W Conway St. Inner Harbor area. Phone 410/685-4703.* (1785-1786) Fine Georgian architecture; mother church of United Brethren. Tours of historic building (Apr-Oct, Sat).

Old Town Mall. *400 N Gay St.* This 150-year-old, brick-lined commercial area has been beautifully refurbished; closed to vehicular traffic. Nearby is

Stirling Street. *1000 block of Monument St, 1 block W of mall.* First community urban "homesteading" venture in the US. Renovated homes date back to the 1830s. Original facades have been maintained; interior rehabilitation ranges in style from the antique to the avant-garde.

Oriole Park at Camden Yards. *333 W Camden St (21201). Phone 410/685-9800.* The crack of the bat and the roar of the crowd signal that the Orioles are home. Opened in 1992 and located just blocks from the Inner Harbor, Camden Yards is considered by many to be the best baseball stadium in the US. With its steel trusses, arched brick façade, and natural turf, the stadium's design is reminiscent of the great ballparks built in the early 1900s. It holds 48,876 fans and memorializes local legends Brooks Robinson, Earl Weaver, and Cal Ripken, Jr. The old B & O Warehouse sits behind right field and has long been a target for batters aiming for a home run. Guests can sit anywhere in the stadium and enjoy an unobstructed view of the game. Tours of the stadium are also available and allow visitors to sit in the dugout, see the press box, and explore the clubhouse. (Season Mar-Sept; tours held mid-Feb-late Dec, daily except on days of afternoon home games)

Otterbein "Homesteading." *Area around S Sharp St, Inner Harbor area.* The original neighborhood dates back to 1785. Houses have been restored.

Patterson Park. *200 S Linwood Ave (21231). Phone 410/396-7931.* Defenses here helped stop British attack in 1814. Breastworks, artillery pieces are displayed.

Peabody Institute of the Johns Hopkins University. *609 N Charles St (21202). In Mt. Vernon Place area. (box office) Phone 410/659-8124.* (1857) 550 students. Music conservatory founded by philanthropist George Peabody; now affiliated with Johns Hopkins. Research and reference collection in library accessible to the public (Mon-Fri; closed holidays). The Miriam A. Friedberg Concert Hall seats 800. Orchestral, recital, and opera performances.

Port Discovery. *35 Market Pl (21202). Phone 410/727-8120.* Port Discovery is three floors and 80,000 square feet of pure imagination. Ranked the fourth best children's museum in the country by *Child* magazine, the museum opened in 1998 in collaboration with Walt Disney Imagineering. Its exhibits are interactive, innovative, and educational. Kids will have a blast exploring the three-story urban tree house. In MPT Studioworks, they can become producers of their own television broadcasts. Sensation Station will overload their senses of sight, sound, and touch. Kids can even travel back to ancient Egypt and uncover the mystery of the pyramids and Pharaoh's tomb. The museum also operates the HiFlyer, a giant helium balloon that's anchored 450 feet above the Inner Harbor. The enclosed gondola holds 20 to 25 passengers and offers a spectacular view of the city. (Memorial Day-Labor Day, daily; rest of year, Tues-Sun; closed Thanksgiving, Dec 25) **$$$$**

The Power Plant. *601 E Pratt St (21202). Phone 410/752-5444.* As its name implies, this commercial complex was once a power plant owned by Baltimore Gas & Electric. Located in the Inner Harbor next to the National Aquarium (See also NATIONAL AQUARIUM), the renovated plant now houses a two-story Barnes & Noble bookstore, a Hard Rock Café, and the original ESPN Zone, a 35,000 square-foot sports-themed restaurant and arcade.

Pride of Baltimore II. *Inner Harbor (21202). Phone 410/752-2490.* This replicated 1812-style Baltimore Clipper is Maryland's goodwill ambassador. The ship has sailed to more than 40 countries in North and South America, Europe, and Asia to promote the state's tourism and economical interests. In 1986, the original *Pride of Baltimore* sank in a storm near Puerto Rico, killing the entire crew. When the *Pride of Baltimore II* is docked in the Inner Harbor, visitors can board for a tour. Day sails and overnight passages between ports are also available. (Daily; closed holidays) **FREE**

Public Works Museum & Streetscape. *751 Eastern Ave, at Inner Harbor East. Phone 410/396-5565.* Museum exhibits the history and artifacts of public works. Located in historic sewage pumping station. Streetscape sculpture outside depicts the various utility lines and ducts under a typical city street, in a walk-through model. (Tues-Sun) **$$**

Sail Baltimore. *1809 Thames St (21231). Phone 410/522-7300.* Because boats are to Baltimore as cows are to farms, Sail Baltimore, a nonprofit organization, informs the public about a variety of citywide boating events that take place throughout the year. Its Web site provides an updated schedule of the different boats and ships that will be visiting the Inner Harbor. It also hosts the Great Chesapeake Bay Schooner Race in October, among other seasonal events.

Senator Theatre. *5904 York Rd (21212). Phone 410/435-8338.* Movie buffs will appreciate the charm and history of the Senator, which *USA Today* rated one of the top theaters in the country. Showing first-run, independent, and classic films, the theater seats 900 and has a 40-foot-wide screen. Listed on the National Register of Historic Places, its architecture is elegant Art Deco. The theater has

also premiered several films by directors John Waters and Barry Levinson, who are Baltimore natives. The theater recently added its own mini "Walk of Fame" outside its entrance. **$$$**

Sherwood Gardens. *Stratford Rd and Greenway, in the residential community of Guilford in northern Baltimore.* More than 6 acres in size, the gardens reach their peak of splendor in late April and early May, when thousands of tulips, azaleas, and flowering shrubs bloom.

⭐ **Star-Spangled Banner Flag House and War of 1812 Museum.** *844 E Pratt St (21202). Phone 410/837-1793.* Open to the public for over 75 years, this museum was the home of Mary Pickersgill, sewer of the flag that Francis Scott Key eternalized in America's national anthem. Although the flag now hangs in the Smithsonian's National Museum of American History, visitors can tour the house to learn about its origins and Pickersgill's life. The house has an adjoining War of 1812 museum, which exhibits military and domestic artifacts and presents an award-winning video. (Tues-Sat) **$**

Top of the World. *401 E Pratt St. World Trade Center, Inner Harbor area.* Observation deck and museum on the 27th floor of the World Trade Center, which was designed by I. M. Pei. Exhibits describe the city's history, famous residents, and the activities of the port. (Daily) **$$**

University of Maryland at Baltimore. *520 W Lombard St (21201). Downtown. Phone 410/706-7820.* 5,476 students. The 32-acre downtown campus includes six professional schools; the University of Maryland Medical System, and the Graduate School. Davidge Hall (1812) is the oldest medical teaching building in continuous use in the Western Hemisphere.

USS Constellation. *301 E Pratt St, Pier 1 (21202). Phone 410/539-1797.* This retired sloop has a proud naval history that spans from the Civil War to World War II. Anchored at Pier 1 in the Inner Harbor, visitors can board the ship for a self-guided audio tour. Kids can participate in the Powder Monkey program, in which they learn what it was like to serve in President Lincoln's navy. In 1999, a restoration project returned the ship to its original Civil War appearance. (Daily; closed Jan 1, Thanksgiving, Dec 25) **$$$**

Vagabond Players. *806 S Broadway. (Box office) Phone 410/563-9135.* Oldest continuously operating "little theater" in US. Recent Broadway shows, revivals, and original scripts are performed. (Fri-Sun)

Walters Art Museum. *600 N Charles St (21201). Phone 410/547-9000.* This museum's collection is so comprehensive that it spans 55 centuries and traces the history of the world from ancient times to the present day. Father and son William and Henry Walters gifted the museum and its numerous holdings to Baltimore, although the New York Metropolitan Museum of Art also coveted it. Located in the historic neighborhood of Mount Vernon and containing more than 30,000 pieces of art, the collection, which is housed in three buildings, is renowned for its French paintings and Renaissance and Asian art. The museum also exhibits Faberge eggs; paintings by the Old Masters, such as Raphael and El Greco; and an impressive assortment of ivories and Art Deco jewelry. Visitors will also want to check out the unique Roman sarcophagus. (Tues-Sun; closed Mon, major holidays) **$$**

Washington Monument. *N Charles St (21202). Charles and Monument sts, in Mt. Vernon Pl area. Phone 410/ 396-1049.* (1815-1842) First major monument to honor George Washington. Museum in base; view city from top. Other monuments nearby honor Lafayette, Chief Justice Roger Brooke Taney, philanthropist George Peabody, lawyer Severn Teackle Wallis, and Revolutionary War hero John Eager Howard.

Special Events

American Craft Council Baltimore-Winter Show. *1 W Pratt St (21201). Phone 410/649-7000. Convention Center.* Craft festival features the works of nearly 800 artisans, with crafts ranging from clay and glass to furniture and toys. Three-day weekend in late Feb. **$$$**

Artscape. *1200 block of Mt. Royal Ave (21217). Phone 877/ BALTIMORE.* This festival celebrates the area's abundance of visual, literary, and performing arts. The three-day event, which occurs in late July, takes place in the "cultural corridor" of the city's Bolton Hill neighborhood. It features live music performances, poetry and fiction readings by regional writers, and even a one-act opera. Past festival performers and guests have included John Waters, Buckwheat Zydeco, Kool & the Gang, and India.Arie. The Artists' Market exhibits and sells the work of more than 140 artists. The festival includes a wide variety of activities for children, which in the past have included a youth Shakespearean performance and an interactive art tent. The event also presents a charity wine-tasting hosted by a regional vineyard. Late July.

Cockpit in Court Summer Theatre. *7201 Rossville Blvd (21237). Phone 410/780-6369. Use Beltway (I-695) exit 34, in Baltimore County. Theater in residence at Essex Community College.* Four separate theaters offer a diverse collection of plays, including Broadway productions, contemporary drama, revues, and Shakespeare. Mid-June-mid-Aug.

Harbor Expo. *3001 Boston St (21224). Phone 410/396-7931.* Boat parades, seafood festival; entertainment; events. Mid-June.

Maryland Film Festival. *107 E Read St (21202). Phone 410/752-8083.* Initiated in 1999, this four-day festival has become a premiere cinema event for Baltimore, presenting more than 120 foreign, domestic, and short films throughout the city's movie houses, including the famous Senator Theater (See also SENATOR THEATER). Most screenings are followed by a discussion with the film's director or producer; past directors in attendance have included Barry Levinson and John Waters. In addition to featuring cutting-edge contemporary movies, its Guest Host Program invites members from the film community to screen and discuss films that have influenced their own work. The festival has also hosted films for children, such as a silent movie version of *Peter Pan* accompanied by an orchestra. The festival's committee holds film-related events in Baltimore throughout the year. Late Apr or early May. **$$$$**

Maryland House and Garden Pilgrimage. *1105-A Providence Rd (21286). Phone 410/821-6933.* More than 100 homes and gardens throughout the state are open. Late Apr-early May.

New Year's Eve Extravaganza. *Convention Center and Inner Harbor. 1 W Pratt St (21201). Phone 410/649-7144.* Parties, entertainment, big bands, fireworks.

Pier 6 Concert Pavilion. *731 Eastern Ave. Pier 6, Inner Harbor area. Phone 410/625-3100 for schedule.* Summertime outdoor concerts and plays at the water's edge. Some covered seating. (June-Sept, evenings) **$$$$**

Pimlico Race Course. *5201 Park Heights Ave (21215). Phone 410/542-9400.* Home to the world-famous Preakness Stakes (See also PREAKNESS STAKES AND CELEBRATION WEEK), this track is well steeped in thoroughbred horseracing tradition. Pimlico features a 70-foot-wide and 1-mile-long track. It can easily meet the needs of horseracing fans with more than 750 betting windows and a clubhouse and two grandstands that can accommodate more than 13,000 people. In the lounge, visitors can view broadcasts of races at other tracks. (Wed-Sun, Apr-June) **$**

Preakness Stakes and Celebration Week. *401 E Pratt St. Statewide festival. Phone 410/837-3030.* The Preakness Stakes, the second jewel in horse racing's Triple Crown, is a time-honored tradition in Baltimore. Every year, on the third Saturday in May, nearly 100,000 people from Maryland and around the world gather at the Pimilico Race Course. Celebration festivities begin one week before the race. The week is packed with activities that include a parade, a hot-air balloon festival, outdoor concerts, boat races, and 5K and 10K runs. On race day, the track's gates open at 8:30 am, with the first races beginning at 11 am. The Preakness itself is the second-to-last race of the day and begins at around 5:30 pm. Visitors looking for a good value and an eye-level view of the horses should reserve seats in the infield. Those willing to spend more money—and dress more formally—should choose seats in the clubhouse or grandstand.

Showcase of Nations Ethnic Festivals. *200 W Lombard St. Various downtown locations. Phone 410/752-8632.* Presenting the food, music, and crafts of a different culture each weekend. June-Sept.

Motels/Motor Lodges

★ ★ **BEST WESTERN HOTEL & CONFERENCE CENTER.** *5625 O'Donnell St (21224). Phone 410/633-9500; toll-free 800/633-9511; fax 410/633-4314. www.bestwestern.com.* 175 rooms, 12 story. S, D $109-$129; under 12 free; each additional $10; suites $129-$229. Crib free. Check-out noon. TV; cable (premium). In-room modem link. Microwaves available. Coffee in rooms. Valet services. Coin laundry. Restaurant 6:30 am-10 pm. Bar. Room service. Exercise equipment, sauna. Game room. Indoor pool, whirlpool, lifeguard. Meeting rooms. Business services. Gift shop. Cr cds: A, C, D, DS, JCB, MC, V.

D ⌨ 🏋 ⛵ SC

★ **DAYS INN.** *100 Hopkins Pl (21201). Phone 410/576-1000; toll-free 800/329-7466; fax 410/576-9437. www.daysinn.com.* 250 rooms, 9 story. S $90-$120; D $100-$130; each additional $10; suites $140-$180; under 12 free; higher rates special events. Crib free. Check-out 11 am. TV; cable (premium). In-room modem link. Some refrigerators; microwaves available. Coffee in rooms. Valet service. Restaurant 6:30 am-10 pm. Bar. Room service. Health club privileges. Pool, poolside service, lifeguard. Garage $8.50. Meeting rooms. Business center. Concierge. Sundries. Cr cds: A, C, D, DS, JCB, MC, V.

D ⌨ ⛵ SC 🏋

★ **HAMPTON INN.** *8225 Town Ctr Dr (21236). Phone 410/931-2200; toll-free 800/426-7866; fax 410/931-2215. www.hamptoninn.com.* 127 rooms, 4 story. Complimentary continental breakfast. Check-out noon, check-in 3 pm. TV; cable (premium). In-room modem link. Laundry services. In-house fitness room. Health club privileges. Outdoor pool. Cr cds: A, C, D, DS, MC, V. **$**

D ⌨ 🏋 ⛵

★ ★ **HOLIDAY INN.** *1800 Belmont Ave (21244). Phone 410/265-1400; toll-free 800/465-4329; fax 410/281-9569. www.holiday-inn.com.* 133 units, 2 story. S, D $89. Crib free. Pet accepted, some restrictions; $25. Check-out noon. TV; cable (premium). In-room modem link. Some refrigerators; microwaves available. Valet services. Coin laundry. Restaurant 6-10 am, 5-9:30 pm; Sat, Sun to 11 am. Bar 5 pm-midnight. Room service. Health club privileges $8. Pool, lifeguard. Meeting rooms. Business services. Sundries. Cr cds: A, C, D, DS, JCB, MC, V.

D 🐾 ⌨ ⛵ SC

★ ★ **HOLIDAY INN SELECT.** *2004 Greenspring Dr (21093). Phone 410/252-7373; toll-free 800/289-4499;* fax 410/561-0182. www.holiday-inn.com. 245 rooms, 5 story. S, D $139; each additional $10; suites $259-$368; family, weekly, weekend, holiday rates. Crib free. Check-out noon. TV; cable (premium). In-room modem link. Microwaves available. Valet services. Coin laundry. Restaurant 6 am-10 pm. Bar; entertainment. Room service. Exercise equipment. Indoor/outdoor pool; whirlpool. Meeting rooms. Business services. Concierge. Gift shop. Cr cds: A, C, D, DS, JCB, MC, V.

D ⌨ 🏋 ⛵ SC

Hotels

★ ★ ★ **BROOKSHIRE INNER HARBOR SUITE HOTEL.** *120 E Lombard St (21202). Phone 410/625-1300; toll-free 800/647-0013; fax 410/649-2635. www.harbormagic.com.* Welcoming guests with the quiet elegance and sophisticated grace of a luxury retreat, this hotel offers a memorable stay. The guest rooms are spacious and handsomely appointed. 97 rooms, 11 story. Apr-Oct: S, D $169-$249; suites $219-$309; each additional $20; children free; weekend rates. Pet accepted, some restrictions; $100 deposit. Complimentary full breakfast. Check-out noon. Check-in noon. TV; cable (premium), VCR available. In-room modem link. Restaurant 6:30-10 am, 5-9 pm. Bar 5-10 pm. Room service. Health club privileges. Exercise equipment. Valet parking $20. Cr cds: A, D, DS, MC, V.

D 🐾 🏋 ⛵ SC

★ ★ **CLARION HOTEL PEABODY COURT.** *612 Cathedral St (21201). Phone 410/727-7101; fax 410/789-3312. www.clarioninn.com.* 104 rooms, 14 story. S, D $149-$169; each additional $10; suites $189-$500; under 18 free; weekend rates; package plans. Complimentary breakfast buffet. Check-out 11 am. TV; cable (premium), VCR available (movies). In-room modem link. Restaurant 6:30-9:30 am; 11 am-2 pm; 5-10 pm; Sun to 9 pm. Bar. Health club privileges. Pool privileges. Parking. Concierge. Restored hotel built in 1927. Marble floors, stairs in lobby. Period furnishings, artwork, crystal chandeliers. Cr cds: A, C, D, DS, JCB, MC, V.

D ⛵ SC

★ ★ **INN AT THE COLONNADE.** *4 W University Pkwy (21218). Phone 410/235-5400; toll-free 800/222-8733; fax 410/235-5572. www.doubletree.com.* With its rich European elegance, this hotel has spacious guest suites, an indoor pool, exercise facilities, and much more. Enjoy fine dining at the award-winning Four West, or see the local aquariums and museums. 3 story, 125 units. S, D $145-$202; each additional $15; suites $167-$475; family rates; weekend plans. Crib free. Pet accepted. Check-out noon. TV; cable (premium). In-room modem link. Balconies. Refrigerators, microwaves available. Coffee in rooms. Valet services. Restaurant 6 am-11 pm. Room service to 10 pm. Exercise equipment. Indoor pool, whirlpool, poolside service, lifeguard. Barber, beauty shop. Meeting room. Business center. Gift shop. Biedermeier-inspired furnishings; extensive collection of 18th-century European masters. Adjacent to Johns Hopkins University. Cr cds: A, C, D, DS, ER, JCB, MC, V.

⬛🏊🎿🛏️🆒🚶

★ ★ ★ **HARBOR COURT HOTEL.** *550 Light St (21202). Phone 410/234-0550; res 800/824-0076; fax 410/659-5925. www.harborcourt.com.* Gracious style is what this hotel is made of. With beautiful guest suites, 24-hour room service, and massage, visitors will have a great experience here. Relax at Hampton's, well known for great service, to experience the ultimate in dining. 200 rooms, 8 story, 25 suites. S, D $270-$340; suites $405-$2,000; under 18 free; weekend rates; some package plans. Crib free. Check-out noon. TV; cable (premium), VCR available, CD player in suites. In-room modem link. Bathroom phones, refrigerators. Coffee in rooms. Restaurant 6:30 am-9 pm; Sun from 7 am (See also HAMPTON'S). Bar 11-2 am; entertainment. Room service 24 hours. Exercise room, massage, sauna. Indoor pool, whirlpool, poolside service, lifeguard. Tennis. Lawn games. Racquetball. Covered parking: self-park $19; valet $25. Airport transportation. Meeting rooms. Business center. Concierge. Elegant retreat located on Inner Harbor; panoramic view of city. Cr cds: A, C, D, DS, MC, V.

⬛🏌️🏊🎿🛏️🚶

★ ★ **HOLIDAY INN.** *301 W Lombard St (21201). Phone 410/685-3500; toll-free 800/465-4329; fax 410/727-6169. www.holiday-inn.com.* 373 rooms, 13 story. Apr-Sept: S, D $219; each additional $10; suites $275; under 19 free; lower rates rest of year. Crib free. Check-out noon. TV; cable (premium). In-room modem link. Coin laundry. Restaurant 6:30 am-11 pm. Bar 11-1 am. Room service. Exercise equipment, sauna. Indoor pool, lifeguard. Garage parking $11/night. Business services. Convention facilities. Concierge. Gift shop. Cr cds: A, C, D, DS, JCB, MC, V.

⬛🏊🎿🛏️🆒

★ ★ ★ **HYATT REGENCY BALTIMORE.** *300 Light St (21202). Phone 410/528-1234; toll-free 800/233-1234; fax 410/685-3362. www.hyatt.com.* For business or pleasure, this grand hotel is conveniently located in Baltimore's Inner Harbor. It's linked by skywalk to the convention center and mall. Amenities also include basketball court, two restaurants, outdoor pool, and 29,000 square feet of meeting space. 511 rooms, 15 story. Memorial Day-late Oct: S, D $125-$363; each additional $25; suites $450-$1,000; under 18 free; weekend plan. Check-out noon. Check-in 3 pm. TV; cable (premium). In-room modem link. Restaurant. Bar; entertainment Fri, Sat. Room service. Supervised children's activities. Exercise

room, sauna. Two pools, one indoor; whirlpool, poolside services available. Tennis. Valet parking $20. Business center. Concierge. Luxury level. Cr cds: A, C, D, DS, ER, JCB, MC, V.

⬛🏌️🎿🛏️🆒🚶

★ ★ ★ **MARRIOTT BALTIMORE INNER HARBOR.** *110 S Eutaw St (21201). Phone 410/962-0202; fax 410/625-7892. www.marriott.com.* With a great location, this hotel is within walking distance to local aquariums, shopping, and site seeing. It also has 14,000 square feet of meeting space and a health club. 534 rooms, 10 story. S, D $179-$259; suites $284-$650; under 18 free; weekend rates. Check-out noon. Check-in 4 pm. TV; cable (premium), VCR available. In-room modem link. Restaurant. Bar; entertainment. Room service. Exercise equipment, sauna. Indoor pool, whirlpool. Business center. Concierge. Luxury level. Opposite baseball stadium at Camden Yards. Cr cds: A, C, D, DS, JCB, MC, V.

⬛🏊🎿🛏️🚶

★ ★ ★ **MARRIOTT BALTIMORE WATERFRONT.** *700 Aliceanna St (21202). Phone 410/385-3000; fax 410/895-1900. www.marriott.com.* 777 rooms, 32 story. S, D $129-$289; under 17 free. Check-out noon, check-in 4 pm. TV; cable (premium). In-room modem link. Restaurant. Bar. Room service. Exercise equipment, sauna. Indoor pool, whirlpool. Business center. Concierge. Luxury level. Cr cds: A, C, D, DS, MC, V.

⬛🏊🎿🛏️🆒🚶

★ ★ **RADISSON HOTEL AT CROSS KEYS.** *100 Village Sq (21210). Phone 410/532-6900; res 800/333-3333; fax 410/532-2403. www.radisson.com.* With stylish French country decorated rooms, this hotel offers tennis, swimming, tanning beds, and much more. Complimentary shuttle service to Baltimore's Inner Harbor and Camden Yards is provided. 148 rooms, 4 story. S, D $139-$189; each additional $15; suites $225-$425; under 17 free; weekend rates. Crib free. Check-out noon. TV; cable (premium). In-room modem link. Some private balconies. Bathroom phones. Restaurant. Bar. Room service. Exercise equipment. Health club privileges. Pool, poolside service, lifeguard. Barber, beauty shop. Meeting rooms. Business services. Cr cds: A, C, D, DS, ER, JCB, MC, V.

⬛🎾🏌️🏊🛏️

★ ★ ★ **RADISSON PLAZA LORD BALTIMORE.** *20 W Baltimore St (21201). Phone 410/539-8400; toll-free 800/333-3333; fax 410/625-1060. www.radisson.com.* Built in 1928, this elegant hotel is a registered historical landmark that continues to welcome guests with attentive service. The handsomely appointed guest rooms offer spectacular views of scenic downtown Baltimore. 458 rooms, 23 story. D $159-$269; each additional $15;

under 17 free; weekend rates. Check-out noon, check-in 3 pm. TV; cable. In-room modem link. Restaurant 6:30 am-10 pm. Bar 11-2 am. Health club privileges. Exercise equipment, sauna. Valet parking. Historic landmark; near harbor. Cr cds: A, C, D, DS, ER, JCB, MC, V.

[D] [⚇] [⚌] [SC]

★ ★ ★ **RENAISSANCE HARBORPLACE HOTEL.** *202 E Pratt St (21202). Phone 410/547-1200; toll-free 800/535-1201; fax 410/539-5780. www.renaissancehotels.com.* Located on the waterfront at Baltimore's scenic Inner Harbor and amidst all of downtown's delights, this hotel offers guests friendly service and elegantly-appointed guest rooms. Nearby attractions include the Gallery, Convention Center, and World Trade Center. 657 rooms, 12 story. Mar-Nov: S, D $169-$249; each additional $20; suites $275-$3,000; under 18 free; weekend rates. Check-out noon. TV; cable (premium), VCR available. In-room modem link. Restaurant. Bar; entertainment. Room service 24 hours. Exercise equipment, sauna. Health club privileges. Indoor pool; whirlpool, poolside service. Garage, valet parking available. Business center. Concierge. Luxury level. Cr cds: A, C, D, DS, ER, JCB, MC, V.

[D] [⚌] [⚇] [⚌] [⚌]

★ ★ ★ **SHERATON INNER HARBOR HOTEL.** *300 S Charles St (21201). Phone 410/962-8300; toll-free 800/325-3535; fax 410/962-8211. www.sheraton.com/Innerharbor.* 357 rooms, 15 story. Mar-June, Sept-Dec: S, D $109-$269; each additional $15; suites $450-$1,600; under 17 free; weekly, weekend rates; lower rates rest of year. Check-out noon. Check-in 3 pm. TV; cable (premium), VCR available (movies). In-room modem link. Restaurant. Bar. Room service. Exercise equipment, sauna. Health club privileges. Valet parking $19. Business center. Concierge. Cr cds: A, C, D, DS, JCB, MC, V.

[D] [⚌] [⚇] [⚌] [SC] [⚌]

★ ★ **TREMONT HOTEL.** *8 E Pleasant St (21202). Phone 410/576-1200; toll-free 800/873-6668; fax 410/244-1154. www.tremontsuiteshotels.com.* 58 kitchen suites, 13 story. S, D $159-$179; each additional $20; under 16 free; weekend rates. Crib free. Pet accepted; $5. Complimentary continental breakfast. Check-out noon. TV; cable, VCR available. Valet services. Restaurant. Bar. Health club privileges. Pool privileges. Valet parking $14. Meeting rooms. Business services. Concierge. Cr cds: A, C, D, DS, JCB, MC, V.

[D] [⚇] [⚌]

★ ★ ★ **WYNDHAM BALTIMORE INNER HARBOR HOTEL.** *101 W Fayette St (21201). Phone 410/752-1100; toll-free 800/996-3426; fax 410/752-0832. www.wyndham.com.* Just fifteen minutes from BWI Airport, this modern, high-rise hotel offers everything one would expect from a luxury hotel. Its grand style and comfort leaves guests feeling pampered. Oversized rooms and a great sports bar add to the overall experience. 732 rooms, 27 story. Apr-Nov: S, D $199-$269; each additional $20; suites $250-$1,500; under 17 free; weekend rates; package plans. Check-out noon. Check-in 4 pm. TV; cable (premium). In-room modem link. Restaurant. Bar. Exercise equipment. Pool, poolside service. Valet parking. Business center. Concierge. Cr cds: A, C, D, DS, ER, JCB, MC, V.

[D] [⚌] [⚇] [⚌] [SC] [⚌]

B&B/Small Inns

★ ★ ★ **ABACROMBIE BADGER BED AND BREAKFAST.** *58 W Biddle St (21201). Phone 410/244-7227; toll-free 888/9-BADGER; fax 410/244-8415. www.badger-inn.com.* Originally an 1880s townhouse, this delightful inn welcomes both business and leisure travelers. Catering to even the most discriminating guest, this wonderful inn envelopes guests with gracious tranquility and serene atmosphere. Nearby delights include the Meyerhoff Symphony Hall, Lyric Opera House, and the start to the fashionable Antique Row. 12 rooms, 4 story. D $88-$155. Children over 10 years only. Complimentary continental breakfast. Check-out 11 am, check-in 4-6 pm. TV. Restaurant. Bar. Turn-of-the-century building; many antique furnishings. Totally nonsmoking. Cr cds: A, D, DS, MC, V.

[⚌]

★ ★ ★ **ADMIRAL FELL INN.** *888 S Broadway, Historic Fell's Point (21231). Phone 410/522-7377; toll-free 800/292-4667; fax 410/522-0707. www.admiralfell.com.* Conveniently located downtown in the scenic historic waterfront, guests will delight in this renovated urban inn. From the custom-designed, Federal-style furnishings and meeting rooms, which offers guests an empowering view of the skyline and harbor, to the warm and attentive service guests are guaranteed to receive, this hotel offers a delight to both the business and leisure traveler. Enjoy a stroll along the quaint brick sidewalks to the numerous antique shops, gourmet restaurants, galleries, and friendly pubs. 83 rooms, 5 story. D $225-$245; each additional $20; under 16 free; weekly rates. Pet accepted, some restrictions. Complimentary continental breakfast. Check-out noon, check-in 4 pm. TV; cable (premium). Dining room noon-10 pm. Bar. Health club privileges. Cr cds: A, MC, V.

[D] [⚇] [⚌] [SC]

★ ★ ★ **CELIE'S WATERFRONT INN.** *1714 Thames St (21231). Phone 410/522-2323; toll-free 800/432-0184; fax 410/522-2324. www.celieswaterfront.com.* Located in the heart of Fell's Point waterfront district, this inn beckons to travelers with its atmospheric seafaring past. Rooms are airy and graced with skylights, offering scenic views of the harbor and well-maintained gardens. 9 rooms, 3 story. D $109-$239; holiday, weekend rates. Children over 10 years only. Complimentary continental breakfast. Check-out 11 am, check-in 3 pm. TV; cable; VCR. In-room modem link. Fireplaces. Health club privileges. Roof deck. Totally nonsmoking. Cr cds: A, DS, MC, V.

D ⊠

★ ★ ★ **HOPKINS INN.** *3404 St. Paul St (21218). Phone 410/235-8600; fax 410/235-7051. www.bichotels .com/hopkinsinn.* This charming bed-and-breakfast is just blocks from the Baltimore International College, and offers guests a delightful stay. Guests will enjoy the handsomely appointed rooms and friendly service. 25 rooms, 4 story. S $99-$129, D $109-$139; each additional $10; weekly, monthly rates. Covered parking $6. TV; cable. Complimentary continental breakfast. Check-out 11 am, check-in 3 pm. Meeting rooms. Business services available. 1920s Spanish Revival building. Rooms individually furnished in variety of styles. Totally nonsmoking. Cr cds: A, C, D, DS, JCB, MC, V.

⊠ SC

★ ★ ★ **INN AT GOVERNMENT HOUSE.** *1125 N Calvert St (21202). Phone 410/539-0566; fax 410/539-0567.* Located in the scenic Mount Vernon historic district, this elegant inn known to welcome Baltimore's visiting dignitaries also enjoys catering the leisure traveler. Comprised of three townhouses and charmingly appointed with an elegant Victorian décor, this inn guarantees a welcoming respite as well as warm and friendly service. 18 rooms, 4 story. S, D $125-$150; weekly rates; Preakness (2-day minimum). TV. Complimentary continental breakfast. Restaurant nearby. Check-out noon, check-in 3-8 pm. Business services available. Part of a complex of several Federal and Victorian mansions and townhouses (1888). Totally nonsmoking. Cr cds: A, C, D, DS, MC, V.

D ⊠ SC

★ ★ **INN AT HENDERSON'S WHARF.** *1000 Fell St (21231). Phone 410/522-7777; toll-free 800/522-2088; fax 410/522-7087. www.hendersonswharf.com.* 38 rooms. Pet accepted. Complimentary continental breakfast. Check-out noon, check-in 3 pm. TV; cable (premium). In-room modem link. Coin laundry. Exercise equipment. 19th-century tobacco warehouse. On waterfront; dockage available. Cr cds: A, C, D, DS, MC, V. **$$**

D ➹ ⟰ ⊠ SC

★ ★ ★ **MR. MOLE BED AND BREAKFAST.** *1601 Bolton St (21217). Phone 410/728-1179; fax 410/728-3379. www.mrmolebb.com.* Built in the 1860s and carefully restored, this charming inn offers guests a truly delightful stay. Charmingly appointed with beautiful 18th- and 19th-century antiques, as well as enchanting with its elegant marble fireplaces and handsomely furnished guest rooms, this inn welcomes guests to relax in this gracious style of living. 5 rooms, 5 story. S, D $119-$175; suites $150-$175; 2-day minimum weekends. Garage parking. Children over 10 years only. Complimentary breakfast. Check-out 11 am, check-in 4-6 pm. Business services available. In-room modem link. Totally nonsmoking. Cr cds: A, D, DS, MC, V.

⊠

Restaurants

★ ★ **ANGELINA'S.** *7135 Harford Rd (21234). Phone 410/444-5545; toll-free 800/272-2225. www.crabcake.com.* Italian, seafood, American menu. Closed Mon; Thanksgiving, Dec 25. Lunch, dinner. Bar. Entertainment Fri. Children's menu. Casual attire. Cr cds: A, DS, MC, V. **$$**

D

★ ★ ★ **ATLANTIC.** *2400 Boston St (21224). Phone 410/675-4565; fax 410/675-8755. www.atlanticrestaurant .com.* Specializes in fresh seafood. Hours: 11 am-3 pm, 5:30-10 pm; Fri, Sat to 11 pm; brunch 11 am-3 pm. Closed major holidays. Reservations accepted. Parking. Wine list. Lunch $6.50-$16; dinner $17-$26. Sun brunch $6-$12. Children's menu. Entertainment. Cr cds: A, C, D, DS, MC, V.

D ⊠

★ **BERTHA'S.** *734 S Broadway (21231). Phone 410/ 327-5795; fax 410/732-1548. www.berthas.com.* Hours: 11:30 am-11 pm; Fri, Sat to midnight; Sun brunch to 2 pm. Closed major holidays. Reservations required for Scottish afternoon tea (Mon-Sat). Bar. Lunch, dinner $5.75-$27.90. Sun brunch $7.50-$8.25. Specializes in mussels, seafood. Eclectic décor. Historic 19th-century building. Entertainment. Cr cds: MC, V.

D

★ ★ ★ **BLACK OLIVE.** *814 S Bond St (21231). Phone 410/276-7141; fax 410/276-7143. www.theblackolive.com.* Greek, Mediterranean, Middle Eastern menu. Hours: 5:30-10 pm; Sun 5-9 pm. Closed major holidays. Dinner $22-$48. Entertainment. Casual attire. Cr cds: A, C, D, DS, MC, V.

D ⊠

★ ★ ★ **BOCCACCIO.** *925 Eastern Ave (21231). Phone 410/234-1322; fax 410/727-6318.* Northern Italian cuisine of the highest caliber is prepared here. Zabaglione is heavenly, and the service is professional and charming. Hours: 11:30 am-2:30 pm, 5-11 pm; Sat from 5 pm; Sun 3-10 pm. Closed most major holidays. Dinner $17.25-$32.50. Bar. Casual attire. Cr cds: A, D, MC, V.

🄳

★ **CAFE HON.** *1002 W 36th St (21211). Phone 410/243-1230; fax 410/243-6461. www.cafehon.com.* Hours: 7 am-9 pm; Fri, Sat to 10 pm; Sun to 8 pm; Sat, Sun brunch 9 am-3 pm. Closed most major holidays. Reservations accepted. Bar. Breakfast $1.25-$6.25, lunch, dinner $3.75-$14.95. Sun brunch $1.75-$8.95. Children's menu. Specialties: crab cakes, meatloaf. Eclectic cafe reminiscent of 1930s Baltimore soda fountain. Totally nonsmoking. Cr cds: A, D, MC, V.

🄳 ⬛

★ ★ ★ ★ **CHARLESTON.** *1000 Lancaster St (21202). Phone 410/332-7373; fax 410/332-8425. www.charlestonrestaurant.com.* Chef-owner Cindy Wolf's stunning, regional American restaurant is one of the most exciting and luxurious dining experiences to be had in Baltimore. This upscale bistro-style room is warmed by an amber glow that makes you feel ten years younger. And the food is even better. Sautéed heads-on gulf shrimp with andouille sausage and Tasso ham with creamy stone-milled grits, a signature dish, is a perfect example of the robust, home-style low-country cooking served here nightly. The restaurant also has an impressive wine program that includes several dozen sparkling wines and a hefty selection of about 400 well-chosen whites and reds from the new world (Australia, South Africa, New Zealand, and Chile) and the old (France, Italy, and Spain). If wine doesn't call you, Charleston offers more than a dozen microbrews and imported beers and a splashy cocktail list that contains some inventive sippers as well as a great variety of classics. American menu. Menu changes daily. Hours: 5:30-10 pm; Fri, Sat to 11 pm. Closed Sun, holidays. Dinner a la carte entrées $26-$32; prix fixe $60. Entertainment. Reservations accepted. Cr cds: A, C, D, DS, MC, V.

🄳 ⬛

★ ★ **CHIAPPARELLI'S OF LITTLE ITALY.** *237 S High St (21202). Phone 410/837-0309; fax 410/783-7985. www.chiapparellis.com.* Southern Italian menu. Hours: 11 am-10 pm; Fri, Sat to midnight. Closed Thanksgiving, Dec 25. Dinner $13-$28. Bar. Children's menu. Built in 1870; original brick walls, oak paneling. Casual attire. Valet parking. 7 dining rooms on 2 levels. Cr cds: A, C, D, DS, MC, V.

★ ★ **CITY LIGHTS.** *301 Light St (21202). Phone 410/244-8811; fax 410/244-8815. www.citylightsseafood.com.* Hours: 11:30 am-10 pm; Fri to 11 pm; Sat to midnight; Sun to 9 pm. Closed Thanksgiving, Dec 24, 25. Seafood menu. Lunch, dinner $11.50-$23.95. Bar. Children's menu. Reservations accepted. Outdoor seating. Cr cds: A, C, D, DS, MC, V.

🄳

★ ★ ★ **DALESIO'S OF LITTLE ITALY.** *829 Eastern Ave (21202). Phone 410/539-1965; fax 410/576-8749. www.dalesios.com.* Northern Italian menu. Hours: 11:30 am-3 pm, 5-10 pm; Sun 4-9 pm. Closed Thanksgiving. Dinner $14-$25. Bar. Casual attire. Valet parking available. Outdoor seating. Own cakes, pasta. Cr cds: MC, V.

🄳

★ ★ ★ **DELLA NOTTE.** *801 Eastern Ave (21202). Phone 410/837-5500; fax 410/837-2600.* Italian menu. Closed Dec 25. Lunch, dinner. Bar. Children's menu. Casual attire. Cr cds: A, D, DS, MC, V. **$$**

🄳

★ ★ **GERMANO'S TRATTORIA.** *300 S High St (21202). Phone 410/752-4515; fax 410/625-6472. www.germanostrattoria.com.* Tuscan, regional Italian menu. Hours: 11:30 am-11 pm; Fri, Sat to midnight. Closed Thanksgiving, Dec 25. Dinner $12.50-$25.95. Bar. Children's menu. Casual attire. Cr cds: A, C, D, DS, ER, MC, V.

🄳

★ ★ ★ **HAMPTON'S.** *550 Light St (21202). Phone 410/234-0550; fax 410/659-5925. www.harborcourt.com.* Located in the Harbor Court Hotel, Hampton's is a luxurious restaurant that serves marvelous seasonal American fare matched by serene and romantic views of Baltimore's Inner Harbor. The kitchen stays true to classic technique, using pristine regional ingredients and clever modern tweaks to add a savvy edge to the plate. Specialties include lobster bisque flecked with chives and mushrooms, seared dry-aged beef tenderloin, and a kickin' horseradish Caesar salad. The wine list is exceptional as well, focusing on small, independent producers and rare vintages that pair up seamlessly with the inspired menu. Nightly live piano and a jazz quartet on the weekends fill the room with an old-world elegance and charm. American menu. Hours: 5:30-10 pm; Sun brunch 10:30 am-2 pm, closed Mon. Dinner $65, Sun brunch $23-$36. Service bar. Jacket required. Reservations required. Valet parking available. Totally nonsmoking. Cr cds: A, D, DS, MC, V.

🄳 ⬛

★ **HENNINGER'S TAVERN.** *1812 Bank St (21231). Phone 410/342-2172. www.henningerstavern.com.* American menu. Hours: 5-10 pm; Fri, Sat to 11 pm. Closed Sun, Mon; Jan 1, Dec 25. Dinner $16.50-$24. Bar to 1 am. Casual attire. Cr cds: A, D, MC, V.

★ ★ **IKAROS.** *4805 Eastern Ave (21224). Phone 410/633-3750.* Hours: 11 am-10 pm; Fri, Sat to 11 pm. Closed Tues; Thanksgiving, Dec 25. Greek, American menu. Service bar. Lunch $4-$9, dinner $8-$15. Specializes in lamb, squid, fresh whole fish. Cr cds: A, D, DS, MC, V.

D

★ ★ **JEANNIER'S.** *105 W 39th St (21211). Phone 410/889-3303; fax 410/889-6813.* Hours: noon-2:30 pm, 5:30-9:30 pm; Fri to 10 pm; Sat 5:30-10 pm; early-bird dinner 5:30-7 pm. Closed Sun; most major holidays. French, continental menu. Bar noon-11 pm. A la carte entrées: lunch $6-$11, dinner $13.95-$25. Complete meals: dinner $14-$25. Specializes in seafood, country French cuisine. Own desserts. Country château décor. Cr cds: A, D, MC, V.

D

★ ★ **JOHN STEVEN, LTD.** *1800 Thames St (21231). Phone 410/327-5561; toll-free 877/732-3460; fax 410/327-0513. www.johnstevensltd.com.* American, eclectic, seafood menu. Hours: 11 am-11 pm; Fri, Sat to midnight. Dinner $12.50-$22. Sushi bar noon-1:30 am. Bar to 2 am; Sun from 10 am. Building built in 1838. Casual attire. Outdoor seating. Cr cds: A, D, MC, V.

D

★ ★ ★ **JOY AMERICA CAFE.** *800 Key Hwy (21230). Phone 410/244-6500; fax 410/244-6363.* "Nothing Without Joy" is the fitting motto at this whimsical restaurant housed on the top floor of Baltimore's unique Visionary Arts Museum. The food is as creative as the décor and many dishes have a Latin flare. Hours: 11:30 am-2:30 pm, 5:30-10 pm; Sun brunch 11 am-4 pm. Closed Mon; Labor Day, Thanksgiving, Dec 25. Reservations accepted. Contemporary American menu. Bar. Lunch $9-$15, dinner $19-$28.50. Sun brunch $11.50-$14. Children's menu. Specialties: chicken and dried cherry dim sum, Thai-grilled rack of lamb. Outdoor seating. View of city and Inner Harbor. Totally nonsmoking. Cr cds: A, C, D, MC, V.

D 🚱

★ ★ **KAWASAKI.** *413 N Charles St (21201). Phone 410/659-7600; fax 410/625-0607. www.kawasaki-restaurant.com.* Japanese menu. Hours: 11:30-2:30 pm, 5-11 pm; Fri to midnight; Sat 5 pm-midnight. Closed Sun;

most major holidays. Dinner $9.50-$19. Bar. Casual attire. Cr cds: A, D, MC, V.

D

★ ★ ★ **LA SCALA.** *1012 Eastern Ave (21202). Phone 410/783-9209; fax 410/783-5949. www.lascaladining.com.* Italian menu. Hours: 4:30-10 pm; Fri, Sat to 11 pm; Sun 2-10 pm. Closed Jan 1, Thanksgiving, Dec 25. Dinner $12.95-$29.95. Bar. Casual attire. Cr cds: A, D, DS, MC, V.

★ ★ **MT. WASHINGTON TAVERN.** *5700 Newbury St (21209). Phone 410/367-6903; fax 410/542-9023. www.mtwashingtontavern.com.* Hours: 11:30 am-10 pm; Sun 10:30 am-10 pm; Sun brunch to 3 pm. Closed Dec 25. Reservations accepted. Bar. Lunch, dinner $6-$24.50. Sun brunch $4.95-$12.95. Children's menu. Specializes in Angus beef, veal chops, shrimp. Entertainment Wed, Sat. Outdoor seating. Tavern atmosphere has varied dining areas. Cr cds: A, D, MC, V.

★ ★ **OBRYCKI'S CRAB HOUSE.** *1727 E Pratt St (21231). Phone 410/732-6399; fax 410/522-4637. www.obryckis.com.* Hours: 11:30 am-11 pm; Sun to 9:30 pm. Closed mid-Dec-Mar. Bar. Lunch $4.95-$13.50, dinner $6.50-$28.95. Children's menu. Specializes in crab. Parking. Family-owned. Cr cds: A, D, DS, MC, V.

D

★ ★ **PIERPOINT.** *1822 Aliceanna St (21231). Phone 410/675-2080; fax 410/563-2855. www.pierpointrestaurant.com.* American menu. Hours: 11:30 am-2 pm, 5-9:30 pm; Fri, Sat 5:30-10:30 pm; Sun 4-9 pm; Sun brunch 10:30 am-1:30 pm. Closed Mon; Jan 1, Dec 25. Dinner $17.50-$25. Bar. Casual attire. Cr cds: A, C, D, DS, ER, MC, V.

★ ★ ★ **THE PRIME RIB.** *1101 N Calvert St (21202). Phone 410/539-1804; fax 410/837-0244. www.theprimerib.com.* It's no surprise that The Prime Rib has been voted the best steakhouse in town—it has been serving consistently good steaks, chops, and seafood for three decades. With an upscale atmosphere, it is known as "the civilized steakhouse." Hours: 5-11:30 pm; Sat to midnight; Sun 4-10:30 pm. Closed Thanksgiving. Dinner $20-$40. Bar. Jacket required. Reservations accepted. Black lacquered walls. Cr cds: A, C, D, MC, V.

D

★ ★ **ROCCO'S CAPRICCIO.** *846 Fawn St (21202). Phone 410/685-2710; toll-free 888/685-2710; fax 410/539-4261.* Northern Italian, Mediterranean menu. Hours: 11:30 am-10:30 pm; Fri, Sat to 11:30 pm. Closed Thanksgiving, Dec 25. Dinner $15.95-$32. Bar. Children's menu. Casual attire. Cr cds: A, DS, MC, V.

★ ★ ★ **RUBY LOUNGE.** *802 N Charles St (21201). Phone 410/539-8051.* This is a sophisticated spot to spend an evening. The elegantly apportioned restaurant and bar are both upscale. The menu presents appetizers and entrées that are a cut above, and the skilled and efficient bar staff whip up fanciful concoctions that are sure to please. American menu. Hours: 5:30-11 pm; Fri, Sat to midnight. Closed Sun, Mon; also most major holidays. Dinner $12-$26. Bar. Casual attire. Valet parking available. Cr cds: A, C, D, DS, MC, V.

★ ★ ★ **RUTH'S CHRIS STEAK HOUSE.** *600 Water St (21202). Phone 410/783-0033; toll-free 800/544-0808; fax 410/783-0049. www.ruthschris.com.* Sizzling hot, custom-aged steaks are the specialty at this branch of the famed, national chain. Portions are big enough to share, and there's a courtesy shuttle to all major, Inner Harbor hotels. Hours: 5-10 pm; Fri, Sat to 11 pm. Closed Jan 1, Super Bowl Sun, Thanksgiving, Dec 25. Dinner $17.95-$32.95. Bar. Upscale furnishings. Cr cds: A, D, DS, MC, V.
D

★ ★ **SOTTO SOPRA.** *405 N Charles St (21201). Phone 410/625-0534; fax 410/625-2642. www.sottosoprainc.com.* Northern Italian menu. Hours: 11:30 am-2:30 pm, 5:30-10:30 pm; Fri, Sat to 11:30 pm; Sun to 9:30 pm. Dinner $16-$28. Entertainment. Casual attire. Cr cds: A, MC, V.
D 🚫

★ ★ ★ **SPIKE AND CHARLIE'S.** *1225 Cathedral St (21201). Phone 410/752-8144. www.spikeandcharlies.com.* Here food is art and there is a dedication to value and creativity. Eclectic culinary creations are served in a ultrachic dinner salon. American, seafood, steak menu. Hours: 5:30-10 pm; Fri, Sat to midnight. Closed Mon; most major holidays. Dinner. Bar. Reservations required. Cr cds: A, D, MC, V. **$$**
D

★ ★ **TIO PEPE.** *10 E Franklin St (21202). Phone 410/539-4675; fax 410/837-7288.* Spanish, continental menu. Hours: 11:30 am-2:30 pm, 5-10:30 pm; Fri to 11:30 pm; Sat 5-11:30 pm; Sun 4-10:30 pm. Closed most major holidays. Lunch $8.75-$15.50, dinner $16.25-$29.50. Bar. Jacket required. Reservations required. Cr cds: A, C, D, DS, ER, MC, V.
D

★ ★ **VELLEGGIA'S.** *829 E Pratt St (21202). Phone 410/685-2620; fax 410/837-5176.* Italian menu. Hours: 11 am-11 pm; Fri to midnight; Sat to 1 am. Closed Dec 24, 25. Dinner $10.25-$21.95. Bar. Children's menu. Casual attire. Cr cds: A, C, D, DS, ER, MC, V.
D

Baltimore/ Washington International Airport Area

See also Baltimore; also see District of Columbia

Services and Information

Information 410/859-7100.

Lost and Found. 410/859-7387.

Weather. 410/936-1212.

Cash machines. Main Terminal, Pier C.

Airlines. Air Aruba, Air Canada, Air Jamaica, America West, American, British Airways, Continental, Delta, El Al, Icelandair, Midway, Northwest, Southwest, United, USAir.

Motel/Motor Lodge

★ **HAMPTON INN.** *829 Elkridge Landing Rd, Linthicum (21090). Phone 410/850-0600; toll-free 800/426-7866; fax 410/691-2119. www.hamptoninn.com.* 139 rooms, 5 story. S, D $94-$114; under 18 free. Crib free. Pet accepted. TV; cable (premium). Complimentary continental breakfast. Restaurant nearby. Check-out noon. Meeting rooms. Business services available. In-room modem link. Valet service. Free airport, train transportation. Refrigerators, microwaves available. Cr cds: A, C, D, DS, ER, JCB, MC, V.
D 🐾 ✈ 🔙 **SC**

Hotels

★ ★ ★ **MARRIOTT BALTIMORE WASHINGTON INTERNATIONAL AIRPORT.** *1743 W Nursery Rd, Linthicum (21240). Phone 410/859-8300; toll-free 800/228-9290; fax 410/691-4555. www.marriott.com.* This hotel caters to the business traveler and delights the leisure traveler with the spacious guest rooms and warm, friendly service. Nearby attractions include the Arundel Mills Outlet Shopping Center, Baltimore Inner Harbor, and National Aquarium. 310 rooms, 10 story. S, D $235-$269; each additional $15; suites $255-$279; under 18 free. Crib free. Check-out noon. TV; cable (premium). In-room modem link. Valet services, coin laundry. Restaurant 6:30 am-10 pm. Bar 4 pm-1:30 am. Room service. Health club privileges. Exercise equipment, massage. Indoor pool, whirlpool. Free airport transportation. Business center. Convention facilities. Gift shop. Luxury level. Cr cds: A, C, D, DS, ER, JCB, MC, V.

D ⛲ ⛷ 🏊 SC 🚶

★ ★ ★ **SHERATON INTERNATIONAL HOTEL ON BWI AIRPORT.** *7032 Elm Rd, Baltimore (21240). Phone 410/859-3300; fax 410/859-0565. www.sheraton.com.* 201 rooms, 2 story. S, D $199-$239; each additional $10; suites $219-$259; under 16 free; weekend rates. Crib free. Check-out noon. TV; cable (premium). In-room modem link. Restaurant 6:30 am-10:30 pm. Bar noon-2 am; entertainment. Room service 24 hours. Exercise equipment. Pool, poolside service, lifeguard. Airport transportation. Meeting rooms. Business services. Sundries. Gift shop. Luxury level. Cr cds: A, C, D, DS, JCB, MC, V.

D ⛲ ⛷ 🏊

All Suite

★ ★ **EMBASSY SUITES.** *1300 Concourse Dr, Linthicum (21090). Phone 410/850-0747; fax 410/850-0895. www.embassysuites.com.* Conveniently located 1.5 miles from the airport, this elegant hotel caters to the business traveler as well as the leisure traveler. Featuring a lush garden atrium, spacious guest rooms, and friendly and attentive service, this hotel welcomes guests with an elegance and an attention to detail that pleases even the most discriminating traveler. 251 suites, 8 story. S $229.95-$259.95; D $249.95-$279.95; each additional $10; under 18 free; weekend rates. Crib free. Complimentary breakfast. Check-out noon. TV; cable (premium). In-room modem link. Bathroom phones, refrigerators, microwaves. Valet services. Restaurant 6:30 am-10 pm; weekends to 11 pm. Bar 11-1 am. Room service. Health club privileges. Exercise equipment, sauna. Indoor pool, whirlpool, lifeguard. Airport transportation. Business center. Convention facilities. Gift shop. Cr cds: A, C, D, DS, ER, JCB, MC, V.

D ⛲ ⛷ 🏊 SC 🚶

Bethesda (C-6)

Also see District of Columbia

Pop 55,277 **Elev** 305 ft **Area code** 301

Information The Greater Bethesda-Chevy Chase Chamber of Commerce, Landow Building, 7910 Woodmont Ave, Suite 1204, 20814; 301/652-4900

Web www.bccchamber.org

A suburb of Washington, D.C., Bethesda is the home of both the National Institutes of Health, research arm of the Public Health Service, and Bethesda Naval Hospital.

What to See and Do

Cabin John Regional Park. *Approximately 3 miles N on MD 355 then W on Tuckerman Ln. Phone 301/299-0024.* This 551-acre park has playgrounds, miniature train ride; nature center; concerts (summer evenings; free); tennis courts, game fields, ice rink, nature trails, picnicking. Fee for some activities. (Daily)

Clara Barton National Historic Site. *5801 Oxford Rd (20812). 3 miles W via MD 191, Goldsboro Rd in Glen Echo. Phone 301/492-6245.* (see DISTRICT OF COLUMBIA)

National Library of Medicine. *8600 Rockville Pike. Phone 301/496-6308.* World's largest biomedical library; rare books, manuscripts, prints; medical art displays. (Mon-Sat; closed holidays and Sat before Mon holidays) Visitors center and guided tour (Mon-Fri, one departure each day). **FREE**

Motel/Motor Lodge

★ ★ **HOLIDAY INN.** *5520 Wisconsin Ave, Chevy Chase (20815). Phone 301/656-1500; fax 301/656-5045. www.holiday-inn.com.* 215 rooms, 12 story. S, D $89-$159; each additional $10; suites $169; under 18 free. Crib free. Pet accepted, some restrictions; $50. Check-out noon. TV; cable (premium), VCR available. In-room modem link. Bathroom phones; microwaves available. Free laundry facilities. Restaurant 6:30 am-11 pm. Bar. Health club privileges. Pool. Meeting rooms. Business center. Gift shop. Cr cds: A, D, DS, JCB, MC, V.

D 🐾 ⛲ 🏊 🚶

Hotel

★ ★ ★ **HYATT REGENCY BETHESDA.** *1 Bethesda Metro Ctr (20814). Phone 301/657-1234; fax 301/657-6453. www.bethesda.hyatt.com.* Guests will delight in all the amenities this hotel has to offer. Located at Metro Center and within steps to restaurants, theaters, and some of the best shopping, this hotel is perfect for both the business and leisure traveler, with a fully equipped health club and rooftop indoor pool, attentive service, and well appointed guest rooms. 390 rooms, 12 story. Check-out noon, check-in 3 pm. TV; cable (premium), VCR available. In-room modem link. Restaurant, bar. Children's activity center. In-house fitness room, sauna. Indoor pool. Covered parking $10; valet $12. Business center. Luxury level. Cr cds: A, C, D, DS, ER, JCB, MC, V. **$$**

D ⛲ ⛷ 🏊 🚶

All Suite

★ ★ ★ **MARRIOTT SUITES BETHESDA.** *6711 Democracy Blvd (20817). Phone 301/897-5600; fax 301/ 530-1427. www.marriotthotels.com.* Whether traveling for business or pleasure, this hotel welcomes guests with spacious and well-appointed guest rooms, some with extravagant marbled baths. Providing all the comforts of home, this hotel offers guests a relaxing stay. Nearby attractions include the Kennedy Center, Mormon Temple, and National Zoo. 274 suites, 11 story. Check-out noon, check-in 4 pm. TV; cable (premium), VCR available. In-room modem link. Restaurant. In-house fitness room. Indoor pool, outdoor pool, whirlpool. Business center. Cr cds: A, C, D, DS, ER, JCB, MC, V. **$$**

D 🏊 🏋 🚭 🏃

Restaurants

★ **AUSTIN GRILL.** *7278 Woodmont Ave (20814). Phone 301/656-1366; fax 301/656-1398. www.austingrill.com.* Hours: 11:30 am-11 pm; Mon to 10 pm; Fri to midnight; Sat 11 am-midnight; Sun 11 am-10 pm; Sat, Sun brunch to 3 pm. Closed Thanksgiving, Dec 24-25. Tex-Mex menu. Bar. Lunch $6-$9, dinner $6-$14. Sat, Sun brunch $5-$7. Children's menu. Specializes in chicken, fresh seafood, vegetarian dishes. Outdoor seating. Contemporary Southwestern motif. Totally nonsmoking. Cr cds: D, MC, V.

D 🚭

★★**BACCHUS BETHESDA.** *7945 Norfolk Ave (20814). Phone 301/657-1722; fax 301/657-4406. www.bacchusrestaurant.com.* Middle Eastern menu. Closed Jan 1, Thanksgiving, Dec 25. Lunch, dinner. Casual attire. Valet parking (dinner). Outdoor seating. Cr cds: A, D, DS, MC, V. **$$**

D

★ **BETHESDA CRAB HOUSE.** *4958 Bethesda Ave (20814). Phone 301/652-3382; fax 301/652-4669. www.bethesdacrabhouse.com.* Hours: 9 am-midnight. Closed Dec 25. Reservations accepted. Wine, beer. A la carte entrées: lunch, dinner $10-$30. Specializes in spiced shrimp, steamed crab, crabcakes. Outdoor seating. Rustic décor; established 1961. Cr cds: MC, V.

★ ★ **BOMBAY DINING.** *4931 Cordell Ave (20814). Phone 301/656-3373; fax 301/656-2535.* Hours: 11:30 am-2:30 pm, 5:30-10 pm; Sat, Sun noon-3 pm, 5:30-10:30 pm. Reservations accepted. Indian menu. Bar. Lunch, dinner $7.95-$15.95. Sat, Sun brunch $9.95. Specializes in tandoori, curries, vegetables. Salad bar. Valet parking (weekends). Cr cds: A, DS, MC, V.

★ ★ **BUON GIORNO.** *8003 Norfolk Ave (20814). Phone 301/652-1400; fax 301/654-5508.* Italian menu. Closed Mon; Jan 1, Easter, Thanksgiving, Dec 25; also mid-Aug-mid-Sept. Dinner. Bar. Valet parking (dinner). Totally nonsmoking. Cr cds: A, C, D, DS, MC, V.

D 🚭

★ ★ **CAFE BETHESDA.** *5027 Wilson Ln (20814). Phone 301/657-3383.* French bistro menu. Closed Mon; major holidays; also Super Bowl Sun. Lunch, dinner. Casual attire. Valet parking. Outdoor seating. Totally nonsmoking. Cr cds: A, D, MC, V. **$$$**

🚭

★ ★ ★ **CESCO TRATTORIA.** *4871 Cordell Ave (20814). Phone 301/654-8333; fax 301/654-8874.* Reminiscent of a Tuscan villa, Cesco Trattoria features breads are baked fresh daily in a wood-burning oven which is visible to diners. Entrees are light, yet hearty, and desserts are simply delicious. Italian menu. Closed major holidays. Lunch, dinner. Bar. Casual attire. Valet parking (dinner). Outdoor seating. Cr cds: A, MC, V. **$$$**

D

★ ★ **DELRAY VIETNAMESE GARDEN.** *4918 Delray Ave (20814). Phone 301/986-0606.* Hours: 11:30 am-2:30 pm, 5-10 pm; Sat, Sun 5-10 pm. Closed major holidays. Reservations required Fri, Sat (dinner). Vietnamese menu. Bar. A la carte entrées: lunch $5.95-$12.75, dinner $7.95-$12.75. Specialties: pinecone fish, nid d'amour, curry. Valet parking weekends. Outdoor seating. Country inn décor. Cr cds: A, V.

D SC

★ ★ **FOONG LIN.** *7710 Norfolk Ave (20814). Phone 301/656-3427; fax 301/215-7985. www.foonglin.com.* Chinese menu. Hours: 11 am-10:30 pm; Fri, Sat to 11 pm. Closed Thanksgiving. Lunch $3.95-$7.95, dinner $3.95-$19.95. Bar. Reservations accepted. Cr cds: A, MC.

D

★ ★ **FRASCATI.** *4806 Rugby Ave (20814). Phone 301/652-9514; fax 301/656-5538. www.ilfrascati.com.* Italian menu. Hours: 11 am-2:30 pm, 4-10:30 pm; Sat from 5 pm; Sun 4-9:30 pm; early-bird dinner Tues-Fri, Sun 4-6:30 pm. Closed Mon; Jan 1, Easter, Dec 25. Lunch $4.75-$6.95, dinner $9.75-$16.95. Reservations accepted, required Fri, Sat. Outdoor seating. Totally nonsmoking. Cr cds: A, C, D, DS, MC, V.

D 🚭

★ ★ **HAANDI.** *4904 Fairmont Ave (20814). Phone 301/718-0121; fax 301/718-0123. www.haandi.com.* Hours: 11:30 am-2:30 pm, 5-10 pm; Fri, Sat to 10:30 pm. Reservations accepted. Indian menu. Bar. Lunch $4.95-$10.95, dinner $7.95-$14.95. Buffet: lunch $7.95. Specialties: tandoori dishes, vegetarian dishes, murg makhini. Totally nonsmoking. Cr cds: A, C, D, MC, V.

D

★ ★ **JEAN-MICHEL.** *10223 Old Georgetown Rd (20814). Phone 301/564-4910; fax 301/569-4912.* Hours: 11:30 am-2:30 pm, 5:30-10 pm; Sat from 5:30 pm; Sun 5:30-8:30 pm. Closed most major holidays; also Sun July-Aug. Reservations accepted. French menu. Service bar. Lunch $9.50-$13.25, dinner $12.95-$21.75. Specialties: mussels marinieres, venison with chestnut puree and cranberry jelly. French décor. Cr cds: A, C, D, MC, V.

D

★ ★ ★ **LA FERME.** *7101 Brookville Rd, Chevy Chase (20815). Phone 301/986-5255; fax 301/951-4450. www. lafermerestaurant.com.* A pretty country house setting is the draw at this comfortable French restaurant. French menu. Closed Mon; Dec 25. Lunch, dinner. Reservations required Fri, Sat dinner. Outdoor seating. Cr cds: A, D, DS, MC, V. **$$**

D

★ ★ ★ **LE VIEUX LOGIS.** *7925 Old Georgetown Rd (20814). Phone 301/652-6816; fax 301/652-8221.* This American and Scandinavian cooking adds to the dining experience. French menu. Closed Sun; Jan 1, Dec 25. Dinner. Casual attire. Free valet parking. Outdoor seating. Cr cds: A, D, DS, MC, V. **$$$**

D

★ **MATUBA.** *4918 Cordell Ave (20814). Phone 301/652-7449; fax 301/365-5991.* Hours: 11:30 am-2:30 pm, 5-10 pm; Fri to 10:30 pm; Sat noon-3 pm, 5-10:30 pm; Sun 5-10 pm. Japanese menu. Wine, beer. Lunch $4.95-$9.95, dinner $6.95-$11.95. Specialties: sushi, chicken teriyaki. Casual décor. Totally nonsmoking. Cr cds: A, C, D, DS, MC, V.

D

★ ★ **MONTGOMERY'S GRILLE.** *7200 Wisconsin Ave (20814). Phone 301/654-3595; fax 301/654-3596.* Hours: 11:30 am-10 pm; Thurs to 11 pm; Fri, Sat to midnight; Sun from 10 am; Sun brunch to 2 pm. Closed Thanksgiving, Dec 25. Bar to 12:30 am; Fri, Sat to 1:30 am. Lunch $5.95-$8.95, dinner $7.95-$14.95. Sun brunch $12.95. Children's menu. Specializes in pasta, fresh grilled seafood, crab cakes. Own baking. Outdoor seating. American pub atmosphere with antique bar, bronze-framed windows, hand-carved woodwork. Totally nonsmoking. Cr cds: A, C, D, DS, MC, V.

★ ★ **NAM'S.** *4928 Cordell Ave (20814). Phone 301/652-2635; fax 301/652-7937.* Hours: 11:30 am-2:30 pm, 5:30-11 pm; Sat 5-11 pm; Sun 5-9:30 pm. Closed Thanksgiving, Dec 25. Reservations accepted. Vietnamese menu. Bar. Lunch $5.50-$8.50, dinner $7.50-$10.95. Specializes in chicken, beef, pork. Contemporary décor. Cr cds: A, MC, V.

★ **NAPA THAI.** *4924 St. Elmo (20814). Phone 301/986-8590; fax 301/986-8490.* Thai menu. Closed July 4, Thanksgiving. Lunch, dinner. Casual attire. Outdoor seating. **$$**

★ **RAKU.** *7240 Woodmont Ave (20814). Phone 301/718-8680; fax 301/718-8683.* Pan-Asian menu. Hours: 11:30 am-10 pm; Fri, Sat to 10:30 pm; Sun to 9 pm. Closed Thanksgiving, Dec 25. Lunch $6.95-$17.95, dinner $12-$19. Children's menu. Casual décor with Asian flair. Outdoor seating. Totally nonsmoking. Cr cds: A, MC, V.

★ ★ **RED TOMATO CAFE.** *4910 St. Elmo Ave (20814). Phone 301/652-4499; fax 301/652-9643. www.redtomato.com.* Hours: 11:30 am-9:30 pm; Thurs to 10 pm; Fri, Sat to 11 pm; Sun 4:30-9 pm. Closed Jan 1, Thanksgiving, Dec 25. Reservations accepted Sun-Thurs. Italian, American menu. Service bar. A la carte entrees: lunch $3.95-$10.95, dinner $5.95-$15.95. Specializes in pasta, pizza. Valet parking Thurs-Sat. Colorful, contemporary pizzeria; large mural, wood-burning pizza oven. Totally nonsmoking. Cr cds: A, D, DS, MC, V.

D

★ ★ ★ **RUTH'S CHRIS STEAKHOUSE.** *7315 Wisconsin Ave (20814). Phone 301/652-7877; fax 301/718-8463. www.ruthschris.com.* Hours: 5-10:30 pm; Sun 4-9:30 pm. Closed Thanksgiving, Dec 25. Dinner $18.95-$35.95. Bar to midnight. Reservations required Fri, Sat dinner. Valet parking available. Lobster tank; cigar lounge. Totally nonsmoking. Cr cds: A, D, DS, MC, V.

D

★ ★ **TEL-AVIV CAFE.** *4869 Cordell Ave (20814). Phone 301/718-9068; fax 301/718-9069.* Mediterranean menu. Closed Yom Kippur, Passover. Lunch, dinner $6.95-$15.95. Bar to 1 am; Fri, Sat to 2 am. Entertainment Tues, Sat. Outdoor seating. Cr cds: A, C, D, MC, V.

D

★ ★ **THYME SQUARE.** *4735 Bethesda Ave (20814). Phone 301/657-9077; fax 301/657-4505.* Hours: 11 am-10 pm; Fri, Sat to 11 pm. Closed Dec 24, 25. Reservations accepted; required Thurs-Sun dinner. Bar. Lunch $5.95-$10.95, dinner $6.95-$18.95. Specializes in seasonal American dishes, vegetarian dishes, fresh seafood. Contemporary décor with extensive murals; open kitchen. Totally nonsmoking. Cr cds: MC, V.

D

★ ★ ★ **TRAGARA.** *4935 Cordell Ave (20814). Phone 301/951-4935; fax 301/951-0401. www.tragara.com.* Tragara is one of Bethesda's most elegant and romantic restaurants, offering satisfying Italian cuisine and impeccable service. Bathed in soft light, with fresh roses on every linen-topped table, Tragara is serene and relaxing—a lovely place to dine and then linger. Tables fill up quickly at lunch and dinner with smartly dressed business executives and stylish quartets of 30-something couples who have no doubt hired baby-sitters for their escape to the civilized land of adults. The impressive Italian kitchen draws them all in with a tempting menu of pastas, fish, meat, and antipasti, but be sure to save room to indulge in the house-made gelato before saying, "Ciao." Italian menu. Closed Jan 1, July 4, Thanksgiving, Dec 25. Lunch, dinner. Casual attire. Valet parking available. Cr cds: A, C, D, MC, V. **$$$**

D

Boonsboro (B-5)

See also Frederick, Hagerstown

Settled 1787 **Pop** 2,803 **Elev** 591 ft **Area code** 301 **Zip** 21713

Information Hagerstown/Washington County Chamber of Commerce, 111 W Washington St; 301/739-2015

Web www.hagerstown.org

What to See and Do

Crystal Grottoes Caverns. *1 mile SW on MD 34. Phone 301/432-6336.* Limestone caverns may be viewed from walkways. Picnicking. Guided tours (Apr-Oct, daily; rest of year, by appointment). **$$$**

Gathland State Park. *8 miles S off MD 67, then 1 mile E, W of Burkittsville off MD 17. Phone 301/791-4767.* On 140 acres. A site once owned by George Townsend, Civil War reporter. Monument built in 1896 to honor Civil War correspondents. Visitor center contains original papers. Picnicking, walking tour, winter sports.

Washington Monument State Park. *13070 Crouse Mill Rd (21657). 3 miles SE off US 40 A. Phone 301/791-4767.* On 147 acres. A 34-foot tower of native stone (1827) was first completed monument to honor George Washington. Views of nearby battlefields, two states (PA and WV). History Center displays firearms and Civil War mementos (by appointment). The Appalachian Trail leads through the park; hiking and picnicking. **FREE**

Restaurant

★ ★ **OLD SOUTH MOUNTAIN INN.** *6132 Old Natl Pike (Alt US 40) (21713). Phone 301/371-5400; fax 301/432-2211. www.oldsouthmountaininn.com.* Hours: 5-9 pm; Sat 11:30 am-2:30 pm, 4-10 pm; Sun 10:30 am-8 pm, brunch to 2 pm. Closed Mon; Dec 25. Reservations accepted; required Sat, Sun. Bar. Lunch $5-$11, dinner $14-$28. Sun brunch $12.95. Children's menu. Specialties: crab cakes, prime rib. Outdoor seating. Founded in 1732; was once a stagecoach stop. Totally nonsmoking. Cr cds: A, C, D, MC, V.

D

Bowie (C-7)

See also College Park, Silver Spring; also see District of Columbia

Pop 50,269 **Elev** 150 ft **Area code** 301 and 204

Information Greater Bowie Chamber of Commerce, 6770 Race Track Rd, Hilltop Plaza, 20715; 301/262-0920. Information is also available from Prince George's Conference & Visitors Bureau, 9475 Lottsford Rd, #130, Landover 20785; 301/925-8300

What to See and Do

Bel Air Mansion. *12207 Tulip Grove Dr. Phone 301/262-6200.* Georgian-style home (circa 1745) was home of Governor Samuel Ogle in the 1700s; later owned by the Woodward family, prominent racehorse breeders in the first half of the 20th century. Tours. (Thurs-Sun afternoons, groups by appointment) **DONATION**

Bel Air Stable. *2835 Belair Dr. Phone 301/262-6200.* Part of famed Bel Air Stud, one of the premier Thoroughbred racing stables of the '30s, '40s, and '50s. Was home to two Triple Crown winners—Gallant Fox and Omaha—and the 1955 Horse of the Year, Nashua. (Thurs-Sun afternoons, groups by appointment) **FREE**

Marietta House Museum. *5626 Bell Station Rd. 3 miles W in Glenn Dale. Phone 301/464-5291.* A modest Federal-style plantation house built by Gabriel Duvall, an associate justice of the US Supreme Court (1811-1835). Tours. (Fri-Sun; also by appointment) **$**

Special Event

Heritage Day. *2614 Kenhill Dr. Bel Air Mansion and Stable. Phone 301/262-6200.* Performance by Congress' Own Regiment; tour of stables and grounds; battle reenactments; demonstrations of colonial crafts. Third Sun in May.

Motel/Motor Lodge

★ **FOREST HILLS MOTEL.** *2901 Crain Hwy, Upper Marlboro (20774). Phone 301/627-3969; fax 301/627-4058.* 13 rooms, shower only. Apr-Oct: S $42-$44; D $46-$49; under 13 free; lower rates rest of year. Crib free. Pet accepted. TV. Check-out 11 am. Some refrigerators. Picnic tables. Cr cds: A, D, DS, MC, V.

D 🐾

Cambridge (D-8)

See also Easton, Salisbury

Founded 1684 **Pop** 10,911 **Elev** 14 ft **Area code** 410 **Zip** 21613

Information Dorchester County Visitors Center, 2 Rose Hill Pl; 410/228-1000 or 800/522-TOUR

Web www.tourdorchester.org

On the Eastern Shore, Cambridge is Maryland's second-largest deep-water port. Boating and fishing opportunities are found in the Choptank and Honga rivers and Chesapeake, Tar, and Fishing bays.

What to See and Do

Blackwater National Wildlife Refuge. *2185 T. Wallace Dr, Rte 1 (21613). 12 miles S via MD 16, 335. Phone 410/228-2677.* Over 20,000 acres of rich tidal marsh, freshwater ponds, and woodlands. One of the chief wintering areas for Canada geese and ducks using the Atlantic Flyway; in fall, as many as 33,000 geese and 17,000 ducks swell the bird population. Also a haven for the bald eagle, the Delmarva fox squirrel, and the peregrine falcon. Scenic drive, woodland trails, photo blind. Visitor center (Daily; closed Thanksgiving, Dec 25). Golden Age, Golden Eagle, and Golden Access passports (see MAKING THE MOST OF YOUR TRIP). **$**

Old Trinity Church, Dorchester Parish. *8 miles SW on MD 16 in Church Creek. Phone 410/228-2940.* (circa 1675) One of the oldest churches in US still holding regular services; faithful restoration of interior. (By appointment) **FREE**

Special Events

Antique Aircraft Fly-In. *1904 Horn Point Road (21613). Dorchester Heritage Museum, 5 miles W on MD 343. Phone 410/228-1899.* Old and new planes on display. Phone 410/228-5530, 410/228-1899, or 800/522-TOUR. Third weekend in May.

National Outdoor Show. *Phone 800/522-TOUR.* Goose and duck calling, log sawing, crab picking, trap setting contests; entertainment. Last weekend in Feb.

Chesapeake and Ohio Canal National Historical Park (C-5)

As early as 1754, the enterprising George Washington, only in his twenties, proposed a system of navigation along the Potomac River valley. His Potowmack Canal Company, organized in 1785, cleared obstructions and built skirting canals to facilitate the transportation of goods from settlements beyond the Allegheny Mountains to the lower Potomac River towns.

The eventual inadequacy of these improvements and the renowned success of the Erie Canal spurred the formation in 1828 of the Chesapeake and Ohio Canal Company, whose purpose was to connect Georgetown with the Ohio Valley by river and canal. On July 4, 1828, President John Quincy Adams led the traditional groundbreaking ceremony declaring, "To subdue the earth is preeminently the purpose of this undertaking." Unfortunately, the earth was not easily subdued. President Adams bent his shovel after several attempts before breaking into an energetic frenzy and successfully getting a shovelful of dirt.

The difficulty of the groundbreaking ceremony foreshadowed the canal's short-lived future as a major transportation artery. Completed in 1850 as far as Cumberland, Maryland (184 1/2 miles from Georgetown), the waterway was used extensively for the transportation of coal, flour, grain, and lumber. Financial and legal difficulties, the decline of commerce after the Civil War, the Baltimore & Ohio Railroad, and the advent of improved roads cut deeply into the commerce of the waterway, and it gradually faded into obsolescence. The canal still had limited commercial use as late as 1924, when a flood destroyed many of the canal locks and nothing was restored.

The unfortunate demise of the C & O Canal is now a blessing for hikers, canoeists, and bikers, who can find access to the towpath along the banks of the waterway. Remaining as one of the least altered of old American canals, the Chesapeake and Ohio is flanked by ample foliage throughout most of its 20,239 acres.

Many points of interest can be seen along the waterway. Exhibits are offered in Cumberland, Georgetown, Hancock, and Williamsport, and at a museum near the Great Falls of the Potomac. At the Great Falls, there are interpretive programs, including self-guiding trails, picnic facilities, and a working lock. Mule-drawn canal boat rides are offered April-October at Georgetown and Great Falls (fee). Camping for hikers and bikers is available throughout the park.

For information about the canal, contact the Chief of Visitor Services, C & O Canal National Historical Park, PO Box 4, Sharpsburg, MD 21782; 301/739-4200. Visitor centers are located in Cumberland, Georgetown, Great Falls, Hancock, and Williamsport.

Chesapeake Bay Bridge Area

The majestic twin spans of the Chesapeake Bay Bridge carry visitors to the Eastern Shore, a patchwork of small picturesque towns, lighthouses, and fishing villages tucked away from the city. Scenic rivers and bays, wildlife, gardens, and wildflowers fill the countryside. The main attractions of any visit, however, are the many fine inns and the restaurants specializing in local seafood.

What to See and Do

Wye Oak State Park. *E on US 50 to Wye Mills. Phone 410/820-1668.* The official state tree of Maryland is in this 29-acre park; it is the largest white oak in the US (108 feet high, 28 feet around) and believed to be over 460 years old; a new tree has been started from an acorn. A restored 18th-century one-room schoolhouse and the Old Wye Mill (late 1600s) are nearby.

Motels/Motor Lodges

★ **COMFORT INN KENT NARROWS.** *3101 Main St, Grasonville (21638). Phone 410/827-6767; toll-free 800/228-5151; fax 410/827-8626. www.comfortinn.com.* 86 units, 4 story, 9 kitchen suites. Apr-Nov: S $66-$126; D $76-$140; each additional $8; kitchen suites $125-$200; under 18 free; higher rates special events; lower rates rest of year. Crib free. TV; cable (premium). Indoor pool; whirlpool. Complimentary continental breakfast. Check-out 11 am. Coin laundry. Meeting rooms. Business services available. Exercise equipment; sauna. Refrigerators, microwaves. Cr cds: A, C, D, DS, ER, JCB, MC, V.

⊼ D ⋈ SC ⛵

★ **COMFORT SUITES CHESTERTOWN.** *160 Scheeler Rd, Chestertown (21666). Phone 410/810-0555; fax 410/810-0286. www.chestertown.com/comfortsuites.* 53 suites, 3 story. Apr-Nov: S, D $69.95-$109.95; under 18 free; lower rates rest of year. Crib available. TV; cable. Indoor pool. Complimentary continental breakfast. Check-out 11 am. Meeting rooms. Business services available. Coin laundry. Health club privileges. Refrigerators, microwaves. Cr cds: A, C, D, DS, MC, V.

D ⋈ SC ⛵

B&Bs/Small Inns

★ ★ **HUNTINGFIELD MANOR.** *4928 Eastern Neck Rd, Rock Hall (21661). Phone 410/639-7779; toll-free 800/720-8788; fax 410/639-2924. www.huntingfield.com.* 6 rooms, 2 story. No room phones. S, D $85-$125; each additional $25; under 3 free. Pet accepted. Complimentary continental breakfast. Check-out noon, check-in 2 pm. Telescope-type house on a working farm that dates back to the middle 1600s. Cr cds: A, MC, V.

D ⋈ 🐾

★ ★ ★ **IMPERIAL HOTEL.** *208 High St, Chestertown (21620). Phone 410/778-5000; toll-free 800/295-0014; fax 410/778-9662. www.imperialchestertown.com.* 13 rooms, 3 story. Check-out 11 am, check-in 3 pm. TV; cable (premium), VCR available. Dining room 11:45 am-2:30 pm, 5:30-close; Sun brunch 11:30 am-3 pm; closed Mon. Built in 1903; Victorian furnishings. Continental breakfast Tues-Sat. Cr cds: A, MC, V.

⚓ D ⋈

★ ★ ★ **INN AT MITCHELL HOUSE.** *8796 Maryland Pkwy, Chestertown (21620). Phone 410/778-6500; fax 410/778-2861. www.chestertown.com/mitchell.* Built in 1743, this elegant and historic manor house welcomes guests with friendly service and a serene atmosphere. Set amidst lush woods and 10 beautiful acres, guests will delight in views of the Stoneybrook Pond and the tranquility of this charming inn. 5 rooms, 2 story. No room phones. Complimentary breakfast. Check-out noon, check-in 3 pm. TV. Dinner available Fri, Sat 7 pm; reservations required. Totally nonsmoking. Cr cds: A, MC, V.

⚓ ⋈

★ ★ **KENT MANOR INN & RESTAURANT.** *500 Kent Manor Dr, Stevensville (21666). Phone 410/643-5757; toll-free 800/820-4511; fax 410/643-8315. www.kentmanor.com.* 24 rooms, 3 story. S, D $135-$215; lower rates mid-week. Crib $15. Complimentary continental breakfast. Check-out 11 am, check-in 3 pm. TV. Restaurant 11:30 am-9 pm; Fri, Sat to 9:30 pm; Sun brunch 10 am-2 pm, 4:30-8 pm. Pool. Meeting rooms. Business services. Built in 1820. On Thompson Creek. Cr cds: A, D, DS, MC, V.

⚓ D ⋈ ⛵

★ ★ **WHITE SWAN TAVERN.** *231 High St, Chestertown (21620). Phone 410/778-2300; fax 410/778-4543. www.chestertown.com/whiteswan.* 6 rooms, 2 suites, 2 story. No room phones. Complimentary continental breakfast. Check-out noon, check-in 3 pm. TV. Health club privileges. Game room. Former house and tavern built in 1733 and 1793; restored with antique furnishings; museum. Cr cds: MC, V. **$$**

D ✈ ⚓ ⋈

Restaurants

★ ★ **FISHERMAN'S INN AND CRAB DECK.** *316 Main St, Kent Narrows (21638). Phone 410/827-8807; fax 410/827-5705. www.fishermansinn.com.* Seafood menu. Closed Dec 24, 25. Lunch, dinner. Bar. Cr cds: A, DS, MC, V. **$$**

D ⊟

★ **HARRIS CRAB HOUSE.** *433 Kent Narrows Way N, Grasonville (21638). Phone 410/827-9500; fax 410/827-9057. www.harriscrabhouse.com.* Seafood menu. Closed Thanksgiving, Dec 25. Lunch, dinner. Bar. Outdoor seating. Gazebo. Cr cds: MC, V. **$**

D ⊟

★ ★ **NARROWS.** *3023 Kent Narrows Way S, Grasonville (21638). Phone 410/827-8113; fax 410/827-8436.* This restaurant specializes in terrific cream of crab and all-lump crab cakes. This is waterfront dining with a spectacular view of the narrows. Specializes in seafood, traditional Maryland recipes. Closed Dec 24, 25. Lunch, dinner, brunch. Bar. Children's menu. Regional Eastern Shore menu. Cr cds: A, C, D, DS, MC, V. **$$**

D

★ ★ **OLD WHARF INN.** *Cannon St, Chestertown (21620). Phone 41/778-3566; fax 410/778-2989.* Hours: 11 am-9 pm; Fri, Sat to 10 pm; Sun from 10 am; Sun brunch to 3 pm. Closed Dec 25. Bar. Lunch $3-$8, dinner $7.25-$19.95. Sun brunch $2.50-$12.25. Children's menu. Specializes in fresh seafood, steak, salad. Outdoor seating. View of river. Cr cds: A, MC, V.

D SC ⊟

★ **WATERMAN'S CRAB HOUSE.** *21055 Sharp St, Rock Hall (21661). Phone 410/639-2261; fax 410/639-2819.* Seafood menu. Closed Thanksgiving; also Jan-Feb. Lunch, dinner. Bar. Children's menu. Outdoor seating. On Rock Hall Harbor. Cr cds: A, DS, MC, V.

D ⊟

Cockeysville (B-7)

See also Baltimore, Towson

Pop 19,388 **Elev** 260 ft **Area code** 410 **Zip** 21030

Information Baltimore County Chamber of Commerce, 102 W Pennsylvania Ave, Suite 402, Towson 21204; 410/825-6200

What to See and Do

★ **Ladew Topiary Gardens.** *3535 Jarrettsville Pike, Monkton (21111). Phone 410/557-9466.* The Garden Club of America once described these gardens as the best in the country. Created by Harvey S. Ladew in the 1930s, the property contains 15 thematic gardens that total 22 acres. In addition to seeing the gardens, visitors can walk a 1.5-mile nature trail that runs through the property or tour the Ladew Manor House, furnished with Ladew's own antique English furniture and fox-hunting memorabilia. (Daily, mid-April–October) **$$$**

Special Event

Point-to-Point Steeplechase. *Phone 410-825-6200.* Three well-known meets on consecutive weekends: **My Lady's Manor.** In Monkton. Mid-Apr. **Grand National.** In Butler; phone 410/666-7777. Mid-Apr. **Maryland Hunt Cup.** In Glyndon; Phone 410/666-7777. Late Apr.

Hotels

★ ★ **COURTYARD BY MARRIOTT.** *221 International Cir, Hunt Valley (21030). Phone 410/584-7070; fax 410/584-8151. www.courtyard.com.* 146 rooms, 3 story. Check-out noon, check-in 3 pm. TV; cable (premium). In-room modem link. Restaurant. Bar. Room service. In-house fitness room. Indoor pool, whirlpool. Cr cds: A, C, D, DS, MC, V. **$**

D ⟲ ⤢ ⊠

★ ★ ★ **MARRIOTT'S HUNT VALLEY INN.** *245 Shawan Rd, Hunt Valley (21031). Phone 410/785-7000; toll-free 800/228-9290; fax 410/785-0341. www.marriott.com.* 390 rooms, 4 story. Pet accepted, some restrictions. Check-out noon, check-in 4 pm. TV; cable (premium). In-room modem link. Restaurant. Bar. Room service. In-house fitness room. Indoor, outdoor pools; whirlpool. Outdoor tennis. Business center. Concierge, luxury level. Cr cds: A, C, D, DS, ER, JCB, MC, V. **$**

D ⟲ ⤢ ⟲ ⊠ SC ⟲

Restaurants

★ ★ ★ **THE MILTON INN.** *14833 York Rd, Sparks (21152). Phone 410/771-4366; fax 410/771-4184. www.miltoninn.com.* This is an old stone house that has been restored for use as a country inn that serves exceptional food in an authentic colonial atmosphere. Many other wonderful appetizers, entrees, sides, and specials to select from. Seafood menu. Closed some major holidays. Dinner. Bar. Children's menu. Outdoor seating. Main part of building circa 1820; one section was stagecoach stop circa 1740. Cr cds: A, D, DS, MC, V. **$**

D

★ ★ ★ **THE OREGON GRILLE.** *1201 Shawan Rd, Hunt Valley (21030). Phone 410/771-0505; fax 410/771-9837. www.theoregongrille.com.* Steakhouses tend to blur together after a while. You find meat, creamed spinach, mashed potatoes, some sort of hash browns, and overpriced cabernets, and that's pretty much the standard formula. It takes a special place to break the cookie-cutter mold. The Oregon Grille succeeds in differentiating itself from the fray by offering not only a terrific selection of impeccably prepared steaks (all beef is dry-aged USDA Prime), but also a creative selection of classic American cuisine, including free-range poultry, fresh seafood, and vibrant first courses that stay true to regional ingredients. But it's not just the food that sets it apart. The attentive, tuxedoed waitstaff succeeds in making every diner in the room feel special, and the décor takes a step back from the typical boys' club. The restaurant, set in a renovated 19th-century stone farmhouse, has four fireplaces and is filled with deep, luxurious banquettes. Its long, rich, mahogany bar is the perfect spot for lingering pre- or post-steak. American menu. Closed Dec 25. Lunch, dinner, Sun brunch. Bar. Jacket required after 5 pm. Outdoor seating. Cr cds: A, C, D, DS, MC, V. **$$$**

D

★ ★ **YORK INN.** *10010 York Rd (21030). Phone 410/666-0006; fax 410/666-7612.* Hours: 11-2 am; Sun brunch 9 am-2 pm. Closed Dec 25. Reservations accepted; required major holidays. Continental menu. Bar to 2 am. Lunch $5.95-$10.95, dinner $11.95-$25.95. Sun breakfast buffet $6.95. Children's menu. Specializes in seafood, steak. Casual dining. Cr cds: A, C, D, DS, ER, MC, V.

D

College Park (C-6)

See also Silver Spring; also see District of Columbia

Pop 24,657 **Elev** 190 ft **Area code** 301 **Zip** 20740

Information Prince George's County Conference & Visitors Bureau, 9200 Basil Ct, #101, Largo 20774; 301/925-8300 or 888/925-8300

Web www.goprincegeorgescounty.com

What to See and Do

College Park Aviation Museum. *1985 Corporal Frank Scott Dr. Phone 301/864-6029 (recording).* World's oldest operating airport, started by Wilbur Wright in 1909 to train two military officers in the operation of aircraft. First airplane machine gun and radio-navigational aids tested here; first air mail and controlled helicopter flights. Museum (daily; closed holidays). **$$**

Greenbelt Park. *6565 Greenbelt Rd, E off Kenilworth Ave, MD 201 exit 23. Phone 301/344-3948.* An 1,100-acre wooded park operated by the National Park Service. Nature trails, picnicking, camping (dump station, showers; 7-day limit Memorial Day-Labor Day; 14-day limit rest of year). Self-registration; first-come, first-served. Standard fees.

NASA/Goddard Visitor Center. *SE on I-95 to Baltimore-Washington Pkwy, exit 22 A Greenbelt, then follow signs. Phone 301/286-8981.* Satellites, rockets, capsules, and exhibits in all phases of space research. (Mon-Fri) **FREE**

University of Maryland. *US 1 (20742). Phone 301/405-1000.* (1865) 35,000 students. Tawes Fine Arts Theater has plays, musicals, concerts, dance, opera, and music festivals. Tours.

Motels/Motor Lodges

★ ★ **COURTYARD BY MARRIOTT.** *6301 Golden Triangle Dr, Greenbelt (20770). Phone 301/441-3311; fax 301/441-4978. www.courtyard.com.* 152 rooms, 4 story. S, D $110; each additional $10; suites $124-$134; under 17 free; weekend, weekly rates. Crib free. TV; cable (premium). Indoor pool; whirlpool, lifeguard. Restaurant 6:30-10 am, 5-10 pm; weekends 6:30 am-midnight. Bar 4-10 pm Mon-Thurs. Check-out noon. Meeting rooms. Business services available. Bellstaff. Valet service. Sundries. Coin laundry. Exercise equipment. Refrigerator in suites; microwaves available. Some balconies. Cr cds: A, C, D, DS, MC, V.

D ➣ ⊀ ⚡ ⊷

★ ★ **HOLIDAY INN.** *10000 Baltimore Ave (20740). Phone 301/345-6700; toll-free 800/465-4329; fax 301/441-4923. www.holiday-inn.com.* 222 rooms in 2 buildings, 4 story. S, D $139; under 18 free. Crib free. TV; cable (premium). Indoor pool; whirlpool, lifeguard. Restaurant 6:30 am-10 pm. Bar 11 am-midnight. Check-out noon. Coin laundry. Meeting rooms. Business center. In-room modem link. Exercise equipment; sauna. Health club privileges. Refrigerators, microwaves available. Cr cds: A, C, D, DS, ER, JCB, MC, V.

D ➣ ⊀ ⊷ SC ⚡

Hotels

★ ★ ★ **MARRIOTT GREENBELT.** *6400 Ivy Ln, Greenbelt (20770). Phone 301/441-3700; toll-free 800/228-9290; fax 301/441-3995. www.marriott.com.* Providing every possible amenity, guests will enjoy a comfortable stay in recently renovated and handsomely appointed guest rooms. 283 rooms, 18 story. S, D $149-$179; kitchen units (minimum stay) $139-$184; family, weekend rates.

Crib free. TV; cable (premium), VCR available. 2 pools, 1 indoor; whirlpool, poolside service, lifeguard. Restaurant. Bar. Check-out noon. Coin laundry. Convention facilities. Business center. In-room modem link. Gift shop. Lighted tennis. Exercise equipment; sauna. Refrigerators, microwaves available. Luxury level. Cr cds: A, C, D, DS, ER, JCB, MC, V.

★ ★ **SHERATON COLLEGE PARK.** *4095 Powder Mill Rd, Beltsville (20705). Phone 301/937-4422; fax 301/ 937-4455. www.sheraton.com.* 206 rooms, 9 story. S, D $109-$129; each additional $7; suites $165; under 18 free; weekend rates; higher rates Cherry Blossom. Crib free. TV; cable (premium). Pool; lifeguard. Restaurant. Bar. Check-out noon. Coin laundry. Meeting rooms. Business services available. In-room modem link. Gift shop. Exercise equipment. Massage. Game room. Refrigerator; microwaves available. Cr cds: A, C, D, DS, JCB, MC, V.

Restaurant

★ ★ **ALAMO.** *5508 Kenilworth Ave, Riverdale (20737). Phone 301/927-8787; fax 301/927-3400.* Hours: 11 am-11 pm. Reservations accepted. Mexican menu. Bar. Lunch $5-$11, dinner $8.30-$12.95. Children's menu. Specializes in tostadas, tacos, enchiladas. Entertainment Fri, Sat. Mexican décor. Cr cds: A, MC, V.

★ ★ **CALVERT HOUSE INN.** *6211 Baltimore Ave, Riverdale (20737). Phone 301/864-5220; fax 301/927-6612. www.calverthouseinn.com.* Seafood, steak menu. Closed Dec 25. Lunch, dinner. Bar. Children's menu. Reservations accepted; required Fri, Sat dinner. Cr cds: A, DS, MC, V. $

★ ★ ★ **CHEF'S SECRET.** *5810 Greenbelt Rd, Greenbelt (20770). Phone 301/345-6101; fax 301/345-6102.* Superb continental seafood courses are served in a most elegant setting. Don't let the small warehouse-like exterior fool you. Hours: 11:30 am-3 pm, 5-9 pm; Fri, Sat to 10 pm; Sun 4-9 pm; early-bird dinner 5-6 pm. Closed Labor Day, Dec 25. Reservations accepted. Continental menu. Service bar. Lunch $7.95-$14.95, dinner $11.95-$17.95. Specializes in seafood, veal, steak. Own desserts. Cr cds: A, DS, MC, V.

★ **SANTA FE CAFE.** *4410 Knox Rd (20740). Phone 301/ 779-1345; fax 301/779-4522. www.santafecafe.com.* Hours: 11 am-midnight. Closed Sun; Thanksgiving, Dec 25. Reservations accepted. Southwestern, American menu. Bar to 1:30 am. Lunch, dinner $3.95-$9.95. Specializes in fajitas, buffalo wings, pizzas. Outdoor seating. Casual Southwestern décor; murals, buffalo heads, Native American rugs. Cr cds: A, D, DS, MC, V.

Columbia

See also Baltimore

Pop 88,254 **Elev** 402 ft **Area code** 410 & 443

Information Howard County Tourism Council, 8267 Main St, PO Box 9, Ellicott City 21041; 410/313-1900 or 800/288-TRIP

Web www.visithowardcounty.com

A planned city built on a tract of land larger than Manhattan Island, Columbia comprises 11 villages surrounding a central downtown service area. Construction of the city began in 1966.

What to See and Do

African Art Museum of Maryland. *5430 Vantage Point Rd, in Historic Oakland at Town Center. Phone 410/730-7105.* Masks, sculptured figures, textiles, basketry, household items, and musical instruments displayed in a 19th-century manor. (Tues-Fri, also Sun afternoons; closed holidays) $

Howard County Center of African-American Culture. *5434 Vantage Point Rd. Phone 410/715-1921.* Contains artifacts and memorabilia depicting images of African-Americans over the last 200 years. Extensive collection of spiritual, jazz, and rap music; more than 2,000 books and periodicals; hands-on exhibit for children. (Tues-Sun; closed holidays) $$

Special Events

Columbia Festival of Arts. *10221 Wincopin Cir.* Music, dance, theater, lakeside entertainment. Ten days in mid-June.

Symphony of Lights. *Phone 410/313-1900.* Animated lighting displays along a 1 1/2-mile park route. Late Nov-early Jan.

Wine in the Woods. *10475 Little Patuxent Pkwy (21044). Symphony Woods at Merriweather Post Pavilion. Phone 410/313-PARK.* Two-day celebration featuring Maryland wines, gourmet food, entertainment, arts and crafts. Third weekend in May.

Hotels

★ ★ ★ **HILTON COLUMBIA.** *5485 Twin Knolls Rd (21045). Phone 410/997-1060; toll-free 800/445-8667; fax*

410/997-0169. www.hilton.com. Located in the heart of Columbia and set amidst a parklike setting, this hotel offers a very relaxing stay. From the exquisitely glassed atrium, to the elegantly appointed guest rooms, this hotel is a delight. 152 rooms, 4 story. S, D $99-$129; each additional $10; suites $175-$250; under 18 free; weekend plans. Crib free. TV; cable (premium), VCR available. Indoor pool; whirlpool. Restaurant. Bar. Check-out 11 am. Meeting rooms. Business services available. In-room modem link. Exercise equipment; sauna. Microwaves available. Cr cds: A, C, D, DS, ER, MC, V.

★ ★ ★ **SHERATON COLUMBIA HOTEL.** 10207 Wincopin Cir (21044). Phone 410/730-3900; toll-free 800/325-3535; fax 410/730-1290. www.sheraton.com. Recognized for its gracious accommodations, superb service and handsomely appointed guest rooms, this hotel is a welcome retreat for both business and leisure travelers. 289 rooms, 3-10 story. S $115-$130; D $130-$145; each additional $10; suites $250-$375; under 12 free; weekend plan. Crib free. Pet accepted, some restrictions; $75 refundable. TV; cable (premium). Pool; poolside service (in season), lifeguard. Restaurant. Bar. Check-out noon. Laundry facilities. Meeting rooms. Business services available. In-room modem link. Gift shop. Health club privileges. Some bathroom phones; microwaves available. Overlooks Lake Kittamaqundi; boat rides, entertainment on lake (summer). Cr cds: A, C, D, DS, MC, V.

Restaurants

★ ★ **CLYDE'S.** 10221 Wincopin Cir (21044). Phone 410/730-2829; fax 410/596-4052. www.clydes.com. Hours: 11:30-2 am; Sun from 10 am; early-bird dinner Mon-Fri 4:30-6 pm; Sun brunch to 4 pm. Closed Dec 25. Reservations accepted (dinner). Bar. Lunch $7-$13, dinner $10-$18. Sun brunch $6-$11. Children's menu. Specializes in seasonal dishes, salmon, crab. Own baking. Outdoor dining. Bistro atmosphere; etched and stained-glass windows; view of lake. Totally nonsmoking. Cr cds: A, C, D, DS, ER, MC, V.

★ ★ ★ **KING'S CONTRIVANCE.** 10150 Shaker Dr (21046). Phone 410/995-0500; fax 410/730-8063. A mansion built in 1900 is the casual setting for this regional seafood restaurant with excellent crab cakes. Landlubbers can feast on rack of lamb, and all can enjoy the house baked goods. Hours: 11:30 am-2 pm, 5:30-9 pm; Fri, Sat 5:30-9:30 pm; Sun 4-8 pm. Reservations accepted; required Dec. Bar. Wine cellar. Lunch $8-$14, dinner $14-$26. Own baking. Enclosed porch dining. Mansion built in 1900. Cr cds: A, D, DS, MC, V.

Crisfield (F-8)

See also Pocomoke City

Pop 2,723 **Elev** 4 ft **Area code** 410 **Zip** 21817

Information Crisfield Area Chamber of Commerce, 906 W Main St, PO Box 292; 410/968-2500

Web www.crisfield.org

What to See and Do

Janes Island State Park. 26280 Alfred Lawson Dr. Approximately 2 miles NE via MD 413, then 1 1/2 miles N on MD 358. Phone 410/968-1565. These 3,147 acres are nearly surrounded by Chesapeake Bay and its inlets. Swimming, fishing, boat ramp (rentals); cabins, camping. Standard fees.

Tangier Island Cruises. 1001 W Main St. Phone 410/968-2338. Trips to the fishing village of Tangier Island, VA. (Mid-may-Oct) $$$$

Tyler's Cruises. Somers Cove Marina. Phone 410/425-2771. The Chelsea's Lane Tyler and the Captain Tyler make approximately one-hour cruises to Smith Island. Bus tour of the two villages that compose the island, with spare time to visit the rest of the island; lunch available (fee). Tour length approximately 4 1/2 hours. (Memorial Day weekend-mid-Oct)

Special Event

National Hard Crab Derby & Fair. 906 W Main St. Phone 410/968-2500. Cooking, crab picking, boat docking contests; crab racing; fireworks and parade. Fri-Sun, Labor Day weekend.

Motel/Motor Lodge

★ ★ **PINES MOTEL.** 127 N Somerset Ave (21817). Phone 410/968-0900; fax 410/968-0900. www.intercom .net/biz/pines. 40 rooms. July-Aug: S $50-$55; D $55-$70; each additional $5; kitchen units $15 additional; under 11 free; higher rates: July 4, Labor Day, special events; lower rates rest of year. TV; cable. Pool. Check-out 11 am. Gift shop. Picnic area. In scenic, wooded section. Cr cds: A, MC, V.

Cumberland (A-2)

Settled 1750 **Pop** 21,518 **Elev** 688 ft **Area code** 301 and 240 **Zip** 21502

Information Allegany County Convention & Visitors Bureau, 13 Canal St; 301/777-5132 or 800/425-2067

Web www.mdmountainside.com

Far to the west in the state, Cumberland is nestled between Pennsylvania and West Virginia. The Potomac River and its tributary, Wills Creek, flow peaceably by this onetime western outpost of the colonies.

British General Edward Braddock was sent here to conquer the French and Native Americans in 1755; unprepared for the wilderness, he met with defeat and death. George Washington, who defended the town in that period, felt the main east-west route would pass through Cumberland eventually. In 1833, the National Road (US 40 Alternate) made the town a supply terminus for overland commerce. The road was extended farther west, the B & O Railroad reached here in 1842, and eight years later came the Chesapeake and Ohio Canal (see CHESAPEAKE AND OHIO CANAL NATIONAL HISTORICAL PARK), bringing prosperous business. Today's economy no longer depends on industry alone but includes services and recreational facilities.

What to See and Do

Dans Mountain State Park. *10 miles W on I-68, then 8 miles S on MD 36, 2 miles SE of Lonaconing. Phone 301/ 463-5564 or 301/777-2139.* On 481 acres. Nearby Dans Rock affords a panoramic view of surrounding region from a height of 2,898 feet. Swimming pool (fee), fishing; picnicking, playground, hiking, sledding.

Fort Cumberland Trail. Walking trail covers several city blocks downtown around the site of Fort Cumberland. Includes boundary markers, narrative plaques.

George Washington's Headquarters. *In Riverside Park, downtown, on Greene St.* (circa 1755) His first military headquarters. Taped narration. **FREE**

Gordon-Roberts House. *218 Washington St, in Victorian Historic District. Phone 301/777-8678.* (circa 1867) Restored 18-room Victorian house with nine period rooms; costumes; research room. (June-Oct, Tues-Sun; rest of year, Tues-Sat) **$$**

Green Ridge State Forest. *28700 Headquarters Dr NE. 21 miles E off I-68 at exit 64. Phone 301/478-3124.* These 44,000 acres of forest land stretch across mountains of western Maryland and occupy portions of Town Hill, Polish Mountain, and Green Ridge Mountain. Abundant wildlife. Fishing, boat launch, canoeing; hiking trails, camping, winter sports. C & O Canal runs through here into 3,118-foot Paw-Paw Tunnel.

The Narrows. Picturesque 1,000-foot gap through Alleghenies (US 40 A) used by pioneers on their way to the West.

Rocky Gap State Park. *12500 Pleasant Valley Rd NE. 6 miles E on I-68, exit 50. Phone 301/777-2138 (camping) or 301/777-2139.* Mountain scenery around 243-acre lake with three swimming beaches. Swimming, fishing, boating (electric motors only; rentals); nature and hiking trails, picnicking, cafe, improved camping (reservations accepted one year in advance), winter activities. Resort; 18-hole golf course. Standard fees. (See SPECIAL EVENTS) **$**

Toll Gate House. *Approximately 6 miles W on US 40 A, in La Vale. Phone 301/777-5905.* (1836) Built to collect tolls from users of Cumberland Rd (National Rd); only remaining toll house in state; restored. (Late May-late Oct, Sat and Sun afternoons; other times by appointment) **$**

Western Maryland Station Center. *13 Canal St (21502). Phone 301/777-5905.* This 1913 railroad station houses Canal Place Authority, Industrial and Transportation Museum; C & O Canal National Historical Park Visitors Center and Allegany County Visitors Center. (Daily; closed holidays) **FREE** This is also the departure point for

> **Western Maryland Scenic Railroad.** *13 Canal St. Phone 301/759-4400 or 800/TRAIN-50.* Excursion train makes scenic trip 17 miles to Frostburg and back. (May-Oct, Tues-Sun; Nov-mid-Dec, weekends)

Special Events

Agricultural Expo and Fair. *Allegany County Fairgrounds. 11490 Moss Ave Ext (21502). Phone 301/729-1200.* Poultry, livestock, carnival, entertainment. Mid-July.

Drumfest. *Greenway Ave Stadium. Phone 301/777-8325.* Drum and bugle corps championship. Last Sat in July.

Rocky Gap Music Festival. *Allegany College. 12401 Willow Brook Rd SE (21502). Phone 888/762-5942.* Features bluegrass and country music; children's activities, crafts, workshops. Fri-Sun, first weekend in Aug.

Street Rod Roundup. *6 miles S on MD 220, at fairgrounds. Phone 301/729-5555.* Hundreds of pre-1950 hot rods on display and in competitions. Labor Day weekend.

Motels/Motor Lodges

★★ **BEST WESTERN BRADDOCK MOTOR INN.** *1268 National Hwy, La Vale (21502). Phone 301/ 729-3300; toll-free 800/528-1234; fax 301/729-3300. www.bestwestern.com.* 107 rooms, 3 story. D $69-$109; each additional $6; under 18 free. Check-out 11 am, check-in 2 pm. TV; cable (premium), VCR available (movies). In-room modem link. Restaurant 7 am-9 pm. Bar 4:30 pm-midnight; Fri, Sat to 1 am; closed Sun. Room service. Exercise equipment, sauna. Game room. Indoor pool, whirlpool, poolside service. Airport transportation. Cr cds: A, C, D, DS, MC, V.

D ⊠ ✕ ⊠ SC

★ **DAYS INN.** *11100 New Georges Creek Rd SW, Frostburg (21532). Phone 301/689-2050; fax 301/689-2050. www.daysinn.com.* 100 rooms, 2 story. May-Oct: S $66-$78; D $71-$83; each additional $5; suites $86; under

18 free; weekly rates; lower rates rest of year. Crib free. Pet accepted; $10. Complimentary continental breakfast. Check-out 11 am. TV; cable. In-room modem link. Some in-room whirlpools. Restaurant nearby. Exercise room. Pool privileges. Cross-country ski 15 miles. Picnic tables. Meeting rooms. Business services. Cr cds: A, C, D, DS, ER, JCB, MC, V.

⌷ 🐾 ⊁ ≈ 🖈 ⊵ 𝗦𝗖

★ ★ **HOLIDAY INN.** *100 S George St (21502). Phone 301/724-8800; toll-free 877/426-4672; fax 301/724-4001. www.holiday-inn.com.* 134 rooms, 5 story. D $89-$109; under 18 free. Pet accepted. Check-out noon. TV; cable (premium), VCR available. In-room modem link. Restaurant 6:30 am-2 pm, 5-10 pm; Sun from 7 am. Bar noon-midnight; Sun from 4 pm; entertainment. Room service. Outdoor pool. Airport transportation. Business center. Cr cds: A, C, D, DS, JCB, MC, V.

⌷ 🐾 ≈ ⊵ 🖈

★ **SUPER 8.** *1301 National Hwy, La Vale (21502). Phone 301/729-6265; toll-free 800/800-8000; fax 301/729-6265. www.super8.com.* 63 rooms, 3 story. D $59-$70. Complimentary continental breakfast. Check-out 11 am. TV. Cr cds: A, C, D, DS, MC, V.

⌷ ⊵ 𝗦𝗖

Hotel

★ ★ **OAK TREE INN.** *12310 Winchester Rd (21502). Phone 301/777-6003; toll-free 800/286-9718.* 82 rooms, 3 story. Pet accepted. Check-out noon, check-in 2 pm. TV; cable (premium). Laundry services. Restaurant. In-house fitness room. Cr cds: A, D, DS, MC, V. **$**

⌷ 🐾 🖈 ⊵

Resort

★ ★ **ROCKY GAP LODGE & GOLF RESORT.** *16701 Lakeview Rd NE, Flintstone (21530). Phone 301/784-8400; toll-free 800/724-0828; fax 301/784-8408.* 220 rooms, 6 story. Check-out 11 am, check-in 3 pm. TV; cable (premium). Restaurant. Bar. Room service. Children's activity center. In-house fitness room. Indoor pool, whirlpool, poolside service. Outdoor tennis. Boats, fishing, hiking. Business center. Cr cds: A, D, DS, MC, V. **$$**

⌷ 🗲 ⛵ ⊁ ≈ 🖈 ⊵

B&B/Small Inn

★ ★ ★ **INN AT WALNUT BOTTOM.** *120 Greene St (21502). Phone 301/777-0003; toll-free 800/286-9718; fax 301/777-8288. www.iwbinfo.com.* At this elegant retreat, guests are offered their choice of two equally charming accommodations. The Georgian-style architecture of the Cowden House welcomes guests with a formal doorway and chimneys at each end, while the Queen Anne-style

Dent House delights guests with the distinctly round turret on the corner. Either place is guaranteed to enchant guests with the history behind it, with their charmingly appointed guest rooms and wonderful antiques. 14 rooms, 4 share bath, 2-3 story, 2 suites. D $89-$114; each additional $15; suites $147-$198. Complimentary full breakfast. Check-out 11 am, check-in 3 pm. TV; cable (premium). Restaurant. Health club privileges. Two buildings (1820, 1890). Totally nonsmoking. Cr cds: A, DS, MC, V.

⊵ 𝗦𝗖

Restaurant

★ ★ **WARNER'S GERMAN RESTAURANT.** *US 220 S McMullen Hwy (21502). Phone 301/729-2361.* German menu. Hours: 11 am-9 pm; Fri, Sat to 10 pm; Sun noon-7 pm. Closed Mon; Jan 1, July 4, Dec 25. Dinner $9-$18. Bar. Children's menu. Casual attire. Outdoor seating. Totally nonsmoking. Cr cds: A, C, D, DS, MC, V.

⌷ ⊵

Easton (D-8)

See also Cambridge, St. Michael's

Settled 1682 **Pop** 11,708 **Elev** 28 ft **Area code** 410 **Zip** 21601

Information Talbot County Chamber of Commerce, PO Box 1366, Easton Plaza Suite 53; 410/822-4653

Web www.talbotchamber.org

What to See and Do

Academy Art Museum. *106 South St. Phone 410/822-0455 or 410/822-ARTS (recording).* Housed in renovated 1820s schoolhouse, Academy exhibits works of local and national artists in permanent collection. Also hosts over 250 visual and performing arts programs annually. (Mon-Sat) **$**

Historical Society of Talbot County. *25 S Washington St. Phone 410/822-0773.* A three-gallery museum in a renovated early commercial building; changing exhibits, museum shop. Historic houses: 1810 Federal town house, 1700s Quaker cabinetmaker's cottage, period gardens; tours. (Tues-Sat) **$$**

Third Haven Friends Meeting House. *405 S Washington St. Phone 410/822-0293.* (1682-1684) One of the oldest frame-construction houses of worship in US. (Daily) **FREE**

Tuckahoe State Park. *13070 Crouse Mill Rd. 5 miles N of Queen Anne, off MD 404. Phone 410/820-1668.* A 60-acre lake and Tuckahoe Creek provide a secluded atmosphere in this 3,800-acre park. The Adkins Arboretum (500 acres)

propagates trees, plants, and shrubs indigenous to Maryland. Fishing, boating; hunting, hiking, picnicking, camping (electric hook-ups, dump station). Standard fees.

Special Events

Eastern Shore Chamber Music Festival. *21 S Harrison St. Various locations. Phone 410/819-0380.* World-class chamber music; young people's concert. Two weeks in June.

Tuckahoe Steam and Gas Show and Reunion. *210 Marlboro Ave. 5 miles N via US 50, opposite Woodlawn Memorial Park. Phone 410/643-6123 or 410/820-9868 (during event).* Old steam and gas engines; antique tractors and cars. Demonstrations in soap and broom making; flour milling. Gas and steam wheat threshing; sawmill working; flea market, crafts, parade, entertainment. Usually weekend after July 4.

Waterfowl Festival. *Downtown and various locations in and around town. Phone 410/822-4606.* Exhibits on waterfowl; pictures, carvings; food. First or second weekend in Nov.

Motels/Motor Lodges

★ **COMFORT INN.** *8523 Ocean Gateway (21601). Phone 410/820-8333; toll-free 800/228-5150; fax 410/820-8436. www.comfortinn.com.* 84 units, 2 story, 15 suites. Mid-Apr-Nov: S, D $79-$99; each additional $8; suites $105; under 18 free; higher rates special events; lower rates rest of year. Crib free. TV; cable (premium). Pool; whirlpool. Complimentary continental breakfast. Check-out 11 am. Meeting rooms. Business services available. In-room modem link. Sundries. Some refrigerators; microwaves available. Picnic tables. Cr cds: A, C, D, DS, JCB, MC, V.

[D] [≈] [≥] [SC]

★ **DAYS INN.** *7018 Ocean Gateway (21601). Phone 410/822-4600; toll-free 800/329-7466; fax 410/820-9723. www.daysinn.com.* 80 rooms, 2 story. Apr-Nov: S $69-$89; D, suites $79-$102; under 18 free; higher rates Waterfowl Festival; lower rates rest of year. Crib free. Pet accepted, some restrictions; $8. TV; cable (premium). Complimentary continental breakfast. Check-out 11 am. Pool; wading pool. Some refrigerators. Cr cds: A, C, D, DS, ER, JCB, MC, V.

[D] [🐾] [≈] [≥] [SC]

★ **HOLIDAY INN EXPRESS.** *8561 Ocean Gateway (21601). Phone 410/819-6500; toll-free 877/327-8661; fax 410/819-6505. www.holiday-inn.com.* 73 rooms, 4 story. Apr-Nov: S, D $109-$129; each additional $8; under 18 free; lower rates rest of year. Crib free. Pet accepted. TV; cable (premium). Indoor pool; whirlpool. Complimentary continental breakfast. Restaurant adjacent open 24 hours. Check-out 11 am. Meeting rooms. Business ser-

vices available. Exercise equipment. Cr cds: A, C, D, DS, JCB, MC, V.

[D] [🐾] [≈] [📺] [≥] [SC]

Hotel

★ ★ ★ **TIDEWATER INN AND CONFERENCE CENTER.** *101 E Dover St (21601). Phone 410/822-1300; toll-free 800/237-8775; fax 410/820-8847. www.tidewaterinn.com.* Ideally located in the historic and scenic district of Easton, this stately inn features elegantly appointed Federal-style guest rooms, a warm and friendly staff, and a level of style and comfort to please even the most discriminating traveler. 114 rooms, 4 story. June-Nov: S $90-$175; D $90-$190; each additional $10; under 13 free; weekly, weekend rates; package plans; higher rates Waterfowl Festival; lower rates rest of year. Crib free. TV; cable (premium), VCR available. Pool; poolside service. Restaurant (See also HUNTER'S TAVERN). Bar 11-2 am; entertainment Fri, Sat, Sun brunch. Check-out noon. Meeting rooms. Business center. In-room modem link. Free valet parking. Airport transportation. Health club privileges. Restored turn-of-the-century hotel. Cr cds: A, C, D, DS, MC, V.

[D] [≈] [≥] [SC] [🏃]

B&B/Small Inns

★ ★ **BISHOP'S HOUSE.** *214 Goldsborough St (21601). Phone 410/820-7290; fax 410/820-7290. www.bishopshouse.com.* 5 rooms, 3 story. No room phone. No elevator. 2-day minimum: S $110; D $120; lower rates mid-week. Children over 13 years only. TV; cable (premium) in main room. Complimentary full breakfast. Check-out 11 am, check-in 4-5 pm. Some whirlpools, fireplaces. Built in 1880; antiques, toys, porcelains. Totally nonsmoking. Cr cds: A, DS, MC, V.

[≥]

★ ★ ★ **ROBERT MORRIS INN.** *314 N Morris St, Oxford (21654). Phone 410/226-5111; fax 410/226-5744. www.robertmorrisinn.com.* This is a family inn that provides quiet, comfortable lodging, great food, and a location that is perfect for exploring the local area. Guests can relax on the beach, visit the marine museum, go biking or antiquing, or play a game of golf or tennis. 35 rooms, 13 rooms with showers only, 2-3 story, 2 kitchen cottages. No room phones. S, D $100-$240. Children over 10 years only. Check-out noon, check-in 3 pm. Private patios, balconies. Dining room 8-10 am, noon-9 pm; winter hours vary. Bar noon-10 pm. Business services. Historic house (1710) built by ships' carpenters. Totally nonsmoking. Cr cds: A, MC, V.

[D] [🦽] [≥]

Restaurant

★ ★ ★ **HUNTER'S TAVERN.** *101 E Dover St (21601). Phone 410/822-1300; fax 410/820-8847. www.tidewaterinn.com.* A hunting theme predominates at this casual tavern-style restaurant, which serves regional specialties, including wild game. Seafood menu. Breakfast $4.95-$10.50, lunch $6.95-$12.50, dinner $12.95-$24.95. Sun brunch $15.70-$18.80. Bar; Fri, Sat 11-2 am. Reservations accepted (dinner). Valet parking available. Outdoor seating. Cr cds: A, C, D, DS, ER, MC, V.

D SC

Elkton (B-8)

See also Havre de Grace

Pop 11,893 **Elev** 30 ft **Area code** 410 **Zip** 21921

Information Elkton Chamber of Commerce, 101 E Main St; 410/398-1640

What to See and Do

Elk Neck State Forest. *4395 Turkey Point Rd (21901). 4 miles W off MD 7, near North East. Phone 410/287-5675.* Has 3,165 acres. Forest wildlife, particularly whitetail deer, can be seen; food plots have been established. Hunting, hiking, bridle trail, picnicking, primitive camping, shooting range, winter sports. Pets allowed.

Elk Neck State Park. *4395 Turkey Point Rd. 14 miles SW via US 40, MD 272, near North East. Phone 410/287-5333.* Park has 2,188 acres of sandy beaches, marshlands and heavily wooded bluffs. Swimming, fishing, boating (launch, rentals); miniature golf (fee), hiking and nature trails, picnicking, concession, winter sports, camping, cabins. Standard fees.

Motels/Motor Lodges

★ **ELKTON LODGE.** *200 Belle Hill Rd (21921). Phone 410/398-9400; fax 410/398-9579.* 32 rooms, 2 story. S $35-$40; D $42-$50; each additional $4; under 15 free. Crib $5. TV; cable (premium). Check-out 11 am. Refrigerators; some microwaves. Cr cds: A, C, D, DS, MC, V.

D 🖼 SC

★ **SUTTON MOTEL.** *405 E Pulaski Hwy (21921). Phone 410/398-3830.* 11 rooms, shower only. No room phones. S $31; D $34-$36; each additional $3. Crib $1. Pet accepted, some restrictions. TV. Check-out 11 am. Cr cds: A, DS, MC, V.

🐾 🖼

B&B/Small Inn

★ ★ **INN AT THE CANAL.** *104 Bohemia Ave, Chesapeake City (21915). Phone 410/885-5995; fax 410/885-3585. www.innatthecanal.com.* 7 rooms, 3 story. Apr-Nov: D $85-$185; each additional $25; 2-day minimum some holidays; lower rates rest of year. Children over 10 years only. Complimentary full breakfast. Check-out 11 am, check-in 2 pm. TV; cable (premium). Lawn games. Mansion built in 1870; antiques. Overlooks Chesapeake and Delaware Canal. Totally nonsmoking. Cr cds: A, C, D, DS, MC, V.

🔧 🖼

Restaurant

★ ★ **SCHAEFER'S CANAL HOUSE.** *208 Bank St, Chesapeake City (21915). Phone 410/885-2200; fax 410/885-2206. www.schaeferscanalhouse.com.* Specializes in seafood. Hours: 8 am-10 pm; weekend hours may vary; Sun brunch 10 am-3 pm. Closed Dec 25. Breakfast $3-$9, lunch $5-$24, dinner $18-$32. Sun brunch $14.95. Bar. Children's menu. Reservations accepted Sun-Fri. Outdoor seating. Cr cds: A, MC, V.

D 🖼

Ellicott City (B-6)

See also Baltimore

Settled 1772 **Pop** 56,397 **Elev** 233 ft **Area code** 410

Information Howard County Tourism Council, 8267 Main St, PO Box 9, 21041; 410/313-1900 or 800/288-TRIP

Web www.visithowardcounty.com

The town was originally named Ellicott Mills for the three Quaker brothers who founded it as the site of their gristmill. Charles Carroll of Carrollton, whose Doughoregan Manor can still be seen nearby, lent financial help to the Ellicotts and the town eventually became the site of ironworks, rolling mills, and the first railroad terminus in the United States. The famous Tom Thumb locomotive race with a horse took place near here. Many of the town's original stone houses and log cabins, on hills above the Patapsco River, have been preserved.

What to See and Do

Ellicott City B & O Railroad Station Museum. *2711 Maryland Ave, at Main St. Phone 410/461-1944 (recording).* Two restored buildings (circa 1830 and 1885) house historic rooms, railroad displays and memorabilia, operating HO model railroad of the first 13 miles of the B & O track, photographs, dioramas. Full-size B & O caboose and museum store. Civil War reenactments of military and civilian life, June-Sept. (May-Sept, Mon, Wed-Sun; rest of year, Mon, Fri-Sun) **$$**

Patapsco Valley State Park. *8020 Baltimore National Pike (21043). NE and SE of town; 5 miles from I-695 exits 12 and 15, 50 yards from I-195 exit 1. Phone 410/461-5005; toll-free 888/432-2267.* Spread across three counties, this great nature and recreational area runs along a 32-mile stretch of the scenic Patapsco River, spans 14,000 acres, and contains five sites. Guests can hike, bike, ride horses, fish, camp, canoe, tube, or picnic. The park also includes the world's largest multiple arched stone railroad bridge, a 300-foot suspension bridge, and a paved hiking trail for the disabled. (Daily) **$**

Special Events

Howard County Fair. *2210 Fairgrounds Rd, West Friendship (21794). Phone 410/442-1022.* Rides, entertainment, concessions, 4-H exhibits, horse-pulling contests, and other events. Early-Aug.

Maryland Sheep and Wool Festival. *In West Friendship. Phone 410/442-1022.* Sheep breeds and other wool-bearing animals; sheepdog demonstration. Crafters sell products related to sheep and wool; spinning, weaving, and sheep-shearing contests; wool dyeing; entertainment. First weekend in May.

Hotel

★ ★ **TURF VALLEY HOTEL AND COUNTRY CLUB.** *2700 Turf Valley Rd (21042). Phone 410/465-1500; fax 410/465-8280. www.turfvalley.com.* 223 rooms, 7 story. 6 villas. Mar-Nov: S $120; D $135; each additional $15; suites $130-$415; villas $650-$700; under 12 free; weekend rates; lower rates rest of year. Crib free. Checkout noon. TV; cable (premium). In-room modem link. Restaurant 6:30 am-10 pm. Bar 4:30-11 pm; Fri, Sat to 2 am; entertainment Fri-Sun. Exercise equipment, steam room. Indoor/outdoor pool; whirlpool, poolside service, lifeguard. 54-hole golf, greens fee $37-$52, pro, putting green, driving range. Tennis. Business services. Convention facilities. Gift shop. Cr cds: A, D, DS, MC, V.

D 🛐 🖋 🛌 🎿 🖼

Restaurants

★ ★ **CRAB SHANTY.** *3410 Plumtree Dr (21042). Phone 410/465-9660; fax 410/750-0154. www.crabshanty.com.* Hours: 11:30 am-2:30 pm, 5-10 pm; Mon, Tues to 9 pm; Sun 2-9 pm. Bar. Lunch $2.95-$9.50, dinner $8.75-$18.95. Children's menu. Specializes in seafood. Cr cds: A, D, DS, MC, V.

D SC

★ **SIDESTREETS.** *8069 Tiber Alley (21043). Phone 410/461-5577; fax 410/750-8096.* Seafood menu. Closed Thanksgiving, Dec 25. Lunch, dinner $5.95-$19.95. Sun brunch $2.95-$7.95. Bar. Totally nonsmoking. Cr cds: A, DS, MC, V.

🖼

★ ★ ★ **TERSIGUEL'S.** *8293 Main St (21043). Phone 410/465-4004; fax 410/461-1421. www.tersiguels.com.* Fine dining in a 19th-century home with six individual dining rooms serving a combination of authentic French-style cooking and rustic country fare. Seasonal cuisine is prepared with fresh vegetables and herbs from their garden and chevre cheese is made daily. French menu. Closed Dec 25. Lunch, dinner. Bar. Historic building; mementos from Brittany, France. Totally nonsmoking. Cr cds: A, C, D, DS, MC, V. **$$**

🖼

Emmitsburg (A-5)

See also Frederick, Hagerstown, Thurmont

Settled 1785 **Pop** 2,290 **Elev** 449 ft **Area code** 301 **Zip** 21727

Information Tourism Council of Frederick County, 19 E Church St, Frederick 21701; 301/228-2888

Web www.visitfrederick.org

What to See and Do

Mount St. Mary's College and Seminary. *3 miles S on US 15. Phone 301/447-6122.* (1808) 1,800 students. Oldest independent Catholic college in US. Liberal arts and sciences. Near the campus is the

National Shrine Grotto of Lourdes. *Phone 301/447-5318.* Replica of the French shrine is 1/3 the size of the original; oldest replica in the Western Hemisphere. Pangborn Memorial Campanile, constructed of native stone and located at the entrance, is 120 feet tall and is surmounted by a 25-foot bronze gold-leaf statue of the Blessed Virgin Mary. (Apr-Oct, daily; rest of year, Tues-Sun) **FREE**

⭐ **Seton Shrine Center.** *333 S Seton Ave. Phone 301/447-6606.* National Shrine of St. Elizabeth Ann Seton, first US female saint, canonized 1975. Includes Stone House (1750), White House (1810), home in which Mother Seton died; video presentation, basilica, museum, and cemetery. (Tues-Sun, or by appointment; closed major holidays; also last two weeks in Jan) **FREE**

B&B/Small Inn

★ ★ **ANTRIM 1844.** *30 Trevanion Rd, Taneytown (21787). Phone 410/756-6812; toll-free 800/858-1844; fax 410/756-2744. www.antrim1844.com.* This country inn is located on 23 acres of property in the Catoctin Mountains. Guest rooms and suites are decorated with antiques. 22

rooms, 3 story, 3-story spiral staircase. No room phones. Complimentary full breakfast. Check-out 11 am, check-in 3 pm. Many fireplaces, in-room whirlpools. Restaurant. Pool; whirlpools. Golf. Tennis. Downhill ski 14 miles; cross-country 15 miles. Lawn games. Airport transportation. Croquet. Antebellum plantation (1844) on 25 acres. Cr cds: A, D, DS, MC, V. **$$$**

D

Restaurant

★ ★ ★ **ANTRIM 1844.** *30 Trevanion Rd, Taneytown (21787). Phone 410/756-6812; fax 410/756-2744. www.antrim1844.com.* This restaurant is known for its superb cuisine. When weather permits, dinner may be served on the veranda overlooking the formal gardens or in the "Smokehouse," with a brick floor and large fireplaces. American, French menu. Closed Jan 1, Dec 25. Dinner. Refined dining in elegant atmosphere; fireplace, piano. Reservations required. Sittings: 7-7:30 pm (hors d'oeuvres served at 6:30 pm). Cr cds: A, C, D, DS, MC, V. **$$$**

D

Frederick (B-5)

See also Hagerstown, Thurmont

Settled 1745 **Pop** 52,767 **Elev** 290 ft **Area code** 301 and 240 **Zip** 21701

Information Tourism Council of Frederick County, 19 E Church St; 301/663-8687 or 800/999-3613

Web www.visitfrederick.org

Home of dauntless Barbara Frietchie, who reportedly spoke her mind to Stonewall Jackson and his "rebel hordes," Frederick is a town filled with history. Named for Frederick Calvert, sixth Lord Baltimore, it is the seat of one of America's richest agricultural counties. Francis Scott Key and Chief Justice Roger Brooke Taney made their homes here. Court House Square was the scene of several important events during the Revolutionary War, including the famed protest against the Stamp Act, in which an effigy of the stamp distributor was burned.

During the Civil War, Frederick was a focal point for strategic operations by both sides. In the campaign of 1862, the Confederacy's first invasions of the North were made at nearby South Mountain and Sharpsburg, at Antietam Creek. Wounded men by the thousands were cared for here. Troop movements continued for the duration of the war; cavalry skirmishes took place in the streets. In July 1864, the town was forced to pay a $200,000 ransom to Confederate General Jubal Early before he fought the Battle of Monocacy a few miles south. Frederick today is an educational center, tourist attraction, location of Fort

Detrick army installation, and home of diversified small industry. A 33-block area has been designated a Historic District.

What to See and Do

Barbara Frietchie House and Museum. *154 W Patrick St. Phone 301/698-0630.* Exhibits include quilts, clothing made by Frietchie, her rocker and Bible, the bed in which she died, and other items; ten-minute film; also garden. (Apr-Sept, Mon, Thurs-Sun; Oct-Nov, Sat and Sun) **$$**

Brunswick Museum. *40 W Potomac St. Phone 301/834-7100.* Furnishings and clothing interpret life in turn-of-the-century railroad town; large HO model train exhibit; gift shop. Special events held on selected weekends. (June-Sept, Thurs-Sun; Apr-May and Oct-late Dec, Sat and Sun; limited hours) **$$**

Gambrill State Park. *8602 Gambrill Park Rd (21702). Phone 301/791-4767.* Park has 1,136 acres with two developed areas. Fishing; nature and hiking trails, picnicking, tent and trailer sites (standard fees). Tea room. Two overlooks.

Historical Society of Frederick County Museum. *24 E Church St. Phone 301/663-1188.* House, built in early 1800s, shows both Georgian and Federal details; leaded side and fanlights, Doric columns inside, double porches in rear, and boxwood gardens. Portraits of early Frederick residents. Genealogy library (Tues-Sat). (Mon-Sat; also Sun afternoons) **$**

Horse-drawn carriage tours. *811 Trail Ave. Phone 301/694-RIDE.* (Daily, by appointment)

Monocacy National Battlefield. *4801 Urbana Pike (21701). 3 miles S on MD 355. Phone 301/662-3515.* On July 9, 1864, Union General Lew Wallace with 5,000 men delayed General Jubal Early and his 23,000 Confederate soldiers for 24 hours, during which Grant was able to reinforce, and save, Washington, D.C. New Jersey, Vermont, Pennsylvania, and Confederate monuments mark the area. **FREE**

Mount Olivet Cemetery. *S end of Market St.* (1852) Monuments mark graves of Francis Scott Key and Barbara Frietchie. Flag flies over Key's grave.

Roger Brooke Taney Home. (1799) **and Francis Scott Key Museum.** *121 S Bentz St. Phone 301/663-8687.* Chief Justice of the US from 1835-1864, Taney was chosen by Andrew Jackson to succeed John Marshall. He swore in seven presidents, including Abraham Lincoln, and issued the famous Dred Scott Decision. He is buried in the cemetery of St. John's Catholic Church at E 3rd and East sts. (Apr-Oct, weekends) **$$**

Rose Hill Manor Children's Museum. *1611 N Market St. Phone 301/694-1648 or 301/694-1650.* Hands-on exhibits of 19th-century family life; carriage museum; colonial herb and fragrant gardens; farm museum; blacksmith

Civil War Sites of Frederick

A well-preserved city of elegant 18th- and 19th-century structures, Frederick should be placed on anyone's tour of important Civil War landmarks. It is an especially appropriate sequel to a visit to nearby Antietam National Battlefield, which has entered the history books as the site on September 17, 1862, of the single bloodiest day of the Civil War. At the end of the battle, thousands of Union wounded ware transported to the small city, where 29 buildings were turned into makeshift hospitals. President Lincoln later praised townsfolk for their humanity. This heritage proved an important factor when Frederick was chosen from among 15 communities vying to be the site of the National Museum of Civil War Medicine. Begin an hour-long, 1-mile walking tour of the city's Historic District at the museum at 48 East Patrick Street. The museum tells the story of radical improvements in medical treatment during the four years of the war, as the divided nation coped with the flood of ill or wounded soldiers on both sides of the Mason-Dixon line. As the museum points out, the use of ambulances and the technique of embalming both emerged during the war. From the museum, walk three blocks west (left) to the reconstructed Barbara Frietchie House & Museum at 154 West Patrick. Frietchie was immortalized in John Greenleaf Whittier's Civil War poem, *Barbara Frietchie*: "Shoot, if you must, this old gray head, But spare your country's flag." According to legend, she waved a Union flag defiantly at "Stonewall" Jackson, who was leading a Confederate army through the city. In truth, she may have waved a flag, but to honor Union troops passing by later. Double back on Patrick Street to Court Street and walk north (left) one block to tour Courthouse Square. On Court Street, opposite City Hall, is the small office where Francis Scott Key, author of "The Star-Spangled Banner," practiced law. Revolutionary War General Lafayette was a guest at 103 Council Street during his ceremonial US tour in 1824. At 119 Record Street, Lincoln visited a wounded general and addressed a crowd from its steps after the Antietam battle. Head east (left) on West Church Street. At No. 108, you'll see a cast-iron model of the pet dog of John Tyler, a pioneer ophthalmologist. The statue was stolen by Confederates seeking to melt it into bullets, but later it was found near an Antietam battlefield. Conclude your tour two blocks east at the Historical Society of Fredericksburg at 24 East Church. A large 1820 home, it is maintained as a house museum furnished with local antiques—appropriately so, because nearby East Patrick Street has been dubbed "Antique Row" for its many antique shops.

shop; log cabin. (Apr-Oct, daily; Nov, Sat and Sun only) **$$**

Schifferstadt. *1110 Rosemont Ave. Phone 301/663-3885.* (1756) Fine example of German colonial farmhouse architecture. Tours of architectural museum. Gift shop. (Apr-mid Dec, Tues-Sun; closed Thanksgiving) **$**

Trinity Chapel. *W Church St, near N Market St.* (1763) Graceful colonial church; Francis Scott Key was baptized here. Steeple houses town clock and ten-bell chimes; chimes play every Sat evening. The chapel is now used as Sunday School for

Evangelical Reformed Church. *15 W Church St. Phone 301/662-2762.* United Church of Christ (1848). Opposite Trinity Chapel. A Grecian-style building modeled after the Erechtheum, with two towers resembling Lanterns of Demosthenes. Here Stonewall Jackson slept through a pro-Union sermon before the Battle of Antietam; Barbara Frietchie was a member.

Special Events

Beyond the Garden Gates Tour. *19 E Church St, downtown. Phone 301/663-8687.* Tour historic and contemporary gardens. Late May.

Fall Festival. *Rose Hill Manor. 1611 N Market St (21701).* Apple butter making, music, crafts demonstrations, tractor pull, hay rides, country cooking. Early Oct.

Great Frederick Fair. *797 E Patrick St (21705). Phone 301/663-5895.* Frederick county fair. Mid-late Sept.

Lotus Blossom Festival. *Lilypons Water Gardens, 6800 Lilypons Rd (21717). 10 miles S via MD 85. Phone 800/999-5459.* Endless blooms of water lilies and lotus, water garden; arts and crafts, food, entertainment, lectures. First double-digit weekend in July.

New Market Days. *2 W Main St. 8 miles E, in New Market. Phone 301/831-6755.* Nostalgic revival of the atmosphere of a 19th-century village; costumed guides, period crafts and events; held in New Market, the town dedicated to being the "Antiques Capital of Maryland." Last full weekend in Sept.

Motels/Motor Lodges

★ **DAYS INN.** *5646 Buckeystown Pike (21704). Phone 301/694-6600; toll-free 800/329-7466; fax 301/831-4242. www.daysinn.com.* 119 rooms, 2 story. Apr-Oct: S, D $56-$75; under 18 free; lower rates rest of year. Crib free. TV; cable (premium). Pool. Playground. Complimentary continental breakfast. Check-out noon. Meeting room. Business services available. Sundries. Refrigerators, microwaves available. Cr cds: A, C, D, DS, JCB, MC, V.

D ⌷ ⌷ SC

★ **FAIRFIELD INN.** *5220 Westview Dr (21703). Phone 301/631-2000; fax 301/631-2100. www.fairfieldinn.com.* 105 rooms, 3 story. May-mid-Oct: S $69-$82; D $69-$87; higher rates special events. Crib free. Complimentary continental breakfast. Check-out noon. TV; cable (premium). Some refrigerators, microwaves. Health club privileges. Exercise equipment. Indoor pool, whirlpool. Business services. Sundries. Cr cds: A, C, D, DS, MC, V.

D ⌷ ⌷ ⌷ ⌷

★ **HAMPTON INN.** *5311 Buckeystown Pike (21704). Phone 301/698-2500; toll-free 800/426-7866; fax 301/695-8735. www.hamptoninn.com.* 160 rooms, 6 story. S, D $69-$100; suites $150; under 18 free. Crib free. Pet accepted, some restrictions; fee. TV; cable (premium). Pool; lifeguard. Complimentary continental breakfast. Restaurant 11:30 am-9 pm. Bar; entertainment. Check-out noon. Coin laundry. Meeting rooms. Business services available. In-room modem link. Sundries. Valet service. Exercise equipment. Health club privileges. Some refrigerators; microwaves available. Cr cds: A, C, D, DS, MC, V.

D ⌷ ⌷ ⌷ ⌷ SC

B&B/Small Inns

★ ★ **CATOCTIN INN.** *3619 Buckeystown Pike, Buckeystown (21717). Phone 301/874-5555; fax 301/831-8102. www.catoctininn.com.* 20 rooms, 3 story. S, D $85-$125; each additional $10; cottages $150; under 2 free; weekly rates; minimum stay holidays; higher rates: weekends, fall foliage. Complimentary breakfast. Check-out noon, check-in 4 pm. TV; cable (premium), VCR available (movies). Fireplaces. Lawn games. Built in the 1780s; parlor with antique sofas. Cr cds: A, C, D, DS, MC, V.

D ⌷ ⌷

★ ★ ★ **INN AT BUCKEYSTOWN.** *3521 Buckeystown Pike, Buckeystown (21717). Phone 301/874-5755; toll-free 800/272-1190; fax 301/831-1355. www.innatbuckeystown.com.* This stately and elegant mansion opened its doors in 1981, and today continues to enchant guests with touches of luxury and the charm of another era. Located in a National Registered Historic Village, this mansion delights with its warm hospitality, Victorian-style décor, and wonderful appointment of collectibles and period pieces. 5 rooms, 3 story. Restaurant (public by reservation) 7:30 pm sitting; closed Sun-Tues. Children over 12 years only. Check-out 11 am, check-in 4 pm. TV; cable (premium), VCR available. Restaurant. Downhill ski 20 miles; cross-country ski 1 mile. Restored Victorian

mansion (1897). Near river. Setups. Totally nonsmoking. Cr cds: A, MC, V. **$$$**

⌷ ⌷

★ ★ ★ **STONE MANOR.** *5820 Carroll Boyer Rd, Middletown (21769). Phone 301/473-5454; fax 301/371-5622. www.stonemanor.com.* This inn offers luxury suites, each decorated with its own unique style and charm. It is located just outside of the town of Fredrick, where visitors will find shopping and restaurants. 6 rooms, 2 story, 5 suites. No room phones. S, D $200; suites $125-$250. TV; VCR available. Complimentary continental breakfast. Restaurant 11 am-2 pm, 6-9 pm; Sun 11 am-2 pm (brunch), 4-7 pm; closed Mon. Room service 24 hours. Check-out 11 am, check-in 2 pm. Business services available. Lawn games. Fireplaces. Balconies. On pond. Stone building built in 1760s; on more than 100 acres of wooded area. Totally nonsmoking. Cr cds: A, DS, MC, V.

D ⌷ ⌷ ⌷

★ ★ ★ **TURNING POINT INN.** *3406 Urbana Pike (21704). Phone 301/831-8232; fax 301/831-8092. www.turningpointinn.com.* This elegant Edwardian estate, built in the early 1900s and lovingly renovated with modern amenities, offers guests a truly delightful and memorable stay. 5 rooms, 2 with shower only, 3 story, 2 kitchen cottages. S, D $75-$95; kitchen cottages $100-$150. Dining room 11:30 am-2 pm, 5:30-9 pm; weekend hours vary; closed Mon. Complimentary full breakfast. Check-out 11 am, check-in 3 pm. TV; cable (premium). Dining room 11:30 am-2 pm, 5:30-9 pm Tues-Sun; weekend hours vary. Business services. Built in 1910. View of Sugarloaf Mountain and adjacent farmland. Cr cds: A, C, D, DS, MC, V.

D ⌷ ⌷ ⌷

Restaurants

★ ★ **BROWN PELICAN.** *5 E Church St (21701). Phone 301/695-5833; fax 301/695-5876.* Hours: 11:30 am-3 pm, 5-9:30 pm; Fri to 10 pm; Sat 5-10 pm; Sun 5-9:30 pm. Closed Jan 1, Thanksgiving, Dec 25; also Super Bowl Sun. Reservations accepted; required Fri, Sat. Continental menu. Bar. Lunch $5.75-$12.95, dinner $12.95-$23.95. Specializes in fresh seafood, pasta, veal. In basement of antebellum bank. Cr cds: A, C, D, DS, MC, V.

D

★ ★ **GABRIEL'S.** *4730 Ijamsville Rd, Ijamsville (21754). Phone 301/865-5500; fax 301/698-9880. www.gabrielsinn.com.* French menu. Closed Mon-Wed; Jan 1. Dinner. Bar. French Provincial inn atmosphere; building constructed in 1862. Reservations required; Fri, Sat. Cr cds: D, DS, MC, V. **$$**

D

★ ★ **TAURASO'S.** *6 East St (21701). Phone 301/663-6600; fax 301/663-6677. www.tauraso.com.* Hours: 11 am-10 pm; Fri, Sat to 11 pm. Closed Dec 25. Reservations accepted. Italian, American menu. Bar to midnight. Lunch $4.95-$8.95, dinner $7.95-$19.95. Specializes in fresh fish, veal, steak. Outdoor seating. In restored factory building (late 1800s). Cr cds: A, D, DS, MC, V.

D

Gaithersburg (C-6)

See also Rockville

Pop 52,613 **Elev** 508 ft **Area code** 301

Information Chamber of Commerce, 9 Park Ave, 20877; 301/840-1400

What to See and Do

Seneca Creek State Park. *11950 Clopper Rd. 2 1/2 miles W of I-270 on MD 117. Phone 301/924-2127.* Stream valley park of 6,109 acres with 90-acre lake. Historic sites with old mills, an old schoolhouse, stone quarries. Fishing, boating (rentals); picnicking, disk golf, hiking, bicycle and bridle trails, winter sports. Standard fees. **$**

Special Event

Montgomery County Agricultural Fair. *16 Chestnut St. Phone 301/926-3100.* One of the East Coast's leading county fairs; emphasis on agriculture, 4-H activities; animal exhibits, home arts; antique farm equipment; tractor pull, horse pull, demolition derby; rodeo; entertainment. Mid-late Aug.

Motels/Motor Lodges

★ **COMFORT INN AT SHADY GROVE.** *16216 Frederick Rd (20877). Phone 301/330-0023; toll-free 800/228-5150; fax 301/258-1950. www.comfortinn.com.* 127 rooms, 7 story. Apr-Oct: S, D $49-$109; each additional $10; under 18 free; monthly rates; lower rates rest of year. Crib free. Pet accepted, some restrictions. TV; cable (premium). Heated pool; lifeguard. Complimentary full breakfast. Restaurant adjacent 11 am-9 pm. Check-out 11 am. Coin laundry. Meeting rooms. Business center. In-room modem link. Valet service. Gift shop. Exercise equipment. Health club privileges. Some refrigerators; microwaves. Picnic tables. Cr cds: A, C, D, DS, ER, JCB, MC, V.

D 🐾 ⊷ ⫟ ⊠ **SC** 🏃

★ ★ **COURTYARD BY MARRIOTT.** *805 Russell Ave (20879). Phone 301/670-0008; fax 301/948-4538. www.courtyard.com.* 203 rooms, 7 story. S $105; D $115; each additional $10; suites $250; weekend rates. Crib free. Check-out noon. TV; cable (premium), VCR available. In-room modem link. Some balconies, refrigerators,

microwaves. Valet services. Coin laundry. Restaurant 6-10 am, 5:30-9:30 pm; Sat 7-11 am; Sun 7 am-noon. Bar 5 pm-midnight. Exercise equipment, steam room. Pool, whirlpool, lifeguard. Lighted tennis. Meeting rooms. Business services. Cr cds: A, C, D, DS, MC, V.

D ⊷ ⫟ 🏌 ⊠

★ **HAMPTON INN.** *20260 Goldenrod Ln, Germantown (20876). Phone 301/428-1300; fax 301/428-9034. www.hamptoninn.com.* 178 rooms, 6 story, 16 kitchen units. S, D $95-$105; kitchen units $129; suites $199; under 18 free; weekend rates. Crib free. TV; cable (premium). Pool. Complimentary continental breakfast. Restaurant 11 am-11 pm. Check-out noon. Coin laundry. Meeting rooms. Business services available. Valet service. Sundries. Exercise equipment; sauna. Health club privileges. Microwaves available. Cr cds: A, C, D, DS, MC, V.

D ⊷ ⫟ 🏌 ⊠

★ ★ **HOLIDAY INN.** *2 Montgomery Village Ave (20879). Phone 301/948-8900; toll-free 800/465-4329; fax 301/258-1940. www.holiday-inn.com.* 301 rooms, 2-8 story. S $114-$124; D $124-$149; suites $300-$350; kitchen units $119-$139; under 18 free. Crib free. Pet accepted, some restrictions. TV; cable (premium). Indoor pool; whirlpool, poolside service, lifeguard. Restaurant 6:30 am-10 pm. Room service to midnight. Bar noon-midnight. Check-out noon. Coin laundry. Convention facilities. Business center. In-room modem link. Bellstaff. Gift shop. Exercise equipment. Game room. Some refrigerators; microwaves available. Balconies. Cr cds: A, C, D, DS, JCB, MC, V.

D 🐾 ⊷ ⫟ ⊠ **SC** 🏃

Hotels

★ ★ ★ **HILTON.** *620 Perry Pkwy (20877). Phone 301/977-8900; toll-free 800/445-8667; fax 301/977-3450. www.hilton.com.* 301 rooms, 12 story. S, D $115-$155; suites $325; under 18 free; weekend rates. Crib free. Pet accepted, some restrictions. TV; cable (premium). Indoor/outdoor pool. Restaurant 6:30 am-11 pm; weekends from 7 am. Bars 11-1 am. Convention facilities. Business services available. In-room modem link. Exercise equipment. Health club privileges. Refrigerators available. Some private patios, balconies. Adjacent to Lake Forest shopping center. Cr cds: A, C, D, DS, ER, JCB, MC, V.

D 🐾 ⊷ ⫟ ⊠ **SC**

★ ★ ★ **MARRIOTT GAITHERSBURG WASHINGTONIAN CENTER.** *9751 Washingtonian Blvd (20878). Phone 301/590-0044; toll-free 800/228-9290; fax 301/212-6155. www.marriott.com.* This hotel is conveniently connected to restaurants, retail stores, and a multiplex theater. 284 rooms, 11 story. S, D $164; suites $250; under 18 free; weekend rates. Crib free. TV; cable (premium). Indoor pool; whirlpool, poolside service, lifeguard. Restaurant 6:30 am-11 pm; weekend hours vary. Bar 4 pm-midnight. Check-out noon. Convention facilities. Business center. In-room modem link. Concierge. Gift shop. Exercise equipment; sauna. Health club privileges. Luxury level. Cr cds: A, C, D, DS, ER, JCB, MC, V.

D ⊠ 🏋 🛠 ≈ **SC** 🚶

All Suite

★ ★ **SPRINGHILL SUITES.** *9715 Washingtonian Blvd (20878). Phone 301/987-0900; fax 301/987-0500. www. springhillsuites.com.* Guests traveling on business or pleasure will find comfort at this all-suites property. Spacious rooms feature a separate area for eating, sleeping, working, and relaxing. 162 suites, 6 story. S, D $69-$139. Crib available. Complimentary continental breakfast. Check-out noon, check-in 3 pm. TV; cable (premium). In-room modem link. Refrigerators, microwaves. Valet services, coin laundry. Exercise room. Indoor pool, whirlpool. Meeting room. Business center. Concierge. Cr cds: A, C, D, DS, MC, V.

⊠ 🏋 🛠 🚶

Restaurants

★ **CHRIS' STEAK HOUSE.** *201 E Diamond Ave (20877). Phone 301/869-6116.* Specializes in beef, pork, seafood. Hours: 11 am-midnight. Closed Sun; also most major holidays. Lunch, dinner. Bar. Children's menu. Football memorabilia. Cr cds: MC, V. **$**

D

★ ★ **FLAMING PIT.** *18701 N Frederick Ave (20879). Phone 301/977-0700; fax 301/840-9633.* Hours: 11:30 am-10 pm; Fri to 11 pm; Sat 4-11 pm; Sun 5-10 pm; early-bird dinner Mon-Fri 4-7 pm. Closed some major holidays. Reservations accepted; required Fri, Sat. Bar to midnight; Fri, Sat to 1 am. Lunch $6.95-$12.95, dinner $13.95-$29.95. Children's menu. Specializes in prime rib, lamb, fresh seafood. Pianist. Skylight; hanging baskets. Original antique fireplaces. Cr cds: A, C, D, DS, MC, V.

D

★ ★ **GOLDEN BULL GRAND CAFE.** *7 Dalamar St (20877). Phone 301/948-3666; fax 301/948-4542.* Specializes in beef, seafood. Closed Dec 25. Lunch $5.50-$10.95, dinner $9.95-$29.95. Bar 11 am-11 pm. Children's menu. Cr cds: A, D, DS, MC, V.

D

★ **IL FORNO PIZZERIA.** *8941 Westland Dr (20877). Phone 301/977-5900; fax 301/977-5902.* Hours: 11 am-10 pm; Fri, Sat to 11 pm. Closed most major holidays. Italian menu. Wine, beer. A la carte entrées: lunch $4.45-$7.95, dinner $10-$15.95. Specializes in pizza, pasta. Outdoor seating. Casual décor. Cr cds: MC, V.

D

★ ★ **PEKING CHEERS.** *519 Quince Orchard Rd (20878). Phone 301/216-2090; fax 301/216-1473. www.thepekingcheers.com.* Hours: 11 am-10:30 pm; Fri, Sat to 11 pm. Reservations accepted. Chinese menu. Service bar. Lunch $4.25-$5.50, dinner $5.95-$11.95. Specializes in: Peking duck, sesame chicken, crispy beef. Casual décor; large murals. Totally nonsmoking. Cr cds: A, D, DS, MC, V.

D ⊠

★ **PEKING SUPREME.** *19204 Montgomery Village Ave, Montgomery Village (20886). Phone 301/963-8088; fax 301/963-8318.* Hours: 11:30 am-9:45 pm; Fri, Sat to 10:45 pm. Closed Thanksgiving. Chinese menu. Bar. Lunch $4.50-$5.50, dinner $6.95-$11.95. Specializes in: Peking-style chicken, crispy beef. Art Deco décor. Cr cds: A, C, D, DS, MC, V.

D

★ **ROY'S PLACE.** *2 E Diamond Ave (20877). Phone 301/948-5548; fax 301/948-4840. www.roysplacerestaurant .com.* Closed Thanksgiving, 25. Lunch, dinner. Bar. Cr cds: A, D, DS, MC, V. **$**

D

★ ★ **SIR WALTER RALEIGH.** *19100 Montgomery Village Ave, Montgomery Village (20886). Phone 301/258-0576; fax 301/590-9357. www.sirwalterraleigh.com.* Closed Dec 25. Lunch, dinner. Bar. Children's menu. Cr cds: A, D, DS, MC, V. **$$**

D

Grantsville (A-2)

See also Cumberland, Oakland

Pop 619 **Elev** 2,300 ft **Area code** 301 **Zip** 21536

Information Garrett County Chamber of Commerce, 15 Visitors Center Dr, McHenry 21541; 301/387-4386

Web www.garrettchamber.com

What to See and Do

Casselman Bridge and State Park. *E of Grantsville on US 40. Contact 349 Headquarters Ln. Phone 301/895-5453.* Single-span stone arch bridge over the Casselman River was built in 1813.

New Germany State Park. *5 miles SE of Grantsville, in Savage River State Forest. Contact 349 Headquarters Ln. Phone 301/895-5453.* A 13-acre lake built on site of a once prosperous milling center. Swimming, fishing, boating; nature, hiking trails, winter sports, picnicking, playground, concession, improved campsites, cabins (fee). **$**

Savage River State Forest. *W and S via US 40 and I-68. Contact 349 Headquarters Ln (21536). Phone 301/895-5453.* Largest of Maryland's state forests comprises about 52,800 acres of near wilderness. A strategic watershed area, the northern hardwood forest surrounds the Savage River Dam. Fishing; hunting, hiking trails, winter sports, primitive camping (permit required).

Springs Museum. *2 miles N via MD 669, PA 669 in Springs, PA. Phone 814/662-4158.* Depicts life of settlers of Casselman Valley; 18th-century farming tools, fossil collection, other exhibits. (Memorial Day-mid-Oct, Wed-Sat afternoons)

Spruce Forest Artisan Village. *177 Casselman Rd. 1 mile E on US 40, near Penn Alps. Phone 301/895-3332.* Original log cabins plus other historic buildings serve as studios for a potter, internationally recognized bird carver, weaver, spinner, stained-glass maker, and other artisans. Buildings (Mon-Sat). Special events (summer; fee). Restaurant. (See SPECIAL EVENTS) **FREE**

Special Events

Springs Folk Festival. *On grounds of Springs Museum (see). Phone 814/662-4158.* Pennsylvania Dutch food, music. First Fri and Sat in Oct.

Spruce Forest Summerfest and Quilt Show. *Spruce Forest Artisan Village. 177 Casselman Rd. Phone 301/895-3332.* More than 200 quilts on display; more than 70 craftspeople demonstrate their various skills. Second full Thurs, Fri, and Sat weekend in July.

Restaurant

★ ★ **PENN ALPS.** *125 Casselman Rd (21536). Phone 301/895-5985; fax 301/895-9542. www.pennalps.com.* Hours: 7 am-8 pm; Sun brunch 10 am-3 pm. Closed Dec 24, 25. Complete meals: breakfast $2.50-$6.95, lunch $4-$7.95, dinner $8.75-$15.95. Sun brunch $8.95. Children's menu. Specializes in Dutch cooking. Salad bar. Colonial décor; 1818 stagecoach stop. Totally nonsmoking. Cr cds: A, DS, MC, V.

Hagerstown (A-5)

See also Boonsboro, Frederick, Thurmont

Settled 1762 **Pop** 36,687 **Elev** 552 ft **Area code** 301 **Zip** 21740

Information Hagerstown/Washington County Tourism Office, 16 Public Sq; 301/791-3246 or 800/228-7829

Web www.marylandmemories.org

Within the city of Hagerstown there is a walking tour with points of interest marked on downtown sidewalks and walking paths in city parks. South Prospect Street is one of the city's oldest neighborhoods, listed on the National Register of Historic Places. The tree-lined street is graced by homes dating back to the early 1800s.

What to See and Do

Antietam National Battlefield. (see) *11 miles S on MD 65.*

Fort Frederick State Park. *18 miles W of junction I-81 and I-70 to Big Pool, then 1 mile SE via MD 56, unnumbered road. Phone 301/842-2155.* Erected in 1756, during French and Indian War, the fort is considered a fine example of a pre-Revolutionary stone fort. Overlooks Chesapeake and Ohio Canal National Historical Park (see); barracks, interior, and wall of fort restored; military reenactments throughout year. Fishing, boating (rentals); nature and hiking trails, picnicking (shelter), playground, unimproved camping. Museum, orientation film, historical programs. Standard fees. Winter hours may vary.

Greenbrier State Park. *21843 National Pike (21713). 6 miles E via US 40. Phone 301/791-4767.* The Appalachian Trail passes near this 1,275-acre park and its 42-acre man-made lake. Swimming (Memorial Day-Labor Day, daily), fishing, boating (rentals; no gas motors); nature and hiking trails, picnicking. Standard fees.

Hagerstown Roundhouse Museum. *300 S Burhans Blvd, across the tracks from City Park. Phone 301/739-4665.* Museum houses photographic exhibits of the seven railroads of Hagerstown; historic railroad memorabilia, tools, and equipment; archives of maps, books, papers, and related items. Gift shop. (Fri-Sun afternoons) (See SPECIAL EVENTS) **$**

Jonathan Hager House and Museum. *110 Key St, in City Park. Phone 301/739-8393.* (1739) Stone house in park setting; authentic 18th-century furnishings. (Apr-Dec, Tues-Sun) **$$**

Miller House. *135 W Washington St. Phone 301/797-8782.* Washington County Historical Society Headquarters. Federal townhouse (circa 1820); three-story spiral staircase; period furnishings; garden; clock, doll, and Bell pottery collections; Chesapeake and Ohio Canal and Civil War exhibits; 19th-century country store display. (Apr-Dec, Wed-Sat; closed holidays; also first two weeks in Dec) **$$**

Washington County Museum of Fine Arts. *91 Key St, in City Park, S on US 11 (Virginia Ave). Phone 301/739-5727.* Paintings, sculpture, changing exhibits; concerts, lectures. (Tues-Sun; closed holidays) **FREE**

Special Events

Alsatia Mummers Halloween Parade Festival. *Phone 301/791-3246.* Sat, weekend closest to Halloween.

Hagerstown Railroad Heritage Days. *300 S Burhans Blvd E. Phone 301/739-4665.* Special events centered on the Roundhouse Museum. Early May.

Halfway Park Days. *Phone 301/791-3246.* Helicopter rides, antique cars, dance bands, flea market, food. Late May.

Jonathan Hager Frontier Craft Day. *110 Key St.* Colonial crafts demonstrated and exhibited. Bluegrass music; food. First weekend in Aug.

Leitersburg Peach Festival. *21378 Leiters Mill Rd.* Peach-related edibles, farmers market, bluegrass music. Second weekend in Aug.

Williamsport C & O Canal Days. *30 W Potomac St.* Arts and crafts, Indian Village, National Park Service activities; food. Late Aug.

Motels/Motor Lodges

★★ **CLARION HOTEL & CONFERENCE CENTER ANTIETAM CREEK.** *901 Dual Hwy (21740). Phone 301/733-5100; fax 301/733-9192. www.clarion.com.* 210 rooms, 5 story. S $62-$69; D $67-$74; each additional $5; suites $95-$200; under 18 free. Crib free. TV; cable (premium). Indoor pool. Restaurant 6:30 am-9:30 pm; Sun to 9 pm. Room service. Bar noon-2 am. Check-out 11 am. Coin laundry. Meeting rooms. Business services available. Free airport transportation. Exercise equipment. Some refrigerators, in-room whirlpools. Cr cds: A, C, D, DS, JCB, MC, V.

D ⌨ ✗ ⛷ ⊠ SC

★★ **DAYS INN.** *900 Dual Hwy (21740). Phone 301/739-9050; toll-free 800/422-2754; fax 301/739-8347. www.daysinn.com.* 140 rooms, 2 story. May-Oct: S $48-$58; D $54-$65; each additional $5; under 18 free; weekend rates; lower rates rest of year. Complimentary continental breakfast. Check-out noon. TV; cable (premium). Laundry services. Restaurant 6:30 am-2 pm, 5-9 pm. Bar 4:30-9:30 pm. Pool. Cr cds: A, C, D, DS, JCB, MC, V.

D ⌨ ⊠ SC

★★ **FOUR POINTS BY SHERATON.** *1910 Dual Hwy (21740). Phone 301/790-3010; toll-free 800/325-3535; fax 301/733-4559. www.fourpoints.com.* 108 rooms, 2 story. S $60-$75; D $64-$79; each additional $6; suites $150; under 18 free. Crib $6. Pet accepted; $50 deposit. TV; cable (premium). Pool; whirlpool. Complimentary continental breakfast. Restaurant 6:30 am-10 pm; Sat, Sun 7 am-9 pm. Room service. Bar 11-2 am. Check-out noon. Meeting rooms. Business services available. Bellstaff. Valet service. Sundries. Free airport transportation. Exercise equipment; sauna. Microwaves available. Cr cds: A, C, D, DS, MC, V.

D ⭭ ⌨ ✗ ⊠ SC

★★ **PLAZA HOTEL.** *1718 Underpass Way (21740). Phone 301/797-2500; toll-free 800/826-4534; fax 301/797-6209. www.plazahotelhagerstown.com.* 163 units, 6 story.

Check-out noon. TV; cable (premium), VCR available. In-room modem link. Restaurant 6:30 am-9 pm. Bar 11 am-11 pm. Room service. Exercise equipment, sauna. Indoor pool, whirlpool. Free airport transportation. Cr cds: A, C, D, DS, JCB, MC, V.

D ⌨ ✗ ⊠ SC

★★ **VENICE INN.** *431 Dual Hwy (21740). Phone 301/733-0830; fax 301/733-4978.* 220 rooms, 2-5 story. Apr-Oct: S $58-$68; D $63-$73; each additional $6; suites $125-$250; under 18 free; lower rates rest of year. Crib $6. Pet accepted, some restrictions. Check-out noon. TV; cable (premium), VCR (movies). Refrigerators, microwaves available. Valet services. Restaurant 6 am-10:30 pm. Bar; entertainment Tues-Sat. Room service. Exercise equipment. Game room. Pool. Beauty shop. Airport transportation. Meeting rooms. Cr cds: A, C, D, DS, MC, V.

D ⭭ ⌨ ✗ ⊠

Restaurants

★ **JUNCTION 808.** *808 Noland Dr (21740). Phone 301/791-3639; fax 301/791-3639.* Hours: 6 am-8:30 pm. Closed Sun; also July 4, Dec 24-26. Reservations accepted. Breakfast $1.50-$4.95, lunch $2.50-$4.25, dinner $4.95-$10.95. Children's menu. Located near railroad tracks. Railroad-theme décor and tapes of actual trains; model trains circle the room at the ceiling. Totally nonsmoking. Cr cds: MC, V.

D SC ⊠

★★ **RED HORSE STEAK HOUSE.** *1800 Dual Hwy (21740). Phone 301/733-3788.* Seafood, steak menu. Closed major holidays. Dinner. Bar. Children's menu. Cr cds: A, D, MC, V. **$**

D

★★ **RICHARDSON'S.** *710 Dual Hwy (21740). Phone 301/733-3660; fax 301/733-3662. www.richardsonrestaurant.com.* Seafood menu. Closed Dec 24 evening, Dec 25. Buffet, breakfast, lunch, dinner. Bar. Children's menu. Cr cds: DS, MC, V. **$**

D

Havre de Grace (B-8)

See also Aberdeen, Elkton

Settled 1658 **Pop** 11,331 **Elev** 52 ft **Area code** 410 and 443 **Zip** 21078

Information Chamber of Commerce, 224 N Washington St, PO Box 339; 410/939-3303 or 800/851-7756

Web www.hdgchamber.com

What to See and Do

Concord Point Lighthouse. *At foot of Lafayette St.* (1827) Built of granite, considered the oldest continuously used lighthouse on the East Coast. It was automated in 1928. (May-Oct, weekends and holidays only) **FREE**

Decoy Museum. *215 Giles St. At the bay. Phone 410/939-3739.* Houses a collection of hand-carved waterfowl decoys and interprets this art form as it applies to the heritage of Chesapeake Bay. (Daily; closed Jan 1, Thanksgiving, Dec 25) (See SPECIAL EVENTS) **$**

Susquehanna State Park. *3318 Rockchrome Hill Rd. Phone 410/557-7994.* A 2,639-acre park. Fishing, boat launch; nature, riding, and hiking trails; cross-country skiing, picnicking, camping (May-Sept; fee). In the park is

Steppingstone Museum. *461 Quaker Bottom Rd. Phone 410/939-2299.* Self-guided tour of museum grounds includes sites of a once working Harford County farm; farmhouse is furnished as a turn-of-the-century country home; nearby shops and barn hold many displays and exhibits of the 1880-1920 period; demonstrations of rural arts and crafts of the period. Also here are blacksmith, woodworking, cooper, and dairy shops. (May-first Sun in Oct, Sat and Sun afternoons) Special events held throughout the year (see SPECIAL EVENTS).

Special Events

Decoy Festival. *215 Giles St (21078). Phone 410/939-3739.* Decoys on display, auction. Carving, gunning, and calling contests. Refreshments. Fri-Sun first weekend in May.

Fall Harvest Festival and Craft Show. *Steppingstone Museum. 461 Quaker Bottom Rd (21078). Phone 410/939-2299.* Features activities related to the harvest and preparation for winter: apple pressing, scarecrow stuffing, and other events. Entertainment. Last full weekend in Sept.

B&B/Small Inns

★★★VANDIVER INN. *301 S Union Ave (21078). Phone 410/939-5200; toll-free 800/245-1655; fax 410/939-5202. www.vandiverinn.com.* This elegant Victorian mansion was built in 1886 and is listed on the National Historic Register. Located just blocks from the Chesapeake Bay, charming antique stores, and numerous water activities, this delightful inn offers a welcome respite from the daily hustle and bustle of life. Guests will delight in everything from the relaxing veranda to the elegantly appointed guest rooms. 9 rooms, 3 story. S, D $75-$105; weekly rates. TV in parlor. Complimentary full breakfast. Check-out 11 am, check-in 4-7 pm. Some fireplaces, balconies. Queen Anne-style mansion (1886); antiques. Chesapeake Bay 2 blocks. Cr cds: A, DS, MC, V.

D ⊠ SC

Restaurants

★★ BAYOU. *927 Pulaski Hwy (US 40) (21078). Phone 410/939-3565; fax 410/939-5396.* Specializes in seafood, veal. Closed Mon; Dec 24-26. Lunch, dinner. Children's menu. Reservations accepted required holidays. Cr cds: A, C, MC, V. **$$**

D

★★ CRAZY SWEDE. *400 N Union Ave (21078). Phone 410/939-5440; fax 410/939-8020. www.crazyswederestaurant.com.* Hours: 11-2 am; Sun brunch 10 am-2:30 pm. Closed Thanksgiving, Dec 25. Reservations accepted; required Fri, Sat. Continental menu. Bar. Lunch $4.25-$6.95, dinner $11.95-$21. Sun brunch $3.50-$9. Children's menu. Specializes in seafood. Cr cds: A, MC, V.

D

La Plata (D-6)

See also Waldorf; also see District of Columbia

Pop 6,551 **Elev** 193 ft **Area code** 301 **Zip** 20646

Information Charles County Chamber of Commerce, 6360 Crain Hwy, phone 301/932-6500; or the Department of Tourism, 301/645-0558

Web www.ccc-md.org

What to See and Do

Doncaster Demonstration Forest. *13 miles W on MD 6, near Doncaster. Phone 301/934-2282.* Heavily forested with yellow poplar, sweet gum, red and white oaks, and pine throughout its 1,477 acres. Hunting, 13 miles of hiking trails, bridle trails, picnic area, cross-country skiing.

Port Tobacco. *3 miles SW on MD 6. Phone 301/934-4313.* Infrared aerial photography and archaeological excavation revealed the site of one of the oldest continuously-inhabited English settlements in North America. Appearing as a Native American village on Captain John Smith's map of the area (1608), the area was colonized by the English as early as 1638. The town was chartered in 1727, and the first courthouse was erected in 1729. Among the remaining buildings are the Chimney House (1765) and Stagg Hall (1732), an original colonial home still a private residence, Burch (Catslide) House (1700), the reconstructed Quenzel Store, and a Federal period courthouse, with the Port Tobacco Museum on the second floor; archeological items on display, replicas of colonial houses; Civil War and John Wilkes Booth exhibits, 30-minute audiovisual film *The Story of Port Tobacco.* (Apr-Dec, Sat and Sun afternoons) **$**

Smallwood State Park. *2750 Sweden Point Rd. 16 miles W via MD 225, 224, near Rison.* Phone 301/743-7613. Restored home of Revolutionary General William Smallwood. Guided tour and historical program during summer. Marina. Boating (launch, rentals), fishing; hiking, picnicking. Retreat house. Park (daily). Standard fees. **$**

Motel/Motor Lodge

★ **BEST WESTERN LA PLATA INN.** *6900 Crain Hwy; Rte 301 (20646).* Phone 301/934-4900; toll-free 800/780-7234; fax 301/934-5389. www.bestwestern.com. 73 rooms, 2 story. S, D $57-$67; each additional $5; suites $90-$105; under 13 free. Complimentary continental breakfast. Check-out noon. TV; cable (premium), VCR available. Laundry services. Restaurant adjacent 11 am-11 pm. Exercise equipment. Pool. Cr cds: A, C, D, DS, MC, V.

D ⚊ 🕴 🏊 SC

Laurel (C-6)

See also Bowie, College Park, Silver Spring

Pop 19,960 **Elev** 160 ft **Area code** 240 and 301

Information Baltimore/Washington Corridor Chamber of Commerce, 312 Marshall Ave, Suite 104; 301/725-4000

Web www.laurel.md.us

What to See and Do

Montpelier Mansion. *9401 Montpelier Dr. 3 miles SE on MD 197 at Muirkirk.* Phone 301/953-1376. (circa 1780) Built and owned for generations by Maryland's Snowden family; Georgian architecture. George Washington and Abigail Adams were among its early visitors. On the grounds are boxwood gardens, an 18th-century herb garden, and a small summer house. Tours; purchase ticket in gift shop. (Mar-Nov, Sun afternoons; groups by appointment; closed holidays) Candlelight tours held in early Dec. **$$**

National Wildlife Visitor Center. *10901 Scarlet Tanager Loop.* Phone 301/497-5760. A 12,750-acre national wildlife refuge and research area. Interactive exhibits focus on global environmental issues, migratory birds, wildlife habitats, and endangered species. Tram tours available of surrounding forests and lakes (weather permitting; fee). Trails. Gift shop. (Daily; closed Dec 25) **FREE**

Special Event

Thoroughbred racing. *Racetrack Rd and Rte 198 (20725). Laurel Race Course, on MD 198. Entrances accessible from northbound or southbound on US 1, I-95, or from Baltimore-Washington Pkwy, MD 198 exit.* Phone 301/725-0400 or 800/638-1859 for current racing schedule.

Motels/Motor Lodges

★ **COMFORT SUITES LAUREL LAKES.** *14402 Laurel Pl (20707).* Phone 301/206-2600; toll-free 800/628-7760; fax 301/725-0056. www.comfortinn.com. 119 rooms, 5 story. S, D $80-$100; each additional $10; suites $95-$125; under 18 free; weekly, weekend rates; higher rates: Cherry Blossom Festival, Memorial Day weekend. Crib free. Pet accepted; $50 refundable. Complimentary continental breakfast. Check-out noon. TV; cable (premium). Refrigerators, microwaves. Valet services. Coin laundry. Exercise equipment. Indoor pool, whirlpool, lifeguard. Airport transportation. Meeting rooms. Business services. Sundries. Cr cds: A, C, D, DS, JCB, MC, V.

D 🐾 ⚊ 🕴 🏊

★ ★ **HOLIDAY INN.** *3400 Fort Meade Rd (20724).* Phone 301/498-0900; toll-free 800/477-7410; fax 301/498-3203. www.holiday-inn.com. 166 rooms, 2 story. S, D $84-$114; each additional $10; under 18 free. Crib free. TV; cable (premium), VCR available. Pool; lifeguard. Restaurant 6:30 am-2 pm, 5-10 pm. Room service from 7 am. Bar 4 pm-midnight. Check-out 11 am. Coin laundry. Meeting rooms. Business services available. In-room modem link. Valet service. Exercise equipment. Health club privileges. Refrigerators, microwaves available. Cr cds: A, C, D, DS, ER, JCB, MC, V.

D ⚊ 🕴 🏊 SC

Leonardtown (E-7)

See also St. Mary's City

Pop 1,896 **Elev** 87 ft **Area code** 301 **Zip** 20650

Information St. Mary's County Division of Tourism, 23115 Leonard Hall Dr, PO Box 653; 301/475-4411 or 800/327-9023

Web www.co.saint-marys.md.us

What to See and Do

Calvert Marine Museum. *14150 Solomons Island Rd. 1 mile SE on MD 5, then 11 miles NE on MD 4, cross bridge and turn right on Solomons Island Rd; follow signs.* Phone 410/326-2042. Museum complex with exhibits relating to the culture and marine environment of Chesapeake Bay and Patuxent River estuary; fossils of marine life; estuarine biology displays, aquariums, touch-tank; maritime history exhibits, includes boat-building gallery. Also here is the restored Drum Point Lighthouse, built in 1883; 1/2 mile S is the JC Lore Oyster House, with exhibits on the area's seafood industry. Gift shop. (Daily; closed Jan 1, Thanksgiving, Dec 25) **$$**

Old Jail Museum. *11 Court House Dr.* Phone 301/475-2467. Local historical exhibits housed in an old jail; also a genealogy library for researchers. A cannon from Leonard Calvert's ship, the *Ark,* is mounted in front. (Tues-Sat; closed holidays; also last week in Dec) **FREE**

Sotterley Plantation. *44300 Sotterley Ln. 9 miles E on MD 245. Phone 301/373-2280.* (circa 1715) Overlooks Patuxent River. Working plantation; house in original condition. Chinese Chippendale staircase, antiques, original pine paneling in three rooms. Farming exhibit. (Grounds open May-Oct, Tues-Sun; individual tours of manor house on weekends; group tours by appointment only) **$$$**

St. Clements Island-Potomac River Museum. *5 miles W via MD 234 to Clements, then 9 miles S on MD 242, in Colton Point. Phone 301/769-2222.* Maryland colonists first landed on the island in 1634. Exhibits trace 12,000 years of local history and pre-history. Museum includes Little Red School House (circa 1821) and country store. Picnic area; fishing and crabbing. (Late Mar-Sept, Mon-Fri, also Sat, Sun afternoons; rest of year, Wed-Sun afternoons; closed holidays)

Special Events

Blessing of the Fleet and Historical Pageant. *St. Clements Island, Potomac River Museum. 38370 Point Breeze Rd. Phone 301/769-2222.* Celebration commemorates first Roman Catholic Mass held on Maryland soil and Governor Leonard Calvert's proclamation of religious freedom. Blessing of oyster and clam fishing fleets. Folk dances, historical exhibits, concerts. Boat rides to the island. First weekend in Oct.

St. Mary's County Fair. *Phone 301/475-2707.* Midway, seafood, horse shows. Late Sept.

St. Mary's County Oyster Festival. *County Fairgrounds. Phone 301/863-5015.* National oyster shucking contest; oyster cook-off, seafood and crafts. Third weekend in Oct.

Oakland (B-1)

Settled 1851 **Pop** 1,930 **Elev** 2,384 ft **Area code** 301 **Zip** 21550

Information Garrett County Chamber of Commerce, 200 S Third St; 301/387-4386

Web www.garrettchamber.com

What to See and Do

Backbone Mountain. *8 miles S on US 219, then W on US 50.* Highest point in the state (3,360 feet).

Deep Creek Lake State Park. *From I-68, 10 miles SE off US 219. General Information and camping reservations Phone 301/387-5563 (reservations accepted up to 1 year in advance).* Approximately 1,800 acres with 3,900-acre man-made lake. Swimming, bathhouse, fishing, boating

(rowboat rentals); nature and hiking trails, picnicking (shelters), playground, concession, improved campsites (fee). **$**

Garrett State Forest. *5 miles NW on County 20. Phone 301/334-2038.* Approximately 6,800 acres. The forest contains much wildlife. Fishing; hunting, hiking and riding trails, winter activities, primitive camping. Forestry demonstration area. Within the forest are

Herrington Manor State Park. *Phone 301/334-9180.* Well-developed 365-acre park with housekeeping cabins, 53-acre lake. Swimming, fishing, boating (launch, rentals); hiking trails, concession, picnicking, cross-country skiing (rentals). Interpretive programs (summer). No pets. Standard fees.

Swallow Falls State Park. *Phone 301/334-9180.* Surrounding 257 acres, the Youghiogheny River tumbles along the park's boundaries, passing through shaded rocky gorges and over sunny rapids. Muddy Creek produces a 52-foot waterfall. Here the last remaining stand of virgin hemlock dwarfs visitors. Fishing; nature trails, hiking, picnicking, improved campsites. Pets at registered campsites only. Standard fees.

Potomac State Forest. *9 miles SE off MD 560, along Potomac River. Phone 301/334-2038.* More than 10,685 acres for hiking, riding, and hunting. Primitive camping. Timber is harvested regularly here and the area is important in the management of watershed and wildlife programs.

Special Events

Autumn Glory Festival. *Phone 301/334-1948.* Celebrates fall foliage. Features arts and crafts, five-string banjo contest, state fiddle contest, western Maryland tournament of bands, parades, antique show. Mid-Oct.

Garrett County Fair. *McHenry Fairgrounds. Phone 301/334-1948.* Early Aug.

McHenry Highland Festival. *Deep Creek Lake in McHenry.* Traditional Scottish and Celtic festival. First Sat in June.

Winterfest. *Deep Creek Lake in McHenry.* Ski races, parade, fireworks. Late Feb or early Mar.

Motels/Motor Lodges

★ **LAKE SIDE MOTOR COURT.** *19956 Garrett Hwy, Oakland (21550). Phone 301/387-5566, ext 2205.* 11 rooms, 1 story. D $68-$75; each additional $4; MAP available. Closed late-Oct-early May. Check-out 11 am, check-in 2 pm. TV; cable. Pool privileges. Cr cds: A, D, DS, MC, V.
D **⛵**

★ **WILL O' THE WISP.** *20160 Garrett Hwy, Oakland (21550). Phone 301/387-5503; fax 301/387-4999. www.*

willothewisp.com. 10 rooms. May-Oct: S, D $62; each additional $4; cottage for 2-6, $468-$900/week; MAP available. Closed rest of year. Crib free. Check-out 11 am. TV. Restaurant adjacent 7 am-2 pm, 5-9:30 pm. Pool privileges. Picnic tables. On lake; private beach, dock. Cr cds: A, DS, MC, V.

⬛ ⬛ ⬛

B&B/Small Inns

★ ★ ★ CARMEL COVE BED AND BREAKFAST.
105 Monastery Way, Swanton (21550). Phone 301/387-0067; fax 301/387-2394. www.carmelcoveinn.com. This bed-and-breakfast was once a monastery and now offers fine accommodations surrounded by beautiful mountains and the clear lake. 10 rooms, 5 with shower only, 2 story, 3 suites. S, D $80-$140; suites $120-$140; ski plans; package plans; weekends, holidays (2-3 day minimum). Children over 12 years only. TV in common room; cable (premium), VCR (movies). Complimentary full breakfast. Check-out 11 am, check-in 4-9 pm. In-room modem link. Luggage handling. Concierge service. Gift shop. Tennis. Cross-country ski 10 miles. Game room. Recreation room. In-room whirlpool, fireplace in suites. Some balconies. Picnic tables, grills. On lake. Built in 1945. Totally nonsmoking. Cr cds: DS, MC, V.

⬛ ⬛ ⬛ ⬛

★ ★ ★ HALEY FARM BED AND BREAKFAST.
16766 Garrett Hwy, Oakland (21550). Phone 301/387-9050; toll-free 888/231-3276. www.haleyfarm.com. 10 rooms, 3 kitchen units, 2 story. Room phone in 4 suites only. D $140-$150; each additional $25; kitchen units $175-$215; golf rates; package plans; weekends, holidays (2-3 day minimum). Children over 12 years only. Complimentary full breakfast. Check-out noon, check-in 3 pm. TV in suites; cable (premium), VCR (movies). Fireplaces. Sauna. Downhill ski 5 miles, cross-country ski on site. Bicycles. Concierge service. Built in 1923; formerly a working farm; near Deep Creek Lake, Swallow Falls, and five state parks. Totally nonsmoking. Cr cds: A, DS, MC, V.

⬛ ⬛ ⬛ ⬛ ⬛

Restaurant

★ ★ POINT VIEW INN.
609 Deep Creek Dr, McHenry (21541). Phone 301/387-5555. www.pointviewinn.com. African, American, seafood menu. Hours: 8 am-10 pm; Sun to 9 pm. Closed Easter, Dec 25. Dinner $10.25-$29. Bar 11-2 am. Entertainment weekends. Children's menu. Casual attire. Patio seating. Cr cds: A, DS, MC, V.

⬛

Ocean City (E-10)

Founded 1869 **Pop** 7,173 **Elev** 7 ft **Area code** 410 **Zip** 21842

Information Chamber of Commerce, 12320 Ocean Gateway; 410/213-0552

Web www.oceancity.org

Deep-sea fishing is highly regarded in Maryland's only Atlantic Ocean resort. The white sand beach, 3-mile boardwalk, amusements, golf courses, and boating draw thousands of visitors every summer.

What to See and Do

⭐ **Assateague Island National Seashore.** *7206 National Seashore Lane (21811).* There are two entrances to Assateague Island National Seashore. Assateague's north entrance is at the end of Route 611, 8 miles south of Ocean City, MD. The south entrance is at the end of Rte 175, 2 miles from Chincoteague, VA. There is no vehicle access between the two entrances on Assateague Island. Vehicles must return to the mainland to access the north or south entrance. For further information, phone 410/641-1441. For camping reservations, phone 800/365-2267. Visitors interested in sandy beaches and wildlife should visit Assateague Island, which is about a four-hour drive from Baltimore. Straddling Maryland and Virginia, it contains a state park and a wildlife refuge. Visitors have their choice of activities: swimming, hiking, canoeing, sea kayaking, biking, camping on the beach, and some of the best surf-fishing on the Atlantic Coast. In addition to the seashore's beauty, guests also come to see the wild horses. According to legend, the horses, which are only the size of ponies, swam to the island from a shipwrecked Spanish galleon. On every last Wednesday and Thursday in July, the world-famous "Pony Penning" event occurs. During this event, the horses swim from the Maryland side of the island to the Virginia side with a crowd of spectators cheering them on. The visitor center offers more information about the horses as well as the seashore's many activities. (Daily; closed Thanksgiving, Dec 25) **$$** Also on the island is

Assateague State Park. *7307 Stephen Decatur Hwy.* Phone 410/641-2120. Has 755 acres with 2 miles of ocean frontage and gentle, sloping beaches. Swimming, fishing, boat launch; picnicking, concession (summer), bicycle and hiking trails, camping (Apr-Oct). Standard fees (summer). **$**

Special Events

Fishing contests and tournaments. *Phone 410/213-0552.* Many held throughout the year. For exact dates contact the Chamber of Commerce.

Harness racing. *10218 Racetrack Rd. Ocean Downs. 4 miles W on US 50. Phone 410/641-0600.* Nightly Tues-Sun. Children with adult only. Late July-Labor Day.

Motels/Motor Lodges

★ **BEST WESTERN FLAGSHIP OCEANFRONT.** *2600 Baltimore Ave (21842). Phone 410/289-3384; toll-free 800/528-1234; fax 410/289-1743. www.bestwestern.com.* 93 rooms, 3 story. Late June-late Aug (3-day minimum weekends): S, D $179-$189; under 13 free; lower rates rest of year. Closed 2 weeks in Dec and weekdays Dec 26-Feb 14. Check-out 11 am. TV; cable (premium), VCR (movies). Laundry services. Exercise equipment, sauna. Game room. Two pools, one indoor; children's pool, whirlpool, poolside service. Lighted tennis. Cr cds: A, C, D, DS, MC, V.

[D] [🏋] [≈] [🎾] [🏊] [SC]

★ ★ **CASTLE IN THE SAND HOTEL.** *3701 Atlantic Ave (21842). Phone 410/289-6846; toll-free 800/552-7263; fax 410/289-9446. www.castleinthesand.com.* 36 rooms, 5 story, 27 cottages, 108 kitchen units. Early July-late Aug: S, D $165-$182; each additional $8; kitchen units $165-$205; cottages $750-$1,295/week; under 12 free; lower rates mid-Apr-early July and late Aug-late Oct. Closed rest of year. Crib $5. TV; cable (premium). Pool; lifeguard. Supervised children's activities (June-Aug); ages 3-12. Restaurant 7:30 am-midnight. Bar 11-2 am; entertainment weekends. Check-out 11 am. Meeting room. Business services available. In-room modem link. Bellstaff. Free airport transportation. Game room. Refrigerators. Some balconies. Cr cds: A, D, DS, MC, V.

[D] [🛎] [≈] [🏊]

★ **CAYMAN SUITES.** *12500 Coastal Hwy (21842). Phone 410/250-7600; toll-free 800/546-0042; fax 410/250-7603. www.caymansuites.com.* 57 suites. July-Aug: suites $179-$209; each additional $10; under 16 free; weekly, mid-week rates; lower rates rest of year. Closed Jan, Feb. Crib $6. TV; cable (premium). Indoor pool. Check-out 11 am. Meeting rooms. Business services available. Bellstaff (in season). Exercise equipment. Microwaves. Balconies. Near beach. Cr cds: A, DS, MC, V.

[D] [≈] [🎾] [🏊] [SC]

★ **COMFORT INN BOARDWALK.** *507 Atlantic Ave (21842). Phone 410/289-5155; toll-free 800/228-5150; fax 410/289-6547. www.comfortinnboardwalk.com.* 84 kitchen units in 2 buildings, 5 story. June-Aug: S, D $164-$209; each additional $10; under 12 free; lower rates Mar-May, Sept-Nov. Closed rest of year. Crib free. TV; cable (pre-mium). Two pools, one indoor. Complimentary continental breakfast. Check-out 11 am. Bellstaff. Balconies. On ocean. Cr cds: A, C, D, DS, ER, JCB, MC, V.

[D] [≈] [🏊] [SC]

★ **EXECUTIVE MOTEL.** *30th St and Baltimore Ave (21843). Phone 410/289-3101; toll-free 800/638-1600. www.executivemotel.com.* 47 rooms, 3 story. No elevator. Memorial Day weekend, July-Labor Day (3-day minimum weekends): S, D $78-$88; each additional $6; under 6 free; lower rates late May-June, after Labor Day-mid-Sept. Closed rest of year. Crib $6. TV; cable. Check-out 11 am. Refrigerators. Cr cds: MC, V.

[D]

★ ★ **GATEWAY RESORT HOTEL.** *4800 Coastal Hwy (21842). Phone 410/524-6500; toll-free 800/382-2582; fax 410/524-5374. www.gatewayoc.com.* 59 kitchen units, 3 story. July-mid-Aug: S, D $195-$230; each additional $10; suites $1,195-$1,285/week; under 6 free; higher rates holiday weekends; lower rates rest of year. Check-out 11 am. TV; cable (premium). Laundry services. Restaurant 11-2 am. Bar; entertainment. Room service. Health club privileges. Pool, children's pool, whirlpool, lifeguard (summer). Lawn games. Cr cds: A, C, D, DS, MC, V.

[≈] [🏊]

★ ★ **HOLIDAY INN.** *6600 Coastal Hwy (21842). Phone 410/524-1600; toll-free 800/638-2106; fax 410/524-1135. www.holiday-inn.com.* 216 kitchen units, 8 story. Memorial Day-Labor Day: S, D $160-$250; each additional $9; under 19 free; higher rates holiday weekends; golf plans; lower rates rest of year. Crib free. TV; cable (premium). Two pools, one indoor; wading pools, whirlpool, poolside service. Supervised children's activities (June-Aug); ages 5-9. Restaurant 7-11:30 am, 5-11 pm. Room service. Bar 5-midnight. Check-out 11 am. Free laundry facilities. Meeting rooms. Business services available. In-room modem link. Bellstaff. Tennis. Exercise equipment; sauna. Game room. Balconies. Picnic tables. On ocean. Cr cds: A, D, DS, JCB, MC, V.

[D] [🏋] [≈] [🎾] [🏊]

★ ★ **HOWARD JOHNSON OCEANFRONT.** *2401 Baltimore Ave (21842). Phone 410/289-9101; fax 410/289-1722. www.hojo.com.* 72 units, 26 kitchen units, 4 story. Late June-Aug: S, D $135-$175; each additional $10; kitchen units $165-$185; under 18 free; lower rates Mar-June, Sept-Oct. Closed rest of year. Check-out 11 am. TV; cable (premium). Restaurant 7 am-6 pm. Pool; whirlpool. Cr cds: A, DS, MC, V.

[D] [🛎] [≈] [🏊]

★ **NASSAU MOTEL.** *6002 Coastal Hwy (21842). Phone 410/524-6451.* 62 rooms, 3 story. No elevator. July-late Aug: S, D $102-$120; each additional $6; higher rates weekends; lower rates Apr-June, late Aug-Oct. Closed rest of year. Crib $5. TV; cable (premium). Pool. Restaurant opposite. Check-out 11 am. Refrigerators, microwaves. Grills. Sun deck. On ocean, beach. Cr cds: A, DS, MC, V.

⊡ 🏖 🏊

★ ★ **PHILLIPS BEACH PLAZA HOTEL.** *1301 N Atlantic Ave (21842). Phone 410/289-9121; toll-free 800/ 492-5834; fax 410/289-3041. www.phillipsbeachplaza.com.* 96 units, 5 story. July-late Aug: S, D $119-$174; each additional $20; kitchen units $154-$194; kitchen suites $200-$230; $20 surcharge weekends; package plans; lower rates rest of year. Crib $10. TV; cable. Restaurant 8 am-1 pm, 5-9:30 pm. Bar 5 pm-2 am; entertainment 6-11 pm. Check-out 11 am. Business services available. Bellstaff. Shopping arcade. On ocean. Cr cds: A, C, D, DS, MC, V.

★ ★ **QUALITY INN.** *3301 Atlantic Ave (21843). Phone 410/289-1234; toll-free 800/228-5151. www.qualityinn.com.* 109 units, 5 story. June-Aug: S, D $158-$235; suites $250-$330; lower rates rest of year. Crib $5. TV; cable, VCR (movies). 2 pools, 1 indoor; wading pool, whirlpool. Restaurant. Check-out 11 am. Sundries. Coin laundry. Business services available. Gift shop. Exercise equipment; sauna. Game room. Some in-room whirlpools. Balconies. Cr cds: A, C, D, DS, MC, V.

⊡ 🏖 🏋 🏊 SC

★ ★ **QUALITY INN OCEANFRONT.** *5400 Coastal Hwy (21842). Phone 410/524-7200; toll-free 800/837-3586; fax 410/723-0018. www.qualityinn.com.* 126 kitchen units, 3-5 story. Memorial Day-Labor Day: S, D $79-$239; each additional $7; under 6 free; weekly rates; package plans; higher rates holidays; lower rates rest of year. Crib free. TV; cable (premium), VCR (movies). Two pools, one indoor; wading pool, whirlpool. Playground. Restaurant 8 am-9 pm. Bar 11 am-11 pm. Check-out 11 am. Free laundry facilities. Business services available. In-room modem link. Bellstaff (summer). Tennis. Exercise equipment; saunas. Game room. Lawn games. Private patios, balconies. Picnic tables, grills. On ocean, swimming beach. Tropical atrium. Cr cds: A, C, D, DS, JCB, MC, V.

⊡ 🏂 🏖 🏋 🏊

★ **RAMADA LIMITED OCEANFRONT.** *Oceanfront and 32nd St (21842). Phone 410/289-6444; toll-free 800/ 837-3589; fax 410/289-0108. www.ramada.com.* 76 kitchen units, 3 story. No elevator. July-Aug: S, D $174-$189; each additional $7; surcharge off-season weekends; lower rates rest of year. Complimentary continental breakfast. Check-out 11 am. TV; cable (premium), VCR (movies). Guest laundry. Pool. Cr cds: A, C, D, DS, ER, JCB, MC, V.

⊡ 🏖 🏊

★ **SAFARI MOTEL.** *1-13th St (21842). Phone 410/289-6411; toll-free 800/787-2183.* 46 rooms in 2 buildings, 3

and 4 story. July-Aug: S, D $119; under 14 free; lower rates mid-Apr-June, Sept-Oct. Closed rest of year. Crib free. Pet accepted, some restrictions; $9/day. TV; cable (premium). Restaurant opposite from 8 am. Check-out 11 am. Bellstaff. Balconies. On ocean. Cr cds: A, C, D, DS, MC, V.

🐾

★ ★ **SAHARA MOTEL.** *19th St and Boardwalk (21842). Phone 410/289-8101; toll-free 800/638-1600; fax 410/289-2894. www.saharamotel.com.* 161 rooms, 5 kitchen units, 3 and 4 story. Late June-mid-Sept: S, D $78-$140; each additional $6; kitchen units $102-$138; lower rates late Apr-late June, late Sept. Closed rest of year. Check-out 11 am. TV. Restaurant 6 am-3 pm. Two pools. Elevator in Tower building. Cr cds: MC, V.

⊡ 🏖

★ **TIDES.** *71st St (21843). Phone 410/524-7100; toll-free 800/638-1600; fax 410/289-3039. www.bestmotels.com.* 54 kitchen units, 3 story. No elevator. Late June-late Aug: S, D $99; each additional $6; under 6 free; higher rates: weekends and holidays (3-day minimum), July-Aug weekdays (2-day minimum), Memorial Day and Labor Day; lower rates May-late June and Sept. Closed rest of year. Crib $5. TV; cable. Pool. Check-out 11 am. Bellstaff (in season). Some balconies. Cr cds: MC, V.

⊡ 🛥 🏖 🏊

Hotels

★ ★ **CLARION RESORT FOUNTAINE BLEAU.** *10100 Coastal Hwy (21842). Phone 410/524-3535; fax 410/524-3834. www.clarioninn.com.* Visitors can enjoy the sunrise and sunset from their well-appointed rooms. The hotel offers a wide range of shops, restaurants, lounges and services, as well as recreational facilities such as a health spa. 250 rooms, 16 story. June-Aug: S, D $230-$300; each additional $15; suites, kitchen units $350; studio rooms $320; condos $1,600-$2,700/weekly; under 17 free; higher rates holiday weekends (3-day minimum); lower rates rest of year. Crib $15. Pet accepted; $20/day. Check-out 11 am. TV; cable (premium), VCR available. In-room modem link. Balconies. Refrigerators. Restaurant 7 am-11 pm. Bar to 2 am; entertainment. Exercise equipment, sauna, steam room. Game room. Heated pool, whirlpool, poolside service in season, lifeguard. Beauty shop. Airport transportation. Meeting rooms. Business center. On ocean, beach. Cr cds: A, C, D, DS, JCB, MC, V.

⊡ 🐾 🛥 🏖 🏋 🏊 🏃

★ ★ ★ **COCONUT MALORIE HOTEL RESORT.** *200 59th St (21842). Phone 410/723-6100; toll-free 800/ 767-6060; fax 410/524-9327. www.coconutmalorie.com.* This resort is found in the wetlands overlooking the Isle of Wight Bay. Guests enter to find a marble lobby with a waterfall before checking into one of the well-appointed guest suites. 85 units, 5 story, 52 suites. Memorial Day-Labor Day: S, D $164-$290; each additional $15; weekly rates; lower rates rest of year. Crib $15. TV; cable (premium), VCR available. Pool; poolside service. Complimentary coffee in rooms. Restaurant adjacent 11 am-11 pm. Check-out noon. Meeting rooms. Business services available. In-room modem link. Concierge. Health club privileges. Refrigerators; many bathroom phones. Balconies. Original Haitian art; antique collection. Footbridge over marsh to dining facilities. Cr cds: A, C, D, MC, V.

★ ★ ★ **THE LIGHTHOUSE CLUB HOTEL.** *56th St in the Bay (21842). Phone 410/524-5400; toll-free 888/371-5400; fax 410/524-3928. www.fagers.com.* Located directly on the Isle of Wight Bay at Fager's Island, this three-story octagonal hotel affords spectacular views of waterfowl in flight and sunsets over the natural wetlands. The elegant, beachy accommodations are decorated with lush greenery, taupe and cream-colored fabrics, blond wood, and marble baths, and all one-bedroom suites include continental breakfast. 23 rooms, 3 story. No elevator. Mid-June-Labor Day (2-day minimum): S, D $184-$285; each additional $15; weekly rates; lower rates rest of year. Crib $15. Complimentary continental breakfast. Check-out noon. TV; cable (premium), VCR available. In-room modem link. Balconies, refrigerators; some fireplaces. In-room whirlpools, bathroom phones. Complimentary coffee in rooms. Restaurant adjacent 11 am-11 pm. Bar 11-2 am, entertainment. Health club privileges. Pool privileges. Meeting room. Business services available. Cr cds: A, C, D, DS, MC, V.

★ ★ ★ **PRINCESS ROYALE OCEANFRONT HOTEL.** *9100 Coastal Hwy (21842). Phone 410/524-7777; toll-free 800/476-9253; fax 410/524-7787. www.princessroyale.com.* This hotel is located on the white sandy beaches of Ocean City. It offers two-room suites and two or three-room condominiums. An Olympic-sized pool is found in a glass atrium overlooking the ocean. Golfers will enjoy the 11 nearby courses. 310 kitchen suites, 5 story. Mid-June-Labor Day: D $109-$299; under 12 free; weekly rates; golf plans; lower rates rest of year. Crib $10. Complimentary coffee in rooms. Check-out 11 am. TV; cable. Balconies. Some in-room whirlpools. Coin laundry. Restaurant 7-2 am. Bar 11-2 am; entertainment. Health club privileges. Exercise equipment, sauna. Game room. On ocean; swimming beach, ocean deck, private boardwalk. Indoor pool, whirlpool, poolside service. 18-hole golf privileges, pro, putting green, driving range.

Lighted tennis. Beauty shop. Business center. Convention facilities. Gift shop. Most suites with ocean view. Cr cds: A, C, D, DS, MC, V.

B&B/Small Inns

★ ★ ★ **BERLIN ATLANTIC.** *2 N Main St, Berlin (21811). Phone 410/641-0189; toll-free 800/814-7672; fax 410/641-4928. www.atlantichotel.com.* Centrally located in Berlin's historic district, this elegant inn is perfect for a relaxing stay and quiet getaway. Guests can relax in rooms fashioned in Victorian antique décor and designed with the guests' comforts in mind. 17 rooms, 3 story. Complimentary full breakfast. Check-out 11 am, check-in 3 pm. TV. Dining room 6-9 pm; Fri, Sat to 10 pm. Bar noon-1 am. Greens fee $30-$35. Restored Victorian hotel (1895). Porch on each floor. 2nd-floor parlor. Cr cds: A, DS, MC, V. **$**

★ ★ **MERRY SHERWOOD PLANTATION.** *8909 Worcester Hwy, Berlin (21811). Phone 410/641-2112; toll-free 800/660-0358; fax 410/641-9528. www.merrysherwood .com.* 8 rooms, 6 with bath. No room phones. Mid-May-mid-Oct: S, D $150-$175; lower rates rest of year. Children over 8 years only. Complimentary full breakfast; afternoon refreshments. Check-out 11 am, check-in 2 pm. Some fireplaces. Built in 1859; on grounds of former plantation; large variety of trees and shrubs. Totally nonsmoking. Cr cds: MC, V.

Restaurants

★ ★ **BONFIRE.** *71st St (21842). Phone 410/524-7171; fax 410/524-4228.* Hours: 5-10 pm; from 4 pm in season; early-bird dinner 4-5 pm. Closed Mon-Thurs in winter. Reservations accepted. Bar to 2 am. Dinner $14.95-$26.95. Seafood buffet $21.95. Children's menu. Specializes in steak, prime rib, seafood. Cr cds: A, C, D, MC, V.

★ ★ **EMBERS.** *2305 Philadelphia Ave (21842). Phone 410/289-3322; fax 410/289-0609. www.embers.com.* Hours: 2-10 pm; also 8 am-noon Memorial Day weekend-Labor Day. Closed Dec-Feb. Reservations accepted. Bar to 2 am. Buffet: breakfast $7.99. Dinner $14-$25. Seafood buffet $22.95. Children's menu. Specializes in fresh seafood, steak, prime rib. Family-owned. Cr cds: A, C, DS, MC, V.

★ ★ ★ **FAGER'S ISLAND.** *201 60th St (21842). Phone 410/524-5500; fax 410/723-2055. www.fagers.com.* The outdoor deck overlooking the bay is the perfect spot to take in a glorious summer sunset. The menu does well with standard and creative seafood preparations, but other classics, like prime rib, are also good. Choose a wine from a list that features over 500 bottles to accompany your meal. Pacific-Rim/Pan-Asian, seafood menu. Lunch, dinner, brunch. Bar. Entertainment. Cr cds: A, D, DS, MC, V. **$$**

D

★ ★ **HANNA'S MARINA DECK.** *306 Dorchester St (21842). Phone 410/289-4411; fax 410/289-6449. www. marinadeckrestaurant.com.* Seafood menu. Closed mid-Oct-Easter. Breakfast, lunch, dinner. Bar. Children's menu. Cr cds: A, DS, V. **$$**

D

★ ★ ★ **HARRISON'S HARBOR WATCH.** *806 S Boardwalk (21842). Phone 410/289-5121.* Breathtaking ocean views, a bountiful raw bar, and fresh seafood keep this enormous restaurant packed on summer weekends. Hours: 5-10 pm; July-Aug from 11:30 am. Closed Mon-Thurs Dec-Mar. Reservations accepted. Bar. Wine list. Dinner $8.95-$24.95. Children's menu. Specializes in fresh seafood, fish. Raw bar. Own breads. View of inlet overlooking Assateague Island. Cr cds: A, D, DS, MC, V.

D

★ ★ ★ **HOBBIT.** *81st St and Bay (21842). Phone 410/524-8100; fax 410/524-5290.* This restaurant serves many of your old favorites, as well as creative new items from time to time. After dinner, browse through the unique gift shop for your Hobbit memorabilia. American, seafood menu. Closed Dec 24-25. Lunch, dinner. Bar. Children's menu. Cr cds: A, DS, MC, V. **$$**

D

★ ★ **OCEAN CLUB.** *49th St (21842). Phone 410/524-7500; fax 410/524-5086.* Specializes in seafood. Closed Dec 25; Mon, Tues off-season; mid Jan-Feb. Breakfast, lunch, dinner. Bar. Entertainment. Children's menu. Cr cds: A, MC, V. **$$**

D

★ ★ **PHILLIPS CRAB HOUSE.** *2004 Philadelphia Ave (21842). Phone 410/289-6821; fax 410/289-2053. www. phillipsoc.com.* Seafood menu. Closed Nov-Mar. Lunch, dinner. Bar. Children's menu. Cr cds: A, D, DS, MC, V. **$$**

D

★ ★ **PHILLIPS SEAFOOD HOUSE.** *14101 Coastal Hwy (21842). Phone 410/250-1200. www.phillipsseafood house.com.* Seafood menu. Closed late-Nov-late-Feb.

Lunch, dinner. Bar. Children's menu. Cr cds: A, D, DS, MC, V. **$$**

D

Pikesville

See also Baltimore

Pop 29,123 **Area code** 410 **Zip** 21208

Motels/Motor Lodges

★ **COMFORT INN.** *10 Wooded Way (21208). Phone 410/484-7700; toll-free 800/732-2458; fax 410/653-1516. www.comfortinn.com.* 103 rooms, 2-3 story. No elevator. S, D $59-$89; under 18 free; weekly, monthly rates. Crib free. Pet accepted. TV; cable (premium). Pool; wading pool, lifeguard. Complimentary continental breakfast. Coffee in rooms. Restaurant adjacent 6:30 am-11:30 pm. Check-out 11 am. Coin laundry. Meeting rooms. Business services available. In-room modem link. Valet service Mon-Fri. Health club privileges. Microwaves available. Cr cds: A, C, D, DS, ER, JCB, MC, V.

D ⚡ ⌦ ⋈ SC

★ ★ **RAMADA INN–BALTIMORE WEST.** *1721 Reisterstown Rd (21208). Phone 410/486-5600; toll-free 800/272-7232; fax 410/484-9377. www.ramada.com.* 108 rooms, 2 story. S, D $69; under 18 free; higher rates Preakness. Pet accepted. Check-out noon. TV; cable (premium). Restaurant 6 am-1 pm, 5-10 pm; Sat, Sun from 7 am. Bar 5 pm-midnight. Room service. Health club privileges. Pool, poolside service. Cr cds: A, C, D, DS, ER, JCB, MC, V.

D ⚡ ⌦ ⋈ SC

Hotel

★ ★ ★ **HILTON PIKESVILLE.** *1726 Reisterstown Rd (21208). Phone 410/653-1100; toll-free 800/445-8667; fax 410/415-6232. www.hilton.com.* This property is located 8 miles from the Baltimore/Washington International Airport, and is a short drive from local attractions like the Inner Harbor. Six indoor tennis courts, and a restaurant and lounge are on site. 171 rooms, 5 story. S $99-$154; D $102-$164; each additional $15; suites $300-$399; weekend plans; family rates. Crib $10. TV; cable (premium), VCR available (movies). Pool; lifeguard. Coffee in rooms. Restaurant 7 am-11 pm. Room service. Bar 11-1 am. Check-out noon. Meeting rooms. Business services available. Bellstaff. Valet service. Gift shop. Barber, beauty shop. Airport transportation. Exercise equipment. Bathroom phones; microwaves available. Cr cds: A, C, D, DS, ER, MC, V.

D ⌦ ⚡ ⋈ SC ⚡

B&B/Small Inn

★ ★ ★ **GRAMERCY BED AND BREAKFAST.** *1400 Greenspring Valley, Stevenson (21153). Phone 410/486-2405; toll-free 800/553-3404; fax 410/486-1765. www.gramercymansion.com.* This property provides elegant accomodations, and is minutes away from downtown Baltimore's shopping, museums, and fine restaurants. 10 rooms, 3 story. Complimentary full breakfast. Check-out noon, check-in 3 pm. TV; VCR (movies). In-room modem link. Pool. Tennis. Lawn games. Tudor-style mansion (1902) on 45-acre wooded estate. Totally nonsmoking. Cr cds: A, DS, MC, V. **$**

Pocomoke City (F-9)

See also Crisfield

Founded 1670 **Pop** 4,098 **Elev** 22 ft **Area code** 410 and 443 **Zip** 21851

Information Pocomoke Chamber of Commerce, 144 Market St; 410/957-1919

Web www.pocomoke.com

Motel/Motor Lodge

★ ★ **QUALITY INN.** *825 Ocean Hwy (21851). Phone 410/957-1300; fax 410/957-9329. www.qualityinn.com.* 64 rooms. Memorial Day-Labor Day: S $60-$75; D $65-$82; each additional $5; under 18 free; higher rates Pony Penning. Crib free. Pet accepted. TV; cable (premium). Pool; wading pool. Complimentary continental breakfast. Check-out 11 am. Business services available. In-room modem link. Some in-room whirlpools, refrigerators. Picnic tables, grills. Cr cds: A, C, D, DS, ER, JCB, MC, V.

B&B/Small Inns

★ ★ **RIVER HOUSE INN.** *201 E Market St, Snow Hill (21863). Phone 410/632-2722; fax 410/632-2866. www.riverhouseinn.com.* 8 rooms, 2 with shower only, 3 story, 1 suite, 1 guest house. No elevators, room phones. Apr-Oct: S, D $100-$175; each additional $20; suite $100; guest house $160; under 16 free; golf rates; package plans; weekends (2-day minimum); lower rates rest of year. Pet accepted, some restrictions. Some refrigerators, microwaves. Fireplaces. In-room whirlpool in suite. Lawn games. Built in 1860. On river. Totally nonsmoking. Cr cds: A, DS, MC, V.

Restaurant

★ **UPPER DECK.** *1245 Ocean Hwy (21851). Phone 410/957-3166.* Hours: 11 am-10 pm; Sun noon-9 pm. Reservations accepted. Bar to 11 am; Sun to 10 pm. Lunch $4.95-$5.95, dinner $7.50-$20. Children's menu. Specializes in local seafood, steak. Own desserts. Antiques. Cr cds: MC, V.

Rockville (C-6)

See also Gaithersburg

Pop 47,388 **Elev** 451 ft **Area code** 240 and 301

Information Chamber of Commerce, 250 Hungerford Dr, Suite L10, 20850; 301/424-9300

Web www.rockvillechamber.org

The second-largest city in the state of Maryland, Rockville is the seat of Montgomery County, located at the north edge of the District of Columbia. The Great Falls of the Potomac are 9 miles south off MD 189. This series of small falls was pretty but unnavigable, so the Chesapeake and Ohio Canal (see CHESAPEAKE AND OHIO CANAL NATIONAL HISTORICAL PARK) was built from Washington, D.C., to Cumberland to simplify travel. Stone locks and levels are still visible. The graves of F. Scott and Zelda Fitzgerald are in St. Mary's Cemetery.

What to See and Do

Beall-Dawson House. *103 W Montgomery Ave. Phone 301/762-1492.* (1815) Federal architecture; period furnishings; library; museum shop; 19th-century doctor's office. Tours guided by docents. (Tues-Sat; also first Sun of month; closed holidays) **$**

Special Event

Hometown Holidays. *Phone 301/424-9300.* Family entertainment. Memorial Day weekend.

Motels/Motor Lodges

★ ★ **COURTYARD BY MARRIOTT.** *2500 Research Blvd (20850). Phone 301/670-6700; fax 301/670-9023. www.courtyard.com.* 147 rooms, 2 story, 13 suites. S, D $120-$135; suites $135-$145; under 12 free; weekly rates. Crib free. TV; cable (premium). Indoor pool; whirlpool, lifeguard. Complimentary coffee. Restaurant 6:30 am-2 pm, 5-10 pm; Sat 7-11 am; Sun 7 am-2 pm. Room service 5-10 pm. Bar 5-11 pm. Check-out 1 pm. Coin laundry. Meeting rooms. Business services available. In-room modem link. Valet service. Sundries. Exercise equipment. Balconies. Refrigerators available. Cr cds: A, C, D, DS, MC, V.

★ ★ **QUALITY INN & SUITES.** *3 Research Ct (20850).* *Phone 301/840-0200; toll-free 800/228-5151; fax 301/258-0160. www.qualityinn.com.* 124 rooms, 3 story, 66 kitchen suites. S, D $99.95-$129.95; each additional $10; kitchen suites $109.95-$139.95; under 18 free; weekend rates. Crib free. TV; cable (premium), VCR available. Complimentary full breakfast. Check-out noon. Meeting rooms. Business center. Valet service. Sundries. Gift shop. Coin laundry. Exercise equipment. Pool; lifeguard. Refrigerators, microwaves, wet bars. Cr cds: A, C, D, DS, JCB, MC, V.

Hotel

★ ★ **DOUBLETREE HOTEL.** *1750 Rockville Pike (20852). Phone 301/468-1100; fax 301/468-0308. www.doubletree.com.* This hotel is only minutes from many attractions of the nation's capital, including great shopping at the White Flint Mall. 315 rooms, 8 story. S, D $159-$169; each additional $10; suites $195-$325; under 19 free; weekly, weekend rates. Crib free. TV; cable (premium). Indoor/outdoor pool; whirlpool, lifeguard. Coffee in rooms. Restaurant 6 am-11 pm. Bar from 11 am; Fri, Sat to 1 am. Check-out noon. Convention facilities. Business center. In-room modem link. Gift shop. Beauty shop. Covered valet parking. Exercise equipment: sauna. Game room. Refrigerators, microwaves available. 8-story atrium; 20-foot waterfall. Gazebo. Luxury level. Cr cds: A, C, D, DS, ER, JCB, MC, V.

All-Suite

★ ★ ★ **WOODFIN SUITES.** *1380 Piccard Dr (20850). Phone 301/590-9880; toll-free 800/237-8811; fax 301/590-9614. www.woodfinsuiteshotel.com.* This property was created with business travelers in mind, but is also well-suited for families and leisure travelers. It offers suites with a separate living room, a fully equipped kitchen, two phones, two TVs and a VCR. 203 suites, 3 story. S, D $165-$230; each additional $15; 2-bedroom suites $275; under 12 free. Crib free. Pet accepted, some restrictions. TV; cable (premium). Pool; whirlpool, lifeguard. Complimentary full breakfast. Restaurant 6-9 am, weekends 7-10 am. Bar 5-10 pm Mon-Thurs. Check-out noon. Meeting rooms. Business center. In-room modem link. Valet service. Sundries. Exercise equipment. Refrigerators, microwaves. Cr cds: A, C, D, DS, ER, JCB, MC, V.

Restaurants

★ **A AND J.** *1319-C Rockville Pike (20852). Phone 301/251-7878.* Chinese menu. Lunch, dinner. Casual attire. Totally nonsmoking. $

★ ★ **ADDIE'S.** *11120 Rockville Pike (20852). Phone 301/881-0081; fax 301/881-0082.* Regional American menu. Eclectic décor; collection of whimsical clocks; wood-burning grill. Closed Sun; Jan 1, Thanksgiving, Dec 25. Lunch, dinner, brunch. Bar. Children's menu. Outdoor seating. Cr cds: A, D, DS, MC, V. $$

★ ★ **ANDALUCIA.** *12300 Wilkens Ave (20852). Phone 301/770-1880. www.tasteandalucia.com.* Mediterranean décor; many plants. Specialties: paella Valenciana, zarzuela costa del sol, fresh seafood. Spanish menu. Closed Mon; Jan 1. Lunch, dinner. Bar. Entertainment. Reservations accepted; required Fri, Sat dinner. Totally nonsmoking. Cr cds: A, D, DS, MC, V. $$

★ ★ **BOMBAY BISTRO.** *98 W Montgomery Ave (20850). Phone 301/762-8798; fax 301/762-8799. www.bombaybistro.com.* Indian, vegetarian menu. Closed Thanksgiving, Labor Day. Lunch, dinner. Casual décor. Cr cds: A, DS, MC, V. $$

★ ★ **COPELAND'S OF NEW ORLEANS.** *1584 Rockville Pike (20852). Phone 301/230-0968; fax 301/230-0949. www.alcopeland.com.* Cajun/Creole, seafood menu. Closed Dec 25. Lunch, dinner. Bar. Children's menu. Cr cds: A, D, DS, MC, V. $

★ **HARD TIMES CAFE.** *1117 Nelson St (20850). Phone 301/294-9720; fax 301/424-7116. www.hardtimes.com.* Hours: 11:30 am-10 pm; Fri, Sat to 11 pm; Sun noon-9 pm. Closed Thanksgiving, Dec 25. Lunch, dinner $4.50-$6. Bar. Children's menu. Cr cds: A, MC, V.

★ ★ **IL PIZZICO.** *15209 Frederick Rd (20850). Phone 301/309-0610; fax 301/340-1227.* Italian, seafood menu. Italian décor. Closed Sun; most major holidays. Lunch, dinner. Bar. Cr cds: A, MC, V. $

★ ★ ★ **NORMANDIE FARM.** *10710 Falls Rd, Potomac (20854). Phone 301/983-8838. www.popovers.com.* The relaxed feeling of being in a country home is part of what makes Normandie Farm a favorite among locals. The continental fare is appetizing, and there is no lack of attention to detail. French, seafood menu. French Provincial décor. Closed Mon. Lunch, dinner, brunch. Bar. Entertainment. Cr cds: A, DS, MC, V. $$

★ ★ ★ **OLD ANGLER'S INN.** *10801 MacArthur Blvd, Potomac (20854). Phone 301/299-9097; fax 301/983-0630.*

www.oldanglersinn.com. In a Tudor-style house that was built in 1860, the rustic dining room is a perfect spot for a cozy evening. In winter, get a table near the fireplace, but in summer the terrace provides a lovely setting. Seafood menu. Closed Mon. Lunch, dinner. Bar. Patio seating overlooking wooded area. Cr cds: A, MC, V. **$$**

★ **RED HOT & BLUE.** *16811 Crabbs Branch Way (20855). Phone 301/948-7333; fax 301/926-7090. www.redhotandblue.com.* Hours: 11 am-10 pm; Fri to 11 pm; Sat noon-11 pm; Sun from noon. Closed Thanksgiving, Dec 25. Bar. Lunch, dinner $5.99-$13.99. Children's menu. Specializes in Memphis pit barbecue, ribs. Outdoor seating. Casual décor; blues memorabilia. Totally nonsmoking. Cr cds: A, D, MC, V.

D ⊠

★ **RICCIUTI'S.** *3308 Olney-Sandy Spring Rd, Olney (20832). Phone 301/570-3388; fax 301/570-5351. www.ricciutis.com.* Italian menu. Closed major holidays. Lunch, dinner. Children's menu. Outdoor seating. Italian décor. Totally nonsmoking. Cr cds: A, DS, MC, V. **$**

D ⊠

★ **SEVEN SEAS.** *1776 E Jefferson St (20852). Phone 301/770-5020; fax 301/770-5083.* Hours: 11:30-1 am. Closed Thanksgiving. Reservations accepted. Chinese, Japanese menu. Bar. Lunch $3.95-$6.50, dinner $7.25-$16.95. Specializes in Szechwan, Taiwan, Shanghai cuisine. Sushi bar. Chinese artwork. Cr cds: A, D, DS, MC, V.

D

★ **SILVER DINER.** *11806 Rockville Pike (20852). Phone 301/770-1444; fax 301/770-1940. www.silverdiner.com.* Hours: 7-2 am; Fri, Sat to 3 am; early-bird dinner Mon-Fri 4-6 pm. Closed Dec 25. Service bar. Breakfast $3.99-$5.99, lunch $5.99-$7.99, dinner $5.99-$9.99. Children's menu. Specialties: meatloaf, chicken pot pie, turkey. 1950s-style diner; jukeboxes. Servers dressed in period clothing. Cr cds: A, C, D, DS, MC, V.

D SC

★★ **TASTE OF SAIGON.** *410 Hungerford Dr (20850). Phone 301/424-7222.* Steak, Vietnamese menu. Closed Thanksgiving, Dec 25. Lunch, dinner. Bar. Outdoor seating. Cr cds: A, D, DS, MC, V. **$$**

D

★★ **THAT'S AMORE.** *15201 Shady Grove Rd (20850). Phone 301/670-9666; fax 301/670-0810. www.thatsamore.com.* Italian menu. Closed Labor Day, Thanksgiving, Dec 25. Lunch, dinner. Bar. Early 20th-century mens' club atmosphere. Stained-glass windows. Cr cds: A, D, DS, MC, V. **$$**

D SC

St. Mary's City (E-7)

See also Leonardtown, Waldorf

Settled 1634 **Pop** 1,300 **Elev** 36 ft **Area code** 240 and 301 **Zip** 20686

Information St. Mary's County Division of Tourism, 23115 Leonard Hall Dr, PO Box 653, Leonardtown 20650; 301/475-4411 or 800/327-9023

Web www.co.saint-marys.md.us

Maryland's first colonists bought a Native American village on this site upon their arrival in the New World under Leonard Calvert. The settlement was the capital and hub of the area until 1694, when the colonial capital was moved to Annapolis. The town gradually disappeared. The city and county are still rich in historical attractions.

What to See and Do

Historic St. Mary's City. *MD 5 and Rosecroft Rd. Phone 301/862-0990 or 800/SMC-1634.* Outdoor museum at site of Maryland's first capital (1634) includes reconstructed State House (1676), replica of the original capitol building; other exhibits include the *Maryland Dove*, replica of a 17th-century ship, and archaeological exhibits. Also seasonal living history programs, a 17th-century tobacco plantation, reconstructed 17th-century inn; visitor center, outdoor cafe. Visitor center (daily; closed Jan 1, Thanksgiving, Dec 25); outdoor museum (fourth weekend Mar-Nov, Wed-Sun). Also here is

> **Margaret Brent Memorial.** *18751 Hogaboom Ln.* Gazebo overlooking the river; memorial to the woman who, being a wealthy landowner, requested the right to vote in the Maryland Assembly in 1648, in order to settle Leonard Calvert's affairs after his death.

Leonard Calvert Monument. *Trinity Churchyard. 18751 Hogaboom Ln.* Monument to Maryland's first colonial governor.

Point Lookout State Park. *11175 Point Lookout Rd. 13 miles S on MD 5. Phone 301/872-5688.* Site of Confederate Monument, the only memorial erected by US government to honor POWs who died in Point Lookout Prison Camp during Civil War (3,384 died here). Swimming, fishing, boating; hiking, picnicking, improved camping (Apr-Oct; self-contained camping units year-round). Nature center. Civil War museum. Standard fees. (May-Sept, weekends) **$$**

Special Events

Crab Festival. *41348 Medley's Neck Rd.* Steamed crabs, other seafood and nonseafood dishes. Arts and crafts, antique and classic car show. First Sun in June.

Maryland Days. *38370 Point Breeze Rd.* Boat rides, seafood, 17th-century militia musters. Third weekend in Mar.

Restaurants

★ **ALOHA.** *2025 MD 235, California (20619). Phone 301/862-4838; fax 301/862-4158.* Hours: 10:30 am-10 pm; Fri to 11 pm; Sat noon-11 pm; Sun noon-9:30 pm. Closed Thanksgiving, Dec 25. Chinese, Japanese menu. Bar. Lunch $4.25-$5.25, dinner $5.95-$19. Complete meals: lunch $4.95, dinner $7.25-$9.95. Buffet: lunch $5.99, dinner $7.99. Children's menu. Specializes in Szechwan, Hunan dishes. Sushi bar. Polynesian atmosphere. Cr cds: A, C, DS. MC, V.

D ⊟

★ **EVANS SEAFOOD.** *16680 Piney Point Rd, St. George Island (20674). Phone 301/994-2299; fax 301/994-2848. www.evansseafood.com.* Hours: 4-10 pm; Sat from noon; Sun noon-9 pm. Closed Mon. Lunch $5.50-$13.95, dinner $8.95-$21.95. Bar. Children's menu. Cr cds: MC, V.

D

St. Michaels (D-8)

Pop 1,193 **Elev** 7 ft **Area code** 410 **Zip** 21663

Information Talbot County Chamber of Commerce, PO Box 1366, Easton Plaza Suite 53, Easton 21601; 410/822-4653

Web www.talbottchamber.org

Chartered in 1804, St. Michaels has become a boating and tourist center with its abundance of shops, marinas, restaurants, bed-and-breakfasts, and country inns. It is a town with many Federal- and Victorian-period buildings.

What to See and Do

Chesapeake Bay Maritime Museum. *Mill St/Navy Point. Phone 410/745-2916.* Waterside museum consists of nine buildings. Includes historic lighthouse, floating exhibits, boat-building shop with working exhibit, ship models, small boats; paintings; waterfowl exhibits; workboats and mechanical propulsion. Special events throughout the year (see SPECIAL EVENT). (Daily) **$$$**

The Footbridge. *109 S Talbot St.* Joins Navy Point to Cherry St. Only remaining bridge of three that once connected the town with areas across the harbor.

The *Patriot*. *Berthed at Chesapeake Bay Maritime Museum. Phone 410/745-3100.* A one-hour narrated cruise on Miles River. Four trips daily. (Apr-Oct)

St. Mary's Square. *In Covington.* Public square laid out in 1770 by Englishman James Braddock. Several buildings date to the early 1800s, including the Cannonball House and Dr. Miller's Farmhouse. The Ship's Carpenter Bell was cast in 1842; across from the bell stand two cannons, one dating from the Revolution, the other from the War of 1812. Also here is

St. Mary's Square Museum. *In Covington. Phone 410/745-9535.* Mid-19th-century home of "half-timber" construction; one of the earliest buildings in St. Michaels. Exhibits of historical and local interest. (First weekend May-last weekend Oct, Sat and Sun; also by appointment) Inquire about the town walking tour brochures. Contact the Town Office.

Special Event

Mid-Atlantic Maritime Festival. *Chesapeake Bay Maritime Museum, in Covington. Phone 410/745-2916 or 410/822-5553.* Nautical celebration with fly-fishing demonstration, skipjack races, boat building contest, boat parade, seafood festival cooking contest. Three days mid-May.

Motel/Motor Lodge

★ **BEST WESTERN ST. MICHAELS MOTOR INN.** *1228 S Talbot St (21663). Phone 410/745-3333; fax 410/745-2906; toll-free 800/528-1234. www.bestwestern.com.* 93 rooms, 2 story. May-mid-Nov: S $75-$96; D $87-$107; each additional $8; under 18 free; lower rates rest of year. Complimentary continental breakfast. Check-out 11 am. TV; cable (premium). Restaurant adjacent 11 am-11 pm. Two pools. Cr cds: A, C, D, DS, MC, V.

D ⊠ SC ⊠

Hotel

★ ★ ★ **ST. MICHAELS HARBOR INN.** *101 N Harbor Rd (21663). Phone 410/745-9001; fax 410/745-9150; toll-free 800/332-8994. www. harbourinn.com.* From this waterfront resort, visitors can take a short stroll down the main road to shops, museums, and historical sites. 46 units, 3 story, 38 suites. May-Oct: S, D, suites $169-$429; under 18 free; higher rates weekends (2-day minimum); lower rates rest of year. Crib $10. Check-out noon. TV; cable (premium). Some balconies. Refrigerator in suites; some in-room whirlpools. Coin laundry. Restaurant, bar 11 am-10 pm. Health club privileges. Exercise equipment. Pool, whirlpool, poolside service. Picnic tables. 60-slip marina. Meeting rooms. Business services. Gift shop. Cr cds: A, C, D, DS, MC, V.

🕊 D ⊠ ⊠

Resorts

★ ★ **HARBOURTOWNE GOLF RESORT AND CONFERENCE CENTER.** *Rte 33 and Martingham Dr (21663). Phone 410/745-9066; fax 410/745-9124; toll-free 800/446-9066. www.harbourtowne.com.* 111 rooms,

1-2 story. Mar-Nov: S, D $155-$175; each additional $10; suites $225-$250; under 12 free; golf plans; lower rates rest of year. Crib free. Check-out 11 am, check-in 3 pm. TV; cable (premium), VCR available. In-room modem link. Private patios, balconies. Refrigerators. Some fireplaces. Dining room 7 am-10 pm. Exercise equipment. Pool, poolside service, lifeguard. Golf, greens fee $55, pro, putting green, driving range. Tennis. Lawn games. Bicycles. Paddle boats. Meeting rooms. Business center. Cr cds: A, C, D, DS, MC, V.

★ ★ ★ **THE INN AT PERRY CABIN.** *308 Watkins Ln (21663). Phone 410/745-2200; fax 410/745-3348; toll-free 800/722-2949. www.perrycabin.com.* The Inn at Perry Cabin marries the charm of a country inn and the intimacy of a private home with the service of a world-class resort. Nestled on the shores of eastern Maryland in the quaint Victorian town of St. Michaels, the inn is a well-heeled country getaway. Built just after the War of 1812, it looks and feels like a gracious manor house. English and early American styles blend in the lovely guest rooms, where mahogany sleigh beds, antiques, and enchanting views of the Miles River warm visitors' hearts. Cycling and nearby golf are popular pastimes, while others do as the locals do and set sail. A definitive British influence is evident throughout the inn, from the high tea and scones with Devonshire cream to the shortbread served at evening turndown, while the bounty of the Chesapeake is celebrated on the menu at the exquisite Sherwood Landing restaurant (see also). 41 rooms, 6 suites, 3 story. S, D $295-$695; suites $695. Children over 10 years only. Complimentary full breakfast. Check-out noon, check-in 3 pm. TV; cable (premium), VCR available (movies). In-room modem link. Dining room. Health club privileges. Exercise equipment, sauna, steam room. Massage. Indoor pool, whirlpool. Outdoor tennis. Lawn games. Business center. Concierge. Dockage. Cr cds: A, C, D, MC, V.

B&Bs/Small Inns

★ **BLACK WALNUT POINT INN.** *Black Walnut Point Rd, Tilghman (21671). Phone 410/886-2452; fax 410/886-2053.* 7 rooms, 3 story. No room phones. D $120-$135; each additional $25, kitchen unit $150. Adults only. Complimentary continental breakfast. Check-out 11, check-in 2-7 pm. TV. Pool, whirlpool. Outdoor tennis, lighted courts. Lawn games. Built in 1843; hand-hewn beams. On Cheasapeake Bay. Cr cds: DS, MC, V. **$$**

★ ★ ★ **CHESAPEAKE WOOD DUCK INN.** *21490 Gibsontown Rd at Dogwood Harbor, Tilghman Island (21671). Phone 410/886-2070; toll-free 800/956-2070.* www.woodduckinn.com. This waterfront Victorian-style bed-and-breakfast was first used as a boarding house, but has since been remodeled to provide comfortable and intimate lodging for visitors to the area. 7 rooms, 3 story. No elevator, room phones. D $129-$189. Children over 14 years only. Complimentary full breakfast. Check-out 11 am, check-in 4-7 pm. TV, cable in main room; VCR. Fireplace. Built in 1890. Water sport privileges. Totally nonsmoking. Cr cds: MC, V.

★ ★ ★ **LAZYJACK INN.** *5907 Tilghman Island Rd, Tilghman Island (21671). Phone 410/886-2215; fax 410/886-2635; toll-free 800/690-5080. www.lazyjackinn.com.* This waterfront home was built in 1855 and is located within walking distance of fine dining and antique shops. It offers spacious rooms, many with views of the water. 4 rooms, 2 story. No room phones. D $140-$175. Children over 12 years only. Complimentary full breakfast. Check-out 11 am, check-in 4-7 pm. TV; VCR in main room. Historic waterfront building (1855). Private yacht for charter. Totally nonsmoking. Cr cds: A, MC, V.

★ ★ ★ **PARSONAGE INN.** *210 N Talbot (21663). Phone 410/745-5519; toll-free 800/394-5519.* This inn is in the National Historic District and colonial seaport of St. Michaels, near the Maritime Museum, fine restaurants, and shops. 8 rooms, 7 with shower only, 2 story. No room phones. May-Oct: D $110-$172; lower rates rest of year. Crib free. TV in some rooms. Complimentary full breakfast. Restaurant adjacent. Check-out 11 am, check-in 2-7 pm. Health club privileges. Balconies. Picnic table, grill. Built in 1883 as private residence; later used as parsonage. Restored and furnished with period reproductions; unique architecture. Totally nonsmoking. Cr cds: MC, V.

★ ★ ★ **WADE'S POINT INN.** *Wades Point Rd (21663). Phone 410/745-2500; fax 410/745-3443; toll-free 888/923-3466. www.wadespoint.com.* This bed-and-breakfast is located just outside historic St. Michaels. It is situated on 120 acres of fields, woodlands, and 1/2 mile of coastline that overlooks Chesapeake bay. The inn is perfect for relaxation or recreation. 28 rooms, 4 kitchen units, 2-3 story. No room phones. D $95-$230; each additional $30; kitchen units $230; under 12 free. Complimentary continental breakfast. Check-out 11 am, check-in 2-8 pm. Located on 120 acres; flower gardens, woods with nature trail. Main building (1819) with new guest house (1989) built in same style. Both buildings are surrounded by fields and Chesapeake Bay. Totally nonsmoking. Cr cds: MC, V.

Restaurants

★ ★ **BAY HUNDRED RESTAURANT.** *6178 Tilghman Island Rd, Tilghman (21671). Phone 410/886-2126; fax 410/886-2455.* Seafood menu. Lunch, dinner, brunch. Entertainment. Children's menu. Outdoor seating. Cr cds: A, DS, MC, V.

D ⊠

★ **BISTRO ST. MICHAELS.** *403 S Talbot St (21663). Phone 410/745-9111; fax 410/745-3447. www.bistrosmichaels.com.* Mediterranean menu. Closed Tues, Wed. Lunch, dinner. Entertainment. Over 100 years old. Cr cds: A, D, DS, MC, V.

D ⊠

★ ★ **THE BRIDGE.** *6316 Tilghman Island Dr, Tilghman (21671). Phone 410/886-2330. www.bridge restaurant.com.* Hours: 11:30 am-9 pm; Fri-Sun to 9:30 pm. Closed Thanksgiving, Dec 25. Reservations required Fri-Sun (dinner). Bar to 2 am. Lunch, dinner $13.95-$19.95. Children's menu. Specializes in seafood, sandwiches, pizza. Parking. Outdoor seating. View of bay. Casual dining. Totally nonsmoking. Cr cds: A, MC, V.

D ⊠

★ **CHESAPEAKE LANDING SEAFOOD.** *23713 St. Michael's Rd (21663). Phone 410/745-9600; fax 410/745-9176.* Seafood menu. Hours: 11 am-9 pm; early-bird dinner 4-6 pm (Mon-Fri). Closed Dec 25. Dinner $9.95-$24.95. Children's menu. Casual attire. Totally nonsmoking. Cr cds: A, DS, MC, V.

D ⊠

★ ★ ★ **SHERWOOD LANDING.** *308 Watkins Ln (21663). Phone 410/745-2200. www.perrycabin.com.* Located in the magnificent, manor-style Inn at Perry Cabin (see also THE INN AT PERRY CABIN) in the Victorian resort town of St. Michaels, Sherwood Landing features eclectic continental cuisine, an international wine list, and thoughtful, knowledgeable service. The restaurant is formal and elegant, swathed in soothing sandy tones, filled with gorgeous flower arrangements, and lined with luxurious tables cloaked in creamy linens and topped with crystal glasses and fine china. The menu takes classic French technique and marries it with regional Chesapeake Bay flair and the best local produce, fish, poultry, and meats. Crispy maple leaf duck leg on celery, chayote, and raisin slaw with carrot-orange vinaigrette; honey-glazed lamb shank with a casserole of Welsh leeks, potatoes, and thyme; and jumbo lump crab with saffron sauce are a few of the signature dishes on the menu. A special treat is the proper English tea served every afternoon, featuring a selection of homemade breads, English scones, Devonshire clotted cream, lemon curd, preserves, and blended teas. French menu. Menu changes seasonally. Hours: 8-10:30 am, 12:30-2:30 pm, 6-10 pm; Sun brunch 11:30 am-2:30 pm; afternoon tea 3-5 pm. Breakfast $27.50, lunch $30, dinner prix fixe (five-course) $69.50. Service bar. Reservations accepted. Valet parking. Totally nonsmoking. High tea $19.50. Cr cds: A, D, DS, MC, V.

D ⊠

★ ★ ★ **HARBOUR LIGHTS.** *101 N Harbor Rd (21663). Phone 410/745-5102. www.harbourinn.com.* This intimate dining room offers professional service, and one of the finest water views on the Eastern Shore. Hours: 7 am-9 pm; Oct-May to 10 pm. Closed Mon, Tues (Dec-mid-Mar). Reservations accepted. Bar. Wine list. Breakfast $5.95-$9.95, lunch $5.95-$11.95, dinner $14.95-$22.95. Specializes in seafood, steaks, chicken. Cr cds: A, D, DS, MC, V.

D

★ **ST. MICHAELS CRAB HOUSE.** *305 Mulberry St (21663). Phone 410/745-3737; fax 410/745-2471. www.stmichaelscrabhouse.com.* Hours: 11 am-10 pm; Fri, Sat to 11 pm. Closed mid-Dec-early Mar. Reservations accepted. Bar. Lunch $4.95-$10.95, dinner $9.95-$17.95. Children's menu. Specializes in fresh seafood, beef, chicken. Outdoor seating. Overlooks harbor. Cr cds: DS, MC, V.

D

★ ★ ★ **208 TALBOT.** *208 N Talbot St (21663). Phone 410/745-3838; fax 410/745-6507. www.208talbot.com.* One of the top dining destinations in quaint St. Michaels, 208 Talbot is full every night with those who appreciate the creative, seasonal approach to seafood and other regional specialties. As an added bonus, the townhouse setting is comfortable and romantic. Hours: 5-10 pm; Sun 5-9 pm; Sun brunch 11 am-2 pm. Closed Mon, Tues; Dec 24, 25. Reservations accepted; required weekends. Bar. Dinner $21-$26. Prix fixe: Sat dinner $48. Sun brunch $9.50-$15.50. Specializes in fresh seafood, rack of lamb. Own pastries, ice cream. Casual gourmet dining in renovated mid-1800s brick house; many antiques; original fireplace. Cr cds: DS, MC, V.

D

Salisbury (E-9)

See also Ocean City

Founded 1732 **Pop** 20,592 **Elev** 33 ft **Area code** 410 and 443 **Zip** 21801

Information Wicomico County Convention & Visitors Bureau, 8480 Ocean Hwy, Delmar 21875; 410/548-4914 or 800/332-TOUR. Information is also available from the Chamber of Commerce, 300 E Main St, PO Box 510, 21803; 410/749-0144

Web www.salisburyarea.com

"Central City of the Eastern Shore" and of the Delmarva Peninsula, Salisbury has a marina on the Wicomico River providing access to Chesapeake Bay. It lies within 30 miles of duck hunting and deep-sea fishing. Gasoline pumps, hydraulic lifts, canned and frozen foods, seafood, and poultry come from this area.

What to See and Do

Mason-Dixon Line Marker. *5 miles N on US 13, 13 A, then 7 miles W on MD 467.* Bears coats of arms of Lord Baltimore and William Penn.

Nassawango Iron Furnace. *3816 Old Furnace Rd. 16 miles S via MD 12 to Old Furnace Rd. Phone 410/632-2032.* One of the oldest industrial sites in Maryland and one of the earliest hot blast mechanisms still intact. The stack was restored in 1966; archaeological excavations were made and a canal, a dike, and a portion of the old waterwheel used in the manufacturing process were found. The remains of the area are undergoing restoration. (Apr-Oct, daily) **$$**

Furnace Town. *3816 Old Furnace Rd.* This 1840s industrial village occupies 22 acres around the iron furnace and also includes six historic structures; a working 19th-century blacksmith shop and broom making shop has demonstrations on selected days; a museum and company store; archaeological excavations; a nature trail and picnic area. Special events take place throughout the season. (Same days and fees as Nassawango Iron Furnace)

Poplar Hill Mansion. *117 Elizabeth St. Phone 410/749-1776.* (circa 1805). Example of Georgian- and Federal-style architecture; Palladian and bull's-eye windows; large brass box locks on doors, woodwork, mantels, and fireplaces. Period furniture; country garden. (Usually Sun afternoons; Tues-Sat by appointment. **$**

Princess Anne. *13 miles SW on US 13.* This town was the home of Samuel Chase, signer of the Declaration of Independence. Buildings of the Colonial and Federal periods are of architectural interest.

Salisbury Zoological Park. *755 S Park Dr. Phone 410/548-3188.* Natural habitats for almost 400 mammals, birds, and reptiles. Major exhibits include bears, monkeys, jaguars, bison, waterfowl. Also exotic plants. (Daily) **DONATION**

Ward Museum of Wildfowl Art. *909 S Schumaker Dr, at Beaglin Park Dr. Phone 410/742-4988, ext 100.* Displays include the history of decoy and wildfowl carving in North America; wildfowl habitats; contemporary wildfowl art. Changing exhibits. Gift shop. (Mon-Sat, also Sun afternoons) **$$**

Motels/Motor Lodges

★ **COMFORT INN.** *2701 N Salisbury Blvd (21801). Phone 410/543-4666; toll-free 800/638-7949; fax 410/749-2639. www.comfortinn.com.* 96 units, 2 story, 24 suites. Mid-May-mid-Sept: S $74.95-$97.95; D $85.95-$108.95; each additional $8; suites $97.95-$120.95; under 18 free; higher rates weekends; lower rates rest of year. Crib available. Pet accepted. TV; cable (premium). Pool privileges. Complimentary continental breakfast. Check-out 11 am. Meeting room. Business services available. Lawn games. Refrigerator, wet bar available. Picnic table, grills. Cr cds: A, C, D, DS, ER, JCB, MC, V.

D 🐾 🏊 SC

★ **HOWARD JOHNSON.** *2625 N Salisbury Blvd (21801). Phone 410/742-7194; toll-free 800/446-4656; fax 410/742-5194. www.hojo.com.* 123 rooms, 2 story. Mid-June-mid-Sept: S $49-$99; D $49-$107; each additional $8; under 18 free; lower rates rest of year. Crib free. Pet accepted, some restrictions. TV; cable (premium). Pool. Complimentary breakfast buffet. Restaurant 6:30-9:30 am. Bar 4:30 pm-midnight. Check-out 11 am. Coin laundry. Meeting rooms. Business services available. Health club privileges. Cr cds: A, C, D, DS, MC, V.

D 🐾 🏊 SC

★ ★ **RAMADA INN AND CONFERENCE CENTER.** *300 S Salisbury Blvd (21801). Phone 410/546-4400; fax 410/546-2528; res 800/800-7617. www.ramada.com.* 156 rooms, 5 story. July-Aug: S, D $87-$135; each additional $10; under 18 free; lower rates rest of year. Crib free. Pet accepted. TV; cable (premium). Indoor pool. Restaurant 6:30 am-2:30 pm, 5:30-10 pm; weekends from 7 am. Room service. Bar 4 pm-2 am; weekends from noon. Check-out noon. Meeting rooms. Business services available. Bellstaff. Free airport transportation. Health club privileges. On river. Cr cds: A, C, D, DS, MC, V.

D 🐾 🏊 SC

B&B/Small Inn

★ ★ ★ **WATERLOO COUNTRY INN.** *28822 Mt. Vernon Rd (21853). Phone 410/651-0883; fax 410/651-5592. www.waterloocountryinn.com.* Built in the 1750s, this waterfront estate offers canoes and bikes to explore the area, and gardens and forests to walk through and relax. 6 rooms, 3 story. Jan-Feb. Children over 9 years only. Complimentary full breakfast. Check-out 11 am. TV. Fireplace in suites. Pool, whirlpool. Golf privileges, greens fee $60. Built in 1750; on 317 acres. Totally nonsmoking. Cr cds: A, DS, MC, V. **$**

D 🐕 🎿 🏊

Silver Spring (C-6)

*See also Bowie, College Park, Rockville;
also see District of Columbia*

Pop 76,540 **Elev** 350 ft **Area code** 240 and 301

Information Chamber of Commerce, 8601 Georgia Ave, Suite 203, 20910; 301/565-3777

Web www.gsscc.org

What to See and Do

Brookside Gardens. *1500 Glenallan Ave. N on MD 97, right on Randolph Rd, right on Glenallan Ave, in Wheaton.* Phone 301/949-8230. A 50-acre display garden with two conservatories, flowering displays; variety of flowering plants in eight gardens; educational programs. (Daily; closed Dec 25) **FREE**

National Capital Trolley Museum. *1313 Bonifant Rd. Northwest Branch Park, about 7 miles N on Bonifant Rd, just off MD 650 in Layhill.* Phone 301/384-6088. Rides on old-time American and European trolleys; exhibits depict history of streetcars. Special events during year. (July-Aug, Sat-Sun and Wed; rest of year, Sat and Sun only; also open Memorial Day, July 4, Labor Day) **$$**

Restaurants

★ ★ **BLAIR MANSION INN.** *7711 Eastern Ave (20912).* Phone 301/588-6646. www.blairmansion.com. Hours: 11:30 am-9 pm; Sat from 5 pm; Sun from 2 pm. Closed Mon. Reservations accepted. Continental, American menu. Bar. Lunch $5.95-$9.95, dinner $9.95-$19.95. Specializes in poultry, beef, crab. Murder mystery dinners Thurs-Sun. 1890s Victorian mansion; gaslight chandelier, 7 fireplaces. Family-owned. Totally nonsmoking. Cr cds: A, DS, MC, V.

D 📶

★ ★ **CRISFIELD.** *8606 Colesville Rd (20910).* Phone 301/588-1572; fax 301/588-1574. Seafood menu. Closed Thanksgiving, Dec 25. Lunch, dinner. Bar. Children's menu. Reservations accepted; required Fri, Sat. Cr cds: A, D, DS, MC, V. **$$**

D

★★★**MRS. K'S TOLL HOUSE.** *9201 Colesville Rd (20910).* Phone 301/589-3500; fax 301/589-0768. www.mrsks.com. Hours: 11:30 am-2:30 pm, 5-9 pm; Fri, Sat to 9:30 pm; Sun 11 am-9 pm; Sun brunch to 1 pm. Closed Mon; Dec 25. Service bar. Complete meals: lunch $11.95, dinner $17.95-$25.50. Sun brunch $15.75. Specializes in regional American cuisine. Century-old tollhouse; antique china, glass. Gardens. Totally nonsmoking. Cr cds: A, C, D, DS, MC, V.

D 📶

★ **VICINO.** *959 Sligo Ave (20910).* Phone 301/588-3372; fax 301/585-8151. Hours: 11:30 am-10:30 pm; Mon to 9:30 pm; Sun 1-9:30 pm. Closed some major holidays. Italian menu. Wine, beer. A la carte entrées: lunch, dinner $6.50-$12. Children's menu. Specializes in pizza, pasta, seafood. Outdoor seating. Casual Italian neighborhood décor. Totally nonsmoking. Cr cds: A, MC, V.
📶

Thurmont (B-5)

See also Frederick, Hagerstown

Settled 1751 **Pop** 5,588 **Elev** 523 ft **Area code** 301 **Zip** 21788

Information Tourism Council of Frederick County, 19 E Church St, Frederick 21701; 301/228-2888 or 800/999-3613

Web www.visitfrederick.org

What to See and Do

Catoctin Mountain National Park. *From Rte 15 North, exit onto Rte 77 West. Go approximately 3 miles and then turn right onto Park Central Rd; the visitor center is on the right.* www.nps.gov/cato/. Located one hour outside Baltimore, this 5,810-acre forest is an easily accessible nature retreat. The park is adjacent to two state parks and Camp David, the weekend mountain home of the US president. If you go, you probably won't see the president, but you will be treated to beautiful overlook views and wildlife as well as scenic hiking trails. The park also offers camping, picnicking areas, fishing, and playgrounds. (Daily; the visitor center is closed on major holidays.) **FREE**

Cunningham Falls State Park. *14039 Catoctin Hollow Rd.* Phone 301/271-7574. 4,950 acres in the Catoctin Mountains. Two recreation areas: Houck, 5 miles W of town, has swimming, fishing, boating (rentals); picnicking, camping, hiking trails that lead to 78-foot falls and scenic overlooks. Manor Area, 3 miles S of town on US 15, has picnicking, camping, playground. Trout fishing in Big Hunting Creek. Ruins of Iron Masters Mansion and the industrial village that surrounded it are also here. (See SPECIAL EVENTS) Standard fees.

Special Events

Catoctin Colorfest. *6602 Foxville Rd.* Phone 301/271-4432. Fall foliage; arts and crafts show. Second weekend Oct.

Maple Syrup Demonstration. *At Cunningham Falls State Park. 14039 Catoctin Hollow Rd (21788).* Phone 301/271-7574. Tree tapping, sap boiling; carriage rides; food; children's storytelling corner. Usually second and third weekend in Mar.

Motel/Motor Lodge

★ ★ ★ **COZY COUNTRY INN THURMONT.** *103 Frederick Rd (21788). Phone 301/271-4301; fax 301/271-4301. www.cozyvillage.com.* This is a small property located near Camp David, many historic sites, and numerous antique shops. 21 units, 3 with shower only, 2 story, 5 cottages. May-Oct: S, D $46-$130; each additional $5; cottages $46-$110; under 12 free; weekly rates. Crib available. Pet accepted. TV; cable (premium), VCR available. Complimentary continental breakfast Mon-Fri. Restaurant 11 am-9 pm; Sat, Sun from 8 am. Room service. Bar 11 am-10 pm. Meeting rooms. Business services available. In-room modem link. Gift shop. Downhill ski 12 miles; cross-country ski 4 miles. Refrigerators; some minibars; microwaves available. Balconies. Picnic tables. Near Camp David; visiting dignitaries have stayed here. Cr cds: A, DS, MC, V.

D 🤚 🐾 🏃 🏊

Restaurant

★ ★ **COZY.** *103 Frederick Rd (MD 806) (21788). Phone 301/271-7373; fax 301/271-4301. www.cozyvillage.com.* Closed Dec 24, 25. Breakfast, lunch, dinner. Bar. Children's menu. Outdoor seating. Cr cds: A, MC, V. **$$**

D

Towson (B-7)

See also Baltimore

Pop 51,793 **Elev** 465 ft **Area code** 410 and 443 **Zip** 21204

Information Baltimore County Chamber of Commerce, 102 W Pennsylvania Ave, Suite 402; 410/825-6200

Web www.baltcountycc.com

What to See and Do

Fire Museum of Maryland. *1301 York Rd, 1 block N of I-695 exit 26 B, in Lutherville. Phone 410/321-7500.* More than 60 pieces of antique firefighting equipment; includes motorized and hand/horse-drawn units from 1822-1957. (May, Sept-Oct, weekends; June-Aug, daily) **$$**

Hampton National Historic Site. *535 Hampton Ln, 1/2 mile off Dulaney Valley Rd; I-695 exit 27 B.* Includes ornate Georgian mansion (circa 1790) (tours), formal gardens, and plantation outbuildings. Gift shop. (Daily; closed Jan 1, Thanksgiving, Dec 25) Tea room open for luncheon (Daily; closed six weeks mid-Jan-early Mar).

Soldiers Delight Natural Environment Area. *5100 Deer Park Rd. 7 miles W on I-695, then W on MD 26, then 5 miles N on Deerpark Rd to overlook. Phone 410/922-3044.* This 1,725-acre park has 19th-century chrome mines; restored log cabin; scenic overlook; hiking and nature trails, picnicking (at visitor center only). It is the only undisturbed serpentine barren in the state. Pets must be on leash.

Towson State University. *8000 York Rd (21252). Phone 410/830-ARTS (Information on entertainment and events).* (1866) 15,000 students. On campus are three art galleries, including Holtzman Art Gallery, with an extensive collection of art media (Sept-May, Tues-Sat). Concerts and sporting events are held in the Towson Center.

Special Event

State Fair. *Timonium Fairgrounds, 3 miles N on York Rd, in Timonium. Phone 410/252-0200.* Ten-day festival of home arts; entertainment, midway; agricultural demonstrations, Thoroughbred horse racing, livestock presentations. Aug-Sept.

Motel/Motor Lodge

★ ★ **DAYS INN.** *9615 Deereco Rd, Timonium (21093). Phone 410/560-1000; toll-free 800/235-3297; fax 410/561-3918. www.daysinn.com.* 146 rooms, 7 story. Apr-Nov: S $49.95-$85; D $55-$90; each additional $5; suites $100-$140; family, holiday rates; lower rates rest of year. Complimentary continental breakfast. Check-out 11 am. TV; cable (premium), VCR. In-room modem link. Laundry services. Restaurant open 24 hours. Bar. Room service 7 am-10 pm. Exercise equipment. Game room. Pool. Cr cds: A, D, DS, JCB, MC, V.

D 🏊 🏃 🏊 SC

Hotel

★ ★ ★ **SHERATON BALTIMORE NORTH.** *903 Dulaney Valley Rd (21204). Phone 410/321-7400; toll-free 800/433-7619; fax 410/296-9534. www.sheraton.com.* 284 rooms, 12 story. S, D $109-$179; each additional $12; suites $350-$450; under 17 free; weekend plans; higher rates Preakness. Crib free. TV; cable (premium). Indoor pool; whirlpool, poolside service, lifeguard. Restaurant 6:30 am-10:30 pm. Bar 11:30-1 am; entertainment. Check-out noon. Convention facilities. Business center. In-room modem link. Gift shop. Free valet parking. Exercise equipment; sauna. Health club privileges. Refrigerators, microwaves available. Cr cds: A, C, D, DS, MC, V.

D 🏊 🏃 🏊 SC 🏃

Restaurants

★ ★ **CAFE TROIA.** *28 W Allegheny Ave (21204). Phone 410/337-0133. www.cafetroia.com.* Hours: 11 am-3 pm, 5-10 pm; Mon 5-10 pm; Fri to 11 pm; Sat 5-11 pm; Sun 5-9 pm. Reservations accepted. Italian menu. Bar. Lunch $4-$12, dinner $9-$22. Specializes in regional Italian dishes. Outdoor seating. Cr cds: A, MC, V.

D

★★★ LIBERATORE'S. *9515 Derreco Rd, Timonium (21093). Phone 410/561-3300; fax 410/561-2404. www.liberatores.com.* With an elegant Mediterranean ambiance, this restaurant serves authentic Italian specialties. Hours: 11 am-10 pm; Fri, Sat to 11 pm; Sun 3-10 pm. Closed most major holidays. Reservations accepted. Italian menu. Bar. A la carte entrées: lunch, dinner $3.95-$14.95. Specializes in pasta, chicken, seafood. Pianist Thurs-Sat. Italian décor. Cr cds: A, D, DS, MC, V.

D

★★ PEERCE'S PLANTATION. *12460 Dulaney Valley Rd, Phoenix (21131). Phone 410/252-3100; fax 410/560-0718. 410/252-3100. www.peerces.com.* Continental menu. Closed Dec 25. Lunch, dinner, brunch. Bar. Children's menu. Jacket. Reservations accepted. Valet parking available. Outdoor seating. Cr cds: A, C, D, DS, MC, V. **$$**

D

★★ ROTHWELL'S GRILLE. *106 W Padonia Rd, Timonium (21093). Phone 410/252-0600; fax 410/252-0946.* Hours: 11:30 am-midnight; Sat, Sun from 5 pm. Closed most major holidays. Reservations accepted (dinner). Bar. Lunch $6-$12, dinner $9-$19. Specializes in fresh meats and fish cooked on wood burning grill. Own baking. Outdoor seating. Casual atmosphere. Cr cds: A, D, DS, MC, V.

D

★★ THAT'S AMORE. *720 Kenilworth Dr (21204). Phone 410/825-5255; fax 410/825-3147. www.thatsamore.com.* Hours: 11:30 am-10:30 pm; Fri to midnight; Sat 4 pm-midnight; Sun 4-9:30 pm. Closed Labor Day, Thanksgiving, Dec 25. Italian menu. Bar. A la carte entrées: lunch $3.50-$10.95, dinner $16-$22. Specializes in seafood. Outdoor seating. Italian vineyard setting. Cr cds: A, DS, MC, V.

D

Waldorf (D-6)

See also La Plata

Pop 22,312 **Elev** 215 ft **Area code** 301

Information Tourism Director, PO Box 2150, La Plata 20646; 301/645-0558 or 800/766-3386

Web www.explorecharlesmd.com

What to See and Do

Cedarville State Forest. *4 miles E off US 301 on Cedarville Rd. Phone 301/856-8987 or 410/974-3771. Schedule varies.* Includes 3,697 acres of woodland, once home of the Piscataway, who settled around the Zekiah Swamp. Fishing; hunting, nature and hiking trails, picnicking. Standard fees.

Farmer's Market and Auction. *29890 Three Notch Rd (20622). 13 miles SE on MD 5. Phone 301/884-3108.* Nearby Amish farms offer fresh baked goods and produce (auction Wed) for sale; more than 90 shops. Antique dealers. (Wed and Sat)

⭐ **John Wilkes Booth Escape Route.** After shooting Abraham Lincoln on April 14, 1865, John Wilkes Booth fled south into Maryland to rendezvous with his accomplice, David Herold, at

Surratt House and Tavern. *9110 Brandywine Rd, Clinton (then Surrattsville). Phone 301/868-1121.* (1852) Where they recovered arms they had hidden there. Though she may have been innocent, Mary Surratt was hanged for conspiracy. Eight period rooms, museum; guides in period costumes; Dec candlelight tours; special events and exhibits throughout the year. (Mar-mid-Dec, Thurs-Sun) **$** Booth and Herold next stopped at

Dr. Samuel A. Mudd House Museum. *3725 Dr. Samuel Mudd Rd. From US 301, take MD 5, then left on MD 205, turn right on Poplar Hill Rd approximately 4 miles, right on Dr. Samuel Mudd Rd, continue to house; sign at entrance. Phone 301/934-8464 or 301/645-6870.* (circa 1830) Where Dr. Mudd set Booth's broken leg, unaware that Booth had just shot the president. Mudd was convicted and imprisoned for life, but pardoned four years later by President Andrew Johnson. Tours conducted by costumed docents, some of whom are Dr. Mudd's descendants. (Apr-Nov, Sat-Sun afternoons and Wed 11 am-3 pm; closed Easter, Thanksgiving) **$$**

Maryland Indian Cultural Center. *16816 Country Ln. Phone 301/372-1932.* Exhibits reflect diverse tribal structures, art, lodging construction, and cultures of Native Americans. (Tues, Thurs, Sun afternoons) **FREE**

Special Event

John Wilkes Booth Escape Route Tour. *9118 Brandywine Rd (20735). Phone 301/868-1121.* Day-long bus tour of Booth's route from Ford's Theatre, Washington, through southern Maryland to site of Garrett's farm, Virginia, with expert commentary. Mid-Apr and early Sept.

Motels/Motor Lodges

★ DAYS INN. *US 301 (20603). Phone 301/932-9200; fax 301/843-9816.* 100 rooms, 3 story. S, D $65-$75; suite $119-$135. Each additional $5; under 18 free. Crib free. Pet accepted; $10. Complimentary continental breakfast. Check-out 11 am. TV; cable (premium). Some in-room whirlpools, refrigerators. Coin laundry. Restaurant adjacent

11 am-10 pm. Meeting room. Business services. Cr cds: A, C, D, DS, JCB, MC, V.

D 🐾 ⊠

★ ★ **HOLIDAY INN.** *45 St. Patrick's Dr (20603). Phone 301/645-8200; toll-free 800/465-4329; fax 301/843-7945. www.holiday-inn.com.* 192 rooms, 3 story, 8 kitchen units. S, D $69-$74; each additional $6; suites, kitchen units $70-$90; under 19 free. Crib free. TV; cable (premium). Pool; lifeguard. Complimentary coffee in rooms. Restaurant 6: 30 am-10 pm. Room service. Bar noon-11 pm. Check-out 11 am. Coin laundry. Meeting rooms. Business services available. In-room modem link. Bellstaff. Valet service. Beauty shop. Health club privileges. Refrigerators, microwaves available. Cr cds: A, C, D, DS, JCB, MC, V.

D ⊠ ⊠ SC

★ **HOWARD JOHNSON EXPRESS INN.** *3125 Crain Hwy (20603). Phone 301/932-5090; toll-free 800/826-4534; fax 301/932-5090. www.hojo.com.* 109 rooms. S, D $55-$65; suites, kitchen units $60-$65; under 18 free. Crib free. Pet accepted; $10. TV; cable (premium), VCR (movies). Pool. Complimentary continental breakfast. Coffee in rooms. Restaurant adjacent 11 am-10 pm. Check-out noon. Meeting rooms. Business services available. Health club privileges. Refrigerators, microwaves available. Picnic tables, grills. Cr cds: A, C, D, DS, JCB, MC, V.

D 🐾 ⊠ ⊠ SC

Westminster (B-6)

See also Baltimore, Frederick

Founded 1764 **Pop** 16,731 **Elev** 717 ft **Area code** 410 and 443

Westminster, a Union supply depot at the Battle of Gettysburg, saw scattered action before the battle. It is the county seat of Carroll County, first in the United States to offer complete rural free delivery mail service (started in 1899 with four two-horse wagons).

Motel/Motor Lodge

★ **BEST WESTERN WESTMINSTER.** *451 WMC Dr (21158). Phone 410/857-1900; fax 410/857-9584. www.bestwesternwestminster.com.* 101 rooms, 1-2 story. May-June: S $69-$89; D $69-$159; each additional $10; under 18 free; weekly rates; monthly rates; higher rates: WMC parents weekend, graduation, Dec 31; lower rates rest of year. Crib free. Pet accepted, some restrictions; $25 refundable. TV; cable. Pool; whirlpool. Complimentary continental breakfast. Check-out 11 am. Meeting rooms. Business services available. Valet service. Some in-room whirlpools; microwaves available. Cr cds: A, C, D, DS, ER, JCB, MC, V.

D 🐾 ⊠ ⊠ SC

Restaurants

★ ★ **JOHANSSON'S.** *4 W Main St (21157). Phone 410/876-0101; fax 410/848-1707.* Seafood menu. Closed Thanksgiving, Dec 25. Lunch, dinner. Bar. Children's menu. English pub atmosphere, originally a nickel-and-dime store; colored glass artwork. Outdoor seating. Cr cds: A, DS, MC, V. **$**

★ ★ **RUDY'S 2900.** *2900 Baltimore Blvd, Finksburg (21048). Phone 410/833-5777. www.rudys2900.com.* Continental menu. Closed Mon; most major holidays. Lunch, dinner. Bar to 10:30 pm. Reservations required Fri, Sat dinner. Vocalist Wed. Cr cds: A, MC, V. **$$**

D

New Jersey

Tree-shaded 18th-century towns and history-hallowed grounds, on which Revolutionary battles were fought, make this state one of dignified beauty and democratic tradition. More than 800 lakes and ponds, 100 rivers and streams, and 1,400 miles of freshly stocked trout streams are scattered throughout its wooded, scenic northwest corner. The swampy meadows west of the New Jersey Turnpike have been reclaimed and transformed into commercial and industrial areas. The Meadowlands, a multimillion-dollar sports complex, offers horse racing, the New York Giants and the New York Jets NFL football teams, the New Jersey Devils NHL hockey team, and the New Jersey Nets NBA basketball team. The coastline, stretching 127 miles from Sandy Hook to Cape May, offers excellent swimming and ocean fishing.

George Washington spent a quarter of his time here as commander-in-chief of the Revolutionary Army. On Christmas night in 1776, he crossed the Delaware and surprised the Hessians at Trenton. A few days later, he marched to Princeton and defeated three British regiments. He then spent the winter in Morristown, where the memories of his campaign are preserved in a national historical park.

New Jersey often is associated only with its factories, oil refineries, research laboratories, and industrial towns. But history buffs, hunters, anglers, scenery lovers, and amateur beachcombers need only to wander a short distance from its industrial areas to find whatever they like best.

When to Go/Climate

Moderate temperatures in spring and fall make these the best times to visit New Jersey. Summers can be hot and humid; winters can be bitterly cold, particularly in the inland mountain areas. Beaches are lovely, and coastal temperatures are often 5°F lower in summer and higher in winter than inland areas.

Population: 7,730,188
Area: 7,504 square miles
Elevation: 0-1,803 feet
Peak: High Point Mountain (Sussex County)
Entered Union: Third of original 13 states (December 18, 1787)
Capital: Trenton
Motto: Liberty and prosperity
Nickname: Garden State
Flower: Purple Violet
Bird: Eastern Goldfinch
Tree: Red Oak
Time Zone: Eastern
Website: www.state.nj.us/travel

AVERAGE HIGH/LOW TEMPERATURES (°F)

Atlantic City

Jan 40/27	May 66/54	Sept 74/62
Feb 42/29	June 74/62	Oct 64/51
Mar 49/36	July 80/68	Nov 55/42
Apr 57/44	Aug 80/68	Dec 46/33

Newark

Jan 38/23	May 72/53	Sept 78/60
Feb 41/25	June 82/63	Oct 67/48
Mar 51/33	July 87/69	Nov 55/39
Apr 62/43	Aug 85/67	Dec 43/29

Parks and Recreation

Water-related activities, hiking, riding, various sports, picnicking, camping, and visitor centers are available in many state parks. There is a $1 per person (12-62 years) walk-in/bicycle fee in some areas; there is a parking fee ($2-$7) in many areas. In most areas, fees are collected Memorial Day weekend-Labor Day weekend; fees are collected year-round at Island Beach (see SEASIDE PARK). No pets in bathing, camping areas or buildings; in other day-use areas, pets must be attended and kept on a 6-foot leash.

Calendar Highlights

APRIL

Tulip Festival *(Cape May). Phone 609/884-5508.* Celebrate Dutch heritage with ethnic foods and dancing, craft show, street fair, garden and house tours.

JUNE

IMB/USET Festival of Champions *(Somerville). Hamilton Farm. Phone 908/234-0555.* Competition of three Olympic equestrian disciplines.

JULY

Night in Venice *(Ocean City). Phone 800/BEACH-NJ.* Decorated boat parade.

OCTOBER

Atlantic City Marathon *(Atlantic City). Phone 609/601-1RUN.*

DECEMBER

Reenactment of Crossing of the Delaware *(Trenton). Washington Crossing State Park.* Departs PA side on the afternoon of Dec 25.

Bathing at inland beaches, Memorial Day-Labor Day; at ocean beaches from mid-June; cabins ($20-$100); campsites ($10-$12), lean-tos ($15); reservations accepted ($7, nonrefundable). Most areas are wild-life sanctuaries. In addition, 1,700 acres of Palisades Interstate Parks (see) on the Hudson are in New Jersey. There are also more than 20 state-owned historic sites (clearly marked); some with museums and guides. For detailed information contact Division of Parks and Forestry, PO Box 404, Trenton 08625; 609/984-0370 or 800/843-6420.

FISHING AND HUNTING

Fishing opportunities abound in New Jersey's fresh and salt waters. No license is required for deep-sea or surf fishing along the 127-mile coastline; *however,* a license is required for taking shellfish. Nonresident clam license: $20; under age 16, $2. A license is required for freshwater fishing for everyone over 16 years of age. Nonresident fishing license: $34; nonresident trout stamp: $20; 7-day nonresident vacation fishing license: $19.50.

Hunting licenses are required for everyone over 10 years of age. Firearm or bow and arrow: nonresident, $135.50 each; small game only: nonresident, 2-day, $36.50; pheasant and quail stamp: $40 (for wildlife management areas only). Hunter Education Course or resident license from previous year required to purchase license. For information contact Department of Environmental Protection, Division of Fish, Game, and Wildlife, PO Box 400, Trenton 08625-0400; 609/292-2965.

Driving Information

Safety belts are mandatory for all persons in front seat of vehicle. Children under 5 years must be in approved passenger restraints anywhere in a vehicle: ages 18 months-5 years may use regulation safety belts in back seat; however, in front seat, children must use approved safety seats; children under 18 months must use approved safety seats anywhere in a vehicle. For further information phone 609/633-9300.

INTERSTATE HIGHWAY SYSTEM

The following alphabetical listing of New Jersey towns in this book shows that these cities are within 10 miles of the indicated Interstate highways. Check a highway map for the nearest exit.

Highway Number	Cities/Towns within 10 Miles
Interstate 78	Clinton, Plainfield, Scotch Plains, Somerville, Union.
Interstate 80	Fort Lee, Hackensack, Hackettstown, Paramus, Parsippany, Rockaway, Saddle Brook, Wayne.
Interstate 95	Elizabeth, Fort Lee, Newark, Trenton, Woodbridge.

Additional Visitor Information

The State Division of Travel and Tourism, PO Box 820, Trenton 08625-0820, phone 609/292-2470 or 800/JERSEY-7, publishes a variety of materials for travelers. There are also two periodicals: *New Jersey Monthly* (write Subscription Department, Box 936, Farmingdale,

NY 11737; phone 888/419-0419); *New Jersey Outdoors* (write Department of Environmental Protection & Energy, CN-402, Trenton 08625).

There are eight tourist welcome centers and numerous information centers in New Jersey. At these centers visitors will find information racks with brochures to help plan trips to points of interest. For a publication with the locations of the centers contact the State Division of Travel and Tourism.

THE AMUSEMENTS OF THE JERSEY SHORE

Pennsylvania Route 40 leads to the Jersey Shore, where you'll find some of the best-known New Jersey resort towns: Atlantic City, Ocean City, and historic Cape May. People of all ages are sure to find something fun to do in Atlantic City. Children will be delighted by Lucy the Margate Elephant, a six-story elephant-shaped building. If you climb Lucy's legs to the observation area on her back, your children can add "riding an elephant" to the things they've done on their summer vacation—and they'll have a great story to share with their classmates when vacation is over! Storybook Land, which includes more than 50 storybook buildings, rides, animals, and a playground will also be a hit with the little ones. A trip to the fantastic world of the Ripley's Believe it or Not Museum may be of more interest to older children. Adults will enjoy the guided tour of Renault Winery, a visit to the Noyes Museum, and the specialty shops and restaurants of Historic Smithville. Still at a loss for entertainment? A visit to one of the recreation areas along the coast is a sure-fire way to please any family member, young or old. Or spend some time at one of the amusement piers where shopping and food provide distraction for even the hardest to please. Other noteworthy attractions include the Marine Mammal Stranding Center & Museum, which also offers dolphin- and whale-watching tours, and Edwin B. Forsythe National Wildlife Refuge. Looking for the wilder side of Atlantic City? Test your luck at one of a dozen casinos where the action never stops and fortunes are won and lost in an instant. It might be safest to stick to the slot machines. . . .

Head south from Atlantic City to Ocean City, a popular family resort where you can enjoy swimming, fishing, and boating on 8 miles of beaches. A walk on the boardwalk bordering the Jersey Shore is an absolute must. Take a ride to the top of the 140-foot-tall Ferris wheel for breathtaking views that stretch for miles. Video arcades, roller coasters, and water slides will keep the kids entertained. In fact, at Li'l Buc's Bay, adults are only admitted if they are accompanied by children—your kids are bound to get a kick out of that! Stop for a snack at one of the outdoor cafes or fill up on sweet goodies like cotton candy and ice cream. After all, you're on vacation!

Cape May, the nation's oldest seashore resort, is at the southernmost tip of New Jersey. History enthusiasts will enjoy exploring Historic Cold Spring Village, a restored 1870 South Jersey farm village with craft shops and demonstrations. Take the ferry across Delaware Bay, or explore on foot with a guided walking tour of the Historic District or a one-hour Ocean Walk tour of area beaches and marine life. As in Atlantic City and Ocean City, there are plenty of opportunities for swimming, boating, and fishing in the Atlantic or in Delaware Bay. **(Approximately 125 miles)**

A NORTHERN NEW JERSEY LOOP

Begin in Fort Lee, just south of the George Washington Bridge at Fort Lee Historic Park, part of Palisades Interstate Park, off of County Route 505 (Hudson Terrace/Main Street). The park's Visitor Center and Museum focuses on the role of Fort Lee in the American Revolution. See a reconstructed 18th-century soldier hut and campsite, reconstructed gun batteries, and beautiful Manhattan views. Turn left, leaving the Historic Park. Go one block and turn left at the stop sign (Main Street). In about 50 yards, an unmarked parking lot appears on the left. Turn into it and follow the narrow roadway, Henry Hudson Drive, down toward the river. Follow this tree-covered, 25-mph lane to its end (about 25 minutes), admiring the river views. Stops can be made at one of the two marinas along the way , where walking trails can be accessed. Henry Hudson Drive ends at exit 2 of the Palisades Parkway. Take the parkway north. At exit 3, State Line Lookout is set on the highest point on the Palisades Cliffs, commanding views of the Hudson River, Westchester County, and beyond. There's hiking, a snack bar, information center, and gift shop.

Follow the Parkway into New York State and turn onto I-87/287 (NY Thruway) North. At Suffern, follow I-287 South back into New Jersey. At exit 57 (Oakland), follow Skyline Drive, which travels over Ramapo Mountain and offers some fun-to-drive, twisting mountain roads. At the end, turn right onto Country Road 511 North. Expansive, picturesque Wanaque Reservoir is on the left. County 511 leads to Ringwood State Park, site of the historic homes Ringwood Manor and Skylands Manor, and the NJ State Botanical Garden. Leaving the park, return to 511 and follow it into Greenwood Lake. Continue straight onto Warwick Turnpike, through Upper Greenwood Lake, skirting Waywayanda State Park (a good place for hiking, mountain biking, or swimming), and up into New York State again. At Route 94, turn south (left), driving back into New Jersey and through the town of Vernon. You'll pass Mountain Creek Resort, a major ski center in winter and water/adventure sports park in summer, a great place to stop with the kids. Continue on Route 94 to Route 23, turn right (north) and go into the town of Sussex. In summertime, Sussex is the site of the annual Sussex Air Show, one of the best small-airport shows of its kind, and the Sussex Horse & Farm Show/NJ State Fair.

If kids are on the ride, detour to Space Farms Zoo & Museum by following County Route 628 West out of Sussex, turning left onto County Route 519. A private attraction, Space Farms offers a fascinating collection of animals, as well as antique cars and farm equipment. Return to (or continue north from Sussex on) Route 23 into High Point State Park, site of the state's highest elevation. Stop here for a picnic, climb the obelisk that marks the state zenith, swim, or camp. Continue on Route 23 North into Port Jervis, NY, and take US 209 South, which follows the upper Delaware River on the Pennsylvania side. In Milford, PA, take US 206 South. At Tuttles Corner, turn right onto County Route 580, then left onto County Route 615 to Peters Valley, an arts and crafts center where artists can be watched as they work. The annual crafts fair here is one of the state's finest and biggest. Return to US 206 at Tuttles Corner; this is the heart of Stokes State Forest, which holds a variety of hiking opportunities. Follow US 206 south into Augusta. In the summer, the New Jersey Cardinals minor league baseball team plays here. At Ross Corner, leave US 206 for Route 15 South, traveling into Lafayette, known for its large number of antique emporia.

Out of Lafayette, follow Route 94 South back to US 206 South, into Stanhope. Here, Waterloo Village offers a living-history look at an iron works and Morris Canal town (circa 1831), a re-created Lenape Indian Village (circa 1625), and a summer-long series of music concerts. Follow County Route 602 into Hopatcong State Park. Lake Hopatcong is the state's largest lake and offers excellent boating and swimming. Follow the local roads around the lake into the village of Hopatcong for some good lakeside dining. From here, take I-80 East back to Fort Lee/New York City. **(Approximately 110 miles)**

A SOUTHERN NEW JERSEY LOOP

From Philadelphia, follow Route 70 East through the suburbs to the junction of Route 72, and turn right onto 72 East. In a few miles, you'll see the entrance to Lebanon State Forest on the left. Stop at the Visitors Center and pick up a park map, and drive north through the park to Whitesbog Village. This is the heart of the famous Jersey Pinelands, and the village, almost a ghost-town, was once a thriving cranberry/blueberry producing community, the place where the blueberry was first commercially grown and processed. Stroll among the old buildings and talk to the folks who are trying to preserve the place—their office is at the main crossroad. Also in Lebanon State Forest is access to the Batona Trail, south Jersey's longest hiking trail, and a variety of places to hike and swim. Return to Route 72, turn right, and then quickly left onto County 563, a local, two-lane, tree-lined road that meanders south past forest and meadows into Wharton State Forest. Passing through the tiny hamlets of Jenkins and Maxwell, turn right onto County Route 542 westbound at Green Bank. Route 542 parallels the picturesque Mullica River. Follow it to Batsto, and stop for a visit to Historic Batsto Village.

Batsto was an ironworks (supplying munitions for the Revolutionary War and the War of 1812) and a glassmaking center. The restored village includes a mansion and several workers' houses, some of which are occupied today by artisans who are happy to show their work. There's a small nature center, as well as picnic grounds, a nature trail, and plenty of hiking, mountain biking (on some 500 miles of unpaved roads), and canoeing. Canoeing can also be done on the Mullica River from the nearby towns of Sweetwater or Pleasant Mills.

Leave Batsto, heading south on County 623, then turn left onto County 643, following the other side of the Mullica River through Sweetwater. At County 612 (Elwood Weekstown Road), turn right on County 563. Turn right at Alternate 511 (Mill Road), and visit the Renault Winery. Renault is a bit "touristy," but their glass collection and very good restaurant (especially for Sunday brunch) make this stop worthwhile. Return to County 563 and turn left. In

Egg Harbor City County 563 will become NJ 50. Continue south to Tuckahoe, then turn right onto NJ 49 West into Millville, home to Wheaton Village. Wheaton Village pays homage to Millville's storied glassmaking heritage with the Museum of American Glass, one of the world's finest collections. The Village also holds the T. J. Wheaton Glass Factory and Crafts & Traders' Row, where glass- and craft-making demonstrations are staged, the Down Jersey Folklife Center, many stores, a miniature train ride, and a long list of special events. A nice motel is on-site.

After Millville, consider a detour to Bivalve. (If not, continue on Route 49 West to Bridgeton.) The local roads pass through bucolic fields producing fruits, vegetables, and ornamentals, as well as dairy, poultry, and swine farms. Follow County 555 South out of Millville to County 553 East (left turn) at the tiny hamlet of Dividing Creek. In slightly less than 4 miles, turn right onto Shell Road, which becomes Lighthouse Road into Bivalve. This tiny spot was once the capital of the oyster industry, and it displays a series of industrial buildings (some half-ruined, some fully-functioning) that create a compelling atmosphere. Return to County 553, turn right into Port Norris, and visit the restored *A. J. Meerwald,* New Jersey's official "tall ship" and an archetype for the heyday of oystering. This is a great chance to explore this little-known facet of New Jersey's heritage.

Follow County 553 back to the west until it reunites with NJ 49. Turn left. Three miles before entering Bridgeton is Berry's Farm Market (739 Shiloh Pike/NJ 49), one of several terrific farm markets in the area. In town, follow the signs to the Bridgeton Historical District on East Broad Street. This is New Jersey's largest historical district, holding some 2,200 Colonial, Victorian, and Federalist buildings. Downtown has paved-brick walkways, and a scenic promenade fronts the river. A 1,100-acre city park has four museums, a zoo, canoe rentals, swimming, and picnicking. A handful of small restaurants and nice shops can be found here, too. Leave Bridgeton on NJ 49, passing through Salem to Fort Mott State Park, a small park is noteworthy because of its fortifications (built in 1896), good walking trails, and picnic grounds. Return to NJ 49, accessing I-295 back to Philadelphia. **(Approximately 180 miles)**

PHILADELPHIA AND WESTERN NEW JERSEY

This drive meanders up New Jersey's western border, following the scenic Delaware River from the greater Philadelphia area through the timberlands of Delaware Water Gap National Recreation Area.

From Philadelphia, follow Route 130 to Route 73 North. Turn left, and make a right onto County Route 543. From here, the drive becomes leisurely, following local roads for quite a distance. The scenic Delaware River is on your left, and the road passes through the small towns of Palmyra, Riverton, and Riverside. It merges with Route 130, a major thoroughfare just south of Burlington. In Burlington, go left onto High Street, the main intersection, and into the Historic District, which dates back to 1677. (Ben Franklin learned the printing trade here.) Walking tours are offered by the Burlington Center (Phone 609/387-8300), and the Burlington County Historical Society is at 457 High Street. Tours are also offered of the James Fenimore Cooper house. Several fine restaurants are found here, including the Café Gallery, which overlooks the river at 219 High Street.

Leave Burlington northbound on County Route 656, which loops alongside the river and comes back to Route 130. Take 130 North into Trenton, the state capital. Among the worthwhile stops in Trenton are the Old Barracks Museum, an original French and Indian War Barracks; the State House, seat of NJ government; the Contemporary Victorian Museum; the War Memorial Theater; and the New Jersey State Museum and Planetarium. For a good meal and jazz, try Joe's Mill Hill Saloon. Leave Trenton on NJ 29 North. Near the junction of I-95 stands the New Jersey State Police Museum and, soon after in Titusville, Washington Crossing State Park. Here, each Christmas Day, Washington's crossing of the Delaware is re-enacted. The park also contains nice walking paths, river views, picnic areas, and historical information. Also in Titusville is the Howell Living History Farm, (101 Hunter Road, just off NJ 29), a circa 1900 horse-powered farm where visitors join in field, barn, and craft programs on weekends.

Continue on NJ 29 northbound into Lambertville. An exceptionally well-maintained historic town with many Federal-style and Victorian buildings, Lambertville is a treasure trove of antiques shopping, fine dining, bed-and-breakfast lodging, and access to the Delaware & Raritan Canal State Park, where walking, boating, canoeing, biking, fishing, cross-country skiing, and picnicking are possible. NJ 29 continues north along the river. In Stockton, the Stockton Inn on Main Street offers pleasant accommodations. The Prallsville Mills at Delaware & Raritan Canal State Park consist of nine structures dating from 1796 and historical exhibits. The Bull's Island Recreation Area offers 30 miles of hiking trails and superb birdwatching. In Frenchtown, Hunterdon House and The Guesthouse at Frenchtown Brown's Old Homestead are two excellent bed-and-breakfast inns, and Poor Richard's Winery offers tours and tastings.

In Frenchtown, jog left on Ridge Street, then right on Harrison Street, which becomes Milford-Frenchtown Road and eventually Frenchtown Road, leading into Milford, site of The Ship Inn, New Jersey's first brew pub and an excellent spot to stop and dine. Follow County Route 627 out of Milford. In Holland Township, the Vollendam Windmill Museum shows its operational gristmill and replica windmills on summer weekends. In Mount Joy, Route 627 veers inland. Follow it to a merge with Route 173, bearing right, then to the junction of I-78 (exit 6). Take I-78 westbound to exit 4, and follow County Route 687 towards Lower Harmony, switching to County Route 519 northbound in Harmony. Follow Route 519 to Belvidere and visit Four Sisters Winery at Matarazzo Farms, which not only produces some surprisingly nice wines, but has an excellent bakery and stages many special events. Also in town is the Pequest River Book Company, which stocks historic local books, and has an art gallery and café.

Continue on Route 519 north until it meets US 46/I-80 at Columbia. Follow I-80 westbound to exit 1, exiting for a visit to the Delaware Water Gap National Recreation Area, a magnificent outdoor wonderland with swimming, fishing, canoeing, tubing, hiking, camping, biking, cross-country skiing, and all manner of other outdoor activities. The Kittatiny Ranger Station offers information, an audio-visual program, and displays, and rangers present impromptu "Terrace Talks" on weekends. Make the trip to Millbrook Village, located about 12 miles north of I-80 along Old Mine Road (the park's main north-south route), a 19th-century settlement in an ongoing process of restoration. **(Approximately 115 miles)**

NORTHERN SHORE TO ATLANTIC CITY

New Jersey has some 130 miles of coastline. This tour covers the shore from Atlantic Highlands to Atlantic City. While many local roads are noted, the main north-south route is the Garden State Parkway (a toll road). At any given time, the local roads can be abandoned for a quick run down the Parkway to the next desired shore point.

Coming out of the New York metro area, access the Parkway south. Leave the Parkway at exit 117, and follow Route 36 into Atlantic Highlands. Just as the highway crosses the bridge into Highlands, you'll see Gateway National Recreation Area on the left. There's a swimming beach here, but the highlights are Sandy Hook Lighthouse, Fort Hancock (including World War II fortifications remnants), and the Visitor Center, which sponsors nature and maritime history programs.

Route 36 continues south through the beach towns of Sea Bright, Monmouth Beach, and Long Branch, then turns inland. Turn right on Route 35. In about 7 1/2 miles, turn right onto Route 33 and head to Ocean Grove. First founded as a religious retreat, Ocean Grove holds a great collection of Victorian architecture. It's also home to the Ocean Grove Auditorium, an extraordinary all-wood structure with one of the world's great organs. Stop in for a bite to eat—or stay the night—at the Manchester Inn & Secret Garden Restaurant. Follow Route 35 south to County 71 and turn right on Jersey Avenue to get to the heart of Spring Lake, which can also be accessed from the Garden State Parkway via exit 98, once known as the Irish Riviera, now known for its extensive collection of fine bed-and-breakfast inns. This is a great place to spend the night.

The next stop is Point Pleasant Beach, a must for those traveling with small children. It's reached by returning to Route 35 South. Turn right on Route 88, then left on Ocean Avenue. Here Jenkinson's Pavilion Boardwalk & Amusement Park is a shore-side heaven for little ones. It has a terrific small aquarium, and its beach, boardwalk, rides, fun house, arcades, restaurants, shops, and miniature golf are all family-oriented.

Moving south, Ocean Avenue becomes Route 35, and travels through a number of shore towns, most of which attract second-home owners or summer-home renters. In about 7 miles, the highway becomes Central Avenue, the main street in Seaside Heights/Seaside Park, a mecca for teens and young adults, filled with amusements, a long boardwalk, and much noise and action. (MTV set up its summer beach house here a few years back.) To the south, Central Avenue becomes the entryway to Island Beach State Park, one of the state's most pristine environments, ideal for those who want the beach without the amusements. The park also has nature trails and hosts excellent nature programs.

Returning north out of the park and into Seaside Heights, turn left onto Route 37, and enter the Garden State Parkway at exit 82. At exit 63, leave the Parkway onto Route 72 East, which leads to Long Beach Island, a collection of small towns that are very popular with vacationers. Turn right onto Route 9 southbound and in about 5 miles, after passing through several towns, enter Tuckerton, site of the Barnegat Bay Decoy and Baymen's Museum, an excellent small museum that preserves maritime history, heritage, and the lifestyle of the Jersey shore and its baymen. Drive south on Route 9 for 10 miles or so into Oceanville. Following the signs, turn left on East Great Creek Road and right onto Lily Lake Road to reach The Noyes Museum of Art, a surprisingly fine facility set almost literally in the middle of nowhere. From the museum, return to East Great Creek Road, turn right, and follow the signs to the Forsythe Wildlife Refuge, a 42,000-acre tract with a beautiful 8-mile wildlife auto trail that reveals magnificent wetlands and ocean views, and has terrific bird-watching.

Return to Route 9 South. At the junction of Route 30 turn left (east) to go into Atlantic City. Famous for its casinos, "AC" is not everyone's cup of tea, but it does offer an excellent race track, a good (albeit small) historical museum, minor league baseball, the Ocean Life Center for Marine Education, the world's most famous boardwalk, and two of the region's best golf courses—Blue Heron Pines Golf Club and the Seaview Marriott Resort. **(Approximately 160 miles)**

Allaire State Park (E-5)

See also Asbury Park, Freehold

What to See and Do

Allaire State Park. *(On County 524 in Howell and Wall Townships) Phone 732/938-2371.* Allaire State Park has more than 3,000 acres and offers a fishing pond for children under 14; multiuse trails, picnic facilities, playground, camping (dump station, summer), and the opportunity to visit a historic 19th-century village (see below). Park (daily). Standard fees when village buildings are open. Contact PO Box 220, Farmingdale 07727; 732/938-2371. Parking fee (Memorial Day-Labor Day, weekends) $2-$5 **$$**

Historic Allaire Village. *524 Allaire Rd. Phone 732/938-2253.* In 1822, James Allaire bought this site as a source of bog ore for his ironworks. The furnace also produced cast-iron items such as hollow-ware pots and kettles, stoves, sadirons, and pipes for New York City's waterworks. Today, visitors can explore the bakery, general store, blacksmith and carpentry shops, worker's houses, the community church, and other buildings still much as they were in 1836. Village grounds and Center (all year); village buildings (Memorial Day-Labor Day, Wed-Sun); special events (Feb-Dec). **FREE**

> **Train Rides.** *Allaire State Rd. Phone 732/938-5524.* Narrow-gauge steam and diesel locomotive rides (Jul-Aug, daily; Mid-Apr-June, Sept-Oct, daily). **$$**

Asbury Park (E-5)

Settled 1871 **Pop** 16,930 **Elev** 21 ft **Area code** 732 **Zip** 07712

Information Greater Asbury Park Chamber of Commerce, 308 Main St, PO Box 649; 732/775-7676

Web www.asburyparkchamber.com

This popular shore resort was bought in 1871 by New York brush manufacturer James A. Bradley and named for Francis Asbury, first American Bishop of the Methodist Episcopal Church. Bradley established a town for temperance advocates and good neighbors. The beach and the three lakes proved so attractive that, by 1874, Asbury Park had grown into a borough, and by 1897, a city. It is the home of the famous boardwalk, Convention Hall, and the Paramount Theatre. In September 1934, the SS *Morro Castle* was grounded off this beach and burned with a loss of 122 lives. Asbury Park became the birthplace of a favorite sweet when a local confectioner introduced "saltwater

taffy" and watched the sales curve rise with the tide. Today, this is a popular resort area for swimming and fishing.

What to See and Do

Stephen Crane House. *508 4th Ave. Phone 732/988-2260.* Early home of the author of *The Red Badge of Courage* contains photos, drawings, and other artifacts. Tours (by appointment). **FREE**

The Stone Pony. *913 Ocean Ave. Phone 732/502-0600.* Legendary nightclub known for unexpected visits from rock musician Bruce Springsteen and others. Includes the Asbury Park Gallery, with a collection of photographs and other memorabilia from the resort town's glory days. (Daily)

Special Events

Concerts at the Great Auditorium. *54 Pitman Ave, Ocean Grove (07756). Phone 732/988-0645.* Pipe organ recitals. Sat, June-Sept.

Horse racing. Monmouth Park. *175 Oceanport Ave in Oceanport via NJ 35 N to NJ 36; or via Garden State Pkwy exit 105, then E on NJ 36. Phone 732/222-5100.* Thoroughbred racing. Wed-Sun, Memorial Day-Labor Day.

Jazz Fest. *1 Municipal Plaza (07712). Phone 732/775-7676 or 732/502-5728.* July.

Metro Lyric Opera Series. *At the Paramount Theatre on the Boardwalk.* Sat evenings, July-Aug.

Ocean Grove House Tour. *50 Pitman Ave, Ocean Grove (07756). Phone 732/774-1869.* Tour of Victorian cottages. July.

Atlantic City (I-4)

See also Ocean City

Settled 1854 **Pop** 40,517 **Elev** 8 ft **Area code** 609

Information Atlantic City Convention & Visitors Authority, 2314 Pacific Ave, 08401; 609/449-7147, 888/ACVISIT, or 800/BOARDWALK

Web www.atlanticcitynj.com

Honeymooners, conventioneers, Miss America, and some 37 million annual visitors have made Atlantic City the best-known New Jersey beach resort. Built on Absecon Island, the curve of the coast shields it from battering northeastern storms while the nearby Gulf Stream warms its waters, helping to make it a year-round resort. A 60-foot-wide boardwalk extends along 5 miles of beaches. Hand-pushed wicker rolling chairs take visitors up and down the Boardwalk. Absecon Lighthouse ("Old Ab"), a well-known landmark, was first lit in 1857 and now stands in an uptown city park.

City Fun Fact—Atlantic City

Atlantic City is where the street names came from for the game of Monopoly.

What to See and Do

Absecon Lighthouse. *Pacific and Vermont aves. Phone 609/449-1360.* Climb the 228 steps to the top of this 1857 lighthouse, designed by Civil War general George Gordon Meade. Tallest lighthouse in New Jersey, third-tallest in US. (July-Aug, daily; Sept-June, Thurs-Mon; closed holidays) **$$**

Atlantic City Boardwalk Hall. *1 Ocean Way (08401). Phone 609/348-7000.* Seats 13,800; special events, concerts, boxing, ice shows, sports events; site of the annual Miss America Pageant.

Edwin B. Forsythe National Wildlife Refuge, Brigantine Division. *9 miles N on US 9. Contact PO Box 72, Great Creek Rd, Oceanville 08231. Phone 609/652-1665.* Wildlife drive; interpretive nature trails (daily). Over the years, more than 200 species of birds have been observed at this 45,000-acre refuge. Public-use area has an 8-mile wildlife drive through diversified wetlands and uplands habitat; most popular in the spring and fall, during the course of the waterbird migration, and at sunset, when the birds roost for the evening. Refuge headquarters (Mon-Fri). **$$**

Fishing. *Contact Atlantic City Party and Charter Boat Association.* Surf and deep-sea fishing. License may be required, check locally. Charter boats (Mar-Nov). Many tournaments are scheduled.

Garden Pier. *Boardwalk and New Jersey Ave. Phone 609/347-5837.* The Atlantic City Art Center and Atlantic City Historical Museum are located here. (Daily) **FREE**

Historic Gardner's Basin. *800 New Hampshire Ave, at N end of city. Phone 609/348-2880.* An 8-acre, sea-oriented park featuring the working lobstermen; Ocean Life Center, eight tanks totalling 29,800 gallons of aquariums, exhibiting more than 100 varieties of fish and marine animals, 10 exhibits featuring themes on the marine and maritime environment. Picnicking. (Daily; closed Jan 1, Thanksgiving, Dec 25)

Historic Town of Smithville and the Village Greene at Smithville. *7 miles W on US 30 to Absecon, then 6 miles N on US 9, at Moss Mill Rd. Phone 609/652-7777 or 609/652-0440.* (1787) Restored 18th-century village with specialty shops and restaurants. Also carousel, train ride, and paddle boats. Village. Special events throughout the year. (daily).

Lucy, the Margate Elephant. *Decateur and Atlantic Ave (08402). S via Atlantic Ave in Margate. Phone 609/823-6473.* The only elephant in the world you can walk through and come out alive. Guided tour and exhibit inside this six-story elephant-shaped building. Built in 1881; spiral stairs in Lucy's legs lead to main hall and observation area on her back. Gift shop. (Mid-June-Labor Day, daily; Apr-mid-June and Sept-Oct, Sat and Sun only) **$$**

Marine Mammal Stranding Center & Museum. *3625 Atlantic-Brigantine Blvd. Over bridge and 2 miles N. Phone 609/266-0538.* One of few marine mammal rescue and rehabilitation centers in US. Injured dolphins, turtles, and other marine animals are brought to center for treatment. Museum offers exhibits on mammal species; recuperating animals can be viewed at center. Dolphin and whale-watch trips available (fee; reservations required). (Mid-June-Labor Day, Tues-Sun, Labor Day-Dec 25, weekends; Dec 25-May, call for schedule) **DONATION**

Noyes Museum. *12 miles NW via US 9, on Lily Lake Rd in Oceanville. Phone 609/652-8848.* Rotating and permanent exhibits of American art; collection of working bird decoys. (Tues-Sun; closed holidays). **$$**

Recreation areas. Beach (Memorial Day-mid-Sept; free), surfing at special areas (daily), boating; bicycling and rolling chairs on Boardwalk (daily), golf, tennis.

Renault Winery. *72 N Bremen Ave (08215). 16 miles W on US 30 in Egg Harbor City. Phone 609/965-2111.* Guided tour (approximately 45 minutes) including wine-aging cellars; press room; antique wine-making equipment; free wine tasting (daily). Restaurants. **$**

The Shops on Ocean One. *Boardwalk at Arkansas Ave. Phone 609/347-8082.* A 900-foot, three-deck shopping pier houses shops, food court, and restaurants. (Daily) **FREE**

Storybook Land. *10 miles W via US 40, 322. Phone 609/641-7847.* More than 50 storybook buildings and displays depicting children's stories; live animals; rides; picnic area, concession. (May-mid-Sept, daily; Mar-Apr and mid-Sept-Thanksgiving, Sat and Sun only) Christmas Fantasy with Lights and visiting with Mr. and Mrs. Santa (Thanksgiving-Dec 30, nightly). Admission includes attractions and unlimited rides. **$$$**

Special Events

Atlantic City Marathon. *Phone 609/601-1RUN.* Mid-Oct.

LPGA Atlantic City Classic. *401 S New York Rd (08201). Phone 609/927-7888.* Late June.

Miss America Pageant. *Atlantic City Boardwalk Hall. 2301 Boardwalk (08401).* Usually first or second weekend after Labor Day.

Motels/Motor Lodges

★ ★ **CLARION HOTEL.** *8029 Black Horse Pike (08232). Phone 609/641-3546; toll-free 800/999-9466; fax 609/641-9740. www.clarionhotel.com.* 110 rooms, 2 story. July-mid-Sept: S, D $85-$125; each additional $10; under 17 free; lower rates rest of year. Check-out 11 am. TV; cable (premium), VCR available. Coin laundry. Restaurant 7 am-10 pm. Service bar. Supervised children's activities (June-Aug) ages 8-15. Exercise room, sauna. Pool, wading pool. Indoor and outdoor tennis, pro. Airport transportation. Meeting rooms. Business services. On bay. Cr cds: A, C, D, DS, JCB, MC, V.

★ **COMFORT INN.** *539 E Absecon Blvd (08201). Phone 609/641-7272; toll-free 800/233-4656; fax 609/646-3286. www.comfortinn.com.* 205 rooms, 7 story. S, D $79-$145; each additional $10; under 18 free. Crib available. Complimentary continental breakfast. Check-out noon. TV; cable (premium). Meeting rooms. Business services. Cr cds: A, C, D, DS, MC, V.

★ **DAYS INN.** *6708 Tilton Rd, Egg Harbor City (08234). Phone 609/641-4500; toll-free 800/329-7466; fax 609/645-8295. www.daysinn.com.* 117 rooms, 5 story. July-mid-Sept: S, D $69-$169; each additional $5; suites $89-$189; kitchen unit $99-$200; under 13 free; family rates; package plans; holidays (2-day minimum); higher rates special events; lower rates rest of year. Crib free. TV; cable (premium), VCR available. Complimentary continental breakfast. Restaurant adjacent 7 am-midnight. Check-out 11 am. Meeting rooms. Business services available. In-room modem link. Coin laundry. Exercise equipment. Pool; lifeguard. Playground. Game room. Some refrigerators, microwaves. Picnic tables. Cr cds: A, C, D, DS, JCB, MC, V.

★ **FAIRFIELD INN.** *405 E Absecon Blvd, Absecon (08201). Phone 609/646-5000; toll-free 800/228-2800; fax 609/383-8744. www.fairfieldinn.com.* 200 rooms, 6 story. S $50-$70; D $110-$150; each additional $10; suites $75-$199; under 18 free. Crib free. Complimentary continental breakfast. Check-out 11 am. TV; cable (premium). In-room modem link. Pool. Meeting rooms. Business services. Cr cds: A, C, D, DS, ER, JCB, MC, V.

★ **HAMPTON INN.** *240 E White Horse Pike (08201). Phone 609/652-2500; toll-free 800/426-7866; fax 609/652-2212. www.hamptoninn.com.* 129 rooms, 4 story. Memorial Day-Labor Day: S, D $65-$109; suites $92-$146; under 18 free; higher rates holidays; lower rates rest of year. Crib free. Complimentary continental breakfast.

Check-out 11 am. TV; cable (premium), VCR available. In-room modem link. Coin laundry. Restaurant adjacent open 24 hours. Pool, whirlpool, lifeguard. Free airport transportation. Meeting rooms. Business services. Cr cds: A, C, D, DS, MC, V.

★ **HAMPTON INN.** *7079 Black Horse Pike (08232). Phone 609/484-1900; toll-free 800/426-7866; fax 609/383-0731. www.hamptoninn.com.* 143 rooms, 6 story. June-Sept: S, D $99; family rates; higher rates: holidays (2-day minimum). Crib free. Complimentary continental breakfast. Check-out 11 am. TV; cable (premium). Meeting room. Business services. Cr cds: A, C, D, DS, MC, V.

★ ★ **HOLIDAY INN.** *111 S Chelsea Ave (08401). Phone 609/348-2200; toll-free 800/548-3030; fax 609/345-5110. www.holidayinnac.com.* 220 rooms, 21 story. Mid-June-Labor Day: S, D $98-$179; each additional $15; under 19 free; lower rates rest of year. Crib available. Check-out 11 am. TV; cable (premium). In-room modem link. Restaurant 7 am-10 pm. Bar 11:30-2 am. Health club privileges. Pool, poolside service. Meeting rooms. Business services. On ocean. Cr cds: A, C, D, DS, MC, V.

★ **SUPER 8.** *229 E US 30; 633 White Horse Pike, Absecon (08201). Phone 609/652-2477; fax 609/748-0666. www.super8.com.* 58 rooms, 2 story. July 4-Aug: S, D $55-$125; suites $80-$150; under 12 free; lower rates rest of year. TV; cable (premium). Restaurant opposite open 24 hours. Check-out noon. Business services available. Refrigerators available. Cr cds: A, C, D, DS, MC, V.

Hotel

★ ★ ★ **SHERATON ATLANTIC CITY CONVENTION.** *2 Miss America Way (08401). Phone 609/344-3535.* 502 rooms, 12 story. S, D $159-$199; suites $250-$450; under 17 free; weekend rates. Crib free. Check-out noon. TV; cable (premium), VCR available. In-room modem link. Refrigerators available. Laundry service. Restaurant 6:30 am-midnight. Bar 11 am-midnight. Exercise equipment. Indoor pool, whirlpool. Meeting rooms. Business center. Concierge. Gift shop. Casino. Cr cds: A, D, DS, MC, V.

Resorts

★ ★ ★ **MARRIOTT SEAVIEW RESORT AND SPA.** *401 S New York Rd, Absecon (08201). Phone 609/652-1800; toll-free 800/932-8000; fax 609/652-2307. www.marriott.com.* A golfer's dream, this hotel is located on 650 acres near Reeds Bay and offers two 18-hole championship golf courses. Other amenities include a full spa nearby, health club, and tennis courts. There are other attractions nearby. 297 rooms; 3 story. May-Nov: S, D $199-$275; suites $250-$700; under 18 free; golf, package plans; lower rates rest of year. Crib free. TV; cable (premium), VCR available (free movies). Two pools, one indoor; whirlpool, poolside service, lifeguard. Dining room 6:30 am-10 pm. Room service. Box lunches. Snack bar. Bar noon-2 am. Check-out 12:30 pm, check-in 4 pm. Coin laundry. Convention facilities. Business center. In-room modem link. Gift shop. Sports director. 8 tennis courts, 4 lighted, pro. 9-hole putting green; golf school. Driving ranges. Recreation room. Game room. Exercise equipment; sauna. Basketball. Volleyball. Minibars; refrigerator, fireplace in suites. Located on 670-acre estate. Cr cds: A, C, D, DS, ER, JCB, MC, V.

★ ★ ★ **RESORTS CASINO HOTEL.** *1133 Boardwalk (08401). Phone 609/344-6000; toll-free 800/336-6378; fax 609/340-7684. www.resortsac.com.* The rooms in this oceanfront casino property have a summery décor with bright plaid comforters and white wood furniture. Fine dining options are numerous highlighting Asian, Italian, and French cuisines, and the Le Palais' Sunday champagne brunch is worth a visit. 662 rooms, 15 story. July-Labor Day: S, D $70-$225; each additional $10; lower rates rest of year. Crib free. TV; cable. Indoor/outdoor pool; whirlpool. Restaurants open 24 hours. Bars open 24 hours. Check-out noon. Convention facilities. Business services available. In-room modem link. Concierge. Shopping arcade. Valet parking. Airport transportation. Exercise equipment; steam rm, sauna. Game room. Bathroom phones. Some balconies. First casino in Atlantic City. Cr cds: A, C, D, DS, MC, V.

Restaurants

★ ★ ★ **BRIGHTON STEAKHOUSE.** *Indiana Ave at Brighton Park (08401). Phone 609/441-4300. www.acsands.com.* In addition to thick cuts of steak, veal, and lamb as well as the usual seafood, this surf 'n' turf spot in the Sands casino also serves up live piano music. American menu. Specialties: chateaubriand, pepper-seared tuna, Brighton seafood harvest. Hours: 5:30-10 pm, closed Tues, Wed. A la carte entrées: dinner $20-$60. Bar noon-3:30 am. Wine list. Reservations required. Tropical décor. Cr cds: A, DS, MC, V.

★ **CAPTAIN YOUNG'S SEAFOOD EMPORIUM.** *2801 Atlantic Ave (08401). Phone 609/344-2001.* Hours: 11:30 am-9 pm; Sat to 10 pm. Closed Thanksgiving, Dec 25.

Lunch $6.25-$9.95, dinner $13.95-$19.95. Bar. Cr cds: A, C, D, DS, MC, V.

★ ★ **CHEF VOLA'S.** *111 S Albion Place (08401). Phone 609/345-2022; fax 609/266-2649.* Italian menu. Closed Mon; Thanksgiving, Dec 24, 25. Dinner. Reservations required. Photographs of celebrities. **$$**

★ ★ **DOCK'S OYSTER HOUSE.** *2405 Atlantic Ave (08401). Phone 609/345-0092; fax 609/345-7893. www.shorecast.com.* Dinner. Bar. Children's menu. Casual atmosphere in family-owned restaurant since 1897. Reservations accepted. Cr cds: A, D, DS, MC, V. **$$**

★ **GRABELS RESTAURANT LOUNGE.** *3901 Atlantic Ave (08401). Phone 609/344-9263; fax 609/344-6433. www.grabels.com.* Continental menu. Closed Dec 24. Dinner. Bar. Piano Wed-Sun. Children's menu. Casual attire. Cr cds: A, MC, V. **$**

★ **IRISH PUB AND INN.** *St. James Pl and Boardwalk (08401). Phone 609/344-9063; fax 606/344-7225. www.theirishpub.com.* American, Irish menu. Irish balladeer Thurs-Sun (summer). Informal, Irish pub atmosphere. Hours: Open 24 hours. Lunch $1.95-$3.95, dinner $2.95-$6.25. Bar. Patio seating.

★ ★ **OLD WATERWAY INN.** *1660 W Riverside Dr (08401). Phone 609/347-1793; fax 609/347-0075. www.oldwaterwayinn.com.* Hours: 5-11 pm. Closed Mon, Tues Oct-Apr. Reservations accepted. Bar. Dinner $15-$24. Children's menu. Specializes in fresh seafood and Cajun specialities. Own pasta. Outdoor seating. Nautical décor. On waterfront; view of skyline. Cr cds: A, D, MC, V.

★ ★ **SCANNICCHIO'S.** *119 S California Ave (08401). Phone 609/348-6378; fax 609/345-5711.* Italian menu. Specializes in veal, fresh seafood. Hours: 4 pm-midnight. Closed most major holidays. A la carte entrées: dinner $12.95-$21.95. Bar. Reservations required. Cr cds: A, D, MC, V.

★ ★ **STEVE AND COOKIE'S BY THE BAY.** *9700 Amherst Ave, Margate (08402). Phone 609/823-1163; fax 609/823-9571. www.steveandcookies.com.* Contemporary American menu. Hours: 5-10 pm; Sat to 11 pm; Sat, Sun 10 am-3 pm. Closed Dec 24, Dec 25. Dinner $12-$27. Bar. Live music. Children's menu. Casual attire. Cr cds: A, D, DS, MC, V.

Basking Ridge

See also Bernardsville

Motel/Motor Lodge

★ ★ **COURTYARD BY MARRIOTT.** *595 Martinsville Rd (07920). Phone 908/542-0300; fax 908/542-0400. www.courtyard.com.* Designed by business travelers, this property is conveniently located and guest rooms feature a large work desk, two dual-line phones, and in-room coffee. 227 rooms, 8 suites, 4 story. S, D $69-$164, suites $149-$189. Check-out noon, check-in 3 pm. TV; cable (premium). In-room modem link. Coin laundry, laundry valet. Restaurant, bar. Room service. Exercise room. Indoor pool. Golf nearby. Cr cds: A, C, D, DS, MC, V.

⊠🛉⊠

Batsto

See also Atlantic City

Area code 609 **Zip** 08037

The Batsto Iron Works, established in 1766, made munitions for the Revolutionary Army from the bog iron ore found nearby. Its furnaces shut down for the last time in 1848. Eighteen years later, Joseph Wharton, whose immense estate totaled nearly 100,000 acres, bought the land. In 1954, the state of New Jersey bought nearly 150 square miles of land in this area, including the entire Wharton tract, for a state forest.

What to See and Do

Atsion Recreation Area. *744 US 206 (08088). Phone 609/268-0444.* Swimming, canoeing; picnicking, camping. Standard fees.

Batsto State Historic Site. *4110 Nesco Rd (main office) (08037). Phone 609/561-3262.* Restored early 19th-century iron and glassmaking community. General store, gristmill, blacksmith shop, wheelwright shop, sawmill, workers' houses, and visitor center are open seasonally to the public. Guided tours of the mansion (fee). Parking fee (Memorial Day-Labor Day, weekends and holidays). **$$$**

Wharton State Forest. *Along US 206 near Atsion. Crossed by NJ 542, 563. Phone 609/561-3262.* Streams wind through 110,000 acres of wilderness. Swimming, fishing, canoeing; limited picnicking, tent and trailer sites, cabins. Standard fees.

Bernardsville (C-4)

See also Morristown

Pop 7,345 **Elev** 400 ft **Area code** 908 **Zip** 07924

What to See and Do

Great Swamp National Wildlife Refuge. *152 Pleasant Plains Rd (07920). 1 mile N on US 202, W on N Maple Ave, 2 miles E on Madisonville Rd, 1 1/2 miles NE on Lee's Hill Rd, then right on Long Hill Rd. Phone 973/425-1222.* Nature trails, boardwalk. Observation blind; wilderness area. More than 200 species of birds, fish, reptiles, frogs, ducks, geese, and fox may be seen in this 7,300-acre refuge. Headquarters (Mon-Fri; closed holidays). Trails and information booth (daily, dawn-dusk). **FREE**

Hotel

★ ★ ★ **SOMERSET HILLS HOTEL.** *200 Liberty Corner Rd, Warren (07059). Phone 908/647-6700; fax 908/647-8053. www.shh.com.* Visitors will find this hotel combines the service of a country inn with the facilities, entertainment, and accommodation expected from a large hotel. It is found in the Watchung Mountains. 111 units, 4 story. S $170; D $180; each additional $10; suites $250-$310; kitchens $145-$185. Crib free. Pet accepted. TV; cable (premium). Pool; poolside service. Restaurant 6:30 am-11 pm. Bar 11:30-2 am. Check-out noon. Meeting rooms. Business center. In-room modem link. Concierge. Gift shop. Tennis privileges. 18-hole golf privileges, pro, putting green, driving range. Exercise equipment. Microwaves available. Nestled in the Watchung Mountains near the crossroads of historical Liberty Corner. Cr cds: A, C, D, MC, V.

ᴅ🐾🛉🎿⛸🏌⊠🛉⊠🛉

B&B/Small Inn

★ ★ ★ **BERNARDS INN.** *27 Mine Brook Rd (07924). Phone 908/766-0002; toll-free 888/766-0002; fax 908/766-4604. www.bernardsinn.com.* This historic property, located in quaint Bernardsville, is a favored retreat for locals looking for a night out. Guest rooms are individually decorated with antiques and reproductions, and are quite roomy. The restaurant serves sophisticated American food in an upscale, clubby setting. 20 rooms, 4 suites, 5 story. S, D $180; suites $190-$215. Crib $10. Complimentary continental breakfast. Check-out 11 am, check-in 4 pm. TV; cable (premium). In-room modem link. Bar. Room service. Health club privileges. Massage. Business services. Luggage handling. Concierge. Cr cds: A, C, D, MC, V.

🛉⊠

Restaurant

★ ★ ★ **THE BERNARDS INN.** *27 Mine Brook Rd (07924). Phone 908/766-0002; fax 908/766-4604. www.bernardsinn.com.* This traditional dining room features chef Edward Stone's creative Contemporary American menu in a rustic, intimate setting that's just a short drive from New York City. Few others can match the graceful, elegant service (or the 8,000-bottle wine cellar). Hours: 11:30 am-3 pm, 5:30-10 pm; Fri, Sat to 11 pm. Closed Sun; some major holidays. Lunch $9-$13, dinner $24-$34. Bar. Jacket (dinner). Reservations accepted; required Fri, Sat. Outdoor seating. Cr cds: A, D, MC, V.

D

Bordentown (F-3)

See also Trenton

Settled 1682 **Pop** 3,969 **Elev** 72 ft **Area code** 609 **Zip** 08505

Information Historical Society Visitors Center, Old City Hall, 13 Crosswicks St, PO Box 182; 609/298-1740

A long and honorable history has left an indelible stamp on this town. Bordentown was once a busy shipping center and a key stop on the Delaware and Raritan Canal. In January 1778, Bordentown citizens filled numerous kegs with gunpowder and sent them down the Delaware River to Philadelphia hoping to blow up the British fleet stationed there. But the plan was discovered, and British troops intercepted the kegs and discharged them. In 1816, Joseph Bonaparte, exiled king of Spain and brother of Napoleon, bought 1,500 acres and settled here.

What to See and Do

Clara Barton Schoolhouse. *142 Crosswicks St. Phone 609/298-0676.* This building was in use as a school in Revolutionary days. In 1851, Clara Barton, founder of the American Red Cross, established one of the first free public schools in the country in this building. (By appointment) **FREE**

Motel/Motor Lodge

★ **DAYS INN.** *1073 Rte 206 (08505). Phone 609/298-6100; toll-free 800/329-7466; fax 609/298-7509. www.daysinn.com.* 131 rooms, 2 story. S, D $95-$105; each additional $10; under 12 free. Crib free. Pet accepted. Check-out 11 am. TV; cable. Coin laundry. Restaurant 6:30-10 am, 5-9 pm. Bar 5 pm-1:30 am. Room service. Pool; lifeguard. Meeting rooms. Business services. Sundries. Cr cds: A, C, D, DS, JCB, MC, V.

D 🐾 🏊 ⛷

Branchville (B-3)

See also Vernon

Pop 845 **Elev** 529 ft **Area code** 201 **Zip** 07826

Information Sussex County Chamber of Commerce, 120 Hampton House Rd, Newton 07860; 201/579-1811

Web www.sussexcountychamber.org

This town in Sussex County is near many attractions in New Jersey's scenic northwest corner.

What to See and Do

Peters Valley. *8 miles NW via US 206, County 560, then S on County 615. Phone 973/948-5200.* Historic buildings in the Delaware Water Gap National Recreation Area (see DELAWARE WATER GAP, PA) serve as residences and studios for professional craftspeople and summer crafts workshops in blacksmithing, ceramics, fine metals, photography, fibers, and woodworking. Contemporary craft store (Seasonal hours). Studios (June-Aug, Sat-Sun afternoons). **FREE**

Space Farms Zoo & Museum. *218 Rte 519. 6 miles N on County 519, in Beamerville. Phone 973/875-5800 or 973/875-3223.* Collection of more than 500 wild animals; early American museum in main building, additional museums on grounds; picnic area, concession; gift shop. Zoo and museum (Apr-Oct). **$$$**

Stokes State Forest. *4 miles N on US 206. Phone 973/948-3820.* Located on the Kittatinny Ridge, this 15,482-acre forest includes some of the finest mountain country in New Jersey. Swimming, fishing; hunting, picnicking, camping. Scenic views from Sunrise Mountain; Tillman Ravine, a natural gorge, is in the southern corner of the park. Standard fees.

Swartswood State Park. *1091 County Rd 619 (07877). 2 miles S on County 519, then continue 2 miles on County 627, left 3 miles on County 521 to Swartswood, left 1 mile on County 622, right on County 619, 1/2 mile to park entrance. Phone 973/383-5230.* A 1,470-acre park on Swartswood Lake. Swimming (Memorial Day-Labor Day), bathhouse, fishing, boating (rentals, Memorial Day-Labor Day); hunting, picnicking, concession, camping. Standard fees.

Special Event

Peters Valley Craft Fair. *Peters Valley.* More than 150 juried exhibitors; demonstrations, music, food. Last weekend in Sept.

Bridgeton (H-2)

See also Millville

Settled 1686 **Pop** 22,771 **Elev** 40 ft **Area code** 856
Zip 08302

Information Bridgeton-Cumberland Tourist Association,
50 E Broad St; 856/451-4802 or 800/319-3379

The city of Bridgeton has been recognized as New Jersey's
largest historic district, with more than 2,200 registered
historical landmarks. There are many styles of architecture
here, some of which date back nearly 300 years.

What to See and Do

City Park. *W Commerce St and Mayor Aitken Dr off NJ
49. Phone 856/451-9208.* A 1,100-acre wooded area with
swimming (protected beaches, Memorial Day-Labor
Day), fishing, boating (floating dock), canoeing. Picnic
grounds, recreation center; zoo. (Daily) Also here is

New Sweden Farmstead Museum. *Phone 856/455-
3230.* Reconstruction of first permanent European
settlement in Delaware Valley. Seven log buildings
including smokehouse/sauna; horse barn, cow and
goat barn, threshing barn; storage house; blacksmith
shop; family residence with period furnishings.
Costumed guides. (May-Labor Day, Wed-Sat, also Sun
afternoons) **$$**

George J. Woodruff Museum of Indian Artifacts.
*Bridgeton Free Public Library, 150 E Commerce St.
Phone 856/451-2620.* Approximately 20,000 local Native
American artifacts, some up to 10,000 years old; clay
pots, pipes, implements. (Mon-Fri afternoons; also by
appointment; closed holidays) **FREE**

Gibbon House. *7 miles SW in Greenwich, on Ye Greate
St. Phone 856/455-4055 or 856/451-8454.* (1730) Site of
New Jersey's only 18th-century tea burning party; genea-
logical research library (Mar-Dec, Wed and Sun). Events
scheduled throughout year. Gibbon House (early Apr-late
Nov, Tues-Sat; closed Sun in July, Aug); tours (weekdays).
DONATION

Old Broad Street Church. *W Broad St and West Ave.*
(1792) Outstanding example of Georgian architecture,
with Palladian window, high-backed wooden pews, wine
glass pulpit, brick-paved aisles, and brass lamps that once
held whale oil.

Parvin State Park. *701 Almond Rd (08318). 7 miles NE off
NJ 77, near Centerton. Phone 856/358-8616.* This 1,125-
acre park offers swimming, bathhouse, fishing, boating,
canoeing (rentals); picnicking, concessions, playgrounds,
camping (dump station), cabins. Standard fees.

Special Event

Concerts. *Riverfront. Phone 856/451-9208.* Performances
by ragtime, military, country and western bands, and oth-
ers. Sun nights. Nine weeks in July-Aug.

Bridgewater (D-4)

See also Somerville

Hotel

★ ★ **MARRIOTT BRIDGEWATER.** *700 Commons
Way. Phone 908/927-9300; fax 908/927-0033. www.
marriott.com.* Relax at the indoor pool or conduct busi-
ness in one of the well-appointed guest rooms; this hotel
caters to both vacationers and business travelers alike.
347 rooms, 8 story, 3 suites. S, D $89-$249. Crib available.
Complimentary coffee in rooms. Check-out noon, check-
in 3 pm. TV; cable (premium). In-room modem link.
Valet services, coin laundry. Restaurant. Room service.
Exercise room. Indoor pool, whirlpool. Meeting rooms.
Business center. Concierge. Gift shop. Cr cds: A, C, D, DS,
MC, V.

Burlington (F-3)

See also Bordentown; Mount Holly, Philadelphia, PA

Settled 1677 **Pop** 9,736 **Elev** 13 ft **Area code** 609, 856
Zip 08016

Information Burlington County Chamber of Commerce,
900 Briggs Rd, Mount Laurel, 08054; 856/439-2520

In 1774, Burlington, along with New York, Philadelphia,
and Boston, was a thriving port. A Quaker settlement, it
was one of the first to provide public education. A 1682
Act of Assembly gave Matinicunk (now Burlington) Island
in the Delaware River to the town with the stipulation that
the revenue it generated would be used for public schools;
that act is still upheld. Burlington was the capital of West
Jersey; the legislature met here, and in the East Jersey capi-
tal of Perth Amboy, from 1681 until after the Revolution.
In 1776, the Provincial Congress adopted the state consti-
tution here.

What to See and Do

Burlington County Historical Society. *457 High St. Phone
609/386-4773.* The society maintains **D. B. Pugh Library,**
in the Corson-Poley Center, genealogical and historical
holdings; Revolutionary War exhibit; **James Fenimore
Cooper House** (circa 1780), birthplace of the famous
author; **Bard-How House** (circa 1740) with period

furnishings; **Captain James Lawrence House,** birthplace of the commander of the *Chesapeake* during the War of 1812 and speaker of the immortal words "Don't give up the ship," contains 1812 objects and costume display. Tour of historic houses (Tues-Sun). **$$**

Friends Meeting House. *340 High St (08016). Phone 609/ 387-3875.* (1784) (By appointment) **$$**

Historic tours. *Leave foot of High St. Phone 609/386-3993.* Guided walking tours of 33 historic sites (1685-1829), eight of which are open to the public. (Daily; no tours Easter, Dec 25) **$$**

Old St. Mary's Church. *W Broad and Wood sts. Phone 609/ 386-0902.* (1703) The oldest Episcopal Church building in the state. (By appointment)

Thomas Revell House. *213 Wood St. Phone 609/386-3993.* (1685) The oldest building in Burlington County. Included in Burlington County Historical Society home tour (see). (By appointment and during Wood Street Fair; see SPECIAL EVENT) **FREE**

Special Event

Wood Street Fair. Re-creation of colonial fair; crafts, antique exhibits; food; entertainment. First Sat after Labor Day.

Restaurant

★ ★ ★ **CAFE GALLERY.** *219 High St (08016). Phone 609/386-6150. www.cafegalleryburlington.com.* Continental menu. Specialties: fresh seafood. Hours: 11:30 am-10 pm; Fri, Sat to 11 pm; Sun brunch 11:30 am-3 pm. Closed most major holidays. Lunch $5.75-$9.75, dinner $14.50-$23.50. Sun brunch $9.75-$18.75. Bar. Children's menu. Reservations accepted. Outdoor seating. Restored Colonial building overlooking Delaware River. Cr cds: A, C, D, MC, V.
D

Caldwell (C-5)

See also Newark, Newark International Airport Area

Pop 7,584 **Elev** 411 ft **Area code** 973 **Zip** 07006

What to See and Do

Grover Cleveland Birthplace State Historic Site. *207 Bloomfield Ave. Phone 973/226-0001.* Built in 1832, this building served as the parsonage of the First Presbyterian Church. It is the birthplace of President Grover Cleveland, the only president born in New Jersey. He lived here from 1837-1841. (Wed-Sun afternoons; closed Jan 1, Thanksgiving, Dec 25, state holidays; reservations recommended) **FREE**

Camden (F-2)

See also Cherry Hill; Philadelphia, PA

Settled 1681 **Pop** 79,904 **Elev** 23 ft **Area code** 856

Camden's growth as the leading industrial, marketing, and transportation center of southern New Jersey dates from post-Civil War days. Its location across the Delaware River from Philadelphia prompted large companies such as Campbell Soup (national headquarters) to establish plants here. Walt Whitman spent the last 20 years of his life in Camden.

What to See and Do

Battleship *New Jersey* Museum Site. *Delaware River. Docked adjacent to the Tweeter Entertainment Center, south of the NJ State Aquarium Phone 866/877-6262.* The United States Navy permanently berthed the USS *New Jersey* (or "Big J"), one of the nation's largest and most decorated battleships, at the Camden Waterfront in 2000 and has transformed it into a floating museum. First launched in 1942, the ship was commissioned for operations during World War II at Iwo Jima and Okinawa. The ship conducted its last mission, to provide fire support to Marines in embattled Beirut, Lebanon, in 1983. Military history buffs will be awed by the guided two-hour tour through this 887-foot, 11-story, 212,000-horsepower, Iowa-class ship. "Big J" is available for special events, retreats, and overnight encampments. **$$$$**

Camden County Historical Society-Pomona Hall. *Park Blvd and Euclid Ave (08103). Phone 856/964-3333.* (1726/ 1788) Brick Georgian house that belonged to descendants of William Cooper, an early Camden settler; period furnishings. Museum exhibits focus on regional history and include antique glass, lamps, toys, and early hand tools; fire-fighting equipment; Victor Talking Machines. Library (fee) has more than 20,000 books, as well as maps (17th century-present), newspapers (18th-20th century), oral history tapes, photographs, and genealogical material. (Tues-Thurs, Sun; closed holidays, also Aug) **$**

New Jersey State Aquarium. *1 Riverside Dr, I-676 exit Mickle Blvd. Phone 856/365-3300.* This home to more than 4,000 fish of some 500 species is just minutes across the Ben Franklin Bridge in Camden, New Jersey, on the Delaware River waterfront. (You can also get there via the Delaware River Aerial Tram, coming soon.) At the aquarium, curious kids can find out how fish sleep and which fish can change from male to female and back again. You will also find exhibits of seals, penguins, sharks, turtles, and tropical fish, as well as elaborate rain forest, water filtration, and conservation awareness displays. (Daily; closed Jan 1, Thanksgiving, Dec 25) **$$$$**

Tomb of Walt Whitman. *Harleigh Cemetery, Haddon Ave and Vesper Blvd.* The vault of the "good gray poet," designed by the poet himself, is of rough-cut stone with a grillwork door.

Walt Whitman Arts Center. *2nd and Cooper sts. Phone 856/964-8300.* Poetry readings, concerts, and gallery exhibits (Oct-May). Children's theater (late June-Aug, Fri). Art gallery; statuary. Center (Mon-Fri).

★ **Walt Whitman House State Historic Site.** *330 Mickle Blvd. Phone 856/964-5383.* The last residence of the poet and the only house he ever owned; he lived here from 1884 until his death on Mar 26, 1892. Contains original furnishings, books, and mementos. (Wed-Sat, also Sun afternoons) **FREE**

Cape May (J-3)

See also Wildwood and Wildwood Crest

Settled 1631 **Pop** 4,034 **Elev** 14 ft **Area code** 609 **Zip** 08204

Information Chamber of Commerce, PO Box 556; 609/884-5508. Welcome Center, 405 Lafayette St; 609/884-9562

Web www.capemaychamber.com

Cape May, the nation's oldest seashore resort, is located on the southernmost tip of the state surrounded by the Atlantic Ocean and Delaware Bay. Popular with Philadelphia and New York society since 1766, Cape May has been host to Presidents Lincoln, Grant, Pierce, Buchanan, and Harrison, as well as notables such as John Wanamaker and Horace Greeley. The entire town has been proclaimed a National Historic Landmark because it has more than 600 Victorian homes and buildings, many of which have been restored. The downtown Washington Street Victorian Mall features 3 blocks of shops and restaurants. Four miles of beaches and a 1 1/4-mile paved promenade offer vacationers varied entertainment. "Cape May diamonds," often found on the shores of Delaware Bay by visitors, are actually pure quartz, rounded by the waves.

What to See and Do

Cape May-Lewes (DE) Ferry. *End of Rte 9 S (08204). Phone 609/889-7200.* Sole connection between southern terminus of Garden State Pkwy and US 13 (Ocean Hwy) on the Delmarva Peninsula. 16-mile, 70-minute trip across Delaware Bay. (Daily) **$$$$**

Cape May INNteriors Tour & Tea. *202 Ocean St (08204). Phone 809/884-5404.* Features a different group of houses each week, visiting five or more bed-and-breakfast inns and guesthouses. Innkeepers greet guests and describe experiences. (Summer, Mon; rest of year, Sat; no tours Dec-Jan) **$$$$**

Combination Tours. *Begin at Emlen Physick Estate (see). Phone 609/884-5404 for schedule.* Approximately two hours; includes trolley tour and guided tour of Physick Estate. (June-Oct, daily; rest of year, Sat and Sun) **$$$**

Emlen Physick Estate. *1048 Washington St. Phone 609/884-5404.* (1879) Authentically restored 18-room Victorian mansion designed by Frank Furness. Mansion is also headquarters for the Mid-Atlantic Center for the Arts. (Daily) **$$**

Historic Cold Spring Village. *720 Rte 9 (08204). 3 miles N via US 109. Phone 609/898-2300.* Restored early 1800s South Jersey farm village; 25 restored historic buildings on 22 acres. Craft shops; spinning, blacksmithing, weaving, pottery, broom making, ship modeling demonstrations; folk art; bakery and food shops; restaurant.(June-Sept, daily) **$$**

Mansions by Gaslight. *Phone 609/884-5404.* Three-hour tour begins at Emlen Physick Estate. Visits four Victorian landmarks: Emlen Physick House (see), the Abbey (1869), Mainstay Inn (1872), and Humphrey Hughes House (1903); shuttle bus between houses. (Mid-June-Sept, Wed evenings; rest of year, holiday and special tours) **$$$$**

Ocean Walk Tours. *Promenade and Beach drs. Phone 609/884-5404.* A 1 1/2-hour guided tour of Cape May's beaches. Guide discusses marine life and history of the beaches, including legends of buried treasure. (May-Sept, Tues-Sat) **$$**

Swimming, fishing, boating. Beaches with lifeguards (fee). Fishing is very good at the confluence of the Atlantic and Delaware Bay. A large harbor holds boats of all sizes; excellent for sailboating and other small-boat activity.

Trolleys. *Phone 609/884-5404.* Half-hour tours on enclosed trolley bus or open-air carriage; three routes beginning at Ocean St opposite the Washington St Mall. (June-Oct, daily; reduced schedule rest of year; no tours Thanksgiving) **$$**

Walking Tours of the Historic District. *Washington St Mall and Ocean St. Phone 609/884-5404.* Begin at Information Booth on Washington St Mall at Ocean St. Three 90-minute guided tours give historical insight into the customs and traditions of the Victorians and their ornate architecture. (June-Sept, daily; reduced schedule rest of year) **$$**

Special Events

Promenade Art Exhibit. July.

Sea & Sky Festival. *513 Washington. Phone 609/884-5508.* Sample Cape May's variety of seafood while colorful kites and blues music fill the air. June.

Cape May: An Architectural Bounty

The Center for the Arts, located at the historic Emlen Physic Estate at 1048 Washington Street (phone 609/884-5404), is a good place to begin a walking tour that explores some of the many (more than 600!) Victorian-era buildings in Cape May. Enjoy the 45-minute house tour, which imparts an excellent, concise history of Cape May. Leaving the estate, turn left, go right onto Madison and, having arrived at the corner of Virginia Street, turn left and walk amid the grid created by Madison, Philadelphia, and Reading Streets as they intersect Virginia, Ohio, Cape May Idaho, Maryland, New York, and New Jersey streets. The entire neighborhood is rich in antique homes.

Having completed as much neighborhood viewing as you want, return to Madison. Turn left onto Sewell, then right onto Franklin. At the corner of Columbia Avenue, note The Clivedon Inn (709 Columbia) on the right. Turn left on Columbia. Here stand the Henry Sawyer Inn (722 Columbia) with its magnificent garden; the Dormer House (800 Columbia), a Colonial Revivalist home; The Inn at Journey's End (710 Columbia); and The Mainstay Inn (635 Columbia), once a gentlemen's gambling house.

Walk toward the ocean on Howard Street. At Beach Drive stands the Hotel Macomber (727 Beach Drive),

built in the Shingle style. Turn right, walk 3 blocks to Ocean Street, turn right and look for the Queen Anne-style Columbia House (26 Ocean Street) and Twin Gables (731 Ocean Street), with its pair of Gothic gables. Go left on Hughes to Decatur, turn right and in 3 short blocks enter the downtown shopping district. Here, along the Washington Street Mall, Lyle Lane, Jackson Street, and Perry Street are dozens of shops, restaurants, and inns. Stop at the corner of the Washington Street Mall and Perry to look at Congress Hal, a gargantuan hotel. At 9 Perry, near Beach Drive, stands the King's Cottage, built in the Mansard style with Stick-style detailing. Another excellent Queen Anne-style building, The Inn at 22 Jackson, is found on Jackson Street parallel to Perry. Nearby, the Virginia Hotel (25 Jackson) serves five-star meals in their upscale dining room. You could also take a meal at the Mad Batter (19 Jackson), a Victorian bed-and-breakfast inn, where breakfast on the veranda is a long-standing Cape May tradition.

For a classic Jersey shore finish, return to the beach (at Jackson and Beach Drive) and stroll along the water's edge, or shop and snack along the Promenade. On a summer's eve, another option is to take in a play performed by the professional Cape May Stage. To reach them, stroll back up Jackson (away from the ocean), past the Washington Street Mall to Lafayette Street. Turn right—the theater is in the Visitor Center.

Tulip Festival. *513 Washington. Phone 609/884-5508.* Celebrate Dutch heritage with ethnic foods and dancing, craft show, street fair, garden and house tours. Apr.

Victorian Week. Tours, antiques, crafts, period fashion shows. Mid-Oct.

Motels/Motor Lodges

★ ★ **COACHMAN'S MOTOR INN.** *205 Beach Ave (08204). Phone 609/884-8463; toll-free 800/357-5828; fax 609/884-2643. www.coachmansmotorinn.com.* 65 rooms, 45 kitchen units, 3 story. No elevator. Late June-Labor Day (3-day minimum holidays): S $70-$160; D $140-$185; each additional $15-20; kitchen units $145-$185; lower rates rest of year. Crib free. Check-out 11 am. TV. Coin laundry. Restaurant 7:30 am-10 pm. Bar; entertainment. Pool, wading pool. Tennis. Lawn games. Basketball. Sun deck. On ocean. Cr cds: A, MC, V.

★ ★ **LA MER MOTOR INN.** *1317 Beach Ave (08204). Phone 609/884-9000; fax 609/884-5004.*

www.lamermotorinn.com. 93 rooms, 4 story, 14 kitchen units July-Labor Day: S $118-$136; D $136-$195; each additional $15; kitchen units to 5, $160-$170; lower rates May-June, after Labor Day-mid-Oct. Closed rest of year. TV; VCR available (movies). Pool; wading pool. Restaurant 5-10 pm. Check-out 11 am. Coin laundry. Business services available. Miniature golf. Some microwaves. Bicycles. Picnic tables, grill. On ocean. Cr cds: A, C, D, DS, MC, V.

★ ★ **MONTREAL INN.** *1019 Beach Dr (08204). Phone 609/884-7011; toll-free 800/525-7011; fax 609/884-4559. www.capemayfun.com.* 70 units, 42 kitchen units, 4 story. Mid-June-mid-Sept: S, D, suites $52-$149; each additional $6-$9; kitchen units $140-$165; lower rates Mar-mid-June, mid-Sept-Dec. Closed rest of year. Crib free. Check-out 11 am. TV; cable (premium). In-room modem link. Balconies. Refrigerators; many microwaves. Valet services, coin laundry. Restaurant 8 am-11 pm. Bar from 11 am. Room service. Exercise equipment, sauna. Game room. On ocean. Heated pool, wading pool, whirlpool, poolside service, lifeguard. Putting green, miniature golf. Picnic tables, grills. Free airport transportation. Business services. Cr cds: A, DS, MC, V.

★ **MOUNT VERNON MOTEL.** *300 Beach Ave, at 1st Ave (08204). Phone 609/884-4665. www.mountvernonmotel. com.* 25 rooms, 12 kitchen units, 2 story. July-Labor Day: S, D $145; each additional $12-$15; kitchen units $148; lower rates Apr-June, after Labor Day-Oct. Closed rest of year. Check-out 11 am. TV; cable (premium). Pool, children's pool. Cr cds: A, MC, V.

★ **PERIWINKLE INN.** *1039 Beach Ave (08204). Phone 609/884-9200. www.periwinkleinn.com.* 50 rooms, 14 kitchen units, 3 story. July-Aug: S, D $130-$152; each additional $15; suites, kitchen units $161-$205; lower rates mid-Apr-June, Sept-mid-Oct. Closed rest of year. Check-out 11 am. TV; cable (premium). Pool, children's pool. Cr cds: A, MC, V.

Hotels

★ ★ **AVONDALE BY THE SEA.** *Beach and Gurney aves (08204). Phone 609/884-2332; toll-free 800/676-7030; fax 609/884-2073. www.avondalebythesea.com.* 46 rooms, 18 suites, 3 story. Late July-early Sept: S, D $180; each additional $15; suites $164-$192; kitchen units $184-$200; package plans; weekends (2-day minimum); lower rates rest of year. Crib free. Complimentary continental breakfast. Check-out 11 am. TV; cable. Balconies. Refrigerators available. Restaurant adjacent 8 am-9 pm. Pool. Concierge. Opposite ocean. Cr cds: A, DS, MC, V.

★ ★ **QUEEN'S HOTEL.** *601 Columbia Ave (08204). Phone 609/884-1613. www.queenshotel.com.* 11 rooms, 2 suites, 3 story. No elevator. Mid-June-mid-Sept: S $110-$210; D $110-$220; each additional $25; suites $155-$250; weekend, weekly rates; weekends, holidays (3-day minimum); lower rates rest of year. Crib free. Check-out 11 am, check-in 3 pm. TV; cable, VCR available. Some balconies. Refrigerators; some microwaves. Bicycles. Meeting rooms. Concierge. One block to ocean. Totally nonsmoking. Cr cds: A, MC, V.

★ ★ ★ **VIRGINIA HOTEL.** *25 Jackson St (08204). Phone 609/884-5700; toll-free 800/732-4236; fax 609/884-1236. www.virginiahotel.com.* This hotel, built in 1879, has been recently remodeled. No detail was overlooked when creating a warm and welcoming environment for guests to relax in and enjoy. Visitors

will find all the expected amenities. 24 rooms, 3 story. No elevator. Memorial Day-Labor Day: S, D $80-$275; each additional $20; under 5 free; weekly rates; lower rates rest of year. Crib free. Complimentary continental breakfast. Check-out noon, check-in 3 pm. TV; VCR (movies $2). In-room modem link. Balconies. In-room whirlpools. Dining room (see also EBBITT ROOM). Bar 5 pm-midnight; Sat, Sun from noon. Room service. Health club privileges. Meeting rooms. Business services. Luggage handling. Concierge. Antique and modern furnishings; amenities. Ocean view from veranda. Cr cds: A, C, D, DS, MC, V.

Resorts

★ ★ **CARROLL VILLA HOTEL.** *19 Jackson St (08204). Phone 609/884-9619; fax 609/884-0264. www.madbatter.com.* 22 rooms, 3 story. Memorial Day-mid-Sept: S, D $110-$185; each additional $20; under 2 free; weekly rates; holidays, weekends (2-3-day minimum); lower rates rest of year. Crib available. Complimentary breakfast. Check-out 11 am, check-in 2 pm. TV in parlor. Restaurant (see MAD BATTER). Business services. Victorian inn (1882); antiques. Cr cds: A, DS, MC, V.

★ ★ **GRAND HOTEL.** *1045 Beach Ave (08204). Phone 609/884-5611; toll-free 800/257-8550; fax 609/898-0341. www.grandhotelcapemay.com.* 160 rooms, 30 suites, 40 kitchen units, 5 story. Late July-Aug: S, D $61-$133; each additional $10; suites $164-$267; kitchen units $151-$267; family rates; package plans; lower rates rest of year. Crib $9. Check-out 11 am. TV; cable. Balconies. Refrigerators; many microwaves. Coin laundry. Restaurant 8 am-10 pm. Bar noon-1 am; entertainment Fri, Sat. Sauna. Game room. Indoor/outdoor pool, wading pool, whirlpool, poolside service, lifeguard. Picnic tables, grills. Beauty shop. Meeting rooms. Business services. Sundries. Gift shop. Cr cds: A, DS, MC, V.

★ ★ **MARQUIS DE LAFAYETTE HOTEL.** *501 Beach Ave (08204). Phone 609/884-3500; toll-free 800/257-0432; fax 609/884-0669. www.marquiscapemay.com.* 73 units, 43 kitchen units, 6 story. July-Labor Day: S $99-$249; $129-$279; each additional $18; kitchen units $259-$339; under 8 free; weekend rates; lower rates rest of year. Crib available. Pet accepted, some restrictions; $20/day. Complimentary full breakfast. Check-out 1 pm. TV. Balconies. Valet services, coin laundry. Bar; entertainment. Restaurant. Pool, poolside service. Meeting rooms. Business services. Bellstaff. Cr cds: A, D, DS, MC, V.

B&B/Small Inns

★ ★ ★ **THE ABBEY B & B.** *34 Gurney St, at Columbia Ave (08204). Phone 609/884-4506; fax 609/884-2379. www.abbeybedandbreakfast.com.* Located only a few short blocks from the beach and local shopping mall, this is a very convenient location for travelers. 14 rooms, 3 story. No room phones, Jan-Mar, Children over 12 years only. Complimentary full breakfast. Check-out 11 am, check-in 2-10 pm. Beach passes, chairs, towels. Lawn games. Gothic-style inn with 60-foot tower; main house built in 1869; cottage built in 1873. Cr cds: DS, MC, V. **$$**

★ **ABIGAIL ADAMS B & B.** *12 Jackson St (08204). Phone 609/884-1371; toll-free 888/827-4354; fax 609/884-7116. www.abigailadamsinn.com.* 6 rooms, 3 story. No elevator. No room phones. Children over 12 years only. Complimentary full breakfast. Check-out 11 am, check-in 2 pm. TV in some rooms; cable. Street parking. Built in 1892. Victorian inn. Totally nonsmoking. Cr cds: A, MC, V. **$$**

★ ★ ★ **ANGEL OF THE SEA.** *5 Trenton Ave (08204). Phone 609/884-3369; toll-free 800/848-3369; fax 609/884-3331. www.angelofthesea.com.* Guests will be pleased with their stay at this quiet Victorian inn. Room sizes range from standard up to the Angel Suite. All rooms are decorated with antiques, have a private bath and color TVs. The inn is across the street from a great beach. 27 rooms, 3 story. No elevator. No room phones. Children over 8 years only. Complimentary full breakfast; afternoon refreshments. Check-out 11 am, check-in 2 pm. TV; cable (premium), VCR available. Concierge service. Authentic Victorian house (1850). A/C July, Aug only. Totally nonsmoking. Cr cds: A, DS, MC, V. **$$**

★ ★ **COLVMNS BY THE SEA B & B.** *1513 Beach Dr (08204). Phone 609/884-2228; fax 609/884-4789. www.colvmnscapemay.com.* 11 air-cooled rooms, 3 story. No room phones. July-Aug: S $150-$260; D $160-$275; each additional $40; weekly rates; lower rates rest of year. Children over 7 years only. Complimentary full breakfast, afternoon refreshments. Check-out 11:30 am, check-in 2 pm. TV; cable. Refrigerators. Bicycles. Library. Victorian furnishings; antiques. On beach. Totally nonsmoking. Cr cds: MC, V.

★ **INN OF CAPE MAY.** *7 Ocean St, at Beach Dr (08204). Phone 609/884-5555; toll-free 800/582-5933; fax 609/884-3871. www.innofcapemay.com.* 37 rooms, 5 story. No room phones. Closed rest of year. Check-out 1 pm. TV. Restaurant, bar. No room service. Pool, poolside service. Cr cds: A, D, DS, MC, V. **$$**

★ ★ ★ **MAINSTAY INN.** *635 Columbia Ave (08204). Phone 609/884-8690. www.mainstayinn.com.* Guests will enjoy their stay in the elegant inn, decorated in Victorian style and class and located by the sea. Each morning a continental breakfast will be served to guests in their suite so they can enjoy it by the fireplace or on the private porch. 9 rooms, 3 story, 7 suites. Mar-Dec (2-3-day minimum): S, D $95-$255; each additional $35. Complimentary afternoon refreshments. Check-out 11 am, check-in 2 pm. Lawn games. Some balconies. Beach passes. Built in 1872 as a gentlemen's gambling house. Totally nonsmoking.

★ ★ ★ **THE QUEEN VICTORIA B & B INN.** *102 Ocean St (08204). Phone 609/884-8702. www.queenvictoria.com.* The property is located near the ocean and blocks from shops and fine dining. Walk through the historic town or take one of the available bicycles from the inn. 17 rooms, 3 story. Complimentary full breakfast. Check-out 11 am, check-in 3 pm. TV; VCR available. Bicycles, beach passes. Cr cds: MC, V. **$$**

★ ★ ★ **THE SOUTHERN MANSION.** *720 Washington St (08204). Phone 609/884-7171; toll-free 800/381-3888; fax 609/898-0492. www.thesouthernmansion.com.* The name says it all. Originally built as a country estate in 1863 by Philadelphia industrialist George Allen, the Victorian décor of this painstakingly restored home has graced the covers of several magazines. This is true transplanted southern hospitality. 24 rooms, 3 story. July-Dec: S, D $140-$350; each additional $35; suite $175-$350; family rates; lower rates rest of year. Children over 8 years only. Complimentary full breakfast. Check-out 11 am, check-in 3 pm. TV; cable, VCR available. In-room modem link. Massage. Picnic tables. Lawn games. Business services. Luggage handling. Concierge service. 5,000 square feet of verandahs, terraces, and solariums; mid-19th century antiques. Totally nonsmoking. Cr cds: A, MC, V.

★ ★ **VICTORIAN LACE INN.** *901 Stockton Ave (08204). Phone 609/884-1772; fax 609/884-0983. www.victorianlaceinn.com.* 5 rooms, 3 story. Closed early Jan-mid-Feb. Complimentary breakfast. Check-out 10 am, check-in 2 pm. TV; cable; VCR. Fireplaces. Built in 1869. Totally nonsmoking. Cr cds: A, MC, V. **$$**

Restaurants

★ ★ **410 BANK STREET.** *410 Bank St (08204). Phone 609/884-2127; fax 609/884-7796. www.410bankstreet.com.* Louisiana French menu. Specialties: grilled fish steaks and prime meats. Hours: 5-10:30 pm. Closed Nov-Apr. A la carte entrées: dinner $22-$28. Children's menu. Restored 1840 Cape May residence. Reservations accepted. Porch and garden seating. Island atmosphere. Setups. Cr cds: A, C, D, DS, MC, V.

★ **ALEATHEA'S.** *7 Ocean Dr (08204). Phone 609/884-5555. www.aleatheas.com.* Hours: 8 am-noon, 5-10 pm; early-bird dinner 5-6 pm (seasonal). Closed most major holidays; also Sept-mid-May. Reservations accepted. Bar to 11 pm. Breakfast $3-$15, dinner $14-$32. Children's menu. Specialties: grilled filet mignon, grilled swordfish, baked salmon. Parking. Property built in 1894; view of ocean. Cr cds: A, D, DS, MC, V.

D

★ ★ **ALEXANDER'S INN.** *653 Washington St (08204). Phone 609/884-2555; fax 609/884-8883. www.alexandersinn.com.* Hours: 6-10 pm; Sun brunch 10 am-1 pm. Closed Mon, Tues; Jan 1, Thanksgiving, Dec 25. Reservations accepted. French menu. Setups. Dinner $27.95-$39.95. Complete meals: dinner $39.95-$57.95. Specializes in rack of lamb, rabbit, Angus beef. Own ice cream. Victorian décor; antiques. Cr cds: A, C, D, DS, MC, V.

★ ★ ★ **EBBITT ROOM.** *25 Jackson St (08204). Phone 609/884-5700; fax 609/884-1236. www.virginiahotel.com.* This intimate dining room inside Cape May's Virginia Hotel, named after the inn's original founders, has been offering a seasonally changing menu for over ten years. American cuisine with Asian influences. Dinner. Bar. Intimate Victorian dining room. Reservations accepted. Valet Parking. Totally nonsmoking. Cr cds: A, C, D, DS, MC, V. **$$**

⊠

★ ★ **FRESCOS.** *412 Bank St (08204). Phone 609/884-0366; fax 609/884-7796. www.beachcomber.com.* Italian menu. Specialties: fresh seafood, pasta, veal. Hours: 5-10:30 pm. Closed Nov-Apr. A la carte entrées: dinner $15-$23.95. Children's menu. Three dining areas in restored Victorian summer cottage. Reservations accepted. Outdoor seating. Cr cds: A, C, D, DS, MC, V.

★ ★ **MAD BATTER.** *19 Jackson St (08204). Phone 609/884-9619. www.madbatter.com.* Contemporary American menu. Closed Sun; most major holidays; Jan. Dinner. Children's menu. Victorian inn (1882). Outdoor seating. Cr cds: A, D, DS, MC, V. **$$**

D

★ ★ **MERION INN.** *106 Decatur St (08204). Phone 609/884-8363. www.merioninn.com.* Hours: noon-2:30 pm, 5-10 pm; early-bird dinner 5-6 pm. Closed Jan-Mar; also Mon-Thurs Apr-May and mid-Oct-Dec. Reservations accepted. Bar. Lunch $5.95-$15.95, dinner $14.95-$32.95. Children's menu. Specializes in stuffed lobster tail, fresh grilled fish, steak. Own desserts. Outdoor seat-

ing. Turn-of-the-century Victorian décor. Built in 1885. Family-owned. Cr cds: A, D, DS, MC, V.

★ ★ **PELICAN CLUB.** *501 Beach Ave (08204). Phone 609/884-3500; fax 609/884-7036. www.pelicanclubcapemay.com.* Hours: 5-10 pm. Closed Dec 24, 25. Reservations accepted. Bar. Complete meals: dinner $12.95-$43. Children's menu. Specializes in lobster, beef tenderloin. Pianist. Valet parking in season. Victorian setting with view of Atlantic Ocean. Cr cds: A, D, DS, MC, V.

D

★ **RUSTY NAIL.** *205 Beach Dr (08204). Phone 609/884-0220. www.coachmansmotorinn.com.* Hours: 7:30-1 am. Closed Nov-mid-Apr. Bar. Complete meals: breakfast $5-$8.50, lunch $6.50-$10. Dinner $9.25-$22. Children's menu. Specializes in crab cakes, prime rib, lemon chicken. Beach décor. Cr cds: A, MC, V.

D

★ ★ ★ **WASHINGTON INN.** *801 Washington St (08204). Phone 609/884-5697; fax 609/884-1620. www.washingtoninn.com.* Insiders know that the intimate cellar is the place for a romantic meal at this historic Victorian inn. Hours: 5-10 pm; hours may vary weekends and off season. Closed Thanksgiving, Dec 24-25. Reservations accepted; required Sat. Continental menu. Bar. Wine cellar. Dinner $17.95-$25.95. Children's menu. Specializes in steak, veal, fresh seafood. Own baking. Patio seating. Former plantation house (1848). Fireside seating. Cr cds: A, D, DS, MC, V.

D

★ ★ **WATER'S EDGE.** *Beach and Pittsburgh aves (08204). Phone 609/884-1717; fax 609/884-1885. www.watersedgerestaurant.com.* Hours: 5-11 pm; hours vary off season. Closed Thanksgiving, Dec 25. Reservations accepted. Bar. A la carte entrées: dinner $19-$28. Children's menu. Specializes in fresh local seafood, free-range veal, Angus steak. Contemporary décor. Patio seating. Ocean view. Cr cds: A, D, DS, MC, V.

D

Cape May Court House (J-3)

See also Cape May, Stone Harbor, Wildwood and Wildwood Crest

Pop 4,704 **Elev** 18 ft **Area code** 609 **Zip** 08210

Information Cape May County Chamber of Commerce, PO Box 74; 609/465-7181

Web www.cmccofc.com

To be accurately named, this county seat would have to be called Cape May Court Houses, for there are two of them—one is a white, 19th-century building now used as a meeting hall.

What to See and Do

Cape May County Historical Museum. *504 N Rte 9 (08210). Shore Rd, 1 mile N on US 9. Phone 609/465-3535.* Period dining room (predating 1820), 18th-century kitchen, doctor's room, military room with Merrimac flag, Cape May diamonds. Barn exhibits; whaling implements; Indian artifacts; pioneer tools; lens from Cape May Point Lighthouse. Genealogical library. (Mid-Apr-Nov, Tues-Sat; rest of year, Sat only) **$**

Cape May County Park. *707 N US 9 (08210). On US 9 at Crest Haven Rd. Phone 609/465-5271.* Zoo has over 100 types of animals. Jogging path, bike trail, tennis courts, picnicking, playground. (Daily) **DONATION**

Leaming's Run Gardens. *1845 N Rte 9 (08210). Approximately 4 miles N on US 9, between Pkwy exits 13 and 17 in Swainton. Phone 609/465-5871.* Amid 20 acres of lawns, ponds, and ferneries are 25 gardens, each with a separate theme. Eighteenth-century colonial farm grows tobacco and cotton; farm animals. (Mid-May-mid-Oct, daily) **$$$**

Victorian houses. Over 600 fine examples of 19th-century architecture located in the area. Information can be obtained at the Chamber of Commerce Information Center, Crest Haven Rd and Garden State Pkwy, milepost 11 (Easter-mid-Oct, daily; rest of year, Mon-Fri; closed holidays).

Motel/Motor Lodge

★ **HY-LAND MOTOR INN.** *38 E Mechanic St (08210). Phone 609/465-7305; fax 609/465-8776. www.hylandmotorinn.com.* 34 rooms, 24 with shower only, 2 story. Mid-June-Sept: S $50-$85; D $55-$89; each additional $10; suite $100-$125; kitchen units $90-$125; under 10 free; lower rates rest of year. Crib $5. Check-out 11 am. TV; cable. Pool. Picnic tables, grill. Business services. Cr cds: A, DS, MC, V.

⧠ ⧠ ⧠ ⧠

B&B/Small Inn

★ ★ ★ **THE DOCTORS INN.** *2 N Main St (08210). Phone 609/463-9330; fax 609/463-9194. www.doctorsinn.com.* This romantic bed-and-breakfast, housed in a renovated 19th-century home, is a good location for a Jersey shore vacation. Walk the winding brick drive up to the wicker-filled porch before settling into one of the antique-filled rooms. 7 rooms, 3 story. Complimentary breakfast. Check-out 11 am, check-in

2 pm. TV; VCR. Built in 1854; pays tribute to physicians and teachers who ministered to the community. Totally nonsmoking. Cr cds: DS, MC, V. **$$**

⧠ ⧠

Chatham

Pop 10,686 **Elev** 244 ft **Area code** 973 **Zip** 07928

Information Township of Chatham, 58 Meyersville Rd; 973/635-4600

Web www.chathamtownship.org

What to See and Do

Great Swamp National Wildlife Refuge. *152 Pleasant Plains Rd (07920). Phone 973/425-1222.* SW of city (see BERNARDSVILLE).

Restaurant

★ ★ ★ ★ **RESTAURANT SERENADE.** *6 Roosevelt Ave (07928). Phone 973/701-0303; fax 973/701-0613. www.restaurantserenade.com.* Owned by husband and wife James and Nancy Sheridan Laird, Restaurant Serenade is a product of love on a number of levels. The couple met at the Ryland Inn, where James was a sous chef and Nancy was an intern. They fell in love and decided to merge their collective passion for fine dining and each other, marrying in 1996 and opening Restaurant Serenade six months later. Both mergers are fairing very well. Restaurant Serenade is a sophisticated and intimate gastronomic temple, with soft-toned walls, dark-wood moldings, and gorgeous flower arrangements that add warmth and serenity to the elegant space. The kitchen shows a deep respect for seasonal, local ingredients, serving innovative, contemporary French cuisine cleverly and deftly tinged with Asian flair. While James consistently dazzles the palate, Nancy welcomes guests with grace. Dining in their care is a delight from start to finish. Hours: noon-2 pm, 6-9:30 pm; Sat 5:30-10 pm. Closed Sun; holidays. Dinner $17-$28. Bar. Jacket required. Reservations required Sat. Cr cds: A, C, D, DS, MC, V.

⧠

Cherry Hill (F-3)

See also Camden, Haddonfield

Pop 69,965 **Elev** 30 ft **Area code** 856

Information Chamber of Commerce, 1060 Kings Hwy N, Suite 200, 08034; 609/667-1600

Web www.cherryhillnj.com

What to See and Do

Barclay Farmstead. *209 Barclay Ln. Phone 856/795-6225.* One of the earliest properties settled in what is now Cherry Hill; origins traced to 1684. The township-owned site consists of 32 acres of open space; restored Federal-style farmhouse; operating forge barn; corn crib; Victorian spring house. Grounds (all year); house tours (Tues-Fri, first Sun each month; and by appointment). **$**

Motels/Motor Lodges

★ ★ **CLARION HOTEL.** *1450 Rte 70 E (08034). Phone 609/428-2300; fax 609/354-7662. www.clarionhotel.com.* 213 rooms, 4 story. S $98-$139; D $108-$159; each additional $10; under 18 free; weekend rates. Crib free. Check-out noon. TV; cable (premium), VCR available. In-room modem link. Microwaves available. Coffee in rooms. Bar 11-2 am. Restaurant. Health club privileges, exercise equipment. Pool. Tennis. Airport transportation. Meeting rooms. Business center. Gift shop. Cr cds: A, C, D, DS, ER, MC, V.

★ ★ **DAYS INN.** *550 Fellowship Rd (08054). Phone 609/235-7400; toll-free 800/329-7466; fax 609/778-9729. www.daysinn.com/mtlaurel.* 150 rooms, 2 story. S, D $52-$99; each additional $10; under 12 free. Check-out noon. TV; cable (premium). In-room modem link. Laundry services. Restaurant, bar. Room service. Health club privileges. Exercise equipment. Pool. Cr cds: A, C, D, DS, MC, V.

★ **HAMPTON INN.** *121 Laurel Oak Rd, Voorhas (08043). Phone 856/346-4500; fax 856/346-2402. www.hamptoninn.com.* 122 rooms, 50 with shower only, 4 story. S, D $88-$95; under 18 free. Crib available. Pet accepted. TV; cable (premium), VCR available. Pool. Complimentary continental breakfast. Restaurant adjacent 11 am-11 pm. Check-out noon. Business services available. In-room modem link. Health club privileges. Refrigerators, microwaves available. Cr cds: A, C, D, DS, MC, V.

★ ★ **HOLIDAY INN.** *Rte 70 and Sayer Ave (08034). Phone 856/663-5300; toll-free 800/465-4329; fax 856/662-2913. www.holiday-inn.com.* 186 rooms, 6 story. S, D $99-$109; each additional $8; under 19 free; weekend rates. Crib free. Pet accepted. Check-out noon. TV; cable (premium), VCR available. In-room modem link. Microwaves available. Valet services, coin laundry. Restaurant (see also RED HOT & BLUE). Bar 11 am-11 pm. Exercise equipment, sauna. Two pools, one indoor, wading pool. Meeting rooms. Business center. Cr cds: A, C, D, DS, ER, JCB, MC, V.

★ **MCINTOSH INN.** *1132 NJ 73 and Church Rd, Mt. Laurel (08054). Phone 856/234-7194; fax 856/231-8516.* 91 rooms, 2 story. S, D $50.95-$65.95. Crib free. TV; cable (premium). Complimentary continental breakfast. Restaurant adjacent open 24 hours. Check-out 11 am. Business services available. Refrigerators, microwaves available. Cr cds: A, C, D, MC, V.

★ ★ **QUALITY INN.** *531 Rte 38 W (08052). Phone 609/235-6400; fax 609/727-1027.* 106 suites, 3 story. S $85-$115; D $95-$135; each additional $5; under 18 free. Crib free. TV; cable (premium); VCR (movies). Pool; wading pool, lifeguard. Playground. Complimentary breakfast, coffee in rooms. Restaurant 6:30 am-10 pm; Sat, Sun 8 am-noon, 5-11 pm. Room service. Bar; entertainment Fri, Sat. Check-out 11 am. Coin laundry. Meeting rooms. In-room modem link. Sundries. Exercise equipment; sauna. Refrigerators, microwaves. Private patios, balconies. Cr cds: A, C, D, DS, JCB, MC, V.

Hotels

★ ★ ★ **HILTON HOTEL.** *2349 W Marlton Pike (08002). Phone 609/665-6666; fax 609/662-3676. www.hilton.com.* This suburban hotel is located only ten minutes from Philadelphia's historic and business districts and is near Garden State Park Race Track and Blockbuster/Sony Musical Entertainment Center. 408 rooms, 14 story. S $119-$209; D $129-$219; each additional $10; suites $350-$650; under 14 free. Crib free. Pet accepted. TV; cable (premium), VCR available. Pool; wading pool. Coffee in rooms. Restaurant 6 am-11 pm. Bar 11-1 am. Check-out noon. Convention facilities. Business center. In-room modem link. Valet service. Exercise equipment. Some refrigerators; microwaves available. Cr cds: A, C, D, DS, ER, JCB, MC, V.

★ ★ ★ **RADISSON.** *915 NJ 73N, Mt. Laurel (08054). Phone 856/234-7300; fax 856/802-3912. www.radisson.com.* This hotel offers a continental breakfast, evening cocktails and hors d'oeuvres, movies, and a 24 hour copy/fax service, as well as recreational facilities such as tennis and basketball courts, a restaurant, and lounge. 283 rooms, 10 story. S, D $99-$109; suites $250-$350; under 17 free. Crib free. Check-out noon. TV; cable (premium). In-room modem link. Some private patios, balconies. Some in-room whirlpools, refrigerators. Microwaves available. Coin laundry. Restaurant 6:30 am-10 pm; Sat, Sun from 7 am. Bar. Health club privileges, exercise equipment. Game room. Pool, poolside service, lifeguard. Golf privileges. Picnic tables. Business services. Convention center/facilities. Gift shop. Luxury level. Cr cds: A, C, D, DS, ER, JCB, MC, V.

Restaurants

★ ★ **CAFFE LA BELLA.** *61 E Main St, Morristown (08057). Phone 856/234-7755.* Italian menu. Closed most major holidays. Lunch $4.25-$13.95, dinner $13.95-$22.95. Sun brunch $10.95. Children's menu. Casual, intimate dining. Reservations required Fri, Sat (dinner). Totally nonsmoking. Cr cds: MC, V.

★ ★ ★ **LA CAMPAGNE.** *312 Kresson Rd (08034). Phone 856/429-7647; fax 856/429-0037. www. lacampagne.com.* This 150-year-old restaurant and farmhouse serves country French cuisine with an emphasis on the Provençal region of Southeast France. Specializes in rack of lamb, seafood, duck. Hours: 11:30 am-2:30 pm, 5-10 pm; Sun brunch 10 am-2 pm. Closed Mon. Lunch $7.50-$15, dinner $40-$50, Sun brunch $25. Children's menu. Reservations accepted. Outdoor seating. Country French décor. Cr cds: A, D, MC, V.

★ ★ **LOS AMIGOS MEXICAN RESTAURANT.** *461 NJ 73, West Berlin (08091). Phone 856/767-5247; fax 856/767-5566. www.losamigosrest.com.* Southwestern menu. Specialties: Southwestern crab cakes, tabasco tequila shrimp. Hours: 5-11 pm; Sat 3-11 pm; Sun 3-10 pm. Closed Mon; some holidays. A la carte entrées: dinner $9.95-$20.95. Bar. Family-owned. Children's menu. Outdoor seating. Fiesta atmosphere; Mexican cantina décor. Cr cds: A, D, MC, V.

★ ★ **MELANGE CAFE.** *1601 Chapel Ave (08002). Phone 856/663-7339. www.melangecafe.com.* Italian, Louisiana menu. Hours: 11 am-10 pm; Fri to 11 pm; Sat 4-11 pm; Sun 2-10 pm. Closed Mon; also July 4, Thanksgiving, Dec 25. Lunch $9-$12, dinner $18-$27. Children's menu. Upscale casual dining. Reservations accepted. Outdoor seating. Totally nonsmoking. Cr cds: A, D, DS, MC, V.

★ **RED HOT & BLUE.** *Rte 70 and Sayer Ave (08034). Phone 856/665-7427; fax 856/665-8204. www.redhotandblue.com.* Hours: 11 am-10 pm; Fri to 11 pm; Sat to midnight; Sun from noon. Closed Easter, Thanksgiving, Dec 25. Reservations accepted (dinner). Bar; Fri, Sat to 2 am. Lunch, dinner $5.50-$13. Children's

menu. Specialties: pulled pork, barbecue pork ribs, beef brisket. Blues Fri, Sat. Casual, Memphis-style barbecue. Cr cds: A, D, DS, MC, V.

★ ★ **SIRI'S THAI FRENCH CUISINE.** *2117 Rte 70W (08002). Phone 856/663-6781; fax 856/663-6128.* Hours: 11:30 am-10 pm; Fri, Sat to 11 pm. Closed some major holidays. Reservations accepted. Thai, French menu. A la carte entrées: lunch $9-$15, dinner $12-$24.95. Specialties: seafood medley, rack of lamb, crispy duck. Parking. Thai décor. Totally nonsmoking. Cr cds: A, D, MC, V.

Clifton (C-5)

Pop 78,682 **Elev** 70 ft **Area code** 973

Information North Jersey Regional Chamber of Commerce, 1033 US 46 E, PO Box 110, 07011; 973/470-9300

Web www.njrcc.org

What to See and Do

Hamilton House Museum. *971 Valley Rd. Phone 973/744-5707.* Early 19th-century sandstone farmhouse with period furniture; country store; exhibits. Open-hearth cooking demonstrations by costumed guides. (Mar-Dec, First Sun each month, Tues-Thurs afternoons; closed holiday weekends) **FREE**

Motels/Motor Lodges

★ ★ **HOWARD JOHNSON.** *680 Rte 3W (07014). Phone 973/471-3800; toll-free 800/466-4656; fax 973/471-2128. www.howardjohnson.com.* 118 rooms, 4 story. D $94-$124; each additional $10; under 18 free; weekend rates. Pet accepted, some restrictions. Check-out noon, check-in 2 pm. TV; cable (premium). In-room modem link. Restaurant, bar. Pool. Cr cds: A, D, DS, MC, V.

★ ★ **RAMADA.** *265 Rte 3E (07014). Phone 973/778-6500; toll-free 800/772-2816; fax 973/778-8724. www.ramada.com.* 225 rooms, 4 story. D $89-$239; each additional $10; under 12 free; weekend rates. Pet accepted. Check-out noon, check-in 3 pm. TV; cable (premium). Restaurant 6:30 am-10 pm; weekends from 7 am. Bar; entertainment. Room service. Exercise equipment, sauna. Indoor pool. Cr cds: A, C, D, DS, JCB, MC, V.

Clinton

See also Flemington

Pop 2,632 **Elev** 195 ft **Area code** 908 **Zip** 08809

What to See and Do

Red Mill Museum Village. *56 Main St, off I-78. Phone 908/735-4101.* Four-story gristmill (circa 1810). Ten-acre park houses education center, quarry and lime kilns, blacksmith shop, general store, one-room schoolhouse, log cabin, machinery sheds, herb garden. Also home of Clinton's landmark red mill. Gift shop. (Apr-Oct, Tues-Sun) Outdoor concerts some Sat evenings in summer (fee). **$$**

Round Valley State Park. *1220 Lebanon Stanton Rd (08833). Off US 22, E of jct I-78; follow signs. Phone 908/236-6355.* A 4,003-acre park. Swimming, fishing, boating; picnicking, concession (Memorial Day-Labor Day), wilderness camping (access to campsites via hiking or boating only). Standard fees.

Spruce Run State Recreation Area. *1 Van Syckles Rd (08809). 3 miles NW off NJ 31. Phone 908/638-8572.* 1,290 acres of water, 600 acres of park. Swimming, fishing, boating (launch, rentals); picnicking, concession, camping (dump station) (Apr-Oct). Standard fees.

Motel/Motor Lodge

★★ **HOLIDAY INN.** *111 Rte 173 (08809). Phone 908/735-5111; toll-free 800/465-4329; fax 908/730-9768. www.holiday-inn.com.* 142 units, 5 story. S $125-$145; D $133-$153; each additional $8; suites $145-$160; under 18 free; weekend rates. Crib free. TV; cable (premium). Indoor pool. Coffee in rooms. Restaurant 6:30 am-11 pm. Room service. Bar 3 pm-midnight; entertainment Tues-Sat. Check-out noon. Meeting rooms. Business center. In-room modem link. Sundries. Exercise equipment. Microwaves available. Some balconies. Cr cds: A, C, D, DS, JCB, MC, V.

B&B/Small Inn

★★ **STEWART INN.** *708 S Main St, Stewartsville (08886). Phone 908/479-6060; fax 908/479-4211. www.bbianj.com/stewartinn.* 7 rooms, 2 story. S, D $95-$135; suite $125-$135. Children over 12 years only. Complimentary full breakfast. Check-out 11 am, check-in 3 pm. TV; VCR available. Pool. Picnic tables, grills. Business services. Stone manor house built in 1770s, set amidst 16 acres of lawns, gardens, woods, stream, and pasture. Trout stream, barns and outbuildings with farm animals. Totally nonsmoking. Cr cds: A, DS, MC, V.

Restaurant

★★ **CLINTON HOUSE.** *2 W Main St (08809). Phone 908/730-9300; fax 908/735-5490. www.theclintonhouse.com.* Hours: 11:30 am-2:30 pm, 5-9:30 pm. Closed Dec 25. Reservations accepted. Bar to midnight. Lunch $6.95-$21.95, dinner $16.95-$26. Children's menu. Specializes in beef, seafood. Built in 1743; former stagecoach stop. Family-owned. Cr cds: A, MC, V.

Eatontown (E-5)

See also Red Bank

Pop 14,008 **Elev** 46 ft **Area code** 732 **Zip** 07724

Motels/Motor Lodges

★★ **HOLIDAY INN.** *700 Hope Rd, Tinton Falls (07724). Phone 732/544-9300; toll-free 800/465-4329; fax 732/544-0570. www.holiday-inn.com.* 171 rooms, 5 story. S, D $99-$159; each additional $10; suites $115-$225; weekend rates. Crib free. Check-out noon. TV; cable (premium). In-room modem link. Refrigerators, microwaves available. Valet services, laundry facilities. Restaurant 6:30 am-11 pm. Bar 11:30-2 am. Room service. Exercise equipment, sauna. Pool, poolside service. Meeting rooms. Business services. Bellstaff. Gift shop. Cr cds: A, C, D, DS, ER, JCB, MC, V.

★ **RED ROOF INN.** *11 Centre Plaza, Tinton Falls (07724). Phone 732/389-4646; toll-free 800/843-7663; fax 732/389-4509. www.redroof.com.* 119 rooms, 3 story. May-Labor Day: S, D $85-$89; each additional $7; under 18 free; lower rates rest of year. Crib free. Pet accepted, some restrictions. TV; cable (premium). Check-out noon. Cr cds: A, C, D, DS, MC, V.

Hotels

★★★ **OCEAN PLACE CONFERENCE RESORT.** *1 Ocean Blvd, Long Branch (07740). Phone 732/571-4000; toll-free 800/411-7321; fax 732/571-3314. www.oceanplace.com.* 254 rooms, 12 story. Memorial Day-Labor Day: S $170-$205; D $190-$225; each additional $20; suites $350-$1,000; family, weekend rates; lower rates rest of year. Crib free. TV; cable (premium), VCR available. Two pools, one indoor; whirlpools, poolside service, lifeguard. Supervised children's activities (mid-May-early Sept), ages 3-12. Restaurants 6:30 am-10 pm; Sat, Sun from 7 am. Bar 11-2 am; entertainment. Check-out noon. Convention facilities. Business center. In-room modem link. Concierge. Shopping arcade. Barber, beauty shop. Free garage parking. Train station transportation. Lighted tennis. Exercise room; sauna, steam room. Massage. Balconies. On ocean. Cr cds: A, C, D, DS, ER, MC, V.

★ ★ ★ **SHERATON EATONTOWN HOTEL.** *Rte 35, at Industrial Way E (07724). Phone 732/542-6500; toll-free 800/544-5064; fax 732/542-6607. www.sheraton.com.* 208 rooms, 6 story. May-Sept: S $154-$164; D $164-$174; each additional $15; suites $364; weekend rates; lower rates rest of year. Crib free. Check-out noon. TV; cable (premium). In-room modem link. Microwaves, refrigerators available. Coin laundry. Restaurant 6:30 am-11 pm. Bar. Health club privileges, exercise equipment. Indoor/outdoor pool, whirlpool. Meeting rooms. Business center. Gift shop. Cr cds: A, C, D, DS, MC, V.

Edison (D-4)

See also Woodbridge

Pop 97,687 **Elev** 95 ft **Area code** 732

Information Chamber of Commerce, 100 Menlo Park, 3rd Fl, PO Box 2103, 08818-2103; 732/494-0300

Web www.edisonchamber.com

Although Thomas A. Edison's house here has been destroyed, Menlo Park and the Edison Memorial Tower stand in tribute to the great American inventor. Here, on December 6, 1877, the 30-year-old Edison invented the phonograph. Two years later, he perfected the first practical incandescent light, designing and constructing various kinds of electrical equipment we now take for granted. His workshop has been moved to the Ford Museum in Dearborn, Michigan. Edison also built the first electric railway locomotive here in 1880; it ran 1 1/2 miles over the fields of Pumptown.

What to See and Do

Edison Memorial Tower and Menlo Park Museum. *37 Christie St, 1/2 mile SW of Garden State Pkwy exit 131 off NJ 27 in Menlo Park. Phone 732/549-3299.* A 131-foot tower topped by a 13 1/2-foot-high electric light bulb stands at the birthplace of recorded sound. Museum contains some of Edison's inventions, including phonographs and lightbulbs (Wed-Sun). **FREE**

Motel/Motor Lodge

★ ★ **COURTYARD BY MARRIOTT.** *3105 Woodbridge Ave (08837). Phone 732/738-1991; fax 732/738-8866. www.courtyard.com.* Designed for both business and pleasure travelers, this property is conveniently located near the New Jersey Convention and Exposition Center, shopping, and restaurants. 146 rooms, 4 suites, 4 story. S, D $69-$149; suites $149-$179. Check-out noon, check-in 3 pm. TV; cable (premium). In-room modem link. Coin laundry, laundry valet. Bar. Exercise room. Indoor pool. Golf nearby. Tennis nearby. Cr cds: A, C, D, DS, ER, JCB, MC, V.

Hotels

★ ★ **CLARION HOTEL.** *2055 Lincoln Hwy (08817). Phone 732/287-3500; fax 732/287-8190. www.clarionhotel.com.* 169 rooms, 5 story. S, D $119-$149; each additional $10; under 18 free; weekend rates. Crib free. TV; cable (premium). Complimentary continental breakfast. Coffee in rooms. Restaurant 7 am-10:30 pm; Fri, Sat to 11 pm. Room service. Bar 11-1 am. Check-out noon. Meeting rooms. Business center. In-room modem link. Bellstaff. Gift shop. Exercise equipment. Refrigerators; microwaves available. Luxury level. Cr cds: A, C, D, DS, JCB, MC, V.

★ ★ ★ **SHERATON EDISON HOTEL RARITAN CENTER.** *125 Raritan Center Pkwy (08837). Phone 732/225-8300; fax 732/225-0037. www.sheraton.com.* 274 rooms, 12 story. S, D $150-$175; suites $325; under 12 free; weekend rates. Crib free. Pet accepted; fee. Complimentary coffee in rooms. Check-out noon. TV; cable (premium). In-room modem link. Coin laundry. Restaurant 6 am-2 pm, 5-10 pm. Bar. Exercise equipment, sauna. Game room. Indoor pool, whirlpool. Business services. Convention center/facilities. Concierge. Gift shop. Cr cds: A, C, D, DS, JCB, MC, V.

Restaurants

★ ★ **CHARLIE BROWN'S.** *222 Plainfield Rd (08820). Phone 732/494-6135; fax 732/494-7257. www.charliebrowns.com.* Hours: 11:30 am-10 pm; Fri, Sat to 10:30 pm; Sun to 9 pm. Closed Dec 25. Lunch $5.29-$8.45, dinner $9.75-$16.99. Bar to 2 am. Children's menu. Outdoor seating. Rustic American décor; stained glass windows; casual setting. Cr cds: A, D, DS, MC, V.

★ ★ **MOGHUL.** *1665-195 Oaktree Center (08820). Phone 732/549-5050; fax 732/540-5052. www.moghul.com.* Hours: noon-3 pm, 5:30-10:30 pm; Fri, Sat to 11 pm; brunch noon-3 pm. Closed Mon. Reservations accepted. North Indian menu. Setups. A la carte entrées: lunch, dinner $8.95-$15.95. Brunch: weekdays $7.95, weekends $9.95. Specializes in chicken, lamb, shrimp. Parking. Elegant décor; Indian artifacts. Cr cds: A, D, DS, MC, V.
D

Elizabeth (D-5)

See also Jersey City, Newark, Newark International Airport Area

Settled 1664 **Pop** 120,568 **Elev** 36 ft **Area code** 908

Information Union County Chamber of Commerce, 135 Jefferson Ave, PO Box 300, 07207; 908/352-0900

More than 1,200 manufacturing industries are located in Elizabeth and Union County. Long before the Revolution, Elizabeth was not only the capital of New Jersey, but also a thriving industrial town. The first Colonial Assembly met here from 1669-92. Princeton University began in Elizabeth in 1746 as the College of New Jersey. More than 20 pre-Revolutionary buildings still stand. Many noteworthy people were citizens of Elizabeth: William Livingston, first governor of New Jersey; Elias Boudinot, first president of the Continental Congress; Alexander Hamilton; Aaron Burr; General Winfield Scott; John Philip Holland, builder of the first successful submarine; and Admiral William J. Halsey. The Elizabeth-Port Authority Marine Terminal is the largest container port in the United States.

What to See and Do

Boxwood Hall State Historic Site. *1073 E Jersey St, 1 1/2 blocks W of US 1. Phone 973/648-4540.* Home of Elias Boudinot, lawyer, diplomat, president (1783) of the Continental Congress and director of the US Mint. Boudinot entertained George Washington here on April 23, 1789, when Washington was on his way to his inauguration. (Mon-Sat; closed Jan 1, Thanksgiving, Dec 25)

First Presbyterian Church and Graveyard. *42 Broad St (07201). Broad St and Caldwell Pl. Phone 908/353-1518.* The first General Assembly of New Jersey convened in an earlier building in 1668. The burned-out church was rebuilt in 1785-1787, and again in 1949. The Reverend James Caldwell was an early pastor. Alexander Hamilton and Aaron Burr attended an academy where the parish house now stands.

Warinanco Park. *Elizabethtown Town Plaza. St. Georges, border of Elizabeth and Roselle. Phone 908/527-4900.* One of the largest Union County parks. Fishing, boating (rentals June-Sept, daily); running track, parcourse fitness

circuit, tennis (late Apr-early Oct), handball, horseshoes, indoor ice skating (early Oct-early Apr, daily). Henry S. Chatfield Memorial Garden features tulip blooms each spring; azaleas and Japanese cherry trees; summer and fall flower displays. Some fees. **FREE**

Flemington (D-3)

See also Clinton, Somerville

Settled 1738 **Pop** 4,200 **Elev** 160 ft **Area code** 908 **Zip** 08822

Information Hunterdon County Chamber of Commerce, 2200 Rte 31, Suite 15, Lebanon 08833; 908/735-5955

Web www.hunterdon-chamber.org

Originally a farming community, Flemington became a center for the production of pottery and cut glass at the turn of the century.

What to See and Do

Black River & Western Railroad. *Center Shopping Area. Phone 908/782-9600.* Excursion ride on old steam train, 11-mile round trip to Ringoes. Picnic area; museum. (July-Aug, Thurs-Sun; Apr-June and Sept-Dec, Sat, Sun and holidays) **$$$**

County Courthouse. *Main St.* (1828) For 46 days in 1935, world attention was focused on this Greek Revival building where Bruno Hauptmann was tried for the kidnapping and murder of the Lindbergh baby.

Fleming Castle. *5 Bonnell St. Phone 908/782-8840.* (1756) Typical two-story colonial house built as a residence and inn by Samuel Fleming, for whom the town is named. DAR headquarters. (By appointment) **DONATION**

Kase Cemetery. *Bonnell St, W of Fleming Castle.* John Philip Kase, Flemington's first settler, purchased a tract from William Penn. His family's crumbling gravestones date from 1774 to 1856. Kase's Native American friend, Chief Tuccamirgan, is also memorialized here.

Special Events

Flemington Agricultural Fair. *150 Rte 31 N (08822). Phone 908/782-2413.* Late Aug-early Sept.

Stock-car racing. *Flemington Fair Speedway. 150 Rte 31 N.* Sat, Apr-Nov.

Motel/Motor Lodge

★ ★ **RAMADA.** *250 Rte 202, at NJ 31 (08822). Phone 908/782-7472; toll-free 888/298-2054; fax 908/782-1975. www.ramada.com.* 104 rooms, 24 kitchen units, 2 story. S $95, D $103; each additional $10; suites $125; kitchen units $114. Crib available. Pet accepted. Complimentary coffee in lobby. Check-out noon. TV; cable (premium). In-room modem link. Microwaves available. Valet services, coin laundry. Restaurant 6:30 am-10 pm. Bar. Pool. Meeting rooms. Cr cds: A, C, D, DS, MC, V.

Restaurants

★ ★ ★ **HARVEST MOON INN.** *1039 Old York Rd, Ringoes (08551). Phone 908/806-6020; fax 908/806-7111. www.harvestmooninn.com.* Hours: 11:30 am-2:30 pm, 5-9:30 pm; Fri to 10 pm; Sat 5-10 pm; Sun 1-8 pm; early-bird dinner Tues-Fri 5-6 pm. Closed Mon; most major holidays. Reservations accepted. Bar. Lunch $5.95-$12.95, dinner $16-$26. Complete meal: dinner $19.97. Specialty: pan-seared tuna. Own baking. Piano bar Fri, Sat. Stone building (circa 1811) with two fireplaces. Cr cds: A, D, DS, MC, V.

★ ★ **UNION HOTEL.** *76 Main St (08822). Phone 908/788-7474; fax 908/788-0135.* Specialties: fresh fish, steak. Hours: 11 am-10 pm; Sun noon-8 pm. Closed some major holidays. Lunch $6-$9.50, dinner $13-$17.50. Bar to midnight. Children's menu. In ornate Victorian hotel (1878) opposite historical county courthouse. Reservations accepted. Cr cds: A, MC, V.

Forked River (G-5)

See also Toms River

Pop 4,914 **Elev** 19 ft **Area code** 609 **Zip** 08731

Restaurant

★ ★ **CAPTAIN'S INN.** *E Lacey Rd (08731). Phone 609/693-3351; fax 609/242-1302.* Continental menu. Closed Dec 25. Breakfast, lunch, dinner. Bar. Entertainment Fri-Sun evenings. Children's menu. Built in 1831. Docking. Cr cds: A, D, MC, V. $

Fort Lee (C-5)

See also Hackensack

Pop 35,461 **Elev** 314 ft **Area code** 201 **Zip** 07024

Information Greater Fort Lee Chamber of Commerce, 2357 Lemoine Ave; 201/944-7575

North and south of the George Washington Bridge, Fort Lee is named for General Charles Lee, who served in the Revolutionary Army under George Washington. Its rocky bluff achieved fame as the cliff from which Pearl White hung in the early movie serial "The Adventures of Pearl White." From 1907-1916, 21 companies and seven studios produced motion pictures in Fort Lee. Stars such as Mary Pickford, Mabel Normand, Theda Bara, and Clara Kimball Young made movies here.

What to See and Do

Fort Lee Historic Park. *Hudson Terr and Palisades Interstate (07024). Phone 201/461-3956.*

Palisades Interstate Parks. *Palisades Interstate Parks Commission, Administration Building, Bear Mountain 10911-0427. Phone 914/786-2701.* This system of conservation and recreation areas extends along the west side of the Hudson River from the George Washington Bridge at Fort Lee, NJ, to Saugerties, NY, and covers 81,008 acres. The main unit is the 51,680-acre tract of Bear Mountain and Harriman state parks. Included in the system are 17 parks and six historic sites. Parks include:

Bear Mountain (5,067 acres) extends westward from the Hudson River opposite Peekskill. Only 45 miles from New York City via the Palisades Interstate Parkway, this is a popular recreation area, with all-year facilities, mainly for one-day visits. Bear Mountain has picnic areas, hiking trails, swimming pool with bathhouse, boating on Hessian Lake, fishing, and an artificial ice rink. Perkins Memorial Drive goes to the top of Bear Mountain, where there is a picnic area and a sightseeing tower. Near the site of Fort Clinton, just west of Bear Mountain Bridge, is Trailside Museums and Wildlife Center, with native animals and exhibit buildings (Daily). $$

Harriman (46,613 acres), southwest of Bear Mountain, consists of wilder country. Fishing, boating, scenic drives, lakes, bathing beaches at Lakes Tiorati, Welch and Sebago; tent camping at Lake Welch and cabins (primarily for family groups) at Lake Sebago. The **Silver Mine Area,** 4 miles west of Bear Mountain, has fishing, boating, picnicking. (All year) Charges for parking and for most activities change seasonally. $$

Motel/Motor Lodge

★ ★ **HOLIDAY INN.** *2339 Rte 4E (07024). Phone 201/944-5000; toll-free 800/465-4329; fax 201/944-0623. www.holiday-inn.com.* 175 rooms, 6 story. S $71-$100; D $81-$100; each additional $10; under 18 free. Crib free. Check-out noon. TV; cable. Restaurant 7 am-1 pm. Bar 5 pm-midnight; closed Sun. Room service. Exercise equipment. Pool. Meeting rooms. Business services. Sundries. Cr cds: A, D, DS, JCB, MC, V.

Hotels

★★★**HILTON FORT LEE GEORGE WASH-INGTON BRIDGE.** *2117 Rte 4 (07024). Phone 201/461-9000; toll-free 800/774-1500; fax 201/585-9807. www.hilton.com.* This hotel is located at the gateway to the "Big Apple," and offers its guests two restaurants, a lounge, a karaoke night club, and a modern fitness center. 236 rooms, 15 story. S, D $139-$189; under 12 free. Crib free. TV; cable (premium), VCR available. Indoor pool; whirlpool. Coffee in rooms. Restaurant 6:30 am-10:30 pm. Room service. Bars 11-1 am. Check-out noon. Meeting rooms. Business center. In-room modem link. Bellstaff. Valet service. Concierge. Gift shop. Covered parking. Cr cds: A, C, D, DS, ER, JCB, MC, V.

D 🛏 🏊 🏋 🏃

★★★**RADISSON HOTEL ENGLEWOOD.** *401 S Van Brunt St (07631). Phone 201/871-2020; toll-free 800/333-3333; fax 201/871-6904. www.radisson.com.* 192 rooms, 9 story. Late Nov-mid Dec: S, D $145-$165; suites $185-$275; weekend rates; lower rates rest of year. Crib free. Pet accepted, some restrictions. Check-out noon. TV; cable (premium), VCR available. Some bathroom phones. Microwaves, refrigerators available. Coffee in rooms. Coin laundry. Restaurant 6:30 am-10 pm. Bar 11:30-1 am. Exercise equipment. Indoor pool. Meeting rooms. Business center. Concierge. Luxury level. Cr cds: A, C, D, DS, ER, JCB, MC, V.

D 🐾 🏊 🏋 🏃

Freehold (E-5)

See also Eatontown, Hightstown, Lakewood

Founded 1715 **Pop** 10,976 **Elev** 154 ft **Area code** 732 **Zip** 07728

Information Western Monmouth Chamber of Commerce, 17 Broad St; 732/462-3030

Web www.wmchamber.com

George Washington and the Revolutionary Army defeated the British under General Sir Henry Clinton at the Battle of Monmouth near here on June 28, 1778. Molly Hays carried water to artillerymen in a pitcher and from that day on she has been known as "Molly Pitcher." Formerly known as Monmouth Courthouse, Freehold is the seat of Monmouth County.

What to See and Do

Covenhoven House. *150 W Main St. Phone 732/462-1466.* (1756) House with period furnishings; once occupied by General Sir Henry Clinton prior to the Battle of Monmouth in 1778. (May-Sept, Tues, Thurs, Sat, and Sun afternoons) **$**

Monmouth County Historical Museum and Library. *70 Court St. Phone 732/462-1466.* Headquarters of Monmouth County Historical Association. Changing exhibits centering on aspects of life in Monmouth county; collections of silver, ceramics, paintings; exhibits on Battle of Monmouth. Museum (Tues-Sat, also Sun afternoons); library (Wed-Sat; both closed holidays). **$**

Turkey Swamp Park. *200 Georgia Rd (07728). 2 miles SW off I-195, exit 22, County 524 to Georgia Rd. Phone 732/462-7286.* An 1,004-acre park with fishing, boating (rentals); hiking trails, ice skating, picnicking (shelter), playfields, camping (Mar-Nov; fee; electric and water hookups). Special events. **FREE**

Special Event

Harness racing. *Rtes 9 and 33. Freehold Raceway. Phone 732/462-3800.* Tues-Sat, mid-Aug-May.

Motel/Motor Lodge

★ **COLTS NECK INN HOTEL.** *6 Rte 537W, Colts Neck (07722). Phone 732/409-1200; fax 732/431-6640.* 49 rooms, 2 story. S $65; D $85; each additional $10; suites $150; under 12 free. TV; cable (premium), VCR available. Complimentary continental breakfast. Restaurant adjacent. Bar. Check-out 11 am. Meeting rooms. Business services available. Refrigerators, microwaves available. Cr cds: A, C, MC, V.

D 🛏 **SC**

Hotel

★★ **FREEHOLD GARDENS HOTEL.** *50 Gibson Place (07728). Phone 732/780-3870; fax 732/780-8725. www.freeholdgardens.com.* 114 rooms, 5 story. S, D $69-$90; each additional $10; under 13 free; higher rates late May-early Sept. Crib free. Pet accepted, some restrictions. Complimentary continental breakfast. Check-out noon. TV; cable. Refrigerators available. Restaurant 5-11 pm. Entertainment Fri, Sat. Health club privileges. Pool. Meeting rooms. Business services. Cr cds: A, C, D, JCB, MC, V.

D 🐾 🏊 🏋

Restaurant

★ **GOLDEN BELL DINER.** *3320 US 9 (07728). Phone 732/462-7259; fax 732/462-7194.* Italian, American menu. Specialties: Golden Bell fisherman's platter, tropical waffle, chicken salad in pita bread. Hours: 6-1 am; Fri, Sat open 24 hours. Lunch $4.95-$8.25, dinner $7-$23. Children's menu. Greenhouse atrium. Cr cds: A, D, DS, MC, V.

D **SC**

Gateway National Recreation Area (Sandy Hook Unit) (D-6)

See also Red Bank

(5 miles E of Atlantic Highlands on NJ 36)

Sandy Hook is a barrier peninsula that was first sighted by the crew of Henry Hudson's *Half Moon* (1609). It once was owned (1692) by Richard Hartshorne, an English Quaker, but has been government property since the 18th century. Fort Hancock (1895) was an important harbor defense from the Spanish-American War through the Cold War era. Among Sandy Hook's most significant features are the Sandy Hook Lighthouse (1764), the oldest operating lighthouse in the United States, and the US Army Proving Ground (1874-1919), the army's first new-weapons testing site.

The park offers swimming (lifeguards in summer), fishing; guided and self-guided walks, picnicking, and a concession. Visitors are advised to obtain literature at the Visitor Center (daily). There is no charge for entrance and activities scheduled by the National Park Service. Parking fee, Memorial Day weekend-Labor Day. (Daily, sunrise-sunset; some facilities closed in winter) Contact Superintendant, PO Box 530, Fort Hancock 07732; 732/872-5970.

What to See and Do

Twin Lights State Historic Site. *NJ 36 and Light House Rd (07732). Phone 732/872-1814.* (1862) A lighthouse built to guide ships into New York harbor; now a marine museum operated by the State Park Service. (May-Oct, daily; rest of year, Wed-Sun) **DONATION**

Restaurants

★ ★ **BAHR'S RESTAURANT & MARINA.** *2 Bay Ave, Highlands (07732). Phone 732/872-1245; fax 732/872-0495. www.bahrs.com.* Hours: 11:30 am-9:30 pm; Fri, Sat to 10:30 pm; Sun to 9 pm; Sun brunch 11 am-2:30 pm. Closed Dec 25. Bar. A la carte entrées: lunch, dinner $12.95-$25.95. Sun brunch $5-$9.95. Children's menu. Specializes in fresh seafood. On waterfront; scenic view of the channel. Family-owned. Cr cds: A, DS, MC, V.
D

★ ★ **DORIS & ED'S.** *348 Shore Dr, Highlands (07732). Phone 732/872-1565; fax 732/872-2299. www.doris-and-eds.com.* Hours: 5-10 pm; Sat to 11 pm; Sun 3-10 pm. Closed Mon, Tues; also Jan-Feb. Dinner $24-$34. Children's menu. Reservations accepted. Cr cds: A, C, D, ER, MC, V.
D

Gibbstown

Pop 3,758 **Elev** 15 ft **Area code** 856 **Zip** 08027

Information Township of Greenwich, 420 Washington St; 856/423-1038 or 856/423-4913

What to See and Do

Hunter-Lawrence-Jessup House. *58 N Broad St. Approximately 7 miles NW via NJ 45, County 534 in Woodbury. Phone 856/848-8531.* (1765) Headquarters of Gloucester County Historical Society. Museum contains 16 rooms of furnishings and memorabilia from 17th- to 19th-century New Jersey. (Mon, Wed, Fri, last Sat-Sun of each month; closed holidays) **$**

Nothnagle Home. *406 Swedesboro Rd. Phone 856/423-0916.* (1638-1643) America's oldest log house. (By appointment) **FREE**

Motel/Motor Lodge

★ ★ **HOLIDAY INN.** *1 Pureland Dr (08085). Phone 856/467-3322; toll-free 800/465-4329; fax 856/467-3031. www.holiday-inn.com.* 149 rooms, 4 story. S, D $79-$129; each additional $10; suites $149-$189; under 18 free. Crib free. Check-out noon. TV; cable (premium), VCR available. In-room modem link. Some balconies. Some refrigerators. Coffee in rooms. Valet services, coin laundry. Restaurant 6:30 am-10 pm. Bar 11 am-midnight, entertainment Mon-Fri. Room service. Exercise equipment. Game room. Indoor pool, whirlpool, poolside service. Meeting rooms. Business services. Bellstaff. Sundries. Cr cds: A, D, DS, JCB, MC, V.
D ⚓ 🏋 ⊠

Hackensack (C-5)

See also Fort Lee, Paterson

Settled 1647 **Pop** 42,677 **Elev** 20 ft **Area code** 201

Information Chamber of Commerce, 190 Main St, 07601; 201/489-3700

Hackensack was officially known as New Barbados until 1921 when it received its charter under its present name, thought to be derived from the Native American word

Hacquinsacq. The influence of the original Dutch settlers who established a trading post here remained strong even after British conquest. A strategic point during the Revolutionary War, the city contains a number of historical sites from that era. Hackensack is the hub for industry, business, and government in Bergen County. Edward Williams College is located here.

What to See and Do

The Church on the Green. *42 Court St, NE corner of the Green, S end of Main St, opposite County Court House. Phone 201/845-0957.* Organized in 1686, the original building was built in 1696 (13 monogrammed stones preserved in east wall), and rebuilt in 1791 in Stone Dutch architectural style. It is the oldest church building in Bergen County. Museum contains pictures, books, and colonial items. Enoch Poor, a Revolutionary War general, is buried in the cemetery. Tours (weekdays on request). **FREE**

Steuben House State Historic Site. *1209 Main St. Approximately 1/4 mile N of NJ 4, in River Edge, overlooking river. Phone 201/487-1739.* (1713) Museum of the Bergen County Historical Society. Enlarged in 1752 as home of Jan and Annetie Zabriskie. The house was confiscated during the Revolutionary War because the Zabriskies were Loyalists; it was given to Baron von Steuben, by the state of New Jersey, as a reward for his military services. The baron later sold it back to the original owners. Colonial furniture, glassware, china; Native American artifacts. (Wed-Sat and Sun afternoons; closed Jan 1, Thanksgiving, Dec 25)

USS *Ling* Submarine. *Docked at Court and River sts. Phone 201/342-3268.* Restored WWII fleet submarine; New Jersey Naval Museum. (Sat-Sun afternoons; closed holidays)

Hotels

★ ★ ★ **HILTON HOTEL.** *650 Terrace Ave, Hasbrouck Heights (07604). Phone 201/288-6100; fax 201/288-4717. www.hilton.com.* 370 rooms, 12 story. D $109-$219; each additional $20; under 17 free; weekend rates. Pet accepted. Check-out 11 am, check-in 3 pm. TV; cable (premium), VCR available. In-room modem link. Restaurant 6:30 am-11 pm. Bar 11-1:30 am, Sat to 2:30 am. Exercise equipment, sauna. Poolside service. Business center. Luxury level. Cr cds: A, C, D, DS, ER, JCB, MC, V.

⊡ ⬛ ⬛ ⬛ ⬛ ⬛ ⬛ ⬛

★ ★ ★ **MARRIOTT GLENPOINTE.** *100 Frank W Burr Blvd, Teaneck (07666). Phone 201/836-0600; toll-free 800/228-9290; fax 201/836-0638. www.marriott.com.* 347

rooms, 15 story. D $99-$219; weekend rates. Check-out noon, check-in 4 pm. TV; cable (premium), VCR available. In-room modem link. Restaurant 6:30 am-10 pm. Bar 11-1 am. Exercise room, sauna. Indoor pool, whirlpool. Business center. Concierge. Near Meadowlands. Cr cds: A, C, D, DS, ER, JCB, MC, V.

⊡ ⬛ ⬛ ⬛ ⬛

Restaurant

★ ★ ★ **STONY HILL INN.** *231 Polifly Rd (07601). Phone 201/342-4085; fax 201/342-1046. www.stonyhillinn.com.* Continental menu. Hours: 11:30 am-3 pm, 5:30-10:30 pm; Sat from 5:30 pm; Sun 2-9 pm. Closed Dec 25. Dinner $15.95-$29.95. Bar to midnight. Entertainment Fri, Sat. Jacket required. Landmark Dutch colonial house (1818); period furnishings. Cr cds: A, D, MC, V.

⊡

Hackettstown (C-3)

Settled circa 1760 **Pop** 10,403 **Elev** 571 ft **Area code** 908 **Zip** 07840

Information Town Hall, 215 Stiger St; 908/852-3130

First called Helm's Mills and then Musconetcong, citizens renamed the town for Samuel Hackett, the largest local landowner. His popularity increased when he provided unlimited free drinks at the christening of a new hotel. Hackettstown is located in the Musconetcong Valley between the Schooleys and Upper Pohatcong mountains.

What to See and Do

Allamuchy Mountain State Park, Stephens Section. *800 Willow Grove St (07840). 1 1/2 miles N of US 46. Phone 908/852-3790 (Stephens).* Allamuchy Mountain State Park (7,263 acres) is divided into three sections. The Stephens Section (482 acres) is developed; the rest (Allamuchy) is natural. Fishing in Musconetcong River; hunting, hiking, picnicking, playground, camping. Standard fees.

Land of Make Believe. *I-80 exit 12, on County 611, in Hope. Phone 908/459-9000.* Amusement park at foot of Jenny Jump Mountain includes the Tornado; Old McDonald's Farm; the Red Baron airplane; Santa Claus at the North Pole; a Civil War train; a maze; water park; hayrides; picnic grove; fudge factory. (Mid-June-Labor Day, daily; Memorial Day weekend-mid-June, weekends; Sept, weekend after Labor Day) **$$$$**

Motel/Motor Lodge

★★ **THE INN AT MILLRACE POND.** *313 Johnsonberg Rd, Rte 519 N, Hope (07844). Phone 908/459-4884; toll-free 800/746-6467; fax 908/459-5276. www. innatmillracepond.com.* 18 rooms, 2 story. D $115-$125; each additional $20. Complimentary breakfast. Check-out noon, check-in 3 pm. TV in some rooms. Restaurant 5-9 pm; Sun 4-7:30 pm. Tennis. Airport transportation. Rooms individually decorated with colonial-style furniture and period reproductions. Cr cds: A, C, D, DS, MC, V.

[D] [⚡] [🐾] [🏊]

Haddonfield

See also Camden, Cherry Hill

Settled circa 1713 **Pop** 11,659 **Elev** 95 ft **Area code** 856 **Zip** 08033

Information Visitor/Information Center, 114 Kings Hwy E; 856/216-7253

Named for Elizabeth Haddon, a Quaker girl of 20 whose father sent her here from England in 1701 to develop 400 acres of land. This assertive young woman built a house, started a colony, and proposed to a Quaker missionary who promptly married her. The "Theologian's Tale" in Longfellow's *Tales of a Wayside Inn* celebrates Elizabeth Haddon's romance with the missionary.

What to See and Do

Greenfield Hall. *343 King's Hwy E (NJ 41). Phone 856/429-7375.* Haddonfield's Historical Society headquarters in old Gill House (1747-1841) contains personal items of Elizabeth Haddon; furniture; costumes; doll collection. Boxwood garden; library on local history. On grounds is a house (circa 1735) once owned by Elizabeth Haddon. (Library, Tues, Thurs mornings; museum, Wed-Fri afternoons, other days by appointment; closed Aug) **$**

Indian King Tavern Museum State Historic Site. *233 King's Hwy E. Phone 856/429-6792.* Built as an inn; state legislatures met here frequently, passing a bill (1777) substituting "State" for "Colony" in all state papers. Colonial furnishings. Guided tours. (Wed-Sun; closed Jan 1, Thanksgiving, Dec 25; also Wed if following Mon or Tues hol) **DONATION**

The Site of the Elizabeth Haddon House. *Wood Lane and Merion Ave.* Isaac Wood built this house in 1842, on the foundation of Elizabeth Haddon's 1713 brick mansion, immediately after it was destroyed by fire. The original

brew house Elizabeth built (1713) and the English yew trees she brought over in 1712 are in the yard. Private residence; not open to the public.

High Point State Park

(7 miles NW of Sussex on NJ 23)

High Point's elevation (1,803 feet), the highest point in New Jersey, gave this 15,000-acre park its name. The spot is marked by a 220-foot stone war memorial. The view is magnificent, overlooking Tri-State—the point where New Jersey, New York, and Pennsylvania meet—with the Catskill Mountains to the north, the Pocono Mountains to the west, and hills, valleys, and lakes all around. Elsewhere in the forests of this Kittatinny Mountain park are facilities for swimming, fishing, boating; nature center, picnicking, and tent camping (no trailers). Standard fees. Phone 973/875-4800.

Hightstown (E-4)

Pop 5,216 **Elev** 84 ft **Area code** 609 **Zip** 08520

Motel/Motor Lodge

★ **RAMADA INN.** *399 Monmouth St, East Windsor (08520). Phone 609/448-7000; toll-free 888/298-2054; fax 609/443-6227. www.ramada.com.* 200 rooms, 4 story. Mid-June-Aug: S, D $79-$129; each additional $10; suite $139-$199; under 12 free; lower rates rest of year. Check-out noon. TV; cable (premium). Restaurant opposite 7 am-10 pm. Bar 5 pm-1 am. Exercise equipment, sauna. Pool. Cr cds: A, C, D, DS, JCB, MC, V.

[D] [≈] [🏋] [🏊] [SC]

Restaurant

★★ **FORSGATE COUNTRY CLUB.** *375 Forsgate Dr, Monroe (08831). Phone 732/521-0070; fax 732/521-0687. www.forsgatecc.com.* Hours: 11:30 am-2 pm, 5-9 pm; Sat from 6 pm; Sun brunch from 10:30 am. Closed Mon; Jan 1, Dec 25. Bar. A la carte entrées: lunch $7.50-$18, dinner $8-$27. Sun brunch $22.95. Specializes in regional American dishes. Country club atmosphere; view of golf course. Cr cds: A, D, MC, V.

[D]

Ho-Ho-Kus

See also Paramus

Pop 4,060 **Elev** 111 ft **Area code** 201 **Zip** 07423

Information Borough of Ho-Ho-Kus, 333 Warren Ave; 201/652-4400

In colonial times, Ho-Ho-Kus was known as Hoppertown. Its present name is derived from the Chihohokies, who also had a settlement on this spot.

What to See and Do

The Hermitage. *335 N Franklin Tpke (07423). Phone 201/445-8311 for exact schedule, including events and productions.* Stone Victorian house of Gothic Revival architecture superimposed on original 18th-century house. Its span of history includes ownership by the Rosencrantz family for more than 150 years. Grounds consist of 5 wooded acres, including a second stone Victorian house. Docents conduct tours of site and the Hermitage. Changing exhibits. Special events held throughout the year. Tours. **$$**

Hoboken

See also Jersey City, Secaucus

Settled 1640 **Pop** 38,577 **Elev** 5 ft **Area code** 201 **Zip** 07030

Information Hoboken Community Development, 94 Washington St; 201/420-2013

In the early 19th century, beer gardens and other amusement centers dotted the Hoboken shore, enticing New Yorkers across the Hudson. John Jacob Astor, Washington Irving, William Cullen Bryant, and Martin Van Buren were among the fashionable visitors. By the second half of the century, industries and shipping began to encroach on the fun. In 1928-29, Christopher Morley and Cleon Throckmorton presented revivals of *After Dark* and *The Black Crook* to enchanted New Yorkers. Hoboken is connected to Manhattan by the PATH rapid-transit system.

What to See and Do

Davidson Laboratory. *Hudson and 7th sts. On the W end of the campus of Stevens Institute of Technology. Phone 201/216-5290.* One of the largest privately owned hydrodynamic labs of its kind in the world. Testing site for models of ships, hydrofoils, the America's Cup participants, and the Apollo command capsule. (Limited public access)

Samuel C. Williams Library. *On the campus of Stevens Institute of Technology. Phone 201/216-5198.* (1969) Special collections including set of facsimiles of every drawing by Leonardo da Vinci; library of 3,000 volumes by and about da Vinci; Alexander Calder mobile; the Frederick Winslow Taylor Collection of Scientific Management. (Academic year)

Stevens Center. *On the campus of Stevens Institute of Technology.* (1962) The 14-story hub of campus. Excellent view of Manhattan from George Washington Bridge to the Verrazano Bridge.

Stevens Institute of Technology. *Castle Point, E of Hudson St between 5th and 9th sts. Phone 201/216-5105.* (1870) 3,600 students. A leading college of engineering, science, computer science management, and the humanities; also a center for research. Campus tours.

Restaurants

★ ★ **BAJA MEXICAN CUISINE.** *104 14th St (07030). Phone 201/653-0610; fax 201/239-9034.* Mexican menu. Hours: 5-10:30 pm; Fri, Sat noon-11:30 pm; Sun noon-10 pm. Closed Jan 1, Thanksgiving, Dec 25. Dinner $8.95-$41.90. Bar. Casual attire. Cr cds: A, D, DS, MC, V.

★ **CAFE MICHELINA.** *423 Bloomfield St (07030). Phone 201/659-3663.* Italian menu. Hours: 11 am-10 pm; Fri to midnight; Sat 3-11 pm; Sun 3-9:30 pm. Closed Mon; most major holidays. Dinner $8.95-$15.95. Casual attire. Cr cds: MC, V.

Ⓓ

★ **GRIMALDI'S.** *133 Clinton St (07030). Phone 201/792-0800. www.grimaldis.com.* Hours: noon-11 pm; Sat, Sun from 2 pm; Tues, Wed from 5 pm. Closed Mon; Easter, Thanksgiving, Dec 25. Italian menu. A la carte entrées: lunch, dinner $11-$16. Specialties: roasted sweet red peppers, sausage pizza, mushroom pizza. Outdoor seating. Cozy, Italian atmosphere; brick oven; two-level dining area. Cr cds: A, C, DS, MC, V.

★ **MARGHERITAS'.** *740 Washington St (07030). Phone 201/222-2400; fax 201/222-3440.* Italian menu. Closed Mon; Easter, Thanksgiving, Dec 25. Lunch, dinner. Cr cds: MC, V.

★ **ODD FELLOWS.** *80 River St (07030). Phone 201/656-9009; fax 201/656-0484. www.oddfellowsrest.com.* Creole/Cajun menu. Hours: 11:30 am-10:30 pm; Thurs-Sat to 11 pm; Sun to 4 pm (brunch). Closed Thanksgiving, Dec 25. Dinner $7.95-$18.95. Bar. Casual attire. Outdoor seating. Blues Thurs, Sun. Cr cds: A, MC, V.

Ⓓ

Jackson (F-4)

See also Lakewood, Toms River

Pop 42,816 **Elev** 138 ft **Area code** 732 **Zip** 08527

Information Chamber of Commerce, 1080 N County Line Rd, PO Box A-C; 732/363-1080

What to See and Do

Six Flags Great Adventure Theme Park/Six Flags Wild Safari Animal Park. *299 Cherry Hill Rd (07054). On NJ 537, 1 mile S of I-195.* Phone 732/928-1821. This family entertainment center includes a 350-acre drive-through safari park with more than 1,200 free-roaming animals from six continents; 125-acre theme park featuring more than 100 rides, shows and attractions. (Late Mar-late Oct; schedule varies). **$$$$**

Jersey City (C-5)

See also Newark, Newark International Airport Area

Settled 1629 **Pop** 240,055 **Elev** 11 ft **Area code** 201

Information Jersey City Cultural Affairs, 1 Chapel Ave, 07305; 201/547-5522

Jersey City's location on the Hudson River, due west of the southern end of Manhattan Island, has aided its growth to such a degree that it is now the second-largest city in New Jersey. New Yorkers across the bay tell time by the Colgate-Palmolive Clock at 105 Hudson Street; the dial is 50 feet across, and the minute hand, weighing 2,200 pounds, moves 23 inches each minute. Jersey City's major links with New York are the 8,557-foot Holland Tunnel, which is 72 feet below water level; the Port Authority Trans-Hudson (PATH) rapid-transit system; and New York Waterways Ferries, which run between Exchange Place, the city's Financial District, and the World Financial Center in lower Manhattan.

What to See and Do

⭐ **Liberty Science Center.** *In Liberty State Park. 251 Phillip St.* Phone 201/200-1000. Four-story structure encompasses Environment, Health, and Invention exhibit areas that feature more than 250 hands-on exhibits. Geodesic dome houses IMAX Theater with a six-story screen. (Daily; closed Thanksgiving, Dec 25) **$$$$**

Liberty State Park. *Morris Pesin Dr (07305). Off NJ Tpke, exit 14B; on the New York Harbor, less than 2,000 feet from the Statue of Liberty. Boat tours and ferry service to Ellis Island and Statue of Liberty are available.* Phone 201/915-3400. Offers breathtaking view of New York City skyline; flag display includes state, historic, and US flags; boat launch;

fitness course, picnic area. Historic railroad terminal has been partially restored. The Interpretive Center houses an exhibit area; adjacent to the Center is a 60-acre natural area consisting mostly of salt marsh. Nature trails and observation points complement this wildlife habitat. (Daily)

Lake Hopatcong

(Approximately 15 miles N and W of Dover via NJ 15 and unnumbered road)

The largest lake in New Jersey, Hopatcong's popularity as a resort is second only to the seacoast spots. It covers 2,443 acres and has a hilly shoreline of approximately 40 miles. The area offers swimming, stocked fishing, and boating.

What to See and Do

Hopatcong State Park. *Southwestern shore of lake, in Landing.* Phone 973/398-7010. A 113-acre park with swimming, bathhouse, fishing; picnicking, playground, and concession. Historic museum (Sun afternoons). Standard fees.

Motels/Motor Lodges

⭐ ⭐ **COURTYARD BY MARRIOTT ARLINGTON.** *15 Howard Blvd, Mt. Arlington (07856).* Phone 973/770-2000; fax 973/770-1287. 134 rooms, 5 story. D $89-$159; each additional $10; under 18 free; weekend rates. Pets accepted. Check-out noon, check-in 3 pm. TV; cable (premium). Restaurant 6:30 am-10 pm. Bar 11-2 am; entertainment Wed, Sat. Room service. Exercise equipment. Indoor pool. Cr cds: A, DS, MC, V.

⬛⬛⬛⬛⬛

⭐ ⭐ **LEDGEWOOD DAYS INN LAKE HOPATCONG.** *1691 Rte 46 West, Ledgewood (07852).* Phone 973/347-5100; fax 973/347-6356. 100 rooms, 2 story. D $69-$99; each additional $10; under 15 free. Complimentary continental breakfast. Check-out 11 am, check-in 2 pm. TV. Restaurant 11:30 am-9:30 pm; Sun 8 am-1 pm. Bar 4 pm-2 am; entertainment Fri, Sat. Room service. Pool; two tennis courts. Cr cds: A, C, D, DS, MC, V.

⬛⬛⬛⬛⬛

Lakewood (F-5)

See also Toms River

Settled 1800 **Pop** 36,065 **Elev** 67 ft **Area code** 732 **Zip** 08701

Information Chamber of Commerce, 395 Rt 70 W, Suite 125; 732/363-0012

A well-known winter resort in the 1890s, many socially prominent New Yorkers such as the Astors, the Goulds, the Rhinelanders, the Rockefellers, and the Vanderbilts maintained large homes on the shores of Lake Carasaljo.

What to See and Do

Ocean County Park #1. *659 Ocean Ave, 1 mile E on NJ 88. Phone 732/370-7380.* The 325-acre former Rockefeller estate. Lake swimming, children's fishing lake; tennis, platform tennis, picnicking (grills), playground, athletic fields. (Daily) Entrance fee (July-Aug, weekends). **$**

Motel/Motor Lodge

★ ★ **BEST WESTERN LEISURE INN.** *1600 Hwy 70 (08701). Phone 732/367-0900; toll-free 800/780-7234; fax 732/370-4928. www.bestwestern.com.* 105 rooms, 2 story. Memorial Day-Sept: S, D $75-$115; each additional $10; lower rates rest of year. Crib free. Check-out 11 am.

TV; cable (premium). In-room modem link. Refrigerators available. Coin laundry. Restaurant 7 am-10 pm. Bar 6-11 pm. Pool. Meeting room. Business services. Cr cds: A, C, D, DS, MC, V.

D ⚓ ⛱ ⛵

Lambertville (E-3)

See also Trenton

Settled 1705 **Pop** 3,868 **Elev** 76 ft **Area code** 609 **Zip** 08530

Information Lambertville Area Chamber of Commerce, 239 N Union St; 609/397-0055

Web www.lambertville.org

Lambertville's Unique Shopping

This tour can cover anywhere from about 1 1/2 miles to many miles, depending on whether you stay within the town proper or extend the walk along the Delaware & Raritan Canal, or even cross the Delaware River into New Hope, Pennsylvania. Lambertville is rich in history, antique shops, fine restaurants, and historic homes. The town has long been the state's shad fishing center, and still celebrates the annual Shad Festival. It was also the country's hairpin-making capital during the early 20th century. Today, Lambertville is a fine antiques and art center. The streets are set out in a grid, with Union and Main Streets running north and south, parallel to the river, and a series of short cross-streets passing between them. A variety of historic homes in the Federalist and Victorian styles can be found here.

Start at the historic Marshall House at 62 Bridge Street. A classic Federalist building, this is the home of the Lambertville Historical Society, which leads one-hour guided walking tours from late June through September, presents a 30-minute film on Lambertville's history, and can supply you with a guide to the town's historic buildings. After visiting the Marshall House, proceed west to Union Street, and head north into the heart of the shopping district. Along this street you'll encounter Phoenix Books at 49 North Union, a treasure trove of rare and out-of-print volumes; the Five and Dime at 40 North Union, which houses an equally fascinating collection of antique toys; and, all along the street, a number of high-quality antique shops and galleries, from The People's Store at the corner of Union and Church streets and Broadmoor Antiques at 6 North Union to the Best of France at 204 North Union, with many others in-between. At the north end of Union (ten blocks north), turn right onto Cherry Street. Follow Cherry to North Main, turn right, and begin weaving among the cross streets between North Union and North Main back to Bridge Street. Along North Main, A Mano Gallery specializes in American crafts, jewelry, and glass, while Almirah focuses on colonial-era Indian antique furniture and gifts. Shopping, window shopping, or gallery hopping are best done on Perry, York, Coryell, Church Bridge, and Ferry streets. More shops can be found on Kline's Court (one block on the left from Bridge Street) and Lambert Lane (just across the canal on the right). From Lambert Lane, cross the footbridge onto Lewis Island, home of Fred Lewis, the state's only commercially licensed freshwater shad fisherman.

Back on Bridge Street, take a break at Lambertville Station, which serves New American cuisine, or return to town for other dining options, including The Fish House at 2 Canal Street for local catches of the day, Anton's at the Swan at 43 South Main Street for upscale dining in a historical building, or the Church Street Bistro at 11 Church Street for intimate dinning.

For those with stamina, add one of the two extended walk options. To get in touch with nature, follow the walking/biking path along the Delaware & Raritan Canal, which travels south for many miles, presenting a bucolic view of the canal and the Delaware River. Another option is to cross the Delaware on the Bridge Street bridge and enter New Hope, Pennsylvania, a treasure trove of antique shops and restaurants.

What to See and Do

John Holcombe House. *260 N Main St.* Washington stayed here just before crossing the Delaware. Privately owned residence.

Marshall House. *62 Bridge St. Phone 609/397-0770.* (1816) James Marshall, who first discovered gold at Sutter's Mill in California in 1848, lived here until 1834. Period furnishings; memorabilia of Lambertville; small museum collection. (May-mid-Oct, weekends or by appointment) **FREE**

Motel/Motor Lodge

★ **WOOLVERTON INN.** *6 Woolverton Rd, Stockton (08559). Phone 609/397-0802; toll-free 888/264-6648; fax 609/397-0987. www.woolvertoninn.com.* 10 rooms, 3 with shower only, 2 suites, 2 story. May-Sept: S, D $90-$140; each additional $35; suites $120-$190; weekends, holidays (2-3 day minimum). Complimentary full breakfast. Check-out 11 am, check-in 3-8 pm. Totally nonsmoking. Cr cds: A, MC, V.

D ⬧ ⬧ ⬧

Hotel

★★★ **INN AT LAMBERTVILLE STATION.** *11 Bridge St (08530). Phone 609/397-4400; toll-free 800/524-1091; fax 609/397-9744. www.lambertvillestation.com.* The actual restored 19th-century train station serves as a new American restaurant next door to this charming inn. Creative, city-themed rooms span the globe, all with Delaware River views. An extensive Sunday champagne brunch is served in the glass-walled Riverside Room. 45 units, 3 story. S, D $85-$95; each additional $15; suites $135. Crib available. TV; cable (premium). Complimentary continental breakfast. Dining room 11:30 am-10 pm. Check-out noon. Meeting rooms. Business services available. Health club privileges. Fireplace in suites. View of Delaware River. Victorian antiques. Cr cds: A, D, MC, V.

D ⬧ SC

B&B/Small Inn

★★ **CHIMNEY HILL FARM ESTATE.** *207 Goat Hill Rd (08530). Phone 609/397-1516; toll-free 800/211-4667; fax 609/397-9353. www.chimneyhill.com.* 12 rooms, 3 story. Children over 12 years only. Complimentary breakfast. Check-out 11 am, check-in 3 pm. Elegant stone and frame manor house built in 1820; furnishings are antiques and period reproductions. Cr cds: A, MC, V. **$$**

SC

Restaurants

★★ **ANTON'S AT THE SWAN.** *43 S Main St (08530). Phone 609/397-1960. www.antonsattheswan.com.* Contemporary American menu. Menu changes monthly. Hours: 6-10 pm; Mon to 9 pm; Sun 4:30-8 pm. Closed Mon; also Jan 1, Dec 25. Dinner $23-$29. Bar 4 pm-1 am; Sun 2-11 pm. Reservations accepted. Cr cds: A, D, DS, MC, V.

★★ **LAMBERTVILLE STATION.** *11 Bridge St (08530). Phone 609/397-8300; fax 609/397-4262. www.lambertvillestation.com.* Hours: 11:30 am-3 pm, 4-10 pm; Fri, Sat to 11 pm; early-bird dinner Mon-Thurs 4-6:30 pm, Fri to 6 pm; Sun brunch 10:30 am-3 pm. Reservations accepted. Bar. Lunch $6.95-$12.50, dinner $13.50-$22.50. Sun brunch $7.25-$11.50. Children's menu. Specializes in rack of lamb, elk. Jazz Sat, Sun. Renovated train station with three dining areas; one dining room is an old station platform. Victorian-style décor. Cr cds: A, D, MC, V.

D

Livingston

Pop 27,391 **Elev** 307 ft **Area code** 973 **Zip** 07039

This suburban community in southwestern Essex County is named for William Livingston, the first governor of New Jersey.

Restaurant

★★ **AFTON.** *2 Hanover Rd, Florham Park (07932). Phone 973/377-1871; fax 973/377-6362.* Hours: 11:30 am-2:30 pm, 5-9 pm; Sun noon-8 pm; Sun brunch 11 am-2 pm. Closed Mon; Dec 25. Bar to 11 pm. Complete meals: lunch $7.95-$12.95, dinner $13.50-$18.50. Sun brunch $12.95. Specializes in prime rib, seafood. Family-owned. Cr cds: A, D, MC, V.

D SC

Long Beach Island

Six miles out to sea, this island is separated from the New Jersey mainland by Barnegat and Little Egg Harbor bays. NJ 72, going east from Manahawkin on the mainland, enters the island at Ship Bottom. The island is no more than three blocks wide in some places, and extends 18 miles from historic Barnegat Lighthouse to the north. It includes towns such as Loveladies, Harvey Cedars, Surf City, Ship Bottom, Brant Beach, and the Beach Havens at the southern tip. The island is a popular family resort with excellent fishing, boating, and other water sports. For swimming, the bay is calm, while the ocean offers vigorous surf.

Tales are told of pirate coins buried on the island, and, over the years, silver and gold pieces occasionally have turned up. Whether they are part of pirate treasure or the refuse of shipwrecks remains a mystery.

What to See and Do

Barnegat Lighthouse State Park. *At the northern end of the island (08006). Phone 609/494-2016.* Barnegat Lighthouse, a 167-foot red and white tower, was engineered by General George G. Meade and completed in 1858. There is a 217-step spiral staircase leading to a lookout that offers a spectacular view. Fishing; picnicking. Park (daily); lighthouse (Memorial Day-Labor Day, daily; May and Labor Day-Oct, weekends only). Standard fees.

Fantasy Island Amusement Park. *320 W 7th St, Beach Haven (08008). Phone 609/492-4000.* Family-oriented amusement park featuring rides and games; family casino arcade. (June-Aug, daily; May and Sept, weekends; schedule varies)

Special Event

Surflight Theatre. *Beach Haven. Beach and Engleside aves. Phone 609/492-9477.* Broadway musicals nightly. Children's theater, Wed-Sat. May-mid-Oct.

Motels/Motor Lodges

★ ★ ★ **THE ENGLESIDE INN.** *30 E Engleside Ave, Beach Haven (08008). Phone 609/492-1251; toll-free 800/762-2214; fax 609/492-9175. www.engleside.com.* 72 units, 37 kitchen units, 3 story. No elevator. July-Labor Day: S, D $150-$225; each additional $12; suites $290-$375; kitchen units $165-$225; lower rates rest of year. Crib available. Pets accepted, some restrictions. Check-out 11 am. TV; cable, VCR (movies $2). Private patios, balconies. Refrigerators. Restaurant, bar. Exercise equipment. Pool, poolside service (in season), lifeguard. Meeting rooms. Business services. Sundries. On beach. Cr cds: A, C, D, DS, MC, V.

⬛ D ⬛ ⬛ ⬛ ⬛

★ **SANDPIPER MOTEL.** *10th St and LBI Blvd, Ship Bottom (08008). Phone 609/494-6909; fax 609/361-2246.* 20 rooms, shower only. July-Aug: S, D $110-$140; each additional $5; higher rates weekends and holidays (3-day minimum); lower rates May-June and Sept-Oct. Closed rest of year. Check-out 11 am. TV; cable. Refrigerators. Restaurant adjacent 4-10 pm. Pool. Ocean 1 block. Cr cds: MC, V.

⬛ ⬛

Resort

★ **SPRAY BEACH INN.** *Ocean and 24th sts, Spray Beach (08008). Phone 609/492-1501; fax 609/492-0504. www.lbinns.com.* 88 rooms, 10 kitchen units, 3 story. Late June-Labor Day: S, D $166-$235; each additional $10; kitchen units $155-$195; lower rates rest of year. Closed Jan. Crib $7. Check-out noon. TV; cable, VCR available. Refrigerators. Restaurant 8 am-2:30 pm, 5-10 pm. Bar 10:30-2 am; entertainment weekends, holidays in season. Heated pool, lifeguard. Business services. Sundries. On beach. Cr cds: A, MC, V.

⬛

B&B/Small Inn

★ ★ ★ **AMBER STREET INN BED & BREAKFAST.** *118 Amber St, Beach Haven (08008). Phone 609/492-1611; fax 609/492-9165. www.amberstreetinn.com.* 6 rooms, 3 story. Children over 10 years only. Complimentary full breakfast. Check-out 11 am, check-in 3 pm. TV in parlor. Restaurant. Built in 1885; antiques. Totally nonsmoking. Cr cds: MC, V.

⬛ ⬛ ⬛ ⬛

Restaurants

★ ★ **BUCKALEW'S.** *101 N Bay Ave, Beach Haven (08008). Phone 609/492-1065; fax 609/492-2975. www.buckalews.com.* Continental menu. Hours: 11:30-1:30 am, closed Dec 25. Breakfast $3.95-$8.95, lunch $3.95-$7.95, dinner $13.95-$22.95. Bar. Bands Tues-Sat. Children's menu. Reservations accepted. Cr cds: A, DS, MC, V.

D

★ ★ **LEEWARD ROOM.** *30 Engleside Ave, Beach Haven (08008). Phone 609/492-5116. www.engleside.com.* Japanese menu. Hours: 8 am-noon, 5-10 pm; Sun brunch 8 am-1:30 pm. Closed Dec 25. Breakfast $2.25-$9.50, lunch $2-$10, dinner $10-$31, Sun brunch $13.95. Bar 5 pm-1 am. Children's menu. Reservations accepted. Cr cds: A, D, DS, MC, V.

D

★ ★ **TUCKER'S.** *Engleside Ave and West St (08008). Phone 609/492-2300; fax 609/492-8160. www.tuckers.com.* Hours: 11:30-2 am; early-bird dinner (seasonal) 5-6 pm. Closed Dec 25. A la carte entrées: lunch $5.95-$11.95, dinner $5.95-$19.95. Bar. Entertainment weekends. Children's menu. Outdoor seating. Cr Cds: A, DC, MC, V.

D

Madison (C-4)

See also Chatham, Morristown

Settled circa 1685 **Pop** 16,530 **Elev** 261 ft **Area code** 973 **Zip** 07940

Information Chamber of Commerce, 155 Main St, PO Box 152; 973/377-7830

For many years, the quiet suburban town of Madison was called the "Rose City" because of the thousands of bouquets produced in its many greenhouses.

What to See and Do

Drew University. *36 Madison Ave (07940). Phone 973/408-3000.* (1867) 2,100 students. A 186-acre wooded campus west of town. College of Liberal Arts, Theological School, and Graduate School. On campus are a Neoclassical administration building (1833), the United Methodist Archives and History Center, and the Rose Memorial Library containing Nestorian Cross collection, government and UN documents and manuscripts, and memorabilia of early Methodism. Tours.

Fairleigh Dickinson University-Florham-Madison Campus. *285 Madison Ave, NJ 124. Phone 973/443-8661.* (1958) 3,889 students. (One of three campuses) On site of Twombly Estate (1895); many original buildings still in use. Friendship Library houses numerous special collections including Harry A. Chesler collection of comic art, and collections devoted to printing and the graphic arts. (Academic year, Mon-Fri; closed school holidays) Tours of campus by appointment.

Museum of Early Trades and Crafts. *9 Main St (07940). Main St (NJ 124) at Green Village Rd. Phone 973/377-2982.* Hands-on look at 18th- and 19th-century artisans. Special events include Bottle Hill Craft Festival (Oct). Tours. (Tues-Sat, also Sun afternoons; closed holidays) **$$**

Special Event

New Jersey Shakespeare Festival. *36 Madison Ave (07940). Phone 973/408-5600 or 973/408-3278.* In residence at Drew University. Professional theater company. Includes Shakespearean, classic, and modern plays; special guest attractions and classic films.(Mid-May-Dec).

Matawan (E-5)

See also Freehold

Pop 8,910 **Elev** 55 ft **Area code** 732 **Zip** 07747

Information Matawan-Aberdeen Chamber of Commerce, PO Box 522; 732/290-1125

What to See and Do

Cheesequake State Park. *300 Gordon Rd (07747). Garden State Pkwy, exit 120, right at first traffic light and right at next traffic light onto Gordon Rd, 1/4 mile to entrance. Phone 732/566-2161.* This 1,300-acre park offers swimming, bathhouse, fishing; nature tours, picnicking, playground, concession, camping (fee; dump station). Standard fees.

Special Event

Concerts. *3215 State Rte 35. PNC Bank Arts Center, at Telegraph Hill Park on the Garden State Pkwy, exit 116. Phone 732-442-9200.* A 5,302-seat amphitheater; lawn area seats 4,500-5,500. Contemporary, classical, pop, and rock concerts. Mid-June-Sept.

Motel/Motor Lodge

★ **WELLESLEY INN.** *3215 NJ 35, Hazlet (07730). Phone 732/888-2800; toll-free 800/444-8888; fax 732/888-2902. www.wellesleyinnandsuites.com.* 89 rooms, 3 story. S $63-$129; D $65-$129; each additional $5; under 18 free. Pet accepted, some restrictions; fee. Complimentary continental breakfast. Check-out 11 am. TV; cable (premium). Health club privileges. Cr cds: A, C, D, DS, JCB, MC, V.

D 🐾 ⊠ SC

Hotel

★ **HAZLET HOTEL.** *2870 NJ 35, Hazlet (07730). Phone 732/264-2400; fax 732/739-9735.* 120 rooms, 2 story. S, D $72-$99; each additional $5. Crib free. Check-out noon. TV; cable (premium). Refrigerators available. Restaurant 6:30 am-10 pm. Health club privileges. Pool, lifeguard. Meeting rooms. Business services. Cr cds: A, D, DS, MC, V.

D ⊟ ⊠

Restaurant

★ ★ **BUTTONWOOD MANOR.** *845 NJ 34 (07747). Phone 732/566-6220; fax 732/566-3801. www.buttonwoodmanor.com.* Hours: 11:30 am-10 pm; Sat to 11 pm; Sun noon-9 pm. Reservations accepted. Bar. Lunch $5.25-$9.95, dinner $11.95-$24.95. Children's menu. Specializes in duckling, steak, fresh seafood. Entertainment Fri, Sat. Lakeside seating. Cr cds: A, D, MC, V.

Ⓓ

Millburn

See also Newark, Newark International Airport Area

Settled 1720s **Pop** 19,765 **Elev** 140 ft **Area code** 973 **Zip** 07041

Information Chamber of Commerce, 343 Millburn Ave, PO Box 651; 973/379-1198

Web www.millburn.com

Once bristling with paper mills and hat factories, Millburn today boasts a thriving downtown with a regional theater, a quiet residential area, and direct access to New York City.

What to See and Do

Cora Hartshorn Arboretum and Bird Sanctuary. *324 Forest Dr S (07078). 2 miles W on Forest Dr in Short Hills. Phone 973/376-3587.* A 17-acre sanctuary with nature trails; guided walks. Stone House Museum with nature exhibits (late Sept-mid-June, Tues, Thurs, and Sat). Grounds (Daily). **FREE**

Paper Mill Playhouse. *Brookside Dr and Old Shore Hills Rd (07041). Phone 973/376-4343 (box office) or 973/379-3636 (information). State Theater of New Jersey.* A variety of plays, musicals, and children's theater (Wed-Sun); matinees (Thurs, Sat, and Sun).

Hotel

★ ★ ★ **HILTON SHORT HILLS.** *41 John F. Kennedy Pkwy (07078). Phone 973/379-0100; toll-free 800/445-8667; fax 973/379-6870. www.hilton.com.* 329 rooms, 7 story. D $159-$399; each additional $30; family, weekend rates. Check-out noon, check-in 3 pm. TV; cable (premium), VCR available. In-room modem link. Restaurant 6:30 am-10:30 pm (see also THE DINING ROOM). Bar 11:30-1:30 am; entertainment. Room service 24 hours.

Exercise room, spa, massage, sauna, steam room. Two pools, one indoor, whirlpool. Valet parking. Business center. Concierge. Luxury level. Cr cds: A, C, D, DS, ER, MC, V.

Ⓓ 🎿 ⚓ 🏋 ✈ 🛂 🚶

Restaurant

★ ★ ★ **THE DINING ROOM.** *41 John F Kennedy Pkwy (07078). Phone 973/379-0100; fax 973/379-6870. www.hilton.com.* American, Continental, French menu. Hours: 6-10:30 pm. Closed Sun. 3-course dinner $62, 4-course dinner $92. Bar. Jacket required. Valet parking. Cr cds: A, D, DS, MC, V.

Ⓓ

Millville (H-2)

See also Bridgeton

Pop 26,847 **Elev** 37 ft **Area code** 856 **Zip** 08332

Information Chamber of Commerce, 4 City Park Drive; 856/825-2600

Web www.millville-nj.com

What to See and Do

Wheaton Village. *1501 Glasstown Rd (08332). 2 miles NE via County 552. Phone 856/825-6800.* Buildings include the Museum of American Glass, which houses an extensive glass collection; working factory where demonstrations of glassmaking are given; general store; restored train station; 1876 one-room schoolhouse. Crafts demonstrations, arcade, shops. Restaurant, hotel. Self-guided tours. (Jan-Feb, Fri-Sun; Mar, Wed-Sun; Apr-Dec, daily; closed holidays) **$$$**

Motel/Motor Lodge

★ ★ **COUNTRY INN.** *1125 Village Dr (08332). Phone 856/825-3100; toll-free 800/456-4000; fax 856/825-1317. www.countryinns.com.* 100 rooms, 2 story. S, D $75; each additional $5; suites $125-$130; under 18 free. Crib free. TV; cable (premium). Heated pool. Restaurant 7 am-9 pm; Fri, Sat to 10 pm. Bar 11-1 am. Meeting rooms. Business services available. Health club privileges. Game room. Some refrigerators. Cr cds: A, C, D, DS, MC, V.

Ⓓ ⚓ 🛂 SC

Montclair

See also Newark, Newark International Airport, Area

Settled 1666 **Pop** 38,977 **Elev** 337 ft **Area code** 973

Information Chamber of Commerce, 26 Park St, Suite 2025, 07042; 973/226-5500

Web www.montclairchamber.org

Originally a part of Newark, the area that includes Montclair was purchased from Native Americans in 1678 for "two guns, three coats, and thirteen cans of rum." The first settlers were English farmers from Connecticut who came here to form a Puritan church of their own. Shortly after, Dutch from Hackensack arrived, and two communities were created: Cranetown and Speertown. The two communities later were absorbed into West Bloomfield.

During the Revolutionary War, First Mountain served as a lookout point and as a barrier, preventing the British from crossing into the Upper Passaic valley. In the early 1800s, manufacturing began, new roads opened and the area grew. In 1856-57, a rail controversy arose: West Bloomfield citizens wanted a rail connection with New York City; Bloomfield residents saw no need for it. In 1868, the two towns separated and West Bloomfield became Montclair. This railroad helped to make Montclair the suburban, residential town it is today. One of the town's schools is named for painter George Inness, who once lived here.

What to See and Do

Eagle Rock Reservation. *1/2 mile W on Bloomfield Ave, then S on Prospect Ave to Eagle Rock Ave in West Orange* (see).

Israel Crane House. *110 Orange Rd. Phone 973/744-1796.* (1796) Federal mansion with period rooms; working 18th-century kitchen; school room; special exhibits during the year. Country Store and Post Office have authentic items; old-time crafts demonstrations. Research library. (June-Aug, Thurs-Sat; Sept-May, Sun afternoons; other times by appointment) **$$**

The Montclair Art Museum. *3 S Mountain Ave at Bloomfield Ave. Phone 973/746-5555.* American art; Native American gallery; changing exhibits. (Tues-Sun; closed holidays Gallery lectures (Sun). Concerts; jazz; film series. **$$**

Presby Iris Gardens. *In Mountainside Park. 474 Upper Mountain Ave (07043). Phone 973/783-5974.* Height of bloom in mid-May or early June.

Morristown (C-4)

See also Madison

Settled circa 1710 **Pop** 18,554 **Elev** 327 ft **Area code** 973

Information Historic Morris Visitors Center, 6 Court St, 07960; 973/631-5151

Web www.morristourism.org

Today, Morristown is primarily residential, but the iron industry, so desperately needed during the Revolutionary War, was responsible for the development of the town and the surrounding county. George Washington and his army spent two winters here, operating throughout the area until the fall of 1781. The first successful experiments with the telegraph were made in Morristown by Samuel F. B. Morse and Stephen Vail. Cartoonist Thomas Nast, writers Bret Harte and Frank Stockton, and millionaire Otto Kahn all lived here. Morristown rises to a 597-foot peak at Fort Nonsense; the Whippany River runs through the town.

What to See and Do

Acorn Hall. *68 Morris Ave. Phone 973/267-3465.* (1853) Victorian Italianate house; original furnishings; reference library; restored garden. (Mon, Thurs, Sun; group tours by appointment; closed holidays) **$$**

Fosterfields Living Historical Farm. *73 Kahdena Rd, off County Rte 510. Phone 973/326-7645.* Turn-of-the-century living history farm (200 acres). Self-guided trail; displays; audiovisual presentations; workshops, farming demonstrations; restored Gothic Revival house. Visitor Center. (Apr-Oct, Wed-Sun) **$$**

Frelinghuysen Arboretum. *53 E Hanover Ave (07962). 1 1/2 miles NE via Morris Ave, Whippany Rd; entrance from E Hanover Ave. Phone 973/326-7600.* Features 127 acres of forest and open fields; natural and formal gardens; spring and fall bulb displays; labeled collections of trees and shrubs; Braille trail; gift shop. Grounds (daily). **FREE**

Historic Speedwell. *333 Speedwell Ave. Phone 973/540-0211.* Home and factory of Stephen Vail, iron master, who in 1818 manufactured the engine for the SS *Savannah*, the first steamship to cross the Atlantic. In 1838, Alfred Vail (Stephen's son) and Samuel F. B. Morse perfected the telegraph and first publicly demonstrated it here in the factory. Displays include period furnishings in the mansion, exhibit on Speedwell Iron Works, exhibits on history of the telegraph; water wheel, carriage house, and granary. Gift shop. Picnic area. (May-Sept, Sun, Thurs; closed July 4) **$$**

Macculloch Hall Historical Museum. *45 Macculloch Ave. Phone 973/538-2404.* Restored 1810 house and garden;

home of George P. Macculloch, initiator of the Morris Canal, and his descendants for more than 140 years. American, European decorative arts from the 18th and 19th centuries. Illustrations by Thomas Nast. Garden. (Wed, Thurs, and Sun afternoons; closed holidays) **$$**

Morris Museum. *6 Normandy Heights Rd. Phone 973/971-3700.* Art, science, and history exhibits; permanent and changing. Musical, theatrical events; lectures and films. (Tues-Sun; closed holidays) Free admission Thurs afternoons. **$$$**

Morristown National Historical Park. (see) *Approximately 3 miles S on US 202.*

Schuyler-Hamilton House. *5 Olyphant Pl. Phone 973/267-4039.* (1760) Former home of Dr. Jabez Campfield. Alexander Hamilton courted Betsy Schuyler here. Period furniture; colonial garden. (Sun afternoons; other times by appointment; closed Easter, Dec 25) **$$**

Hotels

★ ★ ★ **MADISON HOTEL.** *One Convent Rd (07960). Phone 973/285-1800; toll-free 800/526-0729; fax 973/540-8566. www.themadisonhotel.com.* 203 rooms, 4 story. D $89-$229; under 18 free; weekend rates. Complimentary continental breakfast. Check-out noon, check-in 3 pm. TV; cable (premium). In-room modem link. Restaurant 6:30 am-11 pm. Bar 11-2 am, entertainment. Exercise equipment. Indoor pool, whirlpool, poolside service. Golf privileges. Airport transportation. Business center. Concierge. Cr cds: A, C, D, DS, MC, V.

D 🛌 🏋 🛬 SC 🏃

★ ★ ★ **THE WESTIN MORRISTOWN.** *2 Whippany Rd (07960). Phone 973/539-7300; toll-free 800/937-8461; fax 973/984-1036. www.westin.com.* 246 rooms, 6 story. D $164-$261; under 17 free; weekend rates. Check-out 11 am, check-in 3 pm. TV; cable (premium), VCR available. In-room modem link. Laundry services. Restaurant 6:30 am-midnight. Bar 11 am-midnight. Exercise equipment. Pool, whirlpool. Business center. Concierge. Cr cds: A, C, D, DS, JCB, MC, V.

D 🛌 🏋 🛬 🏃

Restaurant

★ ★ **ROD'S STEAK AND SEAFOOD GRILLE.** *Phone 973/539-6666; fax 973/285-0586. www.rodssteakseafoodgrill.com.* Seafood, steak menu. Hours: 11:30 am-11 pm; early-bird dinner 4:30-6 pm; Sun brunch 11 am-3 pm. Closed Dec 25. Dinner $14.95-$34.95. Bar. Entertainment Wed-Sat. Children's menu. Display of authentic Victorian antiques. Casual attire. Valet parking. Cr cds: A, D, DS, MC, V.

D

Morristown National Historical Park (C-4)

See also Bernardsville, Morristown

(Approx 3 miles S of Morristown on US 202)

This national historical park, the first to be established and maintained by the federal government, was created by an Act of Congress in 1933. Its three units cover more than 1,600 acres, all but Jockey Hollow and the New Jersey Brigade Area being within Morristown's limits. The main body of the Continental Army stayed here in the winter of 1779-1780.

Headquarters and museum (daily); Jockey Hollow buildings (summer, daily; rest of year schedule varies, phone ahead; closed Jan 1, Thanksgiving, Dec 25). Contact Chief of Interpretation, Washington Pl, Morristown 07960; 973/539-2085.

What to See and Do

Ford Mansion. *10 Washington Pl (07960). Phone 973/539-2085.* One of the finest early houses in Morristown was built in 1772-74 by Colonel Jacob Ford, Jr., who produced gunpowder for American troops during the Revolutionary War. His widow rented the house to the army for General and Mrs. Washington when the Continental Army spent the winter of 1779-80 here.

Fort Nonsense. *Ann St.* Its name came long after residents had forgotten the real reason for earthworks constructed here in 1777. Overlook commemorates fortifications which were built at Washington's order to defend military supplies stored in the village.

Jockey Hollow. *10 Washington Pl (07960). 5 miles SW of Morristown. Phone 973/539-2085.* The site of the Continental Army's winter quarters in 1779-80 and the 1781 mutiny of the Pennsylvania Line. Signs indicate locations of various brigades. There are typical log huts and an officer's hut, among other landmarks. Demonstrations of military and colonial farm life (summer). Visitor center has exhibits and audiovisual programs.

Wick House. *Jockey Hollow. 30 Washington St (07960).* Farmer Henry Wick lived here with his wife and daughter. Used as quarters by Major General Arthur St. Clair in 1779-1780. Restored with period furnishings.

Mount Holly (F-3)

Settled 1676 **Pop** 10,728 **Elev** 52 ft **Area code** 609 **Zip** 08060

The mountain that gives this old Quaker town its name is only 183 feet high. For two months in 1779, Mount Holly was the capital of the state; today, it is the seat of Burlington County.

What to See and Do

John Woolman Memorial. *99 Branch St. Phone 609/267-3226.* (1783) John Woolman, the noted Quaker abolitionist whose *Journal* is still appreciated today, owned the property on which this small, three-story red brick house was built; garden. Picnicking. (Wed-Fri; also by appointment) **DONATION**

Mansion at Smithville. *801 Smithville Rd. Phone 609/265-5068.* (1840) Victorian mansion and village of inventor/entrepreneur Hezekiah B. Smith; home of the "Star" hi-wheel bicycle. Guided tours (May-Oct, Wed and Sun). Victorian Christmas tours (Dec; fee). **$$**

Mount Holly Library. *307 High St. Phone 609/267-7111.* Chartered in 1765 by King George III, the library is currently housed in Georgian mansion built in 1830. Historic Lyceum contains original crystal chandeliers, blue marble fireplaces, boxwood gardens; archives date to original 1765 collection. (July-Aug, Tues-Thurs; rest of year, Mon-Sat, limited hours) **FREE**

Motels/Motor Lodges

★ **HOWARD JOHNSON.** *NJ 541 at NJ Tpke Exit 5 (08060). Phone 609/267-6550; fax 609/267-2575. www.hojo.com.* 90 rooms, 2 story. S $58-$95; D $60-$102; each additional $7; under 12 free. Crib free. Pet accepted. Check-out noon. TV; cable (premium), VCR available. Coffee in rooms. Restaurant 6 am-11 pm. Bar 5-11 pm. Playground. Sauna. Pool, lifeguard. Meeting rooms. Cr cds: A, D, DS, MC, V.

[D] [⟲] [⌷] [⌷]

★ ★ **QUALITY INN.** *21 Wrightstown/Cookstown Rd, Cookstown (08511). Phone 609/723-6500; toll-free 800/228-5151; fax 609/723-7895. www.qualityinn.com.* 100 rooms, 2 story. May-Sept: S, D $79-$115; each additional $10; suites $125-$175; under 16 free; higher rates holidays; lower rates rest of year. Crib free. Complimentary full breakfast. Check-out 11 am. TV; cable. Refrigerators available. Restaurant 11 am-10 pm. Pool. Business services. Cr cds: A, C, D, DS, ER, JCB, MC, V.

[D] [⌷] [⌷] [SC]

B&B/Small Inn

★ ★ **ISSAC HILLARD HOUSE B&B.** *31 Hanover St, Pemberton (08068). Phone 609/894-0756; toll-free 800/371-0756; fax 609/894-7899.* 4 rooms, 2 story. D $110-$120; each additional $20. Complimentary breakfast. Check-out 11 am, check-in 3 pm. TV. Pool. Victorian house built in mid-18th century. Totally nonsmoking. Cr cds: A, D, DS, MC, V. **$**

[⌷] [⌷]

Restaurants

★ ★ ★ **BEAU RIVAGE.** *128 Taunton Blvd, Medford (08055). Phone 856/983-1999; fax 856/988-1136. www.beau-rivage.com.* The well-trained staff provides guests with attentive tableside service—everything from boning fish to offering helpful suggestions for wine selection. Hours: 11:30 am-2:30 pm, 5:30-9:30 pm; Sat from 5:30 pm; Sun 4-8 pm. Closed Mon; most major holidays; also 2 weeks before Labor Day. Reservations accepted. French menu. Service bar. Wine cellar. A la carte entrées: lunch $12.50-$15, dinner $20-$25. Specialties: beef Wellington, wild game, souffles. Own pastries. Two dining areas, 1 upstairs. Parking; valet weekends. Jacket (dinner). Cr cds: A, D, MC, V.

[D]

★ ★ ★ **BRADDOCK'S TAVERN.** *39 S Main St, Medford Village (08055). Phone 609/654-1604; fax 609/654-8180. www.braddocks.com.* This casual restaurant features traditional American cuisine with European influences. Don't miss the cooking classes held throughout the year. Specializes in fresh seafood, beef, veal. Closed Jan 1, Dec 25. Lunch $5.75-$8.95, dinner $16.95-$26.95. Sun brunch $15.95. Bar. Children's menu. Reservations accepted. Cr cds: A, D, DS, MC, V.

[D]

★ ★ **CHARLEY'S OTHER BROTHER.** *1383 Monmouth Rd (08060). Phone 609/261-1555; fax 609/261-7577. www.charleysotherbrother.com.* Specialties: fresh seafood, steak, prime rib. Hours: 11:30 am-2:30 pm, 5-9:30 pm; Fri, Sat to 10:30 pm; Sun 4-9 pm. Closed Dec 25. Lunch $5.95-$7.95, dinner $15.95-$33. Bar. Children's menu. Reservations accepted. Country setting; Tiffany lamps. Cr cds: A, D, DS, MC, V.

[D] [SC]

Ironbound Newark

Newark, once moribund, is in renaissance, and the city offers a combination of fascinating history, modern facilities, and some of the finest Spanish-Portugese dining anywhere. This walk first covers the historic Ironbound section, named for the surrounding railroads, the settling site for immigrant groups since the 1830s, now home to about 40 ethnic groups. It continues into the resurgent Four Corners/Military Park section.

Start at Pennsylvania Station, built in 1933 and beautifully decorated with Art Deco wall reliefs and ceiling sculptures. Walk east on Market Street, passing diminutive Mother Cabrini Park, site of a bust of Jose Marti, liberator of Cuba. Turn right onto Union Street. In one block, at Ferry Street, Our Lady of Mount Carmel Roman Catholic Church stands opposite at McWhorter Street. Originally opened in 1848, this building is now home to the Ironbound Educational and Cultural Center. Turn left onto Ferry Street. This is the commercial heart of the Ironbound, and is filled with shops and restaurants. Among the eateries of note are Fornos of Spain (47 Ferry Street) Iberia Peninsula Restaurant (63-69 Ferry Street), Iberia Restaurant (82-89 Ferry Street), and Brasilia Restaurant (132 Ferry Street).

Turn right onto Prospect Street. In 1/2-block at Number 76 is the Gothic Revival-style Christ Episcopal Church, completed in 1850. Destroyed by vandalism and fire, it was restored in 1978, and now serves as the Chancery Professional Center. At the corner of Lafayette Street stands St. Joseph's Roman Catholic Church, circa 1858, now called Immaculate Heart of Mary. In the basement are hidden catacombs that are replicas of those found in Rome, complete with crypts featuring wax likenesses of Spanish saints. Turn left on Lafayette and walk six blocks to Van Duren. Turn right two blocks to Independence Park. Covering 12 1/2 acres, this was one of the city's first neighborhood parks (circa 1896). Turn left on New York Avenue, go one block, and turn right on Pulaski Street. Pass East Side High School, and come to St. Casimir's Roman Catholic Church, built in 1919 in the Italian Renaissance style. Continue to Chestnut Street and turn right. Five blocks down the road stand the remains of the Murphy Varnish Company, once comprising six major structures; note the carving of a Roman chariot carrying a can of Murphy Varnish on the west side of the building.

Follow Chestnut under the railroad and across McCarter Highway to Broad Street. Turn right and walk through the business district to the Prudential Building at the heart of the Four Corners Historic District. Among the many historic buildings; the National Newark Building, (744 Broad Street), a 34-story neoclassical structure completed in 1930, and 1180 Raymond Boulevard, another Depression-era skyscraper. In two more blocks, Military Park appears. Walk on the left side of the park to the New Jersey Historical Society (52 Park Place), which has an on-site museum and is next door to the historic Robert Treat Hotel. At the end of the park on Center Street stands the architecturally stunning New Jersey Performing Arts Center. Opened in 1997, it has become a world-renowned performance space. Return on Center Street towards Military Park, turn left on Central Street, and go two blocks to the Newark Museum (49 Washington Street), site of the largest collection of Tibetan art outside Tibet, the Dreyfus Planetarium, and the historic 1885 Ballantine House.

Newark (C-5)

See also Elizabeth, Jersey City

Settled 1666 **Pop** 273,546 **Elev** 146 ft **Area code** 973

Web www.state.nj.us/travel

Once a strict Puritan settlement, Newark has grown to become the largest city in the state and one of the country's leading manufacturing cities. Major insurance firms and banks have large offices in Newark, dominating the city's financial life. Newark was the birthplace of Stephen Crane (1871-1900), author of *The Red Badge of Courage,* and Mary Mapes Dodge (1838-1905), author of the children's book *Hans Brinker, or the Silver Skates.* Newark is also an educational center with Newark College of Rutgers University, College of Medicine and Dentistry of New Jersey, New Jersey Institute of Technology, Seton Hall Law School, and Essex County College.

Transportation

Car Rental Agencies See IMPORTANT TOLL-FREE NUMBERS.

Public Transportation Trains, buses (NJ Transit), phone 973/491-9400.

Rail Passenger Service Amtrak 800/872-7245.

Airport Information

For additional accommodations, see NEWARK INTERNATIONAL AIRPORT AREA, which follows NEWARK.

What to See and Do

Minor Basilica of the Sacred Heart. *89 Ridge St, at Clifton and 6th aves.* French Gothic in design, it resembles the cathedral at Rheims. Hand-carved reredos. (Daily) **DONATION**

The Newark Museum. *49 Washington St. Phone 973/596-6550.* Museum of art and science, with changing exhibitions. American paintings and sculpture; American and European decorative arts; classical art; the arts of Asia, the Americas, and the Pacific; numismatics and the natural sciences. Also here are the Junior Museum, Mini Zoo, Dreyfuss Planetarium, Garden, with its 1784 schoolhouse, and the Newark Fire Museum. Special programs, lectures, concerts; cafe (lunch). (Wed-Sun, afternoons)

New Jersey Historical Society. *52 Park Pl. Phone 973/596-8500.* Museum with collections of paintings, prints, furniture, decorative arts; period room; special exhibitions. Reference and research library of state and local history; manuscripts, documents, maps. (Tues-Sat) **FREE**

New Jersey Performing Arts Center. *1 Center St. Phone 888/GO-NJPAC.* Home of the New Jersey Symphony Orchestra and host to many other performances.

Old Plume House. *407 Broad St. Phone 973/483-8202.* Now the rectory of the adjoining House of Prayer Episcopal Church, it is thought to have been standing as early as 1710, which would make it the oldest building in Newark.

Symphony Hall. *1030 Broad St. Phone 973/643-4550 or 973/643-8009 (box office).* (1925) A 2,811-seat auditorium; home of New Jersey State Opera and the New Jersey Symphony Orchestra; also here is the famous Terrace Ballroom.

The Wars of America. *Military Park, bounded by Broad St, Park Pl, Rector St, Raymond Blvd.* Sculptured bronze group by Gutzon Borglum features 42 human figures representing soldiers in the major conflicts in US history. Other works by Borglum are

Bridge Memorial. *N of Washington Park (Broad St, Washington Pl, and Washington St).* This sculpture of a Native American and a Puritan stands on the site of a colonial marketplace.

Statue of Abraham Lincoln. *Essex County Courthouse, Springfield Ave, and Market St.*

Hotel

★ ★ ★ **HILTON NEWARK GATEWAY.** *One Gateway Center - Raymond Blvd (07102). Phone 973/622-5000; toll-free 800/932-3322; fax 973/824-2188. www.hilton.com.* This hotel has been offering superior service for 20 years. It's found 3 miles from Newark Airport and in the heart of the business district, making it convenient for all travelers. 263 rooms, 8 story. D $129-$289; each additional $10; under 18 free; weekend rates. Check-out noon, check-in 3 pm. TV; cable (premium), VCR available. Restaurant 6:30 am-10 pm; Sat, Sun 7 am-10 pm. Bar 11:30 am-midnight; Fri, Sat to 1 am. Room service. Exercise equipment. Pool. Free airport transportation. Business center. Luxury level. Cr cds: A, C, D, DS, ER, MC, V.

D 🖙 🏋 ✈ 🖎 SC 🏃

Newark International Airport Area

See also Newark

Information 201/961-6000 or 800/247-7433.

Hotels

★ ★ ★ **HILTON NEWARK AIRPORT.** *1170 Spring St, Elizabeth (07201). Phone 908/351-3900; toll-free 800/445-8667; fax 908/351-9556. www.newarkairport.hilton.com.* 378 rooms, 12 story. D $79-$289; each additional $10; under 18 free; weekend rates. Check-out noon, check-in 3 pm. TV; cable (premium), VCR available. In-room modem link. Valet service. Restaurant 6:30 am-11 pm. Bar 4 pm-2 am. Room service 24 hours. Exercise equipment, sauna. Indoor pool, whirlpool. Valet parking. Free airport transportation. Business center. Cr cds: A, C, D, DS, ER, JCB, MC, V.

D 🖙 🏋 ✈ 🏃

★ ★ ★ **MARRIOTT NEWARK AIRPORT.** *Newark International Airport (07114). Phone 973/623-0006; toll-free 800/228-9290; fax 973/623-1419. www.marriott.com.* 598 rooms, 10 story. D $229-$300; under 18 free; weekend rates. Check-out noon, check-in 4 pm. TV; cable (premium), VCR available. Restaurant 6 am-11 pm. Bar 11:30-1:30 am. Room service 24 hours. Exercise equipment, sauna. Indoor/outdoor pool, whirlpool, poolside service. Free airport transportation. Business center. Concierge. Luxury level. Cr cds: A, C, D, DS, JCB, MC, V.

D 🖙 🏋 ✈ 🖎 SC 🏃

New Brunswick (D-4)

Settled 1681 **Pop** 48,573 **Elev** 42 ft **Area code** 732

Information Middlesex County Regional Chamber of Commerce, One Distribution Way, Suite 101, Monmouth Junction 08852; 732/821-1700

New Brunswick, the seat of Middlesex County, is on the south bank of the Raritan River. It is both a college town and a diversified commercial and retail city. Rutgers University, the eighth-oldest institution of higher learning in the country and the only state university with a colonial charter, was founded in 1766 as Queens College, and opened in 1771 with a faculty of one—aged 18. Livingston College, Cook College, and Douglass College (for women), all part of the university, are also located here. One of New Brunswick's most important industries is Johnson and Johnson; its company headquarters are located downtown. Joyce Kilmer, the poet, was born in New Brunswick; his house, at 17 Joyce Kilmer Avenue, is open to visitors.

What to See and Do

Buccleuch Mansion. *George St and Easton Ave, in 78-acre Buccleuch Park.* Phone 732/745-5094. Built in 1739 by Anthony White, son-in-law of Lewis Morris, a colonial governor of New Jersey. Period rooms. (June-Oct, Sun afternoons; closed holidays) Under 10 only with adult. **FREE**

Crossroads Theatre. *7 Livingston Ave.* Phone 732/729-9559. Professional African-American theater company offering plays, musicals, touring programs, and workshops. (Oct-May, Wed-Sun)

Geology Museum. *George and Somerset sts, on the campus of Rutgers—The State University of New Jersey.* Phone 732/932-7243. Displays of New Jersey minerals; dinosaur; mammals, including a mastodon; Egyptian exhibit with mummy. (Mon-Fri; call for weekend/summer hours; closed holidays) **FREE**

George Street Playhouse. *9 Livingston Ave.* Phone 732/246-7717 *(box office, daily except Mon).* Regional theater; six-show season of plays and musicals; touring Outreach program for students. A 379-seat house. Stage II Theater; cafe; cabaret. (Tues-Sun)

Hungarian Heritage Center. *300 Somerset St.* Phone 732/846-5777. Museum of changing exhibits that focus on Hungarian folk life, fine and folk art; library, archives. (Tues-Sun; closed holidays) **DONATION**

Jane Voorhees Zimmerli Art Museum. *George and Hamilton sts, on the campus of Rutgers—The State University of New Jersey.* Phone 732/932-7237. Paintings from early 16th century through the present; changing exhibits. (Tues-Fri, also Sat and Sun afternoons; closed holidays) **$$**

New Jersey Museum of Agriculture. *103 College Farm Rd.* Phone 732/249-2077. Large collection of farm implements; covers three centuries of farming history. Interactive science and history exhibits. (Tues-Sun) **$$**

Rutgers-The State University of New Jersey. *126 College Ave (08901).* Phone 732/932-1766 *(general information)* or 732/932-7881 *(campus tours).* (1766) 50,000 students. Multiple campuses include 30 colleges serving students at all levels through postdoctoral studies; main campus on College Ave.

The Rutgers Gardens. *Ryder's Ln (US 1).* Phone 732/932-8451. Features extensive display of American holly. (Daily) **FREE**

Special Event

Middlesex County Fair. *Cranbury-South River Rd, in East Brunswick.* Phone 732/356-7400. Aug.

Motels/Motor Lodges

★ **CLARION HOTEL.** *11 Cedar Grove Ln, Somerset (08873).* Phone 732/563-1000; toll-free 800/372-9099; fax 732/563-0352. www.clarionsuitesnj.com. 83 suites, 2 story. Suites $185-$205; under 18 free; weekend rates. Complimentary continental breakfast. Check-out noon, check-in 3 pm. TV; cable (premium). In-room modem link. Health club privileges. Cr cds: A, C, D, DS, JCB, MC, V.
D ⛶ SC

★ ★ ★ **HYATT REGENCY NEW BRUNSWICK.** *2 Albany St (08901).* Phone 732/873-1234; toll-free 800/233-1234; fax 732/873-1382. www.hyatt.com. This property is located downtown on a 6-acre lot, midway between New York and Philadelphia. The central location offers easy access to shopping, restaurants and nearby attractions. 304 rooms, 6 story. D $105-$215; under 18 free; weekend rates. Check-out noon, check-in 3 pm. TV; cable (premium). In-room modem link. Restaurant (see also 2 ALBANY). Bar 11-1 am; pianist Thurs-Sat. Exercise equipment, sauna. Indoor pool, whirlpool. Tennis. Business center. Cr cds: A, C, D, DS, JCB, MC, V.
D ⛷ ⛱ ⚘ ⛶ SC ⚘

★ **MCINTOSH INN.** *764 NJ 18, East Brunswick (08816).* Phone 732/238-4900; toll-free 800/444-2775; fax 732/257-2023. www.mcintoshinn.com. 107 rooms, 2 story. D $68.95-$75.95; each additional $3. Complimentary continental breakfast. Check-out 11 am, check-in 3 pm. TV; cable (premium). Cr cds: A, C, D, MC, V.

D

Hotels

★ ★ ★ **DOUBLETREE HOTEL.** *200 Atrium Dr, Somerset (08873). Phone 732/469-2600; toll-free 800/222-8733; fax 732/469-4617. ww.doubletree.com.* This hotel is located in the business district, providing convenient access to shopping, restaurants, and other local attractions. 366 rooms, 6 story. D $99-$209; each additional $10; family, weekend rates. Check-out noon, check-in 3 pm. TV; cable (premium), VCR available. In-room modem link. Restaurant 6:30 am-2 pm. Dining room 5:30-10 pm. Bar 2 pm-1:30 am, entertainment. Exercise equipment. Two pools, one indoor, whirlpool, poolside service. Tennis. Business center. Cr cds: A, C, D, DS, ER, MC, V.

D

★ ★ ★ **HILTON EAST BRUNSWICK.** *3 Tower Center Blvd (08816). Phone 732/828-2000; toll-free 800/445-8667; fax 732/828-6958. www.hilton.com.* 426 rooms, 15 story. D $120-$225; each additional $20; under 18 free; weekend rates. Check-out noon, check-in 3 pm. TV; cable (premium), VCR available. In-room modem link. Restaurant 6:30 am-10:30 pm. Bar 11 am-midnight; weekends to 2 am. Room service 24 hours. Exercise equipment, sauna. Indoor pool, whirlpool. Airport transportation. Business center. Concierge. Luxury level. Cr cds: A, C, D, DS, ER, MC, V.

D

★ ★ ★ **MARRIOTT.** *110 Davidson Ave, Somerset (08873). Phone 732/560-0500; toll-free 800/228-9290; fax 732/560-0817. www.marriott.com.* 442 rooms, 10 story. D $69-$260; each additional $15; under 18 free; weekend rates. Check-out 11 am, check-in 3 pm. TV; cable (premium), VCR available. In-room modem link. Restaurant 6:30 am-10 pm. Bar 11:30 am-midnight; Fri, Sat to 2 am. Exercise room, sauna. Indoor/outdoor pool, whirlpool, poolside service (summer). Tennis. Business center. Concierge. Cr cds: A, C, D, DS, ER, JCB, MC, V.

D

Restaurants

★ ★ **2 ALBANY.** *2 Albany St (08901). Phone 732/867-2300; fax 732/867-1382. www.hyatt.com.* American menu. Hours: 6:30 am-10 pm; Sun brunch 10:30 am-2 pm; early-bird dinner 4:30-6:30 pm (seasonal, Thurs-Sat). Dinner $18-$26. Piano Thurs-Sat. Children's menu. Casual attire. Cr cds: A, D, DS, MC, V.

D

★ ★ **ANTONIA'S.** *40 Livingston Ave (08901). Phone 732/828-7080; fax 732/828-7090.* Italian menu. Hours: 11 am-2 pm, 5-9 pm; Mon 11 am-2 pm. Closed Sat, Sun; also major holidays. Dinner $8.95-$12.95. Bar. Children's menu. Patriotic décor; turn-of-the-century pictures. Casual attire. Cr cds: A, D, DS, MC, V.

D

★ ★ **DELTA'S.** *19 Dennis St (08901). Phone 732/249-1551; fax 732/249-7922. www.deltasrestaurant.com.* Hours: 11:30-1 am; Fri to 2 am; Sat 5 pm-2 am; Sun 3:30-7:30 pm. Closed Jan 1, July 4, Dec 25. Lunch $7-$12, dinner $14.95-$25.95. Bar. Piano, guitar Fri, Sat. Reservations accepted. Street parking. Antiques. Cr cds: A, D, DS, MC, V.

D

★ ★ ★ **THE FROG AND THE PEACH.** *29 Dennis St (08901). Phone 732/846-3216; fax 732/846-4820. www.frogandpeach.com.* Housed in a converted factory, this new American landmark has been in business since 1983. American menu. Hours: 11:30 am-2:30 pm, 5:30-10:30 pm; Sat from 5:30 pm; Sun 4:30-9:30 pm. Closed most major holidays. Dinner $19.50-$37.50. Bar to midnight. Children's menu. Casual attire. Reservations required. Outdoor seating. Factory motif; painted brick walls, exposed duct work. Cr cds: A, D, DS, MC, V.

D

★ ★ ★ **LA FONTANA.** *120 Albany St (08901). Phone 732/249-7500; fax 732/214-1811. www.lafontanaristorante.com.* Executive chef Oscar Romero and partner Jose Akena offer a traditional BYOB Italian experience. After an appetizer, pasta course, salad and meat course (filet mignon, veal, and fish, among the choices), will you have any room for dessert? Italian menu. Hours: 11:30 am-2:30 pm, 5-10 pm; Fri to 11 pm; Sat 5-11 pm. Closed Sun. Dinner $18-$40. Bar. Children's menu. Casual attire. Valet parking. Cr cds: A, D, MC, V.

D

★ ★ **MAKEDA ETHIOPIAN RESTAURANT.** *338 George St (08901). Phone 732/545-5115; fax 732/545-8740. www.makedas.com.* Ethiopian menu. Hours: 11:30 am-10:30 pm; Fri, Sat to midnight; Sun 1-10 pm. Closed most major holidays. Dinner $10.50-$24. Bar 11:30-2 am. Casual attire. Cr cds: A, D, DS, MC, V.

D SC

★ **MARITA'S CANTINA.** *1 Penn Plz (08901). Phone 732/247-3840; fax 732/247-7852.* Mexican, Southwestern menu. Hours: 11:30-2 am; Sun 3-11:30 pm. Closed Easter, Thanksgiving, Dec 25. Dinner $6.95-$13.95. Bar to 2 am. Entertainment Thurs. Children's menu. Casual attire. Outdoor seating. Cr cds: A, D, MC, V.

D

★ ★ **THE OLD BAY.** *61-63 Church St (08901). Phone 732/246-3111; fax 732/246-2049. www.oldbay.com.* French Creole menu. Closed Sun; most major holidays. Lunch $5.45-$8.95, dinner $16.95-$25.95. Bar to 2 am. Entertainment Thurs-Sat. Reservations accepted. Outdoor seating. Cr cds: A, MC, V.

D

★ **RUSTY NAIL.** *US 130S (08902). Phone 732/821-4141; fax 732/821-7856.* American menu. Hours: 11:30 am-10 pm; Sun from noon pm. Dinner $6-$16. Bar to 2 am. Children's menu. Cr cds: A, D, MC, V.

D

★ ★ ★ **STAGE LEFT: AN AMERICAN CAFE.** *5 Livingston Ave (08901). Phone 732/828-4444; fax 732/828-6228. www.stageleft.com.* Hours: 5-11 pm; Fri 11:30 am-2 pm, 5-11 pm; early-bird dinner 5:30-7 pm. Closed Mon; also Jan 1, Memorial Day, Dec 25. Reservations accepted. Bar to 2 am. Wine cellar. A la carte entrées: lunch $9.95-$15.95, dinner $18.95-$26.95. Complete meal: dinner $29. Specializes in chicken, beef, seafood. Valet parking. Outdoor seating. Romantic atmosphere; unique art. Mahogany Art Deco bar. Cr cds: A, MC, V.

D

★ ★ **SZECHWAN GOURMET.** *3 Livingston Ave (08901). Phone 732/846-7878; fax 732/846-3779.* Chinese menu. Hours: 11:30-2 am; summer hours to 11:30 pm. Closed Thanksgiving. Dinner $4.50-$13.95. Casual attire. Cr cds: A, DS, MC, V.

★ ★ **TERESA'S.** *48 Easton Ave (08901). Phone 732/545-3737; fax 732/545-9405.* Hours: 11 am-11 pm; Fri to midnight; Sun 4-10 pm. Closed Easter, Thanksgiving, Dec 25. Reservations accepted. Italian menu. Bar to 2 am. A la carte entrées: lunch $7-$11, dinner $11-$21. Children's menu. Specializes in seafood, pasta. Street parking. Outdoor seating. Cr cds: A, MC, V.

D

Ocean City (I-4)

Pop 15,378 **Elev** 4 ft **Area code** 609 **Zip** 08226

Information Public Relations Department, City of Ocean City, 9th and Asbury Ave; 609/525-9300

Families from all over the country come to this popular resort year after year, as do conventions and religious conferences. In accordance with its founder's instructions, liquor cannot be sold here. Ocean City is an island that lies between the Atlantic Ocean and Great Egg Harbor. It has 8 miles of beaches, more than 2 miles of boardwalk, an enclosed entertainment auditorium on the boardwalk, and excellent swimming, fishing, boating, golf, and tennis.

What to See and Do

Historic House. *1139 Wesley Ave. Phone 609/399-1801.* Furnishings and fashions circa 1920-1930. Tours. (Apr-Dec, Mon-Sat) **DONATION**

Ocean City Historical Museum. *1735 Simpson Ave, at 17th St. Phone 609/399-1801.* Victorian furnishings and fashions; doll exhibit; local shipwreck; historical tours; research library; gift shop. (Mon-Sat) **DONATION**

Special Events

Boardwalk Art Show. International and regional artists. Aug.

Concerts. *Hwy 152 and Hwy 40. Phone 732-316-1095. Music Pier.* Pops orchestra and dance band. Mon-Wed, Sun. Late June-Sept.

Flower Show. *Music Pier.* June.

Hermit Crab Race, Miss Crustacean Contest. *12th St Beach. Phone 609/525-9300 or 800/BEACH-NJ.* Crab beauty pageant, races. Early Aug.

Night in Venice. Decorated boat parade. Mid-July.

Motels/Motor Lodges

★ **DAYS INN.** *7th St and Boardwalk (08226). Phone 609/398-2200; toll-free 800/329-7466; fax 609/391-2050. www.daysinn.com.* 80 rooms, 39 kitchen suites, 4 story. June-Aug: S $70-$180; D $80-$250; each additional $15; kitchen suites $90-$325; weekly rates; higher rates during sporting events; lower rates Apr-May and Sept-Oct. Closed rest of year. Crib free. Check-out 11 am. TV; cable, VCR available (movies). Balconies. Coin laundry. Heated pool, lifeguard. Business services. Bellstaff. Cr cds: A, C, D, DS, MC, V.

D ⛵ ⛱

★ **FORUM MOTOR INN.** *800 Atlantic Ave (08226). Phone 609/399-8700; fax 609/399-8704. www.theforuminnoc. homestead.com.* 61 rooms, 2-3 story. July-Aug (3-day min): S $64-$164; D $64-$204; each additional $8; some weekend rates; lower rates Apr-May, Sept-Oct. Closed rest of year. Check-out noon. TV; cable (premium). Game room. Children's pool. Cr cds: MC, V.

⛷ ⚙ ⛱

★ **HARRIS HOUSE.** *1201 Ocean Ave (08226). Phone 609/399-7800; fax 609/398-8082. www.harrishouse.net.* 74 rooms, 2 story. Late June-Aug: S, D $160-$250; each additional $10; under 12 free; weekly rates; higher rates during holidays (3-day minimum); lower rates late Aug-late Oct and Apr-late June; closed rest of year. Crib free. TV; cable. Heated pool; lifeguard. Complimentary coffee in lobby. Restaurant adjacent. Check-out 11 am. Business services available. Refrigerators, microwaves available. Beach nearby. Cr cds: A, DS, MC, V.

[D] [≈] [≈]

★ ★ **IMPALA ISLAND INN.** *1001 Ocean Ave (08226). Phone 609/399-7500; fax 609/398-4379. www.ochotels.com.* 109 units in 2 buildings, 2 story. July-Aug; S, D $105-$194; kitchen units $1,300-$1,800/week; lower rates rest of year. Crib free. Check-out 11 am. TV; cable. Refrigerators. Restaurant 7 am-9 pm. Room service. Two pools, one heated, wading pool, lifeguard. Meeting rooms. Business services. Sun deck. Cr cds: A, MC, V.

[D] [♨] [≈] [≈]

★ **PAVILION MOTOR LODGE.** *801 Atlantic Ave (08226). Phone 609/399-2600; toll-free 800/523-2552; fax 609/814-0456. www.pavilionmotorlodge.com.* 80 rooms, 3 story. Early July-early Sept (3-day minimum weekends): S, D $80-$160; kitchen units $150; lower rates Mar-June and early Sept-Nov; closed rest of year. Crib available. Check-out 11 am. TV; cable (premium), VCR available (movies). Refrigerators. Coin laundry. Restaurant 7:30 am-9 pm. Room service. Beach. Heated pool, wading pool, poolside service, lifeguard. Business services. Cr cds: A, DS, MC, V.

[≈] [≈] [SC]

Hotels

★ ★ ★ **BEACH CLUB HOTEL.** *1280 Boardwalk (08226). Phone 609/399-8555; www.ochotels.com.* 82 rooms, 3 story. Mid-June-Labor Day: S, D $158-$305; each additional $10; higher rates weekends, May-mid-June, Labor Day-Nov. Closed rest of year. Crib free. Check-out 11 am. TV; cable (premium). Balconies. Refrigerators. Coin laundry. Restaurant 7 am-9 pm. Room service. Health club privileges. Pool, wading pool, lifeguard. Golf privileges. Business services. Bellstaff. Sun deck. Beach. Cr cds: A, MC, V.

[♨] [ⅈ] [≈]

★ ★ **PIER 4 HOTEL.** *Broadway Ave and The Bay (08244). Phone 609/927-9141; toll-free 888/927-9141; fax 609/653-2752. www.pier4hotel.com.* 70 rooms, 8 suites, 4 story. Apr-Dec: S, D $59-$169; each additional $15; suites $89-$225; under 14 free; weekly rates; weekends, holidays

(2-day minimum); higher rates during special events; lower rates rest of year. Crib free. Complimentary continental breakfast, coffee in rooms. Check-out 11 am. TV; cable. Microwaves, refrigerators. Coin laundry. Restaurant adjacent. Health club privileges, exercise equipment. Recreation room. Heated pool, poolside service. Golf privileges. Meeting rooms. Business services. On bay. Cr cds: A, C, D, DS, MC, V.

[D] [♨] [ⅈ] [≈] [ⅈ] [≈]

Resort

★ ★ **PORT-O-CALL HOTEL.** *1510 Boardwalk (08226). Phone 609/399-8812; toll-free 800/334-4546; fax 609/399-0387. www.portocallhotel.com.* 99 rooms, 9 story. June-Sept: S, D $115-$295; each additional $15; penthouse apartment $325-$650; under 18 free; lower rates rest of year. Crib free. Check-out 11 am. TV; cable (premium). In-room modem link. Balconies. Refrigerators. Coffee in rooms. Coin laundry. Restaurant 7 am-2 pm, 5-8 pm; Sun 9:30 am-1:30 pm, 5-8 pm. Room service. Free supervised children's activities (June-Aug). Exercise room, sauna. Pool, lifeguard. Golf privileges. Grills. Airport transportation. Meeting rooms. Business services. Bellstaff. Sundries. On ocean. Cr cds: A, C, D, DS, MC, V.

[D] [♨] [ⅈ] [ⅈ] [≈] [ⅈ] [≈]

All Suite

★ ★ **WILD DUNES INN.** *801 E 10th St (08226). Phone 609/399-2910; fax 609/398-4379. www.ochotels.com.* 28 suites, 2 story. S, D $95-$250; weekends, holidays (3-day minimum). Crib free. Check-out 10 am. TV; cable. Microwaves, refrigerators. Coin laundry. Heated pool, wading pool, lifeguard. Cr cds: A, MC, V.

[D] [♨] [≈]

B&B/Small Inn

★ ★ ★ **SERENDIPITY B&B.** *712 E 9th St (08226). Phone 609/399-1554; toll-free 800/842-8544; fax 609/399-1527. www.serendipitynj.com.* 6 rooms, 2 share bath, 3 story. No room phones. July 4-Labor Day: S $95-$129; D $98-$159; higher rates holidays (3-day minimum); lower rates rest of year. Children over 10 years only. Complimentary full breakfast. Check-out 11 am, check-in 2 pm. TV; cable. Restaurant opposite 7 am-9 pm. Picnic tables. Luggage handling. Renovated inn built in 1912. Ocean City Boardwalk 1/2 block. Totally nonsmoking. Cr cds: A, DS, MC, V.

[♨] [≈]

Paramus (B-5)

Settled 1660 **Pop** 25,737 **Elev** 58 ft **Area code** 201 **Zip** 07652

Information Chamber of Commerce, 58 E Midland Ave, PO Box 325; 201/261-3344

Web www.paramuschamber.com

This old Dutch farm community was an important hub of transportation as long ago as the Revolutionary War; western Paramus became headquarters for the Continental Army as a result. Paramus has grown as a residential community from 4,000 inhabitants in 1946 to its present size.

What to See and Do

New Jersey Children's Museum. *599 Valley Health Plz. Phone 201/262-5151.* Interactive displays in 30 rooms. Including displays on aviation, firefighting, TV studio, hospital. Gift shop. (Daily; closed holidays) **$$$**

Schoolhouse Museum. *650 E Glen Ave, at NJ 17, in Ridgewood. Phone 201/652-4584 or 201/447-3242 (recording).* Exhibits in 1873 schoolhouse depict life from colonial times through 19th century, with emphasis on local history. Native American relics; early maps; Dutch genealogies; farm implements; doll and toy displays; clothing. Tours (by appointment). (May-late Oct, Sun afternoons; closed holidays) **FREE**

Van Saun County Park. *216 Forest Ave, 1 1/2 miles N of NJ 4. Phone 201/262-2627 or 201/262-3771 (zoo).* Fishing lake; bike trail, tennis (fee), horseshoes, shuffleboard, ice-skating, sledding, picnicking, concession, playgrounds, ball fields (permit). Zoo; train, pony rides (fees). Garden surrounding historic Washington Spring; farmyard. Park (daily). **FREE**

Hotel

★ ★ ★ **RADISSON INN PARAMUS.** *601 From Rd (07652). Phone 201/262-6900; toll-free 800/333-3333; fax 201/262-4955. www.radisson.com.* With a complete health and fitness center, an outdoor pool, volleyball courts, and many other recreational facilities, this is a great place to relax. 120 rooms, 2 story. S, D $79-$145; each additional $10; weekend rates. Crib free. Pet accepted, some restrictions. Complimentary coffee in rooms. Check-out noon. TV; cable (premium). In-room modem link. Refrigerators. Coin laundry. Restaurant 6:30 am-10 pm; Sat, Sun from 7 am. Bar. Room service. Meeting rooms. Business services. Cr cds: A, C, D, DS, ER, JCB, MC, V.

⊡ 🐾 🛏 🚫

Park Ridge

Restaurant

★ ★ **VALENTINO'S.** *103 Spring Valley Rd (07645). Phone 201/391-2230; fax 201/391-3646.* Italian menu. Hours: 11:30 am-2:30 pm, 5-10 pm; Fri to 11 pm, Sat 5-11 pm. Closed Sun; some major holidays. Dinner $13.95-$24.95. Bar. Casual attire. Cr cds: A, D, DS, MC, V.

Parsippany

Pop 50,649 **Elev** 282 ft **Area code** 973 **Zip** 07054

Motel/Motor Lodge

★ **HAMPTON INN.** *3535 Rte 46E (07054). Phone 973/263-0095; fax 973/263-6133. www.hamptoninn.com.* 112 rooms, 4 story. D $144-$164; under 18 free; weekend rates. Complimentary continental breakfast. Check-out noon, check-in 3 pm. TV; cable (premium). Exercise equipment, sauna. Business center. Cr cds: A, C, D, DS, MC, V.

⊡ 🕴 🛏 🚶

Hotel

★ ★ ★ **HILTON PARSIPPANY.** *1 Hilton Ct (07054). Phone 973/267-7373; toll-free 800/774-1500; fax 973/984-2896. www.hilton.com.* The Hilton Parsippany is located 25 minutes from the Newark International Airport, 3 miles from New Jersey, and 27 miles from New York. It offers accommodations for business, leisure, and group travelers. 516 rooms, 6 story. D $229-$239; each additional $20; family, weekend rates. Pet accepted, some restrictions. Check-out noon, check-in 3 pm. TV; cable (premium), VCR available. In-room modem link. Restaurant 6:30 am-11 pm; weekends from 7 am. Bar 11-2 am; entertainment. Room service Mon-Thurs. Exercise equipment. Indoor/outdoor pool, whirlpool. Tennis. Airport transportation. Business center. Cr cds: A, C, D, DS, ER, JCB, MC, V.

⊡ 🐾 🛏 🕴 🚫 🚶

Paterson (C-5)

See also Clifton, Wayne

Settled 1711 **Pop** 149,222 **Elev** 100 ft **Area code** 973

Information Great Falls Visitor Center, 65 McBride Ave, across from the Great Falls, 07501-1715; 973/279-9587. Special Events Office, 72 McBride Ave, 07501; 973/523-9201

Named after Governor William Paterson, this city owes its present and historic eminence as an industrial city to Alexander Hamilton. He was the first man to realize the possibility of harnessing the Great Falls of the Passaic River for industrial purposes. As secretary of the Treasury, he helped form the Society for Establishing Useful Manufactures in 1791 and, a year later, was instrumental in choosing Paterson as the site of its initial ventures. Paterson was the country's major silk-producing town in the late 1800s. Today, it is a diversified industrial center. The area surrounding the Great Falls is now being restored and preserved as a historic district. Paterson is the seat of Passaic County.

City Fun Fact–Paterson

The first radio station and broadcast was in Paterson.

What to See and Do

American Labor Museum-Botto House National Landmark. *83 Norwood St, Haledon. Phone 973/595-7953.* The history of the working class is presented through restored period rooms, changing exhibits, and ethnic gardens. Tours, seminars, and workshops are offered. (Wed-Sat afternoons; closed holidays). **$$**

Garret Mountain Reservation. *Rifle Camp Rd and Mountain Ave. Phone 973/881-4994.* A 575-acre woodland park on a 502-foot-high plateau. Fishing pond (stocked with trout), boat dock, rowboats, paddleboats; trails, stables, picnic groves. **FREE**

⭐ **Great Falls Historic District Cultural Center.** *65 McBride. Phone 973/279-9587.* Includes 77-foot-high falls, park and picnic area, renovated raceway system, restored 19th-century buildings. **DONATION** Also here is

Paterson Museum. *Thomas Rogers Building, 2 Market St. Phone 973/881-3874.* Contains shell of original 14-foot submarine invented by John P. Holland in 1878; also his second submarine (31 feet), built in 1881. Paterson-Colt gun collection (1836-1840); mineral display; exhibits on Paterson history, including the silk and locomotive industries; two locomotives; Curtiss-Wright airplane engines; changing art exhibits. (Tues-Sun; closed holidays) **DONATION**

Lambert Castle. *3 Valley Rd. Phone 973/247-0085.* Built by an immigrant who rose to wealth as a silk manufacturer. The 1893 castle of brownstone and granite houses a local-history museum; restored period rooms; art-history gallery; changing exhibits; library (Wed, Fri, Sun; closed holidays). **$$**

Rifle Camp Park. *Rifle Camp Rd in West Paterson. Phone 973/881-4832.* This 158-acre park is 584 feet above sea level. Includes nature and geology trails, nature center with astronomical observatory; walking paths, fitness course. Picnic areas. **FREE**

Plainfield (D-4)

Settled 1685 **Pop** 47,829 **Elev** 118 ft **Area code** 908

Information Central Jersey Chamber of Commerce, 120 W 7th St, #217, 07060; 908/754-7250

Web www.erols.com/cjcc

Plainfield, directly south of the Watchung Mountains, is actually the center of a group of associated towns: Scotch Plains (see), Watchung, North and South Plainfield, Fanwood, Green Brook, Warren Township, Dunellen, Middlesex, and Piscataway, all of which are mainly residential. Plainfield is also home to a number of industries.

What to See and Do

Drake House Museum. *602 W Front St. Phone 908/755-5831.* (1746) General Washington's headquarters in 1777; now the Historical Society of Plainfield headquarters. Period furnishings; diorama depicts Battle of Shorthills. (Sun afternoons) **$$**

Littell-Lord Farmhouse Museum. *31 Horseshoe Rd in Berkeley Heights (07922).* Museum includes a pre-Revolutionary farmstead, 1878 Victorian House, spring house, 1914 pump house, summer kitchen, spring house, corn crib. (Third Sun of each month or by appointment) **DONATION**

Motel/Motor Lodge

★ ★ **HOLIDAY INN.** *4701 Stelton Rd (07080). Phone 908/753-5500; toll-free 877/214-6161; fax 908/753-5500. www.holiday-inn.com.* 173 rooms, 4 story. S, D $149; under 12 free; weekend rates. Crib free. Pet accepted, some restrictions. Check-out 1 pm. TV; cable (premium). In-room modem link. Refrigerators, microwaves available. Coffee in rooms. Valet services, coin laundry. Restaurant 6:30 am-midnight. Bar. Room service. Exercise equipment, sauna. Indoor pool, whirlpool, lifeguard. Meeting rooms. Business services. Cr cds: A, D, DS, JCB, MC, V.

D 🐾 ≈ 🏋

Princeton (E-3)

See also Trenton

Settled 1685 **Pop** 14,203 **Elev** 215 ft **Area code** 609

Information Chamber of Commerce, 216 Rockingham Row, PO Box 431, 08540; 609/520-1776

Web www.princetonchamber.org

In 1776, the first State Legislature of New Jersey met in Princeton University's Nassau Hall. Washington and his troops surprised and defeated a superior British Army in the 1777 Battle of Princeton. From June to November 1783, Princeton was the new nation's capital. Around the same time, Washington was staying at Rockingham in nearby Rocky Hill, where he wrote and delivered his famous "Farewell Orders to the Armies."

Princeton's life is greatly influenced by the university, which opened here in 1756; at that time it was known as the College of New Jersey. In 1896, on the 150th anniversary of its charter, the institution became Princeton University. Woodrow Wilson, the first president of the university who was not a clergyman, held the office from 1902-10. Princeton is also the home of the Institute for Advanced Study, where Albert Einstein spent the last years of his life.

What to See and Do

Bainbridge House. *158 Nassau St. Phone 609/921-6748.* (circa 1766) Birthplace of commander of the USS *Constitution* during War of 1812. Changing exhibits on Princeton history; research library (Tues, Sat; fee), photo archives. Museum shops. Also offers walking tours of historic district (Sun; fee). **FREE**

Kuser Farm Mansion and Park. *10 miles SE via US 206, I-295 to Olden Ave in Hamilton, then 1/2 mile W to Newkirk Ave. Phone 609/890-3630.* Farm and 1890s summer mansion of Fred Kuser; more than 20 rooms open; many original furnishings. Grounds consist of 22 acres with original buildings including coachman's house, chicken house; tennis pavilion; clay tennis court. Park with picnic areas; quoit courts, lawn bowling, walking trails; formal garden, gazebo. Tours (May-Nov, Thurs-Sun; Feb-Apr, Sat and Sun; limited hours, call for schedule and holiday closings); self-guided tour maps of grounds. Special programs, lectures, and video evenings throughout the year. **FREE**

McCarter Theatre. *91 University Pl, on campus of Princeton University (08540).* Professional repertory company performs classical and modern drama; concerts; ballet; other special programs year-round.

Morven. *55 Stockton St. Phone 609/683-4495 for schedule.* (circa 1750) House of Richard Stockton, signer of the Declaration of Independence. Ransacked during Revolutionary War; was frequently visited by General Washington and other colonial leaders. (Apr-Oct, Wed-Fri, Sun).

Nassau Hall. *Princeton University. Phone 609/258-3000.* (1756) Provided all college facilities, classrooms, dormitories, library, and prayer hall for about 50 years. New Jersey's first legislature met here in 1776, and the Continental Congress met here in 1783, when Princeton was the capital. During the Revolution, it served as a barracks and hospital for Continental and British troops.

Princeton Battle Monument. *On Monument Dr, off Stockton St, near Morven.* The work of Frederick W. MacMonnies, this 50-foot block of Indiana limestone commemorates the famous 1777 battle when George Washington's troops defeated the British.

Princeton Cemetery. *Witherspoon and Wigging St (08542). Phone 609/924-1369.* Buried in the Presidents' Plot are 11 university presidents, including Aaron Burr, Sr., Jonathan Edwards, and John Witherspoon. Monument to Grover Cleveland and grave of Paul Tulane, in whose honor Tulane University was named.

Princeton University. *1 Nassau Hall (08544). Phone 609/258-3603.* (1746) 4,500 undergraduate students, 1,650 graduate students. An Ivy League college that has been coeducational since 1969. A campus guide service shows the visitor points of interest on the main campus. (Daily; closed major holidays)

The Putnam Sculptures. *On campus of Princeton University.* One of the largest modern outdoor sculpture showcases in the country, with 19 sculptures on display throughout the campus, including pieces by Picasso, Moore, Noguchi, Calder, and Lipchitz.

Rockingham State Historic Site. *108 County Rd, Sight 18 (08540). 4 miles N on US 206, then 2 miles E on County 518 in Rocky Hill. Phone 609/921-8835.* On this 5-acre site are three buildings: a kitchen, a wash house, and the main building. This was Washington's headquarters Aug 23-Nov 10, 1783, where he wrote his "Farewell Orders to the Armies"; ten rooms with period furnishings. (Wed-Sat, also Sun afternoons; closed holidays) **FREE**

Woodrow Wilson School of Public and International Affairs. *Princeton University (08544). Phone 609/258-4831.* Designed by Minoru Yamasaki; reflecting pool and "Fountain of Freedom" by James Fitzgerald.

Motel/Motor Lodge

★ ★ **RADISSON HOTEL PRINCETON.** *4355 US 1 S (08540). Phone 609/452-2400; fax 609/452-2494. www.princetonol.com/holidayinn.* 242 rooms, 6 story. S, D $99-$179; each additional $10; suites from $225; under 18 free; weekend rates. Crib free. Pet accepted. Check-out noon. TV; cable (premium). Microwaves, refrigerators available. Restaurant 6:30 am-10 pm. Bar 11-1 am. Health club privileges, exercise equipment. Indoor pool. Meeting rooms. Business services. Gift shop. Cr cds: A, C, D, DS, ER, JCB, MC, V.

D ⌂ ⫪ ⊠ SC

Hotels

★ ★ ★ **DORAL FORRESTAL.** *100 College Rd E (08540). Phone 609/452-7800; toll-free 800/222-1131; fax 609/452-7883. www.forrestal.com.* This property is located on 25 wooded acres. The hotel is decorated with turn-of-the-century arts and crafts, but offers its guests all of the modern-day conveniences. 290 rooms, 3-4 story. S, D $125-$185; each additional $10; suites $275-$650; under 18 free; weekend rates. Crib free. TV; cable (premium), VCR available. Indoor pool; whirlpool. Restaurant 7 am-10 pm. Bars 11-1 am. Check-out noon. Convention facilities. Business center. In-room modem link. Gift shop. Free valet parking. Airport transportation. Lighted tennis. Exercise equipment; sauna. Lawn games. Minibars. Contemporary design and furnishings. On 25 wooded acres. Luxury level. Cr cds: A, C, D, DS, MC, V.

D ⌘ ⌂ ⫪ ⼻ ⊠ SC ⫪

★ ★ ★ **HYATT REGENCY PRINCETON.** *102 Carnegie Center (08540). Phone 609/987-1234; fax 609/987-2584. www.hyatt.com.* This hotel is nestled on 16 acres of landscaped property, just 1 mile from the city's business center, and near the Princeton Junction Train Station. Guests receive a complimentary shuttle to anywhere within a 5-mile radius of the property. 348 rooms, 4 story. S $89-$179; D $89-$204; suites $200-$575; under 18 free; weekend rates. Crib free. Check-out noon. TV; cable (premium), VCR available. In-room modem link. Some bathroom phones. microwaves available. Restaurant 6:30 am-10:30 pm. Bar 11-2 am; entertainment Fri-Sun. Health club privileges, exercise equipment, sauna. Indoor/outdoor pool, whirlpool, poolside service. Tennis. Airport transportation. Business center. Gift shop. Cr cds: A, C, D, DS, ER, JCB, MC, V.

D ⌘ ⌂ ⫪ ⊠ ⫪

★ ★ **NASSAU INN.** *10 Palmer Sq (08542). Phone 609/921-7500; toll-free 800/862-7728; fax 609/921-9385. www.nassauinn.com.* Visitors to Princeton University are lucky to have this inn in such a convenient downtown location. Red armchairs, oriental rugs and beamed ceilings create a rustic country charm, and the nightly, fresh-baked chocolate chip cookies are a welcome treat.

216 rooms, 5 story. S $139-$189; D $159-$209; each additional $20; suites $325-$780; under 13 free. Pet accepted. Check-out noon. TV; cable (premium). In-room modem link. Colonial atmosphere, beamed ceilings, fireplaces in public rooms. Restaurant 7 am-10 pm, bar 4 pm-1 am; entertainment Fri, Sat. Exercise equipment. Business center. Cr cds: A, C, D, MC, V.

D ⌨ ⫪ ⊠ ⫪

B&B/Small Inn

★ ★ **PEACOCK INN.** *20 Bayard Ln (08540). Phone 609/924-1707; fax 609/924-0788. www.peacockinn.com.* 17 rooms, 3 story. Pet accepted. Complimentary breakfast buffet. Check-out 11 am, check-in 2 pm. TV in some rooms, lobby; cable (premium). Dining room. Historic late Georgian Colonial house, built in 1775 and relocated from Nassau St to its present site. Two blocks from Princeton University campus. Cr cds: A, MC, V. **$$**

⌨ ⊠

Restaurants

★ ★ **ALCHEMIST AND BARRISTER.** *28 Witherspoon (08540). Phone 609/924-5555; fax 609/921-2634. www.alchemistandbarrister.com.* Specializes in: seafood, steak. Hours: 11:30 am-2:30 pm, 5:30-10 pm; Fri, Sat to 10:30 pm; Sun 11:30 am-3 pm (brunch), 5:30-10 pm. Closed Jan 1, July 4, Dec 25. Lunch $8-$13, dinner $18-$33. Sun brunch $7.95-$13. Bar to 2 am. Reservations accepted. Outdoor seating. Colonial décor. Cr cds: A, D, DS, MC, V.

D

★ **ANNEX.** *128 1/2 Nassau St (08542). Phone 609/921-7555; fax 609/921-7556. www.annexrestaurant.com.* Hours: 11 am-10 pm; early-bird dinner Mon-Thurs 3:30-5:30 pm. Closed Sun; most major holidays. Continental menu. Bar to 1 am. Lunch $4.50-$23, dinner $6.25-$23. Children's menu. Specialties: steak Diane, chicken a la cacciatori, baked stuffed sole with crabmeat. Casual atmosphere. Family-owned. Cr cds: A, D, MC, V.

★ ★ **RUSTY SCUPPER.** *378 Alexander Rd (08540). Phone 609/921-3276; fax 609/924-5170. www.rustyscupperrestaurant.baweb.com.* Closed Dec 25. Lunch $8-$16.95, dinner $18-$35.95. Bar. Children's menu. Reservations accepted. Outdoor seating. Cr cds: A, MC, V.

Ramsey (B-5)

Pop 14,351 **Elev** 373 ft **Area code** 201 **Zip** 7446

What to See and Do

Campgaw Mountain Ski Area. *200 Campgaw Rd (07430). NJ 17 N, exit NJ 202 Suffern, 1.6 miles S on NJ 202, left on*

Darlington Ave 1 block, stay to right, 1 mile on Campgaw Rd in Mahwah. Phone 201/327-7800. Two double chairlifts, T-bar, two rope tows; patrol, school, rentals; snowmaking; cafeteria. Eight runs, longest run 600 feet; vertical drop 275 feet. (Early Dec-mid-Mar, daily) Lighted cross-country trails; half-pipe; cross-country and snowboard rentals; night skiing (Mon-Sat); snow tubing. **$$$$**

James A. McFaul Environmental Center. *3 miles NW off NJ 208 on Crescent Ave in Wyckoff.* Phone 201/891-5571. An 81-acre wildlife sanctuary includes museum with natural history displays, lectures, film programs; woodland trail; waterfowl pond; picnic area. Arboretum and perennial gardens. (Daily; closed morning weekends and holidays)

Motel/Motor Lodge

★ ★ **RAMADA.** *180 Rte 17 S (07430).* Phone 201/529-5880; toll-free 888/298-2054; fax 201/529-4767. www.ramada.com. 151 rooms, 4 story. D $89-$149; each additional $10; under 16 free. Check-out noon, check-in 3 pm. TV; cable (premium). In-room modem link. Restaurant 6:30 am-11 pm. Bar. Room service. Exercise equipment. Indoor pool. Cr cds: A, C, D, DS, JCB, MC, V.

D ⌨ ⅄ ☒ **SC**

Hotels

★ ★ ★ **SHERATON CROSSROADS HOTEL.** *One International Blvd, Rte 17 N (07495).* Phone 201/529-1660; toll-free 800/325-3535; fax 201/529-4709. www.sheraton.com. Choose a room with a garden or a fountain view. This hotel offers an indoor heated pool, tennis courts, two restaurants and two lounges. Golfers will enjoy the nearby courses, and all will enjoy shopping and other attractions close to this hotel. 251 rooms, 22 story. D $229; each additional $10; under 18 free; weekend rates. Pet accepted, some restrictions. Check-out noon, check-in 3 pm. TV; cable (premium). Restaurant 6:30 am-11 pm. Bar noon-2 am; entertainment except Sun. Exercise equipment, sauna. Indoor pool. Tennis. Business center. Concierge. Luxury level. Cr cds: A, C, D, DS, MC, V.

D ⌨ ⌦ ⌨ ⅄ ☒ ⌨

★ ★ **WELLESLEY INN.** *946 NJ 17N (07446).* Phone 201/934-9250; toll-free 800/444-8888; fax 201/934-9719. www.wellesleyinnandsuites.com. 89 rooms, 3 story. D $89-$109; each additional $5; under 18 free; weekend, monthly rates. Pet accepted, some restrictions; fee. Complimentary continental breakfast. Check-out 11 am, check-in 2 pm. TV; cable (premium). Health club privileges. Cr cds: A, C, D, DS, MC, V.

D ⌦ ☒ ☒

Restaurant

★ ★ ★ **CAFE PANACHE.** *130 E Main St (07446).* Phone 201/934-0030. Located near the center of the town,

this restaurant serves upscale French cuisine in an elegant atmosphere. Hours: noon-2 pm, 5-9 pm; Mon to 8 pm; Fri to 10 pm; Sat 5:30-10 pm. Closed Sun; most major holidays. Dinner $24-$34. Casual attire. Totally nonsmoking. Cr cds: A, MC, V.

D ☒

Red Bank (E-5)

Pop 11,844 **Elev** 35 ft **Area code** 732 **Zip** 07701

Red Bank, an historic community on the shores of the Navesink River, includes a central business area with shops, restaurants, brokerage firms, and an antique center.

What to See and Do

Allen House. *400 Sycamore Ave (07702). 2 miles S on NJ 35, at junction Sycamore Ave in Shrewsbury.* Phone 732/462-1466. (circa 1750) Lower floor restored as tavern of the Revolutionary period; traveler's bedrooms upstairs. (Days same as Holmes House) **$**

Holmes-Hendrickson House. *Longstreet Rd in Holmdel, W on NJ 520.* Phone 732/462-1466. (circa 1750) A 14-room Dutch Colonial farmhouse with period furnishings. (May-Sept, Tues, Thurs, Sat-Sun; closed holidays) **$**

Monmouth Museum. *761 Newman Springs Rd. 5 miles W on Newman Springs Rd; on campus of Brookdale Community College in Lincroft.* Phone 732/747-2266. Changing exhibits of art, science, nature, and cultural history; children's hands-on wing. (Tues-Sun; closed holidays) **$$$**

Motel/Motor Lodge

★ ★ **COURTYARD BY MARRIOTT.** *245 Half Mile Rd (07701).* Phone 732/530-5552; toll-free 800/321-2211; fax 732/530-5756. www.courtyard.com. 146 rooms, 3 story. S $119-$129; D $145-$155; weekend rates. Crib free. TV; cable (premium). Indoor pool; whirlpool. Complimentary coffee in rooms. Restaurant 6:30-10 am, 6-10 pm. Bar 6-11 pm. Check-out noon. Coin laundry. Meeting rooms. Business services available. In-room modem link. Valet service. Exercise equipment. Some refrigerators; microwaves available. Balconies. Cr cds: A, C, D, DS, MC, V.

D ⌦ ⅄ ☒ **SC**

Restaurants

★ ★ **2 SENZA RISTORANTE.** *2 Bridge Ave, Building 5 (07701).* Phone 732/758-0999; fax 732/758-9399. www.2senza.com. Italian, Mediterranean menu. Closed Mon. Lunch, dinner. Children's menu. Casual attire. Outdoor seating. **$$**

D

★ ★ **DOWNTOWN CAFE.** *8 West Front St (07701). Phone 732/741-8844. www.dtcafe.com.* American, sushi menu. Dinner, late night. Bar. Casual attire. **$$**

★ **GAETANO'S.** *10 Wallace St (07701). Phone 732/741-1321. www.gaetanosrebank.com.* Italian menu. Lunch, dinner. Casual attire. Outdoor seating. **$$**

Ⓓ

★ **LITTLE KRAUT.** *115 Oakland St (07701). Phone 732/842-4830.* German menu. Closed Mon. Dinner. Bar. Children's menu. Casual attire. Outdoor seating. **$$**

Ⓓ

★ ★ ★ **MOLLY PITCHER INN.** *88 Riverside Ave (07701). Phone 732/747-2500; toll-free 800/221-1372; fax 732/747-2713. www.mollypitcher-oysterpoint.com.* This restaurant is located in a waterfront hotel on the banks of the Navensink river. A la carte entrées: breakfast $2.95-$12.95, lunch $4.95-$12.95. Dinner $6-$30. Jacket required (dinner). Sun brunch $23.95. Bar. Children's menu. Reservations accepted. Cr cds: A, D, MC, V.

Ⓓ

Rutherford

Pop 18,110 **Elev** 100 ft **Area code** 201

What to See and Do

Fairleigh Dickinson University-Rutherford Campus. *W Passaic and Montross aves. Phone 201/692-7032.* (1942) 2,300 students. On campus is the Kingsland House (1670), in which George Washington stayed in August 1783; and the Castle, an 1888 copy of Chateau d'Amboise in France.

New Jersey Devils (NHL). *Continental Airlines Arena. 50 NJ 120N. East Rutherford. Phone 800/NJ-DEVIL.*

Skylands at Ringwood State Park

Skylands is the official state garden of New Jersey. The walking here is largely on marked dirt paths, with some paved drives and paths. Skylands Manor House is the park's centerpiece. A circa 1922 Tudor-style manor house, it holds, among other items of note, an outstanding collection of antique stained-glass medallions set in leaded windows. Guided house tours are offered one Sunday a month from March through December (phone 973/962-9534). In all, the botanical garden covers 96 acres.

Start at the Visitors Center/Carriage House and pick up a self-guiding tour brochure. Walk first to the right (in the general direction of Parking Lot A), skirting the manor house counter-clockwise. The Winter Garden contains New Jersey's largest Jeffery pine, a century-old upright beech, and an elegant weeping beech. The Japanese umbrella pine is distinctive for its dark-green needles. Also on display here are Atlas cedars and an Algerian fir, a tree that produces 7-inch-tall, purple standing cones.

Walk around the house along the lawn to the Terrace Garden. This garden is comprised of five terraces, each with its own particular ambience. The first centers on an octagonal pool with a swan fountain. Its rock garden is filled with a variety of dwarf plants, including a not-so-dwarf-like 20-foot-tall Dwarf Alberta Spruce. Continue past a pair of Sweet Bay Magnolias, especially beautiful during June, to the third level. Here the centerpiece is a rectangular reflecting pool that, in summer, displays water lilies and tropical fish. Surrounding it are a large collection of azaleas and rhododendrons that bloom in many colors. Next comes the Summer Garden, home to annuals and day lilies, followed by the final terrace level, the Peony Garden.

Walk to the left into the Lilac Garden, which peaks in mid-May. Step onto Maple Avenue, the paved lane, and walk back toward the house. On the right, you'll see the Perennial Garden. A constant flow of color is maintained here from March until November. Just beyond that stands the Annual Garden, a frequently-changing formal garden centered on a 16th-century Italian marble well. Move from there to the right, turn around and walk along Crab Apple Vista, a 1,600-foot grassy *allee* (or corridor) of 166 Carmine crab apple trees that erupts into full bloom in early- to mid-May. At the end of the Vista stands a series of sculptures known as the Four Continents Statues and, to the left, a collection of horsechestnut trees.

Turn left at the horsechestnut trees, and another world appears, revealing woodland paths that travel past Swan Ponds and through a bog. Following the interlaced and meandering dirt paths here, you'll see a wetland in which duck families, as well as the occasional frog, can be spotted. The paths also travel through a cactus collection, a wildflower garden, and a heather garden, and end at a colorful and flashy, yet formal, Rhododendron Display Garden. From here, follow East Cottage Road as it winds its way back to the Carriage House.

New Jersey Nets (NBA). *Continental Airlines Arena. 50 NJ 120 in East Rutherford. Phone 201/935-8888.*

Motel/Motor Lodge

★ **FAIRFIELD INN.** *850 Paterson Plank Rd (07073). Phone 201/507-5222; toll-free 800/228-2800; fax 201/507-0744. www.fairfieldinn.com.* 145 rooms, 5 story. D $99-$119. Check-out noon, check-in 3 pm. TV; cable (premium). In-room modem link. Exercise equipment. Cr cds: A, D, DS, MC, V.

D 🛪 🖾

Hotels

★★ **COURTYARD BY MARRIOTT.** *1 Polito Ave, Lyndhurst (07071). Phone 201/896-6666; fax 201/896-1309. www.marriott.com.* 227 rooms, 6 story. D $150-$250; each additional $10; under 18 free; family, weekend, holiday rates. Check-out noon, check-in 3 pm. TV; cable (premium). In-room modem link. Restaurant 6:30 am-midnight. Bar 5 pm-1 am. Health club privileges, exercise room, sauna. Indoor pool, whirlpool. Business center. Cr cds: A, C, D, DS, MC, V.

D 🛌 🛪 🖾 🕴

★★★ **SHERATON MEADOWLANDS HOTEL AND CONFERENCE CENTER.** *2 Meadowlands Plaza (07073). Phone 201/896-0500; toll-free 800/325-3535; fax 201/896-9696. www.sheraton.com.* This hotel is only minutes from Manhattan, and is perfect for business or leisure travelers. A restaurant, sports pub and lounge are available, as well as many recreational facilities. 443 rooms, 21 story. D $99-$265; each additional $20; under 18 free; weekend rates. Pet accepted, some restrictions. Check-out noon, check-in 3 pm. TV; cable (premium), VCR available. In-room modem link. Restaurant 6:30 am-11 pm. Bar noon-2 am. Exercise equipment, sauna. Indoor pool, whirlpool, poolside service. Business center. Concierge. Cr cds: A, C, D, DS, JCB, MC, V.

D 🐾 🛌 🛪 🕴

Salem (H-1)

Founded circa 1675 **Pop** 5,857 **Elev** 19 ft **Area code** 856 **Zip** 08079

Information Salem County Chamber of Commerce, 91A S Virginia Ave, Carneys Point, 08069; 856/299-6699

Web www.salemnjchamber.com

Salem is said to be the oldest English settlement on the Delaware River. The town and its surrounding area have more than sixty 18th-century houses and buildings, as well as many points of historical interest. In the Friends Burying Ground on Broadway is the 600-year-old Salem Oak, under which John Fenwick, the town's founder, signed a treaty with the Lenni-Lenape tribe.

What to See and Do

Alexander Grant House. *79-83 Market St. Phone 856/935-5004.* (1721) Headquarters of Salem County Historical Society. Twenty rooms with period furniture; Wistarburg glass; Native American relics; dolls; paintings; genealogy library; stone barn. (Tues-Fri afternoons; also open the second Sat afternoon of each month) **$$**

Fort Mott State Park. *454 Fort Mott Rd. Phone 856/935-3218.* A 104-acre park at Finns Point; established in 1837 as a defense of the port of Philadelphia. North of the park is Finns Point National Cemetery, where more than 2,500 Union and Confederate soldiers are buried. Fishing, ferry ride, picnicking, playground; overlook.

Special Event

Cowtown Rodeo. *Cowtown 780 Rte 40 Pilesgrove NJ 08098 (08098). 12 miles NE on NJ 45, then 3 miles W on US 40, near Woodstown. Phone 609/769-3200.* PRCA sanctioned. Sat evenings, Memorial Day-late Sept.

Scotch Plains (D-4)

See also Plainfield

Settled 1684 **Pop** 22,732 **Elev** 119 ft **Area code** 908 **Zip** 07076

What to See and Do

Watchung Reservation. *Elizabethtown Town Plaza. 1 mile NE. Phone 908/527-4900.* A 2,000-wooded-acre reservation in the Watchung Mountains includes the 25-acre Surprise Lake. Nature and bridle trails, ice skating, picnic areas, playground. Ten-acre nursery and rhododendron display garden. Also here is

> **Trailside Nature and Science Center.** *452 New Providence Rd in Mountainside. Phone 908/789-3670.* Nature exhibits; special programs; planetarium shows (Sun; fee). Museum (late Mar-mid-Nov, daily; rest of year, weekends only; closed some holidays). Visitor Center with live reptile exhibit (daily, afternoons). Gift shop. Grounds (daily). **FREE**

Restaurant

★★★ **STAGE HOUSE INN.** *366 Park Ave (07076). Phone 908/322-4224; fax 908/322-4225. www.stagehouseinn.com.* A local favorite, this establishment offers lightened versions of classic French dishes, beautifully presented and full of flavor. Guests enjoy the simple, refined atmosphere and the casual patio dining. Specialties: charlotte of Maine crab; pan-roasted cod with crispy potatoes, peas, and black truffle sauce. Hours: 11:30 am-2 pm, 5:30-9 pm; Fri, Sat to 10 pm; Sun 4-8 pm. Closed Mon; Dec 25. A la carte entrées: lunch $8-$18, dinner $21-$29. Bar. Jacket. Outdoor seating. Cr cds: A, DS, MC, V.

D

Seaside Park (F-5)

Pop 2,263 **Elev** 6 ft **Area code** 732 **Zip** 08752

What to See and Do

Island Beach State Park. *S on Central Ave. Phone 732/793-0506.* This strip of land (3,002 acres) is across the water, north of Long Beach Island (see), and faces Barnegat Lighthouse. There are two natural areas (Northern Area and Southern Area) and a recreational zone in the center. Excellent swimming and fishing in Atlantic Ocean (seasonal). Nature tours. Picnicking. (Daily) Standard fees.

Motel/Motor Lodge

★ ★ **WINDJAMMER MOTOR INN.** *1st and Central aves (08752). Phone 732/830-2555.* 39 rooms, 24 kitchen units, 3 story. June-Sept: S, D $100-$135; each additional $10; kitchen units $130; lower rates rest of year. Crib $5. Check-out 11 am. TV; cable. Coin laundry. Restaurant 8 am-7 pm. Bar from 11 am. Beach privileges. Heated pool, poolside service. Cr cds: A, MC, V.

D 🐾 ⚡ 🏊 ⊠

Secaucus

Pop 15,931 **Elev** 12 ft **Area code** 201

Motel/Motor Lodge

★ ★ **HOLIDAY INN.** *300 Plaza Dr (07094). Phone 201/348-2000; toll-free 800/465-4329; fax 201/348-6035. www.holiday-inn.com.* 168 rooms, 8 story. D $159-$189; each additional $10; under 18 free; weekend, monthly rates. Check-out noon, check-in 3 pm. TV; cable (premium). In-room modem link. Restaurant 7 am-11 pm. Bar. Room service. Health club privileges, exercise equipment. Valet parking. Luxury level. Cr cds: A, C, D, DS, JCB, MC, V.

D 🏋 ⊠ **SC**

Somerville (D-4)

See also New Brunswick

Pop 12,423 **Elev** 54 ft **Area code** 908 **Zip** 08876

Information Somerset County Chamber of Commerce, 64 W End Ave, PO Box 833; 908/725-1552

Web www.somersetcountychamber.org

What to See and Do

Duke Gardens. *US 206 S, about 1 1/4 mile S of Somerville Cir. Reservations required; contact Duke Gardens Foundation (Mon-Fri). Phone 908/722-3700.* Features 11 gardens under glass, including colonial, desert, Italian, Asian, English, and tropical (closed Jan 1, Thanksgiving, Dec 25); 45-minute guided tour (Oct-May, daily). No high heels, no cameras.

Golf House—USGA Museum and Library. *US 287 to NJ 512, in Far Hills. Phone 800/223-0041.* Georgian colonial mansion originally designed as private residence by John Russel Pope, now houses exhibits tracing the evolution of golf. Equipment and artifacts donated by golf's greatest champions, including Bobby Jones, Byron Nelson, Jack Nicklaus, and Arnold Palmer. Interactive displays. Library with over 13,000 volumes on golf; USGA Research and Test Center. (Daily; closed holidays)

Old Dutch Parsonage State Historic Site. *38 Washington Pl (08876). Phone 908/725-1015.* (1751) Moved from its original location, this brick building was the home of the Reverend Jacob Hardenbergh from 1758 to 1781. He founded Queens College, now Rutgers University, while residing in this building. Some furnishings and memorabilia on display. (Wed-Sun; closed holidays; hours may vary)

Wallace House State Historic Site. *38 Washington Pl (08876). Phone 908/725-1015.* General and Mrs. Washington made their headquarters here immediately after the house was built in 1778, while the army was stationed at Camp Middlebrook. Period furnishings. (Wed-Sun; closed holidays; hours may vary)

Special Event

IMB/USET Festival of Champions. *Hamilton Farm. Pottersville Rd, Gladstone (07934). Phone 908/234-0555.* Competition of three Olympic equestrian disciplines. Mid- or late June.

Motel/Motor Lodge

★ **DAYS INN.** *118 Rte 206 S, Hillsborough (08844). Phone 908/685-9000; toll-free 800/329-7466; fax 908/*

685-0601. www.daysinn.com. 100 rooms, 2 story. S, D $100-$150; each additional $5; suites $125-$175; under 17 free. Crib free. TV; cable. Complimentary continental breakfast. Check-out 11 am. In-room modem link. Valet service. Pool. Exercise equipment. Some refrigerators; microwaves available. Cr cds: A, C, D, DS, JCB, MC, V.

D ⌨ 🏋 ☒ SC

Restaurant

★ ★ ★ **THE RYLAND INN.** *US 22 W, Whitehouse (08888). Phone 908/534-4011; fax 908/534-6592. www. therylandinn.com.* Using ingredients culled from his 7 acres of gardens, chef-owner Craig Shelton creates a deceivingly simple seasonal French cuisine at this country-estate restaurant. The decor ranges from homey to hunting lodge, and the wine list is long and varied. Hours: 11am-2 pm, 5-9 pm; Fri to 10 pm; Sat 5-10 pm; Sun 5-9 pm. Closed Mon; also first week in Jan. Lunch $13-$16, dinner $26-$36. Eight-course tasting menu: $85. Bar. Piano bar. Jacket required. Valet parking available. Cigar room. Organic garden. Cr cds: A, D, DS, MC, V. **$$$$**

D

Spring Lake (E-5)
See also Asbury Park

Pop 3,567 **Elev** 25 ft **Area code** 732 **Zip** 07762

Motels/Motor Lodges

★ **BELMAR MOTOR LODGE.** *910 NJ 35 10th Ave, Belmar (07719). Phone 732/681-6600; fax 732/681-6604.* 55 rooms, 2 story. Memorial Day-Labor Day: S, D $88-$115; each additional $10; under 14 free; higher rates holidays (3-day minimum); lower rates rest of year. Crib $3. TV; cable (premium). Pool. Restaurant adjacent open 24 hours. Check-out 11 am. Coin laundry. Opposite Belmar Marine Basin. Cr cds: A, C, D, MC, V.

⌨ ☒ SC

★ **COMFORT INN.** *1909 NJ 35 (07719). Phone 732/449-6146; fax 732/449-6556. www.comfortinn.com.* 70 rooms, 2 story. Mid-June-Labor Day: S, D $125-$190; each additional $10; suites from $150; lower rates rest of year. Crib $5. Complimentary continental breakfast. Check-out 11 am. TV. In-room modem link. Microwave, refrigerator in suites. Exercise equipment. Pool, lifeguard. Meeting room. Business services. Cr cds: A, C, D, DS, JCB, MC, V.

D ⌨ 🏋 ☒

★ **DOOLAN'S.** *700 NJ 71, Spring Lake Heights (07762). Phone 732/449-3666; fax 732/449-2601. www.doolans.com.* 60 rooms, 3 story. Memorial Day-Labor Day: S $50-$175; D $55-$275; each additional $10; lower rates rest of year. Crib $5. Complimentary continental breakfast. Check-out 11 am. TV; cable (premium). Restaurant 8-10 am, noon-3 pm, 4:30-10 pm; closed for lunch Sat. Bar; entertainment Wed-Sun. Pool, lifeguard. Meeting rooms. Cr cds: A, C, D, DS, MC, V.

⌨

★ **MARINERS COVE MOTOR INN.** *50 Broadway, Point Pleasant (08742). Phone 732/899-0060; fax 732/701-0260.* 28 rooms, 2 story. Memorial Day-Labor Day: S, D $139-$210; under 16 free; family rates; package plans; weekends, holidays (2-3 day minimum). Check-out 11 am, check-in 2 pm. TV; cable. Refrigerators. Restaurant adjacent 6 am-9 pm. Heated pool. Cr cds: A, DS, MC, V.

🎣 ⌨

★ **POINT BEACH MOTEL.** *Ocean and Trenton Aves, Point Pleasant Beach (08742). Phone 732/892-5100.* 25 rooms, 2 story. Memorial Day-Labor Day: S, D $142-$172; each additional $10; under 8 free; higher rates holidays; lower rates rest of year. Closed Oct-Apr. Crib $10. Check-out 11 am. TV; cable. Refrigerators. Opposite Atlantic Ocean. Heated pool, wading pool. Microwaves available. Cr cds: DS, MC, V.

D 🎣 ⌨ ☒

★ **TRAVELODGE.** *1916 Hwy 35, Wall (07719). Phone 732/974-8400; toll-free 888/515-6375; fax 732/974-8401. www.travelodge.com.* 52 rooms, 2 with shower only. S $44-$124; D $54-$159; each additional $5-$10; under 16 free; higher rates some holiday weekends. Crib free. TV; cable (premium). Pool. Complimentary continental breakfast, coffee in rooms. Check-out 11 am. Business services available. Refrigerators. Cr cds: A, C, D, DS, JC, B, MC, V.

D ⌨ ☒ SC

Hotels

★ ★ **BREAKERS HOTEL.** *1507 Ocean Ave (07762). Phone 732/449-7700; fax 732/449-0161. www.breakershotel.com.* 67 units. Mid-June-Labor Day (holiday weekends 5-day minimum): S, D $180-$390; each additional $30; lower rates rest of year. Crib free. Check-out noon. TV. Refrigerators. Restaurant 8 am-4 pm, 4:30-10 pm. Pool, whirlpool, poolside service, lifeguard. Meeting rooms. Business services. Restored Victorian oceanfront hotel. Cr cds: A, C, D, MC, V.

D ⌨ ☒

★ ★ ★ **HEWITT WELLINGTON HOTEL.** *200 Monmouth Ave (07762). Phone 732/974-1212; fax 732/974-2338. www.hewittwellington.com.* Found lakeside, with a view of the ocean, this Victorian-style hotel was renovated in 1988, yet still keeps its Old World charm and grace. 29 rooms, 17 suites, 3 story. Late June-Labor Day: S, D $150-$220; each additional $40; suites $225-$290; weekly rates; higher rates: weekends (2-day minimum), holidays (3-day minimum); lower rates rest of year. Children over 12 years only. Check-out 11 am. TV; cable. In-room modem link. Some balconies. Refrigerators. Coffee in rooms. Restaurant 5:30-11 pm. Heated pool. Meeting room. Business services. Cr cds: A, D, DS, MC, V.

⬛⬛

B&B/Small Inns

★ ★ **ASHLING COTTAGE.** *106 Sussex Ave (07762). Phone 732/449-3553; toll-free 888/274-5464; fax 732/449-9067. www.ashlingcottage.com.* 11 rooms, 3 story. No room phones, mid Dec-mid-Feb. Complimentary full breakfast. Check-out 11 am, check-in 2 pm. TV in lobby; VCR available (movies). Bicycles. Concierge. Victorian-style frame house (1877). Totally nonsmoking. Cr cds: A, D, MC, V. **$$**

⬛

★ ★ ★ **BAY HEAD GABLES.** *200 Main Ave, Bay Head (08742). Phone 732/892-9844; toll-free 800/984-9536; fax 732/295-2196. www.bayheadgables.com.* This oceanfront bed-and-breakfast sits at the head of Barnegat Beach Island. Its Georgian-style, 150-foot wraparound porch, cedar-shingled facade, and manicured grounds are well regarded in this fashionable area. Point Pleasant Beach is nearby for walking the boardwalk or sunbathing. 11 rooms, 3 story. June-Labor Day: S, D $150-$225; weekly rates; higher rates weekends (2-3-day minimum); open weekends only Apr-June and Labor Day-Dec. Closed rest of year. Complimentary full breakfast. Check-out 11 am, check-in 1 pm. TV in sitting room; cable. Designed by Stanford White in 1914. Totally nonsmoking. Cr cds: A, DS, MC, V.

⬛⬛

★ ★ ★ **CHATEAU INN.** *500 Warren Avenue (07762). Phone 732/974-2000; toll-free 877/974-5253; fax 732/974-0007. www.chateauinn.com.* 38 rooms, 2 story. Late June-Labor Day: S $159-$209; D $179-$259; each additional $15; suites $219-$299; lower rates rest of year. TV; cable (premium), VCR (movies). Private patios. Refrigerators, some fireplaces. Microwaves available. Health club privileges. Beach, pool privileges. Bicycles. Meeting room. Business services. Renovated Victorian hotel (1888). Overlooks parks, lake. Cr cds: A, D, DS, MC, V.

D⬛⬛⬛⬛

★ ★ **THE INN AT THE SHORE.** *301 4th Ave, Belmar (07719). Phone 732/681-3762; fax 732/280-1914. www.theinnattheshore.com.* 10 rooms, 6 share bath. S, D $115-$210; each additional $20; under 12 free. Crib free. Complimentary full breakfast. Check-out noon, check-in 2 pm. In-room modem link. Microwaves, refrigerators available. Business services. Luggage handling. Victorian-style ambience in a house built in 1888; many antiques. Cr cds: A, MC, V.

⬛⬛⬛

★ ★ **NORMANDY INN.** *21 Tuttle Ave (07762). Phone 732/449-7172; toll-free 800/449-1888; fax 732/449-1070. www.normandyinn.com.* 19 rooms, 3 story. June-Sept: S $95-$198; D $179-$346; each additional $20; lower rates rest of year. Crib available. Complimentary full breakfast. TV available; VCR available. Some fireplaces. Bicycles. Business services. Built as a private residence in 1888; 19th-century antiques. Porches. Cr cds: A, C, D, DS, MC, V.

⬛⬛⬛

★ ★ **THE SANDPIPER INN.** *7 Atlantic Ave (07762). Phone 732/449-6060; toll-free 800/824-2779; fax 732/529-3390. www.sandpiperinn.com.* 15 rooms, 8 with shower only, 4 story. Mid-June-early Sept: S, D $199-$279; each additional $50; lower rates rest of year. Children over 16 years only. Complimentary continental breakfast, afternoon refreshments. Check-out noon, check-in 3 pm. TV; cable. Refrigerators. Dining room (see also THE SANDPIPER). Indoor pool. Business services. Victorian inn built in 1888; casual atmosphere in elegant surroundings. Opposite beach. Cr cds: DS, MC, V.

⬛⬛⬛

★ ★ **WHITE LILAC INN.** *414 Central Ave (07762). Phone 732/449-0211; fax 732/974-0568. www.whitelilac.com.* 10 rooms, 2 share bath, 2 1/2 story. No room phones. S, D $125-$325; weekly rates; weekends (2-day minimum); holidays (3-day minimum). Closed Jan. Children over 14 years only. Complimentary full breakfast. Check-out 11 am, check-in 2 pm. TV in some rooms; cable (premium). Some fireplaces. Free train station transportation. Southern accent; built in 1880. Cr cds: A, DS, MC, V.

⬛⬛

Restaurant

★ ★ **THE SANDPIPER.** *7 Atlantic Ave (07762). Phone 732/449-4700; fax 732/449-9825. www.sandpiperrestaurant.com.* Contemporary American menu. Lunch, dinner. Piano Sat. Children's menu. Candlelit dining in Victorian setting. Cr cds: D, MC, V. **$$**

D

Stanhope

See also Lake Hopatcong, Rockaway

Pop 3,584 **Elev** 882 ft **Area code** 973 **Zip** 07874

What to See and Do

Waterloo Village Restoration. *525 Waterloo Rd (07874). I-80 exit 25; follow signs.* Phone 973/347-0900. Known as the Andover Forge during the Revolutionary War, it was once a busy town on the Morris Canal. The 18th-century buildings include Stagecoach Inn, houses, craft barns, gristmill, apothecary shop, general store. Music festival during summer (fee). (Mid-Apr-mid-Nov, Wed-Sun; closed Thanksgiving, Dec 25) **$$$**

Motel/Motor Lodge

★ ★ **CROSSED KEYS INN.** *289 Pequest Rd, Andover (07821).* Phone 973/786-6661; fax 973/786-6485. *www. crossedkeys.com.* 7 rooms, 2 story. D $130-$185; each additional $25; weekends, holidays (2-day minimum). Complimentary full breakfast. Check-out 11 am, check-in 2 pm. TV. Some fireplaces. Game room. Lawn games. Totally nonsmoking. Cr cds: A, MC, V.

B&B/Small Inns

★ ★ ★ **THE WOODEN DUCK B & B.** *140 Goodale Rd, Newton (07860).* Phone 973/300-0395; fax 973/300-0395. *www.woodenduckinn.com.* A shuttered facade and neat little brick steps are a prelude to the residential, lived-in interior of this small bed-and-breakfast in rural Sussex County. All seven guest rooms feature elegant country décor, as well as queen-size beds and modern amenities. 7 rooms, 2 story. D $110-$190; holidays (2-day minimum). Children over 12 years only. Complimentary full breakfast. Check-out 11 am, check-in 2 pm. TV; VCR (movies). In-room modem link. Game room. Pool. Downhill ski 20 miles, cross-country ski on site. Lawn games. Totally nonsmoking. Cr cds: A, DS, MC, V.

Restaurant

★ ★ **THE BLACK FOREST INN.** *249 US 206N (07874).* Phone 973/347-3344; fax 973/347-0176. *www.blackforestinn.com.* German, Continental menu. Hours: 11:30 am-2 pm, 5-10 pm; Sun 1-8 pm. Closed Tues; most major holidays. Dinner $18.50-$26.50. Bar. Casual attire. Cr cds: A, D, MC, V.

Stone Harbor (J-3)

Pop 1,128 **Elev** 5 ft **Area code** 609 **Zip** 08247

Information Stone Harbor Chamber of Commerce, 212 96th St, PO Box 422; 609/368-6101. Cape May County Chamber of Commerce, PO Box 74, Cape May Court House 08210; 609/465-7181

What to See and Do

Wetlands Institute. *1075 Stone Harbor Blvd (08247). 3 miles E off Garden State Pkwy exit 10.* Phone 609/368-1211. Environmental center focusing on coastal ecology. Also includes observation tower; marsh trail; aquarium; films and guided walks (July and Aug, daily). Bookstore. (Mid-May-mid-Oct, daily; rest of year, Tues-Sat; closed Easter, July 4, Thanksgiving; also two weeks late in Dec-early Jan) **$$**

Special Events

Sail into Summer Boat Show. Phone 609/368-6101. Pleasure boating, family entertainment, musicians, food. First weekend in May.

Wings 'n Water Festival. *1075 Stone Harbor Blvd.* Phone 609/368-1211. Arts and crafts, decoys; entertainment; seafood. Third full weekend in Sept.

Motel/Motor Lodge

★ ★ **DESERT SAND RESORT COMPLEX.** *7888 Dune Dr, Avalon (08202).* Phone 609/368-5133; toll-free 800/458-6008; fax 609/368-1849. *www.desertsand.com.* 90 units, 15 suites, 31 kitchen units, 3 story. July-Aug: S $72-123; D $80-$163; each additional $10; suites $163-$205; kitchens $170-$357, weekly rates; higher rates holidays; lower rates mid-Apr-June, Sept-Oct. Closed rest of year. Crib available. Check-out 11 am. TV; cable. Refrigerators. Microwaves available. Coin laundry. Restaurant 8:30 am-10 pm. Bar noon-midnight. Exercise equipment. Two pools, one indoor, whirlpool, lifeguard. Meeting rooms. Business services. Cr cds: MC, V.

Resort

★ ★ ★ **AVALON GOLDEN INN HOTEL & CONFERENCE CENTER.** *7849 Dune Dr (08202).* Phone 609/368-5155; fax 609/368-6112. *www.goldeninn. com.* This is an oceanfront inn with a relaxed atmosphere. Guest rooms are tastefully decorated, food is delicately prepared in the dining room and a wide variety of activities can be found only minutes away. 154 rooms,

76 kitchen units, 3 story. June-Labor Day: S, D $70-$275; each additional $15; suites $245-$345; kitchen units $214-$275; under 12 free; lower rates rest of year. Crib available. Check-out 11 am. TV; cable (premium), VCR (movies). In-room modem link. Balconies. Refrigerators. Restaurant 8 am-11 pm. Bar 11-2 am; entertainment weekends. Room service. Supervised children's activities (mid-June-late Sept). Health club privileges. Heated pool, wading pool, lifeguard, poolside service. Golf privileges. Tennis privileges. Picnic tables. Meeting rooms. Business services. Bellstaff. On beach. Cr cds: MC, V.

[D] [icons]

Toms River (F-5)

Pop 7,524 **Elev** 40 ft **Area code** 732

Information Toms River-Ocean County Chamber of Commerce, 1200 Hooper Ave, 08753; 732/349-0220

What to See and Do

Cooper Environmental Center. *1170 Cattus Island Blvd, E on NJ 37 to Fischer Blvd, follow signs.* Phone 732/270-6960. A 530-acre facility with 3-mile bay front. Boat tours (summer; free); 7 miles of marked trails, picnicking (grills), playground. Nature center. (Daily) **FREE**

Motels/Motor Lodges

★ ★ **HOLIDAY INN.** *290 Rte 37E (08753). Phone 732/244-4052; toll-free 800/465-4329; fax 732/244-4000. www.holiday-inn.com.* 122 rooms, 4 story. Memorial Day-Labor Day: S, D $109-$149; each additional $10; higher rates weekends; lower rates rest of year. Crib free. Check-out noon. TV; cable (premium). Refrigerators. Valet services, coin laundry. Restaurant 6:30 am-10 pm. Bar 11-2 am; entertainment. Room service. Sauna. Game room. Indoor pool, whirlpool, poolside service. Meeting rooms. Business services. Cr cds: A, C, D, DS, MC, V.

[D] [icons] SC

★ ★ **HOWARD JOHNSON.** *955 Hooper Ave (08753). Phone 732/244-1000; fax 732/505-3194. www.tomsriverhojos.com.* 96 rooms, 2 story. S $60-$199; D $70-$229; each additional $10; under 18 free; higher rates some holidays. Pet accepted, some restrictions; fee. Check-out noon. TV; VCR available (movies). In-room modem link. Restaurant 11 am-9 pm. Bar. Indoor/outdoor pool. Cr cds: A, C, D, DS, MC, V.

[D] [icons] SC

★ ★ **QUALITY INN.** *815 W Rte 37 (08755). Phone 732/341-2400; toll-free 800/228-5151; fax 732/341-6469. www.qualityinntr.com.* 100 rooms, 2 story. Memorial Day-Labor Day: S, D $75-$195; each additional $10; suites $129-$229; under 18 free; lower rates rest of year. Crib free. Complimentary continental breakfast. Check-out 11 am. TV; cable. In-room modem link. Refrigerators available. Coffee in rooms. Valet services. Restaurant noon-8 pm. Bar; entertainment. Room service. Playground. Exercise equipment, sauna. Pool, poolside service, lifeguard. Airport transportation. Meeting rooms. Business services. Sundries. Cr cds: A, DS, ER, JCB, MC, V.

[D] [icons] SC

★ ★ **RAMADA.** *2373 Rte 9 (08755). Phone 732/905-2626; toll-free 888/298-2054; fax 732/905-8735. www.ramada.com.* 154 rooms, 48 kitchen units, 3 story. Memorial Day-Labor Day: S $72-$139; D $79-$132; each additional $10; suites $119-$159; under 12 free; lower rates rest of year. Crib free. Complimentary continental breakfast. Check-out noon. TV; cable (premium). In-room modem link. Refrigerators available. Coin laundry. Restaurant 7 am-10 pm. Bar. Room service. Exercise equipment. Game room. Pool, whirlpool, lifeguard. Tennis. Meeting rooms. Business services. Sundries. Cr cds: A, C, D, DS, JCB, MC, V.

[D] [icons]

Restaurant

★ **THE OLD TIME TAVERN.** *Dover Mall Rte 166 (08753). Phone 732/349-2387; fax 732/505-5976. www.theoldtimetavern.com.* Hours: 11:30-1 am; Sun to midnight. Closed Dec 25. Dinner $5.95-$14.95. Bar. Children's menu. Cr cds: A, C, D, MC, V.

[D]

Trenton (E-3)

See also Princeton

Settled 1679 **Pop** 85,403 **Elev** 50 ft **Area code** 609

Information Mercer County Chamber of Commerce, 214 W State St, 08608-1002; 609/393-4143

Web www.mercerchamber.org

The capital of New Jersey since 1790, Trenton is one of the fastest growing business and industrial areas in the country and a leading rubber-manufacturing center since colonial times. After crossing the Delaware on December 26, 1776, George Washington attacked the British-held town eight miles to the northwest.

What to See and Do

Auditorium. *205 W State St, in the New Jersey State Museum.* Lectures; films; music; children's theater. Some fees.

College Art Gallery. *On the campus of The College of New Jersey. Phone 609/771-2652.* (Feb-May and Sept-Dec, Mon-Fri, Sun; closed holidays) **FREE**

College of New Jersey. *4 miles N on NJ 31. Phone 609/771-1855.* (1855) 6,150 students. A 250-acre wooded campus with two lakes. Tours of campus.

Ferry House State Historic Site. *355 Washington Crossing, in Washington Crossing State Park (08560). Phone 609/737-2515.* Building sheltered Washington and some of his men on Dec 25, 1776, after they had crossed the Delaware from the Pennsylvania side. It is believed that the strategy to be used for the attack on Trenton was discussed here. Restored as a living history colonial farmhouse; special programs throughout the year. (Wed-Sun)

Main Building. *In the New Jersey State Museum.* Fine art, cultural history, archaeology and natural science exhibits. (Tues-Sun; closed state holidays) **FREE**

New Jersey State Museum. *205 W State St, adjacent to Capitol. Phone 609/292-6464.* (Tues-Sun; closed holidays). **FREE**

The Old Barracks Museum. *Barrack St, opposite W Front St. Phone 609/396-1776.* One of the finest examples of colonial barracks in the US. Built in 1758-1759, it housed British, Hessian, and Continental troops during the Revolutionary War. Museum contains restored soldiers' squad room; antique furniture; ceramics; firearms; dioramas. Guides in period costumes. (Daily; closed holidays) **$$$**

Planetarium. *205 W State St, in the New Jersey State Museum. Phone 609/292-6303.* One of few Intermediate Space Transit planetaria (duplicates motions of space vehicles) in the world. Programs (weekends; July-Aug, Tues-Sun). Over four years only except children's programs. Tickets 30 minutes in advance. **$$**

Sesame Place. *Rte 1 S to Oxford Valley exit. Phone 215/752-7070.* A family play park featuring characters from *Sesame Street.* **$$$$**

⭐ **Washington Crossing State Park.** *8 miles NW on NJ 29, at 355 Washington Crossing-Pennington Rd, in Titusville. Phone 609/737-0623.* This 996-acre park commemorates the famous crossing on Christmas night, 1776, by the Continental Army, under the command of General George Washington. Continental Lane, at the park, is the road over which Washington's army began its march to Trenton, Dec 25, 1776. Natural trails. Picnicking, playground. Visitor center and nature center (Wed-Sun); open-air summer theater (fee). Standard fees. (See SPECIAL EVENTS)

William Trent House. *15 Market St. Phone 609/989-3027.* (1719) Trenton's oldest house is an example of Georgian architecture. It was the home of Chief Justice William Trent, for whom the city was named. Colonial garden. (Daily, afternoons; closed holidays) **$$**

Special Events

Heritage Days. First weekend in June.

Reenactment of Crossing of the Delaware. *355 Washington Crossing Rd. Washington Crossing State Park.* Departs PA side on the afternoon of Dec 25.

Trenton Kennel Club Dog Show. *Mercer County Central Park.* Early May.

Motel/Motor Lodge

★★ **HOWARD JOHNSON.** *Rte 1 S, Lawrenceville (08648). Phone 609/896-1100; toll-free 800/654-2000; fax 609/895-1325. www.hojo.com.* 104 rooms, 2 story. S $62.50-$88; D $68.50-$110; each additional $10; under 18 free; higher rates special events. Pet accepted. Complimentary continental breakfast. Check-out noon. TV; cable (premium). In-room modem link. Restaurant open 24 hours. Pool. Cr cds: A, C, D, DS, MC, V.

D 🐾 ⛱ ⤐ SC

Restaurants

★★ **DIAMONDS.** *132 Kent (08611). Phone 609/393-1000; fax 609/393-1672. www.diamondsrestaurant.com.* Italian, seafood, steak menu. Hours: 11:30 am-2:30 pm, 4:30 pm-midnight; Sat from 4:30 pm; Sun from 3:30 pm. Closed Thanksgiving, Dec 25. Lunch $7-$15, dinner $16-$33. Bar. Valet parking available. Cr cds: A, C, D, DS, MC, V.

★★ **MARSILIO'S.** *541 Roebling Ave (08611). Phone 609/695-2986; fax 609/695-2986.* Hours: 11:30 am-2 pm, 5-10 pm; Fri, Sat to 11 pm. Closed Sun; most major holidays. Reservations accepted. Italian menu. Bar. Lunch $6.45-$19.95, dinner $12.95-$26. Children's menu. Specializes in veal, chicken. Italian décor. Cr cds: A, MC, V.

D

Vernon

Pop 1,737 **Elev** 564 ft **Area code** 973 **Zip** 7462

Information Vernon Township Municipal Building, 21 Church St; 973/764-4055

What to See and Do

Action Park. *200 NJ 94. Phone 973/827-2000.* Theme park includes 75 self-operative rides, shows and attractions. Action Park has more than 40 water rides, including river rides and Tidal Wave Pool; also Grand Prix race cars, bungee jumping, miniature golf, children's park; food, picnic area. Three daily shows, weekend festival series. (Mid-June-Labor Day, daily; late May-mid-June, Thurs-Sun) **$$$$**

Mountain Creek Ski Resort. *200 NJ 94. Phone 973/827-2000.* Gondola; four quad, triple, double chairlifts; three surface lifts, rope tow; school, rentals; snowmaking; cafeterias, restaurants, bars, night club; nursery. Forty-three runs; vertical drop 1,040 feet. (Dec-Mar, daily) Night skiing. Health spa, country club (daily). **$$$$**

B&B/Small Inn

★★**APPLE VALLEY INN.** *967 Rte 517, PO Box 302, Glenwood (07418). Phone 973/764-3735; fax 973/764-1050. www.applevalleyinn.com.* 7 rooms, 5 share bath, 3 story. No elevator. S, D $110-$150; each additional $25. Complimentary full breakfast. Check-out 11 am, check-in before 9 pm. Premium cable TV in common room; VCR available (movies). Pool. Built in 1831; antiques. Cr cds: A, MC, V.

🔣 🔣 🔣 🔣

Wayne

───────────────────

Pop 54,069 **Elev** 200 ft **Area code** 973 **Zip** 07470

Information Tri-County Chamber of Commerce, 2055 Hamburg Tpke; 973/831-7788

Web www.tricounty.org

Wayne is the home of William Paterson University of New Jersey (1855).

What to See and Do

Dey Mansion. *199 Totowa Rd. Phone 973/696-1776.* (circa 1740) Restoration of Washington's headquarters (1780); period furnishings. Guided tours. Picnic tables. (Wed-Sun; closed holidays) **$**

Mead Van Duyne House. *530 Berdan Ave (07470). Phone 973/694-7192.* Restored Dutch farmhouse.

Ringwood State Park. *(On the New Jersey, New York border) Phone 973/962-7031.* Ringwood State Park lies in upper Passaic County, near the town of Ringwood, within the heart of the Ramapo Mountains. Consisting of 6,196 acres, the park is reached by routes 23 and 511 from the west and Route 17 and Sloatsburg Road from the east. Standard fees are charged for each section Memorial Day-Labor Day. In park is the

Ringwood Manor Section This section features a 51-room mansion containing a collection of Americana; relics of iron-making days (1740); formal gardens. Interpretive tours. Fishing in Ringwood River. Picnic facilities nearby. Tours (Wed-Sun).

Shepherd Lake Section A 541-acre wooded area has trap and skeet shooting all year (fee). The 74-acre Shepherd Lake provides a swimming beach and bathhouse, fishing, boating (ramp). Also available is picnicking (tables and grills).

Skylands Section Located here is a 44-room mansion modeled after an English baronial house (open to the public on select days). The gardens (90 acres) surrounding the manor house comprise the only botanical garden in the state park system (guided tours upon request; phone 973/962-7527). This 1,119-acre section also offers fishing; hunting, hiking, mountain biking.

Terhune Memorial Park (Sunnybank). *Terhune Dr. and Lamereux (07470). 2 1/2 miles N on US 202N. Phone 973/694-1800.* Estate of the late Albert Payson Terhune, author of *Lad, a Dog* and many other books about his collies. Scenic garden; picnic area. (Daily) **FREE**

Van Riper-Hopper (Wayne) Museum. *533 Berdan Ave. Phone 973/694-7192 for schedule and fees.* (circa 1786) Dutch Colonial farmhouse with 18th- and 19th-century furnishings; local historical objects; herb garden; bird sanctuary.

Motels/Motor Lodges

★★ **BEST WESTERN EXECUTIVE INN.** *216-234 Rte 46 E, Fairfield (07004). Phone 973/575-7700; fax 973/575-4653. www.bwfei.com.* 185 rooms, 4 story. D $69-$95.50; each additional $13; under 16 free; family, weekend, weekly, holiday rates. Complimentary full breakfast. Check-out noon, check-in 3 pm. TV; cable (premium), VCR available (movies). In-room modem link. Restaurant 6 am-11 pm. Bar 11-1:30 am; entertainment Thurs-Sun. Room service. Health club privileges, exercise equipment, sauna. Game room. Indoor pool, whirlpool, poolside service. Business center. Cr cds: A, C, D, DS, MC, V.

🔣 🔣 🔣 🔣 🔣

★★ **HOLIDAY INN.** *1 US 46W, Totowa (07512). Phone 973/785-9000; toll-free 800/443-5943; fax 973/785-3031. www.holiday-inn.com.* 157 rooms, 5 story. D $99-$149; each additional $6; under 18 free. Complimentary breakfast. Check-out 1 pm, check-in 1 pm. TV; cable (premium), VCR available. In-room modem link. Restaurant 6:30 am-11 pm Mon-Fri. Room service. Exercise equipment. Pool. Indoor parking. Cr cds: A, C, D, DS, MC, V.

🔣 🔣 🔣 🔣

★★ **HOLIDAY INN.** *334 Rte 46 E, Service Rd (07470). Phone 973/256-7000; toll-free 800/292-6483; fax 973/890-5406. www.holiday-inn.com.* 140 rooms, 2 story. D $89-$115; under 18 free. Check-out noon, check-in 2 pm. TV; cable (premium). In-room modem link. Restaurant 6:30 am-2 pm, 5-10 pm. Bar 11-2 am; 5 pm-12:30 am; entertainment. Room service. Health club privileges. Pool, poolside service. Miniature golf. Cr cds: A, C, D, DS, JCB, MC, V.

🔣 🔣 🔣

★ **WELLESLEY INN.** *1850 NJ 23 and Ratzer Rd (07470). Phone 973/696-8050; toll-free 800/444-8888; fax*

973/696-8050. *www.wellesleyonline.com.* 146 rooms, 2 story. D $94-$104; each additional $10; under 16 free. Pet accepted, some restrictions. Complimentary continental breakfast. Check-out noon, check-in 2 pm. TV; cable (premium). In-room modem link. Laundry services. Pool. Cr cds: A, C, D, DS, MC, V.

D 🐾 ⛱ ⇊ SC

Hotel

★ ★ ★ **RADISSON HOTEL AND SUITES.** *690 Rte 46 E, Fairfield (07004). Phone 973/227-9200; toll-free 800/333-3333; fax 973/227-4308. www.radisson.com.* 256 rooms, 5 story. D $199-$219; each additional $10; under 18 free. Check-out noon, check-in 3 pm. TV; cable (premium), VCR available. In-room modem link. Restaurant 6:30 am-10 pm. Bar 11-1:30 am, entertainment Thurs-Sat. Room service. Exercise equipment, sauna. Indoor pool. Business center. Cr cds: A, C, D, DS, ER, JCB, MC, V.

D ⛱ 🏃 ⇊ 🏃

West Orange (C-5)

See also Newark, Newark International Airport Area

Pop 44,943 **Elev** 368 ft **Area code** 973 **Zip** 07052

Information West Orange Chamber of Commerce, PO Box 83; 973/731-0360

Web www.westorange.com

What to See and Do

Eagle Rock Reservation. *Prospect and Eagle Rock aves (07052). NW via Main St and Eagle Rock Ave. Phone 973/268-3500 or 973/731-3000.* A 644-foot elevation in the Orange Mountains; visitors see a heavily populated area that stretches from the Passaic River Valley east to New York City. Hiking trails, picnicking, bridle paths. Restaurant. (Daily)

⭐ **Edison National Historic Site.** *Main St and Lakeside Ave; Phone 973/736-5050.* Included is

Edison Laboratory. *Main St and Lakeside Ave (07052). Phone 973/736-5050.* Built by Edison in 1887, it was his laboratory for 44 years. During that time, he was granted more than half of his 1,093 patents (an all-time record). Here he perfected the phonograph, motion picture camera, and electric storage battery. One-hour lab tour (no video cameras, strollers) includes the chemistry lab and library; demonstrations of early phonographs. Visitor center has exhibits; films (Daily; closed Jan 1, Thanksgiving, Dec 25). **$**

South Mountain Arena. *560 Northfield Ave (07052). Phone 973/731-3828.* Indoor ice rink. Hockey games, special events.

Turtle Back Zoo. *560 Northfield Ave, 3 miles W on I-280, exit 10, in South Mountain Reservation. Phone 973/731-5800.* This 20-acre park features animals in natural surroundings; sea lion pool; miniature train ride (1 mile). Picnicking, concessions. Gift shop (hours vary). (Daily; closed Thanksgiving, Dec 25; limited schedule Dec-Mar) **$$$**

Restaurants

★ ★ ★ **HIGHLAWN PAVILION.** *Eagle Rock Reservation (07052). Phone 973/731-3463; fax 973/731-0034. www.highlawn.com/home.html.* American menu. Oyster bar. Hours: noon-3 pm, 5:30-10 pm; Fri to 11:30 pm; Sat 5-11:30 pm; Sun 5-9 pm. Closed Dec 24. Dinner $19-$32. Bar to midnight. Located in county park on top of mountain. Jacket required. Valet parking. Outdoor seating. Cr cds: A, C, D, DS, MC, V.

D

★ ★ ★ **THE MANOR.** *111 Prospect Ave (07052). Phone 973/731-2360; fax 973/731-2348. www.themanor restaurant.com.* One of the most well-known (and most formal) restaurants in New Jersey continues to excel at all items on chef Ossama Mickheil's menu, especially the seafood. Try the cilantro-sesame-seed-coated halibut filet, the pan-seared veal tournados or the lobster bisque. American, Continental menu. Hours: noon-2:30 pm, 6-10 pm; Sat 6 pm-midnight; Sun to 8:30 pm. Closed Mon. Dinner $23-$30. Bar to 2 am. Jacket required. Cr cds: A, D, DS, MC, V.

D

Wildwood and Wildwood Crest (J-3)

See also Cape May

Pop 5,463 **Elev** 8 ft **Area code** 609 **Zip** 08260

Information Greater Wildwood Chamber of Commerce, 3306 Pacific Ave, PO Box 823; 609/729-4000

Web www.gwcoc.com

Wildwood's busy boardwalk extends for approximately 2 miles along the 5 miles of protected sandy beach it shares with North Wildwood and Wildwood Crest, two neighboring resorts. The area offers swimming, waterskiing, ocean and bay fishing, boating, sailing; bicycling, golf, tennis, and shuffleboard.

What to See and Do

Boat trips. *Capt Sinn's Dock, 6006 Park Blvd in Wildwood Crest. Phone 609/522-3934.* Sightseeing and whale-watching cruises aboard *Big Flamingo.* (July-Nov, daily) Also aboard the *Big Blue Sightseer.* (June-Sept, daily) *4500 Park Blvd in Wildwood.*

Motels/Motor Lodges

★ ★ **ADVENTURE MOTOR INN.** *5401 Ocean Ave (08260). Phone 609/729-1200; fax 609/523-1485. www.adventurerinn.com.* 104 rooms, 6 story. July-early Sept: S, D $140-$330; each additional $12; under 3 free; higher rates weekends (3-day minimum); lower rates early-Sept-Oct and mid-Apr-June. Closed rest of year. Crib $8. TV; cable. Heated pool; wading pool, lifeguard. Restaurant 7 am-8 pm. Room service. Check-out 11 am. Coin laundry. Meeting rooms. Business services available. Sundries. Gift shop. Game room. Refrigerators; microwaves available. On beach. Cr cds: A, D, DS, MC, V.

★ **AQUARIUS MOTOR INN.** *4712 Ocean Ave (08260). Phone 609/729-0054; toll-free 800/982-1831. www.aquariusmotorinn.com.* 28 rooms, 4 story. S, D $110-$159; under 18 free; weekly, weekend rates; lower rates Apr-June and Sept-Oct. Closed rest of year. Crib free. TV; cable (premium). Heated pool; wading pool. Complimentary coffee in lobby. Restaurant opposite 7 am-11 pm. Check-out 10 am. Coin laundry. Business services available. Refrigerators, microwaves. Balconies. Picnic tables. Opposite beach. Cr cds: A, DS, MC, V.

★ **ARMADA BY THE SEA.** *6503 Ocean Ave (08260). Phone 609/729-3000; toll-free 800/399-3001; fax 609/729-7472. www.armadamotel.com.* 56 rooms, 40 kitchen units, 5 story. Mid-July-Aug: up to 4 persons $166-$189; each additional $10; kitchen units up to 4 persons $163-$290; some lower rates rest of year. Oct-mid-Apr. Check-out 11 am. TV; VCR available (movies). Game room. Children's pool. Cr cds: A, DS, MC, V.

★ **ASTRONAUT MOTEL.** *511 E Stockton Rd (08260). Phone 609/522-6981; fax 609/523-1927. www.beachcomber.com.* 33 kitchen units, 3 story. No elevator. July-early Sept: up to 6 persons $134-$180; lower rates Apr-June, early Sept-mid-Oct. Closed rest of year. Check-out 11 am. TV. Laundry services. Pool, children's pool. Shuffleboard. Cr cds: DS, MC, V.

★ **ATTACHE.** *5707 Ocean Ave (08260). Phone 609/522-0241; fax 609/523-8379. www.attache-motel.com.* 42 rooms, 26 kitchen units, 3 story. Mid-July-late Aug: up to 4 persons $130-$175; each additional $10; kitchen units for 4 persons $130-$215; family rates; lower rates mid-Apr-mid-July, late Aug-mid-Oct. Closed rest of year. Check-out 11 am. TV; VCR available. Guest laundry. Children's pool. Cr cds: A, MC, V.

★ **CAPE COD INN MOTEL.** *6109 Atlantic Ave (08260). Phone 609/522-1177; fax 609/729-2353. www.capecodinnmotel.com.* 50 units, 27 kitchen units, 3 story. Mid-July-mid-Aug: S, D $110; each additional $10; kitchens. Closed rest of year. Check-out 10 am. TV; cable (premium). Laundry services. Game room. Pool, children's pool. Miniature golf. Cr cds: A, DS, MC, V.

★ **CARIBBEAN MOTEL.** *5600 Ocean Ave (08260). Phone 609/522-8292; toll-free 800/457-7040; fax 609/729-3212.* 30 rooms, 9 kitchen units, 2 story. July-Labor Day: up to 4 persons $119; kitchen units for 4 persons $128; lower rates May-June, after Labor Day-Sept. Closed rest of year. Check-out 11 am. TV. Game room. Children's pool. Lawn games. Cr cds: MC, V.

★ **FLEUR DE LIS.** *6105 Ocean Ave (08260). Phone 609/522-0123; fax 609/523-0893. www.fleurdelismotel.com.* 44 rooms, 32 kitchen units, 3 story. Mid-July-late Aug: S $51-$103; D $55-$123; each additional $10; kitchens $149-$184; higher rates weekends (3-day minimum); lower rates mid-Apr-mid-July and Sept-mid-Oct. Closed rest of year. Check-out 11 am. TV. Game room. Pool, children's pool. On beach. Cr cds: MC, V.

★ **IMPERIAL 500 MOTEL.** *6601 Atlantic Ave (08260). Phone 609/522-6063; toll-free 800/522-1255; fax 609/522-7643. www.imperial500.com.* 45 rooms, 26 kitchen units, 3 story. July-Labor Day: S, D for 4, $100-$135; each additional $10; kitchen units $135; lower rates May-June, after Labor Day-Sept. Closed rest of year. Check-out 11 am. TV. Children's pool. Lawn games. Shuffleboard. Cr cds: DS, MC, V.

★ **IVANHOE MOTEL.** *430 E 21st Ave (08260). Phone 609/522-5874; fax 609/523-2323. www.ivanhoemotel.com.* 40 rooms, 2 story. July-Aug: S $98; D $165; each additional $10-$15; family, weekly rates; lower rates rest of year. Crib $8. Check-out 10 am. TV; cable (premium). Some balconies. Microwaves, refrigerators. Coffee in rooms. Coin laundry. Opposite beach. Heated pools, wading pool. Meeting rooms. Business services. Cr cds: A, C, D, DS, MC, V.

★ **JOLLY ROGER MOTEL.** *6805 Atlantic Ave (08260). Phone 609/522-6915; toll-free 800/337-5232; fax 609/522-3767. www.jollyrogermotel.com.* 74 rooms, 3 story. Mid-July-mid-Aug: S, D $102-$121; each additional $7; kitchens $112-$158; under 5 free; weekends, holidays (3-day minimum); lower rates mid-May, late Aug-late Sept. Closed rest of year. Check-out 11 am. TV; cable. Laundry services. Supervised children's activities (July-Aug), ages 4-16. Game room. Pool, children's pool. Tennis. Cr cds: MC, V.

★ **LEVOYAGEUR MOTEL.** *232 E Andrew Ave (08260). Phone 609/522-6407; toll-free 800/348-0846; fax 609/523-1834. www.levoyageurmotel.com.* 33 rooms, 14 kitchen units, 3 story. July-Aug: S $40-$89; D $89-$118; each additional $10; suites $112; kitchens $123; under 5 free; weekly, holiday rates; lower rates rest of year. Closed rest of year. Check-out 10:30 am. TV. Game room. Children's pool. Cr cds: A, DS, MC, V.

★ **MADRID OCEAN RESORT.** *427 E Miami Ave (08260). Phone 609/729-1600; fax 609/729-8483. www.beachcomber.com.* 54 rooms, 24 kitchen units, 5 story. July-Labor Day: S, D $140-$185; each additional $10; suites $165; kitchen units up to 4 persons $175; higher rates weekends; lower rates mid-May-June, after Labor Day-Sept. Closed rest of year. Crib available. Check-out 11 am. TV. Refrigerators. Microwaves available. Coin laundry. Restaurant 7:30 am-9 pm. Recreation room. Heated pool, wading pool. Business services. Sundries. Sun deck. All oceanfront rooms. Cr cds: A, MC, V.

★ **NEW COMPASS MOTEL.** *6501 Atlantic Ave (08260). Phone 609/522-6948; fax 609/729-9363. www.compassmotel.com.* 50 rooms, 25 kitchen units, 3 story. July-Aug: S, D $98-$122; each additional $10; family rates; weekly, weekend rates; higher rates holidays (3-day minimum); lower rates May-June, Sept-Oct. Closed rest of year. Crib $10. Complimentary coffee in rooms. Check-out 11 am. TV; cable. Microwaves, refrigerators. Heated pool, wading pool. Meeting rooms. Business services. Cr cds: A, DS, MC, V.

★ **OCEAN HOLIDAY MOTOR INN.** *6501 Ocean Ave (08260). Phone 609/729-2900; toll-free 800/321-6232; fax 609/523-1024. www.oceanholiday.com.* 56 rooms, 51 kitchen units, 5 story. July-Aug: S, D $70-$170; each additional $10; kitchen units (up to 4 persons) $100-$255; holiday weekends (3-day minimum); lower rates Apr-June, Sept-Oct. Closed rest of year. Check-out 11 am. TV; cable (premium), VCR available. Game room. Pool, children's pool. Cr cds: A, MC, V.

★ **OCEANVIEW.** *7201 Ocean Ave (08260). Phone 609/522-6656; toll-free 800/647-6656; fax 609/522-6793. www.oceanviewmotel.net.* 110 rooms, 36 suites, 61 kitchen units, 4 story. July-Aug: S $105-$145; D $150; each additional $10; suites $130-$150; kitchen units $130-$160; family rates; package plans; lower rates May-June, Sept-Oct. Closed rest of year. Crib $9. Check-out 11 am. TV; cable (premium). Refrigerators. Coin laundry. Restaurant opposite 7 am-9 pm. Supervised children's activities (late June-early Sept). Playground. Game room. Heated pool, wading pool, lifeguard. Miniature golf. Picnic tables, grills. Business services. On beach. Cr cds: DS, MC, V.

★ **PANORAMIC MOTEL AND APTS.** *2101 Surf Ave (08260). Phone 609/522-1181; fax 609/523-2323. www.panoramicmotel.com.* 25 rooms, 2 story. July-Sept: S $65-$98; D $98-$150; each additional $10-$15; family, weekly rates; lower rates rest of year. Crib $8. Complimentary coffee in rooms. Check-out 10 am. TV; cable (premium). Some balconies. Microwaves, refrigerators. Coin laundry. Heated pool, wading pool. Meeting rooms. Business services. On beach. Cr cds: A, C, D, DS, MC, V.

Hotels

★ ★ ★ **PAN AMERICAN HOTEL.** *5901 Ocean Ave (08260). Phone 609/522-6936; fax 609/522-6937. www.panamericanhotel.com.* 78 rooms, 4 story, 39 kitchens Early July-early Sept $165-$175; each additional $12; suites $195-$200; kitchen units $175-$185; lower rates mid-May-early June, early Sept-mid-Oct. Closed rest of year. Crib free. TV; VCR available. Heated pool; wading pool, lifeguard. Sauna. Free supervised children's activities (mid-June-Labor Day); ages 4-10. Restaurant 7:30 am-8 pm. Room service. Check-out 11 am. Meeting room. Coin laundry. Business services available. Sundries. Recreation room. Refrigerators; some microwaves. Sun deck. Balconies. Cr cds: MC, V.

★ ★ ★ **PORT ROYAL HOTEL.** *6801 Ocean Ave (08260). Phone 609/729-2000; fax 609/729-2051. www.portroyalhotel.com.* Take a swim in the hour glass-shaped pool, play with the kids in their own kid pool, or relax in the sun pool side on the patio. Guests will find golf, tennis, boating, fine restaurants, theater, and many more activities nearby. 100 rooms, 50 kitchen units, 6 story. Late June-Labor Day: S $81-$170; D $160-$176; each additional $12; kitchen units for 4 persons $190-$205; lower rates May-late June, after Labor Day-mid-Oct. Closed rest of year. Crib available. Check-out 11 am. TV; VCR available. Balconies. Some microwaves. Coin laundry. Restaurant 7:30 am-8 pm in season. Free supervised children's activities (mid-June-Labor Day); ages 3-10. Sauna. Recreation room, game room in season. Heated pool, wading pool. Meeting room (off-season). Business services. Sundries. Cr cds: MC, V.

🐾 🏊

Resorts

★ ★ **BRISTOL PLAZA RESORT.** *6407 Ocean Ave (08260). Phone 609/729-1234; toll-free 800/433-9731; fax 609/729-9363. www.bristolplazamotel.com.* 55 rooms, 41 kitchen units, 5 story. Mid-July-late Aug: S, D (up to 4) $60-$122; family rates; weekly, weekend, holiday rates; lower rates May-mid-July and late Aug-Oct. Closed rest of year. Crib $10. Complimentary coffee in rooms. Check-out 11 am. TV; cable. Balconies. Refrigerators, many microwaves. Coin laundry. Sauna. Heated pool, wading pool. Picnic tables. Business services. Opposite ocean. Cr cds: DS, MC, V.

🐾 🏊

★ ★ **CRUSADER OCEAN FRONT RESORT.** *6101 Ocean Ave (08260). Phone 609/522-6991; toll-free 800/462-3260; fax 609/522-2280. www.crusaderresort.com.* 61 units, 54 suites, 37 kitchen units, 3 story. July-Aug: S, D $160-$168; each additional $12; kitchen units $166-$245; lower rates Apr-June and Sept-Oct. Closed Nov-Mar. Crib available. Check-out 11 am. TV; cable (premium), VCR available. Some balconies. Microwaves, refrigerators. Coin laundry. Restaurant 7 am-8 pm. Sauna. Game room. Ocean beach; boardwalk. Heated pool, wading pool, lifeguard. Picnic tables. Meeting rooms. Business services. Sundries. Gift shop. Cr cds: A, MC, V.

🅳 🏊 ✈

★ ★ ★ **EL CORONADO MOTOR INN.** *8501 Atlantic Ave (08260). Phone 609/729-1000; toll-free 800/227-5302; fax 609/729-6557. www.elcoronado.com.* 113 rooms, 63 kitchen units, 6 story. July-Aug: S, D $130-$174; each additional $10; kitchen suites $180-$272; under 12 free; weekly, weekend (3-night minimum), holiday rates; lower rates May-June and Sept-Oct. Closed rest of year. Crib available. Check-out 11 am. TV; cable (premium). In-room modem link. Balconies. Microwaves, refrigerators. Coin laundry. Restaurant 7 am-4 pm. Supervised children's activities (July-Aug). Sauna. Game room. Pool, wading pool, whirlpool, poolside service, lifeguard. Meeting rooms. Business services. Gift shop. Cr cds: DS, MC, V.

🐾 🏌 🏊 🖼

★ ★ **NASSAU INN.** *6201 Ocean Ave (08260). Phone 609/729-9077; fax 609/729-2208. www.nassauinnmotel.com.* 56 rooms, 5 story. July-early Sept: S, D $115-$125; each additional $10; kitchens $170-$180; family rates; package plans; lower rates early Sept-mid-Oct and May-June. Closed rest of year. Crib $9. Check-out 11 am. TV; cable. Refrigerators, many microwaves. Coin laundry. Restaurant adjacent 7 am-9 pm. Game room. Heated pool, wading pool. Business services. On beach. Cr cds: DS, MC, V.

🅳 🐾 🏊 🏌

★ **ROYAL HAWAIIAN BEACHFRONT RESORT.** *500 E Orchid Rd (08260). Phone 609/522-3414; fax 609/522-1316. www.royalhawaiianresort.com.* 88 rooms, 56 kitchen units, 5 story. Mid-July-Aug: S, D $103; suites, kitchen units for 4 $129-$229; each additional $10; lower rates mid-May-mid-July, Sept-Oct. Closed rest of year. Crib available. Check-out 11 am. TV; cable (premium). Balconies. Microwaves, refrigerators. Valet services, coin laundry. Playground. Exercise equipment, sauna. Recreation room. Pool, wading pool, lifeguard. Grills. Business services. Sun deck. On ocean. Cr cds: A, DS, MC, V.

🅳 🐾 🏊 🏃

B&B/Small Inn

★ ★ ★ **CANDLELIGHT INN.** *2310 Central Ave (08260). Phone 609/522-6200; toll-free 800/992-2632; fax 609/522-6125. www.candlelight-inn.com.* 10 rooms, 4 story. No room phones, Adults only. Complimentary full breakfast. Check-out 11 am, check-in 1 pm. Some fireplaces. Health club privileges. Lawn games. Queen Anne/Victorian-style house (circa 1905); restored. Large porch with swing and hammocks. Totally nonsmoking. Cr cds: A, DS, MC, V. **$$**

🖼

Restaurant

★ ★ **GARFIELD'S GIARDINO RISTORANTE.**
3800 Pacific Ave (08260). Phone 609/729-0120; fax 609/729-2643. www.garfieldsnj.com. Italian, seafood menu. Dinner. Bar. Entertainment July, Aug. Children's menu. Two seating areas in garden setting. Cr cds: A, D, DS, MC, V. **$$**
D

Woodbridge

Settled 1664 **Pop** 97,203 **Elev** 21 ft **Area code** 732 **Zip** 07095

Information Chamber of Commerce Visitor Center, 52 Main St; 732/636-4040

Here, where the first cloverleaf interchange in the US was constructed in 1929, cross two of the country's busiest roads—the Garden State Parkway and the New Jersey Turnpike. Also in Woodbridge are seaway and river port areas visited by thousands of vessels annually.

What to See and Do

Barron Arts Center. *582 Rahway Ave. Phone 732/634-0413.* Built in 1877 in Romanesque Revival style. Originally the first free public library in Middlesex County, now an arts and cultural center with art exhibits; workshops; lectures; poetry sessions; concerts; special events. Gallery (Sun-Fri; closed holidays). **FREE**

Pennsylvania

From its easternmost tip near Bordentown, New Jersey, to its straight western boundary with Ohio and West Virginia, Pennsylvania's 300-mile giant stride across the country covers a mountain-and-farm, river-and-stream, mine-and-mill topography. Its cities, people, and resources are just as diverse. Philadelphia is a great city in the eastern part of the state, a treasure house of tradition and historical shrines; Pittsburgh is a great city in the western part, a mighty arsenal of industry. In this state are the Pennsylvania Dutch, their barns painted with vivid hex signs; here also are steel mills. Pennsylvania miners dig nearly all the anthracite coal in the United States and still work some of the oldest iron mines in the country. Oil employees work more than 19,000 producing wells, and 55,000 farm families make up 20 percent of the Pennsylvania work force.

Pennsylvania, the keystone of the original 13 states, remains one of the keystones in modern America. A leader in steel and coal production, the state also is a leader in cigar leaf tobacco, apples, grapes, ice cream, chocolate products, mushrooms (nearly half of the United States total), and soft drinks, plus factory and farm machinery, electronics equipment, scientific instruments, watches, textile machines, railroad cars, ships, assorted metal products, and electrical machinery. This fifth most populous state is also a major factor in national politics.

Pennsylvania has been a keystone of culture. The first serious music in the colonies was heard in Bethlehem; today, it resounds throughout the state—Pittsburgh has an acclaimed symphony, as does Philadelphia. There are 140 institutions of higher learning (including the oldest medical school in the United States at the University of Pennsylvania), celebrated art galleries, and hundreds of museums.

Despite its size, all of Pennsylvania is within the motorist's grasp. Its 44,000 miles of state highways, including the 470-mile Pennsylvania Turnpike (pioneer of super-highways), plus 69,363 miles of other roads make up one of the largest road networks in the nation.

Swedes made the first settlement on this fertile land at Tinicum Island in the Delaware River in 1643. The territory became Dutch in 1655 and British in 1664. After Charles II granted William Penn a charter that made him proprietor of "Pennsilvania," this Quaker statesman landed here in 1682 and invested the land with his money, leadership, and fellow Quakers. The Swedes, Finns, and Dutch already in the new land were granted citizenship; soon came Welsh, Germans, Scots, Irish, and French Huguenots. Of these, the Germans left the strongest imprint on the state's personality. Commercial, agricultural, and industrial growth came quickly, and all these resources were contributed to the Revolution. In Pennsylvania, Washington camped at Valley Forge, the Declaration of Independence was signed, and the Constitution drafted.

Population: 11,881,643
Area: 44,892 square miles
Elevation: 0-3,213 feet
Peak: Mount Davis (Somerset County)
Entered Union: Second of original 13 states (December 12, 1787)
Capital: Harrisburg
Motto: Virtue, liberty, and independence
Nickname: Keystone State
Flower: Mountain Laurel
Bird: Ruffed Grouse
Tree: Eastern Hemlock
Fair: (Pennsylvania State Farm Show), January, in Harrisburg
Time Zone: Eastern
Website: www.state.pa.us
Fun Facts:
1. Betsy Ross made the first american flag in Philadelphia.
2. Benjamin Franklin founded the Philadephia Zoo. This was the first zoo in the United States.

Calendar Highlights

JANUARY
Pennsylvania State Farm Show *(Harrisburg)*. *Phone 717/787-5373*. State fair.

FEBRUARY
Chocolate Lovers' Extravaganza *(Hershey)*. *Hotel Hershey. For reservations, phone 800/533-3131*. Everything chocolate—tasting and sampling, chef-taught classes, decorating instruction, and more.

MAY
Devon Horse Show *(Philadelphia)*. *Horse Show Grounds in Devon. Phone 610/964-0550*. One of America's leading equestrian events. More than 1,200 horses compete; country fair; antique carriage drive.

JUNE
Three Rivers Arts Festival *(Pittsburgh)*. *Point State Park. Phone 412/281-8723*. Juried, original works of local and national artists; paintings, photography, sculpture, crafts, and videos; artists' market in outdoor plazas. Ongoing performances include music, dance, and performance art. Special art projects; film festival; food; children's activities.

CoreStates US Pro Cycling Championship *(Philadelphia)*. Longest single-day cycling event in the country—156 miles.

JULY
Civil War Heritage Days *(Gettysburg)*. *Phone 717/334-6274*. Lectures by historians; Civil War collectors' show; entertainment; Civil War book show; firefighters' festival; fireworks.

Folk Festival *(Kutztown)*. *Festival grounds. Phone 215/679-9610*. Celebration of Pennsylvania Dutch folk culture; quilts, music, dancing, and food of Plain and Fancy Dutch. Craftspeople make baskets, brooms, rugs, toleware, and other handcrafts.

AUGUST
Das Awkscht Festival *(Allentown)*. *Macungle Memorial Park. Phone 610/967-2317*. 2,500 antique, classic and special-interest autos; arts and crafts; antique toy show, entertainment, food, fireworks.

Musikfest *(Bethlehem)*. *Nine sites in downtown historic area. Phone 610/861-0678*. Nine-day festival celebrating Bethlehem's rich musical and ethnic heritage. More than 600 performances of all types of music from folk to rock.

SEPTEMBER
Ligonier Highland Games and Gathering of the Clans of Scotland *(Ligonier)*. *Idlewild Park. Phone 724/238-3666*. Sports; massed pipe bands, Highland dancing competitions, Scottish fiddling; sheep dog, wool spinning, and weaving demonstrations; geneology booth, Scottish fair.

Wine Country Harvest Festival *(North East)*. *Gravel Pit Park and Gibson Park. Phone 814/725-4262*. Arts and crafts, bands, buses to wineries, food.

DECEMBER
Army-Navy Football Game *(Philadelphia)*. *John F. Kennedy Memorial Stadium or Veterans Stadium*.

With Philadelphia the capital of the new nation, tides of pioneers pushed west and north to develop far corners of the state. The Civil War brought fresh industrial development, and for the past century Pennsylvania has continued to develop at an ever-quickening industrial pace. Today, the Keystone State is an empire of industry and a storehouse of historic traditions.

When to Go/Climate

Pennsylvania's lands and hill country enjoy typical East Coast seasonal temperatures—hot, humid summers; relatively mild winters; crisp falls; and wet springs. The mountains, however, experience short summers and cold, snowy winters.

AVERAGE HIGH/LOW TEMPERATURES (°F)

Philadelphia

Jan 38/23	**May** 73/53	**Sept** 78/59
Feb 41/25	**June** 82/62	**Oct** 66/47
Mar 52/33	**July** 86/67	**Nov** 55/38
Apr 63/42	**Aug** 85/66	**Dec** 43/28

Pittsburgh

Jan 34/19	**May** 71/48	**Sept** 74/54
Feb 37/20	**June** 79/57	**Oct** 63/42
Mar 49/30	**July** 83/62	**Nov** 50/34
Apr 60/39	**Aug** 81/60	**Dec** 39/24

Parks and Recreation

Water-related activities, hiking, riding, various other sports, picnicking, and environmental interpretive centers, as well as camping, are available in many state parks. More than 116 state parks and 4 environmental centers are scattered throughout the commonwealth. 57 campgrounds offer camping. Seven are open all year; the rest are open from 2nd Fri Apr-3rd Sun Oct or Dec. Occupancy is limited to 2 consecutive weeks; $9-$14 resident, $11-$16 nonresident/night (primitive areas); $11-$14 resident, $13-$16 nonresident/night (modern areas). Cabins (daily and weekly rentals spring, fall, and winter; 1 week only, Fri after Memorial Day-Fri before Labor Day). Boat launching (annually) $10 resident, $15 nonresident. No pets allowed in overnight areas. Write to Bureau of State Parks, PO Box 8551, Harrisburg 17105-8551, for detailed information. Cabin reservations are made by calling the park directly. For other state park information, phone 888/PA-PARKS.

FISHING AND HUNTING

Pennsylvania is one of the country's leading states in the amount of waters open to public and private fishing. There are nearly 5,000 miles of trout streams stocked annually, and many thousands of miles of warm-water streams, plus thousands of acres of lakes with walleye, panfish, muskellunge, and bass. A nonresident fishing license is $35; a 3-day tourist license is $15; a 7-day tourist license is $30. A $5.50 trout/salmon stamp also is required (for trout fishing only). Write to Pennsylvania Fish and Boat Commission, PO Box 67000, Harrisburg 17106-7000, or phone 717/705-7800, for the annual *Summary of Fishing Regulations and Laws,* as well as maps and other useful information.

A license is required to hunt, take, trap, or kill any wild bird or animal in the state. Nonresident hunting license, $101; children 12-16, $41. The license tag must be displayed on the back of outer garment, between the shoulders, at all times. For big-game and turkey hunting and small-game hunting in the fall, 250 square inches of fluorescent orange must be worn on the head, chest, and back combined. For the *Official Digest, Pennsylvania Hunting and Trapping Regulations,* contact the Pennsylvania Game Commission, 2001 Elmerton Ave, Harrisburg 17110-9797, phone 717/787-4250.

Driving Information

Safety belts are mandatory for all persons in the front seat of a vehicle. Children under 4 years must be in an approved passenger restraint anywhere in the vehicle: age 4 and older may use a regulation safety belt; ages 1-3 may use a regulation safety belt in back seat only. Children under 4 years must use an approved safety seat in front seat; under age 1 must use an approved safety seat anywhere in the vehicle. Phone 717/787-6853.

INTERSTATE HIGHWAY SYSTEM

The following alphabetical listing of Pennsylvania towns in this book shows that these cities are within 10 miles of the indicated Interstate highways. Check a highway map for the nearest exit.

Highway Number	Cities/Towns within 10 Miles
Interstate 70	Bedford, Breezewood, Donegal, Greensburg, New Stanton, Somerset, Washington.
Interstate 78	Allentown, Bethlehem, Easton, Hamburg, Kutztown, Lebanon, Shartlesville.
Interstate 79	Conneaut Lake, Edinboro, Erie, Harmony, Meadville, Mercer, Pittsburgh, Washington.
Interstate 80	Belefonte, Bloomsburg, Brookville, Clarion, Clearfield, Danville, Du Bois, Hazleton, Lewisburg, Lock Haven, Mercer, Mount Pocono, Sharon, Shawnee on Delaware, Stroudsburg, Tannersville, White Haven.
Interstate 81	Ashland, Carlisle, Chambersburg, Harrisburg, Hazleton, Scranton, Wilkes-Barre.
Interstate 83	Harrisburg, York.
Interstate 84	Milford, Scranton.
Interstate 90	Erie, North East.
Interstate 95	Bristol, Philadelphia.

Additional Visitor Information

A free visitors guide is available by calling 800/VISIT-PA, at the Pennsylvania Office of Travel, Tourism, and Film Promotion, Department of Community & Economic Development, PO Box 61, Warrendale 15086.

There are 14 state-run traveler information centers in Pennsylvania; visitors who stop by will find information and brochures most helpful in planning stops at points of interest. Their locations are as follows: I-79 Edinboro (southbound), 1 mile S of the Edinboro exit; I-81 Greencastle (northbound), 1 mile N of the Pennsylvania/Maryland border; I-95 Linwood (northbound), 1/2 mile N of the Pennsylvania/Delaware border; I-70 Warfordsburg (westbound), 1 mile from the Pennsylvania/Maryland border; I-80 West Middlesex (eastbound), 1/2 mile E of the Pennsylvania/Ohio border; Neshaminy Welcome Center, Mile Marker 351 (westbound) on the Pennsylvania Turnpike, 7 miles W of the Pennsylvania/New Jersey border, located inside the plaza building; I-78 Easton (westbound), 1 mile W of the Pennsylvania/New Jersey border; Sideling Hill Welcome Center, Mile Marker 172 (eastbound and westbound) on the Pennsylvania Turnpike, 10 miles E of the Breezewood exit, located inside the plaza building; I-81 Lenox (southbound), 4 miles S of the Lenox exit 64; I-83 Shrewsbury (northbound), 1/2 mile N of the Pennsylvania/Maryland border; Zelienople Welcome Center, Mile Marker 21 (eastbound), 21 miles E of the Pennsylvania/Ohio border, located inside the plaza building; I-79 northbound, N of the Pennsylvania/West Virginia line; I-70 Washington County, E of the Pennsylvania/West Virginia line.

Ride with Me—Pennsylvania, Interstate 81 is a 90-minute audio cassette tape that provides information on points of interest along I-81, from New York to Maryland. Topics such as the history of the Pennsylvania Dutch, notable battlegrounds and areas related to the Civil War, and anthracite coal miners are discussed. Contact RWM Associates, PO Box 1324, Bethesda, MD 20817; 301/299-7817.

LAUREL HIGHLANDS

As the name suggests, the Laurel Highlands—spread across the Allegheny Mountains in southwestern Pennsylvania—is a region of lofty wooded ridges, slender farm valleys, splashing streams, and quiet lakes, many boasting swimming beaches. Here and there you come upon covered bridges. George Washington once trod these hills, acquiring the military skills he would need as the Revolutionary War commander. Early on, the beauty of the setting drew many travelers—and continues to do so. Today, the Highlands serve as a year-round playground, where you can raft, kayak, fish, swim, and bicycle. This two-day, 150-mile drive meanders though this appealing setting while visiting several important historic sites. This is a one-way trip between Bedford in the east and Uniontown in the west. You can drive in either direction; we'll begin at Bedford, just off the Pennsylvania Turnpike. Stop in Bedford at the Old Bedford Village, which preserves more than 40 original farm buildings and other structures from bygone days in a village-like cluster. One that catches the eye is the eight-sided frame schoolhouse built nearby in 1851. Called an Eight Square, the octagon shape had a specific purpose: it gave every student an equal share of window light and proximity to the pot-bellied stove in the center. In summer, craftsmen demonstrate blacksmithing, barrel-making, broom-making, and other pioneer skills. From Bedford, take I-99 North to State Route 56 northwest to Johnstown. Two sites here capture the horror of the Johnstown Flood of 1889, which struck the small steel-manufacturing city with a sudden ferocity that left 2,200 people dead. Just east of the city, the National Park Service operates the Johnstown Flood National Memorial. It overlooks the dry basin of what was once a man-made lake that emptied when heavy rains collapsed an earthen dam. In Johnstown itself, the Johnstown Flood Museum illustrates the damage wrought by the flood and Johnstown's determination to rebuild. Ahead on the drive, two reconstructed 18th-century forts, Fort Ligonier in Ligonier and Fort Necessity National Battlefield near Farmington, recount British colonial efforts to wrest the Ohio River Valley west of the Alleghenies from French control. Both forts played a role in the ultimate defeat of the French at Fort Duquesne, which became the site of Pittsburgh. Ligonier is the most imposing of the two forts, but Fort Necessity may be more memorable. To reach it, take Route 271 West from Johnstown to Ligonier, and plan to spend the night there. To reach Fort Necessity, head 2 miles southeast on US 30 to Route 381 to Farmington, and turn right on US 40. At Fort Necessity, a modest ring of stakes thrusting from the earth marks the site of George Washington's only military surrender, a lesson that surely must have aided him two decades later as commander of the Continental Army. The route from Ligonier to Farmington edges past Fallingwater, architect Frank Lloyd Wright's masterpiece on Bear Run. The structure, stair-stepping down a wooded mountainside, combines architecture and nature in a glorious piece of artwork. A stop here is a must, but allow at least three hours to take an escorted tour and to walk the grounds. Exhibits at the Entrance Pavilion explain the construction of the house, built in 1936 as a mountain retreat for a wealthy Pittsburgh department store owner. Inside the house, you'll learn about Wright's daring use of new construction materials and his fascination with the possibilities of space, as well as his idiosyncrasies. Short in stature, Wright designed the house with surprisingly low ceilings. A couple of miles down the road, the village of Ohiopyle is a center for whitewater rafting. Sign up for thrills, or watch helmet-clad rafters arriving or departing on upper and lower stretches of the Youghiogheny River (also called the "Yock"). From Fort Necessity, continue west on US 40 to Uniontown to conclude this tour. **(Approximately 150 miles)**

BUCKS COUNTY

Over the years, literary references to Bucks County, just north of Philadelphia, have been plentiful, and with good reason. This woodland retreat along the Delaware River has been favored by notable Manhattanite literati for decades, including Broadway's Moss Hart and George S. Kaufman, and the acerbic writer Dorothy Parker. Though estate-sized homes are popping up everywhere in the privileged realm, the rumpled landscape still retains the look of a Currier and Ives print. Stately old fieldstone houses stand beneath towering trees, and stalks of ripening corn march across the fields. In fall, pumpkins peek from among patches of vines. Nearby, the wide and peaceful Delaware flows quietly past. A one-day, 75-mile loop drive out of New Hope provides a rewarding glimpse of Bucks County's scenic and cultural appeal. Begin in New Hope, a small town noted as a romantic weekend getaway destination. A colonial-era ferry crossing on the main road between Philadelphia and New York, the town is dotted with old stone structures sandwiched between the river and the Delaware Canal. The shops they house are well worth a look; several feature exquisite hand-made crafts of local and national artisans. Many visitors come simply to stroll the old streets and enjoy the cafes, pubs, and ice cream parlors. You can hike or bicycle on the canal tow path. If you're in town on Saturday or Tuesday morning, drop by Rice's Market on Greenhill Road, a ten-minute drive northwest of New Hope. Set in a 30-acre field, the market is the next best thing to an old-fashioned county fair. More than 200 vendors haul in booths selling merchandise of all kinds—produce, plants and flowers, crafts, furniture pieces, clothing, you name it—often at bargain prices. To see more of the county, return to New Hope and take River Road (State Route 32) north. The road winds alongside the Delaware River for about 25 miles to Kintnersville, providing gorgeous river views the entire way. Quaint river towns, mostly a cluster of old homes, dot the route. In places, the road narrows as it skirts a stone wall. The stretch of road between New Hope and Lumberville passes a river setting that, in the early years of the century, drew a number of landscape artists who formed a colony of Pennsylvania Impressionists in the hamlet of Phillips Mill. You can't miss it; River Road makes a sharp turn here. Today, their work can be seen in a permanent exhibit called "Visual Heritage of Bucks County" at the James A. Michener Art Museum in Doylestown, ahead on this drive. In Kintnersville, take Route 611, the Lackawanna Trail, south to Doylestown. Visit the Michener Museum, which also features a diverting exhibit detailing the Broadway and Hollywood legends who have lived in the county. Save plenty of time for the three fantastical castle-like structures that archeologist and historian Henry Chapman Mercer bequeathed his hometown. Turrets, towers, and parapets adorn the buildings, all built between 1908 and 1916 in a free-form style of reinforced concrete. The Moravian Pottery and Tile Works, which resembles a Spanish-colonial mission, houses Mercer's innovative tile factory. Good-quality artistic tiles are still made here by hand. On the same 70-acre, park-like grounds stands Fonthill, Mercer's 44-room mansion, a fairy-tale creation of strange nooks and crannies adorned with decorative titles from his factory and around the world. A mile away, the seven-story Mercer Museum houses an important collection of furnishings, folk art, and implements of early America. Conclude this drive by returning to New Hope via Routes 202 and 179. **(Approximately 75 miles)**

Allentown (F-12)

See also Bethlehem, Easton, Kutztown, Quakertown (Bucks County)

Founded 1762 **Pop** 106,632 **Elev** 364 ft **Area code** 484 and 610

Information Lehigh Valley Convention & Visitors Bureau, PO Box 20785, Lehigh Valley 18002-0785; 610/882-9200

Allentown, situated in the heart of Pennsylvania Dutch country, is conveniently accessible via a network of major highways. Allentown was originally incorporated as Northamptontown. The city later took the name of its founder, William Allen, a Chief Justice of Pennsylvania. Allentown was greatly influenced by the Pennsylvania Germans who settled the surrounding countryside and helped the city become the business hub for a rich agricultural community.

What to See and Do

Bear Creek Ski Area. *12 miles SW, 4 1/2 miles off PA 100, just N of Hereford. Phone 610/682-7100 or (in PA, ski report).* Four chairlifts, one handle tow, T-bar, two rope tows; 15 slopes; patrol, school, rentals, snowmaking; night skiing and snowboarding; tubing park; restaurant, cafeteria, bar; nursery. Longest run 1 1/2 miles; vertical drop 500 feet. (Dec-mid-Mar, daily) **$$$$**

Blue Mountain. *1660 Blue Mountain Dr. 17 miles N via PA 145, Treichlers exit, at "Y" turn right to Cherryville, and on to Danielsville, to top of Blue Mountain. Phone 610/826-7700; 800/SKI-BLUE.* Seven chairlifts, T-bar; school, rentals, snowmaking; cafeteria, bar, lodge. Vertical drop 1,082 feet. Also 27 trails with day and night skiing. (Dec-Apr, daily) **$$$$**

Cedar Crest College. *100 College Dr. Phone 610/437-4471.* (1867) 1,700 women. An 84-acre campus that includes nationally registered William F. Curtis Arboretum (tours); chapel with stained-glass windows portraying outstanding women in history; art galleries, sculpture gardens, museum, and theater. Campus tours.

Dorney Park and Wildwater Kingdom. *3830 Dorney Park Rd (18104). Phone 610/395-3724.* This amusement and water park is one of the country's oldest. A former fish hatchery, the 200-acre park is home to nearly 100 rides, 11 water slides, and four roller coasters. It's just an hour from Philadelphia, and there are activities here to engage every member of the family. Little ones can discover frog slides, turtle fountains, and squirt guns. Bigger kids can climb, slide, splash, and play on a submarine and an octopus. Older kids (and grownup ones) may want to torpedo through an enclosed tube or float slowly down a 1,600-foot winding river. In addition to rides, there are song and dance revues and 40 food locations, including two air-conditioned, dine-in restaurants. (Daily; closed Nov-Apr) **$$$$**

Frank Buchman House. *117 N 11th St. Phone 610/435-4664.* Constructed in 1892, this three-story row house, typical of Allentown's inner city, is an example of Victorian architecture; period rooms. (Sat and Sun afternoons; also by appointment) **FREE**

George Taylor House and Park. *501 W Hamilton St. 4 miles N off US 22, at Lehigh and Poplar sts in Catasauqua. Phone 610/435-4664.* (1768) House of a signer of the Declaration of Independence; 18th-century restoration period rooms; museum; walled garden. Guided tours. (June-Oct, Sat and Sun afternoons; also by appointment) **$**

Haines Mill Museum. *3600 Dorney Park Rd, Cetronia. 3 miles W via Hamilton St. Phone 610/435-4664.* (circa 1760) Operating gristmill (reconstructed 1909); exhibits portray the development and importance of the gristmill in rural America. (May-Sept, Sat and Sun afternoons; also by appointment; closed holidays) **FREE**

Lehigh County Museum. *501 W Hamilton St. Old Courthouse. Phone 610/435-4664.* Exhibits illustrate economic, social, and cultural history of the county. (Mon-Sat, Sun afternoons; closed holidays) **FREE**

Liberty Bell Shrine. *622 Hamilton, at Church St. Phone 610/435-4232.* Reconstructed Zion's church has shrine in basement area where Liberty Bell was hidden in 1777; contains a full-size replica of the original bell; a 46-foot mural depicts the journey of the bell; other historical exhibits, art collection. (Mon-Sat afternoons; closed holidays) **FREE**

Lock Ridge Furnace Museum. *525 Franklin St. Phone 610/435-4664.* Exhibits on the development of the US iron and steel industry; emphasis on the anthracite-coal-heated iron industry. Located in a reconstructed 19th-century iron furnace. (May-Sept, Sat and Sun afternoons; also by appointment) **FREE**

Muhlenberg College. *2400 W Chew St. Phone 484/664-3100.* (1848) 2,000 students. Founded by the Lutheran Church to honor patriarch of Lutheranism in America. On campus is the Gideon F. Egner Memorial Chapel, an example of Gothic architecture. Also here is the Center for the Arts, a dramatic building designed by renowned architect Philip Johnson, which houses the Muhlenberg Theater Association. Campus tours.

Saylor Park Cement Industry Museum. *245 N 2nd in Coplay. Phone 610/435-4664.* Outdoor historic site featuring remains of cement kilns. (Daily, year-round) **FREE**

Trexler-Lehigh County Game Preserve. *5150 Game Preserve Rd. 4 miles W on US 22, then 6 miles N on US 309, near Schnecksville.* Phone 610/799-4171. A 1,200-acre zoo, petting farm, and wilderness tour that is home to more than 350 animals. Scenic overlooks; picnic area. (Mid-Apr-Oct, daily) **$$$**

Trexler Memorial Park. *Cedar Crest Blvd and Broadway.* Phone 610/437-7628. Spring outdoor bulb display (Apr-May). **Gross Memorial Rose Garden** (at peak second week June) and **Old-Fashioned Garden,** Cedar Pkwy (June-Aug). **Trout Nursery** and Fish-for-Fun stream, Lehigh Pkwy; picnic areas. **West Park,** 16th and Turner. Band concerts (June-Aug). **FREE**

Trout Hall. *414 Walnut St.* Phone 610/435-4664. (1770) Oldest house in city, Georgian Colonial; restored. Period rooms, museum. Guided tours (Apr-May & Sept-Nov, Sat & Sun afternoons; June-Aug, Tues-Sun afternoons; also by appointment; closed holidays) **$**

Troxell-Steckel House and Farm Museum. *6 miles N on PA 145, then 1 mile W on PA 329, at 4229 Reliance St in Egypt.* Phone 610/435-4664. (1756) Stone house is an example of German medieval architecture. Period rooms; museum. Swiss-style bank barn adjacent has exhibits of farm implements, carriages, and sleighs. Guided tours. (June-Oct, Sat and Sun afternoons; also by appointment) **$**

Special Events

Das Awkscht Fescht. *Macungie Memorial Park.* Phone 610/967-2317 (festival) or 610-966-4289 (park office). 2,500 antique, classic, and special-interest autos; arts and crafts; antique toy show, entertainment, food, fireworks. First weekend in Aug.

Drum Corps International-Eastern Regional Championship. *21st and Linden sts.* Phone 610/966-5344. *J. Birney Crum Stadium.* Drum and bugle corps competition. Sept.

Great Allentown Fair. *17th and Chew sts. Fairgrounds.* Phone 610/435-SHOW. Farm and commercial exhibits, rides, games, food, entertainment. Late Aug-early Sept.

Mayfair Festival of the Arts. *Allentown parks.* Phone 610/437-6900. Family arts festival with 150 free musical performances; crafts and food. Mon and Thurs-Sun, Memorial Day weekend.

Motels/Motor Lodges

★ **ALLENWOOD MOTEL.** *1058 Hausman Rd (18104).* Phone 610/395-3707; fax 610/530-8166. 21 rooms. S, D, studio rooms $45-$50; each additional $5. Crib free. Pet accepted. TV; cable. Restaurant nearby. Check-out 11 am. Cr cds: A, DS, MC, V.

⮐ ⊠

★ **COMFORT SUITES.** *3712 Hamilton Blvd (18103).* Phone 610/437-9100; toll-free 800/228-5150; fax 610/437-0221. www.comfortsuites.com. 122 suites, 4 story. Suites $105-$130; each additional $10; under 18 free. Crib free. TV; cable. Complimentary continental breakfast. Restaurant 7-2 am. Room service. Bar; entertainment Thurs-Sat. Check-out noon. Meeting rooms. Business services available. In-room modem link. Sundries. Free airport, train station, bus depot transportation. Exercise equipment. Refrigerators. Cr cds: A, C, D, DS, ER, JCB, MC, V.

D 🏋 ⊠ SC

★ ★ **DAYS INN.** *1151 Bulldog Dr (18104).* Phone 610/395-3731; toll-free 800/329-7466; fax 610/395-9899. www.daysinn.com. 282 rooms, 2 story. May-Oct: S $79.95; D $109; each additional $6; suites $109-$129; under 18 free; weekly rates; package plans; higher rates local festivals; lower rates rest of year. Check-out noon. TV; cable. Laundry services. Restaurant 6:30 am-10 pm. Bar 2 pm-1 am. Game room. Pool, poolside service. Lawn games. Free airport transportation. Cr cds: A, C, D, DS, JCB, MC, V.

D ⇌ ⊠ SC

★ **HAMPTON INN.** *7471 Keebler Way (18106).* Phone 610/391-1500; toll-free 800/426-7866; fax 610/391-0386. www.hamptoninn.com. 124 rooms, 5 story. S, D $89-$129; under 18 free; higher rates special events. Crib free. TV; cable. Complimentary continental breakfast. Restaurant nearby. Check-out noon. Meeting rooms. Business services available. Free airport transportation. Exercise equipment; sauna. Cr cds: A, C, D, DS, MC, V.

D 🏋 ⬚ ⊠ SC

★ **SUPER 8.** *1715 Plaza Ln (18104).* Phone 610/435-7880; toll-free 800/800-8000; fax 610/432-2555. www.super8.com. 82 rooms, 4 story. S, D $74-$95; each additional $5; under 18 free. Crib free. Pet accepted; $5. TV; cable. Complimentary continental breakfast. Restaurant nearby. Check-out 11 am. Business services available. Cr cds: A, C, D, DS, MC, V.

D 🐾 ⊠ SC

Hotels

★ ★ **CLARION HOTEL.** *904 Hamilton Mall (18101).* Phone 610/433-2221; toll-free 800/4-CHOICE; fax 610/433-6455. As an executive-style hotel, this property is a great place to stay for business and leisure travelers. Its location in downtown Allentown is only 6 miles from the ABE International Airport and within walking distance of the Liberty Bell. 224 rooms, 9 story. D $89-$129; each additional $10; suites $145-$250; under 18 free; weekend rates. Check-out 11 am. TV. In-room modem link. Restaurant 6:30 am-10 pm. Bar 11-2 am. Exercise equipment, sauna. Pool. Free airport transportation. Cr cds: A, C, D, DS, JCB, MC, V.

D ⇌ ✈ 🏋 ⊠ SC

★ ★ **FOUR POINTS BY SHERATON.** *3400 Airport Rd (18109). Phone 610/266-1000; toll-free 888/610-2662; fax 610/266-1888.* 147 rooms, 3 story. D $80-$164; each additional $10; suites $115-$145; under 13 free; higher rates NASCAR races. Pets accepted. Check-out noon. TV; cable (premium), VCR available. In-room modem link. Restaurant 6:30 am-10 pm. Bar 11-2 am; entertainment Tues-Sun. Room service. Exercise equipment, sauna. Indoor pool, whirlpool. Cr cds: A, C, D, DS, MC, V.

D ⊷ ⇌ ⅋ ✈ ⊠ SC

B&B/Small Inn

★ ★ ★ **THE GLASBERN INN.** *2141 Pack House Rd (18051). Phone 610/285-4723; fax 610/285-2862. www.glasbern.com.* 37 rooms, 2 story. D $110-$185; each additional $20; suites, kitchen units $120-$355; 2-night minimum special weekends, holidays. Complimentary full breakfast. Check-out noon, check-in 4 pm. TV; VCR available. Fireplaces. Dining room (public by reservation) 6-8 pm. Exercise equipment. Heated pool. Farmhouse, barn, gate house and carriage house built in late 1800s; antiques. Cr cds: A, MC, V.

D ♨ ⇌ ⅋ ⊠

Restaurants

★ ★ **ALADDIN RESTAURANT.** *651 Union Blvd (18109). Phone 610/437-4023; fax 610/437-9841.* Middle Eastern menu. Closed Mon. Lunch, dinner. Children's menu. Casual attire. **$$**

★ ★ **APPENNINO.** *3079 Willow St (18104). Phone 610/799-2727; fax 610/799-2741.* Northern Italian menu. Hours: 5:30-10 pm. Closed Sun; major holidays. Dinner $18.50-$30. Bar. Restored hotel (1800s); imported Italian lamps, chandeliers and tapestry on chairs. Jacket required. Reservations accepted. Cr cds: A, DS, MC, V.

D

★ ★ **BAY LEAF.** *935 W Hamilton St (18101). Phone 610/433-4211; fax 610/433-2652.* Thai menu. Hours: 11:30 am-2 pm, 5-10 pm, Sat from 5 pm. Closed Sun; also major holidays. Lunch $7.95, dinner $14.95-$25.95. Bar. Reservations accepted. Cr cds: A, MC, V.

D

★ ★ **FEDERAL GRILL.** *536 Hamilton St (18101). Phone 610/776-7600; fax 610/776-3660.* Seafood menu. Hours: 11 am-midnight; Sat, Sun brunch 11 am-3 pm. Closed most major holidays. Lunch $5-$15, dinner $13-$24, Brunch $8-$15. Cigar bar. Bar. Reservations required Fri, Sat. Outdoor dining. Cr cds: A, D, DS, MC, V.

D

Altoona (F-6)

See also Ebensburg

Founded 1849 **Pop** 49,523 **Elev** 1,170 ft **Area code** 814

Information Allegheny Mountains Convention & Visitors Bureau, One Convention Center Dr, 16602; 814/943-4183 or 800/842-5866

Web www.alleghenymountains.com

The rough, high Alleghenies ring this city, which was founded by the Pennsylvania Railroad. Altoona expanded rapidly after 1852, when the difficult task of spanning the Alleghenies with track, linking Philadelphia and Pittsburgh, was completed. The railroad shops still offer substantial employment for residents of the city and Blair County, but new and diversified industries now provide the economic base.

What to See and Do

Allegheny Portage Railroad National Site. *110 Federal Park Rd (16641). In Cresson. Phone 814/886-6150.* View authentic Lemon House and original rehabbed Engine House; learn how canal boats were taken over the Allegheny Mountains before the Horseshoe Curve was built. (Daily; closed Dec 25) **$$$**

Baker Mansion Museum. *3500 Oak Ln. Phone 814/942-3916.* (1844-1848) Stone Greek Revival house of early ironmaster; now occupied by Blair County Historical Society. Hand-carved Belgian furniture of the period; transportation exhibits, gun collection, clothing, housewares. (Memorial Day-Labor Day, Tues-Sun; mid-Apr-Memorial Day and Labor Day-Oct, Sat and Sun; closed holidays) **$$**

Canoe Creek State Park. *12 miles E via US 22. Phone 814/695-6807.* Approximately 950-acre park features 155-acre lake. Swimming beach, fishing, boating (launches, rentals); hiking, picnicking (reservations for pavilion), cross-country skiing, sledding, ice boating, ice skating, cabins. Standard fees.

Delgrossos Park. *10 miles N on US 220, in Tipton. Phone 814/684-3538.* More than 30 rides and attractions include antique carousel, miniature golf, and pony rides. Also here are arcade games, picnic pavilions, and restaurant. (May-Sept, Tues-Sun) **$$$$**

Fort Roberdeau. *8 miles NE via US 220, Kettle St exit onto PA 1013. Phone 814/946-0048.* Reconstructed Revolutionary War fort with horizontal logs; contains lead smelter, blacksmith shop, lead miners' hut, barracks, storehouse, officers' quarters, powder magazine. Costumed guides; weekend reenactments. Visitor center. Picnicking, nature trails. (Mid-May-early Oct, Tues-Sun) **$$**

Horseshoe Curve Visitors Center. *5 miles W via well-marked, unnumbered road. Phone 814/946-0834.* World-famous engineering feat, carrying main-line Conrail and Amtrak trains around western grade of 91 feet per mile. Curve is 2,375 feet long and has a central angle of 220 degrees. Funicular runs between interpretive center and observation area. Gift shop. (Apr-Dec, daily) **$$**

Lakemont Park. *700 Park Ave, Frankstown Rd and I-99. Phone 814/949-7275.* An amusement park with more than 30 rides and attractions; home of the nation's oldest wooden roller coaster; water park, miniature golf, entertainment. (May-Sept, daily) **$$$**

Prince Gallitzin State Park. *8 miles NW on PA 36, then 1 1/4 miles NW off PA 53, then W on PA 1026. Phone 814/674-1000 or 814/674-1007 (reservations).* Approximately 6,200 acres; 26 miles of shoreline on 1,600-acre lake. Swimming beach, fishing, boating (rentals, mooring, launching, marina); hiking trails, horseback riding, cross-country skiing, snowmobiling, ice skating, ice fishing, picnicking, snack bar, store, laundry facilities, tent and trailer sites, cabins. Standard fees.

Railroader's Memorial Museum. *1300 9th Ave. Phone 814/946-0834.* Exhibits feature railroad artifacts, art, and theme displays. Railroad rolling stock, steam and electric locomotive collections. (Daily) **$$$**

Wopsononock Mountain. *6 miles NW on Juniata Gap Rd.* Lookout provides view of six-county area from height of 2,580 feet; offers one of the best views in the state.

Special Events

Blair County Arts Festival. *3000 Ivyside Park (16601). Penn State Altoona Campus.* Arts, crafts, hobbies on display. Mid-May.

Keystone Country Festival. *700 Park Ave. Lakemont Park.* Arts and crafts, continuous music; food. Contact Convention and Visitors Bureau for details. Weekend after Labor Day.

Railfest. *1300 9th Ave. Phone 814/946-0834.* A celebration of Altoona's rich rail heritage. Oct.

Motel/Motor Lodge

★ **RAMADA INN.** *1 Sheraton Dr (16601). Phone 814/946-1631; fax 814/946-0785. www.ramada.com.* 215 rooms, 2-3 story. S, D $55-$85; each additional $5; suites $80-$140; under 18 free; some weekend rates; higher rates: football games, ski season. Crib $5. Pet accepted. Complimentary continental breakfast. Check-out noon. TV; cable (premium), VCR available. In-room modem link. Microwaves available. Valet services. Restaurant 6:30 am-2:30 pm, 5:30-10 pm; Sat to 11 pm. Bar 11-2 am. Room service. Exercise equipment. Recreation room. Indoor pool, wading pool, whirlpool, lifeguard. 18-hole golf privileges. Downhill ski 20 miles. Airport transportation. Meeting rooms. Business center. Gift shop. Cr cds: A, C, D, DS, JCB, MC, V.

⬚ ⬚ ⬚ ⬚ ⬚ ⬚ ⬚ SC ⬚

Restaurant

★ ★ ★ **ALLEGRO.** *3926 Broad Ave (16601). Phone 814/946-5216; fax 814/946-4635. www.allegro-restaurant .com.* Locals favor Allegro Ristorante for special occasions due to the candlelit setting and stately ambiance. The Italian food is not innovative, but classic dishes are tried and true. Italian, American menu. Specializes in veal, seafood. Hours: 4-9:30 pm; Sat to 10 pm. Closed Sun; major holidays. Dinner $10.95-$25.50. Bar. Children's menu. Reservations accepted. Cr cds: A, C, D, DS, MC, V.

⬚ SC

Ambridge (F-2)

See also Beaver Falls, Pittsburgh

Founded 1901 **Pop** 7,769 **Elev** 751 ft **Area code** 724 **Zip** 15003

Information Beaver County Recreation & Tourism Department, Brady's Run Park, RD 1, Box 526, Beaver Falls, PA, 15010; 724/891-7030

Web www.co.beaver.pa.us

Founded by and taking its name from the American Bridge Company, this city rests on part of the site of Old Economy Village. In 1825, under the leadership of George Rapp, the Harmony Society established a communal pietistic colony that, for many decades, was important in the industrial life and development of western Pennsylvania. Despite its spiritual emphasis, Old Economy Village enjoyed a great material prosperity; farms were productive, craft shops were busy, and factories made textiles widely acclaimed for their quality. Surplus funds financed railroads and industrial enterprises throughout the upper Ohio Valley. After celibacy was adopted and unwise investments were made, the community's productivity decreased. Officially dissolved in 1905, the remains of the community were taken over by the Commonwealth of Pennsylvania in 1916.

What to See and Do

⬚ **Old Economy Village.** *14th and Church sts. Phone 724/266-4500.* Seventeen original Harmony Society buildings located on 6 acres, restored and filled with furnishings of the community. Included are the communal leader's 32-room Great House, the Feast Hall, the Grotto in the Gardens, wine cellars, a five-story granary, shops, dwellings, and community kitchens. Cobblestone streets link the buildings. Special festivals and events. (Tues-Sun; closed holidays)

Raccoon Creek State Park. *3000 PA 18 (15050). 9 miles W on PA 151, then 7 miles S on PA 18, near Frankfort Springs. Phone 724/899-2200.* Approximately 7,300 acres. Swimming beach, fishing, boating (rentals, mooring, launching); hunting, hiking, horseback riding, cross-country skiing, sledding, snowmobiling, ice skating, ice fishing, snack bar, tent and trailer sites. Nature and historical centers. Standard fees.

Special Event

Nationality Days. Ethnic cultural displays, foods; native music, dancing. Mid-May.

Ashland

See also Hazleton

Pop 3,283 **Elev** 1,000 ft **Area code** 717 **Zip** 17921

Information Schuylkill County Visitors Bureau, 91 S Progress Ave, Pottsville 17901; 717/622-7700 or 800/765-7282

Web www.schuylkill.org

What to See and Do

Museum of Anthracite Mining. *Pine and 17th sts. Phone 570/875-4708.* Museum on geology and technology of mining "hard" coal. (May-Oct, Mon-Sat, also Sun afternoons; rest of year, Tues-Sat, also Sun afternoons; closed holidays) **$$**

Pioneer Tunnel Coal Mine and Steam Lokie Ride. *19th and Oak sts. Phone 717/875-3850 or 717/875-3301.* Tour and explanation of mining in original coal mine tunnel; indoor temperature 52°F. Narrow-gauge steam train ride; picnic park. (call for hours) **$$$**

Beaver Falls (F-1)

See also Ambridge, Harmony

Founded 1806 **Pop** 9,920 **Elev** 800 ft **Area code** 724 **Zip** 15010

Information Beaver County Recreation & Tourism Department, Brady's Run Park, RD 1, Box 526, Beaver Falls, PA, 15010; 724/891-7030

Web www.co.beaver.pa.us

Founded as Brighton, the town changed its name for the falls in the Beaver River. The plates from which US currency is printed are made in Beaver Falls. Geneva College (1848) is located here.

Motels/Motor Lodges

★ **BEAVER VALLEY MOTEL.** *7257 Big Beaver Blvd (15010). Phone 724/843-0630; toll-free 800/400-8312; fax 724/843-1610. www.bvmotel.com.* 27 rooms. S $39.60-$44; D $47-$52; each additional $6; kitchen units $225/week; under 18 free. Crib free. TV; cable (premium). Complimentary coffee in lobby. Check-out 11 am. Business services available. Cr cds: A, DS, MC, V.
D ⊠ SC

★ **CONLEY INN.** *Big Beaver Blvd; RR 18 (15010). Phone 724/843-0630; toll-free 800/345-6819; fax 724/843-9039.* 56 rooms. S $45; D $55; each additional $10; under 12 free; weekly, monthly rates. Pet accepted. TV; cable. Restaurant 5:30-10 pm. Bar. Check-out 11 am. Meeting rooms. Business services available. Refrigerators. Cr cds: A, C, D, DS, MC, V.
⊠ SC

★ ★ **HOLIDAY INN.** *7195 Eastwood Rd (15010). Phone 724/846-3700; toll-free 800/465-4329; fax 724/846-7008. www.holiday-inn.com.* 156 rooms, 3 story. S, D $89; under 18 free. Crib free. Pet accepted. TV. Indoor pool; whirlpool, poolside service, lifeguard. Coffee in rooms. Restaurant 6:30 am-2 pm, 5-10 pm. Bar 11-2 am. Room service. Check-out noon. Meeting rooms. Business services available. In-room modem link. Valet service. Sauna. Miniature golf. Game room. Cr cds: A, C, D, DS, JCB, MC, V.
D ⊠ SC

Bedford (H-6)

Settled 1751 **Pop** 5,417 **Elev** 1,106 ft **Area code** 814 **Zip** 15522

Information Bedford County Conference & Visitors Bureau, 141 S Juliana St; 814/623-1771or 800/765-3331

Web www.bedfordcounty.net

Fort Bedford was a major frontier outpost in pre-Revolutionary War days. After the war, it became an important stopover along the route of western migration and has remained so up until the present. Garrett Pendergrass, the second settler here, built Pendergrass's Tavern, which figures in a number of novels by Hervey Allen.

What to See and Do

Bedford County Courthouse. *230 S Juliana St, Bldg 2. Phone 814/623-4807.* Federal-style building constructed in 1828 has unique hanging spiral staircase; oldest courthouse still in operation in PA. (Mon-Fri; closed holidays) **FREE**

Blue Knob Ski Area. *RR 1. Phone 814/239-5111; 800/458-3403 (snow conditions).* Two triple, two double chairlifts; three platter pulls; patrol, school, rentals; snowmaking; bar, cafeteria; nursery. Longest run approximately 2 miles; vertical drop 1,072 feet. (Dec-Mar, daily) Half-day rates available. **$$$$**

Blue Knob State Park. *10 miles N on US 220, then 8 miles NW on PA 869. Phone 814/276-3576.* Approximately 6,000 acres. Swimming pool, fishing; hunting, hiking, cross-country skiing, snowmobiling, sledding, picnicking, playfield, camping (mid-Apr-mid-Oct). Standard fees.

Fort Bedford Park and Museum. *Fort Bedford Dr, N end of Juliana St, park along Raystown River. Phone 814/623-8891.* Log blockhouse, erected during Bedford's bicentennial. Contains large-scale replica of original fort, displays of colonial antiques and relics, Native American artifacts. (May-late Oct, daily)

Old Bedford Village. *220 Sawblade Rd (15522). Phone 814/623-1156.* More than 40 authentic log and frame structures (1750-1851) house historical exhibits; crafts demonstrations; operating pioneer farm. Many special events throughout the year. (Memorial Day weekend-Labor Day) **$$$**

Shawnee. *132 State Park Rd (15559). 8 miles W on US 30. Phone 814/733-4218.* Approximately 450-acre lake surrounded by 3,840 acres. Swimming beach, fishing, boating (rentals, mooring, launching); hunting, cross-country skiing, snowmobiling, sledding, ice skating, ice fishing, picnicking, playfield, snack bar, camping; tent and trailer sites. Standard fees.

Special Events

Civil War Reenactment. *Old Bedford Village.* Early Sept.

Fall Foliage Festival Days. *141 S Juliana St.* Entertainment, ethnic foods, antique cars, more than 350 craft booths. First two full weekends in Oct.

Motels/Motor Lodges

★ ★ **BEST WESTERN BEDFORD INN.** *4517 Business 220 (15522). Phone 814/623-9006; toll-free 800/752-8592; fax 814/623-7120. www.bestwestern.com.* 105 rooms, 2 story. Apr-Oct: S $49.95; D $59.95; suites $67.95; each additional $10; under 18 free; lower rates rest of year. Crib free. Pet accepted, some restrictions; $50. TV; cable (premium), VCR available (movies). Pool; whirlpool, lifeguard. Restaurant 6:30-11 am, 5-10 pm; Sat, Sun 6:30 am-10 pm. Bar 5 pm-midnight. Check-out noon. Meeting rooms. Gift shop. Exercise equipment; sauna. Game room. Cr cds: A, C, D, DS, MC, V.

★ **ECONO LODGE.** *141 Hillcrest Dr (15522). Phone 814/623-5174; fax 814/623-5455. www.econolodge.com.* 32 rooms, 2 story. May-Oct: S $42-$58; D $46-$65; each additional $6; under 18 free; ski plans; higher rates special events; lower rates rest of year. Crib free. Pet accepted. TV; cable (premium). Bar 4 pm-midnight. Check-out 11 am. Downhill ski 15 miles. Game room. Cr cds: A, C, D, DS, JCB, MC, V.

★ ★ **QUALITY INN.** *4407 Business 220 (15522). Phone 814/623-5188; toll-free 800/228-5050; fax 814/623-0049. www.qualityinn.com.* 66 rooms. May-Nov: S $57-$63; D $63-$69; each additional $6; under 18 free; lower rates rest of year. Crib $4. Pet accepted, some restrictions. TV; cable (premium). Pool. Complimentary continental breakfast. Restaurant 7 am-10 pm. Bar 11 am-11 pm. Check-out 11 am. Meeting rooms. Business services available. Downhill ski 20 miles. Cr cds: A, C, D, DS, ER, JCB, MC, V.

Restaurant

★ ★ **ED'S STEAK HOUSE.** *4476 Business 220 (15522). Phone 814/623-8894; fax 814/623-2643.* Hours: 7 am-9 pm; Fri, Sat to 10 pm. Closed Thanksgiving, Dec 25. Reservations accepted. Bar. Breakfast $2.59-$4.59, lunch $2.99-$5.99, dinner $6.59-$14.99. Children's menu. Specializes in steak, seafood. Family-owned. Cr cds: A, MC, V.

Bellefonte (E-7)

See also State College

Settled 1770 **Pop** 6,395 **Elev** 809 ft **Area code** 814 **Zip** 16823

Information Bellefonte Intervalley Area Chamber of Commerce, Train Station, 320 W High St; 814/355-2917

Web bellefontechamber.org

When the exiled French minister Talleyrand saw the Big Spring here in 1794, his exclamation—"Beautiful fountain"—gave the town its name. Bellefonte is perched on seven hills at the southeast base of Bald Eagle Mountain.

What to See and Do

Black Moshannon State Park. *N via PA 144/150, SW via US 220, then approximately 12 miles W on PA 504. Phone 814/342-5960.* Approximately 3,450 acres. Swimming beach, fishing, boating (rentals, mooring, launching); hunting, hiking, cross-country skiing, snowmobiling, ice skating, ice fishing, ice boating, picnicking, snack bar, tent and trailer sites, cabins. Interpretive program. Standard fees.

Centre County Library and Historical Museum. *200 N Allegheny St. Phone 814/355-1516.* Local historical museum includes central Pennsylvania historical and genealogical books, records. (Mon-Sat; closed holidays) **FREE**

Restaurant

★ ★ **GAMBLE MILL TAVERN.** *160 Dunlap St (16823). Phone 814/355-7764; fax 814/355-1571. www.gamblemill.com.* Continental menu. Specializes in fresh seafood, veal, duck. Hours: 11:30 am-2 pm, 5-8 pm. Closed Sun; Thanksgiving, Dec 25. A la carte entrées: lunch $6-$10, dinner $15-$26. Bar. Restored mill (1786); rustic early American décor. Reservations accepted. Cr cds: DS, MC, V.

Bethlehem (E-13)

See also Allentown, Easton, Quakertown (Bucks County)

Founded 1741 **Pop** 71,329 **Elev** 340 ft **Area code** 484 and 610

Information Bethlehem Tourism Authority, 52 W Broad St, 18018; 610/868-1513 or 800/360-8687

Web www.bethtour.org

The city is famous throughout the world for Bethlehem Steel products, and is also well known for its Bach Festival, for Lehigh University (1865), Moravian College (1807), Musikfest, its historic district, and as "America's Christmas city."

Moravians, members of a very old Protestant denomination that came here to the banks of the Lehigh River, assembled on Christmas Evening 1741 in the only building, a log house that was part stable. Singing a hymn that praised Bethlehem, they found a name for their village. The musical heritage, too, dates from this moment; string quartets and symphonies were heard here before any other place in the colonies.

The opening of the Lehigh Canal in 1829 started industrialization of the area and development of the borough of South Bethlehem (1865), which was incorporated into the city of Bethlehem in 1917.

What to See and Do

Apothecary Museum. *424 Main St, in rear; entry gate next to book shop. Phone 610/867-0173.* Original fireplace (1752), where prescriptions were compounded; collection of artifacts includes retorts, grinders, mortars and pestles,

scales, blown-glass bottles, labels, and a set of Delft jars (1743); herb and flower garden. (By appointment) **$**

Brethren's House. *Church and Main sts. Phone 610/861-3916.* (1748) Early residence and shop area for single men of the Moravian Community. Used as a general hospital by the Continental Army during the Revolutionary War. Now serves Moravian College as its Center for Music and Art.

Central Moravian Church. *40 W Church St (10818).* (1806) Federal-style with hand-carved detail, considered foremost Moravian church in the US. Noted for its music, including a trombone choir in existence since 1754.

God's Acre. *Church and Market sts (18018).* (1742-1910) Old Moravian cemetery following Moravian tradition that all gravestones are laid flat, indicating that all are equal in the sight of God.

Hill-to-Hill Bridge. *Main St, PA 378 over Lehigh River.* Joins old and new parts of the city and provides excellent view of historic area, river, and Bethlehem Steel plant.

Historic Bethlehem Inc's 18th-Century Industrial Quarter. *459 Old York Rd (18018). Ohio Rd and Main St (pedestrian entrance); Old York Rd and Union Blvd (parking lot entrance). Phone 610/691-0603.* Guided tours (July-Aug, Sat; late Nov-late Dec, weekends). (See SPECIAL EVENTS) **$$** Tour of area includes

> **Goundie House.** *501 Main St.* (1810) Restored Federal-style brick house has period-furnished rooms and interpretive exhibits.

> **Luckenbach Mill.** (1869) Restored gristmill contains contemporary craft gallery and museum shop; also the offices of Bethlehem Area Chamber of Commerce and Historic Bethlehem Inc. Interpretive display here is included in guided tour.

> **Springhouse.** (1764) Reconstruction on site of original spring that served Moravian community as a water source from the time of settlement in 1741 until 1912.

> **Tannery.** (1761) Exhibits Moravian crafts, trades, and industries. Includes a working model of the original oil mill.

> **Waterworks.** (1762) with reconstructed 18-foot wooden waterwheel and pumping mechanisms.

Kemerer Museum of Decorative Arts. *427 N New St. Phone 610/691-0603.* Exhibits include art, Bohemian glass, toys, prints, china; regional German folk art from 1750-1900; Federal furniture; period room settings. (Tues-Sun; closed holidays) **$$$**

Lost River Caverns. *726 Durham St, 3 miles SE via PA 412 in Hellertown. Phone 610/838-8767.* Stalagmites, stalactites, other formations. Picnic area; Gilman Museum with rocks and minerals, ancient and modern armor; also jungle garden (free). Thirty-minute guided tours. (Daily; closed Jan 1, Thanksgiving, Dec 25) **$$$**

Moravian Museum (Gemein Haus). *66 W Church St. Phone 610/867-0173.* (1741) This five-story log building is the oldest structure in the city; docents interpret the history and culture of early Bethlehem and the Moravians. 45-minute tour. (Tues-Sun; closed holidays, including Good Friday, Holy Saturday, also Jan)

Old Chapel. *Heckewelder Place, adjacent to Moravian Museum.* (1751) Once called the "Indian chapel" because so many Native Americans attended the services, this stone structure, the second church for the Moravian congregation, is still used frequently. May be toured only in combination with Moravian Museum community walking tour.

Special Events

Bach Festival. *423 Heckewelder Pl. Phone 610/866-4382. Packer Church, Lehigh University campus.* One of the country's outstanding musical events. Famous artists and the Bach Choir of Bethlehem participate. Mid-late May.

Christmas. *52 W Broad St. Phone 610/868-1513 or 800/360-8687.* Bethlehem continues more than two centuries of Christmas tradition with candlelight, music, and a number of special events. Moravians sing their own Christmas songs intermingled with Mozart and Handel. A huge "Star of Bethlehem" shines from the top of South Mountain and the Hill-to-Hill Bridge has special lighting. The community "Putzes," a Moravian version of nativity scenes, are open to the public daily. Thousands of people post their Christmas cards from Bethlehem. Night Light Tours of city's Christmas displays and historical areas are offered (Dec) by the Bethlehem Tourism Authority. Reservations suggested. Thanksgiving-Jan 1.

Live Bethlehem Christmas Pageant. *Phone 610/867-2893.* Scores of volunteers (garbed in biblical costumes) and live animals (including camels, horses, donkey and sheep) join together to re-create the nativity story; narrated. First weekend in Dec.

Moravian College Alumni Association Antiques Show. *1200 Main St. Johnston Hall, Moravian College Campus. Phone 610/861-1366.* Early June.

Musikfest. *25 W 3rd St. Phone 610/861-0678.* Nine-day festival celebrating Bethlehem's rich musical and ethnic heritage. More than 600 performances (most free) of all types of music including folk, big-band, jazz, country-western, chamber, classical, gospel, rock, swing; held at nine different sites in downtown historic area. Also children's activities. Late Aug.

Shad Festival. *Historic Bethlehem's 18th-century Industrial Quarter. Phone 610/691-0603.* Old-fashioned planked shad bake (reservations required for dinner), exhibits, demonstrations. First Sun May.

Motels/Motor Lodges

★ **COMFORT INN.** *3191 Highfield Dr (18020). Phone 610/865-6300; toll-free 800/732-2500; fax 610/865-5074. www.comfortinn.com.* 116 rooms, 2 1/2 story. S $59-$80; D $66-$86; each additional $6; under 18 free; ski plan. Crib free. Pet accepted. Complimentary continental breakfast. Check-out noon. TV; cable, VCR (movies $5). Valet services. Restaurant adjacent. Bar noon-2 am; entertainment Fri, Sat. Business services. Cr cds: A, C, D, DS, ER, JCB, MC, V.

⎮D⎮ 🐾 🌊 📶 SC

★ ★ **HOLIDAY INN.** *3560 Bath Pike; Rtes 512 and 22 (18017). Phone 610/866-5800; toll-free 888/222-8512; fax 610/867-9120. www.holiday-inn.com.* 192 rooms, 2 story. S $110-$115; D $120-$125; each additional $10; under 18 free. Crib free. Check-out noon. TV; cable. In-room modem link. Valet services. Restaurant 6:30 am-10 pm. Bar 11-2 am. Room service. Exercise equipment. Pool, wading pool, lifeguard. Free airport transportation. Meeting rooms. Business center. Gift shop. Cr cds: A, C, D, DS, MC, V.

⎮D⎮ 🏊 🏋 📶 SC 🚶

B&B/Small Inn

★ ★ ★ **WYDNOR HALL INN.** *3612 Old Philadelphia Pike (18015). Phone 610/867-6851; toll-free 800/839-0020; fax 610/866-2062.* 5 rooms, 2 suites, 3 story. No elevator. Complimentary continental breakfast. Check-out 11 am, check-in 2-8 pm. TV. Built in 1895. European-style inn. Totally nonsmoking. Cr cds: A, C, DS, MC, V. **$**

📶

Restaurants

★ ★ **CAFE.** *221 W Broad St (18018). Phone 610/866-1686.* International menu. Specializes in fresh seafood, Thai cuisine, French pastries. Hours: 11 am-2 pm, 5-9 pm. Closed Mon, Sun. Lunch $6-$7, dinner $17-$21.25. Piano Fri, Sat. Reservations required Fri, Sat (dinner). Totally nonsmoking. Cr cds: A, DS, MC, V.

★ ★ **CANDLELIGHT INN.** *4431 Easton Ave (18020). Phone 610/691-7777; fax 610/691-8378.* Continental menu. Specializes in prime rib, steak, seafood. Hours: 11 am-10 pm; Sat from 4 pm; Sun from 10 am. Lunch $5-$14, dinner $19-$35. Bar. Children's menu. Reservations accepted. Cr cds: A, DS, MC, V.

⎮D⎮

★ **EASTERN CHINESE.** *3926 Linden St (18020). Phone 610/868-0299; fax 610/868-1321.* Chinese menu. Hours: 11 am-10 pm. Closed Thanksgiving. Lunch $6-$8, dinner $10-$15. Bar. Reservations required Fri, Sat (dinner). Cr cds: A, C, D, DS, MC, V.

D

★ ★ ★ **INN OF THE FALCON.** *1740 Seidersville Rd (18015). Phone 610/868-6505; fax 610/868-6507. www. innofthefalcon.com.* The landmark status of this charming restaurant is evident from the red shutters, flower-filled window boxes, and rustic stone facade of its home. Chef/owner Shirlee Neumeyer turns out creative dishes in the cozy, authentically furnished dining room. International menu. Hours: 5-9:30 pm. Closed Sun; also major holidays. A la carte entrées: dinner $15-$24. Bar. Building built in 1800s. Reservations required. Cr cds: A, DS, MC, V.

D

★ ★ ★ **MAIN STREET DEPOT.** *61 W Lehigh St (18018). Phone 610/868-7123.* 1979. Hours: 11:30 am-2 pm, 4:30-9:30 pm. Closed Sun; also many major holidays. Specializes in chicken, veal, and seafood. A la carte entrées: lunch $4.50-$7, dinner $18-$32. Bar to midnight. 1873 Victorian railway station; old train pictures, gas chandeliers. Reservations required Fri, Sat (dinner). Cr cds: A, MC, V.

D

★ ★ **MINSI TRAIL INN.** *626 Stefko Blvd (18018). Phone 610/691-5613. www.minsitrail.com.* Greek, American menu. Specializes in seafood, veal, beef. Hours: 11 am-9 pm; Sun brunch 11 am-3 pm. Closed some major holidays. A la carte entrées: lunch $5.95-$9.95, dinner: $8.95-$18.95. Sun brunch 11 am-3 pm. Sun brunch $12.95. Bar. Children's menu. Reservations required Fri, Sat (dinner). Totally nonsmoking. Cr cds: A, MC, V.

D

Bird-in-Hand (H-11)

See also Ephrata, Lancaster

Pop 700 **Elev** 358 ft **Area code** 717 **Zip** 17505

Information Pennsylvania Dutch Convention and Visitors Bureau, 501 Greenfield Rd, Lancaster 17601; 717/299-8901 or 800/723-8824

Web www.800padutch.com

This Pennsylvania Dutch farming village got its name from the signboard of an early inn.

What to See and Do

Amish Village. *1 mile W on PA 340, then 3 miles S on PA 896. Phone 717/687-8511.* Reconstructed and original buildings include blacksmith shop, schoolhouse, operating smokehouse; livestock. Guided tours of Amish farmhouse. (Mar-Dec, daily; rest of year, most weekends; closed week of Thanksgiving, also Dec 25) **$$$**

Bird-in-Hand Farmers' Market. *PA 340 and Maple Ave. Phone 717/393-9674.* Indoor market with a wide variety of Pennsylvania Dutch foods and gifts. (July-Oct, Wed-Sat; Apr-June and Nov, Wed, Fri, and Sat; rest of year, Fri and Sat; closed Jan 1, Thanksgiving, Dec 25)

Folk Craft Center & Museum. *1 1/2 miles W on PA 340, then N on Mt. Sidney Rd, in Witmer. Phone 717/397-3609.* Early 18th-century buildings display tools, household implements, stoneware pottery, toys, Stiegel glass, quilts, coverlets, and early Pennsylvania Dutch memorabilia; log cabin loom house (1762); herb and ornamental gardens; turn-of-the-century woodworking and print shops; audiovisual presentation. (Apr-Nov, daily) **DONATION**

The People's Place. *3513 Old Philadelphia Pike. Phone 717/768-7171.* Arts and heritage center features three-screen documentary on the Amish; interpretive museum with hands-on exhibits; Amish quilt museum. Also bookstore, art gallery. 5 miles E on PA 340, on Main St in Intercourse. (Mon-Sat; closed Jan 1, Thanksgiving, Dec 25)

Weavertown One-Room Schoolhouse. *2916 Old Philadelphia Pike (17505). 1 mile E via PA 340. Phone 717/768-3976 or 717/291-1888 (winter).* Life-size animated re-creation of activities at a one-room schoolhouse. (Early April-Oct, daily; Mar and Nov, weekends) **$$**

Motel/Motor Lodge

★ ★ ★ **BIRD-IN-HAND FAMILY INN.** *2740 Old Philadelphia Pike (17505). Phone 717/768-8271; toll-free 800/665-8780; fax 717/768-1117. www.bird-in-hand.com.* This quiet inn is found in the small town of Bird-in-Hand, and within walking of the local attractions including the general store, farmers market, craft shops and factory outlet stores. 100 rooms, 1-2 story. May-Nov: S $60-$88; D $74-$90; each additional $8; under 16 free; higher rates weekends; lower rates rest of year. Crib $6. TV; cable, VCR available (movies). 2 pools, 1 indoor. Playground. Complimentary coffee in rooms. Restaurant 6 am-9 pm. Check-out 11 am. Coin laundry. Meeting rooms. Business services available. In-room modem link. Sundries. Lighted tennis. Game room. Refrigerators; microwaves available. Picnic tables. Cr cds: A, D, DS, MC, V.

D ⚞ ⚟ ⚠

B&B/Small Inns

★ ★ ★ **GREYSTONE MANOR BED AND BREAKFAST.** *2658 Old Philadelphia Pike (17505). Phone 717/393-4233; fax 717/393-0616. www. 800padutch.com/greystone.html.* This inn was built in the mid-1880s and is used today as a heritage lodging site. Situated on 8 acres of landscaped property, the inn offers guests Victorian charm and style for a relaxing stay. 10 rooms, 6 suites, 3 story. No room phones. S $70-$90; D $75-$95; each additional $15; suites $95-$135; under 2 free; minimum stay holidays, weekends. Closed Jan. Complimentary full breakfast. Check-out 11 am, check-in 3 pm. TV; cable. Victorian mansion built in 1883; Carriage House once a barn (1880s). Totally nonsmoking. Cr cds: MC, V.

D ⊠

★ ★ ★ **VILLAGE INN.** *2695 Old Philadelphia Pike (17505). Phone 717/293-8369; toll-free 800/914-2473; fax 717/768-1117. www.bird-in-hand.com/villageinn.* 11 units, 6 suites, 3 story. Closed early Dec-early Feb. Children over 13 years old only. Complimentary continental breakfast. Check-out noon, check-in 3 pm. TV; cable. Pool privileges. Tennis privileges. Built 1734 as inn on Old Philadelphia Pike. Victorian interior ambience. Cr cds: A, DS, MC, V. **$**

⫽ ⊠ ⊠

Restaurants

★ ★ **AMISH BARN.** *3029 Old Philadelphia Pike (17505). Phone 717/768-8886; fax 717/768-7396. www.amishbarnpa.com.* Pennsylvania Dutch menu. Hours: winter 8 am-7 pm; summer to 9 pm. Closed Jan 1, Dec 25. Dinner $9.95-$16.95. Children's menu. Outdoor seating. Cr cds: A, C, DS, MC, V.

D SC

★ **PLAIN AND FANCY FARM.** *3121 Old Philadelphia Pike (17505). Phone 717/768-4400; fax 717/768-4444. www.plainandfancyfarm.com.* Hours: 11:30 am-8 pm; Sun noon-7 pm. Reservations accepted. Pennsylvania Dutch cuisine. Closed Dec 24, 25. Complete meals: lunch, dinner $15.95-$16.95. Children's menu. Specializes in family-style food. Authentic Amish homestead. Buggy rides available 8 am-dusk. Variety of specialty shops. Family-owned. Totally nonsmoking. Cr cds: A, C, DS, MC, V.

D ⊠

Bloomsburg (E-10)

See also Danville

Settled 1802 **Pop** 12,375 **Elev** 530 ft **Area code** 570 **Zip** 17815

Information Columbia-Montour Visitors Bureau, 121 Papermill Rd; 570/784-8279 or 800/847-4810

Web www.cmtpa.org

Situated on the north bank of the Susquehanna River, Bloomsburg is the county seat of Columbia County. The town was a center of mining, transportation, and industry during the 19th and early 20th centuries. Although manufacturing continues to be the largest employer here, Bloomsburg retains the relaxed atmosphere of earlier days with its lovely scenery and many covered bridges. In nearby Orangeville, 9 miles west on PA 487, Fishing Creek offers trout, bass, and pickerel.

The only incorporated town in the state (all the others are boroughs or cities), Bloomsburg has silk and rayon manufacturers; it also produces architectural aluminum, processed foods, and electronic products. During the Civil War, Union troops came here to crush the "Fishing Creek Confederacy," a group of alleged draft dodgers who were reportedly building fortifications; no fort was found, and the men were released. One of the "Molly Maguire" murder trials was held here. (The Molly Maguires was a miners' society seeking improved conditions through force and violence.)

What to See and Do

Bloomsburg University of Pennsylvania. *400 2nd St (17815). Phone 570/389-4316.* (1839) 6,600 students. On campus are Carver Hall (1867); the Harvey A. Andruss Library (1966); Haas Center for the Arts (1967) with 2,000-seat auditorium and art gallery; McCormick Center for Human Services (1985); Redman Stadium and Nelson Field House. Tours (academic year, Mon-Fri).

Columbia County Historical Society. *410 Main St. 6 miles N on PA 487, in Orangeville. Phone 570/784-1600.* Museum and Edwin M. Barton Library with local history exhibits, pioneer items. (Apr-Oct, Thurs-Sat; closed holidays) **$**

Historic District. *Bounded by West, 5th, 1st, Lake sts (17815). Phone 570/784-7703.* More than 650 structures spanning architectural styles from Georgian to Art Deco. Center of town.

Twin covered bridges. *10 miles N on PA 487.* Believed to be only twin covered bridges in US. More than 20 other covered bridges are in the area.

Special Events

Bloomsburg Fair. *Fairgrounds, W side of town.* Fair held since 1854. Agricultural and industrial exhibits; harness racing. Eight days in late Sept.

Bloomsburg Theatre Ensemble. *226 Center St. Phone 717/784-8181. Alvina Krause Theatre.* Three to four weeks of performances for each of six plays. Main stage Oct-June (special performances rest of year).

Covered Bridge & Arts Festival. *I-80, exit 35.* Tours of covered bridges; apple butter boil; weaving; old-fashioned arts and crafts. Early Oct.

Motels/Motor Lodges

★ **BUDGET HOST PATRIOT INN.** *6305 Columbia Blvd (17815). Phone 570/387-1776; toll-free 800/873-1180; fax 570/387-9611. www.budgethost.com.* 48 rooms. S $42-$48; D $48-$55; each additional $6; under 18 free. Crib free. TV; cable, VCR available (movies). Restaurant adjacent 11 am-9 pm. Bar from 4 pm. Check-out noon. Meeting rooms. Business services available. Health club privileges. Some refrigerators. Cr cds: A, C, D, DS, MC, V.
D ⊗ SC

★ **INN AT BUCKHORN.** *5 Buckhorn Rd (17815). Phone 570/784-5300; toll-free 888/754-6600; fax 570/387-0367. www.pavisnet.com/innatbuckhorn.* 120 rooms, 2 story. S $45-$65; D $50-$70; each additional $5; under 18 free. Pet accepted. Check-out 11 am. TV; cable. Restaurant adjacent 6 am-10 pm. Bar 7-2 am, Sun from 11 am. Cr cds: A, C, D, DS, MC, V.
D ⊗ ⊗

B&B/Small Inns

★ ★ ★ **INN AT TURKEY HILL.** *991 Central Rd (17815). Phone 570/387-1500; fax 570/784-3718. www.innatturkeyhill.com.* 18 rooms, 2 story. D $105-$225. Pet accepted; $15. Complimentary continental breakfast. Check-out noon, check-in 2 pm. TV. In-room modem link. Fireplace in some rooms. Dining room 5-9 pm. Bar. Room service. Airport, bus depot transportation. Old homestead (1839); guest rooms overlook landscaped courtyard; gazebo, lily pond. Cr cds: A, C, D, DS, MC, V.
D ⊗ ⊗ SC

★ ★ **MAGEE'S MAIN STREET INN.** *20 W Main St (17815). Phone 570/784-3200; toll-free 800/331-9815; fax 570/784-5517. www.magees.com.* 8 rooms, 3 story. Pet accepted. Complimentary continental breakfast. Check-out noon. TV. Dining room 7 am-midnight. Bar. Cr cds: A, C, D, DS, MC, V. **$**
D ⊗ ⊗ ⊗ ⊗

Bradford (B-5)

See also Kane, Warren

Settled 1827 **Pop** 9,175 **Elev** 1,442 ft **Area code** 814 **Zip** 16701

Information Bradford Area Chamber of Commerce, 10 Marilyn Horne Way, PO Box 135; 814/368-7115

Web www.bradfordpa.com

When oil was discovered here, the price of land jumped from about six cents to $1,000 an acre; wells appeared on front lawns, in backyards, even in a cemetery. An oil exchange was established in 1877, two years after the first producing well was brought in. Diversified industry now provides the city's economic base. A Ranger District office of the Allegheny National Forest (see WARREN) is located here.

What to See and Do

Bradford Landmark Society. *45 E Corydon St. Phone 814/362-3906.* Headquartered in restored bakery; local history exhibits, period rooms. (Mon, Wed, and Fri; closed holidays) **FREE**

Crook Farm. *On Seaward Ave extension near the Tuna Crossroad. Phone 814/362-3906.* (1848) Original home of Erastus and Betsy Crook; restored to the 1870s period. (May-Sept, Tues-Fri afternoons, also Sat by appointment; closed holidays (See SPECIAL EVENT)

Carpenter Shop. (circa 1870) Reconstruction of original; old hand tools.

Old Barn. (circa 1870) Identical to the original; moved to Crook Farm in 1981 and rebuilt on the site of the original barn.

Old One-Room Schoolhouse #8. (1880) Authentic structure where classes are still held occasionally. **$**

Special Event

Crook Farm Country Fair. *Seaward Ave at Tuna Crossroad. Phone 914 362-3906. Crook Farm.* Arts and crafts, exhibits, entertainment, food. Last weekend in Aug.

Motels/Motor Lodges

★ ★ **DE SOTO HOLIDAY HOUSE.** *515 South Ave (16701). Phone 814/362-4511; fax 814/362-1699.* 70 rooms, 2-3 story. No elevator. S $39-$49; D $47-$53; each additional $4. Check-out noon. TV; cable. Restaurant 7 am-10 pm; Sun to 8 pm. Bar 11-2 am; entertainment. Sauna. Heated pool; whirlpool. Driving range, miniature golf, batting cages. Cr cds: A, C, D, DS, MC, V.
⊗ ⊗

★ ★ **HOWARD JOHNSON.** *100 S Davis St (16701). Phone 814/362-4501; toll-free 800/654-2000; fax 814/362-2709. www.hojo.com.* 120 rooms, 3 story. S $64-$74; D $69-$79; each additional $10; under 12 free. Check-out noon. TV; cable (premium). Restaurant 6:30 am-2 pm, 5-10 pm. Bar 3 pm-1 am. Health club privileges. Pool. Cr cds: A, C, D, DS, JCB, MC, V.
D ⊗ ⊗ SC

B&B/Small Inn

★ ★ ★ **GLENDORN-A LODGE IN THE COUNTRY.** *1000 Glendorn Dr (16701). Phone 814/362-6511; toll-free*

800/843-8568; fax 814/368-9923. www.glendorn.com. This lodge is found tucked away down a mile-and-a-half-long private driveway on 1,280 acres of dense forest, streams and lakes. 4 suites, 6 cabins. Children over 12 years only. Check-out 11 am, check-in 2 pm. TV. Sittings: 9:30 am breakfast, 1 pm lunch, 7:30 pm dinner. Exercise equipment. Game room. Golf privileges. Tennis. Cross-country ski on site. Lawn games. Cr cds: A, MC, V. **$$$$**

Breezewood (H-6)

See also Bedford, Chambersburg

Pop 180 **Elev** 1,356 ft **Area code** 814 **Zip** 15533

Motels/Motor Lodges

★ ★ **BEST WESTERN PLAZA MOTOR LODGE.**
16407 Lincoln Hwy (15533). Phone 814/735-4352; toll-free 800/528-1234; fax 814/735-3036. *www.bestwestern.com.* 89 rooms, 2 story. S $37-$42; D $43-$52; each additional $7. Crib $7. TV; cable (premium). Pool. Restaurant 7 am-10 pm. Check-out 11 am. Meeting room. Cr cds: A, C, D, DS, MC, V.

★ ★ **QUALITY INN.** *16621 Lincoln Hwy (15533).* Phone 814/735-4311; toll-free 800/721-4311; fax 814/735-3433. *www.qualityinn.com.* 50 rooms, 1-2 story. May-Nov: S $43-$76; D $48-$76; each additional $5; family rates; lower rates rest of year. Crib $5. Check-out noon. TV; cable (premium). Coin laundry. Restaurant opposite open 24 hours. Playground. Heated pool, wading pool, lifeguard. Business services. Sundries. Cr cds: A, C, D, DS, ER, JCB, MC, V.

★ **RAMADA INN.** *US Rte 30 and I-70 (15533).* Phone 814/735-4005; toll-free 814/535-4025; fax 814/735-3228. *www.ramada.com.* 125 rooms, 2 story. Apr-Oct: S $57; D $79; under 18 free; lower rates rest of year. Crib available. Pet accepted, some restrictions. TV; cable (premium), VCR available (movies). Indoor pool. Playground. Restaurant 6:30 am-10 pm. Room service. Bar 4 pm-midnight. Check-out noon. Meeting rooms. Business center. In-room modem link. Gift shop. Golf privileges. Exercise equipment. Game room. Some in-room whirlpool. Picnic tables. Cr cds: A, C, D, DS, JCB, MC, V.

Bristol (Bucks County)

See also Philadelphia

Settled 1697 **Pop** 9,923 **Elev** 20 ft **Area code** 215 & 267 **Zip** 19007

Information Bucks County Conference and Visitors Bureau, Inc, 152 Swamp Rd, Doylestown 18901; 215/345-4552 or 800/836-BUCKS

Web www.buckscountycvb.org

Bristol, founded in 1681, was the main thoroughfare from Philadelphia to New York. It has been frequented by famous visitors including Joseph Bonaparte, brother of Napoleon, and General Lafayette. There are homes dating from the 1700s; most of these have been restored.

What to See and Do

Grave of Captain John Green. *St. James Protestant Episcopal Church Burial Ground. Cedar and Walnut sts.* Grave of US Navy captain who piloted the Columbia around the world in 1787-1789 on first such voyage by vessel flying American flag.

Historic Fallsington. *4 Yardley Ave, Fallsington. 5 miles N of PA Tpke, off PA 13.* Phone 215/295-6567. Restored 17th-, 18th-, and 19th-century buildings. Guided tours of 17th-century log house, Burges-Lippincott house, tavern. Also museum store. (See SPECIAL EVENT) (Mid-May-Oct, daily; closed holidays) **$$**

Pennsbury Manor. *5 miles NE at 400 Pennsbury Memorial Rd, off Bordentown Rd.* Phone 215/946-0400. Reconstruction of William Penn's 17th-century country manor; formal and kitchen gardens; livestock. Craft demonstrations; hands-on workshops. (Tues-Sun; closed some holidays) **$$**

Sesame Place. *100 Sesame Rd (19047). Approximately 7 miles N, near Oxford Valley Mall (Langhorne), just N of Philadelphia off I-95 between Philadelphia and Trenton, NJ.* Phone 215/752-7070. Family theme park combines fun with learning. More than 50 outdoor physical play activities develop skills and coordination with kid-powered units. The indoor interactive and science galleries offer games to challenge the mind. Sesame Food Factory: visible kitchen-in-the-round serves wholesome favorites. Mr. Hooper's Emporium: complete shop for all Sesame Street items. Sesame Island area with Caribbean theme; water activities include Big Bird's Rambling River and Sky Splash. Musical revue with Sesame Street characters. (May-Labor Day, daily; after Labor Day-late Oct, weekends only) **$$$$**

Special Event

Fallsington Day. *In Fallsington.* Outdoor fair; restored buildings open; colonial craft demonstrations; entertainment. Second Sat in Oct.

Brookville (D-4)

See also Clarion

Settled 1830 **Pop** 4,230 **Elev** 1,269 ft **Area code** 814 **Zip** 15825

Information Brookville Area Chamber of Commerce, 70 Pickering St; 814/849-8448

What to See and Do

Clear Creek State Park. *8 miles N on PA 36, then 4 miles NE on PA 949.* Contact Park Manager, RD 1, Box 82, Sigel, 15860. Approximately 1,600 acres. Swimming beach, fishing, canoeing; hiking trails, cross-country skiing, picnicking, playing field, camping, cabins (dump station). Nature center; interpretive activities. Standard fees.

Special Event

Western Pennsylvania Laurel Festival. *Phone 814/849-2024.* Third week in June.

Motels/Motor Lodges

★ ★ **DAYS INN.** *US 322 and I-80, exit 13 (15825). Phone 814/849-8001; toll-free 800/329-7466; fax 814/849-9647. www.daysinn.com.* 118 rooms, 3 story. S $40-$60; D $45-$85; each additional $5; under 18 free; higher rates hunting season. Bar 5 pm-midnight; closed Sun. Pet accepted. Check-out noon. TV; cable. Laundry services. Restaurant 6-10 am, 4:30-10 pm; winter from 7 am. Bar 5 pm-midnight; closed Sun. Game room. Heated pool; children's pool, whirlpool, poolside service. Cross-country ski 17 miles. Cr cds: A, C, D, DS, JCB, MC, V.

D 🐾 🏊 ➳ ⛷ SC

★ **HOLIDAY INN EXPRESS.** *235 Allegheny Blvd (15825). Phone 814/849-8381; fax 814/849-8386. www.holiday-inn.com.* 68 rooms, 3 story. S $50-$60; D $57-$67; each additional $7; under 12 free; higher rates hunting season. Crib free. Pet accepted. Complimentary continental breakfast. Check-out noon. TV; cable (premium). Private patios, balconies. Coin laundry. Restaurant adjacent 11 am-11 pm. Meeting room. Business services. Sundries. Cr cds: A, C, D, DS, JCB, MC, V.

D 🐾 🏋 ✈ ⛷

Restaurant

★ ★ **MEETING PLACE.** *209 Main St (15825). Phone 814/849-2557.* Hours: 11 am-8:30 pm, closed Sun, holidays. Breakfast $2-$5, lunch $2.75-$7, dinner $8-$18. Bar. Children's menu. Restored Victorian building (1871); casual dining. Reservations accepted. Cr cds: A, D, DS, MC, V.

D

Bucks County

Bucks County's great natural resources, location, and waterway transportation were known to the Leni-Lenape centuries ago. Dutch explorers, followed by Swedes, English Quakers, and Germans, began to take possession of the area in the 1600s. William Penn established his country estate in this area in the 17th century.

The county's historic importance is highlighted in the central section—it was here that General George Washington crossed the Delaware River with the Continental Army during the Revolutionary War. More recently, artists and writers have settled in and around New Hope, giving rise to the village's fame as an art center. Bucks County's scenic beauty and rich history make it a popular tourist spot.

Following are the places in Bucks County included in this book. For full information on any one of them, see the individual alphabetical listing: Bristol, Doylestown, New Hope, Quakertown, Washington Crossing Historic Park.

Bushkill (E-13)

See also Milford

Pop 900 **Elev** 365 ft **Area code** 570 **Zip** 18324

Information Pocono Mountains Vacation Bureau, 1004 Main St, Stroudsburg 18360; 570/424-6050; for free brochures phone 800/POCONOS

Web www.poconos.org

What to See and Do

Bushkill Falls. *2 miles N off US 209 on local road. Phone 570/588-6682.* Largest series of falls in Pocono Mountains. Main falls have 100-foot drop. Scenic gorge. Fishing, boating; picnicking. Wildlife exhibit of mounted animals and birds of Pennsylvania. (Apr-mid-Nov, daily) **$$$**

Delaware Water Gap. (see) *3 E Main St. Phone 315/386-8133.* **$**

Pocono Indian Museum. *US 209 N. 3 miles S on US 209. Phone 570/588-9338 or 570/588-9164.* Traces history of the Delaware through displays of artifacts, weapons, and tools. Gift shop. (Daily; closed Thanksgiving, Dec 25) **$$**

Butler (E-2)

See also Harmony, Pittsburgh

Settled 1793 **Pop** 15,121 **Elev** 1,077 ft **Area code** 724 **Zip** 16003

Information Butler County Chamber of Commerce, PO Box 1082; 724/283-2222

Web www.butlercountychamber.com

This is a manufacturing city nestled amid rolling hills that were owned by Robert Morris of Philadelphia, financier of the Revolutionary War. The city and county are named for General Richard Butler, who died in the St. Clair Indian Expedition. During the 1930s, the Butler-based American Austin Company—later called American Bantam Company—pioneered the development of small, lightweight cars in America and invented the prototype of the jeep.

What to See and Do

Cooper Cabin. *199 Cooper Rd, in Cabot. Phone 724/283-8116.* (circa 1810) A family homestead on 4 acres with heirlooms and memorabilia; spinning house, spring house, tool shed. Self-guided nature trail and herb garden; live history demonstrations and tours. (Call for hours and events) **$**

Jennings Environmental Education Center. *2951 Prospect Rd (16057). 12 miles N, at junction PA 8, 528, 173. Phone 724/794-6011.* Blazing Star, a relict prairie wildflower, blooms profusely here late July-early Aug. Trails, guided walks, interpretive center; picnicking. (Memorial Day-Labor Day, daily; rest of year, Mon-Fri, some Sun) **FREE**

Moraine State Park. *225 Pleasant Valley Rd (16051). 12 miles NW on US 422. Phone 724/368-8811.* A 3,225-acre lake in a 16,180-acre park. Swimming beaches, fishing, boating (rentals, mooring, launching, marina); hunting, hiking, bicycle trails (rentals), horseback riding, cross-country skiing, snowmobiling, sledding, ice skating, ice fishing, ice boating, picnicking, playground, snack bar, restaurant, cabin rentals. Waterfowl observation area; interpretive programs. Pontoon boat tours. **FREE**

Motels/Motor Lodges

★ **DAYS INN.** *139 Pittsburgh Rd (16001). Phone 724/287-6761; toll-free 800/329-7466; fax 724/287-4307. www.daysinn.com.* 139 rooms, 2 story. S $56-$72; D $62-$77; each additional $6; family rates; golf package plan. Crib free. Pet accepted. TV; cable. Indoor pool; whirlpool, lifeguard. Coffee in rooms. Restaurant 6 am-10 pm. Room service. Bar 3 pm-2 am; Sun 1 pm-midnight; entertainment. Check-out 11 am. Coin laundry. Meeting rooms. Business services available. Valet service. Sundries. Exercise equipment. Game room. Cr cds: A, C, D, DS, MC, V.

★ **MCKEE'S MOTEL.** *930 New Castle Rd (16001). Phone 724/865-2272.* 22 rooms. S $29.68-$33.92; D $41; kitchen units $49; under 5 free; weekly rates. TV; cable. Check-out 11 am. Cr cds: A, DS, MC, V.

Resort

★ ★ **CONLEY RESORT INN.** *740 Pittsburgh Rd (16002). Phone 724/586-7711; toll-free 800/344-7303; fax 724/586-2944. www.conleyresort.com.* 56 rooms, 3 story. No elevator. S $62-$65; D $84-$99; each additional $10; under 18 free; golf plans. Crib free. Check-out 1 pm. TV. Restaurant 7 am-10 pm. Bar 11-2 am; Sun to midnight. Room service. Sauna. Game room, recreation room. Indoor pool; whirlpool, lifeguard. 18-hole golf, greens fee $20-$32, putting green. Tennis. Cross-country ski on site. Meeting rooms. Business services. Sundries. 150-foot indoor water slide. Cr cds: A, DS, MC, V.

B&B/Small Inn

★ ★ ★ **APPLEBUTTER INN.** *666 Centreville Pike (16057). Phone 724/794-1844; toll-free 888/275-3466; fax 724/794-3319. www.pathway.net/applebutterinn.* Built in 1844, this charming inn offers guests a truly delightful stay. Guests are welcomed to relax amongst handsomely appointed guest rooms, including one room boasting an exquisite 1810 four-poster bed complete with a beautiful fish net canopy and antique chest. Make sure to take time to pamper yourself with one of the hot tub, spa, or massage packages. 11 rooms, 2 story. S $59-$79; D $79-$125; each additional $15; higher rates weekends. Adults only. TV. Complimentary full breakfast. Check-out 11 am, check-in 3-8 pm; Fri, Sat 3-10 pm. Sitting room. Massage. Restored brick farmhouse (1844) furnished with antiques; addition 1988. Totally nonsmoking. Cr cds: A, MC, V.

Canadensis

Pop 1,200 **Area code** 570 **Zip** 18325

What to See and Do

Holley Ross Pottery. *S on PA 390, NW on PA 447, on PA 191 N in La Anna. Phone 570/676-3248.* Twenty-minute guided tours with demonstration of pottery making (Mon-Fri). Swinging bridge, park, sawdust trails. (May-mid-Dec, daily) **FREE**

Resort

★ ★ ★ **SKYTOP LODGE.** *1 Skytop (18357). Phone 570/595-7401; toll-free 800/345-7759; fax 570/595-9618. www.skytop.com.* 185 rooms, 40 cottages, 1-4 story. Rates: S, D $395-$650. Gratuity/service charge $30; under 18 free; family, weekend, holiday rates; ski, golf plans; 3-day minimum weekends, holidays; higher rates some holidays; lower rates rest of year. Crib free. Check-out 1 pm, check-in 4 pm. Refrigerators in cottages. Valet services. Grocery, coin laundry 3-5 miles. Dining room. Bar noon-midnight. Room service. Supervised children's activities; ages 4-10. Playground. Exercise room, massage, sauna, steam room. Social director. Sports director. Game room. Recreation room. 2 pools, 1 indoor; wading pool, whirlpool, poolside service, lifeguard. 18-hole golf, pro, greens fee $40, putting green, driving range. Tennis, pro. Downhill, cross-country ski on site. Picnic tables. Lawn games. Bicycle rentals. Boats. Fishing guides, clean and store. Hiking. Sleighing. Tobogganing. Meeting rooms. Business services. Gift shop. On beach. Cr cds: A, C, D, DS, MC, V.

� icons

B&B/Small Inns

★ ★ ★ **BROOKVIEW MANOR INN.** *2960 Rte 447 (18325). Phone 570/595-2451; toll-free 800/585-7974; fax 570/595-5065. www.brookviewmanor.com.* This bed and breakfast offers the traveler an ideal retreat from the workday world. Each room offers a panoramic view of the forest, stream, and mountains. The inn is convenient to many popular Pocono activities, a wide selection of outlet stores, and unique country craft and antiques shops. 10 rooms, 2-3 story. No room phones. Children over 12 years only. Complimentary full breakfast. Check-out noon, check-in 3 pm. TV; cable (premium), VCR available. Totally nonsmoking. Cr cds: A, D, DS, MC, V. **$$**

⚫ icon

★ ★ ★ **CRESCENT LODGE.** *191 Paradise Valley (18326). Phone 570/595-7486; toll-free 800/392-9400; fax 570/595-3452. www.crescentlodge.com.* Nestled in the heart of the Pocono Mountains, guests should be pre-pared to enter a truly elegant country inn, where the welcomes are warm and the ambience is one of pure serenity. Guests will find delight in the charmingly furnished guest rooms, each with its own distinctive flair, with some rooms offering a sunken Jacuzzi as well as private patios and sundecks overlooking the lush and well-maintained grounds. 31 rooms. Mid-June-mid-Sept: S, D $85-$185; each additional $15; suites $172-$275; kitchen cottages $1,000-$1,150/week; EP, MAP, weekly rates; ski plans; lower rates rest of year. Complimentary continental breakfast (except summer). Check-out 11 am, check-in 2 pm. TV; cable (premium), VCR available. Restaurant, bar. Fitness trail. Whirlpool in suites. Tennis. Downhill, cross-country ski 5 miles. Lawn games. Varied accommodations. Same owners for over 40 years. Cr cds: A, D, DS, MC, V.

⚫ icons

★ ★ **PINE KNOB INN.** *RR 447 (18325). Phone 570/595-2532; toll-free 800/426-1460; fax 570/595-6429. www.pineknobinn.com.* 28 rooms. No room phones. Check-out 11 am, check-in 2 pm. TV in library; cable. Outdoor tennis. Downhill, cross-country ski 5 miles. Lawn games. Cr cds: A, DS, MC, V. **$$**

⚫ icons

★ **PUMP HOUSE INN.** *Rte 390 N (18325). Phone 570/595-7501. www.pumphouseinn.com.* 8 rooms, 2 story. Complimentary continental breakfast. Check-out 11 am, check-in 2 pm. Restaurant. Built as stagecoach stop in 1842; furnished in country décor; antiques. Cr cds: C, D, MC, V. **$$**

Restaurant

★ ★ ★ **PUMP HOUSE INN.** *Rte 390 N (18325). Phone 570/595-7501. www.pumphouseinn.com.* Located in a big house in the country—guest rooms are upstairs—the Pump House pleases diners with well prepared American fare and congenial service. There are a variety of specials that change every night. American, French menu. Hours: 5-9 pm; Sun 2:30-8:30 pm. Closed Mon; Dec 25. Lunch, dinner $13.95-$24.95. Bar. Country inn (1842). Cr cds: D, MC, V.

Carbondale (C-12)

See also Hawley, Scranton

Founded 1822 **Pop** 9,804 **Elev** 1,070 ft **Area code** 570 **Zip** 18407

Information Northeast Pennsylvania Convention and Visitors Bureau, 99 Glenmaura National Blvd, Scranton, 18507; 800/229-3526

Web www.visitnepa.org

Carbondale, located in the heart of the northeast Pocono area, has excellent sports facilities. There are 33 lakes within an 8-mile radius and 201 more lakes within 25 miles. One of the first railroad lines in the country was built to haul coal from Carbondale.

What to See and Do

Elk Mountain Ski Center. *NW on PA 106, E on PA 374. Phone 570/679-4400; 800/233-4131 (snow conditions).* At an elevation of 2,693 feet, this is eastern Pennsylvania's highest mountain. Quad, five double chairlifts; patrol, school, rentals; cafeteria, restaurant, bar. Longest run 2 miles; vertical drop 1,000 feet. (Early Dec-late Mar, daily) Half-day rate. **$$$$**

Merli-Sarnoski Park. *Extra 1/2 mile off PA 106. Phone 570/876-1714.* Covers 850 acres of woodlands with 40-acre lake. Swimming beach (lifeguards), fishing (seasonal), boating (launch); hiking trails, picnicking. Winter activities include cross-country skiing, ice skating, ice fishing. (Daily)

Mount Tone Ski Resort. *N via PA 171, E via PA 370 to Lakewood, then S on PA 247 to Lake Como, follow signs. Phone 570/798-2707.* Triple chairlift, T-bar, rope tow, mighty mite; school, rentals; snowmaking; cafeteria; lodge. Vertical drop 450 feet. (Late Dec-mid-Mar) Two mountains, ten trails; also night skiing, cross-country trails. **$$$$**

Carlisle (G-8)

See also Harrisburg

Settled 1720 **Pop** 17,970 **Elev** 478 ft **Area code** 717 **Zip** 17013

Information Greater Area Chamber of Commerce, 212 N Hanover St, PO Box 572; 717/243-4515

Web www.carlislechamber.org

In the historically strategic Cumberland Valley, Carlisle was a vital point for Native American fighting during the Revolutionary and Civil wars.

Carlisle Barracks is one of the oldest military posts in America. Soldiers mounted guard here as early as 1750 to protect the frontier. From here began British campaigns that drove the French from the Ohio Valley and, in 1763, the march to relieve Fort Pitt. In 1794, President Washington reviewed troops assembled to march against the "Whiskey Rebels." Troops went from the Barracks to the Mexican and Civil wars. The famous Carlisle Indian Industrial School, the first nonreservation school, was here until 1918. The Barracks was reopened in 1920 as the Medical Field Service School. It is now the home of the US Army War College.

George Ross, James Wilson, and James Smith, all signers of the Declaration of Independence, lived in Carlisle, as did Molly Pitcher.

What to See and Do

Carlisle Barracks. *22 Ashburn Dr (17013). 1 mile N on US 11. Phone 717/245-3611.* Army War College, senior school in US Army's educational system. Includes the US Army Military History Institute and Hessian Powder Magazine Museum (1777), built by prisoners captured at the Battle of Trenton. The Carlisle Indian Industrial School (1879-1918) was one of the first institutions of higher learning for Native Americans. Also includes the Omar Bradley Museum, containing a collection of personal and military memorabilia of the five-star general. Jim Thorpe and other famous Native American athletes studied here. Military History Institute and the Omar Bradley Museum (Mon-Fri; closed federal holidays). Post/grounds (Daily; closed federal holidays). **FREE**

Cumberland County Historical Society and Hamilton Library Association. *21 N Pitt St. Phone 717/249-7610.* Woodcarvings, furniture, silver, tools, redware, ironware, tall-case clocks, coverlets, paintings by local artisans; mementos of the Carlisle Indian School; special exhibits and programs. Library contains books, tax lists, early photographs, genealogical material. (Tues-Sat, Mon evenings; closed holidays) **FREE**

Dickinson College. *242 W High St (US 11). Phone 717/243-5121.* (1773) 1,900 students. Tenth college chartered in US; President James Buchanan was a graduate. On campus is "Old West" (1804), a building registered as a National Historic Landmark that was designed by Benjamin Henry Latrobe, one of the designers of the Capitol in Washington. Tours of campus. Also here is

> **The Trout Gallery.** *Emil R. Weiss Center for the Arts. Phone 717/245-1711.* Permanent and temporary exhibits. (Sept-mid-June, Tues-Sat) **FREE**

Grave of "Molly Pitcher." *In Old Graveyard, E South St.* (Mary Ludwig Hays McCauley) Soldiers in the Battle of Monmouth (June 1778) gave Molly her nickname because of her devotion to her husband and others who were fighting by bringing them pitchers of water. When her husband was wounded, Molly took his place at a cannon and continued fighting for him.

Huntsdale Fish Hatchery. *195 Lebo Rd (17013). 10 miles SW in Huntsdale. Phone 717/486-3419.* Springs and mountain stream fill tanks and ponds of brown, rainbow, and palomino trout, muskellunge and walleye; visitor center. (Daily) **FREE**

Pine Grove Furnace State Park. *1212 Pine Grove Rd (17234). 10 miles SW on I-81, exit 11, then 8 miles S on PA 233. Phone 717/486-7575.* Standard fees. Park office phone 71. Pre-Revolutionary iron, slate, and brick works were in this area. Approximately 696 acres. Swimming beaches, fishing, boating (rentals, mooring, launching); hunting, hiking, bicycling (rentals), cross-country skiing, ice skating, ice fishing, picnicking, snack bar, store, tent and trailer sites. Visitor center. Lodging available

Special Events

Art Festival and Octoberfest. Oct.

Summerfair. *Downtown Carlisle.* Early July.

Motels/Motor Lodges

★ ★ **APPALACHIAN TRAIL INN.** *1825 Harrisburg Pike (17013). Phone 717/245-2242; toll-free 800/445-6715; fax 717/258-4881.* 200 rooms, 2 story. Apr-Oct: S $42-$52; D $47-$57; each additional $5; suites $85-$125; under 12 free; higher rates car shows; lower rates rest of year. Crib free. Check-out noon. TV; cable (premium). Restaurant 5-2 am. Downhill ski 16 miles. Picnic tables. Business services avialble. Cr cds: A, D, DS, MC, V.

⊡ ⊠

★ ★ **BEST WESTERN CARLISLE.** *1245 Harrisburg Pike (17013). Phone 717/243-5411; toll-free 800/304-1082; fax 717/243-0778. www.bestwestern.com.* 130 rooms, 2 story. S $46.50-$64.50; D $63.50-$77.50; each additional $7; suites $68.50-$140; under 18 free. Crib free. TV; cable (premium), VCR available (movies). Pool; lifeguard. Restaurant 6:30 am-9 pm. Bar 5 pm-1 am. Check-out noon. Meeting rooms. Valet service. Sundries. Health club privileges. Microwaves available. Cr cds: A, C, D, DS, ER, MC, V.

⊡ ⊠ ⊠ SC

★ ★ **CLARION HOTEL.** *1700 Harrisburg Pike (17013). Phone 800/692-7315; fax 717/243-6648. www.clarioncarlisle.com.* 270 rooms. S $62; D $67; each additional $5; suites $110-$173; under 18 free. Crib $10. Pet accepted. TV; cable (premium), VCR available (movies). Indoor pool; whirlpool. Sauna. Restaurant 7 am-9 pm. Room service. Bar 11-2 am. Check-out 11 am. Meeting rooms. Business services available. In-room modem link. Sundries. Gift shop. Tennis. Refrigerators; microwaves available. Cr cds: A, C, D, DS, ER, JCB, MC, V.

⊡ ⊠ ⊠ ⊠ ⊠ SC

★ **DAYS INN.** *101 Alexander Spring Rd (17013). Phone 717/258-4147; toll-free 800/329-7466; fax 717/258-1207. www.daysinn.com.* 130 rooms, 3 story. S $55-$80; D $60-$80; suites $85-$125; each additional $5; under 18 free; higher rates special events. Crib free. TV; cable, VCR available (movies). Pool; lifeguard. Complimentary continental breakfast. Restaurant nearby. Check-out noon. Coin laundry. Meeting room. Business services available.

Sundries. Airport transportation. Exercise equipment. Game room. Some refrigerators. Cr cds: A, C, D, DS, JCB, MC, V.

⊡ ⊠ ⊠ ⊠ SC

★ ★ **HOLIDAY INN.** *1450 Harrisburg Pike (17013). Phone 717/245-2400; toll-free 800/465-4329; fax 717/245-9070. www.holiday-inn.com.* 100 rooms, 2 story. S, D $79; each additional $10; under 18 free; higher rates special events. Crib free. Pet accepted. TV; cable (premium), VCR available. Pool; lifeguard. Restaurant 6:30 am-2 pm, 5-10 pm. Bar 11 am-midnight. Room service. Check-out noon. Coin laundry. Meeting rooms. Business services available. In-room modem link. Valet service. Health club privileges. Cr cds: A, D, DS, JCB, MC, V.

⊡ ⊠ ⊠ ⊠ SC

★ ★ **QUALITY INN.** *1255 Harrisburg Pike (17013). Phone 717/243-6000; fax 717/258-4123. www.qualityinn .com.* 96 rooms, 2 story. S, D $62.99; each additional $5; under 18 free; higher rates special events. Crib free. Pet accepted. Complimentary continental breakfast. Coffee in rooms. Check-out noon. TV; cable (premium). Refrigerators, microwaves available. Valet services, coin laundry. Restaurant adjacent open 24 hours. Bar 5 pm-midnight. Pool, wading pool. Meeting room. Business services. Cr cds: A, C, D, DS, JCB, MC, V.

⊡ ⊠ ⊠ ⊠

★ **SUPER 8.** *1800 Harrisburg Pike (17013). Phone 717/ 249-7000; toll-free 800/800-8000; fax 717/249-9070. www.super8.com.* 112 rooms, 2 story, 16 kitchens S $40-$80; D $45-$90; kitchen units $58; under 12 free; higher rates special events. Crib free. TV; cable. Complimentary coffee in lobby. Restaurant nearby. Check-out 11 am. Coin laundry. Microwaves available. Cr cds: A, D, DS, MC, V.

⊡ ⊠ SC

Resort

★ ★ ★ **ALLENBERRY RESORT INN.** *1559 Boiling Springs Rd (17007). Phone 717/258-3211; toll-free 800/430-5468; fax 717/960-5293. www.allenberry.com.* 69 rooms in lodge, 1 cottage (3-bedroom). S $89; D $109; each additional $15; suites $225; cottage $295; under 17 free; package plans. Crib free. Check-out noon. TV. Dining room 8-10 am, 11 am-2 pm, 5-9 pm, bar 11 am-midnight. Pool, wading pool, whirlpool, lifeguard. Lighted tennis. Airport transportation. Meeting rooms. Business services. On 57 wooded acres, 200-year-old trees; several remodeled limestone buildings date from 1785, 1812. Professional theater. On Yellow Breeches Creek. Cr cds: A, DS, MC, V.

⊡ ⊠ ⊠ ⊠ ⊠

Restaurant

★ ★ ★ **CALIFORNIA CAFE.** *38 W Pomfret St (17013). Phone 717/249-2028; fax 717/249-0330. www.calcaf.com.* French, California menu. 1859 fire station building; French and Florentine artwork in addition to artwork from local gallery. Hours: 11 am-9 pm. Closed Memorial Day weekend, Dec 25. Lunch $4.45-$9.45. Complete meals: dinner $14.95-$23.95. Service bar. Reservations accepted. Cr cds: A, D, DS, MC, V.

D

Chambersburg (H-7)

Settled 1730 **Pop** 17,862 **Elev** 621 ft **Area code** 717 **Zip** 17201

Information Chamber of Commerce, 75 S Second St; 717/264-7101. Information is also available at the Visitors Station, 1235 Lincoln Way E; 717/261-1200

Web www.chambersburg.org

Named for Colonel Benjamin Chambers, a Scottish-Irish pioneer, this is an industrial county seat amid peach and apple orchards. John Brown had his headquarters here. During the Civil War, Confederate cavalry burned down the town, destroying 537 buildings after the citizens refused to pay an indemnity of $100,000.

What to See and Do

Caledonia State Park. *40 Rocky Mountain Rd (17222). 10 miles E on US 30. Phone 717/352-2161.* Confederate General Jubal A. Early came through here during the Civil War and destroyed an iron furnace, which had been producing arms for the Union armies. Approximately 1,100 acres. Swimming pool (fee), fishing; nature and hiking trails, bicycling, 18-hole golf course, cross-country skiing, picnicking, playground, snack bar, tent and trailer sites. Standard fees. (See SPECIAL EVENTS)

Capitol Theatre. *159 S Main St. Phone 717/263-0202.* This 1927 movie house presents performances ranging from classical concerts to big bands; theatrical presentations. Features a 1928 Moller pipe organ. Call for performances and fees.

The Old Jail. *175 E King St. Phone 717/264-6364 or 717/264-1667.* Jail complex (1818) restored and renovated for use as the Kittochtinny Historical Society's Museum and Library. An 1880 cell block houses community cultural activities, art and historical exhibits; other events. Also on grounds are Colonial, Fragrance, and Japanese gardens;

19th-century barn; agricultural museum. Cultural programs (May-Oct). Tours (May-Nov, Thurs-Sat). **FREE**

Special Events

ChambersFest. *75 S 2nd St. Emil R. Weiss Center for the Arts. Caledonia State Park. Phone 717/264-7101.* Civil War festival with crafts, food, reenactments, parade of pets. July.

Franklin County Fair. *5995 Warm Springs Rd. Chambersburg Rod and Gun Club Farm. Phone 717/369-4100.* Arts and crafts displays, needlework, home and dairy products, state turkey-calling contest, tractor pull, agricultural and livestock exhibits, entertainment. Third full week in Aug.

Totem Pole Playhouse. *9555 Golf Course Rd. Phone 717/352-2164. Caledonia State Park.* Resident professional theater company performs dramas, comedies, and musicals in 453-seat proscenium theater. Tues-Sun evenings; matinees Wed, Sat-Sun. June-Aug.

Motels/Motor Lodges

★ **DAYS INN.** *30 Falling Spring Rd (17201). Phone 717/263-1288; fax 717/263-6514. www.daysinn.com.* 107 rooms, 3 story. Apr-Oct: S $46-$60; D $51-$65; each additional $7; suites $70-$85; under 17 free; lower rates rest of year. Crib free. Pet accepted. Complimentary continental breakfast. Check-out 11 am. TV; cable (premium). Restaurant adjacent 6 am-11 pm. Downhill ski 15 miles. Business services available. Cr cds: A, C, D, DS, JCB, MC, V.

D

★ **HAMPTON INN.** *955 Lesher Rd (17201). Phone 717/261-9185; toll-free 800/426-7866; fax 717/261-1984. www.hamptoninn.com.* 124 rooms, 3 story. May-Oct: S, D $64-$72; under 18 free; higher rates special events; lower rates rest of year. Crib free. TV; cable (premium). Complimentary continental breakfast. Coffee in rooms. Restaurant adjacent 6 am-11 pm. Check-out noon. Meeting rooms. Business services available. In-room modem link. Sundries. Exercise equipment. Refrigerators. Cr cds: A, C, D, DS, MC, V.

D SC

★ ★ **QUALITY INN.** *1095 Wayne Ave (17201). Phone 717/263-3400; toll-free 800/465-4329; fax 717/263-8386. www.qualityinn.com.* 139 rooms, 2 story. Apr-Oct: S $59; D $66; each additional $7; under 19 free; weekend rates; golf plan; lower rates rest of year. Crib free. Pet accepted, some restrictions. Check-out noon. TV; cable, VCR available. Some in-room modem links. Valet services. Restaurant 6 am-2 pm, 5-10 pm. Bar. Room service.

Health club privileges. Pool, poolside service, lifeguard. 18-hole golf privileges. Meeting rooms. Business services. Sundries. Cr cds: A, C, D, DS, JCB, MC, V.

[D] [icons] SC

★ ★ **TRAVELODGE.** *565 Lincoln Way E (17201). Phone 717/264-4187; fax 717/264-2446. www.travelodge .com.* 52 rooms, 3 story. S $39-$49; D $45-$57; each additional $7; under 18 free. Pet accepted, some restrictions. Check-out noon. TV; cable (premium). Restaurant 6 am-2 pm, 4:30-9:30 pm. Bar 11 am-2 pm, 4:30-9:30 pm. Room service. Health club privileges. Cr cds: A, C, D, DS, MC, V.

[D] [icons]

B&B/Small Inns

★ ★ ★ **MERCERSBURG INN.** *405 S Main St (17236). Phone 717/328-5231; fax 717/328-3403. www.mercersburginn.com.* Located between the civil war battlefield and other historic sites is this 15-room country inn. Golf courses, tennis facilities, skiing, fly fishing, mountain biking and hiking trails are all located within a short distance. 15 rooms, 3 story. D $135-$275; each additional $25. Complimentary full breakfast. Check-out 11 am, check-in 3 pm. TV. Some fireplaces. Restaurant. Room service. Game room. Totally nonsmoking. Cr cds: DS, MC, V.

[icon]

★ ★ **PENN NATIONAL INN AND GOLF CLUB.** *3809 Anthony Hwy (17237). Phone 717/352-2400; toll-free 800/231-0080; fax 717/352-3926. www.penngolf.com.* 48 rooms, 4 in manor house, 2 story. Mid-Apr-Oct: S $80-$100; D $90-$110; each additional $10-$15; under 18 free; golf package plans; monthly rates; lower rates rest of year. Crib free. Pet accepted, some restrictions. Check-out 11 am. Check-in 2 pm. TV; cable. Refrigerators; microwaves available. Coffee in rooms. Restaurant (Apr-Oct) 7 am-7 pm. Playground. Heated pool. Two 18-hole championship golf courses, greens fee $30-$70, putting green, driving range. Tennis. Business services available. Georgian-style manor house built 1847, additions built 1989 and 2000. Cr cds: A, DS, MC, V.

[D] [icons] SC

Restaurant

★ ★ **COPPER KETTLE.** *1049 Lincoln Way E (US 30) (17201). Phone 717/264-3109.* Hours: 5-9:30 pm; Fri, Sat to 10 pm. Closed Sun; major holidays. Reservations accepted; required Fri, Sat. Bar to midnight. Dinner $8-$21.50. Children's menu. Specializes in seafood, steak, prime rib. Early American décor; antiques. Cr cds: A, D, DS, MC, V.

[D]

Chester (H-13)

See also Kennett Square, King of Prussia, Media, Philadelphia, West Chester

Settled 1643 **Pop** 41,856 **Area code** 484, 610

Information Delaware County Convention & Tourist Bureau, 200 E Estate St, Suite 100, Media 19063; 610/565-3679 or 800/343-3983

The oldest settlement in the state, Chester was established by the Swedish Trading Company as Upland. William Penn came to Upland in 1682 to begin colonization of the land granted to him by King Charles II. He renamed the settlement in honor of Chester, a Quaker center in Cheshire, England. The first Assembly here adopted Penn's Framework of Government, enacted the first laws, and organized the county of Chester—from which Delaware County broke off in 1789. On the Delaware River, 15 miles southwest of Philadelphia, Chester is a busy port and home of shipyards where every type of vessel has been built for the navy and merchant marine.

What to See and Do

Caleb Pusey Home, Landingford Plantation. *15 Race St, in Upland. Phone 610/874-5665.* (1683) Built for manager and agent of Penn's mill; only remaining house in state visited by William Penn. Period furniture. Also on 27 acres of original plantation are a log house (1790), stone schoolhouse-museum (1849), and herb garden. (May-Sept, Sat and Sun afternoons; also by appointment; closed holidays) **FREE**

Morton Homestead. *100 Lincoln Ave in Prospect Park, 4 miles NE on US 13, then SW on PA 420. Phone 610/583-7221.* (circa 1655) Two-part log house built by ancestors of John Morton, signer of Declaration of Independence. Contemporary outdoor exhibits on Pennsylvania's Swedish Period, log-house construction, Morton family. (Wed-Sat) **FREE**

Penn Memorial Landing Stone. *Front and Penn sts.* Marks spot where William Penn first landed Oct 28, 1682.

Swarthmore College. *500 College Ave (19081). 4 miles N on PA 320, in Swarthmore. Phone 610/328-8000.* (1864) 1,320 students. Coeducational; on wooded 330-acre campus are Friends Historical Library and Peace Collection, an art gallery, concert hall, performing arts center, observatory, terraced grass amphitheater, Friends Meeting House, Scott Arboretum, a collection of trees, shrubs, and herbaceous plants throughout campus. Symposia, exhibits, music, and dance programs are open to the public.

Widener University. *3800 Vartan Rd (17110). 14th and Walnut sts. Phone 610/499-4000.* (1821) 7,000 students. On campus are Old Main, a national historic landmark, and the University Art Museum, with a permanent collection of 19th- and 20th-century American Impressionist and European academic art as well as contemporary exhibits (Sept-May, Tues-Sat; June and Aug, Mon-Thurs; closed July). Also here is Wolfgram Memorial Library. Campus tours.

Clarion (D-4)

Founded 1839 **Pop** 8,491 **Elev** 1,491 ft **Area code** 814
Zip 16214

Information Clarion Area Chamber of Business and Industry, 41 S Fifth Ave; 814/226-9161

Web www.clarionpa.com

Once the forests were so thick and tall here that, according to tradition, the wind in the treetops sounded like a distant clarion. That's how the town, county, and river got their names. Today many campers and sports and outdoors enthusiasts enjoy the beauty and recreation that the Clarion area offers.

What to See and Do

Clarion County Historical Society. *18 Grant St. Phone 814/226-4450.* Museum housed in mid-19th century Sutton-Ditz house. Contains exhibits on county industry and business; Victorian bedroom and parlor; genealogical and historical library (researchers may call ahead for appointment other than regular hours); changing exhibits. (Apr-Dec, Tues, Thurs, and Fri afternoons; closed holidays) **FREE**

Cook Forest State Park. *11 miles NE on Clarion to Cook Forest Rd, then 3 miles S on PA 36. Phone 814/744-8407.* Approximately 6,700 acres. Swimming pool (fee), fishing; hunting, hiking, bicycling, horseback riding, cross-country skiing (rentals), snowmobiling, sledding, ice skating, picnicking, tent and trailer sites, cabins (rentals). Nature and historical center. Standard fees.

Tionesta Reservoir. *5 miles NW on US 322, then 20 miles NW on PA 66, in Allegheny National Forest.* (see WARREN)

Special Events

Autumn Leaf Festival. Parade, carnival, autorama, scholarship pageants, concerts, flea market, craft shows. Late Sept-early Oct.

Spring Fling. Concerts, food concessions, games, entertainment. Early May.

Motels/Motor Lodges

★ ★ **DAYS INN.** *24 United Dr (16214). Phone 814/226-8682; fax 814/226-8372. www.daysinn.com.* 150 rooms, 2 story. S $46-$56; D $51-$61; each additional $5; under 18 free; tennis, golf, ski plans; higher rates: Autumn Leaf Festival, hunting season. Pet accepted. Complimentary continental breakfast. Check-out noon. TV; cable (premium). Restaurant 6 am-2 pm, 5-10 pm. Bar 5 pm-2 am; entertainment. Room service. Health club privileges. Golf privileges. Cr cds: A, C, D, DS, JCB, MC, V.

D 🐾 🏋️ 🎿 🏊 🏊

★ ★ **HOLIDAY INN.** *45 Holiday Inn Dr (16214). Phone 814/226-8850; toll-free 800/596-1313; fax 814/226-9055. www.holiday-inn.com.* 122 rooms, 2 story. S, D $69-$94; suites $149; under 20 free. Crib free. Pet accepted. Check-out noon. TV; cable (premium), VCR available (movies). In-room modem link. Indoor balconies. Coffee in rooms. Restaurant 6:30 am-10 pm. Bar 4 pm-1 am. Room service. Sauna. Game room. Indoor pool, lifeguard. 18-hole golf privileges, greens fee $14-$28, putting green. Airport transportation. Meeting rooms. Business services. Cr cds: A, D, DS, JCB, MC, V.

D 🐾 🏋️ 🏊 🏊

★ **SUPER 8.** *I-80 and Rte 68 (16214). Phone 814/226-4550; toll-free 800/800-8000; fax 814/227-2337. www.super8.com.* 99 rooms, 9 kitchens S, D $45-$90; each additional $5; under 18 free; weekly, monthly rates (winter). Crib free. Pet accepted. TV; cable (premium), VCR available (movies). Pool. Complimentary continental breakfast. Coffee in rooms. Restaurant adjacent open 24 hours. Check-out noon. Business services available. In-room modem link. Cr cds: A, C, D, DS, MC, V.

D 🐾 🏊 🏊 **SC**

Clearfield (Clearfield County) (E-6)

Settled 1805 **Pop** 6,631 **Elev** 1,109 ft **Area code** 814
Zip 16830

Information Clearfield Chamber of Commerce, 125 E Market St, PO Box 250; 814/765-7567

The old and important Native American town of Chinklacamoose occupied this site until it was burned in 1757. Coal and clay mining and more than 20 diversified plants producing school supplies, firebrick, fur products, precision instruments, electronic products, and sportswear now occupy what used to be cleared fields. Easy access to other parts of the state and rich river bottom land led to the establishment of the county seat here.

What to See and Do

State Parks.

Parker Dam. *14 miles NW on PA 153, 6 miles off I-80 exit 18, then 2 miles E on unnumbered road. Phone 814/765-0630.* Approximately 950 acres in Moshannon State Forest. Swimming beach, fishing, boating (launch, rentals); hiking, cross-country skiing, snowmobiling, sledding, ice skating, ice fishing, snack bar, tent and trailer sites (electric hookups), cabins. Nature center. Standard fees.

S. B. Elliott. *9 miles N, off PA 153, just N of I-80 exit 18. Phone 814/765-7271 or 814/765-0630.* Approximately 300 acres in the heart of the Moshannon State Forest; entirely wooded; display of mountain laurel in season. Fishing in small mountain streams surrounding the park. Hiking, snowmobile trails, tent and trailer sites, cabins. Standard fees.

Special Events

Central Counties Concerned Sportsmen Annual Show. *Mill Rd and Turnpike Ave. Clearfield County Fairgrounds. Phone 814/765-9495.* Fri-Sun mid-Mar.

Clearfield County Fair. *Mill Rd and Turnpike Ave. Clearfield County Fairgrounds. Phone 814/765-4629.* Late July-early Aug.

Special Events

High Country Arts & Craft Fair. *S. B. Elliott State Park. Phone 814/765-9804.* Sun after July 4.

Laurel Tour. Late June-early July.

Motel/Motor Lodge

★ **DAYS INN.** *PA 879 and I-80 (16830). Phone 814/765-5381; fax 814/765-7885. www.daysinn.com.* 119 rooms, 2 story. S $40-$60; D $46-$80; each additional $6; under 18 free; higher rates special events. Crib free. Pet accepted. Complimentary continental breakfast. Check-out noon. TV; VCR available (movies). In-room modem link. Some refrigerators. Exercise equipment. Pool, lifeguard. Meeting rooms. Business services. Cr cds: A, D, DS, MC, V.

Conneaut Lake (C-2)

See also Edinboro, Meadville

Pop 708 **Elev** 1,100 ft **Area code** 814 **Zip** 16316

Information Crawford County Convention & Visitors Bureau, 211 Chestnut St, Meadville 16335; 814/333-1258 or 800/332-2338

Web www.visitcrawford.org

Located on the largest natural lake in Pennsylvania (929 acres), this resort town has swimming, boating, and excellent fishing for perch, muskellunge, walleye, bass, and crappie.

What to See and Do

Conneaut Cellars Winery. *12005 Conneaut Lake Rd. Phone 814/382-3999.* Tours and tastings. (Daily) **FREE**

Pymatuning Spillway. *2660 Williamsfield Rd. NW via US 6 on N end of reservoir. Phone 724/932-3141.* Part of Pymatuning State Park. When fish are fed bread, they flock so thickly that ducks walk on them. **FREE**

Pymatuning State Park. *2660 Williamsfield Rd. SW via US 322, 1 mile W of Jamestown. Phone 724/932-3141.* Approximately 21,100 acres with 17-mile lake. Swimming beach, fishing, boating (rentals, mooring, launching, marina); hunting, hiking, cross-country skiing, snowmobiling, sledding, ice skating, picnicking, playground, tent and trailer areas along shore, cabins. Waterfowl museum and refuge; fish hatchery. Standard fees.

Wildlife Learning Center. *12590 Hartstown Rd (16424). 9 miles W on US 285, then N on Hartstown-Linesville Rd. Phone 814/683-5545.* Part of Pennsylvania Game Commission; birds and animals indigenous to Pymatuning Reservoir area; bald eagle's nest visible from museum. Educational and interpretive programs. (Apr-mid Oct, Wed-Sun) **FREE**

Connellsville (H-3)

See also New Stanton, Uniontown

Pop 9,146 **Elev** 885 ft **Area code** 724 **Zip** 15425

Information Greater Connellsville Chamber of Commerce, 923 W Crawford Ave; 724/628-5500

Located in an area visited by George Washington and where he owned land, the region has many references to him in place names. The restored Crawford Cabin near the river was the home of Colonel William Crawford, surveyor of these properties and Washington's surveying pupil.

Northwest of town in Perryopolis are many historic restorations. The town square is named for Washington, who some believe planned the design of the town.

What to See and Do

☆ **Fallingwater (Kaufmann Conservation on Bear Run).** *8 miles E on PA 711, then 8 miles S on PA 381, near Mill Run. Phone 724/329-8501.* One of the most famous structures of the 20th century, Fallingwater, designed by Frank Lloyd Wright in 1936, is cantilevered on three levels over a waterfall; interior features Wright-designed furniture, textiles, and lighting, as well as sculpture by modern masters; extensive grounds are heavily wooded and planted with rhododendron, which blooms in early July. Visitor center with self-guided orientation program; concession; gift shop. Guided tours (Mid-Mar-Nov, Tues-Sun; winter, Sat-Sun). No children under six; child-care center. No pets. Reservations required.

Linden Hall. *4 miles S on PA 201, then 1 mile N on PA 819, left on River Rd in Dawson. Phone 724/529-7543, 724/529-2882 or 412/461-2424.* (1913) Conference and convention center in mountaintop mansion, situated in picturesque Laurel Highlands. Swimming, fishing; golf, tennis, walking trail. Guided tours of mansion (Mar-Dec, Mon-Fri; weekends by appointment). **$$$**

Motel/Motor Lodge

★ **MELODY MOTOR LODGE.** *1607 Morrell Ave (15425). Phone 724/628-9600.* 46 rooms. S, D $34-$47; higher rates Labor Day weekend. Crib $5. Pet accepted, some restrictions. TV; cable. Restaurant adjacent 6 am-10 pm. Check-out 11 am. Picnic tables. Cr cds: A, DS, MC, V.

B&B/Small Inn

★ ★ **NEWMYER HOUSE.** *507 S Pittsburgh St (15425). Phone 724/626-0141.* 4 rooms, 1 with shower only, 3 story. No room phones. S, D $125; each additional $10; June-Labor Day weekends (2-day minimum). Children over 12 years only. TV in common room; cable, VCR available (movies). Complimentary full breakfast. Check-out 11 am, check-in 3 pm. Downhill/cross-country ski 20 miles. Many fireplaces. Restored Queen Anne-style mansion built in 1892; antiques. Cr cds: MC, V.

Cornwall (G-10)

See also Ephrata, Hershey, Lancaster, Lebanon, Manheim

Settled 1732 **Pop** 3,486 **Elev** 680 ft **Area code** 717 **Zip** 17016

Information Pennsylvania Rainbow Region Vacation Bureau, 625 Quentin Rd, PO Box 329, Lebanon 17042; 717/272-8555

The Cornwall Ore Banks were a major source of magnetic iron ore for nearly 250 years.

What to See and Do

Cornwall Iron Furnace. *Rexmont Rd at Boyd St. Phone 717/272-9711.* In operation 1742-1883. Open pit mine;

19th-century Miners Village still occupied. Furnace building houses "great wheel" and 19th-century steam engine. Visitor center, exhibits, book store. (Tues-Sun; closed Jan 1, Thanksgiving, Dec 25) **$$**

Historic Schaefferstown. *6 miles SE of Lebanon at junction PA 419, 501, 897. Phone 717/949-2244.* An 18th-century farm established by Swiss-German settlers. Village square with authentic log and stone and half-timber buildings; site of first waterworks in US (1758), still in operation. Schaeffer Farm Museum has Swiss Bank House and Barn (1737); early farm tools; colonial farm garden. The museum north of the square has antiques and artifacts of settlers. (See SPECIAL EVENT) House and museum (open during festivals; also June-Sept, by appointment). **$$**

Special Event

Historic Schaefferstown Events. Events during the year include Cherry Fair, fourth Sat in June; Folk Festival, mid-July; Harvest Fair & Horse Plowing Contest, second weekend in Sept.

Danville (E-10)

See also Bloomsburg, Lewisburg

Pop 4,897 **Elev** 490 ft **Area code** 570 **Zip** 17821

Information Danville Area Chamber of Commerce, 206 Walnut St; 570/275-5200

Web www.danvillepa.org

What to See and Do

Joseph Priestley House. *SW via US 11 in Northumberland at 472 Priestley Ave. Phone 570/473-9474.* (1798) American house of the 18th-century Englishman and Unitarian theologian who, in 1774, isolated the element oxygen. (Tues-Sat; closed most major holidays) **$$**

PP & L Montour Preserve. *700 Preserve Rd (17821). From I-80 exit 33, then PA 54 W to Washingtonville, and NE on local roads. Phone 570/437-3131.* Fishing, boating (no gasoline motors) on 165-acre Lake Chillisquaque. Hiking and nature trails, picnicking. Birds of prey exhibit in visitor center; scheduled programs (Daily, fee for some). **FREE**

Motel/Motor Lodge

★ **QUALITY INN.** *15 Valley West Rd (17821). Phone 570/275-5100; fax 570/275-1886. www.qualityinn.com.* 77 rooms, 2 story. Apr-Oct: S $45-$55; D $50-$65; each additional $5; under 18 free; lower rates rest of year. Check-out noon. TV; cable. In-room modem link. Laundry services. Restaurant adjacent open 24 hours. Game room. Pool. Cr cds: A, C, D, DS, JCB, MC, V.

B&B/Small Inn

★ ★ ★ **PINE BARN INN.** *1 Pine Barn Pl (17821). Phone 570/275-2071; toll-free 800/627-2276; fax 570/275-3248. www.pinebarninn.com.* This quiet inn is only a 20-minute drive from downtown and the lake. Each room features a full bath, some with Jacuzzi tubs. 65 rooms, 1-2 story. D $49-$100; each additional $2; under 16 free. Check-out 1 pm. TV. Restaurant, bar 11 am-midnight, Sun 1-8 pm. Room service. Geisinger Medical Center adjacent. Cr cds: A, C, D, DS, MC, V.

D ⊠

Restaurants

★ **OLD HARDWARE RESTAURANT.** *336 Mill St (17821). Phone 570/275-6615; fax 570/275-4210.* American menu. Closed major holidays. Lunch, dinner, Sun brunch. Children's menu. Casual attire. **$$**

D

★ ★ **PINE BARN INN.** *1 Pine Barn Pl (17821). Phone 570/275-2071; fax 570/275-3248. www.pinebarninn.com.* Hours: 7 am-10 pm; Sun 8 am-8 pm; Sun brunch 11 am-2 pm. Closed major holidays. Reservations accepted. Bar 11 am-midnight; Sun 1-8 pm. Breakfast $3.50-$6.50, lunch $4.50-$9.50, dinner $12-$26. Sun brunch $5-$13. Children's menu. Specializes in New England seafood, steak. Salad bar. Outdoor dining. Converted 19th-century barn. Fireplace. Family-owned. Cr cds: A, D, DS, MC, V.

D

Delaware Water Gap

See also Milford, Pocono Mountains, Stroudsburg

It is difficult to believe that the quiet Delaware River could carve a path through the Kittatinny Mountains, which are nearly 1/4 of a mile high at this point. Conflicting geological theories account for this natural phenomenon, which is part of a national recreation area. The prevailing theory is that the mountains were formed after the advent of the river, rising up from the earth so slowly that the course of the Delaware was never altered.

Despite the speculation about the origin of the gap, there is no doubt about the area's recreational value. A relatively unspoiled area along the river boundary between Pennsylvania and New Jersey, stretching approximately 35 miles from Matamoras to an area just south of I-80, the site of the Delaware Water Gap is managed by the National Park Service.

Trails and overlooks (year-round) offer scenic views. Also here are canoeing and boating, hunting and fishing; camp-ing is nearby at the Dingmans Campground within the recreation area. Swimming and picnicking at Smithfield and Milford beaches. Dingmans Falls and Silver Thread Falls, two of the highest waterfalls in the Poconos, are near here (see MILFORD). Several 19th-century buildings are in the area, including Millbrook Village (several buildings open May-Oct) and Peters Valley (see BRANCHVILLE, NJ). The visitor center is located off I-80 in New Jersey, at Kittatinny Point (Apr-Nov, daily; rest of year, Sat and Sun only; closed Jan 1, Dec 25), phone 908/496-4458 or 717/588-2451. Park headquarters are in Bushkill, PA.

Denver/Adamstown (G-11)

See also Ephrata, Lancaster, Reading

Pop 3,332 **Elev** Denver 380 ft; Adamstown 500 ft **Area code** 717 **Zip** Denver 17517; Adamstown 19501

Information Pennsylvania Dutch Convention and Visitors Bureau, 501 Greenfield Rd, Lancaster 17601; 717/299-8901 or 800/PADUTCH

Web www.800padutch.com

Located near a Pennsylvania Turnpike exit, Denver and Adamstown are in the center of an active antique marketing area, which preserves its Pennsylvania German heritage.

What to See and Do

Stoudt's Black Angus. *Along PA 272 from PA Tpke exit 21 to just beyond Adamstown. Phone 717/484-4385.* More than 350 dealers display quality antiques for sale. (Sun)

Special Event

Bavarian Summer Fest. *SW via PA 272 in Adamstown at Black Angus Bier Garten. Phone 717/484-4385.* Oompah bands, schuhplattler dance groups; Oktoberfest atmosphere. Includes special events, German folklore, German food, displays, shops. (weekends). Fri-Sun, early Aug-Labor Day; Sun only Oct.

Motels/Motor Lodges

★ ★ ★ **BLACK HORSE LODGE & SUITES.** *2180 N Reading Rd (17517). Phone 717/336-7563; toll-free 800/610-3805; fax 717/336-1110. www.blackhorselodge.com.* Located on 10 acres of land, this lodge comprises three buildings, all found next to the outdoor pool. The property offers large suites with the living and bedroom areas separated by French doors, a king size bed and marble bathroom. 74 rooms, 2 story. Mid-Apr-mid-Nov: S $59-$129; D $69-$139; under 13 free; suites $100-$250; weekly, monthly rates; golf plans; lower rates rest of year. Crib free. Pet accepted, some restrictions. Complimentary full breakfast, coffee in rooms. Check-out noon. TV; cable. Private patios, balconies. Many refrigerators; some bathroom phones; microwaves available. Coin laundry. Restaurant from 4 pm; Sun from 11 am. Bar to 11 pm. Pool. Golf privileges. Picnic tables. Business services. Cr cds: A, C, D, DS, MC, V.

★ ★ **HOLIDAY INN.** *1 Denver Rd (17517). Phone 717/336-7541; toll-free 800/437-5711; fax 717/336-0515. www.holiday-inn.com.* 110 rooms, 2 story. June-Oct: S, D $89; each additional $8; under 18 free; higher rates special events; lower rates rest of year. Crib free. TV; cable (premium), VCR available (movies). Pool; poolside service, lifeguard. Restaurant 6:30 am-2 pm, 5-10 pm. Bar 5-10 pm. Room service. Check-out noon. Coin laundry. Meeting rooms. Business services available. In-room modem link. Valet service. Golf privileges. Cr cds: A, C, D, DS, JCB, MC, V.

B&B/Small Inn

★ ★ ★ **INNS OF ADAMSTOWN.** *62 W Main St (19501). Phone 717/484-0800; toll-free 800/594-4808; fax 717/484-1384. www.adamstown.com.* 4 rooms, 2 story. S $71-$139; D $79-$149; weekends (2-day minimum). Children over 12 years only. Complimentary continental breakfast. Check-out 10 am, check-in 3-6 pm. TV; cable. Fireplaces. Health club privileges. Concierge service. Built in 1925; Victorian décor; antiques, family heirlooms. Totally nonsmoking. Cr cds: A, MC, V.

Restaurant

★ ★ ★ **BLACK HORSE.** *2180 N Reading Rd (17517). Phone 717/336-6555; fax 717/336-1110. www.blackhorse lodge.com.* This restaurant is located in the heart of Pennsylvania Dutch country. The adjacent tavern features over 100 microbrews and imported beers, 350 different liquers, and 30 types of premium cigars. Specializes in certified Angus beef, fresh seafood, gourmet desserts. Hours: 5-10 pm; Sun 11:30 am-9 pm. Closed Dec 25. Dinner $14-$42. Bar 4-11 pm; Sun 11 am-10 pm. Children's menu. Casual yet elegant décor with stained-glass windows, antique chandeliers, artwork. Reservations accepted. Cr cds: A, C, D, DS, MC, V.

Donegal (H-4)

See also Connellsville, Greensburg, Ligonier, Somerset

Pop 165 **Elev** 1,814 ft **Area code** 724 **Zip** 15628

What to See and Do

Seven Springs Mountain Resort Ski Area. *12 miles SE of PA Tpke exit 9 on Champion-Trent Rd. Phone 800/452-2223.* Three quad, five triple chairlifts; two rope tows, six-passenger high-speed chair; patrol, school, rentals; snowmaking; cafeteria, restaurant, bar; lodge. Longest run 1 1/4 miles; vertical drop 750 feet. Night skiing. (Dec-Mar, daily) Alpine slide (May-Sept, daily). Hotel and conference center; summer activities include 18-hole golf, tennis, rope course, horseback riding, swimming. **$$$$**

Motel/Motor Lodge

★ **DAYS INN.** *Rte 31 (15628). Phone 724/593-7536; toll-free 800/329-7466; fax 724/593-6165. www.daysinn.com.* 50 rooms, 20 with shower only. S, D $59-$72; each additional $6; under 12 free; higher rates special events. TV; cable (premium). Heated pool. Complimentary continental breakfast. Restaurant nearby. Check-out 11 am. Downhill/cross-country ski 9 miles. Lawn games. Picnic tables. Cr cds: A, MC, V.

Resort

★ ★ ★ **SEVEN SPRINGS MOUNTAIN RESORT.** *777 Waterwheel Dr, Champion (15622). Phone 814/352-7777; toll-free 800/452-2223; fax 814/352-7911. www.7springs.com.* With plenty of accommodations and more activities then one could imagine, this is the perfect stop for vacationers. During the winter months this is an active ski resort, while summer time brings golfer, hikers, and mountain bikers. 385 rooms in 10-story lodge; 20 kitchen chalets, cabins, 1-4 bedroom, 2 story. Lodge: S, D $155; each additional $50; under 17 free; suites $420; kitchen chalets $525; package plans; cabins for 6-25, $520-$895/week; also daily rates (2-day minimum); weekend rates. Crib free. Maid service available in chalets, cabins $5/bed. Check-out noon, check-in 5 pm. TV; VCR available. Many private patios, balconies. Coin laundry. Dining room 7 am-10 pm (see also HELEN'S). Snack bar. Bar 11-2 am. Dancing, entertainment. Free supervised children's activities. Playground. Exercise equipment, sauna, steam room. Sports director. Social director. Recreation room. Heated indoor/outdoor pools (open to public), wading pool, poolside service, lifeguard. Miniature golf. Greens fee $65.90, pro, putting green, driving range. Tennis. Downhill ski on site. Hay rides. Mountain bikes available. Indoor roller skating. Bowling. Beauty shop. Airport transportation. Business services, convention facilities. Outdoor games. Cr cds: DS, MC, V.

Restaurants

★ ★ ★ **HELEN'S.** *777 Waterwheel Dr, Champion (15622). Phone 814/352-7777. www.7springs.com.* The formal service, complete with tableside carving and preparations, is a surprise considering the rural setting. Though the menu changes with the seasons, it leans towards classics. Hours: 6-10 pm; also lunch during ski season. Reservations required. Continental menu. Bar. A la carte entrées: dinner $19-$30. Totally nonsmoking. Cr cds: DS, MC, V.

★ ★ ★ **NINO BARSOTTI'S.** *PA 31. Phone 724/547-2900.* American, Italian menu. Specializes in fresh seafood, steak. Salad bar. Own desserts. Own pasta. Hours: 11 am-3 pm, 5-10 pm; Sat to 11 pm; Sun to 9 pm. Sun brunch 11:30 am-2 pm. Closed Mon; holidays. Lunch $4.95-$9.45, dinner $7.45-$23.45. Sun brunch $7.95. Bar. Salad bar. Family-owned. Children's menu. Reservations accepted Fri, Sat. Valet parking. Cr cds: A, D, DS, MC, V.

Downingtown (H-12)

See also King of Prussia, West Chester

Settled 1702 **Pop** 7,589 **Elev** 244 ft **Area code** 484 and 610 **Zip** 19335

Information Chester County, Exton, 19341; 610/280-6145 or 800/228-9933

Web www.brandywinevalley.com

Settled by emigrants from Birmingham, England, Downingtown honors Thomas Downing, who erected a log cabin here in 1702. The borough was first called Milltown, after the mill built here by Roger Hunt in 1765. The town, with its many historically interesting homes, retains much of its colonial charm. Jacob Eichholtz, a leading early American portrait artist, was born here.

What to See and Do

Hibernia County Park. *1 Park Ave (19320). From US 30 Bypass take PA 82 approximately 2 miles N to Cedar Knoll Rd, then left 1 1/4 miles to park entrance on left. Phone 610/384-0290.* Once the center of an iron works community, it is now the largest of the county parks, encompassing 800 acres of woodlands and meadows. The west branch of the Brandywine Creek, Birch Run, and a pond are stocked with trout; hiking trails, picnicking, tent and trailer camping (dump station). Park features Hibernia Mansion; portions of house date from 1798, period furnishings. Tours of mansion (Memorial Day-Labor Day, Sun; fee). **FREE**

Historic Yellow Springs. *10 miles NE via PA 113, NW on Yellow Springs Rd. Phone 610/827-7414.* From its beginnings as a fashionable spa, this historic village has been everything from a Revolutionary War hospital to an art school. Countryside covers 145 acres with buildings, medicinal herb garden, and mineral springs. Events and educational programs throughout the year (some fees). Self-guided tour. Office (Mon-Fri).

Special Events

Hibernia Mansion Christmas Tours. *1 Park Ave (19320). Hibernia County Park.* First week in Dec.

Old Fiddlers' Picnic. *1 Park Ave (19320). Hibernia County Park.* Second Sat in Aug.

Motel/Motor Lodge

★ ★ **INN AT CHESTER SPRINGS.** *815 N Pottstown Pike (19341). Phone 610/363-1100; toll-free 800/465-4329; fax 610/524-2329.* 225 rooms, 4 story. S, D $109; under 18 free. Crib free. Pet accepted. TV; cable (premium). 2 pools, 1 indoor; poolside service, lifeguard. Coffee in rooms. Restaurant. Room service. Check-out 11 am. Coin laundry. Meeting rooms. Business services available. In-room modem link. Valet service. Gift shop. Airport transportation. Refrigerators, microwaves available. Picnic tables. Cr cds: A, C, D, DS, ER, JCB, MC, V.

Hotel

★ ★ ★ **SHERATON GREAT VALLEY HOTEL.** *707 Lancaster Pike (19355). Phone 610/524-5500. www.sheraton.com.* 198 rooms, 5 story. S, D $195-$250; under 17 free. Crib available. Check-out noon, check-in 3 pm. TV; cable (premium). In-room modem link. Many refrigerators in suites. Minibars. Restaurant 6:30 am-10 pm. Bar to midnight. Exercise equipment. Pool, whirlpool. Meeting rooms. Business center. Concierge. Cr cds: A, C, D, DS, MC, V.

Doylestown (Bucks County) (G-13)

See also Philadelphia, Quakertown (Bucks County)

Settled 1735 **Pop** 8,227 **Elev** 340 ft **Area code** 215 **Zip** 18901

Information Bucks County Conference and Visitors Bureau, 152 Swamp Rd; 215/345-4552 or 800/836-2825

Web www.buckscountycvb.org

Doylestown is the county seat of historic and colorful Bucks County.

What to See and Do

Covered bridges. Descriptive list, map of 11 bridges in Bucks County may be obtained at Bucks County Tourist Commission.

James A. Michener Art Museum. *138 S Pine St. Phone 215/340-9800.* This museum, a former prison modeled after the Eastern State Penitentiary in Philadelphia, is as large as a football field and was named for Doylestown's most famous son, the Pulitzer-Prize winning writer James Michener. He supported the arts and dreamed of a regional art museum dedicated to preserving, interpreting, and exhibiting the art and cultural heritage of the Bucks County region. The museum is home to more than 2,500 paintings, sculptures, drawings, and photographs; stained glass collections; an outdoor gallery paying homage to the local landscape; a café décor; a museum shop; and a research and reference library. (Tues-Sun; closed holidays) **$$**

Mercer Mile. Three reinforced-concrete structures built between 1910-1916 within a 1-mile radius by Dr. Henry Chapman Mercer, archaeologist, historian, world traveler, and tile maker. They include

> **Fonthill Museum.** *525 E Court St. Phone 215/348-9461.* Concrete castle of Henry Chapman Mercer (1856-1930) displays his collection of tiles and prints from around the world. Guided tours (times vary) **$$$**

> **Mercer Museum.** *845 Pine St (18901). Phone 215/345-0210.* In this towering castle built in 1969, visitors will find implements, folk art, and furnishings of early America before mechanization. See a Conestoga wagon, a whaling boat, carriages, and an antique fire engine. Fifty thousand pieces of more than 60 early American crafts and varying trade tools on display. (Daily; closed Jan 1, Thanksgiving, Dec 25) **$$$**

The Moravian Pottery and Tile Works. *Between Court and North sts. Phone 215/345-6722.* This historic landmark is a working history museum in which visitors can witness tiles produced their original handmade manner. Henry Chapman Mercer, a historian, archaeologist, collector, ceramist, and major proponent of the Arts & Crafts movement in America, left behind three historic buildings in his hometown of Doylestown: his home, Fonthill; the Mercer Museum (see also MERCER MUSEUM); and the Moravian Pottery and Tile Works. Visitors will see original installations and selected aspects of current tile production, and may purchase tiles made on site in the tile shop. (Daily; closed holidays) **$**

★ **Pearl S. Buck House.** *520 Dublin Rd, 8 miles NW via PA 611, 313 in Hilltown Township. Phone 215/249-0100.* (1835) House of Pulitzer and Nobel Prize winning author Pearl S. Buck. Original furnishings include desk at which *The Good Earth* was written; memorabilia, Chinese artifacts. Picnicking on grounds. Gift shop. One-hour guided tours (Mar-Dec, Tues-Sun; closed holidays). **$$$**

Motel/Motor Lodge

★ **COMFORT INN.** *678 Bethlehem Pike (18936). Phone 215/361-3600; toll-free 800/228-5150; fax 215/361-7949. www.comfortinn.com.* 84 rooms, 3 story. S $90.95-$129.95; D $95.95-$129.95; each additional $5; suites $124.95-$129.95; under 18 free. Crib free. TV; cable, VCR available (movies). Complimentary continental breakfast. Coffee in rooms. Restaurant nearby. Check-out 11 am. Coin laundry. Meeting room. Business services available. In-room modem link. Valet service. Health club privileges. Microwaves available. Refrigerator, wet bar in suites. Cr cds: A, C, D, DS, JCB, MC, V.

[D] [⊠] [SC]

Du Bois (E-5)

See also Clearfield (Clearfield County)

Settled 1865 **Pop** 8,123 **Elev** 1,420 ft **Area code** 814 **Zip** 15801

Information Du Bois Area Chamber of Commerce, 31 N Brady St; 814/371-5010

At the entrance to the lowest pass of the Allegheny Range, Du Bois is a transportation center—once the apex of huge lumbering operations. Destroyed by fire in 1888, the town was rebuilt on the ashes of the old community and today ranks as one of the 12 major trading centers in the state.

Motels/Motor Lodges

★ **BEST WESTERN INN & CONFERENCE CENTER.** *82 N Park Pl (15801). Phone 814/371-6200; fax 814/371-4608. www.bestwestern.com.* 60 rooms, 3 story. S $47-$57; D $53-$63; each additional $6; under 18 free. Complimentary continental breakfast. Check-out 11 am. TV. Restaurant nearby. Health club privileges. Golf privileges. Cr cds: A, C, D, DS, MC, V.

[icons]

★ **HAMPTON INN.** *RR 8, Box 3A (15801). Phone 814/375-1000; toll-free 800/426-7866; fax 814/375-4668. www.hamptoninn.com.* 96 rooms, 3 story. S $84-$89; D $89-$94; kitchen suite $130; under 18 free; weekly, weekend, holiday rates; golf plans; 2-day minimum Penn State football games. Crib free. Complimentary continental breakfast, coffee in rooms. Check-out noon. TV; cable (premium), VCR available. Refrigerators available. Valet services. Restaurant adjacent. Health club privileges. Exercise equipment. Indoor pool, whirlpool. Cross-country ski 1 mile. Meeting rooms. Business services. Cr cds: A, C, D, DS, MC, V.

[icons]

★ ★ **HOLIDAY INN.** *US 219 and I-80 (15801). Phone 814/371-5100; toll-free 800/959-3412; fax 814/375-0230. www.holiday-inn.com.* 160 rooms, 2 story. S $72-$77; D $78-$84; each additional $6; studio rooms $75; under 18 free. Pet accepted. TV; cable (premium), VCR available. Pool; wading, poolside service, lifeguard. Complimentary coffee in rooms. Restaurant 7 am-2 pm, 5-10 pm. Room service. Bar 5 pm-1 am. Check-out noon. Coin laundry. Meeting rooms. Business services available. In-room modem link. Bellstaff. Free airport transportation. Health club privileges. Cr cds: A, C, D, DS, JCB, MC, V.

[icons]

★ ★ **RAMADA INN.** *I-80 and Rte 255 (15801). Phone 814/371-7070; toll-free 800/272-6232; fax 814/371-1055. www.ramada.com.* 96 rooms, 2-3 story. No elevator. S $53-$65; D $59-$75; each additional $10; suites $80-$150; under 18 free. Pet accepted. Check-out noon. TV; cable (premium), VCR available. Restaurant 6:30 am-1:30 pm, 5:30-10 pm. Bar 5 pm-2 am; entertainment Mon-Sat. Room service. Health club privileges. Indoor pool; poolside service. Golf privileges. Airport transportation. Cr cds: A, C, D, DS, JCB, MC, V.

[icons]

B&B/Small Inn

★ ★ ★ **TOWNE HOUSE INN.** *138 Center St (15857). Phone 814/781-1556; toll-free 800/851-1180; fax 814/834-4449. www.townehouseinn.com.* 57 rooms, 3 story. S $48-$90; D $53-$97; each additional $7. Restaurant 6:30 am-2 pm, 5-9 pm; Sat from 5 pm; closed Sun. Crib $7. Complimentary continental breakfast, coffee in rooms. Check-out 11 am. TV; cable (premium). In-room modem link. Fireplaces. Restaurant 6:30 am-2 pm, 5-9 pm; Sat from 5 pm; closed Sun. Room service. Exercise equipment. Picnic tables. Meeting rooms. Business services. Stained glass, antiques in 7 historic (1890s) townhouses. Cr cds: A, D, DS, MC, V.

[icons]

Easton (F-13)

See also Allentown, Bethlehem

Founded 1752 **Pop** 26,263 **Elev** 300 ft **Area code** 484 and 610 **Zip** 18042

Information Two Rivers Area Chamber of Commerce, 1 S 3rd St, PO Box 637, 18044-0637; 610/253-4211

Web www.eastonareachamber.org

Named by Thomas Penn, one of the proprietors, for the English birthplace of his bride, Easton today is the gateway to the great industrial Lehigh Valley. Lafayette College, with its beautiful campus, and the historic Great Square are of interest. Easton, the seat of Northampton County, is part of a larger metropolitan area, the Lehigh Valley, which also includes Allentown and Bethlehem.

What to See and Do

Canal Museum. *30 Centre Sq (18042). PA 611, 1 mile S of US 22, Two Rivers Landing. Phone 610/250-6700.* Exhibits include photographs, models, documents, and artifacts from the era of mule-drawn canal boats in the 1800s; electronic map and audiovisual programs. Changing exhibits. (Memorial Day-Labor Day, daily; rest of year, Tues-Sun; closed Jan 1, Thanksgiving, Dec 25) **$$$**

The Crayola Factory. *30 Centre Sq (18042). Phone 610/515-8000.* See how crayons and markers are created. Visit Crayola Hall of Fame; enjoy dozens of interactive exhibits featuring the wonders of light and color. Same location and schedule as Canal Museum.

"The Great Square." *Center of business district.* Now called Center Square. Dominated by Soldiers' and Sailors' Monument. Bronze marker shows replica of Old Courthouse, which stood until 1862 on land rented from the Penns for one red rose a year. From Old Courthouse steps, the Declaration of Independence was read on July 8, 1776, when the Easton Flag, the first Stars and Stripes of the united colonies, was unfurled here.

Hugh Moore Park. *S 25th St, 2 miles S of US 22. Phone 610/250-6700.* Restored Lehigh Canal, locks, and locktender's house; mule-drawn canal boat rides (early May-Labor Day, daily; early-late Sept, weekends) Also hiking, picnicking; boat rentals in park. Park (Daily). **FREE**

Lafayette College. *US 22 and US 78 (18042). N side of town. Phone 610/250-5000.* (1826) 2,000 students. Bronze statue of Lafayette by Daniel Chester French in front of college chapel; American historical portrait collection in Kirby Hall of Civil Rights. Tour of campus.

Northampton County Historical Society. *101-107 S 4th St, diagonally opposite Parsons-Taylor House. Phone 610/253-1222.* Changing exhibits; library; museum. (By appointment) **$**

Restaurants

★ ★ **MY LITTLE GYPSY ROSE.** *1600 N Delaware Dr (18040). Phone 610/258-6175; fax 610/258-6176.* American menu. Closed Mon. Dinner. Bar. Outdoor seating. **$$**
Ⓓ

★ ★ **PEARLY BAKER'S ALE HOUSE.** *11 Center Sq (18042). Phone 610/253-9949; fax 610/253-6133.* International menu. Hours: 11:30 am-10 pm. Closed Mon; also many major holidays. Reservations required Fri, Sat (dinner). A la carte entrées: lunch $6-$9, dinner $14-$29. Children's menu. Fri, Sat (dinner). Outdoor dining. Austrian chandelier in main dining room. Cr cds: A, DS, MC, V.
Ⓓ

Ebensburg (F-5)

See also Altoona, Johnstown

Pop 3,091 **Elev** 2,140 ft **Area code** 814 **Zip** 15931

Information Johnstown/Cambria County Convention & Visitors Bureau, 416 Main St, Suite 200, Johnstown 15901-1608; 814/536-7993 or 800/237-8590

Web www.visitjohnstownpa.com

What to See and Do

Allegheny Portage Railroad National Historic Site. Remains of railroad built 1831-1834 to link east and west divisions of the Pennsylvania Mainline Canal. Cars were pulled up ten inclined planes by ropes powered by steam engines. Horses or locomotives pulled the cars over the level stretches of the 36-mile route across the Alleghenies from Hollidaysburg to Johnstown. The Skew Arch Bridge, an engine house exhibit, and the Lemon House, a historic tavern, help tell the story of the Allegheny Portage Railroad. A visitor center (daily; closed Dec 25) has exhib-

its and a 20-minute film. There are ranger-led programs (summer, daily) and costumed demonstrations (summer); picnic area (daily), hiking and cross-country trails.

Portage Station Museum. *400 Lee St, in Portage. Phone 814/736-8918 or 814/736-4343.* This historic station was once a stop on the Pennsylvania Railroad. The first floor, with its original lighting fixtures, oak wainscoting, and woodwork, contains the Master's Office and waiting room. Exhibits on the second floor include artifacts from the newly renovated Mainline Mining Museum. (Wed, Sat and Sun afternoons). **FREE**

Edinboro (B-2)

See also Erie, Meadville

Pop 6,950 **Elev** 1,210 ft **Area code** 814 **Zip** 16412

This is a resort town on Edinboro Lake and the home of Edinboro State College.

What to See and Do

Mountain View Ski Area. *4 miles E on US 6 N, then 3 miles S on PA 86, in Cambridge Springs. Phone 814/734-1641.* Two T-bars, Pomalift; patrol, school, rentals; snowmaking; cafeteria. Longest run 2,500 feet; vertical drop 320 feet. (Dec-Mar, daily) Half-day and evening rates. **$$$$**

Motel/Motor Lodge

★ ★ **RAMADA INN.** *401 W Plum St (16412). Phone 814/734-5650; toll-free 888/449-0344; fax 814/734-7532. www.ramada.com.* 105 rooms, 2 story. S, D $80-$90; each additional $10; package plans. Pet accepted. Check-out noon. TV. Restaurant 6 am-10 pm. Bar 11:30-2 am; entertainment. Room service. Sauna. Indoor pool. Greens fee $18-$24. Downhill ski 7 miles. Cr cds: A, C, D, DS, MC, V.
Ⓓ 🐾 🛗 🏊 🍴 🏊 ➽ SC

B&B/Small Inn

★ ★ ★ **RIVERSIDE INN.** *1 Fountain Ave, Cambridge Springs (16403). Phone 814/398-4645; toll-free 800/964-5173; fax 814/398-8161. www.theriversideinn.com.* Opened in 1885, this inn continues to provide top service to its visitors. The inn is found nestled in a quiet and peaceful area overlooking French Creek. Guests will enjoy golf, swimming, tennis, and many other activities. 74 rooms, 3 story. Closed Jan-mid-Apr. Complimentary full breakfast. Check-out 11 am, check-in 3 pm. TV in suites and sitting room. Dining room 11:30 am-2 pm, 5:30-8:30 pm; Fri, Sat to 10 pm; Sun 11 am-2 pm, 5:30-8:30 pm. Bar. Pool. Golf privileges. Lawn games. Victorian inn (1885) overlooking French Creek. Dinner theater on weekends, matinees weekdays. Cr cds: A, DS, MC, V. **$**
Ⓓ 🐾 🍴 🏌 ➽ ➽

Ephrata (G-11)

See also Bird-in-Hand, Denver/Adamstown, Lancaster, Lebanon, Reading

Settled 1732 **Pop** 13,213 **Elev** 380 ft **Area code** 717 **Zip** 17522

Information Chamber of Commerce, 77 Park Ave, Suite 1; 717/738-9010

Web www.ephrata-area.org

What to See and Do

Ephrata Cloister. *632 W Main St. Phone 717/733-6600.* Buildings stand as a monument to an unusual religious experiment. In 1732 Conrad Beissel, a German Seventh-Day Baptist, began to lead a hermit's life here; within a few years he established a religious community of recluses, with a Brotherhood, a Sisterhood, and a group of married "householders." The members of the solitary order dressed in concealing white habits; the buildings (1735-1749) were without adornment, the halls were narrow, the doorways were low, and board benches served as beds and wooden blocks as pillows. Their religious zeal and charity, however, proved to be their undoing. After the Battle of Brandywine, the cloistered community nursed the Revolutionary sick and wounded, but contracted typhus, which decimated their numbers. Celibacy also contributed to the decline of the community, but the Society was not formally dissolved until 1934. An orientation exhibit and video prepare each visitor for their relaxing journey back through time. Surviving and restored buildings include the Sisters' House, Chapel, Almonry, and eight others. Craft demonstrations (summer). (Mon-Sat; closed holidays) **$$$**

Museum and Library of the Historical Society of Cocalico Valley. *249 W Main St. Phone 717/733-1616.* Italianate Victorian mansion contains period displays; historical exhibits; genealogical and historical research library (fee) on Cocalico Valley area and residents. (Mon, Wed, Thurs, Sat) **FREE**

Special Event

Street Fair. One of largest in the state. Last full week in Sept.

B&B/Small Inns

★ ★ **THE INNS AT DONECKERS.** *318-324 N State St (17522). Phone 717/738-9502; toll-free 800/377-2206; fax 717/738-9554. www.doneckers.com.* 56 rooms, 3 story. D $65-$95. Complimentary continental breakfast. Check-out 11 am, check-in 3 pm. TV in sitting room. Restaurant nearby. Health club privileges. Restored clockmaker's house (1777). Hand-cut stenciling. Cr cds: A, C, D, DS, MC, V.
Ⓓ 🖼

★ ★ **SMITHTON BED & BREAKFAST COUNTRY INN.** *900 W Main St (17522). Phone 717/733-6094. www.historicsmithtoninn.com.* 17 rooms, 3 story. D $85-$170. Complimentary full breakfast. Check-out noon, check-in 3:30 pm. Fireplaces. Restaurant nearby. Concierge. Historic stone inn (1763). Totally nonsmoking. Cr cds: A, MC, V.
Ⓓ 🖼

Restaurant

★ ★ ★ **THE RESTAURANT AT DONECKERS.** *333 N State St (17522). Phone 717/738-9501; fax 717/738-9512. www.doneckers.com.* Guests can opt for formal atmosphere amidst antiques and artwork in the main dining room, or a more casual setting in the bistro. Check for special events, such as theme dinners, wine tastings, and the like. American, French menu. Hours: 11 am-10 pm. Closed Wed, Sun; holidays. Lunch $9.95-$30.95, dinner $23.50-$30.95. Bar. Children's menu. Reservations accepted. Cr cds: A, C, D, DS, MC, V.
Ⓓ

Erie (A-2)

See also North East

Settled 1753 **Pop** 103,717 **Elev** 744 ft **Area code** 814

Information Erie Area Chamber of Commerce, 109 Boston Store Pl, 16501-2312; 814/454-7191

Web www.eriechamber.com

As the third-largest city in the state, and the only Great Lakes port in Pennsylvania, Erie's fine natural harbor on Lake Erie is protected and bounded by Presque Isle peninsula, the site of many historic events. Greater Erie is also one of the nation's mighty industrial centers, with more than 750 highly diversified manufacturing firms and several large industrial parks. The lake and city take their name from the Eriez tribe, who were killed by the Seneca about 1654.

On the south shore of Presque Isle Bay, Commodore Oliver Hazard Perry built his fleet, floated the ships across the sandbars, and fought the British in the Battle of Lake Erie (1813). Fort Presque Isle, built by the French in 1753 and destroyed by them in 1759, was rebuilt by the English, burned by Native Americans, and rebuilt again in 1794 by Americans.

What to See and Do

Bicentennial Tower. *7 Dobbins Landing (16507). Erie's Bayfront, at the foot of State St. Phone 814/455-6055.*

Commemorating Erie's 200th birthday, this 187-foot tower features two observation decks with an aerial view of city, bay, and Lake Erie. Concessions in tower lobby. (Apr-Sept, daily; rest of year, call for schedule; closed holidays) Free admission Tues. **$**

Erie Art Museum. *411 State St. Phone 814/459-5477.* Temporary art exhibits in a variety of media; regional artwork and lectures in the restored Greek Revival Old Customs House (1839). Art classes, concerts, lectures, and workshops are also offered. (Tues-Sat, also Sun afternoons; closed holidays) Free admission Wed. **$**

Erie Zoo. *423 W 38th St, 3 miles N of I-90 State St exit 7. Phone 814/868-3651.* Zoo houses more than 300 animals, including gorillas, polar bears, and giraffes; children's zoo (May-Sept); one-mile tour of grounds on Safariland Express Train (fee). Indoor ice rink (Sept-Mar) **$$**

Firefighters Historical Museum. *428 Chestnut St. Phone 814/456-5969.* More than 1,300 items of firefighting memorabilia are displayed in the old #4 Firehouse. Exhibits include fire apparatus dating from 1823, alarm systems, uniforms, badges, ribbons, helmets, nozzles, fire marks and fire extinguishers; fire safety films are shown in the Hay Loft Theater. (May-Oct, Sat and Sun) **$$**

Gridley's Grave. *1718 E Lake Rd. Lakeside Cemetery. Phone 814/459-8200.* Final resting place of Captain Charles Vernon Gridley, to whom, at the Battle of Manila Bay in 1898, Admiral Dewey said, "You may fire when ready, Gridley." Gridley died in Japan; his body was returned here for burial. Four old Spanish cannons from Manila Harbor, built in 1777, guard the grave. Offers view of peninsula, Lake Erie and entrance to Erie Harbor from cliff by Gridley Circle.

Land Lighthouse. *2 Lighthouse St (16507). Foot of Lighthouse St. Phone 814/452-3937.* (1867) The first lighthouse on the Great Lakes was constructed on this site in 1813.

Misery Bay. *NE corner of Presque Isle Bay.* State monument to Perry; named after Perry defeated British and the fleet suffered cold and privations of a bitter winter.

Presque Isle State Park. *1 Peninsula Dr. N off PA 832. Phone 814/833-7424.* Peninsula stretches 7 miles into Lake Erie and curves back toward city. Approximately 3,200 acres of recreation and conservation areas. Swimming, fishing, boating (rentals, mooring, launching, marina); hiking, birding, trails, cross-country skiing, ice skating, ice fishing, ice boating, picnicking, concessions. Visitor center, environmental education, and interpretive programs.

Waldameer Park & Water World. *220 Peninsula Dr, at entrance to Presque Isle State Park. Phone 814/838-3591.* Rides, midway, kiddieland, water park, picnic area, food, dance pavilion. (Memorial Day-Labor Day, Tues-Sun; open Mon holidays) **$$$$**

Watson-Curtze Mansion. *356 W 6th St. Phone 814/871-5790.* Housed in 1890s Victorian mansion. Museum features regional history and decorative arts exhibits; restored period rooms; changing exhibits (Tues-Sat afternoons; closed holidays). Also planetarium with shows (Sat afternoons). **$$**

Wayne Memorial Blockhouse. *560 E 3rd St. On grounds of State Soldiers' and Sailors' Home. Phone 814/871-4531.* Replica of blockhouse in which General Anthony Wayne died Dec 15, 1796, after becoming ill on a voyage from Detroit. He was buried at the foot of the flagpole; later, his son had the body disinterred and the remains moved to Radnor. (Memorial Day-Labor Day, daily) **FREE**

Motels/Motor Lodges

★ **COMFORT INN.** *8051 Peach St (16509). Phone 814/866-6666; fax 814/864-1367. www.comfortinn.com.* 110 rooms, 2 story, 50 suites. Mid-May-Sept: S $80-$99; D $90-$120; each additional $6; suites $95-$125; under 18 free; higher rates holiday weekends; lower rates rest of year. Crib free. TV; cable (premium), VCR (movies). Heated pool; whirlpool, lifeguard. Complimentary continental breakfast. Coffee in rooms. Restaurant adjacent 6 am-midnight. Check-out noon. Meeting room. Business services available. In-room modem link. Free airport transportation. Exercise equipment. Refrigerator, wet bar in suites. Some balconies. Cr cds: A, C, D, DS, JCB, MC, V.

⊡ 🏊 ⚓ 🖨 SC

★ **ECONO LODGE.** *8050 Peach St (16509). Phone 814/866-5544; toll-free 800/638-7949; fax 814/864-6218. www.econolodge.com.* 97 rooms, 3 story. Late May-Oct: S $79-$109; D $89.95-$149; each additional $10; higher rates special events; lower rates rest of year. Crib free. TV; cable, VCR (movies). Indoor pool; whirlpool. Complimentary continental breakfast. Restaurant adjacent 7-2 am. Check-out noon. Meeting rooms. Business services available. In-room modem link. Sundries. Free airport transportation. Exercise equipment. Some refrigerators, wet bars. Cr cds: A, C, D, DS, JCB, MC, V.

⊡ 🏊 ⚓ 🖨 SC

★ **GLASS HOUSE INN.** *3202 W 26th St (16506). Phone 814/833-7751; toll-free 800/956-7222; fax 814/833-4222. www.glasshouseinn.com.* 30 rooms. June-Labor Day: S, D $65-$92; each additional $7; family rates; lower rates rest of year. Complimentary continental breakfast. Check-out 11 am. TV; cable (premium), VCR available (movies). In-room modem link. Restaurant nearby. Heated pool. Downhill, cross-country ski 20 miles. Cr cds: A, C, D, DS, MC, V.

✈ 🏊 🖨

★ **HAMPTON INN.** *3041 W 12th St (16505). Phone 814/835-4200; toll-free 800/426-7866; fax 814/835-5212. www.hamptoninn.com.* 100 rooms, 3 story. S $71-$105; D $78-$105; under 18 free. Crib available. TV; cable (premium). Heated pool. Complimentary continental breakfast. Restaurant nearby 7 am-10:30 pm. Check-out noon. Business services available. Valet service. Cr cds: A, C, D, DS, MC, V.

[D] [≈] [≧] [SC]

★★ **HOLIDAY INN.** *18 W 18th St (16501). Phone 814/456-2961; toll-free 800/465-4329; fax 814/456-7067. www.holiday-inn.com.* 133 rooms, 4 story. Memorial Day-Labor Day: S, D $69-$94; each additional $6; under 18 free; lower rates rest of year. Crib free. TV; cable (premium). Heated pool; poolside service. Complimentary full breakfast. Coffee in rooms. Restaurant 6:30 am-10 pm. Room service. Bar 11:30-2 am. Check-out noon. Laundry facilities. Meeting rooms. Business center. In-room modem link. Bellstaff. Valet service. Free airport transportation. Exercise equipment. Health club privileges. Cr cds: A, D, DS, JCB, MC, V.

[D] [≈] [术] [≧] [SC] [术]

★ **MOTEL 6.** *7875 Peach St (16509). Phone 814/864-4811; toll-free 800/542-7674; fax 814/868-1277. www.motel6.com.* 83 rooms, 2 story. Late May-Sept: S $59-$89; D $69-$99; each additional $10; under 18 free; package plan; some lower rates rest of year. Crib free. Pet accepted. TV; cable. Indoor pool; wading pool. Complimentary coffee. Restaurant nearby. Check-out noon. Business services available. Coin laundry. Valet service. Free airport transportation. Exercise equipment; sauna. Private patios, balconies. Cr cds: A, C, D, DS, ER, JCB, MC, V.

[D] [☏] [≈] [术] [≧] [SC]

★★ **QUALITY INN & SUITES.** *8040 Perry Hwy (16509). Phone 814/864-4911; toll-free 800/550-8040; fax 814/864-3743. www.qualityinn.com.* 107 rooms, 2 story. S, D $49-$109; each additional $6; under 18 free. Pet accepted. Check-out 11 am. TV; cable. In-room modem link. Restaurant 6:30 am-10 pm. Bar 11-1 am. Room service. Health club privileges. Heated pool. Free airport transportation. Business center. Cr cds: A, C, D, DS, JCB, MC, V.

[D] [☏] [≈] [✕] [≧] [SC] [术]

★★ **RAMADA INN.** *6101 Wattsburg Rd (16509). Phone 814/825-3100; toll-free 800/272-6232; fax 814/825-0857. www.ramada.com.* 122 rooms, 2 story. July-Sept: S, D $80-$90; each additional $8; suites $90-$120; under 18 free; ski, weekend plans; lower rates rest of year. Check-out noon. TV; cable (premium), VCR (movies). In-room modem link. Restaurant 6:30 am-1 pm, 5-10 pm. Bar 5 pm-2 am. Room service. Exercise equipment. Game room. Heated pool; children's pool, whirlpool. Downhill ski 15 miles. Business center. Cr cds: A, C, D, DS, JCB, MC, V.

[D] [≈] [≈] [术] [≧] [SC] [术]

★ **SUPER 8.** *8040 Perry Hwy (16509). Phone 814/864-9200; fax 814/864-3743. www.super8.com.* 93 rooms, 4 story. Apr-Oct: S, D $39-$89; under 18 free; family rates; package plans; higher rates special events; lower rates rest of year. Crib free. Pet accepted, some restrictions. Complimentary continental breakfast. Check-out 11 am. TV; cable (premium). In-room modem link. Some refrigerators, microwaves. Valet services, coin laundry. Restaurant adjacent 6:30 am-10 pm. Game room. Pool privileges. Airport transportation. Business services available. Cr cds: A, D, DS, ER, MC, V.

[D] [☏] [≈] [≧] [SC]

Restaurant

★★ **PUFFERBELLY.** *414 French St (16507). Phone 814/454-1557; fax 814/455-6138. www.pufferbelly.com.* Hours: 11:30 am-9:30 pm; Fri, Sat to 11 pm; Sun to 8 pm; Sun brunch to 3 pm. Closed major holidays. Dinner $8.95-$15.95. Sun brunch. Bar. Restored firehouse (1907). Outdoor seating. Cr cds: A, DS, MC, V.

[D]

Erwinna

See also New Hope

B&B/Small Inn

★★★ **EVERMAY ON THE DELAWARE.** *889 River Rd (18920). Phone 610/294-9100; toll-free 1-877/864-2365; fax 610/294-8249. www.evermay.com.* Built in the 1700s, this inn is situated on 25 acres of pastures, woodlands and gardens, and close to antique shops, galleries, historic sites, parks, and much more. 18 rooms, 4 story. No elevators. D $145-$275; suite $250; guest house $150; weekends (2-day minimum). Children over 13 years only. Complimentary continental breakfast. Check-out noon, check-in 2 pm. TV in common room; VCR available. In-room modem link. Some fireplaces. Restaurant. Game room. Cross-country ski on-site. Lawn games. Built in 1790; classic Federal structure with Victorian antiques. On river. On 25 acres. Totally nonsmoking. Cr cds: A, MC, V.

[⚑] [术] [≈] [≧]

Restaurants

★★★ **EVERMAY.** *889 River Rd (18920). Phone 610/294-9100; toll-free 877/864-2365; fax 610/294-8249. www.evermay.com.* American menu. Hours: 7:30-11 pm.

Closed Mon-Thurs. Dinner $68. Bar. Casual attire. Cr cds: A, MC, V.

★ ★ ★ **GOLDEN PHEASANT INN.** *763 River Rd (PA 32) (18920). Phone 610/294-9595; fax 610/294-9882. www.goldenpheasant.com.* This provincial and romantic weekend hideaway sits nestled between the Delaware River and the Pennsylvania Canal, located an hour and a half from New York City, and 20 minutes outside Philadelphia. Hours: 5:30-10 pm; Sun 11 am-9 pm. Sun brunch 11 am-3 pm. Closed Mon. Reservations accepted. French menu. Bar. Wine cellar. A la carte entrées: dinner $18.95-$24.95. Sun brunch $18.95. Specialties: roast lamb, steak au poivre. Own baking. Restored 1857 inn; dining room in solarium, overlooks canal. Cr cds: A, C, D, DS, MC, V.

SC

Fort Washington

Pop 3,680 **Elev** 250 ft **Area code** 215 **Zip** 19034

Information Valley Forge Convention & Visitors Bureau, 600 W Germantown Pike, Suite 130, Plymouth Meeting 19462; 610/834-1550

Web www.valleyforge.org

What to See and Do

Fort Washington State Park. *500 Bethlehem Pike. Phone 215/646-2942.* Commemorates the site of Washington's northern defense line against the British in 1777. Fishing; hiking, ball fields, picnicking.

The Highlands. *7001 Sheaff Ln. Phone 215/641-2687.* (1796) Late-Georgian mansion on 43 acres built by Anthony Morris, active in both state and federal government. Formal gardens and crenellated walls built circa 1845. Tours. (Mon-Fri) **$$**

Hope Lodge. *1 mile S, 553 Bethlehem Pike. Phone 215/646-1595.* (circa 1745) Colonial Georgian mansion; headquarters for Surgeon General John Cochran after Battle of Germantown. Historic furnishings, paintings, ceramics. (Tues-Sun; closed holidays) **$$**

Restaurant

★ ★ **PALACE OF ASIA.** *285 Commerce Dr (19034). Phone 215/646-2133; fax 215/646-2953. www.palaceofasia .citysearch.com.* Hours: 11:30 am-11 pm; Sat, Sun brunch to 3:30 pm. Closed Dec 24. Reservations required Fri-Sun dinner. Indian menu. Bar. Lunch $6.25-$7.95, dinner $7.95-$15.95. Sat, Sun brunch $3.50-$8.25. Specializes in vegetarian and curry dishes. Own baking. Authentic Indian atmosphere. Cr cds: A, DS, MC, V.

D

Franklin (Venango County) (D-3)

See also Meadville, Oil City, Titusville

Settled 1787 **Pop** 7,212 **Elev** 1,020 ft **Area code** 814 **Zip** 16323

Information Franklin Area Chamber of Commerce, 1259 Liberty St; 814/432-5823

Web www.franklin-pa.org

A series of French and British forts was erected in this area. The last one, Fort Franklin, was razed by local settlers who used the stone and timber in their own buildings. Old Garrison took its place in 1796 and later served as the Venango County Jail. In 1859, James Evans, a blacksmith, made tools to drill an oil well that brought an oil boom to the area. For years, oil was dominant in the area's industries.

What to See and Do

DeBence Antique Music World. *1261 Liberty St. Phone 814/432-5668.* Features nickelodeons, band organs, calliopes, German organs, a variety of music boxes, many other items. Unique "see and hear" museum. Guided tours. (Mid-Mar-Dec, Tues-Sun; closed holidays) **$$$**

Hoge-Osmer House. *Corner of South Park and Elk sts. Phone 814/437-2275.* (circa 1865) Museum owned by Venango County Historical Society; houses displays of materials and artifacts relating to Venango County history; period furnishings, research library. House open (May-Dec, Tues-Thurs and Sat; rest of year, Sat; closed holidays). Inquire for genealogy library hours. **FREE**

Pioneer Cemetery. *Otter and 15th sts.* (1795-1879) Self-guided walking tour booklets can be purchased at the Chamber of Commerce.

Venango County Court House. *1168 Liberty St. Phone 814/ 432-9500.* (1868). Unique styling; contains display of Native American artifacts. (Mon-Fri; closed holidays)

Special Events

Applefest. *Downtown. Phone 814/432-5823.* Apple pie-baking contest; arts and crafts; entertainment; classic car show. Kids Korner. Five-km race; horse-drawn buggy rides. First full weekend in Oct.

Franklin Silver Cornet Band Concerts. *City Park.* Thurs, mid-June-Aug.

Motel/Motor Lodge

★ ★ ★ **FRANKLIN INN.** *1421 Liberty St (16323). Phone 814/437-3031; toll-free 800/535-4052; fax 814/432-7481.* 85 rooms, 6 story. Apr-Sept: S $65; D $70; each additional $5; under 18 free; weekly, monthly rates; lower rates rest of year. Pet accepted, some restrictions. TV; cable. Complimentary continental breakfast. Restaurant 6 am-2 pm, 5-10 pm; Sun 7 am-2 pm. Bar. Check-out 11 am. Business services available. Valet service. Barber, beauty shop. Free airport, bus depot transportation. Exercise equipment. Health club privileges. Some refrigerators. Cr cds: A, D, DS, ER, MC, V.

⊡ 🐾 ⚡ 🎿 ✈ ⊠

B&B/Small Inn

★ ★ **LAMBERTON HOUSE BED AND BREAKFAST.** *1331 Otter St (16323). Phone 814/432-7908.* 5 rooms, 2 story. No room phones. Complimentary full breakfast. Check-out 11 am, check-in 3 pm. TV in drawing room; VCR. Health club privileges. Historic building (1874). Cr cds: A, DS, MC, V. **$**

⊡ ⚓ ⊠ SC

Galeton

See also Wellsboro

Pop 1,325 **Elev** 1,325 ft **Area code** 814 **Zip** 16922

Information Potter County Recreation, PO Box 245, Coudersport 16915; 814/435-2290 or 888-POTTER2

What to See and Do

Ole Bull State Park. *18 miles SW on PA 144. Phone 814/435-5000.* At upper reaches of the Kettle Creek. Site of unsuccessful effort by the famous Norwegian violinist, Ole Bornemann Bull, to establish a colony called "New Norway." Approximately 125 acres. Swimming beach, fishing; hunting, hiking, cross-country skiing, snowmobiling, tent and trailer sites (electric hookups). Interpretive program. Standard fees.

Pennsylvania Lumber Museum. *5660 US 6 W. 10 miles W on US 6. Phone 814/435-2652.* Exhibits on lumbering and its techniques, forest industries, and products; reconstructed lumber camp and sawmill; restored locomotive and log-loader; nature trails, picnicking. Slide show in visitor center. (Apr-Nov, daily; closed holidays (See SPECIAL EVENTS) **$$**

Ski Denton/Denton Hill. *5661 US 6. 10 miles W on US 6. Phone 814/435-2115.* Double, triple chairlifts; two Pomalifts; patrol, school, rentals, snowmaking; cafeteria, restaurant, lodge, cabins. Longest run 1 mile; vertical drop 650 feet. (Dec-Mar, daily) 100 miles of cross-country trails; night skiing; camping. (See SPECIAL EVENTS) **$$$$**

Special Events

Bark Peeler's Convention. *5660 US 6 W. Phone 814/435-2652.* On grounds of Pennsylvania Lumber Museum. Re-creation of old-time festival held by lumber camp workers celebrating the end of the work year. Features many demonstrations, including cross-cut sawing, hewing, bark peeling; entertainment; period music; exhibits. July 4-5.

Germania Old Home Day. *7 miles SE via PA 144 in Germania.* Entertainment. Early Sept.

Woodsmen's Carnival. *Cherry Springs State Park, 12 miles SW on West Branch Rd. Phone 814/435-5010.* Horsepulling and woodcutting competitions; food; displays. First full weekend in Aug.

Gettysburg (I-8)

See also Hanover, York

Founded 1798 **Pop** 7,490 **Elev** 560 ft **Area code** 717 **Zip** 17325

Information Convention & Visitors Bureau, 35 Carlisle St; 717/334-6274

Web www.gettysburg.com

Because of the historical nature of this area and the many attractions in this town, visitors may want to stop in at the Gettysburg Convention & Visitors Bureau for complete information about bus tours, guide service (including a tape-recorded and self-guided tour) and help in planning their visit here.

What to See and Do

A. Lincoln's Place. *571 Steinwehr Ave. Phone 717/334-6049 or 717/334-8003.* Live portrayal of the 16th president; 45 minutes. (Mid-June-Labor Day, Mon-Fri) **$$$**

Eisenhower National Historic Site. (see GETTYSBURG NATIONAL MILITARY PARK)

General Lee's Headquarters. *401 Buford Ave. Phone 717/334-3141.* Robert E. Lee planned Confederate strategy for the Gettysburg battle in this house; contains collection of historical items from the battle. (Mid-Mar-mid-Nov, daily) **$$**

Gettysburg Battle Theatre. *571 Steinwehr Ave. Phone 717/334-6100.* Battlefield diorama with 25,000 figures; 30-minute film and electronic maps program showing battle strategy. (Mar-Nov, daily) **$$$**

Gettysburg: A Town Gripped by War

A three-day Civil War battle in July 1863 unfolded about a mile outside Gettysburg, which was a small rural community at the time. The town also suffered from the battle, and the impact can be seen in a one-hour, 1-mile walking tour that visits several of the well-preserved buildings that witnessed the conflict. Begin at Lincoln Square, the commercial heart of Gettysburg. Abraham Lincoln stayed at the David Wills House, now a small museum at No.12, the night before he gave the "Gettysburg Address" dedicating the nearby National Cemetery. Just outside the door is a life-size statue of Lincoln in somber attire appearing to help a visiting tourist casually dressed in a colorful sweater and cords. Among the townsfolk, it is called the "Perry Como statue," because that's who the tourist looks like. Head south on Baltimore Street to Nos. 242-246, the Jennie Wade Birthplace. Wade, the only civilian to be killed in the battle, is believed to have been shot by a Confederate sharpshooter while baking bread and biscuits for Union troops in her sister's nearby house. That house, on Baltimore Street, is a museum, the Jennie Wade House. Between the two homes, stop at the Schriver house at 309 Baltimore. Built for George Schriver and his family, its garret was occupied by Confederate sharpshooters who poked still-visible holes in the wall for their rifles. Now a museum, the Schriver House details life in the town during and immediately after the battle. Across the street at No. 304, formerly the Methodist parsonage, note the shell near the second-story window in front. The parson's daughter, Laura, was said to have narrowly escaped injury when a shell crashed through the brick wall into her room. Later, the shell was placed in the hole to mark the spot. Return to Lincoln Square via Washington Street. At the corner of West Middle Street, pause in front of the Michael Jacobs House at No. 101. A meteorologist, Jacobs recorded the weather throughout his life, leaving important details to posterity of weather and cloud conditions during the battle.

Gettysburg College. *300 N Washington St (17325). 3 blocks NW of Lincoln Sq off US 15 Business. Phone 717/337-6000.* (1832) 2,000 students. Liberal arts; oldest Lutheran-affiliated college in US. Pennsylvania Hall was used as Civil War hospital; Eisenhower House and statue on grounds. Tour of campus.

Gettysburg Scenic Rail Tours. *Washington St. Phone 717/334-6932.* A 22-mile round trip to Aspers on steam train. Also charter trips and special runs. (June, Thurs-Sun; July-Aug, Tues-Sun; Sept Sat-Sun afternoons) **$$$**

Ghosts of Gettysburg Candlelight Walking Tours. *271 Baltimore St. Phone 717/337-0445.* Armed with tales from Mark Nesbitt's Ghosts of Gettysburg books, knowledgeable guides lead 1 1/4-hour tours through sections of town that were bloody battlefields 130 years ago. (June-Oct, daily evenings; Apr, May, Nov, weekend evenings) **$$$**

Hall of Presidents and First Ladies. *789 Baltimore St, adjacent to National Cemetery. Phone 717/334-5717.* Costumed life-size wax figures of all the presidents; reproductions of their wives' inaugural gowns; "The Eisenhowers at Gettysburg" exhibit. (Mid-Mar-Nov, daily) **$$$**

Land of Little Horses. *125 Glenwood Dr (17325). 5 miles W off US 30, on Knoxlyn Rd to Glenwood Dr; follow signs. Phone 717/334-7259.* A variety of performing horses—all in miniature. Continuous entertainment; indoor arena; exotic animal races. Saddle and wagon rides. Picnic area, snack bar, gift shop. (May-late Aug, daily; Apr, Sept, Oct, weekends) **$$$**

Lincoln Room Museum. *12 Lincoln Sq. Phone 717/334-8188.* Preserved bedroom in Wills House; collection of Lincoln items; huge plaque inscribed with Gettysburg Address, audiovisual display. (Apr-Nov, daily) **$$**

The Lincoln Train Museum. *425 Steinwehr Ave (17325). 1/2 mile S via US 15 on Steinwehr Ave. Phone 717/334-5678.* Museum features more than 1,000 model trains and railroad memorabilia; Lincoln Train Ride—simulated trip of 15 minutes. (Mar-Nov, daily) **$$$**

Lutheran Theological Seminary. *61 Seminary Ridge (17325). Confederate Ave, 1 mile W of Lincoln Sq on US 30. Phone 717/334-6286.* (1826) 250 students. Oldest Lutheran seminary in US; cupola on campus used as Confederate lookout during battle. Old Dorm, now home of Adams County Historical Society, served as hospital for both Union and Confederate soldiers.

National Civil War Wax Museum. *297 Steinwehr Ave. Phone 717/334-6245.* Highlights Civil War era and Battle of Gettysburg. (Mar-Dec, daily; rest of year, Sat and Sun; closed Jan 1, Thanksgiving, Dec 25) **$$**

Schriver House. *309 Baltimore St. Phone 717/337-2800.* Built prior to the Civil War, this two-story brick house was used by Confederate sharpshooters, who knocked still-visible holes in the garret walls through which to aim their weapons. Private owners have restored and furnished the house as a period museum; the 30-minute guided tour details the Schriver family's experience during the battle, as well as the experience of other townspeople. (Apr-Nov, daily; Dec-Mar, weekends) **$$$**

Ski Liberty. *78 Country Club Trail. 9 miles W on PA 116, in Carroll Valley.* Phone 717/642-8282. Two quad, three double chairlifts; J-bar, handle tow; patrol, school, rentals; snowmaking; cafeteria, restaurant, bar; nursery, lodge. Longest run approximately 1 mile; vertical drop 600 feet. (Dec-Mar, daily) **$$$$**

Soldiers' National Museum. *777 Baltimore St.* Phone 717/334-4890. Dioramas of major battles, with sound; Civil War collection. (Mar-Nov, daily; schedule may vary) **$$$**

Special Events

Apple Blossom Festival. *35 Carlisle St. South Mountain Fairgrounds, 8 miles NW.* Early May.

Apple Harvest Festival. *218 Mercer St. South Mountain Fairgrounds.* Demonstrations; arts and crafts; guided tours of orchard, mountain areas. First and second weekends in Oct.

Civil War Heritage Days. Lectures by historians; Civil War collectors' show; entertainment; Civil War book show; firefighters' festival; fireworks. Late June-early July.

Motels/Motor Lodges

★ **BEST INN.** *301 Steinwehr Ave (17325).* Phone 717/334-1188; toll-free 800/237-8466; fax 717/334-1188. *www.bestinn.com.* 77 rooms, 2 story. Apr-Oct: S, D $59-$99; under 18 free; lower rates rest of year. Crib free. Pet accepted, some restrictions. TV; cable (premium), VCR available. Pool; lifeguard. Coffee in rooms. Restaurant adjacent 6:30 am-11 pm. Bar 4 pm-1 am; closed Sun. Check-out noon. Sundries. Free bus depot transportation. Downhill ski 9 miles; cross-country ski adjacent. Private patios. Sun deck. Cr cds: A, C, D, DS, MC, V.

⬜ 🐾 ➤ ⬚ ⬛ SC

★ ★ **BEST WESTERN INN.** *1 Lincoln Sq (17325).* Phone 717/337-2000; toll-free 800/528-1234; fax 717/337-2075. *www.bestwestern.com.* 83 rooms, 6 story, 23 suites. Mid-June-Oct: S, D $88-$125; each additional $5; suites $125-$150; under 16 free; higher rates: graduation, homecoming; lower rates rest of year. Crib free. TV; cable, VCR available (movies). Pool; whirlpool, poolside service, lifeguard. Restaurant 7-10:30 am, 5-9 pm. Bar from 5 pm. Check-out 11 am. Meeting rooms. Business center. In-room modem link. Free garage parking. Tennis privileges. Downhill ski 8 miles. Some refrigerators. Established 1797. Cr cds: A, D, DS, MC, V.

⬜ ➤ 🏌 ⬚ ⬛ SC 🚶

★ ★ **COLLEGE MOTEL.** *345 Carlisle St (17325).* Phone 717/334-6731; toll-free 800/367-6731. 21 rooms. Mid-June-Labor Day: S, D $76; each additional $10; higher rates: weekends, graduation, parents' weekend; lower rates rest of year. TV; cable. Pool; lifeguard. Restaurant nearby. Check-out 11 am. Cr cds: A, MC, V.

⬚ SC

★ **COLONIAL MOTEL.** *157 Carlisle St (17325).* Phone 717/334-3126; toll-free 800/336-3126. 30 rooms, 2 story. Early June-early Sept: S, D $68-$82; each additional $5; under 17 free; higher rates special events; lower rates rest of year. Crib free. TV; cable (premium). Complimentary coffee in lobby. Restaurant nearby. Check-out 11 am. Cr cds: A, MC, V.

SC

★ **COMFORT INN.** *871 York Rd (17325).* Phone 717/337-2400; toll-free 800/221-2222; fax 717/337-0831. *www.choicehotels.com.* 81 rooms, 2 story. June-Aug: S $77-$82; D $87-$90; each additional $6; under 18 free; higher rates: antique car show, college events; lower rates rest of year. Crib free. TV; cable (premium). Indoor pool; whirlpool. Complimentary continental breakfast. Restaurant nearby. Check-out 11 am. Business services available. In-room modem link. Some in-room whirlpools; refrigerator in suites. Cr cds: A, C, D, DS, ER, JCB, MC, V.

⬜ ⬚ ⬛ SC

★ ★ **CROSS KEYS MOTOR INN RESTAURANT.** *6110 York Rd (17350).* Phone 717/624-7778; fax 717/624-7941. 64 rooms, 4 story. Apr-Sept: S $39-$63; D $49-$73; each additional $5; under 12 free; weekly rates; higher rates special events; lower rates rest of year. Crib free. TV; cable, VCR available (movies). Restaurants 6 am-10 pm; Fri, Sat to 11 pm. Room service. Bar 4 pm-2 am. Check-out 11 am. Meeting rooms. Business services available. Gift shop. Golf privileges. Downhill ski 15 miles. Some in-room whirlpools. Cr cds: A, DS, MC, V.

➤ ⬛ SC

★ **DAYS INN.** *865 York Rd (17325).* Phone 717/334-0030; toll-free 800/329-7466; fax 717/337-1002. *www.daysinngettysburg.com.* 112 rooms, 5 story. Apr-Oct: S $59-$98; D $69-$108; each additional $5; under 18 free; ski plans; higher rates special events; lower rates rest of year. Crib free. TV; cable (premium), VCR available. Heated pool; lifeguard. Complimentary coffee in lobby. Restaurant adjacent 6 am-11 pm. Check-out noon. Coin laundry. Meeting rooms. Business services available. In-room modem link. Valet service. Sundries. Downhill ski 10 miles. Exercise equipment. Game room. Microwaves available. Cr cds: A, C, D, DS, JCB, MC, V.

⬜ ➤ ⬚ 🏋 ⬛ SC

★ **HOLIDAY INN EXPRESS.** *869 York Rd (15628).* Phone 717/337-1400; toll-free 800/465-4329; fax 717/337-

0159. *www.holiday-inn.com.* 51 rooms, 2 story. Apr-Oct: S $79-$99; D $89-$109; each additional $10; suites $109-$129; under 19 free; higher rates special events; lower rates rest of year. Crib free. TV; cable (premium). Indoor pool; lifeguard, whirlpool. Complimentary continental breakfast. Restaurant adjacent open 24 hours. Check-out 11 am. In-room modem link. Downhill ski 8 miles. Picnic tables. Cr cds: A, C, D, DS, JCB, MC, V.

[D] [⚑] [≈] [⊠] [SC]

★ **HOMESTEAD MOTOR LODGE.** *1650 York Rd (17325). Phone 717/334-3866.* 10 rooms. June-Oct: S, D $45-$65; each additional $8; lower rates Apr-May, Nov. Closed rest of year. TV. Restaurant nearby. Check-out 10 am. Downhill ski 8 miles. Totally nonsmoking. Cr cds: A, DS, MC, V.

[⚑] [⊠]

★★ **QUALITY INN.** *380 Steinwehr Ave (17325). Phone 717/334-1103; toll-free 800/228-5151. www.gettysburgqualityinn.com.* 109 rooms, 2 story. Apr-Oct: S, D $69-$107; suite $97-$135; under 16 free; lower rates rest of year. Crib free. Pet accepted, some restrictions. TV; cable (premium), VCR available. 2 pools, 1 indoor; lifeguard. Coffee in rooms. Restaurant opposite 6 am-11 pm. Bar 6 pm-1 am. Check-out noon. Coin laundry. Meeting room. Gift shop. Free bus depot transportation. Putting green. Downhill/cross-country ski 8 miles. Exercise equipment; sauna. Balconies. Cr cds: A, C, D, DS, JCB, MC, V.

[D] [⚑] [⚑] [≈] [⊀] [⊠] [SC]

★★ **QUALITY INN.** *401 Buford Ave (17325). Phone 717/334-3141; toll-free 800/228-5050; fax 717/334-1813. www.qualityinn.com.* 41 rooms. June-early Sept: S, D $69-$89; each additional $5; under 17 free; lower rates rest of year. Crib $3. TV; VCR available. Pool. Restaurant 7 am-9 pm. Bar from noon. Check-out noon. Business services available. Downhill ski 6 miles. General Lee's Headquarters (museum) adjacent. Cr cds: A, C, D, DS, ER, JCB, MC, V.

[D] [⚑] [≈] [⊠] [SC]

★ **RED CARPET INN.** *2450 Emmitsburg Rd (17325). Phone 717/334-1345; toll-free 800/336-1345; fax 717/334-5026.* 25 rooms. Apr-early Nov: S, D $35-$69; suites $58-$85; higher rates: spring, fall weekends, college, area events; lower rates rest of year. Crib $5. Complimentary coffee. Check-out 11 am. TV; cable (premium). Microwaves available. Restaurant nearby. Pool. Picnic tables. Cr cds: A, C, D, DS, ER, MC, V.

[≈] [⊠]

All Suite

★★ **JAMES GETTYS HOTEL.** *27 Chambersburg St (17325). Phone 717/337-1334; toll-free 800/900-5275; fax 717/334-2103. www.jamesgettyshotel.com.* 11 kitchen suites, 4 story. D $125-$145. Complimentary continental breakfast. Check-out 11 am, check-in 3 pm. TV; VCR available. Laundry services. Restaurant adjacent 11:30 am-5 pm. Downhill ski 10 miles, cross-country ski 1 mile. Concierge service. Built in 1804. Totally nonsmoking. Cr cds: A, DS, MC, V.

[D] [⚑] [⊠]

B&B/Small Inns

★★★ **BALADERRY INN.** *40 Hospital Rd (17325). Phone 717/337-1342; toll-free 800/220-0025; fax 717/337-1342. www.baladerryinn.com.* 8 rooms, 7 with shower only, 2 story. S $84-$102; D $94-$112; each additional $15; 2-day minimum weekends Apr-Nov. Children over 14 years only. TV in common area; VCR. Complimentary full breakfast. Check-out 11 am, check-in 2 pm. Tennis. Golf privileges. Downhill ski 10 miles; cross-country ski adjacent. Built in 1812; used as a field hospital during the Civil War battle of Gettysburg. Restored; furnished with antiques and reproductions. Cr cds: A, C, D, DS, MC, V.

[⊹] [⚑] [⊁] [⊠] [SC]

★★★ **BATTLEFIELD BED AND BREAKFAST INN.** *2264 Emmitsburg Rd (17325). Phone 717/334-8804; toll-free 888/766-3897. www.gettysburgbattlefield.com.* Built in 1809, this Civil War inn is found on the Gettysburg battlefield. Guests can enjoy a carriage ride, and a historic demonstration with real muskets, cannons and cavalry. 9 rooms, 2 story. No room phones. D $147-$172. Complimentary full breakfast. Check-out 11:30 am, check-in 2:30 pm. TV in sitting room; VCR. Fireplaces. Downhill ski 10 miles. Lawn games. Concierge service. Restored 1809 farmhouse famous for living history activities. Carriage rides. Totally nonsmoking. Cr cds: A, C, D, DS, MC, V.

[⚑] [⊠]

★★ **BRAFFERTON INN.** *44 York St (17325). Phone 717/337-3423.* 10 rooms, 2 story, 2 suites. No room phones. S, D $75-$125; each additional $10; suites $120-$125; higher rates special events. TV in suites. Complimentary full breakfast. Restaurant nearby. Check-out 11 am, check-in 2 pm. First house built in town (1786); antiques. Cr cds: A, DS, MC, V.

[⊠]

★★★ **FARNSWORTH HOUSE INN.** *401 Baltimore St (17325). Phone 717/334-8838; fax 717/334-5862. www.gettysburgaddress.com.* 9 rooms, 2 story. No room phones. Apr-Oct: S $85; D $95; each additional $10. TV in some rooms, sitting room; cable. Complimentary full breakfast. Restaurant (see also FARNSWORTH HOUSE). Check-out 11 am, check-in 3 pm. Business services available. Concierge service. Luggage handling. Downhill ski 7 miles; cross-country ski 1/4 mile. Some in-room whirlpools. Historic house (1810), restored to its

1863 appearance. The uppermost level of the inn was once used by Confederate sharpshooters; more than 100 bullet holes still remain in the south wall of the inn. Daily tours. Cr cds: A, DS, MC, V.

★ ★ ★ **GASLIGHT INN.** *33 E Middle St (17325). Phone 717/337-9100; toll-free 1-800/914-5698; fax 717/ 337-1100.* This bed and breakfast is located in the center of historic Gettysburg, near shopping, restaurants, and local attractions. 9 rooms, 3 story. D $100-$175; each additional $20; 2-day minimum holiday weekends. Children over 10 years only. Complimentary full breakfast. Check-out 11 am, check-in 3 pm. TV; VCR (free movies). In-room modem link. Dining room 6-8 pm (by reservations only). Health club privileges. Concierge service. Italianate house (1872) with original exterior trim. Rooms decorated and named in theme of flowers. Cr cds: A, DS, MC, V.

★ ★ **GETTYSTOWN INN BED & BREAKFAST.** *89 Steinwehr Ave (17325). Phone 717/334-2100; fax 717/ 334-6905. www.dobbinhouse.com.* 5 rooms, 2 story, 1 suite. No room phones. Mar-Nov: S $79-$99, D $85-$105; each additional $6; suite $105; under 12 free; weekly rates; higher rates: holidays (2-day minimum), special events; lower rates rest of year. TV in some rooms; cable. Complimentary full breakfast. Restaurant (see also DOBBIN HOUSE). Check-out 10 am, check-in 2 pm. Downhill ski 7 miles; cross-country ski 1 mile. Refrigerators. Renovated 1860s home; antiques. Overlooks site of Abraham Lincoln's Gettysburg Address. Totally nonsmoking. Cr cds: A, MC, V.

★ ★ **THE HERR TAVERN AND PUBLICK HOUSE.** *900 Chambersburg Rd (17325). Phone 717/334-4332; toll-free 800/362-9849; fax 717/334-3332. www. herrtavern.com.* 16 rooms, 3 story. D $89-$149. Children over 12 years only. Complimentary full breakfast. Check-out 11 am, check-in 4 pm. TV; VCR (movies). Restaurant. Room service. Downhill ski 5 miles. Built in 1815, served as Confederate hospital. Totally nonsmoking. Cr cds: DS, MC, V.

★ ★ **OLD APPLEFORD INN.** *218 Carlisle St (17325). Phone 717/337-1711; toll-free 800/275-3373; fax 717/334-6228.* 10 rooms, 6 with shower only, 3 story. No room phones. Apr-Oct: S $80-$95; D $105-$120; suite $115-$150; 2-day minimum weekends, holidays, special events; lower rates rest of year. Children over 8 years only. Complimentary full breakfast; afternoon refreshments. Restaurant nearby. Check-out 11 am, check-in 2 pm. Concierge service. Downhill ski 7 miles; cross-country ski 15 miles. Health club privileges. Victorian mansion

(1867); many antiques. Totally nonsmoking. Cr cds: A, DS, MC, V.

Restaurants

★ ★ ★ **DOBBIN HOUSE.** *89 Steinwehr Ave (17325).; fax 717/334-6905. www.dobbinhouse.com.* Built for Reverend Alexander Dobbin in 1776, this colonial restaurant is listed on the National Register of Historic Places. Meals are served against a backdrop of traditional 18th-century décor, including stone walls, fireplaces, and carved woodwork. American, seafood menu. Hours: 11:30 am-11 pm. Closed Jan 1, Thanksgiving, Dec 25. Lunch $6.25-$18.95, dinner $18.25-$23.95. Bar. Children's menu. Oldest building in Gettysburg; built 1776. Totally nonsmoking. Cr cds: A, DS, MC, V.

★ ★ ★ **FARNSWORTH HOUSE.** *401 Baltimore St (17325). Phone 717/334-8838; fax 717/334-5862. www. farnsworthhousedining.com.* Hours: 5-9 pm. Closed Jan 1, Thanksgiving, Dec 25. Dinner $13.95-$21.95. Bar. Children's menu. Built in 1810; tour available. Outdoor seating. Cr cds: A, DS, MC, V.

★ **GINGERBREAD MAN.** *217 Steinwehr Ave (17325). Phone 717/334-1100. www.thegingerbreadman.net.* Hours: 11 am-11 pm; Sun to 10 pm. Closed major holidays. Varied menu. Bar. Lunch $4.50-$8.95, dinner $6.95-$18.95. Children's menu. Specializes in NY-style deli sandwiches, Mexican dishes, fresh Maryland crabcakes. Casual, lively atmosphere. Cr cds: A, D, DS, MC, V.

★ ★ **THE HERR TAVERN & PUBLICK HOUSE.** *900 Chambersburg Rd (17325). Phone 717/334-4332; fax 717/334-3332. www.herrtavern.com.* Hours: 11 am-9 pm; Sun from 5 pm. Closed Jan 1, Dec 24, 25. Reservations accepted. Continental menu. Bar. Lunch $3.49-$8.49, dinner $13-$20. Specializes in blackened prime rib, seafood, pasta. Children's menu. Restored antebellum tavern with period art and antiques. Cr cds: A, DS, MC, V.

Gettysburg National Military Park (I-8)

See also Gettysburg, Hanover

The hallowed battlefield of Gettysburg, scene of one of the most decisive battles of the Civil War and immortalized by Lincoln's Gettysburg Address, is preserved by the

National Park Service. The town itself is still a college community, as it was more than a hundred years ago on July 1-3, 1863, when General Robert E. Lee led his Confederate Army in its greatest invasion of the North. The defending Northerners under Union General George Meade repulsed the Southern assault after three days of fierce fighting, which left 51,000 men dead, wounded, or missing.

The Gettysburg National Military Park has more than 35 miles of roads through 5,900 acres of the battlefield area. There are more than 1,300 monuments, markers, and tablets of granite and bronze; 400 cannons are also located on the field.

Visitors may wish to tour the battlefield with a Battlefield Guide, licensed by the National Park Service (two-hour tour; fee). The guides escort visitors to all points of interest and sketch the movement of troops and details of the battle. Or visitors may wish to first orient themselves at the Electric Map at the Visitor Center; then using the park folder, the battlefield can be toured without a guide. Audio cassettes are also available for self-guided tours.

The late President Dwight D. Eisenhower's retirement farm, a National Historic Site, adjoins the battlefield. It is open to the public on a limited-tour basis. All visitors must obtain tour tickets at the tour information center, located at the lobby of the Visitor Center-Electric Map building. Transportation to the farm is by shuttle (fee). For further information contact Gettysburg National Military Park, 97 Taneytown Rd, Gettysburg 17325; 717/334-1124.

What to See and Do

The Angle. Spot where Pickett's Charge was repulsed on July 3, referred to as "high water mark" of the Confederacy.

Culp's Hill. Site of longest sustained fighting during battle.

Cyclorama Center. *Adjacent to visitor center.* Instructive film and exhibits: 356-foot Cyclorama painting of Pickett's Charge. (Daily) **$$**

Devil's Den. Stronghold of Confederate sharpshooters following its capture during action on the second day.

East Cemetery Hill. Rallying point for Union forces on first day of battle. Scene of fierce fighting on evening of second day.

Eisenhower National Historic Site. *97 Taneytown Rd (Visitor Center).* Phone 717/338-9114 (advance tickets) or 717/338-9114 (info). Farm and home of the 34th President of the United States and his wife, Mamie. Tour of grounds and home (1 1/2-2 hours). Self-guided tours explore the farm and skeet range. Reception Center houses exhibits and bookstore; 11-minute video is shown. Access to site is by shuttle only, from the National Park Service Visitor Center. (Daily; closed Jan 1, Thanksgiving, Dec 25) **$$$**

The Eternal Light Peace Memorial. *On Oak Ridge.* Erected in 1938 and dedicated by President Roosevelt to "peace eternal in a nation united."

The Gettysburg National Cemetery. Site of Lincoln's Gettysburg Address.

Little Round Top. Key Union position during second and third days of battle.

Memorials to State Units. Includes Pennsylvania State Monument, with names of more than 34,500 Pennsylvanian soldiers who participated in the battle.

Seminary Ridge. Main Confederate battle line.

☆ **Visitor Center-Electric Map-Gettysburg Museum of the Civil War.** *On PA 134.* Electric map. Visits to the park should begin here. Park information, including a self-guided auto tour, and guides may be obtained at the center. Story of battle told on 750-square-foot electric map surrounded by 525 seats (every 45 minutes; fee). Gettysburg Museum of the Civil War has an extensive collection of Civil War relics (free). (Daily; closed Jan 1, Thanksgiving, Dec 25) **$$**

The Wheatfield and Peach Orchard. Scene of heavy Union and Confederate losses on the second day of fighting.

Whitworth Guns on Oak Hill. Only breech-loading cannon used here.

Greensburg (G-3)

See also Connellsville, Donegal, Ligonier, New Stanton

Founded 1785 **Pop** 15,889 **Elev** 1,099 ft **Area code** 724 **Zip** 15601

Information Laurel Highlands Visitors Bureau, 120 E Main St, Ligonier 15658; 724/238-5661

Web www.laurelhighlands.org

Greensburg was named for Revolutionary General Nathanael Greene.

What to See and Do

Bushy Run Battlefield. *Bushy Run Rd. NW on PA 993.* Phone 724/527-5584. Here, Colonel Henry Bouquet defeated united Native American forces during Pontiac's War on Aug 5 and 6, 1763. The battle lifted the siege of Fort Pitt and was the turning point of the war. Picnicking, park (free), hiking trails. Visitor center exhibits depict battle (Wed-Sun; closed holidays). **$$**

Historic Hanna's Town. *951 Old Salem Rd (15601). 3 miles NE via US 119.* Phone 724/836-1800. Costumed tour guide tells story of Hanna's Town, site of first court west of Alleghenies. Includes reconstructed courthouse, tavern, jail, and stockaded fort; picnic area. (June-Aug, Tues-Sun; May, Sept and Oct, weekends only) **$$**

Lincoln Highway Heritage Corridor. *114 S Market St. Phone 724/238-9030.* A 140-mile stretch of US 30 extending from Greensburg to Chambersburg. Pass through and explore countless historical and recreational areas. Driving guide available (fee). **$**

Westmoreland County Courthouse. *Main and Pittsburgh sts. Phone 724/830-3000.* Building in style of Italian Renaissance; restored in 1982. (Mon-Fri; closed holidays)

Westmoreland Museum of American Art. *221 N Main St. Phone 724/837-1500.* 18th-, 19th-, and early 20th-century American paintings, sculpture, furniture and decorative arts. 19th- and early 20th-century southwestern Pennsylvania paintings. Extensive toy collection. Lectures, guided tours. (Wed-Sun; closed holidays) **DONATION**

Motels/Motor Lodges

★ **COMFORT INN.** *1129 E Pittsburgh St (15601). Phone 724/832-2600; toll-free 800/228-5150; fax 724/834-3442. www.comfortinn.com.* 77 rooms, 3 story. S $66-$110; D $76-$110; each additional $5; suites $81-$147; under 18 free; higher rates special events. Crib free. TV; cable (premium), VCR available (movies). Heated pool. Complimentary continental breakfast. Restaurant nearby. Check-out 11 am. Meeting room. Business services available. Valet service. Health club privileges. Some in-room whirlpools, refrigerators, wet bars; microwaves available. Cr cds: A, C, D, DS, ER, JCB, MC, V.

D ⊷ ⊠ SC

★ ★ **FOUR POINTS BY SHERATON.** *100 Sheraton Dr (Rte 30E) (15601). Phone 724/836-6060; fax 724/834-5640. www.sheraton.com.* 146 rooms, 2 story. S $66-$80; D $71-$85; each additional $5; suites $110-$250; under 17 free; package plans. Crib free. Check-out noon. TV; cable (premium), VCR available. Some refrigerators. Valet service. Restaurant 6:30 am-2 pm, 5-10 pm. Bar 11-2 am; entertainment. Exercise equipment, sauna. Indoor pool. 9-hole golf course, greens fee, putting green, pro shop. Free transportation. Meeting rooms. Business services. Sundries. Cr cds: A, C, D, DS, JCB, MC, V.

D ⊀ ⊷ ⊼ ⊠ SC

★ **KNIGHTS INN.** *1215 S Main St (15601). Phone 724/836-7100; toll-free 800/843-5644; fax 724/837-5390. www.knightsinn.com.* 110 rooms, 10 suites, 11 kitchens May-Oct: S $47.95-$57.95; D $56.95-$73.95; each additional $7; kitchen units $63.95-$75.95; under 18 free; lower rates rest of year. Crib free. TV; cable (premium), VCR available. Pool. Complimentary coffee in lobby. Restaurant adjacent 6 am-11 pm. Check-out noon. Meeting room. In-room modem link. Guest laundry. Refrigerators, microwaves available. Cr cds: A, C, D, DS, MC, V.

⊷ ⊠ SC

★ ★ ★ **MOUNTAIN VIEW INN.** *001 Village Dr (15601). Phone 724/834-5300; toll-free 800/537-8709; fax 724/834-5304. www.mountainviewinn.com.* Found tucked away in the Laurel Highlands, this inn has been providing visitors with superb accommodations and fine dining since 1924. 97 rooms. S $59-$135; D $69-$135; suites $150-$275. TV; cable (premium), VCR available. Pool. Complimentary continental breakfast. Coffee in rooms. Restaurant 7 am-2 pm, 5-9 pm; weekend hours vary. Room service 7:30 am-11 pm. Bar 11 am-midnight; Fri, Sat to 1 am; Sun noon-8 pm. Check-out 11 am. Meeting rooms. Business services available. In-room modem link. Sundries. Exercise equipment. Health club privileges. Antique décor; English and herb gardens; gazebo. Cr cds: A, C, D, DS, MC, V.

D ⊷ ⊼ ⊠ SC

Restaurant

★ ★ **CARBONE'S.** *US 119 (15624). Phone 724/834-3430; fax 724/836-2501. www.carbonepasta.com.* American, Italian menu. Hours: 4:30-9 pm; Fri, Sat to 10 pm. Closed Sun; major holidays. Dinner $8.95-$16.95. Children's menu. Cr cds: A, D, DS, MC, V.

D SC

Hamburg (F-11)

See also Kutztown, Reading, Shartlesville

Founded 1779 **Pop** 4,114 **Elev** 373 ft **Area code** 484 and 610 **Zip** 19526

Information Reading/Berks County Visitors Bureau, 352 Penn St, Reading 19602; 610/375-4085 or 800/443-6610

Web www.readingberkspa.com

Situated on the banks of the Schuylkill River, Hamburg is a center for one of the finest farming sections in Pennsylvania. The town's industries include the manufacture of brooms, iron and steel castings, knitwear, and soft-drink products.

What to See and Do

Blue Rocks. *341 Sousley Rd (19534). 5 miles E on I-78 to Lenhartsville, then 2 miles N on PA 143. Phone 610/756-6366.* Covers 125 acres; pool, fishing (stocked pond); picnicking, two pavilions; hiking, Appalachian Trail; camping, trailer facilities (fee; hookups additional). Game room. **$**

Hawk Mountain Sanctuary. *1700 Hawk Mountain Rd (19529). 11 miles N via PA 61 and 895; follow signs. Phone 610/756-6961.* Hawk and eagle flights visible with binoculars from lookouts mid-Aug-mid-Dec; museum, bookstore. (Daily; closed Jan 1, Thanksgiving, Dec 25) **$$$**

Wanamaker, Kempton & Southern, Inc. *5 miles E on I-78 to Lenhartsville exit, then 5 miles N on PA 143 to Kempton. Phone 610/756-6469.* A 6-mile, 40-minute round trip on steam or deisel train along the Ontelaunee Creek at the foot of Hawk Mountain. Model railroad (Sun), antique shop. Snack bar, picnic area. Steam train (July-Aug and Oct, Sat and Sun afternoons; May and June, Sun afternoons). Diesel train (June and Sept, first and third Sat afternoons only). Also special events throughout the year. **$$**

Hanover (I-9)

See also Gettysburg, York

Founded 1763 **Pop** 14,535 **Elev** 609 ft **Area code** 717 **Zip** 17331

Information Hanover Area Chamber of Commerce, 146 Carlisle St; 717/637-6130

Web www.hanoverchamber.com

Known in early days as "McAllisterstown" (for founder Colonel Richard McAllister) and "Rogue's Harbor" (for lack of law enforcement), Hanover is in the rich Conewago Valley. Here, on June 30, 1863, Confederate General J. E. B. Stuart's cavalry tangled with Union forces under Generals Kilpatrick and Custer. The battle prevented Stuart from reaching Gettysburg in time to function as "the eyes of Lee's army."

Among the products of the town's diversified industry are books, wirecloth, yarns, furniture, industrial machinery, textiles, and foods, including the famous pretzel maker, Snyder's of Hanover.

What to See and Do

Codorus State Park. *1066 Blooming Grove Rd (17331). 3 miles E on PA 216. Phone 717/637-2816.* Approximately 3,300 acres. Swimming pool, fishing in 1,275-acre Lake Marburg, boating (rentals, mooring, launching, marina); hunting, hiking, bridle trails, cross-country skiing, snowmobiling, sledding, ice skating, ice boating, ice fishing, picnicking, mountain biking, snack bar, tent and trailer sites. Standard fees.

Conewago Chapel. *30 Basilica Dr, 2 miles W on PA 116, then 2 miles N. Phone 717/637-2721.* (1741) Oldest stone Catholic church in the US. Designated Sacred Heart Basilica in 1962. Cemetery dates from 1752. (Daily) **FREE**

Neas House Museum. *113 W Chestnut St. Phone 717/632-3207.* Neas House (circa 1783), restored Georgian mansion, serves as local history museum. (May-Nov, Tues-Fri) Special events (spring, summer, late Dec). **FREE**

Utz Quality Foods, Inc. *900 High St. Phone 717/637-6644.* Producers of potato chips and snack foods. Glass-enclosed tour gallery overlooks production area; push-to-talk audio program and closed-circuit TV monitors. (Mon-Thurs; closed holidays) **FREE**

B&B/Small Inn

★ ★ ★ **THE BEECHMONT BED AND BREAKFAST INN.** *315 Broadway (17331). Phone 717/632-3013; toll-free 800/553-7009; fax 717/632-2769. www.thebeechmont.com.* Built in 1834, this bed and breakfast is located just 14 miles outside of Gettysburg. It offers four large guest rooms and three suites, each furnished with fine antiques. Breakfast can be enjoyed in the dining room, on the porch, or in the rooms. 7 rooms, 2 story. D $85-$109; suites $129-$149. Children over 12 years only. Complimentary full breakfast; afternoon refreshments. Check-out 11 am, check-in 3 pm. Federal period house (1834); landscaped courtyard. Cr cds: A, DS, MC, V. ⊠ SC

Harmony (E-2)

See also Butler, Pittsburgh

Founded 1804 **Pop** 937 **Elev** 925 ft **Area code** 724 **Zip** 16037

Information Butler County Chamber of Commerce, 112 Woody Dr, PO Box 1082, Butler, 16003; 724/283-2222

Web www.butlercountychamber.com

First settlement of George Rapp's Harmony Society, Harmony served the colony only until 1814. More than 100 of the original group are buried in Harmonists Cemetery, southeast of town. Several of the Rappite Society's sturdy brick houses still stand in the village.

What to See and Do

Harmony Museum. *218 Mercer St. Phone 724/452-7341.* (1809) Exhibits depict early life under Harmonists and Mennonites; regional history. The Harmony Society was one of America's most successful experiments in communal living. Harmony was the society's first home (1804). Tour. (Tues-Sun afternoons) **$$**

Special Events

Christmas Open House. *218 Mercer St.* Candlelight tour of Harmony Museum, Wagner House and Ziegler log house. Entertainment, refreshments. Contact museum for schedule. Early Dec.

Dankfest. *218 Mercer. Phone 722 452-7341.* Pioneer craft festival held on grounds of Harmony Museum (see).

Crafts, entertainment, tours, refreshments. Contact museum for schedule. Late Aug.

Harrisburg (G-9)

See also Carlisle, Hershey, York

Settled 1718 **Pop** 48,950 **Elev** 360 ft **Area code** 717

Information Capital Regional Chamber of Commerce, 3211 N Front St, 17110-1342, phone 717/232-4099; or the Harrisburg-Hershey-Carlisle Tourism & Convention Bureau, 25 N Front St, 17101, phone 717/231-7788

Web www.harrisburgregionalchamber.org

This midstate metropolis is graced by what many consider the finest capitol building in the nation. Its riverside park (known as City Island), Italian Lake, unique museum, and beautiful Forum are the showplaces; commerce, industry, and politics keep the city going.

The site was viewed in 1615 by Etienne Brulé on a trip down the Susquehanna, but more than a century passed before John Harris, the first settler, opened his trading post here. His son established the town in 1785. It became the seat of state government in 1812; the cornerstone of the first capitol building was laid in 1819.

What to See and Do

Capitol Hill buildings. *N 3rd and Walnut sts. Phone 717/787-6810.* Clustered in a 45-acre complex, the major buildings are

The Capitol. *Main entrance, 3rd and State sts.* (dedicated 1906) Italian Renaissance building covers 2 acres, has 651 rooms; 26,000-ton, 272-foot dome, imitating that of St. Peter's in Rome, dominates city skyline. Includes murals by Abbey and Okley. Tours (daily; closed holidays). **FREE**

Finance Building. Ceiling murals by Maragliotti, Eugene Savage; mural in south vestibule illustrates The Collection of Taxes. (Mon-Fri)

Forum Building. Includes auditorium below constellation-bedecked ceiling; walls review man's progress through time. Main lobby boasts a Maragliotti ceiling. General and law libraries.

North Office Building. Map inscribed on main lobby floor shows state highways, seals of Pennsylvania cities.

South Office Building. Colorful murals by Edward Trumbull depict Penn's Treaty with the Indians and The Industries of Pittsburgh.

The State Museum of Pennsylvania. *N of Capitol Building, 3rd and North sts. Phone 717/787-4978.* A six-story circular building housing four stories of galleries, authentic early country store, Native American life

exhibit, technological and industrial exhibits, collection of antique autos and period carriages; planetarium; natural history and geology exhibits and one of the world's largest framed paintings, Rothermel's The Battle of Gettysburg. Planetarium has public shows (Sat and Sun; fee). (Tues-Sun; closed holidays) **FREE**

Dauphin County Courthouse. *Front and Market sts. Phone 717/255-2741.* Seven imposing courtrooms; outline map on floor of main foyer pictures borough and township boundaries. (Mon-Fri; closed holidays)

Fort Hunter Park. *6 miles N on N Front St.* Historic 37-acre property; site of British-built fort erected in 1754 to combat mounting threats prior to the French and Indian War. In 1787, the land was purchased and became a farm that eventually grew into a self-sufficient village. The Pennsylvania Canal runs through the park; on the grounds are historic buttonwood trees dating from William Penn's time; a 19th-century boxwood garden; herb gardens; paths along the banks of the Susquehanna River; picnic area. Also here are an ice house, springhouse (circa 1800), Centennial barn (1876), and corncrib (1880). Also on the grounds, but not open to the public because of restoration, are the old tavern (1800), and stone stable. Outstanding feature of the park is

Fort Hunter Mansion. *5300 N Front St. Phone 717/599-5751.* Federal-style stone mansion, built in three sections. Front stone portions were built in 1786 and 1814; rear wooden portion built in 1870. Spacious mansion displays period furnishings, clothing, toys, and other artifacts. Guided tours. (May-Dec, Tues-Sun) **$$**

Indian Echo Caverns. *368 Middletown Rd. 10 miles E on US 322, 422, in Hummelstown. Phone 717/566-8131.* Stalagmite and stalactite formations. Picnicking, playground. (Daily, schedule varies; closed Jan 1, Thanksgiving, Dec 25) **$$$**

Italian Lake. *N 3rd and Division sts.* Bordered with flowers, shrubs, and shade trees in summer.

John Harris Mansion. *219 S Front St. Phone 717/233-3462.* Home of city's founder, now Historical Society of Dauphin County headquarters. Stone house has 19th-century furnishings, library (Mon-Thurs; fee), collection of county artifacts. Tours (Mon-Thurs and by appointment). **$$$**

Penn National Race Course. *I-81 exit 28. NE via I-81, exit 28, in Grantville. Phone 717/469-2211.* Live year-round Thoroughbred racing (Wed, Fri-Sun). Nationwide simulcasts (daily). Terrace dining room; gift shop. **$$**

Reservoir Park. *Walnut and N 19th sts.* View of east end of city, five nearby counties.

Riverfront Park. Four miles along Susquehanna River, with park promenade flanking Front St, concrete walk along river.

Rockville Bridge. *4 miles N on US 22.* (1902) A 3,810-foot stone-arch bridge; 48 spans carry four tracks of Penn Central Railroad main line.

Special Events

Eastern Sports & Outdoor Show. *2301 N. Cameron St. State Farm Show Complex. Phone 717/630-2268.* Early-mid-Feb.

Kipona. Boating and water-related activites. Labor Day weekend.

Pennsylvania National Horse Show. *1509 Cedar Cliff Dr. Phone 717/975-3677.* Ten days mid-Oct.

Pennsylvania State Farm Show. *2301 N Cameron. State Farm Show Complex. Phone 717/787-5373.* State fair. Early-mid-Jan.

Motels/Motor Lodges

★ **BAYMONT HARRISBURG-AIRPORT.** *200 N Mountain Rd (17112). Phone 717/540-9339; toll-free 800/428-3438; fax 717/540-9486. www.baymontinns.com.* 66 rooms, 8 suites, 3 story. Apr-Oct: S $57.95-$70.95; D $63.95-$76.95; suites $66.95-$80.95; under 19 free; lower rates rest of year. Pet accepted. Complimentary continental breakfast. Check-out noon. TV; VCR available. In-room modem link. Restaurant nearby. Business center. Cr cds: A, C, D, DS, JCB, MC, V.

D 🐾 🏊 ⌘ SC 🏃

★ ★ **BEST WESTERN HARRISBURG/HERSHEY HOTEL & SUITES.** *300 N Mountain Rd (17112). Phone 717/652-7180; toll-free 800/528-1234; fax 717/541-8991. www.bestwestern.com.* 49 rooms, 2 story. S $50-$80; D $50-$85; each additional $3; under 13 free. Crib $5. Pet accepted. TV; cable (premium). Restaurant 6:30 am-9 pm. Bar 11 am-11 pm. Check-out 11 am. Business services available. In-room modem link. Sundries. Microwaves available. Cr cds: A, C, D, DS, MC, V.

🐾 ⌘ SC

★ **COMFORT INN.** *4021 Union Deposit Rd (17109). Phone 717/561-8100; toll-free 800/253-1409; fax 717/561-1357. www.harrisburgpacomfortinn.com.* 115 rooms, 5 story. June-Oct: S, D $79-$109; under 18 free; higher rates car shows; lower rates rest of year. Crib free. Pet accepted. TV; cable (premium). Heated pool; lifeguard. Complimentary continental breakfast. Coffee in rooms. Restaurant adjacent 6 am-10 pm. Check-out noon. Coin laundry. Meeting rooms. Business services available. Free airport, train station transportation. Health club privileges. Microwaves available. Cr cds: A, C, D, DS, ER, JCB, MC, V.

D 🐾 🏊 ⌘ SC

★ ★ **CROWNE PLAZA.** *23 S 2nd St (17101). Phone 717/234-5021; fax 717/234-6797. www.crowneplaza.com.* 261 rooms, 10 story. S $75-$95; D $85-$105; each additional $10; studio rooms $78-$90; suites $145; under 19 free. TV; cable (premium), VCR available (movies). Indoor pool. Restaurant 6:30 am-2 pm, 5-10 pm. Bar 4:30 pm-1 am. Check-out noon. Meeting rooms. Business services available. In-room modem link. Gift shop. Airport transportation. Exercise equipment. Microwaves available. Rooftop patio. Cr cds: A, C, D, DS, ER, JCB, MC, V.

D 🏊 🏋 ⌘ SC

★ **DAYS INN.** *3919 N Front St (17110). Phone 717/233-3100; toll-free 800/329-7466; fax 717/233-6415. www.daysinn.com.* 116 rooms, 3 story. S $54.99-$69.99; D $54.99-$74.99; each additional $5; under 12 free; higher rates: car shows, farm show. Crib free. TV; cable. Pool; lifeguard. Playground. Complimentary continental breakfast. Restaurant nearby. Check-out noon. Coin laundry. Business services available. In-room modem link. Exercise equipment. Refrigerators, microwaves available. Picnic tables. Cr cds: A, C, D, DS, JCB, MC, V.

D 🏊 🏋 ⌘ SC

★ **HAMPTON INN.** *4950 Ritter Rd (17055). Phone 717/691-1300; fax 717/691-9692. www.hamptoninn.com.* 129 rooms, 4 story. S $79-$84; D $88-$93; under 18 free; ski plan. Crib free. Complimentary continental breakfast. Check-out 11 am. TV; cable (premium), VCR available. In-room modem link. Microwaves available. Coin laundry. Restaurant adjacent 11 am-11 pm. Health club privileges. Exercise equipment. Heated pool, whirlpool, lifeguard. Downhill ski 20 miles. Meeting rooms. Business center. Cr cds: A, C, D, DS, MC, V.

D 🏊 🏊 🏋 ⌘ 🏃

★ **HAMPTON INN.** *4230 Union Deposit Rd (17111). Phone 717/545-9595; toll-free 800/426-7866; fax 717/545-6907. www.hamptoninn.com.* 145 rooms, 5 story. S $68-$80; D $75-$86; under 18 free; higher rates auto shows. Crib available. Complimentary continental breakfast. Check-out noon. TV; cable (premium). Microwaves available. Valet services, coin laundry. Restaurant adjacent open 24 hours. Health club privileges. Exercise equipment. Heated pool, whirlpool, lifeguard. Golf privileges. Downhill ski 15 miles. Meeting rooms. Business services. Cr cds: A, C, D, DS, MC, V.

D 🏊 🍴 🏊 🏋 ⌘ SC

★ ★ **HOLIDAY INN.** *148 Sheraton Dr (17070). Phone 717/774-2721; fax 717/774-2485. www.holilday-inn.com.* 196 rooms, 2 story. May-Oct: S, D $59-$99; each additional $10; suites $160; under 18 free; family, weekend, holiday rates; ski plans; higher rates special events; lower rates rest of year. Crib free. Pet accepted, some restrictions; $10. TV; cable (premium). Indoor pool; whirlpool. Restaurant 6:30 am-2 pm, 5-9 pm; Fri, Sat to 10 pm. Room service. Bar 5 pm-2 am; entertainment. Check-out

11 am. Meeting rooms. Business center. In-room modem link. Bellstaff. Valet service. Coin laundry. Free airport, train station transportation. Exercise equipment. Health club privileges. Game room. Refrigerators, microwaves available. Some balconies. Picnic tables, grills. Luxury level. Cr cds: A, C, D, DS, JCB, MC, V.

⊡ 🐾 ⌚ 🛅 🛩 ⚆ SC 🏃

★ ★ **HOLIDAY INN.** *4751 Lindle Rd (17111). Phone 717/939-7841; toll-free 800/637-4817; fax 717/939-9317. www.holiday-inn.com.* 300 rooms, 4 story. S $109-$139; D $121-$151; each additional $12; under 19 free. Crib free. Check-out 10 am. TV; cable (premium). Private patios, balconies. Valet services. Restaurant 7 am-2 pm, 5-10 pm. Bar 11-2 am. Room service 7 am-10 pm. Health club privileges. Exercise equipment, sauna. Game room. 2 pools, 1 indoor, whirlpool, poolside service, lifeguard. Putting green. Lighted tennis. Free airport transportation. Business services. Convention facilities. Cr cds: A, C, D, DS, JCB, MC, V.

⊡ 🐾 ✈ 🛅 🎿 ⌚ 🛩 ⚆

★ ★ **HOLIDAY INN.** *5401 Carlisle Pike (17055). Phone 717/697-0321; toll-free 800/772-7829; fax 717/697-5917. www.holiday-inn.com.* 218 rooms, 2 story. Feb-Oct: S $93; D $103; each additional $10; suites $125-$200; under 18 free; weekly rates; higher rates special events; lower rates rest of year. Crib free. Pet accepted, some restrictions; $50 deposit. Complimentary continental breakfast, coffee in rooms. Check-out noon. TV; cable (premium). Some in-room whirlpools; microwaves available. Coin laundry. Restaurant 6:30 am-9 pm. Bar 5 pm-2 am; entertainment. Room service. Exercise equipment. Heated indoor/outdoor pool, lifeguard. Miniature golf. Picnic tables. Meeting rooms. Business services. Cr cds: A, C, D, DS, JCB, MC, V.

⊡ 🐾 ⌚ 🛅 🛩 ⚆ SC

★ ★ **HOWARD JOHNSON.** *473 Eisenhower Blvd (17111). Phone 717/564-6300; fax 717/564-4840. www.hojo.com.* 176 rooms, 2 story. S $55-$79; D $62-$89; each additional $8; under 17 free; higher rates Hershey Antique Auto Show. Check-out noon. TV; cable (premium). Restaurant 5 am-midnight. Bar from 11 am. Exercise equipment. Pool, children's pool. Free airport transportation. Business center. Cr cds: A, C, D, DS, MC, V.

⊡ ⌚ 🛅 ✈ 🛩 🏃

★ **RED ROOF INN.** *400 Corp Cir (17110). Phone 717/657-1445; toll-free 800/843-7663; fax 717/657-2775. www.redroof.com.* 110 rooms, 2 story. S $34-$44; D $44-$62; under 18 free. Crib free. Pet accepted. TV; cable (premium). Complimentary coffee in lobby. Restaurant nearby. Check-out noon. Business services available. In-room modem link. Cr cds: A, C, D, DS, MC, V.

⊡ 🐾 🛩 SC

Hotels

★ ★ **FOUR POINTS BY SHERATON.** *800 E Park Dr (17111). Phone 717/561-2800; toll-free 800/644-3144; fax 717/561-8398. www.fourpoints.com.* 174 rooms, 3 story. D $79-$145. Pet accepted, some restrictions. Check-out noon. TV; cable (premium). In-room modem link. Restaurant 6:30 am-10 pm. Bar 11-2 am. Room service. Exercise room, sauna. Game room. Heated pool; whirlpool. Free airport transportation. Cr cds: A, C, D, DS, ER, JCB, MC, V.

⊡ 🐾 ⌚ 🛅 🛩 ⚆ SC

★ ★ ★ **HILTON HOTEL.** *1 N 2nd St (17101). Phone 717/233-6000; fax 717/233-6271. www.hilton.com.* 356 rooms, 15 story. D $129-$199; each additional $10; suites $250-$600; weekend rates. Check-out noon. TV; cable (premium). In-room modem link. Restaurant 6:30 am-11 pm. Bar 11-1 am; entertainment. Health club privileges. Exercise equipment. Indoor pool. Valet parking. Free airport transportation. Concierge. Luxury level. Cr cds: A, D, DS, MC, V.

⊡ ⌚ 🛅 🛩 ⚆

★ ★ ★ **MARRIOTT HARRISBURG.** *4650 Lindle Rd (17111). Phone 717/564-5511; fax 717/564-6173. www.marriott.com.* 358 rooms, 10 story. D $79-$159. Check-out 11 am. TV; cable (premium), VCR available. In-room modem link. Restaurant 6 am-midnight. Bar to 2 am; entertainment. Room service. Exercise equipment, sauna. Game room. Indoor/outdoor pool, whirlpool, poolside service. Free airport transportation. Luxury level. Cr cds: A, C, D, DS, ER, JCB, MC, V.

⊡ ⌚ 🛅 🛩 ⚆

★ ★ **RADISSON PENN HARRIS HOTEL & CONVENTION CENTER.** *1150 Camp Hill Byp (17011). Phone 717/763-7117; toll-free 800/333-3333; fax 717/763-7120. www.radisson.com.* 250 rooms, 2-3 story. No elevator. S $69-$119; D $79-$139; each additional $10; suites $225-$400; under 18 free. Crib free. Pet accepted. TV; cable (premium). Pool; poolside service, lifeguard. Coffee in rooms. Restaurant 6:30 am-10 pm. Room service. Bar noon-2 am. Check-out 11 am. Convention facilities. Business center. In-room modem link. Valet service. Bellstaff. Free airport transportation. Exercise equipment. Some refrigerators. Cr cds: A, C, D, DS, ER, JCB, MC, V.

⊡ 🐾 ⌚ 🛅 🛩 ⚆ SC 🏃

★ ★ **WYNDHAM GARDEN HOTEL.** *765 Eisenhower Blvd (17111). Phone 717/558-9500; toll-free 800/528-1234; fax 717/558-8956. www.wyndham.com.* 167 rooms, 6 story. May-Oct: S, D $89-$119; each additional $10; suites $150; under 19 free; ski plans; weekend rates; higher rates car shows; lower rates rest of year. Crib free. Pet accepted. TV; cable (premium). Heated pool; lifeguard. Coffee in rooms. Restaurant 6 am-2:30 pm, 5-10 pm. Bar

4 pm-midnight. Check-out noon. Meeting rooms. Business services available. In-room modem link. Free airport, train station, bus depot transportation. Downhill ski 20 miles. Exercise equipment. Health club privileges. Refrigerator in suites; microwaves available. Cr cds: A, C, D, DS, ER, JCB, MC, V.

D ⚑ 🏊 ⇌ 🏃 ⊠ SC

Hawley (C-13)

See also Milford, Scranton

Settled 1827 **Pop** 1,303 **Elev** 920 ft **Area code** 570 **Zip** 18428

Information Pocono Mountains Vacation Bureau, 1004 Main St, Stroudsburg 18360; 570/424-6050; for brochures phone 800/POCONOS

Web www.poconos.org

A major attraction in this Pocono resort area is man-made Lake Wallenpaupack, offering summer recreation on the lake, as well as winter recreation nearby.

What to See and Do

Claws 'N Paws Wild Animal Park. *12 miles W via PA 590, near Lake Wallenpaupack.* Phone 570/698-6154. A zoo in the woods with more than 100 species of exotic animals. Petting zoo with tame deer, lambs, and goats. Farmyard area. Parrot, reptile shows; zookeeper talks (schedule varies). Picnicking, snack bar. (May-Oct, daily) **$$$**

Gravity Coach. *W of town on US 6.* Car used on Pennsylvania Gravity Railroad (22 inclined planes between Hawley and Scranton, 1850-1885).

Lake Wallenpaupack. *US 6.* Phone 570/226-2141. One of the largest man-made lakes in state (5,600 acres), formed by damming of Wallenpaupack Creek. Swimming beach (Memorial Day-day before Labor Day; fee), fishing, boating, water sports; ice fishing, camping. Information center, 1/2 mile NW on US 6 at PA 507 (Daily; closed Easter, Thanksgiving, Dec 25). **FREE**

PPL. *Approximately 1 1/2 miles E on US 6.* Phone 570/226-3702. Hydroelectric facilities, dam; recreation area. Superintendent's office has information on campgrounds, hiking trails, picnic groves (Mon-Fri); observation point. (Daily) **FREE**

Promised Land State Park. *12 miles S on PA 390.* Phone 570/676-3428. Approximately 2,950 acres. Swimming beach, fishing, boating (rentals, mooring, launch); hiking, cross-country skiing, snowmobiling, ice skating, ice fishing, picnicking, snack bar, tent and trailer sites, cabins. Nature center, interpretive program. **$$$$**

Tanglwood. *4 miles S via PA 390, off I-84 in Tafton.* Phone 570/226-7669; 888/226-SNOW. Two double chairlifts, two

rope tows, beginner lift; patrol, school, rentals, snowmaking; cafeteria, bar; nursery. Longest run 1 mile; vertical drop 415 feet. Night skiing. (Early Dec-late Mar, daily) Half-day rates. **$$$$**

Motel/Motor Lodge

★ **GRESHAM'S LAKE VIEW MOTEL.** *Rte 6 (18428).* Phone 570/226-4621; fax 570/226-4621. 21 rooms, 2 story. S, D $68-$73; each additional $5; under 5 free; weekly rates; ski plans; lower rates off-season. Crib free. TV; cable. Complimentary coffee in lobby. Restaurant nearby. Check-out 11 am. Downhill/cross-country ski 2 1/2 miles. Balconies. Overlooks Lake Wallenpaupack. Cr cds: A, DS, MC, V.

D ⚓ ⊠

Resort

★★★ **COVE HAVEN HONEYMOON RESORT.** *RR 590 (18438).* Phone 717/226-4506; toll-free 800/233-4141; fax 717/226-4697. 282 units, 3 story. MAP: D $180-$320; weekly rates. Adults only. TV; VCR available (movies $5). Indoor/outdoor pools; whirlpool, poolside service. Bars 11:30-1:30 am; entertainment. Check-out 11 am. Coin laundry. Gift shop. Free bus depot transportation. Indoor tennis. Racquetball. Driving range, indoor miniature golf. Boats, waterskiing. Snowmobiling. Social director. Indoor ice skating and roller skating. Recreation room. Game room. Exercise equipment; saunas. Refrigerators, some balconies. On lake. Cr cds: A, D, DS, MC, V.

D ⚑ ⇌ 🏃 ⚑ ⊠ SC

B&B/Small Inns

★ **FALLS PORT INN & RESTAURANT.** *330 Main Ave (18428).* Phone 570/226-2600; fax 570/226-6409. 9 rooms, 3 story. No room phones. Pet accepted; fee. Complimentary continental breakfast. Check-out 11 am, check-in 1 pm. TV; cable, VCR available. Restaurant, room service. Downhill, cross-country ski 9 miles. Built in 1902 as an inn. Cr cds: A, MC, V. **$**

⚑ ⊠ ⊠

★★★ **ROEBLING INN ON THE DELAWARE.** *155 Scenic Dr (18435).* Phone 570/685-7900; fax 570/685-1718. www.roeblinginn.com. This classic Greek Revival mansion is located at the junction of the Delaware and the Lackawaxen rivers. Many local restaurants are nearby. 6 rooms, 2 story. Complimentary full breakfast. Check-out 11:30 am, check-in 2:30 pm. TV. Downhill, cross-country ski 5 miles. Cr cds: A, DS, MC, V. **$**

⊠ ⊠

★★★ **SETTLERS INN AT BINGHAM PARK.** *4 Main Ave (18428).* Phone 570/226-2993; toll-free 800/833-8527; fax 570/226-1874. www.thesettlersinn.com. 23

rooms, 2 story, 5 suites. Complimentary full breakfast. Check-out noon, check-in 2 pm. In-room modem link. Tudor Revival manor (1927); stone fireplace, sitting rooms with many antiques. Restaurant. Golf course nearby. Downhill ski 8 miles; cross-country ski 1 mile. Airport transportation. Bingham Park opposite. Totally nonsmoking. Cr cds: A, DS, MC, V. **$**

⬛ ⬛ ⬛ ⬛ **SC**

Restaurant

★ ★ ★ **THE SETTLERS INN.** *4 Main Ave (18428). Phone 570/226-2993; fax 570/226-1874. www.thesettlersinn .com.* Specializes in pheasant, seafood, trout. Hours: 11:30 am-2 pm, 5-9 pm, closed Dec 23-25. A la carte entrées: lunch $8-$11, dinner $15-$23. Bar. Children's menu. Dining room of Tudor-style hotel constructed in 1920s. Reservations accepted weekends and July-Aug. Cr cds: A, DS, MC, V.

Ⓓ

Hazleton (E-11)

See also Ashland, Bloomsburg, Jim Thorpe, Wilkes Barre

Settled 1809 **Pop** 23,329 **Elev** 1,660 ft **Area code** 570 **Zip** 18201

Information Greater Hazleton Chamber of Commerce, 1 S Church St, Suite 200; 570/455-1508

Web www.hazletonchamber.org

On top of Spring Mountain, Hazleton calls itself the highest city in Pennsylvania. Rich agricultural land surrounds Hazleton, and its early and rapid economic growth was spurred by the rich anthracite coal reserves found in the area. Although coal dominated the town's economy during the 19th century, today there are many diversified industries located here, producing building materials, textiles, office furniture, business forms, foods and food containers, boxes, heavy fabricated steel, plastics, electronic parts, and other products.

What to See and Do

Eckley Miners' Village. *10 miles NE off PA 940, near Freeland. Phone 570/636-2070.* (Pennsylvania Anthracite Museum Complex) Mining coal patch town (1850s) portrays life in the anthracite region until about 1940. Walking tour (Memorial Day-Labor Day; fee). (Daily; closed holidays) **$$**

National Shrine of the Sacred Heart. *1 1/2 miles NE on US 309, PA 940, in Harleigh section of Hazleton. Phone 570/455-1162.* Large outdoor shrine includes stations of the cross and crucifixion scene; picnic area. (Mar-Oct, daily) **FREE**

Motels/Motor Lodges

★ ★ **BEST WESTERN GENETTI MOTOR LODGE.** *PA 309, RR1 (18201). Phone 570/454-2494; toll-free 800/528-1234; fax 570/455-7793. www.bestwestern.com.* 89 rooms, 3 story. June-Oct: S $55-$65; D $65-$75; each additional $7; suites $130-$150; under 12 free; higher rates special events; lower rates rest of year. Crib free. TV; cable, VCR available (movies). Heated pool; lifeguard. Playground. Complimentary continental breakfast. Check-out 11 am. Coin laundry. Business services available. Valet service. Sundries. Bus depot transportation. Cr cds: A, C, D, DS, MC, V.

⬛ ⬛ **SC**

★ **RAMADA INN.** *Rte 309 N (18201). Phone 570/455-2061; fax 570/455-9387.* 107 rooms, 2 story. S, D, studio rooms $72; under 18 free. Crib free. Pet accepted. Check-out noon. TV; cable. In-room modem link. Restaurant 6 am-10 pm. Bar 5 pm-2 am. Room service. Pool, lifeguard. Meeting rooms. Business services. Sundries. Cr cds: A, C, D, DS, JCB, MC, V.

Ⓓ ⬛ ⬛ ⬛

Hershey (G-10)

See also Cornwall, Harrisburg, Lebanon

Founded 1903 **Pop** 12,771 **Elev** 420 ft **Area code** 717 **Zip** 17033

Information Hersheypark, 100 W Hersheypark Dr; 800/HERSHEY (information) or 800/533-3131 (reservations)

Web www.800hershey.com

One of America's most fascinating success stories, this planned community takes its name from founder M. S. Hershey, who established his world-famous chocolate factory here in 1903, then built a town around it. The streets have names like Chocolate and Cocoa, and streetlights are shaped like chocolate kisses. But there's more than chocolate here. Today, Hershey is known as one of the most diverse entertainment and resort areas in the eastern United States. Hershey is also known as the "golf capital of Pennsylvania," and has a number of well-known golf courses.

What to See and Do

Founders Hall. *801 Spartan Ln. Phone 717/520-2000.* Campus center of Milton Hershey School, noted for its striking rotunda. (Daily; closed holidays)

⭐ **Hershey's Chocolate World.** *800 Hershey Park Dr. Entrance adjacent to Hersheypark. Phone 717/534-4900.* Tour via automated conveyance; simulates steps of chocolate production from cacao bean plantations through chocolate-making in Hershey. Also tropical gardens, shopping village. (Daily; closed Dec 25) **FREE**

Hershey Gardens. *170 Hotel Rd. Phone 717/534-3492.* From mid-June to first frost, 8,000 rose plants bloom on 23 acres. Tulip garden (mid-Apr-mid-May); chrysanthemums and annuals; butterfly house featuring 400-500 butterflies; six theme gardens. (Mid-Apr-Oct, daily) **$$$**

Hershey Museum. *170 W Hershey Park Dr (17033). Near entrance to Hersheypark. Phone 717/534-3439.* Pennsylvania German, Native American, Eskimo collections; displays of Stiegel glass; "Apostolic Clock" depicting life of Christ; Milton Hershey history. (Daily; closed Jan 1, Thanksgiving, Dec 25) **$$** Adjacent is

Hersheypark Arena. *100 Hershey Park Dr. Phone 717/534-3911.* Capacity 10,000; professional hockey, basketball, ice skating, variety shows, concerts.

Hersheypark. *100 W Hershey Park Dr (17033). Phone 800/HERSHEY.* 110-acre theme park includes Rhine Land, Tudor Square, Dutch crafts barn; more than 60 rides include six roller coasters; live family shows. (Mid-May-Labor Day, daily; May and Sept, selected weekends) **$$$$** Also here is

ZooAmerica. *100 W Hershey Park Dr. Phone 717/534-3860.* An 11-acre environmental zoo depicting five climatic regions of North America; home to more than 200 animals. (Daily; closed holidays) Combination admission with Hersheypark available. **$$$**

Hersheypark Stadium/Star Pavilion. *100 W Hershey Park Dr. Phone 717/534-3911.* Stadium seats 25,000, Star Pavilion seats 7,200; sports and entertainment events.

Seltzer's Lebanon Bologna Company. *230 N College St, 3 blocks N of US 422, in Palmyra. Phone 717/838-6336.* Outdoor wooden smokehouses since 1902. (Mon-Sat; closed holidays) **FREE**

Special Events

Antique Automobile Club. National fall rally. Second weekend in Oct.

Chocolate Lovers' Weekend. *Hotel Hershey, 100 Hotel Rd.* Feb.

Christmas Candylane. Hersheypark is transformed into "Christmas Candylane" to mark the beginning of the Christmas season. Mid-Nov-Dec.

Hersheypark Balloonfest. *100 W Hershey Park Dr (17033). Phone 717/534-3900.* Oct.

Motels/Motor Lodges

★ **ADDEY'S INN OF HERSHEY.** *150 E Governor Rd (17033). Phone 717/533-2591; fax 717/533-2591.* 12 rooms. May-Labor Day: S, D $89; each additional $5;

lower rates rest of year. Crib $5. TV; cable (premium). Complimentary coffee in lobby. Check-out 11 am. Picnic tables. Cr cds: A, DS, MC, V.
⌨ SC

★ **BEST WESTERN INN.** *Rte 422 and Sipe Ave (17033). Phone 717/533-5665; toll-free 800/233-0338; fax 717/533-5675. www.bestwestern.com.* 123 rooms, 3 story. No elevator. May-Aug: S, D $99-$159; each additional $10; under 17 free; weekly rates; higher rates special events; lower rates rest of year. Complimentary continental breakfast. Check-out noon. TV; cable (premium), VCR available. In-room modem link. Restaurant nearby. Game room. Pool; whirlpool. Cr cds: A, C, D, DS, ER, JCB, MC, V.
D ⌨ ⌨ SC

★ **DAYS INN.** *350 W Chocolate Ave (17033). Phone 717/534-2162; toll-free 800/329-7466; fax 717/533-6409. www.daysinn.com.* 75 rooms, 4 story. Late June-Aug: S $119-$139; D $129-$149; each additional $6; under 18 free; higher rates antique car shows; lower rates rest of year. Crib free. TV; cable, VCR available (movies). Complimentary continental breakfast. Restaurant opposite 11:30 am-10 pm. Check-out 11 am. Valet service. Free train station, bus depot transportation. Health club privileges. Some refrigerators; microwaves available. Cr cds: A, C, D, DS, JCB, MC, V.
D ⌨ SC

★ ★ **HOLIDAY INN.** *604 Station Rd (17028). Phone 717/469-0661; toll-free 800/465-4329; fax 717/469-7755. www.stayholiday.com.* 195 rooms, 4 story. Memorial Day-mid-Oct: S $119-$179; D $129-$189; each additional $10; suites $195-$295; under 19 free; lower rates rest of year. Crib free. Pet accepted. TV; cable. 2 pools, 1 indoor; whirlpool. Restaurant 6:30 am-10 pm. Room service. Bar 11-2 am; entertainment. Check-out noon. Coin laundry. Meeting rooms. Business center. In-room modem link. Bellstaff. Valet service. Gift shop. Airport, train station, bus depot transportation. Exercise equipment; sauna. Lawn games. Microwaves available. Balconies. Cr cds: A, C, D, DS, ER, JCB, MC, V.
D ⌨ ⌨ ⌨ ⌨ ⌨ SC ⌨

★ **MILTON MOTEL.** *1733 E Chocolate Ave (17033). Phone 717/533-4533; fax 717/533-0369. www.miltonmotel.com.* 34 rooms, 2 story. Mid-May-Labor Day: S $49-$76; D $66-$99; each additional $5; weekly rates Sept-May; higher rates holiday weekends; lower rates rest of year. Check-out 11 am. TV; cable (premium), VCR available. In-room modem link. Restaurant adjacent 11-2 am. Game room. Heated pool. Cr cds: A, D, DS, MC, V.
⌨ ⌨ SC

★ **RODEWAY INN.** *43 W Areba Ave (17033). Phone 717/533-7054; toll-free 800/638-7949; fax 717/533-3405. www.rodeway.com.* 22 rooms, 2 story, 11 kitchens

Mid-June-early Sept: S $79-$198; D $89-$129; each additional $10; kitchen units $125-$198; under 18 free; lower rates rest of year. Crib free. Complimentary continental breakfast, coffee in rooms. Check-out 11 am. TV; cable. In-room modem link. Refrigerators; microwaves available. Restaurant nearby. Indoor pool. Business services. Cr cds: A, C, D, DS, JCB, MC, V.

★ **SIMMONS MOTEL.** *355 W Chocolate Ave (17033). Phone 717/533-9177; fax 717/533-3605. www.simmons motel.com.* 32 rooms, 2 story. June-Oct: S $55-$85; D $65-$95; each additional $5; apartments (1-3 bedroom) $110-$185; kitchen units $95-$110; weekly, family rates; higher rates antique car show; lower rates rest of year. Crib free. TV; cable (premium), VCR available. Complimentary coffee in lobby. Restaurant nearby. Check-out 11 am. Business services available. Health club privileges. Many refrigerators; microwaves available. Picnic tables, grills. Cr cds: A, DS, MC, V.

★ ★ **SPINNERS MOTOR INN.** *845 E Chocolate Ave (17033). Phone 717/533-9157; fax 717/534-1189. www.spinnersinn.com.* 52 rooms, 6 with shower only, 2 story. May-mid-Oct: S $65-$95; D $69-$109; each additional $5; suites $89-$139; under 2 free; golf plans; weekends, holidays (2-day minimum); higher rates special events; lower rates rest of year. Crib $6. TV; cable (premium), VCR available (movies). Heated pool. Complimentary continental breakfast. Restaurant. Bar. Check-out 11 am. Business services available. Game rooms. Some refrigerators, microwaves. Some balconies. Picnic tables. Cr cds: A, C, D, DS, MC, V.

★ **WHITE ROSE MOTEL.** *1060 E Chocolate Ave (17033). Phone 717/533-9876; fax 717/533-6923. www.800hershey.com.* 24 rooms, 2 story. July-Aug: S, D $108; under 18 free; lower rates rest of year. Check-out 11 am. TV; cable (premium). In-room modem link. Restaurant nearby. Health club privileges. Heated pool; lifeguard. Totally nonsmoking. Cr cds: A, DS, MC, V.

Hotel

★ ★ ★ **HERSHEY LODGE & CONVENTION CENTER.** *W Chocolate Ave and University Dr (17033). Phone 717/533-3311; toll-free 800/437-7439; fax 717/534-8666. www.hersheypa.com.* 665 rooms, 1-2 story. D $119-$219; each additional $15; under 18 free; package plans. Check-out 11 am, check-in noon. TV; cable (premium). In-room modem link. Restaurant 7 am-10 pm, also dining room. Bar 11-2 am; entertainment. Free supervised

children's activities (May-early Sept, late Nov-Jan 1). Exercise equipment, sauna. 2 pools, 1 indoor, children's pool, whirlpool, poolside service. Golf on premise, greens fee $60-$120. Lighted tennis. Free airport transportation. Cr cds: A, C, D, DS, ER, JCB, MC, V.

Resort

★ ★ ★ ★ **THE HOTEL HERSHEY.** *100 Hotel Rd (17033). Phone 717/533-2171; toll-free 800/533-3131; fax 717/534-8887. www.hersheypa.com.* Indulge in the delicious world of the Hotel Hershey. This Mediterranean masterpiece of old-world elegance was the realization of a dream for chocolate empire founder Milton Hershey. Perched atop a hill overlooking the town, the Hotel Hershey is a palatial retreat of 300 acres of formal gardens, fountains, and reflecting pools. The hotel impresses visitors of all ages with its signature touches such as evening turndown with chocolate kisses. Its rooms and suites are traditional and refined. Recreational opportunities abound, from 72 holes of golf, 6 miles of nature trails, basketball, volleyball, and tennis courts to the pools and fitness center. Gourmets delight in the Fountain Café, while others enjoy snacks and light meals at the coffeehouse or fireside lounge. The Spa at Hotel Hershey is a wonderfully sinful place, where whipped cocoa baths and chocolate fondue wraps tempt guests. 234 rooms, 5 story. MAP, D $289-$351; each additional $75; under 3 free; EP available; package plans. Check-out noon, check-in 4 pm. TV; VCR available. Restaurant 7 am-11 pm. Bar 11-1 am; entertainment Sat. Room service 24 hours. In-house fitness room, spa, massage, sauna. Indoor, outdoor pools; whirlpool. Golf, greens fee $19-$22. Tennis. Cross-country ski on site. Lawn games. Bicycle rentals. Carriage rides. Nature trails. Valet parking. Business center. Cr cds: A, C, D, DS, MC, V.

B&B/Small Inn

★ ★ **PINEHURST INN BED AND BREAKFAST.** *50 NE Dr (17033). Phone 717/533-2603; toll-free 800/743-9140; fax 717/534-2639. www.pinehursthershey.com.* 12 rooms, 2 story. No room phones. Complimentary full breakfast. Check-out 11 am, check-in 3-6 pm. TV in sitting room. Health club privileges. Airport transportation. Brick mansion built by Milton Hershey for orphaned boys. Totally nonsmoking. Cr cds: MC, V. **$**

Restaurants

★ ★ ★ **CIRCULAR DINING ROOM.** *Hotel Rd (17033). Phone 717/534-8800; toll-free 800/HERSHEY.*

www.hersheypa.com. Contemporary American menu. Hours: 7 am-2 pm, 5:30-10 pm. Breakfast, lunch $7.95-$9.95, dinner $24-$35. Entertainment. Children's menu. Jacket required. Reservations accepted. Cr cds: A, D, DS, MC, V.

★ ★ **DIMITRI'S.** *1311 E Chocolate Ave (17033). Phone 717/533-3403; fax 717/533-1405.* Greek, seafood, steak menu. Hours: 4-11 pm. Closed Sundays. Lunch $3.95-$7.95, dinner $9.95-$32.95. Bar to 2 am. Children's menu. Reservations accepted. Cr cds: A, DS, MC, V.

D

★ ★ **UNION CANAL HOUSE.** *107 S Hanover St (17033). Phone 717/566-0054; fax 717/566-5867. www.unioncanalhouse.com.* Hours: 5-10 pm. Closed Sun; major holidays. Reservations accepted. Continental menu. Bar. Dinner $8.95-$29.95. Children's menu. Three dining areas; fireplace, memorabilia from 1800s. Family-owned. Cr cds: A, D, DS, MC, V.

Honesdale (C-13)

See also Hawley, Scranton

Founded 1826 **Pop** 4,874 **Elev** 980 ft **Area code** 570 **Zip** 18431

Information Wayne County Chamber of Commerce, 303 Commercial St; 570/253-1960 or 800/433-9008

Web www.waynecountycc.com

Named in honor of Philip Hone, a mayor of New York City and first president of the Delaware & Hudson Canal Company, Honesdale was for many years the world's largest coal storage center, shipping millions of tons of anthracite. A gravity railroad brought coal here in winter; in spring it was reshipped by canal boats to tidewater. The Stourbridge Lion, first steam locomotive to operate in the United States (1829), was used by the Delaware & Hudson Canal Company, but when the rail bed proved too weak, mule power replaced the steam engine. Today, Honesdale manufactures textile products, business forms, and furniture, and is surrounded by dairy farms in the beautiful rolling countryside.

What to See and Do

Replica of the Stourbridge Lion. *Main St.* (Original is in Smithsonian Institution) First steam locomotive to operate in the US (1829).

Stourbridge Rail Excursions. Scenic rail excursions from Honesdale to Lackawaxen, centering on the change of seasons, with entertainment and activities. Contact the Chamber of Commerce for schedule, fees.

Triple W Riding Stable. *US 6 through Hawley, left at post office, 3 1/2 miles to "Triple W" sign, turn right. Phone 570/226-2620.* A 181-acre horse ranch in the NE range of Pocono Mountains. Variety of trail rides for beginners or advanced riders; 1/2- and full-day trips; overnight camping trips. Hay and sleigh rides (seasonal; by appointment). (Daily) **$$$$**

Wayne County Historical Society Museum. *810 Main St. Phone 570/253-3240.* Delaware and Hudson-Canal exhibit, Native American exhibit. (Jan-Feb, Sat; Mar-Dec, Wed-Sat; closed Jan 1, Thanksgiving, Dec 25) **$**

Special Event

Wayne County Fair. *545 W Butler St.* Exhibits, livestock, horse racing. First full week in Aug.

Hopewell Furnace National Historic Site

See also Pottstown, Reading

(15 miles SE of Reading via US 422, PA 82 to Birdsboro, then SE on Birdsboro-Warwick Rd/PA 345; 10 miles NE of Tpke Morgantown Interchange)

Hopewell, an early industrial community, was built around a charcoal-burning cold-blast furnace, which made pig iron and many other iron products from 1771-1883. Nearby mines and forests supplied ore and charcoal for the furnace. The National Park Service has restored the buildings, and interpretive programs emphasize the community's role in the history of American industry. Hopewell is surrounded by the approximately 7,330-acre French Creek State Park (see POTTSTOWN).

The Visitor Center has a museum and audiovisual program on ironmaking and community life. Self-guided tour includes: charcoal house, where fuel for furnace was stored; anthracite furnace ruin; waterwheel and blast machinery; casting house, where 16 molders produced up to 5,000 stoves annually; cold-blast charcoal-burning furnace; blacksmith shop; tenant houses; barn for horses and mules transporting charcoal, ore, iron products to market; office store, which was source of staples, clothing, and house furnishings; springhouse, which supplied "refrigeration"; ironmaster's house, home of proprietor or manager. Stove molding and casting demonstrations (late June-Labor Day; fee). Captioned slide program for the hearing impaired; Braille map and large-print pamphlets for the visually impaired; wheelchair access. (Daily; closed winter holidays) Contact the Superintendent, 2 Mark Bird Lane, Elverson 19520; 610/582-8773 or 610/582-2093 (TDD). **$**

Huntingdon (F-7)

See also Altoona, Orbisonia

Founded 1767 **Pop** 6,918 **Elev** 643 ft **Area code** 814
Zip 16652

Information Raystown County Visitors Bureau, 241 Mifflin St; 814/643-3577 or 888/RAYSTOWN

Web www.raystown.org

Founded on the site of an Oneida village in the Juniata Valley, Huntingdon was first called Standing Stone—for a 14-foot etched stone pillar venerated by Native Americans.

What to See and Do

Indian Caverns. *13 miles NW via US 22, PA 45 in Spruce Creek. Phone 814/632-7578 or 814/632-8333.* A 1-mile guided tour; extensive scenic beauty and authentic Native American history; relic room contains artifacts, tablet of picture writing; picnic area. (Apr-Oct, daily) **$$$**

Lincoln Caverns. *3 miles W on US 22. Phone 814/643-0268.* The one-hour tour of two caves includes Frozen Niagara, Diamond Cascade; visitor center and gift shop. (Apr-Nov, daily; Mar and Dec, weekends only) **$$$**

Raystown Lake. *7 miles S on PA 26, follow signs to Hesston. Phone 814/658-3405.* Large man-made lake, with 110 miles of shoreline. Swimming, fishing, boating; hunting, hiking, picnicking, camping. Restaurant. Observation area. Fee for some activities.

Swigart Auto Museum. *US 22 E. 4 miles E on US 22. Phone 814/643-0885.* Changing exhibits of American steam, gas, electric autos. Large collection of nameplates, license plates, and auto memorabilia; picnic area. (Memorial Day-Oct, daily) **$$**

Special Event

Hartslog Day. *7 miles NW via US 22, in Alexandria.* Heritage festival includes crafts, food, music, games. Second Sat in Oct.

Motels/Motor Lodges

★ ★ **DAYS INN.** *US 22 and S 4th St (16652). Phone 814/643-3934; fax 814/643-3005. www.daysinn.com.* 76 rooms, 3 story. S $44-$56; D $49-$61; each additional $5; under 13 free; higher rates special events. Pet accepted; fee. Check-out 11 am. TV; cable. In-room modem link. Restaurant 6 am-10 pm; Fri, Sat to 11 pm. Bar 4:30 pm-2 am. Cr cds: A, C, D, DS, MC, V.

D 🐾 ⌦ SC

★ ★ **HUNTINGDON MOTOR INN.** *US 22 (16652). Phone 814/643-1133; fax 814/643-1331.* 48 rooms, 2 story.

S $37-$40; D $46-$52; each additional $4. Crib free. Pet accepted, some restrictions. Check-out 11 pm. TV; cable. In-room modem link. Balconies. Microwaves available. Restaurant 7 am-9 pm. Bar 4:30 pm-2 am. Meeting rooms. Business services. Cr cds: A, C, D, DS, MC, V.

D 🐾 ⌦

Indiana (F-4)

See also Johnstown

Founded 1805 **Pop** 14,895 **Elev** 1,310 ft **Area code** 724
Zip 15701

Information Indiana County Tourist Bureau, 2334 Oakland Ave, Suite 7; 724/463-7505

Web www.indiana-co-pa-tourism.org

Named after the Native American population in the area, this borough was established on 250 acres donated for a county seat by George Clymer of Philadelphia, a signer of the Declaration of Independence. Indiana University of Pennsylvania (1875) is located here. This is also the birthplace of actor Jimmy Stewart.

What to See and Do

County parks. **Blue Spruce.** *6 miles N off PA 110. Phone 724/463-8636* (park commission). Covers 420 acres. Fishing for bass, perch, catfish, and crappie; boating (rowboat, canoe rentals); winter sports area, picnicking, grills, playground. (Daily) **Pine Ridge.** *US 22 near Blairsville.* Covers 630 acres. Trout fishing; hiking, picnicking. Nature study. (Daily) *SW via* **Hemlock Lake.** *W on PA 286 near Rossiter.* Covers 200 acres. Fishing; small game hunting, hiking, ice skating. Nature study, photography. (Daily)

Jimmy Stewart Museum. *Indiana Public Library Building, third floor, corner of 9th and Philadelphia sts. Phone 724/349-6112 or 800/83-JIMMY.* Highlights the namesake's accomplishments on film, radio, and TV. His roles as a military hero, civic leader, family man, and world citizen are woven into displays, film presentations and gallery talks. Fifty-seat vintage theater. (Daily) **$$**

Yellow Creek State Park. *12 miles E via US 422. Phone 724/357-7913.* Approximately 3,000 acres. Swimming beach, fishing, boating; hunting, hiking, cross-country skiing, snowmobiling, sledding, ice skating, ice fishing, ice boating, picnicking, playground. Standard fees.

Motels/Motor Lodges

★ ★ **BEST WESTERN UNIVERSITY INN.** *1545 Wayne Ave (15701). Phone 724/349-9620; toll-free 888/299-9620; fax 724/349-2620. www.bestwestern.com.* 107

rooms, 2 story. S $55-$65; D $60-$70; each additional $5; under 12 free; higher rates special university events. Crib free. TV; cable (premium). Heated pool. Coffee in rooms. Restaurant 6:30 am-1:30 pm; Sun from 8 am. Check-out noon. Meeting rooms. In-room modem link. Cr cds: A, C, D, DS, MC, V.

D ⛰ ⊠ SC

★ ★ **HOLIDAY INN.** *1395 Wayne Ave (15701). Phone 724/463-3561; toll-free 800/477-3561; fax 724/463-8006. www.holiday-inn.com.* 159 rooms, 2 story. S, D $69-$94; suites $199; family, weekend rates; golf plans; higher rates university events. Crib free. Pet accepted. TV; cable (premium). Indoor pool; whirlpool, poolside service. Coffee in rooms. Restaurant 6:30 am-10 pm; Sat, Sun from 7 am. Room service. Bar 4 pm-2 am; entertainment. Check-out noon. Meeting rooms. Business services available. In-room modem link. Miniature golf. Game room. Sauna. Health club privileges. Cr cds: A, C, D, DS, JCB, MC, V.

D 🐾 ⛰ ⊠ SC

Jenkintown (H-13)

See also Fort Washington, Philadelphia, Willow Grove

Pop 4,478 **Elev** 250 ft **Area code** 215 **Zip** 19046

Information Valley Forge Convention & Visitors Bureau, 600 W Germantown Pike, Suite 130, Plymouth Meeting 19462; 610/834-1550

Web www.valleyforge.org

What to See and Do

Abington Art Center. *515 Meetinghouse Rd. Located in historic Alverthorpe Manor. Phone 215/887-4882.* Contemporary art, sculpture garden (daily, dawn to dusk), gallery and gallery shop. (Tues-Sat) **FREE**

Beth Sholom Synagogue. *Old York and Foxcroft rds, 1 mile S, in Elkins Park. Phone 215/887-1342.* The only synagogue designed by Frank Lloyd Wright. (By appointment) **$$**

Restaurant

★ ★ **STAZI MILANO.** *Township Line and Greenwood Ave (19046). Phone 215/885-9000; fax 215/885-9353. www.stazimilano.com.* Hours: 11:30 am-3 pm, 4-9:30 pm; Fri, Sat 5-10:30 pm; Sun 4-9 pm; early-bird dinner Mon-Thurs 4-6 pm. Italian menu. Bar to midnight; Fri, Sat to 1 am. Lunch $6.95-$10.95, dinner $6.95-$17.95. Specializes in pasta, beef, chicken. In 1931 train station; mahogany railings. Cr cds: A, D, MC, V.

D

Jim Thorpe (E-12)

See also Hazelton

Settled 1815 **Pop** 4,804 **Elev** 600 ft **Area code** 570 **Zip** 18229

Information Carbon County Tourist Promotion Agency Information Center, PO Box 90; 570/325-3673 or 888/JIM-THORPE

The twin towns, Mauch Chunk (Bear Mountain) and East Mauch Chunk, built on the sides of a narrow gorge of the Lehigh River, merged in 1954 and adopted the name of Jim Thorpe, the great Native American athlete. This, together with a "nickel-a-week" plan whereby each man, woman, and child paid five cents to promote the community and attract industry, gave the area (formerly dependent on coal mining) a new lease on economic life. Little has changed in appearance after more than a century; a walking tour will reveal 19th-century architecture.

What to See and Do

Asa Packer Mansion. *Packer Hill. Phone 570/325-3229.* Former showplace home of founder of Lehigh Valley Railroad and Lehigh University, one of state's wealthiest men. Packer's house, treasures, and money were left to the borough. (June-Nov, daily; Apr-May, weekends; first two weeks in Dec) Adjacent is

Jim Thorpe Memorial. *1 mile E on PA 903.* A 20-ton granite mausoleum built in memory of the 1912 Olympic champion. **$$**

Jim Thorpe River Adventures, Inc. *1 Adventure Ln (18229). Phone 570/325-2570 or 570/325-4960.* (Mar-Nov, daily) **$$$$**

Old Jail Museum. *128 W Broadway. Phone 570/325-5259.* Built in 1871, the Old Jail, which was an active prison until Jan 1995, contains 28 original cells, warden's living quarters, and 16 dungeon cells. Famous for hangings of Molly Maguires; one Molly, to claim his innocence, placed his hand on his cell wall and said his hand print would remain forever as a sign of his innocence. The hand print is still on the wall of Cell 17. (Late May-early Nov) **$$**

Pocono Whitewater Adventures. *8 miles NE of Jim Thorpe Bridge on PA 903. Phone 570/325-3655.* Also bike tours. (Mar-Nov, daily) **$$$$**

Stone Row. *Race St, downtown.* Sixteen town houses built by Asa Packer for the engineers on his railroad; reminiscent of Philadelphia's Elfreth's Alley. Some are stores open to the public. Also here is

St. Mark's Church. *Phone 570/325-2241.* Has Tiffany windows and copy of reredos from Windsor Castle. (June-Oct, Wed-Sat afternoons)

Special Events

Fall Foliage Festival. Arts and crafts, food, entertainment. Scenic three-hour train rides. Second weekend in Oct.

Laurel Blossom Festival. Arts and crafts, entertainment, food, steam train rides. Second weekend in June.

B&B/Small Inn

★ ★ ★ **HARRY PACKER MANSION.** *Packer Hill (18229). Phone 570/325-8566. www.murdermansion.com.* This mansion served as a model for the haunted mansion in Disney World. If you are not interested in a Murder Mystery event at the property, there are numerous activities in the area including hiking, biking, and exploring the historical past of the community. 13 rooms, 2 share bath, 2 with shower only, 3 suites, 3 story. S, D $75-$150; package plans; weekends, holidays (2-day minimum); higher rates special events. Pet accepted. Children over 12 years only. Complimentary full breakfast. Check-out 11 am, check-in 4 pm. TV in some rooms; VCR (movies). Valet services. Concierge service. Built in 1871; a second empire mansion used as a model for the haunted mansion in Disney World. Cr cds: A, MC, V.

Restaurant

★ **JT'S STEAK & ALE HOUSE.** *5 Hazard Sq (18229). Phone 570/325-4563; fax 570/325-8231. www.emeraldinjimthorpe.com.* Steak menu. Lunch, dinner. Bar. Casual attire. Outdoor seating. **$$**

D

Johnstown (G-5)

See also Ebensburg, Ligonier

Settled 1800 **Pop** 23,906 **Elev** 1,180 ft **Area code** 814

Information Greater Johnstown/Cambria County Convention & Visitors Bureau, 416 Main St, 15901; 814/536-7993 or 800/237-8590

Web www.visitjohnstownpa.com

On May 31, 1889, a break in the South Fork Dam that impounded an old reservoir 10 miles to the east poured a wall of water onto the city in the disastrous "Johnstown Flood." The death toll rose to 2,209 and property damage totaled $17 million. The city has been flooded 22 times since 1850, most recently in 1977.

Founded by a Swiss Mennonite, Joseph Johns, the city today is the center of Cambria County's iron and steel industry, producing iron and steel bars, railroad cars, parts, and railroad supplies.

What to See and Do

Conemaugh Gap. *Located at the W end of the city.* Gorge, 7 miles long and 1,700 feet deep, cuts between Laurel Hill Ridge and Chestnut Ridge.

Grandview Cemetery. *801 Mill Creek Rd (15905). 1 mile W on PA 271, in Westmont. Phone 814/535-2652.* The 777 unidentified victims of the 1889 flood are buried under blank headstones in the "Unknown Plot."

Inclined Plane Railway. *Vine St and Roosevelt Blvd. Phone 814/536-1816.* Joins Johnstown and Westmont. Ride is on steep (72% grade) passenger incline with 500-foot ascent. Counterbalanced cable cars take 50 passengers and two automobiles each. (Daily; closed Jan 1, Dec 25) **$$**

Johnstown Flood Museum. *304 Washington St. Phone 814/539-1889.* Museum depicts history of Johnstown, with permanent exhibits on 1889 Johnstown Flood; Academy Award-winning film, photographs, artifacts, memorabilia. (Daily; closed holidays) **$$**

Johnstown Flood National Memorial. *Lake Rd. Jct US 219, PA 869. Phone 814/495-4643.* Commemorates 1889 Johnstown Flood; preserved remnants of the South Fork Dam. Visitor center with exhibits, 30-minute movie (Daily; closed Dec 25). **$**

Motels/Motor Lodges

★ **COMFORT INN.** *455 Theatre Dr (15904). Phone 814/266-3678; toll-free 800/228-5150; fax 814/266-9783. www.comfortinn.com.* 117 rooms, 5 story, 27 suites. S $57-$63; D $63-$69; each additional $6; suites $84-$91; kitchen units $94-$99; under 18 free; monthly rates; higher rates special events. Crib free. Pet accepted; $6. TV; cable, VCR (movies). Indoor pool; whirlpool, lifeguard. Complimentary continental breakfast. Restaurant nearby. Check-out noon. Coin laundry. Meeting rooms. Business center. In-room modem link. Sundries. Free airport transportation. Exercise equipment. Health club privileges. Refrigerator, wet bar in suites; microwaves available. Picnic table, grill. Cr cds: A, C, D, DS, ER, JCB, MC, V.

D 🐾 ➰ 🏄 🖿 SC 🏄

★ **SLEEP INN.** *453 Theatre Dr (15904). Phone 814/262-9292; fax 814/262-0486. www.sleepinn.com.* 62 rooms, 58 with shower only, 3 story. S $49-$55; D $55-$61; under 18 free; weekly rates; higher rates: Labor Day, sporting events. Crib free. Pet accepted, some restrictions; $6. TV; cable (premium). Complimentary continental breakfast. Restaurant adjacent 11 am-9 pm. Check-out noon. Meeting room. Business services available. In-room modem link. Airport transportation. Refrigerators, microwaves available. Cr cds: A, C, D, DS, ER, JCB, MC, V.

D 🐾 🖿 SC

Hotel

★ ★ **HOLIDAY INN.** *250 Market St (15901). Phone 814/535-7777; toll-free 800/443-5663; fax 814/539-1393. www.holiday-inn.com.* 164 rooms, 6 story. S, D $72-$89; suites $238-$290; under 18 free. Crib free. Pet accepted, some restrictions. TV; cable (premium). Indoor pool; whirlpool, poolside service, lifeguard. Coffee in rooms. Restaurant 7 am-10 pm. Bar 4 pm-midnight. Check-out noon. Meeting rooms. Business center. In-room modem link. Airport transportation. Exercise equipment; sauna. Health club privileges. Cr cds: A, C, D, DS, JCB, MC, V.

D ➔ ⚓ 🛪 ⇌ SC 🏃

Restaurant

★ ★ **SURF N' TURF.** *100 Valley Pike (15905). Phone 814/536-9250; fax 814/539-4641.* Hours: 4-10 pm; Sun 11 am-8 pm. Closed Dec 25. Bar. Dinner $8.95-$32.95. Children's menu. Specializes in seafood, steak. Salad bar. Pianist Sat. Cr cds: A, D, DS, MC, V.

D SC

Kane (C-5)

See also Clarion, Warren

Settled 1864 **Pop** 4,126 **Elev** 2,000 ft **Area code** 814 **Zip** 16735

Information Seneca Highlands Tourist Association, junction PA 770 W and US 219, PO Box H, Custer City 16725; 814/368-9370

Situated on a lofty plateau, Kane offers hunting, fishing, and abundant winter sports. Summers are cool and winters are bracing. Allegheny National Forest is to the north, west, and south; there are scenic drives through 4,000 acres of virgin timber. General Thomas L. Kane of "Mormon War" fame settled here and laid out the community, which prospered as a lumber and railroad town. General Ulysses Grant was once arrested here for fishing without a license.

What to See and Do

Bendigo State Park. *Glen Hazel Rd.* 9 miles SE on PA 321, then 7 miles S on US 219, then 3 miles NE on unnumbered road. Phone 814/965-2646. Approximately 100 acres. Swimming pool, fishing; sledding. Standard fees.

Kinzua Bridge State Park. *Glen Hazel Rd.* 12 miles E via US 6 in Mt Jewett. Phone 814/965-2646. An approximately 300-acre park surrounds Kinzua Bridge. When built in 1882, it was the highest railroad bridge in the world, taking its 2,053-foot span 301 feet above the Kinzua Creek. Overlooks, picnicking. (Daily) **FREE**

Thomas L. Kane Memorial Chapel. *30 Chestnut St.* Phone 814/837-9729. (1878) Built as a chapel for the new town under the direction of General Kane, a Civil War hero and humanitarian who championed the persecuted Mormons. Visitor center includes film of General Kane's life; small museum. (Tues-Sat) **FREE**

Twin Lakes. *8 miles S of E Kane on PA 321, then 2 miles N on Forest Rd 191, in Allegheny National Forest.* Phone 814/723-5150. Swimming (fee), fishing; hiking, picnicking, camping (fee).

Kennett Square (H-12)

See also West Chester; also see Wilmington, DE

Settled 1705 **Pop** 5,273 **Elev** 370 ft **Area code** 484 and 610 **Zip** 19348

Information Chester County Conference and Visitors Bureau, 400 Exton Sq Pkwy, Exton, 19341; 610/280-6145 or 800/228-9933; or the Southeastern Chester County Chamber of Commerce, 206 E State St, PO Box 395, phone 610/444-0774

Web www.brandywinevalley.com

What to See and Do

Barns-Brinton House. *5 1/2 miles NE on US 1, in Chadds Ford.* Phone 610/388-7376. (1714) Authentically restored 18th-century tavern, now a house museum furnished in the period. Guides in colonial costume offer interpretive tours; domestic art demonstrations. (May-Sept, Sat-Sun; also by appointment) **$$**

Brandywine Battlefield. *2 miles W of junction US 1 and 202, near Chadds Ford.* Phone 610/459-3342. Includes Lafayette's quarters and Washington's headquarters. Here, and around Chadds Ford, the Battle of the Brandywine (1777) took place—a decisive battle for Washington. Visitor center with exhibits; tours of historic buildings; museum shop. Picnicking. (Tues-Sun; closed holidays) **$$**

Brandywine River Museum. *7 miles NE on US 1, in Chadds Ford.* Phone 610/388-2700. Converted 19th-century gristmill houses largest collection of paintings by Andrew Wyeth and other Wyeth family members; also collections of American illustration, still life, and landscape painting. Nature trail, wildflower gardens; restaurant, museum shop, guided tours. (Daily; closed Dec 25) **$$$**

Chaddsford Winery. *5 miles NE on US 1, in Chadds Ford.* Phone 610/388-6221. Tours of boutique winery, housed in renovated old barn; view of production process; tasting room. Tours; tastings. (Schedule varies) **$$**

John Chads House. *7 miles NE via US 1, then 1/4 mile N on PA 100, in Chadds Ford. Phone 610/388-7376.* Stone building (circa 1725) is fine example of early 18th-century Pennsylvania architecture; authentically restored and furnished as a house museum. Narrated tours by guides in colonial costume; baking demonstrations in beehive oven. (May-Sept, Sat-Sun; also by appointment) **$**

⭐ **Longwood Gardens.** *3 miles NE on US 1. Phone 610/388-1000.* Longwood Gardens is a stately horticultural display garden created by Pierre S. du Pont, offering more than 1,000 acres of indoor and outdoor gardens, woodlands, and meadows. Lovers of living things are treated to greenhouses heated year-round, more than 10,000 different types of plants, spectacular fountains, flower shows, and gardening demonstrations. Children's programs are available, as well. The Orangery and Exhibition Hall are centerpieces, with a sunken marble floor flooded with reflective water. (Daily) **$$$**

Motels/Motor Lodges

⭐ **HILTON GARDEN INN.** *815 E Baltimore Pike. Phone 610/444-3515; fax 610/444-4285.* 28 rooms. S $74; D $80; each additional $6; under 12 free; weekly rates (winter). Crib free. TV; VCR available. Check-out noon. Business services available. Cr cds: A, C, D, DS, ER, JCB, MC, V.

D ⊠ SC

⭐⭐ **MENDENHALL HOTEL.** *323 Kennett Pike (19357). Phone 610/388-2100; fax 610/388-1184. www.mendenhallinn.com.* 70 rooms, 3 story. D $119; each additional $20; suites $150-$199; under 12 free. Complimentary continental breakfast. Check-out noon. TV; cable (premium), VCR available. In-room modem link. Bar from 11:30 am. Room service. Exercise equipment. Airport transportation. Business center. Concierge. Cr cds: A, C, D, DS, MC, V.

D 🏋 ⊠ SC 🚶

B&B/Small Inns

⭐⭐⭐ **BRANDYWINE RIVER HOTEL.** *US 1 and SR 100 (19317). Phone 610/388-1200; toll-free 800/274-9644; fax 610/388-1200.* 40 rooms, 2 story. D $125-$169. Pet accepted, some restrictions. Complimentary continental breakfast; afternoon refreshments. Check-out 11 am, check-in 2 pm. TV; cable. Exercise equipment. Airport, train station, bus depot transportation. Specialty shops on site. Cr cds: A, C, D, DS, MC, V.

D 🐾 🏋 ⊠ SC

⭐⭐⭐ **FAIRVILLE INN.** *506 Kennett Pike (19317). Phone 610/388-5900; toll-free 877/285-7772; fax 610/388-5902. www.innbook.com.* 15 rooms, 2 story. D $150-$225; each additional $15. Adults only. Complimentary conti-

nental breakfast. Check-out 11 am, check-in 3 pm. TV; cable. Some fireplaces. Built in 1826; antiques, period décor. View of surrounding countryside. Totally non-smoking. Cr cds: A, DS, MC, V.

D 🏋 ⊠

Restaurants

⭐⭐ **KENNETT SQUARE INN.** *201 E State St (19348). Phone 610/444-5687; fax 610/444-4904. www.kennettinn.com.* Hours: 11:30 am-2:30 pm, 5:30-10 pm; Sun 5-9 pm; Mon, Tues to 9 pm. Closed Jan 1, Dec 25. Lunch $7-$12, dinner $18-$27. Bar 11:30-2 am. Restored country inn (1835). Reservations accepted. Cr cds: A, C, D, MC, V.

D

⭐⭐⭐ **MENDENHALL INN.** *323 Kennett Pike (19357). Phone 610/388-1181; fax 610/388-1184. www.mendenhallinn.com.* Continental menu. Hours: 11:30 am-2:30 pm, 5-9:30 pm; Sun 4-8 pm; Sun brunch 10 am-2 pm. Closed Dec 25. Lunch $6-$15, dinner $18-$29. Brunch. Bar. Children's menu. Reservations required. Valet parking available. Cr cds: A, D, DS, MC, V.

D

⭐⭐⭐ **TERRACE.** *Longwood Gardens (19348). Phone 610/388-6771; fax 610/388-7064. www.longwoodgardens.org.* Located in Longwood Gardens, this restaurant offers a unique blend of regional favorites and American comfort foods. Hours: 11 am-4 pm, 5-9 pm; weekend hours vary; Dec to 7:30 pm. Cafeteria 10 am-4 pm; weekend hours vary; Jan, Feb 10 am-3 pm; Dec 10 am-8 pm. Dining room closed Jan-Mar. Reservations accepted. Bar. Lunch $6.95-$13.95, dinner $9.95-$18.95. Children's menu. Salad bar. Outdoor dining. Admission to Longwood Gardens required. Cr cds: A, C, D, DS, MC, V.

D

King of Prussia

See also Norristown, Philadelphia, West Chester

Settled early 1700s **Pop** 18,511 **Elev** 200 ft **Area code** 484 and 610 **Zip** 19406

Information Valley Forge Convention & Visitors Bureau, 600 W Germantown Pike, Suite 130, Plymouth Meeting 19462; 610/834-1550

Web www.valleyforge.org

Originally named Reeseville for the Welsh family that owned the land, the town changed its name to that of the local inn, which is still standing. The area around the town is full of historic interest.

What to See and Do

Harriton House. *500 Harriton Rd (19010). 6 miles SE via Old Gulph Rd to Harriton Rd, in Bryn Mawr. Phone 610/ 525-0201.* (1704) Early American domestic architecture of the Philadelphia area. Originally 700-acre estate, now 16 1/2 acres. House of Charles Thomson, Secretary of the Continental Congresses; restored to early 18th-century period. Nature park. (Wed-Sat; Sun by appointment; closed holidays) **$**

King of Prussia Mall. *On Rte 202 at Mall Blvd, where the expressway meets the turnpike. Phone 610/265-5727 (Plaza); 610/337-1210 (Court).* The king of malls on the eastern seaboard is located just 18 miles west of central Philadelphia. Bloomingdale's, Neiman Marcus, Nordstrom, Macy's, Lord & Taylor, JCPenney, Sears, and Strawbridge's anchor this mall, and its 365 specialty shops and 40 restaurants will keep you from staying in one place too long. (Daily)

Mill Grove. *Pawlings and Audubon rds (19407). 5 miles NW via US 422 and Audubon Rd, N of Valley Forge National Historic Park, on Pawlings Rd, in Audubon. Phone 610/666-5593.* (1762) Includes 175-acre wildlife sanctuary, developed around the first American home of ornithologist John James Audubon, now a museum. Prints, including complete elephant folio. Hiking trails. (Tues-Sat, also Sun afternoons; closed Jan 1, Thanksgiving, Dec 25) **FREE**

Swiss Pines. *6 miles SW via PA 202, Great Valley exit, on Charlestown Rd in Malvern. Phone 610/933-6916.* Japanese gardens featuring azalea and rhododendron collection; ponds, waterfalls, winding pathway; herb and ground-cover garden. Children under 12 years not permitted. (Mid-Apr-Nov, Mon-Fri, also Sat mornings; closed holidays and inclement weather) **FREE**

Valley Forge National Historical Park. (see) *Just W of town.*

Motels/Motor Lodges

★ **BEST WESTERN THE INN AT KING OF PRUSSIA.** *127 S Gulph Rd; Rte 202 N (19406). Phone 610/265-4500; fax 610/354-8905. www.bestwestern.com.* 2 story. S, D $95-$115; each additional $10; under 12 free. Complimentary continental breakfast. Check-out noon. TV; cable (premium). In-room modem link. Restaurant adj. Health club privileges. Pool. Airport transportation. Cr cds: A, C, D, DS, MC, V.

D ⊷ ⊠

★ **COMFORT INN.** *550 W Dekalb Pike (19406). Phone 610/962-0700; toll-free 800/222-0222; fax 610/962-0218. www.comfortinn.com.* 121 rooms, 5 story. S, D $85-$139; under 18 free; weekend rates. Crib free. TV; cable (premium), VCR available. Complimentary continental breakfast. Check-out noon. Coin laundry. Meeting room.

Business services available. Concierge. Airport transportation. Exercise equipment. Bathroom phones, minibars. Cr cds: A, C, D, DS, ER, JCB, MC, V.

D ⊀ ⊠ **SC**

★ ★ **COURTYARD BY MARRIOTT.** *1100 Drummers Ln (19087). Phone 610/687-6700; fax 610/687-1149. www.courtyard.com.* 150 rooms, 2 story. S, D $79-$144; suites $169; under 16 free; weekly, weekend rates. TV; cable (premium). Indoor pool; whirlpool. Complimentary coffee in rooms. Restaurant 5-10 pm Mon-Thurs; 7-11 am Sat-Sun. Room service Sun-Thurs. Bar 5-10 pm. Check-out 1 pm. Coin laundry. Meeting rooms. Business center. In-room modem link. Valet service. Sundries. Exercise equipment. Refrigerator, microwaves available. Many balconies. Cr cds: A, C, D, DS, MC, V.

D ⊷ ⊀ ⊠ ⊀

★ ★ **HOLIDAY INN.** *260 Mall Blvd (19406). Phone 610/265-7500; toll-free 800/465-4329; fax 610/265-4076. www.holiday-inn.com.* 225 rooms, 5 story. S, D $135; each additional $10; under 19 free. Crib free. TV; cable (premium). Restaurant 6:30 am-9:30 pm. Room service. Bar 11-2 am. Check-out 11 am. Meeting rooms. Business center. In-room modem link. Bellstaff. Valet service. Gift shop. Barber, beauty shop. Health club privileges. Pool privileges. Microwaves available. Cr cds: A, C, D, DS, ER, JCB, MC, V.

D ⊠ **SC** ⊀

★ ★ **HOMEWOOD SUITES.** *12 E Swedesford Rd (19355). Phone 610/296-3500; fax 610/296-1941. www. homewoodsuites.com.* 123 suites, 4 story. May-Nov: suites $134-$194; under 18 free; lower rates rest of year. Crib available. Pet accepted, some restrictions; $150. TV; cable (premium), VCR. Complimentary continental breakfast. Room service. Check-out noon. Meeting rooms. Business services available. In-room modem link. Bellstaff. Valet service. Sundries. Coin laundry. Exercise equipment. Indoor pool; whirlpool, lifeguard. Refrigerators, microwaves. Picnic tables, grills. Cr cds: A, C, D, DS, JCB, MC, V.

D ⊛ ⊷ ⊀ ⊠ **SC**

★ **MCINTOSH INN OF KING OF PRUSSIA.** *260 N Gulph Rd (19406). Phone 610/768-9500; toll-free 800/444-2775; fax 610/768-0225. www.mcintoshinn.com.* 210 rooms, 7 story. S $64.95; D $64.95-$74.95; each additional $5. Crib free. Complimentary continental breakfast. Check-out 11 am. TV; cable (premium). In-room modem link. Refrigerators, microwaves available. Valet service Mon-Fri. Business services available. Cr cds: A, C, D, MC, V.

D ⊠

Hotels

★ ★ ★ **HILTON VALLEY FORGE.** *251 W Dekalb Pike (19406). Phone 610/337-1200; fax 610/337-2224.*

www.hilton.com. 340 rooms, 9 story. S, D $110-$139; each additional $10; suites $139-$500; under 18 free; weekend rates. Crib free. TV; cable (premium), VCR available. Indoor/outdoor pool; whirlpool, lifeguard. Restaurants 6:30 am-11 pm. Bars 11:30-2 am. Check-out noon. Meeting rooms. Business center. In-room modem link. Concierge. Gift shop. Garage parking. Airport, bus depot transportation. Exercise equipment; sauna. Luxury level. Cr cds: A, C, D, DS, ER, JCB, MC, V.

D ⌧ ⌧ ⌧ SC ⌧

★ ★ ★ **RADISSON HOTEL VALLEY FORGE.** *1160 1st Ave (19406). Phone 610/337-2000; fax 610/768-3222. www.radisson.com.* 489 rooms, 15 story. S, D $140-$180; each additional $12; suites $175-$275. Crib. TV; cable (premium), VCR available. Heated pool; whirlpool, poolside service, lifeguard. Restaurant 6:30 am-11:30 pm; weekends to midnight. Bars 11-2 am; entertainment. Check-out noon. Convention facilities. Business center. In-room modem link. Concierge. Airport, train station, bus depot transportation. Exercise equipment; sauna. Wet bar in suites; microwaves available. Cr cds: A, C, D, DS, ER, JCB, MC, V.

D ⌧ ⌧ ⌧ ⌧ ⌧ SC ⌧

★ ★ ★ **WAYNE HOTEL.** *139 E Lancaster Ave (19087). Phone 610/687-5000; toll-free 800/962-5850; fax 610/687-8387. www.waynehotel.com.* Located 18 miles west of Philadelphia, this restored property reflects the elegance of a time past with its wrap-around porch, antique reproduction furnishings, and carpeted, subdued lobby. Individually decorated guest rooms feature voice mail, data ports, and direct dial telephones. 38 rooms, 6 story. S, D $125-$159; each additional $10; suites $159-$189; under 12 free; weekend rates. Crib free. TV; cable (premium). Pool. Complimentary continental breakfast. Restaurant. Bar 11:30 am-midnight. Check-out noon. Meeting rooms. Business services available. In-room modem link. Concierge. Airport, train station transportation. Health club privileges. Microwaves available. Restored Victorian building (1906) with ornate furnishings, antiques. Cr cds: A, D, DS, MC, V.

D ⌧ ⌧ SC

★ ★ **WYNDHAM VALLEY FORGE HOTEL.** *888 Chesterbrook Blvd (19087). Phone 610/647-6700; fax 610/889-9420. www.wyndham.com.* 229 suites, 5 story. Suites $149-$199; each additional $20; under 16 free; weekend rates. Crib free. Check-out noon. TV; cable (premium), VCR available. In-room modem link. Refrigerators, bathroom phones; microwaves available. Restaurant. Bar 11:30 am-midnight; weekends to 1 am. Exercise equipment, sauna. Indoor pool, whirlpool, lifeguard. Tennis privileges. Airport transportation. Meeting rooms. Business services. Gift shop. Cr cds: A, D, DS, MC, V.

D ⌧ ⌧ ⌧ ⌧

Restaurants

★ ★ **BARON'S INNE.** *499 N Gulph Rd (19406). Phone 610/265-2550; fax 610/265-2733. www.creedskop.com.* Hours: 11 am-2:30 pm, 5-10 pm. Closed Sun; major holidays; also first week in July. Reservations accepted. Bar 11 am-10 pm; Sat 5-10 pm. A la carte entrées: lunch $7-$13, dinner $16-$25. Specializes in steak, seafood. Piano Fri, Sat. Parking. Antique chandeliers and furniture. Cr cds: A, C, D, DS, MC, V.

D

★ ★ **LOTUS INN.** *402 W Swedesford Rd (19312). Phone 610/725-8888; fax 610/725-8285.* Chinese, Japanese menu. Hours: 11:30 am-10 pm; Fri to 11 pm; Sat noon-11 pm; Sun from noon, closed Thanksgiving. Lunch $6.95-$14.95, dinner $5.95-$14.95. Bar. Oriental décor; sushi bar. Children's menu. Reservations accepted; required Fri-Sun. Cr cds: A, D, DS, MC, V.

★ ★ ★ **TOWN AND COUNTRY GRILLE.** *888 Chesterbrook Blvd (19087). Phone 610/647-6700; fax 610/964-9086. www.wyndhamvalleyforge.com.* Hours: 7 am-2 pm, 5-10 pm; Fri, Sat to 11 pm. Reservations accepted. Bar. A la carte entrées: breakfast, lunch $6.95-$10.95, dinner $13.95-$22.95. Buffet: breakfast, lunch $8.95-$9.95. Sun brunch $11.95. Children's menu. Specializes in pasta, grilled steak, seafood. Salad bar (lunch buffet). Country furnishings. View of Valley Forge National Park. Cr cds: A, D, DS, MC, V.

D ⌧

★ ★ **WILD ONION.** *900 Conestoga Rd (19010). Phone 610/527-4826; fax 610/527-5051. www.thewildonion.com.* Specializes in fresh seafood, in-season produce. Hours: 11:30 am-11 pm. Lunch $5.25-$7.95, dinner $8.95-$19.95. Bar to 2 am. Children's menu. Reservations accepted. Cr cds: A, D, DS, MC, V.

D

Kulpsville (G-13)

See also Norristown, Philadelphia

Pop 1,200 **Elev** 290 ft **Area code** 215 **Zip** 19443

Information Valley Forge Country Convention & Visitors Bureau, 600 W Germantown Pike, Suite 130, Plymouth Meeting 19462; 610/834-1550

Web www.valleyforge.org

What to See and Do

Morgan Log House. *850 Weikel Rd. E on PA 63, then N on Troxel Rd, E on Snyder Rd and N on Weikel Rd. Phone 215/368-2480.* (1695) Built by the grandfather of General

Daniel Morgan and Daniel Boone, this is the oldest and finest surviving medieval-style log house in the country. Partially restored; authentic early 18th-century furnishings. It exhibits fine, early antiques, including 18th-century Pennsylvania furniture. Guided tours (Apr-Dec, weekends; other times by appointment). **$$**

Restaurant

★ ★ **MAINLAND INN.** *17 Main St (19451). Phone 215/256-8500; fax 215/256-9308.* Specializes in seafood, lamb, game (in season). Hours: 11:30 am-2:30 pm, 5:30-9 pm; Fri to 9:30 pm; Sat 5:30-9:30 pm; Sun (brunch) 11 am-2 pm, 5-8 pm. Closed most major holidays. Lunch $7-$14, dinner $20-$29, Sun brunch $19.95. Bar. Reservations accepted. Cr cds: A, D, MC, V.

Kutztown (F-12)

See also Allentown, Hamburg, Pennsylvania Dutch Area, Reading

Founded 1771 **Pop** 5,067 **Elev** 417 ft **Area code** 484 and 610 **Zip** 19530

Home of a popular folk festival, Kutztown is named for its founder, George Kutz. The town's population includes many descendants of the Pennsylvania Germans.

What to See and Do

Crystal Cave Park. *3 Crystal Cave Rd. 3 miles NW off US 222. Phone 610/683-6765.* Discovered in 1871; crystal formations, stalactites, stalagmites, natural bridges—all enhanced by indirect lighting. Also museum (July-Sept); nature trail; miniature golf (July-Sept; fee); theater. Café, rock shop, gift shop. Tours (Mar-Nov, daily). **$$$**

Special Event

Folk Festival. *Festival grounds. Phone 215/679-9610.* Celebration of Pennsylvania Dutch folk culture; quilts, music, dancing, and food of Plain and Fancy Dutch. Craftspeople make baskets, brooms, rugs, toleware and other handcrafts. Late June-early July.

Restaurant

★ ★ **NEW SMITHVILLE COUNTRY INN.** *10425 Old Rte 22 (19530). Phone 610/285-2987; fax 610/285-2032.* Hours: 11 am-11 pm; Sun 8 am-10 pm. Closed Memorial Day, Labor Day. Breakfast $2.25-$6.75, lunch $4.95-$7.25, dinner $10.95-$18.95. Bar. Children's menu. Originally a post office and general store; fireplace, antiques. Reservations accepted. Fireplace. Cr cds: A, MC, V.

Lancaster (H-10)

See also Bird-in-Hand, Cornwall, Ephrata, Lebanon, Reading, Wrightsville (York County), York

Settled 1721 **Pop** 56,348 **Elev** 380 ft **Area code** 717

Information Pennsylvania Dutch Convention & Visitors Bureau, 501 Greenfield Rd, 17601; 717/299-8901 or 800/723-8824

Web www.800padutch.com

Lancaster blends the industrial modern, the colonial past, and the Pennsylvania Dutch present. It is the heart of the Pennsylvania Dutch Area (see), one of the East's most colorful tourist attractions. To fully appreciate the area, visitors should leave the main highways and travel on country roads, which Amish buggies share with automobiles. Lancaster was an important provisioning area for the armies of the French and Indian and Revolutionary wars. Its crafters turned out fine guns, which brought the city fame as the "arsenal of the Colonies." When Congress, fleeing Philadelphia, paused here on September 27, 1777, the city was the national capital for one day. It was the state capital from 1799-1812.

What to See and Do

Amish Farm and House. *2395 Lincoln Hwy E (17602). 4 1/2 miles E via US 30. Phone 717/394-6185.* Typical Amish farm in operation. Lecture on the Amish and tour through early 19th-century stone buildings furnished and decorated as old-order Amish household; waterwheels, windmill, hand-dug well, carriages, spring wagon, sleighs. (Daily; closed Dec 25) **$$$**

★ **Bube's Brewery.** *102 N Market St, in Mount Joy. Phone 717/653-2056.* Historic brewery built before the Civil War is the only brewery left in the country that has remained intact since the mid-1800s; now operates as a restaurant (see CATACOMBS). Guided tours take visitors 43 feet below the street into the brewery's aging vaults and passages, built from a cave and later part of the Underground Railroad; narrator tells history of brewery and explains methods of producing beer in a Victorian-age brewery. Tours (Memorial Day-Labor Day, daily). Restaurant open all year (free tour included with reservations for Catacombs restaurant). **FREE**

Candy Americana Museum. *48 N Broad St, 5 miles N via PA 501 at Wilbur Chocolate Company, in Lititz. Phone 717/626-3249.* Antique candy production equipment, confectionery molds, unusual candy containers; outlet store. (Mon-Sat; call for hours) **FREE**

Choo-Choo Barn, Traintown, USA. *PA 741 E. E via US 30, then SE on PA 741, in Strasburg. Phone 717/687-7911.* A

1,700-square-foot layout of Lancaster County in miniature, featuring 20 operating trains and more than 150 animated and automated figures and vehicles. Gift shop. Picnicking. (Apr-Dec, daily; closed holidays) **$$**

Dutch Wonderland. *2249 Lincoln Hwy E (17602). 4 miles E via US 30. Phone 717/291-1888.* Family fun park with rides, botanical gardens, diving shows, shops. Monorail (fee). (Memorial Day-Labor Day, daily; Mid-May-Memorial Day and after Labor Day-Oct, Sat and Sun) **$$$$** Adjacent is

> **National Wax Museum of Lancaster County.** *2251 Lincoln Hwy E (17602). Phone 717/393-3679.* Figures re-create Lancaster County's history from the 1700s to present. (Daily; closed Dec 25) **$$$**

Franklin and Marshall College. *Race and College aves (17602). Phone 717/291-3981.* (1787) 1,810 students. Liberal arts college. Rothman Gallery showcases Pennsylvania-German artifacts: quilts, Fraktur, and stoneware. More than 200 varieties of trees, plants, and shrubs on grounds. Tours of campus. Also here are

> **Joseph R. Grundy Observatory.** *Phone 717/291-4136.* Holds 11-inch refractor and 16-inch reflecting telescope demonstrations. **FREE**

> **North Museum of Natural History and Science.** *400 College Ave. Phone 717/291-3941.* General science and natural history; planetarium shows (Sat and Sun); children's Discovery Room; film series; monthly art exhibits. (Tues-Sun) **$$**

Fulton Opera House. *12 N Prince St. Phone 717/394-7133.* (1852) One of the oldest American theaters; many legendary people have performed here. It is believed that more than one ghost haunts the theater's Victorian interior. Professional regional theater; home of community theater, opera and symphony organizations. **$$$$**

Hans Herr House. *1849 Hans Herr Dr, in Willow St. Phone 717/464-4438.* (1719) Example of medieval Germanic architecture; served as an early Mennonite meetinghouse and colonial residence of the Herr family. Mennonite rural life exhibit; blacksmith shop. House tours. (Apr-Nov, Mon-Sat; rest of year by appointment; closed holidays) **$$**

Heritage Center Museum of Lancaster County. *13 King St (17603). Phone 717/299-6440.* (1795) Houses examples of early Lancaster County arts and crafts. Furniture, tall clocks, quilts, needlework, silver, pewter, Fraktur, rifles. (Mid-Apr-early Jan, Tues-Sat) **FREE**

Historic Rock Ford. *881 Rockford Rd. 2 miles S on Rockford Rd, off S Duke St at Lancaster County Park. Phone 717/392-7223.* (1794) Preserved home of General Edward Hand, Revolutionary War commander, member of Continental Congress. (Apr-Oct, Tues-Fri and Sun) **$$**

James Buchanan's Wheatland. *1120 Marietta Ave, 1 1/2 miles W on PA 23. Phone 717/392-8721.* (1828) Residence of President James Buchanan from 1848-1868; restored Federal mansion with period rooms containing American Empire and Victorian furniture and decorative arts. Guided tours (Apr-Oct, daily; Nov, Fri-Mon). Christmas candlelight tours (early Dec). **$$$**

Landis Valley Museum. *2451 Kissel Hill Rd, 2 1/2 miles N, off PA 272. Phone 717/569-0401 or 717/569-9312.* Interprets Pennsylvania German rural life. Largest collection of Pennsylvania German objects in US; craft and living history demonstrations (May-Oct; see SPECIAL EVENTS); farmsteads, tavern, country store among other exhibit buildings. (Mar-Dec, daily; closed holidays) **$$$**

Mennonite Information Center. *2209 Millstream Rd, E on US 30. Phone 717/299-0954.* Tourist information; interpretation of Mennonite and Amish origins, beliefs. Free video. (Mon-Sat; closed Jan 1, Thanksgiving, Dec 25) **FREE** Also here is

> **Hebrew Tabernacle Reproduction.** *2209 Millstream Rd (17602). Phone 717/299-0954.* Tours (Mon-Sat; closed Jan 1, Thanksgiving, Dec 25). **$$**

Mill Bridge Village. *S Ronks and Soudersburg rds. Phone 717/687-8181 or 800/645-2744.* Restored historic colonial mill village with operating water-powered gristmill (1738); covered bridge; country crafts include broommaking, quilting, candlemaking, blacksmithing; quilt log cabin; Amish kitchen exhibit; music boxes and nickelodeons; horse-drawn hay and carriage rides; 1890s playground; picnicking. Amish house and schoolhouse tour available. Oktoberfest (Oct weekends). Camp resort (early Apr-Oct, daily; fee). Village (early Apr-Nov, daily). **$$$**

Muddy Run LLC. *11 miles S on PA 272, then 3 1/2 miles SW on PA 372. Phone 717/284-4325.* Covers 700 acres with 100-acre lake for boating (rentals; no power boats), fishing; picnicking, playgrounds, snack bar, concession, camping. Park (Apr-early Nov).

National Toy Train Museum. *300 Paradise Ln. E via US 30, PA 896, PA 741, to Paradise Ln, in Strasburg. Phone 717/687-8976.* Trains from the 1880s to present; live operating layouts; movies; rare, unusual and specialty trains. (May-Oct, daily; Apr and Nov-Dec, Sat and Sun) **$$**

Robert Fulton Birthplace. *14 miles S via PA 222. Phone 717/548-2679.* Robert Fulton, a great inventor and accomplished artist, is best known for having built the steamboat Clermont, which, in 1807, successfully made a trip up the Hudson River against winds and strong current. This little stone house, where Fulton was born, was nearly destroyed by fire about 1822; now refurbished. (Memorial Day-Labor Day, Sat and Sun) **$**

Sightseeing tours.

Abe's Buggy Rides. *2596 Old Philadelphia Pike, 6 miles E on PA 340, in Bird-in-Hand. Phone 717/392-1794.* A tour through Amish country in an Amish family carriage. (Mon-Sat) **$$$**

Amish Country Tours. *3121 Old Philadelphia Pike (Rte 340) (17505). Phone 717/768-3600.* Tours of Amish farmlands and Philadelphia. **$$$$**

Brunswick Tours. *2102 Lincoln Hwy E. Phone 717/397-7541.* Private guide and auto tape tours. **$$$$**

Historic Lancaster Walking Tour. *100 S Queen St. Phone 717/392-1776.* A 90-minute tour of historic downtown area. Costumed guide narrates 50 points of architectural or historic interest covering 6 square blocks. (Apr-Oct, two tours daily Fri and Sat, one tour daily Mon-Thurs and Sun; rest of year, by appointment) **$$**

Strasburg Railroad. *8 miles SE via US 30, PA 896, PA 741, in Strasburg. Phone 717/687-7522.* Railroad runs 4 1/2 miles to Paradise. Picnic stop. This 160-year-old line uses late 19th-century coaches, various steam locomotives. (Apr-Oct, daily; winter, weekends) **$$$** Adjacent is

Railroad Museum of Pennsylvania. *300 Gap Rd. Phone 717/687-8628.* More than 50 locomotives, freight and passenger cars dating from 1825; audiovisual exhibits; railroading memorabilia. Picnicking. (Apr-Oct, daily; rest of year, Tues-Sun; closed holidays) **$$$**

Sturgis Pretzel House. *219 E Main St, 9 miles N via PA 501, 772 in Lititz. Phone 717/626-4354.* First US commercial pretzel bakery (1861), restored as museum. Early equipment (also modern plant); pretzel-making demonstrations, visitors may try twisting pretzels; outlet store. (Mon-Sat; closed Jan 1, Thanksgiving, Dec 25) **$**

Twin Brook Winery. *Strasburg Rd. 17 miles E via US 30, S on PA 41, E on Strasburg Rd, located in Gap at 5697. Phone 717/442-4915.* Estate winery housed in a restored 19th-century barn offers wine tasting, tours of wine-making facilities, visits to the vineyard; picnic areas. Outdoor concerts (late June-mid-Sept, Sat evenings; fee); special events throughout the year. (Apr-Dec, Mon-Sat, also Sun afternoons; rest of year, Tues-Sat, also Sun afternoons)

The Watch and Clock Museum. *12 miles W via US 30, at 514 Poplar St in Columbia. Phone 717/684-8261.* National Association of Watch and Clock Collectors living museum of timepieces and related tools and memorabilia. Over 8,000 items representing the 1600s to the present. Extensive research library. Special exhibitions. (May-Sept, Tues-Sat, also Sun afternoons; winter schedule varies; closed holidays) **$$**

Special Events

Harvest Days. *2451 Kissel Hill Rd. Phone 717/569-0401. Landis Valley Museum.* Demonstrations of more than 80 traditional craft and harvest-time activities. Columbus Day weekend.

Music at Gretna. *1 Alpha Dr. 15 miles N via PA 72, in Mt. Gretna. Phone 717/964-3836.* Chamber music and jazz; well-known artists. Mid-June-early Sept.

Old Fashioned Sunday. *1120 Marietta Ave. On grounds of Wheatland. Phone 717/392-8721.* Festivities include entertainment, magic show, and 19th-century activities. Mid-May.

Sheep Shearing. *2395 Lincoln Hwy E. Phone 717/394-6185. Amish Farm and House.* Last Thurs and Fri in Apr, first Fri in Oct.

Victorian Christmas Week. *1120 Marietta Ave. On grounds of Wheatland. Phone 717/392-8721.* Early Dec.

Motels/Motor Lodges

★ ★ **BEST INN.** *1492 Lititz Pike (17601). Phone 717/393-0771; fax 717/299-6238. www.bestinn.com.* 160 rooms, 2 story. May-Oct: S, D $95; under 12 free; 2-day minimum stay holidays; lower rates rest of year. Crib free. TV; cable. Pool. Restaurant 6 am-2 pm, 5-10 pm, Sat, Sun 7 am-2 pm. Room service. Bar 5 pm-midnight. Check-out noon. Meeting rooms. Business services available. In-room modem link. Bellstaff. Valet service. Sundries. Health club privileges. Game room. Some refrigerators. Balconies. Cr cds: A, C, D, DS, ER, JCB, MC, V.

[D] [icons] [SC]

★ ★ **BEST WESTERN EDEN RESORT INN & SUITES.** *222 Eden Rd (17601). Phone 717/569-6444; toll-free 800/528-1234; fax 717/569-4208. www.edenresort.com.* 276 rooms, 3 story. June-Nov: S, D $125-$139; each additional $10; suites $129-$249; under 18 free; varied lower rates rest of year. Crib free. Pet accepted. TV; cable (premium). 2 pools, 1 indoor; whirlpool, poolside service, lifeguard. Playground. Restaurant 6:30 am-11 pm; weekends to midnight. Room service. Bar 11-2 am; entertainment. Check-out noon. Meeting rooms. Business center. In-room modem link. Valet service. Free airport transportation. Gift shop. Lighted tennis. Exercise equipment; saunas. Lawn games. Microwaves available. Some balconies. Cr cds: A, C, D, DS, MC, V.

[D] [icons] [SC] [icon]

★ **COUNTRY LIVING INN.** *2406 Old Philadelphia Pike (17602). Phone 717/295-7295; fax 717/295-0994. www.countrylivinginn.com.* 34 rooms, 2 story. July-Oct: S, D $79-$99; each additional $8; higher rates holiday weekends; lower rates rest of year. Check-out noon. TV; cable (premium). Restaurant nearby. Cr cds: MC, V.

[icon]

★ ★ **DAYS INN.** *30 Keller Ave (17601). Phone 717/299-5700; toll-free 800/329-7466; fax 717/295-1907.*

www.kellerinn.com. 193 rooms, 2-3 story. S $76-$81; D $88-$91; each additional $10; under 12 free. Check-out noon. TV; cable (premium). Laundry services. Restaurant 7-11 am, 5-9 pm. Bar noon-midnight. Game room. 2 pools, 1 indoor; children's pool. Tennis. Cr cds: A, C, D, DS, MC, V.

⊠ ⇔ ⊠ ⊠ SC

★★ **GARDEN SPOT MOTEL.** *2291 Lincoln Hwy E (17602). Phone 717/394-4736; fax 717/299-6339.* 19 rooms. S $35-$55; D $40-$62; each additional $5; under 5 free; higher rates holidays. Closed Dec-Mar. Crib $4. TV; cable. Restaurant 7:30-11 am. Check-out 11:30 am. Gift shop. Cr cds: A, DS, MC, V.

⊠

★ **HERSHEY FARM MOTOR INN.** *240 Hartman Bride Rd (17572). Phone 717/687-8635; toll-free 800/827-8635; fax 717/687-8638. www.hersheyfarm.com.* 59 rooms, 2 story. June-Aug: S $84; D $89; each additional $8; suites $104-$109; under 16 free; weekly rates; lower rates rest of year. Complimentary full breakfast. Check-out 11 am. TV; cable (premium). Pool. Cr cds: DS, MC, V.

⊠ ⇔ ⊠ ⊠

★★ **HOLIDAY INN.** *521 Greenfield Rd (17601). Phone 717/299-2551; toll-free 800/465-4329; fax 717/397-0220. www.holiday-inn.com.* 189 rooms, 4 story. Early May-Nov: S, D $79-$109; under 18 free; lower rates rest of year. Crib free. TV; cable (premium). 2 pools, 1 indoor. Restaurant 6:30 am-2 pm, 5-10 pm. Room service. Bar 4 pm-2 am. Check-out noon. Meeting rooms. Business services available. In-room modem link. Valet service. Sundries. Tennis. Exercise equipment. Health club privileges. Microwaves available. Cr cds: A, C, D, DS, ER, JCB, MC, V.

D ⊠ ⇔ ⊠ ⊠ SC

★★ **HOWARD JOHNSON.** *2100 Lincoln Hwy (17602). Phone 717/397-7781; toll-free 800/654-2000; fax 717/397-6340. www.hojo.com.* 112 rooms, 2 story. June-Oct: S $48-$75; D $68-$88; each additional $7; higher rates major holidays; lower rates rest of year. Complimentary continental breakfast. Check-out 11 am. TV; cable (premium). Restaurant 11 am-midnight. Bar from 11 am. Indoor pool. Cr cds: A, C, D, DS, MC, V.

D ⇔ ⊠ SC

★★ **PARK INN.** *24 S Willowdale Dr (17602). Phone 717/293-9500; toll-free 800/524-3817; fax 717/293-8558. www.rockvaleinn.com.* 113 rooms, 2 story. Late June-Nov: S, D $79-$109; each additional $8; under 12 free; lower rates rest of year. Crib free. TV; cable (premium). Pool; lifeguard. Restaurant 7 am-2 pm. Bar noon-midnight. Check-out 11 am. Meeting room. Business services available. Cr cds: A, C, D, DS, ER, JCB, MC, V.

D ⇔ ⊠ SC

★ **RAMADA INN.** *2250 Lincoln Hwy E (17602). Phone 717/393-5499; toll-free 800/867-2623; fax 717/293-1014. www.ramada.com.* 166 rooms, 5 story. Mid-June-Oct: S, D $84-$129; each additional $10; under 18 free; lower rates rest of year. Crib free. Pet accepted, some restrictions. Check-out 11 am. TV; cable. In-room modem link. Balconies. Refrigerators. Coin laundry. Playground. Health club privileges. Sauna. Game room. 2 pools, 1 indoor. 27-hole golf privileges, pro, putting green, driving range. Tennis. Picnic tables. Lawn games. Free airport transportation. Meeting rooms. Business services. Cr cds: A, C, D, DS, ER, JCB, MC, V.

D ⊠ ⊠ ⊠ ⇔ ⊠ SC

★ **WESTFIELD MOTOR INN.** *2929 Hempland Rd (17601). Phone 717/397-9300; toll-free 800/547-1395; fax 717/295-9240. www.westfieldinn.com.* 84 rooms, 2 story. S, D $49-$79; each additional $5; suites $79-$89; under 18 free. Complimentary continental breakfast. Check-out 11 am. TV; cable; VCR available. Laundry services. Restaurant nearby. Pool; lifeguard. Cr cds: A, C, D, DS, MC, V.

D ⇔ ⊠ SC

Hotels

★★ **BRUNSWICK HOTEL.** *N Queen St (17608). Phone 717/397-4801; toll-free 800/233-0182; fax 717/397-4991. www.hotelbrunswick.com.* 222 rooms, 7 story. S $62-$78; D $72-$86; each additional $6; under 17 free; monthly, weekly, weekend rates; golf plan; lower rates Nov-Apr. Crib free. Pet accepted; $100. Check-out noon. TV; cable, VCR available (movies). Refrigerators available. Coin laundry. Restaurant 7 am-1:30 pm, 5:30-9 pm. Bar; entertainment. Exercise equipment. Indoor pool, lifeguard. Free garage parking. Meeting rooms. Business services. Cr cds: A, D, DS, MC, V.

D ⊠ ⇔ ⊠ ⊠

★★ **HILTON GARDEN INN LANCASTER.** *101 Granite Run Dr (17601). Phone 717/560-0880; toll-free 800/445-8667; fax 717/560-5400. www.hilton.com.* 156 rooms, 2 story. D $119-$149. TV; cable (premium). In-room modem link. Laundry services. Restaurant 6:30 am-2 pm, 5-10 pm. Bar 11:30 am-midnight. Exercise equipment. Indoor pool, whirlpool. Business center. Cr cds: A, C, D, DS, ER, JCB, MC, V.

D ⇔ ⊠ ⊠ SC ⊠

Resort

★★ **WILLOW VALLEY RESORT.** *2416 Willow St Pike. (17602). Phone 717/464-2711; toll-free 800/444-1714; fax 717/464-1722. www.willowvalley.com.* 342 rooms, 5 story. Mid-June-early Sept, holiday weekends: S,

D $119-$199; each additional $10; ages 6-12, $5; under 6 free; lower rates rest of year. Check-out noon. TV; VCR available (movies). Free guest laundry. Restaurant 6 am-9 pm. Exercise equipment, sauna. Game room. 3 pools, 2 indoor, whirlpool. Lighted tennis. Free airport transportation. Country view; large landscaped grounds. Cr cds: A, D, DS, MC, V.

[icons]

B&B/Small Inns

★ ★ ALDEN HOUSE BED AND BREAKFAST.
62 E Main St (17543). Phone 717/627-3363; toll-free 800/584-0753; fax 717/627-5428. www.aldenhouse.com. 5 rooms, shower only, 3 suites, 3 story. No room phones. S $90; D $120; each additional $20; suites $105-$120; weekends (2-day minimum); higher rates special events. Children over 10 years only. Complimentary full breakfast. Check-out 11 am, check-in after 3 pm. TV. Restaurant nearby. Concierge service. Built in 1850. Totally nonsmoking. Cr cds: MC, V.

[icon]

★ ★ AUSTRALIAN WALKABOUT INN BED AND BREAKFAST.
837 Village Rd (17537). Phone 717/464-0707; fax 717/464-2501. www.walkaboutinn.com. 5 rooms, 3 suites, 3 story. No room phones. Adults only. Children over 10 years only. Complimentary full breakfast. Check-out 10 am, check-in 3-8 pm. TV; cable (premium). Fireplaces. Lawn games. Brick house with wrap-around porch built in 1925. Totally nonsmoking. Cr cds: A, MC, V. **$$**

[icon]

★ ★ GENERAL SUTTER INN.
14 E Main St (17543). Phone 717/626-2115; fax 717/626-0992. www.generalsutterinn.com. 16 rooms, 3 story. D $63-$110; suite $120-$140. Pet accepted. Check-out noon, check-in 3 pm. TV. Fireplace in parlor. Dining room 7 am-9 pm; Sun 8 am-8 pm. Bar 11 am-11 pm. Built in 1764; antique country and Victorian furniture. Cr cds: A, DS, MC, V.

[icons]

★ ★ ★ HISTORIC STRASBURG INN.
1 Historic Dr, Rte 896 (17579). Phone 717/687-7691; toll-free 800/872-0201; fax 717/687-6098. www.histoicstrasburginn.com. 101 rooms in 5 buildings, 2 story. Apr-Nov: S, D $119-$129; each additional $15; suites $159-$199; under 12 free; lower rates rest of year. Crib $7. Pet accepted; $15. TV; cable, VCR available (movies). Heated pool; whirlpool. Playground. Complimentary full breakfast. Restaurant (see also WASHINGTON HOUSE). Bar 11:30 am-11 pm. Check-out noon. Meeting rooms. Business services available. Gift shop. Exercise equipment; sauna. Lawn games. Balconies. Hot air balloon rides on property (58 acres). Cr cds: A, C, D, DS, MC, V.

[icons]

★ ★ ★ KING'S COTTAGE.
1049 E King St (17602). Phone 717/397-1017; toll-free 800/747-8717; fax 717/397-3447. www.kingscottagebb.com. This bed and breakfast is nestled in the center of scenic Lancaster County. It provides a perfect location for travelers looking to explore Pennsylvania Dutch Country. The inn is a Spanish-style mansion providing a comfortable stay for travelers. 8 rooms. S, D $165-$260. Children over 12 years only. Complimentary full breakfast; afternoon refreshments. Check-out 11 am, check-in 4 pm. TV. Restaurant nearby. Restored Spanish/mission-style house (1913); antiques, fireplaces. Cr cds: DS, MC, V.

[icons]

★ ★ O'FLAHERTY'S DINGELDEIN HOUSE.
1105 E King St (17602). Phone 717/293-1723; toll-free 800/779-7765; fax 717/293-1947. www.dingeldeinhouse.com. 6 rooms, 1 suites, 3 story. No room phones. Complimentary full breakfast. Check-out 11 am, check-in 2:30 pm. TV in common room; cable (premium), VCR available (movies). Free airport transportation. Dutch Colonial mansion built in 1912. Totally nonsmoking. Cr cds: A, DS, MC, V. **$**

[icon]

★ ★ SWISS WOODS BED & BREAKFAST.
500 Blantz Rd (17543). Phone 717/627-3358; toll-free 800/594-8018; fax 717/627-3483. www.swisswoods.com. Each of the seven rooms at this bed and breakfast offers goose down comforters on the beds, natural wood work, and hand-crafted furnishings. Its location puts it near hiking and biking trails, farmers markets, and the lake. 7 rooms, 1 suite, 2 story. Apr-Dec: S, D $125-$185; each additional $15; suite $165; weekends, holidays (2-3 day minimum); lower rates rest of year. Children over 12 years only. Complimentary full breakfast. Check-out 11 am, check-in 3-7 pm. TV in suite and common room; VCR available. Fireplace in suite. Concierge service. Built to resemble Swiss chalet. Totally nonsmoking. Cr cds: A, DS, MC, V.

[icon]

Restaurants

★ ★ ★ CATACOMBS AT BUBE'S BREWERY.
102 N Market St (17552). Phone 717/653-2056; fax 717/653-9337. www.bubesbrewery.com. Hours: 11 am-2 pm, 5:30-9 pm; Fri, Sat to 10 pm; Sun 4:30-9 pm. Closed some major holidays. Reservations accepted. Continental menu. Bar. Lunch $2.95-$7.45. Complete meals: dinner $15.95-$26.95. Specializes in shrimp, roast duck. Entertainment Fri, Sat. Outdoor dining. In old Victorian hotel and brewery (1876); dining areas are located in original bottling plant, original dining rooms of the hotel portion (Victorian décor) and below ground, in the cellars (medieval atmosphere, costumes, entertainment). Guided tours. Cr cds: A, DS, MC, V.

[icon]

★★**D & S BRASSERIE.** *1679 Lincoln Hwy E (17602). Phone 717/299-1694; fax 717/299-4687. www.dandsbrasserie.com.* Hours: 11:30 am-midnight; Sat 4 pm-1 am; Sun 4-10 pm. Closed Thanksgiving, Dec 25. Reservations accepted. Continental menu. Bar. Lunch $3.75-$8.95, dinner $8.95-$33. Specializes in prime rib, pasta, seafood. Outdoor dining. House built in 1925; original woodwork, fireplaces. Cr cds: A, D, DS, MC, V.

D

★★★**LOG CABIN.** *11 Lehoy Forest Dr, Leola, (17540). Phone 717/626-1181; fax 717/626-0969. www.log cabinrestaurant.com.* American menu. Hours: 5-10 pm; Sun 4-9 pm. Closed major holidays. Dinner $15-$35. Bar. Children's menu. Reservations accepted. Entry through covered "kissing" bridge. Cr cds: A, D, MC, V.

D

★★★**OLDE GREENFIELD INN.** *595 Greenfield Rd (17601). Phone 717/393-0668; fax 717/393-0908. www. theoldegreenfieldinn.com.* American menu. Hours: 11 am-2 pm, 5-10 pm; Mon from 5 pm; Sat 8 am-2 pm (brunch), 5-10 pm; Sun 8 am-2 pm (brunch). Closed some major holidays. Dinner $15.95-$38.50. Bar. Children's menu. In restored stone farmhouse; dining available on balcony and in wine cellar. Casual attire. Outdoor dining. Cr cds: A, D, DS, MC, V.

D

★★**WASHINGTON HOUSE.** *1 Historic Dr (17579). Phone 717/687-9211; fax 717/687-5290. www. historicstrasburginn.com.* French menu. Hours: 7 am-2 pm, 5-9:30 pm; Sun 7 am-9:30 pm. Dinner $26-$33. Sun brunch. 24 hour service. Bar 11:30 am-10 pm. Children's menu. Outdoor seating. Cr cds: A, D, DS, MC, V.

D

Lebanon (G-10)

See also Cornwall, Ephrata, Hershey, Lancaster, Pennsylvania Dutch Area

Founded 1756 **Pop** 24,461 **Elev** 460 ft **Area code** 717 **Zip** 17042

Information Pennsylvania Rainbow Region Vacation Bureau, 625 Quentin Rd, PO Box 329; 717/272-8555

This industrial city, steeped in German traditions, is the marketplace for colorful Lebanon County. Many Hessians were confined here after the Battle of Trenton. Today, Lebanon bologna factories and food processing are important to the city's economy. Master planning for redevelopment of city and county combines with the traditional atmosphere to make this a charming community.

What to See and Do

Coleman Memorial Park. *PA 72 and N 12th St (17046). 2 miles N on PA 72, W Maple St. Phone 717/228-4470.* This 100-acre former estate has swimming pool (Memorial Day-Labor Day, daily; fee); tennis courts, athletic fields, picnic facilities. Fee for some activities. Park (Daily). **FREE**

The Daniel Weaver Company. *15th Ave and Weavertown Rd. Phone 717/274-6100 or 800/WEAVERS.* Manufacturers, since 1885, of Weaver's Famous Lebanon Bologna and other wood-smoked gourmet meats; smoked in 100-year-old outdoor smokehouses. Samples. Tours. (Mon-Sat) **FREE**

Fort Zeller. *11 miles E on US 422, then S on PA 419, in Newmanstown. Phone 610/589-4301.* One of state's oldest existing forts; originally built of logs, rebuilt of stone in 1745; has 12-foot-wide Queen Anne fireplace in kitchen. (By appointment) **DONATION**

Middlecreek Wildlife Management Area. *11 miles SE on PA 897 to Kleinfeltersville, then 1 mile S. Phone 717/733-1512.* A 6,254-acre tract provides refuge for waterfowl, forest, and farmland wildlife. Permit and open hunting areas, inquire at visitor center for regulations. Fishing, boating (Feb-Nov); hiking, picnicking. Visitor center (Mar-Nov, Tues-Sun). **FREE**

Stoevers Dam Recreational Area. *943 Miller St (17046). 2 miles N on PA 343. Phone 717/228-4470.* A 153-acre park with 52-acre lake for fishing, boating (electric motors only), canoeing; 1 1/2-mile trail for jogging, hiking, and bicycling; primitive camping (permit only; fee). Nature trails; nature barn (Apr-Oct, Tues-Sun; winter, by appointment). Community park (daily). **FREE**

Stoy Museum of the Lebanon County Historical Society. *924 Cumberland St. Phone 717/272-1473.* Local historical museum containing 30 permanent room and shop displays on three floors of house built in 1773 and used as first county courthouse; research library. Tours. (Mon-Fri, Sun; closed Mon and Sun of holiday weekends) **$$**

Motels/Motor Lodges

★★**LANTERN LODGE MOTOR INN.** *411 N College St (17067). Phone 717/866-6536; toll-free 800/262-5564; fax 717/866-8857. www.thelanternlodge.com.* 83 rooms, 2 story. D $60-$105; each additional $10. Check-out 11 am, check-in 2 pm. TV; cable; VCR available. Restaurant 7 am-10 pm. Room service. Cr cds: A, C, D, DS, MC, V.

D

★★**QUALITY INN.** *625 Quentin Rd (17042). Phone 717/273-6771; toll-free 800/626-8242; fax 717/273-4882. www.qualityinn.com.* 56 hotel rooms, 74 motel rooms, 5 story. Late May-Oct: S $78-$110; D $83-$120; each additional $7; under 18 free; lower rates rest of year. Crib free. TV; cable. Pool; lifeguard. Restaurant 6 am-9 pm. Room service. Bar 11-2 am; entertainment. Check-out noon. Meeting rooms. Business services available. Sundries. Barber. Game room. Cr cds: A, C, D, DS, ER, JCB, MC, V.

D ⚊ ⚊ SC

B&B/Small Inn

★ ★ **SWATARA CREEK INN.** *10463 Jonestown Rd (17003). Phone 717/865-3259. www.swataracreekinn.com.* 10 rooms, 2 with shower only, 1 suite, 3 story. No room phones. Apr-Nov: S $45-$70; D $55-$80; suite $115; family rates; Hershey car show (3-day minimum); lower rates rest of year. Complimentary full breakfast. Restaurant nearby. Check-out 11 am, check-in 3 pm. Concierge service. Gift shop. Refrigerator on 2nd floor. Some balconies. Picnic tables. Victorian mansion built in 1860; country setting. Cr cds: A, D, DS, MC, V.

D ⚊ SC

Lewisburg (E-9)

See also Danville, Williamsport

Settled 1785 **Pop** 5,620 **Elev** 460 ft **Area code** 570 **Zip** 17837

Information Susquehanna Valley Visitors Bureau, Rural Rte 3, 219-D Hafer Rd; 570/524-7234 or 800/525-7320

Web www.svvb.com

Home of Bucknell University (1846), this college community also has light industry. The Native American village of Old Muncy Town was located nearby before the region was opened by Ludwig (Lewis) Doerr.

What to See and Do

Fort Augusta. *1150 N Front St. 9 miles SE on PA 147, in Sunbury. Phone 570/286-4083.* (1757) Museum collection of Northumberland County Historical Society. (Mon, Wed, Fri, afternoons) **FREE**

Packwood House Museum. *15 N Water St. Phone 570/524-0323.* A three-story, 27-room log and frame building begun in the late 18th century. Former hostelry houses a wide-ranging collection of Americana, period furnishings, textiles, and decorative arts. Changing exhibits; museum shop. Tours. (Tues-Sun; closed holidays) **$$**

Slifer House Museum. *1 mile N, on grounds of Riverwoods. Phone 570/524-2245.* Elaborate three-story, 20-room Victorian mansion. First and second floors have been restored, complete with Victorian parlor, dining room, library, and five bedrooms. Gift shop. (Apr-late Dec, Tues-Sun; rest of year, Tues-Fri afternoons, also by appointment; closed holidays) **$$**

Motels/Motor Lodges

★**BEST WESTERN COUNTRY CUPBOARD INN.** *Rte 15 N (17837). Phone 570/524-5500; fax 570/524-4291. www.bestwestern.com.* 106 rooms, 3 story. S $68-$99; D $75-$105; each additional $6; suites $105-$149; under 18 free; higher rates university events. Complimentary continental breakfast. Check-out 11 am. TV; cable. Laundry services. Exercise equipment. Game room. Pool. Cr cds: A, C, D, DS, JCB, MC, V.

D ⚊ 🏃 ⚊

★ **DAYS INN.** *US Rte 15 (17837). Phone 570/523-1171; toll-free 800/329-7466; fax 570/524-4667. www.daysinn.com.* 108 rooms, 2 story. S $55-$69; D $61-$69; each additional $6; under 16 free. Crib free. TV; cable, VCR available (movies). Pool; lifeguard. Check-out noon. Business services available. In-room modem link. Exercise equipment. Cr cds: A, C, D, DS, JCB, MC, V.

⚊ 🏃 ⚊ SC

Restaurant

★ ★ **COUNTRY CUPBOARD.** *101 Hafer Rd (17837). Phone 570/523-3211; fax 570/524-9299.* Hours: 7 am-9 pm. Closed Dec 25. Breakfast $2.25-$5.50, lunch $4.99-$10.99, dinner $6.99-$11.99. Children's menu. Reservations accepted Mon-Fri. Totally nonsmoking. Country dining. Cr cds: DS, MC, V.

D

Lewistown (F-8)

Settled 1754 **Pop** 9,341 **Elev** 520 ft **Area code** 717

Information Juniata Valley Area Chamber of Commerce, 3 W Monument Sq, 17044; 717/248-6713

Surrounded by rich farmland and beautiful forested mountain ranges, Lewistown lies in the scenic Juniata River Valley in the heart of central Pennsylvania. Lewistown retains the charm of its rustic surroundings, which yearly attract thousands of sportsmen and outdoor enthusiasts to the area's fine hunting, fishing, and camping facilities. A large Amish population that thrives on the farmland of the Kishacoquillas Valley has contributed greatly to the area's culture and heritage.

What to See and Do

Brookmere Farm Vineyards. *5369 SR 655 (17004). Approximately 5 miles N via US 322, then SW on PA 655, near Belleville. Phone 717/935-5380.* In 19th-century stone and wood barn. Winery tour, wine tasting; picnicking. (Mon-Sat, also Sun afternoons; closed holidays) **FREE**

Greenwood Furnace State Park. *PA 305 and Broadmountain Rd. 5 miles N on US 322, then 9 miles W on PA 655, then NW on PA 305. Phone 814/667-1800.* Remains of Greenwood Works, last iron furnace to operate in area (circa 1833-1904); restored stack. Approximately 400 acres. Swimming beach, fishing; hiking, snowmobiling, ice skating, ice fishing, picnicking, playground, snack bar, store, tent and trailer sites. Visitor center, interpretive program. Standard fees.

Reeds Gap State Park. *8 miles N off US 322 and unnumbered road. Phone 717/667-3622.* Approximately 200 acres. Swimming pool, fishing; hiking, picnicking, snack bar. Tent sites only.

Motel/Motor Lodge

★ ★ **CLARION HOTEL.** *13015 Furguson Valley Rd (17009). Phone 717/248-4961; toll-free 800/252-7466; fax 717/242-3013. www.clarioninn.com.* 119 rooms, 2 story. S, D $59; each additional $5; under 18 free. Crib free. Pet accepted. TV; cable (premium). Pool; poolside service, lifeguard. Restaurant 6 am-2 pm, 5-10 pm. Room service. Bar 4 pm-midnight. Check-out noon. Meeting rooms. In-room modem link. Valet service. Cr cds: A, C, D, DS, JCB, MC, V.

D 🐾 ⛖ ⛝ SC

Ligonier (G-4)

See also Donegal, Greensburg, Johnstown

Founded 1816 **Pop** 1,695 **Elev** 1,200 ft **Area code** 724 **Zip** 15658

Information Ligonier Valley Chamber of Commerce, Town Hall, 120 E Main St; 724/238-4200

Web www.ligonier.com

Fort Ligonier, built in 1758 by the British, was the scene of one of the key battles of the French and Indian War. It also served as a supply base during Pontiac's War in 1763.

What to See and Do

Compass Inn Museum. *3 miles E on US 30, in Laughlintown. Phone 724/238-4983.* A 1799 stagecoach stop; original log and stone inn authentically restored and furnished; log barn houses. Conestoga wagon and stagecoach; cookhouse with beehive oven and fireplace; blacksmith shop contains working forge. (May-Oct, Tues-Sun) **$$**

Fort Ligonier. *S Market St, on US 30, PA 711. Phone 724/238-9701.* Reconstructed 18th-century British fort; includes buildings with period furnishings. Museum

houses outstanding French and Indian War collection, 18th-century artifacts; introductory film. (May-Oct, daily) (See SPECIAL EVENTS) **$$**

Idlewild Park. *Rte 30 E. Phone 724/238-3666.* Amusement rides; entertainment; picnicking; children's play area; water park. (Memorial Day-late Aug, Tues-Sun) **$$$$** Adjacent is

Story Book Forest. *US 30 E. Phone 724/238-3666.* Admission included with Idlewild Park. Children's park with animals, people, and buildings portraying nursery rhymes. (Memorial Day-late Aug, Tues-Sun)

St. Vincent Archabbey and College. *8 miles W on US 30, in Latrobe. Phone 724/537-4560.* (1846) 1,200 students. Includes Benedictine monastery, seminary, and coeducational liberal arts college. St. Vincent Theatre has performances in theater-in-the-round. Free self-guided tape tours.

Special Events

Fort Ligonier Days. *120 E Main St (15658). Phone 724/238-4200.* Living history program of the French and Indian War. Parade, 150 juried crafters, food, and special events. Usually second weekend in Oct.

Ligonier Highland Games and Gathering of the Clans of Scotland. *Idlewild Park. Phone 724/238-3666.* Sports; massed pipe bands, Highland dancing competitions, Scottish fiddling; sheep dog, wool spinning, and weaving demonstrations; genealogy booth, Scottish fair. First Sat after Labor Day.

Ligonier Ice Fest. *Phone 724/238-4200.* Professional ice sculptures on the Diamond and in front of businesses; collegiate ice-carving competition. Super Bowl weekend, Jan.

Mountain Playhouse. *RR 985 N. 11 miles SE on US 30, then 1/2 mile N on US 985, in Jennerstown. Phone 814/629-9201.* Broadway shows in restored gristmill (1805). Matinees and evening performances. Late May-mid-Oct.

Motel/Motor Lodge

★ ★ **RAMADA INN.** *216 W Loyalhanna St (15658). Phone 724/238-9545; toll-free 800/272-6232; fax 724/238-9803. www.ramada.com.* 66 rooms, 3 story. S, D $65-$95; each additional $6; suites $95-$150; under 12 free; ski plans. Check-out noon. TV; cable (premium), VCR available. In-room modem link. Restaurant 6:30 am-10 pm. Bar 4 pm-2 am. Room service. Health club privileges. Pool. Cr cds: A, DS, MC, V.

D ⛖ ⛝ SC

Limerick (G-12)

See also Norristown, Pottstown, Reading

Pop 800 **Elev** 302 ft **Area code** 484 and 610 **Zip** 19468

Information Valley Forge Convention & Visitors Bureau, 600 W Germantown Pike, Suite 130, Plymouth Meeting 19462; 610/834-1550

Web www.valleyforge.org

What to See and Do

Spring Mountain Ski Area. *6 miles N, off PA 29. Phone 610/287-7900.* Triple, three double chairlifts; two rope tows; patrol, school, rentals; snowmaking; cafeteria, lodge. Longest run 1/2 mile; vertical drop 420 feet. Also camping available (fee; hookups). (Mid-Dec-mid-Mar, daily) **$$$$**

Lock Haven (D-8)

See also Williamsport

Founded 1833 **Pop** 9,149 **Elev** 564 ft **Area code** 570 **Zip** 17745

Information Clinton County Tourist Promotion Agency, Court House Annex, 151 Susquehanna Ave; 570/893-4037

Founded on the site of pre-Revolutionary Fort Reed, the community takes its name from two sources. The lock of the Pennsylvania Canal once crossed the West Branch of the Susquehanna River here, and the town was once a "haven" for the rafts and lumberjacks of nearby logging camps. Near the geographic center of the state, the town today is a center of commerce and small industry.

What to See and Do

Bucktail Natural Area. Scenic area extends from mountain rim to mountain rim for 75 miles from Lock Haven north to Renovo and west to Emporium. Connecting the three towns and weaving through the park is PA 120, an outstanding drive through mountain scenery. Historic site west of Renovo commemorates Bucktail Trail, which served pioneers and Civil War volunteers. Fishing.

Bull Run School House. *Phone 570/893-4037.* (1899) Only remaining one-room schoolhouse in county; fully restored with all of its original equipment, including double desks, schoolmaster's and recitation desks, Waterbury clock, bell. (Hours vary) **FREE**

The Heisey Museum. *362 E Water St. Phone 570/748-7254.* Victorian house museum; early 1800s kitchen; ice house

containing logging, farming, and canal artifacts. (Tues-Fri; also by appointment) **DONATION**

Hyner View. *22 miles NW on PA 120.* At 2,000 feet, "Laurel Drive to the top of the world" provides panoramic view of valley, river, highway and forest. Site of state and national hang gliding competitions.

State parks.

Bald Eagle. *PA 150 and Rte 26 (16841). 13 miles SW off PA 150. Phone 814/625-2775.* A 1,730-acre lake on approximately 5,900 acres. Swimming beach, fishing, boating (rentals, mooring, launching, marina); hunting, hiking, sledding, ice skating, ice boating, picnicking, playground, snack bar, store, tent and trailer sites. Standard fees.

Kettle Creek. *35 miles NW on PA 120 to Westport, then 7 miles N on PA 4001. Phone 570/923-6004.* Approximately 1,600 acres. Winds through beautiful valley developed as tourist area. Swimming beach, fishing, boating (mooring, launching); hunting, hiking, bridle trail, snowmobiling, sledding, ice skating, picnicking, playground, tent and trailer sites (electric hookups). Standard fees.

Special Event

Flaming Foliage Festival. *29 miles NW on PA 120, in Renovo. Phone 570/923-2411.* Includes parade, craft show, and contest for festival queen. Second weekend in Oct.

B&B/Small Inn

★ ★ **VICTORIAN INN BED AND BREAKFAST.** *402 E Water St (17745). Phone 570/748-8688; toll-free 888/653-8688; fax 570/748-2444.* 12 rooms, 2 with shower only, 2 share bath, 2 story. S $55-$60; D $60-$65; each additional $10. Adults only. Pet accepted. TV. Complimentary full breakfast. Restaurant nearby. Check-out 1 pm, check-in 2 pm. Health club privileges. Built in 1859; garden atrium. Cr cds: A, C, D, DS, MC, V.
🐾 🏊

Lumberville

See also New Hope

B&B/Small Inn

★ ★ ★ **1740 HOUSE.** *3690 River Rd Rte 32 (18933). Phone 215/297-5661; fax 215/297-5243. www.1740house .com.* 25 rooms, 2 story. D $165-$225; Weekends (Sat 2-day minimum), holidays (3-4-day minimum). Complimentary buffet breakfast. Check-out noon, check-in 2 pm. Pool.
D 🏊 🏊

Restaurant

★ ★ **CUTTALOSSA INN.** *3478 River Rd (PA 32) (18933). Phone 215/297-5082. www.cuttalossainn.com.* American menu. Closed Sun; Jan 1, Dec 24, 25; also 3 weeks in Jan. Lunch, dinner. Bar. Entertainment in summer except Tues-Sun. Outdoor seating. Cr cds: A, MC, V. **$$**

Manheim (G-10)

See also Cornwall, Lancaster, Lebanon

Founded 1762 **Pop** 4,784 **Elev** 400 ft **Area code** 717 **Zip** 17545

Information Manheim Area Chamber of Commerce, 210 S Charlotte St; 717/665-6330

Web www.manheimchamber.com

Baron Henry William Stiegel founded Manheim and started manufacturing the flint glassware that bore his name. In 1770 he owned the town; by 1774 he was in debtor's prison, the victim of his own generosity and his poor choice of business associates. After his imprisonment, he made a meager living teaching here.

What to See and Do

◼ **Mount Hope Estate & Winery.** *1/2 mile S of exit 20 at junction PA 72 and PA Tpke. Phone 717/665-7021.* Restored sandstone mansion was originally built in the Federal style (circa 1800), then increased its size to 32 rooms with an extension built in 1895, which changed the house's style to Victorian. Turrets, winding walnut staircase, hand-painted 18-foot ceilings, Egyptian marble fireplaces, grand ballroom, crystal chandeliers; greenhouse, solarium, gardens. Wine tasting in billiards room. (Daily; closed Jan 1, Thanksgiving, Dec 25) (See SPECIAL EVENTS) **FREE**

Zion Lutheran Church. *2 S Hazel St, 1 block E of PA 72. Phone 717/665-5880.* (1891) Victorian-Gothic structure built on site of original church; Stiegel donated the ground (1772) in exchange for one red rose from the congregation every year. (Mon-Fri)

Special Events

Pennsylvania Renaissance Faire. *83 Mansion House Rd. Mt. Hope Estate and Winery.* A 16th-century village is created in the acres of gardens surrounding the mansion. Eleven stages include a jousting arena with capacity of 6,000. Highlights include medieval jousting tournament, trial and dunking, human chess match, knighthood ceremonies. Weekends, Aug-mid-Oct.

Rose Festival. Celebration during which Stiegel descendant accepts annual rent of one red rose for church grounds. Second Sun in June.

Mansfield (B-9)

See also Wellsboro

Pop 3,411 **Elev** 1,120 ft **Area code** 570 **Zip** 16933

Information Wellsboro Area Chamber of Commerce, 114 Main St, PO Box 733, Wellsboro 16901; 570/724-1926

Web www.wellsboropa.com

What to See and Do

Cowanesque Lake. *15 miles N on US 15 to Lawrenceville, then 3 1/2 miles W on Bliss Rd. Phone 570/835-5281.* Same facilities as Tioga-Hammond Lakes (see). (May-Sept)

Hills Creek State Park. *Hills Creek Lake. 6 miles W, then N on unnumbered road. Phone 570/724-4246.* Approximately 400 acres. Swimming beach; fishing for muskellunge, largemouth bass, walleye in Hills Creek Lake; boating (rentals, mooring, launching); hiking, sledding, ice skating, ice fishing, picnicking, playground, snack bar, tent and trailer sites, cabins. Interpretive program. Standard fees.

Tioga-Hammond Lakes. *10 miles N on US 15, then 7 miles SW on PA 287. Phone 570/835-5281.* Twin lakes and dams for flood control and recreation. Swimming, fishing, boating; hunting, trails, picnicking, camping (fee; some sites free). (Late Apr-Dec)

Motel/Motor Lodge

★ **COMFORT INN.** *300 Gateway Dr (16933). Phone 570/662-3000; toll-free 800/822-5470; fax 570/662-2551. www.comfortinn.com.* 100 rooms, 2 story. S $49-$75; D $59-$85; each additional $6; under 18 free; golf plans; higher rates seasonal events. Crib available. Pet accepted. TV; cable. Complimentary continental breakfast. Checkout noon. Business services available. Exercise equipment. Cr cds: A, C, D, DS, ER, JCB, MC, V.

⬛ ⬛ ⬛ ⬛ ⬛

Meadville (C-2)

See also Conneaut Lake, Franklin (Venango County)

Settled 1788 **Pop** 13,685 **Elev** 1,100 ft **Area code** 814 **Zip** 16335

Information Crawford County Convention & Visitors Bureau, 211 Chestnut St; 814/333-1258 or 800/332-2338

Web www.visitcrawford.org

David Mead—Revolutionary War ensign, tavernkeeper, and major general in the War of 1812—and his brothers established Mead's Settlement in 1788. Colonel Lewis Walker started manufacture of hookless slide fasteners here; since 1923 these fasteners (now known as "zippers") have been the leading local industry. The city is also a major producer of yarn and thread and is home to many tool-and-die manufacturers.

What to See and Do

Allegheny College. *485 Chestnut St. Phone 814/332-3100.* (1815) 1,850 students. Bentley Hall (1820) is a fine example of Federalist architecture. Also on campus are Bowman, Penelec, and Megahan Art Galleries. Library has colonial, Ida Tarbell, and Lincoln collections. Tours of campus.

Baldwin-Reynolds House Museum. *639 Terrace St. Phone 814/724-6080.* (1841-1843) Restored mansion of Henry Baldwin, congressman and US Supreme Court justice. First and second floors refurbished in period; basement exhibits 19th-century kitchen and Land Office. Also on grounds is 1890 doctor's office. Elaborate landscaping on 3-acre grounds feature pond and icehouse. Tours (Late May-Labor Day, Wed-Sun). **$$**

Colonel Crawford Park. *6 miles NE via PA 86, PA 198. Phone 814/724-6879 (summer) or 814/333-7372 (Memorial Day-Labor Day).* Within park is Woodcock Creek Lake. Swimming (fee), fishing, boating; hunting, nature trail, picnicking, camping (fee). Park (Memorial Day-Labor Day, daily). **FREE**

Erie National Wildlife Refuge. *10 miles E on PA 27. Phone 814/789-3585.* Over 250 species of birds, as well as woodchuck, white-tailed deer, fox, beaver, and muskrat are found on this 8,777-acre refuge. Fishing and hunting permitted, regulations at refuge office; nature and ski trails, overlook, photo blind. (Daily). **FREE**

Special Event

Crawford County Fair. *Phone 814/337-2154.* Third week in Aug.

Motel/Motor Lodge

★ **DAYS INN.** *18360 Conneaut Lake Rd (16335). Phone 814/337-4264; toll-free 800/329-7466; fax 814/337-7304. www.daysinn.com.* 163 rooms, 2 story. S $65-$85; D $70-$86; each additional $6; under 18 free; higher rates special events. Crib free. Pet accepted. TV; cable (premium), VCR available (movies). Indoor pool; whirlpool. Restaurant 7 am-2 pm, 5-10 pm; Sun 7 am-2 pm. Bar 3 pm-2 am. Check-out 11 am. Coin laundry. Meeting rooms. Business services available. Cr cds: A, C, D, DS, JCB, MC, V.

Media (H-13)

See also Chester, Kennett Square, King of Prussia, Philadelphia, West Chester

Pop 5,533 **Area code** 484 & 610

Information Delaware County Convention & Visitors Bureau, 200 E State St, Suite 100, 19063; 610/565-3679 or 800/343-3983

What to See and Do

Franklin Mint Museum. *4 miles SW on US 1. Phone 610/459-6168.* Houses original works by Andrew Wyeth and Norman Rockwell; collectibles on display include books, dolls, jewelry, furniture; artworks in porcelain, bronze, pewter, crystal, and precious metals; one of the world's largest private mints. (Daily; closed holidays) **FREE**

Newlin Mill Park. *7 miles SW via US 1, in Glen Mills. Phone 610/459-2359.* Park with operating stone gristmill (1704), furnished miller's house (1739), springhouse, blacksmith shop; milling exhibit. Tours, picnicking, fishing, nature trails. (Daily) **$**

Ridley Creek State Park. *S on US 1, then N on PA 352. Phone 610/892-3900.* Approximately 2,600 acres of woodlands and meadows. Fishing; hiking, bicycling, sledding, picnicking, playground. Within park is

Colonial Pennsylvania Plantation. *Phone 610/566-1725.* A 200-year-old farm is a living history museum that re-creates the life of a typical farm family of the late 1700s. Period tools and methods are used to perform seasonal and daily chores. Tours (Tues-Fri, by appointment). Visitors may participate in some activities. (Mid-Apr-Nov, Sat and Sun) **$$**

Tyler Arboretum. *515 Painter Rd (19063). Phone 610/566-5431.* Approximately 650 acres of ornamental and native plants. Outdoor "living museum" with a 20-mile system of trails; special fragrant garden and bird garden; notable trees planted in the 1800s; bookstore. Guided walks and educational programs each week. **$$**

Restaurant

★ ★ **D'IGNAZIO'S TOWNE HOUSE.** *117 Veterans Sq (19063). Phone 610/566-6141; fax 610/566-3840. www.townehouse.com.* Italian, seafood menu. Hours: 11:30 am-3 pm, 4:30-10 pm; Fri, Sat to 10:30 pm; Sun 4-8:30 pm. Bar to midnight; Fri, Sat to 1 am; Sun 4-9 pm. Closed Dec 25. A la carte entrées: lunch $6-$12, dinner $10-$20. Bar to midnight; Fri, Sat to 1 am; Sun 4-9 pm. Children's menu. Reservations accepted. Singing maitre'd. Cr cds: A, C, D, DS, MC, V.

[D]

Mercer (D-2)

See also Franklin(Venango County)

Settled 1795 **Pop** 2,391 **Elev** 1,270 ft **Area code** 724 **Zip** 16137

Information Mercer Area Chamber of Commerce, PO Box 473; 724/662-4185

What to See and Do

Magoffin House Museum. *119 S Pitt St. Phone 724/662-3490.* (1821) Houses collection of Native American artifacts, pioneer tools, furniture, children's toys, clothing; military items. Some original furnishings; memorabilia. Special collection of artifacts from John Goodsell's trip to the North Pole with Peary in 1908-1909, as well as early maps, historic records; restored print shop. Office of Mercer County Historical Society is located in the Anderson House, just off Court House Square. (Tues-Sat; closed holidays) **FREE**

Wendell August Forge, Inc. *10 miles SE on PA 58, in Grove City at 620 Madison Ave. Phone 724/458-8360.* Creators of hand-hammered aluminum, bronze, copper, pewter, sterling silver, and glass and crystal items hand-cut on stone wheel lathe; also limited-edition collectors' items. Gift shop. Self-guided tours (15-30 minutes). (Daily; closed holidays) **FREE**

Special Event

Penn's Woods West-Folk & Arts Festival. *545 W Butler St. Mercer Area High School. Phone 412/662-1490.* Fine arts and country crafts. 130 artisans, live entertainment and demonstrations, children's activities, home-cooked food. Mid Feb.

Motel/Motor Lodge

★ ★ **HOWARD JOHNSON.** *835 Perry Hwy (16137). Phone 724/748-3030; toll-free 800/542-7674; fax 724/748-3484. www.hojo.com.* 102 rooms, 2 story. S $67; D $71-$74; each additional $6; suites $105-$125; under 18 free; higher rates special events. Pet accepted. Check-out noon. TV; cable (premium), VCR available. In-room modem link. Restaurant 6 am-midnight. Bar. Room service. Exercise equipment, sauna. Amish craft shop in lobby. Cr cds: A, C, D, DS, MC, V.

⊡ 🐾 ⇌ 🏋 🖼

Restaurant

★ ★ **CHADAGAN'S.** *8399 Sharon Mercer Rd (16137). Phone 724/662-4533; fax 724/662-2855. www.chadagans .com.* Hours: 3-10 pm; Fri, Sat 11:30 am-11 pm; Sun 11 am-8 pm. Closed Mon; major holidays. Bar. Complete meals: dinner $6.95-$13.95. Children's menu. Specializes in seafood, prime rib. Rustic atmosphere; in converted barn (1872). Cr cds: A, DS, MC, V.

⊡ 🆂🅲

Milford (D-14)

See also Bushkill, Delaware Water Gap

Settled 1733 **Pop** 1,104 **Elev** 503 ft **Area code** 570 **Zip** 18337

Information Pocono Mountains Vacation Bureau, 1004 Main St, Stroudsburg 18360; 570/424-6050; for free brochures phone 800/POCONOS

Web www.poconos.org

The borough of Milford was settled by Thomas Quick, a Hollander. Noted forester and conservationist Governor Gifford Pinchot lived here. His house, Grey Towers, is near the town.

What to See and Do

Canoeing, rafting, kayaking, and tubing. *S to Dingmans Ferry via US 209, then 1/2 mile E via PA 739 S, at Dingmans Ferry toll bridge. Phone 570/828-2338 or 800/FLOAT-KC.* Kittatinny Canoes. Trips travel down the Delaware River. Camping. (Mid-Apr-Oct, daily)

Dingmans Falls and Silver Thread Falls. *8 miles S and W on US 209 near Dingmans Ferry. Phone 570/588-2451.* Part of Delaware Water Gap National Recreation Area (see). Two of the highest waterfalls in the Pocono Mountains; many rhododendrons bloom in July. **FREE**

Grey Towers. *151 Grey Tower Dr (18337). Phone 570/296-6401.* (1886) A 100-acre estate originally built as summer house for philanthropist James W. Pinchot; became residence of his son, Gifford Pinchot, "father of American conservation," governor of Pennsylvania and first chief of USDA Forest Service. Now site of Pinchot Institute for Conservation Studies. Tours. (Memorial Day weekend-Labor Day weekend, daily; after Labor Day-Veterans Day, afternoons Mon and Fri-Sun; rest of year, by appointment; occasionally closed for conferences. **DONATION**

Motels/Motor Lodges

★ ★ **BEST WESTERN INN AT HUNT'S LANDING.** *120 Rte 6 (18336). Phone 570/491-2400; toll-free 800/308-2378; fax 570/491-2422. www.bestwestern.com.* 108 rooms, 4 story. May-Oct: S $69-$75; D $77-$85; each additional $6; suites $115-$125; under 12 free; lower rates rest of year. Crib free. Pet accepted. TV; cable. Indoor pool; lifeguard. Sauna. Restaurant 6:30 am-9 pm; Fri, Sat to 10 pm; Sun from 7 am. Bar 4-11 pm; entertainment. Check-out 11 am. Coin laundry. Meeting rooms. Business services available. In-room modem link. Sundries. Gift shop. Game room. Lawn games. Cr cds: A, C, D, DS, MC, V.

⟦D⟧ ⟦⟧ ⟦⟧ ⟦⟧ ⟦⟧ ⟦SC⟧

★ **MYER MOTEL.** *600 Rtes 6 and 209 (18337).* Phone *570/296-7223; toll-free 800/764-6937. www.myermotel.com.* 19 cottages, 1 kitchen unit. S $40-$50; D $45-$70; each additional $5; kitchen unit $90. Pet accepted, some restrictions. Check-out 11 am. TV; cable. Restaurant nearby. Lawn games. Cr cds: A, C, D, DS, MC, V.

⟦⟧ ⟦⟧ ⟦⟧ ⟦SC⟧

B&B/Small Inns

★ **BLACK WALNUT BED & BREAKFAST COUNTRY INN.** *179 Fire Tower Rd (18337).* Phone *570/296-6322; fax 570/296-7696. www.theblackwalnutinn.com.* 12 rooms, 2 story. No A/C. Check-out 11 am, check-in 2 pm. TV in sitting room; movies. Tudor-style stone house; marble fireplace. Dining room 8:30-10 am; 5:30-9 pm; closed Mon-Thurs. 160-acre estate on the bank of a 5-acre stocked pond; paddleboats, rowboats. Cr cds: A, MC, V. **$**

⟦⟧ ⟦⟧

★ ★ ★ **CLIFF PARK INN.** *155 Cliff Park Rd (18337).* Phone *570/296-6491; toll-free 800/225-6535; fax 570/296-3982. www.cliffparkinn.com.* This is an inn and golf course located on 500 acres overlooking the Delaware River. The inn offers rooms in the main building and guest cottages. Nearby activities include cross-country skiing, hiking trails, swimming, and more. 18 rooms, 1-3 story. In-room modem link. Some fireplaces. Dining room 8-10 am, noon-3 pm, 6-9 pm. Greens fee $15-$26. Cross-country ski. Hiking trails. Classic country inn; originally a farmhouse built 1820. Near Delaware River. Screened porches. Cr cds: A, C, D, DS, MC, V. **$**

⟦⟧ ⟦⟧ ⟦⟧ ⟦SC⟧

★ ★ **PINE HILL FARM BED AND BREAKFAST.** *181 Pine Hill Farm Rd (18337).* Phone *570/296-5261. www.pinehillfarm.com.* 6 rooms, 2 story. No room phones. Children over 12 years old only. Complimentary full breakfast. Check-out 11 am, check-in 3 pm. TV in some rooms and sitting room. Fireplaces. Cross-country ski on site. Located atop hill overlooking the Delaware River. Includes 268 acres of fields and forests, with 5 miles of 1800s logging trails for walking, birdwatching. Cr cds: DS, MC, V. **$$**

⟦⟧ ⟦⟧

Mount Pocono

See also Pocono Mountains

Pop 2,742 **Elev** 1,840 ft **Area code** 570 **Zip** 18344

Information Pocono Mountains Vacation Bureau, Inc, 1004 Main St, Stroudsburg 18360; 570/424-6050; for brochures phone 800/POCONOS

Web www.poconos.org

One of the many thriving resort communities in the heart of the Pocono Mountains, Mount Pocono offers recreation year-round in nearby parks, lakes, and ski areas.

What to See and Do

Gouldsboro State Park. *10 miles N on PA 611 and I-380, then NE on PA 507.* Phone 570/894-8336. Approximately 2,800 acres; 250-acre lake. Swimming beach, fishing, boating (rentals, mooring, launching); hunting, hiking, ice skating, ice fishing.

Memorytown, USA. *Grange Rd. 2 miles E via PA 940.* Phone 570/839-1680. Old-time village includes hex shop, country store, store with artifacts; ice-cream parlor; paddle-boats; entertainment; lodging, restaurant, and tavern. Summer festivals. Fee for some activities. (Daily) **FREE**

Mount Airy Lodge Ski Area. *42 Wood Land (18344). Just E of town via PA 940 to PA 611.* Phone 800/441-4410. Two double chairlifts; patrol, school, rentals, snowmaking; cafeteria, restaurant, bar, nursery, lodge. Longest run 1,800 feet; vertical drop 250 feet. Also country trails. (Mid-Dec-late Mar) **$$$$**

Pocono Knob. *1 1/2 miles E on Knob Rd.* Excellent view of surrounding countryside.

Tobyhanna State Park. *5 miles N on PA 611, then NE on PA 423.* Phone 570/894-8336. Approximately 5,440 acres with 170-acre lake. Swimming beach; fishing, hunting; boating (rentals, mooring, launching). Hiking, biking; country skiing. Snowmobiling, ice skating, ice fishing. Tent and trailer sites. Standard fees.

Motels/Motor Lodges

★ ★ **MEMORYTOWN.** *HC 1, Box 10 (18344).* Phone 570/839-1680; fax 570/839-5846. 30 rooms, all with shower only. No A/C. No room phones. May-Oct: S $109; D $118-$138; each additional $70; family rates; package plans; holidays 2-day minimum; higher rates special events; lower rates rest of year. Pet accepted. TV; cable. Complimentary continental breakfast; full breakfast weekends. Restaurant 11 am-8 pm. Check-out 11 am, check-in 3 pm. Gift shop. Downhill ski 10 miles; cross-country ski on site. Playground. Game room. Lawn games. Some fireplaces. Picnic tables. On lake. Built in 1890; antiques. Country store, farmhouse on premises. Cr cds: A, D, DS, MC, V.

★ **SUPER 8.** *Rte 611 (18344). Phone 570/839-7728; fax 570/839-7728. www.super8.com.* 37 rooms. May-Sept: S $58-$135; D $65-$135; each additional $5; lower rates rest of year. Crib free. Check-out 11 am. TV; cable. Private patios. Restaurant 6 am-10 pm. Playground. Pool, whirlpool. Downhill ski 5 miles. Picnic tables. Business services available. Sundries. Cr cds: A, D, DS, MC, V.

Resorts

★ ★ ★ **CAESARS PARADISE STREAM.** *Rte 940 (18344). Phone 570/839-8881; fax 570/839-1842. www. caesarsparadisestream.com.* 164 rooms. MAP: D $260-$335; weekly rates. Check-out 11, check-in 3 pm. TV; cable, VCR available (movies $5). Some fireplaces. Bar noon-2 am. Entertainment. Snack bar. Room service limited hours. Exercise equipment, sauna. Social director. Game room. 2 pools, 1 indoor, whirlpool, poolside service, lifeguard. Miniature golf. Tennis. Lawn games. Bicycles. Boats, paddleboats. Hiking trails. Snowmobiles available. Business services. Concierge. Sundries. Couples only. Archery. Cr cds: A, D, DS, MC, V.

★ ★ ★ **POCONO MANOR INN AND GOLF CLUB.** *Rte 314 (18349). Phone 570/839-7111; toll-free 800/233-8150; fax 570/839-0708. www.poconomanor.com.* 190 rooms in inn, 65 in 2 lodges. MAP: S $119; D $198; each additional $50; under 8 free; higher rates special events. Crib $7. Service charge. Check-out 11 am, check-in 4 pm. TV. In-room modem link. Dining room (public by reservation) 7:30-9 am, noon-1 pm, 6:30-8:30 pm. Bar 11-2 am; entertainment. Room service. Free supervised children's activities. Exercise equipment, sauna. Social director. Sports director. Recreation room. Indoor/outdoor pool, poolside service, lifeguard. 36-hole golf, pro, putting green, driving range. Tennis, pro. Bicycles. Artificial ice rink, sleigh rides. Business services. Trapshooting. Indoor, outdoor games. Extra fee for some activities. On 3,100-acre mountain estate. Cr cds: A, D, MC, V.

B&B/Small Inns

★ ★ ★ **FRENCH MANOR.** *Huckleberry Rd, South Sterling (18460). Phone 570/676-3244; toll-free 800/523-8200; fax 570/676-9786. www.thefrenchmanor.com.* 9 rooms, 3 story. No room phones. S, D $165-$180. Adults only. TV in sitting room. Indoor pool privileges. Dining

room (public by reservation; jacket required) 8:30-10 am, noon-2 pm, 6-9 pm. Room service. Check-out 11 am, check-in 2 pm. Airport, bus depot transportation. Cross-country ski on premises. French chateau-style; Spanish slate roof; patio; 38-foot high dining room with beamed ceilings; Great Hall has 2 floor-to-ceiling fireplaces. Antiques. Cr cds: A, DS, MC, V.

★ ★ ★ **STERLING INN.** *Rte 191, South Sterling (18460). Phone 570/676-3311; toll-free 800/523-8200; fax 570/676-9786. www.thesterlinginn.com.* 54 suites, 3 story. MAP: S $75-$95, D $140-$160; suites, cottages $190-$220; family, weekly rates; ski, golf plans; lower rates mid-week. Check-out 11 am, check-in 4 pm. TV in some rooms; cable. Some fireplaces. Dining room. Indoor pool, whirlpool. Golf on premise. Tennis. Downhill ski 10 miles, cross-country ski on site; rentals. Lawn games, sleighing/sleigh rides. Airport, bus depot transportation. Built in 1850s; country and Victorian suites. Cr cds: A, DS, MC, V.

Restaurants

★ **TAVERN BY THE LAKE.** *HC 1, Box 10 (18344). Phone 570/839-1680. fax 570/839-5846.www.memorytown .net.* Hours: 11 am-8 pm; Fri to midnight; Sat to 2 am. A la carte entrées: lunch, $5.50-$16.95, dinner $6.99-$18.99. Bar. Reservations required Sat (dinner). Outdoor dining. Cr cds: A, D, DS, MC, V.

★ **TOKYO TEAHOUSE.** *RR 940 (18346). Phone 570/ 839-8880; fax 570/839-1888. www.poconobest.com.* Japanese menu. Specializes in sushi, steak takiki. Hours: 11:30 am-10 pm. Closed Tues in July, Aug. Lunch $4.95-$7, dinner $8.75-$28.95. Reservations accepted. Cr cds: A, MC, V.

New Castle (E-1)

See also Beaver Falls, Harmony

Settled 1798 **Pop** 26,309 **Elev** 860 ft **Area code** 724

Information Lawrence County Tourist Promotion Agency, Celli Central Station, 229 S Jefferson, 16101; 724/654-8408

Web www.lawrencecounty.com/tourism

At the junction of the Shenango, Mahoning, and Beaver rivers, this was long an important Native American trading center; the Delawares used it as their capital. Today the fireworks and plastics industries have become an integral part of the community.

What to See and Do

Greer House. *408 N Jefferson. Phone 724/658-4022.* Turn-of-the-century restored mansion houses the Lawrence County Historical Society. Museum has extensive Shenango and Castleton china collections, Sports Hall of Fame, fireworks room. Archives; workshops and speakers. (Tues-Sat; also by appointment) **DONATION**

Hoyt Institute of Fine Arts. *124 E Leasure Ave. Phone 724/652-2882.* Cultural arts center housed in two early 20th-century mansions on 4 acres of landscaped grounds; permanent art collection, changing exhibits, period rooms, performing arts programs, classes. Tours. (Tues-Sat; closed major holidays) **DONATION**

Living Treasures Animal Park. *On US 422. Phone 724/924-9571.* Pet and feed over 100 species from around the world. (Memorial Day-Labor Day, daily; May, Sept, Oct, weekends) **$$$**

McConnell's Mill State Park. *12 miles E via US 422. Phone 724/368-8091 or 724/368-8811.* Approximately 2,500 acres. Century-old mill surrounded by beautiful landscape and scenery. Fishing, hunting; whitewater boating. Hiking. Picnicking, store. Historical center, interpretive program. Standard fees.

Scottish Rite Cathedral. *614 Center Ave. Phone 724/654-6683.* On hillside; six 32-foot columns dominate city's skyline. Large auditorium; cathedral; ballroom. Local Masonic headquarters. Tours (by appointment). **$**

Motel/Motor Lodge

★ **COMFORT INN.** *1740 New Butler Rd (16101). Phone 724/658-7700; fax 724/658-7727. www.comfortinn.com.* 79 rooms, 13 suites, 2 story. S $66-$72; D $78-$88; each additional $6; suites $96-$124; under 18 free; weekly, weekend rates; higher rates: July 4, Dec 31. Crib free. Pet accepted, some restrictions; $6/day. Complimentary continental breakfast. Check-out noon. TV; cable. Some refrigerators. Valet services. Restaurant nearby. Exercise equipment, sauna. Meeting room. Business services. Cr cds: A, C, D, DS, ER, JCB, MC, V.

D ➤ ⌘ ✕ ⊠

New Hope (G-14)

See also Doylestown (Bucks County)

Founded 1681 **Pop** 2,252 **Elev** 76 ft **Area code** 215 and 267 **Zip** 18938

Information Information Center, 1 W Mechanic St, PO Box 633, phone; 215/862-5880 or Bucks County Conference and Visitors Bureau, Inc, 152 Swamp Rd, Doylestown 18901, phone 215/345-4552 or 800/836-2825

Web www.buckscountycvb.org

The river village of New Hope was originally the largest part of a 1,000-acre land grant from William Penn to Thomas Woolrich of Shalford, England. In the 20th century the area gained fame as the home of artists and literary and theatrical personalities.

What to See and Do

Bucks County River Country. *Phone 215/297-5000.* On the Delaware River; two- to four-hour canoeing, rafting, tubing and kayaking trips; one-day outings to full vacation trips. (May-Oct). **$$$$**

Coryell's Ferry. *22 S Main St. Phone 215/862-2050.* Passenger and charter rides aboard the *Major William C. Barnett,* a 65-foot Mississippi-style sternwheel riverboat, on the Delaware River. (Memorial Day-Labor Day, daily; call for extended season) **$$$**

Ghost Tours. *Main and Ferry sts. Phone 215/957-9988.* Follow a lantern-led walk to learn about the area's ghosts. (Oct, Fri and Sat evenings; June-Sept, Sat evening only) **$$$**

New Hope & Ivyland Railroad. *W Bridge St, adjacent to Delaware Canal. Phone 215/862-2332.* A 9-mile, 50-minute narrated train ride through Bucks County. Reading Railroad passenger coaches from the 1920s depart from restored 1890 New Hope Station. Gift shop. (Early Apr-Nov, daily; Dec, special Santa Train Fri-Sun; rest of year, weekends) **$$$**

Parry Barn. *S Main St, opposite mansion.* (1784). Owned by New Hope Historical Society; operated as commercial art gallery. **FREE**

Parry Mansion Museum. *S Main and Ferry sts. Phone 215/862-5652 or 215/862-5460.* (1784). Restored stone house built by Benjamin Parry, prosperous merchant and mill owner. Eleven rooms on view, restored and furnished to depict period styles from late 18th to early 20th centuries. (May-Dec, Fri-Sun; also by appointment) **$$**

Peddler's Village. *5 miles S on US 202 in Lahaska. Phone 215/794-4000.* This 18th-century-style country village with 42 acres of landscaped gardens and winding brick paths makes a great day trip from Philadelphia. Browse through a selection of more than 70 specialty shops for handicrafts, toys, accessories, leather goods, collectibles, and gourmet foods. Take the kids for a ride on an antique carousel, or take advantage of the many free family events and seasonal festivals. (Daily; closed Jan 1, Thanksgiving, Dec 25) Also in village is

> **Carousel World.** *Phone 215/794-8960.* Learn about history of the carousel in turn-of-the-century park. Antique carousel rides. Gift shop. (Daily) **$**

Washington Crossing Historical Park. *7 miles S on PA 32.* (see).

Special Events

New Hope Arts and Crafts Festival. *Phone 215/862-5880.* Contemporary and traditional crafts. Painting, photography, sculpture. Oct.

Scarecrow Festival. *Peddler's Village. Phone 215/794-4000.* Scarecrow making, pumpkin painting. Jack-o-lantern and gourd art contest. Square dancing, entertainment. Sept.

Teddy Bear's Picnic. *Peddler's Village. Phone 215/794-4000.* Teddy bear vendors, parades, competitions. "Bear clinic" for hurt bears. Appraisals. Music. July.

B&B/Small Inns

★ ★ ★ **1870 WEDGWOOD INN OF NEW HOPE.** *111 W Bridge St (18938). Phone 215/862-3936; fax 215/862-3937. www.1870wedgwoodinn.com.* 12 rooms, 2 story. Some room phones. D $95-$199; each additional $20; suites $150-$225. Pet accepted. Complimentary full breakfast. Check-out 11 am, check-in 3 pm. Some fireplaces. Health club privileges. Lawn games. Concierge service. Built 1870; antiques, large Wedgwood collection. Carriage rides. Totally nonsmoking. Cr cds: A, MC, V.

D 🐾 🛟 🖼 SC

★ ★ ★ **AARON BURR HOUSE.** *80 W Bridge St (18938). Phone 215/862-2343; fax 215/862-3937. www.new-hope-inn.com.* 5 rooms, 2 suites, 2 story. D $95-$199. Pet accepted. Complimentary full breakfast. Check-out 11 am, check-in 2 pm. TV in sitting room; VCR available. Fireplace in suites. Restaurant nearby. Health club privileges. Downhill ski 2 miles, cross-country ski adjacent. Lawn games. Concierge. Built in 1873. Swimming privileges. Totally nonsmoking. Cr cds: MC, V.

D 🐾 🛟 🖼 🖼 SC

★ ★ ★ **BARLEY SHEAF FARM BED & BREAKFAST.** *5281 York Rd, Holicong (18928). Phone 215/794-5104; fax 215/794-5332. www.barleysheaf.com.* 15 rooms, 3 story. Complimentary full breakfast. Check-out 11 am, check-in 2 pm. TV in sitting room; cable; VCR available. In-room modem link. Pool. Lawn games. Thirty-acre farmhouse; built in 1740. Room phones available. Totally nonsmoking. Cr cds: A, MC, V. **$$**

D 🛟 🖼 🖼

★ ★ **CENTRE BRIDGE INN.** *2998 N River Rd (18938). Phone 215/862-2048; fax 215/862-3244. www.centrebridgeinn.com.* 9 rooms, 2 story. No room phones. D $80-$150; each additional $15. Complimentary continental breakfast. Check-out noon, check-in 3 pm. TV; cable. Fireplace. Restaurant (see also CENTRE BRIDGE INN). Bar. Business services. Sitting room and terrace overlook river. Cr cds: A, MC, V.

🛟 🖼 SC

★ ★ ★ **FOX AND HOUND BED AND BREAKFAST.** *246 W Bridge St (18938). Phone 215/862-5082; toll-free 800/862-5082; fax 215/862-5082. www.foxhoundinn.com.* 8 rooms, 3 story. Some room phones. D $85-$170; weekend rates. Pet accepted. Children over 12 years only. Complimentary continental breakfast; full breakfast on weekends. Check-out 11 am, check-in 2 pm. TV available; cable. Health club privileges. Stone manor house built in 1850. Cr cds: A, MC, V.

🐾 🛟 🖼

★ ★ ★ **GOLDEN PHEASANT INN.** *763 River Rd (18920). Phone 610/294-9595; fax 610/294-9882. www.goldenpheasant.com.* 6 rooms, 2 story. No room phones. Pet accepted; fee. Complimentary continental breakfast. Check-out noon, check-in 3 pm. TV. Restaurant. Cr cds: A, C, D, DS, MC, V. **$$**

🐾 🛟 🖼

★ ★ ★ **GOLDEN PLOUGH INN.** *SR 202, Lahaska (18931). Phone 215/794-4004; fax 215/794-4008. www.peddlersvillage.com.* 72 rooms, 2-3 story. Complimentary continental breakfast. Check-out 11 am, check-in 3 pm. TV; cable. In-room modem link. Restaurant. Health club privileges. Cr cds: A, C, D, DS, MC, V. **$$**

D 🖼 SC

★ ★ ★ **HOLLILEIF BED & BREAKFAST.** *677 Durham Rd (SR 413) (18940). Phone 215/598-3100.* 5 rooms, 3 story. No room phones. D $85-$160; each additional $20. TV in some rooms; cable, VCR available (free movies). Complimentary full breakfast; afternoon refreshments. Check-out 11:30 am, check-in 3 pm. Business services available. Lawn games. 18th-century house; antiques, fireplace. Totally nonsmoking. Cr cds: A, DS, MC, V.

🖼

★ ★ **HOTEL DU VILLAGE.** *2535 N River Rd (18938). Phone 215/862-9911; fax 215/862-9788. www.hotelduvillage.com.* 20 rooms, 2 story. No room phones. Complimentary continental breakfast. Check-out 11 am, check-in after 2 pm. Dining room. Bar. Pool. Tennis. Small Tudor-style country inn on spacious grounds; former estate. Cr cds: A, D. **$**

D 🛟 🏃 🖼 🖼

★ **INN AT PHILLIPS MILL.** *2590 N River Rd (18938). Phone 215/862-2984; fax 215/862-0530.* 4 rooms, 1 suite, 3 story. Closed Jan. Check-out 1 pm, check-in 2 pm. Fireplaces. Dining room (see also INN AT PHILLIPS MILL). Room service. Pool. Built in 1750 as stone barn; antiques, fireplaces. Cr cds: A, MC, V. **$**

🖼 🖼

★ ★ ★ **INN TO THE WOODS.** *150 Glenwood Dr (18977). Phone 215/493-1974; toll-free 800/574-1974; fax 215/493-7592. www.inn-bucks.com.* 6 rooms, 3 story. Children over 12 years only. Complimentary full breakfast; afternoon refreshments. Check-out 11 am, check-in 3 pm. TV; cable, VCR available (movies). In-room modem link. Some fireplaces. Cross-country ski 1 mile. On 10 acres of forest with hiking trails. Concierge service. Totally nonsmoking. Cr cds: A, DS, MC, V. **$$**

★ **LOGAN INN.** *10 W Ferry St (18938). Phone 215/862-2300; fax 215/862-3931. www.loganinn.com.* 16 rooms, 3 story. S, D $75-$150; each additional $17; under 3 free; weekly, weekday rates; holidays (3-day minimum). Complimentary continental breakfast. Check-out 11 am, check-in 3-10 pm. TV; cable. Restaurant 11 am-11 pm. Downhill, cross-country ski 5 miles. On canal; built in 1722. One of the oldest inns in US. Cr cds: A, D, DS, MC, V.

★ ★ ★ **MANSION INN.** *9 S Main St (18938). Phone 215/862-1231; fax 215/862-0277. www.themansioninn.com.* 15 rooms, 5 suites, 3 story. No elevator. D $195-$245; suites $245-$300; minimum stay 2-3 days. Children over 16 years only. Complimentary full breakfast. Check-out 11 am, check-in 2 pm. TV; cable (premium). In-room modem link. Fireplaces. Restaurant nearby. Health club privileges. Pool. Cross-country ski 15 miles. Concierge service. Built (1865); Victorian décor. Totally nonsmoking. Cr cds: A, MC, V.

★ ★ ★ **PINEAPPLE HILL BED AND BREAKFAST.** *1324 River Rd (18938). Phone 215/862-1790; toll-free 888/866-8404. www.pineapplehill.com.* 8 rooms, 3 story. May-Dec: S $75-$135; D $85-$145; each additional $30; suites $115-$165; weekly rates; weekends (2-day minimum); package plans; lower rates rest of year. Complimentary full breakfast; afternoon refreshments. Check-out 11 am, check-in 3 pm. TV; VCR available. Health club privileges. Pool. Cross-country ski on site. Lawn games. Concierge service. Built in 1790. On river. Totally nonsmoking. Cr cds: A, DS, MC, V.

★ ★ ★ **TATTERSALL INN.** *16 Cafferty N River Rd, Point Pleasant (18950). Phone 215/297-8233; toll-free 800/297-4988; fax 215/297-5093. www.tattersallinn.com.* 6 rooms, 2 story. Complimentary full breakfast; afternoon refreshments. Check-out 11 am, check-in 3 pm. Some fireplaces. House (1740); porches, marble fireplace, antiques. Cr cds: A, DS, MC, V. **$**

★ ★ ★ **WHITEHALL INN.** *1370 Pineville Rd (18938). Phone 215/598-7945; toll-free 888/379-4483; fax 215/598-0378.* 5 rooms, 1 suite, 3 story. No room phones. Complimentary full breakfast. Check-out 11 am, check-in after 3 pm. Many fireplaces. Health club privileges. Pool. Downhill ski 7 miles, cross-country ski on-site. Lawn games. Concierge service. Built in 1794; set on 12 rolling acres. Totally nonsmoking. Cr cds: A, C, D, DS, MC, V. **$$**

Restaurants

★ ★ **CENTRE BRIDGE INN.** *2998 N River Rd (18938). Phone 215/862-2048; fax 215/862-3244. www.centrebridgeinn.com.* American menu with French influences. Closed Mon; Dec 25. Lunch, dinner, Sun brunch. Bar. Entertainment Sat. Valet parking Sat. Outdoor seating. Cr cds: MC, V. **$$$**

★ ★ **COCK N' BULL.** *US 202 and 263, Lahaska (18931). Phone 215/794-4000; fax 215/794-4001. www.peddlersvillage.com.* Steak menu. Salad bar. Hours: 11 am-3 pm, 5-9 pm; Fri to 10 pm; Sat 4-10 pm; Sun 4-8 pm; Sun brunch 9:30 am-2:30 pm. Closed Jan 1, Dec 25. Dinner $14.95-$35.95. Bar. Casual attire. Reservations required (dinner). Cr cds: A, C, D, DS, MC, V.

★ ★ **INN AT PHILLIPS MILL.** *2590 N River Rd (18938). Phone 215/862-9919; fax 215/862-0530.* French country menu. Hours: 5:30-9:30 pm; Fri, Sat to 10 pm. Closed Dec 25; also Jan 1. Dinner $15-$25. Entertainment Fri, Sun. Casual attire. Reservations required Sat. Outdoor dining in garden setting.

★ ★ ★ **ODETTE'S.** *S River Rd (18938). Phone 215/862-2432; fax 215/862-2142. www.odettes.com.* Hours: 11:30-2 am; Sun brunch 10:30 am-1:30 pm. Reservations accepted; required holidays. Continental menu. Bar. Wine list. A la carte entrées: lunch $7.50-$10, dinner $15-$24. Sun brunch $15.95. Children's menu. Specializes in veal chops, salmon. Pianist. Valet parking. Built in 1794 as bargeman's inn; overlooks Delaware River; memorabilia of Odette Myrtil Logan of *South Pacific* fame. Cr cds: A, D, DS, MC, V.

★ **SPOTTED HOG.** *US 202 and 263 (18931). Phone 215/794-4000; fax 215/794-4008. www.peddlersvillage.com.* Hours: 7 am-11 pm; Sun to 9 pm. Bar to midnight; Fri, Sat to 1 am; Sun to 10 pm. Closed Thanksgiving, Dec 25. Breakfast $2.95-$7.25, lunch $3.25-$18.95, dinner $3.25-$19.95. Children's menu. Cr cds: A, C, D, DS, MC, V.

New Stanton (G-3)

See also Connellsville, Greensburg

Pop 1,906 **Elev** 980 ft **Area code** 724 **Zip** 15672

Information Laurel Highlands Visitors Bureau, Town Hall, 120 E Main St, Ligonier 15658; 724/238-5661

Web www.laurelhighlands.org

What to See and Do

L. E. Smith Glass Co. *1900 Liberty St. Phone 724/547-3544 for tour schedule.* Reproductions of several styles of antique handcrafted glass. Tours. Children under six years not admitted on tour. (Mon-Fri; closed first two weeks July) **FREE**

Motels/Motor Lodges

★ ★ **DAYS INN.** *127 W Byers Ave (15672). Phone 724/925-3591; toll-free 800/329-7466; fax 724/925-9859. www.daysinn.com.* 135 rooms, 3 story. S $47-$55; D $49-$60; each additional $6; under 18 free. Check-out 11 am. TV; cable (premium). Laundry services. Restaurant 6-11 am, 4-10 pm; Sat, Sun from 7 am. Bar 4 pm-midnight; entertainment. Exercise equipment. Pool; lifeguard. Cr cds: A, DS, MC, V.

⊡ ⛱ 🏋 ⅁ SC

★ **HOWARD JOHNSON.** *112 W Byers Ave (15672). Phone 724/925-3511; toll-free 800/446-4656.* 87 rooms, 2 story. Mid-May-Sept: S $38-$79; D $45-$79; each additional $5; under 18 free; lower rates rest of year. Crib free. TV; cable (premium), VCR available (movies). Heated pool. Playground. Complimentary continental breakfast. Check-out noon. Business services available. In-room modem link. Valet service. Refrigerators, microwaves available. Cr cds: A, C, D, DS, MC, V.

⊡ ⛱ ⅁ SC

Norristown (H-13)

See also King of Prussia, Kulpsville, Philadelphia

Founded 1704 **Pop** 31,282 **Elev** 130 ft **Area code** 484 & 610

Information Valley Forge Convention and Visitors Bureau, 600 W Germantown Pike, Suite 130, Plymouth Meeting 19462; 610/834-1550

Web www.valleyforge.org

William Penn, Jr., owner of the 7,600-acre tract around Norristown, sold it to Isaac Norris and William Trent for 50 cents an acre in 1704. It became a crossroads for colo-

nial merchants and soldiers; Washington's army camped nearby. Dutch, German, Swedish, Welsh, and English immigrants left their mark on the city. Today Norristown, still a transportation hub, houses many industries and serves as a county government center.

What to See and Do

Elmwood Park Zoo. *1661 Harding Blvd. Phone 610/277-3825.* Features extensive North American waterfowl area; cougars, bobcats, bison, elk; outdoor aviary; birds of prey; children's zoo barn; museum with exhibit on animal senses. (Daily; closed Jan 1, Thanksgiving, Dec 25) **$$**

Peter Wentz Farmstead. *10 miles NW via US 202, W via PA 73 on Schultz Rd, in Worcester. Phone 610/584-5104.* Restored and furnished mid-18th-century country mansion, twice used by Washington during the Pennsylvania campaign. More than 70 acres with demonstration field and crops of the period. Slide presentation; reconstructed 1744 barn with farm animals. (Tues-Sun; closed holidays) **FREE**

Valley Forge National Historical Park. (see) *NW on US 422 to Trooper, then S.*

Hotel

★ ★ ★ **SHERATON BUCKS COUNTY HOTEL.** *400 Oxford Valley Rd (19047). Phone 215/547-4100. www.sheraton.com.* 187 rooms, 15 story. S, D $225-$275; under 17 free. Crib available. Check-out noon, check-in 3 pm. TV; cable (premium). In-room modem link. Minibars; many refrigerators in suites. Restaurant 6:30 am-10 pm. Bar to midnight. Exercise equipment. Indoor pool, whirlpool. Meeting rooms. Business center. Concierge. Cr cds: A, C, D, DS, MC, V.

⛱ 🏋 🏃

B&B/Small Inn

★ ★ ★ **WILLIAM PENN INN.** *US 202 and Sumneytown Pike, Gwynedd (19436). Phone 215/699-9272; fax 215/699-4808. www.williampenninn.com.* 4 rooms, 3 suites, 2 story. S, D $115-$150; suites $135-$180. TV; cable (premium). Complimentary continental breakfast. Restaurant (see also WILLIAM PENN INN). Room service. Check-out 11 am, check-in 1 pm. Business services available. In-room modem link. Luggage handling. Refrigerators, minibars. Continuous operation since 1714; antiques. Totally nonsmoking. Cr cds: A, C, D, DS, MC, V.

⊡ ⅁

Restaurants

★ ★ ★ **THE JEFFERSON HOUSE.** *2519 DeKalb Pike (19401). Phone 610/275-3407; fax 610/275-1275.*

www.thejeffersonink.com. American menu. Hours: 11:30 am-2:30 pm, 4:30-10 pm; Sun noon-8 pm; Sun brunch to 4 pm; early-bird dinner Mon-Sat 4-6 pm. Closed most major holidays. Lunch $5.50-$16.95, dinner $12.50-$32. Brunch. Bar to 2 am. Children's menu. Manor house set on extensive, landscaped grounds; former Buckland estate. Cr cds: A, D, MC, V.

D

★ ★ **WILLIAM PENN INN.** *US 202 and Sumneytown Pike, Gwynedd (19436). Phone 215/699-9272; fax 215/699-4808. www.williampenninn.com.* Continental menu. Specializes in seafood, roast rack of lamb, prime rib. Hours: 11:30 am-3 pm, 5-10 pm; Fri, Sat to 11 pm; Sun 2-8 pm; early-bird dinner Mon-Sat 5-6:30 pm; Sun brunch 10 am-2 pm. Closed Dec 25. Lunch $10-$15, dinner $18-$30. Sun brunch $18.95. Bar. Originally built as a tavern (1714); antiques. Reservations accepted. Cr cds: A, C, D, DS, MC, V.

D

North East (A-3)

See also Erie

Settled 1794 **Pop** 4,601 **Elev** 801 ft **Area code** 814 **Zip** 16428

Information Chamber of Commerce, 21 S Lake St; 814/725-4262

When Pennsylvania bought from the federal government the tract containing North East in 1778, the state gained 46 miles of Lake Erie frontage, a fine harbor, and some of the best Concord grape country in the nation.

What to See and Do

Winery tours.

    Heritage Wine Cellars. *12162 E Main Rd. Phone 814/725-8015.* Guided tours; wine tastings. (Daily; closed some holidays) **FREE**

    Mazza Vineyards. *11815 E Lake Rd. Phone 814/725-8695.* Guided tours; wine tastings. (Daily; closed some holidays) **FREE**

    Penn-Shore Vineyards and Winery. *10225 E Lake Rd. Phone 814/725-8688.* Guided tours; wine tastings. (Daily; closed some holidays) **FREE**

Special Events

Cherry Festival. Concessions, rides, games, parade. Mid-July.

Wine Country Harvest Festival. *21 S Lake St. Phone 814/725-4262. Gravel Pit Park and Gibson Park.* Arts and crafts, bands, buses to wineries, food. Last full weekend in Sept.

Oil City (C-3)

See also Franklin (Venargo County), Titusville

Pop 11,504 **Elev** 1,000 ft **Area code** 814 **Zip** 16301

Spreading on both sides of Oil Creek and the Allegheny River, Oil City was born of the oil boom. Oil refining and the manufacture of oil machinery are its major occupations today. Nearby are natural gas fields. Seven miles northwest stood the famous oil-boom town of Pithole. In 1865, it expanded from a single farmhouse to a population of more than 10,000 in five months as its first oil well brought in 250 barrels a day.

Motel/Motor Lodge

★ ★ **HOLIDAY INN.** *1 Seneca St (16301). Phone 814/677-1221; fax 814/677-0492. www.holiday-inn.com.* 106 rooms, 5 story. S, D $65; each additional $5; suites $75-$99; family rates. Crib free. Pet accepted. Check-out noon. TV; cable. In-room modem link. Coffee in rooms. Valet services. Restaurant 6:30 am-2 pm, 5-9 pm. Bar 5 pm-2 am, Sun from 1 pm. Room service. Health club privileges. Heated pool. Cross-country ski 2 miles. Meeting rooms. Business services. Cr cds: A, D, DS, MC, V.

D ◓ ⊠ ⊠

Orbisonia

See also Chambersburg, Huntingdon

Pop 425 **Elev** 640 ft **Area code** 814 **Zip** 17243

What to See and Do

East Broad Top Railroad. *On US 522. Phone 814/447-3011.* The oldest surviving narrow-gauge railroad east of the Rockies. Train ride (70 minutes); fascinating old equipment, opposite is buildings. Picnic area. (June-Oct, weekends only) **$$$**

    Rockhill Trolley Museum. *1/2 mile W off US 522, on PA 994, in Rockhill Furnace. Phone 814/447-9576.* Old-time trolleys; car barn and restoration shop tours. A 2-mile ride on Shade Gap Electric Railway. Gift shop. (Memorial Day-Oct, weekends) **$$**

Pennsylvania Dutch Area

See also Allentown, Bird-in-Hand, Ephrata, Kutztown, Lancaster, Lebanon, Manheim, Reading

From the Rhineland and Palatinate of Germany came great migrations of settlers to Pennsylvania in the 18th century, first near Philadelphia and then moving West. Because they retained their customs and speech and developed beautiful and bountiful farms, the Pennsylvania Dutch (corruption of the German *Deutsch*) country is one of the state's greatest tourist attractions. There are all degrees of conservatism among these descendants of German immigrants, ranging from the Amish to the Brethren, but all share tremendous vigor, family devotion, love of the Bible, and belief in thrift and hard work.

Many of the "plain people"—the Amish, Old Order Mennonites, and Bretren (Dunkards)—live today much as they did a century ago. Married men wear beards, black coats, and low-crowned black hats; women wear bonnets and long, simple dresses. They drive horses and buggies instead of cars, work long hours in the fields, shun the use of modern farm machinery, and turn to the Bible for guidance. Despire their refusal to use machinery they are master farmers. (They were among the first to rotate crops and practice modern fertilization methods.) Their harvests are consistently among the best in the country.

Many of the Amish regard photographs as "graven images"; visitors should not take pictures of individuals without their permission.

Philadelphia (H-13)

Founded 1682 **Pop** 1,517,550 **Elev** 45 ft **Area code** 215 & 267

Information Convention & Visitors Bureau, 1515 Market St, 19102; 215/636-3300

Web www.pcvb.org

Suburbs Bristol, Chester, Fort Washington, Jenkintown, Kennett Square, King of Prussia, Media, Norristown, West Chester, Willow Grove; also Wilmington, DE and Camden, NJ.

The nation's first capital has experienced a rebirth in the past few decades. Philadelphia has successfully blended its historic past with an electricity of modern times, all the while keeping an eye on the future. In the mid-18th century, it was the second-largest city in the English-speaking world. Today, Philadelphia is the second-largest city on the East Coast and the fifth largest in the country. Here, in William Penn's City of Brotherly Love, the Declaration of Independence was written and adopted, the Constitution was molded and signed, the Liberty Bell was rung, Betsy Ross was said to have sewn her flag, and Washington served most of his years as president.

This is the city of "firsts," including the first American hospital, medical college, women's medical college, bank, paper mill, steamboat, zoo, sugar refinery, daily newspaper, US mint, and public school for black children (1750).

The first Quakers, who came here in 1681, lived in caves dug into the banks of the Delaware River. During the first year 80 houses were raised; by the following year William Penn's "greene countrie towne" was a city of 600 buildings. The Quakers prospered in trade and commerce, and Philadelphia became the leading port in the colonies. Its leading citizen for many years was Benjamin Franklin —statesman, scientist, diplomat, writer, inventor, and publisher.

The fires of colonial indignation burned hot and early in Philadelphia. Soon after the Boston Tea Party, a protest rally of 8,000 Philadelphians frightened off a British tea ship. In May 1774, when Paul Revere rode from Boston to Philadelphia to report Boston's harbor had been closed, all of Philadelphia went into mourning. The first and second Continental Congresses convened here, and Philadelphia became the headquarters of the Revolution. After the Declaration of Independence was composed and accepted by Congress the city gave its men, factories, and shipyards to the cause. But British General Howe and 18,000 soldiers poured in on September 26, 1777, to spend a comfortable and social winter here while Washington's troops endured the bitter winter at Valley Forge. When the British evacuated the city, Congress returned. Philadelphia continued as the seat of government until 1800, except for a short period when New York City held the honor. The Constitution of the United States was written here, and President George Washington graced the city's halls and streets.

Since those historic days, Philadelphia has figured importantly in the politics, economy, and culture of the country. Here, national conventions have nominated presidents. During four wars the city has served as an arsenal and a shipyard. More than 1,400 churches and synagogues grace the city. There are over 25 colleges, universities, and professional schools in Philadelphia as well. Fine restaurants are in abundance, along with exciting nightlife to top off an evening. Entertainment is offered by the world-renowned Philadelphia Orchestra, theaters, college and professional sports, outstanding parks, recreation centers, and playgrounds. Shoppers may browse major department stores, hundreds of specialty shops, and antique shopping areas.

For 10 blocks between the Delaware River and 9th Street lies a history-rich part of Philadelphia. Here are the shrines of American liberty: Independence Hall, the Liberty Bell Pavilion, and many other historical sites in and around Independence National Historical Park.

Additional Visitor Information

There is also a visitor center at 3rd & Chestnut sts, operated by the National Park Service. (Daily) Phone 215/597-8975 or 215/597-8974 for information on park attractions.

The Visitors Center of the Philadelphia Convention and Visitors Bureau, 16th St & John F. Kennedy Blvd, 19102, has tourist information and maps (daily; closed Thanksgiving, Dec 25). Phone 215/636-1666 or 800/537-7676.

Transportation

Car Rental Agencies. See IMPORTANT TOLL-FREE NUMBERS.

Public Transportation. Subway and elevated trains, commuter trains, buses, trolleys (SEPTA), phone 215/580-7800.

Rail Passenger Service. Amtrak 800/872-7245.

Airport Information

Philadelphia International Airport. Information 215/937-6800 or 800/PHL-GATE; lost and found 215/937-6888; weather 215/936-1212.

What to See and Do

Academy of Music. *Broad and Locust sts. Phone 215/893-1935. (1857).* City's opera house, concert hall; home of Philadelphia Orchestra, Philly Pops, Opera Company of Philadelphia and Pennsylvania Ballet.

Academy of Natural Sciences Museum. *1900 Benjamin Franklin Pkwy. Phone 215/299-1000. (1812).* Dinosaurs, Egyptian mummies, animal displays in natural habitats, live animal programs, hands-on children's museum. (Daily; closed Jan 1, Thanksgiving, Dec 25) **$$$**

African-American Museum Philadelphia. *701 Arch St. Phone 215/574-0380.* Built to house and interpret African-American culture. Changing exhibits; public events include lectures, workshops, films and concerts. (Tues-Sun; closed Jan 1, Thanksgiving, Dec 25) **$$$**

American Swedish Historical Museum. *1900 Pattison Ave. Phone 215/389-1776.* From tapestries to technology, the museum celebrates Swedish influence on American life. Special exhibits on the New Sweden Colony. Research library, collections. (Tues-Sun; closed holidays) **$$**

Arch Street Meetinghouse. *320 Arch St. Phone 215/627-2667. (1804).* Perhaps the largest Friends meetinghouse in the world. Exhibits, slide show, tours. (Daily except Sun; closed Jan 1, Thanksgiving, Dec 25) **DONATION**

Atwater Kent Museum. *15 S 7th St. Phone 215/685-4830.* Artifacts depicting Philadelphia's history; 321 *Saturday Evening Post* covers produced by artist and illustrator Norman Rockwell between 1916 and 1975. (Mon, Wed-Sun)

Balch Institute for Ethnic Studies. A multicultural library, archive, museum, and education center that promotes intergroup understanding using education; 300 years of US immigration are documented here. Features "Peopling of Pennsylvania," as well as changing exhibits. (Mon-Sat; closed holidays) **$$**

Betsy Ross House. *239 Arch St. Phone 215/686-1252.* Where the famous seamstress is said to have made the first American flag. Upholsterer's shop, memorabilia. Flag Day ceremonies, June 14. (Apr-Oct, daily; Tues-Sun rest of year; closed Jan 1, Thanksgiving, Dec 25) **DONATION**

Blue Cross River Rink. *Columbus Blvd at Spring Garden St. Phone 215/925-RINK.* Few outdoor ice skating rinks are as well located as this one along the Delaware River. Visitors have a great vantage point from which to view the Benjamin Franklin Bridge and the Philadelphia skyline. This Olympic-size rink, at 200 feet x 85 feet, can accommodate 500 skaters. After a hearty skate, warm yourself in the heated pavilion, which features a video game area and concessions. (Daily, Nov-mid Mar) **$$**

Burial Ground of Congregation Mikveh Israel. *Spruce and 8th sts. (1738).* Graves of Haym Salomon, Revolutionary War financier, and Rebecca Gratz, probable model for "Rebecca" of Sir Walter Scott's Ivanhoe.

Centipede Tours. *1315 Walnut St. Phone 215/735-3123.* Candlelight strolls (1 1/2 hours) through historic Philadelphia and Society Hill areas led by guides in 18th-century dress; begins and ends at City Tavern. (Mid-May-mid-Oct, Fri-Sat) Reservations preferred. **$$**

Christ Church. *2nd and Market sts. Phone 215/922-1695.* (Episcopal). Patriots, Loyalists, and heroes have worshiped here since 1695. Sit in pews once occupied by Washington, Franklin, and Betsy Ross. (Mar-Dec, daily; rest of year, Wed-Sun; closed Jan 1, Thanksgiving, Dec 25) **FREE**

Christ Church Burial Ground. *5th and Arch sts. Phone 215/922-1695.* Resting place of Benjamin Franklin, his wife, Deborah, and six other signers of the Declaration of Independence. (Call for hours)

City Hall. *Broad and Market sts. Phone 215/686-2840.* A granite statue of William Penn stands 510 feet high above the heart of the city on top of this municipal building, which is larger than the Capitol. It is known as Penn Square, and was designated by Penn as the location for a building of "publick concerns." It also functions as Philadelphia's City Hall. It is one of the finest examples of French Second-Empire architectural style and a sculptural achievement. Constructing this building with the tallest statue (37,000 feet) in the world on its top took 30 years. Penn's famous hat is more than 7 feet in diameter, and the brim creates a 2-foot-wide track. There are more than 250 sculptures around this marble, granite, and limestone structure, 20 elevators, and a four-faced, 50-ton clock. Tower tours take place every 15 minutes between 9:30 am-4:30 pm. (Mon-Fri; closed holidays)

Civil War Library and Museum. *1805 Pine St. Phone 215/735-8196.* Four-story brick 19th-century town house filled with 18,000 books and periodicals dealing with events leading up to the American Civil War, the war itself, and early Reconstruction. Unique collection of arms, uniforms, flags of the period, memorabilia and artifacts begun in 1888 by former officers of the Union Army. Exhibits on Lincoln, Grant, and Meade; also the Navy Room and the Armory. (Thurs-Fri; closed holidays) **$$**

Edgar Allan Poe National Historic Site. *532 N 7th St.* Where Poe lived before his move to New York in 1844. The site is the nation's memorial to the literary genius of Edgar Allan Poe. Exhibits, slide show, tours, and special programs. (June-Oct, daily; rest of year, Wed-Sun; closed Jan 1, Dec 25)

Electric Factory. *421 N 7th St (19123). Phone 215/569-9400.* This all-ages live music venue offers accessibility to lesser-known bands, although Tori Amos, Garbage, Brian Setzer, and other well-known artists have played here. Because it can accommodate 3,000 people, it can feel crowded; there is no seating on the main level. But early arrivers can position themselves at bar tables in the upstairs balcony overlooking the stage. (Daily)

Elfreth's Alley. *126 Elfreth's Alley (19106). Phone 215/574-0560.* Philadelphians still live in these Georgian and Federal-style homes along cobblestoned Elfreth's Alley, the nation's oldest continued-use residential street. A few homes have been converted into museums, offering guided tours, a quaint gift shop, and handcrafted memorabilia. Culture and architecture appreciators will pick up all sorts of historical facts through photos and the collections. (Mar-Oct, Mon-Sat, Sun afternoons; Nov-Feb, Thurs-Sat, Sun afternoons) **$**

⭐ **Fairmount Park.** *4231 N Concourse Dr (19131). Begins at Philadelphia Museum of Art, extends NW on both sides of Wissahickon Creek and Schuylkill River. Phone 215/685-0000.* At 8,900 acres, Fairmount Park is the largest city park in America. The park can please the very active and the moderately active, as well as the artistically and historically inclined. It is home to 100 miles of beautifully landscaped paths for walking and horseback riding. Cyclists love to bike along the Pennypack and Wissa-

hickon trails. Walkers stroll or power-hike in Valley Green alongside the ducks. Inline skaters and rowing and sculling enthusiasts at Boathouse Row enjoy the sights along the Schuykill River on Kelly Drive. Within the park are the Philadelphia Zoo (see also PHILADELPHIA ZOO), the Shofuso Japanese House, the Philadelphia Museum of Art (see also PHILADELPHIA MUSEUM OF ART), the outdoor festival center Robin Hood Dell, and the Philadelphia Orchestra's summer amphitheater (Mann Music Center) (see also PHILADELPHIA ORCHESTRA), as well as 127 tennis courts and numerous picnic spots. The park contains America's largest collection of authentic colonial homes, features majestic outdoor sculptures, and includes Memorial Hall, the only building remaining from the 1876 Centennial Exhibition. (Daily) In park are

Boathouse Row Rowing Regattas. *On E bank of river. Phone 215/978-6919 for rowing, regatta schedules.* The Schuylkill River along Kelly Drive beckons competitive rowers. Powerboats are not allowed on this scenic 28-mile river. With Fairmount Park surrounding the 14 historic boathouses where the boats are kept and the Art Museum as a backdrop, it is among the most picturesque rowing courses in the world. Several well-attended events take place here from spring into fall, including the Stotesbury Cup Regatta, the Dad Vail Regatta, the Head of the Schuylkill Regatta, Independence Day Regatta, and the Schuylkill Navy Regatta. **FREE**

Colonial Mansions. *Phone 215/684-7922.* Handsome 18th-century dwellings in varying architectural styles, authentically preserved and furnished, include Mount Pleasant (1761) (Tues-Sun); Cedar Grove (1756) (Tues-Sun); Strawberry Mansion (1797) (Tues-Sun); Sweetbriar (1797) (Mon, Wed-Sun); Lemon Hill (1799) (Wed-Sun); Woodford (1756) (Tues-Sun); Laurel Hill (1760) (Wed-Sun). Further details and guided tours from Park Houses office at Philadelphia Museum of Art. **$**

Japanese Exhibition House. *Horticultural Dr. Fairmount Park Horticulture Center. Phone 215/878-5097.* Re-creates a bit of Japan, complete with garden, pond, bridge. (May-Labor Day, Tues-Sun; Labor Day-Oct, Sat and Sun) **$**

Philadelphia Zoo. *3400 W Girard Ave. Located at the corner of 34th St and Girard Ave in Fairmount Park Phone 215/243-5707.* The Philadelphia Zoo may have been America's first zoo—it was home to the nation's first white lions and witnessed its first successful chimpanzee birth—but you'll see no signs of old age here. Over the last century, the zoo has transformed itself into much more. The zoo is a preservation spot for rare and endangered animals, as well as a garden and wildlife destination point. Lovers of living things will appreciate the opportunity to see 1,600 live animals, from red pandas to Rodrigues fruit bats, in realistic re-creations of their natural habitats. Inclined to reach out and touch? Take a pony, camel, or elephant ride, feed nectar to a parrot in a walk-through aviary, or engage with a playful wallaby. Prefer less hands-on contact? Pedal a boat around Bird Lake. If you are happier at arm's length, pretend that you're a giraffe and explore a four-story tropical tree or take a soaring balloon 400 feet up on the country's first passenger-carrying Zooballoon. (Daily; closed Jan 1, Jun 12, Thanksgiving, Dec 24-25, Dec 31) **$$$$**

Robin Hood Dell East. *1600 Arch St (19103).* (See SPECIAL EVENTS)

Fireman's Hall Museum. *147 N 2nd St.* Phone 215/923-1438. Collection of antique firefighting equipment; displays and exhibits of fire department history since its beginning in 1736; library. (Tues-Sat; closed holidays) **DONATION**

First Presbyterian Church. *201 S 21st St.* Phone 215/567-0532. This more than 300-year-old church was designed in the Victorian Gothic style, combining French and English medieval Gothic cathedral motifs with massive details, flamboyant decoration, and mixed materials, including granite, sand-toned brick, six types of marble, terra cotta, and stone. No plaster was used anywhere within the original building, a matter of some architectural significance toward the end of the 19th century. **FREE**

The Five Spot. *5 S Bank St (19106).* Phone 215/574-0070. Originally opened as a swing club during the late-1990s "swing trend," The Five Spot is now a live music and dance club that features everything from rock music and live DJs to salsa and swing. The club hosts a live cabaret act called the Peek-a-boo Revue the first Saturday of every month, as well as Latin salsa on Thursdays, open-mike nights on Tuesdays (where many musicians claim to have gotten their start), and weekly swing lessons. (Daily) **$**

Fort Mifflin. *Fort Mifflin Rd and Enterprise Ave (19153). From I-95 S take exit 13 to Island Ave, left at stop sign, follow signs. From I-95 N take exit 10, pass the airport, turn right at Island Avenue and follow the road around; turn right onto Fort Mifflin Road.* Phone 215/685-4192. Fort Mifflin is a complex of 11 restored buildings that bring the area's only existing fort to life. It was a Revolutionary War fort strategically located in the Delaware River at the mouth of the Schuylkill. Here, you can climb into a bombproof enclosure used to shelter troops; witness the uniform and weapons demonstrations that take place throughout the year; explore the four-foot-thick walls of the Arsenal, soldiers' barracks, officers' quarters, and blacksmith's shop; or simply enjoy the spectacular view of Philadelphia and the Delaware from the Northeast Bastion. Self-guided and one-hour guided tours are available. (Apr-Nov, Wed-Sun) **$$**

Franklin Institute Science Museum. *20th St and Ben Franklin Pkwy.* Phone 215/448-1200. This 300,000-square-foot science museum complex and memorial hall brings biology, earth science, physics, mechanics, aviation, astronomy, communications, and technology to life with a variety of highly interactive exhibits honoring Philadelphia's mechanical inventor Ben Franklin. (A 30-foot marble statue of Franklin sits in a Roman Pantheon-inspired chamber known as the Benjamin Franklin National Memorial.) The kids can play tic-tac-toe with a strategically adept computer, climb into the cockpit of an Air Force jet trainer, experiment with the laws governing flight, or test water quality in the Mandell Center, located in a 38,000-square-foot garden. Stargazers can witness the birth of the universe, see galaxies form, or discover wondrous nebulae under the Fels Planetarium dome. Budding physicists and bike fanatics will appreciate the 28-foot-high bicycle perched on a 1-inch cable demonstrating gyroscopic stability in the Sky Bike exhibit. And every member of the family can lose themselves in the 56-speaker sounds and larger-than-life-size images at the Tuttleman IMAX Theater. (Daily; closed major holidays) **$$$$**

Franklin Mills Mall. *I-95 and Woodhaven Rd, 15 minutes north of center-city Philadelphia; daily shuttle bus available.* Phone 215/632-1500. Bargain hunters will feel like they've hit the jackpot in the more than 200 discount stores in this mega-shopping complex, just 15 miles outside center-city Philadelphia, which touts itself as "Pennsylvania's most visited attraction." Shoppers will find outlets of such well-known retailers as Kenneth Cole, Tommy Hilfiger, Casual Corner, The Gap, Old Navy, Nine West, Neiman Marcus, Saks Fifth Avenue, and Marshalls. There is no sales tax on apparel in Pennsylvania, which makes slashed prices even more appealing. Two food courts, seven restaurants, and a 14-screen movie theater will engage any non-shoppers in the group. If you don't want to fight for a parking spot, take advantage of the daily shuttle services from area hotels, airport, and train stations. (Daily)

Free Library. *Logan Sq, 19th and Vine sts.* Phone 215/686-5322. Large central library with over 9 million indexed items in all fields. Rare books, maps, theater scripts, and orchestral scores; automobile reference collections; changing exhibits. (Memorial Day-Labor Day, Tues-Sun; rest of year, daily; closed holidays) **FREE**

Germantown. Includes

> **Cliveden.** *6401 Germantown Ave, between Johnson and Cliveden sts.* Phone 215/848-1777. (1767) A 2 1/2-story stone Georgian house of individual design built as summer home by Benjamin Chew, Chief Justice of colonial Pennsylvania. On Oct 4, 1777, British soldiers used house as a fortress to repulse Washington's attempt to recapture Philadelphia. Used as Chew

family residence for 200 years; many original furnishings. A National Trust for Historic Preservation property. (Apr-Dec, Thurs-Sun afternoons; closed Easter, Thanksgiving, Dec 25) **$$$**

Deshler-Morris House. *5442 Germantown Ave. Phone 215/596-1748.* (1772-1773) Residence of President Washington in the summers of 1793, 1794; period furnishings, garden. (Wed-Sun afternoons, or by appointment; closed holidays) **$**

Stenton House. *18th and Courtland sts. Phone 215/329-7312.* (1723-1730) Mansion built by James Logan, secretary to William Penn. Excellent example of Pennsylvania colonial architecture, furnished with 18th- and 19th-century antiques. General Washington spent Aug 23, 1777, here and General Sir William Howe headquartered here for the Battle of Germantown. colonial barn, gardens, kitchen. (Apr-Dec, Tues-Sat afternoons; rest of year, by appointment; closed holidays) **$$**

Gloria Dei Church National Historic Site ("Old Swedes"). *Columbus Blvd and Christian St, 8 blocks S of Chestnut. Phone 215/389-1513.* (1700) State's oldest church. Memorial to John Hanson, president of the United States under Articles of Confederation. (Daily)

Gray Line bus tours. *3101 Orthodox St. Phone 215/744-1100 or 800/220-3133.*

Haverford College. *10 miles W on US 30, in Haverford. Phone 610/896-1000.* (1833) 1,138 students. Founded by members of the Society of Friends. The 204-acre campus includes Founders Hall; James P. Magill Library; Arboretum; Morris Cricket Library and Collection (by appointment only; phone 610/896-1162). Tours of arboretum and campus.

Historical Society of Pennsylvania. *1300 Locust St. Phone 215/732-6200.* Museum exhibit features first draft of Constitution, 500 artifacts and manuscripts, plus video tours of turn-of-the-century urban and suburban neighborhoods. Research library and archives house historical and genealogical collections. (Tues-Sat; closed holidays) **$$**

Historic Bartram's Garden. *54th St and Lindbergh Blvd. Phone 215/729-5281.* Pre-Revolutionary home of John Bartram, the royal botanist to the colonies under George III, naturalist and plant explorer. The 18th-century stone farmhouse (fee), barn, stable, and cider mill overlook the Schuylkill River. Museum shop. (Apr-Dec, daily; rest of year, Wed-Fri afternoons; closed holidays) **$**

⭐ **Independence National Historical Park.** *3rd and Chestnut sts. Phone 215/597-8974.* The park has been called "America's most historic square mile." The Independence Visitor Center at 6th & Marker sts has a tour map, information on all park activities and attractions, and a 30-minute film entitled *Independence.* Unless otherwise indicated, all historic sites and museums in the park are open daily and are free.

Independence Square. *(Known as State House Yard in colonial times) Bounded by Chestnut, Walnut, 5th and 6th sts.* Contains Independence Hall, Congress Hall, Old City Hall and Philosophical Hall.

Declaration House. *701 Market St.* Reconstructed house on site of writing of Declaration of Independence by Thomas Jefferson; two rooms Jefferson rented have been reproduced. Short orientation and movie about Jefferson, his philosophy on the common man and the history of the house.

⭐ **The Liberty Bell.** *Market and 5th sts. Phone 215/597-8974.* "Proclaim liberty throughout all the land unto all the inhabitants thereof," reads the inscription on this irreparably damaged, 2,000-pound historic bell housed in its own exhibit pavilion. An international icon and one of the most venerated stops in Independence Park, the bell is a representation of the fragile but enduring nature of the republic it reflects. This mostly copper symbol of religious freedom, the abolitionist movement, and independence is believed to hang from its original yoke. (Daily) **FREE**

Independence Hall. *5th and Chestnut sts. Phone 215/597-8974.* Built in the mid 1700s, Independence Hall is the site of the first public reading of the Declaration of Independence. It also played host to large political rallies during the country's founding years. It is considered a fine example of Georgian architecture. Visitors often find the Hall a good first stop for their tour of Independence National Historic Park, which includes the Liberty Bell, Congress Hall, Old City Hall, and Carpenter's Hall. The building is open for tours only. Admission by tour only. (Daily) **FREE** Beside Independence Hall is

Congress Hall. *6th and Chestnut sts.* Congress met here during the last decade of the 18th century. House of Representatives and Senate chambers are restored. On the other side of Independence Hall is

Old City Hall. *5th and Chestnut sts.* (1789) Built as City Hall, but was also home of first US Supreme Court, 1791-1800. Exterior restored. Interior depicts the judicial phase of the building. Nearby is

Philosophical Hall. *5th St side of Square.* (1785-1789) Home of the American Philosophical Society, oldest learned society in America (1743), founded by Benjamin Franklin. Not open to public. Across 5th St is

Library Hall. *5th and Library sts.* Reconstruction of Library Company of Philadelphia (1789-1790) building is occupied by library of American Philosophical Society. Open to scholars. (Mon-Fri) To the NE is

Franklin Court. *Between Market and Chestnut sts, in block bounded by 3rd and 4th Sts.* The site of Benjamin

Franklin's house has been developed as a tribute to him; area includes working printing office and bindery, underground museum with multimedia exhibits, an archaeological exhibit, and the B. Franklin Free Post Office. One-half block S is

Carpenters' Hall. *320 Chestnut St.* (1770) Constructed as guild hall; meeting site of First Continental Congress (1774). Historical museum since 1857; still operated by Carpenters Co. Contains original chairs; exhibits of early tools. Adjacent is

New Hall Military Museum. *4th and Chestnut sts.* This reconstruction houses the US Marine Corps Memorial Museum, featuring exhibits on the early history of the Marines, and the Army-Navy Museum. Also in Carpenter's Court is

Museum Shop (Pemberton House). Reconstruction of Quaker merchant's house; now shop with items relating to historic sites. Nearby is

The First Bank of the United States. *3rd and Walnut sts.* (1797-1811). Organized by Alexander Hamilton; country's oldest bank building; exterior restored. Closed to public. Walk approximately 1/2 block S to

Bishop White House. *309 Walnut St.* (1786-1787) House of Bishop William White, first Episcopal Bishop of Pennsylvania. Restored and furnished. Tours. Free tickets at park's Visitor Center. **$** One block W is

Todd House. *4th and Walnut sts.* (1775) House of Dolley Payne Todd, who later married James Madison and became First Lady; 18th-century furnishings depict middle-class Quaker family life. Tours. Free tickets at park's Visitor Center. Retrace steps 1 block to

The Merchant's Exchange. *3rd and Walnut sts.* Designed by William Strickland, one of the East's finest examples of Greek Revival architecture. Exterior restored; now houses regional offices of the National Park Service. Closed to public. Proceed E on Dock St to

Thaddeus Kosciuszko National Memorial. *3rd and Pine sts.* Phone 215/597-1785 (TDD); 215/597-8974 (voice). House of Polish patriot during his second visit to US (1797-1798). He was one of the 18th century's greatest champions of American and Polish freedom and one of the first volunteers to come to the aid of the American Revolutionary Army. Exterior and second-floor bedroom have been restored. (Daily)

Independence Seaport Museum. *211 S Columbus Blvd. Take I-95 to exit 20. At the traffic light turn left onto Columbus Blvd (aka Delaware Ave.). Pass the Hyatt Regency Philadelphia at Penn's Landing on the right; the next building is the Museum. Turn right into the museum just before the bridge. The circular driveway leads to the* entrance to the Penn's Landing parking lot. Phone 215/413-8615. Maritime enthusiasts of all ages will appreciate the creative interactive exhibits about the science, history, and art of boat building along the region's waterways at the Independence Seaport Museum. Oral histories of the men and women who have lived and worked here take visitors through immigration, commerce, defense, industry, and the recreational aspects of boats. You can watch how builders assemble a boat, walk (or crawl) through a full-size replica of a Delaware River Shad Skiff, or pull shapes through a 10-foot tank of water to examine drag-affecting speed. Or you can chart a course for Penn's Landing or learn about navigation as you travel beneath a three-story replica of the Ben Franklin Bridge and make your way along a model of the Delaware River. (Daily; closed Jan 1, Thanksgiving, Dec 25) **$$**

John Heinz National Wildlife Refuge at Tinicum. *86th and Lindbergh Blvd. S via I-95, W PA 291 exit, right on Bartram Ave, left on 84th St, left on Lindbergh Blvd.* Phone 215/365-3118 or 610/521-0662. Largest remaining freshwater tidal wetland in the state, protecting more than 1,000 acres of wildlife habitat. Area was first diked by Swedish farmers in 1643; Dutch farmers and the colonial government added dikes during the Revolutionary War. More than 280 species of birds and 13 resident mammal species. Hiking, bicycling, nature observation, canoeing on Darby Creek, fishing. (Daily) **FREE**

Laff House Comedy Club. *221 South St (19147).* Phone 215/440-4242. This humor hub located on the city's artsy and alternative South Street hosts comedy events all week. There are Open Mic nights ($5), Comedy Spotlights ($10), and comedy competitions. Laff Club attracts up-and-comers as well as established comics such as Dave Attell of Comedy Central's "Insomniac."

Manayunk. *Take 76 from the city center to Manayunk exit 338. At the bottom of the ramp, turn left and cross the Green Ln bridge to the traffic light, which is Main St, and turn right into Manayunk.* This historic district, just 7 miles from Center City, makes a great destination point or place to hang out. Appreciators of old things will marvel over the rail lines, canal locks, and old textile mills dotting this quaint town. Joggers, walkers, hikers, and off-road cyclists will enjoy traveling the towpath that edges the town while their shop-a-holic counterparts check out the more than 70 boutiques and galleries. The word *Manayunk* is derived from the Lenape Indian word *manaiung*, which means "where we go to drink," after the canal that flows into town, and this town offers a selection of charming watering holes. Serious shoppers will find collectibles, furnishings, crafts, clothing, and accessories that you can't find just anywhere.

Masonic Temple. *1 N Broad St. Phone 215/988-1917.* Philadelphia's Masonic Temple was designed for the Fraternal Order of Freemasons, of which Benjamin Franklin and George Washington were members. The interior houses seven different halls, including the Gothic Hall, Oriental Hall, and the better-known Egyptian Hall. It showcases treasures of freemasonry, including a book written by Franklin and a Masonic apron of Washington's. A tour helps illuminate the mysteries of this unusual religious order. (Mon-Sat) **FREE**

Morris Arboretum of the University of Pennsylvania. *Northwestern and Stenton aves. Approximately 12 miles NW in Chestnut Hill. Phone 215/247-5777.* (1887). Public garden with more than 14,000 accessioned plants on 166 acres; special garden areas such as Swan Pond, Rose Garden, and Japanese gardens. Tours (Sat and Sun afternoon; one each day) (Daily; closed major holidays) **$$$**

Mummer's Museum. *1100 S 2nd St (19147). Phone 215/336-3050.* Participatory exhibits and displays highlighting the history and tradition of the Mummer's Parade (see SPECIAL EVENTS). Costumes and videotapes of past parades. Free outdoor string band concerts (May-Sept, Tues evenings, weather permitting); 20 string bands, different every week. (Tues-Sun; closed Mon, major holidays, and Sun in July-Aug) **$**

Museum of American Art of the Pennsylvania Academy of the Fine Arts. *118 N Broad St. Phone 215/972-7600.* Oldest art museum and school in US; housed in restored Victorian building by architect Frank Furness. Outstanding permanent collection of three centuries of American art; rotating exhibits. Guided tours (Tues-Sun; closed major holidays). **$$$**

Mütter Museum. *19 S 22nd St. Phone 215/563-3737.* This collection of one-of-a-kind, hair-raising medical curiosities includes President Cleveland's jawbone; the thorax of John Wilkes Booth; a plaster cast of Siamese twins; human bones shattered by bullets; a liver in a jar; and a drawer full of buttons, coins, and teeth removed from human stomachs without surgery. Located at the esteemed College of Physicians of Philadelphia, the gallery holds an internationally revered collection of creepy anatomical and pathological specimens, medical instruments, and illustrations. (Mon-Sun; closed Jan 1, Thanksgiving, Dec 25) **$$$**

National Museum of American Jewish History. *Independence Mall East, 55 N 5th St. Phone 215/923-3811.* The museum presents experiences and educational programs that preserve, explore, and celebrate the history of Jews in America. (Daily except Sat; limited hours Fri and Sun; closed Jan 1, Thanksgiving, also Jewish holidays) **$$**

Old Pine Street Presbyterian Church. *412 Pine St. Phone 215/925-8051.* (1768) Colonial church and graveyard, renovated in 1850s in Greek Revival style. (Daily)

Old St. Mary's Church. *252 S 4th St, between Locust and Spruce sts. Phone 215/923-7930.* (1763) Commodore John Barry, "father of the US Navy," is interred in graveyard behind the city's first Catholic cathedral. (Daily)

Old St. George's United Methodist Church. *235 N 4th St. Phone 215/925-7788.* (1769) Oldest Methodist Church in continuous service in US. Colonial architecture; collection of Methodist memorabilia; has only Bishop Asbury bible and John Wesley chalice cup in America. (Daily)

The Opera Company of Philadelphia. *510 Walnut St. Phone 215/928-2100.* Academy of Music. Oct-Apr.

Penn's Landing. *Columbus Blvd and Spruce St.*

> **Gazela of Philadelphia.** *Columbus Blvd. Phone 215/218-0110.* (1883) Portuguese square-rigger, tall ship. (call for hours)

> **USS Olympia.** *Columbus Blvd and Walnut St. Phone 215/925-5439.* Commodore Dewey's flagship during Spanish-American War; restored. Naval museum has weapons, uniforms, ship models, naval relics of all periods. Also here is WWII submarine, USS *Becuna.* (Daily; closed holidays) **$$$**

Pennsylvania Academy of Fine Arts. *118 N Broad St. Phone 215/972-7600.* This is the nation's oldest art museum and school of fine arts. Within the Gothic Victorian structure are paintings, works on paper, and sculptures by American artists ranging from colonial masters to contemporary artists. Many of the nation's finest artists, including Charles Willson Peale, Mary Cassatt, William Merritt Chase, and Maxfield Parrish, were founders, teachers, or students here. (Tues-Sat) **$$$**

Pennsylvania Ballet. *1101 S Broad St. Phone 215/336-2000.* This company with a George Balanchine influence includes a varied repertoire of ballets ranging from classics like *The Nutcracker* to original works. Performances are held at the Academy of Music and the Merriam Theatre.

Pennsylvania Hospital. *8th and Spruce sts.* (1751) First in country, founded by Benjamin Franklin.

Pentimenti Gallery. *133 N 3rd St. Phone 215/625-9990.* Exhibiting works of art in all modes ranging from figurative to abstract by local, regional, and international artists. (Wed-Sat)

Philadelphia Carriage Company. *500 N 13th St. Phone 215/922-6840.* Guided tours via horse-drawn carriage covering Society Hill and other historic areas; begin and end on 5th St at Chestnut. (Daily, weather permitting; closed Dec 25) **$$$$**

Professional sports.

> **Philadelphia Eagles (NFL).** *Broad St and Pattison Ave. Phone 215/463-2500.* Team plays at NovaCare Complex.

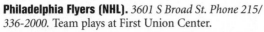

Philadelphia Flyers (NHL). *3601 S Broad St. Phone 215/ 336-2000.* Team plays at First Union Center.

Philadelphia Phillies (MLB). *3501 S Broad St. Phone 215/463-6000.* Team plays at Veterans Stadium.

Philadelphia 76ers (NBA). *3601 S Broad St. Phone 215/ 339-7676.* Team plays at First Union Center.

Philadelphia History Museum—The Atwater Kent. *15 S 7th St. Phone 215/685-4830.* Hundreds of fascinating artifacts, toys and miniatures, maps, prints, paintings and photographs reflecting the city's social and cultural history. (Wed-Mon; closed holidays) **$$**

Philadelphia Museum of Art. *26th St and Benjamin Franklin Pkwy (19130). Take I-676 west to the Benjamin Franklin Pkwy exit (22nd St, museum area), on the right side. At the end of the exit ramp, turn right onto 22nd St and move into the far left lane. Turn left onto the outside lanes of the parkway toward the museum, follow the Art Museum signs, and turn left at the stoplight. Follow this to the west entrance of the museum, where limited parking is available. Phone 215/763-8100.* Modeled after a Greco-Roman temple, this massive museum amplifies the beauty of more than 300,000 works of art, and offers spectacular natural views. From the top of the steps outside (made famous by Sylvester Stallone in the movie *Rocky*), visitors discover a breathtaking view of the Benjamin Franklin Parkway toward City Hall. Inside, the collections span 2,000 years and many more miles. There's a lavish collection of period rooms, a Japanese teahouse, a Chinese palace hall, and a celebrated selection of Oriental carpets. Art lovers will also find East Asian art costumes, Indian and Himalayan pieces, European decorative arts, Medieval sculptures, Renaissance paintings, Impressionist and Post-Impressionist paintings, and modern and contemporary works in many media. (Tues-Sun; closed holidays) **$$**

Philadelphia Orchestra. *260 S Broad St # 1600. Phone 215/893-1999.* The internationally renowned Philadelphia Orchestra has distinguished itself as a leading American orchestra through a century of acclaimed performances, historic international tours, and best-selling recordings. Performances are held at The Kimmel Center for the Performing Arts at Broad and Spruce Streets; the Mann Center for the Performing Arts, 52nd Street and Parkside Avenue; Saratoga Performing Arts Center in upstate New York; and annually at New York's Carnegie Hall.

Philadelphia Soft Pretzel. The famous Philadelphia soft pretzel is not your average hard, crunchy plastic-wrapped snack. You know you're getting the real deal when you are handed this hand-rolled, freshly baked, coarsely salted, buttery, golden-brown comfort food in a paper bag. A Philadelphia pretzel's texture is as vital as its taste: that means not too dry (read: stale) and certainly not too moist. Aficionados claim that Amish girls in hairnets sell the best ones at Fishers in Reading Terminal Market. But

serious pretzel hunters can also find these chewy twists of dough, considered to be the country's oldest snack food, in food carts at city intersections, family-owned restaurants, and the airport. Try one with a dollop or two of yellow—not Dijon—mustard.

Philadelphia Theatre Company. *Plays and Players Theatre, 1714 Delancey St. Phone 215/568-1920.* Four contemporary American plays per season. Oct-June.

Please Touch Museum for Children. *210 N 21st St. Phone 215/963-0667.* A group of artists, educators, and parents conceived of this award-winning, interactive exploratory learning center for children ages 1 to 7 in 1976. The safe, hands-on learning laboratory has since become a model for children's museums nationwide. Story lovers will enjoy having tea with the Mad Hatter or hanging out with Max in the forest "where the wild things are." Children who don't want to sit still can board the life-sized bus or shop at the miniature supermarket. The ones who like to get their hands dirty can engage in science experiments. Creature lovers can interact with fuzzy human-made barnyard animals. And the entertainment-minded can see themselves on television or audition for a news anchor position. (Daily) **$$$**

Reading Terminal Market. *12th and Arch sts. Phone 215/922-2317.* The nation's oldest continuously operating farmers market is alive and well—and thriving—in downtown Philadelphia. An indoor banquet for the senses, the market offers an exhilarating array of baked goods, meats, poultry, seafood, produce, flowers, and Asian, Middle Eastern, and Pennsylvania Dutch foods. Locals recommend the family-run stands, three of which are descendants of the original market. (Mon-Sat)

Rita's Water Ice. *235 South St (19147). Phone 215/629-3910.* The best water ice is not a solid and not quite a liquid, and visitors to Philadelphia will find it at Rita's. With locations throughout the city and surrounding area, Rita's is the city's favorite for frozen water ice, offering a changing selection of smooth, savory water ice, as well as ice cream and gelati. (Daily)

Rittenhouse Square. *1800 Walnut St (19103).* In the blocks that surround this genteel urban square in Philadelphia's most fashionable section of town are exclusive shops, restaurants, and cafés. Discover what's new at chic boutiques—Francis Jerome, Sophy Curson, Nicole Miller, or Ralph Lauren—or experience department store shopping of old at the historic Wanamaker's building, which is now a Lord & Taylor.

Rodin Museum. *22nd St and Franklin Pkwy. Phone 215/ 763-8100.* This museum, built in the Beaux Arts style, houses more than 200 sculptures created by Auguste Rodin (1840-1917) and is considered the largest collection of his works outside his native France. "The Thinker," Rodin's most famous piece, greets visitors outside at the gateway to the museum. Tours available. (Tues-Sun; closed holidays) **$$**

Schuylkill Center for Environmental Education. *8480 Hagy's Mill Rd.* Phone 215/482-7300. A 500-acre natural area with more than 7 miles of trails; discovery room; gift shop/bookstore. (Daily; closed holidays) **$$**

Sesame Place. *100 Sesame Rd (19047). 20 miles NE via I-95 to Levittown exit (25 E). Follow signs for the Oxford Valley Mall on the US 1 Bypass.* (See BRISTOL)

Shopping.

9th Street Italian Market. *9th St between Wharton and Fitzwater (19147).* Phone 215/923-5637. Stroll through this outdoor market and you'll get more than a just a whiff of Italy. Sip on Italian gourmet coffee, inhale imported cheeses, or treat yourself to a cannoli. With more than 100 merchants selling their wares, this is the largest working outdoor market in the US, calling this neighborhood home for more than a century. But there's local flavor here as well. Pinch a Jersey tomato, stop for a famous soft pretzel, or take home fresh-baked Amish bread. And if you want to sit for a while, there are plenty of choices for every budget, from fine Italian dining to lunch counters to an outdoor snack tent. **FREE**

Antique Row. *9th and Pine sts.* Dozens of antique, craft and curio shops.

The Bourse. *5th St, across from Liberty Bell Pavilion.* (1893-1895) Restored Victorian building houses shops and restaurants.

The Gallery. *10th and Market sts.* Phone 215/925-7162. Concentration of 250 shops and restaurants in four-level mall with glass elevators, trees, fountains, and benches.

Jeweler's Row. *7th and Sansom sts.* Largest jewelry district in the country other than New York City. More than 300 shops, including wholesalers and diamond cutters.

Shops at the Bellevue. *200 Broad St.* Phone 215/875-8350. Beaux Arts architecture of the former Bellevue Stratford Hotel has been preserved and transformed; it now contains offices, a hotel, and a four-level shopping area centered around an atrium court. (Mon-Sat)

South Street District. *From the Schuylkill Expy, take the South St exit east. From the Center City area, it's 5 blocks south of Market St.* Phone 215/413-3713. On South Street, the young and hip will enjoy the search for thrift store finds, the aroma of incense, the light refracting from crystals, and a fashion show of the pierced and tattooed sort. The rest can rifle through dusty rare books, cruise the art galleries, or try on every manner of hat. These blocks at the southern boundary of the city—as well as the numbered streets just off of it—are chock full of offbeat shops, cafés, street musicians, and water ice stands, all within walking distance of Penn's Landing and Society Hill. For a Philadelphia signature treat, visitors of all tastes should not miss the legendary Jim's Steaks for cheesesteaks.

Society Hill Area. *7th and Lombard sts (19106). Area between the Delaware River and Washington Square (5th St), bounded by Walnut St to the north and Lombard St to the south.* Secret parks, cobblestone walkways, and diminutive alleys among beautifully restored brick colonial townhomes make this historic area a treasure for visitors. A popular daily 30-minute walking tour will inspire history fans as well architecture lovers. Highlights along the way include a courtyard designed by famed architect I. M. Pei; gardens planted by the Daughters of the American Revolution; a sculpture of Robert Morris, one of the signers of the Declaration of Independence; Greek Revival-style architecture now home to the National Portrait Gallery; and the burial ground of Revolutionary War soldiers. Admire the gardens, immerse yourself in the history of Independence National Historical Park, or stroll through the exquisitely landscaped Washington Square Park. In the summer months, the area hosts outdoor arts festivals in Headhouse Square. It's also home to some of Philadelphia's finest restaurants. In this area are

Athenaeum of Philadelphia. *219 S 6th St.* Phone 215/925-2688. Landmark example of Italian Renaissance architecture (1845-1847); restored building has American neoclassical-style decorative arts, paintings, sculpture; research library; furniture and art from the collection of Joseph Bonaparte, King of Spain and older brother of Napoleon; changing exhibits of architectural drawings, photos and rare books. Tours by appointment. (Mon-Fri; closed holidays) **FREE**

Physick House. *321 S 4th St.* Phone 215/925-7866. (1786) House of Dr. Philip Sung Physick, "father of American surgery," from 1815-1837. Restored Federal-style house with period furnishings; garden. (Thurs-Sun afternoons) **$$**

Powel House. *244 S 3rd St.* Phone 215/627-0364. (1765) Georgian townhouse of Samuel Powel, last colonial mayor of Philadelphia and first mayor under the new republic. Period furnishings, silver and porcelain; garden. Tours (Thurs-Sun afternoons; closed holidays). **$$**

St. Peter's Church. *3rd and Pine sts.* (1761 Episcopal) (1761) Georgian colonial architecture; numerous famous people buried in churchyard.

Temple University. *Cecil B. Moore Ave and Broad St.* Phone 215/204-7000. (1884) 33,000 students. Undergraduate, professional, and research school. Walking tours of campus.

The Trocadero Theatre. *1003 Arch St (19107). Phone 215/922-LIVE.* This former 1870s opera house hosted vaudeville, burlesque, and Chinese movies before it became the beautiful, contemporary live music venue that it is today. The theater, which includes upstairs and downstairs seating, now hosts many well-known rock and pop artists, as well as the annual eight-hour Philadelphia Pop Festival held in June, which highlights local bands. Recently, it has gone back to one of its previous incarnations—a movie house. On "Movie Mondays," the theater holds free screenings (on its original screen) of such classic movies as Apocalypse Now and Escape from New York.

University of Pennsylvania. *32nd and Walnut (19104). Phone 215/898-5000.* (1740) 23,000 students. On campus are the restored Fisher Fine Arts Library (phone 215/898-8325), Annenberg Center for performing arts (phone 215/898-6791); University Museum of Archaeology and Anthropology and Institute of Contemporary Art, located at 36th and Sansom sts (Wed-Sun; phone 215/898-7108; fee). Also here is

> **University of Pennsylvania Museum of Archaeology and Anthropology.** *3rd and Spruce sts. Phone 215/898-4000.* World-famous archaeological and ethnographic collections developed from the museum's own expeditions, gifts and purchases; features Chinese, Near Eastern, Greek, ancient Egyptian, African, Pacific, and North, Middle and South American materials; library. Restaurant, shops. (Tues-Sun; closed holidays, also Sun in summer) **$$**

US Mint. *5th and Arch sts. On Independence Mall. Phone 215/408-0114.* Produces coins of all denominations. Gallery affords visitors an elevated view of the coinage operations. Medal making may also be observed. Audiovisual, self-guided tours. Rittenhouse Room on the mezzanine contains historic coins, medals and other exhibits. (July-Aug, daily; rest of year, Mon-Fri; closed Jan 1, Thanksgiving, Dec 25) **FREE**

Wagner Free Institute of Science. *Montgomery and 17th sts. Phone 215/763-6529.* Victorian science museum with more than 50,000 specimens illustrating the various branches of the natural sciences. Dinosaur bones, fossils, reptiles, and rare species are all mounted in the Victorian style. Reference library and research archives. (Tues-Fri) **FREE**

Walnut Street Theatre. *9th and Walnut sts. Phone 215/574-3550.* (1809) America's oldest theater. The Walnut Mainstage offers musicals, classical and contemporary plays. Two studio theaters provide a forum for new and avant-garde works.

Washington Square. *Walnut St from 6th St.* Site where hundreds of Revolutionary War soldiers and victims of the yellow fever epidemic are buried. Life-size statue of Washington has tomb of Revolutionary War's Unknown Soldier at its feet. Across the street is

Philadelphia Savings Fund Society Building. *Walnut and 8th sts.* (1816) Site of oldest savings bank in US. Not open to public.

Wok N' Walk Tours of Philadelphia Chinatown. *Located at the corner of 10th and Arch sts in center city Philadelphia. Phone 215/928-9333.* Considered one of the best culinary tours in the country, Joseph Poon's Wok N' Walk Tour is rich with Chinese history and culture as well as calories. This two-and-a-half-hour tour begins at Poon's Asian restaurant. (Be sure to try Chef Poon's trademark potato carvings.) Walkers are treated to a tai chi demonstration, Poon's state-of-the-art kitchen, and a vegetable carving lesson. Along the tour, you visit a Chinese herbal medicine expert, a fortune cookie factory, and a Chinese noodle shop; see exotic fish and places of worship; and, best of all, snack on free samples from a Chinese bakery in one of the city's more vibrant ethnic communities. (Daily) **$$$$**

Special Events

American Music Theater Festival. *123 S Broad St (19109). Phone 215/893-1570.* Repertory includes new opera, musical comedy, cabaret-style shows, revues, and experimental works. Mainstage productions Mar-June.

Army-Navy Football Game. *John F. Kennedy Memorial Stadium or Veterans Stadium.* First Sat in Dec.

The Book and the Cook. *1528 Walnut St. (19102). Phone 215/686-3662.* Sample fine cuisine as world-famous cookbook authors team up with the city's most respected chefs to create culinary delights. Wine tastings, market tours, film festival. Mar.

CoreStates US Pro Cycling Championship. *Broad and Walnut sts.* At 156 miles, it's the longest (and richest) single-day cycling event in the country. Mid-June.

Delaware Valley First Fridays. First Fridays is a citywide cultural event that takes place at rotating venues with alternating formats on the first Friday of every month, with socializing and networking as goals. Galleries, shops, theaters, restaurants, and sidewalks in the Old City area along Second and Third streets from Market to Race have hosted record label release parties, live concerts, comedy shows, children's festivals, fashion shows, and vendor expositions. Proceeds go to African-American charitable organizations. First Fri of every month.

Devon Horse Show. *Approximately 20 miles NW via US 30, at Horse Show Grounds, in Devon. Phone 610/964-0550.* One of America's leading equestrian events. More than 1,200 horses compete; country fair; antique carriage drive. Nine days beginning Memorial Day weekend.

Elfreth's Alley Fete Days. *126 Elfreth's Alley (19106). Phone 215/574-0560.* Homes open to public, costumed guides, demonstrations of colonial crafts; food, entertainment. Second weekend in June.

Fairmount Park Historical Christmas Tours. *2600 Benjamin Franklin Pkwy (19130). Phone 215/684-7922.* Period decorations in 18th-century mansions. Early Dec.

Head House Open Air Craft Market. *Pine and 2nd sts, in Society Hill area in Head House Sq (19147).* Crafts demonstrations, children's workshops. Sat and Sun, June-Aug.

Horse racing. *3001 Street Rd. Phone 215/639-9000.* Flat racing at Philadelphia Park, Richlieu and Street rds in Bensalem.

Mann Center for the Performing Arts. *123 S Broad St # 1930. Phone 215/546-7900.* Orchestra performs late June-July, Mon, Wed and Thurs. Also popular music attractions. June-Sept.

Mummer's Parade. *Phone 215/336-3050.* The Mummer's Parade is Philadelphia's version of New Orleans' Mardi Gras or Spain's Carnival. It is an annual tradition to dress in outlandish costumes and noisily parade down the streets of Philadelphia on New Year's Day (the word *mummer* comes from an old French word that means to wear a mask). Jan 1.

PECO Energy Jazz Festival. *2301 Market St (19101). Phone 800/537-7676.* Jazz concerts around the city. Four days mid-Feb.

Penn Relays. *Field is at the corner of 33rd and South sts. Phone 215/898-6151.* These races originally served as a way to dedicate Franklin Field to the University of Pennsylvania. That was in 1895. Today, the Penn Relays hold the record for being the longest uninterrupted amateur track meet in the country. Thousands of men and women, ranging in age from 8 to 80, have competed. More than 400 races take place, one every five minutes, to keep spectators glued. Last weekend in Apr. **$$$**

The Philadelphia Flower Show. *Pennsylvania Convention Center, 12th and Arch sts (19107). Phone 215/988-8899.* The country's first formal flower show took place here in 1829 in the city's Masonic Hall on Chestnut Street. More than 150 years later, exotic and rare flowers are still on display in this town, but in a new location: the Pennsylvania Convention Center. Flower lovers will be dazzled by more than 275,000 flowers from Africa, Germany, Japan, England, France, Holland, Italy, and Belgium. Early Mar. **$$**

Philadelphia Open House. *325 Walnut St. Phone 215/928-1188.* House and garden tours in different neighborhoods; distinguished selection of over 150 private homes, gardens, historic sites. Many tours include lunches, candlelight dinners, or high teas. Late Apr-mid-May.

Robin Hood Dell East. *33rd and Ridge sts, in Fairmount Park. Phone 215/685-9560.* Top stars in outdoor popular music concerts. July-Aug.

Thanksgiving Day Parade. *Franklin Parkway. Phone 215/878-9700.* Giant floats; celebrities.

Motels/Motor Lodges

★★ **BEST WESTERN CENTER CITY HOTEL.** *501 N 22nd St (19130). Phone 215/568-8300; fax 215/557-0259. www.bestwestern.com.* 183 rooms, 3 story. S $109-$119; D $119-$139; each additional $10; suites $150; under 18 free. Pet accepted, some restrictions. Check-out noon. TV; cable (premium). In-room modem link. Valet services. Restaurant 6:30 am-10 pm. Bar 11-2 am. Exercise equipment. Pool, lifeguard. Meeting rooms. Business services. Gift shop. Cr cds: A, C, D, DS, MC, V.

D 🐾 ⚊ 🏋 ⚟

★ **BEST WESTERN HOTEL PHILADELPHIA NORTHEAST.** *11580 Roosevelt Blvd (19116). Phone 215/464-9500; fax 215/464-8511. www.bestwestern.com.* 100 rooms, 2 story. S, D $70-$125; under 18 free. Complimentary continental breakfast. Check-out 11 am. TV; cable (premium). Bar from 5 pm. Exercise equipment. Pool. Lawn games. Cr cds: A, C, D, DS, JCB, MC, V.

D ⚊ 🏋 ⚟

★ **COMFORT INN.** *100 N Christopher Columbus Blvd (19106). Phone 215/627-7900; toll-free 800/228-5150; fax 215/238-0809. www.comfortinn.com.* 185 rooms, 10 story. S, D $99-$169; each additional $10; suites $159-$199; under 18 free; higher rates holidays. Crib free. Complimentary continental breakfast. Check-out 11 am. TV. In-room modem link. Coffee in rooms. Restaurant nearby. Bar 5 pm-2 am. Health club privileges. Airport transportation. Meeting rooms. Business services. View of Delaware River. Cr cds: A, C, D, DS, ER, JCB, MC, V.

D ⚟ SC

★★ **COURTYARD BY MARRIOTT.** *21 N Juniper St (19107). Phone 215/496-3200; fax 215/496-3696. www.courtyard.com.* 498 rooms, 21 suites, 15 story. S, D $89-$225, suites $250. Check-out noon, check-in 3 pm. TV. In-room modem link. Coin laundry, valet service. Restaurant. Bar. Room service. Indoor pool. Business center. Concierge. Cr cds: A, C, D, DS, MC, V.

⚊ ⚟ 🏋

★★ **DAYS INN.** *2015 Penrose Ave (19145). Phone 215/755-6500; toll-free 800/537-8483; fax 215/465-7517. www.daysinn.com.* 224 rooms, 17 story. S $99-$129; D $109-$139; each additional $10; under 18 free; weekly, weekend, holiday rates; higher rates special events. Crib free. Pet accepted, some restrictions; $35. TV; cable (premium). Heated pool; wading pool, poolside service. Complimentary coffee in rooms. Restaurant 6:30 am-10 pm. Bar 11-2 am. Check-out noon. Coin laundry. Meeting rooms. Business services available. In-room modem link. Gift shop. Free airport, train station transportation. Tennis privileges. 18-hole golf privileges. Exercise equipment. Some refrigerators; microwaves available. Cr cds: A, C, D, DS, ER, JCB, MC, V.

★ ★ **HOLIDAY INN.** *400 Arch St (19106). Phone 215/923-8660; toll-free 800/843-2355; fax 215/923-4633. www.holiday-inn.com.* 364 rooms, 8 story. S, D $99-$169; suites $199-$250; under 12 free; weekend rates. Crib free. Check-out 11 am. TV; cable (premium). Coin laundry. Restaurant 6:30 am-10 pm. Bar 11-1 am, Sun from noon. Health club privileges. Rooftop pool. Garage $10. Meeting rooms. Business center. Sundries. Gift shop. Cr cds: A, C, D, DS, JCB, MC, V.

★ **HOLIDAY INN EXPRESS.** *1305 Walnut St (19107). Phone 215/735-9300; toll-free 800/465-4329; fax 215/732-2682. www.holiday-inn.com.* 166 rooms, 20 story. S, D $115-$145; each additional $10; under 19 free. Crib $10. Complimentary continental breakfast. Check-out 1 pm. TV; cable (premium). In-room modem link. Health club privileges. Pool. Garage $15. Meeting rooms. Business services. Cr cds: A, C, D, DS, JCB, MC, V.

★ **RODEWAY INN.** *1208 Walnut St (19107). Phone 215/546-7000; toll-free 800/887-1776; fax 215/546-7573. www.rodeway.com.* 25 rooms, 22 with shower only, 6 suites, 7 story. S, D $69-$189; each additional $10; suites $125. Crib free. Complimentary continental breakfast. Check-out noon, check-in 3 pm. TV; cable. In-room modem link. Restaurant nearby. Health club privileges. Parking adjacent $9. Business services available. Walking distance from Pennsylvania Convention Center. Built in 1890s; Early American décor. Cr cds: A, C, D, DS, JCB, MC, V.

Hotels

★ ★ **ADAM'S MARK HOTEL.** *4000 City Line Monument Rd (19131). Phone 215/581-5000; toll-free 800/444-2326; fax 215/581-5069. www.adamsmark.com.* 515 rooms, 23 story. S, D $99-$224; each additional $25; suites $179-$925; under 18 free; weekend, weekly rates. Crib $15. Check-out noon. TV. In-room modem link. Refrigerators. Restaurant. Bar; entertainment. Exercise equipment, sauna, steam room. Indoor/outdoor pool; whirlpool, poolside service. Barber, beauty shop. Airport transportation. Business center. Convention facilities. Gift shop. Cr cds: A, C, D, DS, MC, V.

★ ★ ★ **BUTTONWOOD SQUARE.** *2001 Hamilton St (19130). Phone 215/569-7000; toll-free 888/456-7626; fax 215/569-7040. www.kormancommunities.com.* 185

suites, 23 story. D $129-$209; under 18 free; weekend rates. Check-out 11 am, check-in 3 pm. TV; cable (premium). In-room modem link. Restaurant 6:30-2 am. Bar. Exercise equipment. Pool, whirlpool, poolside service. Free garage parking. Cr cds: A, D, MC, V.

★ ★ **CROWNE PLAZA.** *1800 Market St (19103). Phone 215/561-7500; fax 215/561-4484. www.crowneplaza.com.* 445 rooms, 25 story. S $149-$215; D $195-$225; each additional $10; suites $475; under 19 free; weekend rates. Crib free. Pet accepted. Check-out noon. TV; cable (premium). In-room modem link. Microwaves available. Coin laundry. Restaurant 6 am-2 am. Bar from 11 am. Health club privileges. Exercise equipment. Pool. Garage fee. Airport transportation. Convention facilities. Concierge. Gift shop. Cr cds: A, C, D, DS, ER, JCB, MC, V.

★ ★ **DOUBLETREE HOTEL.** *9461 Roosevelt Blvd (19114). Phone 215/671-9600; toll-free 800/354-4332; fax 215/464-7759. www.doubletree.com.* 188 rooms, 6 story. S, D $89-$119; suites $175; under 17 free; weekend rates. Crib free. Check-out 11 am. TV; cable. In-room modem link. Some refrigerators; microwaves available. Coin laundry. Restaurant 6 am-10 pm. Bar 5-11 pm. Exercise equipment. Indoor pool. Meeting rooms. Business center. Sundries. Gift shop. Cr cds: A, C, D, DS, ER, JCB, MC, V.

★ ★ **DOUBLETREE HOTEL.** *Broad and Locust sts (19107). Phone 215/893-1600; toll-free 800/222-8733; fax 215/893-1663. www.doubletree.com.* 434 rooms, 26 story. D $119-$269; each additional $10; suites $239-$339; under 18 free; weekend rates; higher rates New Year's holidays. Check-out noon. TV; cable (premium), VCR available. In-room modem link. Restaurant 6:30 am-11 pm; Fri, Sat to midnight. Bar to 1 am. Health club privileges. Exercise equipment, sauna, steam room. Indoor pool, whirlpool. Airport transportation. Concierge. Luxury level. Cr cds: A, C, D, DS, ER, JCB, MC, V.

★ ★ **DOUBLETREE HOTEL.** *640 W Germantown Pike (19462). Phone 610/834-8300; fax 610/879-4242. www.doubletree.com.* 252 suites, 7 story. S, D $230-$250; family, weekend rates. Crib $10. Check-out noon. TV; cable, VCR available. In-room modem link. Some private patios, balconies. Bathroom phones, refrigerators, minibars, microwaves. Coin laundry. Restaurant 6:30 am-10 pm. Bar. Exercise equipment, sauna. Indoor pool, wading pool, whirlpool, poolside service. Airport transportation. Meeting rooms. Business services. Gift shop. Cr cds: A, C, D, DS, ER, JCB, MC, V.

★ ★ ★ ★ **FOUR SEASONS HOTEL PHILADEL-PHIA.** *1 Logan Sq (19103). Phone 215/963-1500; toll-free 800/332-3442; fax 215/963-9506. www.fourseasons.com/philadelphia.* Philadelphia's rich heritage comes alive at the Four Seasons Hotel. Located on historic Logan Square, the hotel puts the city's museums, shops, and businesses within easy reach. The eight-story Four Seasons is a Philadelphia institution in itself, from its dramatic Swann Fountain to its highly rated Fountain Restaurant (see also FOUNTAIN RESTAURANT), considered one of the better dining establishments in town. The rooms and suites are a celebration of federalist décor, and some accommodations incorporate little luxuries like deep soaking tubs and high-speed Internet access. City views of the Academy of Natural Science, Logan Square, and the tree-lined Benjamin Franklin Parkway provide a sense of place for some guests, while other rooms offer tranquil views over the inner courtyard and gardens. The Four Seasons spa focuses on nourishing treatments, while the indoor pool resembles a tropical oasis with breezy palm trees and large skylights. 364 rooms, 8 story. Pet accepted. Check-out noon, check-in 3 pm. TV; cable (premium), VCR available. In-room modem link. Laundry services. Room service 24 hours. Restaurant, bar. Babysitting services available. In-house fitness room, spa, massage, sauna. Indoor pool; whirlpool, poolside service. Business center. Concierge. Cr cds: A, C, D, DS, ER, JCB, MC, V. **$$$$**

⬜ 🏊 🏊 🎿 🖥 🏃

★ ★ ★ **HILTON PHILADELPHIA AIRPORT.** *4509 Island Ave (19153). Phone 215/365-4150; fax 215/937-6382. www.hilton.com.* 334 rooms, 9 story. D $89-$189; suites $325; studio rooms $150; under 18 free; weekend rates. Pet accepted, some restrictions. Check-out noon. TV; cable (premium). In-room modem link. Restaurant 6 am-11 pm. Bar 11-2 am. Room service 24 hours. Exercise equipment. Indoor pool, whirlpool. Free airport transportation. Business center. Luxury level. Cr cds: A, C, D, DS, ER, JCB, MC, V.

⬜ 🏊 🏊 🎿 ✈ 🖥 🏃

★ ★ ★ **HYATT REGENCY PHILADELPHIA AT PENN'S LANDING.** *201 S Columbus Blvd (19106). Phone 215/928-1234; toll-free 800/233-1234; fax 215/521-6600. www.hyatt.com.* 363 rooms, 22 story. D $119-$320. Check-out noon, check-in 3 pm. TV; cable (premium). In-room modem link. Restaurant 6:30 am-10 pm. Bar to midnight. Exercise equipment. Indoor pool, whirlpool. Business center. Concierge. Cr cds: A, C, D, DS, JCB, MC, V.

🏊 🎿 🏃

★ ★ ★ **LATHAM HOTEL.** *135 S 17th St (19103). Phone 215/563-7474; toll-free 877/528-4261; fax 215/568-0110. www.lathamhotel.com.* This charming hotel is a favorite of guests looking for an intimate setting in downtown Philly. Conveniently located, it is just blocks away from Independence Hall and the Pennsylvania Convention Center. 139 rooms, 14 story. D $109-$219; each additional $10; suites $219-$329; under 18 free; weekend, holiday rates. Check-out noon. TV; cable (premium), VCR available (movies). In-room modem link. Restaurant 6:30 am-10:30 pm. Bar 11:30-2 am. Health club privileges. Exercise equipment. Pool privileges. Valet parking $14. Business center. Concierge. European ambience in intimate, boutique-style hotel. Cr cds: A, C, D, DS, MC, V.

⬜ 🏊 🎿 🖥 SC 🏃

★ ★ ★ **LOEWS PHILADELPHIA HOTEL.** *1200 Market St (19107). Phone 215/627-1200; fax 215/231-7312. www.loewshotels.com.* 583 rooms, 32 story. D $175-$275; under 17 free. Check-out noon, check-in 3 pm. TV; cable (premium). In-room modem link. Restaurant 6:30 am-10 pm. Bar to midnight. Exercise room, sauna. Indoor pool, whirlpool. Business center. Concierge. Cr cds: A, D, DS, MC, V.

🏊 🎿 🏃

★ ★ ★ **MARRIOTT PHILADELPHIA AIRPORT.** *One Arrivals Rd (19153). Phone 215/492-9000; toll-free 800/228-9290; fax 215/492-6799. www.marriott.com.* 424 rooms, 15 story. D $195-$250; under 17 free. Check-out noon, check-in 3 pm. TV; cable (premium). In-room modem link. Restaurant 6:30 am-10 pm. Bar to midnight. Exercise equipment. Indoor pool, whirlpool. Business center. Concierge. Cr cds: A, C, D, DS, MC, V.

🏊 🎿 ✈ 🏃

★ ★ ★ **MARRIOTT PHILADELPHIA DOWN-TOWN.** *1201 Market St (19107). Phone 215/625-2900; toll-free 800/228-9290; fax 215/625-6000. www.marriott.com.* 1,408 rooms, 20 story, 76 suites. D $289-$309; suites $450-$5,000; under 12 free; weekend, holiday rates. Check-out noon. TV; cable (premium), VCR available. In-room modem link. Restaurant 6:30-1:30 am. Bar 11-2 am. Exercise equipment, sauna. Indoor pool, children's pool, whirlpool. Valet parking $23. Business center. Concierge. Luxury level. Cr cds: A, C, D, DS, ER, JCB, MC, V.

⬜ 🏊 🎿 🖥 SC 🏃

★ ★ ★ **MARRIOTT PHILADELPHIA WEST.** *111 Crawford Ave (19428). Phone 610/941-5600; toll-free 800/237-3639; fax 610/941-4425. www.marriott.com.* This hotel is located just miles from the Valley Forge National Park, Philadelphia Zoo, Museum of Art, and the Franklin Institute, as well as many other local points of interests. 286 rooms, 17 story. S $179-$189; D $199-$209; each additional $30; suites $375; weekend, holiday rates. Crib free. Check-out noon. TV; cable (premium), VCR available. In-room modem link. Microwaves available. Restaurant 6 am-11 pm. Bar. Exercise room, sauna. Indoor pool, whirlpool, poolside service, lifeguard. Airport transportation. Business services. Convention facilities.

Concierge. Gift shop. Luxury level. Atrium deck. 1 block from Schuylkill River. Cr cds: A, C, D, DS, MC, V.

[D] [icons] [SC]

★ ★ ★ **OMNI HOTEL AT INDEPENDENCE PARK.** 401 Chestnut St (19106). Phone 215/925-0000; fax 215/925-1263. www.omnihotels.com. 150 rooms, 14 story. D $169-$259. Check-out 11 am. TV; cable (premium), VCR available. In-room modem link. Restaurant, bar 3-11 pm; entertainment Tues-Sat. Room service 24 hours. Exercise equipment, sauna. Indoor pool, whirlpool. Valet parking (fees). Business center. Concierge. Cr cds: A, C, D, DS, ER, JCB, MC, V.

[D] [icons] [SC] [icon]

★ ★ ★ **PARK HYATT PHILADELPHIA AT THE BELLEVUE.** Broad and Walnut sts (19102). Phone 215/893-1234; toll-free 800/228-9000; fax 215/732-8518. www.hyatt.com. 172 rooms, 5 story. D $159-$370. Check-out 11 am. TV; cable (premium), VCR. In-room modem link. Restaurant 7 am-11 pm, bar 11-1 am. Room service 24 hours. Health club privileges. Massage, sauna. Indoor pool privileges; whirlpool. Business center. Concierge. Cr cds: A, C, D, DS, MC, V.

[D] [icons] [SC] [icon]

★ ★ ★ **PENN'S VIEW HOTEL.** Front and Market sts (19106). Phone 215/922-7600; toll-free 800/331-7634; fax 215/922-7642. www.pennsviewhotel.com. 54 rooms, 5 story. D $165-$250; under 12 free; weekend rates. Complimentary continental breakfast. Check-out noon, check-in 3 pm. TV. In-room modem link. Fireplaces. Dining room. Health club privileges. Airport transportation. Concierge. Built 1828; Old World elegance. Overlooks Delaware River. Cr cds: A, C, D, ER, JCB, MC, V.

[D] [icon] [SC]

★★**RADISSON HOTEL.** US 1 at Old Lincoln Hwy (19053). Phone 215/638-8300; fax 215/638-4377. www.radisson.com. Conveniently located just 3 miles from the Northeast Philadelphia Airport and 10 miles from the Williowgrove Airport, this hotel is perfect for the business traveler. 282 rooms, 6 story. S, D $109-$159; suites $250; under 18 free; family rates. Complimentary coffee in rooms. Check-out noon. TV; cable. In-room modem link. Some refrigerators. Coin laundry. Restaurant 6:30 am-10 pm; Sun 7 am-noon, 5-10 pm. Bar noon-2 am; exercise equipment. Indoor/outdoor pool; poolside service, lifeguard. Barber, beauty shop. Business services. Convention facilities. Concierge. Gift shop. Atrium. Cr cds: A, D, DS, MC, V.

[D] [icons]

★ ★ ★ **THE RADISSON PLAZA WARWICK HOTEL.** 1701 Locust St (19103). Phone 215/735-6000; toll-free 800/333-3333; fax 215/790-7766. www.radisson.com. 545 rooms, 21 story. D $159-$235; each additional $15; suites $185-$390; studio rooms $185; apartment $195; under 12 free; weekend rates. Check-out noon. TV; cable (premium), VCR available. In-room modem link. Restaurant 6:30 am-midnight. Bar 11-2 am. Health club privileges. Concierge. Cr cds: A, C, D, DS, ER, JCB, MC, V.

[D] [icon] [SC]

★ ★ ★ **RADNOR HOTEL.** 591 E Lancaster Ave (19087). Phone 610/688-5800; toll-free 800/537-3000; fax 610/341-3299. www.radnorhotel.com. 171 rooms, 4 story. S $139; D $149; each additional $10; suites $199; under 16 free. Crib free. Check-out noon. TV; cable (premium), VCR available. In-room modem link. Microwaves available. Restaurant. Bar 11-2 am; entertainment weekends. Room service 24 hours. Health club privileges. Exercise equipment. Game room. Pool, wading pool, lifeguard. Airport transportation. Meeting rooms. Business center. Luxury level. Cr cds: A, C, D, DS, ER, JCB, MC, V.

[D] [icons] [SC] [icon]

★ ★ ★ **RENAISSANCE PHILADELPHIA AIR-PORT HOTEL.** 500 Stevens Dr (19113). Phone 610/521-5900; toll-free 888/887-7951; fax 610/521-4362. www.renaissancehotels.com. 351 rooms, 12 story. D $105-$189; suites $175; under 18 free; weekend packages. Check-out noon. TV. In-room modem link. Restaurant 6:30 am-2 pm, 5-11 pm. Bar 2 pm-midnight. Exercise equipment. Game room. Indoor pool, whirlpool, poolside service. Free airport transportation. Business center. Cr cds: A, C, D, DS, ER, JCB, MC, V.

[D] [icons] [icon]

★ ★ ★ ★ **THE RITTENHOUSE HOTEL.** 210 W Rittenhouse Sq (19103). Phone 215/546-9000; toll-free 800/635-1042; fax 215/732-3364. www.rittenhousehotel.com. The Rittenhouse Hotel is a jewel in the heart of Philadelphia. This intimate hotel occupies a particularly enviable address across from the leafy Rittenhouse Square and among the prestigious townhouses of this exclusive area. The accommodations are among the most spacious in the city and are decorated with a sophisticated flair. Guests at The Rittenhouse are treated to the highest levels of personalized service. Fitness and business centers cater to travelers visiting for work or pleasure, while the Adolf Biecker Spa and Salon pampers and primps its clients in a peaceful setting. From the mood-lifting décor of the gracious Cassatt Lounge and the striking contemporary style of Lacroix to the rowing memorabilia of Boathouse Row Bar and the traditional steakhouse feel of Smith & Wollensky, the Rittenhouse Hotel also provides memorable dining experiences to match every taste. 98 rooms, 9 story. Pet accepted. Check-out 1 pm, check-in 3 pm. TV; cable (premium), VCR available. In-room modem link. Restaurant, bar; entertainment. Room service. Babysitting services available. In-house fitness room, sauna, steam room, spa, massage. Indoor pool. Business center. Garage; valet parking. Concierge. Cr cds: A, C, D, DS, MC, V. **$$$**

⊡🐾🏊🏄🏋🎿🏃

★ ★ ★ ★ **THE RITZ-CARLTON, PHILADELPHIA.**
Ten Avenue of the Arts (19102). Phone 215/523-8000; toll-free 888/505-3914; fax 215/568-0942. www.ritzcarlton.com. The Ritz-Carlton breathes new life into a magnificent historic building in the center of Philadelphia's downtown business district. This one-time home to Girard and Mellon Banks was designed in the 1900s by the architectural firm of McKim, Mead, and White, and was inspired by Rome's Pantheon. Marrying historic significance with trademark Ritz-Carlton style, this Philadelphia showpiece boasts handsome and striking décor. Impressive marble columns dominate the lobby, where guests can pause for reflection over light meals in the Rotunda. The rooms and suites are the last word in luxury, while Club Level accommodations transport guests to heaven with a private lounge filled with five food and beverage selections daily. Dedicated to exceeding visitors' expectations, The Ritz-Carlton even offers a pillow menu, a bath butler, and other unique services. Dining options are plentiful, and the Sunday jazz brunch is a local favorite. 330 rooms, 31 story. Pet accepted. Check-out noon, check-in 3 pm. TV; cable (premium). In-room modem link. Restaurant, bar. In-house fitness room. Business center. Concierge. Cr cds: A, C, D, DS, ER, JCB, MC, V. **$$$**

🐾🏄🏋🎿🏃

★ ★ ★ **SHERATON PHILADELPHIA AIRPORT HOTEL.** *4101 Island Ave (19079). Phone 215/365-6600; toll-free 800/362-3535; fax 215/365-6035. www.sheraton.com.* 178 rooms, 5 story. S, D $69-$149; each additional $20; under 18 free. Check-out noon. TV; cable (premium), VCR available. Restaurant 6 am-2 pm, 5 pm-midnight; Sat to noon. Bar 1 pm-midnight. Health club privileges. Pool. Free airport transportation. Cr cds: A, C, D, DS, MC, V.

⊡🏊🏄🎿SC

★ ★ ★ **SHERATON RITTENHOUSE SQUARE HOTEL.** *227 S 18th St (19103). Phone 215/546-9400; toll-free 800/325-3535; fax 215/875-9457. www.sheratonrittenhouse.com.* 193 rooms, 4 suites, 16 story. Mar-June, Sept-Nov: S, D $279; suites $450-$575; under 17 free; lower rates rest of year. Complimentary continental breakfast. Check-out noon, check-in 3 pm. TV; cable (premium), VCR available. Restaurant 6:30 am-1 pm. Bar. Room service 24 hours. Supervised children's activities. Exercise equipment. Valet parking available. Free airport transportation. Business center. Cr cds: A, C, D, DS, MC, V.

⊡🏄🎿SC🏃

★ ★ ★ **SHERATON SOCIETY HILL HOTEL.** *One Dock St (19106). Phone 215/238-6000; toll-free 800/325-*

3535; fax 215/238-6736. www.sheraton.com.* Located in downtown Philadelphia, this hotel is conveniently located near Independence Hall, Society Hill, the Liberty Bell, the Philadelphia Zoo, and the Pennsylvania Convention Center. 378 rooms, 4 story. D $99-$310. Check-out noon. TV; cable (premium), VCR available. In-room modem link. Restaurant 6:30 am-2 pm, 5-10 pm. Bar noon-2 am. Room service 24 hours. Exercise room, massage, sauna. Indoor pool, children's pool, whirlpool, poolside service. Concierge. Cr cds: A, C, D, DS, ER, JCB, MC, V.

⊡🏊🏄🎿SC

★ ★ ★ **SHERATON SUITES PHILADELPHIA AIRPORT.** *4101 Island Ave (19153). Phone 215/365-6600; toll-free 800/222-8733; fax 215/492-9858. www.sheraton.com.* This hotel is located in the heart of Philadelphia's business district near Restaurant Row and the Pennsylvania Convention Center. 251 suites, 8 story. S, D $185-$205; each additional $15; under 18 free; weekend rates. Crib free. TV; cable (premium), VCR available. Indoor pool; whirlpool, lifeguard. Coffee in rooms. Restaurant 6 am-11 pm. Bar noon-2 am. Check-out noon. Meeting rooms. Business center. In-room modem link. Gift shop. Free airport transportation. Exercise equipment; sauna, steam room. Bathroom phones. Refrigerators, minibars; microwaves available. Cr cds: A, C, D, DS, JCB, MC, V.

⊡🏊🏄🏋🎿🎿SC🏃

★ ★ ★ **SHERATON UNIVERSITY CITY.** *36th and Chestnut sts (19104). Phone 215/387-8000. www.sheraton.com.* 374 rooms, 15 story. S, D $139-$165; under 17 free. Crib available. Check-out noon, check-in 3 pm. TV; cable (premium). In-room modem link. Minibars; many refrigerators in suites. Restaurant 6:30 am-10 pm. Bar to midnight. Exercise equipment. Pool, whirlpool. Meeting rooms. Business center. Concierge. Cr cds: A, C, D, DS, MC, V.

🏊🏄🏃

★ ★ ★ **SOFITEL.** *120 S 17th St (19103). Phone 215/569-8300; fax 215/569-1492. www.sofitel.com.* 306 rooms, 14 story. S, D $199-$299; under 17 free. Pet accepted. Check-out noon, check-in 3 pm. TV; cable (premium). In-room modem link. Restaurant 6:30 am-10 pm. Bar to midnight. Exercise equipment. Pool, whirlpool. Business center. Concierge. Cr cds: A, C, D, DS, ER, JCB, MC, V.

🐾🏊🏄🏃

★ ★ ★ **THE WESTIN PHILADELPHIA.** *99 S 17th St (19103). Phone 215/563-1600; toll-free 800/937-8461; fax 215/567-2822. www.westin.com.* Located near Restaurant Row and the Pennsylvania Convention Center, this stately hotel exudes old-fashioned elegance despite its fairly recent opening. Guest rooms are modestly sized but extremely comfortable with plush-down bedding and an attractive, European-style décor. Afternoon tea in the relaxing lobby lounge and fine, French cuisine at The Grill Room are both wonderful culinary experiences. 290 rooms, 16 suites, 15 story. S $350; D $370; suites $480; each additional $20; under 12 free. Crib available. Complimentary coffee in rooms, newspaper. Check-out noon, check-in 3 pm. TV; cable (premium). Dry cleaning. Restaurant 6:30 am-10 pm. Bar. Room service 24 hours. Exercise privileges. Valet parking available. Business center. Conference center. Concierge service. Gift shop. Cr cds: A, C, D, DS, ER, JCB, MC, V.

★ ★ **WYNDHAM FRANKLIN PLAZA HOTEL.** *2 Franklin Plaza (19103). Phone 215/448-2000; fax 215/448-2864. www.wyndham.com.* 758 rooms, 26 story. S, D $189-$209; each additional $20; suites $400-$1,300; under 18 free; weekend rates. Crib free. Complimentary coffee in rooms. Check-out noon. TV; cable (premium). In-room modem link. Refrigerators. Restaurant 6 am-11 pm. Bar 11-1 am. Exercise room, massage, sauna, steam room. Indoor pool, whirlpool, poolside service. Tennis. Barber, beauty shop. Garage $17. Business center. Convention facilities. Cr cds: A, C, D, DS, ER, MC, V.

B&B/Small Inns

★ **LA RESERVE CENTER CITY BED & BREAKFAST.** *1804 Pine St (19103). Phone 215/735-1137; toll-free 800/354-8401; fax 215/735-0582. www.centercitybed.com.* 8 rooms, 5 share bath, 3 suites, 4 story. No room phones. S, D $60-$100; suites $95. Crib available. TV in common room; cable (premium), VCR available (movies). Complimentary full breakfast. Restaurant nearby. Check-out, check-in times vary. Business services available. Luggage handling. Concierge service. Street parking. Many fireplaces; microwaves available. Built in 1868. Victorian décor; antiques. Totally nonsmoking. Cr cds: A, MC, V.

★ ★ **TEN-ELEVEN CLINTON.** *1011 Clinton St (19107). Phone 215/923-8144; fax 215/923-5757.* 8 rooms, 7 kitchen units, 3 story. No elevators. S, D, kitchen units $125-$175; each additional $15; weekends (2-day minimum). Crib free. Pet accepted, some restrictions. TV; cable, VCR (movies). Complimentary continental breakfast. Complimentary coffee in rooms. Restaurant nearby. Check-out noon, check-in 3 pm. Business services available. In-room modem link. Luggage handling. Concierge service. Coin laundry. Street parking. Health club privileges. Some fireplaces, balconies. Built in 1836; enclosed courtyard. Totally nonsmoking. Cr cds: A, MC, V.

★ ★ **THOMAS BOND HOUSE.** *129 S 2nd St (19106). Phone 215/923-8523; toll-free 800/845-2663;*

fax 215/923-8504. 12 rooms, 4 suites, 2 story. No elevator. S, D $95-$175; each additional $15; suites $175. Complimentary continental breakfast; afternoon refreshments. Check-out noon, check-in 3-9 pm. TV. Restaurant nearby. Health club privileges. Airport transportation. Business services. Restored guest house (1769) built by Dr. Thomas Bond, founder of the country's first public hospital. Individually decorated rooms. Cr cds: A, D, DS, MC, V.

Restaurants

★ ★ ★ **AZALEA.** *401 Chestnut St (19106). Phone 215/925-0000; fax 215/925-1263. www.omnihotelindependencepark.com.* Just a block from historic Independence Hall and the Liberty Bell, this restaurant at the Omni Hotel Independence Park is a restful spot to enjoy a meal. The décor is stylishly eclectic, and executive chef Peter Paul Meyer's menus are rooted in classic French technique, and feature contemporary touches and international accents. Dishes range from comfortingly rich (house-made herb spaetzle baked with Gruyere and Emmantal cheeses and assorted summer vegetables) to heart-healthy (mustard-glazed salmon over golden whipped potatoes with a sauce ver jus and baby bok choy). American menu. Hours: Mon-Fri 6:30-10:30 am, 11:30 am-2 pm, 5:30-9 pm; Fri to 9:30 pm; Sat 7-11 am, 5:30-10 pm; Sun 7-9:30 am, 10 am-2 pm. Dinner $21-$36. Bar. Casual attire. Valet parking. Cr cds: A, D, DS, MC, V.

★ **BERLENGAS.** *4926 N 5th St (19120). Phone 215/324-3240.* Hours: noon-midnight. Closed Wed. Reservations required Fri-Sun dinner. Portuguese menu. Bar 10 am-midnight. A la carte entrées: lunch, dinner $10-$25. Specializes in seafood. Jacket. Intimate atmosphere. Cr cds: MC, V.

★ **BILLY WONG.** *50 S 2nd St (19106). Phone 215/829-1128.* Chinese menu. Dinner. Bar. **$$$**

★ ★ ★ **BLUE ANGEL.** *706 Chestnut St (19106). Phone 215/925-6889; fax 215/925-9591. www.theblueangel.com.* From the Parisian zinc bar to the milk glass ceiling tiles inset with stained-glass blue angels this French bistro is named for, few restaurants in the country have gone to such great lengths to achieve authenticity. Everything in this Philadelphia favorite is from the 1920s—right down to the mosaic-tiled floor. Likewise, the menus are full of examples of "cuisine traditionnelle." Try the frog leg fricassee or the crisp duck rillete bric with foie gras filling and Perigord truffle sauce. Steak au poivre comes with Blue Angel's signature pommes frites. Contemporary classics such as Chilean seabass with vegetable couscous and vanilla-mango beurre blanc are equally good. Get a reservation—this place can fill up fast.

French bistro menu. Menu changes seasonally. Hours: 11:30 am-3 pm, 5-11 pm; Fri, Sat to midnight; Sun to 10 pm. Closed holidays. Dinner $11-$26. Entertainment. Casual attire. Cr cds: A, D, MC, V.

D

★ ★ **BOOKBINDER'S.** 215 S 15th St (19102). Phone 215/545-1137; fax 215/732-2560. Seafood menu. Closed Thanksgiving, Dec 25. Lunch, dinner. Bar. Children's menu. Casual attire. Cr cds: A, C, D, DS, MC, V. **$$$**

D

★ ★ ★ ★ **BRASSERIE PERRIER.** 1619 Walnut St (19103). Phone 215/568-3000; fax 215/568-7855. www.brasserieperrier.com. Brasserie Perrier, the less formal, younger sibling of Le Bec-Fin, is a terrific spot for first-rate modern French fare with Italian and Asian influences. While the menu is more reasonably priced than the one at its more refined relative, the quality here remains just as high. In traditional French brasserie style, you'll find plats du jour, steak frites, and frisee aux lardons among other perfectly prepared standards. The kitchen also departs from the traditional brasserie-style menu, offering a fantastic selection of sweet and savory fondues (a ton of fun to share as an appetizer or for dessert), as well as creative takes on pasta and entrées painted with eclectic flavors from around the globe. The impressive wine list is mostly French, although some American bottles are also featured. The modern Art Deco dining room is warmed by plush banquettes, vintage silver leaf ceilings, light cherry wood, and golden lighting, making it a wonderful choice for many occasions, from an after-work drink to a lunch meeting. French menu with Italian and Asian influences. Closed holidays. Lunch, dinner. Bar. Reservations required. Valet parking. Outdoor seating. Totally nonsmoking. Cr cds: A, D, DS, MC, V. **$$$**

D

★ ★ **BRIDGET FOY'S SOUTH STREET GRILL.** 2nd and South sts (19147). Phone 215/922-1813; fax 215/922-6551. www.bridgetfoys.com. Hours: 11:30 am-midnight; Fri, Sat to 1 am. Closed Thanksgiving, Dec 25. Lunch $10-$12.95, dinner $12-$20. Bar to 2 am. Reservations accepted. Outdoor seating. Cr cds: A, D, DS, MC, V.

★ ★ ★ **BUDDAKAN.** 325 Chestnut St (19106). Phone 215/574-9440; fax 215/574-8994. www.buddakan.com. Slick, sexy, and spectacular, Buddakan is one of Philadelphia's hottest spots for dining, drinking, and lounging. Whether you're seated in the shadow of the restaurant's 10-foot gilded Buddha at the elevated communal table or at one of the other more intimate tables for two in chairs backed with black-and-white photo portraits, you will never guess that this den of fabulousness was once a post office. If your mail carrier were feasting on Buddakan's brand of splashy Asian fusion fare, like lobster fried rice

with Thai basil and saffron and crisp thin pizza topped with seared tuna and wasabi, you can be sure that the mail would never arrive on time. Entrées are meant for sharing and arrive steamy and fragrant, arranged with a minimalist, Zenlike artistry. The wine and sake list is impressive, as is the lengthy selection of house cocktails. A nice way to kick off the evening is with the signature Buddalini, a sexy sipper made from Champagne, Cointreau, and fresh mango juice. Modern Asian menu. Hours: 11:30 am-2 pm, 5-11 pm; Fri, Sat to midnight. Closed most major holidays. Dinner $15-$28. Casual attire. Cr cds: A, C, D, MC, V.

D

★ ★ ★ **CIRCA.** 1518 Walnut St (19102). Phone 215/545-6800; fax 215/545-7683. www.circarestaurant.com. This hip eatery is decorated with antiques and has fresco cathedral ceilings in its banquet hall. The maitre d' greets you from a Gothic-style church pulpit, and there is a 45-foot mahogany bar. Hours: 11:30 am-2:30 pm, 5-10 pm; Thurs, Sat to 11 pm; Mon from 5 pm; Sun 4:30-9 pm. Closed Jan 1, Dec 25. Reservations accepted. Bar. Wine list. Lunch $7-$13, dinner $16-$29. Menu changes seasonally. Valet parking. Former bank lobby; cathedral ceilings. Seating in authentic bank vault. Cr cds: A, D, MC, V.

D

★ ★ **CITY TAVERN.** 138 S 2nd St (19106). Phone 215/413-1443; fax 215/413-3043. www.citytavern.com. Hours: 11:30 am-9 pm; Fri, Sat to 10 pm. Lunch $9.95-$14.95, dinner $17.95-$27.95. Bar. Entertainment Sat. Children's menu. Historical colonial tavern (1773). Reservations accepted. Outdoor dining (in season). Cr cds: A, D, DS, MC, V.

★ ★ **CUVEE NOTRE DAME.** 1701 Green St (19130). Phone 215/765-2777. Hours: 11:30-2 am; Sun brunch 11:30 am-2:30 pm. Closed Thanksgiving, Dec 25. Reservations accepted. Belgian menu. Bar. A la carte entrées: lunch $5-$10, dinner $16-$22. Sun brunch $15. Children's menu. Specializes in mussels, duck. Outdoor dining. Belgian atmosphere. Cr cds: A, D, DS, MC, V.

D

★ ★ **DARK HORSE.** Head House Sq (19147). Phone 215/928-9307; fax 215/928-0232. www.dickensinn.com. Hours: 11:30 am-3 pm, 5-10 pm; Sat to 10:30 pm; Sun 4:30-9 pm; Sun brunch 11 am-2:30 pm. Closed Mon; Jan 1, Dec 25. Reservations accepted. Continental menu. Bar 11:30-2 am; Mon from 5 pm. A la carte entrées: lunch $8-$12, dinner $17-$20. Sun brunch $8-$12. Children's menu. Specializes in fish and chips. In historic Harper House (1788); Victorian décor; artwork imported from England. Cr cds: A, C, D, DS, MC, V.

D

★ ★ ★ **DEUX CHEMINEES.** *1221 Locust St (19107). Phone 215/790-0200; fax 215/790-0202. www.deuxchem.com.* This formal restaurant, whose name means "two fireplaces," occupies two 1890s townhouses, both on the National Register of Historic Places. Guests can choose one of several elegantly appointed dining rooms in which to enjoy the market-inspired menu. Hours: 5:30-8:30 pm; Sat to 9 pm. Closed Sun, Mon; major holidays. Reservations accepted. French menu. Service bar. Wine cellar. Prix fixe: dinner $85. Specialties: rack of lamb, crab soup. Menu changes daily. Own baking. Chef-owned. Totally nonsmoking. Cr cds: A, D, MC, V.

★ **DIMITRI'S.** *795 S 3rd St (19147). Phone 215/625-0556.* Hours: 5:30-11 pm; Sun 5-10 pm. Closed Easter, Thanksgiving, Dec 24, 25. Mediterranean menu. Setups. A la carte entrées: $13.50-$17.50. Specializes in seafood, lamb. Cr cds: A, D, MC, V.

★ ★ **DINARDO'S.** *312 Race St (19106). Phone 215/925-5115; fax 215/592-1112. www.dinardos.com.* Hours: 11 am-10 pm; Fri, Sat to 11 pm; Sun 3-9 pm. Closed Easter, Thanksgiving, Dec 25. Bar. Lunch $7-$10, dinner $15-$25. Children's menu. Specializes in seafood. Historic building (1740). Cr cds: A, C, D, MC, V.

[D]

★ **FAMOUS 4TH STREET DELI.** *700 S 4th St (19147). Phone 215/922-3274; fax 215/922-7097. www.famouscookies.com.* Family owned since 1923, this Jewish delicatessen is worth a stop for a corned beef, roast beef, roast turkey brisket, or smoked fish sandwich. But it's the freshly baked award-winning cookies that put the Famous in "Famous 4th Street Deli." These large, chunky cookies come in chocolate chip, chocolate walnut, peanut butter, and oatmeal raisin. Hours: 7:30 am-6 pm; Sun to 4 pm. Closed Rosh Hashana, Yom Kippur. Breakfast $2-$9, lunch $3.50-$10. Delicatessen fare. Cr cds: A, D, DS, MC, V.

★ ★ **FELICIA'S.** *1148 S 11th St (19147). Phone 215/755-9656; fax 215/755-6056.* Hours: 11:30 am-10:30 pm. Closed Mon; most major holidays. Reservations accepted; required Fri-Sun. Italian menu. Bar. Lunch $20, dinner $36. Specializes in ricotta gnocci, veal chops. Own desserts. Valet parking. Cr cds: A, D, DS, MC, V.

[D]

★ ★ **FORK.** *306 Market St (19106). Phone 215/625-9425; fax 215/625-9435. www.forkrestaurant.com.* American menu. Hours: 11:30 am-2:30 pm, 5:30-10:30 pm; Fri, Sat to 11:30 pm; Sun brunch Sat 5:30-11:30 pm; Sun 11 am-2:30 pm. Closed some major holidays. Dinner $15-$24. Bar 11:30-2 am. Children's menu. Outdoor dining. Cr cds: A, D, DS, MC, V.

[D]

★ ★ ★ **THE FOUNDERS.** *Broad and Walnut sts (19102). Phone 215/790-2814; fax 215/731-0342. www.hyatt.com.* The formal setting, including a rotunda overhead, huge arched windows, an amazing city view, and statues of the city's founding fathers, makes this restaurant a place for special events. Hours: 6:30 am-10:30 pm; Sun, Mon 6:30 am-2:30 pm; Sun brunch 10:30 am-2 pm. Reservations accepted. French menu. Bar 11-2 am. Wine cellar. Complete meals: breakfast $9.50-$12.50, dinner $45-$70. A la carte entrées: lunch $9.50-$16.50, dinner $24-$36. Sat, Sun brunch $34.50. Entertainment. Valet parking. Rotunda with sweeping views of city. Elegant turn-of-the-century décor. Jacket (dinner). Cr cds: A, D, DS, MC, V.

[D]

★ ★ ★ **FOUNTAIN RESTAURANT.** *1 Logan Sq (19103). Phone 215/963-1500; fax 215/963-9506. www.fourseasons.com/philadelphia.* The wine list at The Fountain, the stunning flagship restaurant of the Four Seasons Hotel (see also FOUR SEASONS HOTEL PHILADELPHIA), weighs as much as a light barbell. If you need to work your biceps, it makes for a good substitute. The extensive list—covering all of France as well as Germany, Italy, the United States, Australia, New Zealand, and South America—is just one of the highlights of dining here. Other highlights include refined service and an exquisitely prepared menu of seasonal, contemporary American fare. The kitchen often serves ingredients from local producers and includes the farms' names on the menu, so you'll know which farmer planted your baby greens and where your beets were picked. This thoughtfulness adds to the experience by giving you a real sense of connection to the food and the care that is taken to find the best ingredients. As you'll see here, the best ingredients really do make a difference. Plates return to the kitchen spotless, and portions are easily manageable. The staff is also concerned that their diners' specific dietary restrictions are accommodated. Vegetarian items are available on request, and the kitchen offers several selections that are marked "nutritionally balanced, healthier fare." If you choose one of these "lighter" options, you can definitely opt for the heavenly chocolate soufflé for dessert. Since it is a house specialty, you really should make a point of having it regardless of what you decide to eat for dinner. *Secret Inspector's Notes:* The dining room at The Fountain is just lovely, ideal for a special occasion or business dinner. Consult the fantastic sommelier for wine assistance, but in case it's an off-evening, be prepared for absent-minded staff and food that on occasion lacks interesting flavor and textural excitement. Continental menu with French Provençal influence. Breakfast, lunch, dinner, Sun brunch. Bar. Entertainment. Children's menu. Jacket required. Valet parking. Cr cds: A, D, DS, MC, V. **$$$$**

[D]

★ **GENO'S.** *1219 S 9th St (19147). Phone 215/389-0659; fax 215/389-4166. www.genosteaks.com.* Hours: open 24 hours. Closed Dec 24, Dec 25. Lunch, dinner $5.50.

D

★ ★ **ITALIAN BISTRO.** *211 S Broad St (19107). Phone 215/731-0700; fax 215/731-0702. www.italianbistro.com.* Hours: 11 am-11 pm; weekends 12:30 pm-midnight. Closed Thanksgiving, Dec 25. Bar. Complete meals: lunch $8-$12, dinner $8-$18. Children's menu. Cr cds: A, D, DS, MC, V.

D

★ ★ ★ ★ **JAKE'S RESTAURANT.** *4365 Main St (19127). Phone 215/483-0444; fax 215/487-7122. www.jakesrestaurant.com.* Chef-owner Bruce Cooper's chic regulars make a habit of staying all night, savoring his unique brand of stylish, regional American food. While at the bar, go for one of Jake's wild house cocktails or take a chance on a unique microbrew. The kitchen is in sync with its customers' desire for both fun and flavor in their food. For instance, on a recent visit, the prix fixe menu was titled "Jake's Clam Bake." Currently, it is offered Sunday through Thursday nights and features a popular four-course clam bake-style shellfish menu paired with wine. New American menu. Lunch, dinner, Sun brunch. Bar. Reservations required. Totally nonsmoking. Cr cds: A, C, D, MC, V. **$$$**

D

★ ★ **JOSEPH POON.** *1002 Arch St (19107). Phone 215/928-9333; fax 215/928-9368. www.josephpoon.com.* Hours: 11:30 am-10:30 pm; Fri to 11:30 pm; Sat 2:30-11:30 pm; Sun 2:30-10 pm. Closed Mon; Thanksgiving, Dec 25; also Chinese New Year's. Bar. Cr cds: A, D, DS, MC, V. **$$**

D

★ ★ ★ **KANSAS CITY PRIME.** *4417 Main St, Manayunk (19127). Phone 215/482-3700; fax 215/483-1515. www.kansascityprime.com.* Exclusive rights (in Philadelphia) to Japanese Kobe beef guarantee exceptional quality in the red meat department, and the chef's seafood and game selections are equally pleasing. Hours: 5:30-11 pm; Fri, Sat to midnight; Sun 5-10 pm. Closed Thanksgiving. Bar to 2 am. Casual attire. Cr cds: A, D, DS, MC, V. **$$$**

D

★ ★ **KNAVE OF HEARTS.** *230 South St (19147). Phone 215/922-3956.* Closed Dec 25. Bar. Lunch, dinner, Sun brunch. Cr cds: A, MC, V. **$**

★ ★ ★ **LACROIX AT THE RITTENHOUSE.** *210 West Rittenhouse Sq (19103). Phone 212/790-2533.* Set in the stately Rittenhouse Hotel, Lacroix is a restaurant of understated elegance featuring the haute culinary creations of chef Jean-Marie Lacroix. The kitchen plays up fresh local ingredients with a delicate French hand, while guests dine in posh, sophisticated luxury and enjoy transporting views of the charming Rittenhouse Square. For an intimate dinner party, consider the private dining room that can seat up to 18 guests. French menu. Breakfast, lunch, dinner. Bar. Children's menu. Jacket required. **$$$**

D

★ ★ ★ **LA FAMIGLIA.** *8 S Front St (19106). Phone 215/922-2803; fax 215/922-7495. www.la-famiglia.com.* Occupying the shell of a Colonial tea warehouse since 1976, this Society Hill Italian restaurant is just one of the Sena-family operations. The classic menu includes items such as Vitello Papa Sena's, a combination of veal picante, involtino, and Capri. The dining room is elegant, filled with paintings and family collectibles, and the wine cellar is one of the finest in the country. Italian menu. Own pasta, desserts. Hours: noon-2 pm, 5:30-9:30 pm; Sat 5:30-10 pm; Sun 5-9 pm. Closed Mon; holidays; also last week Aug. Reservations required. Bar. A la carte entrées: lunch $22, dinner $18-$45. Valet parking. Jacket. Cr cds: A, D, DS, MC, V.

★ ★ ★ **LE BAR LYONNAIS.** *1523 Walnut St (19102). Phone 215/567-1000; fax 215/557-7494. www.lebecfin.com.* In what is essentially the basement of the celebrated Le Bec-Fin is this charming bar with wood paneling and formal fabric upholstery. Though it feels more like a bar than a restaurant, the delicious French fare comes from the same kitchen as it does upstairs, at a fraction of the cost. Closed Sun; major holidays. Lunch, dinner. Bar. Cr cds: A, D, DS, MC, V. **$$$$**

★ ★ ★ ★ ★ **LE BEC-FIN.** *1523 Walnut St (19102). Phone 215/567-1000; fax 215/568-1151. www.lebecfin.com.* Still sparkling from its recent renovation, George Perrier's Le Bec-Fin, which opened in 1970, remains a shining star for elegant haute cuisine of the French variety. Perrier unveiled his better-than-ever culinary temple after closing the restaurant for one month. During that time, he had architects, draftsmen, designers, and painters working around the clock to transform the Louis XVI-style room into a "turn-of-the-century Parisian dining salon." Indeed, the room is a bastion of civility with fresh flowers, tawny-toned carpeting, amber lighting, and finely dressed tabletops. In addition to the stunning physical changes to the space, the menu has been treated to a warm wave of fresh air. Perrier's talented team brings out the brilliance in classic dishes while offering several new creations that are destined to be classics. Perrier's signature crab cake with haricot verts has remained on the menu through the renovation. It joins an exciting menu divided between Les

Entrées (appetizers); an impressive and unusual selection of Les Poissons (fish), depending on availability; and an equally terrific assortment of Les Viandes (meats), also listed according to season and availability. Le Cave, as the restaurant's wine cellar is known, has also seen improvement. The list has been expanded from 200 to 700 bottles and includes many sought-after vintages and rare selections from private collections. Reborn, Le Bec-Fin is better than ever. *Secret Inspector's Notes:* The service here is as warm and attentive as you could imagine. Each guest's wants and needs are consistently attended to, and the staff manages to keep the interaction fun and light while achieving the utmost professionalism. French menu. Closed Sun; holidays. Lunch, dinner. Bar. Jacket required. Valet parking (dinner). Cr cds: A, D, DS, MC, V. **$$$$**

D

★ **MANAYUNK BREWING AND RESTAURANT.** *4120 Main St (19127).* Phone 215/482-8220; fax 215/482-3555. www.manayunkbrewery.com. Hours: 11 am-11 pm; Sun to 3 pm. Lunch $7.25-$12, dinner $9.50-$22.50. Entertainment. Children's menu. Reservations accepted. On the river. Cr cds: A, DS, MC, V.

D

★ **MANAYUNK DINER.** *3720-40 Main St (19127).* Phone 215/483-4200; fax 215/483-0840. American menu with Greek influences. Breakfast, lunch, dinner, late night. Bar. Children's menu. Casual attire. Outdoor seating. **$$**

D

★ ★ **MICHAEL'S.** *824 S 8th St (19147).* Phone 215/922-3986; fax 215/922-3294. www.michaelsristorante.com. Hours: 5-11 pm; Sun 3-10 pm. Closed Mon. Reservations accepted. Italian menu. Bar. Specializes in veal chops, gnocchi. Valet parking. Exposed brick, stucco walls; statuary in alcoves. Bronze, glass chandeliers. Cr cds: A, MC, V. **$$**

★ ★ ★ **MONTE CARLO LIVING ROOM.** *150 South St (19147).* Phone 215/925-2220; fax 215/925-9956. Rounding the corner on this, their showcase restaurant's 20th year, Giorgio Giuliani and Umberto Degli Estosti recently completed an extensive remodel. The resulting ambience in the 45-seat dining room and club upstairs is elegant, warm, and welcoming. The chef's weekly-changing menus represent fine contemporary Mediterranean cuisine at its best. A starter duet of foie gras and sweetbreads is coupled with Firelli pears and aged balsamic vinegar, and in the entrée section, the roasted lamb is fragrant with sage and paired with cranberry beans and Barolo sauce. Cheese course selections are well thought out, and the desserts are creative. Northern Italian menu. Hours: 6-10:30 pm; Fri, Sat 5:30-11 pm; Sun 5-9 pm. Closed major holidays. Dinner $27-$32. Bar. Jacket required. Reservations accepted. Cr cds: A, D, MC, V.

★ ★ ★ **MOONSTRUCK.** *7955 Oxford Ave (19111).* Phone 215/725-6000; fax 215/722-7177. www.moonstruck restaurant.com. This solid Northern Italian eatery can become crowded on weekend nights. Most of the time, though, the staff makes every effort to create an intimate dining experience. Italian menu. Hours: 5-9 pm; Fri, Sat to 10 pm; Sun 4:30-8 pm. Closed Jan 1, July 4, Dec 25. Dinner $18-$25. Cr cds: A, MC, V.

★ ★ ★ **MORIMOTO.** *723 Chestnut St (19106).* Phone 215/412-9070; fax 215/413-9075. www.morimotorestaurant .com. Japanese menu. Closed Jan 1, Thanksgiving, Dec 25. Lunch, dinner. Bar. Reservations required. **$$$**

D

★ **NAIS CUISINE.** *13-17 W Benedict Ave (19083).* Phone 610/789-5983. Hours: 5-9 pm; weekends to 10 pm. Reservations accepted; required Fri, Sat. French menu with Thai influence. A la carte entrées: $14.25-$24.75. Specializes in roast duckling, snow pea salad. Cr cds: A, D, DS, MC, V.

D

★ ★ **OPUS 251.** *251 S 18th St (19103).* Phone 215/735-6787; fax 215/735-6170. www.opus251.citysearch .com. Elegantly set in the historic Waterhill Mansion in the center of Philadelphia. Both the interior and courtyard provide a welcomed decadent retreat from the city. Opus promises European-style opulence complete with its fashionable clientele and attentive service. Hours: 11 am-2:30 pm, 5-10 pm; Fri, Sat to 11 pm; Sun 4:30-8:30 pm; Sun brunch 11 am-2:30 pm. Closed Mon; Memorial Day, Thanksgiving, Dec 25. Reservations accepted. Bar. Wine cellar. Lunch $15, dinner $30. Sun brunch $8-$17. Own baking, ice cream. Outdoor dining. Casually elegant dining in Philadelphia Art Alliance; arched windows, European garden. Cr cds: A, D, MC, V.

★ ★ ★ **OVERTURES.** *609 E Passyunk Ave (19147).* Phone 215/627-3455. Chef/proprietor Peter LamLein has been creating his finely tuned menus of French/Mediterranean fare for Philadelphians for more than a decade. The setting is elegantly Empire, with murals on the garden room walls and additional paintings by pastry chef Ron Weisberg throughout. There's a nice selection of á la carte dishes, including an appetizer of fresh anchovies in lemon oil with garlic and roasted peppers, and an entrée of veal sweetbreads in hazelnut crumbs with orange Cognac sauce. But the best values are LamLein's fixed-price menus—$50 for four courses and $20.04 (the price matches the year) for three courses—three nights a week. Bring your own alcoholic beverages, as there is no bar. Fresh juices and mixers are stocked, however, and the waitstaff will uncork and pour your wines. Mediterranean menu. Hours: 6-10:30 pm. Closed Mon, holidays. Dinner $11-$30. Reservations required. Cr cds: A, D, DS, MC, V.

D

★ ★ ★ **THE PALM.** *200 S Broad St (19102). Phone 215/546-7256; fax 215/546-3088. www.thepalm.com.* Hours: 11:30 am-11 pm; Sat from 5 pm; Sun 4:30-9 pm. Closed most major holidays. Lunch $10-$25, dinner $19-$60. Bar. Valet parking available. Counterpart of famous New York restaurant. Caricatures of celebrities. Cr cds: A, D, DS, MC, V.

D

★ ★ **PALOMA.** *6516 Castor Ave (19149). Phone 215/533-0356. www.palomarestaurant.com.* Hours: 5-10 pm; Fri, Sat to 9:30 pm; Sun to 8 pm. Closed Mon; Dec 25. Reservations accepted. French/Mexican menu. Bar. Dinner $14-$33. Children's menu. Own baking. Intimate atmosphere with modern European décor. Cr cds: A, D, DS, MC, V.

D

★ ★ ★ **PANORAMA RISTORANTE.** *14 N Front St (19106). Phone 215/922-7800; fax 215/922-7642. www.pennsviewhotel.com.* Located right at the bridge to Penn's Landing in a building that's on the National Register of Historic Places, Panorama is part of the Penn's View Hotel. The cuisine is gutsy old-world Italian, featuring dishes such as paillard of beef rolled in garlic, cheese, egg, and herbs, slow-cooked in tomato sauce, and served with house-made gnocchi. But it's wine that this place is known for. Daily wine lists offer from 22 to 26 different flights (five wines per flight), plus dozens more by-the-glass options. The quality—made possible by the restaurant's cruvinet preservation and dispensing system—is exceptional, earning Panorama numerous "Best Wines by the Glass" awards from national food magazines. Northern Italian menu. Hours: Mon-Fri noon-2:30 pm, 5:30-10 pm; Fri to 11 pm; Sat 5:30-11 pm; Sun 5-9 pm. Closed most major holidays. Dinner $18-$26.95. Bar. Casual attire. Cr cds: A, MC, V.

D

★ ★ ★ **PASION!.** *211 S 15th St (19102). Phone 215/875-9895; fax 215/875-9935. www.pasionrestaurant.com.* The upscale tropical décor is the perfect backdrop for the lusty Nuevo Latino cooking of Guillermo Pernot. Servers are extremely knowledgeable about the food and eager to please. Latin menu. Hours: 11:30 am-2:30 pm, 5-10 pm; Fri, Sat to 11 pm; Sun 5-9 pm. Closed major holidays. Dinner $18-$29. Casual attire. Cr cds: A, D, DS, MC, V.

D

★ ★ **PHILADELPHIA FISH.** *207 Chestnut St (19106). Phone 215/625-8605; fax 215/625-9529. www.philadelphia fish.com.* Seafood menu. Hours: 11:30 am-10:30 pm; Fri to midnight; Sat noon-midnight; Sun 4-10:30 pm. Closed

Thanksgiving, Dec 25. Dinner $16.50-$21. Bar to 2 am. Children's menu. Casual attire. Outdoor dining. Cr cds: A, DS, MC, V.

D

★ ★ **PLOUGH & THE STARS.** *123 Chestnut St (19106). Phone 215/733-0300; fax 215/829-1097. www.ploughstars.com.* This upscale Irish pub is situated in a spectacular location in a beautiful historically preserved building with 245-foot ceilings, molded Corinthian columns, and dramatic 16-foot windows. Plan to stop here for Irish tea and scones after a day of touring Philadelphia's historic places, as it's just a few blocks from art galleries and several movie theaters as well as the Liberty Bell, Independence Hall, and Penn's Landing. Pints of Guinness and shepherd's pie are the specialties of the house, made more festive around the roaring fireplace or, in good weather, outdoors. Contemporary Irish menu. Hours: 11:30-2:30 pm, 5-10 pm; Fri-Sat 5-10:30 pm, Sun 5-9 pm; Sat-Sun brunch. Dinner $14.75-$22. Bar. Children's menu. Reservations accepted. Outdoor seating. Cr cds: A, D, DS, MC, V.

D

★ ★ **POD.** *3636 Sansom St (19104). Phone 215/387-1803. www.podphiladelphia.com.* Pan-Asian menu. Specializes in sushi, edamame ravioli, lobster rolls. Hours: 11:30 am-11 pm; Fri 11:30 am-midnight; Sat 4 pm-midnight; Sun 4-10 pm. Reservations accepted. Wine list. Bar. Lunch $9-$15; dinner $20-$40. Conveyor belt sushi bar. Cr cds: A, D, MC, V.

D

★ ★ **RANGOON BURMESE RESTAURANT.** *112 N 9th St (19107). Phone 215/829-8939; fax 215/629-2370. www.chinatown.com.* Hours: 11:30 am-9 pm; Fri to 10 pm; Sat 1-10 pm; Sun from 1 pm. Closed Thanksgiving. Reservations accepted. Burmese menu. Bar. Lunch $9.50-$12.50, dinner $9.50-$21.50. Specializes in salads, curry dishes, appetizers. Authentic Burmese atmosphere. Totally nonsmoking. Cr cds: MC, V.

D

★ **THE RESTAURANT SCHOOL.** *4207 Walnut St (19104). Phone 215/222-4200.* Continental menu. Seasonal menu. Hours: 5:30-10 pm. Closed Sun, Mon; also during student breaks. Dinner $13.50. Bar. Unique dining experience in a "restaurant school." Consists of two buildings: a restored 1856 mansion is linked by a large atrium dining area to a new building housing the kitchen and classrooms. Cr cds: A, DS, MC, V.

D

★ ★ ★ **ROUGE.** *205 S 18th St (19103). Phone 215/732-6622; fax 215/732-0561. www.mealticket.org.* This glorious dining room is packed with a see-and-be-seen crowd. Fashionable visitors dine on bistrolike cuisine in distressed-leather chairs and loveseats reminiscent of the 1920s. American bistro menu with French and Asian influences. Closed Dec 25. Lunch, dinner. Sat, Sun brunch. Late night. Bar. Casual attire. Outdoor seating. Cr cds: A, D, MC, V. **$$$**

★ ★ ★ **THE SALOON.** *750 S 7th St (19147). Phone 215/627-1811; fax 215/627-6765.* The charming décor—Tiffany lamps, wood paneling and the like—has not changed much since this restaurant opened over 30 years ago. Italian menu. Hours: 11:30 am-2 pm, 5-10 pm; Sat to midnight. Closed Sun; holidays. Lunch $18-$28. Dinner $15-$34. Bar. Reservations accepted. Cr cds: A.

D

★ ★ **SERRANO.** *20 S 2nd St (19106). Phone 215/928-0770; fax 215/928-0805. www.tinangel.com.* Hours: 5-10:30 pm; Fri, Sat to 11:30 pm; Sun 4-10 pm. Closed major holidays. Reservations accepted. International menu. Bar. A la carte entrées: dinner $10-$20. Own desserts. Entertainment Wed-Sat. Theatrical décor with puppets and tapestries from around the world. Cr cds: A, D, DS, MC, V.

D

★ ★ **SONOMA.** *4411 Main St (19127). Phone 215/483-9400; fax 215/487-7894. www.sonomarestaurant.com.* California menu. Closed Thanksgiving. Lunch, dinner. Bar. Children's menu. Casual attire. Valet parking. Outdoor seating. Cr cds: A, DS, MC, V. **$$$**

D

★ **SOUTH STREET DINER.** *140 South St (19147). Phone 215/627-5258; fax 215/629-3954.* Greek menu. Hours: Open 24 hours. Closed Dec 25. Breakfast $4.50-$7, lunch $5-$7.50, dinner $7.75-$15.95. Bar. Children's menu. Outdoor seating. Cr cds: A, DS, MC, V.

D

★ ★ **STEPHEN'S.** *1415 City Line Ave (19096). Phone 610/896-0275.* Northern Italian menu. Specializes in grilled Dover sole, double veal chop. Own pasta. Hours: 11:30 am-2:30 pm, 5-10 pm; Fri, Sat 5-11 pm; Sun from 4 pm. Closed Jan 1, Dec 25. A la carte entrées: lunch $7-$25, dinner $7-$25. Bar. Display of wine bottles; Original art. Reservations accepted; required Fri, Sat. Valet parking. Cr cds: A, MC, V.

D

★ ★ ★ **STRIPED BASS.** *1500 Walnut St (19102). Phone 215/732-4444; fax 215/732-4433. www.mealticket.org.* Striped Bass makes quite a visual impression. Set in a former brokerage house, the room boasts towering 30-foot ceilings, red marble columns, potted palms, terra cotta-colored walls, and a high-energy open kitchen. It is a breathtaking room. Luckily, the treat for the eyes extends to the stomach. The menu, a loving showcase of virtually every fish in the sea, changes daily. If it once swam, you'll find it on the menu. (But if you're hungry for meat, head elsewhere. This is not the place for steak.) A magnificent raw bar tempts you with briny oysters, sweet clams, and plump, juicy shrimp. Don't hesitate to indulge here, but save room for the Raw Fish selection: a shimmering array of tartars, ceviches, and carpaccios deliciously tinged with Asian (wasabi, ginger, miso), Latin American (cilantro, chilies, lime), and Italian (olive oil, herbs, pine nuts) flavors. If you're feeling flush, a caviar sampler includes 30 grams each of sevruga, osetra, and beluga. Caviar or not, you'll find no losers on this menu. With global flair drawing inspiration from Cuba to Provence, the kitchen deftly demonstrates fish that can be as exciting and have as much personality as meat, if not more. *Secret Inspector's Notes:* The room and atmosphere at Striped Bass are still as impressive and awe-inspiring as ever, but the food and service may have gone downhill in the last few years of its long reign as one of Philadelphia's top tables. The incredibly renovated bank building is still worthy of a visit, with the proper expectations. Seafood menu. Menu changes daily. Closed holidays. Lunch, dinner. Bar. Reservations required. Valet parking. Cr cds: A, MC, V. **$$$**

D

★ ★ ★ **SUSANNA FOO.** *1512 Walnut St (19102). Phone 215/545-2666; fax 215/546-9106. www.susannafoo.com.* Thanks to the plethora of greasy Chinese takeout joints, Chinese food has been much maligned over the years. But at Susanna Foo, a Zenlike dining oasis, the delicious, traditional cuisine of China sheds its unfortunate reputation and gains the respect it deserves. For the past 20 years, chef/owner Susanna Foo has been dressing up the dishes of her native land with sophisticated French flair and modern, global accents. Foo's dim sum can be a meal on their own, and that's a wonderful way to approach dinner here, as long as you order the stellar signature Hundred Corner crabcakes. The entrées area equally mouthwatering, especially the famous tea-smoked Peking duck breast. You may never be able to order takeout again. Chinese, French menu. Hours: 11:30 am-2:30 pm, 5-10 pm; Fri, Sat to 11 pm; Sun 5-9 pm. Closed holidays. Lunch $24.95, dinner $7-$35. Bar. Jacket. Reservations accepted; required Sat. Valet parking. Cr cds: A, DS, MC, V.

D

★ **SWANKY BUBBLES.** *10 S Front St (19106). Phone 215/928-1200; fax 215/928-1308. www.swankybubbles.com.* Pan-Asian menu. Dinner, late night. Bar. Outdoor seating. **$$**

★ ★ ★ **SWANN CAFE.** *1 Logan Sq (19103). Phone 215/963-1500; toll-free 866/516-1100; fax 215/963-9562. www.fourseasons.com/philadelphia.* Located in the lobby of the Four Seasons Hotel, this comfortable cafe specializes in fine liquors and wines, and serves an impeccable afternoon tea. American menu. Lunch, dinner. Bar. Entertainment. Children's menu. Casual attire. Valet parking. Cr cds: A, D, DS, MC, V. **$$$**

D

★ ★ **TRUST.** *121-127 S 13th St (19107). Phone 215/ 629-1300; fax 215/629-1200. www.trustrestaurant.com.* American bistro, Mediterranean menu. Lunch, dinner, late night. Bar. Casual attire. Outdoor seating. **$$**

D

★ ★ **UMBRIA.** *7131 Germantown Ave (19119). Phone 215/242-6470.* Hours: 6-9 pm. Closed Sun-Tues; major holidays. Reservations accepted. Eclectic menu. A la carte entrées: dinner $19.95-$26.95. Blackboard menu changed daily. Totally nonsmoking. Cr cds: A, MC, V.

★ ★ ★ **VETRI.** *1312 Spruce St (19107). Phone 215/732-3478; fax 215/732-3487. www.vetriristorante.com.* The chef cooks soulful, Italian food each night for a few lucky diners at this quaint, townhouse dining room. The romantic space is intimate and cozy, tucked away on a quiet street. Italian cuisine. Hours: 6 pm-midnight. Closed Sun, holidays. Dinner $18-$38. Casual attire. Cr cds: A, DS, MC, V.

★ ★ **WHITE DOG CAFE.** *3420 Sansom St (19104). Phone 215/386-9224; fax 215/386-1185. www.whitedog.com.* Hours: 11:30 am-2:30 pm, 5:30-10 pm; Fri, Sat 5:30-11 pm; Sun 5-10 pm; Sat, Sun brunch 11 am-2:30 pm. Closed Thanksgiving, Dec 25. Reservations accepted. Bar. A la carte entrées: lunch $7-$12, dinner $16-$24. Sat, Sun brunch $7-$11. Children's menu. Specializes in beef, chicken. Own desserts. Outdoor seating. Former house (circa 1870) of author Madame Blavatsky, founder of the Theosophical Society. Cr cds: A, D, DS, MC, V.

★ ★ ★ **ZANZIBAR BLUE.** *200 S Broad St (19102). Phone 215/732-4500; fax 215/732-4550. www.zanzibarblue.com.* This noisy beneath-the-street venue is considered a major stop on the jazz circuit. It blends Southern-styled (as well as some Latin and French) fine dining with a plush, low-lit downstairs jazz club and bar. With live jazz seven nights a week, it draws locally, nationally, and internationally known artists. Eclectic/International menu. Dinner. Bar. **$$$**

D

★ ★ **ZESTY'S.** *4376 Main St (19127). Phone 215/483-6226. www.zestys.com.* Greek, Italian menu. Lunch, dinner. Bar. Children's menu. Casual attire. Outdoor seating. **$$$**

D

★ ★ **ZOCALO.** *3600 Lancaster Ave (19104). Phone 215/895-0139.* Contemporary Mexican menu. Specialties: handmade corn tortillas. Hours: noon-10 pm; Fri to 11 pm; Sat 5:30-11 pm; Sun 4-9 pm. Closed holidays. Lunch $5-$12, dinner $14-$20. Bar. Reservations accepted. Outdoor seating. Cr cds: A, D, DS, MC, V.

Pittsburgh (G-2)

See also Ambridge, Beaver Falls, Connellsville, New Stanton, Washington

Settled 1758 **Pop** 334,563 **Elev** 760 ft **Area code** 412

Information Greater Pittsburgh Convention & Visitors Bureau, 425 6th Ave 30th Floor 15219; 800/366-0093

Web www.visitpittsburgh.com

Pittsburgh has had a remarkable renaissance to become one of the most spectacular civic redevelopments in America, with modern buildings, clean parks, and community pride. In fact, it has been named "all-American city" by the National Civic League. The new Pittsburgh is a result of a rare combination of capital-labor cooperation, public and private support, enlightened political leadership, and imaginative, venturesome community planning. Its $1-billion international airport was designed to be the most user-friendly in the country.

After massive war production, Pittsburgh labored to eliminate the 1930s image of an unsophisticated mill town. During the 1950s and 1960s Renaissance I began, a $500-million program to clean the city's air and develop new structures such as Gateway Center, the Civic Arena, and Point State Park. The late 1970s and early 1980s ushered in Renaissance II, a $3-billion expansion program reflecting the movement away from industry and toward high technology.

Today, Pittsburgh has completed this dramatic shift from industry to a diversified base including high technology, health care, finance, and education, and continues its transition to a services-oriented city.

Pittsburgh's cultural personality is expressed by the Pittsburgh Symphony Orchestra, Pittsburgh Opera, Pittsburgh Ballet, Phipps Conservatory, and the Carnegie Museums of Pittsburgh, which include the Museum of Natural History and Museum of Art. The city has 25 parks, 45 "parklets," 60 recreation centers, and 27 swimming pools.

Born of frontier warfare in the shadow of Fort Pitt, the city is named after the elder William Pitt, the great British statesman. Its strategic military position was an important commercial asset, and Pittsburgh soon became a busy river port and transit point for the western flow of pioneers.

Industry grew out of the West's need for manufactured goods; foundries and rolling mills were soon producing nails, axes, frying pans, and shovels. The Civil War added tremendous impetus to industry, and by the end of the war, Pittsburgh was producing half the steel and one-third of the glass made in the country. Such captains of industry and finance as Thomas Mellon, Andrew Carnegie, and Henry Clay Frick built their industrial empires in Pittsburgh. The American Federation of Labor was born here (1881); the city has been the scene of historic clashes between labor and management.

World War I brought a fresh boom to the city, as well as changes in its industrial character. It was a vast arsenal for the Allies during World War II.

Additional Visitor Information

For additional accommodations, see PITTSBURGH INTERNATIONAL AIRPORT AREA, which follows PITTSBURGH.

For additional information about Pittsburgh, contact the Greater Pittsburgh Convention and Visitors Bureau, 425 6th Ave, 30th Floor, 15219 (Mon-Fri); 412/281-7711 or 800/366-0093. A Visitor Information Center is along Liberty Ave, adjacent to 4 Gateway Center (Mar-Dec, daily; rest of year, Mon-Sat). Other centers can be found in the Carnegie Library's Mount Washington branch and on the University of Pittsburgh's campus, Log Cabin, Forbes Ave. For a schedule of events in Pittsburgh, 24-hour visitor information, phone 800/366-0093.

Transportation

Car Rental Agencies See IMPORTANT TOLL-FREE NUMBERS.

Public Transportation Subway and surface trains, buses (Port Authority of Allegheny County). Phone 412/442-2000.

Rail Passenger Service Amtrak 800/872-7245.

What to See and Do

Alcoa Building. *425 6th Ave.* Pioneer in aluminum for skyscraper construction, exterior work was done from inside; no scaffolding was required. Draped in aluminum waffle, 30 stories high; considered to be one of the country's most daring experiments in skyscraper design.

Allegheny County Courthouse. *Grant St and 5th Ave.* One of the country's outstanding Romanesque buildings, the 2-square-city-block structure was designed by Henry Hobson Richardson in 1884. (Mon-Fri; closed holidays) **FREE**

Andy Warhol Museum. *117 Sandusky St. Phone 412/237-8300.* The most comprehensive single-artist museum in the world. More than 500 works. (Tues-Sun) **$$$**

Benedum Center for the Performing Arts. *719 Liberty Ave. Phone 412/456-6666.* Expansion and restoration of the Stanley Theater, a movie palace built in 1928. Gilded plasterwork, 500,000-piece crystal chandelier and a nine-story addition to backstage area make this an exceptional auditorium with one of the largest stages in the country. The center is home to Pittsburgh Ballet Theatre, the Pittsburgh Dance Council, the Pittsburgh Opera, and Civic Light Opera. Free guided tours (by appointment).

Boyce Park Ski Area. *18 miles E on I-376 to Plum exit (16B); follow signs to park. Phone 724/733-4656.* Beginner-intermediate slopes; two double chairlifts; two surface lifts; patrol, school, rentals, snowmaking; cafeteria. Longest run, 1/4 mile; vertical drop, 160 feet. Night skiing. (Dec-Mar, daily) **$$$$**

Carnegie Mellon University. *5000 Forbes Ave (15213). Adjacent to Schenley Park. Phone 412/268-2000; 412/268-5052.* (1900) 7,900 students. Founded by Andrew Carnegie. Composed of seven colleges. Tours of campus.

⭐ **The Carnegie Museums of Pittsburgh.** *4400 Forbes Ave. Phone 412/622-3360.* Public complex built by industrialist Andrew Carnegie. (Daily except Mon; closed holidays) **$$** Includes

Library of Pittsburgh. Central branch contains more than 4 1/2 million books. Houses first department of science and technology established in a US public library.

Museum of Art. Possibly America's first modern art museum, as Carnegie urged the gallery to exhibit works dated after 1896. Collection of Impressionist and Post-Impressionist paintings; Hall of Sculpture; Hall of Architecture; films, videos.

Museum of Natural History. Houses one of the most complete collections of dinosaur fossils. Exhibits include Dinosaur Hall, Polar World, Hillman Hall of Minerals and Gems, the Walton Hall of Ancient Egypt; changing exhibits.

Music Hall. Home to Mendelssohn Choir, Pittsburgh Chamber Music Society and River City Brass Band. Elaborate gilt and marble foyer; walls of French eschallion, 24 pillars made of green stone and a gold baroque ceiling.

The Carnegie Science Center. *One Allegheny Ave, on Ohio River. Phone 412/237-3400.* Learning and entertainment complex has over 40,000 square feet of exhibit galleries that demonstrate how human activities are affected by science and technology. USS *Requin,* moored in front of the center, is a WWII diesel-electric submarine; tours (40 minutes) demonstrate the electronic, visual, and voice communication devices on board. Henry Buhl Jr. Planetarium and Observatory is a technologically sophisticated interactive planetarium with control panels at

Oakland, the City Beautiful

Once known as the "Forge of the Universe," industrial Pittsburgh was a smoky, pulsating mill town that fed the fortunes of such corporate giants as Carnegie, Westinghouse, and Mellon. Since then, the city has cleansed its air and its reputation to rank as one of America's most delightful big cities. Before this renaissance, Pittsburgh's 19th-century elite created a second city just 3 miles east of downtown called Oakland. A sparkling cultural and educational center, it was an antidote to the blue-collar grime from which many of them profited. Under the patronage of Andrew Carnegie and others Oakland became, as historians have described it, "The City Beautiful, a lavish fantasy of parks and monumental structures housing museums and universities. This one-hour, 1-mile tour is an introduction to this rich heritage bequeathed to the public. To explore it fully might take days. Begin on the steps of The Carnegie at 4400 Forbes Avenue. An immense gray building, it is shared by the Museum of Art and the Museum of Natural History. Born to a poor family in Scotland in 1835, founder Carnegie came to the United States with his parents at age 12. Starting his career as telegraph messenger, he went on to make a fortune in steel. A generous man, he gave The Carnegie to the city. For the Museum of Art, he sought contemporary artworks, thus creating what is considered the first museum of modern art in America. It boasts a fine collection of impressionists. Acquiring Jurassic Age fossils, Carnegie put the Museum of Natural History in the paleontology business. The Hall of Dinosaurs is particularly impressive. Across Forbes Avenue is the Foster Memorial, where composer Stephen Collins Foster is cited for the "beautiful ideals' given voice in his enduring music. Soaring above the memorial is the University of Pittsburgh's 42-story Tower of Learning, one of the largest academic buildings in the world. It was built in the early 1930s as a symbol of power and achievement. A ten-minute walk away in adjacent Schenley Park is Phipps Conservatory on Schenley Drive (west from the Carnegie), an elegant Beaux-Art greenhouse that is believed to be the largest in the country. When it opened in 1893, it was one of the nation's first large-scale enclosed botanical gardens. Conclude your tour by strolling among its many exhibits, from tropical flowers to a major assortment of bonsai.

every seat. Also here are the 350-seat OMNIMAX Theater and the Health Sciences Amphitheater. Restaurant, gift shop. (Daily; closed Dec 25) **$$$$**

County parks. South Park. *Phone 412/350-2455 (county park info and permits) or 412/835-4809 (administration south park). 12 miles S on PA 88.* **North Park,** *14 miles N on PA 19. Boyce Park, 14 miles E on I-376, US 22.* **Settler's Cabin Park,** *9 miles W on I-279, US 22.* Swimming; fishing; boating. Bicycling (rentals), ball fields; golf, tennis. Cross-country skiing, ice skating (winter, daily). Picnicking. Parks open daily. Fees for activities. Attractions for each park vary.

⭐ **Fallingwater.** *27 miles S on PA 51, 10 miles E on PA 201 to Connellsville, 8 miles E on PA 711, then 8 miles S on PA 381, near Mill Run.* (See CONNELLSVILLE)

⭐ **The Frick Art and Historical Center.** *7227 Reynolds St. For tour schedule and info, phone 412/371-0600.* Museum complex built on grounds of estate once belonging to industrialist Henry Clay Frick; gardens, carriage house museum, greenhouse, cafe and restored children's playhouse that now serves as a visitor's center. (Tues-Sun; closed holidays) **FREE** Also on grounds are

Clayton, the Henry Clay Frick Home. *7227 Reynolds St.* A restored four-story Victorian mansion with 23 rooms; only remaining house of area in East End once known as "Millionaire's Row." Some original décor and personal mementos of the Fricks. Tours; reservation recommended. **$$$**

The Frick Art Musuem. *7227 Reynolds St. Phone 412/371-0600.* Collection of Helen Clay Frick, daughter of Henry Clay Frick, includes Italian Renaissance, Flemish, and French 18th-century paintings and decorative arts. Italian and French furniture, Renaissance bronzes, tapestries, Chinese porcelains. Also changing exhibits; concerts, lectures. **FREE**

Frick Park. *Beechwood Blvd and English Ln. Phone 412/422-6536.* Covers 476 acres, largely in natural state; nature trails wind through ravines and over hills; also nature center (2005 Beechwood Blvd), tennis courts, picnic areas, playgrounds. Park (Daily). **FREE**

Gateway Center. *420 Fort Duquesne Blvd (15222). Covers 23 acres adjacent to Point State Park. Phone 412/392-6000.* Complex includes four skyscrapers of Trizec Properties, Inc. Gateway Center Plaza, a 2-acre open-air garden over underground parking garage, has lovely walks, three fountains, more than 90 types of trees and 100 varieties of shrubs and seasonal flowers. (Mon-Fri; closed holidays)

Hartwood. *12 miles N via PA 8, at 215 Saxonburg Blvd. Phone 412/767-9200.* (1929). A 629-acre re-creation of English country estate; Tudor mansion with many antiques; formal gardens, stables. Tours (Tues-Sun; closed holidays). Also music and theater events during summer. **$$**

⭐ **Inclines.** (Hill-climbing trolleys). Travel to the top of Mount Washington for an excellent view of Golden Triangle, where the Allegheny and Monongahela rivers join to form the Ohio River.

Duquesne Incline. *Lower station, W Carson St, opposite the fountain, SW of Fort Pitt Bridge; upper station, 1220 Grandview Ave, in restaurant area.* Phone 412/381-1665. Built 1877; restored and run by community effort; observation deck. (Daily) Free parking at lower station. **$**

Monongahela Incline. *Station on W Carson St near Station Sq and Smithfield St Bridge.* Phone 412/442-2000. Panoramic views from observation deck. (Daily) **$**

James L. Kelso Bible Lands Museum. *616 N Highland, on grounds of Pittsburgh Theological Seminary.* Phone 412/362-5610. Artifacts and displays from the ancient Near East, especially Palestine. (Call for hours) **FREE**

Kennywood Park. *4800 Kennywood Blvd, in W Mifflin. 8 miles SE on PA 837.* Phone 412/461-0500. Combines modern rides with rides from traditional streetcar parks, popular at the turn of the 20th century. Lost Kennywood, with lagoon, Victorian-era buildings, shopping. Gardens, picnic groves. (Mid-May-Labor Day, daily) **$$$$**

Mellon Arena. *In Golden Triangle, 66 Mario Lemieux Pl.* This $22-million all-weather amphitheater accommodates 17,500 people. Retractable roof can fold up within 2 1/2 minutes.

Museum of Photographic History. *531 E Ohio.* Phone 412/231-7881. Photo gallery and museum. Selections from 100,000 antique photographic images. (Mon-Sat; closed major holidays) **$$**

National Aviary. *Allegheny Commons West, approximately 1 mile W of downtown.* Phone 412/323-7235. The Aviary is home to one of the world's premier bird collections and is the only indoor bird facility independent of a larger zoo in North America. A veritable jungle of colorful, amusing and exotic birds. (Daily; closed Dec 25) **$$**

Pittsburgh Children's Museum. *10 Children's Way.* Phone 412/322-5058. Hands-on exhibits. Hands-on silk-screen studio; storytelling; regularly scheduled puppet shows; live performances; two-story climber. (Memorial Day-Labor Day, daily; rest of year, Tues-Sat, also Sun afternoons) **$$**

Professional sports.

Pittsburgh Penguins (NHL). *66 Mario Lemieux Pl.* Phone 412/323-1919. Team plays at Mellon Arena.

Pittsburgh Pirates (MLB). *115 Federal St.* Phone 412/323-5000. Team plays at PNC Park.

Pittsburgh Steelers (NFL). *600 Stadium Circle.* Phone 412/432-7800. Team plays at Heinz Field.

The Pittsburgh Zoo. *1 Wild Place (15260). NE on Highland Ave in Highland Park area.* Phone 412/665-3639. Over 70 acres containing over 6,000 animals, children's farm (late May-Oct), discovery pavilion, reptile house, tropical and Asian forests, African savanna and aqua zoo. Merry-go-round and train rides (fee). Highland Park covers 75 acres and has tennis courts, picnic grounds, shelters (some require permit), twin reservoirs, swimming pool (fee). (Daily; closed Dec 25) **$$$**

Point State Park. *Fort Duquesne and Fort Pitt blvds.* Phone 412/471-0235. "Point" where the Allegheny and Monongahela rivers meet to form the Ohio; 36 acres. Giant fountain symbolizes joining of rivers. There are military drills with fifes and drums, muskets and cannon (May-Labor Day; some Sun afternoons). In the park are

Block House of Fort Pitt. Last remaining building of original fort (1767). (Wed-Sun) **FREE**

Fort Pitt Museum. *101 Commonwealth Pl.* Phone 412/281-9284. Built on part of original fort. Exhibits on early Pittsburgh and Fort Pitt; military struggles between France and Britain for western Pennsylvania and the Old Northwest Territory. (Wed-Sun; closed some holidays) **$$**

PPG Place. *Market Sq.* Designed by Philip Johnson, this is Pittsburgh's most popular Renaissance II building. PPG Place consists of six separate buildings designed in a postmodern, Gothic skyscraper style. Shopping and a food court can be found in Two PPG Place.

Riverview Park. *2 miles N on US 19.* Covers 251 acres. Swimming pool (mid-June-Labor Day, daily, fee); tennis courts (Apr-Nov, daily); picnic shelter (May-Sept, permit required). Also playgrounds, parklet; nature, jogging trail. Fee for some activities. In the park is

Allegheny Observatory. *159 Riverview Ave (15214).* Phone 412/321-2400. Slides, tour of building. Maintained by University of Pittsburgh. Children under 12 years only with adult. Reservation required. (Apr-Oct, Thurs-Fri; closed holidays) **FREE**

Rodef Shalom Biblical Botanical Garden. *4905 5th Ave.* Phone 412/621-6566. The natural world of ancient Israel is re-created here in settings that specialize in plants of the Bible. A waterfall, desert, and stream all help simulate the areas of the Jordan, Lake Kineret, and the Dead Sea. Tours (by appointment). Special programs and exhibits. (June-mid-Sept, Mon-Thurs, Sat-Sun; Sat hours limited) **FREE**

Sandcastle Water Park. *1000 Sandcastle Dr (15120). Approximately 5 miles SE of downtown via I-376 and PA 837.* Phone 412/462-6666. The city's down-by-the-riverside water park has 15 slides, adult and kiddie pools;

boardwalk; food. (First Sat June-Labor Day, daily; closed holidays) **$$$$**

Schenley Park. *5000 Forbes Ave (15217). Adjacent Carnegie-Mellon University. Phone 412/687-1800.* Covers 456 acres; picnic areas; 18-hole golf course, lighted tennis courts; swimming pool; ice skating (winter); softball fields, running track; nature trails; bandstand (summer; free). Fee for some activities. (Daily) Also in park is

Phipps Conservatory. *1 Schenley Park (15213). Phone 412/622-6914.* Constantly changing array of flowers; tropical gardens; outstanding orchid collection. Children's Discovery Garden with interactive learning opportunities. Seasonal flower shows (see SPECIAL EVENTS). (Tues-Sun) **$$$**

The Senator John Heinz Regional History Center. *1212 Smallman St. Phone 412/454-6000. In Chatauqua Ice Warehouse (1898).* Preserves 300 years of region's history with artifacts and extensive collection of archives, photos. Houses the Historical Society of Western Pennsylvania. Library (Tues-Sat). (Daily; closed Jan 1, Thanksgiving, Dec 25) **$$$**

Sightseeing tours.

Guided Bus and Walking Tours. *1 Station Sq, Suite 450 (15219). Phone 412/471-5808.* Offered through the Pittsburgh History and Landmarks Foundation. **$$**

Sightseeing USA/Lenzner Coach USA. *110 Lenzner Ct (15143). Phone 412/741-2720, 412/761-7000 or 800/342-2349.*

Soldiers and Sailors Memorial Hall and Military History Museum. *4141 5th Ave at Bigelow Blvd. Phone 412/621-4253.* Auditorium has Lincoln's Gettysburg Address inscribed above stage; flags, weapons, uniforms, memorabilia from US wars. (Tues-Fri, also Sat and Sun afternoons; closed most major holidays) **$$**

Station Square. *450 Landmarks Bldg, 1 Station Sq, along Monongahela River across from downtown, via Smithfield St Bridge. Phone 412/471-5808.* This 40-acre area features shopping, dining, and entertainment in and among the historic buildings of the P & LE Railroad. Shopping in warehouses that once held loaded railroad boxcars. (Daily; closed some holidays)

Tour-Ed Mine and Museum. *748 Bull Creek Rd (15084). 20 miles NW via PA 28 (Allegheny Valley Expy) to Tarentum, then 1/4 mile W via Red Belt W. Phone 724/224-4720.* Complete underground coal mining operation; sawmill; furnished log house (1789); old company store; historical mine museum; shelters; playground. (May-Labor Day week, daily) **$$$**

Two Mellon Bank Center. *Grant St and 5th Ave.* Formerly the Union Trust Building, its Flemish-Gothic style was modeled after a library in Louvain, Belgium. Interior has a glass rotunda.

University of Pittsburgh. *5th Ave and Bigelow Blvd. Phone 412/624-4141. (1787)* 33,000 students. Tours of Nationality Rooms in Cathedral of Learning (weekends; fee). Campus of 70 buildings on 125 acres. Buildings include

Cathedral of Learning. *4200 5th Ave (15260). Phone 412/624-6000. (1935).* Unique skyscraper of classrooms, stretching its Gothic-Moderne architecture 42 floors high (535 feet); vantage point on 36th floor. Surrounding a three-story Gothic commons room are an Early American Room and 24 Nationality Rooms, each reflecting the distinctive culture of the ethnic group that created and furnished it. Tours (Daily; closed holidays). **$$**

Heinz Chapel. *5th and Bellefield aves (15260). E of Cathedral of Learning. Phone 412/624-4157.* Tall stained-glass windows; French Gothic architecture. (Mon-Thurs, Sat-Sun; closed holidays) **FREE**

Henry Clay Frick Fine Arts Building. *104 Frick Fine Arts (15260). Schenley Plaza. Phone 412/648-2400.* Glass-enclosed cloister; changing exhibits; art reference library. (Sept-mid-June, daily; rest of year, Mon-Fri; closed university holidays, also Dec 24-Jan 2) **FREE**

Stephen Foster Memorial. *4301 Forbes Ave (15260). Phone 412/624-4100.* Auditorium/theater. Collection of the Pittsburgh-born composer's music and memorabilia. Said to be one of the most elaborate memorials ever built to a musician. (Mon-Sat, also Sun afternoons; closed holidays)

USX Tower. *Grant St and 7th Ave.* Once known as the US Steel Building, it is 64 stories high, and the tallest building in Pittsburgh. Ten exposed triangular columns and an exterior paneling of steel make up its construction.

Special Events

Folk Festival. *105 Mall Blvd (15146). Pittsburgh Expo Mart, Monroeville.* Food of many nations; arts and crafts; folk music, dancing. Memorial Day weekend.

Phipps Conservatory Flower Shows. *1 Schenley Dr. Phone 412/622-6914. Schenley Park.* Spring, summer, fall, and holidays.

Pittsburgh/Shop 'N Save Three Rivers Regatta. *Point State Park.* Water, land, and air events; water shows and speedboat races. Last weekend in July and first weekend in Aug.

Pittsburgh Irish Festival. *1 Station Sq (15219). Phone 412/422-1113. I. C. Light Amphitheatre, Station Square.* Irish foods, dances, and entertainment. Early or mid-Sept.

Pittsburgh Public Theater. *621 Penn Ave. Phone 412/316-1600.* City's largest resident professional company. Sept-June.

Pittsburgh Symphony Orchestra. *600 Penn Ave, Heinz Hall for the Performing Arts. Phone 412/392-4900.* Classical, pop, and family concerts. Sept-May.

Three Rivers Arts Festival. *707 Penn Ave. Phone 412/281-8723. Point State Park, Gateway Center, USX Tower, PPG Place.* Juried, original works of local and national artists: paintings, photography, sculpture, crafts and videos; artists' market in outdoor plazas. Ongoing performances include music, dance, and performance art. Special art projects; film festival; food; children's activities. Early-mid-June.

Motels/Motor Lodges

★ **BEST WESTERN PARKWAY CENTER INN.** *875 Greentrée Rd (15220). Phone 412/922-7070; toll-free 800/528-1234; fax 412/922-4949. www.bestwestern.com.* 138 rooms, 6 story. S, D $69-$108; kitchen units $118; under 12 free; weekend rates. Complimentary breakfast. Check-out noon. TV; cable (premium). In-room modem link. Exercise equipment, sauna. Indoor pool. Free airport transportation. Cr cds: A, C, D, DS, ER, MC, V.

🅓 🖼 🕆 🖼 SC

★ **COUNTRY INN & SUITES.** *5311 Campbells Run Rd (15205). Phone 412/788-8400; fax 412/788-2577. www.countryinns.com.* 152 rooms, 26 suites, 3 story. S, D $79-$94; each additional $10; suites $109-$114; under 18 free; lower rates Fri, Sat. Complimentary buffet breakfast. Check-out noon. TV; cable (premium). In-room modem link. Restaurant adjacent 11 am-11 pm. Exercise equipment. Whirlpool. Free airport transportation. Cr cds: A, C, D, DS, MC, V.

🅓 🕆 🖼

★ **HAMPTON INN.** *555 Trumbull Dr (15205). Phone 412/922-0100; fax 412/921-7631. www.hamptoninn.com.* 132 rooms, 6 story. June-Nov: S $79-$99; D $79; under 18 free; weekend rates; lower rates rest of year. Crib free. Pet accepted. Complimentary continental breakfast. Check-out noon. TV; cable (premium). In-room modem link. Valet services. Restaurant nearby. Health club privileges. Picnic tables. Free airport transportation. Meeting rooms. Business services. Cr cds: A, C, D, DS, ER, JCB, MC, V.

🅓 🐾 🖼

★ **HAMPTON INN.** *1550 Lebanon Church Rd (15236). Phone 412/650-1000; fax 412/650-1001. www.hamptoninn.com.* 70 rooms, 3 story. S, D $94; under 18 free; higher rates: holidays, football games. Crib free. Check-out noon. TV; cable (premium). In-room modem link. Some in-room whirlpools, refrigerators, microwaves. Restaurant nearby. Heated pool, lifeguard. Meeting rooms. Business services. Cr cds: A, C, D, DS, JCB, MC, V.

🅓 🖼 🖼 SC

★ **HAWTHORN SUITES.** *700 Mansfield Ave (15205). Phone 412/279-6300; toll-free 800/331-3131; fax 412/279-4993. www.hawthornsuitespittsburgh.com.* 151 suites, 2 story. S $79-$119; D $109-$149; weekly, monthly rates. Pet accepted, some restrictions; $50 and $6/day. Complimentary full breakfast. Check-out noon. TV; cable (premium). Fireplaces. Health club privileges. Pool, whirlpool. Airport transportation. Chalet-style buildings. Cr cds: A, C, D, DS, ER, JCB, MC, V.

🅓 🐾 🖼 🖼 SC

★ ★ **HOLIDAY INN.** *180 Gamma Dr (15238). Phone 412/963-0600; fax 412/963-7852. www.holiday-inn.com.* 223 rooms, 2 story. S, D $109; suites $150; under 18 free. Check-out noon. TV; cable (premium). In-room modem link. Refrigerator in suites; microwaves available. Restaurant 6 am-10 pm; Sat, Sun from 7 am. Bar 11-2 am; Sun 1 pm-1 am. Room service. Exercise equipment. Heated pool, poolside service, lifeguard. Airport transportation. Meeting rooms. Business services. Cr cds: A, C, D, DS, JCB, MC, V.

🅓 🖼 🕆

★ ★ **HOLIDAY INN.** *915 Brinton Rd (15221). Phone 412/247-2700; toll-free 800/465-4329; fax 412/371-9619. www.holiday-inn.com.* 177 rooms, 11 story. Apr-Oct: S, D $89.95-$120; suites $150; under 18 free; weekend, holiday rates; lower rates rest of year. Crib free. Pet accepted. Check-out noon. TV; cable (premium). Some refrigerators; microwaves available. Valet services, coin laundry. Restaurant 6:30 am-10 pm. Bar 5 pm-1 am; entertainment Fri, Sat. Room service. Health club privileges. Indoor pool, lifeguard. Meeting rooms. Business services. Cr cds: A, D, DS, ER, JCB, MC, V.

🅓 🐾 🖼 🖼 SC

★ ★ **HOLIDAY INN.** *401 Holiday Dr (15220). Phone 412/922-8100; toll-free 800/465-4329; fax 412/922-6511. www.holiday-inn.com.* 200 rooms, 4 story. S, D $104-$148; each additional $10; under 18 free. Crib free. Pet accepted. Check-out noon. TV; cable, VCR available. In-room modem link. Private patios. Valet services. Restaurant 6:30 am-10 pm; Fri, Sat to 11 pm. Bar 11-2 am; Sun from 1 pm; entertainment. Room service. Health club privileges. Exercise equipment. Heated pool, poolside service, lifeguard. Free airport transportation. Meeting rooms. Business services. Sundries. Cr cds: A, C, D, DS, JCB, MC, V.

🅓 🐾 🖼 🕆 🖼 SC

★ ★ **HOLIDAY INN.** *2750 Mosside Blvd (15146). Phone 412/372-1022; toll-free 800/465-4329; fax 412/373-4065. www.holiday-inn.com.* 188 rooms, 4 story. S, D $109.95-$115.95; under 19 free; package plans. Crib free. Pet accepted. Check-out noon. TV; cable (premium).

In-room modem link. Some in-room whirlpools; microwaves available. Valet services, coin laundry. Restaurant 6:30 am-2 pm, 5-10 pm. Bar 11-2 am; Health club privileges. Exercise equipment. Pool. Meeting rooms. Business services. Sundries. Cr cds: A, C, D, DS, ER, JCB, MC, V.

D 🐾 ⌘ 🏋 ⊠ SC

★ ★ **HOLIDAY INN.** *4859 McKnight Rd (15237). Phone 412/366-5200; toll-free 800/465-4329; fax 412/366-5682. www.holiday-inn.com.* 147 rooms, 7 story, 19 suites. S, D $99-$109; each additional $10; suites $109-$139; under 18 free. Crib free. TV; cable (premium). Heated pool; poolside service, lifeguard. Restaurant 6:30 am-10 pm; Sun from 7 am. Room service. Bar 11 am-11 pm; entertainment Sat. Check-out noon. Coin laundry. Meeting rooms. Business services available. In-room modem link. Valet service. Sundries. Health club privileges. Refrigerator in suites; microwaves available. Cr cds: A, C, D, DS, JCB, MC, V.

D ⌘ ⊠ SC

★ ★ **RAMADA INN.** *699 Rodi Rd (15235). Phone 412/244-1600; toll-free 800/272-6232; fax 412/829-2334. www.ramada.com.* 152 rooms, 3 story. No elevator. S $112-$122; D $122-$132; each additional $10; under 18 free; weekend plan. Check-out 11 am. TV. In-room modem link. Restaurant 6:30 am-2 pm, 5:30-10 pm; Fri, Sat 6-11 pm. Bar 4:30 pm-midnight; Fri to 1 am; Sat noon-1 am; Sun 4:30-11 pm; entertainment Sat. Room service. Health club privileges. Sauna. Indoor pool, whirlpool, poolside service. Airport transportation. Cr cds: A, C, D, DS, JCB, MC, V.

D ⌘ ⊠ SC

★ ★ **RAMADA INN.** *1 Bigelow Sq (15219). Phone 412/281-5800; toll-free 800/225-5858; fax 412/281-4208. www.ramada.com.* 308 kitchen suites, 20 story. S, D $99-$189; under 16 free; package plans. Crib free. Complimentary continental breakfast. Check-out noon. TV; cable, VCR available. In-room modem link. Coin laundry. Restaurant 6:30-1 am; weekends 7 am-midnight. Bar 11-1 am. Exercise room, sauna. Indoor pool. Beauty shop. Convention facilities. Cr cds: A, C, D, DS, JCB, MC, V.

D ⌘ 🏋 ⊠ SC

★ **RED ROOF INN.** *6404 Steubenville Pike (15205). Phone 412/787-7870; fax 412/787-8392. www.redroof.com.* 120 rooms, 2 story. S, D $45.99-$59.99; under 18 free. Crib free. Pet accepted, some restrictions. Check-out noon. TV; cable (premium). Business services. Cr cds: A, C, D, DS, MC, V.

D 🐾 ⊠

Hotels

★ ★ **FOUR POINTS BY SHERATON.** *1 Industry Ln (15275). Phone 724/695-0002; fax 724/695-7262. www.sheraton.com.* 140 rooms, 4 story. S $109; D $119; each additional $10; suites $109-$119; under 18 free; weekend, holiday rates. Crib free. TV; cable (premium). Pool; wading pool, lifeguard. Restaurant 6:30 am-2 pm, 5-10 pm. Bar 4 pm-midnight. Check-out noon. Meeting rooms. Business center. In-room modem link. Free airport transportation. Exercise equipment. Some refrigerators. Cr cds: A, C, D, DS, ER, JCB, MC, V.

D ⌘ 🏋 ⊠ SC 🏃

★ ★ ★ **HILTON PITTSBURGH.** *600 Commonwealth Pl (15222). Phone 412/391-4600; fax 412/594-5161. www.hilton.com.* 713 rooms, 24 story. S $154-$219; D $134-$254; each additional $20; suites $350-$1,500; studio rooms $109; under 12 free; weekend plans. Crib free. Pet accepted, some restrictions. Check-out noon. TV; cable (premium). In-room modem link. Minibars; some bathroom phones. Coffee in rooms. Restaurant 6:30 am-11:30 pm. Bar 11-2 am; entertainment. Exercise equipment. Garage; valet parking. Airport transportation. Meeting rooms. Business center. Concierge. Luxury level. Cr cds: A, C, D, DS, ER, JCB, MC, V.

D 🐾 🏋 ⊠ 🏃

★ ★ ★ **MARRIOTT PITTSBURGH CITY CENTER.** *112 Washington Pl (15219). Phone 412/471-4000. www.marriott.com.* 402 rooms, 11 story. S, D $195-$250; under 17 free. Crib available. Check-out noon, check-in 3 pm. TV; cable (premium). In-room modem link. Many refrigerators in suites. Restaurant 6:30 am-10 pm. Bar to midnight. Exercise equipment. Indoor pool. Meeting rooms. Business center. Concierge. Cr cds: A, C, D, DS, ER, JCB, MC, V.

⌘ 🏋 🏃

★ ★ ★ **OMNI WILLIAM PENN HOTEL.** *530 William Penn Pl (15219). Phone 412/281-7100; fax 412/553-5252. www.omnihotels.com.* 596 rooms, 24 story. S, D $204-$214; each additional $20; suites $400-$2,200; under 18 free; weekend rates. Crib free. Check-out noon. TV; cable (premium), VCR available. Restaurant 6:30 am-10 pm. Bar 11-2 am. Room service 24 hours. Health club privileges. Exercise equipment. Valet parking $19.50. Airport transportation. Business center. Convention facilities. Gift shop. Historic, landmark hotel. Cr cds: A, C, D, DS, JCB, MC, V.

D 🏋 ⊠ 🏃

★ ★ **RADISSON HOTEL PITTSBURGH GREEN TREE.** *101 Radisson Dr (15205). Phone 412/922-8400; toll-free 800/525-5902; fax 412/922-8981. www.radisson.com.* 467 rooms, 7 story. S, D $109-$129;

suites $150-$275; weekend rates; package plans. Crib free. Pet accepted. Check-out noon. TV; cable (premium), VCR available. In-room modem link. Many minibars. Valet services. Restaurant 6:30 am-midnight. Bar 11-2 am; entertainment. Health club privileges. Exercise equipment, sauna. Recreation room. 3 pools, 1 indoor, whirlpool, poolside service, lifeguard. Barber, beauty shop. Free airport transportation. Meeting rooms. Business services. Sundries. Gift shop. Luxury level. Cr cds: A, C, D, DS, ER, JCB, MC, V.

[D] [icons] [SC]

★ ★ ★ RENAISSANCE PITTSBURGH HOTEL.

107 6th St (15222). Phone 412/562-1200; fax 412/992-2010. www.renaissancehotels.com. 300 rooms, 14 story. Check-out 1 pm, check-in 4 pm. TV; cable (premium). In-room modem link. Restaurant, bar. Exercise equipment. Indoor whirlpool. Business center. Concierge. Cr cds: A, D, DS, MC, V. **$$**

[icons]

★ ★ ★ SHERATON STATION SQUARE HOTEL.

7 Station Square Dr (15219). Phone 412/261-2000; toll-free 800/255-7488; fax 412/261-2932. www.sheraton.com. 292 rooms, 15 story. S $149-$170; D $149-$185; each additional $15; suites $225-$600; under 18 free; weekend rates. Crib free. TV; cable (premium), VCR available. Indoor pool; whirlpool, lifeguard. Coffee in rooms. Restaurant 6 am-midnight. Bar 11-2 am; entertainment. Check-out noon. Meeting rooms. Business center. In-room modem link. Shopping arcade. Train station, bus depot transportation. Exercise equipment. Health club privileges. On riverfront. Luxury level. Cr cds: A, C, D, DS, ER, JCB, MC, V.

[D] [icons] [SC] [icon]

★ ★ ★ THE WESTIN CONVENTION CENTER PITTSBURGH.

1000 Penn Ave (15222). Phone 412/281-3700; fax 412/227-4500. www.westin.com. 616 rooms, 26 story. Pet accepted. Check-out noon, check-in 3 pm. TV; cable (premium). In-room modem link. Room service 24 hours. Restaurant, bar. Babysitting services available. In-house fitness room, spa, sauna, steam room. Indoor pool, whirlpool. Business center. Concierge. Cr cds: A, C, D, DS, ER, JCB, MC, V. **$**

[D] [icons] [SC] [icon]

B&B/Small Inns

★ ★ ★ APPLETREE BED AND BREAKFAST.

703 S Negley Ave (15232). Phone 412/661-0631; fax 412/661-7525. www.appletreeb-b.com. 8 rooms, 3 story. MAP: S, D $140-$190; each additional $15; suite $190; weekend plans; holidays (2-3-day minimum). Children over 12 years only. Complimentary full breakfast. Check-out 11 am, check-in 3-6 pm. TV; VCR available. In-room modem

link. Fireplaces. Health club privileges. Business services. Concierge service. Historic building (1884). Totally nonsmoking. Cr cds: A, DS, MC, V.

[icon] [SC]

★ ★ ★ INN AT OAKMONT.

300 Rte 909 (15139). Phone 412/828-0410; fax 412/828-1358. www.pittsburghbnb.com. 8 rooms, 1 with shower only, 2 story. S $105; D $135-$155; each additional $10. Complimentary full breakfast. Coffee in library. Check-out 11 am, check-in 2 pm. TV; VCR available. Balconies. Restaurant nearby. Exercise equipment. Business services. Concierge service. Totally nonsmoking. Cr cds: A, DS, MC, V.

[D] [icons]

★ ★ ★ PRIORY INN.

614 Pressley St (15212). Phone 412/231-3338; fax 412/231-4838. www.thepriory.com. 24 rooms, 3 story. S, D $112; each additional $12; suites $134-$155; lower rates weekends. Complimentary continental breakfast. Check-out 11 am, weekends noon, check-in 3 pm. TV; cable. Meeting rooms. Business services. European-style inn with fountain and floral arrangements in courtyard. Previously a haven for Benedictine monks (1888). Cr cds: A, C, D, DS, MC, V.

[D] [icon] [SC]

★ ★ ★ SHADYSIDE BED AND BREAKFAST.

5516 Maple Heights Rd (15232). Phone 412/683-6501; fax 412/683-7228. www.bnb.lm.com. 8 rooms, 2 share bath, 3 story. No elevator. MAP: S, D $115-$140. TV in sitting room; cable (premium), VCR, (movies). Complimentary continental breakfast. Restaurant nearby. Check-out noon, check-in 3 pm. Concierge service. Luggage handling. Health club privileges. Microwaves available. Billiard room, library. Cr cds: A, D, DS, MC, V.

[icon]

Restaurants

★ ★ 1902 LANDMARK TAVERN.

24 Market Sq (15222). Phone 412/471-1902. American menu. Specializes in steaks, fresh seafood, pasta. Hours: 11:30 am-11 pm; Fri, Sat to 11 pm. Closed Sun; holidays. Lunch $7.95, dinner $18.95. Bar to 2 am. Restored tavern (1902); ornate tin ceiling, original tiles. Reservations accepted. Cr cds: A, D, DS, MC, V.

[D]

★ ★ ★ CAFE ALLEGRO.

51 S 12th St (15203). Phone 412/481-7788; fax 412/481-4520. www.cafeallegropittsburgh.com. The romantic ambience of the several intimate dining areas draws crowds to this South Side Mediterranean restaurant. Try uncomplicated dishes like fish cooked en papillote and pastas. Italian menu. Hours: 5-10 pm; Fri, Sat to 11 pm. Closed major holidays. Dinner $18-$26. Bar. Valet parking available. Cr cds: A, D, MC, V.

[D]

★ ★ **CAFE AT THE FRICK.** *7227 Reynolds St (15208). Phone 412/371-0600; fax 412/371-6030. www.frickart.org.* Hours: 11 am-5 pm; Sun noon-6 pm; high tea from 3 pm. Closed Mon; most major holidays. Lunch $7.95-$10, dinner. Outdoor seating. Totally nonsmoking. Cr cds: A, D, DS, MC, V.

D

★ ★ ★ **CARLTON.** *500 Grant St (15219). Phone 412/391-4099; fax 412/391-4240. www.thecarltonrestaurant.com.* Hours: 11:30 am-2:30 pm, 5-10 pm; Fri to 11 pm; Sat 5-11 pm. Closed Sun; major holidays. Reservations accepted. Continental menu. Bar. Wine list. Lunch $10.95-$15.95, dinner $19.95-$32.95. Children's menu. Specializes in charcoal-grilled seafood, prime steak, veal. Own pastries. Parking. Cr cds: A, D, DS, MC, V.

D

★ ★ ★ **CASBAH.** *229 S Highland Ave (15206). Phone 412/661-5656; fax 412/661-0616. www.bigburrito.com.* Mediterranean menu. Closed most major holidays. Lunch, dinner. Bar. Casual attire. Outdoor seating. Cr cds: A, D, DS, MC, V. **$**

D

★ ★ **CHEESE CELLAR CAFE & BAR.** *25 Station Sq (15219). Phone 412/471-3355; fax 412/281-0549.* Hours: 11 am-11 pm; Fri, Sat to midnight; Sun 10 am-10 pm. Closed Thanksgiving, Dec 25. Reservations accepted Sun-Thurs. Continental menu. Bar to 2 am. Sun breakfast $5.95-$6.50; lunch $6.95-$10.95, dinner $12.95-$18.95. Children's menu. Specializes in cheese and chocolate fondue. Outdoor seating. Rustic décor. Cr cds: A, D, DS, MC, V.

D

★ ★ **CHINA PALACE.** *5440 Walnut St (15232). Phone 412/687-7423; fax 412/687-5555.* Chinese menu. Closed July 4, Labor Day, Thanksgiving. Lunch, dinner. Bar. Casual attire. Cr cds: A, D, DS, MC, V. **$$**

D

★ ★ **THE CHURCH BREW WORKS.** *3525 Liberty Ave (15201). Phone 412/688-8200; fax 412/688-8201. www.churchbrew.com.* Regional American menu. Specializes in buffalo steak, wood-fired oven pizza, Pittsburgh pierogie. Closed Thanksgiving, Dec 25. Dinner $7-$25. Bar. Brewery. Brew-pub in 1902 church; vaulted ceiling, stained-glass windows. Outdoor seating. Cr cds: A, D, DS, MC, V.

D

★ ★ ★ **CLIFFSIDE.** *1208 Grandview Ave (15211). Phone 412/431-6996.* Hours: 5-9:30 pm; Fri, Sat to 11 pm. Closed major holidays. Reservations accepted. Continental menu. Bar. Dinner $18-$25. Specializes in fresh seafood, chicken, veal. Pianist. Valet parking. Contemporary décor in older building (1897). Cr cds: A, D, DS, MC, V.

★ ★ ★ **COMMON PLEA.** *308 Ross St (15219). Phone 412/281-5140; fax 412/281-6856. www.commonplea.citysearch.com.* With its dark paneling, glass wall, and subdued lighting, this restaurant caters to the legal crowd. Seafood menu. Closed major holidays. Lunch $10, dinner $20. Valet parking (dinner). Bar. Reservations accepted. Cr cds: A, D, MC, V.

★ ★ ★ **D'IMPERIO'S.** *3412 William Penn Hwy (15235). Phone 412/823-4800; fax 412/823-4804.* Reserve ahead for Friday night al fresco dining in summer. Otherwise, go for traditional Italian favorites accompanied by opera and Italian crooners. American, Italian menu. Hours: 11:30 am-3 pm, 5-10 pm; Mon, Sat from 5 pm. Closed Sun; most major holidays. Lunch, dinner $13-$38. Bar. Children's menu. Cr cds: A, D, DS, MC, V.

D

★ **DAVE AND ANDY'S ICE CREAM PARLOR.** *207 Atwood St (15213). Phone 412/681-9906.* Hours: 11:30 am-10 pm; Sat, Sun from noon. Closed holidays. 1930s look; some counters. **$**

D

★ ★ **GEORGETOWN INN.** *1230 Grandview Ave (15211). Phone 412/481-4424.* Hours: 11 am-3 pm, 5 pm-midnight; Fri, Sat to 1 am; Sun 4-10 pm. Closed most holidays. Reservations accepted. Bar. Lunch $7-$8, dinner $18-$31.95. Specializes in steak, fresh seafood. Panoramic view of city. Cr cds: A, D, DS, MC, V.

D

★ ★ ★ **GRAND CONCOURSE.** *1 Station Sq (15219). Phone 412/261-1717; fax 412/261-6041. www.muer.com.* Continental menu. Hours: 11:30 am-2:30 pm, 4:30-10 pm; Sat 4:30-11 pm; Sun 4:30-9 pm; early-bird dinner 4:30-6 pm; Sun brunch 10 am-2:30 pm. Closed Dec 25. Lunch $7-$20, dinner $25-$30, Sun brunch $18.95. Bar. Children's menu. Converted railroad station. Outdoor seating. Cr cds: A, D, DS, MC, V.

D SC

★ ★ **INDIA GARDEN.** *328 Atwood St (15213). Phone 412/682-3000; fax 412/682-3130. www.indiagarden.net.* Indian menu. Buffet $8.95. Lunch $8.95. Dinner. Reservations accepted. Indian décor, chairs. Cr cds: A, D, DS, MC, V.

D

★ ★ **KAYA.** *2000 Smallman St (15222). Phone 412/261-6565; fax 412/261-1526. www.bigburrito.com.* Closed some major holidays. Dinner $18-$34. Bar. Outdoor seating. Carribean menu. Cr cds: A, D, DS, MC, V.

D

★ ★ **LE MONT.** *1114 Grandview Ave (15211). Phone 412/431-3100; fax 412/431-1204. www.lemontpittsburgh.com.* Hours: 5-11:30 pm; Sun 4-10 pm. Closed major holidays. Reservations accepted. Contemporary American menu. Bar to midnight. Wine list. A la carte entrées: dinner $27-$50. Specializes in variety of wild game dishes, flaming desserts. Own baking. Pianist Fri, Sat. Valet parking. Atop Mount Washington; panoramic view of city. Cr cds: A, D, DS, MC, V.

[D]

★ ★ ★ **LE POMMIER.** *2104 E Carson St (15203). Phone 412/431-1901. www.lepommier.com.* French menu. Closed Sun; some major holidays. Lunch, dinner. Bar. Located in oldest storefront in area (1863). Valet parking Fri, Sat. Outdoor seating in season. Cr cds: A, D, DS, MC, V. **$**

[D]

★ ★ **MAX'S ALLEGHENY TAVERN.** *537 Suismon St (15212). Phone 412/231-1899; fax 412/231-5099. www. maxsalleghenytavern.com.* Hours: 11 am-midnight; Sun to 10 pm. Closed most major holidays. German menu. Bar. A la carte entrées: lunch $4.25-$7.95, dinner $5.95-$13.95. Specializes in jagerschnitzel, kase spatzle, sauerbraten. Tavern with German memorabilia and collection of photographs. Cr cds: A, D, DS, MC, V.

[D]

★ ★ **MONTEREY BAY FISH GROTTO.** *1411 Grandview Ave (15211). Phone 412/481-4414; fax 412/481-4448. www.montereybayfishgrotto.com.* Menu changes daily. Lunch, dinner. Entertainment. Children's menu. Cr cds: A, D, DS, MC, V. **$$**

[D]

★ ★ **PASTA PIATTO.** *736 Bellefonte St (15232). Phone 412/621-5547; fax 412/621-2164.* Northern Italian menu. Closed major holidays. Lunch, dinner. Bar. Children's menu. **$**

★ ★ **PENN BREWERY.** *800 Vinial St, Troy Hill (15212). Phone 412/237-9402; fax 412/237-9406. www.pennbrew.com.* German menu. Hours: 11 am-midnight; Fri, Sat to 1 am. Closed Sun; holidays. Lunch $5-$12, dinner $8-$15. Bar. Entertainment Tues-Sat. Children's menu. Restored 19th-century brewery, German beer hall-style communal dining. Outdoor seating. Cr cds: A, DS, MC, V.

[D]

★ ★ ★ **PICCOLO MONDO.** *661 Andersen Dr (15220). Phone 412/922-0920; fax 412/922-0921. www.piccolo-mondo.com.* Hours: 11:30 am-10 pm; Sat to 4-11 pm. Closed Sun except Mother's Day; some holidays. Reservations accepted. Northern Italian menu. Bar. Wine list. Lunch $7.50-$13, dinner $14-$24. Children's menu. Specializes in fresh fish, veal. Own desserts. Parking. Jacket. Cr cds: A, D, DS, MC, V.

[D]

★ ★ ★ **POLI.** *2607 Murray Ave (15217). Phone 412/521-6400. www.polisince1921.com.* The Poli family has been operating this Italian seafood restaurant for three generations, and pride themselves on serving the freshest fish possible. Seafood, Italian menu. Closed Mon; Thanksgiving, Dec 25. Lunch, dinner. Bar. Children's menu. Casual attire. Valet parking available. Cr cds: A, D, DS, MC, V. **$$**

[D]

★ **PRIMANTI BROTHERS.** *46 18th St (15222). Phone 412/263-2142. www.primantibros.com.* American, deli, Italian menu. Closed some major holidays. Dinner $4.50-$4.75. Cr cds: A, MC, V.

★ ★ ★ **RICO'S.** *1 Rico Ln (15237). Phone 412/931-1989; fax 412/931-2293. www.ricosrestaurant.com.* Italian, American menu. Specializes in fresh seafood, veal. Hours: 11:45 am-2:45 pm, 4-10:30 pm; Fri, Sat 4-11:30 pm. Closed Sun; holidays. Lunch $8.50-$13.50, dinner $16.50-$32. Bar to midnight. Wine cellar. Jacket. Valet parking. Old World atmosphere; Italian lithographs. Cr cds: A, D, DS, MC, V.

[D]

★ ★ **SEVENTH STREET GRILLE.** *130 7th St (15222). Phone 412/338-0303; fax 412/281-0577. www. seventhstreetgrille.com.* Hours: 11:30 am-9 pm; Fri, Sat to 11 pm; Sun to 8 pm. Closed most major holidays. Reservations accepted. Continental menu. Bar. Lunch $8-$10, dinner $16-$18. Specializes in grilled seafood, prime rib. Cr cds: A, D, DS, MC, V.

[D]

★ ★ ★ **SOBA.** *5847 Ellsworth Ave (15232). Phone 412/362-5656; fax 412/361-4318. www.bigburrito.com.* Pan-Asian menu. Dinner. Bar. Reservations accepted. Outdoor seating. Cr cds: A, D, DS, MC, V. **$$**

[D]

★ ★ ★ **STEELHEAD GRILL.** *112 Washington Pl (15219). Phone 412/394-3474; fax 412/394-1017. www.steelhead-grill.com.* Menu changes seasonally. Hours: 6:30 am-2 pm, 5-10 pm; Sat, Sun 6:30 am-2 pm, 5-11 pm. Reservations accepted. Wine list. Lunch $5-$11; dinner $15-$31. Children's menu. Entertainment. Cr cds: A, C, D, DS, ER, JCB, MC, V.

[D] [SC]

★ ★ **SUSHI TWO.** *2122 E Carson St (15203). Phone 412/431-7874; fax 412/431-7864. www.sushi2-too.com.* Japanese menu. Closed Thanksgiving. Lunch $5.95-$11.50, dinner $10.95-$40.95. Bar. Reservations accepted. Contemporary Japanese décor. Cr cds: A, D, DS, MC, V.

[D]

★ ★ ★ **TAMBELLINI.** *860 Saw Mill Run Blvd (15226). Phone 412/481-1118; fax 412/481-7565. www.tambellini.com.* Guests should come hungry when visiting Louis Tambellini's place just outside of Pittsburgh. Prime steaks, veal chops, pastas, and seafood dishes await the anxious diner; vegetarian dishes are also available. Continental menu. Hours: 11:30 am-10 pm. Closed Sun; Jan 1, Thanksgiving, Dec 25. Lunch $7.95-$9.50, dinner $14.50-$18.95. Bar. Children's menu. Valet parking (dinner). Cr cds: A, D, DS, MC, V.

D

★ ★ **TESSARO'S.** *4601 Liberty Ave (15224). Phone 412/682-6809.* American, Mexican, seafood menu. Hours: 11 am-midnight. Closed Sun; holidays. Lunch $6-$8, dinner $12-$25. Bar. Casual décor has pressed tin ceiling (circa early 1900s), paddle ceiling fans, fireplaces. Cr cds: A, C, D, DS, MC, V.

D

★ ★ **THAI PLACE.** *5528 Walnut St (15232). Phone 412/687-8586; fax 412/687-7970.* Thai menu. Lunch, dinner. Bar. Casual attire. Cr cds: A, D, DS, MC, V. **$$**

D

★ ★ ★ **TIN ANGEL.** *1200 Grandview Ave (15211). Phone 412/381-1919; fax 412/381-6270. www.tinangel.com.* Located in a prime spot on Grandview Avenue, Tin Angel boasts wonderful views of downtown Pittsburgh in a candlelit setting. Hours: 5-10 pm. Closed Sun; holidays. Reservations accepted. Bar. Wine list. Complete meals: $36-$59. Specializes in steak and seafood. Cr cds: A, D, DS, MC, V.

Pittsburgh International Airport Area

See also Pittsburgh

Services and Information

Information. 412/472-3525 or 412/472-3526.

Lost and Found. 412/472-3500.

Weather. 412/936-1212.

Cash Machines. Landside Terminal, entrance; Airside Terminal, throughout concourses in Passenger Service Centers.

Airlines. American, British Airways, Continental, Delta, Northwest, United, USAir.

Motels/Motor Lodges

★ **AIRPORT PLAZA HOTEL.** *1500 Beers School Rd, Coraopolis (15108). Phone 412/264-7900; fax 412/262-3229. www.plazaairport.com.* 193 rooms, 2 story. S, D $59; under 18 free. Pet accepted; $50 refundable. Complimentary deluxe continental breakfast. Check-out noon. TV; cable (premium). In-room modem link. Exercise equipment. Whirlpools. Free airport transportation. Cr cds: A, C, D, DS, MC, V.

★ **HAMPTON INN.** *1420 Beers School Rd, Coraopolis (15108). Phone 412/264-0020; toll-free 800/426-7866; fax 412/264-3220. www.hamptoninn.com.* 129 rooms, 5 story. S, D $79-$99; under 18 free. Crib free. Pet accepted. Complimentary continental breakfast. Check-out noon. TV; cable (premium). Valet services. Health club privileges. Free airport transportation. Meeting rooms. Business services. Cr cds: A, C, D, DS, ER, MC, V.

★ **LA QUINTA INN.** *1433 Beers School Rd, Coraopolis (15108). Phone 412/269-0400; toll-free 800/687-6667; fax 412/269-9258. www.laquinta.com.* 127 rooms, 3 story. S $84.99; D $94.99; suites $94.99-$104.99; under 18 free. Crib free. Pet accepted. Complimentary continental breakfast. Check-out noon. TV; cable. In-room modem link. Valet services, coin laundry. Free airport transportation. Business services. Sundries. Cr cds: A, C, D, DS, MC, V.

★ **RED ROOF INN.** *1454 Beers School Rd, Coraopolis (15108). Phone 412/264-5678; fax 412/264-8034. www.redroof.com.* 119 rooms, 3 story. S $49.99-$59.99; D $54-$64; each additional $6; under 18 free. Crib free. Pet accepted. TV; cable (premium). Check-out noon. Coin laundry. Meeting room. Business services available. Valet service. Free airport transportation. Cr cds: A, C, D, DS, MC, V.

Hotels

★ ★ **CROWNE PLAZA.** *1160 Thorn Run Rd, Coraopolis (15108). Phone 412/262-2400; fax 412/264-9373. www.crowneplaza.com.* 193 rooms, 9 story. S $69-$129; D $69-$139; each additional $10; suites $109-$150; under 18 free; weekend rates. Crib free. Check-out noon. TV; cable (premium). In-room modem link. Restaurant 6:30 am-1:30 pm, 5-10 pm; Sat, Sun 7 am-11 pm. Bar 11-2 am; entertainment weekends. Exercise equipment. Pool, lifeguard. Airport transportation. Meeting rooms. Business center. Concierge. Luxury Level. Cr cds: A, C, D, DS, JCB, MC, V.

★ ★ ★ **HYATT REGENCY PITTSBURGH INTERNATIONAL AIRPORT.** *1111 Airport Blvd (15231).* *Phone 724/899-1234. www.hyatt.com.* 336 rooms, 11 story. S, D $79-$179; under 17 free. Crib available. Check-out noon, check-in 3 pm. TV; cable (premium). In-room modem link. Minibars; many refrigerators in suites. Restaurant 6:30 am-10 pm. Bar to midnight. Exercise equipment. Indoor pool. Meeting rooms. Business center. Concierge. Cr cds: A, C, D, DS, JCB, MC, V.

Restaurant

★ ★ ★ **HYEHOLDE.** *190 Hyeholde Dr, Moontownship (15108). Phone 412/264-3116; fax 412/264-5723. www.hyeholde.com.* Don a jacket and tie for this longstanding outpost of English-country elegance 20 minutes from downtown Pittsburgh. The game and seafood menu and manor-like setting of rich tapestries, exposed wood beams, and candlelight are a popular choice for special events. Continental menu. Hours: 11:30 am-2 pm, 5-10 pm; Sat from 5 pm. Closed Sun; major holidays. Lunch $9.50-$13, dinner $19.50-$36. Valet parking available. Patio dining. Herb garden. Cr cds: A, C, D, DS, MC, V.

Pocono Mountains

See also Bushkill, Canadensis, Hawley, Mildord, Mount Pocono, Shawnee on Delaware

(Northeast Pennsylvania resort area)

Information Pocono Mountains Vacation Bureau, 1004 Main St, Stroudsburg 18360; 717/424-6050; for free brochures phone 800/POCONOS

Web www.poconos.org

The Pocono Mountains area in northeast Pennsylvania extends north from Wind Gap and Delaware Water Gap into Pike, Carbon, Monroe, and Wayne counties. Within its 2,400 square miles almost every form of recreation can be found.

This scenic country with 500 lakes, including Lake Wallenpaupack (see HAWLEY), has hundreds of accommodations and is a well-established resort area. Visitors, many of whom return year after year, take advantage of the large plush resorts, smaller family-run resorts, housekeeping cottage resorts, camping resorts, country inns, and bed and breakfasts. There is primitive, forested country for those who wish to rough it. For the hunter, there are deer, bear, wildcat, and fox. For the freshwater angler, there are black bass, trout, pickerel, and walleye.

Summer offers boating, swimming, hiking, horseback riding, mountain biking, golf, theaters, and a host of other diversions. In the autumn, there is a magnificent display of foliage, as well as heritage festivals and country fairs. The first snowfall brings skiing, snowboarding, snow tubing, ice skating, sleigh rides, tobogganing, and snowmobiling.

The name "Pocono" was probably taken from the Native American *pocohanne,* meaning a stream between the mountains. Settled in the mid-1700s, the Poconos yielded iron and, later, coal. The lakes and forest still retain their charm. The land "between the mountains" is as inviting as it always has been.

Port Allegany (B-6)

See also Bradford

Settled 1816 **Pop** 2,355 **Elev** 1,481 ft **Area code** 814 **Zip** 16743

Information Chamber of Commerce, 22 Church St; 814/642-2181

Native Americans called this spot "canoe place" because here on the portage route between the Allegheny and Susquehanna headwaters they paused to build canoes. Early settlers followed their route. Soon after the town was established, lumbering operations reached their peak; later industrial expansion included coal mining and tanning. In the late 1890s, the borough became the center of a boom resulting from the discovery of natural gas and glass sand.

What to See and Do

Eldred World War II Museum. *201 Main St (16731). 15 miles N on PA 155, 5 miles N on PA 446, in Eldred. Phone 814/225-2220.* Exhibits include battle maps, posters, dioramas with narrative, periscope, video history. Centerpiece is "Remembering the Women Behind the Front Lines" exhibit. Library. (Tues, Thurs, Sat, Sun) **FREE**

Sizerville State Park. *19 miles S on PA 155, in Sizerville. Phone 814/486-5605.* Approximately 385 acres. Swimming pool; fishing, hunting; cross-country skiing, snowmobiling. Picnicking, playground, snack bar. Tent and trailer sites. Standard fees.

Motel/Motor Lodge

★ **MIDTOWN MOTEL.** *111 N Main St (16743). Phone 814/642-2575.* 25 rooms, 2 story. S $40-$49; D $44-$54; each additional $5. Crib $5. TV; cable (premium). Restaurant opposite 6 am-11 pm. Check-out 11 am. Cr cds: A, D, DS, MC, V.

Pottstown (G-12)

See also Limerick, Norristown, Reading

Settled 1701 **Pop** 21,859 **Elev** 160 ft **Area code** 610 **Zip** 19464

Information TriCounty Area Chamber of Commerce, 135 High St; 610/326-2900

Web www.tricopa.com

An iron forge operating in 1714 at Manatawny Creek, about 3 miles north of Pottstown, was the first industrial establishment in the state. The borough was established by John Potts, an ironmaster, on land William Penn had earlier deeded to his son, John. Today, the community is the commercial and cultural hub for an area with a population of 130,000. Nearly 200 modern industries are located here.

What to See and Do

Boyertown Museum of Historic Vehicles. *85 S Walnut St (19512). 7 miles N via PA 100, 73, in Boyertown, on Walnut St. Phone 610/367-2090.* Collection of over 100 antique autos, trucks, sleighs, buggies, and bicycles. Also includes the Hill, which was among the first gasoline-powered cars. (Tues-Sun) **$$**

French Creek State Park. *843 Park Rd (19520). 9 miles W on PA 724, then 4 miles S on PA 345. Phone 610/582-9680.* Approximately 7,330 acres, two lakes. Boating (rentals, mooring, launching), fishing. Swimming pool. Hiking trails. Playground, disc golf. Ice fishing. Picnicking. Tent and trailer sites, cabins. Standard fees. Also here is

Hopewell Furnace National Historic Site. (see)

Merritt's Museum of Childhood. *907 Ben Franklin Hwy W. 1 mile W on US 422, in Douglassville. Phone 610/385-3408.* Antique toys, costumed figures, furnishings; gift shop in lobby. (Mon, Wed-Sun; closed holidays) **$$** Admission includes

Mary Merritt Doll Museum. *843 Ben Franklin Hwy W (19518). Phone 610/385-3809.* Antique dolls and toys dating from 1725 to 1900. (Mon, Wed-Sun; closed holidays)

Pottsgrove Manor. *W King St and PA 100. Phone 610/326-4014.* (1752) Newly restored house of John Potts, 18th-century ironmaster and founder of Pottstown; outstanding example of early Georgian architecture and furniture. Includes recently discovered slave quarters and Potts's office. Slide orientation. Museum shop. (Tues-Sun; closed holidays) **FREE**

Ringing Rocks Park. *1500 Ringing Rocks Park (19464). 3 miles N off PA 663. Phone 610/323-6560.* Roller skating (Fri-Sun; fee); nature trails, picnicking, interesting rock formations. (Daily) **FREE**

Special Event

Duryea Day Antique & Classic Auto Show. *28 Warwick St. Boyertown Community Park.* Antique autos, trucks, and other vehicles; displays, arts and crafts, flea market with automotive memorabilia, activities, Pennsylvania Dutch food. Labor Day weekend.

Motels/Motor Lodges

★ **COMFORT INN.** *Rte 100 and Shoemaker Rd (19464). Phone 610/326-5000; toll-free 800/879-2477; fax 610/970-7230. www.pottstownpacomfortinn.com.* 121 rooms, 4 story. S, D $79-$109; each additional $7; under 18 free; golf plans; weekend rates. Crib free. Pet accepted. TV; cable (premium). Heated pool; lifeguard. Complimentary continental breakfast. Restaurant adjacent 6 am-11 pm. Room service. Check-out noon. Coin laundry. Meeting rooms. Business services available. In-room modem link. Free bus depot transportation. Health club privileges. Refrigerators, microwaves available. Cr cds: A, C, D, DS, ER, JCB, MC, V.

D 🐾 🏊 ✈ 🚭 SC

★ **HOLIDAY INN EXPRESS.** *1600 Industrial Hwy (19464). Phone 610/327-3300; toll-free 800/386-0031; fax 610/327-9447. www.hiexpottstownpa.com.* 120 rooms, 4 story. S, D $69; each additional $5; suites $122; under 19 free; weekly, holiday rates; higher rates special events. Crib free. Pet accepted. Complimentary continental breakfast. Check-out noon. TV; cable (premium), VCR available (movies). In-room modem link. Refrigerators, microwaves available. Valet services. Room service. Health club privileges. Pool. Meeting rooms. Business services. Sundries. Cr cds: A, D, DS, JCB, MC, V.

D 🐾 🏊 🚭

B&B/Small Inn

★ ★ ★ **TWIN TURRETS INN.** *11 E Philadelphia Ave (19512). Phone 610/367-4513; toll-free 877/877-7897; fax 610/369-7898. www.twinturrets.com.* 10 rooms, 3 story. Children over 12 years preferred. Complimentary full breakfast. Check-out 11 am, check-in 1 pm. TV; cable (premium), VCR available. Health club privileges. Business center. Original Boyer mansion built in 1850; antiques and original art. Totally nonsmoking. Cr cds: A, D, DS, MC, V. **$**

🚭 SC 🏋

Restaurants

★ ★ ★ **COVENTRY FORGE INN.** *3360 Coventryville Rd (19465). Phone 610/469-6222; fax 610/469-1909.* The region's first French restaurant is still its best. Housed in one of the oldest homes in the country, this dining establishment is a bit tricky to find, but worth the drive. Hours:

5:30-9 pm; Sat 5-10 pm. Reservations accepted. Closed Mon, Sun except Mother's Day; Jan 1, Dec 25. French menu. Bar. Wine cellar. A la carte entrées: dinner $16.95-$25.95. Prix fixe: (Sat) dinner $39.50. Own baking. Built in 1717; antiques. Cr cds: A, DS, MC, V.

★ ★ ★ **GRACIE'S 21ST CENTURY CAFE.** *Mana Tawny Rd (19548). Phone 610/323-4004. www.gracies 21stcentury.com.* Contemporary American menu. Hours: 5:30-10:30 pm. Closed Thanksgiving, Dec 25, July 4. A la carte entrées: dinner $25-$35. Bar from 5:30 pm. Reservations required Sat (dinner). Valet parking. Outdoor seating. Ultramodern facility. Cr cds: A, MC, V.

Ⓓ

Quakertown (Bucks County) (G-13)

See also Allentown, Bethlehem, Doylestown (Bucks County), Pottstown

Founded 1715 **Pop** 8,931 **Elev** 500 ft **Area code** 215 **Zip** 18951

Information Upper Bucks County Chamber of Commerce, 2170 Portzer Rd; 215/536-3211 or Bucks County Conference and Visitors Bureau, 152 Swamp Rd, Doylestown 18901, phone 215/345-4552 or 800/836-2825

Web www.ubcc.org

Once a station on the Underground Railroad, Quakertown today still retains some of its colonial appearance. In 1798, angered by what they considered an unfair federal tax and incited by one John Fries, Quakertown housewives started greeting tax assessors with pans of hot water. The "hot water" rebellion cooled down when federal troops arrived, but the town switched political parties (from Federalist to Jeffersonian) almost en masse.

What to See and Do

Mennonite Heritage Center. *565 Yoder Rd, 4 miles S of PA 309 on PA 113, in Harleysville. Phone 215/256-3020.* An interpretive video and exhibits including quilts, Pennsylvania German Fraktur, furniture, books, deeds, and clothing show the history of local Mennonites through three centuries. (Tues-Sun) **DONATION**

Restaurant

★ **LA PIAZZA CAFE.** *1408 W Broad St (18951). Phone 215/536-2452; fax 215/536-7538.* Hours: 11 am-11 pm. Closed most major holidays. Reservations required Fri, Sat (dinner). Italian menu. A la carte entrées: lunch $5.95, dinner $7.50-$12.95. Buffet: lunch $7.95, dinner $10.95.

Children's menu. Specializes in chicken, pizza, pasta. Parking. Cr cds: A, D, DS, MC, V.

Ⓓ

Reading (G-11)

See also Denver/Adamstown, Hamburg, Kutztown, Lancaster, Pottstown

Founded 1748 **Pop** 81,207 **Elev** 260 ft **Area code** 484 & 610

Information Reading & Berks County Visitors Bureau, 352 Penn St 19602; 610/375-4085 or 800/443-6610

Web www.readingberkspa.com

A city of railroads and industry famous for its superb pretzels, Reading (RED-ing) was the second community in the United States to vote a Socialist government into office; however, the city has not had such a government for many years. Love of music and the thrift and vigor of the "Dutch" are reflected in the character of this unofficial capital of Pennsylvania Dutch land.

William Penn purchased the land now occupied by Reading from the Lenni-Lenape Native Americans and settled his two sons, Thomas and Richard, on it. They named it Reading (fern meadow) for their home in England. During the Revolution, the citizens of Reading mustered troops for the Continental army, forged cannon, and provided a depot for military supplies and a prison for Hessians and British. The hundreds of skilled German craftspeople, plus canal and railroad transportation, ignited Reading's industrial development. Today, some of the world's leading industries continue to headquarter here.

What to See and Do

Berks County Heritage Center. *2201 Tulpehocken Rd (19610). 4 miles N via PA 183, then W onto Red Bridge Rd. Phone 610/374-8839 or 610/372-8939.* Historical interpretive complex. Here are the Gruber Wagon Works (1882), where finely crafted wagons were produced for farm and industry; Wertz's Red Bridge (1867), the longest single-span covered bridge in the state; Deppen Cemetery, with graves of Irish workers who died of "swamp fever" while building the Union Canal; C. Howard Hiester Canal Center, with its collection of canal artifacts. Tours of wagon works and canal center; orientation slide program. (May-Oct, Tues-Sun) **$$**

Conrad Weiser Homestead. *14 miles W via US 422. Phone 610/589-2934.* (1729) Restored and furnished house of colonial "ambassador" to the Iroquois nation; springhouse; gravesite; visitor center; picnicking in 26-acre park. (Wed-Sun) **$$**

Daniel Boone Homestead. *400 Daniel Boone Rd (19508). 7 miles E on US 422 to Baumstown, then N on Boone Rd. Phone 610/582-4900.* Birthplace of Daniel Boone in 1734. Approximately 570 acres; includes Boone House, barn, blacksmith shop, and sawmill. Picnicking. Nature trails. Youth camping. Visitor's center. (Tues-Sun; closed some holidays) **$$**

Historical Society of Berks County. *940 Centre Ave. Phone 610/375-4375.* Local history exhibits; decorative arts, antiques, transportation displays. (Tues-Sat; closed most holidays) **$$**

Koziar's Christmas Village. *782 Christmas Village Rd. 12 miles N via PA 183, in Bernville. Phone 610/488-1110.* Valley set aglow with over 500,000 Christmas lights; Wishing Well Lane; two barns filled with handmade items, decorations; theme exhibits, Santa's Post Office. (Thanksgiving-Dec) **$$$**

Mid-Atlantic Air Museum. *Reading Regional Airport, at PA 183 and Van Reed Rd. Phone 610/372-7333.* Aviation museum dedicated to the preservation of vintage aircraft; planes are restored to flying condition by volunteers. Collection of 40 airplanes and helicopters; 20 on public display, including Martin 4-0-4 airliners, B-25 bomber, and others. (Daily; closed Jan 1, Thanksgiving, Dec 25) **$$**

Outlet Shopping. *801 N 9th St (19604). Phone 610/375-4085 or 800/443-6610.* More than 300 factory outlet stores can be found at five different shopping complexes. Contact Visitors Bureau.

Reading Public Museum and Art Gallery. *500 Museum Rd. Phone 610/371-5850.* In 25-acre Museum Park with stream. Exhibits of art and science. (Tues-Sun; closed most major holidays) **$$** Adjacent is

> **Planetarium.** *500 Museum Rd (19611). Phone 610/371-5854.* Changing exhibits. Starand laser light shows. **$$**

Motels/Motor Lodges

★ ★ **BEST WESTERN DUTCH COLONY INN & SUITES.** *4635 Perkiomen Ave (19606). Phone 610/779-2345; toll-free 800/828-2830; fax 610/779-8348. www.bestwestern.com.* 71 rooms, 2 story. May-Nov: S $58-$83; D $63-$88; each additional $5; under 18 free; lower rates rest of year. Crib $5. Pet accepted, some restrictions; $5. Check-out noon. TV; cable. Balconies. Microwaves available. Valet services, coin laundry. Restaurant (see also ANTIQUE AIRPLANE). Bar 11-2 am. Room service. Health club privileges. Pool, lifeguard. Lawn games. Meeting rooms. Business services. Sundries. Cr cds: A, C, D, DS, MC, V.

D ⬛ ⬛ ⬛

★ **COMFORT INN.** *2200 Stacy Dr (19605). Phone 610/371-0500; toll-free 800/228-5150; fax 610/478-9421. www.comfortinn.com.* 60 rooms, 2 story. Apr-Oct: S $55-$70; D $55-$75; each additional $5; under 18 free;

weekly rates; higher rates: car shows, antique shows; lower rates rest of year. Crib free. TV; cable (premium), VCR. Complimentary continental breakfast. Restaurant nearby. Check-out 11 am. Meeting rooms. Business services available. In-room modem link. Valet service. Free airport transportation. Exercise equipment. Some refrigerators; microwaves available. Cr cds: A, C, D, DS, ER, JCB, MC, V.

D ⬛ ⬛ SC

★ **ECONO LODGE.** *635 Spring St (19610). Phone 610/378-5105; fax 610/373-3181. www.econolodge.com.* 84 rooms, 4 story. Mar-Nov: S, D $58-$85; each additional $5; under 18 free; higher rates: Keystone Nationals, Antique weekends; lower rates rest of year. Crib free. Pet accepted; $5/day. TV; cable (premium). Complimentary continental breakfast. Check-out 11 am. Business services available. Sundries. Coin laundry. Exercise equipment. Many refrigerators, microwaves. Cr cds: A, C, D, DS, JCB, MC, V.

D ⬛ ⬛ ⬛ SC

★ ★ **HOLIDAY INN.** *6170 Morgantown Rd (19543). Phone 610/286-3000; toll-free 800/339-0264; fax 610/286-1920. www.holiday-inn.com.* 191 rooms, 4 story. S $79-$99; D $89-$109; each additional $5; under 18 free. Crib $10. Pet accepted, some restrictions. TV; cable (premium). Indoor pool; whirlpool. Restaurant 6:30 am-2 pm, 5-10 pm; Sat, Sun from 5 pm. Room service. Bar 5 pm-1 am. Check-out noon. Meeting rooms. Business center. In-room modem link. Sundries. Exercise equipment. Some refrigerators. Cr cds: A, C, D, DS, JCB, MC, V.

D ⬛ ⬛ ⬛ ⬛ SC ⬛

★ ★ **INN AT READING.** *1040 N Park Rd (19610). Phone 610/372-7811; toll-free 800/383-9713; fax 610/372-4545. www.innatreading.com.* 250 rooms, 1-2 story. S, D $79-$129; suites $99-$129; each additional $10; under 18 free; some weekend rates. Crib free. TV; cable (premium). Pool; poolside service, lifeguard. Restaurant 6:30 am-10 pm. Room service. Bar 11-1 am; entertainment. Check-out 11 am. Meeting rooms. Business center. In-room modem link. Bellstaff. Valet service. Free airport, bus depot transportation. Exercise equipment. Refrigerators. Picnic tables. Cr cds: A, C, D, DS, MC, V.

D ⬛ ⬛ ⬛ SC ⬛

★ **RAMADA INN.** *2545 N 5th St (19605). Phone 610/929-4741; toll-free 888/929-9234; fax 610/929-5237. www.ramada.com.* 138 rooms, 2 story. S $55-$175; D $60-$175; each additional $10; under 18 free; some weekend rates. Crib free. Check-out noon. TV; cable (premium). In-room modem link. Refrigerators, microwaves. Valet services. Restaurant 6:30-10:30 am, 5-9 pm. Bar 5-11:30 pm. Room service. Pool. Meeting rooms. Business services. Sundries. Cr cds: A, C, D, DS, MC, V.

D ⬛ ⬛

Hotel

★ ★ **READING HOTEL.** *1741 W Papermill Rd (19610).* *Phone 610/376-3811; toll-free 800/325-3535; fax 610/375-7562.* 254 rooms, 5 story. S, D $79-$139; each additional $10; suites $185-$195; studio rooms $140-$150; under 18 free; some weekend rates. Crib free. Pet accepted; $50. TV; cable (premium), VCR available. Indoor pool; whirlpool, poolside service, lifeguard. Restaurant 6:30 am-10:30 pm. Room service. Bar 11:30-2 am; entertainment. Check-out noon. Meeting rooms. Business services available. In-room modem link. Bellstaff. Gift shop. Free airport, bus depot transportation. Putting green. Exercise equipment; sauna. Massage. Health club privileges. Some bathroom phones; microwaves available. Cr cds: A, C, D, DS, JCB, MC, V.

D 🐾 ⊠ 🏋 ⊠ SC

Restaurants

★ ★ **ALPENHOF BAVARIAN.** *903 Morgantown Rd (19607). Phone 610/373-1624; fax 610/373-8040. www.alphenhofonline.com.* American, German menu. Hours: 11:30 am-2 pm, 5-8:30 pm; Mon to 2 pm; Sat to 9 pm; Sun 11:30 am-7 pm. Closed Jan 1, Dec 25. Lunch $3.45-$6.95, dinner $11.95-$18.95. Bar. Reservations accepted. Outdoor seating. Cr cds: A, MC, V.

D

★ ★ **ANTIQUE AIRPLANE.** *4635 Perkiomen Ave (19606). Phone 610/779-2345; fax 610/779-8348.* Closed Jan 1, Dec 25. Breakfast, lunch, dinner. Bar. Children's menu. Casual elegance; aviation theme. Cr cds: A, D, DS, MC, V. **$**

★ ★ ★ **GREEN HILLS INN.** *2444 Morgantown Rd (19607). Phone 610/777-9611.* French American Menu. Hours: 5-9 pm. Closed Sun. A la carte entrées: dinner $17.50-$28.95. Reservations accepted. Cr cds: A, MC, V.

D

Scranton (D-12)

See also Carbondale, Pocono Mountains, Wilkes Barre

Settled 1771 **Pop** 76,415 **Elev** 754 ft **Area code** 570

Information Northeast Pennsylvania Convention and Visitors Bureau Montage Mountain Rd; 570/963-6363 or 800/22-WELCOME

Web www.visitnepa.org

The first settlers here found a Monsey Native American village on the site. In 1840, George and Seldon Scranton built five iron furnaces using the revolutionary method of firing with anthracite coal instead of charcoal. Manufacture of iron and steel remained an important industry until 1901,

when the mills moved to Lake Erie to ease transportation problems.

After WWII, Scranton thoroughly revamped its economy when faced with depletion of the anthracite coal mines, which for more than a century had fired its forges. Scranton's redevelopment drew nationwide attention and served as a model for problem cities elsewhere. Today, Scranton is the home of electronic and printing industries and is host to several major trucking firm terminals.

What to See and Do

Catlin House. *232 Monroe Ave. Phone 570/344-3841.* (1912) Headquarters of Lackawanna Historical Society; period furnishings (colonial-1900s), historic exhibits, antiques; research library (fee). Tours available (fee). (Tues-Fri, also Sat afternoons; closed holidays) **FREE**

Lackawanna County Stadium. *235 Montage Mountain Rd. Exit 51 off I-81. Phone 570/969-2255.* Open-air stadium/civic arena seats 11,000. Home of AAA baseball, high school and college football and marching band competitions. (Apr-Nov)

Montage Ski Area. *1000 Montage Mountain Rd. S on I-81, exit 51, follow signs. Phone 570/969-7669.* Quad, double, three triple chairlifts; school, rentals; snowmaking; bar, restaurant; lodge. Vertical drop 1,000 feet. Night skiing. More than 130 acres of trails set in 400 acres of mountainside. (Early Dec-late Mar, daily) Summer activities include water slides, batting cages, amphitheater (June-Labor Day). **$$$$**

Nay Aug Park. *Arthur Ave and Mulberry St. Phone 570/348-4186.* More than 35 acres with memorials to pioneer days. Picnicking; swimming pool (fee); walking trail; refreshment stands; and the "Pioneer," a gravity railroad car dating back to 1850; weekend concerts (summer). (Daily) In park is

Anthracite Heritage Museum. *Keyser Ave and Bald Mountain Rd (18504). McDade Park. Phone 570/963-4804.* History and culture of anthracite region. Other affiliated parts of the complex are the Iron Furnaces; Museum of Anthracite Mining (see ASHLAND), with emphasis on the technology of the industry, and the 19th-century miners' village of Eckley, near Hazleton (see). (Daily; closed some holidays) **$$**

Everhart Museum. *1901 Mulberry St (18510). Phone 570/346-7186.* Permanent collections includes 19th- and 20th-century American art; Dorflinger glass; Native American, Asian, and primitive art; natural history displays, including Dinosaur Hall. Gift shop. (Tues-Sun; closed holidays) **$$**

Lackawanna Coal Mine Tour. *McDade Park. Phone 570/963-MINE or 800/238-7245.* Underground coal mine 300 feet below ground shows world of anthracite miners. Conditions are authentic (damp, dark, slippery, and cold); dress appropriately. Above-ground facilities include a "shifting shanty" exhibit room with photo-mural graphic displays, mine artifacts, and video presentations; gift shop; restaurant. (Apr-Nov, daily; closed Thanksgiving) **$$$**

Scranton Iron Furnaces. *159 Cedar Ave. Phone 570/963-3208.* Partially restored site of four anthracite-fired iron furnaces built 1848-1857 and used until 1902. Visitor center, outdoor exhibits. Self-guided tours (Daily). Guided tours (late May-early Sept, Mon-Thurs). **FREE**

Steamtown National Historic Site. Site with large collection of steam locomotives and other memorabilia located in an authentic freight yard. Steam train ride through yard (Memorial Day-Dec; daily). 25-mile train excursion (July 4-mid-Oct, Sat and Sun).

Motels/Motor Lodges

★ ★ **CLARION HOTEL.** *300 Meadow Ave (18505). Phone 570/344-9811; toll-free 800/347-1551; fax 570/344-7799. www.clarioninn.com.* 125 rooms, 6 story. S $59-$69; D $69-$79; each additional $10; suites $135-$150; under 13 free; higher rates special events. Crib free. TV; cable (premium). Pool; lifeguard. Restaurant 6 am-10 pm. Room service. Bar 11-2 am; entertainment Tues-Sun. Check-out noon. Meeting rooms. Business services available. Valet service. Free airport, bus depot transportation. Cr cds: A, C, D, DS, JCB, MC, V.

D ⚫ 🏊 ⛖ **SC**

★ **DAYS INN.** *1226 O'Neill Hwy (18512). Phone 570/348-6101; toll-free 888/246-3297; fax 570/348-5064. www.daysinn.com.* 90 rooms, 4 story. S $59.99-$83.99; D $61.99-$99.99; suites $78.99-$99.99; under 17 free; weekend, holiday rates; higher rates Pocono NASCAR. Crib free. Pet accepted; $3. Complimentary continental breakfast. Check-out 11 am. TV; cable (premium), VCR available. Refrigerators. Valet services. Restaurant adjacent open 24 hours. Business services. Cr cds: A, C, D, DS, JCB, MC, V.

D ⚫ ⛖

★ **HAMPTON INN.** *22 Montage Mountain Rd (18507). Phone 570/342-7002; toll-free 800/426-7866; fax 570/342-7012. www.hamptoninn.com.* 129 rooms, 4 story. S $72-$82; D $77-$87; suites $90-$175; under 19 free; weekend rates; ski plans; higher rates: NASCAR, holidays. Crib free. TV; cable (premium). Indoor pool; whirlpool. Complimentary continental breakfast. Check-out noon. Meeting rooms. Business services available. Valet service. Sundries. Free airport, bus depot transportation. Downhill ski 2 miles. Exercise equipment. Picnic tables. Cr cds: A, C, D, DS, MC, V.

D ⚫ 🏊 🏋 ✈ ⛖ **SC**

★ ★ **HOLIDAY INN.** *200 Tigue St (18512). Phone 570/343-4771; fax 570/343-5171. www.holiday-inn.com.* 139 rooms, 2-3 story. S, D $79-$89; each additional $10; suites $145-$175; under 18 free; some weekend rates; ski plan. Crib free. Pet accepted. Check-out noon. TV; cable. In-room modem link. Valet services. Restaurant 6:30 am-10 pm. Bar noon-2 am. Room service. Pool. Meeting rooms. Business services. Cr cds: A, D, DS, JCB, MC, V.

D ⚫ 🏊 ⛖

★ ★ ★ **INN AT NICHOLS VILLAGE.** *1101 Northern Blvd (18411). Phone 570/587-1135; toll-free 800/642-2215; fax 570/586-7140. www.nicholsvillage.com.* This inn is made of four separate buildings surrounded by a courtyard garden. Both an indoor pool and a sauna are available for guests to enjoy along with two family restaurants and one fine dining room. 135 rooms, 4 story. S, D $98-$150; each additional $10; under 18 free. Crib free. TV; cable. Indoor pool; lifeguard. Restaurant 6 am-10 pm. Room service. Bar 5-11 pm. Check-out noon. Meeting rooms. Business services available. In-room modem link. Sundries. Free airport transportation. Exercise equipment; sauna. Recreation room. 12 acres include over 1,000 rhododendrons; forestland. Cr cds: A, C, D, DS, MC, V.

D 🏊 🏋 ⛖ **SC**

Hotel

★ ★ **RADISSON LACKAWANNA STATION HOTEL SCRANTON.** *700 Lackawanna Ave (18503). Phone 570/342-8300; toll-free 800/333-3333; fax 570/342-0380. www.radisson.com.* 145 rooms, 6 story. S $99; D $109; each additional $10; suites $119-$300; studio rooms $109; package plans. Crib free. TV; cable. Restaurant 7 am-10 pm. Bar 11-2 am. Check-out noon. Meeting rooms. Business services available. In-room modem link. Gift shop. Free airport, bus depot transportation. Downhill/cross-country ski 4 miles. Exercise equipment; sauna, steam room. Whirlpool. Some refrigerators, in-room whirlpools. Located in historic Lackawanna train station building. Cr cds: A, C, D, DS, ER, JCB, MC, V.

D 🏊 🏋 ⛖ **SC**

Resort

★ ★ **SHADOWBROOK RESORT.** *615 Rte 6 E (18657). Phone 570/836-2151; toll-free 800/955-0295; fax 570/836-5655. www.shadowbrookresort.com.* 73 rooms, 3 story. S $50-$85; D $60-$95; each additional $12; kitchen units $80-$90; under 12 free. Crib $8/day. Complimentary continental breakfast. Check-out noon, check-in 2 pm. TV; cable (premium). Balconies. Some refrigerators. Coin laundry 2 miles. Restaurant 6 am-10 pm. Bar

11-2 am; entertainment Wed, Fri-Sun. Room service 5-8 pm. Exercise room, sauna, steam room. Sports director. Game room. Pool, poolside service, lifeguard. Golf, 18-hole, pro. Picnic tables. Hiking. Meeting rooms. Business services. Gift shop. Cr cds: A, C, D, DS, MC, V.

Restaurant

★ **COOPER'S SEAFOOD HOUSE.** *701 N Washington Ave (18509). Phone 570/346-6883; fax 570/346-8049. www.coopers-seafood.com.* Hours: 11 am-midnight. Closed holidays. Complete meals: lunch $5.99-$9.99, dinner $9.99-$28.99. Bar 4 pm-1 am; Sun to 11 pm. Pianist, vocalist Tues-Sun. Children's menu. Nautical décor. Cr cds: D, MC, V.

Shamokin Dam

Settled 1790 **Pop** 1,502 **Elev** 500 ft **Area code** 570 **Zip** 17876

Motel/Motor Lodge

★ ★ **INN OF SHAMOKIN DAM.** *Rtes 11 and 15 (17876). Phone 570/743-1111; fax 570/743-1190.* 151 rooms, 2 story. S $50-$60; D $55-$70; each additional $5; under 18 free. Pet accepted. Check-out noon. TV; cable. In-room modem link. Restaurant 7 am-9 pm. Bar from 5 pm. Pool; lifeguard. Cr cds: A, C, D, DS, MC, V.

B&B/Small Inn

★ ★ ★ **INN AT NEW BERLIN.** *321 Market St (17855). Phone 570/966-0321; toll-free 800/797-2350; fax 570/966-9557. www.newberlin-inn.com.* 9 rooms, 2 story. Complimentary full breakfast. Check-out noon, check-in 3 pm. Restaurant 10 am-2 pm, 4:30-8:30 pm; closed Mon, Tues. Cr cds: A, DS, MC, V. **$**

Sharon (D-1)

See also Mercer

Settled 1802 **Pop** 16,328 **Elev** 998 ft **Area code** 724 **Zip** 16146

Information Mercer County Convention & Visitors Bureau, 50 N Water Ave, 16146; 724/748-5315 or 800/637-2370

Web www.mercercountypa.org

In the heart of the rich Shenango Valley, Sharon is a busy industrial city that started with a lonely mill on the banks of the Shenango River. Steel, fabrication of steel products, and manufacture of electric transformers are a major part of the economic base. The Shenango Dam and its reservoir are northeast of town, near Sharpsville, and offer many recreational activities.

What to See and Do

Shenango Lake. *2442 Celly Rd (16148). 6 miles N of I-80, PA 18. Phone 724/646-1115 (camping); 724/962-7746 or 724/646-1124 (general info).* Swimming, waterskiing; fishing, hunting; boating (ramps). Picnicking. More than 300 tent and trailer sites (mid-May-Labor Day; rest of Sept, reduced number of sites; electric hookups additional).

Special Event

The Small Ships Review. *101 Chestnut Ave. Phone 724/981-3123. Downtown.* Parade of ships, entertainment, fireworks, food. July.

Motel/Motor Lodge

★ **COLLINS MOTEL.** *4036 E State St (16148). Phone 724/981-6150.* 13 rooms, shower only. S $39-$49; D $42-$55; each additional $6; higher rates special events. Crib $6. TV; cable. Restaurant nearby. Check-out 10 am. Gift shop. 9-hole golf privileges. Some refrigerators. Cr cds: MC, V.

B&B/Small Inn

★ ★ ★ **TARA COUNTRY INN.** *2844 Lake Rd (16113). Phone 724/962-2992; toll-free 800/782-2803; fax 724/962-3250. www.tara-inn.com.* 27 rooms, 2 story. Adults only. Check-out noon, check-in 3 pm. TV; cable. In-room modem link. Dining rooms 11 am-8 pm. 2 pools, 1 indoor. Business center. Croquet court. Cr cds: A, DS, MC, V. **$$$**

Restaurants

★ ★ **HOT ROD CAFE MONTICELLO.** *101 Chestnut St (16146). Phone 724/981-3123; fax 724/981-1504. www.quakersteakandlube.com.* Specializes in char-grilled steak. Closed Mon. Dinner. Bar. Entertainment Thurs-Sun. Children's menu. Three dining rooms in a converted, restored railroad depot. Outdoor seating. Cr cds: A, D, DS, MC, V. **$**

★ **QUAKER STEAK & LUBE.** *101 Chestnut St (16146). Phone 724/981-WING; fax 724/981-1504. www. quakersteakandlube.com.* Hours: 11-1 am; Thurs-Sat to

2 am; Sun noon-1 am. Bar. Lunch $3.99-$12, dinner $5.50-$18. Children's menu. Specializes in chicken wings, steak, hamburgers. Outdoor seating. Former gas station; vintage automobiles, license plates, memorabilia. Casual dining. Cr cds: A, D, DS, MC, V.

D

Shartlesville

See also Hamburg, Reading

Pop 300 **Elev** 560 ft **Area code** 610 **Zip** 19554

What to See and Do

Roadside America. *109 Roadside Dr. Just off US 22, Shartlesville, exit I-78. Phone 610/488-6241.* This miniature "village" consists of O-gauge trains, villages and scenes, with 66 miniature displays re-creating 200 years of life in rural America. Started in 1903, displays now cover 6,000 square feet. (Daily; closed Dec 25) **$$**

Restaurants

★ **BLUE MOUNTAIN FAMILY RESTAURANT.** *I-78 (19554). Phone 610/488-0353; fax 610/488-0500.* Continental menu. Salad bar. Hours: 6:30 am-10 pm. Closed Jan 1, Dec 25. Breakfast $1.95-$4.95, lunch $2.75-$6.95, dinner $5.95-$12.95. Bar. Children's menu. Reservations accepted. Cr cds: A, DS, MC, V.

D

★ **HAAG'S HOTEL.** *Main and Third sts (19554). Phone 717/362-3476.* Hours: 7:30 am-7:30 pm. Closed Dec 25. Reservations accepted. Bar 11 am-midnight. Complete meals: breakfast $1.75-$6.50, lunch $4.75-$7, dinner $7-$13. Buffet: breakfast $6.50, lunch, dinner $13. Specializes in Pennsylvania Dutch cooking, family-style dinners. Own pies. In former hotel (1914); Early American décor. Cr cds: MC, V.

D

Shawnee on Delaware

See also Bushkill, Stroudsburg

Pop 400 **Elev** 320 ft **Area code** 717 **Zip** 18356

Information Pocono Mountains Vacation Bureau Inc, 1004 Main St, Stroudsburg 18360; 717/424-6050; for free brochures, phone 800/POCONOS

Web www.poconos.org

What to See and Do

Delaware Water Gap. (see) *Phone 315/229-5261.*

Shawnee Mountain Ski Area. *Hollow Rd. 6 miles N on I-80, exit 52, follow signs. Phone 570/421-7231.* Quad, triple, seven double chairlifts; patrol, school, rentals; snowmaking; cafeteria, bar; nursery. 23 slopes and trails; longest run 1 mile; vertical drop 700 feet. (late Nov-Mar, daily) Night skiing. Half-day rates. **$$$$**

Shawnee Place Play & Water Park. *Hollow Rd. I-80, exit 52, Rte 209 N and follow signs. Phone 570/421-7231.* Kids can jump in a pool of plastic balls, swing on a cable glide, climb on cargo nets, glide down water slides, and splash in a wading pool. Magic shows, picnics, video games, snack bar. (Mid-June-early Sept, daily; Late May-mid-June, weekends only). **$$$**

Resort

★★ **SHAWNEE INN.** *1 River Rd (18356). Phone 570/424-4000; toll-free 800/742-9633; fax 570/424-9168. www.shawneeinn.com.* 103 rooms, 3 story. MAP, May-Oct: S $129; D $179; suites $50 additional; kitchen units (Nov-Apr) $120; EP: S, D $89-$115; under 8 free; some weekly, weekend rates; higher rates Christmas holidays; lower rates rest of year. Crib free. Service charge 10%. Check-out noon, check-in 4 pm. TV; cable, VCR available. Coin laundry. Dining room 7 am-9 pm. Snack bar. Bar hours vary. Entertainment. Supervised children's activities. Playground. Social director, game room, recreation room. 4 pools, 1 indoor; wading pool, lifeguard. 27-hole golf, pro, putting green, driving range, miniature golf. Lighted tennis, pro (summer). Downhill/cross-country ski 3 miles. Picnics. Lawn games. Meeting rooms. Cr cds: A, C, D, DS, MC, V.

D ⚓ ⚐ ≯ ⚑ ⚒ ≈ SC

Somerset (H-4)

See also Johnstown, Ligonier

Settled 1773 **Pop** 6,762 **Elev** 2,190 ft **Area code** 814 **Zip** 15501

Information Somerset County Chamber of Commerce, 601 N Center Ave; 814/445-6431

Web www.shol.com/smrst/somrst.htm

Somerset, a county seat, is also the marketing place for farms, lumber mills, and coal mines in the area. James Whitcomb Riley described the countryside in his poem *'Mongst the Hills of Somerset*. The county offers fishing, swimming, boating, hiking, biking, camping, skiing, and ice skating.

What to See and Do

Hidden Valley Ski Area. *12 miles W of PA Tpke Somerset exit 10; 8 miles E of PA Tpke Donegal exit 9, on PA 31. Phone 814/443-8000; 800/443-SKII (snow conditions).* Six chairlifts, beginner's lift; patrol, school, rentals; snowmaking; cafeteria, restaurant, bars; nursery. Longest run 5,280 feet; vertical drop 610 feet; 28 slopes (Dec-Mar, daily). 30 miles of cross-country trails (rentals). Night skiing. Shuttle service. Conference center, lodging. Year-round facilities, activities. **$$$$**

Kooser State Park. *9 miles NW on PA 31. Phone 814/445-8673.* Approximately 220 acres. Four-acre lake with fishing; swimming beach (Memorial Day-Labor Day). cross-country skiing, sledding. Picnicking. Tent and trailer sites, cabins. Standard fees.

Laurel Hill State Park. *1454 Laurel Hill Park Rd (15501). 8 miles W on PA 31, then SW on unnumbered road. Phone 814/445-7725.* Approximately 3,900 acres. Swimming beach, snack bar; boating (mooring, launching). Hiking, hunting; snowmobiling, ice fishing. Picnicking. Tent and trailer sites. Standard fees.

Mount Davis. *26 miles S on US 219 to Salisbury, then W on unnumbered road. Phone 724/238-9533.* Highest point in state (3,213 feet).

Somerset Historical Center. *10649 Somerset Pike (15501). 5 miles N on PA 985. Phone 814/445-6077.* Museum exhibits on rural life; outdoor display includes log house, log barn, covered bridge, sugarhouse. Bus tour (fee). (Tues-Sat; closed most holidays) **$$**

Special Events

Farmers' and Threshermen's Jubilee. *9 miles SW via PA 281, in New Centerville. Phone 814/926-3142.* Equipment demonstrations; tractor-pulling, horseshoe-pitching, tobacco-spitting contests; antique car show and flea market; food. Early Sept.

Maple Festival. *120 Meyers Ave. Phone 814/634-0213.* Festival Park. Apr.

Mountain Craft Days. *10649 Somerset Pike. Phone 814/445-6077.* Somerset Historical Center. More than 150 traditional craft demonstrations; antique exhibits; entertainment. Early Sept.

Somerfest. *214 Harrison Ave. Phone 814/443-2433.* Laurel Arts/Phillip Dressler Center for the Arts. German festival: dancing, competitions, entertainment, food, tours. Mid-July.

Springs Folk Festival. *Rte 669, between Salisbury, PA (US 219) and Grantsville, MD (US 40, I-68 exit 19) (15562). Phone 814/662-4158 or 814/662-4298.* Crafts demonstrations include bread baking, wheat weaving, basket and broom making, candle dipping, quilt stitching; entertainment featuring banjo and fiddle music; pioneer exhibits on forest trail; maple sugaring, apple butter boiling, log hewing; museum adjacent with antique tools, furnishings, historical artifacts. Early Oct.

Motels/Motor Lodges

★ **BUDGET HOST INN.** *799 N Center Ave (15501). Phone 814/445-7988; toll-free 800/283-4678.* 28 rooms, 2 story. S $33-$35; D $45-$55; each additional $5. Crib $4. Pet accepted. TV; cable (premium). Restaurant nearby. Check-out 11 am. Downhill ski 10 miles; cross-country ski 13 miles. Cr cds: A, C, D, DS, MC, V.

⊡ ⊠ ⊠ **SC**

★ **DOLLAR INN.** *1146 N Center Ave (15501). Phone 814/445-2977; toll-free 800/250-1505; fax 814/443-6205.* 16 rooms. S $25-$40; D $30-$50; each additional $5; under 10 free; weekly, weekend rates; higher rates special events. Crib $5. Pet accepted, some restrictions; $5. TV; cable (premium). Restaurant nearby. Check-out 11 am. Business services available. Some refrigerators. Cr cds: A, D, DS, MC, V.

⊡ ⊠ **SC**

★ **ECONOMY INN.** *1138 N Center Ave (15501). Phone 814/445-4144; fax 814/445-3763. www.a-1economyinn.com.* 19 rooms. S $35-$45; D $40-$95; each additional $5; under 12 free; higher rates: special events, ski season. TV; cable (premium), VCR. Indoor pool. Playground. Complimentary continental breakfast. Restaurant nearby. Check-out 11 am. Coin laundry. Exercise equipment. Game room. Refrigerators, microwaves. Cr cds: A, DS, MC, V.

⊡ ⊠ ⊠ **SC**

★ **KNIGHTS INN.** *585 Ramada Rd (15501). Phone 814/445-8933; fax 814/443-9745. www.knightsinn.com.* 112 rooms, 10 kitchen units. S $39.95-$59.95; D $46.95-$69.95; each additional $10; kitchen units $43.95-$52.95; under 18 free; weekly rates; higher rates Dec-Mar weekends. Crib free. Pet accepted, some restrictions. TV; cable (premium), VCR available (movies). Pool. Restaurant nearby. Check-out noon. Coin laundry. Business services available. Downhill ski 15 miles. Cr cds: A, C, D, DS, MC, V.

D ⊡ ⊠ ⊠ ⊠

★ **RAMADA INN.** *215 Ramada Rd (15501). Phone 814/443-4646; fax 814/445-7539. www.ramada.com.* 152 rooms, 2 story. S $64-$78; D $74-$88; each additional $10; suites $95-$125; under 18 free; some weekend rates. Crib free. Pet accepted. Check-out noon. TV; cable (premium). Valet service. Restaurant 6:30 am-2 pm, 5-10 pm; Sun 7-11 am. Bar 2 pm-2 am; Sun to 9 pm; entertainment Tues-

Sat. Room service. Health club privileges. Sauna. Game room. Indoor pool, whirlpool, poolside service, lifeguard. Downhill/cross-country ski 12 miles. Meeting rooms. Business services. Sundries. Cr cds: A, D, DS, MC, V.

Resort

★ ★ ★ **HIDDEN VALLEY RESORT CONFERENCE CENTER.** *1 Craighead Dr (15502). Phone 814/443-6454; toll-free 800/458-0175; fax 814/443-1907. www.hiddenvalleyresort.com.* 206 units, some A/C, 2-3 story. Mid-Dec-mid-Mar: S $120-$180; D $222-$350; each additional $30; under 13 free; ski, golf packages; MAP available; lower rates rest of year. Crib free. TV; cable (premium). 4 pools, 1 indoor; whirlpool, lifeguard. Playground. Supervised children's activities (June-Sept). Dining rooms 7 am-10 pm. Bars 11-1 am; entertainment. Check-out noon, check-in 4 pm. Grocery. Package store. Convention facilities. Business services available. Bellstaff. Valet service. Gift shop. Airport transportation. Sports director. Lighted tennis, pro. 18-hole golf, greens fee $49-$59, pro, putting green, driving range. Boats. Downhill/cross-country ski on site. Hiking. Social director. Exercise equipment; sauna. Fireplaces; microwaves available. Balconies. Picnic tables. Located in scenic Laurel Highlands mountain area. Cr cds: A, C, D, DS, MC, V.

B&B/Small Inns

★ ★ ★ **BAYBERRY INN BED AND BREAKFAST.** *611 N Center Ave (15501). Phone 814/445-8471.* 11 rooms, shower only, 2 story. No A/C. No room phones. S $40-$50; D $45-$55; each additional $10; suite $75; minimum stay some holiday weekends. Children over 12 years only. TV in sitting room; VCR. Complimentary continental breakfast; afternoon refreshments. Restaurant nearby. Check-out 11 am, check-in 3 pm. Luggage handling. Concierge service. Downhill/cross-country ski 18 miles. Brick house built 1902. Cr cds: A, DS, MC, V.

★ ★ ★ **INN AT GEORGIAN PLACE.** *800 Georgian Place Dr (15501). Phone 814/443-1043; fax 814/443-6220. www.theinnatgeorgianplace.com.* 11 rooms, 2 suites, 3 story. S, D $95-$145; each additional $10; suites $170-$185. Children over 5 years only. Pet accepted, some restrictions. TV; cable (premium), VCR (movies). Complimentary full breakfast. Restaurant noon-4 pm. Room service. Check-out noon, check-in 3 pm. Business services available. Luggage handling. Valet service. Concierge service. Downhill/cross-country ski 12 miles. Some fireplaces. Georgian mansion built in 1915; chandeliers, marble foyer. Cr cds: A, D, DS, MC, V.

Restaurants

★ **COUNTRY COTTAGE.** *2817 New Centerville Rd (15557). Phone 814/926-4078.* Hours: 10:30 am-9 pm. Closed major holidays. Breakfast $2.50-$4.25, lunch $2.50-$4.50, dinner $4.95-$6.95. Children's menu. Cr cds: A, D, MC, V.

★ ★ **OAKHURST TEA ROOM.** *2409 Glades Pike (15501). Phone 814/443-2897; fax 814/445-3781. www.oakhursttearoom.com.* Early American décor. Closed Mon; Dec 25. Lunch, dinner, brunch. Bar. Children's menu. Outdoor seating. Cr cds: A, D, MC, V. **$**

★ ★ **PINE GRILL.** *800 N Center Ave (15501). Phone 814/445-2102; fax 814/443-6043.* Closed Dec 25. Breakfast, lunch, dinner. Bar. Children's menu. Opened 1941. Cr cds: A, MC, V. **$**

State College (F-7)

Settled 1859 **Pop** 38,420 **Elev** 1,154 ft **Area code** 814

Information Centre County Convention & Visitors Bureau, 800 E Park Ave, 16803; 814/231-1400 or 800/358-5466

Web www.visitpennstate.org

The home of Pennsylvania State University and principally concerned with services to this institution, this borough is near the geographic center of the state. In the beautiful Nittany Valley, State College is surrounded by farmland famous for its production of oats and swine. Iron ore was discovered just east of town in 1790, and many iron furnaces later sprang up.

What to See and Do

Columbus Chapel–Boal Mansion Museum. *4 miles E on US 322, in Boalsburg. Phone 814/466-6210.* The mansion has been the Boal family home since 1789 and includes original furnishings, china, tools, and weapons. Colonel Theodore Davis Boal, who outfitted his own troop for World War I, lived here. The 16th-century chapel belonged to the family of Christopher Columbus in Spain and was brought here in 1909 by Boal relatives. It contains religious items and Renaissance and baroque art, as well as an admiral's desk and explorer's cross that belonged to Columbus himself. Summer concerts on grounds. (May-early-Oct, Tues-Sun) **$$$**

Mount Nittany Vineyard & Winery. *7 miles E on US 322, E on PA 45, N on Linden Hall Rd. Phone 814/466-6373.*

Stone-faced, chalet-style building nestled on southern slopes of Mount Nittany. Tasting room offers variety of wines and view of large pond, vineyard, and mountains. Group tastings (by appointment). (Fri-Sun; closed holidays, also Jan) **FREE**

Penn's Cave. *222 Penns Cave Rd (16828). NE on PA 26, SE on PA 144, then 5 miles E of Centre Hall on PA 192. Phone 814/364-1664.* A one-hour, 1-mile boat trip through cavern; stalactites, stalagmites; plus ride-through wildlife park. Picnic area; visitor center; gift shop; snack bar. (Mid-Feb-Nov, daily) **$$$$**

Pennsylvania Military Museum. *4 miles E on US 322, in Boalsburg. Phone 814/466-6263.* On grounds of 28th Division Shrine; dioramas; battle exhibits and equipment from the Revolutionary War to the present. Audiovisual program; military bookstore. (Tues-Sun; closed holidays) **$$**

Pennsylvania State University. *College and Atherton sts (16802). On US 322 in University Park. Phone 814/865-4700.* (1855) 41,000 students. Approximately 760 major buildings on a 15,984-acre campus; it is the land grant institution of Pennsylvania. On campus are

> **Ag Hill, The College of Agriculture.** Showplace for state's dairy industry including the dairy center, off Park Rd near stadium, with five herds of cows, automatic milking equipment (daily). The creamery, Curtain Rd, has retail salesroom for cheeses, milk, cream, ice cream (Daily; closed holidays). Also test flower gardens off Park Rd near East Halls (July-Sept). **FREE**

> **Earth and Mineral Sciences Museum.** *Steidle Building on Pollock Rd. Phone 814/865-6427.* Exhibitions of ores, gems, and fossils; automated displays; art gallery. (Mon-Fri; closed holidays) **FREE**

> **Old Main.** *E of Mall near Pollock Rd. Phone 814/865-2501.* (1929) Present building, on site of original Old Main (1863), uses many of the original stones; topped by lofty bell tower. Here are Henry Varnum Poor's land grant frescoes. (Mon-Fri; closed holidays) **FREE**

Whipple Dam State Park. *10 miles S on PA 26, then 1 mile E on unnumbered road. Phone 814/667-3808.* Approximately 250 acres. Swimming beach; fishing, hunting; boating (launching, mooring). Hiking. Snowmobiling, ice skating, ice fishing. Picnicking, snack bar. Standard fees.

Special Events

Central Pennsylvania Festival of the Arts. *403 S Allen St #201. Phone 814/237-3682.* Open-air display of visual and performing arts; indoor exhibits; demonstrations of arts and crafts; food booths. Mid-July.

Centre County Grange Fair. *237 Hoffer St (16828). PA 144S, at Grange Park in Centre Hall. Phone 814/364-9674.* Exhibits, livestock show, rides, concessions, entertainment. Last week in Aug.

Memorial Day Celebration. *1402 S Atherton St. Phone 814/231-1400. In Boalsburg.* Celebrate the holiday in the birthplace of Memorial Day.

Motels/Motor Lodges

★ ★ ★ **AUTOPORT MOTEL & RESTAURANT.** *1405 S Atherton St (16801). Phone 814/237-7666; toll-free 800/932-7678; fax 814/237-7456. www.autoport.statecollege. com.* 86 rooms, 12 kitchen units, 3 story. S $55-$65; D $59-$69; each additional $5; suites $69-$85; under 16 free; weekly, weekend rates; higher rates special events. Crib free. Check-out 11 am. TV; cable (premium), VCR available (movies). In-room modem link. Coin laundry. Restaurant 6 am-11 pm; dining room 11:30 am-2 pm, 5-10 pm. Bar 11-2 am; Sun to midnight; entertainment Wed-Sat. Heated pool, lifeguard. Downhill ski 4 miles. Meeting rooms. Business services. Sundries. Cr cds: A, D, DS, MC, V.

⬚ ⬚ ⬚ ⬚

★ ★ **DAYS INN.** *240 S Pugh St (16801). Phone 814/238-8454; toll-free 800/258-3297; fax 814/237-1607. www.daysinn.com.* 184 rooms, 6 story. S $59-$115; D $69-$115; each additional $10; suites $150; under 18 free; some weekend rates; higher rates special events. Pet accepted, some restrictions; $10. Complimentary continental breakfast Mon-Fri. Check-out noon. TV. In-room modem link. Restaurant 6:30 am-midnight; Sun from 7 am. Bar 11-2 am; entertainment. Room service. Exercise room, sauna. Game room. Indoor pool. Free airport transportation. Business center. Cr cds: A, C, D, DS, JCB, MC, V.

⬚ ⬚ ⬚ ⬚ ⬚ ⬚

★ **HAMPTON INN.** *1101 E College Ave (16801). Phone 814/231-1590; fax 814/238-7320. www.hamptoninn.com.* 121 rooms, 3 story. S $59-$74; D $66-$81; suites $71-$78; under 18 free; ski, golf plans. Crib free. TV; cable (premium). Heated pool; lifeguard. Complimentary continental breakfast. Restaurant adjacent. Meeting room. Valet service. Sundries. Airport transportation. Downhill/cross-country ski 5 miles. Picnic tables. Cr cds: A, C, D, DS, MC, V.

⬚ ⬚ ⬚ ⬚

★ ★ **RAMADA INN.** *1450 S Atherton St (16801). Phone 814/238-3001; toll-free 800/465-4329; fax 814/237-1345. www.ramada.com.* 288 rooms, 2 story. S $72-$79; D $78-$85; each additional $7; suites $175; under 19 free. Pet accepted. Check-out noon. TV; cable (premium). In-room modem link. Restaurant 7 am-10 pm; Fri, Sat to 11 pm. Bar 11 am-midnight. Room service. Health club privileges. Exercise equipment. Game room. 2 pools; lifeguard. Cr cds: A, C, D, DS, JCB, MC, V.

⬚ ⬚ ⬚ ⬚ ⬚ ⬚

★ **RODEWAY INN.** *1040 N Atherton St (16803). Phone 814/238-6783; toll-free 800/228-2000; fax 814/238-4519. www.rodeway.com.* 29 rooms, 3 with shower only, 2 story. S $39-$69; D $44-$69; each additional $5; under 16 free; weekly rates; higher rates special events. Crib $6. TV; cable. Restaurant nearby. Check-out 11 am. Some refrigerators. Cr cds: A, C, D, DS, JCB, MC, V.

🖼 SC

★ **STEVENS MOTEL.** *1275 N Atherton St (16803). Phone 814/238-2438; fax 814/238-7548.* 18 rooms, 17 with shower only, 2 story. S $33-$38; D $38-$48; each additional $4; family rates; higher rates special events (2-day minimum). Crib $4. TV; cable (premium). Check-out 11 am. Downhill ski 4 miles; cross-country ski 1 mile. Cr cds: A, D, DS, MC, V.

🖼 🖼 SC

Hotel

★ ★ **ATHERTON HOTEL.** *125 S Atherton St (US 322 Business) (16801). Phone 814/231-2100; toll-free 800/832-0132; fax 814/237-1130. www.atherton.statecollege.com.* This inn is located 1/2 mile from Penn State. The Anthropology Museum, Historic Boalsburg Village, and Palmer Museum of Art are also nearby. 150 rooms, 7 story. S $75-$95; D $85-$105; each additional $10; suites $165; under 18 free; higher rates special events. Crib free. Check-out noon. TV; cable (premium). In-room modem link. Some in-room whirlpools; refrigerator, microwave in suites. Valet services. Restaurant 5 am-10 pm. Bar 2 pm-2 am. Health club privileges. Downhill ski 6 miles. Free garage parking. Free airport transportation. Meeting rooms. Business services. Cr cds: A, C, D, DS, ER, MC, V.

🖼 🖼 🖼 SC

Resort

★ ★ **TOFTREES RESORT.** *1 Country Club Ln (16803). Phone 814/234-8000; toll-free 800/458-3602; fax 814/238-4404. www.toftrees.com.* 113 units, 22 suites, 3 story. Apr-mid-Oct: S $99-$150; D $125-$170; each additional $15; suites $150-$250; AP, MAP available; golf plans; some weekend rates; lower rates rest of year. Crib available. TV; cable (premium), VCR available. Heated pool; lifeguard. Dining rooms 6:30 am-10 pm. Bar from 11 am; entertainment. Check-out noon, check-in 3 pm. Business services available. In-room modem link. Free airport transportation. Tennis, pro. 18-hole golf, pro, putting green, driving range. Exercise equipment. Refrigerators; microwaves available. Balconies. Mediterranean décor. Cr cds: A, C, D, DS, MC, V.

🖼 🖼 🖼 🖼 🖼 🖼 🖼 SC

B&B/Small Inns

★ ★ ★ **CARNEGIE HOUSE.** *100 Cricklewood Dr (16803). Phone 814/234-2424; toll-free 800/229-5033; fax 814/231-1299. www.cmagic.com/ch/.* 22 rooms, 2-3 story. S, D $125-$175; suites $250-$275; under 6 free. TV; cable (premium), VCR. Complimentary continental breakfast. Dining room 6:30-10 am, 11:30 am-1:30 pm, 5:30-9 pm. Check-out 11 am, check-in 3 pm. Business services available. In-room modem link. Luggage handling. Gift shop. Free airport transportation. Downhill ski 6 miles; cross-country ski adjacent. Minibar; some microwaves. Décor and ambiance is reminiscent of Scotland. Cr cds: A, MC, V.

🖼 🖼 🖼

★ ★ ★ **NITTANY LION INN.** *200 W Park Ave (16803). Phone 814/865-8500; toll-free 800/233-7505; fax 814/865-8501. www.pshs.psu.edu.* 237 rooms, 3 story. Check-out noon, check-in 3 pm. TV; VCR available. In-room modem link. Dining room, bar. Exercise equipment. Free airport transportation. Located on the main campus of Penn State. Cr cds: A, D, DS, MC, V. **$**

🖼 🖼 🖼

Restaurants

★ ★ **TAVERN.** *220 E College Ave (16801). Phone 814/238-6116. www.thetavern.com.* Hours: 5-10:30 pm; Sun to 8:30 pm. Closed major holidays. Dinner $6.95-$18.45. Bar 4 pm-12:30 am. Children's menu. Cr cds: A, C, D, DS, MC, V.

🖼

★ ★ ★ **VICTORIAN MANOR.** *901 Pike St, Lemont (16851). Phone 814/238-5534; fax 814/237-7890.* Each individually decorated dining room in this Victorian house offers a charming setting for a lovely meal. Continental menu. Closed Mon; Jan 1, Memorial Day, Labor Day, Dec 25. Dinner. Historic building (1891). Victorian décor. Totally nonsmoking. Cr cds: A, MC, V. **$$**

🖼

Stroudsburg (E-13)

See also Easton, Pocono Mountains

Settled 1769 **Pop** 5,756 **Elev** 430 ft **Area code** 570 **Zip** 18360

Information Pocono Mountains Vacation Bureau, Inc, 1004 Main St; phone 570/424-6050; for free brochures, phone 800/POCONOS

Web www.poconos.org

This is a center for the Pocono Mountains resort area and the surrounding rural community. It is the Monroe County seat.

What to See and Do

Alpine Mountain Ski Area. *6 miles N via PA 191, 447 N, just outside Analomink.* Phone 570/595-2150; 800/233-8240. Two quad, one double chairlift; patrol, school, rentals; snowmaking; lodge, restaurant, bar; child-care center. Vertical drop 500 feet. 21 trails and slopes. Night skiing. (Dec-Mar, daily) **$$$$**

Canoeing. *Phone 570/421-0180.* Canoe trips on the Delaware River; equipment provided; also transportation to and from the river. (May-Oct) Contact Chamberlain Canoes, PO Box 155, Minisink Hills 18341; **$$$$**

Quiet Valley Living Historical Farm. *1000 Turkey Hill Rd (18360). 3 1/2 miles SW on US 209 Business, then 1 1/2 miles S (follow signs).* Phone 570/992-6161. A log house (1765) with kitchen and parlor added 1892; 12 other original or reconstructed buildings. Demonstrations of seasonal farm activities. Farm animals, garden, gift shop. Guided tours with costumed guides, 1 1/2-2 hours. (Late June-Labor Day, Tues-Sun) **$$$**

Stroud Mansion. *900 Main St (18360).* Phone 570/421-7703. (18th century). Built by founder of city; houses Historical Society of Monroe County. Historical artifacts, genealogical records. Tours. (Tues-Fri, also Sun afternoons; closed major holidays) **$**

Motels/Motor Lodges

★ ★ **BEST WESTERN POCONO INN.** *700 Main St (18360).* Phone 570/421-2200; toll-free 888/508-2378; fax 570/421-5561. www.bestwestern.com. 90 rooms, 4 story. S, D $74-$109; each additional $10; higher rates special events. Crib free. Check-out 11 am. TV; cable, VCR available (movies). Restaurant, bar 11:30-2 am; entertainment. Room service. Game room. Indoor pool, whirlpools. Meeting rooms. Business services. Cr cds: A, C, D, DS, MC, V.

⬛🏊🖥

★ **BUDGET MOTEL.** *I-80, exit 51 (18301).* Phone 570/424-5451; toll-free 800/233-8144; fax 570/424-0389. www.budmotel.com. 115 rooms, 2-3 story. No elevator. S $33.90-$48; D $48-$66; higher rates: special events, holidays, some weekends. Crib free. Pet accepted; $20 deposit. TV; cable, VCR available (movies). Restaurant 7-11 am, 5-10 pm. Bar 4 pm-midnight. Check-out 11 am. Business services available. In-room modem link. Game room. Cr cds: A, C, D, DS, MC, V.

⬛🐾🖥

★ ★ **CLARION HOTEL.** *1220 W Main St (18360).* Phone 570/424-1930; toll-free 800/777-5453; fax 570/424-5909. www.choicehotels.com. 133 rooms, 2 story. S, D $85-$99; each additional $10; suites $120-$130; under 18 free; some weekend rates. Crib free. TV; cable. Pool; poolside service. Sauna. Restaurant 7 am-10 pm. Room service.

Bars 11-2 am; entertainment. Check-out 11 am. Meeting rooms. Business services available. In-room modem link. Bellstaff. Sundries. Game room. Balconies. Cr cds: A, C, D, DS, JCB, MC, V.

🏊🖥 **SC**

★ ★ **SHANNON INN.** *US Rte 209 and State Rte 447 (18301).* Phone 570/424-1951; toll-free 800/424-8052; fax 570/424-7782. 120 rooms, 2 story. S $60-$90; D $65-$95; each additional $5; under 18 free; (2-day minimum) holidays; higher rates NASCAR races. Crib free. TV; cable. Indoor pool. Complimentary continental breakfast. Restaurant 4 pm-2 am. Room service. Bar; entertainment Fri, Sat. Check-out 11 am. Coin laundry. Meeting rooms. Business services available. In-room modem link. Valet service. Sundries. Downhill/cross-country ski 4 miles. Some refrigerators. Picnic tables. Cr cds: A, D, DS, MC, V.

🎿🏊🖥 **SC**

Resort

★ ★ ★ **CAESARS POCONO PALACE RESORT.** *Rte 209 (18335).* Phone 570/588-6692; fax 570/588-0754. www.caesarspoconosresorts.com. 189 units, 155 suites. MAP: S, D, suites $195-$350; weekly rates. Adults only. Check-out 11 am, check-in 3 pm. TV; cable, VCR available (movies $5). Some balconies. Refrigerators. Dining room 8:30-11 am; 6-8 pm. Bar from 11:30 am; entertainment. Room service. Exercise equipment, sauna. Game room, recreation room. 2 pools, 1 indoor; whirlpool. 9-hole golf, pro, putting green, driving range. Downhill ski 3 miles; cross-country on site. Lawn games. Marina, paddle boats, snowmobiles, ice skating. Volleyball. Business services. Gift shop. Softball field. Archery. On lake. Cr cds: A, C, D, DS, MC, V.

⬛⛳🏊🎿🖥

Restaurants

★ **ARLINGTON DINER.** *834 N 9th St (18360).* Phone 570/421-2329. Hours: 6 am-10 pm; Fri, Sat to 11 pm; Sun 7 am-10 pm. Closed Jan 1, Thanksgiving, Dec 25. Dinner $5.75-$11.50. Children's menu. Cr cds: V.

⬛ **SC**

★ **BEAVER HOUSE.** *1001 N 9th St (18360).* Phone 570/424-1020; fax 570/424-9665. www.beaverhouse.com. Hours: 11:30 am-9:30 pm; Sat to 10:30 pm; Sun noon-8 pm. Closed Dec 25. Reservations accepted. Bar. Complete meals: lunch $4.95-$8.95, dinner $12.50-$31.95. Specializes in seafood, prime rib. Many antiques; Tiffany lamps, trophies, bottles, stained glass, clocks. Family-owned. Cr cds: A, D, DS, MC, V.

⬛

★ **BROWNIE'S IN THE BURG.** *700 Main St (18360).* Phone 570/421-2200. Hours: 11 am-10 pm; Fri, Sat to

11 pm. Bar. Lunch $3.95-$9.95, dinner $8.95-$23.95. Family-owned. Cr cds: A, D, DS, MC, V.

D

★ **LEE'S.** *PA 611 (18321). Phone 570/421-1212. www.leesrestaurant.com.* Chinese, Japanese menu. Hours: noon-9 pm; Sat 2-10 pm; Sun 1-9:30 pm. Closed Thanksgiving. Lunch, dinner $6.50-$12.95. Bar. Reservations required Fri-Sun. Cr cds: A, D, DS, MC, V.

★ ★ **SARAH STREET GRILL.** *550 Quaker Alley (18360). Phone 570/424-9120; fax 570/424-9535. www. sarahstreetgrill.com.* American menu. Lunch, dinner. Bar. Children's menu. Casual attire. Outdoor seating. **$$**

★ ★ **STONEBAR INN.** *PA 209 (18360). Phone 570/992-6634; fax 570/992-6884. www.stonebarinn.com.* Hours: 5-10 pm; Fri, Sat to 11 pm; Sun from 4 pm. Closed most major holidays. Dinner $12.95-$25.95. Bar. Children's menu. Reservations required Fri, Sat. Outdoor seating. Fireside dining. Cr cds: A, D, MC, V.

D

Tannersville

See also Pocono Mountains, Stroudsburg

Pop 1,200 **Elev** 890 ft **Area code** 570 **Zip** 18372

Information Pocono Mountains Vacation Bureau Inc, 1004 Main St, Stroudsburg 18360; 570/424-6050; for free brochures, phone 800/POCONOS.

Web www.poconos.org

What to See and Do

Camelback Ski Area. *Camelback Rd. 3 1/2 miles W off I-80, exit 45, in Big Pocono State Park. Phone 570/629-1661; 800/233-8100 (mid-atlantic states, ski report).* Two quad, three triple, seven double chairlifts, surface lift; patrol, school, rentals; snowmaking; cafeteria, restaurant, bar; nursery. Longest run 1 mile; vertical drop 800 feet. Night skiing. (Late Nov-late Mar, daily) 33 trails. Alpine slide, water slides, swimming pool, bumper boats, entertainment (mid-June-Labor Day, daily; mid-May-mid-June and Labor Day-Oct, weekends only). Single and combination tickets. **$$$$**

Resort

★ ★ **CAESAR'S POCONO RESORTS.** *Rte 611, Brookdale Rd (28374). Phone 570/839-8844; toll-free 800/233-4141; fax 570/839-2414. www.caesarspoconoresorts. com.* 127 rooms in 8 buildings, 1-2 story. June-Sept, MAP: S $106-$215; D $190-$250; each additional $55; suites $230-$360; under 5 free; weekly plans; holiday plans (3-day minimum); higher rates holidays and theme weekends; lower rates rest of year. Crib free. Check-out

11 am, check-in 3 pm. TV; cable, VCR available (movies). Balconies. Some refrigerators. Valet services, coin laundry. Restaurant 8:30-11:30 am, 5:30-8 pm. Bar noon-2 am; entertainment. Room service. Supervised children's activities (seasonal); from 5 years. Playground. Exercise room, massage, sauna. Sports director. Social director. Game room, recreation room. 2 pools, 1 indoor; wading pool, whirlpool, poolside service, lifeguard. 9-hole golf privileges, putting green, driving range. Lighted tennis. Downhill ski 3 miles; cross-country ski 17 miles. Picnic tables. Lawn games. Bicycles. Beach, boats. Hiking. Snowmobiles, sleighing, tobogganing. Meeting rooms. Business services. Gift shop. On lake. Cr cds: A, C, D, DS, MC, V.

D ⛷ 🏊 🎿 ⛳ ≈ 🏃 ✈ SC

Restaurant

★ **BARLEY CREEK BREWING COMPANY.** *Camelback Rd and Sullivan's Trail (18372). Phone 570/629-9399. www.barleycreek.com.* American menu. Lunch, dinner, late night. Bar. Children's menu. Casual attire. Outdoor seating. **$$**

D

Titusville (C-3)

See also Franklin (Venango County), Meadville, Oil City

Settled 1796 **Pop** 6,146 **Elev** 1,199 ft **Area code** 814 **Zip** 16354

Information Titusville Area Chamber of Commerce, 202 W Central Ave; 814/827-2941

Titusville spreads from the banks of Oil Creek, so called because of the oil that appeared on its surface. Edwin L. Drake drilled the first successful oil well in the world on Aug 27, 1859. Overnight, Titusville became the center of the worldwide oil industry.

What to See and Do

Drake Well Museum. *East Bloss and Allen St Ext. 1 mile SE of PA 8. Phone 814/827-2797.* Site of world's first oil well; operating replica of Drake derrick and engine house; picnic area. Museum contains dioramas, working models, life-size exhibits depicting history of oil. (May-Oct, daily; Nov-Apr, Tues-Sat, also Sun afternoons) **$$**

Resort

★ ★ **CROSS CREEK RESORT.** *Rte 8 S (16354). Phone 814/827-9611; toll-free 800/461-3173; fax 814/827-2062. www.crosscreekresort.com.* 94 rooms, 1-2 story. May-Oct: S $95-$110; D $100-$120; each additional $10; suites $120-$140; under 12 free; golf plan; lower rates rest of year. Crib free. TV; cable. Heated pool; lifeguard. Restaurant 7 am-2 pm, 6-10 pm. Bar 11-2 am; entertainment. Check-out 2 pm. Meeting rooms. In-room modem link. Gift shop. Tennis. 27-hole golf, greens fee $28-$33, putting green. Some private patios, balconies. Cr cds: A, D, DS, MC, V.

⧉ 🛏️ 🐾 ≋ ⊠

Towanda (C-10)

See also Mansfield, Scranton

Settled 1794 **Pop** 1,131 **Elev** 737 ft **Area code** 570 **Zip** 18848

Information Endless Mountains Visitors Bureau, 712 Rte 6E, Tunkhannock 18657-9232; 570/836-5431 or 800/769-8999

Web www.endlessmountains.org

On the north branch of the Susquehanna River, Towanda takes its name from a Native American word meaning "where we bury the dead."

In 1793, the Asylum Company purchased 1,600 acres of these wild valleys as a refuge for Marie Antoinette of France, should she escape to America. "La Grande Maison," a queenly house, was built. French noblemen settled here and a thriving community (called Azilum) was planned. The colony was unsuccessful and most of its founders returned to France. Many of their descendants, however, still live in Bradford County.

What to See and Do

David Wilmot's Burial Place. *William and Chestnut sts. Riverside Cemetery.* Congressman (1845-1851), senator (1861-1863), leader of the Free Soil Party, Wilmot introduced the Wilmot Proviso in Congress, which would have required the US to outlaw slavery in any lands purchased from Mexico. This was an important factor in the dissension between North and South that led to the Civil War.

French Azilum. *Rte 456. 8 miles SE via US 6, PA 187. Phone 570/265-3376.* Site of colony for refugees from the French Revolution (1793-1803). Three cabins with crafts, tool exhibits; log cabin museum (1793); Laporte House (1836), built by son of one of colony's founders, reflects elegant French influence. Special events. Guided tours. (June-Aug, Wed-Sun; May, Sept-Oct, Sat and Sun) **$$**

Tioga Point Museum. *724 S Main St in Athens. 17 miles N off US 220, on PA 199, Spalding Memorial Building. Phone 570/888-7225.* Mementos of French Azilum; Civil War, Stephen Foster and Native American exhibits; historical displays of early canals and steam railroad. (Tues, Thurs and Sat; closed holidays) **DONATION**

Valley Railroad Museum. *15 miles N off US 220, in Sayre on S Lehigh Ave. Phone 570/888-1881.* Century-old Lehigh Valley passenger station houses museum with displays of railroad memorabilia and railroad exhibit of Lehigh Valley in miniature; gift shop. (Tues-Sun; closed holidays) **$$**

Motels/Motor Lodges

★ ★ **BEST WESTERN GRAND VICTORIAN INN.** *255 Spring St (18840). Phone 570/888-7711; toll-free 800/627-7972; fax 570/888-0541. www.bestwestern.com.* 100 rooms, 4 story. S $83-$86; D $93-$96; each additional $10; suites $154; under 12 free; weekend package. Crib $10. Check-out 11 am. TV; cable. In-room modem link. Balconies. Restaurant 6:30 am-9 pm; Fri, Sat to 10 pm. Bar; entertainment Fri, Sat. Room service. Exercise room, sauna, steam room. Indoor pool, whirlpool, lifeguard. 18-hole golf privileges. Lighted tennis. Meeting rooms. Business services. Sundries. Cr cds: A, C, D, DS, MC, V.

⧉ 🛏️ 🐾 ≋ 🏋️ ⊠ SC

★ ★ **TOWANDA MOTEL & RESTAURANT.** *383 York Ave (18848). Phone 570/265-2178; fax 570/265-9060.* 48 rooms. S $39-$65; D $43-$70; each additional $5; under 12 free. Pet accepted. Check-out noon. TV; cable. Restaurant 6 am-9:30 pm; Sat, Sun from 7 am. Bar 3 pm-2 am. Pool. Cr cds: A, DS, MC, V.

⧉ 🐾 ≋ ⊠

Uniontown (H-3)

See also Connellsville

Settled 1768 **Pop** 12,422 **Elev** 999 ft **Area code** 724 **Zip** 15401

Information Laurel Highlands Visitors Bureau, 120 E Main St, Ligonier 15658; 724/238-5661

Web www.laurelhighlands.org

Coal and its byproducts made Uniontown prosperous, but with the decline in coal mining the city has developed a more diversified economic base. First known as Union, this city has been the Fayette County seat since 1784. General Lafayette and his son, George Washington de Lafayette, came on a visit after the Revolutionary War and were welcomed by Albert Gallatin, one-time senator and secretary of the Treasury. Uniontown was a hotbed of the Whiskey Rebellion, and federal troops were sent here in 1794.

What to See and Do

Braddock's Grave. *200 Caverns Park Rd (15437).* Granite monument marks burial place of British General Edward Braddock, who was wounded in battle with French and

Native American forces on July 9, 1755, and died four days later.

Fort Necessity National Battlefield. *1 Washington Pkwy (15437).* The site of Washington's first major battle and the opening battle of the French and Indian War (1754). This land was known as the Great Meadows. A portion was later purchased by Washington, who owned it until his death. A replica of the original fort was built on the site following an archaeological survey in 1953. Picnic area (mid-spring-late fall). Nearby and included in admission is

>   **Visitor Center.** Exhibits on battle at Great Meadows; audiovisual program. (Daily; closed Dec 25) Overlooking Fort Necessity is

Friendship Hill National Historic Site. *15 miles S on US 119 to PA 166.* Preserves the restored home of Albert Gallatin, a Swiss immigrant who served his adopted country, in public and private life, for nearly seven decades. Gallatin made significant contributions to our young Republic in the fields of finance, politics, diplomacy, and scholarship. He is best known as the Treasury Secretary under Jefferson and Madison. Exhibits, audiovisual program, and audio tour provide information on Albert Gallatin. (Daily; closed Dec 25)

Jumonville Glen. *200 Caverns Park Rd (15437). 7 miles from Fort Necessity, 2 1/2 miles N of US 40 on Summit Rd.* Site of skirmish between British and French forces that led to the battle at Fort Necessity. (Mid-Apr-mid-Oct)

Laurel Caverns. *5 miles SE on US 40, then 5 miles S on marked road. Phone 724/438-3003.* Colored lighting; unusual formations. Indoor miniature golf. Repelling (fee). Guided tours. Exploring trips. (May-Oct, daily) **$$$$**

Ohiopyle State Park. *Dinner Bell Rd. 10 miles SE on US 40, then 6 miles NE off PA 381. Phone 724/329-8591.* Approximately 18,700 acres of overlooks, waterfalls. Fishing, hunting; whitewater boating. Hiking, bicycling. Cross-country skiing, snowmobiling, sledding. Picnicking, playground, snack bar. Tent and trailer sites. Nature center, interpretive program. Standard fees.

River tours. Whitewater rafting on the Youghiogheny River; some of the wildest and most scenic in the eastern US. Cost includes equipment and professional guides. Age limits are imposed because of level of difficulty.

>   **Laurel Highlands River Tours.** *PO Box 107, Dept PM, Ohiopyle (15470) Sherman St. Phone 724/329-8531 or 800/472-3846.* **$$$$**

>   **Mountain Streams & Trails Outfitters.** *Phone 724/329-8810 or 800/723-8669.* Also on the Youghiogheny, Big Sandy, Cheat and Tygart's Valley rivers. Also rentals of whitewater rafts, canoes, trail bikes. **$$$$**

>   **White Water Adventurers.** *PO Box 31, Ohiopyle (15470). Phone 800/WWA-RAFT.* **$$$$**

>   **Wilderness Voyageurs.** *PO Box 97, Ohiopyle (15470). Phone 800/272-4141.* Trips on the lower and middle Youghiogheny. Also bicycle, canoe rentals; kayak and canoe lessons. **$$$$**

Motels/Motor Lodges

★ ★ **HOLIDAY INN.** *700 W Main St (15401). Phone 724/437-2816; toll-free 800/465-4329; fax 724/437-3505. www.holiday-inn.com.* 179 rooms, 2 story. Under 18 free; package plans; higher rates Labor Day weekend. Crib free. Pet accepted, some restrictions. TV; cable (premium), VCR available. Indoor pool; whirlpool, poolside service, lifeguard. Sauna. Restaurant 6:30 am-2 pm, 4:30-10 pm. Room service from 7 am. Bar 3 pm-2 am; entertainment. Check-out 11 am. Meeting rooms. Business services available. In-room modem link. Valet service. Sundries. Lighted tennis. Miniature golf. Recreation room. Game room. Lawn games. Microwaves available. Some balconies. Cr cds: A, C, D, DS, JCB, MC, V. **$**

[D] [pet] [X] [pool] [X] **SC**

★ ★ **LODGE AT CHALK HILL.** *Rte 40 E (15421). Phone 724/438-0168; toll-free 800/833-4283; fax 724/438-1685. www.thelodgeatchalkhill.com.* 60 units, 6 suites, 6 kitchen units. Higher rates: July 4, Memorial Day, Labor Day, Dec 31; lower rates rest of year. Crib free. Pet accepted, some restrictions; $10. Complimentary continental breakfast. Check-out noon. TV; cable (premium), VCR available. Balconies. Restaurant opposite 7 am-9 pm. Picnic tables. Meeting rooms. Business services. Cr cds: A, DS, JCB, MC, V. **$**

[D] [pet] [X] [X]

Resorts

★ ★ ★ ★ **NEMACOLIN WOODLANDS RESORT.** *1001 Lafayette Dr, Farmington (15437). Phone 724/329-8555; toll-free 800/422-2736; fax 724/329-6153. www.nemacolin.com.* Tucked away in the scenic Laurel Highlands, this comprehensive resort is the sort of place you go to rediscover your inner child. Young and old alike delight in the multitude of recreational opportunities available here, from the Hummer driving club, equestrian center, and shooting academy to the adventure center, culinary classes, and art museums. Grand European style defines the accommodations at Chateau LaFayette, while the Lodge maintains a rustic charm. Families enjoy spacious townhouses, while luxury homes add a touch of class to group travel. Dining also runs the gamut from fine gourmet meals to casual fare. 220 rooms, 60 condo units (1-2 bedroom), 4 and 5 story. Under 17 free; AP, MAP available; weekly rates; golf plans; lower rates rest of year. Crib free. Check-out noon, check-in 3 pm. TV; cable (premium), VCR available. In-room modem link. Balconies. Microwave in condos. Bathroom phones. Minibars; many refrigerators. Valet services, laundry facilities in condos. Dining room 6 am-midnight. Snack bar. Bar noon-2 am; entertainment. Room service 24 hours. Supervised children's activities; ages 4-12. Playground. Exercise room, massage, sauna. Social director. Sports director. Game room, recreation room. 4 pools, 2 indoor; whirlpools, poolside service, lifeguard. Miniature golf. Two 18-hole golf courses, greens fee (includes cart) $69-$109. Lighted tennis, pro. Downhill/cross-country ski on site. Picnics. Lawn games. Bicycle rentals. Boats. Hiking. Sleighing, tobogganing. Business services. Convention facilities. Concierge. Situated on 1,250 acres with seven lakes; landing strip. Equestrian center; surrey rides all year. Cr cds: A, C, D, MC, V. **$$$**

D ⚓ 🏌 ⛷ 🎿 🏋 ➤ 🏊 🛅 🏃 ☃ **SC**

★ ★ ★ **SUMMIT INN RESORT.** *101 Skyline Dr, Farmington (15437). Phone 724/438-8594; fax 724/438-3917. www.summitinnresort.com.* 100 rooms, 3 story. No elevator. Family rates; golf plan, MAP available (2-day minimum); some weekend rates; lower rates mid-Apr-June, after Labor Day-early Nov. Closed rest of year. Crib $10. Check-out noon, check-in 4 pm. TV; cable, VCR available (movies). Dining room (public by reservation) 8-11 am, noon-3 pm, 5-9 pm. Bar 11-1 am. Entertainment. Room service. Exercise equipment. Social director. Recreation room. Indoor/outdoor pool; whirlpool, lifeguard. 9-hole golf, greens fee $8.50, pro, putting green. Tennis. Picnic tables. Business services. Gift shop. Built in 1907. Atop Mount Summit. Cr cds: A, DS, MC, V. **$**

D 🏋 🏌 ➤ 🏊 🏃 ☃ **SC**

B&B/Small Inn

★ ★ ★ **INNE AT WATSON'S CHOICE.** *234 Balsinger Rd (15401). Phone 724/437-4999; toll-free 888/820-5380. www.watsonschoice.com.* 7 rooms, shower only, 2 story. Weekly rates; weekends, holidays (2-day minimum). Adults only. Complimentary full breakfast. Check-out 11 am, check-in after 3 pm. TV in common room; cable (premium), VCR available (movies). Many fireplaces. Guest laundry. Downhill ski 10 miles; cross-country ski 10 miles. Picnic tables. Concierge service. Gift shop. Built in 1820; German architecture. Totally nonsmoking. Cr cds: A, DS, MC, V. **$**

D ➤ 🛅

Restaurant

★ ★ ★ **COAL BARON.** *7606 National Pike (15401). Phone 724/439-0111. www.coalbaron.com.* This 20-year-old restaurant is located 2 miles outside of town and offers a broad, continental menu. A painting of a coal tipple adorns the dining room wall, in honor of

the establishment's name. Continental menu. Hours: 4-11 pm; Sun noon-8 pm. Closed Mon; Dec 24-25. Lunch, dinner $14-$20.95. Bar. Children's menu. Jacket required. Valet parking available. Cr cds: A, D, DS, MC, V.

D

Valley Forge National Historical Park (H-13)

See also King of Prussia, Philadelphia

(3 miles N of PA Tpke, interchange 24)

Information Superintendent, PO Box 953, Valley Forge 19482; 610/783-1077.

Web www.nps.gov/vafo

Two thousand soldiers died here from hunger, disease, and cold, but General George Washington and his beleaguered army ultimately triumphed over the British in 1778. Today, Valley Forge has come to symbolize American perseverance and sacrifice on a lush, 3,600-acre hilly expanse with rich historical significance and beautiful scenery. Visitors can tour the park by car or bus and see Washington's restored stone headquarters, log soldier huts, bronze statues and monuments, and weapons and equipment used during the American Revolution. You can even learn how Washington's soldiers were taught to load and fire their muskets. The visitors' center features exhibits, artifacts, a gift shop, and an 18-minute film. Actively inclined history buffs will enjoy choosing from a 16-mile walking trail, 10-mile horse trails, a bike path, or a 10-mile self-guided tour. Picnic areas are available as well. (Daily; closed Dec 25)

What to See and Do

National Memorial Arch. Built in 1917 to commemorate Washington's army. Inscribed in the arch is a quote from General Washington: "Naked and starving as they are, we cannot enough admire the incomparable patience and fidelity of the soldiery."

Soldier Life Program. Interpreters present programs detailing camp life of the Continental Army soldier (offered at various times during the year).

Tours.

Auto Tape Tour. *Phone 610/783-5788.* Self-guided tour dramatizes Washington's winter encampment. (2-hour tape rental, May-Oct, daily) Bookstore. **$$$**

Bus Tour. *Phone 610/783-5788.* Narrated tour (approximately 90 minutes) includes stops at historic sites.

(June-Labor Day, tour departures every 1/2-hour; Labor Day-Oct, weekends only) Tours leave from Visitor Center. **$$$**

Visitor Center. *Jct PA 23 and N Gulph Rd, just inside park. Phone 610/783-1077.* Information, exhibits, audiovisual program, tour maps. Bus tours depart from here. (Daily)

Washington Headquarters. Park staff will provide information about the house where Washington lived for six months and which served as military headquarters for the Continental Army during that time. (Daily) Fee charged Apr-Nov. **$**

Washington Memorial Chapel. *On PA 23. Phone 610/783-0120.* Private property within park boundaries. Stained-glass windows depict the story of the New World, its discovery and development; hand-carved oak choir stalls, Pews of the Patriots, and Roof of the Republic bearing the State Seal of all the states. Also part of the chapel is the 58 cast-bell Washington Memorial National Carillon, with bells honoring states and territories. **FREE**

Restaurants

★ ★ ★ **KENNEDY-SUPPLEE MANSION.** *1100 W Valley Forge Rd (19406). Phone 610/337-3777; fax 610/337-3567. www.kennedysupplee.com.* Hours: 11:30 am-2 pm, 5:30-11 pm; Sat from 5:30 pm. Closed Sun; some major holidays. Reservations accepted. Continental menu. Bar; pianist Fri, Sat. A la carte entrées: lunch $8-$16, dinner $22-$30. Specializes in French, northern Italian cuisine. Valet parking. Eight dining rooms in mansion (1850s). Crystal chandeliers, original artwork. Jacket (dinner). Cr cds: A, DS, MC, V.

D

★ ★ ★ **KIMBERTON INN.** *Kimberton Rd, Kimberton (19442). Phone 610/933-8148; fax 610/935-3430. www.kimbertoninn.com.* Continental menu. Specializes in fresh seafood. Hours: 5:30-9:30 pm; Sun to 8:30 pm; Sun brunch 11 am-2 pm. Closed Mondays. Dinner $19.95-$29.95. Sun brunch $21.95. Bar. Reservations accepted. Tavern (1796) on 4 1/2 acres of gardens. Cr cds: A, C, D, DS, MC, V.

D

★ ★ **SEVEN STARS INN.** *263 Hoffecker Rd (19460). Phone 610/495-5205; fax 610/495-5340. www.sevenstarsinn.com.* Specializes in prime rib, seafood, veal. Hours: 4:30-10 pm; weekends to 11 pm; Sun 3-7 pm. Closed Mon; most major holidays. Complete meals: dinner $23-$33. Bar. Children's menu. Reservations accepted. Cr cds: D, MC, V.

D

Warren

Founded 1795 **Pop** 10,259 **Elev** 1,200 ft **Area code** 814 **Zip** 16365

Information Warren County Chamber of Commerce, 308 Market St, PO Box 942; 814/723-3050; or Travel Northern Alleghenies, 315 Second St, at the point, PO Box 804, 814/726-1222

Web www.warrenpachamber.com

At the junction of the Allegheny and Conewango rivers, Warren is the headquarters and gateway of the famous Allegheny National Forest. Named for General Joseph Warren, American patriot killed in the Battle of Bunker Hill, the town was once the point where great flotillas of logs were formed for the journey to Pittsburgh or Cincinnati.

What to See and Do

Allegheny National Forest. *222 Liberty St (16365). Phone 814/723-5150.* More than 510,000 acres S and E on US 6, 62, located in Warren, Forest, McKean, and Elk counties. Black bear, whitetail deer, wild turkey, a diversity of small birds and mammals; streams and reservoirs with trout, walleye, muskellunge, northern pike, and bass; rugged hills, quiet valleys, open meadows, dense forest. These lures, plus swimming, boating, hiking, camping, and picnicking facilities, draw more than 2 million visitors a year. Hundreds of campsites; fees are charged at some recreation sites. In forest are

Buckaloons Recreation Area. *Klondike. 6 miles W on US 6. Phone 814/362-4613 or 814/368-8116 (TTY).* Site of former Native American village on the banks of the Allegheny River. Boat launching. Picnicking. Camping (fee). Seneca Interpretive Trail.

Kinzua Dam and Allegheny Reservoir. *1205 Kinzua Rd (16365). Phone 814/726-0661, 814/362-4613 or 814/726-0164 (24-hour fishing hotline).* Dam (179 feet high, 1,897 feet long) with 27-mile-long lake. Swimming; fishing; boating (ramps, rentals; fees). Picnicking, overlooks. Camping (fee). Kinzua Dam Visitor Center has displays. Kinzua Point Information Center, 4 miles NE of dam, phone 814/726-1291. Some fees. 3 miles SE on US 6, then 6 miles E on PA 59. (It is possible that the PA 59 bridge, 1 1/2 miles E of Kinzua Dam, will be closed; phone ahead for information.)

Chapman State Park. *RR 1. 7 miles SE on US 6, then W at light in Clarendon. Phone 814/723-0250.* Approximately 800 acres. Lake and creek stocked with trout and bass. Swimming beach; fishing, hunting; boating (rentals, mooring, launching). Hiking. Cross-country skiing, snowmobiling, sledding, ice skating, ice fishing. Picnicking, snack bar. Tent and trailer sites available (some with electric; fee). Interpretive program.

Washington (G-2)

Founded 1781 **Pop** 15,268 **Elev** 1,120 ft **Area code** 724 **Zip** 15301

Information Washington County Tourism Promotion Agency, Franklin Mall, 1500 W Chestnut St; 724/228-5520 or 800/531-4114

Web www.washpatourism.org

Originally a Native American village known as Catfish Camp, the village of Bassettown became Washington during the Revolution. During the Whiskey Rebellion the town was a center of protest against the new federal government's tax; arrival of federal troops quieted the rebellious farmers. Washington and Jefferson College (1781) is located here.

What to See and Do

David Bradford House. *175 S Main St. Phone 724/222-3604.* (1788) Restored frontier home of a leader of the Whiskey Rebellion. (May-mid-Dec, Wed-Sat, limited hours, also Sun afternoons)

LeMoyne House. *49 E Maiden St. Phone 724/225-6740.* (1812) Abolitionist's home, built by the LeMoyne family, was a stop on the underground railroad; period furnishings, paintings, library; gardens; museum shop. Administered by Washington County Historical Society. (Jan-Feb, Tues-Fri; Mar-Dec, Tues-Sat) **$$**

Magna Entertainment Corporation. *4 miles N on US 19. Phone 724/225-9300.* Harness racing. Parimutuel betting. (Tues, Thurs-Sat evenings) Simulcasts (daily).

Meadowcroft Museum of Rural Life. *19 miles NW via PA 18, 50, in Avella. Phone 724/587-3412.* A 200-acre outdoor museum complex that preserves the history of life on the land in Western Pennsylvania. General store, restored log houses, one-room schoolhouse, blacksmith shop, and archaeology exhibit. (May-Oct, Wed-Sun) **$$$**

Pennsylvania Trolley Museum. *1 Museum Rd (15301). I-79 N, exit 41 (Meadowlands), follow signs.* Museum displays include more than 35 trolley cars dating from 1894. Scenic trolley ride; car barn and trolley-restoration shop; visitor center and gift shop with exhibit, video presentation and picnic area. (June-Aug, daily; Apr-May and Sept-Dec, weekends) **$$$**

Motels/Motor Lodges

★ **ECONO LODGE.** *1385 W Chestnut St (15301). Phone 724/222-6500; fax 724/222-6501. www.econolodge.com.* 62

rooms, 1-2 story. S $40-$60; D $48-$68; each additional $6; under 18 free; higher rates special events. Crib free. TV; cable (premium). Complimentary continental breakfast. Check-out 11 am. Business services available. Bellstaff. Airport transportation. Picnic tables. Cr cds: A, C, D, DS, JCB, MC, V.

⬛ ⬛ SC

★ ★ **HOLIDAY INN.** *340 Racetrack Rd (15301). Phone 724/222-6200; toll-free 800/465-4329; fax 724/228-1977. www.holiday-inn.com.* 138 rooms, 7 story. S, D $99-$109; each additional $6; under 18 free. Crib free. Pet accepted, some restrictions. TV; cable (premium), VCR available. Pool; whirlpool, poolside service, lifeguard. Restaurant 6:30 am-10 pm. Room service. Bars 11-2 am; entertainment. Check-out noon. Meeting rooms. Business services available. In-room modem link. Airport transportation. Exercise equipment; sauna. Microwaves available. Private patios. Meadows Racetrack adjacent. Cr cds: A, C, D, DS, ER, JCB, MC, V.

⬛ ⬛ ⬛ ⬛ ⬛ SC

★ **MOTEL 6.** *1283 Motel 6 Dr (15301). Phone 724/223-8040; fax 724/228-6445. www.motel6.com.* 102 rooms. S $35.99; D $42.39; each additional $6; under 18 free. Crib free. Pet accepted. Check-out noon. TV; cable (premium). Restaurant adjacent open 24 hours. Pool. Cr cds: A, C, D, DS, MC, V.

⬛ ⬛ ⬛ ⬛

★ **RED ROOF INN.** *1399 W Chestnut St (15301). Phone 724/228-5750; fax 724/228-5865. www.redroof.com.* 110 rooms, 2 story. May-Oct: S $35.99-$45.99; D $42.99-$64.99; each additional $6; under 18 free; lower rates rest of year. Crib free. Pet accepted, some restrictions. TV; cable (premium). Check-out noon. Cr cds: A, C, D, DS, MC, V.

⬛ ⬛ ⬛

Washington Crossing Historic Park (Bucks County) (G-14)

See also Doylestown (Bucks County), New Hope, Philadelphia

(Two sections: Bowman's Hill, 2 miles S of New Hope on PA 32, and Washington Crossing, 7 miles S of New Hope on PA 32)

Information Superintendent, PO Box 103, Washington Crossing, 18977; 215/493-4076.

In a blinding snowstorm on Christmas night 1776, George Washington and 2,400 soldiers crossed the Delaware River from the Pennsylvania shore and marched to Trenton, surprising the celebrating Hessian mercenaries and capturing the city. Washington's feat was a turning point of the Revolutionary War. Park (Tues-Sun; closed holidays). $2-$5

What to See and Do

Bowman's Hill Wildflower Preserve. *Located in southeastern PA in Bucks County, about 40 miles northeast of Philadelphia. Phone 215/862-2924.* If you'd like to explore outside the city, Bowman's Hill Wildflower Preserve is a great place to start. Pennsylvania's native plants come into focus at this 100-acre preserve located 40 miles northeast of Philadelphia. Hike or walk along a beautiful woodland, meadow, creek, or arboretum. Botanic enthusiasts will discover 1,000 species of trees, shrubs, ferns, vines, and herbaceous wildflowers. If you're an animal lover, don't forget to bring binoculars to watch for frogs. Photographers can catch a magnified moment in the display gardens. There are many contemplative places for meditation and study, scenic picnic spots, and several historic sites within hiking distance. Then head 5 miles south to Washington Crossing Historic Park (215/493-4076), where George Washington crossed the Delaware River in 1776. Bowman's Hill Tower, a lookout commemorating the American Revolution, offers a view of the Delaware River and rolling countryside 1 mile on foot or by car (215/862-3155). Nearby is New Hope, a perfect place for antiquing, art gallery hopping, shopping, or taking a mule barge ride on the Delaware Canal. (Daily; Closed Jan 1, Thanksgiving, Dec 25) **$$**

Washington Crossing.

   Concentration Valley. Where Washington assembled troops for raid on Trenton.

   Area of Embarkation. Marked by tall granite shaft supporting Washington's statue.

   McConkey Ferry Inn. (1752) Restored as historic house. Sold in 1777 to Benjamin Taylor, whose descendents established the 19th-century village of Taylorsville.

   Memorial Building. *Phone 215/493-4076.* Near Point of Embarkation. Houses copy of Emanuel Leutze's painting, Washington Crossing the Delaware. Movie shown five times a day.

   Memorial Flagstaff. *Bowman's Hill.* Marks graves of unknown Continentals who died during encampment. **$$**

Special Event

The Crossing. *Phone 215/493-4076.* Reenactment of Washington's crossing of the Delaware River, Christmas night in 1776. Dec.

Wellsboro

See also Galeton, Mansfield

Settled 1799 **Pop** 3,328 **Elev** 1,311 ft **Area code** 570 **Zip** 16901

Information Wellsboro Area Chamber of Commerce, 114 Main St, PO Box 733; 570/724-1926

Web www.wellsboropa.com

Wellsboro is the gateway to Pennsylvania's "canyon country." Settled largely by New Englanders, it is sustained by an assortment of industries. The area yields coal, natural gas, hardwoods, maple syrup, and farm products.

What to See and Do

Auto tours. There are more than a million acres of forests, mountains, and streams to be explored. The Wellsboro Area Chamber of Commerce has published a map of three tours.

   Red Arrow Tour. Follows PA 660 SW 10 miles from Wellsboro to Leonard Harrison State Park. Lookout Point, near the parking area, has large picnic area nearby. Path winds 1 mile from park to bottom of gorge, through shady glens, past waterfalls.

   White Arrow Tour. Leads from the Switchbacks (1 1/2 miles W of Bradley Wales Park), 3 miles S to Leetonia, once a prosperous lumber village, now occupied by State Forest Rangers; then W & N to Cushman View, Wilson Point Rd, Lee Fire Tower, Cedar Run Mountain Rd and US 6; approximately 75 miles.

   Yellow Arrow Tour. Leads from Leonard Harrison State Park, back on PA 660, NW on PA 362, then 1/4 mile W on US 6 to Colton Point Rd for views of the canyon and Four Mile Run Country. At Colton Point State Park (observation points, picnic shelters, fireplaces) the arrows follow Pine Creek S on old lumbering railroad tracks, converted into roadways called the "Switchbacks," to Bradley Wales Park overlooking Tiadaghton, the next lookout point on Pine Creek. From here continue S on W Rim Rd to Blackwell. From Blackwell, NE on PA 414 to Morris, then N on PA 287 to Wellsboro—a circle of 65 miles.

Robinson House Museum. *120 Main St. Phone 570/724-6116.* (circa 1820) Houses turn-of-the-century artifacts; genealogical library. (Mon-Fri afternoons) **FREE**

Ski Sawmill Family Resort. *Oregon Hill Rd, 16 miles S via PA 287. Phone 570/353-7521; 800/532-SNOW.* Chairlift, three T-bars; patrol, school, rentals; snowmaking; cafeteria, restaurant, bar. Longest run 3,250 feet; vertical drop 515 feet. (Dec-Mar, daily) Year-round activities. **$$$$**

Special Event

Pennsylvania State Laurel Festival. *114 Main St.* Week-long event includes parade of floats, marching musical and precision units, antique cars, laurel queen contestants; crowning of the queen; arts and crafts; children's pet and hobby parade, exhibits and displays. Mid-June.

Motels/Motor Lodges

★ **CANYON MOTEL.** *18 East Ave (16901). Phone 570/724-1681; toll-free 800/255-2718; fax 570/724-1681. www.canyonmotel.com.* 28 rooms. S $28-$45; D $32-$49; each additional $5; under 12 free; golf, ski package plans. Crib $5. Pet accepted. TV; cable. Heated pool; lifeguard. Playground. Complimentary continental breakfast. Check-out 11 am. Business services available. In-room modem link. Downhill/cross-country ski 17 miles. Refrigerators. Picnic tables, grills. Cr cds: A, C, D, DS, MC, V.

D 🐾 🏊 ⛆ ⛷ SC

★ **PENN WELLS LODGE.** *4 Main St (16901). Phone 570/724-3463; toll-free 800/545-2446; fax 570/724-2270.* 55 rooms, 2 story. S $53-$61; D $61-$69; each additional $5; under 18 free. Check-out noon. TV; cable. Exercise room, sauna. Indoor pool, whirlpool. Downhill, cross-country ski 17 miles. Cr cds: A, D, DS, MC, V.

D 🏊 🏋 ⛷ ⛆

★ **SHERWOOD MOTEL.** *2 Main St (16901). Phone 570/724-3424; toll-free 800/626-5802; fax 570/724-5658. www.sherwoodmotel.org.* 42 rooms, 1-2 story. S $37; D $49-$54; each additional $5; under 10 free; golf, ski package plans. Crib $5. Pet accepted; $5. TV; cable. Heated pool; lifeguard. Playground. Check-out 11 am. Business services available. In-room modem link. Downhill/cross-country ski 17 miles. Refrigerators. Cr cds: A, DS, MC, V.

D 🐾 🏊 🏋 ⛷ ⛆

Hotel

★★ **PENN WELLS HOTEL & LODGE.** *62 Main St (16901). Phone 570/724-2111; toll-free 800/545-2446; fax 570/724-3703. www.pennwells.com.* 73 rooms. Late May-Oct, hunting season: S $30-$40; D $40-$49; each additional $5; suites $55-$60; under 18 free; golf plans; lower rates rest of year. Check-out noon. TV; cable. Restaurant 7 am-1:30 pm, 5-10 pm. Bar 11:30-1 am; entertainment Fri, Sat. Exercise room, sauna. Indoor pool, whirlpool. Downhill, cross-country ski 17 miles. Built in 1869; high ceilings, oak and cherry woodwork, antiques, early Americana. Cr cds: A, DS, MC, V.

D 🏊 🏋 ⛷ ⛆

B&B/Small Inn

★★ **KALTENBACH'S BED AND BREAKFAST.** *Stony Fork Rd (16901). Phone 570/724-4954; toll-free 800/772-4954. www.kaltenbachsinn.com.* 10 rooms, 2 suites. Complimentary full breakfast. Check-out 11 am, check-in noon. TV; cable (premium). Restaurant. Greens fee $35. Downhill ski 12 miles; cross-country ski 20 miles. 5 room phones. Totally nonsmoking. Cr cds: A, C, D, DS, MC, V. **$**

D ⛆ 🏋 🎿 ⛆

West Chester (H-12)

See also Chester, Kennett Square, King of Prussia, Media, Philadelphia

Founded 1788 **Pop** 17,861 **Elev** 459 ft **Area code** 484 & 610

Information Chester County Tourist Bureau, 601 Westtown Rd, Suite 170, 19382; 610/344-6365 or 800/228-9933

Web www.brandywinevalley.com

In the heart of three Pennsylvania Revolutionary War historic sites—Brandywine, Paoli, and Valley Forge—West Chester today is a university and residential community with fine examples of Greek Revival and Victorian architecture.

What to See and Do

Brinton 1704 House. *5 miles S just off US 202, Oakland Rd, in Dilworthtown. Phone 302/478-2853.* Stone house built by Quaker farmer William Brinton, authentically restored and furnished. (May-Oct, Sat, Sun; also by appointment) **$**

Motels/Motor Lodges

★ **ABBEY GREEN MOTOR LODGE.** *1036 Wilmington Pike (19382). Phone 610/692-3310; fax 610/431-0811. www.abbeygreen.com.* 6 rooms. S $49-59; D $59-$69; each additional $5; cottages with kitchen $59-$69; weekly rates. Crib free. Pet accepted. TV; cable (premium). Restaurant nearby. Check-out 11 am. Business services available. Gift shop. Refrigerators; some fireplaces; microwaves available. Picnic tables, grill. Cr cds: A, C, D, DS, MC, V.

D 🐾 ⛆

★★ **BEST WESTERN.** *Rtes 322 and 1 (19331). Phone 610/358-9381; toll-free 800/522-0070; fax 610/358-9381. www.concordville.com.* 116 rooms, 5 story, 25 suites. S $110; D $125; each additional $15; suites $160-$195; under 12 free. Crib free. Complimentary continental breakfast. Check-out noon. TV; cable, VCR available. In-room modem link. Refrigerator in suites, mini bars. Valet services. Restaurant (see also YE OLDE CONCORD-VILLE INN). Bar. Exercise room, sauna. Indoor pool, whirlpool, lifeguard. Beauty shop; spa. Meeting rooms. Business services. Gift shop. Cr cds: A, C, D, DS, MC, V.

D ⊷ 🕏 🔌 SC

★ ★ **HOLIDAY INN.** *943 S High St (19382). Phone 610/692-1900; toll-free 800/465-4329; fax 610/692-5598. www.holiday-inn.com.* 143 rooms, 3 story. S, D $85-$105; each additional $10; suites $109-$129; kitchen suites $129-$149; under 17 free. Crib free. TV; cable (premium), VCR available. Pool; lifeguard. Restaurant 6:30 am-10 pm. Room service. Bar 4 pm-2 am. Check-out noon. Coin laundry. Meeting rooms. Business services available. In-room modem link. Valet service. Airport transportation. Lawn games. Exercise equipment. Microwaves available. Cr cds: A, C, D, DS, JCB, MC, V.

D ⊷ 🕏 ✈ 🔌 SC

B&B/Small Inn

★ ★ ★ **DULING-KURTZ HOUSE & COUNTRY INN.** *146 S Whitford Rd (19341). Phone 610/524-1830; fax 610/524-6258. www.duling-kurtz.com.* This small inn is located within walking distance to shopping, the train station, and more. 15 rooms, 5 suites, 3 story. Complimentary continental breakfast. Check-out 11 am, check-in 3 pm. TV; cable (premium). Restaurant. Room service. Built in 1783; period furniture, sitting room. Cr cds: A, C, D, DS, MC, V. **$**

🔌

Restaurant

★ ★ ★ **YE OLDE CONCORDVILLE INN.** *US 1 and US 322 (19331). Phone 610/459-2230; fax 610/459-1446. www.concordville.com.* Hours: 11 am-10 pm; Sun to 8 pm; early-bird dinner 4-5:30 pm. Closed Dec 25. Reservations accepted. Continental menu. Bar to 2 am. Wine cellar. Lunch $5.50-$9.95; dinner $14.95-$24.95. Children's menu. Specializes in crab cakes, prime rib. Outdoor seating. Family-owned. Cr cds: A, C, D, DS, MC, V.

D

West Middlesex

Pop 929 **Elev** 840 ft **Area code** 724 **Zip** 16159

Motel/Motor Lodge

★ ★ **HOLIDAY INN.** *3200 S Hermitage Rd (16159). Phone 724/981-1530; toll-free 800/465-4329; fax 724/981-1518. www.holiday-inn.com.* 180 rooms, 3 story. S, D $79.95; under 19 free; golf plans. Crib free. Pet accepted. TV; cable (premium). Heated pool; poolside service, lifeguard. Playground. Restaurant 6:30 am-10 pm; Dec-Mar 6:30 am-2 pm, 5-10 pm. Room service. Bar 11-2 am; entertainment. Check-out 11 am. Coin laundry. Meeting rooms. Business services available. In-room modem link. Valet service. Game room. Cr cds: A, C, D, DS, ER, JCB, MC, V.

D ⊷ ⊷ 🔌 SC

Hotel

★ ★ **RADISSON HOTEL SHARON.** *I-80 and Rte 18 (16159). Phone 724/528-2501; toll-free 800/333-3333; fax 724/528-2306. www.radisson.com.* 153 rooms, 3 story. S $80-$90; D $88-$98; each additional $8; suites $150-$200; under 12 free; weekend rates. Crib free. Pet accepted. TV; cable. Indoor pool; whirlpool, poolside service, lifeguard. Restaurant 6:30 am-10 pm. Room service. Bar 11-2 am; entertainment Wed, Fri, Sat. Check-out 11 am. Coin laundry. Meeting rooms. Business services available. Bellstaff. Valet service. Gift shop. Sundries. Exercise equipment; sauna. Game room. In-room whirlpools. Refrigerator in suites. Cr cds: A, C, D, DS, ER, JCB, MC, V.

D ⊷ ⊷ 🕏 🔌 SC

White Haven

See also Hazleton, Jim Thorpe, Pocono Mountains, Wilkes Barre

Pop 1,182 **Elev** 1,221 ft **Area code** 570 **Zip** 18661

Information Pocono Mountains Vacation Bureau, 1004 Main St, Stroudsburg 18360, phone 570/424-6050; for free brochures, phone 800/POCONOS

Web www.poconos.org

What to See and Do

Hickory Run State Park. *6 miles S on PA 534 off I-80, exit 41. Phone 570/443-0400.* Approximately 15,500 acres of scenic area. Swimming beach; fishing, hunting; hiking; cross-country skiing, snowmobiling, sledding, ice skating, ice fishing. Picnicking, playground, snack bar, store. Tent and trailer sites. Standard fees.

Ski areas.

Big Boulder. *Rte 940 and Moseywood Rd. 1 mile E off PA 903 in Lake Harmony. Phone 570/722-0100.* Five double, two triple chairlifts; patrol, school, rentals; snowmaking; cafeteria, bar; nursery, lodge. Night skiing. Longest run approximately 3/4 mile; vertical drop 475 feet. (Dec-Mar, daily) **$$$$**

Jack Frost. *Rte 940. 6 miles E on PA 940. Phone 570/ 443-8425.* Two triple, five double chairlifts; patrol, school, rentals; snowmaking; cafeteria, restaurant, bar; nursery. Longest run approximately 1/2 mile; vertical drop 600 feet. (Dec-Mar, daily) Half-day rate. **$$$$**

Motels/Motor Lodges

★ **COMFORT INN.** *Rte 940 (18661). Phone 570/443-8461; fax 570/443-7988. www.comfortinn.com.* 123 rooms, 6 story. S, D $70; each additional $10; under 18 free; ski plans. Crib free. TV; cable. Pool. Restaurant adjacent 6 am-midnight. Bar 11-2 am. Check-out noon. Meeting rooms. Business services available. Downhill/cross-country ski 4 miles. Hiking trails. Game room. Cr cds: A, C, D, DS, JCB, MC, V.

⊠ ⤢ ⬿ SC

★ **RAMADA INN.** *Rte 940, Lake Harmony (18624). Phone 570/443-8471; toll-free 800/251-2610; fax 570/ 443-0326. www.poconoramada.com.* 138 rooms, 2 suites, 4 story. Jan-Feb and mid-June-Columbus Day: S $90-$120; D $95-$130; each additional $10; under 18 free; higher rates NASCAR races; lower rates rest of year. Crib free. Pet accepted; $50 deposit. TV; cable. Indoor pool; poolside service, lifeguard. Sauna. Restaurant 7 am-10 pm. Room service. Bar 4 pm-midnight. Check-out noon. Meeting room. Business services available. Gift shop. Valet service. Coin laundry. Airport transportation. Golf privileges, greens fee $40, pro, putting green, driving range. Downhill/cross-country ski 4 miles. Game room. Lawn games. Some refrigerators. Picnic tables. Cr cds: A, C, D, DS, JCB, MC, V.

D ⤿ ⤢ ⬿ ⊠

Resort

★ ★ ★ **MOUNTAIN LAUREL RESORT AND SPA.** *I-80 at PA Tpke NE exit (18661). Phone 570/443-8411; fax 570/443-5518. www.mountainlaurelresort.com.* 250 rooms, 3 story. MAP: S $134; D $188/person; each additional $10; suites $150; under 13 free; golf plan; some weekend rates; higher rates holidays. Crib free. Check-out noon, check-in 4 pm. TV; cable, VCR available (movies). Coin laundry. Dining room 6-9 pm. Bar 11-2 am; entertainment. Supervised children's activities. Playground. Exercise room, sauna. Social director. Sports director. Game room. 2 pools, 1 indoor; whirlpool, poolside service, lifeguard. 18-hole golf, greens fee from $44 (including cart), driving range, putting green, miniature golf. Four lighted tennis courts. Downhill ski 5 miles. Picnic tables. Snacks, picnics. Airport transportation. Meeting rooms. Business center. Archery. Nursery. Movies. Cr cds: A, MC, V.

D ⤿ ⟡ ⤡ ⟊ ⟟ ⤢ ⊠ ⟟ ⟊ ⟡

Restaurant

★ ★ ★ **POWERHOUSE.** *I-80, exit 273 (18661). Phone 570/443-4480; fax 570/443-7784. www.powerhouse eatery.com.* Exposed pipes and valves let diners remember the history of Powerhouse's building while they dine on Italian specialties. Italian, American menu. Closed Dec 24, 25. Bar. Located in old power plant. Reservations accepted. Cr cds: A, MC, V. **$$**

D

Wilkes Barre (D-11)

See also Hazleton, Pocono Mountains, Scranton, White Haven

Founded 1769 **Pop** 43,123 **Elev** 550 ft **Area code** 570

Information Northeast Pennsylvania Convention & Visitors Bureau, 99 Glenmaura National Blvd, Scranton, 18507; 800/22WELCOME

Web www.visitnepa.org

Named in honor of two members of the British Parliament who championed individual rights and supported the colonies, Wilkes-Barre (WILKS-berry) and the Wyoming Valley were settled by pioneers from Connecticut. Pennsylvania and Connecticut waged the Pennamite-Yankee War, the first phase ending in 1771 with Connecticut in control of the valley. It was later resumed until Connecticut relinquished its claims in 1800. Wilkes-Barre was burned by the Native Americans and Tories during the Revolution and again by Connecticut settlers protesting the Decree of Trenton (1782), in which Congress favored Pennsylvania's claim to the territory. Discovery of anthracite coal in the valley sparked the town's growth after Judge Jesse Fell demonstrated that anthracite could be burned in a grate without forced draft.

Motels/Motor Lodges

★ ★ **BEST WESTERN EAST MOUNTAIN INN & SUITES.** *2400 E End Blvd (18702). Phone 570/822-1011; toll-free 800/528-1234; fax 570/822-6072. www.bestwestern.com.* 156 rooms, 24 suites, 7 story. S $87-$92; D $92-$97; each additional $5; suites $115-$120; under 13 free; ski, golf plans; higher rates special events. Crib free. TV; cable, VCR available (movies). Indoor pool; whirlpool, poolside service, lifeguard. Restaurant 6 am-11 pm. Bar 11-1 am; entertainment Tues-Sun. Check-out noon. Coin laundry. Meeting rooms. Business services available. In-room modem link. Free airport, train station, bus depot transportation. Tennis privileges. Downhill ski 10 miles.

Exercise equipment; sauna. Game room. Refrigerator, wet bar in suites. Balconies. Cr cds: A, C, D, DS, ER, MC, V.

⬜ ⬜ ⬜ ⬜ ⬜ ⬜ SC

★ ★ **BEST WESTERN GENETTI HOTEL & CONVENTION CENTER.** *77 E Market St (18701). Phone 570/823-6152; toll-free 800/833-6152; fax 570/820-8502. www.bestwestern.com.* 72 rooms, 16 suites, 5 story. Apr-Dec: S $74-$79; D $79-$89; each additional $10; suites $89-$99; under 12 free; higher rates NASCAR races; lower rates rest of year. Crib free. Pet accepted; $25. Check-out 11 am. TV; cable, VCR available (movies). Valet services, coin laundry. Restaurant 7 am-2 pm, 5-9 pm. Bar 4 pm-2 am; entertainment. Room service. Pool, poolside service. Downhill/cross-country ski 12 miles. Meeting rooms. Business services. Cr cds: A, C, D, DS, MC, V.

⬜ ⬜ ⬜ ⬜

★ **HAMPTON INN.** *1063 Hwy 315 (18702). Phone 570/825-3838; toll-free 800/426-7866; fax 570/825-8775. www.hamptoninn.com.* 123 rooms, 5 story. May-Oct: S $55-$65; D $65-$75; under 18 free; ski plans; higher rates: car races, Dec 31; lower rates rest of year. Crib free. Pet accepted. Complimentary continental breakfast. Check-out noon. TV; cable. In-room modem link. Mon-Fri. Downhill ski 10 miles. Meeting room. Business services. Cr cds: A, C, D, DS, ER, MC, V.

⬜ ⬜ ⬜ ⬜ SC

★ ★ **HOLIDAY INN.** *880 Kidder St (18702). Phone 570/824-8901; toll-free 888/466-9272; fax 570/824-9310.* 120 rooms, 2 story. S, D $69-$120; each additional $10; studio rooms $75; package plans. Pet accepted. TV; cable. Pool; wading pool, poolside service. Restaurant 6:30-1 am. Room service. Bar noon-2 am. Check-out noon. Meeting rooms. Business services available. In-room modem link. Bellstaff. Sundries. Downhill ski 10 miles. Cr cds: A, C, D, DS, ER, JCB, MC, V.

⬜ ⬜ ⬜ ⬜ ⬜ SC

Resort

★ ★ ★ **WOODLANDS INN & RESORT.** *1073 Hwy 315 (18702). Phone 570/824-9831; toll-free 800/762-2222; fax 570/824-8865. www.woodlandresort.com.* 179 rooms, 25 apartments, 9 story. S $69-$107; D $79-$107; each additional $10; package plans; weekend rates. Crib $5. TV; cable. 2 pools, 1 indoor; whirlpool, poolside service, lifeguard. Restaurant 7 am-11 pm. Room service. Bar 11-2 am; entertainment, dancing. Check-out noon. Meeting rooms. Business services available. Bellstaff. Sundries. Barber, beauty shop. Free airport transportation. Lighted tennis. Exercise room; sauna. Game room. Recreation room. Lawn games. Private patios, balconies. Cr cds: A, C, D, DS, MC, V.

⬜ ⬜ ⬜ ⬜ ⬜ SC

B&B/Small Inn

★ ★ **PONDA-ROWLAND BED AND BREAKFAST.** *RR 1, Box 349 (84532). Phone 570/639-3245; toll-free 888/855-9966; fax 570/639-5531. www.pondarowland.com.* 5 rooms, 2 story. No room phones. S, D $70-$95; each additional $25; under 3 free; holidays (2-day minimum). Crib free. 2 cable TVs. Playground. Complimentary full breakfast. Check-out noon, check-in 1 pm. Business services available. Refrigerators. Picnic tables. On 130-acre farm. Country antiques. Totally nonsmoking. Cr cds: A, DS, MC, V.

⬜ ⬜

Restaurants

★ ★ **BLACK ROCK BREWING CO.** *380 Coal St (18702). Phone 570/270-7625; fax 570/270-7630. www.blackrockbrewing.com.* American menu. Lunch, dinner, late night. Bar. Children's menu. Casual attire. Outdoor seating. **$$**

★ ★ ★ **SABER ROOM.** *94 Butler St (18702). Phone 570/829-5743; fax 570/829-5311.* Courteous service is found at this fine-dining establishment. Hours: 11 am-2:30 pm, 5-11 pm; Sat from 5 pm. Closed Sun, Easter, July 4. Reservations accepted, required holidays. Continental menu. Bar. Wine list. A la carte entrées: lunch $3.95-$8.95, dinner $10.95-$21.95. Specializes in veal, seafood. Family-owned. Cr cds: A, DS, MC, V.

⬜

Williamsport (D-9)

Settled 1795 **Pop** 30,706 **Elev** 528 ft **Area code** 570 **Zip** 17701

Information Lycoming County Tourist Promotion Agency, 454 Pine St; 800/358-9900

Now famous as the birthplace of Little League baseball, Williamsport once was known as the "lumber capital of the world." In 1870, a log boom extended 7 miles up the Susquehanna River; 300 million feet of sawed lumber were produced each year. When the timber was exhausted the city developed diversified industry and remained prosperous. The historic district of Williamsport, known as "millionaire's row," includes homes of former lumber barons.

What to See and Do

Hiawatha. *I-180, Reach Rd exit, in Susquehanna State Park. Phone 800/248-9287.* Sightseeing trips down Susquehanna River aboard replica of an old-fashioned paddlewheel riverboat. Public cruises (May-Oct, Tues-Sun).

Little League Baseball International Headquarters. *Rte 15. 1 mile S on US 15. Phone 570/326-1921.* Summer baseball camp and Little League World Series Stadium are here. (Mon-Fri; closed holidays) **FREE** Adjacent is

Little League Baseball Museum. *Rte 15. 1 mile S on US 15. Phone 570/326-3607.* (Memorial Day-Labor Day, daily; rest of year, Mon, Thurs-Sun; closed Jan 1, Thanksgiving, Dec 25) **$$**

Little Pine State Park. *15 miles SW via US 220, then 13 miles N via PA 44 and Legislative Rte 4001. Phone 570/753-6000.* Approximately 2,000 acres. Swimming beach; fishing, hunting; boating (ramps, mooring); cross-country skiing, snowmobiling, sledding, ice skating, ice fishing. Picnicking, playground, store. Tent and trailer sites (electric hook-ups). Interpretive program.

Thomas T. Thaber Museum of the Lycoming County Historical Society. *858 W 4th St. Phone 570/326-3326.* Exhibits on regional history from 10,000 B.C. to present. Exhibits include Native American, frontier era; canals, steam fire engine and hose cart; military history; general store, blacksmith shop, woodworker's shop, gristmill, crafts and industry; Victorian parlor and furnished period rooms; wildlife, sports and Little League; lumber business. (May-Oct, daily; rest of year, Tues-Sun; closed major holidays) **$$** Within the museum is

Shempp Toy Train Collection. Extensive toy train collection. More than 350 train sets on display, including the entire Lionel collection. Two detailed running displays allow visitors to start trains, blow whistles. Twelve unique trains include an American Flyer #3117 and Lionel "Super #381."

Special Events

Little League World Series. Teams from all over the world compete. Third week in Aug.

Lycoming County Fair. *20 miles SE via US 220, at Hughesville Fairgrounds.* More than 50 acres of amusements, commercial displays, livestock judging, demolition derbies, grandstand entertainment, food. Mid-July.

Victorian Sunday. House tours, flower show, entertainment. Second Sun in June.

Motels/Motor Lodges

★**ECONO LODGE.** *2019 E 3rd St (17701). Phone 570/326-1501; fax 570/326-9776. www.econolodge.com.* 99 rooms, 2 story. S $45-$50; D $50-$55; each additional $5; higher rates Little League World Series. Crib free. Pet accepted. Check-out noon. TV; cable (premium). Valet service. Restaurant 6 am-8 pm. Bar 6 pm-2 am; entertainment Tues-Sat. Meeting rooms. Business services. Cr cds: A, C, D, DS, JCB, MC, V.

🄳 🐾 ✈ ⬍

★ ★ **HOLIDAY INN.** *1840 E 3rd St (17701). Phone 570/326-1981; toll-free 800/369-4572; fax 570/323-9590. www.holiday-inn.com.* 170 rooms, 2 story. S, D $64-$79; each additional $10; under 18 free; higher rates Little League World Series. Crib free. Pet accepted, some restrictions. Check-out 11 am. TV; cable. In-room modem link. Coin laundry. Restaurant 6:30-1 am. Bar 11-1:30 am. Room service. Pool, lifeguard. Meeting rooms. Business services. Cr cds: A, C, D, DS, JCB, MC, V.

🄳 🐾 ≋ ⬍

★ ★ **QUALITY INN.** *234 Montgomery Pike (17701). Phone 570/323-9801; toll-free 800/221-2222; fax 570/322-5231. www.qualityinn.com.* 115 rooms, 3 story. No elevator. S $55; D $61; each additional $7; suites $85-$90; under 18 free. Crib $4. TV; cable. Pool; poolside service, lifeguard. Restaurant 6:30 am-1:30 pm, 5-10 pm. Room service. Bar 4:30 pm-2 am; entertainment Wed, Fri, Sat. Check-out noon. Business services available. Valet service. Sundries. Airport, bus depot transportation. Game room. Cr cds: A, C, D, DS, ER, JCB, MC, V.

🄳 ≋ ⬍ **SC**

Hotels

★ ★ ★ **GENETTI HOTEL & SUITES.** *200 W 4th St (17701). Phone 570/326-6600; toll-free 800/321-1388; fax 570/326-5006. www.genetti.com.* 206 rooms, 42 suites, 10 story. S $29.95-$59, D $35.95-$65.95, each additional $6, suites $75.95-$139; under 10 free; higher rates Little League World Series; weekly rates; golf plans. Crib free. Pet accepted. Check-out 11 am. TV; cable (premium), VCR available. Some refrigerators. Coin laundry. Restaurant 6:30 am-10 pm. Bar 11-2 am; entertainment Fri, Sat. Exercise equipment. Pool, poolside service. Downhill ski, 20 miles. Barber, beauty shop. Free airport transportation. Meeting room. Business services. Cr cds: A, C, D, DS, MC, V.

🄳 🐾 ✈ ≋ 🏃

★ ★ **RADISSON HOTEL WILLIAMSPORT.** *100 Pine St (17701). Phone 570/327-8231; toll-free 800/325-3535; fax 570/322-2957. www.radisson.com.* This hotel is conveniently located near the Williamsport Regional Airport. 148 rooms, 5 story. S, D $85-$95; suites $150; under 18 free. Crib free. Pet accepted. TV; cable. Indoor pool. Restaurant 6:30 am-10 pm. Room service. Bar 11:30-2 am; DJ Tues-Sat. Check-out noon. Meeting rooms. Business services available. Bellstaff. Free airport transportation. Downhill/cross-country ski 18 miles. Some refrigerators. Whirlpool in suites. Cr cds: A, C, D, DS, ER, JCB, MC, V.

🄳 🐾 ✈ ≋ **SC**

Willow Grove

See also Philadelphia

Pop 35 **Elev** 310 ft **Area code** 215 & 267 **Zip** 19090

What to See and Do

Bryn Athyn Cathedral. *1000 Cathedral Rd. 3 miles N of PA Tpke, exit 27 on PA 611 N, then 4 miles E on County Line Rd to PA 232, in Bryn Athyn. Phone 215/947-0266.* Outstanding example of Gothic architecture. Free guided tours (Apr-Nov, Tues-Sun). On grounds adjacent is

Glencairn Museum. *1001 Cathedral Rd, at PA 232. Phone 215/938-2600.* Romanesque building features medieval sculpture and one of the largest privately owned collections of stained glass in the world; also Egyptian, Greek, Roman, ancient Near East, and Native American collections. (Mon-Fri by appointment) **$$**

Graeme Park. *859 County Line Rd (19044). 5 miles N on PA 611. Phone 215/343-0965.* (1722) A fine example of Georgian architecture; stone house built by Sir William Keith, colonial governor of colony 1717-1726. Tours. (Wed-Sun; closed holidays) **$$**

Motels/Motor Lodges

★ ★ **COURTYARD BY MARRIOTT.** *2350 Easton Rd (19090). Phone 215/830-0550; toll-free 800/321-2211; fax 215/830-0572. www.courtyard.com.* 149 rooms, 3 story. S, D $159; suites $170-$180; weekly, weekend rates. Crib free. TV; cable (premium), VCR available (movies). Indoor pool; whirlpool. Restaurant 6:30-10 am; Sat, Sun 7-11:30 am. Bar 5-10 pm Mon-Sat. Check-out noon. Coin laundry. Meeting rooms. Business services available. In-room modem link. Valet service. Airport transportation. Exercise equipment. Refrigerators; microwaves available. Cr cds: A, C, D, DS, MC, V.

[D] [⇌] [大] [⇘] [SC]

★ **HAMPTON INN.** *1500 Easton Rd (19090). Phone 215/659-3535; fax 215/659-4040. www.hamptoninn.com.* 150 rooms, 5 story. S, D $119-$139; under 18 free; weekend rates. Crib free. TV; cable (premium). Complimentary continental breakfast. Restaurants nearby. Check-out noon. Meeting rooms. Business services available. In-room modem link. Valet. Airport transportation. Exercise equipment; sauna. Health club privileges. Some refrigerators; microwaves available. Cr cds: A, C, D, DS, MC, V.

[D] [大] [⇘] [SC]

B&B/Small Inn

★ ★ ★ **JOSEPH AMBLER INN.** *1005 Horsham Rd (19454). Phone 215/362-7500; fax 215/361-5924.*

www.josephamblerinn.com. 37 rooms, 2-3 story. Complimentary full breakfast. Check-out 11 am, check-in 3 pm. TV; VCR available. In-room modem link. Restaurant. Private parking. Business center. Four buildings built 1734-1820; antiques. Cr cds: A, C, D, DS, MC, V. **$$**

[D] [⇘] [大]

Restaurant

★ ★ **CASABLANCA.** *1111 Easton Rd (18976). Phone 215/343-7715; fax 215/328-0774. www.casablancarestaurants.com.* Moroccan menu. Hours: 5-1 am. Dinner $24. Children's menu. Reservations required. Cr cds: A, D, DS, MC, V.

[D]

Wrightsville

See also Bird-in-Hand, Lancaster, Pennsylvania Dutch Area, York

Pop 2,223 **Elev** 306 ft **Area code** 717 **Zip** 17368

Information York County Visitors Information Center, 1618 Toronita St, York 17402; 717/848-4000 or 800/673-2429

Web www.yorkpa.org

What to See and Do

Donegal Mills Plantation & Inn. *5 miles N via US 30, PA 441, 772, in Mt Joy (Lancaster Co). Phone 717/653-2168.* (1800). Historic village and resort dating from 1736. Mansion, bake house, gardens; restaurant and lodging (year-round). Plantation tours (Mar-Dec, Sat and Sun afternoons). **$$**

York (H-9)

See also Hanover, Harrisburg, Lancaster, Pennsylvania Dutch Area, Wrightsville

Founded 1741 **Pop** 40,862 **Elev** 400 ft **Area code** 717

Information Convention and Visitors Bureau, 1 Market Way East, PO Box 1229, 17405, phone 800/673-2429; or the Visitors Information Center, 1618 Toronita St, 17402, phone 717/843-6660

Web www.yorkpa.org

York claims to be the first capital of the United States. The Continental Congress met here in 1777 and adopted the Articles of Confederation, using the phrase "United States of America" for the first time. The first Pennsylvania town founded west of the Susquehanna River, York was—and is still—based on an agricultural and industrial economy. The city is dotted with 17 historical markers and 35 brass or bronze tablets marking historical events or places. There are more than 10 recreation areas in the county.

What to See and Do

Bob Hoffman Weightlifting Hall of Fame. *3300 Board Rd (17402). 4 miles N via I-83, exit 11; at York Barbell Co corporate headquarters. Phone 717/767-6481.* Weightlifting section honors Olympic weightlifters, powerlifters, bodybuilders, and strongmen; displays include samples of Iron Game artifacts, memorabilia, and photos. (Mon-Sat; closed holidays) **FREE**

Central Market House. *34 W Philadelphia St. Phone 717/848-2243.* Opened in March 1888. Over 70 vendors offer fresh produce, homemade baked goods, regional handcrafts, and specialty items. (Tues, Thurs, Sat; closed holidays) **FREE**

Fire Museum of York County. *757 W Market St. Phone 717/843-0464.* Turn-of-the-century firehouse preserves two centuries of firefighting history; from leather bucket brigades to hand-drawn hose carts and pumps, horse-drawn equipment, and finally to motorized equipment; artifacts and memorabilia; fire chief's office and firefighter's sleeping quarters are re-created, complete with brass slide pole. (Apr-Oct, Sat and second Sun every month; also by appointment; closed holidays) **$**

Friends Meeting House. *135 W Philadelphia St. Phone 717/843-2285.* (1766) Original virgin pine paneling; restored. Regular meetings are still held here. (By appointment) **FREE**

Gifford Pinchot State Park. *2200 Rosstown Rd (17339). 14 miles NW on PA 74 to Rossville, then NE on PA 177. Phone 717/432-5011.* Approximately 2,300 acres; 340-acre lake. Fishing, hunting; boating (rentals, mooring, launching). Hiking. Cross-country skiing, ice skating, ice fishing, ice boating. Picnicking, store. Tent and trailer sites, cabins. Nature center, interpretive center. Standard fees.

Harley-Davidson, Inc. *1425 Eden Rd, 2 miles E on US 30. Phone 717/848-1177.* Guided tour through motorcycle assembly plant and the Rodney Gott Antique Motorcycle Museum. Children under 12 and cameras not permitted on plant tour. Plant and museum combination tour (Mon-Fri); museum tour (Sat). **FREE**

Historical Society of York County. *250 E Market St. Phone 717/848-1587.* Includes library with genealogical records (Tues-Sat; fee for nonmembers). Museum features exhibits on the history of York County. Combination ticket for all historic sites maintained by the society. (Daily; closed most major holidays) **$** Sites include

Bonham House. *152 E Market St. Phone 717/848-1587.* (circa 1875). Historic house reflects life in late 19th century. (By appointment; closed most holidays) **$**

General Gates' House. *157 W Market St (enter on N Pershing Ave).* (1751) It was here that Lafayette gave a toast to Washington, marking the end of a movement to replace him. Also here are Golden Plough Tavern (1741), one of the earliest buildings in York, which reflects the Germanic background of many of the settlers in its furnishings and half-timber architecture, and the Bobb Log House (1811), furnished with painted and grained furniture. (Tues-Sat; closed holidays) **$$**

Ski Roundtop. *925 Roundtop Rd (17339). 12 miles NW on PA 74, then 1/2 mile N on PA 177 to Mt Airy Rd, then to Roundtop Rd, follow signs. Phone 717/432-9631 or 800/767-4766 (snow report).* Triple, two double chairlifts, two quad, two J-bars, one magic carpet, two tubing lifts; patrol, school, rentals; snowmaking; cafeteria; nursery. Longest run 4,100 feet; vertical drop 600 feet. (Mid-Nov-mid-Mar, daily) **$$$$**

Warrington Friends Meeting House. *14 miles NW on PA 74.* (1769; expanded in 1782) Fine example of early Quaker meetinghouse.

York County Colonial Court House. *W Market and Pershing aves. Phone 717/848-1587.* Replica of 1754 original. Exhibits include multimedia presentation of Continental Congress's adoption of the Articles of Confederation, audiovisual story of 1777-1778 historic events; original printer's copy of Articles of Confederation, historic documents, and artifacts. Tours. (Daily) **$**

Special Event

River Walk Art Festival. *1 Market Way W. Along Codorus Creek at York County Colonial Court House.* Late Aug.

Motels/Motor Lodges

★ **BEST WESTERN WESTGATE INN.** *1415 Kenneth Rd (17404). Phone 717/767-6931; toll-free 800/528-1234; fax 717/767-6938. www.bestwestern.com.* 105 rooms, 3 story. S $57-$83; D $68-$93; each additional $5; under 18 free. Complimentary continental breakfast. Check-out noon. TV; cable (premium), VCR available (movies). In-room modem link. Health club privileges. Cr cds: A, C, D, DS, JCB, MC, V.

D ⊷ SC

★ **BUDGET HOST INN.** *1162 Haines Rd (17402). Phone 717/755-1068; toll-free 800/283-4678; fax 717/757-5571. www.budgethost.com.* 40 rooms, 1-2 story. S $34-$35; D $36-$50; each additional $4; under 12 free. Crib $2. TV; cable, VCR available (movies $5). Check-out 11 am. Some refrigerators; microwaves available. Cr cds: A, D, DS, MC, V.

⊷

★ **HAMPTON INN.** *1550 Mt Zion Rd (17402). Phone 717/840-1500; toll-free 800/426-7866; fax 717/840-1567. www.hamptoninn.com.* 144 rooms, 5 story. S $79-$83; D $87-$91; suites, kitchen units $95-$103; under 18 free. Crib free. TV; cable (premium), VCR available. Heated pool. Coffee in rooms. Complimentary continental breakfast. Check-out 11 am. Coin laundry. Meeting rooms. In-room modem link. Sundries. Exercise equipment. Refrigerator in suites. Picnic tables. Cr cds: A, C, D, DS, MC, V.

D ⚊ 🏋 🖼 SC

★ ★ **HOLIDAY INN.** *334 Arsenal Rd (17402). Phone 717/845-5671; fax 717/845-1898. www.holiday-inn.com.* 100 rooms, 2 story. S, D $69-$79; under 18 free. Crib free. Check-out noon. TV; cable (premium). Microwaves available. Valet services. Restaurant 6 am-2 pm, 5:30-10 pm. Bar 5 pm-midnight. Room service. Health club privileges. Pool. Meeting rooms. Business services. Sundries. Cr cds: A, D, DS, JCB, MC, V.

D ⚊ 🖼

★ ★ **HOLIDAY INN.** *2000 Loucks Rd (17404). Phone 717/846-9500; toll-free 800/465-4329; fax 717/764-5038. www.holiday-inn.com.* 181 rooms, 2 story. S, D $72-$98; under 18 free. Crib $10. Pet accepted. TV; cable (premium). 2 pools, 1 indoor; whirlpool, poolside service, lifeguard. Playground. Restaurant 6:30 am-9:30 pm. Room service. Bar 3 pm-2 am. Check-out 11 am. Meeting rooms. Business services available. Bellstaff. Valet service. Miniature golf. Exercise equipment; sauna. Cr cds: A, C, D, DS, JCB, MC, V.

D 🐾 ⚊ 🏋 🖼 SC

★ ★ **QUALITY INN.** *2600 E Market St (17402). Phone 717/755-1966; toll-free 800/228-5151; fax 717/755-6936. www.qualityinn.com.* 110 rooms, 2 story. S, D, studio rooms $69-$79; under 18 free. Crib free. TV; cable (premium). Pool; lifeguard. Restaurant 6 am-2 pm, 5:30-10 pm. Room service 7:30 am-9:30 pm. Bar 4 pm-midnight. Check-out noon. Business services available. In-room modem link. Valet service. Sundries. Free airport transportation. Health club privileges. Refrigerators, microwaves available. Cr cds: A, C, D, DS, JCB, MC, V.

D ⚊ 🖼 SC

Hotel

★ ★ ★ **YORKTOWNE HOTEL.** *48 E Market St (17405). Phone 717/848-1111; toll-free 800/233-9324; fax 717/854-7678. www.yorktowne.com.* Open since 1925, this hotel has hosted such guests as Eleanor Roosevelt, Mickey Mantle, Lucille Ball, and Richard Nixon. 122 rooms, 8 story. S $52-$89; D $59-$96; each additional $7; suites $95-$225. Crib free. TV; cable (premium). Restaurants 6:30-2 am. Bar from 11 am. Check-out noon. Meeting rooms. Business services available. In-room modem link. Gift shop. Barber. Free valet parking. Airport transportation. Exercise equipment. Health club privileges. Some in-room whirlpools; microwaves available. Cr cds: A, D, DS, MC, V.

D 🏋 🖼 SC

Restaurants

★ ★ ★ **ACCOMAC INN.** *6330 S River Dr (17368). Phone 717/252-1521; fax 717/252-5711. www.accomac.com.* Continental, French menu. Hours: 5:30-9:30 pm; Sun 4-8:30 pm; Sun brunch 11 am-2:30 pm. Closed Dec 25. Dinner $21.75-$32.25, Sun brunch $22.95-$28.95. Bar. Reconstructed historic building (1775) on banks of river. Reservations accepted. Porch dining. Cr cds: A, MC, V.

D

★ ★ **SAN CARLO'S.** *333 Arsenal Rd US 30 (17402). Phone 717/854-2028; fax 717/846-2983. www.sancarlos restaurants.com.* Continental menu. Hours: 4-9:30 pm; Fri, Sat to 10 pm. Dinner $9.95-$18.95. Bar. Entertainment. Children's menu. Renovated 175-year-old barn; original fieldstone walls. Cr cds: A, MC, V.

D

Virginia

Settled by Elizabethans and named for their Virgin Queen, the first of the Southern states still retains a degree of the graceful courtliness that reached its peak just before the Civil War. Evidence of strong ties with the past are apparent in the Old Dominion. More than 1,600 historical markers dot its 55,000 miles of paved roads. More than 100 historic buildings are open all year; hundreds more welcome visitors during the statewide Historic Garden Week (usually the last week in April).

Permanent English settlement of America began in Jamestown in 1607 and started a long line of Virginia "firsts": the first legislative assembly in the Western Hemisphere (1619); the first armed rebellion against royal government (Bacon's Rebellion, 1676); the first stirring debates, in Williamsburg and Richmond, which left pre-Revolutionary America echoing Patrick Henry's inflammatory "Give me liberty, or give me death!" Records show that America's first Thanksgiving was held December 4, 1619, on the site of what is now Berkeley Plantation.

To Virginia the nation owes its most cherished documents—Thomas Jefferson's Declaration of Independence, George Mason's Bill of Rights, James Madison's Constitution. From here came George Washington to lead the Revolution and to become the first of eight US presidents to hail from Virginia.

Ironically, the state so passionately involved in creating a new nation was very nearly the means of its destruction. Virginia was the spiritual and physical capital of the Confederacy; the Army of Northern Virginia was the Confederacy's most powerful weapon, General Robert E. Lee its greatest commander. More than half the fighting of the Civil War took place in Virginia; and here, in the courthouse of the quaint little village of Appomattox, the war finally came to an end.

When chartered in 1609, the Virginia territory included about one-tenth of what is now the United States; the present state ranks 36th in size, but the remaining area is remarkably diverse. Tidewater Virginia—the coastal plain—is low, almost flat, arable land cut by

Population: 6,377,000
Area: 40,767 square miles
Elevation: 0-5,729 feet
Peak: Mount Rogers (between Smyth, Grayson Counties)
Entered Union: Tenth of original 13 states (June 25, 1788)
Capital: Richmond
Motto: Thus always to tyrants
Nickname: Old Dominion
Flower: American Dogwood
Bird: Cardinal
Fair: Late September-Early October in Richmond
Time Zone: Eastern
Website: www.virginia.org

rivers and bays into a magnificent system of natural harbors. It was vital to commerce and agriculture in the early days. Today it is still important commercially (the Hampton Roads port is one of the world's great naval and shipbuilding bases) and is a perennial lure to vacationers as well.

Inland lies the gentle rolling Piedmont, covering about half the state. Here is Virginia's leading tobacco area; it also produces apples, corn, wheat, hay, and dairy products. The world's largest single-unit textile plant is in Danville; the Piedmont also manufactures shoes, furniture, paper products, clay, glass, chemicals, and transportation equipment.

West of the Piedmont rise the Blue Ridge Mountains; high, rugged upland plateaus occur to the south. Further west is the Valley of Virginia, a series of fertile valleys. Best known is the Shenandoah, which contains some of the richest—and once bloodiest—land in the nation. Civil War fighting swept the valley for four years; Winchester changed hands 72 times.

To the southwest are the Appalachian Plateaus, a rugged, forested region of coal mines. Here the splendid outdoor drama, *Trail of the Lonesome Pine*, romanticized by the novelist John Fox, is performed.

Calendar Highlights

APRIL

International Azalea Festival *(Norfolk). Phone 757/664-6620. Downtown and Norfolk Botanical Garden.* To honor NATO. Parade, coronation ceremony, air show (held at Norfolk Naval Air Station), events, concerts, fair, ball, entertainment.

Garden Week *(Charlottesville). For more information, phone Garden Club of Virginia/Richmond headquarters 804/644-7776.* Some fine private homes and gardens in the area are open.

Garden Week in Historic Lexington *(Lexington). Phone 540/463-3777.* Tour of homes and gardens in the Lexington and Rockbridge County areas.

MAY

Jamestown Weekend *(Jamestown, Colonial National Historical Park). Phone 757/229-1733.* Original Jamestown site. Commemorates arrival of first settlers in 1607; special tours and activities.

JUNE

Natural Chimneys Jousting Tournament *(Harrisonburg). Phone 540/350-2510. Natural Chimneys Regional Park.* America's oldest continuous sporting event, held annually since 1821. "Knights" armed with lances charge down an 80-yard track and attempt to spear 3 small rings suspended from posts.

Red Cross Waterfront Festival *(Alexandria). Phone 703/549-8300.* Commemorates Alexandria's maritime heritage. Features "tall ships," blessing of the fleet, river cruises, races, arts and crafts, exhibits, food, variety of music; fireworks.

JULY

Pony Penning *(Chincoteague). For more information, phone Chincoteague Chamber of Commerce, 757/336-6161.* The "wild" ponies are rounded up on Assateague Island, then swim the inlet to Chincoteague, where foals are sold at auction before the ponies swim back to Assateague. Carnival amusements.

SEPTEMBER

Publick Times *(Williamsburg). Phone 757/220-7645 or 800/246-2099. Colonial Williamsburg.* Recreation of colonial market days; contests, crafts, auctions, military encampment.

Virginia State Fair *(Richmond). Phone 804/228-3200.* Animal and 4-H contests, music, horse show, carnival.

OCTOBER

Blue Ridge Folklife Festival *(Martinsville). Phone 540/365-4415. Blue Ridge Farm Museum.* Gospel, blues, and string band music; traditional regional crafts; regional foods; quilt show, antique autos, steam and gas-powered farm equipment. Sports events include horse-pulling and log-skidding contests, coon dog swimming and treeing contests.

DECEMBER

Christmas Candlelight Tour *(Fredericksburg). Contact Visitor Center, phone 540/373-1776 or 800/678-4748.* Historic homes open to the public; carriage rides; Christmas decorations and refreshments of the colonial period.

For the vacationer today, the state offers colonial and Civil War history at every turn, seashore and mountain recreation year-round, such natural oddities as caverns in the west and the Dismal Swamp in the southeast, and the Skyline Drive (see SHENANDOAH NATIONAL PARK), one of the loveliest scenic drives in the East.

When to Go/Climate

Virginia summers can be hot and humid, marked by brief, powerful thunderstorms; winter snows are common in the mountains. Moderate temperatures, light rainfall, verdant flowering gardens, and brilliant foliage make spring and fall the best seasons to visit.

AVERAGE HIGH/LOW TEMPERATURES (°F)

Richmond

Jan 46/26	**May** 78/54	**Sept** 81/59
Feb 49/28	**June** 85/63	**Oct** 71/47
Mar 60/36	**July** 88/68	**Nov** 61/38
Apr 70/45	**Aug** 87/66	**Dec** 50/30

Roanoke

Jan 44/25	**May** 76/53	**Sept** 79/57
Feb 47/27	**June** 83/60	**Oct** 68/45
Mar 58/36	**July** 86/65	**Nov** 58/37
Apr 67/44	**Aug** 85/64	**Dec** 48/29

Parks and Recreation

Water-related activities, hiking, various other sports, picnicking and visitor centers, as well as camping, are available in many of these areas. State park facilities and services are operated on a seasonal basis. Parking for noncampers, $1.50-$2.50/car/day, Memorial Day-Labor Day. Admission to State Historical Parks $1.25; children $1. Swimming, boat rentals, cafes, and concessions, Memorial Day-Labor Day; fees for activities. Pets are allowed in camping and cabins, but must be kept inside at night. At all other times pets must be on a leash not longer than 6 feet. Facilities for the disabled at many parks.

Tent and trailer campgrounds are available in 19 state parks generally from March-November; maximum stay is 2 weeks. $11/site/night, $19.25 at Seashore (up to 6 persons, 1 vehicle); electricity and water $15/site/night where available. Reservations may be made 180 days-1 week in advance (see below for addresses). Seven parks offer housekeeping cabins (May-Sept). Douthat (see CLIFTON FORGE) has a guest lodge for 15. Reservations for campsites are accepted beginning in late March Campsite and cabin reservations may be made by phoning 800/933-PARK or 804/225-3867. Booklets with details on each park may be obtained from the Virginia Department of Conservation & Recreation, 203 Governor St, Suite 213, Richmond 23219. A campground directory is available from Virginia Tourism Corporation, 901 E Byrd St, Richmond 23219. Phone 804/786-4484.

HUNTING AND FISHING

Saltwater fishing on ocean, bay, river, or creek is a major sport. Virginia is blessed with many miles of shoreline: 120 miles on the Atlantic Ocean, 300 miles on Chesapeake Bay, and 1,300 miles of tidal shores. There is no closed season for saltwater fishing except for striped bass. There are some species size and bag limits. No license is required to fish in ocean waters or seaside of the eastern shore, but a license is required to fish in the Chesapeake and tidal tributaries. Information concerning size limits and bag limits on saltwater game fish may be obtained from the Virginia Marine Resources Commission, PO Box 756, Newport News 23607; phone 800/937-9247. The Commonwealth of Virginia sponsors an annual Saltwater Fishing Awards Program (see VIRGINIA BEACH), open to the public. Contact Virginia Saltwater Fishing Tournament, 968 S Oriole Dr, Suite 102, Virginia Beach 23451. Phone 757/491-5160.

Freshwater fishing is excellent in many of the state's large reservoirs and rivers for such species as largemouth and smallmouth bass, landlocked striped bass, muskie, and a wide variety of panfish. Lake Anna, Smith Mountain Lake, Lake Gaston, James River, Lake Moomaw, and Buggs Island Lake are nationally known for excellent bass and landlocked striped bass fishing. Nonresident license: $30; $30 additional for license for trout in designated stocked waters. Five-day license to fish statewide, $6; other special fees. Fishing in a national forest requires an additional fishing/hunting stamp, $3.

Hunting for upland game and migratory waterfowl in season. Nonresident license: $60; 3-day license: $30; bear, deer, turkey, $60 additional; nonresident muzzleloader license, $25; nonresident special archery license to hunt during special archery season, $25. Hunting in a national forest requires an additional fishing/hunting stamp, $3. There is a 50¢ issuance fee for all licenses. For fishing and hunting regulations and information write Department of Game and Inland Fisheries, 4010 W Broad St, Richmond 23230, or phone 804/367-1000.

Driving Information

Safety belts are mandatory for all persons in front seat of vehicle. Children under 4 years must be in approved safety seats anywhere in vehicle. For further information, phone 804/367-0538.

INTERSTATE HIGHWAY SYSTEM

The following alphabetical listing of Virginia towns in this book shows that these cities are within 10 miles of the indicated Interstate highways. Check a highway map for the nearest exit.

Highway Number	Cities/Towns within 10 Miles
Interstate 64	Ashland, Charlottesville, Chesapeake, Clifton Forge, Covington, Hampton, Jamestown, Lexington, Newport News, Norfolk, Portsmouth, Richmond, Staunton, Virginia Beach, Waynesboro, Williamsburg, Yorktown.
Interstate 66	Alexandria, Arlington County, Fairfax, Falls Church, Front Royal, Manassas, McLean.
Interstate 77	Wytheville.
Interstate 81	Abingdon, Blacksburg, Bristol, Front Royal, Harrisonburg, Lexington, Marion, Natural Bridge, New Market, Radford, Roanoke, Salem, Staunton, Strasburg, Winchester, Woodstock, Wytheville.
Interstate 85	Petersburg, South Hill.

Interstate 95   Alexandria, Arlington, County, Ashland, Emporia, Fairfax, Falls Church, Fredericksburg, Hopewell, McLean, Petersburg, Richmond, Springfield, Triangle.

Additional Visitor Information

Recreational and tourist information, including travel guides, brochures, and maps, is available from the Virginia Tourism Corporation, 901 E Byrd St, Richmond 23219; phone 800/932-5827. Virginia Department of Transportation, 1401 E Broad St, Richmond 23219, phone 804/786-2838, offers an official state map.

There are ten welcome information centers in Virginia at the following locations: the northern end of the state, on I-81 in Clear Brook, and on I-66 in Manassas; at the northeastern side, on I-95 in Fredericksburg; around the bay area on the eastern side, on US 13 in New Church; around the southerly border, on I-95 in Skippers, and on I-85 in Bracey; in the southwest part of the state, on I-81 in Bristol, and I-77 in Lambsburg; and on the western side, on I-64 in Covington, and on I-77 in Rocky Gap.

GEORGE WASHINGTON'S PLANTATIONS

Ask any historically knowledgeable American to name George Washington's home, and the answer you would expect is Mount Vernon, just south of Alexandria, Virginia, but this is only partly correct. In his youth, Washington lived on two other plantations—both of which, like Mount Vernon, honor the country's first president. Each unique home tells a different aspect of his life. All three can be visited in a one-day, 170-mile round-trip. Make sure to get an early start, and begin in Alexandria, a Potomac River port long before the Capitol at Washington, DC was conceived. Paralleling the Potomac, the scenic Mount Vernon Parkway winds south for about 10 miles to Mount Vernon, a sprawling estate Washington inherited at the age of 20 from a half-brother. Here, you can tour his stately white mansion, enjoy the Potomac views as he surely did, walk among the 18th-century farm fields and gardens, and pay homage at his and Martha's tombs. At Mount Vernon, you'll learn about Washington the farmer, the soldier, and the statesman, an imposing man of laudable qualities. Plan to spend much of the morning at the estate. About noon, head south to Washington's two childhood homes to get to know the youth who became the "father of his country." Your first stop is Popes Creek Plantation, which is officially called George Washington Birthplace National Monument. From Mount Vernon, take State Route 235 West to US 1 South and follow the signs to I-95 South to Fredericksburg—about 40 miles. In Fredericksburg, take State Route 3 east for about 36 miles. Make a left turn onto State Route 204, which ends at the plantation in about 2 miles. This is where Washington was born on February 22, 1732. Unlike Mount Vernon, nothing remains of the original house except a few foundation bricks and grand Potomac River views. And yet the 550-acre park—re-created in part as a colonial farm with fields, pastures, and livestock—does a fine job of exploring Washington's origins. His great-grandfather John, an English seaman, settled in the area in 1657, prospered, and was eventually buried in the park. You can tour Memorial House, a Colonial-style farmhouse similar to one that might have stood on the property in 1732. Nearby are other reconstructed period farm buildings and a large herb garden. Walking trails trace the river's shoreline past a grove of towering cedars, and a shaded picnic area is provided. Packing a picnic is a good idea since the park has no food service. Plan on staying about 90 minutes here, giving yourself time to return to Fredericksburg and Ferry Farm, where Washington's family moved when he was six. At the city outskirts, bear right onto Business Route 3. A sign to Ferry Farm will indicate a U-Turn at a stoplight. It is at Ferry Farm that Washington might have chopped down a cherry tree—wild cherries still grow on the property—and where he might have tossed a coin across the Rappahannock River. Archeological digs, sometimes open to visitors, are underway, and a small museum describes the life of Washington as a lad on these hilly, wooded acres. Return to Alexandria via Route 3 and I-95 North. Conclude your day there with dinner in early-American style at Gadsby's Tavern, built in 1792. **(Approximately 170 miles)**

NORTHERN VIRGINIA WINE COUNTRY

Fifteen years ago, a tour of Virginia's Wine Country would have struck wine connoisseurs as preposterous. But that was then. The state now counts more than 60 wineries, many of them producing award-winning vintages. Even California, home to some of America's most notable wines, is taking notice because several of Virginia's winemakers are producing new and different wines from grapes not yet grown on the West Coast. In recent years, wine-tasting has become an inviting pastime for weekenders. Fortunately, many of the wineries are clustered conveniently to make a visit to three or four in half a day quite practical, though many visitors combine a sampling tour with a stay in a country inn that serves Virginia wines. Part of the fun of visiting Virginia's wineries is that they tend to be located in out-of-the-way corners of the countryside. To get to them, you have to negotiate winding back roads over which you might not otherwise travel. This one-day, 150-mile tour from Fairfax County (a Washington, DC suburb) traverses the scenic foothills of the Blue Ridge Mountains. Here and there it edges Shenandoah National Park, where a detour of a few miles will take you to one of the lofty overlooks along Skyline Drive, the famed ridge-top parkway. Begin in the tour on I-66 West just north of Fairfax City. Near Manassas, stop at the Visitor Information Center to pick up the latest edition of *Virginia Wineries Festival and Tour Guide*. It lists the operating hours of the tasting rooms, many of which are open daily, some only on weekends. If Civil War history interests you, stop briefly at Manassas National Battlefield Park, which commemorates the first major clash between the North and South. At Gainesville, head south on US 29 past Culpeper to the village of Leon; the Prince Michel Vineyards will be on the right. A visit begins with a self-guided tour of the wine-making facility. This French-owned facility produces a very nice Chardonnay. Its gourmet restaurant, serving lunch and dinner, overlooks acres of vineyards draped across rolling hills. From St. Michel, continue south on US 29 to Madison, and turn right onto State Route 231 North. For about 20 miles, this stretch of the road is a Virginia Scenic Byway. On your left, the high, forested ridge rising overhead is Shenandoah National Park. On both sides of the road, stately plantation homes carry descriptive names. Just south of Sperryville, pick up US 522 North. In Sperryville, browse the sprawling Sperryville Antiques Market and stop for a bite—or at least a peek—at The Appetite Repair Shop, a café in used-auto motif. A "Sub in a Hub" is a sandwich served in a hub cap. Continue north on US 522 toward Front Royal, turning right at Route 635. For about a mile, the road glides beneath towering trees; Oasis Winery is on the right. Oasis is best known for its sparkling wines. After your visit to Oasis, return to US 522 and continue north to Front Royal. Head east (right) on Route 55 to Linden. Turn right onto Route 638 and proceed 2 miles to Linden. Perched atop a small hill, its outdoor deck offers gorgeous Blue Ridge views. Linden is one of Virginia's finest wineries, and one of the prettiest. Linden's Seyval, a dry white wine, is popular with wine fanciers looking for something new. Return to Route 55 and turn west (left) 1 mile to the entrance to I-66. Take I-66 east back to Fairfax City. **(Approximately 150 miles)**

Abingdon (I-4)

See also Bristol, Marion

Settled circa 1770 **Pop** 7,780 **Elev** 2,069 ft **Area code** 540 **Zip** 24210

Information Abingdon Convention & Visitors Bureau, 335 Cummings St; 800/435-3344

Web www.abingdon.com

Daniel Boone passed through this area in 1760 and dubbed it Wolf Hill after a pack of wolves from a nearby cave disturbed his dogs. Wolf Hill had long been a crossing for buffalo and Native Americans; Boone later used it for his own family's westward migration. Later, Black's Fort was built here and the community adopted that name. Now known as Abingdon, this summer resort in the Virginia Highlands just north of Tennessee is the Washington County seat, Virginia's largest burley tobacco market, and a livestock auction center.

What to See and Do

Grayson Highlands State Park. *35 miles SE on US 58.* Phone 276/579-7092. Within this 4,935-acre park are rugged peaks, some more than 5,000 feet; alpine scenery. Hiking, horse trails, picnicking, camping, visitor center, interpretive programs, pioneer life displays (June-Aug). Adjacent to Mount Rogers National Recreation Area (see MARION). (Daily) Standard fees.

White's Mill. *12291 White's Mill Rd.* Phone 276/676-0285. Old gristmill and general store, still in operation. (Wed-Sat) **$**

Special Events

Barter Theatre. *133 W Main St. US 11 off I-81, in former Town Hall.* Phone 540/628-3991. America's oldest, longest-running professional repertory theater. Founded during the Depression on the theory that residents would barter their abundant crops for first-rate professional entertainment. Designated State Theatre of Virginia in 1946. Barter Players perform Mar-Dec. Children's theater June-Aug.

Virginia Highlands Festival. *208 W Main St (24210).* Exhibits, demonstrations of rustic handicrafts; plays, musical entertainment; historical reenactments; historic house tours, antique market. Early-mid-Aug.

Motels/Motor Lodges

★ **ALPINE MOTEL.** *882 E Main St (24212).* Phone 540/628-3178; fax 540/628-4247. 19 rooms. S, D $38-$56; each additional $5; under 12 free; higher rates special events. Crib $2. Check-out 11 am. TV; cable. Restaurant nearby. Business services. View of mountains. Cr cds: A, DS, MC, V.

🆚

★ **COMFORT INN.** *170 Old Jonesboro Rd (24210).* Phone 540/676-2222. www.comfortinn.com. 80 rooms, 2 story. S, D $55-$150; each additional $6; under 18 free; higher rates special events. Crib free. TV; cable (premium), VCR available. Pool. Complimentary continental breakfast. Check-out noon. Business services available. Cr cds: A, C, D, DS, ER, JCB, MC, V.

D 🛏 🆚 SC

★★ **DAYS INN.** *887 Empire Dr SW (24210).* Phone 540/628-7131; fax 540/628-7158. 105 rooms, 2 story. S, D $38-$48; each additional $2; under 12 free; higher rates special events. Crib $5. TV; cable (premium). Restaurant 7 am-10 pm. Check-out 11 am. Business services available. Balconies. Cr cds: A, C, D, DS, JCB, MC, V.

D 🆚 SC

Restaurants

★★ **THE DINING ROOM.** *150 W Main St (24210).* Phone 540/628-9151; fax 540/628-8885. Warm hospitality pervades the experience at this Southern-style dining establishment. Innovative cuisine inspired by regional fare gives rise to sophisticated comfort food. An extensive wine list includes rare vintages, and the formal, stately décor sets the tone for a gracious dinner. Hours: 6:30-10 am, 11:30 am-2 pm, 5-9 pm; Fri to 10 pm; Sat 7-10 am, 11:30 am-2 pm, 5-10 pm; Sun 7-10 am, 5-9 pm; Sun brunch 11:30 am-2 pm. Reservations accepted. Bar. Breakfast $4-$8, lunch $6-$9.95, dinner $15-$25. Sun brunch $16.95. Specialties: Virginia trout, tenderloin of beef. Own baking. Cr cds: A, C, D, DS, MC, V.

D SC

★★ **THE TAVERN.** *222 E Main St (24210).* Phone 540/628-1118; fax 540/628-5795. Hours: 11 am-10 pm. Closed Dec 25. Reservations accepted. Continental menu. Bar. Lunch $5.95-$7.25, dinner $14.95-$25.95. Specialties: Kassler rippchen, Wiener schnitzel, stuffed filet mignon. Two-story building (1779); colonial décor with fireplace in each of the three dining rooms. Cr cds: A, DS, MC, V.

Alexandria (D-11)

See also Arlington County (Ronald Reagan Washington-National Airport Area), Fairfax, Falls Church; also see Washington, DC

Settled 1670 **Pop** 128,283 **Elev** 52 ft **Area code** 703

Information Convention/Visitors Association, 421 King St, 22314-3209; 703/838-4200

Web www.funside.com

A group of English and Scottish merchants established a tobacco warehouse at the junction of Hunting Creek and the "Potowmack" River in the 1740s. The little settlement prospered and 17 years later surveyor John West, Jr. and his young assistant, George Washington, arrived and "laid off in streets and 84 half-acre lots" the town of Alexandria. Among the first buyers on the July morning in 1749 when the lots were offered for public sale were Lawrence Washington and his brother Augustus, William Ramsay, the Honorable William Fairfax, and John Carlyle. Erecting handsome townhouses, these gentlemen soon brought a lively and cosmopolitan air to Alexandria with parties, balls, and horse racing. It was also the home town of George Mason and Robert E. Lee and home to George Washington.

In 1789, Virginia ceded Alexandria to the District of Columbia, but in 1846, the still Southern-oriented citizens asked to return to the Old Dominion, which Congress allowed.

During the Civil War, Alexandria was cut off from the Confederacy when Union troops occupied the town to protect Potomac River navigation. Safe behind Union lines, the city escaped the dreadful destruction experienced by many other Southern towns. After the war, even with seven railroads centering here for transfer of freight, Alexandria declined as a center of commerce and was in trade doldrums until about 1914, when the Alexandria shipyards were reopened and the Naval Torpedo Station was built. Today, it has developed into a trade, commerce, transportation, and science center. More than 250 national associations are based here.

What to See and Do

Alexandria Black History Resource Center. *638 N Alfred St. Phone 703/838-4356.* Photographs, letters, documents, and artifacts relate history of African Americans in Alexandria. (Tues-Sat; closed holidays) **DONATION**

The Athenaeum. *201 Prince St. Phone 703/548-0035.* Greek Revival structure (1851) built as bank, now houses Fine Arts Association. Art shows, dance performances. (Wed-Fri and Sat-Sun afternoons; closed holidays)

Atlantic Kayak. *1201 N Royal St (22314). Phone 703/838-9072; toll-free 800/297-0066.* See the capital's sights from a new perspective: as a kayaker on the Potomac. Atlantic Kayak runs short trips that include a brief lesson; all equipment is included, and no experience is required. Sunset and moonlight tours are an especially beautiful way to view DC's monuments. Another outing takes you to the Dyke Marsh Wildlife Area, where you'll see ospreys, great blue herons, and other birds. There's even a tour with fireworks viewing on July 4. (Apr-Oct, daily)

Doorways to Old Virginia. *Phone 703/548-0100.* Offers guided walking tours of historic district. (Mar-Oct, Fri-Sun, evenings) Departs from Ramsay House. **$$$**

Fort Ward Museum and Historic Site. *4301 W Braddock Rd. Phone 703/838-4848.* Restored Union Fort from Civil War; museum contains Civil War collection. Museum (Tues-Sun; closed Jan 1, Thanksgiving, Dec 25). Park, picnicking (daily to sunset). **FREE**

George Washington Masonic National Memorial. *101 Callahan Dr, W end of King St. Phone 703/683-2007.* American Freemasons' memorial to their most prominent member, this 333-foot-high structure houses a large collection of objects that belonged to George Washington, which were collected by his family or the masonic lodge where he served as the first master. Guided tours explore a replica of Alexandria-Washington Lodge's first hall, a library, museum, and an observation deck on the top floor. (Daily; closed Jan 1, Thanksgiving, Dec 25) **FREE**

Gunston Hall. *18 miles S on US 1, then 4 miles E on VA 242 in Lorton at 10709 Gunston Rd. Phone 703/550-9220.* (1755-1759) The 550-acre estate of George Mason, framer of the Constitution, father of the Bill of Rights. Restored 18th-century mansion with period furnishings; reconstructed outbuildings; display of historic livestock on working farm; museum; boxwood gardens on grounds; nature trail; picnic area; gift shop. (Daily; closed Jan 1, Thanksgiving, Dec 25) **$$$**

King Street. *In Old Town.* Street is lined with trendy restaurants, shops, and fine antique stores.

Mount Vernon. (see.) *9 miles S on Mount Vernon Memorial Hwy.*

Pohick Bay Regional Park. *6501 Pohick Bay Dr, in Lorton. Phone 703/339-6104.* Near Gunston Hall. Activities in this 1,000-acre park include swimming (Memorial Day-Labor Day), boating (ramp, rentals, fee); 18-hole golf, miniature and Frisbee golf, camping (7-day limit; electric hookups available; fee), picnicking. Park (all year). Fee charged for activities. **$$$**

Pohick Episcopal Church. *9301 Richmond Hwy, 16 miles S on US 1 in Lorton. Phone 703/550-9449.* (1774) The colonial parish church of Mount Vernon and Gunston Hall. Built under supervision of George Mason and George Washington; original walls; interior fully restored. (Daily) **FREE**

Sightseeing boat tours. *Phone 703/684-0580.* Tours of Alexandria waterfront. Contact the Potomac Riverboat Company. **$$$**

Torpedo Factory Arts Center. *105 N Union St. Phone 703/838-4565.* Renovated munitions plant houses artists' center with more than 160 professional artists of various media. Studios, cooperative galleries, school. Also home of Alexandria Archaeology offices, lab, museum; phone 703/838-4399. (Daily; closed holidays) **FREE**

⭐ **Walking tour of historic sites.** *221 King St, at Fairfax St. Phone 703/838-4200.* Start at Visitors Center in

Ramsay House (circa 1725). Oldest house in Alexandria and later used as a tavern, grocery store, and cigar factory. Here, vistors can obtain special events information and a free visitors guide, as well as purchase "block tickets" good for reduced admission to three of the city's historic properties. Guided walking tours, depart from here (spring-fall, weather permitting). The Bureau also issues free parking permits, tour and highway maps, and hotel, dining, and shopping information. (Daily; closed Jan 1, Thanksgiving, Dec 25) 1 block N on Fairfax St is

Carlyle House. *121 N Fairfax St. Phone 703/549-2997.* (1753) This stately stone mansion built in Palladian style was the site of a 1755 meeting between General Edward Braddock and five British colonial governors to plan the early campaigns of the French and Indian War. (Tues-Sun; closed holidays) **$$** 1 1/2 blocks S on Fairfax St is

Stabler-Leadbeater Apothecary Museum. *105 S Fairfax St. Phone 703/836-3713.* (1792) Largest collection of apothecary glass in its original setting in the country; more than 1,000 apothecary bottles. Original building is now a museum of early pharmacy; collection of old prescriptions, patent medicines, scales, other 18th-century pharmacy items. George Washington, Robert E. Lee, and John Calhoun were regular customers. (Daily; closed Jan 1, Thanksgiving, Dec 25) 2 blocks S on Fairfax St is

Old Presbyterian Meeting House. *321 S Fairfax St. Phone 703/549-6670.* (1774) Tomb of the unknown soldier of the Revolution is in churchyard. (Mon-Fri) **FREE** 1/2 block N, then 3 blocks W on Duke St is

Lafayette House. *301 S St. Asaph St.* Fine example of Federal architecture. House was loaned to Lafayette for his last visit to America (1825). (Private) Walk 2 blocks N to Prince St, then left on Prince to SW corner of Prince and Washington sts to

The Lyceum. *201 S Washington St. Phone 703/838-4994.* Museum, exhibitions; Virginia travel information (limited). (Daily; closed Jan 1, Thanksgiving, Dec 25) **FREE** 2 blocks N on Washington St is

Christ Church. *118 N Washington St. Phone 703/549-1450.* (1773) Washington and Robert E. Lee were pewholders. Fine Palladian window; interior balcony; wrought-brass and crystal chandelier brought from England. Structure is extensively restored but changed little since it was built. Exhibit, gift shop at Columbus St entrance. (Mon-Sat, also Sun afternoons; closed holidays; also for weddings, funerals) 1 block E on Cameron St is

Home of General Henry "Light Horse Harry" Lee. *611 Cameron St.* (Private) 3 blocks N, 1 block W, left on Oronoco St is

Lee-Fendall House. *614 Oronoco St. Phone 703/548-1789.* (1785) Built by Phillip Richard Fendall and lived in by Lee family for 118 years. Both George Washington and Revolutionary War hero "Light Horse Harry" Lee were frequent visitors to the house. Remodeled in 1850, the house is furnished with Lee family belongings. (Tues-Sun; weekend hours may vary; closed holidays) **$$** Proceed 1/2 block E to

Boyhood Home of Robert E. Lee. *607 Oronoco St.* Federalist architecture. Famous guests include Washington and Lafayette. 3 blocks E, then 3 blocks S on Royal St is

Gadsby's Tavern Museum. *134 N Royal St. Phone 703/838-4242.* (1770, 1792) Famous hostelry frequented by Washington and other patriots. Combines two 18th-century buildings; interesting architecture. (Tues-Sun; closed holidays) **$$**

Special Events

George Washington Birthday Celebrations. Events include race, Revolutionary War reenactment; climaxed by birthday parade on federal holiday. Feb.

House tours. *221 King St. Phone 703/838-4200.* Fine Colonial and Federalist houses are opened to the public: Historic Garden Week (Apr); Hospital Auxiliary Tour of Historic Houses (Sept); Scottish Christmas Walk (Dec). Tickets, additional information at Alexandria Convention/Visitors Association.

Red Cross Waterfront Festival. *123 N Alfred St. Phone 703/549-8300.* Commemorates Alexandria's maritime heritage. Features "tall ships," blessing of the fleet, river cruises, races, arts and crafts, exhibits, food, variety of music; fireworks. June.

Scottish Christmas Walk. *Phone 800/388-9119.* Parade, house tour, concerts, greens and heather sales, dinner/dance to emphasize city's Scottish origins. First Sat in Dec.

Virginia Scottish Games. *221 King St. Phone 703/838-4200.* Athletic competition, Highland dance and music, antique cars, displays, food. Fourth weekend in July.

Motels/Motor Lodges

★ **BEST WESTERN.** *615 1st St (22314). Phone 703/739-2222; toll-free 800/528-1234; fax 703/549-2568. www.bestwestern.com.* 151 rooms, 2 story. Apr-June, Sept-Oct: S $89; D $99; each additional $10; kitchen units $109; under 18 free; weekend, holiday rates; lower rates rest of year. Pet accepted; $50 deposit and $10/day. Complimentary continental breakfast. Check-out noon. TV; cable (premium). In-room modem link. Restaurant adjacent 6:30 am-11 pm. Health club privileges. Pool;

lifeguard. Free airport transportation. Cr cds: A, C, D, DS, MC, V.

⬛ ♨ ➳ ✈ 🏊 **SC**

★ **BEST WESTERN MOUNT VERNON.** *8751 Richmond Hwy (22309). Phone 703/360-1300; toll-free 800/528-1234; fax 703/799-7713. www.bestwestern.com.* 132 rooms, 5 story. Mar-Oct: S $77-$82; D $82-$87; each additional $5; suites $110-$120; under 18 free; lower rates rest of year. Complimentary continental breakfast. Check-out 11 am. TV; cable (premium). Restaurant nearby. Exercise equipment. Cr cds: A, C, D, DS, MC, V.

⬛ 🛩 🏊 **SC**

★ ★ **COURTYARD BY MARRIOTT.** *2700 Eisenhower Ave (22314). Phone 703/329-2323; fax 703/329-6853; res 800/321-2211. www.courtyard.com.* 176 rooms, 8 story. Apr-May, Oct-Nov: S $169; D $179; suites $220; under 12 free; higher rates Cherry Blossom Festival; lower rates rest of year. Crib free. TV; cable (premium). Restaurant 6:30-10 am, 5-10 pm; Sat, Sun 7-11 am, 5-10 pm. Room service from 5 pm. Bar 4 pm-midnight. Check-out noon. Meeting rooms. Business services available. Valet service. Sundries. Free train station transportation. Exercise equipment. Whirlpool. Some refrigerators, microwaves, balconies. Cr cds: A, C, D, DS, JCB, MC, V.

⬛ 🛩 🏊 🏊

★ **HAMPTON INN.** *4800 Leesburg Pike (22302). Phone 703/671-4800; toll-free 800/426-7866; fax 703/671-2442. www.hamptoninn.com.* 130 rooms, 4 story. S $95; D $95-$105. Crib free. TV; cable (premium). Pool. Complimentary continental breakfast. Coffee in rooms. Check-out noon. Business services available. In-room modem link. Valet service. Exercise equipment. Health club privileges. Cr cds: A, C, D, DS, MC, V.

⬛ 🏊 🛩 🏊 **SC**

★ ★ **HOLIDAY INN.** *480 King St (22314). Phone 703/549-6080; toll-free 800/465-4329; fax 703/684-6508. www.holiday-inn.com.* 227 rooms, 6 story. Mar-June, Sept-Oct: S $149-$199; D $169-$209; each additional $20; suites $275-$350; under 18 free; weekend rates; lower rates rest of year. Crib free. Pet accepted, some restrictions. Garage $7/day. TV; cable (premium). Indoor pool; lifeguard. Complimentary coffee in rooms. Restaurant 6:30 am-11 pm. Bars 11 am-midnight. Check-out noon. Coin laundry. Meeting rooms. Business center. In-room modem link. Concierge. Gift shop. Free airport transportation. Exercise equipment; sauna. Refrigerators, minibars, microwaves available. Some balconies. Cr cds: A, C, D, DS, ER, JCB, MC, V.

⬛ ♨ 🏊 🛩 🏊 **SC** 🏊

★ ★ **RADISSON HOTEL OLD TOWN ALEXANDRIA.** *901 N Fairfax St (22314). Phone 703/683-6000; fax 703/683-5750. www.radisson.com.* 258

rooms, 12 story. S, D $139-$179; each additional $10; under 18 free; weekend rates. Crib free. TV; cable (premium). Pool; lifeguard. Coffee in rooms. Restaurant 6 am-10 pm. Bar 11-1 am. Check-out noon. Business services available. In-room modem link. Gift shop. Free airport transportation. Health club privileges. Refrigerators, microwaves available. Cr cds: A, C, D, DS, ER, JCB, MC, V.

⬛ 🏊 🏊 **SC**

Hotels

★ ★ **HILTON ALEXANDRIA MARK CENTER.** *5000 Seminary Rd (22311). Phone 703/845-1010; toll-free 800/333-3333; fax 703/845-7662. www.hilton.com.* 495 rooms, 30 story. S, D $125-$195; each additional $20; suites $250-$800; under 16 free; weekly rates; weekend packages. Crib free. Covered parking $4/day, valet parking $10. TV; cable (premium), VCR available (free movies). Indoor/outdoor pool; whirlpool. Restaurant 6 am-11 pm. Bars 11-1 am. Check-out noon. Convention facilities. Business center. In-room modem link. Gift shop. Barber, beauty shop. Free airport transportation. Tennis. Exercise equipment; sauna. Game room. Refrigerators; some bathroom phones. Whirlpool in some suites. Located on 50 wooded acres with nature preserve. Luxury level. Cr cds: A, C, D, DS, ER, JCB, MC, V.

⬛ 🍴 🏊 🛩 🏊 🏊 **SC** 🏊

★ ★ ★ **MORRISON HOUSE.** *116 S Alfred St (22314). Phone 703/838-8000; toll-free 800/367-0800; fax 703/684-6283. www.morrisonhouse.com.* The quaint, brick-lined streets of charming Old Town Alexandria are a perfect match for the historical flavor of the Morrison House. Just down the river from the Capitol, this Federal-style mansion presents visitors with a peaceful alternative to the bustling city. Decorative fireplaces, four-poster mahogany beds, and silk sofas define the guest rooms, all furnished in early American décor. The amenities are decidedly 21st century, however, with oversized marble bathrooms and luxurious Frette linens. The Grille attracts a smart casual set with its clubby ambience and live piano music, but it is the exceptional Elysium that is not to be missed. Menus are banished here, the dishes determined by the chef's conversations with each patron. Diners sip Champagne and fine wines as he concocts creative, personalized meals. Rather like having a private chef for the evening, this is truly a singular experience. 45 rooms, 5 story. Check-out noon, check-in 3 pm. TV; cable (premium), VCR available. In-room modem link. Room service 24 hours. Restaurant, dining room. Bar; entertainment Thurs-Sat. Babysitting services available. Health club privileges. Covered parking. Cr cds: A, C, D, MC, V. **$$**

⬛ 🏊

★ ★ **WASHINGTON SUITES ALEXANDRIA.** *100 S Reynolds St (22304). Phone 703/370-9600; fax 703/370-0467. www.washingtonsuiteshotel.com.* 225 kitchen suites, 9 story. S, D $125-$260; each additional $10; under 18 free; weekend rates. Crib $10. Pet accepted; $10/day. TV; cable (premium). Pool; lifeguard. Complimentary continental breakfast. Restaurant 6:30-9:30 am, 5-10 pm. Bar from 5 pm. Check-out noon. Coin laundry. Meeting rooms. Business center. Exercise equipment. Health club privileges. Microwaves. Some balconies. Cr cds: A, C, D, DS, MC, V.

D ⬛ ⬛ ⬛ ⬛ ⬛ ⬛

All Suite

★ ★ ★ **SHERATON SUITES ALEXANDRIA.** *801 N St. Asaph St (22314). Phone 703/836-4700; toll-free 800/325-3535; fax 703/548-4514. www.sheraton.com.* Located just 2 miles from National Airport and the Pentagon, this hotel offers amenities for both business and leisure travelers. 247 suites, 10 story. Apr-May: S, D $220; under 12 free; weekend, holiday rates; lower rates rest of year. Crib free. Pet accepted. Garage parking $7. TV; cable (premium). Indoor pool; whirlpool, lifeguard. Complimentary coffee in rooms. Restaurant 6:30 am-11 pm; weekends from 7 am. Bar. Check-out 1 pm. Guest laundry. Meeting rooms. Business services available. In-room modem link. Gift shop. Free airport transportation. Exercise equipment. Refrigerators; microwaves available. Luxury level. Cr cds: A, C, D, DS, ER, JCB, MC, V.

D ⬛ ⬛ ⬛ ⬛ ⬛ SC

Restaurants

★ **THE ALAMO.** *100 King St (22314). Phone 703/739-0555; fax 703/549-8441.* Hours: 11:15-2 am. Closed Thanksgiving, Dec 25. Reservations accepted. Nouvelle Southwestern menu. Bar. Lunch $4.95-$8.95, dinner $8.95-$16.95. Specializes in ribs, steak, chicken. Entertainment. In 1871 Corn Exchange Building. Cr cds: A, MC, V.

★ ★ **BILBO BAGGINS.** *208 Queen St (22314). Phone 703/683-0300; fax 703/683-1857. www.bilbobaggins.net.* Continental menu. Hours: 11:30 am-10:30 pm; Sun 11 am-9:30 pm; early-bird dinner Mon-Thurs 5:30-6 pm; Sun brunch 11 am-2:30 pm. Closed Dec 25. Lunch $6.95-$9.95, dinner $10.95-$19.95. Sun brunch $7.95-$9.95. Bar. Upstairs in 1898 structure; stained glass, skylights. Cr cds: A, D, DS, MC, V.

D

★ ★ **BLUE POINT GRILL.** *600 Franklin St (22314). Phone 703/739-0404; fax 703/684-1853. www.suttongourmet.com.* Hours: 11:30 am-10 pm; Fri, Sat to 11 pm; Sun 11 am-3 pm (brunch), 5-9 pm. Closed 3-5:30 pm Oct-May; also Dec 25. Lunch $7-$15, dinner $15-$24. Sun brunch $8.50-$11.95. Outdoor seating. Cr cds: A, DS, MC, V.

D

★ ★ **CALVERT GRILLE.** *3106 Mt. Vernon Ave (22305). Phone 703/836-8425; fax 703/836-0539.* Breakfast $2.95-$6.50, lunch $5.25-$8.95, dinner $5.95-$11.95. Sat, Sun brunch $6.95-$12.95. Bar. Children's menu. Cr cds: A, D, DS, MC, V.

D

★ ★ **CHART HOUSE.** *1 Cameron St (22314). Phone 703/684-5080; fax 703/684-7364. www.chart-house.com.* Contemporary American menu. Lunch, dinner, Sun brunch. Bar. Children's menu. Reservations required Fri-Sun. Cr cds: A, D, DS, MC, V. **$$**

D

★ ★ ★ **CHEZ ANDRE.** *10 E Glebe Rd (22305). Phone 703/836-1404; fax 703/836-2530.* Choose from three different dining rooms at this restaurant that has been family owned for over 36 years. French menu. Hours: 11 am-2:30 pm, 5-9:30 pm; Sat from 5 pm. Closed Sun; major holidays. Lunch $8.95-$15.50, dinner $13.95-$22.95. Bar. Reservations required on Fri, Sat. Cr cds: A, D, MC, V.

★ ★ **COPELAND'S OF NEW ORLEANS.** *4300 King St (22302). Phone 703/671-7997; fax 703/578-1082. www.alcopeland.com.* Cajun, Creole, American menu. Closed Thanksgiving, Dec 25. Lunch, dinner, Sun brunch. Bar. Children's menu. Outdoor seating. Cr cds: A, D, DS, MC, V. **$**

D

★ ★ **EAST WIND.** *809 King St (22314). Phone 703/836-1515; fax 703/836-2380.* Hours: 11:30 am-2:30 pm, 5:30-10 pm; Fri to 10:30 pm; Sat 5:30-10:30 pm; Sun 5:30-9:30 pm. Closed major holidays. Reservations accepted. Vietnamese menu. Bar. Lunch $5.95-$7.95, dinner $7.95-$15.50. Specialty: charbroiled shrimp and scallops. Own desserts. Original Vietnamese paintings and panels. Cr cds: A, D, DS, MC, V.

★ ★ **ECCO CAFE.** *220 N Lee St (22314). Phone 703/684-0321; fax 703/684-1785. www.eccocafe.com.* American, Italian menu. Hours: 11 am-11 pm; Mon to 10 pm; Fri, Sat to midnight; Sun 4-10 pm; Sun brunch 11:30 am-3 pm. Closed Thanksgiving, Dec 25. Lunch $6.95-$9.95, dinner $10.95-$16.95. Sun brunch $7.95-$11.95. Bar. In restored 1890s warehouse building; eclectic décor. Cr cds: A, D, DS, MC, V.

D

★ ★ ★ **ELYSIUM.** *116 S Alfred St (22314). Phone 703/838-8000; toll-free 800/367-0800; fax 703/684-6283. www.morrisonhouse.com.* Have you ever dreamed of having a chef of your very own—someone who would come to your table and say something like, "Good evening. So

nice to see you. What would you like me to make for you this evening?" Open your eyes. This is not a dream. You are at Elysium, a magical restaurant in the Morrison House hotel in historic Alexandria, where you create your very own "Flight of Food" based on what the chef has purchased from local markets and farmers that very day. Instead of a dinner menu, you'll be presented with a wine list (a nice big one with lots of terrific international choices) and then a personal visit from the chef to discuss what you're in the mood to eat. He'll give you the list of ingredients, and you work together to develop the menu. It's very interactive and very exciting. This is living. After dinner, a butler will escort you to the parlor for an after-dinner drink or a wonderful, aromatic pot of special-blend loose tea made for the Morrison House. Eclectic, continental menu. Closed Jan 1. Breakfast, dinner. Bar. Children's menu. Casual attire. Cr cds: A, D, MC, V. **$$$**
D

★ **FACCIA LUNA.** *823 S Washington St (22314). Phone 703/838-5998. www.faccialuna.com.* American, Italian menu. Hours: 11:30 am-11 pm; Fri, Sat to midnight; Sun from noon. Closed some major holidays. Lunch $5.75-$8, dinner $9-$14.50. Bar. Children's menu. Outdoor seating. Totally nonsmoking. Cr cds: A, MC, V.
D

★ ★ **FISH MARKET.** *105 King St (22314). Phone 703/836-5676; fax 703/836-4659. www.fishmarketold town.com.* Closed Thanksgiving, Dec 25. Lunch $3.95-$12.95, dinner $4.25-$16.25. Bar. In restored 18th-century warehouse built of bricks carried to New World as ballast in ship's hold; nautical décor. Outdoor seating. Cr cds: A, D, MC, V.

★ ★ **GADSBY'S TAVERN.** *138 N Royal St (22314). Phone 703/548-1288; fax 703/548-5324. www.gadsbys.org.* Hours: 11:30 am-3 pm, 5:30-10 pm; Sun brunch 11 am-3 pm. Closed Jan 1, Dec 25. Reservations accepted; required Fri, Sat. Lunch $6.95-$8.95, dinner $14.95-$22.95. Sun brunch $6.75-$9.95. Children's menu. Specialties: Sally Lunn bread, George Washington's favorite duck, English trifle. Strolling minstrels. Outdoor seating. Built 1792; Georgian architecture; Colonial décor and costumes. Gadsby's Tavern Museum adjacent. Totally nonsmoking. Cr cds: A, D, MC, V.
D

★ ★ **GERANIO.** *722 King St (22314). Phone 703/548-0088; fax 703/548-0091. www.geranio.net.* A roaring fireplace and stylish décor create a comfortable blend of old and new at this innovative restaurant. Regional favorites make up the diverse and gratifying menu. Italian, Mediterranean, seafood menu. Hours: 11:30 am-2:30 pm, 6-10:30 pm; Sat from 6 pm; Sun

5:30-9:30 pm. Closed some major holidays. Lunch $6.95-$10.25, dinner $15-$26. Bar. Reservations required on Fri, Sat. Cr cds: A, D, MC, V.
D

★ **HARD TIMES CAFE.** *1404 King St (22314). Phone 703/683-5340; fax 703/683-8801. www.hardtimes.com.* Hours: 11 am-10 pm; Fri, Sat to 11 pm; Sun noon-10 pm. Closed some major holidays. Lunch, dinner $3.95-$5.75. Housed in former church; rustic décor; collection of state flags. Cr cds: A, MC, V.
D

★ ★ **IL PORTO.** *121 King St (22314). Phone 703/836-8833; fax 703/836-8835. www.ilportoristorante.com.* A very skilled kitchen staff turns out classic dishes at this cozy restaurant, a local favorite for 25 years. Set in a renovated warehouse, the atmosphere is just as rustic as the food. Northern Italian menu. Closed Thanksgiving. Lunch, dinner. Bar. Children's menu. Casual attire. Reservations required. Cr cds: A, MC, V. **$$**
D

★ ★ ★ **LA BERGERIE.** *218 N Lee St (22314). Phone 703/683-1007; fax 703/519-6114. www.labergerie.com.* A historic brick warehouse is the setting for this restaurant that is a local favorite. Pleasant, tuxedoed waiters serve classic, often-forgotten dishes from the Basque region. Hours: 11:30 am-2:30 pm, 5:30-10:30 pm. Closed Sun except Mother's Day; major holidays. Reservations accepted; required Fri, Sat. French, American menu. Service bar. Lunch $10.95-$14.95, dinner $14.95-$24.95. Specializes in fresh seafood. Own pastries. Restored 1890s warehouse. Cr cds: A, D, DS, MC, V.
D

★ ★ **LANDINI BROTHERS.** *115 King St (22314). Phone 703/836-8404; fax 703/549-2211. www. landinibrothers.com.* Hours: 11:30 am-11 pm; Sun 3-10 pm. Closed major holidays. Reservations accepted; required Fri, Sat. Italian menu. Bar. A la carte entrées: lunch $9-$13, dinner $13.50-$24.95. Specializes in veal, pasta, fresh fish. 1790s building. Cr cds: A, D, DS, MC, V.
D

★ ★ **LE GAULOIS.** *1106 King St (22314). Phone 703/739-9494; fax 703/739-9496.* French menu. Closed major holidays. Lunch, dinner. Casual attire. Reservations required. Outdoor seating. Cr cds: A, D, DS, MC, V. **$$**
D

★ ★ **LE REFUGE.** *127 N Washington St (22314). Phone 703/548-4661.* French menu. Hours: 11:30 am-2:30 pm, 5:30-10 pm; early-bird dinner 5:30-7 pm. Closed Sun; some major holidays. Lunch $15.95. Dinner $15.95-

$28.95. Bar. Reservations required on Fri, Sat. Cr cds: A, D, DS, MC, V.

★ **MANGO MIKE'S.** *4580 Duke St (22304). Phone 703/823-1166; fax 703/370-4424. www.mangomikes.com.* Caribbean menu. Closed Thanksgiving, Dec 25. Lunch, dinner, Sun brunch. Bar to 2 am. Children's menu. Outdoor seating. Cr cds: A, D, DS, MC, V. **$**

D

★★ **MONROE'S.** *1603 Commonwealth Ave (22301). Phone 703/548-5792; fax 703/548-5914.* Hours: 5-10 pm; Fri, Sat to 11 pm; Sun 5-9 pm; Sun brunch 9:30 am-2 pm. Closed most major holidays. Reservations accepted; required Fri, Sat. Italian menu. Bar. Dinner $8.50-$16.95. Sun brunch $3.95-$10.95. Children's menu. Specialties: tonno alla livornese, bowtie pasta with crab meat, aged Angus beef. Own pastries. Outdoor seating. Contemporary trattoria with large murals. Totally nonsmoking. Cr cds: A, DS, MC, V.

D

★★ **R. T.'S.** *3804 Mt. Vernon Ave (22305). Phone 703/684-6010; fax 703/548-0417. www.rts.com.* Creole/Cajun menu. Closed some major holidays. Lunch, dinner. Bar. Children's menu. Cr cds: A, D, DS, MC, V. **$$**

D

★★ **SANTA FE EAST.** *110 S Pitt St (22314). Phone 703/548-6900; fax 703/519-0798. www.santafeeast.com.* Southwestern menu. Hours: 11:30 am-10 pm; Fri, Sat to 11 pm; Sun 11 am-10 pm. Closed July 4, Thanksgiving, Dec 25. Lunch $5.95-$9.95, dinner $8.95-$18.75. Sun brunch $5.25-$7.25. Bar. In historic (1790) building. Outdoor seating. Fountain in courtyard. Cr cds: DS, MC, V.

D

★★ **SCOTLAND YARD.** *728 King St (22314). Phone 703/683-1742; fax 703/683-6989. www.scotlandyardrestaurant.com.* Scottish menu. Hours: 6-8 pm. Closed Mon; Thanksgiving. Dinner $12.95-$24.95. Service bar. Reservations required on Fri, Sat. Totally nonsmoking. Cr cds: A, MC, V.

D

★ **SOUTH AUSTIN GRILL.** *801 King St (22314). Phone 703/684-8969; fax 703/519-0126. www.austingrill.com.* Mexican menu. Hours: 11:30 am-11 pm; Mon to 10 pm; Fri to midnight; Sat 11 am-midnight; Sun 11 am-10 pm; Sat, Sun brunch to 3 pm. Closed Thanksgiving, Dec 24, 25. Lunch $6.95-$13.95. Dinner $6.95-$13.95. Sat, Sun brunch $4.95-$6.95. Bar. Children's menu. Cr cds: A, D, DS, MC, V.

D

★★ **TAVERNA CRETEKOU.** *818 King St (22314). Phone 703/548-8688. www.tavernacretekou.com.* Greek, seafood menu. Hours: 11:30 am-2:30 pm, 5-10:30 pm; Sat noon-11 pm; Sun 5-9:30 pm; Sun brunch 11 am-3 pm. Closed Mon; some major holidays. Lunch $5.95-$14.95. Dinner $11.95-$24.95, Sun brunch $14.95. Bar. Entertainment. Reservations required on Fri, Sat. Outdoor seating. Cr cds: A, MC, V.

★★ **TEMPO.** *4231 Duke St (22304). Phone 703/370-7900; fax 703/370-7902. www.temporestaurant.com.* Hours: 11:30 am-2:30 pm, 5:30-10 pm; Sun to 9 pm; Sun brunch to 2:30 pm. Closed most major holidays. Reservations accepted; required Fri, Sat dinner. Italian, French menu. Bar. Lunch $8.95-$10.95, dinner $11.95-$16.95. Sun brunch $5.95-$10.95. Specialties: linguini with lobster, lamb chops with fresh herbs. Outdoor seating. Modern décor with cathedral windows, original artwork. Cr cds: A, D, DS, MC, V.

D SC

★★ **THAI HUT.** *408 S Van Dorn St (22304). Phone 703/823-5357; fax 703/823-2931.* Hours: 11 am-10 pm; Fri to 11 pm; Sat noon-11 pm; Sun noon-9:30 pm. Closed Thanksgiving, Dec 25. Thai menu. A la carte entrées: lunch, dinner $6.95-$11.95. Complete meals (Mon-Fri): lunch $5.95. Specialties: curries, pad Thai, drunken noodles. Parking. Modern décor; Thai artwork. Cr cds: A, D, MC, V.

D

★★ **UNION STREET PUBLIC HOUSE.** *121 S Union St (22314). Phone 703/548-1785; fax 703/548-0705. www.usphalexandria.com.* Closed Thanksgiving, Dec 25. Lunch, dinner $5.50-$16.95. Sun brunch $4.95-$8.95. Bar to 1:15 am. Oyster raw bar. Children's menu. In sea captain's house and warehouse (circa 1870). Cr cds: A, D, DS, MC, V.

★★ **VILLA D'ESTE.** *600 Montgomery St (22314). Phone 703/549-9477; fax 703/549-8809. www.villadesterestaurant.com.* Italian menu. Hours: 11:30 am-2:30 pm, 5-10 pm; Fri, Sat to 10:30 pm; Sun 5-9 pm. Closed major holidays. Lunch $12.95-$15.95. Dinner $15.95-$27.95. Bar. Reservations required on Fri, Sat. Cr cds: A, MC, V.

D

★★ **WHARF.** *119 King St (22314). Phone 703/836-2834; fax 703/836-3028. www.wharfrestaurant.com.* Seafood menu. Hours: 11 am-10:30 pm; Fri, Sat to 11 pm. Closed Jan 1, Thanksgiving, Dec 25. Lunch $5.95-$9.95, dinner $14.95-$23.95. Bar. Children's menu. Late 18th-century building. Cr cds: A, D, DS, MC, V.

D

Appomattox Court House National Historical Park (G-8)

See also Lynchburg

(3 miles NE of Appomattox on VA 24)

The series of clashes between General Ulysses S. Grant and General Robert E. Lee that started with the Battle of the Wilderness (May 5, 1864) finally ended here on Palm Sunday, April 9, 1865, in the little village of Appomattox.

A week earlier, Lee had evacuated besieged Petersburg and headed west in a desperate attempt to join forces with General Johnston in North Carolina. Ragged and exhausted, decimated by desertions, without supplies, and beset by Union forces at every turn, the once-great Army of Northern Virginia launched its last attack at dawn on April 9. By 10 am, it was clear that further bloodshed was futile; after some difficulty in getting a message to Grant, the two antagonists met in the parlor of the McLean House. By 3 pm, the generous surrender terms had been drafted and signed. The war was over. Three days later, 28,231 Confederate soldiers received their parole here.

The 1,743-acre park includes the village of Appomattox, restored and reconstructed to appear much as it did in 1865. Uniformed park rangers or interpreters in period dress answer questions about the residents and events. (Daily; closed holidays Nov-Feb) Golden Eagle Passport accepted (see MAKING THE MOST OF YOUR TRIP). Audiovisual programs, Braille guide folders, audio guide, and large-print folder available for the hearing and visually impaired. For further information contact the Superintendent, PO Box 218, Appomattox 24522; 804/352-8987. **$$**

What to See and Do

⭐ **Appomattox Courthouse Building.** Reconstructed building houses visitor center, museum; audiovisual slide program (every half hour, second floor). Self-guided tour of village begins here and includes

Clover Hill Tavern and outbuildings. (1819) Oldest structure in village; bookstore, rest rooms.

Confederate Cemetery.

County jail. (1870) Furnished.

McLean House and outbuildings. Reconstruction of house where Generals Lee and Grant met on April 9, 1865.

Meek's Store and Meek's Storehouse. With period furnishings.

Stacking of Arms. On the fourth anniversary of the firing on Fort Sumter, which triggered the outbreak of war, Confederate soldiers laid down their weapons here.

Woodson Law Office. With period furnishings.

Holliday Lake State Park. *9 miles NE of Appomattox on VA 24, then 6 miles SE via VA 626, 692. Phone 434/248-6308.* Approximately 250 acres in Buckingham-Appomattox State Forest. Swimming beach, bathhouse, fishing, boating (launch, rentals) on 150-acre lake; hiking trails, picnicking, concession, tent and trailer sites. Visitor center, interpretive programs. Standard fees. Park (daily); most activities, including camping (Memorial Day-Labor Day).

Arlington County (Ronald Reagan Washington-National Airport Area) (D-11)

See also Alexandria, Fairfax, Falls Church, McLean; also see Washington, DC

Originally a part of the District of Columbia laid out for the capital in 1791, Arlington County, across the Potomac River from Washington, was returned to Virginia in 1846. The community is the urban center of northern Virginia.

Web www.co.arlington.va.us

Services and Information

Airlines. America West, American, American Eagle, Continental, Delta, Midwest Express, Northwest, United, USAir.

Transportation

Car Rental Agencies. See IMPORTANT TOLL-FREE NUMBERS.

Public Transportation. Subway trains and buses (Metro Transit System), phone 202/962-1234. Information 202/637-7000.

Rail Passenger Service. Amtrak 800/872-7245.

Airport Information

Ronald Reagan Washington-National Airport. Information 703/417-8000; lost and found 703/417-8560; weather 202/936-1212; cash machines at Main Terminal, main level near Travelers Aid.

City Fun Facts—Arlington

The Pentagon building in Arlington is the largest office building in the world.

What to See and Do

Arlington Farmers' Market. *N Courthouse Rd and N 14th St. Adjacent to Arlington County Courthouse. Phone 703/ 228-6423.* Irresistibly fresh berries, peaches, and heirloom tomatoes are just some of the pleasures available at this lively market, which has been featuring the produce of farmers within 125 miles of Arlington since 1979. Don't miss the grass-fed meats, specialty goat cheeses, and unusual varieties of familiar fruits and vegetables (one longtime vendor grows 35 different types of apples). Expect a great selection in any season at this year-round market: more than 30 producers are on hand on a typical Saturday. (Sat)

⭐ **Arlington National Cemetery.** *Phone 703/979-0690.* The solemn grounds of Arlington National Cemetery are a profoundly stirring sight. Gentle hills are studded as far as the eye can see with white stones marking the graves of more than 260,000 Americans who served in the nation's military, from the American Revolution to more recent conflicts. Many visitors stop at the Tomb of the Unknowns, which contains the unidentified remains of servicemen killed in the world wars and the Korean conflict and provides quiet tribute to anonymous sacrifice. Most also pay their respects at the eternal flame marking the granite-paved gravesite of President John F. Kennedy and his wife, Jacqueline, and that of Robert F. Kennedy nearby. These graves are situated on a grassy slope below Arlington House, the elegantly columned mansion that was Civil War general Robert E. Lee's home for 30 years and is now maintained as a public memorial to him. **FREE** Here are

Arlington House, the Robert E. Lee Memorial. *Phone 703/557-0613.* National memorial to Robert E. Lee. Built between 1802 and 1818 by George Washington Parke Custis, Martha Washington's grandson and foster son of George Washington. In 1831 his daughter, Mary Anna Randolph Custis, married Lieutenant Robert E. Lee; six of the seven Lee children were born here. As executor of the Custis estate, Lee took extended leave from the US Army and devoted his time to managing and improving the estate. It was the Lee homestead for 30 years before the Civil War. On April 20, 1861, following the secession of Virginia, Lee made his decision to stay with Virginia. Within a month, the house was vacated. Some of the family possessions were moved for safekeeping, but most were stolen or destroyed when Union troops occupied the house during the Civil War. In 1864, when Mrs. Lee could

not appear personally to pay property tax, the estate was confiscated by the federal government; a 200-acre section was set aside for a national cemetery. (There is some evidence that indicates this was done to ensure the Lee family could never again live on the estate.) G. W. Custis Lee, the general's son, later regained title to the property through a Supreme Court decision and sold it to the US government in 1883 for $150,000. Restoration of the house to its 1861 appearance was begun in 1925. The Classic Revival house is furnished with authentic pieces of the period, including some Lee family originals. From the grand portico with its six massive, faux-marble Doric columns there is a panoramic view of Washington, DC. (Daily; closed Jan 1, Dec 25)

Memorial Amphitheatre. This impressive white marble edifice is used for ceremonies such as Memorial Day, Easter sunrise, and Veterans Day services.

Tomb of the Unknowns. On November 11, 1921, the remains of an unknown American soldier of WWI were entombed here. A memorial was erected in 1932 with the inscription "Here rests in honored glory an American soldier known but to God." On Memorial Day 1958, an unknown warrior who died in WWII and another who died in the Korean War were laid beside him. On Memorial Day 1984, an unknown soldier from the Vietnam War was interred here. Sentries stand guard 24 hours a day; changing of the guard is every hour on the hour Oct-Mar, every 30 minutes Apr-Sept.

Crystal City Shops. *Crystal Dr between 15th and 23rd sts. Phone 703/922-4636.* Crystal City, a mixed-use residential and commercial development, has an underground shopping complex and a lot of street-level activity. It's currently being upgraded to provide more of a "Main Street" feel, with outdoor cafés and other seating as well as improved landscaping and opportunities for window-shopping. You'll find jewelry and gift shops, men's and women's apparel, books, and home furnishings, as well as a Japanese steakhouse, two American steakhouses, and a Legal Sea Foods. (Daily)

Fashion Centre at Pentagon City. *1100 S Hayes St (22202). Off I-395 at junction S Hayes St and Army-Navy Dr, S of the Pentagon. Phone 703/415-2400.* The presence of the Ritz-Carlton Hotel dictates a glamorous tone at this huge, glittering mall, anchored by Macy's and Nordstrom and home to more than 150 other tantalizing shops and restaurants. Of-the-moment women's fashions and accessories are everywhere—don't miss bebe, Betsey Johnson, and MAC Cosmetics. For home furnishings, check out Crate & Barrel and Williams-Sonoma; Bang & Olufsen is here, too, if your needs are aural. Recover from strenuous browsing at the skylit food court. (Daily; closed Thanksgiving, Dec 25)

Iwo Jima Statue. *On Arlington Blvd, near Arlington National Cemetery.* Marine Corps War Memorial depicts raising of the flag on Mount Suribachi, Iwo Jima, February 23, 1945; this is the largest sculpture ever cast in bronze. Sunset Parade concert with performances by US Marine Drum and Bugle Corps, US Marine Corps Color Guard, and the Silent Drill Team (late May-late Aug, Tues evenings).

★ **The Newseum.** *1101 Wilson Blvd. Phone 888/ NEWSEUM or 703/284-3700.* This 72,000-square-foot interactive museum of news takes visitors behind the scenes to see and experience how and why news is made. Be a reporter or newscaster; relive great news stories through multimedia exhibits; see today's news as it happens on a block-long video wall. (Wed-Sun; closed holidays) **FREE**

> **Freedom Park.** Nearly 1,000 feet in length, park occupies never-used bridge. Features memorial to journalists killed in line of duty and various icons of freedom.

The Pentagon. *Bounded by Jefferson Davis Hwy, Washington Blvd, and I-395. Phone 703/695-1776.* With some 6 million square feet of floor area, this is one of the largest office buildings in the world; houses offices of the Department of Defense. Guided tour (1 1/2 hours) with a walk of about 1 1/2 miles includes movie, *Hall of Heroes;* Flag Corridor; *Time/Life* Art Collection (Mon-Fri; closed holidays). Tour window located on concourse near the Metrorail subway or by entering at Corridor One, South Parking entrance. A valid picture ID must be presented at tour registration; visitors must stay on the tour once it begins. Cameras are allowed. Accommodations for the disabled available with 48-hour advance notice. **FREE**

Sur La Table. *1101 S Joyce St, Suite B-20 (22202). Phone 703/414-3580.* In the 1970s, Seattle spawned this clearinghouse for hard-to-find kitchen gear, and it soon became known as a source for cookware, small appliances, cutlery, kitchen tools, linens, tableware, gadgets, and specialty foods. Sur La Table has since expanded to include cooking classes, chef demonstrations, and cookbook author signings, as well as a catalog and online presence. Cooking connoisseurs discover such finds as cool oven mitts, zest graters, copper whisks, onion soup bowls, and inspired TV dinner trays. (Daily)

Special Events

Arlington County Fair. *3308 S Stafford St. Phone 703/920-4556 or 703/228-6400.* Countywide fair; arts, crafts, international foods, children's activities. Aug.

Army 10-miler. *Phone 202/685-3361.* America's largest 10-mile road race, attracting thousands of military and civilian runners. Early Oct.

Marine Corps Marathon. *Starts and ends near the intersection of Rte 110 and Marshall Dr. Phone toll-free 800/786-8762.* Cheer on your favorite runner at the Marine Corps Marathon—with 16,000 contestants participating, there will be awesome physiques to admire everywhere you look. The 26-mile, 385-yard route starts and ends near the Iwo Jima Memorial and winds through Arlington, Georgetown, and DC passing the Capitol, the Pentagon, and other inspiring sights along the way. The Marine Corps Marathon 5K race, organized in conjunction with the Special Olympics competition, starts at the Memorial at 9:10 am. Late Oct. **FREE**

Memorial Day Service. *Arlington National Cemetery.* Presidential wreath laying ceremony at Tomb of the Unknowns; music. Memorial Day.

Motels/Motor Lodges

★ ★ **BEST WESTERN KEY BRIDGE.** *1850 Fort Myer Dr (23692). Phone 703/522-0400; toll-free 800/528-1234; fax 703/524-5275. www.bestwestern.com.* 178 rooms, 11 story. S $129; D $139; suites $149-$169; under 12 free. Crib free. Pet accepted. TV; cable (premium). Pool. Restaurant 6:30 am-2 pm, 5-10 pm. Check-out noon. Meeting rooms. Business services available. Exercise equipment. Health club privileges. Some refrigerators; microwaves available. Cr cds: A, C, D, DS, MC, V.

[D] [icons] [SC]

★ ★ **COMFORT INN.** *1211 N Glebe Rd (22201). Phone 703/247-3399; toll-free 800/228-5150; fax 703/524-8739. www.comfortinn.com.* 126 rooms, 3 story. Mar-Oct: S, D $120; suites $135; under 18 free; weekend rates; lower rates rest of year. Complimentary continental breakfast. Check-out 11 am. TV; cable (premium). In-room modem link. Restaurant 6:30 am-10:30 pm. Bar 4-11 pm. Room service. Pool privileges. Cr cds: A, C, D, DS, ER, JCB, MC, V.

[D] [icons] [SC]

★ ★ **COURTYARD BY MARRIOTT CRYSTAL CITY.** *2899 Jefferson Davis Hwy (22202). Phone 703/549-3434; toll-free 800/321-2211; fax 703/549-7440. www.courtyard.com.* 272 rooms, 14 story. S, D $154-$169; each additional $15; suites $200-$250; under 12 free. Crib free. Garage parking $9. TV; cable (premium), VCR available. Indoor pool; whirlpool, lifeguard. Complimentary coffee in rooms. Restaurant 6-10 am, 5 pm-midnight; weekends 7 am-noon, 5 pm-midnight. Room service 5-10 pm. Bar 4 pm-midnight. Check-out 1 pm. Coin laundry. Meeting rooms. Business services available. In-room modem link. Valet service. Sundries. Free airport transportation. Exercise equipment. Health club privileges. Some refrigerators, wet bars; microwaves available. Cr cds: A, C, D, DS, ER, JCB, MC, V.

[D] [icons] [SC]

★ ★ **COURTYARD BY MARRIOTT ROSSLYN.** *1533 Clarendon Blvd (22209). Phone 703/528-2222; toll-free 800/321-2211; fax 703/528-1027. www.courtyard.com.* 162 rooms, 10 story, 18 suites. Apr-June, Aug-Oct: S $154; D $164; each additional $10; suites $174-$184; under 12 free; weekend rates; lower rates rest of year. Crib free. Garage parking $6.50 Sun-Thurs; Fri, Sat free. TV; cable (premium). Indoor pool; whirlpool, lifeguard. Complimentary coffee in rooms. Restaurant 6:30-10 am, 5-11 pm. Room service from 5 pm. Bar from 5 pm. Check-out noon. Business services available. Valet service. Sundries. Coin laundry. Exercise equipment. Health club privileges. Some refrigerators; microwaves available. Many balconies. Cr cds: A, C, D, DS, JCB, MC, V.

[D] [≈] [🏃] [≈] [SC]

★ ★ **HAMPTON INN & SUITES CRYSTAL CITY.** *2000 Jefferson Davis Hwy (22202). Phone 703/920-8600; toll-free 800/329-7466; fax 703/920-2840. www. hamptoninn.com.* 247 rooms, 8 story. Mar-June, Sept-Nov: S $127-$160; D $137-$170; each additional $10; under 16 free; weekend, holiday rates; lower rates rest of year. Check-out 11 am. TV; cable (premium). In-room modem link. Restaurant 6 am-2 pm, 5-10 pm; weekends 7 am-noon, 5-10 pm. Bar 4:30-10 pm. Room service. Exercise equipment. Pool; lifeguard. Garage parking. Free airport transportation. Cr cds: A, C, D, DS, JCB, MC, V.

[D] [≈] [🏃] [✕] [≈] [SC]

★ ★ **HOLIDAY INN.** *2650 Jefferson Davis Hwy (22202). Phone 703/684-7200; fax 703/684-3217. www.holiday-inn.com.* 279 rooms, 11 story. Apr-July, Sept-Oct: S $89-$159; D $89-$169; under 10 free; suites $210-$230; under 18 free; weekend rates; lower rates rest of year. Crib free. Garage, in/out parking $9. TV; cable. Complimentary coffee in rooms. Restaurant 6 am-11 pm. Bar 4-11 pm. Check-out noon. Meeting rooms. Business center. In-room modem link. Gift shop. Coin laundry. Free airport, train station transportation. Exercise equipment. Health club privileges. Pool; lifeguard. Balconies. Cr cds: A, C, D, DS, ER, JCB, MC, V.

[D] [≈] [🏃] [≈] [🏃]

★ ★ **QUALITY HOTEL.** *1200 N Court House Rd (22201). Phone 703/524-4000; toll-free 800/221-2222; fax 703/522-6814. www.qualityhotelarlington.com.* 392 rooms, 1-10 story. S $69.95-$125.95; D $75.95-$135.95; each additional $10; suites $109.95-$169.95; under 18 free; package plans. Crib free. Pet accepted, some restrictions. TV; cable (premium). Pool; lifeguard. Coffee in rooms. Restaurant 6:30 am-2 pm, 5-9:30 pm. Bar 4-10 pm. Check-out noon. Coin laundry. Convention facilities. Business services available. In-room modem link. Concierge. Gift shop. Exercise equipment; sauna. Microwaves available. Balconies. Luxury level. Cr cds: A, C, D, DS, ER, JCB, MC, V.

[D] [🐾] [≈] [🏃] [≈] [SC]

★ ★ **QUALITY INN IWO JIMA.** *1501 Arlington Blvd (22209). Phone 703/524-5000; toll-free 800/228-5151; fax 703/522-5484. www.qualityinn.com.* 141 rooms, 1-3 story. Mar-Nov: S, D $95-$105; each additional $10; weekend, family rates; higher rates special events; lower rates rest of year. Crib free. TV; cable (premium), VCR available. Indoor pool; poolside service, lifeguard. Restaurant (in season) 6:30 am-10 pm; Sat, Sun from 7 am. Room service. Bar. Check-out noon. Coin laundry. Meeting rooms. Business services available. In-room modem link. Bellstaff. Sundries. Exercise equipment. Health club privileges. Refrigerators, microwaves available. Some balconies. Cr cds: A, C, D, DS, ER, JCB, MC, V.

[D] [≈] [🏃] [≈] [SC]

Hotels

★ ★ **CROWNE PLAZA WASHINGTON-NATIONAL AIRPORT.** *1489 Jefferson Davis Hwy (22202). Phone 703/416-1600; fax 703/416-1615. www. basshotels.com/crowneplaza.* 308 rooms, 11 story. S, D $189; each additional $10; suites $199-$209; under 18 free; weekend, holiday rates. Crib free. Pet accepted, some restrictions; $25 deposit. Garage $8/day. TV; cable (premium). Pool; lifeguard. Coffee in rooms. Restaurant 6 am-10 pm; Sat, Sun from 7 am. Bar 11 am-midnight. Check-out noon. Meeting rooms. Business center. In-room modem link. Gift shop. Free airport transportation. Exercise equipment. Refrigerators available. Cr cds: A, C, D, DS, JCB, MC, V.

[D] [🐾] [≈] [🏃] [✕] [≈] [SC] [🏃]

★ ★ **DOUBLETREE HOTEL.** *300 Army Navy Dr (22202). Phone 703/416-4100; toll-free 800/222-8733; fax 703/416-4126. www.doubletreehotels.com.* Located ideally in the Crystal City area, this hotel is close to the airport and within walking distance of a major shopping mall. The Metro system is also close at hand and will take guests quickly to all the sights of Washington, DC. 632 rooms, 265 suites, 15 story. S, D $190; suites $200-$375; under 18 free; weekend rates. Crib free. Pet accepted, some restrictions. Garage $10; valet $12. TV; cable (premium). Indoor pool; lifeguard. Coffee in rooms. Restaurant 6:30 am-11 pm. Bar 11-2 am; entertainment. Check-out noon. Convention facilities. Business center. In-room modem link. Concierge. Gift shop. Free airport transportation. Exercise room; sauna. Health club privileges. Bathroom phones; some refrigerators; microwaves available. Some balconies. Luxury level. Cr cds: A, C, D, DS, ER, JCB, MC, V.

[D] [🐾] [≈] [🏃] [✕] [≈] [SC] [🏃]

★ ★ ★ **HILTON ARLINGTON AND TOWERS.** *950 N Stafford St (22203). Phone 703/528-6000; toll-free 800/468-3571; fax 703/812-5127. www.hilton.com.* This hotel is part of the Balliston Metro Center and is close to shopping and the National Science Foundation. 209 rooms, 7 story.

S $180-$200; D $200-$220; suites $240; under 18 free; weekend rates. Crib free. TV; cable (premium). Indoor pool; whirlpool, lifeguard. Restaurant 6:30 am-10 pm. Bar 4 pm-midnight. Check-out 1 pm. Meeting rooms. Business services available. In-room modem link. Concierge. Gift shop. Health club privileges. Metro stop in building. Luxury level. Cr cds: A, C, D, DS, ER, JCB, MC, V.

★ ★ ★ **HYATT ARLINGTON.** *1325 Wilson Blvd (22209). Phone 703/525-1234; toll-free 800/233-1234; fax 703/875-3393. www.arlingtonhyatt.com.* This hotel is located across the bridge from Washington and close to Arlington National Cemetery. 304 rooms, 16 story. Pet accepted, some restrictions. Check-out noon, check-in 3 pm. TV; cable (premium), VCR available. In-room modem link. Free guest laundry. Restaurant. Bar. Babysitting services available. In-house fitness room. Health club privileges. Business center. Cr cds: A, C, D, DS, ER, JCB, MC, V. **$$**

★ ★ ★ **HYATT REGENCY CRYSTAL CITY.** *2799 Jefferson Davis Hwy (22202). Phone 703/418-1234; toll-free 800/233-1234; fax 703/418-1289. www.hyatt.com.* Located across the Potomac River from Washington, DC and within walking distance to Georgetown University. 685 rooms, 20 story. Check-out noon. TV; cable (premium), VCR available. In-room modem link. Restaurant. Bar. Babysitting services available. In-house fitness room. Health club privileges. Exercise equipment, sauna. Pool, whirlpool, poolside service, lifeguard. Airport transportation. Business center. Concierge. Cr cds: A, C, D, DS, ER, JCB, MC, V. **$$**

★ ★ ★ **MARRIOTT CRYSTAL CITY AT REAGAN NATIONAL AIRPORT.** *1999 Jefferson Davis Hwy (22202). Phone 703/413-5500; toll-free 800/228-9290; fax 703/413-0192. www.marriott.com.* This hotel focuses on the comfort of its guests whether their stay is for business or pleasure. The hotel is convenient to the airport and the Metrorail for easy travel to all of DC. 343 rooms, 12 story. Check-out 1 pm, check-in 4 pm. TV; cable (premium), VCR available. In-room modem link. Restaurant. Bar. Babysitting services available. In-house fitness room. Health club privileges. Sauna. Indoor pool, whirlpool. Valet parking $15/day. Free airport transportation. Business center. Concierge. Luxury level. Cr cds: A, C, D, DS, ER, JCB, MC, V. **$$**

★ ★ ★ **MARRIOTT CRYSTAL GATEWAY.** *1700 Jefferson Davis Hwy (22202). Phone 703/920-3230; toll-free 800/228-9290; fax 703/271-5212. www.marriott.com.* This hotel is just minutes from Washington National Airport. With easy access to the mass transit system, guests are close

to the many attractions of Washington, DC, and several activities are nearby. 697 story, 16 story. Pet accepted, some restrictions. Check-out 1 pm, check-in 4 pm. TV; cable (premium). In-room modem link. Restaurant. Bar. Babysitting services available. In-house fitness room. Health club privileges. Sauna. Indoor/outdoor pool; whirlpool, lifeguard. Free airport transportation. Business center. Concierge. Luxury level. Original artwork. Cr cds: A, C, D, DS, ER, JCB, MC, V. **$$**

★ ★ ★ **MARRIOTT KEY BRIDGE.** *1401 Lee Hwy (22209). Phone 703/524-6400; fax 703/524-8964. www.marriott.com.* Just minutes from Washington, DC and the airport, this hotel has many amenities for guests. 584 rooms, 2-14 story. S, D $199-$209; suites $225-$500; weekend rates. Crib free. Garage $8/day. TV; cable (premium), VCR available. Indoor/outdoor pool; whirlpool, poolside service, lifeguard. Coffee in rooms. Restaurant (See also J. W.'S STEAKHOUSE). Bar noon-2 am; entertainment Thurs-Sat. Check-out 1 pm. Convention facilities. Business center. In-room modem link. Concierge. Gift shop. Barber, beauty shop. Exercise equipment; sauna. Health club privileges. Refrigerators, microwaves available. Some balconies. Overlooks Washington across Potomac River. Luxury level. Cr cds: A, C, D, DS, ER, JCB, MC, V.

★ ★ ★ ★ **THE RITZ-CARLTON, PENTAGON CITY.** *1250 S Hayes St (22202). Phone 703/415-5000; fax 703/415-5061; res 800/241-3333. www.ritzcarlton.com.* Five minutes from Washington National Airport, The Ritz-Carlton, Pentagon City provides its guests with an effortless way to visit the capital region. Although businesses, monuments, and other attractions are only minutes away, visitors leave the hectic pace behind when staying here. Tailored elegance is the hallmark of this hotel, and the guest rooms are no exception. Feather beds and Egyptian cotton linens make demanding travelers loyal fans; updated technology is a boon for business travelers; and club-level accommodations take pampering to another level. Massages and personal fitness assessments are available at the fitness center, and the indoor access to the area's popular Fashion Centre puts smiles on the faces of devoted shoppers. Afternoon tea takes on a whimsical edge with the Winnie-the-Pooh children's tea service in the Lobby Lounge, and The Grill never ceases to delight diners with its all-day dining. 366 rooms, 18 story. Pet accepted. Check-out noon, check-in 3 pm. TV; cable (premium), VCR available (movies). In-room modem link. Restaurant. Bar; entertainment. Children's activity center. Babysitting services available. In-house fitness room, massage, sauna, steam room. Indoor pool, whirlpool. Valet parking. Business center. Concierge, luxury level. Cr cds: A, C, D, DS, ER, JCB, MC, V. **$$$**

★ ★ ★ **SHERATON CRYSTAL CITY HOTEL.** *1800 Jefferson Davis Hwy (22202). Phone 703/486-1111; toll-free 800/325-3535; fax 703/769-3970. www.sheraton.com.* This hotel is just 1 mile from Washington National Airport. Shopping, as well as many sites and activities of Washington are close by. 210 rooms, 15 story. Check-out 1 pm, check-in 3 pm. TV; cable (premium). In-room modem link. Restaurant. Bar; entertainment. In-house fitness room, sauna. Pool; lifeguard. Free airport transportation. Business center. Luxury level. Cr cds: A, C, D, DS, MC, V. **$$**

D 🏊 ✕ ✈ 🆉 SC 🏃

All Suite

★ ★ **EMBASSY SUITES.** *1300 Jefferson Davis Hwy (22202). Phone 703/979-9799; fax 703/920-5947. www.embassysuites.com.* This hotel has the typical atrium structure with gardens. Convenient to downtown Washington and close to the airport, this property is in the center of Crystal City. 267 suites, 11 story. Feb-June, Sept-Nov: S $179-$209; D $189-$219; each additional $10; under 12 free; weekend rates; lower rates rest of year. Crib free. Parking $10. TV; cable (premium). Heated pool; lifeguard. Complimentary full breakfast. Restaurant 11 am-2 pm, 5-10 pm. Room service to midnight. Bar to midnight. Check-out noon. Meeting rooms. Business services available. In-room modem link. Gift shop. Free airport transportation. Exercise equipment. Health club privileges. Refrigerators. Atrium lobby. Cr cds: A, C, D, DS, ER, JCB, MC, V.

D 🍴 🖥 🏊 ✕ ✈ 🆉

Extended Stay

★ ★ **RESIDENCE INN BY MARRIOTT.** *550 Army Navy Dr (22202). Phone 703/413-6630; fax 703/418-1751. www.residenceinn.com.* 299 kitchen suites, 17 story. S, D $170-$235; weekend, weekly rates. Crib free. Garage parking $10/day. TV; cable (premium). Indoor pool; whirlpool, lifeguard. Complimentary continental breakfast. Restaurant nearby. Check-out noon. Meeting rooms. Business services available. Concierge. Coin laundry. Free airport transportation. Exercise equipment. Health club privileges. Refrigerators, microwaves. Picnic tables. Cr cds: A, C, D, DS, ER, JCB, MC, V.

D 🏊 ✕ 🆉

Restaurants

★ ★ **ALPINE.** *4770 Lee Hwy (22207). Phone 703/528-7600; fax 703/528-7625. www.alpinerestaurantaol.com.* Italian menu. Closed Mon; most major holidays. Lunch, dinner. Bar. Cr cds: A, D, MC, V. **$$**

D

★ ★ **BISTRO BISTRO.** *4021 S 28th St (22206). Phone 703/379-0300; fax 703/931-1036. www.bistro-bistro.com.* Closed Thanksgiving, Dec 24, 25. Lunch, dinner, Sun brunch. Bar. Outdoor seating. Cr cds: A, D, DS, MC, V. **$**

D

★ **CAFE DALAT.** *3143 Wilson Blvd (22201). Phone 703/276-0935.* Vietnamese menu. Closed July 4, Thanksgiving, Dec 25; also Chinese New Year. Lunch, dinner. Totally nonsmoking. Cr cds: MC, V. **$**

★ ★ **CARLYLE GRAND CAFE.** *4000 S 28th St (22206). Phone 703/931-0777; fax 703/931-9420. www.greatamericanrestaurants.com/carlyle/em.htm.* Closed Thanksgiving, Dec 25. Lunch, dinner, Sun brunch. Bar. Outdoor seating. Totally nonsmoking. Cr cds: A, MC, V. **$$**

★ **COWBOY CAFE.** *4792 Lee Hwy (22207). Phone 703/243-8010. www.washingtonpost.com/cowboycafe.* Specialties: hamburgers, breakfast dishes. Hours: 11 am-11 pm; Fri to midnight; Sat 9 am-midnight; Sun 9 am-9 pm. Breakfast $2.99-$6.50, lunch, dinner $2.75-$8.25. Bar to midnight; Fri, Sat to 1 am; Sun 11 am-9 pm. Musicians Thurs-Sat. Casual, Western décor. Cr cds: A, D, DS, MC, V.

D

★ **FACCIA LUNA.** *2909 Wilson Blvd (22201). Phone 703/276-3099. www.faccialuna.com.* Hours: 11 am-11 pm; Fri, Sat to midnight; Sun noon-11 pm. Closed Thanksgiving, Dec 24, 25. Italian menu. Bar. Lunch $4.95-$5.95, dinner $7.75-$14.95. Children's menu. Specializes in pasta, pizza. Outdoor seating. Upscale trattoria. Cr cds: A, D, MC, V.

D

★ ★ ★ **THE GRILL.** *1250 S Hayes St (22202). Phone 703/412-2760; fax 703/415-5061. www.ritzcarlton.com.* The Grill at the Ritz-Carlton offers upscale American classics in a warm, clubby dining room decked out in mahogany wood. It features a warm fireplace and fresh flowers. The Grill's formal yet inviting atmosphere makes it ideal for all sorts of gatherings, whether business, pleasure, or both. The seasonal menu features lots of pin-up worthy dishes. Lobster, filet mignon, foie gras, caviar, and oysters are in attendance in abundance, giving those in need of culinary luxury an easy and delicious fix. Weekends are busy for The Grill, as it houses one of the best brunches in the area. American, continental menu. Breakfast, lunch, dinner, brunch. Children's menu. Casual attire. Valet parking available. Tea 3-5 pm; $14-$26. Cr cds: A, D, DS, MC, V. **$$**

D

★ ★ **J. W.'S STEAKHOUSE.** *1401 Lee Hwy (22209). Phone 703/524-6400; fax 703/524-8964.* Seafood, steak menu. Hours: 5-10 pm; Fri to 11 pm; Sat 6-11 pm; Sun 5:30-9:30 pm; Sun brunch 10 am-2:30 pm. Closed Jan 1. Dinner $18.95-$28.95. Sun brunch $25.95-$27.95. Bar. Reservations required on July 4. Cr cds: A, D, DS, MC, V.

[D]

★ ★ **LA COTE D'OR CAFE.** *6876 Lee Hwy (22213). Phone 703/538-3033; fax 703/573-0409. www.lacotedor.com.* Hours: 11:30 am-3 pm, 5:30-11 pm; Sun brunch 11 am-3 pm. Closed Jan 1, Dec 25. Reservations accepted. French menu. Bar. Lunch $5.95-$12.95, dinner $18.75-$22.95. Sun brunch $7.95-$11.50. Specializes in seafood, veal. Outdoor seating. French décor. Cr cds: A, D, MC, V.

[D]

★ ★ **LITTLE VIET GARDEN.** *3012 Wilson Blvd (22201). Phone 703/522-9686.* Vietnamese menu. Closed Thanksgiving, Dec 25. Lunch, dinner. Bar. Outdoor seating. Cr cds: A, D, MC, V. **$**

[D]

★ **MATUBA.** *2915 Columbia Pike (22204). Phone 703/521-2811.* Japanese menu. Lunch, dinner. Cr cds: A, MC, V. **$**

★ ★ **QUEEN BEE.** *3181 Wilson Blvd (22201). Phone 703/527-3444; fax 703/525-2750.* Vietnamese menu. Lunch $3.95-$7.50, dinner $6.50-$9.95. Totally nonsmoking. Cr cds: A, C, D, MC, V.

[D]

★ ★ **R. T.'S SEAFOOD KITCHEN.** *2300 Clarendon Blvd (22201). Phone 703/841-0100; fax 703/841-0597. www.seafoodkitchen.com.* Cajun menu. Closed Jan 1, July 4, Thanksgiving, Dec 25. Lunch $7.95-$10.95, dinner $11.95-$17.95. Bar to midnight. Children's menu. Outdoor seating. Cr cds: A, D, DS, MC, V.

[D]

★ **RED HOT AND BLUE.** *1600 Wilson Blvd (22209). Phone 703/276-8833. www.redhotandblue.com.* Specializes in Memphis pit barbecue dishes. Closed Thanksgiving, Dec 25. Lunch, dinner. Bar. Memphis blues memorabilia. Cr cds: A, D, DS, MC, V. **$$**

[D]

★ **SILVER DINER.** *3200 Wilson Blvd (22201). Phone 703/812-8667; fax 703/812-8669.* Hours: 7 am-midnight; Thurs to 1 am; Fri, Sat to 3 am; Sat, Sun brunch 7 am-2 pm. Closed Dec 25. Breakfast $2.99-$7.99, lunch $4.99-$7.99, dinner $6.99-$12.99. Sat, Sun brunch $5.99-$7.99. Children's menu. Cr cds: A, D, DS, MC, V.

[D] [SC]

★ ★ **TIVOLI.** *1700 N Moore St (22209). Phone 703/524-8900; fax 703/524-4971. www.tivolirestaurant.net.* Hours: 11:30 am-2:30 pm, 5:30-10 pm; Sat from 5:30 pm; early-bird dinner Mon-Sat 5:30-6:30 pm. Closed Sun; major holidays. Reservations accepted; required Fri, Sat. Italian menu. Bar 11:30 am-midnight. Lunch $8.50-$11.50; dinner $12.50-$23.50. Specializes in pasta, seafood, veal. Contemporary décor. Cr cds: A, D, DS, MC, V.

[D]

★ **VILLAGE BISTRO.** *1723 Wilson Blvd (22209). Phone 703/522-0284; fax 703/522-7797.* Continental menu. Closed Thanksgiving, Dec 25. Lunch, dinner. Bar. Outdoor seating. Monet prints on walls. Cr cds: A, DS, MC, V. **$**

[D]

★ ★ **WOO LAE OAK.** *1500 S Joyce St (22202). Phone 703/521-3706; fax 703/521-0014. www.woolaeoak.com.* Korean menu. Closed Jan 1. Lunch, dinner $8-$20. Cr cds: A, DS, MC, V.

[D]

Ashland (G-10)

See also Richmond

Founded 1858 **Pop** 6,619 **Elev** 221 ft **Area code** 804 **Zip** 23005

Information Ashland/Hanover Visitor Information Center, 112 N Railroad Ave; 804/752-6766 or 800/897-1479

Web www.vatc.org

Ashland was founded when the president of the Richmond, Fredericksburg, and Potomac Railroad bought land here. He dug a well, struck mineral water, and started a health resort—Slash Cottage (wilderness acres were called "slashes"). A thriving village grew up and took the name of Henry Clay's Kentucky estate. In 1866, the railroad company gave land to the Methodist Church and induced the church to move Randolph-Macon College here. A section of early 1900s houses along the railroad tracks has been set aside as a historic district.

What to See and Do

Paramount's Kings Dominion. *16000 Theme Pkwy. 1 mile E on VA 54, then 7 miles N on I-95 in Doswell. Phone 804/876-5561; toll-free 800/553-PASS.* A 400-acre family theme park consisting of six theme areas, including Water Werks; Action Epic Theatre; the Anaconda, a looping roller coaster that passes through an underwater tunnel;

also Shockwave stand-up roller coaster; The Outer Limits roller coaster; 33-story likeness of the Eiffel Tower with panoramic view; whitewater raft ride; live entertainment; shops. (late May-Aug, daily; late Mar-late May and Sept-Oct, weekends) **$$$$**

Patrick Henry Home "Scotchtown". *11 miles NW via VA 54, 671, County 685 (Scotchtown Rd), left onto Chiswell Ln. Phone 804/227-3500.* (1719) Also girlhood home of Dolley Madison; fine Colonial architecture. (May-Oct, Wed-Sat; Apr, weekends; also by appointment) **$$**

Randolph-Macon College. *204 Henry St. 1 mile W of I-95. Phone 804/752-7305.* (1830) 1,100 students. Coeducational, liberal arts, Methodist-affiliated college. Historic buildings include Washington-Franklin Hall, Old Chapel, and Pace Hall. **FREE**

Motels/Motor Lodges

★ ★ **BEST WESTERN HANOVER HOUSE.** *10296 Sliding Hill Rd (23005). Phone 804/550-2805; toll-free 800/528-1234; fax 804/550-3843. www.bestwestern.com.* 93 rooms, 2 story. Apr-mid-Oct: S $38-$68; D $51-$68; each additional $5; under 12 free; higher rates special events; lower rates rest of year. Crib free. TV; cable. Pool. Restaurant 6:30 am-9 pm. Check-out noon. Coin laundry. Meeting rooms. Business services available. Exercise equipment. Some balconies. Cr cds: A, C, D, DS, MC, V.

★ **COMFORT INN.** *101 N Cottage Green Dr (23005). Phone 804/752-7777; fax 804/798-0327. www.comfortinn.com.* 126 rooms, 2 story. Memorial Day-Labor Day: S, D $59-$89; each additional $5; suites $120; under 18 free; lower rates rest of year. Crib free. TV; cable. Pool. Complimentary continental breakfast. Restaurant adjacent open 24 hours. Check-out noon. Coin laundry. Business services available. Exercise equipment; sauna. Some refrigerators. Cr cds: A, C, D, DS, ER, JCB, MC, V.

★ ★ **QUALITY INN.** *810 England St (23005). Phone 804/798-4231; fax 804/798-9074. www.qualityinn.com.* 56 rooms, 2 story. S, D $45-$98; under 18 free; higher rates some weekends. Crib free. TV; cable (premium). Pool; wading pool. Restaurant 6 am-10 pm. Room service. Bar. Check-out 11 am. Coin laundry. Meeting rooms. Business services available. Valet service. Exercise equipment. Private patios, balconies. Cr cds: A, C, D, DS, ER, JCB, MC, V.

B&B/Small Inn

★ ★ ★ **HENRY CLAY INN.** *114 N Railroad Ave (23005). Phone 804/798-3100; toll-free 800/343-4565; fax 804/752-7555. www.henryclayinn.com.* Guests will enjoy this inn, with its relaxed slow pace, whether it be for romantic pleasure or business. The inn has reproduction antique furniture and guests will be able to make leisurely visits to the historic areas of Williamsburg, Charlottesville, and Fredericksburg. 11 rooms, 3 story. S, D $90-$115; each additional $15; suite $145; higher rates special events. Complimentary continental breakfast. Check-out 11 am, check-in 2 pm. TV; cable. In-room modem link. Dining room 7-9 am; weekends also 11 am-2:30 pm, 6-9 pm. Authentic reproduction of Georgian Revival inn. Totally nonsmoking. Cr cds: A, MC, V.

Restaurants

★ ★ **IRONHORSE.** *100 S Railroad Ave (23005). Phone 804/752-6410; fax 804/752-6441.* American menu. Hours: 11:30 am-2:30 pm, 5:30-9 pm; Mon to 2:30 pm; Fri, Sat to 10 pm. Closed Sun; some major holidays; also week after Jan 1 and week after July 4. Lunch $5-$19, dinner $15-$30. Bar to midnight. Entertainment. Reservations accepted. Cr cds: A, DS, MC, V.

★ **SMOKEY PIG.** *212 S Washington Hwy (23005). Phone 804/798-4590; fax 804/798-4590.* Hours: 11 am-9 pm; Sun from noon. Closed Mon; major holidays. Bar. Lunch $3.45-$13.99, dinner $3.88-$16.95. Children's menu. Specializes in pit-cooked meats, seafood, ribs. Cr cds: A, MC, V.

Basye

See also Luray, New Market, Woodstock

Pop 200 **Elev** 1,354 ft **Area code** 540 **Zip** 22810

Information Bryce Resort, PO Box 3; 540/856-2121

Web www.bryceresort.com

What to See and Do

Bryce Resort. *1982 Fairway Dr. On VA 263.*

    Summer. *Phone 540/856-2121.* Fishing, swimming, boating; horseback riding, golf, tennis, hiking, grass skiing. Fee for activities.

Winter. *Phone 540/856-2121.* Skiing. Two double chairlifts, three surface lifts; patrol, school, rentals; snowmaking; ski shop; restaurant, cafeteria, bar. Longest run 2,750 feet; vertical drop 500 feet. Night skiing. (Mid-Dec-mid-Mar, daily) **$$$$**

Motel/Motor Lodge

★ ★ **BEST WESTERN SHENANDOAH VALLEY.** *250 Conickville Blvd, Mount Jackson (22842). Phone 540/477-2911; toll-free 800/528-1234; fax 540/477-2392. www.bestwestern.com.* 98 rooms, 2 story. June-Oct: S $60; D $70; each additional $4; lower rates rest of year. Crib free. Pet accepted. TV; cable. Pool; wading pool. Playground. Restaurant 6 am-midnight. Bar 5-10 pm. Check-out 11 am. Meeting rooms. Business services available. Sundries. Gift shop. Tennis. Game room. Cr cds: A, C, D, DS, MC, V.

⒟ 🐾 🖙 ⛱ 🏊 SC

B&B/Small Inn

★ ★ ★ **WIDOW KIP'S COUNTRY INN.** *355 Orchard Dr, Mount Jackson (22842). Phone 540/477-2400; toll-free 800/478-8714. www.widowkips.com.* This restored 1830 Victorian home is set on 7 acres of rural countryside with a view of the Shenandoah River and the valley. 5 rooms. No room phones. Pet accepted. Complimentary full breakfast. Check-out 11 am, check-in 3 pm. TV; in sitting room, cottages; cable (premium). Some fireplaces. Pool. Bicycles. Federal-style saltbox house (1830). Victorian furnishings, handmade quilts. Totally nonsmoking. Cr cds: MC, V.

🐾 🐾 ⛱ 🏊 SC

Big Stone Gap (H-2)

See also Breaks Interstate Park, Wise

Founded 1888 **Pop** 4,856 **Elev** 1,488 ft **Area code** 540 **Zip** 24219

Information Lonesome Pine Tourist Information Center, 619 Gilley Ave, PO Box 236; 540/523-2060

This rugged mountain country gave John Fox, Jr., his inspiration for *Trail of the Lonesome Pine* and *Little Shepherd of Kingdom Come.* The town lies at the junction of three forks of the Powell River, which cuts a pass through Stone Mountain.

What to See and Do

John Fox, Jr., House & Museum. *117 Shawnee Ave. Phone 276/523-2747 or 276/523-1235.* Occupied from 1888 by the author of *Trail of the Lonesome Pine* and *Little Shepherd of Kingdom Come,* best-selling novels of the early 1900s. Memorabilia and original furnishings. Guided tours (June-Sept, Tues-Sun; Oct, weekends).

June Tolliver House. *Jerome St and Clinton Ave, junction US 23, 58 A. Phone 276/523-1235.* Heroine in *Trail of the Lonesome Pine* lived here; period furnishings; now an arts and crafts center; restored 1890 house. (June-late Dec, Tues-Sun) **FREE**

Natural Tunnel State Park. *VA 871. 18 miles SE, off US 23. Phone 276/940-2674.* Consists of 648 acres. Giant hole chiseled through Purchase Ridge by Stock Creek; pinnacles or "chimneys." Railroad and stream are accommodated in this vast tunnel—100 feet or more in diameter, 850 feet long. Tunnel, visitor center with exhibits. Swimming, pool, fishing; hiking, picnicking, concession, camping, tent and trailer sites (Memorial Day-Labor Day). Interpretive programs. Chairlift. Park (daily); tunnel and most activities (Memorial Day-Labor Day; daily). Standard fees.

Southwest Virginia Museum. *10 W 1st St. Phone 540/523-1322.* Four-story mansion contains exhibits dealing with life in southwestern Virginia during original coal boom of the 1890s; also Native Americans of the area and early pioneers. (Memorial Day-Labor Day, daily; Mar-late May and early Sept-Dec, Tues-Sun; closed Thanksgiving, Dec 25) **$$**

Special Event

Trail of the Lonesome Pine. June Tolliver Playhouse, adjacent to June Tolliver House. For reserved seats phone 540/523-1235. Outdoor musical drama. Thurs-Sat, late June-Labor Day.

Blacksburg (H-6)

See also Radford, Roanoke, Salem

Founded 1798 **Pop** 39,573 **Elev** 2,080 ft **Area code** 540 **Zip** 24060

Information Blacksburg Regional Chamber of Commerce, 1995 S Main St, Suite 901; 540/522-4503 or 800/288-4061

Web www.blacksburg-chamber.com

The Washington and Jefferson national forests, which lie to the northwest, provide a colorful backdrop of azaleas, flowering dogwood, and redbud in spring and brilliant hardwoods in fall. Virginia Polytechnic Institute and State University is a source of employment for the town. The forests' Blacksburg Ranger District office is located here.

What to See and Do

Mountain Lake. *20 miles NW on US 460, VA 700.* A resort lake, particularly inviting in late June and early July, when azaleas and rhododendron are in bloom.

Smithfield Plantation. *460 Bypass and Rd 314. 1/4 mile W off US 460 bypass, at VA Tech exit. Phone 540/231-3947.* (1773) Restored pre-Revolutionary house; original woodwork. Home of Colonel William Preston and three governors. Architectural link between Tidewater and Piedmont plantations of Virginia and those of the Mississippi Valley. Grounds restored by Garden Club of Virginia. (Apr-Nov, Thurs-Sun afternoons) **$$**

Motels/Motor Lodges

★ ★ **BEST WESTERN RED LION INN.** *900 Plantation Rd (24060). Phone 540/552-7770; toll-free 800/528-1234; fax 540/552-6346. www.bestwestern.com.* 104 rooms, 1-2 story. S $49-$54; D $64-$68; each additional $6; suites $139; under 18 free; higher rates university events. Crib free. Check-out noon. TV; cable, VCR available. Valet services. Restaurant 7 am-10 pm. Bar 4:30 pm-2 am. Room service. Playground. Pool; poolside service. Tennis. Cross-country ski 15 miles. Picnic tables. Lawn games. Meeting rooms. Business services. Sundries. On 13 acres. Cr cds: A, C, D, DS, MC, V.

[D] [icons] SC

★ **COMFORT INN.** *3705 S Main St (24060). Phone 540/951-1500; toll-free 800/228-5150; fax 540/951-1530. www.comfortinn.com.* 80 rooms, 4 story. S $57-$65; D $62-$67; each additional $5; suites $85; under 18 free; higher rates special events. Crib free. Pet accepted. TV; cable (premium), VCR available. Pool. Complimentary continental breakfast. Restaurant adjacent 6 am-10 pm. Check-out 11 am. Business services available. In-room modem link. Valet service. Exercise equipment. Microwaves available. Cr cds: A, C, D, DS, ER, JCB, MC, V.

[D] [icons] SC

★ **DAYS INN.** *2635 Roanoke, Christiansburg (24073). Phone 540/382-0261; toll-free 800/329-7466; fax 540/382-0365. www.daysinn.com.* 122 rooms, 2 story. S $46-$84; D $54-$84; each additional $5; under 18 free; higher rates: special events. Crib free. Pet accepted. TV; cable (premium). Pool. Playground. Complimentary continental breakfast. Check-out noon. In-room modem link. Cr cds: A, C, D, DS, JCB, MC, V.

[D] [icons] SC

★ ★ **FOUR POINTS BY SHERATON.** *900 Price's Fork Rd (24060). Phone 540/552-7001; toll-free 800/325-3535; fax 540/552-0827. www.sheraton.com.* 148 rooms, 2 story. S, D $89-$169; each additional $10; suites $199; under 18 free. Crib free. TV; cable (premium). 2 pools, 1 indoor; wading pool. Complimentary coffee in lobby. Restaurant 7 am-2 pm, 5-9 pm. Bar noon-2 am; entertainment. Check-out noon. Meeting rooms. Business services available. In-room modem link. Valet service. Health club privileges. Tennis. Cr cds: A, C, D, DS, ER, JCB, MC, V.

[D] [icons] SC

★ **HAMPTON INN.** *50 Hampton Blvd, Christiansburg (24073). Phone 540/382-2055; fax 540/382-4515. www.hamptoninn.com.* 125 rooms, 2 story. S $57; D $70; under 18 free; higher rates: weekends, university graduation, football games. Crib free. TV; cable (premium). Pool. Restaurant opposite 6 am-10 pm. Check-out 11 am. Coin laundry. Business services available. Microwave available. Cr cds: A, C, D, DS, ER, MC, V.

[D] [icons]

★ ★ **RAMADA INN.** *3503 Holiday Ln (24060). Phone 540/951-1330; toll-free 800/684-9628; fax 540/951-4847. www.ramada.com.* 98 rooms, 2 story. S $55-$65; D $60-$70; each additional $5; suites $135; under 12 free; higher rates: university graduation, football weekends. Pet accepted. Check-out noon. TV; cable (premium). Some in-room steam baths. Restaurant 6:30 am-2 pm, 5-10 pm. Bar. Room service. Pool; children's pool. Cross-country ski 20 miles. Cr cds: A, C, D, DS, MC, V.

[D] [icons]

B&B/Small Inn

★ ★ ★ **OAKS VICTORIAN INN.** *311 E Main St, Christiansburg (24073). Phone 540/381-1500; toll-free 800/336-6257; fax 540/381-3036. www.bbhost.com/theoaksinn.* This Queen Anne Victorian (1889) is home to seven historic oak trees, one of which is the largest white oak in the area. Built in 1889, the inn provides guests with many amenities including down comforters and claw foot bathtubs to name a few. 7 rooms, 3 story. S $85-$125; D $115-$150; lower rates Jan-Mar. Children over 14 years only. TV; cable (premium). Whirlpool. Complimentary full breakfast; afternoon refreshments. Restaurant nearby. Check-out noon, check-in 4 pm. Business services available. In-room modem link. Valet service. Airport transportation. Health club privileges. Refrigerators; some fireplaces. Balconies. Totally nonsmoking. Cr cds: A, DS, MC, V.

[icon]

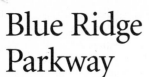

Blue Ridge Parkway

See also Roanoke, Waynesboro

Elev 649-6,050 ft; average 3,000 ft

Winding 469 mountainous miles between the Shenandoah and Great Smoky Mountains national parks (about 217 miles are in Virginia), the Blue Ridge Parkway represents a different concept in highway travel. It is not an express highway (speed limit 45 miles per hour) but a road intended for leisurely travel. All towns are bypassed. Travelers in a hurry would be wise to take state and US routes, where speed limits are higher.

The parkway follows the Blue Ridge Mountains for about 355 miles, then winds through the Craggies, Pisgahs, and Balsams to the Great Smokies. Overlooks, picnic and camp sites, visitor centers, nature trails, fishing streams and lakes, and points of interest are numerous and well-marked.

Accommodations are plentiful in cities and towns along the way. Food availability is limited on the parkway.

The parkway is open all year, but the best time to drive it is between April and November. Some sections are closed by ice and snow for periods in winter and early spring. Fog may be present during wet weather. The higher sections west of Asheville to Great Smoky Mountains National Park and north of Asheville to Mount Mitchell may be closed January through March due to hazardous driving conditions.

For maps, pamphlets and detailed information contact Superintendent, 199 Hemphill Road, Asheville, NC 28803; 828/298-0398.

What to See and Do

Camping. Tent and trailer sites at **Otter Creek, Peaks of Otter, Roanoke Mountain, Rocky Knob, Doughton Park, Julian Price Memorial Park, Linville Falls, Crabtree Meadows,** and **Mount Pisgah.** (May-Oct) 14-day limit, June-Labor Day. No electricity; pets on leash only; water shut off with first freeze, usually late Oct. Primitive winter camping at Linville Falls when roads are passable.

Fishing. Rainbow, brook, brown trout and smallmouth bass in streams and lakes. State licenses required.

Folk Art Center. *Mile 382, Blue Ridge Pkwy (24174).* Craft Guild Headquarters, sales, parkway travel information, park ranger. (Daily)

Horseback Riding. *Mile 292.7, Blue Ridge Pkwy.* 20 miles of trails in Moses H. Cone Memorial Park. Horses for hire at Blowing Rock, NC.

Interpretive programs. *Miles 60.8, 86, 169, 241.1, 297.1, 316.3, 340, and 408.6, Blue Ridge Pkwy.* Outdoor talks (mid-June-Labor Day) at Otter Creek (mile 60.8), Peaks of Otter (mile 86), Rocky Knob (mile 169), Doughton Park (mile 241.1), Price Park (mile 297.1), Linville Falls (mile 316.3), Crabtree Meadows (mile 340), and Mount Pisgah (mile 408.6). Obtain schedules at Parkway Visitor Centers.

Northwest Trading Post. *Mile 258.6, Blue Ridge Pkwy (24174).* Country store sells native handicrafts.

Parkway Craft Center. *Mile 294, Blue Ridge Pkwy, Blowing Rock, NC.* (See BLOWING ROCK, NC)

Self-guided trails. Moderate grades. Walks take from five minutes to one hour. Trails on the parkway include

Cascades Trail. *Mile 272, Blue Ridge Pkwy.* Leads to waterfall.

Cone Park Trail. *Mile 294, Blue Ridge Pkwy.* Manor house wild garden.

Craggy Gardens Trail. *Mile 364.6, Blue Ridge Pkwy.* Traverses high mountain "gardens."

Elk Run Trail. *Mile 86, Blue Ridge Pkwy.* Forest, plant, animal community.

Flat Rock Trail. *Mile 308.2, Blue Ridge Pkwy.* Magnificent valley and mountain views.

Greenstone Trail. *Mile 8.8, Blue Ridge Pkwy.* Of geologic interest.

Linville Falls Trail. *Mile 316.4, Blue Ridge Pkwy.* Views of falls, Linville River Gorge.

Mabry Mill Trail. *Mile 176, Blue Ridge Pkwy.* Old-time mountain industry.

Mountain Farm Trail. *Mile 5.8, Blue Ridge Pkwy.* Typical mountain farm, reconstructed.

Richland Balsam Trail. *Mile 431, Blue Ridge Pkwy.* Spruce-fir forests. Highest spot on parkway.

Rocky Knob Trail. *Mile 168, Blue Ridge Pkwy.* Leads to overlook of Rock Castle Gorge.

Trail of the Trees. *Mile 63.6, Blue Ridge Pkwy.* Leads to overlook of James River.

★ **Visitor Centers.** Exhibits, travel information, interpretive publications. Centers (daily during peak travel season) include

Craggy Gardens Visitor Center. *Mile 364.6, Blue Ridge Pkwy.* 5,892-foot elevation. Natural history exhibits, naturalist. (Mid-June-Labor Day, daily; May-mid-June, early Sept-Oct, weekends)

Humpback Rocks Visitor Center. *Mile 5.8, Blue Ridge Pkwy.* Pioneer mountain farm, park ranger.

James River Wayside. *Mile 63.6.* Story of James River and Kanawha Canal, park ranger.

Linn Cove Information Center. *Mile 304.*

Mabry Mill. *Mile 176, Blue Ridge Pkwy.* Old-time mountain industry, including tannery exhibits, picturesque mill, blacksmith shop.

Museum of North Carolina Minerals. *Mile 331, Blue Ridge Pkwy.* (Daily, winter hours vary; closed holidays)

Peaks of Otter Visitor Center. *Mile 86, Blue Ridge Pkwy.* Wildlife exhibits, park ranger.

Rocky Knob Information Station. *Mile 169, Blue Ridge Pkwy.* Information, exhibits, park ranger.

Waterrock Knob Information Center. *Mile 451, Blue Ridge Pkwy.* Panoramic views, visitor information, exhibits, publications.

Motel/Motor Lodge

★ ★ ★ **PEAKS OF OTTER LODGE.** *Mile Post 86, Blue Ridge Pkwy, Bedford (2423).* Phone 540/586-1081; fax 540/586-4420; toll-free 800/542-5927. www.peaksofotter.com. Nestled between two mountains that make up the Peaks of Otter, this lodge overlooks Abbott Lake. Each room has a view of the lake and the Sharp Top Mountains. 63 rooms, 2 story. Mar-Nov: S $67; D $72; each additional $6.25; suites $85-$100; under 16 free; MAP rest of year. Crib free. TV in lobby. Restaurant (see PEAKS OF OTTER). Bar 5-11 pm. Check-out noon. Meeting room. Business services available. Sundries. Gift shop. Private patios, balconies. Scenic view. Cr cds: MC, V.

🚻 D 🎿 🛇

Resort

★ ★ ★ **DOE RUN LODGE RESORT AND CONFERENCE CENTER.** *Blue Ridge Pkwy, Fancy Gap (24343).* Phone 540/398-2212; toll-free 800/325-6189; fax 540/398-2833. www.doerunlodge.com. Located along Blue Ridge Parkway, this true nature-lover's retreat with its fresh, clean mountain air will truly be delightful. Enjoy the beautiful scenery with deer and wildlife roaming in the forest with the scent of blossoms filling the air. 47 kitchen suites, 1-2 story. No elevator. May-Oct: kitchen suites $119-$250; each additional $18; under 15 free; package plans; lower rates rest of year. Crib free. Pet accepted; $45 deposit. Complimentary coffee in rooms.

Check-out noon. TV; VCR (movies $3). Balconies. Restaurant. Bar; entertainment Fri, Sat. Sauna. Heated pool; poolside service. 18-hole golf privileges, greens fee, pro, putting green, driving range. Lighted tennis. Picnic tables. Lawn games. Meeting rooms. Business services. Sundries. Cr cds: A, MC, V.

D 🐾 🎿 🛇 SC

B&B/Small Inn

★ ★ **THE OSCEOLA MILL COUNTRY INN.** *Hwy 56, Steele's Tavern (24476)* Phone 540/377-6455; fax 540/377-5148. www.osceolamill.com. 12 rooms, 1-2 story. No room phones. Complimentary full breakfast. Check-out 11 am, check-in 2 pm. Pool. In renovated 1849 mill, mill store, and restored 1873 miller's house. Totally nonsmoking. Cr cds: MC, V.

D 🛇 🛇

Restaurants

★ ★ **PEAKS OF OTTER.** *Mile Post 86, Blue Ridge Pkwy (24523).* Phone 540/586-9263; fax 540/586-4420. www.peaksotter.com. Breakfast, lunch, dinner, Sun brunch. Bar. Children's menu. Cr cds: MC, V. **$$**

D

Booker T. Washington National Monument (H-7)

See also Roanoke

(Approximately 18 miles S on VA 116 from Roanoke to Burnt Chimney, then continue 6 miles E on VA 122)

The 1861 property inventory of the Burroughs plantation listed, along with household goods and farm implements, the entry "1 Negro boy (Booker)—$400." Freed in 1865, the boy and his family moved to Malden, West Virginia. There, while working at a salt furnace and in coal mines, the youngster learned the alphabet from *Webster's Blueback Spelling Book.* Later, by working at the salt furnace before school, then going to work at the mine after school, he got the rudiments of an education. When he realized that everyone else at the school roll call had two names, he chose Washington for his own.

At age 16, he started the 500-mile trip from Malden to Hampton Institute, where he earned his way. He taught at Malden for two years, attended Wayland Seminary, and returned to Hampton Institute to teach. In July 1881, he started Tuskegee Institute in Alabama with 30 pupils, two run-down buildings, and $2,000 for salaries. When Washington died in 1915, the Institute had 107 buildings, more than 2,000 acres, and was assessed at more than $500,000.

The 224-acre monument includes most of the original plantation. A 1/4-mile self-guided plantation trail passes reconstructed farm buildings, a slave cabin, crops, and animals of the period; there is also a 1 1/2-mile, self-guided Jack-O-Lantern Branch nature trail. Picnic facilities. Visitor Center has an audiovisual program, exhibits depicting his life (Daily; closed Jan 1, Thanksgiving, Dec 25). Phone 540/721-2094. **FREE**

Breaks Interstate Park (H-3)

See also Wise

(7 miles SE of Elkhorn City, KY and 8 miles N of Haysi, VA on KY-VA 80)

Where the Russell Fork of the Big Sandy River plunges through the mountains is called the "Grand Canyon of the South," the major focus of this 4,600-acre park on the Kentucky-Virginia border. From the entrance, a paved road winds through an evergreen forest and then skirts the canyon rim. Overlooks provide a spectacular view of the "Towers," a huge pyramid of rocks. Within the park are extraordinary rock formations, caves, springs, a profusion of rhododendron and, of course, the 5-mile-long, 1,600-foot-deep gorge.

The visitor center houses historical and natural exhibits, including a coal exhibit (Apr-Oct, daily). Laurel Lake is stocked with bass and bluegill. Swimming pool, pedal boats; hiking, bridle, and mountain bike trails, picnicking, playground, camping (Apr-Oct, fee); motor lodge, cottages (year-round), restaurant, gift shop. Park (daily); facilities (Apr-late Dec, daily). Contact Breaks Interstate Park, PO Box 100, Breaks, VA 24607. Phone 276/865-4413 or 800/982-5122. **$**

Motel/Motor Lodge

★ ★ **BREAKS INTERSTATE.** *Rte 1, Breaks (24607). Phone 540/865-4414; fax 540/865-5561; toll-free 800/982-5122. www.breakspark.com.* 34 rooms, 1-2 story. Apr-Dec: S $66.03; D $74.55; each additional $8; cottages $350/week. Closed late Dec-Mar. Crib free. TV; cable. Pool; wading pool, lifeguard. Restaurant 7 am-9 pm. Check-out

11 am. Meeting room. Sundries. Gift shop. Balconies. Picnic tables, grills. Bicycle rentals. Woodland setting; overlooks Breaks Canyon. Hiking trails, picnic shelters. Cr cds: A, DS, MC, V.

[icons]

Bristol (I-3)

See also Abingdon

Founded 1771 **Pop** 17,367 **Elev** 1,680 ft **Area code** 540 (VA); 423 (TN) **Zip** 24201 (VA); 37620 (TN)

Information Chamber of Commerce, 20 Volunteer Pkwy, TN, or PO Box 519, VA 24203; 423/989-4850

Web www.bristolchamber.org

Essentially a city in two states, Bristol is actually two cities—Bristol, Tennessee and Bristol, Virginia—sharing the same main street and the same personality. Each has its own government and city services. Together they constitute a major shopping center. Named for the English industrial center, Bristol is an important factory town in its own right. These cities carry on the pioneer tradition of an ironworks established here about 1784 which made the first nails for use on the frontier.

What to See and Do

Bristol Caverns. *5 miles SE on US 435, off I-81. Phone 423/878-2011.* Unusual rock formations seen from lighted, paved walkways winding through caverns and along an underground river. Guided tours every 20 minutes. Picnic area. (Daily; closed Easter, Dec 25) **$$$**

Rocky Mount Historic Site. *200 Hyder Hill Rd. 11 miles SW on US 11 E. Phone 423/538-7396.* Features the 2 1/2-story log house (1770) that served from 1790 to 1792 as capital under William Blount, governor of the Territory of the United States South of the River Ohio. Restored to its original simplicity; 18th-century furniture. On grounds are restored log kitchen, slave cabin, barn, blacksmith shop, and smokehouse. (Daily; closed Thanksgiving, Dec 21-Jan 5; also weekends Jan, Feb) **$$**

Special Event

Bristol Motor Speedway. *2801 US 11 E. 5 miles S on US 11 E. Phone 423/764-1161.* Apr, June, and Aug.

Motels/Motor Lodges

★ **BUDGET HOST INN.** *1209 W State St (24201). Phone 540/669-5187; fax 540/466-5848. www.budgethost.com.* 24 rooms. S, D $28.50-$80; each additional $4;

under 12 free; weekly rates. Check-out 11 am. TV; cable (premium). Restaurant nearby. Business services. Cr cds: A, DS, MC, V.

⊠

★ **COMFORT INN.** *2368 Lee Hwy (24201). Phone 540/466-3881; toll-free 800/228-5150; fax 540/466-6544. www.comfortinn.com.* 60 rooms, 2 story. Apr-Oct: S, D $65-$195; each additional $5; suites $125-$225; under 18 free; higher rates special events; lower rates rest of year. Crib free. TV; cable (premium). Pool. Complimentary continental breakfast. Restaurant nearby. Check-out 11 am. Business services available. Cr cds: A, C, D, DS, JCB, MC, V.

D ⇔ ⊠ SC

★ **LA QUINTA INN.** *1014 Old Airport Rd (24201). Phone 540/669-9353; fax 540/669-6974. www.laquintainn. com.* 123 rooms, 4 story. June-Sept: S $59-$79; D $69-$89; each additional $10; suites $95-$105; under 18 free; higher rates race cars; lower rates rest of year. Crib free. Pet accepted. Complimentary continental breakfast. Check-out noon. TV; cable (premium), VCR available. In-room modem link. Restaurant nearby. Pool. Meeting rooms. Business services. Cr cds: A, C, D, DS, MC, V.

D ⇔ ⊠

★ ★ **RAMADA INN.** *2221 Euclid Ave (24201). Phone 540/669-7171. www.ramada.com.* 123 rooms, 2 story. S, D $55-$95; each additional $4; under 18 free; higher rates special events. Check-out noon. TV. Restaurant 7 am-2 pm; 5-9 pm. Bar from 5 pm. Room service. Pool. Cr cds: A, C, D, DS, JCB, MC, V.

D ⇔ ⊠

★ **RED CARPET INN.** *15589 Lee Hwy (24202). Phone 540/669-1151.* 60 rooms, 2 story. June-Oct: S, D $48-$74; each additional $5; higher rates special events; lower rates rest of year. Crib free. Pet accepted, some restrictions. TV; cable (premium). Pool. Check-out noon. Microwaves available. Cr cds: A, D, DS, MC, V.

D ⇔ ⇔ ⇔ ⇔ ⊠

★ **SUPER 8.** *2139 Lee Hwy (24201). Phone 540/466-8800. www.super8.com.* 62 rooms, 3 story. S, D $46-$64; each additional $6; under 12 free; higher rates car races. Crib free. Pet accepted. TV; cable. Restaurant nearby. Check-out 11 am. Business services available. Some refrigerators, microwaves. Picnic tables. Cr cds: A, C, D, DS, MC, V.

D ⇔ ⊠

Restaurants

★ **ATHENS STEAK HOUSE.** *105 Goodson St (24201). Phone 540/466-8271.* Hours: 4-10:30 pm. Closed Sun; major holidays. Greek, American menu. Bar. Dinner $7.95-$20.45. Specializes in lobster tail, steak. Cr cds: MC, V.

D

★ ★ **VINEYARD.** *603 Gate City Hwy (24201). Phone 540/466-4244; fax 540/466-4196.* Hours: 7 am-10 pm; Fri, Sat to 11 pm. Closed July 4, Dec 24, 25. Reservations accepted weekends. Italian, American menu. Bar. Breakfast $3.95-$6.95, lunch $4.95-$7.95. Complete meals: dinner $8.25-$25. Specializes in fresh seafood, veal. Salad bar. Cr cds: A, D, DS, MC, V.

D

Brookneal (H-8)

See also Lynchburg, South Boston

Settled circa 1790 **Pop** 1,259 **Elev** 560 ft **Area code** 804 **Zip** 24528

What to See and Do

Patrick Henry National Memorial (Red Hill). *3 miles E on VA 40, 2 miles S on VA 600 and 619. Phone 434/376-2044.* Last home and burial place of Patrick Henry. Restoration of family cottage, cook's cabin, smokehouse, stable, kitchen. Patrick Henry's law office. Museum and gift shop on grounds. Interpretive video. (Daily; closed Jan 1, Thanksgiving, Dec 25) **$$$**

Cape Charles (H-13)

See also Hampton, Newport News, Norfolk, Portsmouth, Virginia Beach

Pop 1,134 **Elev** 10 ft **Area code** 757 **Zip** 23310

Information Chesapeake Bay Bridge & Tunnel District, Public Relations Department, PO Box 111; 757/331-2960, ext 20

Web www.cbbt.com

The Chesapeake Bay Bridge-Tunnel (17.6 miles long) leads from Cape Charles (12 miles south of the town) to Virginia Beach/Norfolk. There is a scenic stop, gift shop, restaurant, and fishing pier (bait available). **Note:** Noncommercial vehicles entering with compressed gas containers are limited to (a) two nonpermanently-mounted containers with a maximum individual capacity of 105 pounds water or 45 pounds LP gas each, or one container with a maximum capacity of 60 pounds LP gas; or (b) not more than two permanently-mounted containers with a total capacity of 200 gallons water when LP gas is used as a motor fuel. One-way passenger car toll. **$$**

B&B/Small Inn

★ ★ **WILSON-LEE HOUSE BED AND BREAK-FAST.** *403 Tazewell Ave (23310). Phone 757/331-1954; fax 757/331-8133. www.wilsonleehouse.com.* 6 rooms. Children over 12 years only. Complimentary full breakfast. Check-out 11 am, check-in 4-6 pm. Cable TV in common room; VCR available (movies). Street parking. Built in 1906. Totally nonsmoking. Cr cds: A, MC, V. **$**

Cape Henry Memorial (H-13)

See also Norfolk, Virginia Beach

(10 miles E of Norfolk on US 60)

The first English settlers of Jamestown landed here on April 26, 1607. They claimed the land for England, stayed four days, named their landing spot for Henry (then Prince of Wales and oldest son of King James I), and put up a cross.

A cross put up by the Daughters of the American Colonists in 1935 marks the approximate site of the first landing. An interpretive display describes the Battle of the Capes, a sea battle fought between England and France in 1781 and a prelude to the Battle of Yorktown. Nearby is Cape Henry Lighthouse, first lighthouse in the United States authorized and built by the federal government (1791). The memorial is in Fort Story Military Reservation.

Centreville (D-10)

All Suite

★ ★ **SPRINGHILL SUITES.** *5920 Trinity Pkwy (20120). Phone 703/815-7800; toll-free 888/287-9400. www.springhillsuites.com; fax 703/815-4100.* Guests looking for spacious and functional accommodations will enjoy suites that feature a separate area for eating, sleeping, working, and relaxing. 136 rooms, 4 story. Suites $94-$144. Crib available. Complimentary continental breakfast. Check-out noon, check-in 3 pm. TV; cable (premium). In-room modem link. Refrigerators, microwaves. Valet

services. Coin laundry. Restaurant nearby. Exercise equipment. Indoor pool, whirlpool. Meeting room. Business services. Cr cds: A, C, D, DS, MC, V.

Restaurants

★ ★ **SWEETWATER TAVERN.** *14250 Sweetwater Ln (22020). Phone 703/449-1100; fax 703/449-1108. www.sweetwater1-gar.com.* Specializes in hickory-fired Angus beef, fresh seafood, chops. Hours: 4:30-11 pm; Mon to 10 pm; Fri, Sat noon-1 am; Sun noon-10 pm; early-bird dinner Mon-Thurs to 6 pm. Closed Thanksgiving, Dec 25. Lunch $8-$12, dinner $13-$22. Bar. Microbrewery. Children's menu. Totally nonsmoking. Cr cds: A, DS, MC, V.

★ **WINFIELD'S.** *5127 Westfield Blvd (20120). Phone 703/803-1040; fax 703/803-6310.* Hours: 11 am-midnight; Fri, Sat to 1:30 am; Sun to 9 pm. Closed major holidays. Reservations accepted; required Fri, Sat dinner. Bar. Lunch $5.25-$8.50, dinner $7.95-$14.95; Children's menu. Specializes in fresh seafood, steaks. Outdoor seating. Sports bar; informal dining. Cr cds: A, D, MC, V.

Charlottesville (F-9)

See also Waynesboro

Founded 1762 **Pop** 45,049 **Elev** 480 ft **Area code** 804

Information Charlottesville/Albemarle Convention & Visitors Bureau, jct I-64 and VA 20, PO Box 178, 22902; 804/977-1783

Web www.charlottesvilletourism.org

Thomas Jefferson was born here, as was the University of Virginia, which he founded and designed. Ash Lawn-Highland, which was James Monroe's home, and Monticello are southeast of the city.

In the gently rolling terrain of Albemarle County, Charlottesville is almost at the center of Virginia; it is the trading center for a widespread area. In colonial times, tobacco was the dominant product. Today, wheat, beef and dairy herds, riding and race horses, peaches, frozen foods, electronic products, light industry, and mountains of native Albemarle pippin apples invigorate the economy.

What to See and Do

Albemarle County Courthouse. *Court Sq.* North wing was used in 1820s as a "common temple" shared by Episcopalian, Methodist, Presbyterian, and Baptist sects, one Sun a month to each but with all who wished attending each Sun. Jefferson, Monroe, and Madison worshiped here.

⭐ **Ash-Lawn Highland.** *1000 James Monroe Pkwy. 4 1/4 miles SE on County 795. Phone 434/293-9539.* (1799) Built on a site personally selected by Thomas Jefferson, this 535-acre estate was the home of President James Monroe (1799-1823). The estate is now owned by Monroe's alma mater, the College of William and Mary. This early 19th-century working plantation offers guided tours of the house with Monroe possessions, spinning and weaving demonstrations, old boxwood gardens, peacocks, picnic spots. Special events include Summer Music Festival (June-Aug) of arts, evening concerts, children's shows (Sat), Plantation Days Weekend, spring and Christmas programs. (Daily; closed Jan 1, Thanksgiving, Dec 25) **$$$**

George Rogers Clark Memorial. *W Main and Jefferson Park Ave (22906).* Brother of William Clark and soldier on the frontier, this intrepid explorer who opened up the Northwest Territory was an Albemarle County native son.

Historic Michie Tavern. *683 Thomas Jefferson Pkwy (22902). 1 mile S on VA 20. Phone 434/977-1234.* (circa 1784) Located near Jefferson's Monticello. Visitors dine on hearty Midday Fare in the Tavern's Ordinary where servers in period attire greet them. Afterwards, a tour of the original tavern features living history where guests participate in 18th-century activities including a lively Virginia dance. (Daily; closed Jan 1, Dec 25) **$$$**

Lewis and Clark Monument. *Ridge and Main sts.* Memorial to Jefferson's secretary, Meriwether Lewis, who explored the Louisiana Territory with his friend William Clark.

⭐ **Monticello.** *2 miles SE on VA 53. Phone 434/984-9822.* Located on a mountaintop, this is one of the most beautiful estates in Virginia and is considered a classic of American architecture. Monticello was designed by Thomas Jefferson and built over the course of 40 years, symbolizing the pleasure he found in "putting up and pulling down." Jefferson moved into the first completed outbuilding of his new home in 1771, though construction continued until 1809. Most of the interior furnishings are original. Tours of the restored orchard, vineyard, 1,000-foot-long vegetable garden, and Mulberry Row, once the site of plantation workshops. Jefferson died at Monticello on July 4, 1826, and was buried in the family cemetery. The Thomas Jefferson Memorial Foundation maintains the house and gardens. (Daily; closed Dec 25) **$$$$** Approximately 2 miles W of here is

Monticello Visitors Center. *VA 20 S and I-64. Phone 434/984-9822.* Personal and family memorabilia; architectural models and drawings; *Thomas Jefferson:*

The Pursuit of Liberty, a 35-minute film, shown twice daily. (Daily; closed Dec 25) **FREE**

Robert E. Lee Monument. *1st and Jefferson sts.*

Shenandoah National Park. *(see) 20 miles W on VA 250 to Afton, then N on Skyline Dr.*

Stonewall Jackson on Little Sorrel. *Adjacent to courthouse.* By Charles Keck.

University of Virginia. *914 Emmet St N (22903). W end of Main St. Phone 434/924-1019.* (1819) 18,100 students. Founded by Thomas Jefferson and built according to his plans. Handsome red brick buildings with white trim, striking vistas, smooth lawns, and ancient trees form the grounds of Jefferson's "academical village." The serpentine walls, one brick thick, which Jefferson designed for strength and beauty, are famous. Room 13, West Range, occupied by Edgar Allan Poe as a student, is displayed for the public. Walking tours start at the Rotunda (Daily; closed three weeks mid-Dec-early Jan). **FREE**

Walking tour. *VA 20. Phone 434/977-1783.* The Charlottesville/Albemarle Information Center, located on VA 20 S in the Monticello Visitors Center Building, has information for a walking tour of historic Charlottesville.

Wintergreen Resort. *W on US 250 to VA 151, then S to VA 664, turn right, follow signs (approximately 4 1/2 miles). Phone 434/325-2200.* Quad, three triple, double chairlifts; patrol, school, rentals, snow making; lodge (see RESORTS); nursery. Twenty runs; longest run 1 1/2 miles; vertical drop 1,003 feet. (Dec-Mar, daily) Night skiing. Summer activities include fishing, boating; golf, tennis, horseback riding. **$$$$**

Special Events

Dogwood Festival. Parade, lacrosse and golf tournaments, carnival. Nine days mid-Apr.

Founder's Day. (Jefferson's Birthday) Commemorative ceremonies. Apr 13.

Garden Week. Some fine private homes and gardens in the area are open. Mid-Apr.

Motels/Motor Lodges

⭐ **BEST WESTERN.** *1613 Emmet St (22906). Phone 434/296-5501; toll-free 800/528-1234; fax 434/977-6249. www.bestwestern.com.* 104 rooms, 1-2 story. D $68-$76; each additional $6; under 18 free; Pet accepted some restrictions. Check-out noon, check-in 3 pm. TV; cable (premium). Pool; children's pool. Cr cds: A, C, D, DS, MC, V.

D 🐾 ⇌ ⇌ SC

★ **BEST WESTERN CAVALIER INN.** *105 Emmet St N (22903). Phone 434/296-8111; fax 434/296-3523. www.bestwestern.com.* 120 rooms, 5 story. D $79-$135; each additional $8; under 18 free. Pet accepted. Complimentary continental breakfast. Check-out noon, check-in 3 pm. TV; cable (premium). Outdoor pool. Free airport transportation. Business center. Cr cds: A, C, D, DS, MC, V.

D ⊛ ⊠ ⊠ ⅀

★★ **COURTYARD BY MARRIOTT.** *638 Hillsdale Dr (22901). Phone 434/973-7100; res 800/321-2211; fax 434/973-7128. www.courtyard.com.* 161 rooms, 3 story. D $79-$109; under 18 free. Check-out noon, check-in 3 pm. TV; cable (premium), VCR available. In-room modem link. Coin laundry. Bar 5-10 pm. Indoor pool; whirlpool. Free airport transportation. Cr cds: A, C, D, DS, MC, V.

D ⊠ ⊠

★★ **DAYS INN.** *1600 Emmet St N (22901). Phone 434/293-9111; toll-free 800/329-7466; fax 434/977-2780. www.daysinn.com.* 129 rooms, 3 story. D $60-$90; each additional $10; under 18 free. Pet accepted. Check-out noon, check-in 2 pm. TV; cable (premium). In-room modem link. Restaurant 7 am-10 pm; Fri, Sat to 11 pm. Bar 10-1 am. Room service. Health club privileges, exercise equipment. Pool; wading pool, children's pool. Free transportation. Cr cds: A, C, D, DS, JCB, MC, V.

D ⊛ ⊠ ⅄ ⊠ SC

★★ **ENGLISH INN OF CHARLOTTESVILLE.** *2000 Morton Dr (22903). Phone 434/971-9900; toll-free 800/786-5400; fax 434/977-8008. www.wytestone.com.* 88 suites, 3 story. D $64-$74; each additional $6; under 18 free. Complimentary breakfast buffet. Check-out noon, check-in 2 pm. TV; cable (premium). Sauna. Indoor pool. Airport transportation. Cr cds: A, C, D, DS, MC, V.

D ⊠ ⊠ SC

★ **HAMPTON INN.** *2035 India Rd (22901). Phone 434/978-7888; fax 434/973-0436. www.hamptoninn.com.* 123 rooms, 5 story. D $75-$90; under 18 free. Complimentary continental breakfast. Check-out noon, check-in 2 pm. TV; cable (premium). Health club privileges. Pool. Free airport transportation. Cr cds: A, C, D, DS, MC, V.

D ⊠ ⊠

★★ **HOLIDAY INN.** *1200 5th St SW (22902). Phone 434/977-5100; toll-free 800/465-4329; fax 434/293-5228. www.holiday-inn.com.* 132 rooms, 6 story. D $90-$130; each additional $10; under 18 free. Check-out noon, check-in 2 pm. TV; cable (premium). Restaurant 6:30-10:30 am, 5-10 pm. Bar to 11 pm. Room service. Exercise room. Game room. Outdoor pool; children's pool. Cr cds: A, D, DS, JCB, MC, V.

D ⊠ ⅄ ⊠ SC

★★ **RAMADA INN.** *2097 Inn Dr (22911). Phone 434/977-3300. www.ramada.com.* 100 rooms, 2 story. D $50-$70; each additional $10; under 17 free. Complimentary continental breakfast. Check-out noon, check-in 2 pm. TV; cable (premium), VCR available. Restaurant 7 am-10 pm. Bar 5-10 pm. Room service. Game room. Pool. Cr cds: A, C, D, DS, MC, V.

D ⊠ ⊠ SC

Hotels

★★ **DOUBLETREE HOTEL.** *990 Hilton Heights Rd (22901). Phone 434/973-2121; toll-free 800/494-7596; fax 434/978-7735. www.doubletree.com.* Close to the historic sites, this hotel services both the leisure and business traveler. The Blue Ridge Parkway, with its many activities, is nearby. 247 rooms, 9 story. D $99-$149; each additional $10. Check-out noon, check-in 3 pm. TV; cable (premium), VCR available. In-room modem link. Restaurant 6:30 am-10:30 pm. Bar 5:30-11 pm. Room service 6:30 am-11 pm. Exercise equipment. Indoor/outdoor pool; whirlpool, poolside service. Tennis. Free airport depot transportation. Cr cds: A, C, D, DS, ER, JCB, MC, V.

D ⊨ ⊠ ⅄ ⊠

★★★ **OMNI CHARLOTTESVILLE HOTEL.** *235 W Main St (22902). Phone 434/971-5500; toll-free 800/843-6664; fax 434/979-4456. www.omnihotels.com.* Located on a downtown mall, this hotel is within walking distance to the government buildings. 211 rooms, 6 story. D $120-$160; each additional $15; under 18 free. Pet accepted, some restrictions. Check-out noon, check-in 3 pm. TV; cable (premium). Restaurant 6:30 am-10 pm. Bar 11-1 am. Exercise room, sauna. Indoor, outdoor pools; whirlpool. Free covered parking. Cr cds: A, C, D, DS, JCB, MC, V.

D ⊛ ⊠ ⅄ ⊠ SC

Resorts

★★★ **BOAR'S HEAD INN.** *W Rte 250 (22903). Phone 434/296-2181; toll-free 800/476-1988; fax 434/972-6024. www.boarsheadinn.com.* Located in the Blue Ridge Mountains, this resort welcomes guests to visit the past as well as enjoy the present. Guests can visit past presidential homes, stroll through local wineries, or enjoy a panoramic view by hot-air balloon. 171 rooms, 4 story. D $174-$188; each additional $10; under 18 free. Check-out noon, check-in 4 pm. TV; cable (premium), VCR available. In-room modem link. Dining room. Bar 2 pm-midnight. Supervised children's activities (mid-June-Labor Day), ages 5-16. Exercise equipment, sauna. 3 pools, poolside service. Golf. Lighted outdoor, indoor tennis. Bicycles.

Airport transportation. Business center. Concierge, Local landmark; 1834 gristmill. Cr cds: A, D, DS, MC, V.

[icons]

★ ★ ★ **WINTERGREEN RESORT.** *Rte 664, Wintergreen (22958). Phone 434/325-2200; toll-free 800/266-2444; fax 434/325-8003. www.wintergreenresort.com.* 315 kitchen units, 2-3 story. Dec-Mar: S, D $137-$191; lower rates rest of year; family, golf, ski, tennis plans; lower rates rest of year. Crib available. TV; cable (premium), VCR available (movies). 6 pools, 1 indoor; wading pool, whirlpools, lifeguards. Playground. Supervised children's activities, ages 3-12. Restaurants. Box lunches, snack bar, picnics. Bar. Check-out 11 am, check-in 4 pm. Convention facilities. Business center. Shopping arcade. Airport, train station transportation. Indoor tennis, pro. Two 18-hole golf courses, greens fee $55-$99, pro, putting green, driving range. Downhill ski on site. Rowboats, canoes. Nature programs. Bicycles. Entertainment, movies. Exercise room. Some fireplaces. Private patios, balconies. Picnic tables. Cr cds: A, DS, MC, V.

[icons]

B&B/Small Inns

★ ★ **200 SOUTH STREET INN.** *200 W South St (22902). Phone 434/979-0200; fax 434/979-4403. www.southstreetinn.com.* 24 rooms, 3-4 story. D $125-$220; each additional $20; under 16 free. Complimentary continental breakfast. Check-out 11 am, check-in 2 pm. TV. Some fireplaces. Health club privileges. Built 1856; antiques. Cr cds: A, C, D, MC, V.

[icons]

★ ★ ★ **CLIFTON–THE COUNTRY INN.** *1296 Clifton Inn Dr (22911). Phone 434/971-1800; fax 434/971-7098, res 888/971-1800. www.cliftoninn.com.* Set on 100 acres in the Virginia countryside, Clifton appeals to the gallant gentleman or the Southern belle in all visitors. This gracious antebellum mansion, constructed in 1799 by Thomas Jefferson's daughter and her husband, is closely tied to the history of Charlottesville, yet it maintains a contemporary attraction. Imbued with character, the inn is a decorator's showpiece. The light-filled rooms have a *joie de vivre* best expressed by the exuberant colors and talented juxtaposition of plaid, floral, and striped prints. Gauzy linens and canopy-draped beds set a romantic mood, and picture or bay windows feature enchanting views of the countryside. The restaurant's 4,000-bottle wine cellar delights oenophiles, and diners are equally satisfied by the splendid nouvelle cuisine. A dedication to excellence is evident throughout the property, and the attentive service works magic to satisfy any demand. 14 rooms, 8 suites, 1-2 story. Apr-Nov: S, D $150-$265; each additional $75-$133; suites $225-$315; weekends (2-day minimum); lower rates rest of year. Complimentary full breakfast. Check-out 11 am, check-in 3-5 pm. Fireplaces. Restaurant 6:30-11 pm. Pool; whirlpool. Lighted tennis. Lawn games. Totally nonsmoking. Cr cds: A, DS, MC, V.

[icons]

★ ★ ★ **INN AT MONTICELLO.** *1188 Scottsville Rd (22902). Phone 434/979-3593; fax 434/296-1344. www.innatmonticello.com.* Guests can choose to relax by a fireplace in winter or sit on the porch in summer at this country manor house built in the mid-1800s. Guest rooms are decorated with period antiques and reproductions. 5 rooms, 2 story. No room phones. D $150-$175; each additional $25. Children over 12 years only. Complimentary full breakfast. Check-out 11 am, check-in 4 pm. Totally nonsmoking. Cr cds: MC, V.

[icon]

★ ★ ★ **PROSPECT HILL PLANTATION INN.** *2887 Poindexter Rd, Louisa (23093). Phone 540/967-0844; toll-free 800/277-0844; fax 540/967-0102. www.prospecthill.com.* This romantic 1732 manor house is set on 50 acres of lawn. 13 rooms, 2 with shower only, 6 suites, 2 story. No room phones. MAP: S $200-$300; D $285-$380; each additional $50; suites $325-$420; under 5 free. Closed Dec 24 evening, Dec 25. Pool. Complimentary full breakfast; afternoon refreshments. Dining room, 1 sitting: 7 pm; Fri, Sat 8 pm. Check-out 11 am, check-in 3 pm. Meeting room. Business services available. Bellstaff. Lawn games. Many refrigerators; some in-room whirlpools. Cr cds: A, C, D, DS, JCB, MC, V.

[icons]

★ ★ ★ **SILVER THATCH INN.** *3001 Hollymead Dr (22911). Phone 434/978-4686; fax 434/973-6156. www.silverthatch.com.* Built in 1780, this clapboard home is full of history and is one of the oldest buildings in the area. 7 rooms, 2 story. No room phones. D $130-$170; each additional $25. Children over 12 years only. Complimentary breakfast. Check-out 11 am, check-in 3 pm. Dining room Tues-Sat 5:30-9 pm. Pool. Original building dates to 1780 (built by captured Hessian soldiers), additions in 1812 and 1937. Totally nonsmoking. Cr cds: A, C, D, MC, V.

[icons]

Restaurants

★ ★ **ABERDEEN BARN.** *2018 Holiday Dr (22901). Phone 434/296-4630; fax 434/979-6397. www.aberdeenbarn.com.* Seafood, steak menu. Hours: 5 pm-midnight; Sun to 10 pm. Closed Thanksgiving,

Dec 25. Dinner $16-$34. Bar. Entertainment. Children's menu. Reservations accepted. Cr cds: A, D, MC, V.

D

★ ★ **C & O.** *515 E Water St (22902). Phone 434/971-7044; fax 434/963-4789. www.candorestaurant.com.* Eclectic/International, French menu. Hours: 5 pm-2 am. Closed some major holidays. A la carte entrées: dinner $14-$25. Bar. Reservations accepted. Cr cds: A, MC, V.

★ ★ **CARMELLO'S.** *400 Emmet St (22903). Phone 434/977-5200.* Northern Italian menu. Hours: 5-10 pm. Closed Jan 1, Dec 25. Dinner $11-$25. Bar. Reservations accepted. Cr cds: A, C, D, DS, MC, V.

D

★ ★ **HARDWARE STORE.** *316 E Main St (22902). Phone 434/977-1518; toll-free 800/426-6001; fax 434/979-7555.* Hours: 11 am-9 pm; Fri, Sat to 10 pm; winter hours vary. Closed Sun; some major holidays. Reservations accepted. Eclectic menu. Lunch, dinner $6-$18. Specializes in burgers, chicken, sandwiches. Outdoor seating. In 1890s hardware store; vintage signs displayed. Cr cds: A, D, MC, V.

D

★ ★ **IVY INN.** *2244 Old Ivy Inn (22903). Phone 434/977-1222; fax 434/977-1377. www.ivyinnrestaurant.com.* Hours: 5-9:30 pm. Closed Sun. Reservations required. Dinner $18-$27. Sun brunch $8-$13. Specializes in regional cuisine. Outdoor seating. Victorian-style house (1804); fireplaces. Totally nonsmoking. Cr cds: A, D, MC, V.

★ ★ **L'AVVENTURA.** *220 W Market St (22902). Phone 804/977-1912; fax 804/977-8458. www.vinegarhilltheatre. com.* Country Italian menu. Hours: 5:30-10 pm. Closed Sun-Tues; Thanksgiving, Dec 25. Dinner $13-$20. Bar. Entertainment. Outdoor seating. Cr cds: A, MC, V.

D

★ ★ **MAHARAJA.** *139 Zan Rd (22901). Phone 434/973-0440.* Indian, seafood, vegetarian menu. Hours: noon-2 pm, 5-10 pm; Mon from 5 pm. Closed Jan 1, Thanksgiving, Dec 25. A la carte entrées: dinner $11-$14. Bar. Casual décor; Indian pictures, urns. Reservations accepted. Outdoor seating. Totally nonsmoking. Cr cds: A, C, D, DS, MC, V.

D

★ ★ ★ **OLD MILL ROOM.** *US 250 W (22905). Phone 804/972-2230; fax 804/972-6024. www.boarsheadinn.com.* This dining room is located in the Boars Head Inn at the University of Virginia. Entrées are served with vegetables from their own garden. Contemporary American menu. Hours: 7-10 am, 11:30 am-1:30 pm, 6-9:30 pm; Sat, Sun 7-10:30 am, 11:30 am-1:30 pm; 6-9 pm; Sun brunch 11 am-2 pm. Dinner $24-$33. Bar 4 pm-midnight. Salad

bar. Children's menu. 19th-century décor with mahogany woodwork, fireplaces, framed artwork. Reservations accepted. Valet parking. Outdoor seating. Cr cds: A, D, DS, MC, V.

D

★ ★ **ROCOCO'S.** *2001 Commonwealth Dr (22901). Phone 434/971-7371; fax 434/971-4058. www.rococos.com.* Italian, seafood menu. Hours: 11 am-4 pm; Sat 5-10 pm; Sun 11 am-3 pm. Closed Dec 25. Dinner $10-$20, Sun brunch. Children's menu. Cr cds: A, D, DS, MC, V.

D

★ ★ **SCHNITZELHOUSE.** *2208 Fontaine Ave (22903). Phone 434/293-7185; fax 434/293-3719.* Hours: 5-9:30 pm. Closed Sun, Mon; major holidays; 1 week in Jan, also 1 week in July. Reservations accepted. Swiss, German menu. Bar. Complete meals: dinner $12.95-$29. Children's menu. Specializes in veal. Parking. Alpine décor. Cr cds: A, MC, V.

Chesapeake (H-12)

See also Norfolk, Portsmouth, Virginia Beach

Pop 199,184 **Elev** 12 ft **Area code** 757

Information Public Communications Department, 306 Cedar Rd, PO Box 15225, 23328; 757/382-6241

Web www.chesapeake.va.us

This city is located in the heart of the Hampton Roads area, at the northeastern boundary of the Great Dismal Swamp National Wildlife Refuge (see).

What to See and Do

> ### City Fun Facts—Chesapeake
>
> Opened in 1964, the Chesapeake Bay Bridge-Tunnel is 18 miles long and has two bridges and two mile-long tunnels. It extends over the mouth of Chesapeake Bay and connects the cities of Cape Charles and Norfolk.

Northwest River Park. *1733 Indian Creek Rd, off Battlefield Blvd (VA 168). Phone 757/421-3145 or 757/421-7151.* Approximately 8 miles of hiking/nature trails wind through this 763-acre city park. Fishing, boating, canoeing (ramp, rentals); picnicking (shelters), playground, nine-hole miniature golf, camping, tent and trailer sites (Apr-Dec, daily; fee; hookups, dump station). Shuttle tram. (Daily; closed Jan 1, Dec 25) Fragrance trail for the visually impaired. **FREE**

Special Event

Chesapeake Jubilee. *City Park. 1500 Mount Pleasant Rd.* National and regional entertainment, carnival, food booths, fireworks. Third weekend in May.

Motels/Motor Lodges

★ **DAYS INN.** *1433 N Battlefield Blvd (23320). Phone 757/547-9262; fax 757/547-4334. www.daysinn.com.* 90 rooms, 2 story. May-Sept: S, D $55-$95; each additional $5; under 12 free; weekly rates (off-season); lower rates rest of year. Complimentary continental breakfast. Check-out 11 am. TV; cable (premium), VCR available (movies). Some refrigerators, microwaves. Restaurant adjacent open 24 hours. Health club privileges. Pool. Business services. Cr cds: A, C, D, DS, JCB, MC, V.

D 🔀 🔀

★ **FAIRFIELD INN.** *1560 Cross Ways Blvd (23320). Phone 757/420-1300; fax 757/366-0608. www.fairfieldinn .com.* 113 rooms, 3 story. D $69-$109; under 18 free; higher rates special events. Complimentary continental breakfast. Check-out noon, check-in 3 pm. TV; cable (premium). In-room modem link. Exercise equipment. Pool. Business center. Cr cds: A, C, D, DS, ER, JCB, MC, V.

D 🔀 🏋 🔀 🏃

★ **HAMPTON INN.** *701 A Woodlake Dr (23320). Phone 757/420-1550; fax 757/424-7414. www.hamptoninn.com.* 120 rooms, 4 story. Memorial Day-Labor Day: S, D $79-$159; higher rates summer weekends; lower rates rest of year. Suites $99-$199. Complimentary continental breakfast. Check-out noon. TV; cable (premium). In-room modem link. Restaurant adjacent 6:30 am-10 pm. Health club privileges. Pool. Cr cds: A, C, D, DS, MC, V.

D 🔀 🔀

★ ★ **HOLIDAY INN.** *725 Woodlake Dr (23320). Phone 757/523-1500; toll-free 800/465-4329; fax 757/523-0683. www.holiday-in.com.* 258 rooms, 7 story. D $105-$149; each additional $10; under 18 free. Check-out noon, check-in 2 pm. TV; cable (premium). In-room modem link. Laundry services. Restaurant 6:30 am-10:30 pm. Bar 11 am-midnight. Room service. Exercise equipment, sauna. Indoor pool, whirlpool. Free airport transportation. Cr cds: A, C, D, DS, JCB, MC, V.

D 🔀 🏋 🔀 SC

★ **SUPER 8.** *3216 Churchland Blvd (23321). Phone 757/686-8888. www.super8.com.* 59 rooms, 3 story. May-Sept: S $44.88-$50.88; D $56.88-$68.88; each additional $6; suites $68.88-$76.88; under 16 free; weekly rates; higher rates special events; lower rates rest of year. Crib free. Pet accepted, some restrictions. TV; cable (premium). Complimentary continental breakfast. Restaurant opposite 6 am-midnight. Check-out 11 am. Meeting rooms. Business services available. In-room modem link. Cr cds: A, C, D, DS, JCB, MC, V.

D 🐾 🔀 SC

★ **WELLESLEY INN.** *721 Conference Center Dr (23320). Phone 757/366-0100; toll-free 800/444-8888; fax 757/366-0396.* 122 rooms, 4 story. D $49-$119; each additional $10; under 18 free. Pet accepted; fee. Complimentary continental breakfast. Check-out noon, check-in 3 pm. TV; cable (premium). In-room modem link. Laundry services. Health club privileges. Pool. Cr cds: A, C, D, DS, ER, JCB, MC, V.

D 🐾 🔀 🔀 SC

All Suite

★ **COMFORT SUITES.** *1550 Crossways Blvd (23320). Phone 757/420-1600; toll-free 800/428-0562; fax 757/420-0099. www.comfortinn.com.* 123 suites, 3 story. D $89-$149; each additional $7; under 18 free. Complimentary continental breakfast. Check-out 11 am, check-in 3 pm. TV; cable (premium), VCR (movies $5). Exercise equipment, sauna. Pool, whirlpool. Cr cds: A, C, D, DS, JCB, MC, V.

D 🔀 🏋 🔀

Restaurants

★ ★ **KYOTO.** *1412 Greenbriar Pkwy (23320). Phone 757/420-0950; fax 757/420-0692.* Japanese menu. Sushi bar. Hours: 11 am-2 pm, 5-10 pm; Sun 4-9 pm. Closed July 4, Thanksgiving, Dec 25. Lunch $4.50-$13, dinner $10.50-$24.95. Bar. Children's menu. Reservations accepted. Cr cds: A, D, DS, MC, V.

D

★ ★ **LOCKS POINTE.** *136 N Battlefield Blvd (23320). Phone 757/547-9618; fax 757/548-3229. www.lockspointe. com.* Seafood menu. Hours: 11:30 am-3 pm, 5-10 pm; Sat from 5 pm; Sun 10:30 am-9 pm; Sun brunch to 3 pm. Closed Mon; Dec 24, 25. Lunch $4.50-$6.95, dinner $12.95-$21.95. Sun brunch $7.95. Bar. Entertainment. Children's menu. Outdoor seating. On Intracoastal Waterway; dockage. Cr cds: A, MC, V.

D

Chincoteague (F-14)

Founded 1662 **Pop** 4,317 **Elev** 4 ft **Area code** 757 **Zip** 23336

Information Chamber of Commerce, 6733 Maddox Blvd, PO Box 258; 757/336-6161

Web www.chincoteaguechamber.com

Chincoteague oysters, wild ponies, and good fishing are the stock in trade of this small island, connected with Chincoteague National Wildlife Refuge by a bridge and to the mainland by 10 miles of highway (VA 175, from US 13), causeways, and bridges.

The oysters, many of them grown on the hard sand bottoms off Chincoteague from seed or small oysters brought from natural beds elsewhere, are among the best in the East. Clams and crabs are also plentiful. Commercial fishing has always been the main occupation of the islanders, but now, catering to those who fish for fun is also important economically.

Chincoteague's wild ponies are actually small horses but when full-grown are somewhat larger and more graceful than Shetlands. They are thought to be descended from horses that swam ashore from a wrecked Spanish galleon, their limited growth caused by generations of marsh grass diet.

What to See and Do

⭐ **Assateague Island.** *6550 Coach's Ln.* Accessible by bridge from town. Includes Chincoteague National Wildlife Refuge and Virginia unit of Assateague Island National Seashore. A 37-mile barrier island, Assateague's stretches of ocean and sand dunes, forest, and marshes create a natural environment unusual on the East coast. Sika deer, a variety of wildlife and countless birds, including the peregrine falcon (autumn), can be found here, but wild ponies occasionally roaming the marshes offer the most exotic sight for visitors. Nature and auto trails; interpretive programs. Swimming (bathhouse), lifeguards in summer, surf fishing; camping, hike-in and canoe-in camp sites and day-use facilities. Picnicking permitted in designated areas; cars are limited to designated roads. No pets allowed. Obtain information at Toms Cove Visitor Center (spring-fall, daily) and at Chincoteague Refuge Visitor Center (daily). Access for disabled to all facilities. Contact the Chief of Interpretation, Assateague Island National Seashore, Rte 611, 7206 National Seashore Ln, Berlin, MD 21811; phone 410/641-1441 or 410/641-3030 (camping). (See OCEAN CITY, MD) Also contact Refuge Manager, Chincoteague National Wildlife Refuge, PO Box 62, 23336; 757/336-6122. **$$**

NASA Visitor Center. *5 miles S on VA 175 on Wallops Island. Phone 757/824-1344 or 757/824-2298.* Showcases world of past, present, and future flight. Features moon rock brought from *Apollo 17* mission; scale models of space probes, satellites, and aircraft; displays of current and future NASA projects; full-scale aircraft and rockets; films on space and aeronautics. Model rocket demonstrations (Mar-Nov, first Sat; June-Aug also third Sat, weather permitting). Picnic facilities. Gift shop. (July 4-Labor Day, daily; Sept-Nov and Mar-June, Mon and Thurs-Sun; closed holidays) **FREE**

Oyster and Maritime Museum of Chincoteague. *7125 Maddox Blvd. Phone 757/336-6117.* Museum contains diorama, aquarium, shellfish industry interpretation. Also has the Wyle Maddox Library. (May-Aug, daily; Sept-Oct, Sat and Sun) **$$**

Refuge Waterfowl Museum. *7059 Maddox Blvd. Phone 757/336-5800.* Rotating displays of antique decoys and hunting tools. Decoy making and waterfowl art. Call ahead for hours. (Daily; closed Dec 25) **$$**

Sightseeing tours. Captain Barry's Back Bay Cruises & Expeditions. *Phone 757/336-6508 for information.* Includes Bird Watch Cruise, Back Bay Expedition, Champagne Sunset Cruise, Moonlight Excursions, and Fun Cruise. Trips vary from one to four hours. Reservations recommended. **$$$$**

Special Events

Chincoteague Power Boat Regatta. *Phone 757/336-6161.* Late June.

Easter Decoy & Art Festival. *Phone 757/336-6161.* Easter weekend.

Oyster Festival. *6733 Maddox Blvd.* Columbus Day weekend.

Pony Penning. *Phone 757/336-6161.* The "wild" ponies are rounded up on Assateague Island, then swim the inlet to Chincoteague, where foals are sold at auction before the ponies swim back to Assateague. Carnival amusements. Last Wed and Thurs in July.

Waterfowl Week. *8231 Beach Rd.* National Wildlife Refuge open to vehicles during peak migratory waterfowl populations. Late Nov.

Motels/Motor Lodges

★ **BIRCHWOOD.** *3650 Main St (23336). Phone 757/336-6133; fax 757/336-6535.* 41 rooms. Apr-Nov: S, D $43-$89; each additional $5; kitchen units $58-$97.

Closed rest of year. Crib $5. TV; cable. Pool. Playground. Complimentary coffee in lobby. Check-out 11 am. Coin laundry. Refrigerators. Cr cds: A, DS, MC, V.

⬜ 🔧 🌐 🏊 ♿

★ **COMFORT INN.** *25297 Lankford Hwy, Onley (23418). Phone 757/787-7787; fax 757/787-4641. www.comfortinn.com.* 80 units, 10 suites, 2 story. Mid-May-mid-Sept: S $62; D $69; each additional $5; suites $69-$83; under 18 free; lower rates rest of year. Crib free. TV; cable. Pool. Complimentary continental breakfast. Restaurant adjacent 11 am-9:30 pm. Check-out 11 am. Business services available. In-room modem link. Exercise equipment. Refrigerators; microwaves available. Cr cds: A, C, D, DS, JCB, MC, V.

⬜ 🔧 🏊 🏋 ♿

★ **DRIFTWOOD MOTOR LODGE.** *7105 Maddox Blvd (23336). Phone 757/336-6557; toll-free 800/553-6117; fax 757/336-6558. www.driftwoodmotorlodge.com.* 53 rooms, 3 story. Mid-June-early Sept: S, D $86-$91; each additional $7; under 12 free; weekend, holiday rates; lower rates rest of year. Check-out 11 am. TV; cable (premium). Restaurant nearby. Pool. At entrance to Assateague National Seashore. Cr cds: A, C, D, DS, MC, V.

🏊 ♿

★ ★ ★ **ISLAND MOTOR INN.** *4391 Main St (23336). Phone 757/336-3141; toll-free 800/832-2925; fax 757/336-1483.* This waterfront location is within walking distance of shops, restaurants, and art galleries. All rooms have a private balcony and the activities of boats on Chincoteague Bay can be watched from an observation deck. 60 units, 16 suites, 3 story. Mid-June-Labor Day: S, D $92-$150; suites $133-$150; under 16 free; lower rates rest of year. Crib $5. TV; cable (premium). 2 pools, 1 indoor; whirlpool. Restaurant 6:30-11:30 am. Room service. Check-out 11 am. Guest laundry. Meeting rooms. Business services available. In-room modem link. Sundries. Exercise room. Refrigerators. Bathroom phone in suites. Balconies. Picnic tables, grills. On bay. Cr cds: A, C, D, DS, MC, V.

⬜ 🔧 🏊 🏋 ♿ SC

★ **LIGHTHOUSE INN.** *4218 Main St N (23336). Phone 757/336-5091; toll-free 800/505-5257.* 17 rooms, 1-2 story. June-Aug: S, D $59-$75; each additional $6; minimum stays holidays, special events; lower rates rest of year. Crib $6. TV; cable. Pool; whirlpool. Complimentary coffee in rooms. Restaurant nearby. Check-out 11 am. Health club privileges. Refrigerators, microwaves. Picnic tables, grill. Cr cds: MC, V.

🏊 ♿ SC

★ **MARINER MOTEL.** *6273 Maddox Blvd (23336). Phone 757/336-6565; toll-free 800/221-7490; fax 757/336-5351. www.esva.net/~motel.* 92 rooms, 2 story. Mid-June-mid-Sept: S, D $54-$95; each additional $5; suites $95; under 12 free; weekly rates; holidays (2-day minimum); higher rates special events; lower rates rest of year. Closed Dec-Feb. Crib $5. Complimentary continental breakfast. Check-out 11 am. TV; cable. Many refrigerators; some microwaves. Coin laundry. Restaurant adjacent 5-10 pm. Playground. Pool. Picnic tables. Meeting rooms. Business services. Sundries. Cr cds: A, D, DS, MC, V.

⬜ 🔧 🏊 ♿

★ **REFUGE MOTOR INN.** *7058 Maddox Blvd (23336). Phone 757/336-5511; toll-free 800/544-8469; fax 757/336-6134. www.refugeinn.com.* 70 units, 2 suites, 2 story. June-Aug: S, D $92-$202; each additional $10; under 12 free; higher rates special events; lower rates rest of year. Check-out 11 am. TV; cable. Laundry services. Exercise equipment, sauna. Indoor/outdoor pool; whirlpool. Bicycle and beach gear rentals. Near wildlife refuge and national seashore. Chincoteague ponies on grounds. Cr cds: A, C, D, DS, MC, V.

⬜ 🏊 🏋 ♿

★ **SEA SHELL.** *3720 Willow St (23336). Phone 757/336-6589; fax 757/336-0641.* 46 rooms, 1-2 story. Mid-June-early Sept: S, D $66-$74; each additional $4; suites, kitchen cottages $550-$600/week; 2-day minimum weekends, 3-day minimum holidays; lower rates Apr-mid-June, mid-Sept-Oct, Thanksgiving. Closed rest of year. Crib $3. TV; cable. Pool. Complimentary coffee in rooms. Restaurant nearby. Check-out 11 am. Business services available. Refrigerators; microwaves available. Picnic tables. Cr cds: A, DS, MC, V.

⬜ 🏊 ♿

★ **SUNRISE MOTOR INN.** *4491 Chicken City Rd (23336). Phone 757/336-6671; toll-free 800/673-5211; fax 757/336-3752.* 24 units. Mid-June-early Sept: S $66; D $70; each additional $5; kitchen units $540-$575/week; under 12 free; lower rates mid-Mar-mid-June, early Sept-Nov. Closed rest of year. Crib free. TV; cable. Pool. Playground. Complimentary coffee in lobby. Restaurant nearby. Check-out 11 am. Business services available. Refrigerators. Picnic tables, grills. Cr cds: A, C, D, DS, MC, V.

⬜ 🏊

★ **WATERSIDE MOTOR INN.** *3761 S Main St (23336). Phone 757/336-3434; fax 757/336-1878. www.intercom.net/local/chincoteague/hot/water.html.* 45 rooms, 3 story. Mid-June-mid-Sept (2-day minimum): S,

D $95-$150; each additional $5; suites (3-day minimum) $155; under 12 free; lower rates rest of year. Check-out 11 am. TV; cable (premium). Laundry services. Restaurant nearby. Exercise equipment. Pool, whirlpool. Tennis. On saltwater river; marina. Cr cds: A, C, D, DS, MC, V.

B&B/Small Inns

★★★ **CEDAR GABLES SEASIDE INN.** *6095 Hopkins Ln (23336). Phone 757/336-6860; fax 757/336-1291. www.cedargable.com.* This is a waterfront bed and breakfast inn overlooking Oyster Bay and the Chincoteague Wildlife Refuge. All rooms open to waterfront decks with breathtaking views of Assateague Island. The rooms have cable TV and fireplaces, and there are jacuzzis, and a swimming pool on the property. Nearby guests can enjoy the beach, wildlife refuge, fishing, biking, and hiking. 4 rooms, 3 story. Closed 1 week late Dec. Children over 14 years only. Complimentary full breakfast; refreshments. Check-out 11 am, check-in 3 pm. TV; cable (premium), VCR (movies). In-room modem link. Fireplaces. Heated pool; whirlpool. On channel. Contemporary seaside location. Cr cds: A, DS, MC, V. **$$**

★★★ **CHANNEL BASS INN.** *6228 Church St (23336). Phone 757/336-6148; toll-free 800/249-0818; fax 757/336-6599. www.channelbass-inn.com.* Originally built in 1892 as a private home, it was converted to a small hotel in the 1920s. Today, it offers uniquely appointed guest rooms, some with views of the Chincoteague Bay. A traditional English afternoon tea and full breakfast are included. The inn's proximity to the nearby Assateague Island makes it a perfect getaway for birdwatchers and nature lovers. 6 rooms, 3 story. Closed rest of year. Children over 8 years only. Complimentary full breakfast. Check-out 11 am, check-in 2 pm. Built in 1892. Assateague Wildlife Refuge nearby. Totally nonsmoking. Cr cds: A, DS, MC, V. **$$**

★★ **THE GARDEN AND THE SEA INN.** *4188 Nelson Rd, New Church (23415). Phone 757/824-0672; toll-free 800/824-0672. www.gardenandseainn.com.* This lovely Victorian inn offers romantically decorated rooms. The complimentary breakfast can be enjoyed in either the dining room overlooking the gardens or in the garden by the lily pond. 8 rooms. No room phones. Dec-Apr, pet accepted. Complimentary continental breakfast; afternoon refreshments. Check-out 11 am, check-in 3 pm. Restaurant. Pool. Concierge service. Built as Bloxom's

Tavern (1802) and adjacent farmhouse. Cr cds: A, DS, MC, V. **$$**

★★ **MISS MOLLY'S INN.** *4141 Main St (23336). Phone 757/336-6686; toll-free 800/221-5620; fax 757/336-0600. www.missmollys-inn.com.* 7 rooms, 2 share bath, 3 story. Children over 8 years only weekends. Complimentary full breakfast. Check-out 11 am, check-in 2 pm. In historic building (1886); library, sitting room; antiques. Near saltwater bay. Marguerite Henry stayed here while writing *Misty of Chincoteague.* Cr cds: A, DS, MC, V. **$**

★★ **WATSON HOUSE.** *4240 Main St (23336). Phone 757/336-1564; toll-free 800/336-6787; fax 757/336-5776. www.watsonhouse.com.* 6 rooms, 2 story. No room phones. Dec-Apr, Children over 10 years only. Complimentary full breakfast; afternoon refreshments. Check-out 11 am, check-in 2 pm. Health club privileges. Bicycles. Victorian residence (1874). Totally nonsmoking. Cr cds: MC, V. **$**

Restaurants

★ **DON'S SEAFOOD.** *4113 Main St, Chincoteague Island (23336). Phone 757/336-5715. www.donsseafood.com.* Hours: 7 am-9 pm. Closed mid-Jan-late Mar. Lunch $3.95-$4.95, dinner $9.95-$15.95. Bar. Entertainment Wed, Fri, Sat in summer. Children's menu. View of channel. Cr cds: D, DS, MC, V.

★★ **THE GARDEN AND THE SEA INN.** *4188 Nelson Rd, New Church (23415). Phone 757/824-0672. www.gardenandseainn.com.* This casual respite in a Victorian inn specializes in fresh dishes: just-caught seafood and produce from local farms. Entrées of elegant fare are accompanied by rich, flavorful sauces. French, seafood menu. Closed Mon-Wed; also Dec-Mar. Dinner. Intimate dining room in historic country inn. Reservations accepted. Cr cds: A, DS, MC, V. **$$**

★ **STEAMERS SEAFOOD.** *6251 Maddoc Blvd (23336). Phone 757/336-5478.* Hours: 5-9 pm. Closed Nov-Apr. Wine, beer. Dinner $10.95-$19.95. Children's menu. Specializes in steamed crabs and shrimp. Nautical theme. Cr cds: DS, MC, V.

Clarksville (I-9)

See also South Boston, South Hill

Pop 1,329 **Elev** 359 ft **Area code** 804 **Zip** 23927

Information Clarksville Lake Country Chamber of Commerce, 105 2nd St, PO Box 1017; 804/374-2436

Web www.kerrlake.com/chamber

What to See and Do

Occoneechee State Park. *1 1/2 miles E on US 58. Phone 434/374-2210.* Approximately 2,700 acres under development; long shoreline on John H. Kerr Reservoir (Buggs Island Lake). Fishing, boat launching; hiking, picnic shelters, tent and trailer sites (hookups, season varies). Amphitheater; interpretive programs. Standard fees. (Daily)

Prestwould. *429 Prestwould Dr. 2 miles N on US 15. Phone 434/374-8672.* (1795) Manor house built by Sir Peyton Skipwith; rare French scenic wallpaper; original and period furnishings; restored gardens. (Mid-April–Oct, daily; rest of year, by appointment) **$$$**

Special Events

Native American Heritage Festival and Powwow. *105 2nd St. Phone 804/374-2436. Occoneechee State Park.* Native American music, dances, crafts. Second weekend in May.

Virginia Lake Festival. *105 2nd St. Phone 804/374-2436.* Juried arts and crafts show, beach music, dancers, gymnasts. Fun Run, antique car show, sailboat race, hot-air balloons. Food vendors. Third weekend in July.

Motels/Motor Lodges

★ **LAKE MOTEL.** *101 Virginia Ave (23927). Phone 804/374-5500; fax 804/374-0108. www.conradusa.com/lakemotel.* 84 rooms, 3 suites, 2 story. Mid-May-mid-Sept: S, D $53-$68; each additional $5; suites $65-$90; under 12 free; lower rates rest of year. Pet accepted. TV; cable. Pool. Restaurant adjacent 6 am-10 pm. Bar 5 pm-1 am. Check-out 11 am. Meeting room. Business services available. Free airport transportation. Refrigerators available. Picnic tables, grills. On lake; swimming. Cr cds: A, MC, V.

D 🐾 🛄 🖾 SC

★★ **QUALITY INN.** *103 2nd St (23927). Phone 804/374-5023; fax 804/374-0900; res 800/228-5151.* 50 rooms, 8 suites, 2 story. Feb-Oct: S, D $69-$79; each additional $5; suites $79-$95; under 18 free; weekends, holidays (2-3-day minimum); higher rates lake festival; lower rates rest of year. Crib $5. Pet accepted; $10. TV; cable (premium). Complimentary continental breakfast. Restaurant

nearby. Check-out 11 am. Meeting rooms. Business services available. In-room modem link. Valet service. Sundries. Pool. Refrigerators, microwaves. On lake. Cr cds: A, C, D, DS, MC, V.

D 🐾 🖾 🖾

Clifton

Restaurants

★★ **HEART-IN-HAND.** *7145 Main St (20124). Phone 703/830-4111; fax 703/803-9028. www.heartinhandrestaurant.com.* Hours: 11 am-2:30 pm, 6-9:30 pm; Sun 5-8 pm; Sun brunch 11 am-3 pm. Closed most major holidays. Lunch $5.95-$12.95, dinner $14.95-$22.95. Sun brunch $6.95-$12.95. Converted general store (circa 1870). Reservations accepted. Outdoor seating. Totally nonsmoking. Cr cds: A, D, DS, MC, V.

D

★★★ **HERMITAGE INN.** *7134 Main St (20124). Phone 703/266-1623; fax 703/968-0259. www.hermitageinnrestaurant.com.* A historic clapboard inn is the setting for an intimate dining experience. Mediterranean menu. Closed Mon, Tues; Jan 1, July 4. Lunch, dinner. Service bar. Located in 1869 clapboard hotel. Reservations accepted. Cr cds: A, C, D, DS, MC, V. **$$$**

D

Clifton Forge (G-7)

See also Covington, Lexington, Warm Springs

Settled 1878 **Pop** 4,289 **Elev** 1,079 ft **Area code** 540 **Zip** 24422

Information Alleghany Highlands Chamber of Commerce, 501 E Ridgeway St; 540/862-4969

Web members.aol.com/ahchamber

The town, named after a tilt-hammer forge that operated profitably for almost a hundred years, is at the southern tip of the Shenandoah Valley just west of the Blue Ridge Parkway.

What to See and Do

C & O Historical Society Archives. *312 E Ridgeway St, opposite terminal building. Phone 540/862-2210.* Includes C & O Railroad artifacts, old blueprints for cars and engines, books, models, collection of photos. (Mon-Sat; closed holidays) **FREE**

Douthat State Park. *8 miles N on VA 629. Phone 540/862-7200 or 540/862-8100.* Nearly 4,500 acres, high in the Allegheny Mountains, with 50-acre lake. Swimming beach, bathhouse, trout fishing (fee/day), boating (Memorial Day-Labor Day; rentals, some electric and water hookups, launching, electric motors only); hiking, self-guided trails, picnicking, restaurant, concession, camping (fee), tent and trailer sites (Mar-Sept; no hookups), cabins (all year). Visitor center, interpretive programs. Standard fees. (Daily) **FREE**

Iron Gate Gorge. *2 miles S on US 220.* Perpendicular walls of rock rise from banks of Jackson River. James River Division of C & O Railroad and US 220 pass through gorge. Restored chimney of old forge is here.

Colonial National Historical Park (H-12)

Made up of four independent areas—Cape Henry Memorial, Colonial Parkway, Jamestown (see all three), and Yorktown Battlefield (see YORKTOWN)—this is where America as we know it began. Jamestown, Yorktown, and Williamsburg (not a National Park Service area) are connected by the Colonial Parkway. Each of these areas is described in this book under its own name. Abundant in natural as well as historical wealth, the park boundaries enclose more than 9,000 acres of forest woodlands, marshes, shorelines, fields, and a large variety of wildlife.

Colonial Parkway

See also Colonial National Historical Park, Jamestown (Colonial National Historical Park), Williamsburg, Yorktown

The Colonial Parkway is a 23-mile link between the three towns that formed the "cradle of the nation"—Jamestown, Williamsburg, and Yorktown. It starts at the Visitor Center at Jamestown, passes through Williamsburg (the Colonial Williamsburg Information Center is near the north underpass entrance), and ends at the Visitor Center in Yorktown.

At turnouts and overlooks along the route, information signs note such historic spots as Glebeland, Kingsmill, Indian Field Creek, Powhatan's Village, Fusilier's Redoubt, and others. A free picnic area is provided during the summer at Ringfield Plantation, midway between Williamsburg and Yorktown.

The parkway is free to private vehicles. Commercial vehicles are not permitted. Speed limit is 45 miles per hour. There are no service stations.

Covington (G-7)

See also Clifton Forge, Hot Springs

Founded 1833 **Pop** 6,303 **Elev** 1,245 ft **Area code** 540 **Zip** 24426

Information Alleghany Highlands Chamber of Commerce, 501 E Ridgeway St, Clifton Forge 24422; 540/862-4969

Web members.aol.com/ahchamber

Named for its oldest resident, Covington developed from a small village on the Jackson River. It is located in the western part of Virginia known as the Allegheny Highlands. The James River Ranger District office of the Washington and Jefferson national forests is located here.

What to See and Do

Humpback Bridge. *3 miles W just off US 60/I-64.* Erected in 1857, this 100-foot-long structure was made of hand-hewn oak held together with locustwood pins. In use until 1929, it is now maintained as part of a 5-acre state highway wayside and is the only surviving curved-span covered bridge in the US.

Lake Moomaw. *13 miles N via US 220, VA 687, follow signs to Gathright Dam. Phone 540/962-2214.* The 12-mile-long lake has a rugged shoreline of more than 43 miles set off by towering mountains. Surrounded by the Gathright Wildlife Management Area and portions of the Washington and Jefferson national forests. Boating, swimming, fishing, waterskiing; picnicking, camping (fee). Visitor center. (Apr-Oct, daily) **$**

Motels/Motor Lodges

★ ★ **BEST WESTERN MOUNTAIN VIEW.** *820 E Madison St (24426). Phone 540/962-4951; toll-free 800/465-4329; fax 540/965-5714. www.bestwestern.com.* 79 rooms, 2 story. S $52-$69; D $66-$79; each additional $8; under 18 free. Crib free. Pet accepted; $10. TV; cable (premium). Pool; wading pool. Coffee in rooms. Restaurant 6 am-2 pm, 5-10 pm. Room service. Check-out 11 am. Meeting rooms. Business services available. In-room modem link. Bellstaff. Valet service. Some refrigerators. Cr cds: A, C, D, DS, ER, JCB, MC, V.

D 🐾 ⬄ ⬃ **SC**

★ ★ **COMFORT INN.** *203 Interstate Dr (24426). Phone 540/962-2141; toll-free 800/228-5150; fax 540/965-0964.*

99 units, 32 suites, 2 story. S $67-$76; D $76-$86; each additional $9; suites $76-$86; under 18 free. Pet accepted; fee. Check-out 11 am. TV; cable (premium), VCR (movies $4). Laundry services. Restaurant 7 am-midnight. Bar 4 pm-2 am. Pool, whirlpool. Cr cds: A, C, D, DS, ER, JCB, MC, V.

D ⬛ ⬛ ⬛ SC

B&B/Small Inn

★ ★ ★ **MILTON HALL BED AND BREAKFAST INN.** *207 Thorny Ln (24426). Phone 540/965-0196; fax 540/962-8232.* Built in 1874, this Gothic English manor is now an elegant bed and breakfast. The property and its formal English gardens sit on 44 acres of mostly wooded land, adjoining the George Washington National Forest. At the forest, guests can enjoy hiking, horseback riding, fishing, and hunting. 6 rooms, 2 story. No room phones. Pet accepted. Complimentary full breakfast. Check-out noon, check-in 3 pm. TV in some rooms, sitting room; cable (premium). Lawn games. Historic country manor house (1874) on 44 acres adjacent George Washington National Forest. Some room phones. Cr cds: DS, MC, V. **$$**

⬛ SC

Culpeper (E-10)

See also Orange, Warrenton

Founded 1748 **Pop** 9,664 **Elev** 430 ft **Area code** 540 **Zip** 22701

Information Chamber of Commerce, 133 W Davis St; 540/825-8628

Volunteers from Culpeper, Fauquier, and Orange counties marched to Williamsburg in 1777 in answer to Governor Patrick Henry's call to arms. Their flag bore a coiled rattlesnake with the legends "Don't Tread on Me" and "Liberty or Death."

In the winter of 1862-1863, churches, homes, and vacant buildings in Culpeper were turned into hospitals for the wounded from the battles of Cedar Mountain, Kelly's Ford, and Brandy Station. Later, the Union Army had headquarters here.

Today, Culpeper is a light industry and trading center for a five-county area, with a healthy agriculture industry.

What to See and Do

Dominion Wine Cellars. *1 Winery Ave, 2 miles S on VA 3. Phone 540/825-8772.* Tours and tasting. (Daily; closed holidays) **FREE**

Motels/Motor Lodges

★ **COMFORT INN.** *890 Willis Ln (22701). Phone 540/825-4900; toll-free 800/228-5150; fax 540/825-4904. www.comfortinn.com.* 49 rooms, 2 story. Apr-Oct: S $65; D $74; each additional $7; under 18 free. Crib free. Pet accepted, some restrictions; $5. TV; cable (premium). Pool. Complimentary continental breakfast. Check-out 11 am. Business services available. In-room modem link. Refrigerators, microwaves available. Cr cds: A, C, D, DS, JCB, MC, V.

D ⬛ ⬛ ⬛ SC

★ ★ **HOLIDAY INN.** *791 James Madison Rd S (22701). Phone 540/825-1253; toll-free 800/465-4329; fax 540/825-7134. www.holiday-inn.com.* 159 rooms, 2 story. S, D $74; under 19 free. Crib free. Pet accepted, some restrictions. TV; cable (premium). Pool; wading pool. Complimentary coffee in rooms. Restaurant 6 am-2 pm, 5-10 pm. Room service. Bar 2 pm-12:30 am. Check-out noon. Coin laundry. Meeting rooms. Business services available. In-room modem link. Valet service. Sundries. Refrigerators available. Cr cds: A, C, D, DS, JCB, MC, V.

D ⬛ ⬛ ⬛ SC

B&B/Small Inn

★ ★ ★ **FOUNTAIN HALL BED AND BREAKFAST.** *609 S East St (22701). Phone 540/825-8200; toll-free 800/298-4748; fax 540/825-7716. www.fountainhall.com.* This charming bed and breakfast is located on the foothills of the Blue Ridge Mountains in historic downtown Culpeper. The Colonial Revival house (1859) was converted and now offers uniquely decorated rooms. Guests can relax in one of the spacious parlors or go off to discover some of the many neighboring historic sites, bike trails, or scenic countryside. 6 rooms, 2 story. S, D $85-$150; suites $150; Oct, some holidays (2-day minimum). Complimentary continental breakfast; afternoon refreshments. Check-out 11 am, check-in 2 pm. In-room modem link. Some fireplaces, in-room whirlpools. Health club privileges. Lawn games. Totally nonsmoking. Cr cds: A, C, D, DS, MC, V.

D ⬛

Guest Ranch

★ ★ **GRAVES' MOUNTAIN LODGE.** *VA 670, Syria (22743). Phone 540/923-4231; fax 540/923-4312. www.gravesmountain.com.* 40 rooms, 13 cottages, 8 kitchen units. AP, mid-Mar-Nov: S $57-$92; D $65-$98/person; kitchen cottages $110-$230; higher rates Oct. Closed rest of year. Crib free. Pet accepted. Check-out 11 am, check-in 3 pm. Some fireplaces; refrigerators, microwaves available. Coin laundry. Dining room (public by reservation)

8:30-9:30 am, 12:30-1:30 pm, 6:30-7:30 pm. Playground. Recreation room. Pool; wading pool, lifeguard. Golf privileges, greens fee $45. Tennis. Picnic tables. Lawn games. Meeting rooms. Business services. Cr cds: DS, MC, V.

Restaurant

★ ★ ★ **PRINCE MICHEL.** *154 Winery Ln, Leon (22725). Phone 540/547-9720. www.princemichel.com.* Meals are served on gold-rimmed china in a refined setting to create a romantic dining experience. Hours: noon-2 pm, 6-9 pm; Sun 11 am-2:30 pm. Closed Mon-Wed; most major holidays; also Dec 25-mid-Jan, mid-June-mid-July. Reservations accepted. French menu. Service bar. Wine list. Complete meal: lunch $25-$35; dinner $70, Sat $80. Specialties: venison in red wine sauce, medallions of lamb, hot foie gras with apples. Outdoor seating. Parking. Located at vineyard. Cr cds: A, DS, ER, MC, V.

Danville (I-8)

See also Martinsville, South Boston

Founded 1792 **Pop** 48,411 **Elev** 500 ft **Area code** 804

Information Danville Area Chamber of Commerce, 635 Main St, PO Box 1538, 24543; 804/793-5422.

Web www.danvillechamber.com

This textile and tobacco center blends the leisurely pace of the Old South with the modern tempo of industry. It is one of the nation's largest brightleaf tobacco auction markets. Dan River, Inc., houses the largest single-unit textile mill in the world; other major industries are also located here. Nancy Langhorne, Viscountess Astor, the first woman to sit in the British House of Commons, was born in Danville in 1879.

What to See and Do

⭐ **Chatham.** *17 miles N via US 29. Phone 434/432-1650.* Self-guided walking tour information for town and county may be obtained at the Chamber of Commerce, 38 Main St, Chatham 24531. Founded in 1777, this county seat of Pittsylvania County has many historically interesting houses, schools, and public buildings: **Hargrave Military Academy** (1909) with the Owen R. Cheatham Chapel and Yesteryear Hall (museum); **Chatham Hall** (1894) with Renaissance Chapel, stained-glass windows of women, and St. Francis mural in Commons Building; **Old Clerk's Office** (1813) restored as museum; **Courthouse**

(1853) in Greek Revival style with delicate plaster ceiling frescoes and portraits; **Emmanuel Episcopal Church** (1844) with Gothic interior and signed Tiffany windows; and **Sims-Mitchell House** (1860s). Also of interest are the Educational and Cultural Center with planetarium and museum; antique shops, restaurants, trolley diners, and many private houses, several of which offer overnight accommodations.

Danville Museum of Fine Arts and History. *975 Main St. Phone 434/793-5644.* Home of Major W. T. Sutherlin; built 1857. President Jefferson Davis and his cabinet fled to Danville after receiving news of General Lee's retreat from Richmond. It was during this time that the Sutherlin mansion served as the last capital of the Confederacy. Victorian restoration in historical section of house (parlor, library, and Davis bedroom). Rotating art exhibits by national and regional artists. (Tues-Fri, also Sat and Sun afternoons; closed holidays, also Dec 24-Jan 2) **FREE**

Danville Science Center. *677 Craghead St. Phone 434/791-5160.* Hands-on museum for the entire family. Located in a restored Victorian train station. (Daily; closed Thanksgiving, Dec 25) **$$**

Tobacco auctions. *635 Main St. Phone 434/793-5422.* Several huge warehouses ring with the chants of tobacco auctioneers. (Aug-early-Nov, Mon-Thurs; closed Labor Day, Columbus Day, Veterans Day) **FREE**

"Wreck of the Old 97" Marker. *On Riverside Dr (US 58) between N Main and Locust Ln overpass.* Site of celebrated train wreck (September 27, 1903), made famous by a folk song.

Special Events

Danville Harvest Jubilee. *125 S Floyd St. Phone 804/799-5200.* Celebration of tobacco harvest season. Mid-Sept.

Festival in the Park. *125 S Floyd St. Phone 804/799-5200.* Arts, crafts, entertainment. Third weekend in May.

Motels/Motor Lodges

★ **COMFORT INN.** *100 Tower Dr (24540). Phone 804/793-2000; fax 804/792-4621. www.comfortinn.com.* 118 rooms, 20 suites, 6 story. S $69-$74; D $77-$82; each additional $8; suites $89-$97; under 18 free. Crib available. Check-out noon. TV; cable (premium). Coffee in rooms. Valet services. Coin laundry. Restaurant 6:30 am-midnight. Bar from 11 am. Room service. Health club privileges. Pool. Meeting rooms. Business services. Cr cds: A, C, D, DS, JCB, MC, V.

★ **HOLIDAY INN EXPRESS.** *2121 Riverside Dr (24540). Phone 804/793-4000; fax 804/799-5516. www.holiday-inn.com.* 98 rooms, 3 story. S $58-$60; D $64-$66; each additional $6; under 16 free. Crib free. Complimentary continental breakfast. Check-out noon. TV; cable (premium). Bathroom phones; some refrigerators. Restaurant adjacent 6 am-10 pm. Health club privileges. Pool. Golf privileges. Meeting room. Business services. Deck overlooking river. Cr cds: A, C, D, DS, JCB, MC, V.

⊡ 🛠 ⛱ 🖼

★ **INNKEEPER-DANVILLE WEST.** *3020 Riverside Dr (24541). Phone 804/799-1202; toll-free 800/466-5337; fax 804/799-9672.* 118 rooms, 2 story. S $40.99-$52.99; D $50.99-$70.99; each additional $5. Crib free. Complimentary continental breakfast. Check-out noon. TV; cable (premium). Restaurant adjacent 6 am-midnight. Health club privileges. Pool; whirlpool. Business services. Cr cds: A, C, D, DS, MC, V.

⊡ ⛱ 🖼

★ **STRATFORD INN.** *2500 Riverside Dr (24540). Phone 804/793-2500; fax 804/793-6960.* 151 rooms, 2 story. S, D $58-$75; each additional $7; suites $93-$165; under 18 free. Crib free. Pet accepted. TV; cable (premium). Heated pool; wading pool, whirlpool. Complimentary full breakfast. Restaurant 6 am-2 pm, 5-10 pm. Room service. Bar to midnight. Check-out noon. Coin laundry. Meeting rooms. Business services available. In-room modem link. Valet service. Sundries. Exercise equipment. Health club privileges. Cr cds: A, C, D, DS, MC, V.

⊡ 🐾 ⛱ 🏃 🖼 SC

Dulles International Airport Area (D-11)

See also Fairfax

Services and Information

Information. 703/419-8000.

Lost and Found. 703/572-2954.

Weather. 703/260-0307.

Airlines. Aeroflot, Air Canada, Air France, All Nippon, American, ANA, British Airways, Continental, Continental Express, Delta, Delta Connection, Japan Airlines, KLM, Luftansa, Northwest, Qantas, Saudi Arabia Airways, Swissair, TACA, Transbrasil, United, United Express, USAir, Western Pacific.

What to See and Do

Reston Town Center. *Adjacent Dulles Toll Rd (VA 267) at Reston Pkwy in Reston. Phone 703/709-8500.* A 20-acre urban development incorporating elements of a traditional town square. Includes more than 50 retail shops and restaurants, movie theater complex, office space, and hotel. (See SPECIAL EVENTS)

Special Events

Fountain Square Holiday Celebration. *Reston Town Center* (see). Choral groups, puppeteers, magicians, ice shows, dancers, parade. Thanksgiving-Dec 24.

Fountain Square Ice Rink. *Reston Town Center* (see). Outdoor public ice rink. Mid-Nov-mid-Mar.

Northern Virginia Fine Arts Festival. *Reston Town Center* (see). Art sale, children's activity area, barbecue. Mid-May.

Oktoberfest. *Reston Town Center* (see). Biergarten with authentic German music, food. Mid-Sept.

Summer Concerts. *Reston Town Center* (see). Sat evenings June-Aug; also Thurs evenings in July.

Taste of the Town. Selected restaurants offer sample-size specialties. Last weekend in June.

Motels/Motor Lodges

★ **COMFORT INN.** *200 Elden St, Herndon (20170). Phone 703/437-7555; toll-free 800/228-5150; fax 703/437-7572. www.comfortinn.com.* 103 rooms, 3 story. S, D $119-$169; under 19 free; weekend plans. TV; cable (premium). Complimentary continental breakfast. Restaurant adjacent 11 am-10 pm. Check-out 11 am. Meeting room. Business services available. Valet service. Free airport transportation. Exercise equipment. Refrigerators; microwaves available. Cr cds: A, C, D, DS, ER, JCB, MC, V.

⊡ 🏃 ✈ 🖼 SC

★★ **COURTYARD BY MARRIOTT.** *533 Herndon Pkwy, Herndon (22070). Phone 703/478-9400; toll-free 800/321-2211; fax 703/478-3628. www.courtyard.com/iadhc.* 146 rooms, 3 story. S $129; D $139; suites $149; under 16 free; weekend rates. Crib free. TV; cable (premium). Indoor pool; whirlpool, lifeguard. Restaurant 6-10 am, 5-10 pm; weekends 7-11 am, 5-10 pm. Bar 5-10 pm. Check-out noon. Coin laundry. Meeting rooms. Business services available. In-room modem link. Sundries. Valet service. Free airport transportation. Exercise equipment. Refrigerators, microwaves available. Cr cds: A, C, D, DS, MC, V.

⊡ ⛱ 🏃 🖼 SC

★★ **COURTYARD BY MARRIOTT.** *3935 Center-view Dr, Chantilly (20151). Phone 703/709-7100; toll-free 800/321-2211; fax 703/709-8672. www.courtyard.com.* 149 rooms, 3 story. S $105; D $125; suites $129; under 12 free; weekly rates; higher rates special events. Crib free. TV; cable (premium). Indoor pool; whirlpool, lifeguard. Complimentary coffee in rooms. Restaurant 6-10 am; Sat, Sun 7 am-noon. Restaurant opposite 11 am-midnight. Room service 5-10 pm. Check-out noon. Coin laundry. Meeting rooms. Business services available. In-room modem link. Valet service. Sundries. Free airport transportation. Exercise equipment. Microwaves available. Balconies. Picnic tables. Cr cds: A, C, D, DS, MC, V.

[D] [⇌] [犬] [⊠] [SC]

★★ **DAYS INN.** *2200 Centreville Rd, Herndon (20170). Phone 703/471-6700; toll-free 800/329-7466; fax 703/742-8965. www.daysinn.com.* 205 rooms, 4 story. Apr-June, Sept-Oct: S, D $74-$139; each additional $10; under 18 free; weekend, monthly rates; lower rates rest of year. Complimentary continental breakfast. Check-out noon. TV; cable (premium). In-room modem link. Restaurant 6-1 am. Bar. Exercise equipment. Pool, whirlpool. Free airport transportation. Cr cds: A, C, D, DS, JCB, MC, V.

[D] [⇌] [犬] [✈] [⊠] [SC]

★★ **HOLIDAY INN.** *1000 Sully Rd, Sterling (20166). Phone 703/471-7411; fax 703/709-0785. www.holiday-inn.com.* 296 rooms, 2 story. S, D $160; suites $179-$209; each additional $10; under 18 free; weekend rates. Crib free. Pet accepted, some restrictions. TV; cable (premium). Indoor pool; whirlpool, lifeguard. Restaurant 6:30 am-10:30 pm. Room service to midnight. Bars 11-1:30 am, Sun to midnight; entertainment. Check-out noon. Coin laundry. Meeting rooms. Business center. In-room modem link. Bellstaff. Gift shop. Valet service. Free airport transportation. Exercise equipment; sauna. Refrigerators, microwaves available. Game room. Cr cds: A, C, D, DS, JCB, MC, V.

[D] [⊛] [☂] [⌣] [⇌] [犬] [⊠] [⊀]

★ **HOLIDAY INN EXPRESS.** *485 Elden St, Herndon (20170). Phone 703/478-9777; fax 703/471-4624. www.holiday-inn.com.* 115 rooms, 4 story. S, D $99-$129; each additional $6; under 19 free. Crib free. Pet accepted, some restrictions. Complimentary continental breakfast. Check-out 11 am. TV; cable (premium). Refrigerators, microwaves available. Valet services. Restaurant nearby. Exercise equipment. Free airport transportation. Meeting room. Business center. Cr cds: A, C, D, DS, JCB, MC, V.

[D] [⊛] [犬] [⊠] [⊀]

Hotels

★★★ **HYATT DULLES.** *2300 Dulles Corner Blvd, Herndon (20171). Phone 703/713-1234; fax 703/713-3410.* www.hyatt.com. Located in an industrial park adjacent to the Dulles International Airport and 30 minutes from downtown Washington, DC, this hotel welcomes business and leisure travelers. 317 rooms, 14 story. S $189; D $214, suites $300-$700; weekly, weekend rates. Crib free. TV; cable (premium), VCR available. Indoor pool; whirlpool, lifeguard. Restaurant 6 am-midnight. Bar from noon; pianist. Check-out noon. Business center. In-room modem link. Gift shop. Free airport transportation. Exercise equipment; sauna. Refrigerators, microwaves available. Cr cds: A, C, D, DS, JCB, MC, V.

[D] [⇌] [犬] [⌣] [✈] [⊠] [⊀]

★★★ **HYATT REGENCY RESTON.** *1800 President's St, Reston (22190). Phone 703/709-1234; toll-free 800/233-1234; fax 703/709-2291. www.hyatt.com.* Located in the heart of Fairfax County's technology hub, this property offers resortlike ambiance in a suburban setting. 514 rooms, 12 story. S $215; D $235; each additional $25; suites $275-$550; under 18 free; weekend rates. Crib free. Check-out noon. TV; cable (premium), VCR available. In-room modem link. Restaurant (See MARKET STREET BAR AND GRILL). Bar 11:30-2 am; entertainment Fri-Sun. Exercise room, sauna. Indoor pool; whirlpool, poolside service, lifeguard. Golf privileges. Tennis privileges. Garage parking; valet (fee). Free airport transportation. Business center. Convention center/facilities. Concierge. Luxury level. Cr cds: A, C, D, DS, ER, JCB, MC, V.

[D] [🏌] [⌣] [⇌] [犬] [✈] [⊠] [SC] [⊀]

★★★ **MARRIOTT SUITES DULLES WORLDGATE.** *13101 Worldgate Dr, Herndon (20170). Phone 703/709-0400; toll-free 800/228-9290; fax 703/709-0426. www.marriott.com.* 253 suites, 11 story. S $175; D $190; under 18 free; weekend rates. Crib free. TV; cable (premium), VCR available. Indoor/outdoor pool; whirlpool, lifeguard. Complimentary coffee in lobby. Restaurant 6:30 am-10:30 pm. Bar to 11 pm. Check-out noon. Free guest laundry. Meeting rooms. Business services available. In-room modem link. Free garage parking. Free airport transportation. Exercise equipment; sauna. Health club privileges. Refrigerators, wet bars; microwaves available. Cr cds: A, C, D, DS, ER, JCB, MC, V.

[D] [⇌] [犬] [✈] [⊠] [SC]

★★★ **SHERATON RESTON HOTEL.** *11810 Sunrise Valley, Reston (20191). Phone 703/620-9000. www.sheraton.com.* 301 rooms, 5 story. S, D $195-$250; under 17 free. Crib available. Check-out noon, check-in 3 pm. TV; cable (premium). In-room modem link. Minibars; many refrigerators in suites. Restaurant 6:30 am-10 pm. Bar to midnight. Exercise equipment. Pool; whirlpool. Meeting rooms. Business center. Concierge. Cr cds: A, C, D, DS, ER, MC, V.

[⇌] [犬] [⊠] [⊀]

Resort

★ ★ ★ MARRIOTT WESTFIELDS RESORT AND CONFERENCE CENTER. *14750 Conference Center Dr, Chantilly (20151). Phone 703/818-0300; fax 703/818-3655. www.marriott.com.* Whether you are away on business or vacation, this hotel will accommodate all of your needs. The rooms are beautifully decorated and welcoming. 340 rooms, 4 story. S $195; D $215; each additional $20; suites $295-$695; under 12 free; MAP, AP available; weekend rates. Crib free. Pet accepted, some restrictions; $50 deposit. Complimentary coffee in lobby. Check-out 1 pm, check-in 3 pm. TV; cable (premium), VCR available. In-room modem link. Balconies. Minibars; some in-room whirlpools; refrigerators available. Valet services. Restaurant (See PALM COURT). Bar 11-1 am; entertainment. Room service 6-1 am. Health club privileges. Exercise room, massage, sauna, steam room. Sports director. 2 pools, 1 indoor; whirlpool, poolside service, lifeguard. 18-hole golf, greens fee $85. Lighted tennis, pro. Picnic tables. Lawn games. Bicycles. Hiking. Valet parking. Free airport transportation. Business center. Convention center/facilities. Concierge. Gift shop. Cr cds: A, C, D, DS, MC, V.

Extended Stay

★ ★ RESIDENCE INN BY MARRIOTT. *315 Elden St, Herndon (20170). Phone 703/435-0044; fax 703/437-4007. www.residenceinn.com.* 168 kitchen units, 2 story. S, D $135-$174; weekend rates. Crib free. Pet accepted; $100 nonrefundable and $6/day. Complimentary continental breakfast. Check-out noon. TV; cable (premium), VCR available (movies). In-room modem link. Microwaves. Valet services. Coin laundry. Restaurant opposite 6:30 am-10 pm. Playground. Health club privileges. Pool; whirlpool, lifeguard. Lighted tennis. Picnic tables. Business services. Sundries. Cr cds: A, C, D, DS, ER, JCB, MC, V.

Restaurants

★ ★ CLYDE'S. *11905 Market St, Reston (20190). Phone 703/787-6601; fax 703/787-0390. www.clydes.com.* American, seafood menu. Hours: 11 am-midnight; Fri, Sat to 1 am; Sun 10 am-10 pm; early-bird dinner Mon-Fri 4:30-6 pm; Sun brunch to 4 pm. Closed Dec 25. Lunch $5.95-$13.95, dinner $5.95-$18.95, Sun brunch $5.95-$13.95. Bar to 2 am. Outdoor seating. Cr cds: A, D, MC, V.

★ ★ FORTUNE. *1428 N Point Village Ctr, Reston (20194). Phone 703/318-8898; fax 703/318-8990.* Chinese menu. Specializes in dim sum, seafood, traditional Hong Kong dishes. Hours: 11 am-10:30 pm; Fri, Sat to 11:30 pm. A la carte entrées: dinner $7-$20. Service bar. Reservations accepted; required Fri, Sat dinner. Cr cds: DS, MC, V.

★ ★ IL CIGNO. *1617 Washington Plaza N, Reston (20190). Phone 703/471-0121; fax 703/471-4259. www.ilcigno.com.* Northern Italian menu. Hours: 1:30 am-2:30 pm, 5:30-10 pm. Hours: Sun 5-9 pm. Closed holidays. Lunch $8.95-$17.95, dinner $13.95-$25.95. Bar. Reservations accepted; required Fri, Sat. Outdoor seating overlooking Lake Anne. Cr cds: A, C, D, MC, V.

★ ★ ★ MARKET STREET BAR AND GRILL. *1800 Presidents St, Reston (20190). Phone 703/709-6262; fax 703/709-6244. www.msbg.net.* Fresh, local ingredients are used to produce the delicious cuisine. Contemporary American, Asian menu. Hours: 6:30 am-2:30 pm, 5:30-10 pm; Fri, Sat to 10:30 pm; Sun to 9:30 pm. Breakfast $4.50-$7.95, lunch $6.95-$14.95, dinner $13.75-$22.75. Sun brunch $17.95. Bar. Entertainment Fri-Sun. Reservations required Fri, Sat. Valet parking available. Outdoor seating. Cr cds: A, D, DS, MC, V.

★ ★ ★ PALM COURT. *14750 Conference Ctr Dr (20151). Phone 703/818-3522; fax 703/818-0363.* Housed in the Westfield Marriott, this restaurant's menu is a throwback to the days of tableside dining. The buffet-style Sunday brunch is an extravaganza with tuxedo-clad waiters, mimosas, and an unending array of sweets. Continental menu. Specializes in fresh seafood, game. Hours: 7 am-2 pm, 6-10 pm; Sun brunch 10:30 am-2 pm. Breakfast $6-$11.95, lunch $5.75-$15.95. Dinner $24.95-$75. Sun brunch $30. Reservation required Fri, Sat, Sun brunch. Bar 11-1 am. Children's menu. Valet parking available. Cr cds: A, D, DS, MC, V.

★ ★ ★ RUSSIA HOUSE. *790 Station St, Herndon (20170). Phone 703/787-8880; fax 703/319-1765. www.russiahouserestaurant.com.* The décor is contemporary with Russian artwork displayed. Continental, Russian menu. Closed most major holidays. Lunch, dinner. Bar. Cr cds: A, MC, V. **$$**

★ ★ SIAM ASIAN BISTRO. *328 Elden St, Herndon (20170). Phone 703/742-8881; fax 703/437-5967.* Hours: 11:30 am-10 pm; Fri to 10:30 pm; Sat noon-10:30 pm; Sun noon-9:30 pm; early-bird dinner Sun-Thurs 4:30-6:30 pm. Closed Dec 25. Reservations accepted; required Fri, Sat dinner. Asian, Thai menu. Bar. Lunch $6.95-$7.95, dinner $9.95-$12.95. Specialties: pad Thai, Thai

curry. Own desserts. Outdoor seating. Contemporary Thai décor with light woods, etched glass. Cr cds: A, D, DS, MC, V.

D

★ **TORTILLA FACTORY.** *648 Elden St, Herndon (20172). Phone 703/471-1156; fax 703/318-0390.* Mexican menu. Closed most major holidays. Lunch, dinner. Children's menu. Own tortillas. Cr cds: A, D, DS, MC, V. **$**

D SC

Eastville (G-13)

Restaurant

★ ★ ★ **EASTVILLE MANOR.** *6058 Willow Oak Rd (23347). Phone 757/678-7378; fax 757/678-9005. www.eastvillemanor.com.* Chef/owner William Scalley and his wife Melody preside over this 1886 Victorian country inn and restaurant located in a tiny, rural town. Community produce and fish and herbs from the backyard garden make their way onto the creative, internationally inspired menu. Hours: 5:30-9 pm. Closed Sun, Mon; also Tues Sept-May. Reservations accepted. Contemporary American menu. Wine list. A la carte entrées: dinner $11.95-$17.95. Children's menu. Specializes in fresh seafood, beef tenderloin, pasta. Menu changes monthly. Own baking. Cr cds: MC, V.

D

Emporia (I-10)

Pop 5,665 **Elev** 110 ft **Area code** 804 **Zip** 23847

Motels/Motor Lodges

★ **BEST WESTERN EMPORIA.** *1100 W Atlantic St (23847). Phone 804/634-3200; toll-free 800/528-1234; fax 804/634-5459. www.bestwestern.com.* 99 rooms, 2 story. Apr-Sept: S, D $45-$75; each additional $5; under 18 free; lower rates rest of year. Pet accepted. Complimentary continental breakfast. Check-out 11 am. TV; cable (premium). In-room modem link. Restaurant opposite 6 am-10 pm. Exercise equipment. Pool. Cr cds: A, C, D, DS, MC, V.

D ⇥ ⊶ ⅄ ⊠ SC

★ **COMFORT INN.** *1411 Skippers Rd (23847). Phone 804/348-3282; toll-free 800/228-5150. www.comfortinn. com.* 96 rooms, 2 story. S $48.95-$62.95; D $56.95-$62.95; each additional $4; family rates. Crib $2. Pet

accepted. TV; cable (premium). Heated pool. Playground. Complimentary continental breakfast. Restaurant adjacent 6 am-11 pm; Fri, Sat 5 am-midnight. Business services available. In-room modem link. Cr cds: A, C, D, DS, ER, JCB, MC, V.

D ⇥ ⊶ ⊠ SC

★ **DAYS INN.** *921 W Atlantic St (23847). Phone 804/634-9481; fax 804/348-0746. www.daysinn.com.* 122 rooms, 2 story. June-Sept: S $45-$55; D $65-$75; each additional $6; under 18 free; lower rates rest of year. Crib free. Pet accepted. TV; cable (premium). Complimentary full breakfast. Restaurant nearby. Check-out noon. Business services available. Sundries. Coin laundry. Pool. Cr cds: A, C, D, DS, JCB, MC, V.

D ⇥ ⊶ ⊠

★ **HAMPTON INN.** *1207 W Atlantic St (23847). Phone 804/634-9200; toll-free 800/426-7866; fax 804/348-0071. www.hamptoninn.com.* 115 rooms, 2 story. S $59-$65; D $69-$77; under 18 free. Crib free. Pet accepted. TV; cable (premium). Pool. Complimentary continental breakfast. Restaurant nearby. Check-out 11 am. Cr cds: A, C, D, DS, MC, V.

D ⇥ ⊶ ⊠ SC

Fairfax (D-11)

See also Alexandria, Arlington County (Ronald Reagan Washington-National Airport Area), Falls Church, McLean; also see Washington, DC

Pop 21,498 **Elev** 447 ft **Area code** 703

Information Fairfax County Convention & Visitors Bureau, 8300 Boone Blvd, Suite 450, Tyson's Corner-Vienna 22182; 703/790-3329, 703/550-2450 (visitor center), or 800/7-FAIRFAX

Web www.visitfairfax.org

What to See and Do

County parks. *Phone 703/324-8700.* For additional information contact Fairfax County Park Authority, 12055 Government Center Pkwy, Suite 927, 22035.

Burke Lake. *7315 Ox Rd (22039). 6 miles S on VA 123, in Fairfax Station. Phone 703/323-6601.* Consists of 888 acres. Fishing, boating (ramp, rentals); picnicking, playground, concession, miniature train, carousel (summer, daily; early May and late Sept, weekends), 18-hole and par-three golf, camping (May-Sept; 7-day limit). Beaver Cove Nature Trail; fitness trail. Fee for activities. (Daily) **$$**

Lake Fairfax. *1400 Lake Fairfax Dr (20190). On VA 606 near Leesburg Pike in Reston.* Phone 703/471-5415. Pool, boat rentals, fishing, excursion boat; picnicking, carousel, miniature train (late May-Labor Day, daily), camping (Mar-Dec; 7-day limit; electric additional fee). Fee for activities. (Daily)

George Mason University. *4400 University Dr.* Phone 703/993-1000. (1957) 24,000 students. State-supported, started as branch of University of Virginia. Performing Arts Center features concerts, theater, dance; Fenwick Library maintains largest collection anywhere of material pertaining to Federal Theatre Project of the 1930s. Research Center for Federal Theatre Project contains 7,000 scripts, including unpublished works by Arthur Miller, sets and costume designs, and oral history collection of interviews with former Federal Theatre personnel. (Mon-Fri; closed holidays)

Regional parks. Phone 703/352-5900 or 703/352-3165 (TTY). Contact Northern Virginia Regional Park Authority, 5400 Ox Rd, Fairfax Station 22039.

Algonkian. *47001 Fairway Dr (20165). 6 miles NE on VA 123 to VA 7, then 9 miles NW to Cascades Pkwy N, then 3 miles N near Sterling.* Phone 703/450-4655. An 800-acre park on the Potomac River; swimming (Memorial Day-Labor Day, fee), fishing, boating (ramp); golf, miniature golf, picnicking, vacation cottages, meeting and reception areas. **FREE**

Bull Run. *7700 Bull Run Dr (20121). From Beltway I-66 W, exit at Centreville, W on US 29 3 miles to park sign.* Phone 703/631-0550. Consists of 1,500 acres. Themed swimming pool (Memorial Day-Labor Day, daily; fee); camping (one to four persons, fee; electricity available; reservations accepted), concession, picnicking, playground, miniature golf, Frisbee golf, public shooting center, nature trail. (Mid-Mar-Dec) **$$$**

Meadowlark Botanical Gardens. *9750 Meadowlark Gardens Ct. 6 miles N off VA 123.* Phone 703/255-3631. Lilac, wildflower, herb, hosta, native plants and landscaped gardens on 95 acres. Includes three ponds; water garden; gazebos; trails. Visitor center. (Daily) Children under 7 free. **$$**

Sully. *3601 Sully Rd (20151). 10 miles W on US 50, then N on VA 28 (Sully Rd), near Chantilly.* Phone 703/437-1794. (1794) Restored house of Richard Bland Lee, brother of General "Light Horse Harry" Lee; some original furnishings; kitchen-washhouse, log house store, smokehouse on grounds. Guided tours. (Mon, Wed-Sun; closed Jan 1, Thanksgiving, Dec 25) **$$**

Special Events

Antique Car Show. *3601 Sully Rd.* Four hundred antique cars, flea market, and music. June.

Barns of Wolf Trap. *1624 Trap Rd, Vienna (22182). 3/4 mile S of Wolf Trap Farm Park.* Phone 703/938-2404. A 350-seat theater with chamber music, recitals, mime, jazz, folk, theater, and children's programs. For schedule contact the Barns, 1635 Trap Rd, Vienna 22182. Late Sept-early May.

Quilt Show. *3601 Sully Rd.* Quilts for sale, quilting demonstrations, and antique quilts on display. Sept.

Wolf Trap Farm Park for the Performing Arts. *1624 Trap Rd. In Vienna, 8 miles NE on VA 123, then W on US 7 to Towlston Rd (Trap Rd), then follow signs.* Phone 703/255-1900. Varied programs include ballet, musicals, opera, classical, jazz, and folk music. Filene Center open theater seats 3,800 under cover and 3,000 on lawn. Picnicking on grounds, all year. Also free interpretive children's programs, July-Aug. For schedules and prices contact Wolf Trap Foundation, 1624 Trap Rd, Vienna 22182. Late May-Sept.

Motels/Motor Lodges

★ **COMFORT INN.** *11180 Main St (22030).* Phone 703/591-5900; toll-free 800/228-5150; fax 703/273-7915. www.comfortinn.com. 205 rooms, 90 kitchen units, 6 story. Mid-Mar-mid-Nov: S, D $89-$109; kitchen units $89-$129; under 18 free; higher rates special events; lower rates rest of year. Crib free. TV; cable (premium), VCR available (movies). Complimentary continental breakfast. Restaurant 11 am-10 pm. Room service. Bar to 11 pm. Check-out 11 am. Meeting rooms. Business services available. Bellstaff. Valet service. Sundries. Gift shop. Coin laundry. Free airport, train station transportation. Exercise equipment. Two pools, one indoor; lifeguard. Game room. Some in-room whirlpools; microwaves available. Cr cds: A, C, D, DS, JCB, MC, V.

D ⛆ ⍓ ⊠ SC

★ ★ **COURTYARD BY MARRIOTT.** *11220 Lee-Jackson Hwy (22030).* Phone 703/273-6161; fax 703/273-3505. www.courtyard.com. 144 rooms, 3 story. S, D $109-$119; suites $134-$154; under 13 free; package plans. Crib free. TV; cable (premium), VCR available. Indoor pool; whirlpool, lifeguard. Restaurant 6:30-10 am; Sat 7-11 am; Sun 7 am-noon. Bar 5-10 pm. Check-out noon. Coin laundry. Meeting rooms. Business services available. In-room modem link. Valet service. Sundries. Exercise equipment. Health club privileges.

Some refrigerators; microwaves available. Private patios, balconies. Cr cds: A, C, D, DS, JCB, MC, V.

⊡ ⊠ ⊼ ⊠ SC

★ **HAMPTON INN.** *10860 Lee Hwy (22030). Phone 703/385-2600; fax 703/385-2742. www.hamptoninn.com.* 86 rooms, 5 story. S, D $82-$99; under 18 free. Crib free. TV; cable (premium). Complimentary continental breakfast. Restaurant adjacent 7 am-11 pm. Check-out noon. Meeting rooms. Business services available. In-room modem link. Exercise equipment. Health club privileges. Some refrigerators, wet bars; microwaves available. Cr cds: A, C, D, DS, MC, V.

⊡ ⊼ ⊠ SC

★ ★ **HOLIDAY INN.** *11787 Lee-Jackson Memorial Hwy (22033). Phone 703/352-2525; fax 703/352-4471. www.holiday-inn.com.* 312 rooms, 6 story. S, D $129-$149; each additional $10; under 19 free; package plans. Crib free. Pet accepted. TV; cable (premium), VCR available. Indoor pool; lifeguard. Restaurant 6:30 am-midnight. Bar; entertainment. Check-out noon. Coin laundry. Convention facilities. Business center. In-room modem link. Concierge. Gift shop. Exercise equipment; sauna. Health club privileges. Game room. Refrigerators available. Balconies. Luxury level. Cr cds: A, D, DS, JCB, MC, V.

⊡ ⊜ ⊠ ⊼ ⊼ ⊠ ⊼

Hotel

★ ★ ★ **HYATT FAIR LAKES.** *12777 Fair Lakes Cir (22033). Phone 703/818-1234; toll-free 800/233-1234; fax 703/818-3140. www.hyatt.com.* Minutes from the Washington Dulles Airport, this striking high-rise hotel in the wooded Fair Lakes Office Park offers large guest rooms. This property features a column-free ballroom and a towering atrium lobby. 316 rooms, 14 story. S, D $169-$199; each additional $25; suites $199-$475; under 18 free; weekend rates. Crib free. TV; cable (premium), VCR available. Indoor pool; whirlpool, lifeguard. Restaurant 6:30 am-11 pm; Fri, Sat to midnight. Bar 11:30-1 am; entertainment. Check-out noon. Convention facilities. Business center. In-room modem link. Free airport, train station transportation. Exercise equipment; sauna. Health club privileges. Refrigerators, microwaves available. Cr cds: A, C, D, DS, ER, JCB, MC, V.

⊡ ⊠ ⊼ ⊠ SC ⊼

B&B/Small Inn

★ ★ ★ **THE BAILIWICK INN.** *4023 Chain Bridge Rd (22030). Phone 703/691-2266; toll-free 800/366-7666; fax 703/934-2112. www.bailiwickinn.com.* A restored Federal-style inn (1800), this majestic bed and breakfast offers individually decorated guest rooms, all graciously appointed with antiques. Each room is named after a famous Virginian and includes a small library of books dedicated to the namesake. 14 rooms, some with shower only, 4 story. No elevator. S, D $140-$310. TV; VCR available. Complimentary full breakfast. Restaurant (See BAILWICK INN). Check-out 11 am, check-in 2 pm. Health club privileges. Some in-room whirlpools, fireplaces. The first Civil War skirmish occured here in June of 1861. Totally nonsmoking. Cr cds: A, MC, V.

⊡ ⊠ SC

Restaurants

★ ★ **ARTIE'S.** *3260 Old Lee Hwy (22030). Phone 703/273-7600; fax 703/273-9433. www.greatamericanrestaurant.com.* Closed Thanksgiving, Dec 25. Lunch $7-$17, dinner $7-$27. Sun brunch $7.25-$9.95. Bar. Cr cds: A, MC, V.

⊡

★ ★ ★ **BAILIWICK INN.** *4023 Chain Bridge Rd (22030). Phone 703/691-2266; fax 703/934-2112. www.bailiwickinn.com.* This Federal-style inn and restaurant, on the National Register of Historic Places, offers French-American cuisine in a quaint, romantic space. Visit for one of the seasonal wine dinners or for traditional-English high tea in one of the intimate parlors. American, Mediterranean, seafood menu. Hours: Wed, Thurs, Sun seatings 6:30, 7:30, 8:30 pm; Fri, Sat seatings 6, 8:30 pm; Fri lunch noon-2 pm. Closed Mon, Tues. Lunch $8-$35. Dinner $59-$69. In restored inn (1800). Reservations required. Outdoor seating. Totally nonsmoking. Cr cds: A, MC, V.

SC

★ **BLUE OCEAN.** *9440 Main St (22031). Phone 703/425-7555; fax 703/425-8274. www.blueocean-sushi.com.* Hours: 11:30 am-2:30 pm, 5-10 pm; Fri to 10:30 pm; Sat noon-2:30 pm, 5-10:30 pm; Sun from 5 pm. Closed most major holidays. Reservations accepted. Japanese menu. Service bar. Lunch $7.95-$9.95, dinner $9.50-$17.95. Specialties: sushi, teriyaki, sukiaki. Salad bar. Authentic Japanese décor; sushi bar. Cr cds: A, MC, V.

⊡

★ ★ **BOMBAY BISTRO.** *3570 Chain Bridge Rd (22030). Phone 703/359-5810; fax 703/359-5811. www.bombaybistro.com.* Hours: 11:30 am-2:30 pm, 5-10 pm; Fri, Sat to 10:30 pm; Sat, Sun brunch noon-3 pm. Closed Thanksgiving. Indian menu. Bar. A la carte entrées: lunch, dinner $5.95-$11.95. Buffet (Mon-Fri) $6.95. Sat, Sun brunch $8.95. Specializes in tandoori, vegetarian dishes. Outdoor seating. Indian décor. Cr cds: A, D, DS, MC, V.

⊡

★ ★ **CONNAUGHT PLACE.** *10425 North St (22030). Phone 703/352-5959; fax 703/591-2568. www.connaught placerestaurant.com.* Indian menu. Closed Thanksgiving, Dec 25. Buffet, lunch, dinner, Sat, Sun brunch. Bar. Sitar Fri, Sat. Cr cds: A, D, DS, MC, V. **$**

[D]

★ **P. J. SKIDOO'S.** *9908 Lee Hwy (22030). Phone 703/591-4515; fax 703/591-5407. www.pjskidoos.com.* Closed Thanksgiving, Dec 25. Lunch, dinner, Sun brunch. Bar. Entertainment Tues, Thurs-Sat. Children's menu. Cr cds: A, MC, V. **$**

Falls Church (D-11)

See also Alexandria, Arlington County (Ronald Reagan Washington-National Airport Area), Fairfax, McLean; also see Washington, DC

Pop 10,377 **Elev** 340 ft **Area code** 703

Information Greater Falls Church Chamber of Commerce, 417 W Broad St, PO Box 491, 22040-0491; 703/532-1050

Web www.fallschurchchamber.org

Falls Church is a pleasant, cosmopolitan suburb of Washington, DC, just over the Arlington County line, graced with many interesting old houses. This was a crossover point between the North and the South through which pioneers, armies, adventurers, and merchants passed.

What to See and Do

The Falls Church. *115 E Fairfax St at Washington St, on US 29. Phone 703/532-7600.* (1769) Episcopal. This building replaced the original wooden church built in 1732. Served as a recruiting station during the Revolutionary War; abandoned until 1830; used during the Civil War as a hospital and later as a stable for cavalry horses. Restored according to original plans with gallery additions in 1959. (Mon-Fri, Sun; closed holidays) Worship services Wed noon and Sun at 8 am and noon. **FREE**

Fountain of Faith. *7400 Lee Hwy (22042). In National Memorial Park. Phone 703/560-4400.* Memorial dedicated to the four chaplains—two Protestant, one Jewish, one Catholic—who were aboard the USS *Dorchester* when it was torpedoed off Greenland in 1943. They gave their life jackets to four soldiers on deck who had none.

Hotel

★ ★ ★ **MARRIOTT FAIRVIEW PARK.** *3111 Fairview Park Dr (22042). Phone 703/849-9400; toll-free 800/228-9290; fax 703/849-8692. www.marriott.com.* Sitting on a park-like setting, this property offers jogging paths through woods and around a lake. 394 rooms, 15 story. S $189; D $199; suites $250-$500; under 16 free. Crib free. TV; cable (premium), VCR available. Indoor/outdoor pool; whirlpool, poolside service, lifeguard. Restaurant 6:30 am-10 pm; Fri, Sat 7 am-11 pm. Bar 11-2 am. Check-out noon. Coin laundry. Convention facilities. Business center. In-room modem link. Concierge. Gift shop. Exercise equipment; sauna. Some bathroom phones, balconies. Luxury level. Cr cds: A, C, D, DS, ER, JCB, MC, V.

[D] [≈] [⊼] [⊠] [SC] [⋔]

Extended Stay

★ ★ **RESIDENCE INN BY MARRIOTT.** *8125 Gatehouse Rd (22042). Phone 703/573-5200; fax 703/573-8100. www.residenceinn.com.* With a convenient location, this property has easy access to many area companies and is only 12 miles from Washington, DC. 159 kitchen suites, 4 story. S, D $104-$179. Pet accepted, some restrictions. Complimentary buffet breakfast. Check-out noon, check-in 3 pm. TV; cable (premium). In-room modem link. Some fireplaces. Coin laundry, laundry valet. Exercise room. Outdoor pool. Golf nearby. Tennis nearby. Cr cds: A, C, D, DS, ER, JCB, MC, V.

[⋔] [≈] [⊼] [⊠]

Restaurants

★ ★ **BANGKOK STEAKHOUSE.** *926 W Broad St #A (22046). Phone 703/534-0095; fax 703/534-3096. www.bangkokbluesrestaurant.com.* Hours: 11 am-10 pm; weekends to 11 pm. Reservations accepted. Thai, Laotian menu. Lunch $3.95-$8.95, dinner $6.50-$9.25. Lunch buffet $5.95. Specialties: spicy Thai beef noodle, tom yam gung, kaeng seafood combo. Parking. Asian décor. Cr cds: A, D, DS, MC, V.

★ ★ ★ **DUANGRAT'S.** *5878 Leesburg Pike (22041). Phone 703/820-5775; fax 703/820-6206. www.duangrats. com.* This modern restaurant has held its own in the face of constant competition. The classic dishes are good, the dressed-up room is very pleasant and several preparations are definite stars. Thai menu. Specialties: pad Thai noodles, Thai curry, crispy fish with chili sauce. Display of Thai headdresses and masks. Hours: 11:30 am-2:30 pm, 5-10 pm; Fri to 11 pm; Sat 11:30 am-11 pm; Sun 11:30 am-10 pm. Lunch $6.95-$8.95, dinner $9.95-$18.95. Bar. Reservations accepted. Cr cds: A, D, MC, V.

[D]

★ ★ ★ **HAANDI.** *1222 W Broad St (VA 7) (22046). Phone 703/533-3501; fax 703/533-3502. www.haandi.com.* The accolades are plentiful for this fine dining restaurant that is renowned as one of the best in the region. The depth of flavor and unique spices found in each dish are unmatched. Hours: 11:30 am-2:30 pm, 5-10 pm; weekends to 10:30 pm. Closed Dec 25. Reservations accepted Sun-Thurs. Northern Indian menu. Service bar. Lunch $5.95-$10.95, dinner $7.95-$14.95. Specializes in barbecued meats, chicken, vegetarian dishes. Parking. Totally nonsmoking. Cr cds: A, C, D, DS, ER, MC, V.

D

★ ★ **PANJSHIR.** *924 W Broad St (22046). Phone 703/536-4566. www.enterit.com/panjshir566.htm.* Hours: 11 am-2 pm, 5-10 pm; Sun 5-9 pm. Closed July 4, Thanksgiving, Dec 25. Afghan menu. Bar. Lunch $6.50-$7.25, dinner $9.95-$13.25. Specializes in kebab, palows, vegetarian dishes. Parking. Totally nonsmoking. Cr cds: A, MC, V.

★ ★ **PEKING GOURMET INN.** *6029 Leesburg Pike (VA 7) (22041). Phone 703/671-8088; fax 703/671-5912. www.pekinggourmet.com.* Northern Chinese menu. Specialties: Peking duck, beef Szechuan, striped bass Peking style. Hours: 11 am-10:30 pm; Fri, Sat to midnight. Closed Thanksgiving. Lunch $6.25-$13.45, dinner $8.45-$24.95. Service bar. Reservations accepted; required Fri, Sat. Parking. Asian antiques and screens; 300-year-old jade Buddha; original artwork. Favorite of Washington politicians. Cr cds: A, MC, V.

D

★ ★ **PILIN THAI.** *116 W Broad St (VA 7) (22046). Phone 703/241-5850; fax 703/241-7556. www.yp.washing tonpost.com/e/v/wasdc/0013/82/84/.* Hours: 11:30 am-10 pm; Fri, Sat to 11 pm; Sun 5-9 pm. Closed some major holidays. Reservations accepted; required Fri, Sat dinner. Thai menu. Bar. Lunch $4.95-$6.95, dinner $7.95-$13.95. Specialties: spicy, crispy catfish; pad Thai; pad gra prow talay. Parking. Cr cds: A, D, DS, MC, V.

★ ★ **SECRET GARDEN BEEWON.** *6678 Arlington Blvd (22042). Phone 703/533-1004; fax 703/533-1056.* Korean, Japanese menu. Closed Jan 1. Lunch, dinner. Bar. Reservations required Fri, Sat. Cr cds: A, C, D, DS, MC, V. **$$**

★ **SIR WALTER RALEIGH INN.** *8120 Gatehouse Rd (22042). Phone 703/560-6768; fax 703/560-7134.* Closed Dec 25. Lunch, dinner. Bar. Children's menu. Cr cds: A, C, D, DS, MC, V. **$**

D

Farmville (H-9)

See also Keysville

Pop 6,845 **Elev** 304 ft **Area code** 804 **Zip** 23901

Longwood College's Jeffersonian buildings provide architectural interest in downtown Farmville.

What to See and Do

Sailor's Creek Battlefield Historic State Park. *State Rtes 307 N and 17 (23966). 9 miles E on US 460, then 7 miles NE on VA 307 and 2 miles N on VA 617. Phone 804/392-3435.* Site of last major battle of Civil War on April 6, 1865, preceding Lee's surrender at Appomattox by three days. Auto tour. **FREE**

Motels/Motor Lodges

★ **COMFORT INN.** *US 15 and US 460 Bypass (23901). Phone 804/392-8163; toll-free 800/228-5150; fax 804/392-1966. www.comfortinn.com.* 51 rooms, 2 story. S $53-$59; D $56-$62; each additional $6; under 18 free; higher rates special events. TV; cable (premium), VCR available. Pool. Check-out noon. Business services available. Cr cds: A, C, D, DS, ER, MC, V.

D ⚊ ⬚ SC

★ **DAYS INN.** *2011 S Main St (23901). Phone 804/392-6611; fax 804/392-9774. www.daysinn.com.* 60 rooms, 2 story. S $53; D $59; under 18 free; family, weekend, weekly rates; higher rates: homecoming weekend, graduation. Crib free. Complimentary continental breakfast. Check-out 11 am. TV; cable (premium). Valet services. Restaurant opposite 11 am-9 pm. Pool. Picnic tables. Business services. Sundries. Cr cds: A, C, D, DS, JCB, MC, V.

D ⚊ ⬚

Fredericksburg (F-10)

See also Triangle

Settled 1727 **Pop** 19,279 **Elev** 61 ft **Area code** 540

Information Visitor Center, 706 Caroline St, 22401; 540/373-1776 or 800/678-4748.

Web www.fredericksburgvirginia.net

One of the seeds of the American Revolution was planted here when a resolution declaring independence from Great Britain was passed on April 29, 1775. Here is where

George Washington went to school, where his sister Betty lived, and his mother, Mary Ball Washington, lived and died. James Monroe practiced law in town. Guns for the Revolution were manufactured here, and four of the most savage battles of the Civil War were fought nearby.

Captain John Smith visited the area in 1608 and gave glowing reports of its possibilities for settlement. In 1727, the General Assembly directed that 50 acres of "lease-land" be laid out and the town called Fredericksburg, after the Prince of Wales.

Ships from abroad sailed up the Rappahannock River to the harbor—ampler then than now—to exchange their goods for those brought from "upcountry" by the great road wagons and river carriers. The town prospered.

The Civil War left Fredericksburg ravaged. Situated midway between Richmond and Washington, it was recurringly an objective of both sides; the city changed hands seven times and the casualties were high.

Even so, many buildings put up before 1775 still stand. Proudly aware of their town's place in the country's history, the townspeople keep Fredericksburg inviting with fresh paint, beautiful lawns, and well-kept gardens.

What to See and Do

Belmont (The Gari Melchers Estate and Memorial Gallery). *224 Washington St. Phone 540-654-1843.* Residence from 1916 to 1932 of American-born artist Gari Melchers (1860-1932), best known for his portraits of the famous and wealthy, including Theodore Roosevelt, William Vanderbilt, and Andrew Mellon, and as an important impressionist artist of the period. The artist's studio comprises the nation's largest collection of his works, housing more than 1,800 paintings and drawings. The site is a registered National and State Historic Landmark and includes a 27-acre estate, frame house built in the late 18th century and enlarged over the years, and a stone studio built by Melchers. Owned by the state of Virginia, Belmont is administered by Mary Washington College. (Daily; closed holidays) **$$$**

Confederate Cemetery. *William St and Washington Ave.* There are 2,640 Confederate Civil War soldiers buried here, some in graves marked "Unknown."

Fredericksburg Area Museum (Town Hall). *907 Princess Anne St. Phone 540/371-3037.* (1814) Museum and cultural center interpret the history of Fredericksburg area from its first settlers to the 20th century. Changing exhibits. Children's events. (Daily; closed Jan 1, Thanksgiving, Dec 25) **$$**

Fredericksburg's Presidential Legacy

Midway between Washington and Richmond, the old colonial river port of Fredericksburg earned the dubious nickname of "battlefield city" in the Civil War, as the site of four major battles between 1862 and 1864. As a result, many visitors overlook its colonial antecedents and its unique status as the hometown of both George Washington and James Monroe, who were born not far away. This 1-hour, 1-mile stroll down its quiet tree-shaded streets is an introduction to this presidential legacy. Begin by visiting the Fredericksburg Visitor Center at 706 Caroline Street. Walk north along Caroline Street, the Historic District's attractive main street, which is lined with interesting shops and cafes. At George Street, turn left 1 block to Charles Street, and then go right to 908 Charles, the James Monroe Museum. As a young man, Monroe practiced law in an office on this site. The museum displays rich pieces of furniture he took with him to the White House as the country's

fifth president. Continue north on Charles Street to Lewis Street and turn left onto Washington Avenue. Turn right a half block to Kenmore Plantation, the lovely mansion and garden at 2101 Washington. Built in 1752, it was the home of Betty Lewis, who was George Washington's sister, and her husband Fielding Lewis, a financier and gun manufacturer who aided the Revolutionary cause. The house is particularly noted for its richly decorated, hand-molded ceilings. From Kenmore, retrace your steps on Lewis Street for 3 blocks to Charles Street. At 1200 Charles Street stands the Mary Washington House, which George Washington bought for his mother in 1772 so she could be more easily looked after by daughter Betty. Though busy George, who lived 40 miles north at Mount Vernon, was a dutiful son, his mother often accused him of neglect, a story told at the museum. Continue east on Lewis to Caroline Street, and turn north (left) to the Rising Sun Tavern at 1306, the tour's conclusion. Built in 1760 as a private home by Charles Washington, George's younger brother, it has been restored to the 18th-century tavern it became in 1792.

Fredericksburg Masonic Lodge #4, AF and AM. *Princess Anne and Hanover sts.* Phone 540/373-5885. Washington was initiated into this Lodge November 4, 1752; the building, dating from 1812, contains relics of his initiation and membership; authentic Gilbert Stuart portrait; 300-year-old Bible on which Washington took his Masonic oath. (Mon-Sat, also Sun afternoons; closed Jan 1, Thanksgiving, Dec 25) **$**

George Washington Birthplace National Monument. (see)

George Washington's Ferry Farm. *268 Kings Hwy (22405). 1 mile E on VA 3.* Phone 540/370-0732. Site of George Washington's boyhood home. Once a tobacco plantation, it now serves as an archaeological dig and nature preserve. Guided tours. (Daily) **$**

Hugh Mercer Apothecary Shop. *1020 Caroline St.* Phone 540/373-3362. This 18th-century medical office and pharmacy offers exhibits on the medicine and methods of treatment used by Dr. Hugh Mercer before he left to join the Revolutionary War as brigadier general. Authentic herbs and period medical instruments. (Daily; closed holidays) **$$**

James Monroe Museum. *908 Charles St.* Phone 540/654-1043. As a young lawyer, James Monroe lived and worked in Fredericksburg from 1786 to 1789, and even served on Fredericksburg's City Council. This museum houses one of the nation's largest collections of Monroe memorabilia, articles, and original documents. Included are the desk bought in France in 1794 during his years as ambassador and used in the White House for signing of the Monroe Doctrine, formal attire worn at Court of Napoleon, and more than 40 books from Monroe's library; also garden. The site is a National Historic Landmark owned by the Commonwealth of Virginia and administered by Mary Washington College. (Daily; closed holidays) **$$**

Kenmore. *1201 Washington Ave.* Phone 540/373-3381. (1752) Considered one of finest restorations in Virginia; former home of Colonel Fielding Lewis, commissioner of Fredericksburg gunnery, who married George Washington's only sister, Betty. On an original grant of 863 acres, Lewis built a magnificent home; three rooms have full decorative molded plaster ceilings. Diorama of 18th-century Fredericksburg. (Daily; closed Jan, Feb, holidays) **$$$**

Mary Washington College. *1301 College Rd (22401).* Phone 540/654-1000 or 800/468-5614. (1908) 3,700 students. Coeducational liberal arts and sciences institution that offers historic preservation, computer science, and business administration. College also includes 275 acres of open and wooded campus; red brick, white-pillared buildings. President of the college occupies Brompton (private), house built in 1830 on land sold to Fielding Lewis in 1760 and expanded by a later owner, Colonel John Lawrence Marye. Campus tours.

Mary Washington House. *1200 Charles St.* Phone 540/373-1569. Bought by George for his mother in 1772; she lived here until her death in 1789. Here she was visited by General Lafayette. Some original furnishings. Boxwood garden. (Daily; closed holidays) **$$**

Mary Washington Monument. *Near "Meditation Rock."* Where Mrs. Washington often went to rest and pray and where she is buried.

Masonic Cemetery. *George and Charles sts.* One of nation's oldest Masonic burial grounds.

Old Slave Block. *William and Charles sts.* Circular block of sandstone about 3 feet high from which ladies mounted their horses and slaves were auctioned in antebellum days.

Presbyterian Church. *SW corner of Princess Anne and George sts.* Phone 540/373-7057. (1833) Cannonballs in the front pillar and other damages inflicted in 1862 bombardment. Pews were torn loose and made into coffins for soldiers. Clara Barton, founder of the American Red Cross, is said to have nursed wounded here. A plaque to her memory is in the churchyard. Open on request (Mon-Fri, Sun).

Rising Sun Tavern. *1306 Caroline St.* Phone 540/371-1494. (circa 1760) Washington's youngest brother Charles built this tavern, which became a social and political center and stagecoach stop. Restored and authentically refurnished as an 18th-century tavern; costumed tavern staff, English and American pewter collection. (Daily; closed holidays) **$$**

St. George's Episcopal Church and Churchyard. *NE corner of Princess Anne and George sts.* Phone 540/373-4133. Patrick Henry, uncle of the orator, was the third rector. Headstones in the churchyard bear the names of illustrious Virginians. (Daily)

St. James House. *1300 Charles St.* Phone 540/373-1569. Frame house built in 1760s, antique furnishings, porcelain and silver collections; landscaped gardens. (Open Historic Garden Week in Apr and first week in Oct; other times by appointment) **$**

Visitor Center. *706 Caroline St.* Orientation film; information; obtain walking tour brochure and combination tickets here.

Special Events

Christmas Candlelight Tour. *604 William St # A.* Historic homes open to the public; carriage rides; Christmas decorations and refreshments of the Colonial period. First weekend in Dec.

Historic Garden Week. Private homes open. Usually third week in Apr.

Market Square Fair. Entertainment, crafts demonstrations, food. Mid-May.

Quilt Show. Exhibits at various locations. Demonstrations and sale of old and new quilts. Sept.

Motels/Motor Lodges

★ **BEST WESTERN CENTRAL PLAZA.** *3000 Plank Rd (22401). Phone 540/786-7404; toll-free 800/528-1234; fax 540/785-7415. www.bestwestern.com.* 76 rooms, 2-3 story. Mar-Oct: S $48-$55; D $55-$63; each additional $4; under 12 free; higher rates special events. Pet accepted, some restrictions. Complimentary continental breakfast. Check-out noon. TV; cable (premium). Laundry services. Restaurant nearby. Health club privileges. Cr cds: A, C, D, DS, MC, V.

🄳 🐾 ⌔ SC

★ **COMFORT INN.** *5422 Jefferson Davis Hwy (22407). Phone 540/898-5550; toll-free 800/221-2222; fax 540/891-2861. www.comfortinn.com.* 125 rooms, 5 story. Mid-Mar-Aug: S, D $62-$74; each additional $6; under 18 free; lower rates rest of year. Crib free. Complimentary continental breakfast. Check-out noon. TV; cable (premium). In-room modem link. Valet services. Restaurant adjacent 6 am-10 pm. Exercise equipment, sauna. Indoor pool; whirlpool. 18-hole golf privileges, greens fee, pro, putting green, driving range. Meeting rooms. Business services. Sundries. Cr cds: A, C, D, DS, ER, JCB, MC, V.

🄳 🍴 ⌖ ⌔ SC

★ ★ **ECONO LODGE.** *2802 Plank Rd (22404). Phone 540/786-8361; toll-free 800/553-2666; fax 540/786-8811. www.econolodge.com.* 129 rooms, 2 story. S $45-$57; D $50-$62; each additional $5; suites $75-$100; under 18 free. Pet accepted; fee. Check-out 1 pm. TV; cable. In-room modem link. Restaurant 6 am-10 pm. Room service 11 am-9 pm. Health club privileges. Pool. Cr cds: A, C, D, DS, ER, JCB, MC, V.

🄳 🐾 ⌖ ⌔ SC

★ ★ **HOLIDAY INN.** *564 Warrenton Rd (22405). Phone 540/371-5550; fax 540/373-3641. www.holiday-inn.com.* 150 rooms, 2 story. June-Aug: S $52; D $67; each additional $5; under 18 free; lower rates rest of year. Crib free. Check-out noon. TV; cable (premium). Refrigerators available. Valet services. Coin laundry. Restaurant 6-10 am, 5-9:30 pm. Bar 4 pm-2 am; entertainment Fri, Sat. Room service. Exercise equipment. Two pools, one indoor; whirlpool. Meeting rooms. Business services. Sundries. Cr cds: A, D, DS, JCB, MC, V.

🄳 ⌖ ⌔

★ ★ **RAMADA INN.** *5324 Jefferson Davis Hwy (22408). Phone 540/898-1102; toll-free 800/2RAMADA; fax 540/898-2017. www.ramada.com.* 195 rooms, 2 story. S, D $65-$100; each additional $6; under 18 free. Crib free. Pet accepted. TV; cable (premium). Indoor pool; whirlpool. Restaurant 6:30 am-1 pm, 5-9:30 pm. Room service. Bar 4 pm-2 am; entertainment Wed-Sat. Check-out noon. Coin laundry. Meeting rooms. Business services available. In-room modem link. Bellstaff. Sundries. Valet service. Exercise equipment. Game room. Cr cds: A, C, D, DS, JCB, MC, V.

🄳 🐾 ⌖ ⌔ SC

★ **SUPER 8.** *557 Warrenton Rd (22405). Phone 540/371-8900; fax 540/372-6958. www.super8.com.* 80 rooms, 3 story, 10 kitchen units. S, D $62.96-$69.95; each additional $5; kitchen units $69.95; under 18 free; weekly rates. Crib free. Complimentary continental breakfast. Check-out 11 am. TV; cable (premium). In-room modem link. Some in-room whirlpools. Restaurant adjacent open 24 hours. Exercise equipment, sauna. Indoor pool, whirlpool. Business services. Cr cds: A, D, DS, MC, V.

🄳 ⌖ ⌔

Hotel

★ ★ ★ **HOLIDAY INN.** *2801 Plank Rd (22404). Phone 540/786-8321; toll-free 800/465-4329; fax 540/786-3957. www.holiday-inn.com.* 195 rooms, 3 story. S, D $79-$129; each additional $10; suites $150-$275; under 18 free. Crib free. Pet accepted. Check-out noon. TV; cable (premium). Private patios, balconies. Refrigerators available. Valet services. Restaurant 6:30 am-10 pm. Bar 11:30-2 am; entertainment Mon-Sat. Room service. Health club privileges. Exercise equipment. Pool, wading pool, poolside service, lifeguard. Golf privileges. Tennis. Picnic tables. Lawn games. Airport transportation. Meeting rooms. Business services. Sundries. Gift shop. Cr cds: A, C, D, DS, ER, JCB, MC, V.

🄳 🐾 🍴 ⌖ ⌔ SC

B&B/Small Inns

★ ★ **FREDERICKSBURG COLONIAL INN.** *1707 Princess Anne St (22401). Phone 540/371-5666.* 39 rooms, 2 story. S, D $55; each additional $6; suites $75-$85; under 12 free. Crib free. TV; cable. Complimentary continental breakfast. Check-out 11 am, check-in 2 pm. Meeting rooms. Health club privileges. Refrigerators. Built 1928; antiques. Totally nonsmoking. Cr cds: A, MC, V.

🄳 ⌔ SC

★ ★ **KENMORE INN.** *1200 Princess Anne St (22401). Phone 540/371-7622; fax 540/371-5480. www.kenmoreinn. com.* 9 rooms, 2 story. Complimentary continental breakfast. Check-out 11 am, check-in 2 pm. TV in lounge; cable. In-room modem link. Fireplace, canopy bed in some rooms. Dining room 11:30 am-2:30 pm, 5:30-9:30 pm. Bar. Health club privileges. Structure built late 1700s; in historic district. Cr cds: A, C, D, MC, V. **$$** D ⬜ SC

★ ★ **RICHARD JOHNSTON INN.** *711 Caroline St (22401).* Phone 540/899-7606. 9 rooms, 2 suites, 3 story. No room phones. Complimentary continental breakfast. Check-out 11 am, check-in 2-6 pm. Built in 1787. In historic district. Totally nonsmoking. Cr cds: A, MC, V. **$** ⬜

Restaurants

★ ★ **LA PETITE AUBERGE.** *311 William St (22401).* Phone 540/371-2727. American, French menu. French café décor. Specializes in fresh seafood, seasonal specialties, beef. Hours: 11:30 am-2:30 pm, 5:30-10 pm; early-bird dinner Mon-Thurs 5:30-7 pm. Closed Sun; major holidays. A la carte entrées: lunch $6.50-$13.95, dinner $9.95-$26.95. Bar. Reservations accepted. Outdoor seating. Cr cds: A, MC, V. D

★ ★ ★ **RENATO.** *422 William St (22401).* Phone 540/371-8228; fax 540/371-2311. www.renatos1.com. In the center of old town, this cozy dining room offers an extensive menu. All breads, pasta, and pastries are made fresh daily on the premises. Italian menu. Hours: 11:30 am-2 pm, 4:30-10 pm; Sat, Sun from 4:30 pm. Closed most major holidays. Lunch $5.95-$10.95, dinner $9.95-$24.95. Bar. Cr cds: A, MC, V. D

Fredericksburg and Spotsylvania National Military Park (D-6)

See also Fredericksburg

What to See and Do

Chancellorsville Visitor Center. *120 Chatham Ln (22405).* 7 miles W of I-95 on VA 3. Phone 540/786-2880. Slide program, museum with exhibits; dioramas. (Daily; closed Jan 1, Dec 25) **$$**

Chatham Manor. *120 Chatham Ln (22405).* Phone 540/371-0802. Georgian brick manor house, owned by a wealthy planter, was converted to Union headquarters during two of the battles of Fredericksburg. The house was eventually used as a hospital where Clara Barton and Walt Whitman nursed the wounded. (Daily; closed Jan 1, Dec 25) **$$**

Fredericksburg Visitor Center. *Lafayette Blvd (US 1) and Sunken Rd.* Phone 540/373-6122. Information and directions for various parts of park. Tours should start here. (Daily; closed Jan 1, Dec 25) **$$** Center includes

Fredericksburg National Cemetery. *Lafayette Blvd and Sunken Rd.* More than 15,000 Federal interments; almost 13,000 unknown.

Museum. *1900 E Kanawha (22401).* Slide program, diorama, exhibits. (Same days as Visitor Center) **$$**

Old Salem Church. *1 mile W of I-95 on VA 3.* (1844) Building used as a field hospital and refugee center. Scene of battle on May 3-4, 1863.

Stonewall Jackson Shrine. *120 Chatham Ln (22405).* 12 miles S on I-95 to Thornburg exit, then 5 miles E on VA 606 to Guinea. Phone 804/633-6076. Plantation office where on May 10, 1863, Confederate General Jackson, ill with pneumonia and with his shattered left arm amputated, murmured, "Let us cross over the river, and rest under the shade of the trees," and died. (Mid-June-Labor Day, daily; Apr-mid-June, after Labor Day-Oct, Mon, Tues, Fri-Sun; rest of year, Mon, Sat-Sun) **$$**

Front Royal (D-9)

See also Winchester, Woodstock

Founded 1788 **Pop** 13,589 **Elev** 567 ft **Area code** 540 **Zip** 22630

Information Chamber of Commerce of Front Royal-Warren County, 414 E Main St; 540/635-3185 or 800/338-2576

Web www.frontroyal.com

Once known as Hell Town for all the wild and reckless spirits it attracted, Front Royal was a frontier stop on the way to eastern markets. The present name is supposed to have originated in the command, "Front the royal oak," given by an English officer to his untrained mountain militia recruits.

Belle Boyd, the Confederate spy, worked here extracting military secrets from Union officers. It is said that she invited General Nathaniel Banks, whose regiment was occupying the town, and his officers to a ball once. Later she raced on horseback to tell General Jackson what she had learned. The next morning (May 23, 1862), the Confederates attacked and captured nearly all of the Union troops, providing Jackson one of his early victories in the famous Valley Campaign.

Front Royal was a quiet little village until the entrance to Shenandoah National Park (see) and the beginning of Skyline Drive opened in 1935, just 1 mile to the south. With millions of motorists passing through every year, the town has grown rapidly. The production of automotive finishes, limestone, and cement contributes to the town's economy, but the tourism industry remains one of its largest.

What to See and Do

Belle Boyd Cottage. *101 Chester St, behind Ivy Lodge. Phone 540/636-1446.* Relocated to its present site, the two-story cottage has been restored to reflect life in Front Royal between 1840 and 1860. For a two-year period during the Civil War, Belle Boyd stayed in this cottage while visiting relatives and used the opportunity to spy on Union troops occupying the town. This modest dwelling was also used to house wounded soldiers of both armies. (Mid-Apr-Oct, Mon-Fri, weekends by appointment; closed holidays) **$**

Skyline Caverns. *10344 Stonewall Jackson Hwy (22630). 1 mile S on US 340. Phone 540/635-4545 or 800/296-4545.* Extensive, rare, intricate flowerlike formations of calcite (anthodites); sound and light presentation; 37-foot waterfall; clear stream stocked with trout (observation only). Electrically lighted; 54°F year-round. Miniature train provides trip through surrounding wooded area (Mar-mid-Nov, daily, weather permitting). Snack bar; gift shop. Cavern tours start every few minutes. (Daily) **$$$**

Sky Meadows State Park. *11012 Edmonds Ln (20144). 20 miles E on US 66, 7 miles N on VA 17. Phone 540/592-3556.* A 1,862-acre park. Fishing pond; hiking and bridle trails, picnicking, primitive walk-in camping. Visitor center; programs. (Daily) Standard fees. **$$**

Warren Rifles Confederate Museum. *95 Chester St. Phone 540/636-6982.* Historic relics and memorabilia of War between the States. (Mid-Apr-Oct, daily; rest of year, by appointment) **$$**

Special Events

Festival of Leaves. Arts and crafts, demonstrations; historic exhibits; parade. Second weekend in Oct.

Virginia Mushroom and Wine Festival. Mushrooms, wine, and cheese. Entertainment. Third Sat in May.

Warren County Fair. Entertainment, livestock exhibits and sale, contests. First week in Aug.

Warren County Garden Tour. Garden Club sponsors tours of historic houses and gardens. Last week in Apr.

Motel/Motor Lodge

★ ★ QUALITY INN. *10 S Commerce Ave (22630). Phone 540/635-3161; toll-free 888/821-4488; fax 540/635-6624. www.qualityinn.com.* 107 rooms, 3 story. Sept-Oct: S $58-$85; D $68-$85; each additional $9; under 18 free; higher rates special events; lower rates rest of year. Crib free. TV; cable (premium), VCR available (movies). Pool. Restaurant 6 am-9 pm; weekends to 10 pm. Check-out 11 am. Meeting rooms. Business services available. In-room modem link. Gift shop. Lawn games. Refrigerators, microwaves available. Cr cds: A, C, D, DS, ER, MC, V.

[D] [⌖] [⌖] [SC]

B&B/Small Inn

★ ★ ★ CHESTER HOUSE. *43 Chester St (22630). Phone 540/635-3937; toll-free 800/621-0441; fax 540/636-8695. www.chesterhouse.com.* This property, built in 1905, is located 1 mile from Skyline Drive, where there are scenic drives and hiking trails. 5 rooms, 2 story. Children over 12 years only. Complimentary full breakfast. Check-out 11 am, check-in 3 pm. TV in lounge. Health club privileges. Lawn games. Georgian-style mansion built 1905. Cr cds: A, MC, V. **$$**

Galax (I-5)

See also Wytheville

Settled 1904 **Pop** 6,837 **Elev** 2,382 ft **Area code** 540 **Zip** 24333

Information Galax-Carroll-Grayson Chamber of Commerce, 405 N Main St; 540/236-2184

Galax is named for the pretty evergreen with heart-shaped leaves that florists use in various arrangements. It grows in the mountainous regions around Galax and is gathered for sale all over the United States. Nearby are three mountain passes: Fancy Gap, Low Gap, and Piper's Gap.

What to See and Do

Jeff Matthews Memorial Museum. *606 W Stuart Dr (24333). Phone 276/236-7874.* Two authentically restored log cabins (1834 and 1860s). Relocated to present site and furnished with items used in the period in which the cabins were inhabited. Also houses collection of photos of Civil War veterans, artifacts and memorabilia of the area;

covered wagon; farm implements. Restored log cabin used as a blacksmith's shop. (Wed-Sun) **FREE**

Recreation. Swimming, boating, fishing on New River; hunting and hiking. Canoeing and other activities can be found at

> **Cliffview Trading Post.** *442 Cliffview Rd (24333).* Phone 276/238-1530. Bike rentals (Tues-Sat; closed Thanksgiving, Dec 25) and horse rentals (Apr-Nov, Tues-Sat); trail rides in New River Trail State Park.

Special Event

Old Fiddler's Convention. *Felts Park.* Folk songs, bands, and dancing. Second week in Aug.

George Washington Birthplace National Monument (F-11)

See also Fredericksburg, Montross

(38 miles E of Fredericksburg on VA 3, then 2 miles E on VA 204)

George Washington, first child of Augustine and Mary Ball Washington, was born February 11, 1732 (celebrated February 22 according to the new-style calendar) at his father's estate on Popes Creek on the south shore of the Potomac. The family moved in 1735 to Little Hunting Creek Plantation (later called Mount Vernon), then in 1738 to Ferry Farm near Fredericksburg.

The 538-acre monument includes much of the old plantation land. (Daily; closed Jan 1, Dec 25) **$$**

What to See and Do

Family burial ground. *1732 Popes Creek Rd (22443). 1 mile NW on Bridges Creek.* Phone 804/224-1732. Site of 1664 home of Colonel John Washington, first Washington in Virginia and great-grandfather of the first president. Washington's ancestors are buried here.

Memorial House. *1732 Popes Creek Rd (22443). Phone 804/224-1732.* Original house burned (1779) and was never rebuilt. The Memorial House is not a replica of the original; it represents a composite of typical 18th-century Virginia plantation house. Bricks were handmade from nearby clay. Furnishings are typical of the times. Near house is

Colonial farm. *1732 Popes Creek Rd (22443). Phone 804/224-1732.* "Living" farm designed to show 18th-century Virginia plantation life; livestock, colonial garden, several farm buildings, furnished colonial kitchen, household slave quarters, and spinning and weaving room.

Picnic area. *1732 Popes Creek Rd (22443). Phone 804/224-1732.* 1/4 mile N of house.

Visitor Center. *1732 Popes Creek Rd (22443). Phone 804/224-1732.* Orientation film; museum exhibits. **$**

Gloucester (G-12)

See also Newport News, Williamsburg, Yorktown

Founded 1769 **Pop** 900 **Elev** 70 ft **Area code** 804 **Zip** 23061

Information Chamber of Commerce, PO Box 296; 804/693-2425.

In the spring, acres of daffodil blooms make this area a treat for the traveler. This elm-shaded village is the commercial center of Gloucester (GLOSS-ter) County. There are many old landmarks and estates nearby, including the birthplace of Walter Reed, at the junction of VA 614 and 616.

What to See and Do

County Courthouse. *6489 Main St (23061). On US 17 Business. Phone 804/693-4042.* (18th century) Part of Gloucester Court House Circle Historic District. Portraits of native sons in the courtroom; plaques memorializing Nathaniel Bacon, leader in the rebellion of 1676, first organized resistance to British authority, and Major Walter Reed, surgeon and conqueror of yellow fever. (Mon-Fri; closed holidays) **FREE** Nearby are Debtors Prison, the pre-Revolutionary Botetourt Building, and the

> **Roswell Historic Ruins.** *6549 Main St. Phone 804/693-2585.* Three-story Georgian mansion's brickwork was put in place over 250 years ago. Majestic ruins hint at projecting pavilions, arched windows, and stone-capped chimney stacks. Tours by appointment. (Apr-Oct, Sun; winter by appointment) **FREE**

Virginia Institute of Marine Science, College of William and Mary. *1208 Greate Rd. Gloucester Point. Phone 804/684-7000.* Small marine aquarium and museum display local fish, and invertebrates; marine science exhibits; bookstore. (Mon-Fri; closed holidays) **FREE**

Restaurant

★ ★ **SEAWELL'S ORDINARY.** *3968 George Washington Hwy (23131). Phone 804/642-3635; fax 804/642-6588. www.seawellsordinary.com.* Continental menu. Closed Mon, Tues; Jan 1, July 4, Dec 24, Dec 25. Dinner, Sun brunch. Bar. Built in 1712; became country tavern (1757); was frequented by Washington, Jefferson, Lafayette. Outdoor seating. Cr cds: A, D, MC, V. **$$**

Great Dismal Swamp National Wildlife Refuge (I-12)

See also Cheaspeake, Portsmouth

Harriet Beecher Stowe found Virginia's Dismal Swamp a perfect setting for her antislavery novel *Dred* (1856); modern hunters, fishermen, and naturalists find the area fits their ambition just as well. From its northern edge just southwest of Norfolk, the swamp stretches almost due south like a great ribbon, 25 miles long and 11 miles wide. Centuries of decaying organic matter have created layers of peat so deep that fires would sometimes smolder under the surface for weeks.

Creation of the refuge began in 1973 when the Union Camp Corporation donated 49,100 acres of land to the Nature Conservancy, which in turn conveyed it to the Department of Interior. The refuge was officially established through the Dismal Swamp Act of 1974 and is managed for the primary purpose of protecting and preserving a unique ecosystem. The refuge now consists of over 107,000 acres of forested wetlands that have been greatly altered by drainage and logging operations.

Near the center is Lake Drummond, 3,100 acres of juniper water, which is water that combines the juices of gum, cypress, and maple with a strong infusion of juniper or white cedar. The chemical mix added by the tree resins results in a water that remains sweet, or fresh, indefinitely. In the days of long sailing voyages, when ordinary water became foul after a few weeks, this "dark water" was highly valued.

The Great Dismal Swamp has also been commercially exploited for its timber, particularly cypress and cedar. A company organized by George Washington and several other businessmen bought a large piece of the swamp and used slave labor to dig the Dismal Swamp Canal, which both facilitated drainage of timber land and provided a transportation route in and out of the swamp.

Animal and bird life continues to abound in this eerie setting. There are white-tailed deer and rarely observed black bear, foxes, bobcats—and a large number of snakes, including copperheads, cottonmouths, and rattlesnakes. Birding is popular in the swamp from April-June; the peak of spring migration is mid-April-mid-May.

For further information contact Refuge Manager, PO Box 349, Suffolk 23439-0349. Phone 757/986-3705.

Hampton (H-12)

See also Newport News, Norfolk, Portsmouth, Virginia Beach

Settled 1610 **Pop** 146,437 **Elev** 12 ft **Area code** 757

Information Hampton Visitor Center, 710 Settlers Landing Rd, 23669; 757/727-1102 or 800/800-2202

Web www.hampton.va.us/tourism

Hampton is the oldest continuously English-speaking community in the United States (Jamestown, settled in 1607, is a national historical park, but not a town). The settlement began at a place then called Kecoughtan, with the building of Fort Algernourne as protection against the Spanish. In the late 1600s and early 1700s the area was harassed by pirates. Finally in 1718, the notorious brigand Blackbeard was killed by Lieutenant Robert Maynard and organized piracy came to an end here.

Hampton was shelled in the Revolutionary War, sacked by the British in the War of 1812, and burned in 1861 by retreating Confederates to prevent its occupation by Union forces. Only the gutted walls of St. John's Church survived the fire. The town was rebuilt after the Civil War by its citizens and soldiers. Computer technology, manufacturing, aerospace research, and commercial fishing are now big business here.

Langley Air Force Base, headquarters for the Air Combat Command, Fort Monroe, headquarters for the US Army's Training and Doctrine Command, and the NASA Langley Research Center are located here.

What to See and Do

Air Power Park and Aviation History Center. *413 W Mercury Blvd, US 258. Phone 757/727-1163.* Over 50 indoor and outdoor exhibits feature real fighter aircraft, missiles, and rockets; local aviation history and model aircraft exhibits. Picnicking, playground. (Daily; closed Jan 1, Thanksgiving, Dec 25) **FREE**

Bluebird Gap Farm. *60 Pine Chapel Rd. Phone 757/727-6739.* This 60-acre farm includes barnyard zoo; indigenous wildlife such as deer and wolves; antique and modern farm equipment and farmhouse artifacts. Picnicking, playground. (Wed-Sun; closed holidays) **FREE**

Buckroe Beach. *22 Lincoln St (23669). 4 miles E on VA 351, foot of E Pembroke Ave on Chesapeake Bay. Phone 757/ 727-6347.* Swimming; public park, concerts. Lifeguards (Memorial Day-Labor Day). **FREE**

Fort Monroe. *3 miles SE via Mercury Blvd, Ingalls Rd.* First fort here was a stockade called Fort Algernourne (1609); the second, Fort George, though built of brick, was destroyed by a hurricane in 1749; present fort was completed about 1834. **FREE** Here are

Casemate Museum. *20 Bernard Rd (23651). Phone 757/788-3391.* Provides insight on heritage of the fort, Old Point Comfort, and the Army Coast Artillery Corps. Museum offers access to a series of casemates and a walking tour of the fort. Jefferson Davis casemate contains cell in which the Confederacy's president was confined on false charges of plotting against the life of Abraham Lincoln. Museum features Civil War exhibits, military uniforms, and assorted artwork, including three original Remington drawings, along with audiovisual programs. Scale models of coast artillery guns and dioramas represent the role of the coast artillery from 1901 to 1946. (Daily; closed Jan 1, Thanksgiving, Dec 25) **FREE**

Chapel of the Centurion. (1858) One of the oldest churches on the Virginia peninsula. Woodrow Wilson worshiped here occasionally. **FREE**

Hampton Carousel. *602 Settlers Landing Rd, downtown, on waterfront. Phone 757/727-6381 or 757/727-6347 (Parks & Rec Dept).* (1920) Completely restored in 1991, antique carousel is housed in its own pavilion and features 48 hand-carved horses. (Apr-Sept, Mon-Sat, also Sun afternoons; Oct-Nov, daily, weather permitting; Dec 1-15, weekends) **$**

Hampton University. *Cemetery Rd and Frissell Ave (23669). E end of Queen St, 1/4 mile off I-64 exit 267. Phone 757/727-5253.* (1868) 6,100 students. Founded by Union Brigadier General Samuel Chapman Armstrong, chief of the Freedman's Bureau, to prepare the youth of the South, regardless of color, for the work of organizing and instructing schools in the Southern states; many blacks and Native Americans came to be educated. Now Virginia's only coeducational, nondenominational, four-year private college. The Hampton choir is famous. It "sang up" a building, Virginia-Cleveland Hall, in 1870 on a trip through New England and Canada, raising close to $100,000 at concerts. On campus are

Emancipation Oak. The Emancipation Proclamation was read here.

Museum. *Cemetery Rd and Frissell Ave. Huntington Building.* Collection of ethnic art; Native American and African artifacts; contemporary African-American works; paintings by renowned artists. (Daily; closed school holidays) **FREE**

Miss Hampton II Harbor Cruises. *764 Settlers Landing Rd. Phone 757/722-9102.* Narrated three-hour cruise includes a stop at Fort Wool, a Civil War island fortress. (Apr-Oct) **$$$$**

Settlers Landing Monument. *1/2 mile S, on grounds of the Veterans Affairs Medical Center between Hampton River and Mill Creek, off I-64 exit 268.* Marks approximately site of first settlers' landing near Strawberry Banks in 1607. Painting by Sidney King depicts visit to Kecoughtan by colonists en route to Jamestown. (Daily) **FREE**

St. John's Church and Parish Museum. (1728) *W Queens Way and Franklin St. Phone 757/722-2567.* Fourth site of worship of Episcopal parish established in 1610. Bible dating from 1599; communion silver from 1618; Colonial Vestry Book; taped historical message. (Daily)

Virginia Air and Space Center and Hampton Roads History Center. *600 Settlers Landing Rd (23669). Downtown, off I-64 exit 267. Phone 757/727-0900; 800/296-0800.* Exhibits show the historical link between Hampton Roads' seafaring past and spacefaring future. Exhibits include 19 full-sized air- and spacecraft, the Apollo 12 Command Module, a moon rock, and rare NASA artifacts. Films shown in 283-seat IMAX theater (daily). Gift shop. (daily; closed Thanksgiving, Dec 25) **$$$**

Special Events

Hampton Bay Days. *Phone 757/727-6122.* Arts and crafts, rides, science exhibits; entertainment. Mid-Sept.

Hampton Cup Regatta. *Phone 800/800-2202.* Inboard hydroplane races. Mid-Aug.

Hampton Jazz Festival. *1000 Coliseum Dr. Hampton Coliseum. Phone 757/838-4203.* Three days late June.

Motels/Motor Lodges

★ ★ **COURTYARD BY MARRIOTT.** *1917 Coliseum Dr (23666). Phone 757/838-3300; res 800/321-2211; fax 757/838-6387. www.courtyard.com.* 158 rooms, 3 story. June-Sept: S, D $75-$99; each additional $10; suites $90-$129; under 18 free; higher rates jazz festival; lower rates rest of year. Check-out noon. TV; cable (premium). In-room modem link. Bar Mon-Thurs 6-10 pm. Exercise equipment. Pool; whirlpool. Cr cds: A, C, D, DS, MC, V.

D ⚓ **𝕏** ⟷ **SC**

★ **HAMPTON INN.** *1813 W Mercury Blvd (23666).* *Phone 757/838-8484; res 800/426-7866; fax 757/826-0725.* *www.hamptoninn.com.* 131 rooms, 6 story. D $89-$104. Pet accepted, some restrictions. Complimentary continental breakfast. Check-out noon, check-in 3 pm. TV; cable (premium). In-room modem link. Exercise equipment. Pool privileges. Cr cds: A, C, D, DS, MC, V.

★ ★ **HOLIDAY INN.** *1815 W Mercury Blvd (23666).* *Phone 757/838-0200. www.holiday-inn.com.* 390 rooms, 2-4 story. S, D $89-$109; suites $189-$225; weekend rates; higher rates Jazz Festival. Check-out 11 am. TV; cable (premium). In-room modem link. Restaurant 6 am-10 pm. Bar 11 am-midnight. Room service to 11 pm. Exercise equipment, sauna. Game room. Two pools, one indoor; whirlpool. Free airport transportation. Business center. Cr cds: A, D, DS, ER, JCB, MC, V.

★ ★ **RADISSON HOTEL HAMPTON.** *700 Settlers Landing (23669). Phone 757/727-9700; fax 757/722-4557.* *www.radisson.com.* Located on the waterfront in downtown Hampton, this hotel is conveniently located between Williamsburg and Virginia Beach and is close to business and leisure districts and military bases. 177 rooms, 9 story. D $89-$189; each additional $10; under 18 free; weekend rates. Check-out noon, check-in 3 pm. TV; cable (premium). In-room modem link. Restaurant 6:30 am-10 pm. Bar 11-2 am. Exercise equipment. Pool, whirlpool, poolside service. Free airport transportation. Luxury level. On Hampton River. Cr cds: A, C, D, DS, ER, JCB, MC, V.

Restaurant

★ **SAMMY AND NICK'S.** *2718 W Mercury Blvd (23666). Phone 757/838-9100; fax 757/838-9612.* Steak menu. Hours: 11 am-11 pm; Sat, Sun from 7 am. Closed Thanksgiving, Dec 25. Dinner $3.95-$14.95. Bar. Children's menu. Casual attire. Reservations accepted. Cr cds: A, D, DS, MC, V.

Harrisonburg (E-8)

See also Luray, New Market, Staunton

Founded 1780 **Pop** 40,468 **Elev** 1,352 ft **Area code** 540

Information Harrisonburg-Rockingham Convention and Visitors Bureau, 10 E Gay St, 22802; 540/434-2319

Web www.hrcvb.org

Originally named Rocktown due to the limestone outcroppings prevalent in the area, Harrisonburg became the county seat of Rockingham County when Thomas Harrison won a race against Mr. Keezle of Keezletown, 3 miles east. They had raced on horseback to Richmond to file their respective towns for the new county seat. Harrisonburg is noted for good hunting and fishing, recreational opportunities, beautiful scenery, and turkeys. The annual production of more than 5 million turkeys, most of them processed and frozen, has made Rockingham County widely known. This is a college town with three 4-year universities. Much of the Washington and Jefferson national forests are here.

What to See and Do

Caverns. There are several caverns within 24 miles of Harrisonburg. They include

Grand Caverns Regional Park. *Dogwood Ave. 12 miles S on I-81, then 6 miles E on VA 256 in Grottoes. Phone 540/249-5705.* Known for its immense underground chambers and spectacular formations. Visited by Union and Confederate troops during the Civil War. Unique shield formations. Electrically lighted; 54°F. Park facilities include swimming pool; tennis courts, miniature golf, picnic pavilions, hiking and bicycle trails. Guided tours. (Apr-Oct, daily; Mar, weekends) **$$$$**

Shenandoah Caverns. *24 miles N on US 11.* (See NEW MARKET)

Eastern Mennonite University. *1200 Park Rd (22802). 2 miles NW on VA 42. Phone 540/432-4000.* (1917) 1,350 students. Many Mennonites live in this area. On campus is an art gallery, planetarium (shows by appointment, free), natural history museum, and the Menno Simons Historical Library, containing many 16th-century Mennonite volumes (school year, Mon-Sat). Campus tours.

George Washington and Jefferson National Forests. *10 miles W on US 33. Contact Forest Headquarters, 5162 Valleypointe Pkwy, Roanoke 24019-3050. Phone 540/265-5100.* Consist of approximately nearly 2 million acres. Swimming; fishing for trout, bluegill, and bass; hunting for deer, bear, wild turkey, and small game; riding trails, camping, picnicking. Scenic drives past Crabtree Falls, hardwood forests, and unusual geologic features. Overlooks of Shenandoah Valley. Part of Appalachian Trail crosses forest. Fees are charged at some recreation sites. Trails for the visually impaired. **FREE**

James Madison University. *800 S Main St (22807). Phone 540/568-3621.* (1908) 15,000 students. Interesting old bluestone buildings. Campus tours through Visitor Center phone 540/568-5681. On campus is

Miller Hall Planetarium and Sawhill Art Gallery. *800 S Main (22807). Phone 540/568-3621 for schedules.* **FREE**

Lake Shenandoah. *3 miles E.*

Lincoln Homestead. *9 miles N on VA 42.* Brick house, the rear wing of which was built by Abraham Lincoln's grandfather, and where his father was born. Main portion of the house was built about 1800 by Captain Jacob Lincoln. (Private)

Natural Chimneys Regional Park. *15 miles SW off VA 42 in Mt Solon. Phone 540/350-2510.* Seven colorful and massive rock towers rise 120 feet above the plain. Pool; picnic facilities, camping (fee; limited Nov-Feb), bicycle and nature trails, playground. Park (daily). **$$**

Shenandoah National Park. (see) *24 miles E on US 33.*

Shenandoah River. Good bass fishing.

Shenandoah Valley Folk Art and Heritage Center. *115 Bowman Rd. Phone 540/879-2681.* Featured is the Stonewall Jackson Electric Map that depicts his Valley Campaign of 1862. The 12-foot vertical relief map fills an entire wall and lets visitors see and hear the campaign, battle by battle. Also displays of Shenandoah Valley history, artifacts. (Mon-Sat; closed holidays) **$$**

Silver Lake. *5 miles SW on VA 42 in Dayton.*

Virginia Quilt Museum. *301 S Main St. Phone 540/433-3818.* Resource center for the study of quilts and quilting. (Mon, Thurs-Sat, also Sun afternoons; closed holidays) **$$**

Special Events

Natural Chimneys Jousting Tournament. *94 Natural Chimneys Ln. Natural Chimneys Regional Park.* America's oldest continuous sporting event, held annually since 1821. "Knights" armed with lances charge down an 80-yard track and attempt to spear three small rings suspended from posts. Each knight is allowed three rides at the rings, thus a perfect score is nine rings. Ties are run off using successively smaller rings. Third Sat in June and in Aug.

Rockingham County Fair. *4808 S Valley Pike (22801).* Mid-Aug.

Motels/Motor Lodges

★ **COMFORT INN.** *1440 E Market St (22801). Phone 540/433-6066; fax 540/433-0793. www.comfortinn.com.* 60 rooms, 2 story. S, D $70-$80; each additional $10; under 18 free. Crib free. Pet accepted, some restrictions. Complimentary continental breakfast. Check-out noon. TV; cable (premium). Pool. Business services. Cr cds: A, C, D, DS, JCB, MC, V.

⧉ D 🐾 ⇌ ⊠

★ **DAYS INN.** *1131 Forest Hill Rd (22801). Phone 540/433-9353; toll-free 800/329-7466; fax 540/433-5809. www.daysinn.com.* 89 rooms, 4 story. June-Oct: S $55; D $68; each additional $5; under 17 free; ski plan; higher rates special events, weekends (2-day minimum); lower rates rest of year. Crib free. Pet accepted; $5/day. Complimentary continental breakfast. Check-out 11 am. TV; cable (premium). Refrigerators, microwaves available. Valet services. Restaurant adjacent 11 am-11 pm. Health club privileges. Indoor pool, whirlpool. 27-hole golf privileges, greens fee $30, pro, putting green, driving range. Downhill ski 12 miles. Meeting rooms. Business services. Sundries. Cr cds: A, C, D, DS, JCB, MC, V.

D 🐾 ⊠ 🍴 ⇌ ⊠ SC

★★ **FOUR POINTS BY SHERATON.** *1400 E Market St (22801). Phone 540/433-2521; toll-free 800/708-7037; fax 540/434-0253. www.fourpoints.com.* 140 rooms, 5 story. S, D $99-$109; each additional $10; under 18 free. Crib free. Pet accepted. TV; cable (premium). Indoor pool; wading pool, whirlpool, poolside service. Restaurant 6:30-2 pm, 5-10 pm. Room service. Bar 11-2 am; entertainment. Check-out noon. Meeting rooms. Business services available. In-room modem link. Bellstaff. Valet service. Exercise equipment; sauna. Health club privileges. Some bathroom phones; refrigerators, microwaves available. Cr cds: A, C, D, DS, ER, JCB, MC, V.

D 🐾 ⇌ 🏋 ⊠ SC

★ **HAMPTON INN.** *85 University Blvd (22801). Phone 540/432-1111; toll-free 800/426-7866; fax 540/432-0748. www.hamptoninn.com.* 164 rooms, 4 story. May-Oct: S, D $68-$78; under 19 free; higher rates university events; lower rates rest of year. Crib free. TV; cable (premium). Pool. Complimentary continental breakfast. Restaurant nearby. Check-out noon. Meeting rooms. Business services available. In-room modem link. Valet service. Sundries. Health club privileges. Refrigerators, microwaves available. Cr cds: A, C, D, DS, MC, V.

D ⇌ ⊠ SC

★ **HOWARD JOHNSON.** *605 Port Republic Rd (22801). Phone 540/434-6771; fax 540/434-0153. www.hojo.com.* 134 rooms, 2 story. Mar-Nov: S $44.95-$54.95; D $44.95-$59.95; each additional $5; higher rates some university events; lower rates rest of year. Crib free. Pet accepted. TV; cable (premium). Pool; wading pool. Restaurant 6 am-9 pm. Check-out noon. Business services available. Refrigerators available. Private patios, balconies. Cr cds: A, D, DS, MC, V.

D 🐾 ⇌ ⊠

★★ **VILLAGE INN.** *4979 S Valley Pike (22801). Phone 540/434-7355; toll-free 800/736-7355. www.shenandoah.org/villageinn.* 36 rooms. S $43; D $49-$59;

each additional $5; kitchen units $64. Crib free. Pet accepted. TV; cable (premium), VCR available (movies). Pool. Playground. Restaurant 7-10 am, 5:30-9 pm; closed Sun. Check-out noon. Meeting room. Business services available. Sundries. Health club privileges. Lawn games. Many in-room whirlpools. Picnic tables. Cr cds: A, C, D, DS, MC, V.

D ⛄ ☕ ✑

Hopewell (H-11)

See also Petersburg, Richmond, Surry, Williamsburg

Founded 1613 **Pop** 22,354 **Elev** 50 ft **Area code** 804 **Zip** 23860

Information Hopewell Area-Prince George Chamber of Commerce, 210 N 2nd Ave; 804/458-5536

The second permanent English settlement in America has been an important inland port since early times, having a fine channel 28 feet deep and 300 feet wide. It was the birthplace of statesman John Randolph of Roanoke. Edmund Ruffin, an early agricultural chemist who fired the first shot at Fort Sumter, was born near here.

"Cittie Point," at the junction of the James and Appomattox rivers, finally became one of Virginia's big cities during World War I when an E. I. du Pont de Nemours Company dynamite plant on Hopewell Farm supplied guncotton to the Allies.

What to See and Do

City Point Unit of Petersburg National Battlefield. (see) *Jct Cedar Ln and Pecan Ave.* Phone 804/458-9504. Grant's headquarters during the siege of Petersburg and largest Civil War supply depot. Includes Appomattox Manor, home to one family for 340 years; Grant's headquarters were on the front lawn. Many other buildings. (Daily; closed holidays) **$**

Flowerdew Hundred. *1617 Flowerdew Hundred Rd. 10 miles SE on VA 10.* Phone 804/541-8897 or 804/541-8938. Outdoor museum on the site of an early English settlement on the south bank of the James River. Originally inhabited by Native Americans, settled by Governor George Yeardley in 1618. Thousands of artifacts dating from the prehistoric period through the present have been excavated and are on exhibit in the museum. A replicated 19th-century detached kitchen and working 17th-century-style windmill are open to visitors. Exhibits, interpretive tours. Picnicking. (Apr-Nov, Sat and Sun or by appointment; rest of year, by appointment) **$$**

Merchants Hope Church. *11500 Merchants Hope Rd (23860). 6 miles E on VA 10, then 1/2 mile S on VA 641.* Phone 804/458-6197. (1657) Given the name of a plantation that was named for a barque plying between Virginia and England. The exterior has been called the most beautiful colonial brickwork in America. Oldest operating Protestant church in the country. (Open by request) **DONATION**

Special Events

Hooray for Hopewell Festival. *Downtown.* Arts and crafts, food, entertainment, children's rides. Third weekend in Sept.

Prince George County Heritage Fair. *Flowerdew Hundred.* Arts and crafts; educational exhibits and demonstrations; music, food, children's rides, hayrides. Last weekend in Apr.

Motels/Motor Lodges

★ **HOLIDAY INN EXPRESS.** *4911 Oaklawn Blvd (23860).* Phone 804/458-1500; fax 804/458-9151. www.holiday-inn.com. 115 rooms, 50 kitchen suites; 2 story. S $50-$75; D $50-$95; each additional $5; kitchen suites $62-$100; under 18 free; higher rates special events. Crib free. TV; cable, VCR available (movies). Pool; whirlpool. Complimentary continental breakfast. Restaurant nearby. Check-out 11 am. Coin laundry. Business services available. Exercise equipment; sauna. Refrigerators. Cr cds: A, C, D, DS, ER, JCB, MC, V.

D ☕ 🏋 ✑

★ **INNKEEPER.** *3952 Courthouse Rd (23860).* Phone 804/458-2600; toll-free 800/466-6337; fax 804/458-1915. 104 rooms, 3 story. S $52.99-$79.99; D $55.99-$79.99; each additional $5. Crib free. TV; cable. Pool. Complimentary continental breakfast. Restaurant adjacent 6:30 am-11 pm. Check-out noon. Coin laundry. Meeting rooms. Business services available. In-room modem link. Refrigerators; microwaves available. Cr cds: A, C, D, DS, MC, V.

D ☕ ✑ SC

Hot Springs (F-7)

See also Clifton Forge, Covington, Warm Springs

Pop 300 **Elev** 2,238 ft **Area code** 540 **Zip** 24445

A Ranger District office of the Washington and Jefferson national forests is located here.

What to See and Do

The Homestead. *On US 220.* Phone 800/838-1766. Double chairlift, T-bar, J-bar, baby rope tow; patrol, school, rentals; snowmaking; cafeteria, bar. Ice curling, ice-skating rink (Thanksgiving-Mar). **$$$$**

Motel/Motor Lodge

★ **ROSALOE MOTEL.** *590 N Rte 220 (24445). Phone 540/839-5373; fax 540/839-4625. www.rosaloe.com.* 14 rooms. D $60-$80. Check-out 11 am, check-in 3 pm. TV; cable (premium). Downhill ski 3 miles. Cr cds: A, C, D, DS, MC, V.

Resort

★ ★ ★ **THE HOMESTEAD.** *US 220 (24445). Phone 540/839-1766; toll-free 800/838-1766; fax 540/839-7556. www.thehomestead.com.* Founded ten years before the American Revolution, The Homestead is one of America's greatest resorts. For more than two centuries, presidents and other notables have flocked to this idyllic mountain resort on 15,000 acres in the scenic Allegheny Mountains. Mindful of its historical obligations, the resort carefully adds creature comforts to the traditional accommodations. From the fresh mountain air and natural hot springs to the legendary championship golf, this Georgian-style resort is the embodiment of a restorative retreat. A leading golf academy sharpens skills, while three courses challenge players. History abounds at the resort; for example, America's oldest continuously played tee is located here at the Old Course. Guests take to the waters as they have done for 200 years, while the spa incorporates advanced therapies for relaxation and rejuvenation. Eight restaurants tempt guests with a variety of options, from continental cuisine in formal settings to fun flavors in relaxed environments. 513 rooms, 4-12 story. Apr-Oct: S, D $212-$306; suites $372-$810; family rates; MAP available; ski, golf, tennis plans; some seasonal rates; some lower rates rest of year. Service charges: 15% for daily housekeeping and 15% at all dining outlets. Check-out noon, check-in 4 pm. TV; cable. Dining room 7-10 am, 11:30 am-4 pm, 6-9:30 pm. Bar 11 am-midnight. Room service 7 am-midnight. Supervised children's activities, ages 3-12. Exercise equipment. Game room. Spa, mineral pool. Two pools, one indoor; lifeguard. Three 18-hole golf courses, greens fee $100-$150, cart $15/person, putting greens, driving range. Tennis. Downhill, cross-country skiing on site. Lawn games. Hiking, horseback trails. Skating. Airport, railroad station, bus depot transportation. Business center. Snowboarding. Movies. Afternoon tea. Skeet and trap shooting. Cr cds: A, C, D, DS, MC, V.

B&B/Small Inn

★ ★ **VINE COTTAGE INN.** *US 220 (24445). Phone 540/839-2422; toll-free 800/410-9755. www.vinecottageinn.com.* 15 rooms, 7 share bath, 3 story. No elevator, room phones. D $65-$90; each additional $15-$20. Closed 2 weeks in Mar. Pet accepted, some restrictions; fee. Complimentary full breakfast. Check-out noon, check-in 3 pm. TV in common room; VCR available. Downhill ski 1 mile. Built in 1894; family-oriented Victorian inn. Totally nonsmoking. Cr cds: A, C, D, DS, MC, V.

Restaurants

★ **COUNTRY CAFE.** *Rte 220 S (24445). Phone 540/839-2111.* American menu. Hours: 7 am-9 pm; Sun to 2 pm. Closed Mon; major holidays. Dinner $7-$14. Children's menu. Cr cds: MC, V.

★ ★ **SAM SNEAD'S TAVERN.** *Main St (24445). Phone 540/839-7666. www.thehomestead.com.* American, seafood menu. Hours: 5:30-9:30 pm; Sun to 9 pm. Dinner $8-$29. Reservations required. Cr cds: A, MC, V.

Irvington (G-12)

See also Lancaster

Pop 673 **Elev** 31 ft **Area code** 804 **Zip** 22480

What to See and Do

Historic Christ Church. *420 Christ Church Rd. 2 1/2 miles W, off VA 200. Phone 804/438-6855.* (1735) Built by Robert Carter, ancestor of eight governors of Virginia, two presidents, three signers of the Declaration of Independence, a chief justice, and many others who served the country with distinction. Restored; original structure and furnishings, triple-decker pulpit. Built on site of earlier wooden church (1669); family tombs. Tours. (Apr-Nov, daily) **FREE** On the grounds is

Carter Reception Center. Narrated video presentation; museum with artifacts from Corotoman, home of Robert Carter, and from the church construction; photographs of the restoration. Guides. (Apr-Nov, daily) **FREE**

Motel/Motor Lodge

★ **WHISPERING PINES MOTEL.** *Rte 3, White Stone (22578). Phone 804/435-1101.* 29 rooms. S, D $59-$69; each additional $5. Crib $5. TV; cable. Pool; wading pool. Restaurant nearby. Check-out 11 am. Sundries. Picnic tables. On wooded grounds. Cr cds: A, MC, V.

Resort

★ ★ ★ **TIDES INN.** *480 King Carter Dr, White Stone (22480). Phone 804/438-5000; fax 804/438-5222. www. tidesinn.com.* 106 rooms, 23 suites. S, D $195-$325; suites $350-$850; under 10 free; EP available; golf plans; higher rates some weekends. Closed rest of year. Crib free. Pet accepted, some restrictions. Check-out 1 pm, check-in 4 pm. Two pools, one saltwater, one heated; poolside service. TV; cable (premium), VCR available (free movies). Valet services. Coin laundry. Three restaurants. Bar noon-11 pm. Free supervised children's activities (late June-Labor Day), ages 5-12. Playground. Exercise equipment, sauna. Game room, recreation room. 18-hole championship golf; greens fee $25-$40, pro, putting green, driving range, 9-hole complimentary executive course. Lighted tennis. Meeting rooms. Business services available. Balconies, refrigerators, minibars. Gift shop. Lawn games, Bicycles. Marina, cruises, boat rental. Cr cds: A, D, DS, MC, V.

Jamestown (Colonial National Historical Park) (H-12)

See also Colonial Parkway, Newport News, Surry, Williamsburg, Yorktown

On May 13, 1607, in this unpromising setting, the first permanent English settlement in the New World was founded. From the beginning, characteristics of the early United States were established—self-government, industry, commerce, and the plantation system. The 104 men and boys who landed here that day and the people who followed them forecast the varied origins of the American populace. There were English, Germans, Africans, French, Italians, Poles, and Irish.

The *Susan Constant* (120 tons), the *Godspeed* (40 tons), and the *Discovery* (20 tons) brought the settlers here after a landing at Cape Henry. Thus, 20 years after the tragic failure to establish a colony at Roanoke Island and 13 years before the Pilgrims landed at Plymouth, Massachusetts, the English succeeded in settling in America.

The landing was not auspicious. Captain John Smith, ablest man in the group, was in chains; most of the others possessed a singular ineptitude for existing in a strange, hostile wilderness. Smith's ability and driving personality soon made him the acknowledged leader. For about a year he kept the bickering at a minimum, and the establishment of a colony was well under way.

The London Company, under whose patronage the colonists had set forth, continued to send "gentlemen" and adventurers to reinforce the colony. The second such shipment (September 1608) elicited the famous "Smith's rude answer" to company demands for gold and assorted riches. He wrote in part, "I entreat you rather send but thirty carpenters, husbandmen, gardeners, fishermen, blacksmiths, masons, and diggers up of trees, roots . . . than a thousand of such as we have: for except we be able both to lodge them and feed them, the most will consume with want of necessaries before they can be made good for anything."

Good for anything or not, this little band made glass in 1608, introduced the first commercial tobacco cultivation in 1612, and produced the country's first representative legislative body in 1619. In the earliest years, clapboards (some of which were shipped back to England) were made here, and later bricks, fishing nets, pottery, a variety of tools, and other items needed in the colony.

The first Africans were brought to the colony in 1619 on a Dutch privateer. They were probably indentured servants, pledged to work until their passage had been paid off. This was a common arrangement at the time.

There was not an easy day for any of the colonists for years. Crops failed and rats ate the corn. Until John Rolfe married Pocahontas, daughter of Chief Powhatan, in 1614, the Native Americans were suspicious and unfriendly. Disease plagued the settlers. The winter of 1609-1610 was called the "starving time." The 350-person colony was reduced to about 60 emaciated, defeated survivors who decided to give up and return to England. The June 1610 arrival of Lord de la Warre with reinforcements and supplies dissuaded them. Then the colony began to build and hope returned.

When Jamestown became a Royal Colony in 1624, feeling against personal (and often high-handed) government began to mount. By 1676 there was open revolt, led by Nathaniel Bacon, the younger. Bacon's forces finally burned the town, calling it a "stronghold of oppression." It was partially rebuilt but decline was inevitable, in part due to the damp, unhealthy climate of the area. The statehouse burned in 1698 and in 1699 the government moved to Middle Plantation and renamed it Williamsburg. By Revolutionary War days Jamestown was no longer an active community. About the same time, the James River washed away the sandy isthmus and the site became an island.

Nothing of the 17th-century settlement remains above ground except the Old Church Tower. Since 1934, however, archaeological exploration by the National Park Service has made the outline of the town clear. Cooperative efforts by the Park Service and the Association for the Preservation of Virginia Antiquities (which owns 22.5 acres of the island, including the Old Church Tower) have exposed foundations and restored streets, property ditches, hedgerows, fences, and the James Fort site from 1607. Markers, recorded messages, paintings, and monuments are everywhere. Entrance station (daily; closed Dec 25). Contact the Superintendent, PO Box 210, Yorktown 23690; phone 757/898-3400. Jamestown Island entrance fee $5/adult (over age 16); Golden Access, Age, and Eagle passports accepted (see MAKING THE MOST OF YOUR TRIP).

What to See and Do

Confederate Fort. *Near Old Church Tower.* (1861) One of two Civil War fortifications on the island.

Dale House. *1367 Colonial Pkwy (23081).* Archaeological laboratory. A viewing area is open to the public.

First landing site. *Colonial Historic Pkwy and Jamestown Rd (23185).* Fixed by tradition as point in river, about 200 yards from present seawall, upriver from Old Church Tower.

Glasshouse. *Colonial National Historic Pkwy and Jamestown Rd (23185).* Colonists produced glass here in 1608. Demonstration exhibits, glassblowing (daily; closed Dec 25).

James Fort site. *Colonial Historic Pkwy and Jamestown Rd (23185).* Excavation of first fort (1607) can be viewed between seawall and Old Church Tower.

Jamestown Settlement. *31 Rte S Jamestown Rd. Adjacent to historic Jamestown. Phone 757/253-4838; toll-free 888/593-4682.* Living history museum re-creates the first permanent English settlement in New World. Recalls early-17th-century Jamestown with full-scale reproductions of ships which arrived in 1607 and the triangular James Fort. Powhatan Indian Village depicts Native American culture encountered by English colonists. Museum complex features orientation film, changing gallery, and three exhibit galleries focusing on the history of Jamestown and the Powhatan. Food service available. Combination ticket with Yorktown Victory Center (see YORKTOWN) available. (Daily; closed Jan 1, Dec 25) **$$$$**

Memorial Church. *Colonial National Historic Pkwy and Jamestown Rd (23185).* Built in 1907 by the National Society of the Colonial Dames of America over foundations of original church. Within are two foundations alleged to be of earlier churches, one from 1617 that housed first assembly.

"New Towne." *1367 Colonial Pkwy (23081).* Area where Jamestown expanded around 1620 may be toured along "Back Streete" and other original streets. Section includes reconstructed foundations indicating sites of Country House, Governor's House, homes of Richard Kemp, builder of one of the first brick houses in America, Henry Hartwell, a founder of College of William and Mary, and Dr. John Pott and William Pierce, who led the "thrusting out" of Governor John Harvey in 1635.

Old Church Tower. Only standing ruin of the 17th-century town. Believed to be part of first brick church (1639). Has 3-foot-thick walls of handmade brick.

Tercentenary Monument. *Located near Jamestown Visitor Center.* Erected by US (1907) to commemorate 300th Jamestown anniversary. Other monuments include Captain John Smith statue (by William Couper), Pocahontas Monument (by William Ordway Partridge), House of Burgesses Monument (listing members of first representative legislative body in America).

Trails. Three- and five-mile auto drives provide access to entire area. Visitor center has 45-minute auto drive and town site tape tours available.

Visitor Center. *Colonial National Historic Pkwy and Jamestown Rd (23185).* Guide leaflets, introductory film, and exhibits. Post office. (Daily; closed Dec 25)

Special Events

First Assembly Day. *Jamestown, the original town site.* Commemorates first legislative assembly in 1619. Late July.

Jamestown Weekend. *Jamestown, the original town site.* Commemorates arrival of first settlers in 1607; special tours and activities. Mid-May.

Keswick

See also Charlottesville

Resort

★ ★ ★ ★ **KESWICK HALL AT MONTICELLO.** *701 Club Dr (22947). Phone 434/979-3440; toll-free 800/ASHLEY-1; fax 434/977-4171. www.keswick.com.* Keswick Hall inspires its guests with its stately Italianate architecture and serenely beautiful setting. The 600-acre estate, set at the foot of the Blue Ridge Mountains, introduces visitors to a rarefied world of luxury and comfort. Individually designed, the guest rooms reflect a modern interpretation of early American style through the use of overstuffed furniture, club chairs, Aubusson carpets, and canopied four-poster beds. Views over the magnificent formal gardens are particularly coveted. Guests choose from three fantastic restaurants or enjoy the privacy of room service. The rolling hills of the Shenandoah Valley invite exploration and the historic halls of Monticello are only minutes away, but this resort also entices its guests with a variety of recreational opportunities. The members-only Keswick Hall, adjacent to the hotel, presents an exclusive opportunity for guests to enjoy its indoor/outdoor pool, tennis courts, fitness facility, spa services, and 18-hole Arnold Palmer golf course. 48 rooms, 3 suites, 1-3 story. S, D $295-$785; weekends (2-day minimum). Check-out noon. Check-in 3 pm. TV; VCR available. Restaurant. Room service 24 hours. Exercise room, sauna. Indoor/outdoor pool; whirlpool. 18-hole golf, greens fee $40-$100. Lawn games. Free airport, train station transportation. Concierge service. Cr cds: A, C, D, DS, JCB, MC, V.

Restaurant

★ ★ ★ **MAIN DINING ROOM.** *701 Club Dr (22947). Phone 434/979-3440; fax 434/977-4171. www.keswick.com.* A feast for the eyes best describes the chef's classically inspired culinary creations. And most appropriate given the lush atmosphere of this formal dining room with its "Trompe d'oeuil" wall murals and expansive garden views. Continental menu. Hours: 6:30-9:30 pm; Sun to 11:30 am-2:30 pm (brunch). Dinner $22-$32. Entertainment Fri-Sun. Elegant dining in Victorian setting; murals, fireplaces, antiques. Reservations required. Valet parking available. Totally nonsmoking. Cr cds: A, MC, V.

Keysville (H-9)

Pop 817 **Elev** 642 ft **Area code** 804 **Zip** 23947

What to See and Do

Twin Lakes State Park. *15 miles NE on US 360, then 1 1/2 miles NW off VA 613. Phone 434/392-3435.* More than 250 acres of state forest; two lakes. Swimming, bathhouse, fishing, boating (rentals, launching, electric motors only); hiking, bicycle, and self-guided trails; picnicking, playground, concession, camping, hook-ups, tent and trailer sites, cabins (Mar-Dec); pavilion. Standard fees.

Motel/Motor Lodge

★ **SHELDON'S MOTEL.** *1450 Four Locust Hwy (23947). Phone 804/736-8434; fax 804/736-9402. www.sheldonshospitality.com.* 40 rooms, 2 story. S $35.95-$50; D $41.95-$50; each additional $6. Crib $6. Pet accepted. TV; cable (premium). Restaurant 6:30 am-10 pm. Check-out noon. Business services available. Some refrigerators; microwaves available. Cr cds: A, DS, MC, V.

Lancaster (G-12)

See also Irvington

Pop 150 **Elev** 89 ft **Area code** 804 **Zip** 22503

The family of Mary Ball Washington, mother of George Washington, were early settlers of this area. Washington's maternal ancestors are buried in the churchyard of St. Mary's Whitechapel Church 5 miles west of Lancaster.

What to See and Do

Lancaster County Courthouse Historic District. Sycamore trees surround this area around the antebellum courthouse (1860). Marble obelisk is one of the first monuments erected to Confederate soldiers (1872).

Mary Ball Washington Museum and Library Complex. *8346 Mary Ball Rd. Phone 804/462-7280.* Contains the Old Clerk's Office (1797), the Old Jail (1819), Lancaster House (1800), the headquarters and main museum building. Also Virginia genealogical research center. (Wed-Sat, Tues by appointment) **$**

St. Mary's Whitechapel Church. *5 miles W on VA 622.* (1740-1741) Church where Mary Ball and her family worshiped; many of the tombstones bear the Ball name.

B&B/Small Inn

★ ★ **INN AT LEVELFIELD.** *10155 Mary Ball Rd (22503). Phone 804/435-6887; fax 804/435-7440. www.innatlevelefields.com.* 6 rooms, 2 story. No room phones. Complimentary full breakfast. Check-out 11 am, check-in 3 pm. Pool. Lawn games. Antebellum landmark homestead (1857) with double-tiered portico and four massive chimneys; 1,000-foot entrance drive. Located on 54 acres with 12 acres of lawn and 42 acres of timberland bounded by stream. Cr cds: A, MC, V. **$**

Leesburg (D-10)

See also Arlington County (Ronald Reagan Washington-National Airport Area) McLean; also see Washington, DC

Founded 1758 **Pop** 28,311 **Elev** 352 ft **Area code** 703

Information Loudoun Tourism Council, 108-D South St SE, 20175; 703/771-2170 or 800/752-6118

Web www.visitloudoun.org

Originally named Georgetown for King George II of England, this town was later renamed Leesburg, probably after Francis Lightfoot Lee, a signer of the Declaration of Independence and a local landowner. Leesburg is located in a scenic area of rolling hills, picturesque rural towns, and Thoroughbred horse farms, where point-to-point racing and steeplechases are popular.

What to See and Do

Ball's Bluff Battlefield. *N via US 15.* One of the smallest national cemeteries in the US marks site of third armed engagement of Civil War. On October 21, 1861, four Union regiments suffered catastrophic losses while surrounded by Confederate forces; the Union commander, a US senator and presidential confidant, was killed here along with half his troops, who were either killed, wounded, captured, or drowned while attempting to recross the Potomac River. Oliver Wendell Holmes, Jr., later to become a US Supreme Court justice, was wounded here.

Loudoun Museum. *16 Loudoun St SW. Phone 703/777-7427.* Century-old restored building contains exhibits and memorabilia of the area; audiovisual presentation "A Special Look at Loudoun." Brochures, information about Loudoun County; walking tours; self-guided tour booklets (fee). (Daily; closed Thanksgiving, Dec 25; also Jan) **$**

Morven Park. *Old Waterford Rd, 1 mile N of Leesburg. Phone 703/777-2414.* Originally the residence of Thomas Swann, early Maryland governor, the estate was enlarged upon by Westmoreland Davis, governor of Virginia from 1918 to 1922. The 1,200-acre park includes a 28-room mansion, boxwood gardens, Winmill Carriage Museum with more than 70 horse-drawn vehicles, Museum of Hounds and Hunting with video presentation and artifacts depicting the history of fox hunting, and Morven Park International Equestrian Center (see SPECIAL EVENTS). (Apr-Nov, Fri-Mon afternoons) **$$$**

Oatlands. *20850 Oatlands Plantation Ln (20175). 6 miles S on US 15. Phone 703/777-3174.* (1803) A 261-acre estate; Classical Revival mansion, built by George Carter, was the center of a 5,000-acre plantation; house was partially remodeled in 1827, which was when the front portico was added. Most of the building materials, including bricks and wood, came from or were made on the estate. Interior furnished with American, English, and French antiques; reflects period between 1897 and 1965 when the house was owned by Mr. and Mrs. William Corcoran Eustis, prominent Washingtonians. Formal garden has some of the finest boxwood in US. Farm fields provide equestrian area for races and horse shows. (Early Apr-Dec, daily; closed Thanksgiving, Dec 24, 25)

Vineyard and Winery Tours. *Phone toll-free 800/752-6118.* For a list of area winery tours contact the Loudoun Tourism Council, 108-D South St SE.

Waterford. *3 miles NW on VA 7, 1/4 mile on VA 9, then 2 miles N on VA 662. Phone 703/771-2170.* Eighteenth-century Quaker village, designated a National Historic Landmark, has been restored as a residential community. An annual homes tour (first full weekend in Oct) has craft demonstrations, exhibits, traditional music. Waterford Foundation has brochures outlining self-guided walking tours. **$**

Special Events

August Court Days. *108 South St SE. Phone 703/771-2170 or 800/752-6118.* Reenactment of the opening of the 18th-century judicial court. Festivities resemble a country fair with craft demonstrations, games, entertainers on the street. Third weekend in Aug.

Christmas at Oatlands. *20850 Oatlands Plantation Ln.* Candlelight tours, 1800s decorations, refreshments. Mid-Nov-Dec, Sat evenings.

Homes and Gardens Tour. Sponsored by Garden Club of Virginia. Late Apr.

Loudoun Hunt Pony Club Horse Trials. *4173 Tutt Ln. Phone 703/777-2890. Held at Morven Park International Equestrian Institute, Morven Park.* Competition in combined training: dressage, cross-country, and stadium jumping. Late Mar.

Sheep Dog Trials. *20850 Oatlands Plantation Ln. Oatlands.* May.

Wine Festival. *17263 Southern Planter Ln. Phone 202/537-0961. Morven Park.* Many wineries participate; includes seminar for home/commercial wine growers; grape-stomping, waiters' race, jousting tournament, music, wine tastings, awards presentations. Mid-July.

Motels/Motor Lodges

★ **DAYS INN.** *721 E Market St (20176). Phone 703/777-6622; toll-free 800/329-7466; fax 703/777-4119. www.daysinn.com.* 81 rooms, 2 story. Mar-Oct: S, D $65; each additional $6; under 12 free; lower rates rest of year. Crib free. Pet accepted, some restrictions; $6. TV; cable (premium). Complimentary continental breakfast. Restaurant nearby. Check-out noon. Coin laundry. Business services available. Cr cds: A, C, D, DS, JCB, MC, V.

🄳 🐾 🛰 SC

★ ★ **HOLIDAY INN.** *1500 E Market St (20176). Phone 703/771-9200; toll-free 800/272-6232; fax 703/771-1575. www.holiday-inn.com.* 126 rooms, 2 story. S, D $99-$159; each additional $10; suites $159; under 16 free. Crib free. Pet accepted. TV; cable (premium). Pool. Restaurant 6:30 am-2 pm, 5-10 pm. Bar 4 pm-midnight. Check-out noon. Coin laundry. Meeting rooms. Business services available. Free airport transportation. Exercise equipment. Colonial mansion (1773). Cr cds: A, C, D, DS, ER, JCB, MC, V.

🄳 🐾 🛰 🏃 🛰 SC

Resort

★ ★ ★ **LANSDOWNE RESORT.** *44050 Woodridge Pkwy (20176). Phone 703/729-8400; toll-free 800/541-4801; fax 703/729-4096. www.lansdowneresort.com.* Comprising a nine-story tower and two five-story wings, this hotel offers guests a full-service experience. Aside from the woodland views from the guest rooms, guests can enjoy the many amenities. 305 units, 9 story. S $149-$209; D $169-$229; suites $275-$700; under 18 free; weekend rates; golf plans. Crib free. Check-out noon. TV; cable (premium). In-room modem link. Balconies. Refrigerators available. Restaurant 6 am-midnight. Bar; entertainment Wed-Sun. Supervised children's activities, ages 3-12. Exercise room, massage, sauna, steam room. Two pools, one indoor; whirlpool, poolside service, lifeguard. 18-hole golf, greens fee $85-$95, pro, putting green, driving range. Lighted tennis. Racquetball. Picnic tables. Lawn games. Bicycle rentals. Airport transportation. Business center. Convention center/facilities. Concierge. Gift shop. Cr cds: A, C, D, DS, MC, V.

🄳 ⬚ 🛉 ⬚ ⇌ 🛉 ⬚ SC 🛉

B&B/Small Inns

★ ★ **LEESBURG COLONIAL INN.** *19 S King St (20175). Phone 703/777-5000; toll-free 800/392-1332; fax 703/777-7000. www.leesburgcolonialinn.com.* 10 rooms, 2 story. S $58-$150; D $68-$150; under 10 free. Pet accepted, some restrictions. Complimentary full breakfast. Check-out noon, check-in 2 pm. TV; cable. Fireplaces. Restaurant. Room service. Health club privileges. Free airport transportation. Historic building (1759) built of same stone as Capitol in DC. Cr cds: A, C, D, DS, MC, V.

🖐 ⬚ SC

★ ★ **LITTLE RIVER INN.** *39307 John Mosby Hwy, Aldie (20105). Phone 703/327-6742; fax 703/327-6645. www.aldie.com.* 9 rooms, 3 share bath, 2 story. Some room phones. Children under 10 years in cottages only. Complimentary full breakfast. Check-out noon, check-in 3 pm. Pool privileges. Built in 1810. In foothills of Bull Run Mountains. Cr cds: A, DS, MC, V. **$**

🄳 ⬚

★ ★ ★ **NORRIS HOUSE INN.** *108 Loudoun St SW (20175). Phone 703/777-1806; toll-free 800/644-1806; fax 703/771-8051. www.norrishouse.com.* Located in the historic district of Leesburg, this rambling colonial house dates from 1760. Filled with antiques and plenty of charm, both the common rooms and guest rooms are comfortable and relaxing. The Stone House Tea Room serves an elegant afternoon tea. 6 rooms, 3 story. Complimentary full breakfast. Check-out noon, check-in 4-8 pm. Most rooms with fireplace. Lawn games. Airport transportation. Built in 1760. Totally nonsmoking. Cr cds: A, C, D, DS, MC, V. **$**

⬚

Restaurants

★ ★ **GREEN TREE.** *15 S King St (20175). Phone 703/777-7246; fax 703/777-7000.* Hours: 11:30 am-10 pm; Sun brunch 11:30 am-4 pm. Reservations accepted. Service bar. Lunch $6.95-$11.95, dinner $14.95-$24.95.

Sun brunch $14.95. Specialties: Robert's Delight (beef dish), Jefferson's Delight (calf's liver soaked in milk). Own baking. Authentic 18th-century recipes. Windows open to street. Fireplaces. Strolling musician Fri-Sat. Cr cds: A, C, D, DS, MC, V.

★ ★ **LAUREL BRIGADE INN.** *20 W Market St (20176). Phone 703/777-1010; fax 703/777-9001. www.laurelbrigade.com.* Hours: 11:30 am-2 pm, 5:30-8:30 pm; Fri, Sat to 9 pm; Sun 8 am-11 am, noon-7 pm. Closed Mon. Reservations accepted; required holidays. Service bar. Lunch $4-$10, dinner $9.50-$20. Complete meals: lunch $11-$14.50, dinner $12.50-$25. Children's menu. Specializes in chicken, beef, seafood. Outdoor seating. Oldest section dates from 1759; colonial décor, stone walls, fireplace. Family-owned. Cr cds: A, DS, MC, V.

SC

★ ★ **LEESBURG COLONIAL INN.** *19 S King St (20175). Phone 703/777-5000; fax 703/777-9001. www. leesburgcolonialinn.com.* Continental menu. Specializes in beef, seafood. Lunch, dinner. Bar. Children's menu. Reservations accepted. Outdoor seating. Cr cds: A, C, D, DS, MC, V. **$$**

🄳

Lexington (G-7)

See also Clifton Forge, Natural Bridge

Founded 1777 **Pop** 6,867 **Elev** 1,060 ft **Area code** 540 **Zip** 24450

Information Visitors Bureau, 106 E Washington St; 540/463-3777

Web www.lexingtonvirginia.com

Lexington was home to two of the greatest Confederate heroes: Robert E. Lee and Thomas J. "Stonewall" Jackson. Both are buried here. Sam Houston, Cyrus McCormick, and James Gibbs (inventor of the sewing machine) were born nearby.

Set in rolling country between the Blue Ridge and Allegheny mountains, this town is the seat of Rockbridge County. Lexington is known for attractive homes, trim farms, fine old mansions, and two of the leading educational institutions in the Commonwealth: Washington and Lee University and Virginia Military Institute.

What to See and Do

Goshen Pass. *19 miles NW on VA 39.* Scenic mountain gorge formed by Maury River. Memorial to Matthew Fontaine Maury is here.

Lexington Carriage Company. *106 E Washington St. Phone 540/463-5647.* Approximately 45-minute narrated horse-drawn carriage tours of historic Lexington. Groups of ten or more by appointment only. (Apr-Oct, daily, weather permitting) Tours depart across street from Visitor Center. **$$$$**

Stonewall Jackson House. *8 E Washington St. Phone 540/463-2552.* Only home owned by Confederate General Stonewall Jackson, restored to its appearance of 1859-1861. Many of the furnishings were once owned by Jackson. Interpretive slide presentation and guided tours (1/2 hour). Restored gardens; shop. (Daily; closed holidays) **$$**

Stonewall Jackson Memorial Cemetery. *White and Main Sts.* General Jackson and more than 100 other Confederate soldiers are buried here.

Virginia Horse Center. *487 Maury River Rd. VA 11 N to VA 39 W. Phone 540/463-2194.* For schedule of events, contact PO Box 1051. Sprawling across nearly 400 acres, the Center provides a versatile site for numerous horse-related functions year-round: shows, clinics, auctions, festivals. Fees vary.

Virginia Military Institute. *On US 11. Phone 540/464-7207.* (1839) 1,300 cadets. State military, engineering, sciences, and arts college. Coeducational since 1997. Stonewall Jackson taught here, as did Matthew Fontaine Maury, famed naval explorer and inventor. George Catlett Marshall, a general of the army and author of the Marshall Plan, was a graduate. Mementos of these men on display in VMI museum (daily; closed Jan 1, Thanksgiving, Dec 24-31). Dress parade (most Fri afternoons, weather permitting). **FREE** Located on the S end of the parade ground is

> **George C. Marshall Museum.** *VMI Parade Ground. Faces parade ground. Phone 540/463-7103.* (1964) Displays on life and career of the illustrious military figure and statesman (1880-1959); WWI electric map and recorded narration of WWII; Marshall Plan; gold medallion awarded with his Nobel Prize for Peace (1953). (Daily; closed Jan 1, Thanksgiving, Dec 25) **$$**

Washington and Lee University. *W Washington St. Phone 540/463-8400.* (1749) 2,137 students. Liberal arts university situated on an attractive campus with white colonnaded buildings; also includes Washington and Lee Law School. Founded as Augusta Academy in 1749; became Liberty Hall in 1776; name changed to Washington Academy in 1798 after receiving 200 shares of James River Canal Company stock from George Washington, and then to Washington College. General Robert E. Lee served as president from 1865-1870; soon after Lee's death in 1870 it became Washington and Lee University. On campus is

Lee Chapel. Robert E. Lee is entombed here. Also houses Lee family crypt and museum, marble "recumbent statue" of Lee, portions of art collection of Washington and Lee families. Lee's office remains as he left it. (Daily; closed holidays) **FREE**

Special Events

Garden Week in Historic Lexington. *106 E Washington St. Phone 540/463-3777.* Tour of homes and gardens in the Lexington, Rockbridge County area. Late Apr.

Holiday in Lexington. *Phone 540/463-3777.* Parade, plays, children's events. Early Dec.

Lime Kiln Arts Theater. *14 S Randolph St. Phone 540/463-3074.* Professional theatrical productions and concerts in outdoor theater. Memorial Day-Labor Day.

Motels/Motor Lodges

★ ★ **BEST WESTERN INN AT HUNT RIDGE.** *Willow Springs Rd (24450). Phone 540/464-1500; toll-free 800/464-1501. www.bestwestern.com.* 100 rooms, 3 story, 10 suites. Apr-Oct: S $69.95-$87.95; D $79.95-$92.95; each additional $8, suites $92.95; under 12 free; higher rates special events; lower rates rest of year. Crib free. Pet accepted, some restrictions. TV; cable (premium). Indoor/outdoor pool. Restaurant 7 am-10 pm. Room service. Bar to midnight. Check-out 11 am. Coin laundry. Meeting rooms. Business services available. In-room modem link. Health club privileges. Refrigerator, microwave in suites. Cr cds: A, C, D, DS, MC, V.

D 🐾 🏊 ⛳

★ **COMFORT INN VIRGINIA HORSE CENTER.** *US 11 and I-64 (24450). Phone 540/463-7311; toll-free 800/628-1956; fax 540/463-4590. www.comfortinn.com.* 80 rooms, 4 story. Apr-Nov: S $64.95-$76.95; D $64.95-$85; each additional $5; under 18 free; lower rates rest of year. Crib free. Pet accepted. TV; cable (premium). Indoor pool. Complimentary continental breakfast. Restaurant adjacent 6 am-11 pm. Check-out 11 am. Coin laundry. Business services available. Sundries. Cr cds: A, C, D, DS, ER, JCB, MC, V.

D 🐾 🏊 ⛳ **SC**

★ **DAYS INN.** *325 W Midland Trail (24450). Phone 540/463-2143; fax 540/463-2143. www.daysinn.com.* 53 rooms, 10 kitchen units. S $47.95-$57.95; D $55.95-$65.95; each additional $5. Crib free. Pet accepted, some restrictions. Check-out 11 am. TV; cable (premium). Some bathroom phones, refrigerators. Picnic tables. Business services. View of mountains. Cr cds: A, C, D, DS, MC, V.

D 🐾 ⛳ ⚡ ⛳

★ **HOLIDAY INN EXPRESS.** *US 11 and I-64 (24450). Phone 540/463-7351; toll-free 800/465-4329; fax 540/463-7351. www.holiday-inn.com.* 72 rooms, 2 story. S $75; D $85; each additional $10; under 18 free. Crib free. Pet accepted. TV; cable (premium). Complimentary continental breakfast. Check-out 11 am. Business services available. In-room modem link. View of mountains. Cr cds: A, C, D, DS, ER, JCB, MC, V.

D 🐾 🛰 SC

★ **HOWARD JOHNSON.** *2836 N Lee Hwy (24450). Phone 540/463-9181; toll-free 800/654-2000; fax 540/464-3448. www.hojo.com.* 100 rooms, 5 story. S $50-$65; D $55-$75; each additional $7; under 18 free; higher rates special events. Crib free. Pet accepted. TV; cable (premium). Pool. Restaurant 6 am-8 pm. Check-out noon. Coin laundry. Meeting room. Business services available. Gift shop. Balconies. Private patios. On hill; panoramic view of mountains. Cr cds: A, C, D, DS, ER, JCB, MC, V.

D 🐾 🛰 🛰 SC

★ **RAMADA INN.** *US 11 and I-64 (24450). Phone 540/463-7311; fax 540/464-3639. www.ramada.com.* 80 rooms, 4 story. May-Oct: S $60; D $70; each additional $6; under 19 free; weekly, weekend rates; higher rates special events; lower rates rest of year. Crib free. Pet accepted. TV; cable (premium). Indoor pool. Restaurant 6 am-2 pm, 5-10 pm. Room service. Bar 5-10 pm. Check-out noon. Meeting rooms. Business services available. Sundries. Cr cds: A, D, DS, MC, V.

D 🐾 🛰 🛰

★ **TRAVELODGE.** *2809 N Lee Hwy (24450). Phone 540/463-9131; toll-free 800/521-9131; fax 540/463-7448. www.travelodge.com.* 150 rooms, 3 story. May-Oct: S, D $50-$85; each additional $5; under 18 free; lower rates rest of year. Crib free. TV; cable (premium). Pool. Restaurant adjacent 6 am-9 pm. Check-out 11 am. Meeting rooms. Microwaves available. Cr cds: A, C, D, DS, MC, V.

D 🛰 🛰 SC

B&B/Small Inns

★ ★ **ALEXANDER WITHROW INN.** *3 W Washington St (24450). Phone 540/463-2044; fax 540/463-7262. www.lexingtonhistoricinns.com.* 4 story. S $85-$130; D $100-$145; each additional $15; family rates. Complimentary continental breakfast. Check-out noon, check-in 2 pm. TV. Pool privileges. Built in 1809. Cr cds: DS, MC, V.

D 🛰 🛰

★ ★ ★ **HUMMINGBIRD INN.** *30 Wood Ln, Goshen (24439). Phone 540/997-9065; toll-free 800/397-3214; fax 540/997-0289. www.hummingbirdinn.com.* Located on the edge of Shenandoah Valley, near Goshen Pass, this historic bed and breakfast is made for relaxing. Sit on the wraparound veranda, sleep late in one of the individually decorated rooms, or unwind with a day of trout fishing nearby. 4 rooms, 2 story. No room phones. Pet accepted; fee. Children over 12 years only. Complimentary full breakfast. Check-out 11 am, check-in 3 pm. TV in common room. Some in-room whirlpools, fireplaces. Lawn games. Victorian Carpenter Gothic villa built in 1780. On river. Totally nonsmoking. Cr cds: A, DS, MC, V. **$**

🐾 ⬆ 🛰 SC

★ ★ ★ **INN AT UNION RUN.** *325 Union Run (24450). Phone 540/463-9715; toll-free 800/528-6466; fax 540/463-3526. www.unionrun.com.* This Federal-style farmhouse was built in 1883, in the heart of the Shenandoah Valley, just 3 miles from historic Lexington, Virginia. In addition to the guest rooms in the main building and carriage house (built in 1992), the inn features a fine dining room. 8 rooms, 2 story. Children over 10 years only. Complimentary full breakfast. Check-out 11 am, check-in 3 pm. TV in common room; cable (premium). Restaurant. Room service. Lawn games. View of mountains. Cr cds: A, MC, V. **$**

D ⬆ 🛰 SC

★ ★ **MAPLE HALL COUNTRY INN.** *3111 N Lee Hwy (24450). Phone 540/463-6693; fax 540/463-2114. www.lexingtonhistoricinns.com.* 21 rooms, 3 story. Complimentary continental breakfast. Check-out noon, check-in 2 pm. TV; cable; VCR available. In-room modem link. Dining room 5:30-9 pm. Pool. Tennis. Lawn games. Plantation house built 1850; period furnishings. Cr cds: DS, MC, V. **$**

D ⬆ 🏌 🛰 🛰

★ ★ ★ **STEELES TAVERN MANOR.** *US 11, Steeles Tavern (24476). Phone 540/377-6444; toll-free 800/743-8666; fax 540/377-5937. www.steelestavern.com.* Built in 1916, this Georgian manor home offers guests a relaxing vacation spot with afternoon tea and sherry, nearby trout fishing, and beautiful green landscaping. Guest rooms feature refrigerators with complimentary soda, double Jacuzzis, and snack baskets. 5 rooms, 2 story. No room phones. Children over 13 years only. Complimentary full breakfast; afternoon refreshments. Check-out 11 am, check-in 3 pm. TV; VCR (movies). In-room whirlpools; some fireplaces. On 55 acres. Panoramic view. Cr cds: DS, MC, V. **$$**

⬆ 🛰 SC

Restaurants

★ **REDWOOD.** *898 N Lee Hwy (24450). Phone 540/463-2168.* Hours: 7 am-10 pm. Closed Dec 25. Breakfast $2.50-$4.50, lunch $3-$6, dinner $4.50-$9. Children's menu. Specializes in seafood, steak, chicken. Family restaurant with home-style cooking; casual atmosphere. Cr cds: V.

D

★ ★ ★ **WILLSON-WALKER HOUSE.** *30 N Main St (24450). Phone 540/463-3020; fax 540/464-1635. www.willsonwalker.com.* The service is as gracious as one might expect at this historic antebellum mansion. Dress is casual but the food is not. The contemporary southern-style menu includes many elegant variations of American fare. Closed Sun, Mon; Jan 1, Thanksgiving, Dec 24, 25; also Sat lunch Dec-Mar. Lunch, dinner, brunch. Children's menu. In restored Greek Revival house (1820) located in downtown historic district; period antiques. Outdoor seating. Cr cds: A, DS, MC, V. **$$**

D

Luray (E-9)

See also Basye, Front Royal, Harrisonburg, New Market

Founded 1812 **Pop** 4,871 **Elev** 789 ft **Area code** 540 **Zip** 22835

Information Page County Chamber of Commerce, 46 E Main St; 540/743-3915

Web www.luraypage.com

The name of this town is of French origin; its fame comes from the caverns discovered here in 1878. Situated at the junction of US 211 and US 340, Luray is 9 miles away from, and within sight of, Shenandoah National Park (see) and Skyline Drive. Headquarters of the park are here. There are three developed recreation areas north and west of town in Washington and Jefferson national forests.

What to See and Do

⭐ **Luray Caverns.** *970 US 211/340 W. Phone 540/743-6551.* One of the largest caverns in the east. Huge underground rooms (one is 300 feet wide, 500 feet long, with a 140-foot ceiling) connected by natural corridors and paved walkways are encrusted with colorful rock formations, some delicate as lace, others massive. In one chamber is the world's only "stalacpipe" organ, which produces music of symphonic quality from stone formations. Indirect lighting permits taking of color photos within caverns. Temperature is 54°F. One-hour guided tours start about every 20 minutes. (Daily)**$$$$** Fee includes

Car and Carriage Museum. Exhibits include 140 restored antique cars, carriages, and coaches featuring history of transportation from 1625.

Luray Singing Tower. *970 US 211/340 W. Phone 540/743-6551.* Houses 47-bell carillon; largest bell weighs 7,640 lbs. Features 45-minute recitals by celebrated carillonneur. (June-Aug, Tues, Thurs, and Sun evenings; Mar-May and Sept-Oct, weekend afternoons) In park adjacent to caverns. **FREE**

Luray Zoo. *1087 US 211 W. 1/2 mile W on US 211. Phone 540/743-4113.* Features large reptile collection, exotic animals, and tropical birds; petting zoo; live animal shows; life-sized dinosaur reproductions. Gift shop. (Mid-Apr-Oct, daily) **$$$**

Massanutten One-room School. *In Lawn Park. Contact Chamber of Commerce.* Restored and furnished as it was in the 1800s. Period displays and pictures. (By appointment) **FREE**

Shenandoah National Park. (see) *9 miles E on US 211, then S on Skyline Dr.*

Special Events

Mayfest Street Festival. *46 E Main St.* Entertainment, crafts. Third Sat in May.

Page County Heritage Festival. Arts and crafts exhibits. Self-guided tour of churches and old homes. Columbus Day weekend.

Motels/Motor Lodges

★ ★ **BEST WESTERN INTOWN OF LURAY.** *410 W Main St (22835). Phone 540/743-6511; fax 540/743-2917; res 800/526-0942. www.bestwestern.com.* 40 rooms, 2 story. Apr-Nov: S, D $43-$94.50; each additional $5; under 18 free; lower rates rest of year. Crib $4. Pet accepted; $20/day. TV; cable (premium). Pool. Playground. Restaurant 6 am-2 pm, 5-9 pm. Room service. Check-out noon. Business services available. Lawn games. Cr cds: A, C, D, DS, MC, V.

D ⛾ ⊠ SC

★ ★ **BIG MEADOWS LODGE.** *Skyline Dr (22835). Phone 540/999-2221; fax 540/999-2011; res 800/999-4714. www.visitshenandoah.com.* 92 units: 62 motel rooms, 20 lodge rooms, 10 cabins. No A/C. Mid-May-Nov 1: lodge S, D $65-$80; motel S, D $85-$95; cabins $70-$80; suites $130-$140; each additional $5; under 16 free. Closed rest of year. Crib free. TV in some rooms. Playground. Restaurant 7:30-10 am, noon-2 pm, 5:30-8:30 pm. Box lunches. Bar 4-11 pm; entertainment. Check-out noon. Business services available. Gift shop. Private patios, balconies. Panoramic view of Shenandoah Valley. Cr cds: A, DS, MC, V.

D ⛾ ⛾ ⊠

★ ★ ★ **CABINS AT BROOKSIDE.** *2978 US 211 E (22835). Phone 540/743-5698; toll-free 800/299-2655; fax 540/743-1326. www.brooksidecabins.com.* The privacy and seclusion of your own log cabin is the draw to this vacation development located 4 1/2 miles from the entrance to Skyline Drive. The cabins have a plush country décor, front porches, and are set into the woods. A cozy restaurant on the property serves homestyle food. 9 cottages. No room phones. Feb-Nov: S $75-$145; D $135-$150; each additional $5-$10; kitchen suite $150-$185; lower rates rest of year. Crib available. Restaurant adjacent 7 am-8:30 pm. Check-out noon. Sundries. Some fireplaces, in-room whirlpools; refrigerators available. Cr cds: A, C, D, DS, MC, V.

D

★ **DAYS INN.** *138 Whispering Hill Rd (22835). Phone 540/743-4521; toll-free 800/329-7466; fax 540/743-6863. www.daysinn.com.* 101 rooms, 2 story. Apr-Oct: S, D $69-$130; each additional $5; under 16 free; lower rates rest of year. Crib free. TV; cable, VCR available (movies). Pool. Restaurant 6:30 am-2 pm, 5-9 pm. Bar 5 pm-1 am; entertainment weekends. Check-out noon. Meeting rooms. Business services available. Health club privileges. Miniature golf. Game room. Some in-room whirlpools; refrigerators, microwaves available. Picnic tables. Cr cds: A, C, D, DS, JCB, MC, V.

D ⊷ ⚡ ⊠ SC

★ **LURAY CAVERNS MOTEL.** *832 W Main (22835). Phone 540/743-4531; fax 540/743-7088. www.luraycaverns. com.* 64 rooms. S, D $57-$74; each additional $7; under 16 free; TV; cable. Pools. Restaurants nearby. Business services available. Views of Blue Ridge Mountains. Cr cds: A, DS, MC, V.

D ⊷

★ ★ **MIMSLYN INN.** *401 W Main St (22835). Phone 540/743-5105; toll-free 800/296-5105; fax 540/743-2632. www.svta.org/mimslyn.* 49 rooms, 2 with shower only, 11 suites, 3 story. Mid-June-Oct: S $94; D $104; suites $144-$164; under 18 free; lower rates rest of year. Crib free. Pet accepted; $10 deposit. TV; cable. Restaurant 7-10 am, 11:30 am-2 pm, 5-9 pm. Check-out noon. Business services available. Gift shop. Health club privileges. Art gallery, antique shop. Built 1930 in style of antebellum mansion. Cr cds: A, DS, MC, V.

🔊 ⊠ SC

★ ★ **SKYLAND LODGE.** *Skyline Dr (22835). Phone 540/999-2211; toll-free 800/999-4714; fax 540/999-2231.* 177 rooms. No A/C. Apr-Nov: S, D $48-$105; each additional $5; suites $112-$160; under 16 free. Closed rest of year. Crib free. TV available. Playground. Restaurant 7:30 am-8:30 pm. Box lunches available. Bar 3-11:30 pm. Check-out noon. Meeting rooms. Business services available. Sundries. Gift shop. Private patios. Balconies. Cr cds: A, DS, MC, V.

D ⚓ ⚡ ⊠ ⊠

B&B/Small Inns

★ ★ ★ **JORDAN HOLLOW FARM INN.** *326 Hawksbill Park Rd, Stanley (22851). Phone 540/778-2285; toll-free 888/418-7000; fax 540/778-1759. www. jordanhollow.com.* Find serene relaxation at this restored, colonial horse farm. Some guest rooms feature beautiful vista views of the Blue Ridge Mountains. The Shenandoah Valley location offers many outdoor recreations, not the least of which is simply taking in the scenery. 20 rooms in 2 buildings, 1-2 story. S $85-$130; D $110-$154; each additional $25; under 6 free. Crib free. TV in some rooms; cable. Complimentary full breakfast. Dining room 8:30-10 am, 5:30-9:30 pm. Bar. Check-out noon, check-in 3 pm. Business services available. Some in-room whirlpools. Converted 45-acre horse farm; sun deck with view of Blue Ridge Mountains. Totally nonsmoking. Cr cds: C, D, DS, MC, V.

⚡ ⊠

★ ★ ★ **MAYNEVIEW BED AND BREAKFAST.** *439 Mechanic St (22835). Phone 540/743-7921; fax 540/743-1191. www.mayneview.com.* This lovely inn is nestled in the heart of the Shenandoah Valley and has a wonderful wraparound porch. Visitors can take day trips to the famous Luray Caverns, the New Market Battlefield, and several antique shops. 5 rooms, 3 story. No elevator, room phones. Complimentary full breakfast; afternoon refreshments. Check-out noon, check-in 3 pm. Victorian building (1865). Cr cds: A, DS, MC, V. **$$**

⊠ SC

★ ★ ★ **WOODRUFF HOUSE BED AND BREAKFAST.** *330 Mechanic St (22835). Phone 540/743-1494; fax 540/743-1722. www.bbonline.com/va/woodruff.* Three 1800s Victorian houses make up this bed and breakfast located near many local attractions including the Shenandoah National Park, Luray Caverns, and the George Washington National Forest. 5 rooms, 3 story. No room phones. Children over 10 years only. Check-out noon, check-in 3 pm. Health club privileges. Victorian house (1830, 1890); antiques. Totally nonsmoking. Cr cds: DS, MC, V. **$$$**

⊠

Restaurants

★ **BROOKSIDE.** *2978 US 211 E (22835). Phone 540/743-5698; fax 540/743-1326. www.brooksidecabins.com.* Specializes in steak, spaghetti, seafood. Steak menu. Hours: 7 am-8:30 pm; Fri, Sat to 9 pm. Closed mid-Dec-mid-Jan. Buffet breakfast $6.95, dinner $7.50-$14.95. Salad bar. Children's menu. Reservations accepted. Cr cds: A, D, DS, MC, V.

D

★ ★ **PARKHURST.** *2547 US 211 W (22835). Phone 540/743-6009; fax 540/743-7009. www.shentel.net/rainbow hill.* Seafood, steak menu. Hours: 1 am-10 pm; winter hours vary. Closed some major holidays. Lunch $4.75-$8.50, dinner $5.95-$17.95. Bar. Cr cds: A, C, D, DS, MC, V.

D

Lynchburg (G-8)

Settled 1757 **Pop** 65,269 **Elev** 795 ft **Area code** 804

Information Visitors Information Center, 12th and Church sts, 24504; 804/847-1811 or 800/732-5821

Lynchburg is perched on hills overlooking the James River, which was for many years its means of growth. Today, the city is home to more than 3,000 businesses and diversified industries. Educational institutions located here include Lynchburg College, Randolph-Macon Women's College, and Liberty University.

One of the first buildings in the town was a ferry house built by John Lynch. The same enterprising young man later built a tobacco warehouse, probably the first one in the country. During the Civil War, Lynchburg was important as a supply base and hospital town. In June 1864, General Jubal A. Early successfully defended the town from an attack by Union forces. More than 2,200 Confederates are buried in the Confederate Cemetery, located in the Old City Cemetery.

What to See and Do

Anne Spencer House. *1313 Pierce St. Phone 434/845-1313.* House of noted poet, only black woman and only Virginian to be included in *Norton Anthology of Modern American and British Poetry*. On grounds is Spencer's writing cottage "Edan Kraal." Many dignitaries have visited here. Museum with artifacts, memorabilia, period antique furnishings; formal garden. (House by appointment; gardens daily) **$$**

Appomattox Court House National Historical Park. (see) *21 miles E on US 460.*

Blackwater Creek Natural Area. *In center of city.* Ruskin Freer Nature Preserve (115 acres) includes trails with plants; athletic area; bikeway winds past wildflower area and historical sites, ending downtown; Creekside Trunk Trail, natural grass trail with typical Piedmont species of plants, moist ravines, north-facing rocky bluffs. (Daily) **FREE**

Fort Early. *Memorial and Fort aves.* Defense earthwork for Lynchburg's closest battle during the Civil War. Confederates under General Jubal A. Early turned back forces under General David Hunter in 1864. (Daily) **FREE**

Jefferson's Poplar Forest. *Poplar Forest Dr and Fox Hall Rd. SW of Lynchburg on US 221, then left on VA 811 and left again on VA 661 in Bedford County. Phone 434/525-1806.* Designed and built by Thomas Jefferson as a personal retreat; begun in 1806. Restoration in progress; house unfurnished. (Apr-Nov, daily; closed Thanksgiving) **$$$**

Old Court House Museum. *901 Court St. Phone 434/847-1459.* (1855) Restored to original Greek Revival appearance. Three galleries have exhibits on early history of the area, highlighting Quaker settlement and role of tobacco; restored mid-19th-century courtroom. (Daily; closed holidays) **$**

Pest House Medical Museum. *Old City Cemetery, 4th and Taylor sts. Phone 434/847-1465.* The 1840s white frame medical office of Quaker physician Dr. John Jay Terrell has been joined with Pest House quarantine hospital to typify the standard of medicine during the late 1800s. Original medical instruments include operating table, hypodermic needle, clinical thermometer, and chloroform mask. Period furnishings on one side duplicate Dr. Terrell's office during the Civil War; other side represents quarantine hospital for Confederate soldiers in which Dr. Terrell volunteered to assume responsibility. Window displays with audio description. Tours (by appointment). (Daily) **FREE**

Point of Honor. *112 Cabell St. Phone 804/847-1459.* (1815) Restored mansion on Daniel's Hill above the James River, built by Dr. George Cabell, Sr., physician to Patrick Henry. Federalist style with octagon bay facade and finely crafted interior woodwork; period furnishings; gardens and grounds being restored. (Daily; closed holidays) **$$**

Randolph-Macon Women's College. *2500 Rivermont Ave. Phone 434/947-8000.* (1891) 748 women. A 100-acre campus on historic Rivermont Ave near James River. First college for women in the South granted a Phi Beta Kappa chapter. Campus is interesting mixture of architecture including Vincent Kling design for Houston Chapel. Tours (by appointment). On campus is

Maier Museum of Art. *2500 Rivermont Ave (24503).* *Phone 804/947-8136.* Collection is representative of 19th- and 20th-century American painting. Artists include Thomas Hart Benton, Edward Hicks, Winslow Homer, James McNeil Whistler, Mary Cassatt, and Georgia O'Keeffe. Changing exhibits. (Academic year, Tues-Sun afternoons) **FREE**

Riverside Park. Rivermont Ave. (Daily) **FREE** In park is

Packet Boat *Marshall.* Mounted on a stone base, this boat carried the remains of Stonewall Jackson home to Lexington; for many years packets were the principal mode of transportation along the James River and Kanawha Canal.

South River Meeting House. *5810 Fort Ave. Phone 804/239-2548.* Completed in 1798, the stone building remained the site of Quaker worship and activity until the 1840s. John Lynch, founder of Lynchburg, and other early leaders of community are buried in adjacent historic cemetery. (Daily; closed holidays) **FREE**

Motels/Motor Lodges

★ **BEST WESTERN OF LYNCHBURG.** *2815 Candlers Mountain Rd (24502). Phone 804/237-2986; toll-free 800/528-1234. www.bestwestern.com.* 87 rooms, 2-3 story. S $59; D $69; each additional $8; under 12 free; higher rates: homecoming, graduation. Complimentary continental breakfast. Check-out 11 am. TV; cable (premium). In-room modem link. Restaurant adjacent 11 am-midnight. Room service. Health club privileges. Pool. Cr cds: A, C, D, DS, MC, V.

D ⊶ ⇘ SC

★ **COMFORT INN.** *3125 Albert Lankford Dr (24501). Phone 804/847-9041; fax 804/847-8513. www.comfortinn. com.* 120 rooms, 5 story. S $71-$85; D $76-$90; each additional $5; suites $151-$170; under 18 free; higher rates: homecoming, graduation. Crib free. Pet accepted. TV; cable (premium), VCR available. Complimentary full breakfast. Restaurant nearby. Check-out noon. Meeting rooms. Business services available. Free airport, train station transportation. Health club privileges. Pool. Some refrigerators, microwaves. Balconies. Picnic tables, grills. Cr cds: A, C, D, DS, JCB, MC, V.

D ◀ ⊶ ⇘

★ **DAYS INN.** *3320 Candlers Mountain Rd (24502). Phone 804/847-8655; toll-free 800/846-3297; fax 804/846-3297. www.daysinn.com.* 131 rooms, 5 story. S, D $64-$74; each additional $8; under 17 free. Crib free. TV; cable (premium). Pool. Playground. Restaurant 6 am-2 pm, 5 pm-midnight. Room service. Check-out noon. Meeting

rooms. Business services available. In-room modem link. Valet service. Sundries. Free airport, train station, bus depot transportation. Health club privileges. Microwaves available. Private patios, balconies. Cr cds: A, C, D, DS, JCB, MC, V.

D ⊶ ⇘ SC

★ **ECONO LODGE.** *2400 Stadium Dr (24501). Phone 804/847-1045; fax 804/846-0086. www.econolodge.com.* 48 rooms, 2 story. S $39.95-$55; D $55-$80. Crib free. Check-out 11 am. TV; cable (premium). Continental breakfast. Restaurant nearby. Business services. Cr cds: A, C, D, DS, JCB, MC, V.

D ⇘

★ **HAMPTON INN.** *5604 Seminole Ave (24502). Phone 804/237-2704; fax 804/239-9183. www.hamptoninn.com.* 65 rooms, 2 story. S $61-$67; D $71-$77; under 18 free; higher rates Randolph-Macon graduation. Crib available. Complimentary continental breakfast. Check-out noon. TV; cable (premium). Restaurant adjacent 10:30 am-midnight. Health club privileges. Business services. Sundries. Cr cds: A, C, D, DS, MC, V.

D ⇘

★ ★ **HOLIDAY INN SELECT.** *601 Main St (24505). Phone 804/528-2500; fax 804/528-0062. www.holiday-inn.com.* 243 units, 8 story. S, D $72; each additional $10; suites $85-$110; under 17 free. Crib free. Pet accepted. Check-out noon. TV; cable (premium). In-room modem link. Some bathroom phones, refrigerators; microwaves available. Restaurant 6:30 am-10 pm. Bar 3 pm-1 am. Exercise equipment. Pool; poolside service. Free airport transportation. Meeting rooms. Business services. Cr cds: A, C, D, DS, JCB, MC, V.

D ◀ ⊶ 🛉 ⇘

★ **HOLIDAY INN EXPRESS.** *5600 Seminole Ave (24501). Phone 804/237-7771; fax 804/239-0659. www.holiday-inn.com.* 104 rooms, 3 story. S $49.99-$55.99; D $54.99-$59.99; each additional $5; under 16 free. Crib free. Complimentary continental breakfast. Check-out noon. TV; cable (premium). Microwaves available. Valet services. Restaurant nearby. Health club privileges. Pool. Meeting room. Cr cds: A, C, D, DS, JCB, MC, V.

🔧 ⊶ ⇘

★ **HOWARD JOHNSON.** *US 29 N, Madison Heights (24572). Phone 804/845-7041; fax 804/845-4718. www.hojo.com.* 70 rooms, 2 story. S, D $46-$77; each additional $7; under 18 free. Crib free. Check-out noon. TV; cable (premium). Private patios, balconies. Microwaves available. Valet services. Coin laundry. Restaurant 6 am-

10 pm. Pool; wading pool. Free airport transportation. Business services. Sundries. Cr cds: A, C, D, DS, MC, V.

Hotel

★ ★ ★ **HILTON LYNCHBURG.** *2900 Candlers Mountain Rd (24502). Phone 804/237-6333; fax 804/ 237-4277; res 800/221-4982. www.hilton.com.* Located at the foot of the Blue Ridge Mountains, this hotel sits on a unique 10-acre landscaped and wooded spread. The Natural Bridge, one of the seven natural wonders of the world, is easily accessible. 168 rooms, 5 story. S $85-$120; D $105-$140; each additional $20; suites $186; family rates. Crib free. Check-out 11 am. TV; cable (premium). Microwaves available; bathroom phone in suites. Valet services. Restaurant 6:30 am-2 pm, 5:30-10 pm. Bar 11-1:30 am; entertainment. Room service. Exercise equipment, sauna. Indoor pool, whirlpool. Free airport transportation. Meeting rooms. Business center. Sundries. Gift shop. Cr cds: A, C, D, DS, ER, JCB, MC, V.

B&B/Small Inn

★ ★ ★ **1880'S MADISON HOUSE.** *413 Madison St (24504). Phone 434/528-1503. www.madisonhousebb.com.* This 1880s restored Victorian bed and breakfast is located in the Garland Hill historic district. An ornate, cast iron front porch welcomes guests, and the house features antiques and a library full of books including many on the Civil War. Guests can relax in the garden with a good book and refreshments. 4 rooms, 2 story. Complimentary full breakfast. Check-out 11 am, check-in 3-6 pm. TV; cable (premium). Some fireplaces. Free airport, train station transportation. Victorian mansion (1880); antiques. Totally nonsmoking. Cr cds: A, MC, V. **$**

Restaurants

★ ★ **CROWN STERLING.** *6120 Fort Ave (24502). Phone 434/239-7744.* Closed Sun; major holidays. Dinner. Cr cds: A, D, DS, MC, V. **$$**

★ ★ ★ **SACHIKO'S PORTERHOUSE.** *126 Old Graves Mill Rd (24502). Phone 804/237-5655; fax 804/237-2934.* This restaurant has been in business for 25 years. American menu. Hours: 5:30-10 pm. Closed Sun; some holidays. Dinner $10.95-$25. Bar. Cr cds: A, DS, MC, V.

★ **T. C. TROTTER'S.** *2496 Rivermont Ave (24503). Phone 434/846-3545.* Closed Mon; Thanksgiving, Dec 25. Lunch, dinner. Bar. Children's menu. Outdoor seating. Cr cds: A, D, DS, MC, V. **$**

Madison (E-9)

See also Charlottesville

Restaurant

★ ★ **BERTINE'S NORTH CARIBBEAN.** *206 S Main St (22727). Phone 540/948-3463.* Caribbean menu. Specialties: jerk chicken, steak on a hot rock, blackened swordfish. Hours: 6-9 pm. Closed Tues-Thurs; also Easter, Dec 25. Dinner $9.85-$21. Beer, wine. Reservations accepted. Outdoor seating. Caribbean décor. Cr cds: DS, MC, V.

Manassas (E-10)

See also Arlington County (Ronald Reagan Washington-National Airport Area) Fairfax, Falls Church, Triangle; also see Washington, DC

Pop 35,135 **Elev** 321 ft **Area code** 703

Information Prince William County/Manassas Conference & Visitors Bureau, 14420 Bristow Rd, 20112; 703/792-4254 or 800/432-1792

Web www.visitpwc.com

Though the Native Americans who had lived in this area for thousands of years were driven out under a treaty in 1722, settlement remained concentrated along the Potomac River until the coming of the railroad in 1858. The Manassas rail junction was vital to the South, and many troops were stationed along this line of communication. Control of this junction led to two major battles nearby (see MANASSAS (BULL RUN) NATIONAL BATTLEFIELD PARK).

What to See and Do

The Manassas Museum. *9101 Prince William St. Phone 703/368-1873.* Museum features collections dealing with Northern Virginia Piedmont history from prehistoric to modern times, with special emphasis on Civil War. (Tues-Sun; closed holidays) **$$**

Special Event

Prince William County Fair. *9101 Prince William St. Phone 703/368-0173.* Carnival, entertainment, tractor pull, exhibits, contests. Mid-Aug.

Motels/Motor Lodges

★ ★ **BEST WESTERN BATTLEFIELD INN.** *10820 Balls Ford Rd (20109). Phone 703/361-8000; toll-free 800/528-1234; fax 703/361-8000. www.bestwestern.com.* 121 rooms, 2 story. S $54-$89; D $64-$89; each additional

$10; under 18 free. Crib free. Pet accepted; $10/day. TV; cable (premium). Pool. Complimentary continental breakfast. Restaurant 5-10 pm; closed Sun. Room service. Bar to midnight, Fri, Sat to 2 am; entertainment Tues-Sat. Check-out 11 am. Meeting rooms. Business services available. In-room modem link. Valet service. Sundries. Health club privileges. Refrigerators, microwaves available. Cr cds: A, C, D, DS, MC, V.

D 🔁 🏊 🖼️ SC

★ ★ **BEST WESTERN.** *8640 Mathis Ave (20110). Phone 703/368-7070; toll-free 800/258-7177; fax 703/368-7292. www.bestwestern.com.* 60 rooms, 2 story. Apr-Oct: S, D $59-$79; under 18 free; higher rates: special events, holiday weekends; lower rates rest of year. Crib free. Complimentary continental breakfast. Check-out 11 am. TV; cable (premium). Refrigerators, microwaves; some in-room whirlpools. Coin laundry. Restaurant adjacent 4 pm-2 am. Whirlpool. Sauna. Business services. Cr cds: A, C, D, DS, MC, V.

D 🖼️

★ ★ **COURTYARD BY MARRIOTT.** *10701 Battleview Pkwy (20109). Phone 703/335-1300; toll-free 800/321-2211; fax 703/335-9442. www.courtyard.com.* 149 rooms, 3 story. S, D $89-$98; each additional $5; suites $100-$115; under 18 free. Crib free. TV; cable (premium). Indoor pool; whirlpool. Restaurant 6:30-10 am, 5-10 pm; Sat, Sun 7 am-noon. Bar. Check-out noon. Coin laundry. Meeting rooms. Business services available. In-room modem link. Valet service. Sundries. Exercise equipment. Health club privileges. Refrigerators, microwaves available. Balconies. Cr cds: A, C, D, DS, MC, V.

D 🏊 🎿 🖼️ SC

★ **DAYS INN.** *10653 Balls Ford Rd (20109). Phone 703/368-2800; toll-free 800/329-7466; fax 703/368-0083. www.daysinn.com.* 120 rooms, 2 story. S $56; D $62; each additional $6; under 18 free. Crib free. TV; cable (premium). Pool. Complimentary continental breakfast. Check-out 11 am. Coin laundry. Business services available. Health club privileges. Refrigerators available. Cr cds: A, C, D, DS, JCB, MC, V.

D 🏊 🖼️ SC

★ ★ **HOLIDAY INN.** *10800 Vandor Ln (20109). Phone 703/335-0000; fax 703/361-8440. www.holiday-inn.com.* 158 rooms, 5 story. S $125; D $130; under 12 free. Crib free. Pet accepted, some restrictions; deposit. TV; cable (premium). Pool. Restaurant 6-11 am, 6-11 pm. Room service. Bar 4-11 pm; Fri, Sat to midnight. Check-out noon. Coin laundry. Meeting rooms. Business services available. In-room modem link. Valet service. Exercise equipment. Health club privileges. Refrigerators, microwaves available. Near Manassas (Bull Run) Battlefield. Cr cds: A, C, D, DS, JCB, MC, V.

D 🔁 🏊 🎿 🖼️

★ **RED ROOF INN.** *10610 Automotive Dr (20109). Phone 703/335-9333; fax 703/335-9342; res 800/733-7663. www.redroof.com.* 119 rooms, 3 story. S $52.99-$68.99; D $57.99-$72.99; under 18 free; higher rates: Cherry Blossom, holiday weekends. Crib free. Pet accepted, some restrictions. Check-out noon. TV; cable (premium). Restaurant adjacent 6-2 am. Business services. Sundries. Cr cds: A, C, D, DS, MC, V.

D 🔁 🖼️

★ **SUPER 8.** *8691 Phoenix Dr (22110). Phone 703/369-6323; toll-free 800/800-8000; fax 703/369-9206. www.super8.com.* 78 rooms, 3 story. S $42-$50; D $47-$55; each additional $5; under 18 free. Crib free. TV; cable (premium). Complimentary continental breakfast. Restaurant adjacent 6 am-11 pm. Check-out 11 am. Business services available. Some in-room whirlpools; microwaves available. Cr cds: A, C, D, MC, V.

D 🖼️ SC

Restaurants

★ ★ ★ **CARMELLO'S AND LITTLE PORTUGAL.** *9108 Center St (20110). Phone 703/368-5522; fax 703/369-9874. www.carmellos.com.* Italian and Portuguese cuisine are beautifully combined to create generous contemporary dishes. The restaurant's intimate atmosphere makes it a popular spot for special occasions. Northern Italian, Portuguese menu. Closed most major holidays. Lunch, dinner. Bar. Children's menu. Located in two-story brick storefront. Cr cds: A, C, D, DS, MC, V. **$$**

D

★ ★ **JAKE'S.** *9412 Main St (20110). Phone 703/330-1534; fax 703/335-6934. www.jakesofmanassas.com.* Hours: 11 am-10 pm; Thurs-Sat to 12:30 am; Sun from noon. Contemporary American menu. Bar to 1:30 am. Lunch, dinner $5.25-$18.95. Specializes in fresh seafood, hamburgers, sandwiches. Salad bar. Own desserts, ice cream. Jazz Sat. Outdoor seating. Two-level dining; jazz memorabilia. Cr cds: A, DS, MC, V.

D

★ ★ ★ **PANINO.** *9116 Mathis Ave (20110). Phone 703/335-2566; fax 703/257-6394.* Although off the beaten track, this chef-owned and operated restaurant has, for the past ten years, offered perhaps the best regional Italian cuisine outside the Beltway. Only the freshest of ingredients are used. Northern Italian menu. Closed Sun; major holidays. Lunch, dinner. Reservations required Fri, Sat dinner. Cr cds: A, D, DS, MC, V. **$**

D

Manassas (Bull Run) National Battlefield Park (D-10)

See also Falls Church, Manassas

(26 miles SW of Washington, DC, at junction US 29, VA 234)

This 5,000-acre park was the scene of two major Civil War battles. More than 26,000 men were killed or wounded here in struggles for control of a strategically important railroad junction.

The first major land battle of the war (July 21, 1861) was fought here between poorly trained volunteer troops from both North and South. The battle finally resolved itself into a struggle for Henry Hill, where "Stonewall" Jackson earned his nickname. With the outcome in doubt, Confederate reinforcements arrived by railroad from the Shenandoah Valley and turned the battle into a rout.

Thirteen months later (August 28-30, 1862), in the second battle of Manassas, Robert E. Lee outmaneuvered and defeated Union General John Pope and cleared the way for a Confederate invasion of Maryland.

Contact Park Superintendent, 6511 Sudley Rd, Manassas 22110; phone 703/361-1339. Park (daily; closed Dec 25). **$**

What to See and Do

Chinn House Ruins. *6511 Sudley Rd (20109).* The house served as a field hospital in both engagements and marked the left of the Confederate line at First Manassas; also the scene of Longstreet's counterattack at Second Manassas.

Dogan House. *6511 Sudley Rd (20109).* An original structure at Groveton, a village around which the battle of Second Manassas was fought.

Stone Bridge. *6511 Sudley Rd (20109).* Where Union artillery opened the Battle of First Manassas; it afforded an avenue of escape for the Union troops after both First and Second Manassas.

Stone House. *6511 Sudley Rd (20109). Phone 703/361-1339.* Originally a tavern (circa 1848), used as field hospital in both battles. (Summer, daily)

Unfinished Railroad. *6511 Sudley Rd (20109).* Fully graded railroad bed, never completed, behind which Stonewall Jackson's men were positioned during the second battle.

Visitor Center. *6511 Sudley Rd (20109). On Henry Hill, just N of I-66 off VA 234. Phone 703/361-1339.* Hill affords view of much of the first battlefield. Information; self-guided tours start here (walking tour of First Manassas, directions for driving tour of Second Manassas). Markers throughout park explain various aspects of battles. Ranger-conducted tours (summer). In same building is

Battlefield Museum. *6511 Sudley Rd (20109).* Exhibits reflect incidents of battles; audiovisual presentations offer orientation. (Daily; closed Dec 25)

Marion (H-4)

See also Abingdon, Wytheville

Founded 1835 **Pop** 6,349 **Elev** 2,178 ft **Area code** 540 **Zip** 24354

Information Chamber of Commerce of Smyth County, 124 W Main St, PO Box 924; 540/783-3161

Web www.swanva.net/smythcoc.htm

This popular vacation spot is surrounded by Washington and Jefferson national forests, abounding in game and birds, near a state park, and high enough to promise an invigorating climate. The seat of Smyth County, it was named for General Francis Marion, known during the American Revolution as the "Swamp Fox."

What to See and Do

George Washington and Jefferson National Forests. (See HARRISONBURG) SE of town via VA 16 is the

Mount Rogers National Recreation Area. *3714 VA 16 (24354). Phone 276/783-5196.* A 140,000-acre area that includes Mount Rogers, the state's highest point (5,729 feet), mile-high open meadows known as "balds," and a great variety of animals and plants. Swimming, fishing; hunting, camping (fee at some areas), four visitor centers, approximately 400 miles of hiking, bicycle, and bridle trails. Mount Rogers Scenic Byway (auto); Virginia Creeper Trail (hikers, bicycles, horses) follows an abandoned railroad grade through spectacular river gorges. Adjacent to New River Trails State Park (see ABINGDON). Visitor Center (Daily all year) (Mid-May-Mid-Sept, daily; rest of year, Mon-Fri) Some fees.

Hungry Mother State Park. *2854 Park Blvd (24354). 3 miles N on VA 16. Phone 276/781-7400.* More than 2,180 acres amid the mountains with a 108-acre lake; panoramic views. Swimming beach, bathhouse, fishing, boating (rentals, launching, electric motors only); hiking, self-guided trails, picnicking, restaurant, concession, tent and trailer sites (electrical hookups, late Mar-Dec), cabins (year round). Hilltop visitor center, interpretive programs. Standard fees. **$**

Special Events

Chilhowie Apple Festival. Mid-Sept.

Hungry Mother Arts and Crafts Festival. *2854 Park Blvd (24354). Hungry Mother State Park.* Mid-July.

Whitetop Ramp Festival. Mid-May.

Motel/Motor Lodge

★ **BEST WESTERN MARION.** *1424 N Main St (24354). Phone 540/783-3193; toll-free 800/528-1234; fax 540/783-3193. www.bestwestern.com.* 79 rooms, 1-2 story. S $54-$68, D $59-$72; under 18 free. Crib free. TV; cable (premium). Pool. Complimentary continental breakfast. Restaurant 5:30-9:30 pm. Room service. Bar 5 pm-midnight; closed Sun. Check-out noon. Meeting rooms. Business services available. Valet service. Some microwaves. Cr cds: A, C, D, DS, JCB, MC, V.

Martinsville (I-7)

Founded 1793 **Pop** 15,416 **Elev** 1,020 ft **Area code** 540

Information Martinsville-Henry County Chamber of Commerce, 115 Broad St, PO Box 709, 24114; 540/632-6401

Web www.neocomm.net/~mhccoc

Martinsville was named for Joseph Martin, a pioneer who settled here in 1773. Henry County takes its name from Patrick Henry, who lived here. When Henry County Court first opened in October 1776, 640 residents pledged an oath of allegiance to the United States; 40 refused to renounce allegiance to England. Located near the beautiful Blue Ridge Mountains, this community is home to Bassett Furniture and E. I. du Pont de Nemours.

What to See and Do

Blue Ridge Farm Museum. *VA 40 in Ferrum. Phone 540/365-4415.* Presents the heritage of mountain region through reconstructed farmsteads and "folklife galleries." Authentic buildings from 1800 German heritage farm, include log house, kitchen, blacksmith shop, and barn. Costumed interpreters demonstrate farm and household chores. Special events (fees). (Mid-May-mid-Aug, weekends; rest of year, by appointment) **$$**

Fairy Stone State Park. *VA 346. 21 miles NW via US 220/ VA 57, VA 346. Phone 276/930-2424.* Consists of 4,570 acres, with a 168-acre lake adjoining Philpott Reservoir. Nestled in the foothills of the Blue Ridge Mountains, this park is named for the "fairy stones" (staurolites) found near the southern tip of its boundary. Swimming beach, bathhouse, fishing, boating (launch, rentals, electric motors only); hiking and bicycle trails, picnic shelters, concession, cafe, tent and trailer sites (dump station, electrical hookups), cabins (Mar-Dec). Visitor center, evening programs. Standard fees. (Daily)

Philpott Lake. *1058 Philpott Lake Rd (24055). Just NE of Fairy Stone State Park. Phone 276/629-2703.* State's fourth-largest lake, formed by Philpott Dam, a US Army Corps of Engineers project. Swimming, skin diving, waterskiing, boating, fishing; hunting, hiking, picnicking; four camping areas (Apr-Oct), one area free, some fees.

Virginia Museum of Natural History. *1001 Douglas Ave. Phone 276/666-8600.* State museum focuses on preservation, study, and interpretation of Virginia's natural heritage. Features visual and hands-on exhibits; includes a computer-animated triceratops dinosaur and a life-size ground sloth model. Special events during the year include Earth Day (Apr) and Virginia Indian Festival (Sept). (Mon-Sat; closed holidays) **FREE**

Special Events

Blue Ridge Folklife Festival. *Held at Blue Ridge Farm Museum. Phone 540/365-4415.* Gospel, blues, and string band music; traditional regional crafts; regional foods; quilt show, antique autos, steam and gas-powered farm equipment. Sports events include horse-pulling and log-skidding contests, coon dog swimming and treeing contests. Late Oct.

Stock car races. *Phone 540/956-3151. Martinsville Speedway. 3 miles S.* Miller Genuine Draft 300, mid-Mar. Hanes 500, late Apr. Goody's 500, late Sept. Taco Bell 300, mid-Oct.

Motels/Motor Lodges

★ ★ **BEST WESTERN MARTINSVILLE INN.** *1755 Virginia Ave (24112). Phone 540/632-5611; toll-free 800/528-1234; fax 540/632-1168. www.bestwestern.com.* 97 rooms, 20 suites, 2 story. S $48; D $54; each additional $10; suites $49-$59; under 12 free; package plans. Crib free. Pet accepted. TV, cable (premium). Pool; wading pool. Restaurant 6 am-10 pm; Sat, Sun from 7 am. Room service. Bar 4 pm-midnight. Check-out noon. Coin laundry. Meeting rooms. Business services available. In-room modem link. Valet service. Sundries. Exercise equipment. Microwave available. Cr cds: A, C, D, DS, ER, MC, V.

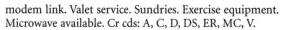

★ ★ **DUTCH INN.** *2360 Virginia Ave, Collinsville (24078). Phone 540/647-3721; toll-free 800/800-3996; fax 540/647-4857. www.dutchinns.com.* 150 rooms, 2 story. S $48-$60; D $56-$66; each additional $6; suites $88-$125; studio rooms $55-$75; under 16 free; higher rates race weeks. Crib free. Pet accepted. Check-out noon. TV; cable (premium). In-room modem link. Many bathroom phones, refrigerators; microwaves available. Valet services. Restaurant 6 am-10:30 pm. Bar 4 pm-midnight; Fri, Sat to 2 am. Room service. Exercise equipment, sauna. Pool; whirlpool, poolside service. 18-hole golf privileges. Meeting rooms. Business services. Sundries. Cr cds: A, C, D, DS, MC, V.

McLean

See also Arlington County (Ronald Reagan Washington-National Airport Area), Fairfax, Falls Church, Tysons Corner; also see Washington, DC and Rockville, MD

Pop 38,929 **Elev** 300 ft **Area code** 703

Information Fairfax County Convention & Visitors Bureau, 8300 Boone Blvd, Suite 450, Tyson's Corner 22182; 703/790-3329 or 800/7-FAIRFAX

Web www.visitfairfax.org

What to See and Do

Claude Moore Colonial Farm. *6310 Georgetown Pike (22101). 2 miles E on VA 193 (Georgetown Pike). Phone 703/442-7557. At Turkey Run.* Demonstration of 1770s low-income working farm; costumed interpreters work with crops and animals using 18th-century techniques. (Apr-mid-Dec, Wed-Sun weather permitting; closed Thanksgiving) **$**

Colvin Run Mill Historic Site. *10017 Colvin Run Rd (22066). 3 miles W via VA 123, then 5 miles NW via VA 7, on Colvin Run Rd in Great Falls. Phone 703/759-2771.* Tours of historical gristmill. General store, miller's house exhibit, barn and grounds (free). (Mar-Dec, Mon and Wed-Sun; rest of year, weekends; closed Jan 1, Thanksgiving, Dec 25) **$$**

Great Falls Park. *Phone 703/285-2965.* Spectacular natural beauty is only 15 miles from the nation's capital at Great Falls Park, where the usually peaceful Potomac River narrows into a series of dramatically cascading rapids and 20-foot waterfalls before heading through Mather Gorge. Enjoy the view from a scenic overlook, and then explore some of the park's 15 miles of trails, which take you past the remains of the Patowmack Canal, part of an 18th-century engineering project backed by George Washington, among others. (Daily 7 am-dark; closed Dec 25) **$**

Motel/Motor Lodge

★ ★ **HOLIDAY INN.** *1960 Chain Bridge Rd (22102). Phone 703/893-2100; fax 703/356-8218.* 316 rooms, 9 story. S, D $179-$194; each additional $15; family rates; weekend rates. Crib free. TV; cable (premium). Indoor pool; whirlpool. Restaurant 6:30 am-10 pm. Bar; entertainment. Check-out 1 pm. Conference facilities. Business center. In-room modem link. Gift shop. Airport transportation. Exercise equipment. Balconies. Cr cds: A, D, DS, JCB, MC, V.

Restaurants

★ ★ **CAFE OGGI.** *6671 Old Dominion Dr (22101). Phone 434/442-7360. www.cafeoggi.com.* Italian menu. Closed major holidays. Lunch, dinner. Reservations required Fri, Sat dinner. Cr cds: A, D, DS, MC, V. **$$**

★ ★ **CAFE TAJ.** *1379 Beverly Rd (22101). Phone 703/827-0444; fax 703/827-2707. www.washingtonpost.com/indianrestaurants.* Hours: 11:30 am-2:30 pm, 5:30-10 pm; Fri, Sat to 10:30 pm. Closed July 4. Reservations accepted. Indian menu. Bar. Lunch $8.95-$10.95, dinner $8.95-$14.95. Lunch buffet (Mon-Fri) $8.99. Specialties: tandoori chicken tikka, prawns masala. Outdoor seating. Modern décor. Cr cds: A, C, D, DS, MC, V.

★ ★ **DA DOMENICO.** *1992 Chain Bridge Rd (22102). Phone 703/790-9000.* Hours: 11:30 am-11 pm; Sat from 5 pm. Closed Sun; major holidays. Reservations accepted; required Fri, Sat. Northern Italian menu. Bar. Lunch $7.95-$9.95, dinner $9.95-$23.95. Specializes in veal chop, seafood, fresh pasta. Parking. Italian garden décor. Cr cds: A, D, DS, MC, V.

★ ★ ★ **DANTE.** *1148 Walker Rd, Great Falls (22066). Phone 703/759-3131; fax 703/759-0457. www.danterestaurant.com.* A historic Victorian home is the setting for this restaurant. Northern Italian menu. Hours: 11:30 am-2:30 pm, 5:30-10:30 pm; Sat from 5:30 pm; Sun 4-9 pm. Closed some major holidays. A la carte entrées: lunch $9.25-$14.50, dinner $16-$27. Bar. Children's menu. Converted country house. Reservations accepted; required Fri, Sat. Patio dining. Cr cds: A, C, D, DS, MC, V.

★ ★ **J GILBERT'S STEAKHOUSE.** *6930 Old Dominion Dr (22101). Phone 703/893-1034; fax 703/893-1036.* Hours: 11 am-10 pm; Fri, Sat to 10:30 pm; Sun 10:30 am-9 pm; early-bird dinner 4-6 pm; Sun brunch 10:30 am-2 pm. Closed Dec 25. Bar to midnight. Lunch $5.99-$10.95, dinner $5.99-$18.95. Children's menu. Specializes in steak, pasta, seafood. Outdoor seating. Parking. Fireplaces. Cr cds: A, D, DS, MC, V.

D

★ ★ **J. R'S GOODTIMES.** *8130 Watson St (22102). Phone 703/821-0546; fax 703/356-9426. www.jrsbeef.com.* Seafood menu. Hours: 11:30 am-3 pm, 5-10:30 pm; Fri to 11 pm; Sat 5-11 pm; Sun 5-9 pm. Closed most major holidays. Lunch $6-$12, dinner $15.50-$26. Bar. Reservations accepted; required Fri, Sat. Cr cds: A, D, DS, MC, V.

D

★ ★ **KAZAN.** *6813 Redmond Dr (22101). Phone 703/734-1960; fax 703/734-9636.* Middle Eastern décor. Turkish menu. Specializes in seafood, lamb. Hours: 11 am-2:30 pm, 5-10 pm; Sat 5-10:30 pm. Closed Sun. Dinner $11.95-$21.95. Service bar. Children's menu. Reservations accepted. Totally nonsmoking. Cr cds: A, D, MC, V.

D

★ ★ ★ **L'AUBERGE CHEZ FRANCOIS.** *332 Springvale Rd, Great Falls (22066). Phone 703/759-3800. www.laubergechezfrancois.com.* Rich, hearty dishes at this Alsatian-themed restaurant are served by dirndl-clad waitresses and waiters in red vests. Hours: 5:30-9:30 pm; Sun 1:30-8 pm. Closed Mon; Jan 1, July 4, Dec 25. Reservations required. French menu. Service bar. Wine cellar. Table d'hôte: dinner $36-$44. Prix fixe: dinner $25-$26 (Tues-Thurs, Sun). Specialties: salmon souffle de l'Auberge; le saute gourmandise Papa Ernest; la choucroute royale garnie comme en Alsace. Own baking, ice cream. Outdoor seating. Chef-owned. Jacket. Totally nonsmoking. Cr cds: A, C, D, DS, MC, V.

D

★ ★ ★ **LE RELAIS.** *1025-I Seneca Rd, Great Falls (22066). Phone 703/444-4060. www.lerelaisonline.com.* French menu. Closed Mon. Lunch, dinner. Bar. Outdoor seating. **$$$**

D

★ ★ **PULCINELLA.** *6852 Old Dominion Dr (22101). Phone 703/893-7777; fax 703/893-0208. www.pulcinella.com.* Italian menu. Hours: 11:30 am-10:45 pm; Sat, Sun from noon. Closed Thanksgiving, Dec 25. Lunch $4.25-$13.95, dinner $9.50-$16.95. Bar. Italian décor. Cr cds: A, D, MC, V.

D

★ ★ ★ **SERBIAN CROWN.** *1141 Walker Rd, Great Falls (22066). Phone 703/759-4150; fax 703/759-1010. www.serbiancrown.com.* Russian and French cuisine are fearlessly combined to create an elegant menu. Hours: 5:30-10 pm; Thurs, Fri noon-2:30 pm; Sun 4-9 pm. Reservations accepted; required Fri-Sun. Russian, Serbian menu. Bar. Wine list. A la carte entrées: lunch $8.95-$19.50, dinner $17.50-$26. Prix fixe: dinner $26, $39. Specialty: kulebiaka. Extensive vodka selection. Own pastries. Piano bar Tues, Fri, Sat. Gypsy music Wed-Sun. Parking. Intimate atmosphere; antique Russian paintings. Enclosed, heated terrace dining. Family-owned. Cr cds: A, C, D, DS, MC, V.

D

★ ★ **TACHIBANA.** *6715 Lowell Ave (22101). Phone 703/847-1771. www.j-netusa.com/com/tachibana/.* Hours: 11:30 am-2 pm, 5-10 pm; Fri to 10:30 pm; Sat noon-2:30 pm, 5-10:30 pm; Sun 12:30-3 pm, 4:30-9 pm. Closed some major holidays. Reservations accepted Mon-Thurs. Japanese menu. Service bar. Lunch $6.50-$15, dinner $8.95-$30. Complete meals: dinner $16.50-$30. Specialties: sushi, sashimi, soft-shell crab tempura (in season). Parking. Circular dining room. Totally nonsmoking. Cr cds: A, C, D, DS, MC, V.

D

Monterey

See also Staunton, Warm Springs

Pop 158 **Elev** 2,881 ft **Area code** 540 **Zip** 24465

Information Highland County Chamber of Commerce, PO Box 223; 540/468-2550

Special Event

Highland County Maple Festival. *Phone 540/468-2550.* Tours of sugar camps producing maple syrup and maple sugar products. Juried craft show; food, entertainment. Mar 13-14 and 20-21.

B&B/Small Inn

★ ★ **HIGHLAND INN.** *Main St (24465). Phone 540/468-2143; toll-free 888/466-4682; fax 540/468-3143. www.highland-inn.com/.* 18 rooms, 3 story. No A/C. Check-out 11 am, check-in 2 pm. TV; cable (premium). Dining room. Bar. Victorian building furnished with period antiques. Built 1904. Cr cds: A, DS, MC, V. **$**

⊠ SC

Montross

Pop 315 **Elev** 149 ft **Area code** 804 **Zip** 22520

What to See and Do

Stratford Hall Plantation. *VA 3 E and VA 214 (22558). 6 miles N on VA 3 to Lerty, then E on VA 214. Phone 804/493-8038.* Boyhood home of Richard Henry Lee and Francis Lightfoot Lee and birthplace of General Robert E. Lee. Center of restored, working plantation is monumental Georgian house built circa 1735, famous for its uniquely grouped chimney stacks. Interiors span approximately 100-year period and feature a Federal-era parlor and neoclassical paneling in the Great Hall. Flanking dependencies include kitchen, plantation office, and gardener's house. Boxwood garden; 18th- and 19th-century carriages; working mill; visitor center with museum, video presentations. Plantation luncheon (daily). (Daily; closed Jan 1, Thanksgiving, Dec 25) **$$$**

Westmoreland State Park. *5 miles NW on VA 3, then N on VA 347. Phone 804/493-8821.* Approximately 1,300 acres on Potomac River. Sand beach, swimming pool, bathhouse, fishing, boating (ramp, rentals); hiking trails, picnicking, playground, concession, camping, tent and trailer sites (Mar-Nov; dump station, electrical hookups), cabins (Mar-Dec). Visitor center, evening programs. Standard fees.

Mount Vernon (E-11)

See also Alexandria, Fairfax, Springfield; also see Washington, DC

(16 miles S of Washington, DC on George Washington Memorial Pkwy)

What to See and Do

Grist Mill Historical State Park. *3 miles W on VA 235. Phone 703/780-3383.* This mill was reconstructed in 1930 on original foundation of a mill George Washington operated on Dogue Run. Visitor center, programs. (Memorial Day-Labor Day, daily) **$**

Potomac Spirit. *Phone 202/554-7447.* Offers round-trip, Potomac River cruises from Washington, DC to Mount Vernon. The five-hour excursion is sufficient for a complete tour of house, gardens, and tomb (late Mar-early June, one trip daily; early June-late Aug, two trips daily).

Woodlawn Plantation. *9000 Richmond Hwy, Alexandria. 3 miles W of George Washington Pkwy on US 1. Phone 703/780-4000.* (1800-1805) In 1799, George Washington gave 2,000 acres of land as a wedding present to Eleanor Parke Custis, his foster daughter, who married his nephew, Major Lawrence Lewis. Dr. William Thornton, first architect of the US Capitol, then designed this mansion. The Lewises entertained such notables as Andrew Jackson, Henry Clay, and the Marquis de Lafayette. The house was restored in the early 1900s and later became the residence of a US senator; 19th-century period rooms; many original furnishings. Formal gardens. (Mar-Dec, daily; closed Jan-Feb, Thanksgiving, Dec 25) A National Trust for Historic Preservation property. **$$$** Also here is

Frank Lloyd Wright's Pope-Leighey House. *Phone 703/780-4000.* (1940) Erected in Falls Church in 1940, the house was disassembled (due to the construction of a new highway) and rebuilt at the present site in 1964. Built of cypress, brick, and glass, the house is an example of Wright's "Usonian" structures, which he proposed as a prototype of affordable housing for Depression-era middle-income families; original Wright-designed furniture. (Mar-Dec, daily; closed Jan-Feb, Thanksgiving, Dec 25) A National Trust for Historic Preservation property. Combination ticket for both houses available. **$$$**

Restaurant

★ ★ **MOUNT VERNON INN.** *On grounds of Mt. Vernon (22121). Phone 703/780-0011; fax 703/780-1704. www.mountvernon.org.* Lunch, dinner. Bar. Children's menu. Waiters in colonial costume. Hand-painted murals of colonial scenes. Cr cds: A, DS, MC, V. **$$**

Nassawadox

See also Cape Charles

Restaurant

★ **LITTLE ITALY.** *10277 Rogers Dr, Nassawadox (23413). Phone 757/442-7831; fax 757/442-3634. www.francolittle italy.com.* Italian menu. Closed Sun; most major holidays. Lunch, dinner. Bar. Children's menu. Former country grocery store. **$**
Ⓓ

Natural Bridge (G-7)

See also Lexington

Founded 1774 **Pop** 200 **Elev** 1,078 ft **Area code** 540 **Zip** 24578

Information Natural Bridge of Virginia, US 11 and VA 130, PO Box 57; 540/291-2121 or 800/533-1410

Web www.naturalbridgeva.com

Native Americans worshiped at the stone bridge nature formed across a deep gorge; town and county were both named after it. The limestone arch, 215 feet high, 90 feet long, and 150 feet wide in some places, attracted the interest of Thomas Jefferson, who purchased the bridge and 157 surrounding acres from King George III for 20 shillings, about $2.49, in 1774. Fully appreciative of this natural wonder, Jefferson built a cabin for visitors and installed caretakers. His guest book reads like a colonial "Who's Who." Surveyed by George Washington and painted by many famous artists, the bridge easily accommodates US 11. The Glenwood Ranger District of the Washington and Jefferson National Forests has its office in Natural Bridge.

What to See and Do

Cave Mountain Lake Recreation Area. *7 miles S via VA 130, right on VA 759, then right on Forest Service Rd 781 in George Washington and Jefferson national forests. Phone 540/291-2189 or 540/265-6054.* Swimming; picnicking, camping (fee). (May-Oct) **$$**

Natural Bridge. *Jct US 11 and VA 130; I-81, exit 175 or 180. Phone 540/291-2121 or 800/533-1410.* Self-guided tours (one hour). (Daily) **$$$** Ticket includes entrance to

> **Caverns of Natural Bridge.** *US 11 and I-81 (24578).* More than 300 feet below ground on three levels; streams, hanging gardens of formations, flowstone cascade, totem pole, colossal dome, and more. One-mile guided tour (one hour). (Mar-Nov, daily) **$$$**

> **Drama of Creation.** Musical presentation, viewed from beneath Natural Bridge, includes light show cast under and across arch. (Nightly) **$$$**

Natural Bridge Wax Museum. *70 Wert Faulkner Hwy. US 11 and VA 130.* (Daily). Wax figures depicting local history; self-guided factory tours. **$$$**

Natural Bridge Zoo. *US 11. I-81 between exits 175 and 180. Phone 540/291-2420.* State's largest and most complete zoo with over 400 reptiles, birds, and mammals. Petting area; safari shop; picnic grounds. (Mar-Nov, daily) **$$$**

Motel/Motor Lodge

★ ★ **WATTSTULL COURT.** *130 Arcadia Rd, Buchanan (24066). Phone 540/254-1551.* 26 rooms. S, D $40-$48; each additional $3. Pet accepted. Check-out 11 am. TV. Restaurant 6 am-10 pm. Pool, children's pool. Panoramic view of Shenandoah Valley. Cr cds: MC, V.

Hotel

★ ★ **NATURAL BRIDGE.** *US Hwy 11 (24578). Phone 540/291-2121; toll-free 800/533-1410; fax 540/291-1551.* *www.naturalbridgeva.com.* 180 rooms in hotel and inn. S, D $59-$129; under 18 free. Crib free. TV; cable. Indoor pool. Restaurant 7 am-9:30 pm. Bar 4-10 pm. Check-out noon. Meeting rooms. Business services available. Gift shop. Tennis. Miniature golf. Game room. Cr cds: A, D, DS, MC, V.

New Market (E-9)

See also Basye, Harrisonburg, Luray

Settled 1761 **Pop** 1,637 **Elev** 1,060 ft **Area code** 540 **Zip** 22844

Information Shenandoah Valley Travel Association, PO Box 1040; 540/740-3132

Web www.svta.org

New Market, situated in the Shenandoah Valley, gained its niche in Virginia history on May 15, 1864, when, in desperation, Confederate General Breckinridge ordered the cadets from Lexington's Virginia Military Institute to join the battle against the forces of General Franz Sigel. The oldest was just 20, but they entered the fray fearlessly, taking prisoners and capturing a battery. Their heroism inspired the Confederate defeat of Sigel's seasoned troops.

What to See and Do

Bedrooms of America. *9386 Congress St, I-81 exit 264. Phone 540/740-3512.* Authentic furnishings from William and Mary through Art Deco periods. Antique dolls. Gift shop. (Daily; closed Dec 25) **$**

Endless Caverns. *1800 Endless Caverns Rd. Via I-81, exit 257 or 264, then approximately 3 miles on US 11 to entrance. Phone 540/896-CAVE.* Lighted display of unusual rock formations; stalagmites and stalactites, columns, shields, flowstone and limestone pendants, presented in natural color. Temperature 55°F summer and winter. Camping. Guided tours (75 minutes). (Daily; closed Dec 25) **$$$**

New Market Battlefield State Historical Park. *8895 Collins Dr. 1 mile N of I-81 exit 264. Phone 540/740-3101.* Site of Civil War Battle of New Market (May 15, 1864), in which 257 VMI cadets played a decisive role. Original Bushong farmhouse and outbuildings restored, period furnishings. Hall of Valor; exhibits; films. Scenic overlooks, walking tour. (Daily; closed Jan 1, Thanksgiving, Dec 24, 25) Also here is

> **New Market Battlefield Military Museum.** *9500 George R. Collins Dr, 1/4 mile N of I-81 exit 264. Phone 540/740-*

8065. Located on actual site of Battle of New Market, the museum houses a private collection of more than 2,000 military artifacts and genuine, personal artifacts of the American soldier from 1776 to the present. Includes uniforms, weapons, battlefield diaries, medals, mementos; film (30 minutes). Bookshop has more than 500 titles, some antique. Union and Confederate troop position markers are on museum grounds. (Mid-Mar-Nov, daily) **$$$**

Shenandoah Caverns. *261 Caverns Rd (22847). 4 miles N, off I-81 exit 269.* Phone 540/477-3115. Elevator lowers visitors 60 feet to large subterranean rooms, fascinating rock formations; snack bar, picnic areas. Interior a constant 54°F. (Daily; closed Dec 25) **$$$$**

Motels/Motor Lodges

★ **BUDGET INN.** *2192 Old Valley Pike (22844).* Phone 540/740-3105; toll-free 800/296-6835; fax 540/740-3108. *www.budgetinn.com.* 14 rooms, 5 with shower only. Mid-Apr-mid-Nov: S $24-$34; D $28-$44; each additional $3; under 12 free; higher rates special events; lower rates rest of year. Crib $3. Pet accepted, some restrictions. TV; cable (premium). Playground. Restaurant nearby. Check-out 11 am. Business services available. Refrigerators. Picnic tables. Cr cds: A, C, D, DS, MC, V.

⬗ ⬗ **SC**

★ ★ **QUALITY INN SHENANDOAH VALLEY.** *162 W Old Cross Rd (22844).* Phone 540/740-3141; toll-free 800/638-7949; fax 540/740-3250. *www.qualityinn.com.* 101 rooms, 2 story. May-Oct: S $55-$70; D $70-$85; each additional $6; lower rates rest of year. Crib free. TV; cable (premium); VCR available. Pool. Sauna. Playground. Restaurant 6:30 am-9 pm. Room service. Check-out noon. Coin laundry. Meeting rooms. Business services available. In-room modem link. Gift shops. Game room. Miniature golf. Cr cds: A, C, D, DS, ER, JCB, MC, V.

D ⬗ ⬗ **SC**

Resort

★ **SHENVALEE GOLF RESORT.** *9660 Fairway Dr (22844).* Phone 540/740-3181; fax 540/740-8931. *www.shenvalee.com.* 42 rooms, 1-2 story. Apr-Oct: S $55; D $62-$66; each additional $12; under 13 free; golf plan; lower rates rest of year. Crib free. Check-out 1 pm. TV; cable. Balconies. Refrigerators. Restaurant 6:15 am-9 pm; Sun to 8 pm. Bar 4:30 pm-midnight; weekends to 2 am. Pool; wading pool. 27-hole golf privileges, greens fee $22-$25, putting green, driving range. Tennis. Picnic tables. Meeting rooms. Business services. On 200 acres. Cr cds: A, C, D, DS, MC, V.

D ⬗ ⬗ ⬗ ⬗

Newport News (H-12)

See also Hampton, Norfolk, Portsmouth, Virginia Beach, Yorktown

Settled 1619 **Pop** 180,150 **Elev** 25 ft **Area code** 757

Information Visitor Center, 13560 Jefferson Ave, 23603; 757/886-7777 or 888/4-WE-R-FUN

Web www.newport-news.org

One of the three cities (also see NORFOLK and PORTSMOUTH) that make up the Port of Hampton Roads, Newport News has the world's largest shipbuilding company, Newport News Shipbuilding. Fourteen miles long and 40 feet deep, Hampton Roads is one of the world's finest natural harbors, formed by the James, York, Elizabeth, and Nansemond rivers as they pass into Chesapeake Bay. The largest ships are accommodated at Newport News docks; huge tonnages of coal, ore, tobacco, and grain are shipped from the port annually. During the two World Wars it was a vitally important point of embarkation and supply. The area still has many important defense establishments.

Newport News is located on the historic Virginia Peninsula between Williamsburg and Virginia Beach. The peninsula contains Hampton, Yorktown, Jamestown, and Williamsburg. Some of the earliest landings in this country were here. The name of the town is said to derive from the good "news" of the arrival of Captain Christopher Newport, who brought supplies and additional colonists to the settlement at Jamestown.

What to See and Do

Fort Eustis. *213 Calhoun St (23604). Public Affairs Office (Building 213). NW end of city on Mulberry Island, I-64 exit 250 A.* Phone 757/878-4920. Headquarters of US Army Transportation Center. Self-guided auto tour available; brochures at **FREE** On grounds is

US Army Transportation Museum. *1387 Jackson Ave (23604).* Phone 757/878-1115. Depicts development of Army transportation from 1776 to the present; "flying saucer," amphibious vehicles, trucks, helicopters. Gift shop. (Tues-Sun; closed holidays) **FREE**

Historic Hilton Village. *I-64 exit 263 A, at Warwick Blvd and Main St.* Listed on the National Register of Historic Places, this village was built between 1918-1920 to provide wartime housing for workers at Newport News Shipbuilding. Architecturally significant neighborhood features 500 English cottage-style homes and antique and specialty shops. **FREE**

Mariners' Museum. *100 Museum Dr (23606). Warwick and J. Clyde Morris blvds, Newport News, VA 23606. From Williamsburg, take I-64 E to exit 258 A. Travel 2 1/2 miles S on J. Clyde Morris Blvd. and the Museum entrance is straight ahead. Phone 757/596-2222.* Exhibits and displays represent international nautical history; ship models, figureheads, scrimshaw, paintings, decorative arts, and small craft. Age of Exploration Gallery chronicles advancements in shipbuilding, ocean navigation, and cartography that led to early transoceanic exploration. The Chesapeake Bay Gallery exhibits Native American artifacts, workboats, racing shells, multimedia exhibits, a working steam engine, and hundreds of artifacts and photos that tell the story of this body of water. The Crabtree Collection of Miniature Ships showcases 16 detailed miniatures that illustrate the evolution of the sailing ship. Small craft gallery showcases vessels from five continents. A short film, *Sea Power Beyond the Horizon,* shows the historic and modern importance of the sea. Historical interpreters; research library; museum shop. A 550-acre park on the James River features 5-mile Noland Trail with 14 pedestrian bridges; picnic area. Guided tours. (Daily; closed Thanksgiving, Dec 25) **$$$**

Newport News Park. *13560 Jefferson Ave (23603). Jct VA 105, 143, I-64 exit 250 B. Phone 757/886-7912.* Facilities of this 8,065-acre park include freshwater fishing, canoes, paddleboats, boat rentals; history and nature trails, bicycle paths (rentals), archery, arboretum, discovery center, picnicking, Civil War earthworks, 188 campsites. (All year) Some fees. **$$$$**

Peninsula Fine Arts Center. *101 Museum Dr, I-64 exit 258 A. Phone 757/596-8175.* Changing bimonthly exhibits ranging from national traveling exhibitions to regional artists; classes, workshops, and special events. Children's hands-on activity area; museum shop. (Daily; closed holidays) **$$**

Virginia Living Museum. *524 J. Clyde Morris Blvd (23601). From Williamsburg take I-64 E to exit 258 A and go S on J. Clyde Morris Blvd. Approximately 2 miles. Phone 757/595-1900.* Exhibits on natural science; wildlife, all native to Virginia, living in natural habitats; indoor and outdoor aviaries; aquariums; wildflower gardens; planetarium with daily shows; observatory; children's hands-on Discovery Center. (Daily; closed holidays) **$$**

Virginia War Museum. *9285 Warwick Blvd in Huntington Park, on US 60, I-64 exit 263 A. Phone 757/247-8523.* More than 60,000 artifacts, including weapons, uniforms, vehicles, posters, insignias, and accoutrements relating to every major US military involvement from the Revolutionary War to the Vietnam War. Military history library and film collection. Civil War tours and educational programs available. (Mon-Sat, also Sun afternoons; closed Jan 1, Thanksgiving, Dec 25). **$$**

Motels/Motor Lodges

★ **COMFORT INN.** *12330 Jefferson Ave (23602). Phone 757/249-0200; toll-free 800/368-2477; fax 757/249-4736. www.comfortinn.com.* 124 rooms, 3 story. D $99; each additional $7; under 18 free. Pet accepted. Complimentary continental breakfast. Check-out noon, check-in 2 pm. TV; cable (premium). In-room modem link. Laundry services. Health club privileges. Pool. Free airport transportation. Cr cds: A, C, D, DS, ER, JCB, MC, V.

⬛ 🔧 ⬛ ⬛ **SC**

★ **HAMPTON INN.** *12251 Jefferson Ave (23602). Phone 757/249-0001; fax 757/249-3911. www.hamptoninn.com.* 120 rooms, 30 suites, 4 story. Memorial Day-Labor Day: S, D $79-$99; suites $109-$124; under 18 free; higher rates special events; lower rates rest of year. Complimentary continental breakfast. Check-out noon. TV; cable (premium). In-room modem link. Some fireplaces; Restaurant opposite open 24 hours. Pool. Free airport transportation. Business center. Cr cds: A, C, D, DS, MC, V.

⬛ ⬛ ✈ ⬛ 🚶

Hotel

★ ★ ★ **OMNI NEWPORT NEWS HOTEL.** *1000 Omni Blvd (23606). Phone 757/873-6664; toll-free 800/843-6664; fax 757/873-1732. www.omnihotels.com.* An upscale, suburban hotel located in Newport News central business district. 187 rooms, 9 story. D $89-$159; each additional $10; under 17 free. Check-out 11 am, check-in 3 pm. TV; cable (premium), VCR available. In-room modem link. Restaurant 6:30 am-11 pm. Bar 11-2 am; piano bar Mon-Sat. Exercise equipment, sauna. Indoor pool, whirlpool, poolside service. Business center. Cr cds: A, C, D, DS, JCB, MC, V.

⬛ ⬛ 🏋 ⬛ **SC** 🚶

Restaurants

★ ★ **AL FRESCO.** *11710 Jefferson Ave (23606). Phone 757/873-0644; fax 757/873-2355.* French, Vietnamese menu. Hours: 11 am-2:30 pm, 5-10 pm; Mon to 9 pm; Sat from 5 pm. Closed Sun; major holidays. Lunch $5.25-$6.75, dinner $9.95-$18.95. Bar. Cr cds: A, DS, MC, V.

⬛

★ ★ **DAS WALDCAFE.** *12529 Warwick Blvd (23606). Phone 757/930-1781.* German menu. Hours: 5-10 pm; Sat from 4 pm; Sun to 9 pm. Closed Mon; holidays. Dinner

$9.25-$14.25. Bar. Reservations accepted. Cr cds: A, D, MC, V.

★ ★ **HERMAN'S HARBOR HOUSE.** *663 Deep Creek Rd (23606). Phone 757/930-1000; fax 757/930-3831.* Seafood menu. Hours: 11:30 am-2:30 pm, 5-10 pm; Sat from 5 pm; Sun brunch 11:30 am-3 pm. Closed Dec 25. Dinner $12.95-$18.95. Bar. Casual attire. Reservations accepted. Cr cds: A, DS, MC, V.

D SC

★ ★ **PORT ARTHUR.** *11137 Warwick Blvd (23601). Phone 757/599-6474; fax 757/595-7599.* Chinese menu. Hours: 11:30 am-10 pm; Fri, Sat to 10:30 pm; Sun noon-10 pm; Sun buffet noon-3 pm, 5:30-9 pm. Closed Thanksgiving, Dec 25. Dinner $7.50-$13.95. Bar. Children's menu. Casual attire. Cr cds: A, DS, MC, V.

Norfolk (H-12)

Founded 1682 **Pop** 243,403 **Elev** 12 ft **Area code** 757

Information Norfolk Convention and Visitors Bureau, 232 E Main St, 23510; 757/664-6620 or 800/368-3097

Web www.norfolkcvb.com

Suburbs Chesapeake, Hampton, Newport News, Portsmouth, Virginia Beach. (See individual alphabetical listings.)

This city is part of the Port of Hampton Roads. It is a bustling trade center and has many historic, cultural, and resort areas nearby to attract the tourist. Harbor tours depart from Norfolk's downtown waterfront.

In 1682, the General Assembly bought from Nicholas Wise, a pioneer settler, 50 acres on the Elizabeth River for "ten thousand pounds of tobacco and caske." By 1736, the town that developed was the largest in Virginia. On January 1, 1776, Norfolk was shelled by the British and later burned by the colonists to prevent a British takeover. The battle between the *Merrimac* and the *Monitor* in Hampton Roads in March 1862 was followed by the fall of the city to Union forces in May of that year. In 1883, the first shipment of coal to the port by the Norfolk and Western Railway (now Norfolk Southern) began a new era of prosperity for the city.

Norfolk and Portsmouth are connected by bridge tunnels and a pedestrian ferry. Norfolk houses the largest naval facility in the world. It is also headquarters for the United States Navy's Atlantic Fleet and NATO's Allied Command Atlantic. Norfolk has shipbuilding and ship repair companies, consumer and industrial equipment manufacturers, and food-processing plants. The city ships coal, tobacco, grain, seafood, and vegetables. It is also the region's cultural center, home to the Virginia Opera, Virginia Symphony, Virginia Waterfront International Arts Festival, and Virginia Stage Company.

Old Dominion University (1930), Virginia Wesleyan College (1967), Norfolk State University (1935), and Eastern Virginia Medical School (1973) are located here. This area is also the headquarters for year-round resort activities. Within a 50-mile radius are ocean, bay, river, and marsh fishing and hunting; nearby there are 25 miles of good beaches. The 17.6-mile-long Chesapeake Bay Bridge-Tunnel between Norfolk and the Delmarva Peninsula opened in 1964; toll for passenger cars is $10, including passengers.

Transportation

Car Rental Agencies. See IMPORTANT TOLL-FREE NUMBERS.

Public Transportation. Buses (Tidewater Regional Transit), phone 757/640-6300.

Rail Passenger Service. Amtrak 800/872-7245.

Airport Information

Norfolk International Airport. Information 757/857-3351; lost and found 757/857-3344; weather 757/666-1212.

What to See and Do

American Rover. *Waterside Marina, Waterside Dr exit off I-264. Phone 757/627-SAIL.* This 135-foot, three-masted topsail passenger schooner cruises the "smooth waters" of Hampton Roads historical harbor; spacious sun decks; below-deck lounges; concessions. Tour passes historic forts, merchant and US Navy ships. Some tours pass the naval base (inquire for tour schedule). (Apr-mid-Oct, two- and three-hour tours daily)

***Carrie B* Harbor Tours.** *Departs from the Waterside. (Also see PORTSMOUTH) Phone 757/393-4735.* Replica of 19th-century riverboat takes narrated 90-minute tour of naval shipyard and inner harbor (Apr-Oct, daily); narrated 2 1/2-hour tour of naval base (Apr-Oct, daily); 2 1/2-hour sunset cruise to Hampton Roads and naval base (June-Labor Day, daily).

Chrysler Museum of Art. *245 W Olney Rd, at Mowbray Arch. Phone 757/664-6200.* Art treasures representing nearly every important culture, civilization, and historical period of the past 4,000 years. Photography gallery; fine collection of Tiffany decorative arts and glass, includes the 8,000-piece Chrysler Institute of Glass. (Wed-Sun; closed holidays) **$$$**

General Douglas MacArthur Memorial. *City Hall Ave and Bank St. Phone 757/441-2965.* Restored former city hall (1847) where MacArthur is buried. Nine galleries contain memorabilia of his life and military career. There are three other buildings on MacArthur Square: a theater where a film biography is shown, a gift shop, and the library/archives. (Daily; closed Jan 1, Thanksgiving, Dec 25) **DONATION**

Hermitage Foundation Museum. *7637 North Shore Rd. Phone 757/423-2052.* Guided tours of fine arts museum in Tudor-style mansion. Collections of tapestries, Chinese bronzes and jade, ancient glass. (Daily; closed Jan 1, Thanksgiving, Dec 25) **$$**

Hunter House Victorian Museum. *240 W Freemason St. Phone 757/623-9814.* Built in 1894 and rich in architectural details, the house contains the Hunter family's collection of Victorian furnishings and decorative pieces, including a Renaissance Revival bedchamber suite, a nursery with children's playthings, an inglenook, and stained-glass windows; lavish period reproduction floor and wall coverings, lighting fixtures, and drapery. Also exhibited is a collection of early-20th-century medical memorabilia. Tours begin every 30 minutes. (Apr-Dec, Wed-Sat, also Sun afternoons; closed Jan 1, Thanksgiving, Dec 25). **$$**

Moses Myers House. *331 Bank St. Phone 757/333-6283.* (1792) Excellent example of Georgian architecture; many pieces of original furniture, silver and china. (Apr-Dec, Tues-Sun; rest of year, Tues-Sat; closed holidays) **$$**

Nauticus—The National Maritime Center. *1 Waterside Dr (23510). Phone 757/664-1000; toll-free 800/664-1080.* Interprets aspects from marine biology and ecology to exploration, trade, and shipbuilding. Interactive computer exhibits allow visitors to navigate a simulated ocean voyage, design a model ship, pilot a virtual reality submarine, and view actual researchers at work in two working marine laboratories. Active US Navy ships and scientific research vessels periodically moor at Nauticus and open to visitors. Also 350-seat, 70mm wide-screen theater; shark petting tank. (Memorial Day-Labor Day, daily; rest of year, Tues-Sun; closed Jan 1, Thanksgiving, Dec 24 and 25). **$$$** Also here is

Hampton Roads Naval Museum. *1 Waterside Dr (23510). Phone 757/444-8971.* Interprets the extensive naval history of the Hampton Roads area; including detailed ship models, period photographs, archaeological artifacts, and a superior collection of naval prints and artwork. (Daily; closed Jan 1, Thanksgiving, Dec 25) **FREE**

Norfolk Botanical Garden. *6700 Azalea Garden Rd, adjacent Norfolk International Airport. Phone 757/441-5830.* Azaleas, camellias, rhododendrons, roses (May-Oct), dogwoods, and hollies on 155 acres. Japanese, Colonial, perennial, and rose gardens; flowering arboretum; Hill of Nations; fragrance garden for the visually impaired; picnicking, restaurant, and gift shop; tropical pavilion. Flowering displays best from early Apr-Oct. Gardens (daily; closed special events). Information center (daily; closed Jan 1, Dec 25). Narrated boat ride (30 minutes) and tram tours (mid-Mar-Labor Day, daily; through Oct weekends, trams only). **$$$**

Norfolk Naval Base and Norfolk Naval Air Station. *Hampton Blvd and I-564. Phone 757/444-7955 or 757/640-6300.* The largest naval installation in the world. Ship visitors should check in at the Naval Base Pass Office on Hampton Blvd, opposite Gate 5. Naval base tours are also offered. Tour buses from Tour and Information Office, 9079 Hampton Blvd (Apr-Oct, daily). **$$**

Spirit of Norfolk. *Departs from the Waterside. Phone 757/625-1748.* Harbor cruise aboard 600-passenger cruise ship. Captain's narration highlights the harbor's famous landmarks, including Waterside Festival Marketplace, Portsmouth Naval Hospital, Old Fort Norfolk, Blackbeard's hiding place, Norfolk Naval Base, and downtown area's dynamic skyline. Luncheon cruise (Tues-Sun); evening dinner cruise (Tues-Sun); moonlight party cruise (Fri-Sat, in season).

St. Paul's Episcopal Church. *201 St. Paul's Blvd, at City Hall Ave. Phone 757/627-4353.* (1739) Only building to survive burning of Norfolk in 1776. (Tues-Fri, also by appointment) **DONATION**

Virginia Zoological Park. *3500 Granby St. Phone 757/441-5227.* A combination zoo, park, and conservatory. Playground, tennis courts, basketball courts; picnic area, concession. (Daily; closed Jan 1, Dec 25). **$$**

Waterside Festival Marketplace. *333 Waterside Dr.* A waterfront pavilion creating a lively marketplace with more than 90 shops, restaurants. (Daily; closed Thanksgiving, Dec 25) Bordering the Waterside are the city's marina and dock areas, where harbor tour vessels take on passengers.

Town Point Park. *120 W Main St. Phone 757/441-2345.* Home to Norfolk Festevents, the park hosts more than 100 free outdoor concerts, parties, dances, movies, and festivals each year.

Willoughby-Baylor House. *601 E Freemason St. Phone 757/664-6200.* (1794) Restored townhouse with period furnishings; herb and flower garden adjacent. (By appointment; inquire at Moses Myers House) **$$**

Special Events

Harborfest. *120 W Main St (23510). Phone 757/441-2149. Town Point Park, downtown waterfront on Wayside Dr.* Sailboat and speedboat races, tall ships, ship tours, water-skiing, military demonstrations, entertainment, children's activities, fireworks, seafood. First full weekend in June.

International Azalea Festival. *Downtown and Norfolk Botanical Garden.* To honor NATO. Parade, coronation ceremony, air show (held at Norfolk Naval Air Station), events, concerts, fair, ball, entertainment. Late Apr.

Virginia Children's Festival. *120 W Main St (23510). Phone 757/441-2149. Town Point Park.* More than 200 educational, creative, and interactive activities; entertainment. Early Oct.

Virginia Opera. *160 E Virginia Beach Blvd (23510). Phone 757/623-1223. Harrison Opera House and other select locations.* Statewide opera company; traditional and contemporary works. Features young American artists. Oct-Apr.

Virginia Symphony. *Chrysler Hall and other select locations. Phone 757/892-6366.* Five performance series. Sept-May.

Virginia Waterfront International Arts Festival. *Phone 757/664-6492.* Eighteen days of classical and contemporary music, dance, visual arts and theater performances. Late Apr-mid-May.

Motels/Motor Lodges

★ ★ **BEST WESTERN CENTER INN.** *235 N Military Hwy (23502). Phone 757/461-6600; toll-free 800/237-5517; fax 757/466-9093. www.bestwestern.com.* 154 rooms, 2 story. D $69-$129; each additional $10; under 13 free; holidays (3-day minimum), Jazz Festival. Check-out noon, check-in 3 pm. TV; cable (premium), VCR available (movies). In-room modem link. Laundry services. Restaurant 6 am-2 pm, 5-10 pm; Sat, Sun from 7 am. Bar. Room service. Exercise equipment, sauna. Two pools, one indoor; whirlpool. Free airport transportation. Near airport. Cr cds: A, C, D, DS, MC, V.

⬚ D ⬚ 🏊 ⬚ 🏋 ⬚ SC

★ **BEST WESTERN HOLIDAY SANDS INN & SUITES.** *1330 E Oceanview Ave (23503). Phone 757/583-2621; toll-free 800/525-5156; fax 757/587-7540.* 95 kitchen units, 5 story. Memorial Day-Labor Day: S, D $50-$95; each additional $5; suites $85-$105; kitchen units $70-$95; under 12 free; lower rates rest of year. Complimentary continental breakfast. Check-out 11 am. TV; cable (premium). Laundry services. Exercise equipment. Heated pool. Free airport transportation. Cr cds: A, C, D, DS, MC, V.

D 🛄 🏊 🏋 ⬚ SC

★ **COMFORT INN.** *8051 Hampton Blvd (23505). Phone 757/451-0000; fax 757/451-8394 res 800/228-5150. www.comfortinn.com.* 120 rooms, 2 story. D $69-$119; each additional $5; under 18 free. Complimentary continental breakfast. Check-out 11 am, check-in 3 pm. TV; cable (premium). In-room modem link. Laundry services. Indoor pool, whirlpool. Cr cds: A, C, D, DS, JCB, MC, V.

D 🏊 🏋 ⬚

★ **ECONO LODGE.** *9601 4th View St (23503). Phone 757/480-9611; fax 757/480-1307. www.econolodge.com.* 71 rooms, 3 story. Mid-May-Labor Day: S $54.95; D $64.95; each additional $5; kitchen units $69.95; under 18 free; weekly rates; higher rates: some holidays, special events; lower rates rest of year. Pet accepted, some restrictions; $50 deposit. Complimentary continental breakfast. Check-out 11 am. TV; cable (premium), VCR available. Laundry services. Exercise equipment. Ocean; fishing pier. Cr cds: A, C, D, DS, JCB, MC, V.

D 🐾 🏋 ⬚

★ **HAMPTON INN.** *1450 N Military Hwy (23502). Phone 757/466-7474; toll-free 800/426-7866. www.hamptoninn.com.* 130 rooms, 2 story. Late May-early S-$65-$69; D $69-$139; under 18 free; lower rates rest of year. Check-out noon. TV; cable (premium). In-room modem link. Restaurant opposite 7 am-11 pm. Health club privileges. Pool. Free airport transportation. Cr cds: A, C, D, DS, MC, V.

D 🏊 🏋 ⬚

★ **SUPER 8.** *7940 Shore Dr (23518). Phone 757/588-7888; toll-free 800/800-8000; fax 757/588-7888. www.super8.com.* 74 units, 10 kitchen units, 3 story. June-Labor Day: S, D $46.95-$66; suites, kitchen units $72.88-$89.47; higher rates: July 4, Labor Day; lower rates rest of year. Crib free. TV; cable (premium). Complimentary continental breakfast. Restaurant nearby. Check-out 11 am. Business services available. Some refrigerators, microwaves. Cr cds: A, C, D, DS, MC, V.

D ⬚ SC

Hotels

★ ★ **CLARION HOTEL.** *345 Granby St (23510). Phone 757/622-6682; toll-free 888/402-6682; fax 757/623-5949.* 125 rooms, 8 story. Pet accepted. Check-out noon, check-in 3 pm. TV; cable (premium). In-room modem link. Restaurant. Bar. In-house fitness room, health club privileges. Cr cds: A, C, D, DS, JCB, MC, V. **$**

D 🐾 ⬚ 🏋

★ ★ **DOUBLETREE HOTEL.** *880 N Military Hwy (23502). Phone 757/461-9192; toll-free 800/933-9600; fax 757/461-8290. www.doubletreehotel.com.* This hotel is conveniently located in Norfolk's Military Circle Mall, close to the Virginia Beach oceanfront, military installations, and historic downtown Norfolk. 208 rooms, 14 story. D $74-$123; each additional $10; under 18 free; weekend rates. Check-out noon, check-in 3 pm. TV; cable (premium). Restaurant 6:30 am-10:30 pm. Bar 11-1 am. Exercise equipment. Pool. Free airport transportation. Business center. Cr cds: A, C, D, DS, ER, JCB, MC, V.

⊡ ⇌ 🛪 ⇙ SC 🚶

★ ★ ★ **HILTON NORFOLK AIRPORT.** *1500 N Military Hwy (23502). Phone 757/466-8000; toll-free 800/422-7474; fax 757/466-8802. www.norfolkhilton.com.* Conveniently located 2 miles from Norfolk International Airport, this hotel is ideal for those visiting the business district or military installations. 254 rooms, 6 story. D $109-$179; each additional $15; under 18 free; package plans. Check-out 1 pm, check-in 3 pm. TV; cable (premium). In-room modem link. Restaurant 6:30 am-midnight. Bar 4 pm-1 am; entertainment. Exercise equipment, sauna. Pool, whirlpool, poolside service. Lighted tennis. Free airport transportation. Luxury level. Cr cds: A, C, D, DS, ER, JCB, MC, V.

⊡ 🏌 ⇌ 🛪 ✈ ⇙ SC

★ ★ ★ **MARRIOTT NORFOLK WATERSIDE.** *235 E Main St (23510). Phone 757/627-4200; toll-free 800/228-9290; fax 757/628-6466. www.marriott.com.* Located in the heart of downtown Norfolk, this property is adjoining the Waterside Convention Center. 405 rooms, 24 story. Check-out 11 pm, check-in 4 pm. TV; cable (premium). In-room modem link. Laundry services. Restaurant. Bar. In-house fitness room, sauna. Game room. Indoor pool, whirlpool. Garage parking $8; valet $10. Business center. Concierge, luxury level. Cr cds: A, C, D, DS, ER, JCB, MC, V. **$$**

⊡ ⇌ 🛪 ⇙ SC 🚶

★ ★ ★ **SHERATON NORFOLK WATERSIDE HOTEL.** *777 Waterside Dr (23510). Phone 757/622-6664; toll-free 800/325-3535; fax 757/625-8271. www.sheraton. com.* Adjacent to Waterside Marketplace on the Elizabeth River, this landmark hotel affords great views of the harbor and downtown skyline. 445 rooms, 10 story. Pet accepted; fee. Check-out noon, check-in 3 pm. TV; cable (premium), VCR available. In-room modem link. Restaurant. Bar; entertainment. Room service to midnight. Health club privileges. Pool; poolside service. Valet parking $9.50. Business center. Luxury level. Dockage. On harbor. Cr cds: A, C, D, DS, JCB, MC, V. **$**

⊡ 🐾 ⇌ ⇙ SC 🚶

B&B/Small Inn

★ ★ ★ **PAGE HOUSE.** *323 Fairfax Ave (23507). Phone 757/625-5033; toll-free 800/599-7659; fax 757/623-9451. www.pagehouseinn.com.* This Georgian Revival mansion (1898), originally a family home and completely renovated in 1990, is located in the fashionable Ghent historic district. It offers distinctly decorated guest rooms. 7 rooms, 3 suites, 3 story. Check-out 11 am, check-in 2-9 pm. TV; cable (premium), VCR available. In-room modem link. In-house fitness room. Children under 12 years only by reservations. Totally nonsmoking. Cr cds: A, MC, V. **$$**

⇙ 🚶

Restaurants

★ ★ **BAKER'S CRUST.** *330 W 21st St (23517). Phone 757/625-3600; fax 757/625-1855. www.bakerscrust.com.* Steak menu. Lunch, dinner. Bar. Entertainment. Children's menu. Casual attire. Outdoor seating. Cr cds: A, DS, MC, V. **$**

⊡ ⇙

★ **THE BANQUE.** *1849 E Little Creek Rd (23518). Phone 757/480-3600; fax 757/583-9622.* Hours: 6 pm-2 am. Closed Mon; Thanksgiving, Dec 24-25. Reservations accepted. Bar. A la carte entrées: dinner $5.95-$14.95. Specializes in prime rib, shrimp. Entertainment. Western décor. Cr cds: A, DS, MC, V.

⊡ SC

★ ★ **FREEMASON ABBEY.** *209 W Freemason St (23510). Phone 757/622-3966; fax 757/490-7678. www.cvent.net/restaurants/cvi/freemason/.* American, seafood menu. Lunch, dinner, Sun brunch. Bar. Children's menu. Renovated church (1873); many antiques. Casual attire. Cr cds: A, D, DS, MC, V. **$**

⊡

★ ★ ★ **LA GALLERIA.** *120 College Pl (23510). Phone 757/623-3939; fax 757/623-9108.* Fine cuisine is the mainstay of this refreshingly cosmopolitan restaurant. All of the delectable desserts are made in-house. Hours: 11:30 am-2:30 pm, 5:30-11:30 pm; Mon to 11 pm; Fri, Sat to midnight. Closed Sun; Thanksgiving, Dec 25. Reservations accepted. Italian menu. Bar 11:30 am-2:30 pm, 4:30 pm-2 am. Lunch $3.95-$7.95, dinner $11.95-$19.95. Children's menu. Specialty: salmon La Galleria. Own baking, pasta. Valet parking. Outdoor seating. Modern décor. Cr cds: A, D, MC, V.

⊡

★ ★ **MONASTERY.** *443 Granby St (23510). Phone 757/625-8193; fax 757/437-0513.* Czech, Eastern European menu. Closed Mon; Easter, Thanksgiving, Dec 25; also July-Aug. Lunch, dinner. Bar. Reservations required Fri, Sat. Cr cds: A, C, D, DS, MC, V. **$$**

D

★ ★ ★ **SHIP'S CABIN.** *4110 E Ocean View Ave (23518). Phone 757/362-4659; fax 757/362-0627. www.shipscabin.com.* Only the freshest seafood is served, thanks to the proprietor's years in the boating business. A popular option is the "mix and match" menu: choose a tailored combination of fish, preparation method, and sauce to accompany. The atmosphere is casual, in keeping with its beach setting. Hours: 5:30-9:30 pm; Fri, Sat to 10:30 pm; Sun 5-9 pm. Reservations accepted. Bar. Wine list. Dinner $12.95-$18.95. Specializes in grilled fish and meat. Own baking. Parking. Fireplaces. Outdoor seating. View of Chesapeake Bay. Cr cds: A, DS, MC, V.

D SC

★ ★ **UNCLE LOUIE'S.** *132 E Little Creek Rd (23505). Phone 757/480-1225; fax 757/480-3540. www.unclelouies. com.* Closed Thanksgiving, Dec 25. Breakfast, lunch, dinner. Bar. Entertainment Wed, Sat. Children's menu. Cr cds: A, D, DS, MC, V. **$$**

D

Orange (F-9)

See also Charlottesville, Culpepper

Founded 1749 **Pop** 4,123 **Elev** 521 ft **Area code** 540 **Zip** 22960

This is the seat of Orange County, named for William, Prince of Orange, in 1734. Located in the Piedmont (foothills) of the Blue Ridge Mountains, Orange was settled by Germans under the leadership of Alexander Spotswood between 1714 and 1719.

This is riding and hunting country, drawing its livelihood from farming, livestock, and light industry. There are many antebellum houses in the county.

What to See and Do

James Madison Museum. *129 Caroline St. Phone 540/672-1776.* Exhibits commemorating Madison's life and his contributions to American history; also Orange County history and Hall of Agriculture that includes an 18th-century homestead. (Mar-Nov, daily; rest of year, Mon-Fri) **$$**

Montpelier. *4 miles SW, on VA 20. Phone 540/672-0006.* Residence of James Madison, fourth president of the US. Madison was the third generation of his family to live on this extensive plantation. He inherited Montpelier and enlarged it twice. After his presidency he and Dolley Madison retired to the estate, which Mrs. Madison sold after the president's death to pay her son's gambling debts. In 1901, the estate was bought by William du Pont, who enlarged the house, added many outbuildings, including a private railroad station, built greenhouses, and planted gardens. Today, under the stewardship of the National Trust for Historic Preservation, a long-term research and preservation project, "The Search for James Madison," has begun. Self-guided tours of arboretum, nature trails, and formal garden. (Daily; closed Jan 1, Thanksgiving, Dec 25; also first Sat in Nov) **$$$**

B&B/Small Inns

★ ★ ★ **HIDDEN INN.** *249 Caroline St (22960). Phone 540/672-3625; toll-free 800/841-1253; fax 540/672-5029. www.hiddeninn.com.* This inn is located close to Monticello, Montpelier, and Skyline drive and offers activities that include biking, hiking, antique shopping, boating, and fishing. Four buildings make up the inn with the main house being over 100 years old. It was built by descendents of Thomas Jefferson. Verandahs wrap around the building and look out over the wooded gardens. 10 rooms, 2 story, 4 buildings. S $59-$89; D $79-$129; each additional $20; suites $139-$169. TV in living room. Complimentary full breakfast; afternoon refreshments. Check-out noon, check-in 3 pm. Business services available. Health club privileges. Some in-room whirlpools. Balconies. Each room individually decorated; some with canopy bed, fireplace. Late 19th-century residence; on 7 1/2 wooded acres. Totally nonsmoking. Cr cds: A, MC, V.

★ ★ **HOLLADAY HOUSE.** *155 W Main St (22960). Phone 540/672-4893; toll-free 800/358-4422; fax 540/672-3028. www.holladayhousebandb.com.* 6 rooms, 3 story. Complimentary full breakfast. Check-out 11 am, check-in 3 pm. TV in some rooms; cable. Fireplace, whirlpool. Restaurant. Federal-style residence (circa 1830). Totally nonsmoking. Cr cds: A, DS, MC, V. **$**

Pearisburg (H-6)

See also Blacksburg, Radford

Pop 2,729 **Elev** 1,804 ft **Area code** 540 **Zip** 24134

What to See and Do

Walnut Flats. *110 Southpark Dr. 11 miles S on VA 100, then 10 1/2 miles W on VA 42 to County 606, N 1 mile to County*

201, 2 1/2 miles. Phone 540/552-4641. Fishing in Dismal Creek; hunting (in season), hiking, primitive camping. Dismal Falls and Flat Top Mountain are here. **FREE** Approximately 1/2 mile from here on County 201 is

White Pine Horse Camp. *Phone 540/552-4641.* Primitive camping, horse trails. **FREE**

White Rocks Recreation Area. *VA 635 and VA 613. In George Washington and Jefferson national forests. Phone 540/552-4641.* Fishing in Big Stony Creek; hunting (in season), hiking, camping (fee). (Apr-Nov)

Petersburg (H-11)

See also Hopewell, Richmond

Settled 1645 **Pop** 33,740 **Elev** 87 ft **Area code** 804

Information Petersburg Visitors Center, 425 Cockade Alley, 23803; 804/733-2402 or 800/368-3595

This city, Lee's last stand before Appomattox (1864-1865), was settled in 1645 when the General Assembly authorized construction of Fort Henry at the falls of the Appomattox River. In 1784, three separate towns united to become the single city of Petersburg.

British troops under Generals Benedict Arnold and William Phillips occupied the town in 1781; on May 24 that same year Cornwallis started the journey to his surrender at Yorktown. Between the Revolutionary War and Civil War, the town was a popular stopping place with a social life that, for a time, eclipsed that of Richmond.

Physically untouched during the early years of the Civil War (though the town sent 17 companies to the front), Petersburg, in 1864, was the scene of Lee's final struggle against Grant. In April 1865, when Lee's supply routes were finally cut and he was forced to evacuate the city, the Confederacy collapsed. A week later Lee surrendered at Appomattox.

The shattered city made a new start after the war, showing amazing recuperative powers; in 1870, Petersburg had 20 more industries than there had been in 1850. Today, besides being a storehouse of colonial and Civil War history, Petersburg is a thriving industrial city.

What to See and Do

Appomattox River Park. *Western part of town, on River Rd. Phone 804/733-2394.* A 137-acre park with canal for canoeing or fishing; access to rapids; picnic area. (Mid-Apr-Oct, daily)

Blandford Church and Cemetery. *321 S Crater Rd.* Church (1735) and cemetery (1702); since 1901 a memorial to the Confederacy, has 15 Tiffany stained-glass windows. (Daily; closed holidays) **$$**

Centre Hill Mansion. *Center Hill.* (1823) Federalist mansion visited by Presidents Tyler, Lincoln, and Taft. Chandeliers, finely detailed carvings; antiques, 1886 Knabe Art grand piano with hollywood inlaid on rosewood. (Daily; closed holidays) **$$**

Farmers Bank. *19 Bollingbrook St.* (1817) Banking memorabilia including original plates and press for printing Confederate currency. Tours depart from Visitor Center, Old Market Square. (Apr-Oct, daily) **$$**

Fort Lee. *3 miles NE on VA 36.* Army training center in WWI and WWII. Here is

US Army Quartermaster Museum. *Blvg 5218, Ave A (23801). Phone 804/734-4203.* Uniforms, flags, weapons, equestrian equipment from 200 years of military service. Civil War and Memorial rooms. (Tues-Sun; closed Jan 1, Thanksgiving, Dec 25) **FREE**

Lee's Retreat. *Phone 800/6-RETREAT.* A 98-mile driving tour follows route of General Robert E. Lee's retreat from Petersburg to Appomattox. Roadside pull-overs, signs, and audio interpretation at important Civil War sites. For brochures, maps, and audio tapes, contact the Petersburg Visitors Center. **FREE**

Lee Memorial Park. *Southern part of town, off Johnson Rd. Phone 804/733-2394.* Facilities of this 864-acre park include lake (launch fee), fishing (fee; license required); game fields and courts (fee), picnic area. (Daily; lake facilities closed mid-Oct-mid-Apr) Also here is

USSSA Softball Hall of Fame Museum. *3935 S Crater Rd, 1 mile off I-95. Phone 804/732-4099.* Honors outstanding persons in amateur softball. Numerous displays, exhibits, photographs; 7-minute film. (Daily; closed holidays) **$**

Pamplin Park Civil War Site. *6125 Boydton Plank Rd. Phone 804/861-2408.* Site of General Ulysses S. Grant's decisive victory over Confederate forces in 1865. This 422-acre park includes battle trails, reconstructed soldier huts, plantation home. Interpretive Center, and museum. Guided tours available. (Daily; closed Jan 1, Thanksgiving, Dec 25)

National Museum of the Civil War Soldier. *6125 Boydton Plank Rd (23803).* Exhibit on the Civil War's common soldier, one of the country's largest Civil War bookshops. Gift shop; restaurant.

Poplar Grove (Petersburg) National Cemetery. *S off I-85.* On self-guided tour of Petersburg National Battlefield (see). Of 6,315 graves, 4,110 are unidentified.

Siege Museum. *15 W Bank St. Phone 804/733-2402.* Greek Revival building houses exhibits describing the ten-month Civil War siege of Petersburg. Film *The Echoes Still Remain,* with Joseph Cotten, is shown every hour on the hour. (Daily; closed holidays) **$$**

St. Paul's Episcopal Church. *110 N Union between W Washington and Tabb sts. Phone 804/733-3415.* (1856) Lee worshiped here during the siege of Petersburg (1864-1865). Open on request (Mon-Thurs).

Trapezium House. *Market and High sts.* (1817) Built by eccentric Irish bachelor Charles O'Hara in the form of a trapezium, with no right angles and no parallel sides. O'Hara is said to have believed the superstitions of his West Indian servant, who thought that ghosts and evil spirits inhabited right angles. Tours depart from Siege Museum, 15 W Bank St. (Apr-Oct, daily) **$$**

Motels/Motor Lodges

★ ★ **BEST WESTERN STEVEN KENT.** *12205 S Crater Rd (23805). Phone 804/733-0600; fax 804/862-4549. www.bestwestern.com.* 138 rooms, 1-2 story. S, D $45.95-$69.95; each additional $5; under 18 free. Crib $5. Pet accepted; $5. Check-out 11 am. TV; cable (premium). In-room modem link. Some refrigerators. Coin laundry. Restaurant 5:30 am-10 pm. Bar noon-midnight. Playground. Pool; wading pool. Miniature golf. Lighted tennis. Picnic tables. Lawn games. Business services. Sundries. Cr cds: A, C, D, DS, MC, V.

D 🐾 🛌 🏊 🖾

★ **DAYS INN.** *12208 S Crater Rd (23805). Phone 804/733-4400; toll-free 877/512-4400; fax 804/861-9559. www.thedaysinn.com/petersburg.* 155 rooms, 2 story. S, D $65-$70; each additional $5; kitchen suites $75-$80. Crib free. Pet accepted; $5. Check-out 11 am. TV; cable (premium). In-room modem link. Refrigerators, microwaves. Coin laundry. Restaurant adjacent 5:30 am-10 pm. Playground. Exercise equipment. Pool; wading pool. Putting green. Meeting rooms. Business services. Sundries. Cr cds: A, C, D, DS, JCB, MC, V.

D 🐾 🏊 🕴 🖾

Restaurant

★ **ALEXANDER'S.** *101 W Bank St (23803). Phone 804/733-7134.* American, Greek, Italian menu. Hours: 9 am-9 pm; Mon, Tues to 3:30 pm. Closed Sun; Jan 1, Thanksgiving, Dec 25; also week of July 4. Breakfast $1.50-$4.55. Lunch $4.50-$6.85. Dinner $6.99-$12.99. Children's menu. In old town storefront.

D

Petersburg National Battlefield (H-11)

See also Hopewell, Petersburg, Richmond

The campaign that spelled doom for the Confederacy occurred in a huge 40-mile semicircle around Richmond and Petersburg at the price of 70,000 Union and Confederate casualties.

After his unsuccessful attempt to take Richmond by frontal assault (at Cold Harbor, June 3, 1864), General Grant withdrew and attacked Petersburg. After four days of fighting and failing to capture the city, Grant decided to lay siege. Petersburg was the rail center that funneled supplies to Lee and Richmond.

The siege lasted ten months, from June 15, 1864, to April 2, 1865, with the two armies in almost constant contact. When Petersburg finally fell, Lee's surrender was only a week away.

The park, more than 2,700 acres, preserves Union and Confederate fortifications, trenches, and gun pits. Another unit of the battlefield, Five Forks Unit, is located 23 miles to the west. Park (daily). Living history programs daily during summer. Access for the disabled includes several paved trails and ramps to the Visitor Center. For further information contact the Superintendent, 1539 Hickory Hill Rd, Petersburg 23803-4721; phone 804/732-3531. Golden Eagle, Golden Age, and Golden Access Passports honored (see MAKING THE MOST OF YOUR TRIP).

What to See and Do

Battery 5. *Rte 36 and I-95 (23801).* Strongest original Confederate position, captured on opening day of battle. From here "the Dictator," a Union mortar, shelled Petersburg, 2 1/2 miles away. A similar mortar is nearby.

Battery 8. *Rte 36 and I-95 (23801).* Confederate artillery position captured and used by Union as Fort Friend.

Battery 9. *Rte 36 and I-95 (23801).* Confederate position on original line. Site of reconstructed Union camp and living history programs.

City Point Unit. (See HOPEWELL)

Colquitt's Salient. Section of Confederate defense line.

The Crater. Hole remaining after Union troops tunneled beneath Confederate artillery position and exploded four tons of powder (July 30, 1864). The resulting breach in Confederate lines failed as a major breakthrough. Several special monuments in vicinity.

First Maine Monument. Memorial to Maine dead in greatest regimental loss in a single action of the war.

Five Forks Unit. *1539 Hickory Hill Rd (23803). Approximately 6 miles SW via VA 613 (White Oak Rd), to junction Dinwiddie Courthouse Rd (VA 627) and Wheeler Pond Rd (VA 645). Phone 804/265-8244.* (1,115 acres) This road junction, beyond Lee's extreme right flank, led to the only remaining Confederate supply line, the South Side Railroad. The Battle of Five Forks (April 1, 1865) saw Union forces under General Philip H. Sheridan smash Confederates commanded by General George Pickett and gain access to the tracks beyond. On April 2, Grant ordered an all-out assault, crumbling Lee's right flank. Only a heroic stand by Confederate forces at Fort Gregg held off the Union advance while Lee evacuated Petersburg on the night of April 2. Visitor contact station (summer). **FREE**

Fort Haskell. One of the points where Union troops stopped a desperate attempt by Lee to break the siege.

Fort Stedman. Lee's "last grand offensive" concentrated here (March 25, 1865). The battle lasted four hours; the Confederates failed to hold their breakthrough.

Gracie's Dam. Site of one of several Confederate dams intended to flood area between lines.

Harrison's Creek. First Grant (June 1864), then Lee (March 1865) had advances checked here.

Spring Garden. Heaviest Union artillery concentration during Battle of Crater was along this ridge.

Visitor Center. *Off VA 36.* Information, exhibits; maps for self-guided tours. (Daily; closed Jan 1, Dec 25) Self-guided tour starts near center building.

Portsmouth (H-12)

See also Chesapeake, Hampton, Newport News, Norfolk, Virginia Beach

Founded 1752 **Pop** 100,565 **Elev** 15 ft **Area code** 757

Information Portsmouth Convention and Visitors Bureau, 505 Crawford St, Suite 2, 23704; 757/393-5327 or 800/767-8782

Web www.portsmouth.va.us

Connected to Norfolk by two bridge tunnels and a pedestrian ferry that cross the Elizabeth River, Portsmouth is part of the great Hampton Roads port, unrivaled for commercial shipping and shipbuilding activity. It is also the headquarters of the United States Coast Guard Atlantic Fleet.

In Gosport, long a part of Portsmouth, Andrew Sprowle, a Scot, built a marine yard in 1767 which became in turn a British naval repair station and, after the Revolutionary War, a federal navy yard. Now called the Norfolk Naval Shipyard, it is the largest naval shipyard in the world. The *Chesapeake,* sister of the *Constitution* and one of the US Navy's first warships, was built here. So was the *Merrimac,* which was seized by the Confederates, changed into an ironclad in 1861, and rechristened the *CSS Virginia.* The oldest drydock (1831) here is still in use.

What to See and Do

***Carrie B* Harbor Tours.** *Departs from Portside, 6 Crawford Pkwy. Phone 757/393-4735 for details. (Also see NORFOLK).* Replica of 19th-century riverboat makes narrated tour (90-minutes) of naval shipyard and inner harbor (Apr-Oct, daily); narrated tour (2 1/2 hours) of naval base and Hampton Roads (Apr-May and Sept-Oct, daily); sunset cruise (2 1/2 hours) to Hampton Roads and naval base (June-Labor Day, daily).

Hill House. *221 North St. Phone 757/393-0241.* Headquarters of the Portsmouth Historical Association. Built in early 1820s, this four-story English basement-style (with a raised basement) house contains original furnishings collected by generations of the Hill family. In near-original condition, the house has undergone only limited renovation through the years. Garden restored. (Apr-Dec, Wed, Sat and Sun) **$**

Historic houses. *6 Crawford Pkwy (23704). Phone 757/393-5111.* Portsmouth has over 300 years of history represented by more than 20 examples of colonial, Federal, and antebellum houses. Among them is the Nivison-Ball House (circa 1730-1750), 417 Middle St, where Andrew Jackson and General Lafayette were entertained. *These houses are private and may be viewed only from the exterior.* Obtain Olde Towne Portsmouth walking tour brochures with map and descriptions of churches, homes, and old buildings from the Visitor Center at High St Landing.

Monumental United Methodist Church. *450 Dinwiddie St, 1 block N of High St. Phone 757/397-1297.* (1772) Methodist. Oldest Methodist congregation in the South; history room. Guided tour (Mon-Fri, by appointment; closed holidays).

⭐ **The Portsmouth Museums.** *221 High St (23704). Phone 757/393-8983.* Located in a 4-block radius, the museum complex has facilities housing artistic, educational, and historic exhibits. Museums (Memorial Day-Labor Day daily; closed Jan 1, Thanksgiving, Dec 25). Includes

Children's Museum of Virginia. *221 High St.* More than 60 interactive activities in 12 areas; planetarium. (Mid-June-Labor Day, Mon-Sat, also Sun afternoons) **$$**

Court House Galleries. *420 High St.* Changing exhibits. **$**

Lightship Museum. *London Slip and Water St.* Built in 1915, commissioned in 1916 as *Lightship 101*, it served 48 years in Virginia, Delaware, and Massachusetts. Retired in 1964 and renamed *Portsmouth*. **$**

Naval Shipyard Museum. *2 High St, on Elizabeth River.* Thousands of items of naval equipment, plus flags, uniforms, prints, maps, and models, including models of the CSS *Virginia*; the *US Ship-of-the-line Delaware*, built in Portsmouth; and the first ship drydocked in the US. **$**

Trinity Church. *500 Court St. Phone 757/393-0431.* Episcopal. Oldest church building (1762) and parish in Portsmouth. Legend says the church bell cracked while ringing out news of Cornwallis' surrender; it was later recast. Confederate Memorial window. Commodore James Barron, many colonial patriots are buried here. Open on request (Mon-Fri); office behind church in parish hall.

Hotels

★ ★ **HOLIDAY INN.** *8 Crawford Pkwy (23704). Phone 757/393-2573; toll-free 800/456-2811; fax 757/399-1248.* 222 rooms, 4 story. D $83-$113; each additional $10; under 19 free; weekend rates. Pet accepted. Check-out 11 am, check-in 4 pm. TV; cable (premium). In-room modem link. Laundry services. Restaurant 6:30 am-10 pm. Bar noon-2 am. Room service. Exercise equipment. Pool. Dockage, marina adjacent. Cr cds: A, D, DS, JCB, MC, V.

D ⬛ 🏊 🍴 ⬛

★ ★ ★ **RENAISSANCE PORTSMOUTH HOTEL.** *425 Water St (23704). Phone 757/673-3000. www.renaissancehotels.com.* 254 rooms, 16 story. S, D $89-$350; under 17 free. Suites $250-$1200. Check-out noon, check-in 3 pm. TV; cable (premium). In-room modem link. Restaurant 6:30 am-10 pm. Bar to midnight. Exercise equipment. Indoor pool; whirlpool. Business center. Concierge. Cr cds: A, C, D, DS, ER, JCB, MC, V.

🏊 🍴 ⬛ 🏃

Restaurants

★ ★ **CAFE EUROPA.** *319 High St (23704). Phone 757/399-6652.* Continental, Mediterranean menu. Hours: 11:30 am-2 pm, 5-9:30 pm; Fri, Sat to 10:30 pm. Closed Sun, Mon; most major holidays. Dinner $13.25-$18.95. Bar. Casual attire. Reservations accepted. Cr cds: MC, V.

D

★ **THE CIRCLE.** *3010 High St (23707). Phone 757/397-8196; fax 757/399-3074.* Steak menu. Hours: 8 am-10 pm; Fri, Sat to 11 pm; Sun brunch noon-9 pm. Closed Christmas. Dinner $9.95-$26.95. Bar. Children's menu. Casual attire. Reservations accepted. Rotunda dining room with extensive buffet. Cr cds: D, DS, MC, V.

D

Radford (H-6)

See also Blacksburg, Salem

Settled 1756 **Pop** 15,859 **Elev** 1,820 ft **Area code** 540 **Zip** 24141

Information Chamber of Commerce, 1126 Norwood St; 540/639-2202

Web www.radfordchamber.com

What to See and Do

Claytor Lake State Park. *4400 State Park Rd (24084). On VA 660, 6 miles SW, just S of I-81 exit 101. Phone 540/674-5492.* Consists of 472 acres in wooded hills adjacent to 5,000-acre lake. Swimming, sand beach, bathhouse, fishing, boating (ramp, rentals, marina); hiking and bridle trails, picnicking, concession, tent and trailer sites (electrical hookups, Apr-Sept), cabins (Mar-early Dec). Visitor center, interpretive programs. Standard fees. Park office and visitor center in Howe House (1876-1879), built on land once settled by Dunkers (Dunkards), a religious sect that fled persecution in Germany in the 1720s.

Radford University. *801 Norwood St. On US 11, I-81 exit 109. Phone 540/831-5324.* (1910) 9,142 students. Flossie Martin Gallery in Powell Hall houses visual arts with an emphasis on regional and contemporary; changing exhibits. Corinna de la Burde Sculpture Court, adjacent to the gallery, is an open-air museum displaying large-scale sculpture; changing exhibits, and permanent installations. Archives in the McConnell Library contain pamphlets, campus information, local history, oral history of Appalachia, and rare books. Greenhouse (daily). Dedmon Center, a recreation-convocation complex, features air-supported roof, arena seating 5,600; swimming pool; indoor tennis and handball courts. (Daily)

Special Event

The Long Way Home. *Contact PO Box 711; phone 540/639-0679.* Outdoor historical drama by Earl Hobson Smith depicts the true story of Mary Draper Ingles, survivor of the 1755 Draper's Meadow Massacre, and her heroic 850-mile flight to warn settlers of Native American attacks. Thurs-Sun, evenings, Mid-June-Aug.

Motels/Motor Lodges

★ ★ **BEST WESTERN RADFORD INN.** *1501 Tyler Ave (24141). Phone 540/639-3000; toll-free 800/628-1955; fax 540/633-0251. www.bestwestern.com.* 72 rooms, 2 story. S $60-$80; D $72-$90; each additional $5; under 18 free; higher rates university events. Crib free. Pet accepted. TV; cable (premium). Indoor pool; wading pool, whirlpool. Check-out noon. Business services available. Sundries. Exercise equipment; sauna. Bathroom phones; some refrigerators. Cr cds: A, C, D, DS, MC, V.

D 🐾 🏊 🎿 🖎 SC

★ **COMFORT INN.** *4424 Cleburne Blvd, Dublin (24084). Phone 540/674-1100; toll-free 800/638-7949; fax 540/674-2644. www.comfortinn.com.* 98 rooms, 2 story. S $56-$72; D $61-$78; each additional $6; under 18 free; higher rates university events. Crib free. TV; cable (premium). Pool. Complimentary continental breakfast. Restaurant adjacent 5-10 pm. Check-out noon. Meeting room. Business services available. Valet service. Sundries. Some in-room whirlpools; microwaves available. Cr cds: A, C, D, DS, ER, JCB, MC, V.

D 🏊 🖎 SC

★ **DOGWOOD LODGE.** *7073 Lee Hwy (24141). Phone 540/639-9338.* 15 rooms. S $28; D $33-$36; each additional $5; higher rates university events. Crib $5. Pet accepted. TV; cable (premium). Restaurant nearby. Check-out 11 am. Cr cds: DS, MC, V.

🐾

★ **EXECUTIVE MOTEL.** *7498 Lee Hwy (24143). Phone 540/639-1664; toll-free 888/393-8483; fax 540/633-1737.* 27 rooms, 13 with shower only, 2 story. Apr-Nov: S $32.50-$36.50; D $36.50-$46.50; under 12 free; higher rates special events; lower rates rest of year. Crib free. Pet accepted, some restrictions; $4. Check-out 11 am. TV; cable (premium), VCR. Refrigerators; microwaves available. Restaurant adjacent 6 am-11 pm. Health club privileges. Cr cds: A, C, D, DS, MC, V.

D 🐾 ♿ 🖎

Richmond (G-10)

See also Ashland, Hopewell, Petersburg

Settled 1607 **Pop** 197,790 **Elev** 150 ft **Area code** 804

Information Convention and Visitors Bureau, 550 E Marshall St, 23219; 804/782-2777 or 800/370-9004

Web www.richmondva.org

There have been few dull moments in Richmond's history. Native Americans and settlers fought over the ground on which it now stands. In 1775, Patrick Henry made his "liberty or death" speech in St. John's Church, and in 1780, the city was named capital of the state. At that time Virginia extended all the way to the Mississippi. British soldiers plundered it brutally in the Revolutionary War. As the capital of the Confederacy from 1861-1865, it was constantly in danger. Finally, in 1865, the city was evacuated and retreating Confederate soldiers burned the government warehouse; a portion of the rest of the city also went up in flames.

However, Richmond did survive. As Virginia's capital, it proudly exemplifies the modern South. It is a city industrially aggressive yet culturally aware, respectful of its own historical background yet receptive to new trends in architecture and modes of living. Richmond esteems both the oldest monuments and the newest skyscrapers.

Tobacco and tobacco products, paper and paper products, aluminum, chemicals, textiles, printing and publishing, and machinery contribute to the city's economy. Richmond is also an educational center; Virginia Commonwealth University, Virginia Union University, and the University of Richmond are based here.

What to See and Do

17th Street Market. *17th St between E Main and E Market sts.* Farmers market built on site of Native American trading village. Seasonal produce, flowers, holiday greens. (Daily)

6th Street Marketplace. *6th St between Coliseum and Grace St, downtown.* Restored area of shops, restaurants, entertainment.

Agecroft Hall. *Cary St exit off I-195, turn onto N Thompson Ave, then right on Cary to Malvern, then left on Cantebury to 4305 Sulgrave Rd. Phone 804/353-4241.* Half-timbered Tudor manor built in the late 15th century near Manchester, England. Disassembled, brought here, and rebuilt during the late 1920s in a spacious setting of formal gardens and grassy terraces overlooking the James River. English furnishings from 16th and 17th centuries. Audiovisual presentation explains history of house. (Tues-Sun; closed holidays) **$$**

⭐ **Capitol Square.** *Ninth and Grace St. (23224). Bounded by Broad, Governor, Bank, and 9th sts, downtown. Phone 804/784-5736.*

> **Equestrian Statue of Washington.** *9th and Grace sts.* By Thomas Crawford; cast in Munich over an 18-year period. Base features allegorical representations of six famous Revolutionary War figures from Virginia.

Richmond's Historical Legacy

Richmond was the Civil War "Capital of the Confederacy," and this aspect of its past can easily be recalled on a two-hour, 2-mile walking tour of the city center. The city also enjoys other, less-troubling claims to historical fame, which will be pointed out along the way. Begin this walk at the Virginia State Capitol, designed in 1785 by Thomas Jefferson, himself a state governor, in the style of a classical temple. Surrounded by Capitol Square's expanse of well-tended lawn, it displays such majesty that it still commands the eye despite the modern-day structures that surround it. Step inside the Rotunda to see the famous life-size statue of George Washington, the only one executed of him from life. From Capitol Square, walk north (right) on 9th Street across Broad Street to the neighborhood once known as Court End, which now bustles with students and faculty of the Medical College of Virginia. At 818 East Marshall Street (intersecting 9th) stands the most important residence of Court End, the home of John Marshall, the distinguished chief justice of the US Supreme Court from 1801 to 1835. Built in 1790, the two-story brick house where he lived for 45 years is a museum dedicated to his memory. Though it's a 7-block detour, head west on Marshall Street to 2nd Street and turn north (right) 2 blocks to 110 East Leigh Street, the Maggie Walker National Historic Site. A museum, the modest two-story brick home on a quiet residential street honors a black woman of impressive ability. Despite physical handicaps, Walker became America's first female bank president, establishing the Penny Savings Bank in 1903 as a way of helping local blacks during the Jim Crow period. Double back via Marshall Street past the John Marshall House, to the Valentine Museum at 1015 East Clay Street. A small, innovative museum with a contemporary outlook, it focuses on the people and history of Richmond. Conclude the tour a block down the street at 12th and East Clay at the adjacent Museum of the Confederacy and the White House of the Confederacy. Not surprisingly, the museum emphasizes Southern leaders, featuring mementos of General Robert E. Lee. The White House, a neoclassical mansion built in 1818, recounts the home life during the Civil War of Confederate President Jefferson Davis and his wife Varina.

Governor's Mansion. *9th and Grace sts (23219). E of State Capitol. Phone 804/371-2642.* (1813) This two-story Federal-style house was built after the capital was moved from Williamsburg. Oldest governor's mansion in the US still in use as a governor's residence. Tours (by appointment). **FREE**

State Capitol. *9th and Grace sts, Capitol Sq. Phone 804/698-1788.* (1785-1788) Modeled after La Maison Carrée, an ancient Roman temple at Nímes, France, the Capitol was designed by Thomas Jefferson. In this building, where America's oldest continuous English-speaking legislative bodies still meet, is the famous Houdon statue of Washington. The rotunda features the first interior dome in the US; here Aaron Burr was tried for treason, Virginia ratified the Articles of Secession, and Robert E. Lee accepted command of the forces of Virginia; the Confederate Congress also met in the building. (Mon-Sat, also Sun afternoons; closed Jan 1, Thanksgiving, Dec 25) Also on Capitol Square are

Virginia State Library and Archives. *800 E Broad St. Phone 804/692-3500.* Outstanding collection of books, maps, manuscripts. (Mon-Sat; closed holidays) **FREE**

Carytown. *W Cary St, between Boulevard St and I-95.* Eight blocks of shops, restaurants, theaters adjacent to historic Fan neighborhood.

Church Hill Historic Area. *Main and 21st sts. Bounded by Broad, 29th, Main, and 21st sts, E of Capitol Sq.* Neighborhood of 19th-century houses, more than 70 of which predate Civil War. Some Church Hill houses are open Historic Garden Week (see SPECIAL EVENTS). In the center of Church Hill is

Edgar Allan Poe Museum. *1914 E Main St. Phone 804/648-5523.* Old Stone House portion is thought to be oldest structure in Richmond (1737). Three additional buildings house Poe mementos; James Carling illustrations of "The Raven"; scale model of Richmond of Poe's time. Guided tours. (Tues-Sun; closed some major holidays). **$$$**

St. John's Episcopal Church. *25th and Broad sts. Phone 804/648-5015.* (1741) Where Patrick Henry delivered his stirring "liberty or death" speech. Reenactment of Second Virginia Convention (late May-early Sept, Sun). Guided tours. (Daily; closed holidays)

City Hall Observation Deck. *900 E Broad St. Phone 804/646-7000.* Eighteenth-floor observation deck offers panoramic view of the city, including Capitol grounds, James River, and Revolutionary and Civil War-era buildings contrasted with modern skyscrapers. (Mon-Fri) **FREE** Across the street is the old **City Hall** (1886-1894), a restored Gothic Revival building featuring an elaborate central court with arcaded galleries.

⭐ **The Fan and Monument Avenue.** *Main and Belvidere sts. Bounded by Franklin St and Monument Ave, Boulevard, Main, and Belvidere sts. Phone 804/643-3589.* Named for the layout of streets that fan out from Monroe Park toward the western part of town. Historical neighborhood has restored antebellum and turn-of-the-century houses, museums, shops, restaurants, and famed Monument Ave. The fashionable boulevard, between Lombard and Belmont sts, is dotted with imposing statues of Generals Lee, Stuart, and Jackson, of Jefferson Davis, and of Commodore Matthew Fontaine Maury, inventor of the electric torpedo. Within the area are

Richmond Children's Museum. *2626 W Broad St. Phone 804/474-2667; 877/295-2667.* Exhibits on arts, nature, and the world around us designed for children 2-12 years old; many hands-on exhibits. (July-Aug, daily; rest of year, Tues-Sun; closed holidays) **$$**

Science Museum of Virginia. *2500 W Broad St, N of Monument Ave. Phone 804/864-1400.* Hands-on museum. Major exhibits include aerospace, computers, electricity, visual perception, physical phenomena, and astronomy, and Foucault pendulum. The Ethyl Universe Planetarium Space Theater features Omnimax films and planetarium shows (inquire for schedule). (Tues-Sun; closed Thanksgiving, Dec 25)

Virginia Historical Society. *428 N Boulevard St. Phone 804/358-4901.* Comprehensive collection of Virginia history housed in Museum of Virginia History with permanent and changing exhibits, and Library of Virginia History with historical and genealogical research facilities. (Mon-Sat, museum also Sun afternoons; closed holidays) **$$**

Virginia Museum of Fine Arts. *Boulevard St and Grove Ave. Phone 804/340-1400.* America's first state-supported museum of art. Collections of paintings, prints, sculpture from major world cultures; Russian Imperial Easter eggs and jewels by Faberge; decorative arts of the Art Nouveau and Art Deco movements; sculpture garden; changing exhibits. Cafeteria. (Tues-Sun; closed holidays) **FREE**

Federal Reserve Money Museum. *701 E Byrd St, downtown, on first floor of bank. Phone 804/697-8000.* Exhibits of currency, include rare bills; gold and silver bars; money-related artifacts. (Open by appointment only; closed holidays) **FREE**

Historic Richmond Tours. *707 E Franklin St. Phone 804/649-0711.* Offers guided van tours with pickup at Visitor Center and major hotels (daily); reservations required. Also guided walking tours (Apr-Oct, daily; fee). **$$$$**

Hollywood Cemetery. *412 S Cherry St (23220). At Albemarle St. Phone 804/648-8501.* (1847) James Monroe, John Tyler, Jefferson Davis, other notables, and 18,000 Confederate soldiers are buried here; audiovisual program (Mon-Fri). (Daily 8 am-5 pm; walking tours Apr-Oct, Mon-Sat at 10 am) **FREE**

Jackson Ward. *Broad and Belvidere sts. Bounded by I-95, 7th, Broad, and Belvidere sts.* Historic downtown neighborhood that was home to many famous black Richmonders, including Bill "Bojangles" Robinson. Area has numerous 19th-century, Greek Revival, and Victorian buildings with ornamental ironwork that rivals the wrought iron of New Orleans. Within the ward are

Bill "Bojangles" Robinson Statue. *Corner of Leigh and Adams sts.* Memorial to the famous dancer who was born at 915 N 3rd St.

Black History Museum and Cultural Center. *Clay St. Phone 804/780-9093.* Limited editions, prints, art, photographs; African memorabilia; Sam Gilliam collection. (Tues-Sun 10 am-5 pm). **$$**

Maggie Walker National Historic Site. *600 N 2nd St. Phone 804/771-2017.* Commemorates life and career of Maggie L. Walker, daughter of former slaves, who overcame great hardships to become successful in banking and insurance; early advocate for women's rights and racial equality. Two-story, red brick house was home to her family 1904-1934. (Mon-Sat; closed Jan 1, Thanksgiving, Dec 25) **FREE**

John Marshall House. *818 E Marshall St. Phone 804/648-7998.* (1790) Restored house of famous Supreme Court justice features original woodwork and paneling; family furnishings, and mementos. (Tues-Sun; closed holidays) Combination ticket available for Marshall House, Valentine Museum, Museum of the Confederacy, White House of the Confederacy.

Kanawha Canal Locks. *12th and Byrd sts, downtown. Phone 804/780-0107 (walking tour) or 840/649-2800 (cruise tour).* Impressive stone locks were part of nation's first canal system, planned by George Washington. Narrated audiovisual presentation explains workings of locks and canal. Picnic grounds. (Mon-Sat) **FREE**

Meadow Farm Museum. *12 miles NW via I-95 N, I-295 W, Woodman Rd S exit, at Courtney and Mountain rds. Phone 804/501-5520. (General Sheppard Crump Memorial Park)* Living history farm museum depicting rural life in the 1860s. Orientation center, farmhouse, barn, outbuildings, crop demonstration fields, 1860s doctor's office. Also a 150-acre park with picnic shelters, playground. (Mar-Dec, Tues-Sun) **$**

Monumental Church. *1224 E Broad St, N of Capitol Sq.* (1812) Located on the Medical College of Virginia campus of Virginia Commonwealth University. Octagonal domed building designed by Robert Mills, architect of the Washington Monument. Commemorative structure was built on site where many prominent persons, including the governor, perished in a theater fire in 1811. Interior closed. Behind the church is the distinctive Egyptian Building (1845).

Museum of the Confederacy. *1201 E Clay St, N of Capitol Sq. Phone 804/649-1861.* Contains the nation's largest collection of Confederate military and civilian artifacts, including uniforms, equipment, flags, personal belongings of Jefferson Davis, Robert E. Lee, and J. E. B. Stuart, documents, manuscripts, and artwork. (Daily; closed Jan 1, Thanksgiving, Dec 25) **$$$**

Paddlewheeler *Annabel Lee.* *Departs from Intermediate Terminal. Phone 804/377-2020 or 800/752-7093.* Triple-decked, 350-passenger, 19th-century-style riverboat cruises the James River. Narrated tour; entertainment. Lunch, brunch, dinner, and plantation cruises. (Apr-Dec, at least one cruise Tues-Sun)

Parks. *Phone 804/780-5733.* For general information contact the Department of Parks and Recreation.

Bryan. *Bellevue Ave and Hermitage Rd.* A 279-acre park, 20 acres of which are an azalea garden with more than 55,000 plants (best viewed late Apr-mid-May). Picnic facilities, tennis courts. **FREE**

James River. *W 22nd St and Riverside Dr.* Five sections. Fishing, pedestrian bridges with overlook of James River, whitewater canoe and inner-tube accesses; bird-watching, wildlife sanctuary, self-guided tours, bicycle and hiking trails, visitor center with display, information station, interpretive programs. **FREE**

Lewis Ginter Botanical Garden. *1800 Lakeside Ave, in Lakeside. Phone 804/262-9887.* Victorian-era estate features the Grace Arents Garden and the Henry M. Flagler Perennial Garden; seasonal floral displays; emphasis on daffodils, daylilies, azaleas, and rhododendrons. (Daily) **$$$**

Maymont. *1700 Hampton St at Pennsylvania Ave. Phone 804/358-7166.* Dooley mansion, late Victorian in style, houses art collection and decorative arts exhibits (Tues-Sun; fee). Also here are formal Japanese and Italian gardens, an arboretum, a nature center with wildlife habitat for native species, an aviary, a children's farm, and a working carriage collection. (Daily) **FREE**

Pocahontas State Park. *10301 State Park Rd (23838). S on US 10, then W on VA 655. Phone 804/796-4255.* More than 7,000 acres; Swift Creek Lake. Swimming, pool, bathhouse, fishing, boating (launch, rentals, electric motors only); hiking trails, bicycle path (rentals), picnicking, concession, tent and trailer sites (seasonal), group cabins. Nature center; evening interpretive programs (summer). Standard fees. (Daily)

William Byrd. *Boulevard St and Idlewood Ave.* Includes 287 acres of groves, artificial lakes, picnic areas. Tennis courts, softball fields, fitness course. Amphitheater (June-Aug). Virginia's WWI memorial, a 240-foot, pink brick carillon tower.

Plantation Tours. *401 E Marshall St (23220). Phone 804/783-7450.* The Richmond-Petersburg-Williamsburg area has many fine old mansions and estates. Some are open most of the year; others only during Historic Garden Week (see SPECIAL EVENTS). The Metro Richmond Visitors Center has maps, information folders, suggestions. (Daily)

Shockoe Slip. *11 S 12th St. E Cary St between 12th and 14th sts, downtown.* Restored area of historic buildings and gaslit cobblestone streets; shopping, restaurants, galleries.

St. Paul's Church. *815 E Grace St, W of Capitol Sq. Phone 804/643-3589.* Episcopal. Established in 1843, the church survived the Civil War intact. It was here that Jefferson Davis received news of Lee's retreat from Petersburg to Appomattox. Beginning in 1890 the church added many fine stained-glass windows, including eight from the Tiffany studios. Sanctuary ceiling features decorative plasterwork interweaving Greek, Hebrew, and Christian motifs around a central panel. A Tiffany mosaic of da Vinci's *Last Supper* surmounts the altar. (Daily; closed holidays)

Valentine Museum. *1015 E Clay St, N of Capitol Sq. Phone 804/649-0711.* Traces history of Richmond. Exhibits focus on city life, decorative arts, costumes and textiles, industrial and social history; tour of restored 1812 Wickham House. Lunch served in walled garden (Apr-Oct). (Daily; closed holidays). **$$**

Virginia Aviation Museum. *5701 Huntsman Rd in Sandston, at Richmond International Airport. Phone 804/236-3622.* Exhibits and artifacts on the history of aviation, with emphasis on Virginia pioneers. (Daily; closed Thanksgiving, Dec 25) **$$**

Virginia House. *4301 Sulgrave Rd, 1/2 mile off VA 147 (Cary St), in Windsor Farms. Phone 804/353-4251.* A Tudor building constructed of materials from Warwick Priory (built in England in 1125 and rebuilt in 1565 as a residence); moved here in 1925. West wing is modeled after Sulgrave Manor, at one time the home of Lawrence Washington. Furniture, tapestries, and paintings from 15th to 20th centuries. Formal gardens. Tours by appointment only except during Historic Garden Week (see SPECIAL EVENTS). (Fri-Sun, otherwise by appointment; closed holidays) **$$**

Virginia War Memorial. *621 S Belvidere St, downtown at N end of Robert E. Lee Bridge.* Honors Virginians who died in WWII, Korean, and Vietnam wars. Mementos of battles; eternal flame; more than 12,000 names engraved on glass and marble walls. (Daily) **FREE**

White House of the Confederacy. *12th and E Clay sts, N of Capitol Sq.* Phone 804/649-1861. Classical Revival house (1818) used by Jefferson Davis as his official residence during period when Richmond was capital of the Confederacy. Abraham Lincoln met with troops here during Union occupation of the city. Restored to prewartime appearance; original furnishings. (Daily; closed Jan 1, Thanksgiving, Dec 25) **$$**

Wilton. *215 S Wilton Rd off Cary St, 8 miles W. Phone 804/282-5936.* (1753) Georgian mansion built by William Randolph III. Fully paneled, authentic 18th-century furnishings. Headquarters of National Society of Colonial Dames in Virginia. (Tues-Sun; closed holidays Open during Historic Garden Week (see SPECIAL EVENTS). **$$**

Special Events

Historic Garden Week in Virginia. *12 E Franklin St. Phone 804/644-7776.* Many private houses and gardens of historic or artistic interest are opened for this event, which includes more than 200 houses and gardens throughout the state. Tours. Mid-late Apr.

June Jubilee. *Downtown.* Performing and visual arts festival with ethnic foods, folk dances, music, crafts. First weekend in June.

Richmond Newpapers Marathon. Last Sun in Oct.

Virginia State Fair. *600 E Laburnum Ave (23222). Phone 804/228-3200.* Animal and 4-H contests, music, horse show, carnival. Late Sept-Oct 1.

Motels/Motor Lodges

★★ **COURTYARD BY MARRIOTT.** *6400 W Broad St (23230). Phone 804/282-1881; fax 804/288-2934. www.courtyard.com.* 145 rooms, 3 story. S, D $119; suites $149; weekend rates. Crib free. TV; cable (premium). Pool; whirlpool. Restaurant. Bar. Check-out noon. Coin laundry. Business services available. In-room modem link. Valet service. Sundries. Exercise equipment. Some refrigerators. Cr cds: A, C, D, DS, MC, V.

⊡ ≈ ⫯ ⬛

★ **FAIRFIELD INN.** *7300 W Broad St (23294). Phone 804/672-8621; toll-free 800/228-2800; fax 804/755-7155. www.fairfieldinn.com.* 124 rooms, 2 story. S, D $61-$89; each additional $5; suites $129; under 18 free. Crib $10. TV; cable (premium). Complimentary continental breakfast. Restaurant adjacent 11-2 am. Check-out noon. Business services available. Valet service. In-room modem link. Pool; sundeck. Refrigerator, microwave in suites. Picnic tables. Cr cds: A, C, D, DS, ER, JCB, MC, V.

⊡ ≈ ⬛ SC

★ **HAMPTON INN.** *10800 W Broad St, Glen Allen (23060). Phone 804/747-7777; fax 804/747-7069. www.hamptoninn.com.* 136 rooms, 5 story. D $98-$140; each additional $7; under 18 free. Complimentary continental breakfast. Check-out noon, check-in 3 pm. TV; cable (premium). In-room modem link. Exercise equipment. Pool. Cr cds: A, C, D, DS, MC, V.

⊡ ≈ ⫯ ⬛

★ **LA QUINTA INN.** *6910 Midlothian Tpke (23225). Phone 804/745-7100; toll-free 800/531-5900; fax 804/276-6660. www.laquintainn.com.* 130 rooms, 3 story. S, D $58-$65; each additional $5; under 18 free. Crib free. Pet accepted, some restrictions. TV; cable (premium). Pool. Complimentary continental breakfast. Restaurant adjacent. Check-out noon. Business services available. In-room modem link. Cr cds: A, C, D, DS, MC, V.

⊡ ⬛ ≈ ⬛ SC

★ **QUALITY INN.** *8008 W Broad St (23294). Phone 804/346-0000; fax 804/527-0284. www.qualityinn.com.* 191 rooms, 6 story. Apr-Oct: S, D $79-$149; each additional $10; under 18 free; lower rates rest of year. Pet accepted, fee. Complimentary continental breakfast. Check-out 11 am. TV; cable (premium). In-room modem link. Restaurant nearby. Exercise room. Pool. Cr cds: A, C, D, DS, ER, JCB, MC, V.

⊡ ⬛ ≈ ⫯ ⬛ SC

★ **RED ROOF INN.** *4350 Commerce Rd (23234). Phone 804/271-7240; fax 804/271-7245; res 800/843-7663. www.redroof.com.* 108 rooms, 2 story. S $35.99-$49.99; D $42.99-$65.99; under 18 free; higher rates race weekends. Pet accepted. TV; cable (premium). Restaurant nearby. Check-out noon. Business services available. Some refrigerators, microwaves. Cr cds: A, C, D, DS, MC, V.

⊡ ⬛ ⬛

Hotels

★★★ **THE BERKELEY HOTEL.** *1200 E Cary St (23219). Phone 804/780-1300; toll-free 888/780-4422. www.berkeleyhotel.com.* This hotel opened in 1988 but appears to be a property of days gone by. It is located at the crossroads of the business district and Historic Shockoe Slip. Dark wood paneling adorns the lobby and dining room. Dramatic windows to the ceiling give it a European appearance and diners get a view of the Slip's cobblestone and lamplights. 56 rooms, 6 story. S $145-$180; D $125-$210; each additional $15; under 18 free; weekend rates. Suite $650. Check-out noon. TV; cable (premium), VCR available. In-room modem link. Restaurant 7 am-2 pm, 6-10 pm; Fri, Sat to 11 pm; Sun to 9 pm. Bar 11:30 am-2 pm, 5:30 pm-midnight. Health club privileges. Valet parking $10. Concierge. Cr cds: A, C, D, DS, MC, V.

🄳 ⊠ 🆂🅲

★ ★ ★ **CROWNE PLAZA.** *555 E Canal St (23219). Phone 804/788-0900; fax 804/788-0791. www. richmondcrowneplaza.com.* Just 9 miles from Richmond International Airport, this hotel is situated in the heart of the historic district and minutes from area attractions such as Shockoe Slip, Sixth Street Market Place, museums, theaters, and fine dining. 299 rooms, 16 story. Apr-June, Sept-Oct: S, D $179; each additional $10; suites $249-$895; under 18 free; weekend rates; lower rates rest of year. Garage, valet parking. Crib free. TV; cable (premium). Heated indoor pool; whirlpool. Restaurant 6 am-11 pm. Room service 6 am-midnight. Bar 4 pm-midnight; weekends to 1 am. Check-out noon. Convention facilities. Business center. In-room modem link. Concierge. Gift shop. Valet service. Exercise equipment; sauna. Health club privileges. Luxury level. Cr cds: A, C, D, DS, JCB, MC, V.

🄳 ⇌ 🄵 ⊠ 🅉 🉆

★ ★ ★ **HILTON RICHMOND AIRPORT.** *5501 Eubank Rd, Sandston (23150). Phone 804/226-6400; toll-free 800/445-8667; fax 804/226-1269. www.hilton.com.* This hotel is just 40 minutes from Colonial Williamsburg and directly across from the Richmond International Airport. Area attractions include Kings Dominion, Busch Gardens, Richmond Coliseum, Aviation Museum, and the Museum of the Confederacy. 160 rooms, 5 story, 122 suites. S, D $79-$159; family, weekend rates. Crib free. TV; cable (premium). Pool; whirlpool. Restaurant 6:30 am-10 pm. Room service 24 hours. Bar 11 am-midnight. Check-out noon. Meeting rooms. Business services available. In-room modem link. Bellstaff. Valet service. Sundries. Free airport transportation. Exercise equipment. Volleyball. Some balconies. Luxury level. Cr cds: A, C, D, DS, ER, JCB, MC, V.

🄳 ⇌ 🉆 ⊠ 🆂🅲

★ ★ ★ ★ ★ **THE JEFFERSON HOTEL.** *101 W Franklin St (23220). Phone 804/788-8000; toll-free 800/424-8014; fax 804/225-0334. www.jefferson-hotel.com.* The Jefferson Hotel is an institution in the heart of Richmond.

Imaginations run wild at this historic landmark, dating to 1895. It's easy to conjure a beautifully dressed debutante gliding down the hotel's sweeping staircase, or influential politicians having a heated debate under the impressive marble-style columns. The guest rooms are furnished in a traditional style defined by antique reproductions and fine art, while modern amenities and inimitable Southern hospitality ensure the comfort of all guests. Pedigreed residents take afternoon tea here. TJ's provides a casual setting for fine dining with local dishes like oyster chowder and peanut soup. The hotel's star restuarant is Lemaire, with its sparkling ambience and refined menu. 264 rooms, 9 story. Pet accepted. Check-out noon, check-in 3 pm. TV; cable (premium), VCR available. In-room modem link. Room service 24 hours. Restaurant. Bar. Children's activity center. Babysitting services available. In-house fitness room. Indoor pool. Valet parking. Business center. Concierge. Cr cds: A, C, D, DS, JCB, MC, V. **$$$**

🄳 🐾 ⇌ 🉆 ⊠ 🆂🅲 🚶

★ ★ ★ **MARRIOTT RICHMOND.** *500 E Broad St (23219). Phone 804/643-3400; fax 804/788-1230; res 800/228-9290. www.marriott.com.* 410 rooms, 17 story. D $99-$149; each additional $10; under 18 free; weekend rates. Check-out noon, check-in 3 pm. TV; cable (premium). In-room modem link. Laundry services. Restaurant 6:30 am-10 pm. Bar 11-1 am. Exercise equipment, sauna. Game room. Indoor pool, whirlpool, poolside service. Business center. Concierge. Luxury level. Cr cds: A, C, D, DS, JCB, MC, V.

🄳 ⇌ 🉆 ⊠ 🚶

★ ★ ★ **OMNI RICHMOND HOTEL.** *100 S 12th St (23219). Phone 804/344-7000; fax 804/648-1029. www.omnihotels.com.* This contemporary hotel is located in the center of the financial and historic district and features views of the scenic James River. 369 rooms, 19 story. Mid-Apr-mid-June, mid-Sept-mid-Nov: S $139; D $109-$219; each additional $15; suites $209-$450; under 18 free; package plans; lower rates rest of year. Check-out noon. TV; cable (premium). In-room modem link. Restaurant 6:30 am-11 pm. Bar noon-1 am. Health club privileges. Indoor pool; poolside service. Business center. Concierge. Luxury level. Cr cds: A, C, D, DS, MC, V.

🄳 ⇌ ⊠ 🉆

★ ★ **SHERATON RICHMOND WEST HOTEL.** *6624 W Broad St (23230). Phone 804/285-2000; toll-free 800/228-9000; fax 804/288-3961. www.starwood/sheraton/richmondwest.com.* This hotel has guest rooms that are conveniently located to the Richmond airport. 372 rooms, 3-8 story. Check-out noon, check-in 3 pm. TV; cable (premium), VCR available. In-room modem link. Restaurant. Bar; entertainment. Room service. Babysitting services available. In-house fitness room. Indoor, outdoor pools. Outdoor tennis. Airport transportation. Business center. Luxury level. Cr cds: A, C, D, DS, JCB, MC, V. **$$**

D ⟡ ⇌ ✈ ✕ ⤳ SC ⟰

All Suites

★ **AMERISUITES.** *4100 Cox Rd, Glen Allen (23060). Phone 804/747-9644; toll-free 800/833-1516; fax 804/ 346-9320. www.amerisuites.com.* 126 suites, 6 story. D $79-$129; under 18 free. Complimentary continental breakfast. Check-out noon, check-in 3 pm. TV; cable (premium). Laundry services. Exercise equipment. Pool. Business center. Cr cds: A, C, D, DS, JCB, MC, V.

D ⇌ ⟰ ⤳ SC ⟰

★ ★ **EMBASSY SUITES.** *2925 Emerywood Pkwy (23294). Phone 804/672-8585; toll-free 800/362-2779; fax 804/672-3749. www.embassy-suites.com.* 224 suites, 8 story. S, D $119-$185; each additional $20; under 18 free. Crib free. TV; cable (premium). Indoor pool; whirlpool. Complimentary full breakfast. Restaurant 11 am-10 pm. Bar to 11 pm. Check-out noon. Coin laundry. Meeting rooms. Business center. In-room modem link. Gift shop. Exercise equipment; sauna. Refrigerators, microwaves; wet bars. Cr cds: A, C, D, DS, JCB, MC, V.

D ⇌ ⟰ ⟰ ⤳ SC

B&B/Small Inns

★ ★ **EMMANUEL HUTZLER HOUSE.** *2036 Monument Ave (23220). Phone 804/353-6900. www.bensonhouse.com.* 4 rooms, 3 story. S $105-$140; D $115-$160. Children over 12 years only. TV; cable. Complimentary full breakfast. Restaurant nearby. Check-out noon, check-in 4 pm. Luggage handling. Health club privileges. Built 1914; antiques. Totally nonsmoking. Cr cds: A, D, DS, MC, V.

⤳

★ ★ **LINDEN ROW INN.** *100 E Franklin St (23219). Phone 804/783-7000; fax 804/648-7504 toll-free 800/348-7424. www.lindenrowinn.com.* 68 rooms, 8 suites; 4 story. S, D $79-$139; additional $10; suites $149-$189. Complimentary continental breakfast. Check-out 11 am, check-in 3 pm. TV; cable (premium). In-room modem link. Dining room (public by reservation) 11 am-2:30 pm, 5:30-10 pm. Room service. Health club privileges. Concierge. In block of Greek Revival rowhouses

(1847), around courtyard thought to be playground of Edgar Allan Poe; antique and period furnishings and décor. Cr cds: A, D, DS, MC, V.

⤳

★ **THE PATRICK HENRY INN.** *2300 E Broad St (23223). Phone 804/225-0477.* 3 rooms. Apr-June, Oct-Nov: S $95-$135; D $115-$135; each additional $10; family, weekly, weekend rates; holiday weekends (2-day minimum); higher rates special events; lower rates rest of year. TV; cable. Complimentary continental breakfast. Check-out noon, check-in 3 pm. Luggage handling. Street parking. Refrigerators. Greek Revival antebellum row house (circa 1855); garden patio, carriage house. Cr cds: A, MC, V.

SC

Extended Stay

★ ★ **RESIDENCE INN BY MARRIOTT.** *2121 Dickens Rd (23230). Phone 804/285-8200; fax 804/285-2530; res 800/331-3131. www.residenceinn.com.* 80 kitchen suites, 2 story. S, D $119-$159; monthly, weekly, weekend rates. Crib free. Pet accepted, some restrictions; $50. Complimentary continental breakfast. Check-out noon. TV; cable (premium), VCR available (movies). In-room modem link. Private patios, balconies. Refrigerators, microwaves; many fireplaces. Valet services. Coin laundry. Pool; whirlpool. Tennis. Volleyball. Picnic tables. Meeting room. Business services. Cr cds: A, C, D, DS, ER, JCB, MC, V.

D ⟡ ⟡ ⇌ ⤳

Restaurants

★ ★ **ACACIA.** *3325 W Cary St (23221). Phone 804/ 354-6060; fax 804/354-6062. www.acaciarestaurant.com* Hours: 11:30 am-9:30 pm. Closed Sun. Lunch $5.95-$9.95, dinner $10.50-$24.95. Entertainment. In an old renovated church. Cr cds: A, D, DS, MC, V.

D ⤳

★ ★ **AMICI.** *3343 W Cary St (23221). Phone 804/353-4700; fax 804/278-6291. www.amiciristorante.net.* Northern Italian menu. Hours: 11:30 am-2:30 pm, 5:30-10 pm; Fri, Sat to 11 pm; Sun from 5:30 pm. Closed major holidays. Lunch $7.95-$12.95, dinner $13.95-$23.95. Bar. Outdoor seating. Cr cds: A, D, DS, MC, V.

★ **BYRAM'S LOBSTER HOUSE.** *3215 W Broad St (23230). Phone 804/355-9193. www.byrams.com.* Continental, Greek, seafood menu. Hours: 11:30 am-10 pm; early-bird dinner Mon-Fri 3:30-6 pm. Closed Jan 1, Dec 25. Lunch $3.95-$13.95. Dinner $8.95-$25.95. Bar. Cr cds: A, D, DS, MC, V.

SC

★ ★ **CABO'S CORNER BISTRO.** *2053 W Broad St (23220). Phone 804/355-1144.* Seafood menu. Closed Sun, Mon. Dinner. Bar. Casual attire. Cr cds: A, MC, V. **$$**

Ⓓ

★ ★ **CAFE MANDOLIN.** *1309 W Main St (23220). Phone 804/355-8558.* International menu. Closed Sun, Mon. Lunch, dinner. Bar. Casual attire. Outdoor seating. Cr cds: A, D, MC, V. **$$**

Ⓓ

★ **CAFFE DI PAGLIACCI.** *214 N Lombardy St (23220). Phone 804/353-3040; fax 804/358-2509. www.caffedipagliacci .com.* Italian menu. Hours: 5-10 pm; Fri, Sat to 11 pm. Closed Mon; major holidays. Sun brunch. Bar. Casual attire. Dinner: $8.95-$19.95. Cr cds: A, C, D, DS, MC, V.

★ ★ ★ **THE DINING ROOM AT THE BERKE-LEY HOTEL.** *1200 E Cary St (23219). Phone 804/225-5105; fax 804/343-1885. www.berkleyhotel.com.* Located in a European-style hotel, this handsomely decorated dining room serves elegant, immpecably prepared meals in an atmosphere that is sophististicated, tranquil, and sedate. Many fine Virginia products are served and classical preparation prevails. Hours: 7 am-10 pm. Breakfast $6.25-$9.75, lunch $7.95-$13.95, dinner $24.95-$34.95. Entertainment. Children's menu. Reservations accepted. European ambiance. Cr cds: A, C, D, DS, MC, V.

Ⓓ

★ **FAROUK'S HOUSE OF INDIA.** *3033 W Cary St (23221). Phone 804/355-0378. www.faroukshouseofindia. com.* Indian menu. Hours: 11:30 am-3 pm, 5:30-10:30 pm. Lunch $5-$8.95, dinner $8.95-$12. Cr cds: A, D, DS, MC, V.

Ⓓ ⓈⒸ

★ ★ **HALF WAY HOUSE.** *10301 Jefferson Davis Hwy (23237). Phone 804/275-1760.* Hours: 11:30 am-2 pm, 5:30-9 pm; Sat, Sun from 5:30 pm. Lunch $9-$18. Dinner $25-$35. Bar. Antique-furnished manor house (1760) was stop on Petersburg stagecoach line until late 19th century; hosted Washington, Lafayette, Patrick Henry, Jefferson, among others. Used as a Union headquarters during 1864 siege of Richmond. Cr cds: A, D, DS, MC, V.

★ ★ **HELEN'S.** *2527 W Main St (23220). Phone 804/358-4370; fax 804/358-4553.* Menu changes weekly. Hours: 5:30-9:30 pm. Closed Mon, major holidays. Reservations accepted. Wine list. Dinner $18-$24. Entertainment. Cr cds: A, MC, V.

★ ★ ★ **KABUTO JAPANESE HOUSE OF STEAK.** *8052 W Broad St (23294). Phone 804/747-9573.* Japanese menu. Hours: 11:30 am-2 pm, 5-9:30 pm; Fri to 10 pm; Sat 4:30-10 pm; Sun 4-10 pm. Closed Thanksgiving,

Dec 25. Lunch $8.50-$12.25, dinner $14-$25. Bar. Children's menu. Cr cds: A, D, DS, MC, V.

Ⓓ

★ ★ **LA PETIT FRANCE.** *2108 Maywill St (23230). Phone 804/353-8729; fax 804/353-4692. www.lapetitefrance. net.* French menu. Closed Sun, Mon; major holidays; also last 2 weeks in Aug. Lunch $8.95-$13.95, dinner $18.50-$29.95. Children's menu. Jacket (dinner). Cr cds: A, D, DS, MC, V.

Ⓓ

★ ★ ★ **LEMAIRE.** *101 W Franklin (23220). Phone 804/788-8000; fax 804/344-5162. www.jefferson-hotel.com.* Old-world fine dining comes to life at Lemaire, located in the historic Jefferson Hotel (see also). The restaurant is named for Etienne Lemaire, who served as maitre d' to President Jefferson and was widely credited for introducing the fine art of cooking with wines to America. His love of food and wine is continued at Lemaire, where contemporary Southern cooking goes upscale with French accents, homegrown herbs, featherweight sauces, and seasonal ingredients. Professional and friendly service and quiet, intimate surroundings make dining at Lemaire a delight. American menu. Closed Memorial Day. Breakfast, lunch, dinner. Bar. Children's menu. Jacket required. Valet parking available. Seven small dining rooms. Cr cds: A, D, DS, MC, V. **$$$**

Ⓓ

★ **MILLIE'S.** *2603 E Main St (23223). Phone 804/643-5512; fax 804/648-4321. www.milliesdiner.com.* Thai menu. Hours: 11 am-10:30 pm; Sat 10 am-10:30 pm; Sun 9 am-3 pm, 5:30-9:30 pm. Closed Mon. Lunch $6-$11, dinner $16.95-$25.95. Sun brunch. Entertainment. In front of old tobacco warehouses, huge collection of old 45 singles with mini-jukeoxes in booths. Cr cds: A, DS, MC, V.

Ⓓ 🚭

★ **O'TOOLES.** *4800 Forest Hill Ave (23225). Phone 804/233-1781; fax 804/232-1737.* Hours: 11-2 am; Sun to midnight. Closed Dec 24, 25. Bar. Lunch $3.75-$8, dinner $4.25-$12.95. Children's menu. Specializes in seafood, steak, barbecued dishes. Pianist. Parking. Irish pub décor. Family-owned. Cr cds: A, MC, V.

Ⓓ

★ ★ ★ **THE ORIGINAL BOOKBINDER'S.** *2306 E Cary St (23223). Phone 804/643-6900; fax 804/643-6690. www.oldoriginalbookbinders.com.* Specializes in steak, seafood. Hours: 4:30-10 pm; Sun to 9 pm. Closed major holidays. Reservations accepted. Bar. Wine list. Complete meals: dinner $16.95-$35. Children's menu. Valet parking. Family-owned. Cr cds: A, D, DS, MC, V.

★ ★ **PEKING PAVILION.** *1302 E Cary St (23219). Phone 804/649-8888; fax 804/649-8147.* Chinese menu. Hours: 11:30 am-2:15 pm, 5-9:30 pm; Fri to 10:30 pm; Sat 5-10:30 pm; Sun brunch 11:30 am-2 pm. Closed Thanksgiving. Lunch $5.20-$8.55, dinner $6.75-$23.95. Sun brunch $9.95. Bar. Cr cds: A, MC, V.

★ ★ **RIVAH BISTRO.** *1417 E Cary St (23219). Phone 804/344-8222.* French Bistro menu. Lunch, dinner. Bar. Children's menu. Casual attire. Outdoor seating. **$$**

D

★ ★ ★ **RUTH'S CHRIS STEAK HOUSE.** *11500 Huguenot Rd (23113). Phone 804/378-0600; fax 804/378-0776. www.sizzlingsteak.com.* Located in the historic Bellgrade Plantation House, the offering is fine dining with elegant southern hospitality. Dine on the patio or in a private room with period furnishings. For those seeking a ribeye or New York strip, this restaurant definitely lives up to its name as the home of serious steaks. Hours: 5-10 pm; Fri, Sat to 11 pm; Sun to 9 pm. Closed some major holidays. Reservations accepted. Bar. A la carte entrées: dinner $19.95-$32.95. Specializes in steak, lobster. Organist Tues-Sun. Parking. Outdoor seating. Cr cds: A, D, DS, MC, V.

D

★ ★ **SAM MILLER'S WAREHOUSE.** *1210 E Cary St (23219). Phone 804/644-5465; fax 804/644-5470. www.sammillers.com.* Seafood menu. Hours: 11 am-11 pm; Sun 10 am-10 pm. Closed Labor day, Dec 25. Dinner $15.95-$26.95. Children's menu. In historic district; display of antique mirrors. Casual attire. Reservations accepted. Lobster tank. Cr cds: A, D, DS, MC, V.

★ ★ **SKILLIGALEE.** *5416 Glenside Dr (23228). Phone 804/672-6200; fax 804/755-1312. www.skilligalee.com.* Hours: 11:30 am-4 pm, 5-10 pm; Fri to 10:30 pm; Sat 5-10:30 pm; Sun 5-9 pm. Closed Thanksgiving, Dec 25. Bar. A la carte entrées: lunch $5.95-$11.95, dinner $15.95-$25.95. Children's menu. Specializes in fresh seafood, soups. Raw bar. Own salad dressing. Parking. Nautical décor with fireplace. Family-owned. Cr cds: A, DS, MC, V.

D

★ **STRAWBERRY STREET CAFE.** *421 Strawberry St (23220). Phone 804/353-6860; fax 804/358-3569. www.strawberrystreetcafe.com.* Specializes in crab cakes, chicken pot pie, salad bar. Hours: 11:30 am-10:30 pm; Fri to midnight; Sat 11 am-midnight; Sun 10 am-10:30 pm. Reservations accepted. Wine list. Lunch $5.50-$9.50; dinner $7.95-$16.95. Children's menu. Entertainment. Stained glass throughout restaurant. Cr cds: A, MC, V.

★ **TANGLEWOOD ORDINARY.** *2210 River Rd, Maidens (23102). Phone 804/556-3284. www.ordinary.com.* Traditional Southern menu. Specializes in chicken, roast beef, seasoned vegetables, ham. Hours: 5-9 pm; Sun noon-8 pm. Closed Mon-Tues; some major holidays. Complete meals: dinner $12. Beer, wine. Casual dining in log cabin building. Reservations accepted; required Wed. Collection of *The Saturday Evening Post* dating from 1913. Totally nonsmoking.

★ ★ **TOBACCO COMPANY.** *1201 E Cary St (23219). Phone 804/782-9555; fax 804/788-8913. www.thetobaccocompany.com.* Hours: 11:30 am-2:30 pm, 5:30-10:30 pm; Sun 11 am-2:30 pm, 5:30-9:30 pm. Closed Jan 1, Dec 25. Lunch $5.95-$9.95, dinner $17.95-$28.95. Sun brunch $4.95-$15.95. Bar 11:30-2 am. In former tobacco warehouse (circa 1880); built around skylit atrium with antique cage elevator; many unusual antiques. Reservations accepted weekend (dinner). Cr cds: A, D, DS, JCB, MC, V.

D

★ **TRAK'S.** *9115 Quioccasin Rd (23229). Phone 804/740-1700; fax 804/740-1700.* Greek, Italian, Mediterranean menu. Hours: 11 am-10 pm; Fri, Sat to 11 pm. Closed Sun; also some major holidays. Lunch $6.49-$9.10. Dinner $10.95-$23.95. Children's menu. Cr cds: A, D, DS, MC, V.

D

★ ★ **YEN CHING.** *6601 Midlothian Tpke (23225). Phone 804/276-7430. www.yenchingdining.com.* Hours: 11:30 am-9:30 pm; Fri, Sat to 11 pm. Closed Thanksgiving. Reservations required. Chinese menu. Bar. Lunch, dinner $7.95-$22.95. Specializes in Hunan and Szechuan dishes. Parking. Chinese tapestries and art. Cr cds: A, MC, V.

D

Richmond National Battlefield Park

See also Ashland, Richmond

(Headquarters located at 3215 E Broad St, in Chimborazo Park)

Web www.nps.gov

A total of seven Union drives on Richmond, the symbol of secession, were made during the Civil War. Richmond National Battlefield Park, 770 acres in ten different units, preserves sites of the two efforts that came close to success—McClellan's Peninsula Campaign of 1862 and Grant's attack in 1864.

Of McClellan's campaign, the park includes sites of the Seven Days' Battles at Chickahominy Bluffs, Beaver Dam Creek, Gaines' Mill (Watt House), and Malvern Hill. Grant's campaign is represented by the battlefield at Cold Harbor, where on June 3, 1864, Grant hurled his army at fortified Confederate positions, resulting in 7,000 casualties in less than one hour. Confederate Fort Harrison, Parker's Battery, Drewry's Bluff (Fort Darling), and Union-built Fort Brady are also included. Park (Daily; closed Jan 1, Thanksgiving, Dec 25).

What to See and Do

Main Visitor Center. *In Chimborazo City Park. 3215 E Broad St, on US 60 E in Richmond. Phone 804/226-1981.* Information, exhibits, film, slide program. (Daily; closed Jan 1, Thanksgiving, Dec 25) **FREE** From here start

Self-guided tour. Auto drive (60 miles) with markers, maps, recorded messages providing background, detailed information for specific places. Visitors may select own route, including all or part of the drive.

Other Visitor Centers. *Cold Harbor, 16 miles NE on VA 156 (daily, unstaffed) and Fort Harrison, 10 miles SE on VA 5 and Battlefield Park Rd* (June-Aug, daily). **FREE**

Roanoke (H-7)

See also Salem

Settled 1740 **Pop** 94,911 **Elev** 948 ft **Area code** 540

Information Roanoke Valley Convention & Visitors Bureau, 114 Market St, 24011; 540/342-6025 or 800/635-5535

Web www.visitroanokeva.com

Roanoke was incorporated in 1882 when it became a junction of the Norfolk and Western Railway and the Shenandoah Valley Railroad. Before that, the town was called Big Lick (salt marshes in the area attracted big game).

It is the cultural, industrial, commercial, convention, and medical center for western Virginia. Manufactured products include railroad cars, fabricated steel, fabrics, apparel, furniture, flour, wood products, electronic equipment, plastics, cosmetics, and locks.

Set in the Shenandoah Valley between the Blue Ridge and the Allegheny mountains, it is near the outdoor attractions of the huge Washington and Jefferson national forests (see HARRISONBURG) and the Blue Ridge Parkway (see).

What to See and Do

Blue Ridge Parkway. (see) *6 miles E on US 460 or 3 miles S on US 220.* Runs on crest of mountains both north and south of Roanoke. Narrow in parts; limited restaurants. Beautiful seasonal views from overlooks.

Center in the Square. *1 Market Sq, downtown. Phone 540/342-5700.* Restored 20th-century furniture warehouse housing five independent cultural organizations: three museums, including Art Museum of Western Virginia, and two professional theater companies (see SPECIAL EVENTS). (Tues-Sun; closed holidays) Also here are

History Museum of Western Virginia. *1 Market Sq SE. Phone 540/342-5770.* Permanent exhibits deal with Roanoke history from days of Native Americans to present. Archives, library (by appointment). (Tues-Sun; closed holidays) **$**

Science Museum of Western Virginia & Hopkins Planetarium. *1 Market Sq (24011). Phone 540/342-5710.* Museum contains hands-on exhibits in the natural and physical sciences: animals of land and ocean, computers, TV weather station. Workshops, programs, and classes for children and adults; special exhibits. Hopkins Planetarium shows films. (Tues-Sun; closed holidays) **$$$**

George Washington and Jefferson National Forests. (see HARRISONBURG)

Mill Mountain Zoological Park. *Off US 220/I-581 and Blue Ridge Pkwy. Phone 540/343-3241.* Zoo sits atop Mill Mountain; offers picnic areas with magnificent views of city and valley. (Daily; closed Dec 25) **$$$**

Virginia's Explore Park. *3900 Rutrough Rd SE. Miles 115 on Blue Ridge Pkwy. Phone 800/842-9163.* This 1,300-acre living history museum and nature center features re-created frontier settlement that depicts life in western Virginia in 1671, 1740, and 1850. Six miles of hiking trails. Picnic areas. (May-Oct, Wed-Sun) **$$$**

Virginia Museum of Transportation. *303 Norfolk Ave, downtown. Phone 540/342-5670.* Vehicles from the past and present. Large steam, diesel, and electric locomotive collection. Aviation exhibits; model of miniature traveling circus. Hands-on exhibits. (Mar-Dec, daily; rest of year, Wed-Sun; closed holidays) **$$$**

Special Events

Festival in the Park. *119 Park Ave (23510). Phone 757/625-1445.* Art exhibits, crafts, sports, food, parade, entertainment. Two weekends beginning the Fri before Memorial Day.

Mill Mountain Theatre. *1 Market Sq SE (24011).* For reservations phone 540/342-5740. *Center in the Square.* Musicals, comedies, dramas. Nightly Tues-Sun; Sat, Sun matinees. Regular season, Oct-Aug.

Virginia State Championship Chili Cookoff. *City Market. Contact Roanoke Special Events Committee, 210 Reserve*

Ave SW, 24016. Phone 540/342-4716. Teams compete to represent Virginia in World Cook-off. Samples, entertainment. First Sat in May.

Motels/Motor Lodges

★ ★ **BEST INN.** *501 Orange Ave (24016). Phone 540/342-8961; toll-free 800/237-8466; fax 540/342-3813.* 150 rooms, 2 story. S, D $39.95-$89.95. Complimentary breakfast buffet. Check-out noon. TV; cable (premium), VCR available. In-room modem link. Restaurant 7 am-9 pm. Bar from 5 pm. Pool, children's pool. Cr cds: A, C, D, DS, ER, JCB, MC, V.

D ⇌ ⊠ SC

★ ★ **CLARION HOTEL.** *2727 Ferndale Dr NW (24017). Phone 540/362-4500; toll-free 800/228-5050; fax 540/362-4506. www.clarionhotel.com.* 154 rooms, 5 story. S $89-$129; D $99-$129; each additional $10; under 18 free; weekend rates. Crib free. Pet accepted; $50 deposit. TV; cable (premium). Indoor/outdoor pool; whirlpool. Restaurant 6 am-10:30 pm. Room service. Bar 11:30 am-11 pm. Check-out noon. Meeting rooms. Business services available. In-room modem link. Bellstaff. Valet service. Sundries. Free airport transportation. Lighted tennis. 18-hole golf privileges. Exercise equipment. Bathroom phones. Picnic tables, grills. Cr cds: A, C, D, DS, ER, JCB, MC, V.

D ⇌ ⛷ ➤ ⊼ ✈ ⊠ SC

★ **COLONY HOUSE MOTOR LODGE.** *3560 Franklin Rd SW (24014). Phone 540/345-0411.* 69 rooms, 2 story. S $46; D $58-$68; each additional $5; under 13 free. Crib available. TV; cable. Complimentary continental breakfast. Restaurant adjacent 11 am-10 pm. Check-out 11 am. Meeting rooms. Business services available. Valet service. Health club privileges. Pool. Bathroom phone, in-room whirlpool, refrigerator in suites. Cr cds: A, C, D, DS, MC, V.

D ⇌ ⊠ SC

★ **DAYS INN.** *8118 Plantation Rd (24019). Phone 540/366-0341; toll-free 800/329-7466; fax 540/366-3935. www.daysinn.com.* 123 rooms, 2 story. S $45-$60; D $55-$65; each additional $6; suites $80; under 12 free. Crib available. TV; cable (premium), VCR available. Pool. Restaurant 6-10:30 am, 5-10 pm. Bar 4:30-11 pm. Check-out noon. Meeting rooms. Business services available. In-room modem link. Valet service. Free airport transportation. Cr cds: A, C, D, DS, JCB, MC, V.

D ⇌ ⊠ SC

★ **HAMPTON INN.** *6621 Thirlane Rd (24019). Phone 540/265-2600; fax 540/366-2091. www.hamptoninn.com.* 79 rooms, 2 story. S $70-$72; D $76-$80; suites $103; under 18 free; higher rates: graduation, sporting events. Crib free. Valet parking $20. TV; cable (premium), VCR. Restaurant nearby. Check-out 11 am. Meeting rooms. Business services available. Valet service. Sundries. Coin laundry. Free airport transportation. Exercise equipment. Heated pool. Refrigerators, microwaves; some bathroom phones; in-room whirlpool in suites. Cr cds: A, C, D, DS, MC, V.

D ⇌ ⊼ ⊠

★ **HAMPTON INN.** *3816 Franklin Rd SW (24014). Phone 540/989-4000; fax 540/989-0250. www.hamptoninn. com.* 59 rooms, 2 story. May-Nov: S $58-$62; D $68-$72; family rates; higher rates special events. Crib free. Complimentary continental breakfast. Check-out 11 am. TV; cable (premium), VCR available. In-room modem link. Some refrigerators, microwaves. Valet services. Coin laundry. Restaurant adjacent 10:30 am-9 pm; weekends from 8 am. Health club privileges. Meeting room. Business services. Cr cds: A, C, D, DS, MC, V.

D ⊠

★ ★ **HOLIDAY INN.** *6626 Thirlane Rd NW (24019). Phone 540/366-8861; toll-free 800/465-4329; fax 540/366-1637. www.holiday-inn.com/hotels/roaap.* 161 rooms, 2 story. S, D $74-$85; under 18 free; weekend, special event rates. Crib free. Check-out noon. TV; cable (premium), VCR available. In-room modem link. Some bathroom phones. Valet services. Coin laundry. Restaurant 6 am-10 pm. Bar. Room service. Health club privileges. Pool; wading pool. Airport transportation. Meeting rooms. Business services. Sundries. Cr cds: A, C, D, DS, JCB, MC, V.

D ⇌ ⊼ ⊠ SC

★ ★ **HOLIDAY INN.** *4468 Starkey Rd (24014). Phone 540/774-4400; toll-free 888/228-5040; fax 540/774-1195. www.holiday-inn.com.* 196 rooms, 5 story. S, D $88-$102; suites $128-$153; under 18 free; weekend rates. Crib free. Pet accepted; $10. TV; cable (premium). Pool; poolside service. Restaurant 6:30 am-10 pm. Room service. Bar 4 pm-2 am; entertainment. Check-out noon. Meeting rooms. Business services available. In-room modem link. Bellstaff. Valet service. Concierge. Free airport, bus depot transportation. Golf privileges. Health club privileges. Some wet bars; microwaves available. Luxury level. Cr cds: A, C, D, DS, JCB, MC, V.

D ➤ ⇌ ⊠

★ **RAMADA INN.** *1927 Franklin Rd SW (24014). Phone 540/343-0121; fax 540/342-2048. www.ramada.com.* 127 rooms, 4 story. S $58; D $64; each additional $7; under 18 free; higher rates special events. Pet accepted. Complimentary full breakfast. Check-out noon. TV;

cable. In-room modem link. Coin laundry. Restaurant 11:30 am-2:30 pm, 4:30-9:30 pm. Bar 4:30 pm-2 am. Health club privileges. Pool. Meeting rooms. Business services. Sundries. Near river. Cr cds: A, C, D, DS, JCB, MC, V.

[icons]

★ **SLEEP INN.** *4045 Electric Rd (24014). Phone 540/ 772-1500; toll-free 800/628-1929; fax 540/772-1500.* 103 rooms, shower only, 2 story. No elevator. S $55.95-$60.95; D $60.95-$65; each additional $6; under 18 free. Crib free. TV; cable (premium), VCR. Complimentary continental breakfast. Restaurant nearby. Check-out noon. Meeting room. Business services available. In-room modem link. Valet service. Health club privileges. Microwaves available. Cr cds: A, C, D, DS, ER, JCB, MC, V.

[icons] SC

★ **TRAVELODGE.** *2619 Lee Hwy S, Troutville (24175). Phone 540/992-6700; toll-free 800/578-7878; fax 540/992-3991. www.travelodge.com/troutville109699.* 108 rooms. S $45; D $52; each additional $6; kitchen units $45; under 18 free; weekly rates. Crib free. Pet accepted; $6. TV; cable (premium). Pool. Playground. Complimentary continental breakfast. Restaurant nearby. Check-out 11 am. Meeting rooms. Business services available. Some refrigerators, microwaves. Cr cds: A, D, DS, MC, V.

[icons] SC

Hotels

★ ★ ★ **DOUBLETREE ROANOKE HOTEL AND CONFERENCE CENTER.** *110 Shenandoah Ave (24016). Phone 540/985-5900; toll-free 800/22TREE; fax 540/853-8290.* This vintage 1882 hotel has been lovingly restored to its rich, 19th-century elegance and is listed in the National Register of Historic Places. It has all that one would desire in a hotel and conference center. It is just a short walk across the Market Square Bridge to downtown Roanoke. 332 rooms, 7 story. S $119-$145; D $129-$155; each additional $10; suites $165-$450; under 18 free; weekend, holiday rates; higher rates: graduation, football. Crib free. Check-out noon. TV; cable (premium). In-room modem link. Some refrigerators, fireplaces. Restaurant 6:30 am-10 pm; Sat from 7 am; Sun 7 am-9 pm. Bar 11 am-midnight; Fri, Sat to 1 am; entertainment Fri, Sat. Exercise equipment. Pool; whirlpool. Golf privileges, pro, putting green, driving range. Tennis privileges. Valet parking $5. Free airport transportation. Business center. Convention center/facilities. Gift shop. Cr cds: A, C, D, DS, ER, JCB, MC, V.

[icons] SC

★ ★ **PATRICK HENRY HOTEL.** *617 S Jefferson St (24011). Phone 540/345-8811; toll-free 800/303-0988; fax 540/342-9908. www.patrickhenryroanoke.com.* This

Virginia historic landmark provides guests with all the modern conveniences. Close by is shopping, dining, and entertainment. 117 kitchen units, 10 story. S $99; D $109; each additional $10; suites $125-$250; under 18 free; monthly rates. Crib available. Complimentary continental breakfast. Check-out noon. TV; cable (premium). In-room modem link. Refrigerators; microwaves available. Guest laundry. Restaurant 11:30 am-11 pm. Bar 4 pm-2 am. Health club privileges. Barber, beauty shop. Free airport transportation. Meeting rooms. Business services. Cr cds: A, C, D, DS, JCB, MC, V.

[icons]

★ ★ **WYNDHAM ROANOKE AIRPORT HOTEL.** *2801 Hershberger Rd NW (24017). Phone 540/563-9300; fax 540/366-5846; res 800/996-3426. www.wyndham.com.* 320 rooms, 8 story. S, studio rooms $74-$134; D $84-$150; each additional $10; suites $210-$250; under 18 free; golf, weekend rates. Crib free. Pet accepted, some restrictions; $10. Check-out noon. TV; cable (premium), VCR available. Private patios, balconies. Some refrigerators. Restaurant 6:30 am-10 pm. Bar 11-1 am. Exercise equipment, sauna. 2 pools, 1 indoor; whirlpool, poolside service. Lighted tennis. Free airport transportation. Business services. Convention center/facilities. Concierge. Gift shop. Luxury level. Cr cds: A, C, D, DS, ER, JCB, MC, V.

[icons]

B&B/Small Inn

★ ★ **CLAIBORNE HOUSE.** *185 Claiborne Ave, Rocky Mount (24151). Phone 540/483-4616. www.claibornehouse .net.* 5 rooms, 2 story. Some room phones. S, D $75-$125. TV in some rooms; cable (premium). Complimentary full breakfast. Check-out 11 am, check-in 3 pm. Business services available. Game room. Built in 1895; Victorian-style décor. Totally nonsmoking. Cr cds: MC, V.

[icon]

Restaurants

★ ★ **BILLY'S RITZ.** *102 Salem Ave SE (24011). Phone 540/342-3937.* Three dining areas with eclectic décor. Steak menu. Hours: 5-10:30 pm; Fri, Sat to midnight. Closed most major holidays; Jan 1-16. Dinner $13-$28. Bar. Outdoor seating. Cr cds: A, D, DS, MC, V.

[icon]

★ ★ **KABUKI JAPANESE STEAK HOUSE.** *3503 Franklin Rd SW (24014). Phone 540/981-0222; fax 540/ 342-0406.* Japanese menu. Closed some major holidays; also Jan 2, Super Bowl Sun. Dinner. Bar. Children's menu. Reservations required Fri, Sat. Cr cds: A, D, DS, MC, V. **$$**

[icon]

★ ★ ★ **LIBRARY.** *3117 Franklin Rd (24014). Phone 540/985-0811; fax 540/345-6588.* Not only is this 1785 New England-style mansion a historic landmark, but it has served the likes of George Washington and a host of other presidents. Hours: 6 pm-midnight. Closed Sun; major holidays. Reservations accepted. French, American menu. Bar. Wine cellar. Dinner $12.95-$29.95. Specialties: roast rack of lamb, Dover sole, steak Diane. Own pastries. Parking. Antique books on display. Jacket. Cr cds: A, D, DS, MC, V.

D

Salem (H-7)

See also Roanoke

Founded 1802 **Pop** 24,747 **Elev** 1,060 ft **Area code** 540 **Zip** 24153

Information Salem/Roanoke County Chamber of Commerce, 9 N College Ave, PO Box 832; 540/387-0267

Salem, part of the industrial complex of the Roanoke Valley, shares with Roanoke the beautiful setting between the Blue Ridge and Allegheny mountains. Historic markers throughout Salem indicate the city's colonial heritage.

What to See and Do

Dixie Caverns. *5753 W Main St (24153). Off I-81 at exit 132. Phone 540/380-2085.* Stalactites in lofty chambers; modern lighting system makes 45-minute tour comfortable as well as interesting. Pottery shop and mineral shop (all year). Camping facilities (fee). (Daily; closed Dec 25) **$$$**

Roanoke College. *221 College Ln. Off I-81. Phone 540/375-2282.* (1842) 1,750 students. One of the few Southern colleges to remain open during the Civil War. Many historic buildings, some antebellum. Olin Hall, fine arts building, has theater, art gallery, and sculptures. Excellent exhibit of paintings, photographs, and other items concerning Mary, Queen of Scots (by appointment only; phone 540/375-2487). Tours.

Motels/Motor Lodges

★ ★ **HOLIDAY INN.** *1671 Skyview Rd (24153). Phone 540/389-7061; toll-free 800/465-4329; fax 540/389-7060. www.holiday-inn.com.* 102 rooms, 3 story. S, D $52-$89; each additional $6; under 19 free. Crib free. TV; cable (premium). Pool; wading pool. Complimentary continental breakfast. Restaurant 6:30 am-2 pm, 5-10 pm. Room service. Check-out noon. Meeting rooms. Business

services available. In-room modem link. Bellstaff. Valet service. Sundries. Cr cds: A, C, D, DS, ER, JCB, MC, V.

D ⌷ ⌷ SC

★ **HOLIDAY INN EXPRESS.** *1535 E Main St (24153). Phone 540/986-1000; toll-free 800/465-4329; fax 540/986-0355. www.holiday-inn.com.* 70 rooms, 3 story. S $55; D $60-$65; each additional $7; under 19 free. Crib free. TV; cable (premium), VCR available (movies). Complimentary continental breakfast. Check-out 11 am. Business services available. In-room modem link. Sundries. Exercise equipment. Refrigerators, microwaves. Cr cds: A, D, DS, JCB, MC, V.

D ⌷ ⌷ SC

★ ★ **QUALITY INN.** *179 Sheraton Dr (24153). Phone 540/562-1912; toll-free 800/459-4949; fax 540/562-0507. www.qualityinn.com.* 120 rooms, 2 story. S $51-$57; D $54-$61; each additional $6; under 18 free. Crib free. Pet accepted, some restrictions; $6. TV; cable (premium), VCR available. Pool. Complimentary continental breakfast. Restaurant 5-9 pm. Bar 5 pm-11 pm. Check-out 11 am. Meeting rooms. Coin laundry. Business services available. Airport transportation. Putting green. Exercise equipment. Balconies. Cr cds: A, C, D, DS, JCB, MC, V.

D ⌷ ⌷ ⌷ ⌷ ⌷

Restaurant

★ **SHANGHAI.** *1416 Colorado St (24153). Phone 540/389-4151; fax 540/389-7049.* Chinese menu. Closed Thanksgiving, Dec 25. Lunch, dinner, Sun brunch. Bar. Children's menu. Cr cds: A, D, DS, MC, V. **$**

D

Shenandoah National Park (E-9)

See also Front Royal, Luray, New Market, Waynesboro

About 450 million years ago, the Blue Ridge was at the bottom of a sea. Today, it averages 2,000 feet above sea level; some 300 square miles of the loveliest Blue Ridge area are included in Shenandoah National Park.

The park is 80 miles long and 2–13 miles wide. Running its full length is the 105-mile Skyline Drive. Main entrances are the North Entrance (Front Royal), from I-66, US 340, US 522, and VA 55; Thornton Gap Entrance (31.5 miles south), from US 211; Swift Run Gap Entrance (65.7 miles south), from US 33; and the South Entrance (Rockfish Gap), from I-64, US 250, and the Blue Ridge Parkway (see). The drive, twisting and turning along the crest of the Blue Ridge, is one of the finest scenic trips in the East. Approximately 70 overlooks give views of the Blue Ridge, the Piedmont, and, to the west, the Shenandoah Valley and the Alleghenies.

The drive offers much, but the park offers more. Exploration on foot or horseback attracts thousands of visitors who return again and again. Most of the area is wooded, predominantly in white, red, and chestnut oak, with hickory, birch, maple, hemlock, tulip poplar, and nearly 100 other species scattered here and there. At the head of Whiteoak Canyon are hemlocks that are more than 300 years old. The park bursts with color and contrast in the fall, which makes this season particularly popular with visitors. The park is a sanctuary for deer, bears, foxes, and bobcats, along with more than 200 varieties of birds.

Accommodations are available in the park, with lodges, motel-type units, and cabins at Big Meadows and Skyland and housekeeping cabins at Lewis Mountain. For reservations and rates (which vary), contact ARA-MARK Virginia Sky-Line Company, Inc, PO Box 727, Luray 22835-9051; phone 800/999-4714. Nearby communities provide a variety of accommodations. In the park, there are restaurants at Panorama, Skyland, and Big Meadows; light lunches and groceries are available at Elkwallow, Big Meadows, Lewis Mountain, and Loft Mountain waysides.

The park is open all year; lodge and cabin accommodations, usually Mar-Dec; phone ahead for schedule. Skyline Drive is occasionally closed for short periods during Nov-Mar. As in all national parks, pets must be on a leash. The speed limit is 35 miles per hour. $10 per car per week, annual permit $20; Golden Age, Golden Access, and Golden Eagle Passports are accepted (see MAKING THE MOST OF YOUR TRIP).

Park Headquarters is 5 miles east of Luray on US 211. Detailed information and pamphlets may be obtained by contacting the Superintendent, Shenandoah National Park, 3655 US 211 E, Luray 22835; phone 540/999-3500.

What to See and Do

Camping. *Phone 800/365-CAMP.* First-come, first-served tent and trailer sites (no hookups) at Mathews Arm, Lewis Mountain, and Loft Mountain. Big Meadows requires reservations. Fourteen-day limit. Campers must register and check out. (Spring-fall) Write Park Superintendent, 3655 US 211 E, Luray 22835, for information. **$$$$**

Fishing. Trout. Regulations and directions at entrance stations, Dickey Ridge, Panorama, Big Meadows, and Loft Mountain. State or 5-day nonresident license necessary.

Hiking. The 500 miles of trails include 101 miles of Appalachian Trail. Along the trail, which winds 2,100 miles from Maine to Georgia, are numerous side trails to mountaintops, waterfalls, and secluded valleys. Trail crosses Skyline Dr at several points and can be entered at many overlooks. Overnight backcountry use requires a permit. No open fires are allowed. Regulations and permits may be obtained at any park entrance station, visitor center, or at Park Headquarters. Backcountry may be closed during periods of high fire danger. Visitor Centers and lodges post schedules of evening programs and ranger-led hikes. Self-guided walks ranging from 1/2 to two hours are at Dickey Ridge (Mile 4.6), Skyland (Mile 1.7), Big Meadows (Mile 51.1), Lewis Mountain (Mile 57.5), and Loft Mountain (Mile 79.5).

Interpretive program. Guided walks, illustrated campfire talks. (Usually mid-June-mid-Oct; rest of year, on a limited basis) Obtain schedule at Park Headquarters, entrance stations, visitor centers, and concessions.

Picnicking. Near Dickey Ridge Visitor Center, Elkwallow, Pinnacles, Big Meadows, Lewis Mountain, South River, Loft Mountain.

⭐ **Points of special interest on Skyline Drive.** (Mile posts are numbered north to south, starting at Front Royal. Periods of operation are estimated—phone ahead.)

Big Meadows. *Mile 51.1.* (3,500 feet) Accommodations, restaurant; store, gas; tent and trailer sites; picnic grounds; nature trail. (Usually Apr-Nov)

Byrd Visitor Center. *Mile 51.* Exhibits, information, book sales, orientation programs, maps. (Usually Apr-Nov, daily)

Dickey Ridge Visitor Center. *Mile 4.6.* Exhibits, programs, information, book sales; picnic grounds. (Usually Apr-Nov, daily)

Elkwallow. *Mile 24.1.* (2,445 feet) Picnic grounds; food, store. (May-Oct, daily)

Lewis Mountain. *Mile 57.5.* (3,390 feet) One- and two-bedroom cabins with heat; tent and trailer sites; picnic grounds, store. (Usually May-Oct)

Loft Mountain. *Mile 79.5.* (3,380 feet) Picnicking, camping (May-Oct); wayside facility; gas, store (May-Oct).

Loft Mountain Information Center. *Mile 79.5.* Exhibits, information; programs, nature trail. (Usually May-Nov)

Marys Rock Tunnel. *Mile 32.4.* (2,545 feet) Drive goes through 600 feet of rock (clearance 13 feet).

Panorama. *Mile 31.5, at junction US 211.* (2,300 feet) Dining room, gift shop. Trail to Marys Rock. Closed in winter.

Motels/Motor Lodges

★ **BEST WESTERN INN.** *260 Rowe Rd (24401). Phone 540/885-1112; toll-free 800/752-9471. www. bestwestern.com.* 80 rooms, 4 story. May-Oct: S $62-$75; D $72-$85; each additional $8; under 18 free; family rates; higher rates: graduation, fall foliage; lower rates rest of year. Complimentary continental breakfast. Check-out 11 am. TV; cable. Restaurant adjacent 6:30 am-9 pm. Indoor pool. Cr cds: A, C, D, DS, JCB, MC, V.

D ⌨ ⌦ SC

★ **BUDGET HOST INN.** *3554 Lee-Jackson Hwy, Greenville (24401). Phone 540/337-1231; fax 540/337-0821.* 32 rooms, 2 story. May-Nov: S $35-$45; D $45-$75; each additional $6; under 12 free; weekly rates; lower rates rest of year. Crib free. Pet accepted, some restrictions; $6. TV; cable (premium). Pool; wading pool. Playground. Complimentary continental breakfast. Restaurant nearby. Check-out 11 am. Refrigerators. Private patios, balconies. Picnic tables. Cr cds: A, D, DS, MC, V.

◀ ⌨ ⌦ SC

★ **COMFORT INN.** *1302 Richmond Ave (24401). Phone 540/886-5000; fax 540/886-6643. www.comfortinn.com.* 98 rooms, 5 story. May-Oct: S $67-$114; D $77-$114; each additional $10; under 18 free; higher rates special events; lower rates rest of year. Crib available. Pet accepted, some restrictions. Complimentary continental breakfast. Check-out 11 am. TV; cable (premium). Refrigerators, microwaves. Restaurant adjacent open 24 hours. Pool. Business services. Cr cds: A, C, D, DS, JCB, MC, V.

D ◀ ⌨ ⌦

★ ★ **HOLIDAY INN.** *I-81; Hwy 275 (24401). Phone 540/248-6020; toll-free 800/465-4329; fax 540/248-2902. www.holidayinnstaunton.com.* 116 rooms, 4 story. Mid-Mar-mid-Nov: S, D $79-$89; suites $95; under 17 free; golf plans; lower rates rest of year. Crib free. TV; cable (premium). Indoor/outdoor pool; poolside service. Restaurant 6 am-10 pm. Room service. Bar 4 pm-11 pm; entertainment. Check-out noon. Meeting rooms. Business services available. In-room modem link. Valet service. Sundries. Free airport transportation. Lighted tennis. 18-hole golf, greens fee $25, pro, putting green, driving range. Exercise equipment. Refrigerator, wet bar in suites. Some balconies. Cr cds: A, C, D, DS, ER, JCB, MC, V.

D ⛷ ⌥ ⌨ ⌧ ⌦ SC

★ ★ **SHONEY'S MOTOR INN.** *I-81 and Rte 250 (24402). Phone 540/885-3117; toll-free 800/222-2222; fax 540/885-5620.* 91 rooms, 2 story. S $48; D $55; each additional $6; under 18 free. Complimentary continental breakfast. Check-out noon. TV; cable (premium). Restaurant 6 am-11 pm; Fri, Sat to 1 am. Exercise equipment, sauna. Indoor pool, whirlpool. Cr cds: A, C, D, DS, ER, MC, V.

D ⌨ ⌧ ⌦ SC

B&B/Small Inns

★ ★ **BELLE GRAE INN.** *515 W Frederick St (24401). Phone 540/886-5151; fax 540/886-6641. www.bellegrae.com.* 14 rooms, 2 story. Some room phones. Children over 12 years only. Complimentary full breakfast. Check-out 11 am, check-in 3 pm. TV in most rooms. Fireplaces. Dining room. Golf privileges. Airport transportation. 1870s restored Victorian mansion. Each room individually decorated. Cr cds: A, MC, V. **$**

D ⌥ ⌦ SC

★ ★ **FREDERICK HOUSE.** *28 N New St (24401). Phone 540/885-4220; toll-free 800/334-5575; fax 540/885-5180. www.frederickhouse.com.* 23 rooms, 2 story. Complimentary full breakfast. Check-out 11 am, check-in 3 pm. TV. Health club privileges. Golf privileges. Encompasses 6 adjacent townhouses built 1810-1919. Totally nonsmoking. Cr cds: A, D, DS, MC, V. **$$**

⌥ ⌦ SC

★ ★ **THORNROSE HOUSE.** *531 Thornrose Ave (24401). Phone 540/885-7026; toll-free 800/861-4338; fax 540/885-6458. www.thornrosehouse.com.* 5 rooms, 2 story. No room phones. Complimentary full breakfast. Check-out 11 am, check-in 3 pm. Georgian Revival house (1912); wrap-around veranda. Opposite park. Totally nonsmoking. Cr cds: A, MC, V. **$**

⌦

Restaurants

★ **THE PULLMAN RESTAURANT.** *36 Middlebrook Ave (24401). Phone 540/885-6612; fax 540/885-6774. www.thepullman.com.* Seafood menu. Closed major holidays. Lunch, dinner, Sun brunch. Entertainment. Children's menu. Cr cds: A, DS, MC, V. **$**

D

★ **ROWE'S.** *74 Rowe Rd (24401). Phone 540/886-1833; fax 540/886-0910. www.mrsrowes.com.* Closed some major holidays. Breakfast, lunch, dinner. Children's menu. Reservations accepted. Cr cds: D, MC, V. **$**

D SC

Strasburg (D-9)

See also Front Royal, Winchester, Woodstock

Founded 1761 **Pop** 4,017 **Elev** 578 ft **Area code** 540 **Zip** 22657

Information Chamber of Commerce, PO Box 42; 540/465-3187

Lying at the base of Massanutten Mountain and on the north fork of the Shenandoah River, Strasburg was founded in 1761 by German settlers. Prospering in the early 19th century as a center of trade and flour milling, the village later became identified with the manufacture of high quality pottery, earning the nickname "Pottown" after the Civil War. The town's location on the Manassas Gap Railroad and the Shenandoah Valley Turnpike gave Strasburg a pivotal role in Stonewall Jackson's Campaign of 1862. The first western Virginia town to be served by two railroads, Strasburg became prominent after 1890 as a railroad town, manufacturing center, and home of printing and publishing businesses.

Today Strasburg, located near the entrance to the Skyline Drive, offers historical and cultural museums. It attracts visitors with its antebellum and Victorian architecture and its burgeoning art community. The town calls itself the "antique capital of Virginia" because of its many antique shops.

What to See and Do

Belle Grove. *336 Belle Grove Rd (22645). 4 miles N on US 11. Phone 540/869-2028.* (1794) The design of this limestone mansion reflects the influence of Thomas Jefferson. Used as Union headquarters during the Battle of Cedar Creek, October 19, 1864. Unusual interior woodwork; herb garden in rear. Guided tours. (Apr-Oct, daily) A National Trust for Historic Preservation property. (See SPECIAL EVENTS) **$$$**

Hupp's Hill Battlefield Park and Study Center. *33229 Old Valley Pike. I-81 to exit 298, S 1/2 mile on US 11. Phone 540/465-5884.* Former campsite for six different Civil War generals' troops, now a museum and hands-on interpretive center. Artifacts, documents, exhibits. Guided battlefield tours (by appointment; fee). (Daily; closed holidays) **$$**

Strasburg Museum. *440 E King St. Phone 540/465-3175.* Blacksmith, cooper, and potter shop collections; displays from colonial homes; relics from Civil War and railroad eras; Native American artifacts. Housed in Southern Railway Depot. (May-Oct, daily) **$**

Special Events

Battle of Cedar Creek Reenactment. *8437 Valley Pike (22645). Phone 830/278-2016. Belle Grove.* Mid-Oct.

Mayfest. Celebration of town's German heritage with parade, entertainment and arts, crafts, antiques, and foods fairs. Third weekend in May.

Wayside Theatre. *7853 Main St. On US 11, I-81 exit 302. Phone 540/869-1776.* Professional performances. Wed-Sun. Reservations required. Late May-mid-Oct and Dec.

B&B/Small Inns

★ ★ ★ **HOTEL STRASBURG.** *213 S Holliday St (22657). Phone 540/465-9191; toll-free 800/348-8327;* *fax 540/465-4788. www.hotelstrasburg.com.* Queen Anne, Renaissance Revival and Eastlake-style antiques make up many of the furnishings of this Victorian-style hotel. Guests are welcome to explore each room looking at the antiques as most are available for purchase. 29 rooms, 3 story. Complimentary continental breakfast (Mon-Fri). Check-out 11 am, check-in 2 pm. TV. Restaurant. Bar. Health club privileges. Victorian building. Cr cds: A, C, D, DS, MC, V. **$$**

⊠ SC

★ ★ ★ **WAYSIDE INN–MIDDLETOWNE.** *7783 Main St, Middletown (22645). Phone 540/869-1797; fax 540/869-6038. www.waysideofva.com.* Operating since 1797, this inn is located in the Shenandoah Valley at the foot of the Massanutten Mountains. Canopied beds, English, French, and Oriental antiques, brocades, chintzes, and silks decorate the property. Fresh cuisine is prepared and served in seven different dining rooms. 22 rooms, 3 story. Check-out 11 am, check-in 2 pm. TV; cable. Restaurant. Bar 11 am-midnight. Boating, swimming nearby. An inn since 1797. Restored Colonial-era building. Cr cds: A, D, DS, MC, V. **$**

D SC

Restaurants

★ ★ ★ **HOTEL STRASBURG.** *213 S Holliday St (22657). Phone 540/465-9191; fax 540/465-4788. www.hotelstrasburg.com.* The inn's ornate Victorian lobby gives way to an invitingly cozy country restaurant, where locals and travelers alike dine on fine wines and elegant cuisine. Continental menu. Hours: 11:30 am-2:30 pm, 5-9 pm; Fri, Sat 8 am-2:30 pm, 5-10 pm; Sun 8 am-9 pm. Dinner $7.95-$23.95, Sun brunch $8.95. Bar from 11 am. Children's menu. Reservations accepted; required Sat. Totally nonsmoking. Cr cds: A, D, DS, MC, V.

★ ★ **WILKINSON'S TAVERN.** *7783 E Main St (US 11), Middletown (22645). Phone 540/869-1797; fax 540/869-6038.* Hours: 7 am-3 pm, 5-9 pm; Fri, Sat to 10 pm; Sun 8 am-3:30 pm, 5-9 pm; Sun brunch 11:30 am-3:30 pm. Reservations accepted; required Sat. Bar 11 am-midnight. Breakfast $2.75-$6.95, lunch $4.95-$8.95, dinner $14.95-$21.95. Sun brunch $14.95. Children's menu. Specializes in fresh seafood, chicken, vegetarian dishes. In restored colonial-era inn; many antiques. Cr cds: A, D, DS, MC, V.

SC

Surry

See also Colonial Parkway, Jamestown (Colonial National Historical Park), Newport News, Williamsburg

Pop 262 **Elev** 122 ft **Area code** 757 **Zip** 23883

What to See and Do

Chippokes Plantation State Park. *695 Chippokes Park Rd. 6 miles E via VA 10, 634. Across James River from Jamestown.* Phone 757/294-3625 *(park) or* 757/294-3439 *(museum).* Plantation continuously operated since 1619. Approximately 1,600 acres. Swimming pool, fishing; hiking and bicycle paths, interpretive tour road, picnicking, concession. Visitor center, programs. Tours of mansion, carriage house, kitchen, and formal gardens (Memorial Day-Labor Day, Wed-Sun; Apr-Oct weekends). (See SPECIAL EVENT) Farm and Forestry Museum (Memorial Day-Labor Day, Wed-Sun; Apr-Oct, weekends). Standard fees. **$**

Special Event

Pork, Peanut, and Pine Festival. *Chippokes Plantation.* Pork products, peanuts, crafts, pine decorations. Third weekend in July.

Tangier Island

Settled 1666 **Pop** 604 **Elev** 3 ft **Area code** 757 **Zip** 23440

Bought from Native Americans for two overcoats, Tangier was first settled by a mainland family named West. In 1686, John Crockett moved here with his four sons and four daughters. They were later joined by a few other families. Descendants of these families now populate the island. Life is simple and lacks most urban complexities. Most of the men are anglers, oystering and clamming in one season, crabbing in another.

This tranquil little island (approximately 4 miles long) is 12 miles out in Chesapeake Bay. The island offers good duck hunting, fishing, swimming, and relaxation. There is an airfield here, and there are excursion boats from Reedville and Onancock, Virginia, and Crisfield, Maryland. Accommodations include a boarding house, Chesapeake House, with seven rooms, family-style meals. Contact PO Box 194; phone 757/891-2331 for reservations.

Tappahannock (F-11)

See also Lancaster, Montross, Richmond

Founded 1680 **Pop** 2,068 **Elev** 22 ft **Area code** 804 **Zip** 22560

Information Chamber of Commerce, PO Box 481; 804/443-5241

Bartholemew Hoskins patented the first land here in 1645. Following his lead, others came and a small village

soon sprang up, known at that time as Hobbes His Hole. Formally chartered in 1682 as New Plymouth, the town was to experience yet another name change. Built around the Rappahannock River, which means "running water," the town port became known as Tappahannock or "on the running water." Four hundred men gathered here in 1765 to protest the Stamp Act.

Today the area around Prince and Duke streets and Water Lane of Tappahannock has been declared a historic district. Highlights include the beautifully renovated Ritchie House, the Anderton House, once used for the prizing of tobacco into hogsheads, and Scot's Arms Tavern.

Motels/Motor Lodges

★ **DAYS INN.** *Rte 17 Tappahannock Blvd (22560).* Phone 804/443-9200; toll-free 800/329-7466; fax 804/443-2663. www.daysinn.com. 60 rooms, 2 story. S, D $44-$49; each additional $6; under 12 free. Crib free. TV; cable. Complimentary continental breakfast. Check-out 11 am. Business services available. Cr cds: A, C, D, DS, MC, V.
ⓓ ⊠ SC

★ **SUPER 8.** *US 17 and 360 (22560).* Phone 804/443-3888; fax 804/443-3888. www.super8.com. 43 rooms, 2 story. Apr-Sept: S $49.88; D $55.88; each additional $5; under 12 free; lower rates rest of year. Pet accepted. Check-out 11 am. TV; cable. Some refrigerators. Restaurant opposite 6 am-11 pm. Meeting rooms. Business services. Cr cds: A, C, D, DS, MC, V.
ⓓ ⊷ ⊠

Restaurant

★ ★ **LOWERY'S SEAFOOD RESTAURANT.** *US 17 and 360 (22560).* Phone 804/443-4314; fax 804/443-4474. www.lowerysrestaurant.com. Seafood menu. Closed Dec 25. Lunch, dinner. Own salad dressing. Cr cds: A, D, MC, V. **$$**
ⓓ

Triangle (E-11)

See also Alexandria, Fredericksburg; also see Washington, DC

Pop 5,500 **Elev** 150 ft **Area code** 703 **Zip** 22172

Information Prince William County/Manassas Conference & Visitors Bureau, 8609 Sudley Rd, Suite 105, Manassas 20110; 703/396-7130

Web www.visitpwc.com

Quantico Marine Corps Base is 3 miles east of town.

What to See and Do

Marine Corps Air-Ground Museum. *715 Broadway St. 2 miles E, in OCS area on Quantico Marine Corps Base. Phone 703/640-7965.* Chronological presentation of the Marine Corps Air-Ground Team's role in American history; artifacts on exhibit include aircraft, engines, armor, tracked and wheeled vehicles, artillery, small arms, uniforms, dioramas, and photographs in pre-WWII aviation hangars. (Apr-late Nov, Tues-Sun) **FREE**

Prince William Forest Park. *From I-95, 1/4 mile W on VA 619. www.nps.gov/prwi.* Consists of 18,000 acres. Hiking, bicycling, picnicking, camping (14-day limit; no hookups; fee; group cabins by reservations only), trailer campground off VA 234 (fee; hookups, showers, laundry). Naturalist programs. (Daily)

Tysons Corner

See also Arlington County (Ronald Reagan Washington-National Airport Area), Fairfax, Falls Church, McLean; also see Washington, DC

Pop 18,540 **Area code** 703

Information Fairfax County Convention & Visitors Bureau, 8300 Boone Blvd, Suite 450, Tysons Corner 22182; 703/790-3329 or 800/7-FAIRFAX

Web www.visitfairfax.org

This Virginia suburban area of Washington, DC, is the location of one of the largest shopping centers in the nation.

Motel/Motor Lodge

★ **COMFORT INN.** *1587 Spring Hill Rd, Vienna (22182). Phone 703/448-8020; toll-free 800/828-3297; fax 703/448-0343. www.comfortinntysons.com.* 250 rooms, 3 story. S, D $115.95-$125.95; each additional $5; suites $125.95-$145.95; under 18 free. Crib free. Pet accepted, some restrictions; $25 deposit. TV; cable (premium). Pool; lifeguard. Complimentary continental breakfast. Check-out noon. Coin laundry. Meeting rooms. Business services available. In-room modem link. Valet service. Free airport transportation. Health club privileges. Refrigerators, microwaves available. Cr cds: A, C, D, DS, ER, JCB, MC, V.

🄳 🏌 ⚊ ⊠ SC

Hotels

★ ★ ★ **HILTON.** *7920 Jones Branch Dr, McLean (22102). Phone 703/847-5000; toll-free 800/932-3322; fax 703/761-5100. www.hilton.com.* Located close to the famous shopping area of Tyson Corners, this hotel has a glass-domed and vaulted atrium lobby and piano music for the enjoyment of guests. 458 rooms, 9 story. S $150-$210; D $170-$230; each additional $20; suites $375-$1,750; package plans. Crib free. TV; cable (premium), VCR available (free movies). Indoor pool; lifeguard. Restaurant 6:30 am-11 pm. Room service 6-2 am. Bar 11-2 am; entertainment. Check-out noon. Convention facilities. Business center. In-room modem link. Gift shop. Exercise equipment; sauna. Minibars; refrigerators available. Atrium lobby; marble floors, fountain. Luxury level. Cr cds: A, C, D, DS, ER, JCB, MC, V.

🄳 ⚊ 🏌 ⊠ SC 🚶

★ ★ ★ **MARRIOTT.** *8028 Leesburg Pike, Vienna (22182). Phone 703/734-3200; toll-free 800/228-9290; fax 703/734-5763. www.marriott.com.* This property is located in the heart of Tysons Corner, next to a major shopping mall. 390 units, 15 story. S, D $184-$199; suites $375; family rates; weekend packages. Crib free. TV; cable (premium). Indoor pool; whirlpool, poolside service, lifeguard. Restaurant 6:30 am-11 pm. Bar 4:30 pm-1 am; Fri to 2 am; Sat 7 pm-2 am; closed Sun. Check-out noon. Convention facilities. Business center. In-room modem link. Gift shop. Coin laundry. Some covered parking. Exercise equipment; sauna. Refrigerators available. Luxury level. Cr cds: A, C, D, DS, ER, JCB, MC, V.

🄳 ⚊ 🏌 ⊠ SC 🚶

★ ★ ★ ★ **THE RITZ-CARLTON.** *1700 Tyson's Blvd, McLean (22102). Phone 703/506-4300; toll-free 800/241-3333; fax 703/506-2694. www.ritzcarlton.com.* The Ritz-Carlton, Tysons Corner is northern Virginia's premier hotel. Only 12 miles from Washington, DC, this hotel offers an escape from the daily grind. The guest rooms are tastefully appointed with a stylishly refined aesthetic, and windows look out over the city or the Blue Ridge Mountains. Culinary works of art are created each day at the Maestro Restaurant. Its sensational contemporary Italian cuisine is complemented by the casually elegant décor, the open kitchen design allows guests to watch as the chef prepares their flavorful meals. Visitors to the Ritz-Carlton Day Spa check their worries at the door, and proper primping and pampering are the order of the day. Rose body wraps and hot stone therapy are just two of the wonderful signature treatments to be experienced here. Others opt for retail therapy and hit the more than 230 stores at the adjacent Tysons Galleria and Tysons Mall. 398 rooms, 24 story. Pet accepted. Check-out noon, check-in 3 pm. TV; cable (premium), VCR available. In-room modem link. Room service 24 hours. Restaurant. Bar; entertainment. Babysitting services available. In-house fitness room, spa, massage, sauna. Indoor pool, whirlpool. Valet parking. Business center. Concierge. Luxury level. Cr cds: A, C, D, DS, ER, JCB, MC, V. **$$**

🄳 🏌 ⚊ 🏌 ⊠ 🚶

Restaurants

★ ★ **AARATHI.** *409 Maple Ave E, Vienna (22180). Phone 703/938-0100; fax 703/319-0111.* Indian menu. Specializes in tandoori, curry, and vegetarian dishes. Hours: 11:30 am-2:30 pm, 5:30-10 pm; Fri, Sat to 10:30 pm. Closed July 4, Dec 25. Dinner $8-$14. Service bar. Reservations accepted; required Fri, Sat dinner. Cr cds: A, D, DS, MC, V.

D

★ ★ **BISTRO 123.** *246 E Maple Ave, Vienna (22180). Phone 703/938-4379; fax 703/255-9042. www. bistro123vienna.com.* French menu. Closed Sun. Lunch, dinner. Bar. Outdoor seating. Cr cds: A, MC, V. **$$**

D

★ ★ **BONAROTI.** *428 Maple Ave E, Vienna (22180). Phone 703/281-7550; fax 703/281-7587.* Hours: 11:30 am-3 pm, 5-10:30 pm; Sat 5-11 pm. Closed Sun; some major holidays. Reservations accepted. Italian menu. Bar. Lunch $8.95-$13.95, dinner $13.95-$22.95. Children's menu. Specializes in veal, pasta, seafood. Own pastries, pasta. Italian art. Totally nonsmoking. Cr cds: A, D, MC, V.

★ ★ **CLYDE'S.** *8332 Leesburg Pike, Vienna (22182). Phone 703/734-1901; fax 703/790-1422. www.clydes.com.* Hours: 11-2 am; Sun brunch 10 am-4 pm. Reservations accepted. Bar. A la carte entrées: lunch $4.95-$10.95, dinner $6.50-$15.50. Children's menu. Specializes in pasta, seafood, sandwiches. Parking. Original art collection. Cr cds: A, C, D, DS, MC, V.

D

★ ★ **HUNAN LION.** *2070 Chain Bridge Rd, Vienna (22182). Phone 703/734-9828; fax 703/893-2972. www.hunanlion.com.* Hours: 11:30 am-10:30 pm; Fri, Sat to 11 pm. Closed Thanksgiving. Reservations accepted. Chinese menu. Bar. Lunch $6-$8, dinner $6-$10.50. Specialties: triple delicacy prawns, orange beef, General Tso's chicken. Parking. Cr cds: A, D, DS, MC, V.

D

★ ★ ★ **LA PROVENCE.** *144 W Maple Ave, Vienna (22180). Phone 703/242-3777; fax 703/242-3983.* French Provençal menu. Hours: 11:30 am-2:30 pm, 5:30-10 pm. Closed Sun; most major holidays. Lunch $9.95-$13.95, dinner $18.95-$25.95. Bar. Reservations accepted; required Fri, Sat dinner. Totally nonsmoking. Cr cds: A, D, DS, MC, V.

D

★ ★ ★ **LE CANARD.** *132 Branch Rd, Vienna (22180). Phone 703/281-0070; fax 703/255-3465. www.lecanard restaurant.com.* The formal interior of dark red fabrics and mahogany wood sets the tone for an elegantly traditional dining experience. Rich, sumptuous dishes are followed by unique flaming specialty coffees. French menu. Lunch, dinner. Bar. Piano bar. Reservations required Fri, Sat. Cr cds: A, D, DS, MC, V. **$$**

D

★ ★ ★ **MAESTRO.** *1700 Tysons Blvd (22102). Phone 703/506-4300; fax 703/917-5499. www.maestro restaurant.com.* The exceedingly lavish décor goes hand-in-hand with the grandiose cuisine and service. Several of the fusion-inspired items are prepared tableside with the finest ingredients. The beautifully sculpted desserts are a must. Specializes in seafood, lamb chops, prime aged beef. A la carte entrées: dinner $72-$112. Sun brunch $45. Hours: 6:30 am-10 pm; Sat, Sun 1-4:30 pm; Sun brunch 10:30 am-2:30 pm. Children's menu. Reservations accepted. Valet parking available. Cr cds: A, D, DS, MC, V.

D

★ ★ **MARCO POLO.** *245 Maple Ave W, Vienna (22180). Phone 703/281-3922; fax 703/281-3926. www.marcopolo restaurant.com.* Continental, Italian, seafood menu. Hours: 11:30 am-10:30 pm; Fri, Sat to 11 pm; early-bird dinner Thurs 5:30-7:30 pm. Closed Sun except Mother's Day. Buffet lunch (Tues-Fri) $8.25, dinner (Thurs) $14.50. Lunch $6-$9, dinner $11-$18. Service bar. Reservations accepted. Cr cds: A, DS, MC, V.

D

★ ★ ★ **MORTON'S OF CHICAGO.** *8075 Leesburg Pike, Vienna (22182). Phone 703/883-0800; fax 703/883-0673. www.mortons.com.* Consistent with expectations, this outlet serves the same famed entrées as its sister restaurants. The tableside menu presentation reveals generous portions and high-quality ingredients. A warm, club-like atmosphere is the backdrop for a succulent meal. Seafood menu. Specializes in steak, seafood. Hours: 11:30 am-2:30 pm, 5:30-11 pm; Sat from 5:30 pm; Sun 5-10 pm. Closed major holidays. A la carte entrées: dinner $24.-$69.95. Bar. Jacket required. Reservations accepted; required Thurs-Sat. Valet parking. Cr cds: A, D, MC, V.

D

★ ★ ★ **NIZAM'S.** *523 Maple Ave W, Vienna (22180). Phone 703/938-8948; fax 703/938-0453. www. nizamsrestaurant.com.* Doner kebob, otherwise known as gyros, is the legendary mainstay of this refined Turkish restaurant. Thin, tender slices of marinated, spit-roasted lamb nestle inside soft pita bread in a dish that rivals anything Istanbul could turn out. Service is polished and attentive. Hours: 11 am-3 pm, 5-10 pm; Sat 5-11 pm; Sun 4-9 pm. Closed Mon; also Jan 1, Thanksgiving, Dec 25.

Lunch $5.25-$10.50, dinner $12.50-$19.50. Bar. Reservations accepted; required Fri, Sat. Totally nonsmoking. Cr cds: A, D, MC, V.

D **SC**

★ ★ **PANJSHIR II.** *224 W Maple Ave, Vienna (22180).* *Phone 703/281-4183; fax 703/281-4183.* Specializes in kebabs, saffron rice, vegetarian dishes. Hours: 1:30 am-2 pm, 5-10 pm; Sun 5-9 pm. Closed Mondays; Jan 1, July 4, Thanksgiving Day. Lunch $7.50-$7.95, dinner $10.95-$15.95. Bar. Reservations accepted. Cr cds: A, MC, V.

D

★ ★ ★ **RITZ-CARLTON, THE RESTAURANT.** *1700 Tyson's Blvd (22102). Phone 703/506-4300. www.ritzcarlton.com.* Specializes in seafood, lamb chops, prime aged beef. Hours: 6:30 am-2 pm, 6-9 pm. Reservations accepted. Wine list. A la carte entrées: breakfast $9-$16; lunch: $9-$24; dinner: $18-$40. Sun brunch $45. Children's menu. Entertainment: harpist. Valet parking. Cr cds: A, D, DS, MC, V.

★ ★ **TARA THAI.** *226 Maple Ave W, Vienna (22180). Phone 703/255-2467; fax 703/255-2867. www.tarathai.com.* Hours: 11:30 am-3 pm, 5-10 pm; Fri to 11 pm; Sat noon-3:30 pm, 5-11 pm; Sun noon-3:30 pm, 5-10 pm. Closed Dec 25. Reservations accepted; required Fri, Sat dinner. Thai menu. Bar. Lunch $3.95-$7.95, dinner $6.95-$12.95. Specializes in fresh seafood, grilled fish. Parking. Underwater ocean décor. Totally nonsmoking. Cr cds: A, D, DS, MC, V.

D

★ ★ **THAT'S AMORE.** *150 Branch Rd SE, Vienna (22180). Phone 703/281-7777; fax 703/281-4132. www.thatsamore.com.* Italian menu. Closed Labor Day, Thanksgiving, Dec 25. Lunch, dinner. Bar. Cr cds: A, D, DS, MC, V. **$$$**

D

★ **WU'S GARDEN.** *418 Maple Ave E, Vienna (22180). Phone 703/281-4410; fax 703/281-3418.* Chinese menu. Closed Thanksgiving. Lunch, dinner. Bar. Cr cds: A, D, DS, MC, V. **$**

D

Virginia Beach (H-13)

See also Chesapeake, Hampton, Newport News, Norfolk, Portsmouth

Pop 425,257 **Elev** 12 ft **Area code** 757

Information Visitor Information Center, 2100 Parks Ave, 23451; 757/437-4882 or 800/446-8038

Web www.vbfun.com

For those who seek year-round recreation, Virginia Beach is the answer. A renovated resort area with a 3-mile boardwalk and 28 miles of oceanfront and bay beaches offer visitors myriad activities: surfing, swimming, fishing, boating, waterskiing; in-line skating, bowling, tennis, golf, bicycling, and an amusement park and arcade games.

After a full day, there's nothing like dinner and a night out. Virginia Beach delivers with many fine restaurants serving fresh seafood, and nightclubs, concerts, and theaters catering to all musical tastes. With activities for all ages and hundreds of places to stay in all price ranges, Virginia Beach is one of the most popular resorts on the East Coast.

What to See and Do

Adam Thoroughgood House. *1636 Parish Rd. Phone 757/431-4000.* (circa 1680) One of the oldest remaining brick houses in US; restored, furnished; restored gardens. (Apr-Dec, Tues-Sun; rest of year, Tues-Sat; closed holidays) **$$**

Association for Research and Enlightenment. *67th St and Atlantic Ave. Phone 757/428-3588.* Headquarters for study and research of work of psychic Edgar Cayce. Visitor Center has bookstore, library, displays, ESP-testing machine, movie, and daily lecture. (Daily; closed Thanksgiving, Dec 25) **FREE**

Contemporary Art Center of Virginia. *2200 Parks Ave. Phone 757/425-0000.* This 32,000-square-foot facility is devoted to presentation of 20th-century art through exhibitions, education, performing arts, and special events. (Mon-Sat, Sun afternoons; closed holidays) **$$**

First Landing/Seashore State Park. *2500 Shore (23451). 5 miles N on US 60 at Cape Henry. Phone 757/412-2300.* More than 2,700 acres with lagoons, cypress trees, and sand dunes. Swimming at own risk, fishing, boating (ramp); hiking, bicycle, and self-guided nature trails; picnicking, tent and trailer sites (Mar-Nov; fee), 20 cabins (open all year round). Visitor center, interpretive programs. Access for disabled to nature trail. (Daily) Standard fees. **$$**

Fishing. *Linkhorn Bay and Rudee Inlet.* In the Lynnhaven and Rudee Inlets for channel bass, speckled trout, spots, croakers, flounder, and whiting in season; in the Back Bay area, 18 miles S on VA 615, for largemouth black bass, pickerel, and perch. Pier fishing and surf casting from piers jutting into the Atlantic and piers in the Chesapeake Bay. Reef, deep-sea, and Gulf Stream fishing from charter boats, for sea bass, weakfish, flounder, cobia, bonito, tuna, marlin, false albacore, blue, and dolphin. Lake and stream fishing at Lake Smith, Lake Christine, and the inland waterways of the Chesapeake and Albemarle Canal. Crabbing for blue crabs in Lynnhaven waters, Linkhorn

Bay, and Rudee Inlet. (No license or closed season for saltwater fishing.)

Francis Land House Historic Site and Gardens. *3131 Virginia Beach Blvd, on the S side of the boulevard, between Rosemont Rd and Lynnhoven Pwky. Phone 757/431-4000.* Late 18th-century plantation home features period rooms, special exhibits, gardens, and museum gift shop. (Tues-Sat, also Sun afternoons; closed holidays) **$$**

Lynnhaven House. *4405 Wishart Rd. Phone 757/460-1688.* (circa 1725). This stately story-and-a-half masonry structure is a well-preserved example of 18th-century architecture and decorative arts. (May and Oct, weekends only; June-Sept, Tues-Sun) **$$**

Motor World Your Place to Race. *700 S Birdneck Rd. Phone 757/422-6419.* Park includes go-carts, arcade. Also a 36-hole miniature Shipwreck Golf Course, batting cages, and large Children's Zone. (May-early Sept, daily)

Norwegian Lady Statue. *25th St and Boardwalk.* A gift to Virginia Beach from the people of Moss, Norway. The statue commemorates the tragic wreck of the Norwegian bark *Dictator* off the shores of Virginia Beach in 1891.

Ocean Breeze Water Park. *849 General Booth Blvd. Phone 800/678-WILD; 757/422-4444 (recording).* "Get wet, get wild" at this Caribbean paradise with slides, wave pool, rapids, and children's water amusements (mid-May-early Sept, daily). **$$$$**

Old Cape Henry Lighthouse and Memorial Park. *On Fort Story, an active army base. 6 miles N on US 60.* First US-government-built lighthouse (circa 1791).

Old Coast Guard Station. *24th St and Atlantic Ave. Phone 757/422-1587.* Former Coast Guard Station (1903); visual exhibits of numerous shipwecks along the Virginia coastline tell of past bravery and disaster. "The War Years" exhibit relates United States Coast Guard efforts during WWI and WWII. Photographs, ship models, artifacts. Gift shop. (Memorial Day-Sept, daily; rest of year, Tues-Sun; closed holidays) **$$**

Virginia Marine Science Museum. *717 General Booth Blvd, 2 miles S of resort area. Phone 757/425-FISH.* Live animals, interactive exhibits, six-story screen, 300-seat **IMAX 3-D** theater. Exhibits include ocean aquarium with sharks, large fish; sea turtle aquarium; seal and other habitats; aviary; salt marsh preserve; touch tank; river room; garden. (Daily; closed Thanksgiving, Dec 25) **$$$**

Special Events

Boardwalk Art Show. Works by more than 350 artists from US and abroad. Mid-June.

East Coast Surfing Championship. *8437 Valley Pike (22645). Phone 830/278-2016.* Fourth weekend in Aug.

Neptune Festival. *265 Kings Grand Rd (23452).* Last two weeks in Sept.

Pungo Strawberry Festival. *916 Princess Anne Rd.* Sat and Sun of Memorial Day weekend.

Virginia Saltwater Fishing Tournament. *968 S Oriole Dr. Phone 757/491-5160.* The Commonwealth of Virginia sponsors this annual program. No entry fee or registration requirements; open to everyone who fishes in tournament waters and complies with tournament rules. For information contact Virginia Saltwater Fishing Tournament, 968 S Oriole Dr, Suite 102, 23451. Mar-Dec.

Winter whale-watching boat trips. *Phone 757/437-4882.* Mon, Wed, Fri-Sun. Jan-Mar.

Motels/Motor Lodges

★ **COMFORT INN.** *2015 Atlantic Ave (23451). Phone 757/425-8200; toll-free 800/443-4733; fax 757/425-6521. www.comfortinn.com.* 83 kitchen suites, 10 story. Mid-June-mid-Aug: S, D $165-$225; each additional $10; under 12 free; lower rates rest of year. Crib free. Complimentary continental breakfast. Check-out 11 am. TV; cable (premium). In-room modem link. Private patios. Refrigerators, microwaves. Restaurant adjacent 6:30 am-10 pm. Exercise equipment. Indoor pool, whirlpool. Business center. On ocean. Cr cds: A, C, D, DS, JCB, MC, V.

★ **COMFORT INN.** *2800 Pacific Ave (23451). Phone 757/428-2203; toll-free 800/441-0684; fax 757/422-6043. www.comfortinn.com.* 135 rooms, 7 story. Memorial Day-Labor Day: S, D $109-$159; each additional $10; under 15 free; family rates; lower rates rest of year. Crib free. TV; cable (premium). Indoor/outdoor pool; whirlpool. Complimentary continental breakfast. Restaurant opposite 11 am-11 pm. Check-out 11 am. Coin laundry. Meeting rooms. Business services available. In-room modem link. Bellstaff. Valet service. Exercise equipment. Game room. Some refrigerators; microwaves available. Cr cds: A, C, D, DS, ER, JCB, MC, V.

★ ★ **COURTYARD BY MARRIOTT.** *5700 Greenwich Rd (23462). Phone 757/490-2002; toll-free 800/321-2211; fax 757/490-0169. www.courtyard.com.* 146 rooms, 3 story. Memorial Day-Labor Day: S, D $75-$99; suites $110-$120; under 12 free; weekly, weekend rates; lower rates rest of year. Crib free. TV; cable (premium). Pool; whirlpool. Bar. Check-out noon. Business services available. In-room modem link. Valet service. Exercise equipment. Some refrigerators. Cr cds: A, C, D, DS, JCB, MC, V.

★ **DAYS INN.** *3107 Atlantic Ave (23451). Phone 757/428-7233; toll-free 800/292-3297; fax 757/491-1936. www.thedays.com/virginiabeach06421.* 121 units, 8 story. Late June-early Sept: S, D $135-$225; each additional $10; under 12 free; golf plans; lower rates rest of year. Crib free. Pet accepted; $10. Check-out 11 am. TV; cable (premium). In-room modem link. Balconies. Some refrigerators; microwaves available. Coin laundry. Restaurant 7-11 am, noon-2 pm, 6-10 pm. Bar from 5 pm. Room service. Indoor pool, whirlpool. Golf privileges. Meeting rooms. Business services. On ocean; beach. Cr cds: A, C, D, DS, MC, V.

[D] [icons] [SC]

★ **ECONO LODGE.** *2109 Atlantic Ave (23451). Phone 757/428-2403; fax 757/422-2530. www.econolodge.com.* 55 rooms, 10 story. Complimentary continental breakfast. Check-out 11 am, check-in 3 pm. TV; cable (premium). In-room modem link. Beach. Indoor pool. Free parking. Cr cds: A, C, D, DS, JCB, MC, V. **$**

[D] [icons]

★ **FAIRFIELD INN.** *4760 Euclid Rd (23462). Phone 757/499-1935. www.fairfieldinn.com.* 134 rooms, 3 story. Mid-May-Labor Day: S, D $62-$95; under 18 free; lower rates rest of year. Crib free. Complimentary continental breakfast. Check-out noon. TV; cable (premium). In-room modem link. Restaurant nearby. Pool. Business services. Cr cds: A, C, D, DS, MC, V.

[D] [icons]

★ **HAMPTON INN.** *5793 Greenwich Rd (23462). Phone 757/490-9800; toll-free 800/426-7866; fax 757/490-3573. www.hamptoninn.com.* 122 rooms, 4 story. June-Aug: S $64-$76; D $66-$76; under 18 free; higher rates special events; lower rates rest of year. Crib free. TV; cable (premium). Pool. Complimentary continental breakfast. Restaurant adjacent 6:30 am-11 pm. Check-out noon. Meeting room. Business services available. In-room modem link. Exercise equipment. Microwaves available. Cr cds: A, C, D, DS, MC, V.

[D] [icons] [SC]

★ ★ **HOLIDAY INN.** *21st and Atlantic Ave (23451). Phone 757/491-1500; toll-free 800/882-3224; fax 757/491-1945. www.holiday-inn.com.* 150 rooms, 12 story. June-Sept: S, D $99-$199; each additional $10; under 18 free; lower rates rest of year. Check-out 11 am. TV; cable (premium). In-room modem link. Balconies. Refrigerators; microwaves available. Restaurant 6:30 am-10 pm. Bar 11 am-10 pm. Room service. Indoor pool, whirlpool. Meeting rooms. Business services. On ocean; swimming beach. Cr cds: A, DS, MC, V.

[D] [icons]

★ ★ **HOLIDAY INN.** *2607 Atlantic Ave (23451). Phone 757/491-6900; fax 757/491-2125. www.holiday-inn.com.* 143 rooms, 18 kitchen suites, 10 story. Mid-June-Labor Day: S, D $159-$199; each additional $10; kitchen suites $199-$219; under 17 free; family rates; weekly rates; higher rates special events. Crib free. TV; cable (premium). Indoor pool; whirlpool. Restaurant 7 am-10 pm. Room service. Bar 5-10 pm. Check-out 11 am. Meeting rooms. Business services available. In-room modem link. Bellstaff. Valet service. Coin laundry. Exercise equipment. Refrigerators; some in-room whirlpools, microwaves. Balconies. On beach. Cr cds: A, D, DS, JCB, MC, V.

[D] [icons]

★ ★ **HOLIDAY INN.** *3900 Atlantic Ave (23451). Phone 757/428-1711; toll-free 800/942-3224; fax 757/425-5742. www.holiday-inn.com.* 266 rooms, 55 kitchen units, 7 story, Mid-June-Labor Day: S, D $149-$189; suites $184-$249; each additional $10; under 19 free. Crib free. TV; cable (premium). Indoor/outdoor pool; poolside service (summer). Free supervised children's activities (Memorial Day-Labor Day), ages 3-12. Restaurant 6:30 am-2 pm, 5-11 pm (in season), to 10 pm rest of year. Room service. Bar 4-11 pm. Check-out 11 am. Meeting rooms. Business services available. Bellstaff. Gift shop. Exercise equipment. Refrigerators. Balconies. On ocean. Cr cds: A, C, D, DS, ER, JCB, MC, V.

[D] [icons] [SC]

★ ★ **HOLIDAY INN.** *5655 Greenwich Rd (23462). Phone 757/499-4400; toll-free 800/567-3856; fax 757/473-0517. www.holiday-inn.com.* 328 rooms, 6 story. S, D $99-$129; suites $289. Crib free. Check-out noon. TV; cable (premium). In-room modem link. Valet services. Restaurant 6:30 am-10 pm. Bar 11 am-10 pm. Room service. Exercise equipment, sauna. 2 pools, 1 indoor; whirlpool. Free airport transportation. Business services. Convention center/facilities. Concierge. Cr cds: A, D, DS, JCB, MC, V.

[D] [icons]

★ ★ **QUALITY INN.** *705 Atlantic Ave (23451). Phone 757/428-8935; toll-free 800/445-8667; fax 757/425-2769. www.qualityinn.com.* 120 rooms, 6 story. Memorial Day-Labor Day: S $165; D $175; each additional $10; under 18 free; lower rates rest of year. Crib free. TV; cable (premium), VCR available. Indoor/outdoor pool; whirlpool, poolside service. Restaurant 7 am-midnight. Room service to 10 pm. Bar noon-1:30 am. Check-out 11 am. Meeting rooms. Business services available. In-room modem link. Bellstaff. Valet service. Exercise equipment; sauna. Lawn games. On ocean; beach. Cr cds: A, C, D, DS, ER, JCB, MC, V.

[icons] [SC]

★★★ **RAMADA INN.** *5700 Atlantic Ave (23451). Phone 757/428-7025; toll-free 800/265-3032; fax 757/321-2468. www.ramada.com.* Located right on the ocean in what locals refer to as the North End, this hotel provides guests with spectacular views. Explore the beach or rent a bike, boat, or jet ski. 216 rooms, 17 story. May-Sept: S, D $165-$210; suites $230-$280; each additional $10; under 18 free; lower rates rest of year. TV; cable (premium), VCR available. Indoor/outdoor pool; whirlpool, poolside service, lifeguard in season. Supervised children's activities (mid-June-Labor Day), ages 5-11. Restaurant 7 am-10 pm. Bar 3 pm-1 am. Check-out 11 am. Meeting rooms. Business center. In-room modem link. Concierge. Gift shop. Exercise equipment; sauna. Many refrigerators, microwaves. Balconies. On ocean; oceanfront deck, swimming beach. Most rooms with ocean view. Luxury level. Video games. Cr cds: A, C, D, DS, MC, V.

[symbols]

★★ **SEA GULL MOTEL.** *2613 Atlantic Ave (23451). Phone 757/425-5711; toll-free 800/426-4855; fax 757/425-5710. www.vabeach.com/seagull.* 51 units, 9 kitchen units, 4 story. Memorial Day-Labor Day: S, D $120-$138; each additional $10; kitchen units $130-$155; family, weekly rates; lower rates rest of year. Crib $5. TV; cable (premium). Indoor pool; whirlpool, poolside service. Restaurant 7 am-10 pm, seasonal. Room service. Bar. Check-out 11 am. Business services available. Refrigerators. On ocean, swimming beach. Cr cds: DS, MC, V.

[symbols]

Hotels

★★ **CLARION HOTEL.** *4453 Bonney Rd (23462). Phone 757/473-1700; toll-free 800/847-5202; fax 757/552-5778. www.clarionhotel.com.* 149 rooms, 8 story. Memorial Day-Labor Day: S, D $89-$159; each additional $10; suites, studio rooms $109-$159; under 12 free; lower rates rest of year. Crib free. TV; cable (premium). Indoor pool; whirlpool, poolside service. Restaurant 6:30-10:30 pm; Sat, Sun 7:30-11:30 pm. Bars 5-10 pm. Meeting rooms. Business center. In-room modem link. Exercise equipment; sauna. Some refrigerators, microwaves. Cr cds: A, C, D, DS, ER, JCB, MC, V.

[symbols]

★★ **DOUBLETREE HOTEL.** *1900 Pavilion Dr (23451). Phone 757/422-8900; toll-free 800/333-3333; fax 757/425-8460. www.doubletree.com.* Adjacent to the Virginia Beach Pavilion Convention Center and only 6 blocks from the beach, this hotel offers amenities for both leisure and business travelers. 292 rooms, 12 story. Late May-early Sept: S, D $159; each additional $10;

suites $165-$395; under 17 free; weekend rates; lower rates rest of year. Crib free. TV; cable (premium). Indoor pool. Restaurant 6:30 am-2 pm, 5-10 pm. Bar from 4 pm; entertainment. Check-out 11 am. Convention facilities. Business center. In-room modem link. Gift shop. Tennis. Exercise equipment; sauna, steam room. Some refrigerators. Cr cds: A, C, D, DS, ER, JCB, MC, V.

[symbols]

★★★ **FOUNDERS INN.** *5641 Indian River Rd (23464). Phone 757/424-5511; toll-free 800/926-4466; fax 757/366-0613. www.foundersinn.com.* Sitting on 26 manicured acres, this Georgian-style inn has a southern-colonial décor and a unique combination of intimate charm and extensive meeting space. 249 rooms. Memorial Day-Labor Day: S, D $89-$159; each additional $15; suites $159-$700; lower rates rest of year; family, weekly rates; golf plans. Crib free. Check-out noon. TV; cable (premium), VCR available (movies). In-room modem link. Balconies. Bathroom phones, refrigerators. Restaurant 6 am-10 pm; dinner theatre. Room service to 11 pm. Supervised children's activities (Memorial Day-Labor Day), ages 3-17. Playground. Exercise room, sauna. 2 pools, 1 indoor; lifeguard (summer). Golf privileges, greens fee $29-59, pro. Lighted tennis, pro. Picnic tables. Lawn games. Bicycle rentals. Indoor racquetball court. Free valet parking. Free airport transportation. Meeting rooms. Business center. Concierge. Cr cds: A, D, DS, MC, V.

[symbols]

★★★ **SHERATON OCEANFRONT HOTEL.** *Oceanfront at 36th St (23451). Phone 757/425-9000. www.sheraton.com.* 204 rooms, 15 story. S, D $175-$225; under 17 free. Crib available. Check-out noon, check-in 3 pm. TV; cable (premium). In-room modem link. Mini-bars; many refrigerators in suites. Restaurant 6:30 am-10 pm. Bar to midnight. Exercise equipment. Pool; whirlpool. Meeting rooms. Business center. Concierge. Cr cds: A, C, D, DS, ER, MC, V.

[symbols]

Resorts

★★ **OCEAN SANDS RESORT.** *2207 Atlantic Ave (23451). Phone 757/428-5141; toll-free 800/874-8661; fax 757/422-8436. www.oceansandsresort.com.* This oceanfront property offers brightly colored rooms and a variety of leisure recreations. 105 rooms, 14 story. Check-out 10 am, check-in 4 pm. TV; cable (premium). In-room modem link. Restaurant. In-house fitness room, spa. Indoor pool, whirlpool. Airport transportation. Beach. Cr cds: A, D, DS, MC, V. **$**

[symbols]

★ ★ ★ **VIRGINIA BEACH RESORT & CONFER-ENCE CENTER.** *2800 Shore Dr (23451). Phone 757/481-9000; toll-free 800/422-4747; fax 757/496-7429. www.virginiabeachresort.com.* This year-round resort is located on the quiet North End of Virginia Beach overlooking Chesapeake Bay. 295 suites, 8 story. Memorial Day-Labor Day: S, D $165-$344; each additional $10; under 18 free; lower rates rest of year. Crib free. Check-out 11 am. TV; cable (premium). In-room modem link. Balconies. Refrigerators, microwaves. Coin laundry. Restaurant 6:30 am-11 pm. Bar. Supervised children's activities (Memorial Day-Labor Day), ages 4-14. Exercise equipment, sauna. Indoor/outdoor pool; whirlpool, poolside service. Golf privileges. Tennis privileges. Bicycles. Airport transportation. Business center. Convention center/facilities. Gift shop. On bay. Private beach. Cr cds: A, C, D, DS, MC, V.

D 👶 🖈 ⚓ 🏊 ⛹

Restaurants

★ **ALDO'S.** *1860 Laskin Rd (23454). Phone 757/491-1111; fax 757/491-0597. www.gohamptonroad.com.* Italian, seafood menu. Hours: 11 am-11 pm; Fri, Sat to 12:30 am; Sun 4-11 pm. Closed Thanksgiving, Dec 25. Lunch $6.99-$27. Dinner $6.99-$27. Bar. Entertainment. Children's menu. Outdoor seating. Cr cds: A, MC, V.

D

★ ★ **BLUE PETE'S SEAFOOD AND STEAK.** *1400 N Muddy Creek Rd (23456). Phone 757/426-2005; fax 757/721-3792.* Seafood menu. Closed Monday. Dinner. Bar. Children's menu. Located on creek in wooded area. Outdoor seating. Cr cds: A, DS, MC, V. **$$$**

D

★ ★ **COASTAL GRILL.** *1427 N Great Neck Rd (23454). Phone 757/496-3348. www.coastalgrill.com.* Closed most major holidays. Dinner. Bar. Children's menu. Cr cds: A, MC, V. **$$**

D

★ **CUISINE AND COMPANY.** *3004 Pacific Ave (23451). Phone 757/428-6700; fax 757/428-0138. www.cuisineandcompany.com.* Continental menu. Closed Jan 1, Thanksgiving, Dec 25. Lunch, dinner. Cr cds: A, D, MC, V. **$**

D

★ ★ **DUCK-IN RESTAURANT AND GAZEBO.** *3324 Shore Dr (23451). Phone 757/481-0201; fax 757/481-9780. www.duck-in.com.* Where can you find the best place in Virginia Beach to eat and drink simply and cheaply and then kick back? Try this eatery. For beach combers looking for a watering hole on the shore, this is the top pick. Try the fired popcorn shrimp and other seafood entrées, made simple and fresh. Seafood menu. Lunch, dinner. Entertainment. Children's menu. Cr cds: A, C, D, DS, MC, V. **$$**

D

★ ★ **IL GIARDINO.** *910 Atlantic Ave (23451). Phone 757/422-6464; fax 757/422-1175. www.ilgiardino.com.* Italian menu. Closed Thanksgiving, Dec 25. Dinner. Bar. Entertainment in season. Children's menu. Valet parking. Outdoor seating. Cr cds: A, D, DS, MC, V. **$$**

D

★ ★ **INLET.** *3319 Shore Dr (23451). Phone 757/481-7300; fax 757/481-0625. www.theinletrestaurant.com.* Seafood menu. Lunch, dinner, Sun brunch. Bar. Children's menu. Valet parking. Outdoor seating. Lobster tank. On Lynnhaven Inlet; 2-story saltwater aquarium in dining area. Cr cds: A, D, MC, V. **$$**

D

★ ★ **THE LIGHTHOUSE.** *1st St and Atlantic Ave (23451). Phone 757/428-7974; fax 757/422-9914. www.thelighthouseva.com.* Lunch, dinner, brunch. Bar. Children's menu. Outdoor seating. Cr cds: A, D, DS, MC, V. **$$**

D SC

★ ★ **LUCKY STAR.** *1608 Pleasure House Rd (23455). Phone 757/363-8410; fax 757/460-4714.* Hours: 5:30-10 pm. Closed Sun; some major holidays. Dinner $5.50-$20. Bar. Reservations required on Fri, Sat. Totally nonsmoking. Cr cds: A, MC, V.

D

★ ★ **LYNNHAVEN FISH HOUSE.** *2350 Starfish Rd (23451). Phone 757/481-0003; fax 757/481-3474. www.lynnhavenfishhouse.net.* Seafood menu. Closed Thanksgiving, Dec 25. Lunch, dinner. Bar. Children's menu. Valet parking. Lobster tank. On Lynnhaven fishing pier. Cr cds: A, C, D, DS, MC, V. **$$**

D

★ **PUNGO GRILL.** *1785 Princess Anne Rd (23456). Phone 757/426-6655.* Regional American, Continental menu. Closed Mon; Thanksgiving, Dec 24, 25; also Jan-Feb. Lunch, dinner. Bar. Children's menu. Outdoor seating. Dining room on enclosed porch of 1919 Aladdin house. Cr cds: D, DS, MC, V. **$$**

D

★ ★ **RUDEE'S.** *227 Mediterranean Ave (23451). Phone 757/425-1777; fax 757/425-5107. www.rudees.com.*

Seafood, steak menu. Hours: 11 am-midnight. Closed Thanksgiving, Dec 25. Lunch $5.95-$34.95, dinner $5.95-$34.95, Sun brunch $4.95-$9.95. Bar. Children's menu. Nautical décor; casual atmosphere. Valet parking available. Outdoor seating. On inlet; transient slips available for boats. Cr cds: A, D, DS, MC, V.

D

★ **WATERMAN'S.** *415 Atlantic Ave (23451). Phone 757/428-3644; fax 757/428-6452. www.watermans.com.* Seafood menu. Hours: 11 am-10 pm; Fri, Sat to 11 pm. Closed Thanksgiving, Dec 24 evening, 25. Lunch $5.95-$14.95, dinner $6.27-$25.95. Bar. Children's menu. Outdoor seating. Cr cds: A, D, DS, MC, V.

D SC

Warm Springs (F-7)

See also Clifton Forge, Covington, Hot Springs, Monterey

Pop 425 **Elev** 2,260 ft **Area code** 540 **Zip** 24484

Nestled at the foot of Little Mountain (3,100 feet), the spring wildflowers and groves of fall foliage make Warm Springs a very scenic spot for sightseeing, hiking, or water activities. Visitors also enjoy walking tours to view the many historic buildings.

B&B/Small Inn

★ ★ ★ **INN AT GRISTMILL SQUARE.** *Rte 619 (24484). Phone 540/839-2231; fax 540/839-5770. www.gristmillsquare.com.* This inn is comprised of five restored 19th-century buildings including a gristmill and blacksmith shop. 15 rooms. Complimentary continental breakfast. Check-out noon, check-in 2 pm. TV. In-room modem link. Some fireplaces. Restaurant. Bar. Sauna. Pool. Tennis. Downhill ski 5 miles. Airport transportation. Cr cds: DS, MC, V. **$**

Restaurant

★ ★ ★ **WATERWHEEL.** *Rte 619 (24484). Phone 540/839-2231; fax 540/839-5770. www.gristmillsquare.com.* A restored gristmill circa 1900 is the very rustic setting for what is sure to be a unique dining experience. Guests venture to the wine cellar to make their selection directly from the bins. Hours: 6-9 pm; Fri, Sat to 10 pm; Sun brunch 11 am-2 pm. Reservations accepted. Contemporary American menu. Bar. Wine list. Dinner $18-$24. Specializes in fresh local trout, veal, homegrown vegetables. Own baking. Parking. Totally nonsmoking. Cr cds: A, MC, V.

Warrenton (E-10)

See also Culpepper, Fairfax, Front Royal, Manassas

Pop 6,670 **Elev** 560 ft **Area code** 540 **Zip** 20186

Information Warrenton-Fauquier County Visitor Center, 183 A Keith St; 540/347-4414 or 800/820-1021

Web www.fauquierchamber.org

The seat of Fauquier County, Warrenton was named for General Joseph Warren, who fought at Bunker Hill in the Revolutionary War. The town is situated in the valley of the Piedmont near the foothills of the Blue Ridge Mountains and is known for its cattle and Thoroughbred horse farms. Many old buildings and houses provide for an interesting walking tour of the town.

Special Event

Flying Circus. *Intersecting streets Morrisville Rd and Brookes Store Dr. Phone 540/439-8661.* Flying shows of the barnstorming era, from comedy acts to precision and stunt flying. Rides, picnic area. Sun. May-Oct.

Motels/Motor Lodges

★ **COMFORT INN.** *7379 Comfort Inn Dr (20187). Phone 540/349-8900; fax 540/347-5759. www.comfortinn. com.* 97 rooms. May-Oct: S, D $59-$79; each additional $8; suites $99-$125; under 18 free; mid-week rates; lower rates rest of year. Crib free. Pet accepted, some restrictions; $10/day. TV; cable (premium). Pool. Complimentary continental breakfast. Check-out 11 am. Coin laundry. Meeting room. Business services available. In-room modem link. Exercise equipment. Health club privileges. Refrigerators; microwaves available. Whirlpool in some suites. Cr cds: A, C, D, DS, JCB, MC, V.

D 🛎 ⇌ 🏌 ⊠

★ **HAMPTON INN.** *501 Blackwell Rd (20186). Phone 540/349-4200; toll-free 800/426-7866; fax 540/349-0061. www.hampton-inn.com.* 101 rooms, 2 story. S, D $64-$79; under 18 free. Crib free. Pet accepted. TV; cable (premium), VCR (movies). Pool. Complimentary continental breakfast. Check-out noon. Meeting rooms. Business services available. Coin laundry. Exercise equipment. Refrigerators, microwaves available. Picnic tables, grill. Cr cds: A, C, D, DS, MC, V.

D 🛎 ⇌ 🏌 ⊠ SC

Restaurant

★ ★ **NAPOLEON'S.** *67 Waterloo St (20186). Phone 540/347-1200. www.napoleonsrestaurant.com.* Continental menu. Specializes in veal, fresh fish, hand-cut beef. Hours: 11 am-midnight; Fri, Sat to 1 am. Closed Dec 25. Lunch $5.75-$7.95, dinner $9.95-$16.50. Bar. Reservations accepted. Outdoor seating. Historic 1838 mansion owned by Confederate General Eppa Hunton. Attractive flower gardens. Cr cds: A, D, DS, MC, V.

Washington (E-10)

See also Warrenton

Founded 1796 **Pop** 183 **Elev** 690 ft **Area code** 540 **Zip** 22747

The oldest of more than 25 American towns to be named after the first president, this town was surveyed in 1749 by none other than George Washington himself. The streets remain laid out exactly as surveyed and still bear the names of families who owned the land on which the town was founded. It is romantically rumored that Gay Street was named by the 17-year-old Washington after the lovely Gay Fairfax.

The town, seat of Rappahannock County, is situated in the foothills of the Blue Ridge Mountains, which dominate the western horizon.

What to See and Do

Mount Vernon. (see).

B&B/Small Inns

★ ★ **BLEU ROCK INN.** *12567 Lee Hwy (22747). Phone 540/987-3190; fax 540/987-3193. www.bleurockinn. com.* 5 rooms, 2 story. No room phones. S, D $125-$195. Closed Mon, Tues; Jan 1, Dec 24, 25. Complimentary full breakfast. Restaurant (See also BLEU ROCK INN). Check-out 11 am, check-in 3 pm. Business services available. Balconies. Restored farmhouse (1899) on lake; rustic setting; vineyard. Cr cds: A, C, D, DS, MC, V.

★ ★ ★ ★ ★ **THE INN AT LITTLE WASHINGTON.** *309 Main St (22747). Phone 540/675-3800; fax 540/675-3100.* Savvy epicureans book a room—and a table—at The Inn at Little Washington. Just far enough away from the nation's capital and tucked away in a sweet village in the foothills of the Blue Ridge Mountains, The Inn offers visitors a taste of the good life. Urban warriors are swayed by the Victorian charms of the public and private rooms, and the pastoral setting in Virginia's hunt country soothes even the most frayed nerves. Sophisticated without being pretentious, this romantic country house's amiable staff welcomes visitors with the comforts of home, including a delightful afternoon tea with scones and tartlets. Tempting as it may be to indulge, guests save their appetites for the evening's superlative cuisine. Many make special trips just for the talented chef's award-winning and artfully prepared meals, although lucky guests recount their memorable feasts while ensconcing themselves in one of the inn's lovely rooms. 14 rooms, 2 story. S, D $290-$495; each additional $50; suites $440-$580; higher rates Fri, Sat, holidays, May, and Oct. Inn closed Tues (except May and Oct); also Dec 24, 25. Complimentary continental breakfast. Check-out noon, check-in 3 pm. Restaurant (See THE INN AT LITTLE WASHINGTON). Bar. Bicycles. Airport transportation. Cr cds: MC, V.

★ ★ ★ **MIDDLETON INN.** *176 Main St (22747). Phone 540/675-2020; toll-free 800/816-8157; fax 540/675-1050.* This country estate is historic and was built in 1850 by Middleton Miller who designed and manufactured the Confederate uniform of the Civil War. The inn faces the Blue Ridge Mountains and the original slaves' quarters have been converted into a two-story guest cottage. 4 rooms, 2 with shower only, 1 cottage, 2 story. S, D $195-$375; 2-day minimum holiday weekends, Oct; higher rates Oct. Children over 12 years only. TV; cable (premium), VCR available (movies). Complimentary full breakfast; afternoon refreshments. Restaurant nearby. Check-out 11 am, check-in 3 pm. Luggage handling. Business services available. Lawn games. Federal-style house built 1850; rural setting. Totally nonsmoking. Cr cds: A, MC, V.

★ ★ **SYCAMORE HILL HOUSE AND GARDENS.** *110 Menefee Mountain Ln (22747). Phone 540/675-3046.* 3 rooms, 1 with shower only, 2 story. No room phones. S, D $115-$165; higher rates: weekends, holidays, month of Oct (2-day minimum). Children over 12 years only. Complimentary full breakfast; afternoon refreshments. Check-out 11 am, check-in 2 pm. Business services available. Luggage handling. Lawn games. On top of hill, view of mountains. Gardens. Totally nonsmoking. Cr cds: MC, V.

Restaurants

★ ★ ★ **BLEU ROCK INN.** *12567 Lee Hwy (22747). Phone 540/987-3190. www.bleurockinn.com.* This country-inn farmhouse is located on 80 acres of rolling hillside overlooking the Blue Ridge Mountains and adjoining vineyards. It is a great place to stop between Harrisonburg and DC. American, French menu. Closed Mon, Tues;

Dec 25. Dinner, brunch. Outdoor seating. Totally non-smoking. Cr cds: A, D, DS, MC, V. **$$**

★ ★ **FOUR AND TWENTY BLACKBIRDS.** *650 Zachary Taylor Hwy, Flint Hill (22627). Phone 540/675-1111.* Closed Mon, Tues; July 4, Dec 25; also 1st 2 weeks of Jan and Aug. Dinner, Sun brunch. Entertainment. Originally built in 1910 as carpenter's shop. Totally non-smoking. Cr cds: MC, V. **$$**

★ ★ ★ ★ **THE INN AT LITTLE WASHINGTON.** *309 Main St (22747). Phone 540/675-3800; fax 540/675-3100.* Opulent, luxurious, romantic, mind-altering, and magnificent: these are just a handful of adjectives that come to mind after experiencing dinner at The Inn at Little Washington. Set in the foothills of the Blue Ridge Mountains, the Inn's dining room is heavy with charm, appointed with rich draperies, tasseled lampshades, and vases overflowing with elaborate flower arrangements. As for the food, it's spectacular. Chef Patrick O'Connell has amassed almost every culinary award in existence. (He must have a separate house for all his plaques and trophies.) For the wonderful opportunity to be a guinea pig in his gifted presence, you will fork over a tidy sum, but your financial indulgence will be well rewarded. Plates are breathtaking, assembled from pristine seasonal ingredients that sparkle and balanced flavors that dazzle. Seasonal dishes that should be considered required eating include the crab cake "sandwich" with fried green tomatoes and tomato vinaigrette; the sesame-crusted Chilean seabass with baby shrimp, artichokes, and grape tomatoes; the rabbit braised in apple cider with wild mushrooms and garlic mashed potatoes; and, for dessert, the pistachio and white chocolate ice cream terrine with blackberry sauce. An amazing wine list will give you the right buzz to match your meal. To make matters even better, coddling is a specialty of the house, so be prepared to have your every whim catered to with grace and warmth. Hours: 6-9:30 pm; Sat 5:30-10 pm; Sun from 4 pm. Closed Tues (except in May and Oct), Dec 24, 25. Dinner prix fixe: $88-$116. Reservations accepted; required Fri, Sat. Valet parking available. Cr cds: MC, V.

D

Waynesboro (F-8)

See also Charlottesville

Settled circa 1739 **Pop** 19,520 **Elev** 1,300 ft **Zip** 22980

Information Waynesboro Augusta County Chamber of Commerce, 301 W Main St; 540/949-8203

Waynesboro is at the southern end of the Skyline Drive and the northern end of the Blue Ridge Parkway.

What to See and Do

P. Buckley Moss Museum. *150 P. Buckley Moss Dr. Phone 540/949-6473.* Museum's exhibits and programs examine the symbolism and aesthetic ideas of one of America's most notable living artists. (Mon-Sat; closed Jan 1, Thanksgiving, Dec 25) **FREE**

Shenandoah National Park. (see). *1 mile E to Skyline Dr.*

Shenandoah Valley Art Center. *600 W Main St. Phone 540/949-7662.* Art galleries, studios. Working artists; performing arts. (Tues-Sun) **DONATION**

Sherando Lake Recreation Area. *16 miles SW on Blue Ridge Pkwy, in George Washington and Jefferson national forests. Phone 540/942-5965 (summer) or 540/261-6105.* Facilities include 21-acre lake with sand beach and bathhouses, swimming, fishing; picnicking, camping (Apr-Oct, fee). Amphitheater, campfire programs. (Apr-Nov, daily) **$$**

Special Event

Fall Foliage Festival. First and second weekends in Oct.

Motels/Motor Lodges

★ **DAYS INN.** *2060 Rosser Ave (22980). Phone 540/943-1101; toll-free 800/943-1102; fax 540/949-7586. www.daysinn.com.* 98 rooms, 2 story. May-Oct: S $45-$75; D $50-$85; each additional $5; higher rates fall foliage, graduation; lower rates rest of year. Crib free. Pet accepted; $6. TV; cable (premium). Pool. Restaurant adjacent 6 am-midnight. Check-out 11 am. Meeting rooms. Business services available. Valet service. Game room. Lawn games. Microwaves available. Picnic tables. Cr cds: A, C, D, DS, JCB, MC, V.

D ⊙ ▬ ⊠ 🖈 ⊠

★ ★ **INN AT AFTON.** *US 250 and I-64 (22980). Phone 540/942-5201; toll-free 800/860-8559; fax 540/943-8746. www.comet.net/nelsoncty.* 118 rooms, 2-3 story. No elevator. May-Oct: S $60-$76; D $63-$81; each additional $7; under 18 free; higher rates special events; lower rates rest of year. Crib free. Pet accepted. TV. Heated pool. Restaurant 7 am-2 pm, 5-10 pm. Room service. Bar 5 pm-12:30 am; entertainment Fri, Sat. Check-out noon. Meeting rooms. Business services available. Valet service. Downhill ski 18 miles. Cr cds: A, C, D, DS, JCB, MC, V.

D ⊙ ▬ ⊠ ⊠ SC

★ ★ **QUALITY INN.** *640 W Broad St (22980). Phone 540/942-1171; fax 540/942-4785. www.comfortinn.com.* 75 rooms. S $45-$59; D $52-$69; each additional $5; under 18 free. Crib free. Pet accepted, some restrictions. TV; cable (premium). Pool; wading pool. Check-out noon. Business services available. Valet service. Downhill ski 20 miles. Health club privileges. Microwaves available. Cr cds: A, C, D, DS, ER, JCB, MC, V.

[D] [icons] [SC]

B&B/Small Inn

★ ★ ★ **IRIS INN.** *191 Chinquapin Dr (22980). Phone 540/943-1991; fax 540/942-2093. www.irisinn.com.* This inn overlooks the Shenandoah Valley and is near the Blue Ridge Mountains. The great room, with its 28-foot stone fireplace and a large mural of the wildlife in the mountains, is a central focus. A full and hearty breakfast is included as well as a "bottomless" cookie jar. 9 rooms, 2 story. S $75-$90; D $80-$100; each additional $20; suites $130-$140; weekend rates (2-day minimum). TV. Complimentary full breakfast. Check-out 11 am, check-in 3 pm. Balconies. Wooded setting overlooking Shenandoah Valley. Totally nonsmoking. Cr cds: MC, V.

[D] [icon]

Williamsburg (H-12)

See also Colonial Parkway, Jamestown (Colonial National Historical Park), Newport News, Surry, Yorktown

Settled 1633 **Pop** 11,998 **Elev** 86 ft **Area code** 757

Information Chamber of Commerce, 201 Penniman Rd, PO Box 3620, 23187; 757/229-6511

Web www.williamsburgcc.com

After the Native American massacre of 1622, this Virginia colony built a palisade across the peninsula between the James and York rivers. The settlement that grew up around the palisade was called Middle Plantation and is now the site of Colonial Williamsburg.

Middle Plantation figured prominently in Bacon's Rebellion against Governor Berkeley. In 1693, it was chosen as the site of the College of William and Mary, and in 1699, the seat of Virginia government was moved here. The capitol was built to replace the Jamestown statehouse, which had burned the year before. Renamed in honor of William III of England, the new capital gradually became a town of about 200 houses and 1,500 residents. For 81 years, Williamsburg was the political, social, and cultural capital of Virginia.

The colony's first successful printing press was established here by William Parks, and in 1736 he published Virginia's first newspaper. The capitol was the scene of such stirring colonial events as Patrick Henry's Stamp Act speech (1765).

The First Continental Congress was called from here by the dissolved House of Burgesses in 1774. Two years later, the Second Continental Congress was boldly led by delegates from Virginia to declare independence; George Mason's Declaration of Rights, which became the basis for the first ten amendments to the Constitution, was adopted here.

Williamsburg's exciting days came to an end in 1780 when the capital was moved to Richmond for greater safety and convenience during the Revolutionary War. For a century and a half it continued as a quiet little college town, its tranquility interrupted briefly by the Civil War. In 1917, when a munitions factory was built near the town and cheap housing for the factory's 15,000 workers was hastily erected, Williamsburg seemed destined to live out its days in ugliness.

In 1926, however, John D. Rockefeller, Jr. and Dr. W. A. R. Goodwin, rector of Bruton Parish Church, who saw the town as a potential treasurehouse of colonial history, shared the broad vision that inspired the restoration of Williamsburg. For more than 30 years, Rockefeller devoted personal attention to the project and contributed funds to accomplish this nonprofit undertaking.

Today, after many years of archaeological and historical research, the project is near completion. The Historic Area, approximately a mile long and a half-mile wide, encompasses most of the 18th-century capital. Eighty-eight of the original buildings have been restored; 50 major buildings, houses, and shops and many smaller outbuildings have been reconstructed on their original sites; 45 of the more historically significant buildings contain more than 200 exhibition rooms, furnished either with original pieces or reproductions and open to the public on regular seasonal schedules.

Visitors stroll Duke of Gloucester Street and mingle with people in 18th-century attire. Craftsmen at about 20 different shops ply such trades as wigmaking and blacksmithing, using materials, tools, and techniques of pre-Revolutionary times.

Williamsburg is beautiful year-round. November through March is an excellent time to visit, when it is less crowded and the pace is more leisurely; some holiday weekends may be busy. The Historic Area is closed to private motor vehicles 8 am-10 pm.

What to See and Do

Abby Aldrich Rockefeller Folk Art Center. *York St. 1/2 block SE of capitol.* Outstanding collection of American folk art. Items in this collection were created by artists not trained in studio techniques, but who faithfully recorded aspects of everyday life in paintings, sculpture, needlework, ceramics, toys, and other media.

America's Railroads on Parade. *1915 Pocahontas Trail, in Village Shops at Kingsmill. Phone 757/220-8725.* More than 4,000 square feet of model train layouts. Hands-on exhibits, gift shop. (Daily; closed Jan 1, Thanksgiving, Dec 25) **$$**

Brush-Everard House. Home of early mayor, with programs on slave life.

Bruton Parish Church. *331 Duke of Gloucester St. Just W of Palace Green. Phone 757/229-2891.* One of America's oldest Episcopal churches, in continuous use since 1715. Organ recitals (Mar-Dec, Tues and Sat). (Daily; no tours during services)

Busch Gardens Williamsburg. *1 Busch Gardens Blvd (23187). 3 miles E on US 60. Phone 757/253-3000; toll-free 800/343-7946.* European-style theme park on 360 acres features re-created 17th-century German, English, French, Italian, Scottish, and Canadian villages. Attractions include more than 30 thrill rides, including Drachen Fire roller coaster, one of the nation's largest; 3-D movie *Haunts of the Olde Country,* with in-theater special effects; live shows, antique carousel, celebrity concerts, miniature of Le Mans racetrack, and rides for small children. Theme restaurants; shops. Transportation around the grounds by sky ride or steam train. A computer-operated monorail links the park with the Anheuser-Busch Hospitality Center; brewery tour. (Mid-Apr-Aug, daily; late Mar-mid-Apr and Sept-Oct, weekends) **$$$$**

The Candle Factory. *Phone 757/564-3354.* Open since 1965. The Candle Factory produces over 6 million soaps and candles each year. Family owned and operated, third generation. You can watch while soaps and candles are made. (Daily; closed Jan 1, Thanksgiving, Dec 25)

The Capitol. *E end of Duke of Gloucester St.* House of Burgesses met here (1704-1779); scene of Patrick Henry's speech against Stamp Act.

Carriage and wagon rides. A drive through Historic Area in carriage or wagon driven by costumed coachman. General admission ticket holders may make reservations on day of ride at Lumber House ticket office. (Daily, weather permitting) **$$$**

Children's Tours. Special programs, tours, and experiences exclusively for children and families are offered in the summer.

College of William and Mary. *Richmond Rd. W end of Duke of Gloucester St. Phone 757/221-4000.* (1693) 7,000 students. America's second-oldest college (only Harvard is older). Initiated honor system, elective system of studies, schools of law, modern languages; second to have school of medicine (all in 1779). Phi Beta Kappa Society founded here (1776). On campus are

Earl Gregg Swem Library. Houses College Museum. Large display honoring the college's 300th anniversary. (Mon-Fri; closed holidays)

Muscarelle Museum of Art. *Jamestown Rd. Phone 757/221-2700.* Traveling displays and exhibitions from an extensive collection. (Wed-Sun; closed holidays) **FREE**

Wren Building. Oldest (1695-1699, restored 1928) academic building in America; designed by the great English architect Sir Christopher Wren. Tours (Daily). **FREE**

Colonial Parkway. The Colonial Parkway is a 23-mile link between the three towns that formed the "cradle of the nation"—Jamestown, Williamsburg, and Yorktown. It starts at the Visitor Center at Jamestown, passes through Williamsburg (the Colonial Williamsburg Information Center is near the north underpass entrance), and ends at the Visitor Center in Yorktown.

At turnouts and overlooks along the route, information signs note such historic spots as Glebeland, Kingsmill, Indian Field Creek, Powhatan's Village, Fusilier's Redoubt, and others. A free picnic area is provided during the summer at Ringfield Plantation, midway between Williamsburg and Yorktown.

The parkway is free to private vehicles. Commercial vehicles are not permitted. Speed limit is 45 miles per hour. There are no service stations.

⭐ **Colonial Williamsburg Visitor Center.** *Colonial Pkwy and VA 132. Contact the Colonial Williamsburg Foundation, PO Box 1776, 23187. Phone 757/220-7645; toll-free 800/246-2099.* Ticket sales, sightseeing information; orientation film; lodging and dining assistance; bookstore; transportation. Center (daily).

Courthouse. *Duke of Gloucester St, E of Palace Green.* County and city business was conducted here from 1770 until 1932. The interior has been carefully restored to its original appearance. Visitors often participate in scheduled reenactments of court sessions.

DeWitt Wallace Decorative Arts Gallery. *Phone 757/220-7724; toll-free 800/447-8679.* Modern museum adjoining Public Hospital, features exhibits, lectures, films, and related programs centering on British and American decorative arts of the 17th to early 19th centuries. (Fri-Wed) **$$$$**

Disabled Visitor Information. *Phone toll-free 800/246-2099.* Efforts are made to accommodate the disabled while still retaining the authenticity of colonial life. Many buildings have wheelchair access once inside, but it should be noted that most buildings are reached by steps. The Visitor Center has a list detailing accessibility of each building; wheelchair ramps may be made available at some buildings. In addition, there are wheelchair rentals and parking. A hands-on tour of several historic trades may be arranged for the visually impaired and sign language tours are available with advance notice.

Evening entertainment. Colonial Williamsburg presents "rollicking 18th-century plays" throughout the year; wide variety of cultural events, concerts, and historical reenactments (fees vary). Chowning's Tavern offers colonial "gambols" (games), music, entertainment and light food and drink (evenings).

Go-Karts Plus. *6910 Richmond Rd, Rte 60 W (23187). Phone 757/564-7600.* This 8-acre park has four go-kart tracks that appeal to various ages and driving skills, as well as bumper cars and boats, a miniature golf course, and an arcade. Admission is free; tickets must be purchased for activities. (Memorial Day weekend through Labor Day, daily 11 am-11 pm; shorter hours in spring and fall; closed Nov-late Mar)

Governor's Palace and Gardens. *N end of Palace Green.* Residence of Royal Governor, one of the most elegant mansions in colonial America; set in 10-acre restored gardens. **$$$$**

Haunted Dinner Theater. *5363 Richmond Rd. Phone 757/258-2500; toll-free 888/426-3746.* Help unravel a murder mystery—tame enough for little ones—while feasting on a 71-item, all-you-can-eat dinner buffet at Capt. George's World Famous Restaurant. Performances are held Wed-Sun evenings at 7 pm. **$$$**

Historic trades. Craftsmen in 18th-century costume pursue old trades of apothecary, printer, bookbinder, silversmith, wigmaker, shoemaker, blacksmith, harnessmaker, cabinetmaker, miller, milliner, gunsmith, wheelwright, basketmaker, cook, cooper, and carpenter.

James Geddy House. Once home of a prominent silversmith with working brass, bronze, silver, and pewter foundry.

Lanthorn Tour. *Phone toll-free 800/246-2099.* A costumed interpreter conducts evening walking tour of selected shops that are illuminated by candlelight. (Mar-Dec, daily) **$$$**

The Magazine. *Duke of Gloucester St, 1 block E of Palace Green.* Arsenal and military storehouse of Virginia Colony; authentic arms exhibited.

The Music Theatre of Williamsburg. *7575 Richmond Rd. Phone 757/564-0200; toll-free 888/687-4220.* This 752-seat theater, which opened in 1998, features ever-changing shows that appeal to and are appropriate for all ages. Call for the performance schedule. **$$$$**

Peyton Randolph House. (1716) Home of president of First Continental Congress. Rochambeau's headquarters prior to Yorktown campaign.

Play Booth Theater. Scenes from 18th-century plays in open-air theater. Open to all Colonial Williamsburg ticket holders. (Spring-fall, daily)

Public Gaol. Where debtors, criminals, and pirates (including Blackbeard's crew) were imprisoned.

Public Hospital. Reconstruction of first public institution in the English colonies devoted exclusively to treatment of mental illness.

Raleigh Tavern. Frequent meeting place for Jefferson, Henry, and other Revolutionary patriots; a social center of the Virginia Colony.

Ride with Me to Williamsburg. *Phone 301/299-7817 or 800/840-7433.* Informative and entertaining 90-minute audiocassette describes events from Williamsburg's colorful colonial, revolutionary, and Civil War past. The town's famous restoration is summarized by one of the architects who worked on the project. Contact RWM Associates, PO Box 1324, Bethesda, MD 20817.

Shirley Pewter Shop. *Phone 757/229-5356; toll-free 800/550-5356.* This shop features Williamsburg's own brand of pewter, "Shirley Pewter." Items available include dinnerware, oil lamps, and tableware. Many items can be engraved. (Daily)

Shopping. Superior wares typical of the 18th century are offered in nine restored or reconstructed stores and shops; items include silver, jewelery, herbs, candles, hats, and books. Two craft houses sell approved reproductions of the antiques on display in the houses and museums.

Skate Park. *5301 Longhill Rd (23187). Phone 757/259-3200.* A great, safe place for inline skating, skateboarding, and biking. The park is open to ages 9 and up, and all skaters and bikers must wear protective gear. (Nov-Mar, closed Mon, Tues, Thurs; rest of year, daily) **$$**

Special focus and orientation tours. Orientation tours (30 minutes) for first-time visitors; special tours (90 minutes), called history walks, include African-American life, gardens, religion, and women of Williamsburg. Reservations are available at any ticket sales location.

Ticket information. *102 Information Center Dr (23185). Phone 800/246-2099 for exact prices.* An admission ticket is necessary to enjoy the full scope of Colonial Williamsburg. Three types of general admission tickets are available: The **Basic Ticket** provides admission on the Colonial Williamsburg transportation system and entrance to the exhibits in the Historic Area for one day. (This ticket does *not* provide admission to the Governor's Palace, the DeWitt Wallace Decorative Arts Gallery, Carter's Grove, or the Abby Aldrich Rockefeller Folk Art Center.) The **Patriot's Pass** (valid for one year) provides admission on the transporation system and entrance to all historic buildings, colonial houses, craft shops, Governor's Palace, Carter's Grove, DeWitt Wallace Decorative Arts Gallery, Abby Aldrich Rockefeller Folk Art Center, and historical film. Ticket prices vary. **$$$$**

Water Country USA. *176 Water Country Pkwy (23187). Phone 757/253-3350; toll-free 800/343-SWIM.* This park, the mid-Atlantic's largest water park, features water slides, thrill rides, and live entertainment. A retro surf theme sets a festive mood. If you're interested in visiting Busch Gardens as well, which is just 3 miles from Water Country USA, you can save money by purchasing a Bounce Pass, which gains you admission to both parks. (May, early-mid-Sept, weekends from 10 am; Jun-Aug, daily from 10 am) **$$$$**

Wetherburn's Tavern. One of the most popular inns of the period.

Wythe House. Home of George Wythe, America's first law professor, teacher of Jefferson, Clay, and Marshall. This was Washington's headquarters before siege of Yorktown, Rochambeau's after.

York River State Park. *5526 Riverview Rd (23188). 8 miles NW via I-64, exit 231 B, then 1 mile N on VA 607 to VA 606 E. Phone 757/566-3036.* A 2,500-acre park along the York River and its related marshes. Includes the Taskinas Creek National Estuarine Research Reserve. Fishing, boating (launch), canoe trips; hiking and bridle trails, picnicking, interpretive center, programs, nature walks. (Daily) Standard fees.

Special Events

18th-Century Comedy. *5363 Richmond Rd (Williamsburg Lodge Auditorium). Phone 800/HISTORY.* Sat nights, Mar-Dec.

Antiques Forum. *102 Information Center Dr (23185). Phone 800/447-8679. Colonial Williamsburg.* Mid-Feb.

Colonial Weekends. *Phone 800/246-2099.* Package weekends on 18th-century theme, features introductory lecture, guided tours, banquet at Colonial Williamsburg. Jan-early Mar.

Fife and Drum Corps. *Intersecting streets Carter's Grove, S. England St. Phone 757/220-7453. Colonial Williamsburg.* Performances in the Historic Area. Sat, Apr-Oct.

Garden Symposium. *102 Information Center Dr (23185). Phone 800/447-8679. Colonial Williamsburg.* Lectures and clinics. Last week in Apr.

Learning Weekend. *Phone 830/278-2016. Colonial Williamsburg.* Family-oriented weekend of discovery on a single topic. Mar.

Living History Programs. *1340 S Pleasant Valley Rd (22601). At Colonial Williamsburg.* Includes *An Assembly,*

Cross or Crown, and *Cry Witch!* Varying schedule weekly. Spring, summer, and fall.

Military Drill. *Intersecting streets Duke of Gloucester and Colonial sts (Market Sq Green). Phone 757/229-6511.* Costumed weekly drill by Williamsburg Independent Company. Mid-Mar-Oct.

Prelude to Independence. *102 Information Center Dr (23185). Phone 800/447-8679. Colonial Williamsburg.* Mid-May.

Publick Times. *102 Information Center Dr (23185). Phone 800/447-8679. Colonial Williamsburg.* Re-creation of colonial market days; contests, crafts, auctions, military encampment. Labor Day weekend.

Traditional Christmas Activities. *102 Information Center Dr (23185). Phone 800/447-8679. Colonial Williamsburg.* Featuring grand illumination of city; fireworks. Dec.

Washington's Birthday Celebration. *8437 Valley Pike (22645). Phone 830/278-2016. Colonial Williamsburg.* President's Day weekend.

Motels/Motor Lodges

★ ★ **COURTYARD BY MARRIOTT.** *470 Mclaws Cir (23185). Phone 757/221-0700; toll-free 800/446-9244; fax 757/221-0741. www.courtyard.com.* 151 rooms, 4 story. Memorial Day-Labor Day: S, D $135-$145; suites $175-$195; lower rates rest of year. Crib free. TV; cable (premium). Indoor/outdoor pool; whirlpool. Bar 5-10 pm. Check-out noon. Coin laundry. Meeting rooms. Business services available. In-room modem link. Valet service. Concierge. Sundries. Exercise equipment. Game room. Refrigerator in suites. Balconies. Cr cds: A, C, D, DS, MC, V.

⊡ ⇌ ⌘ ⊠ SC

★ **GOVENORS INN.** *506 N Henry St (23185). Phone 757/229-1000; toll-free 800/447-8679; fax 757/229-7019.* 200 rooms, 3 story. May-Aug: S, D $89; family rates; lower rates rest of year. Closed Jan-mid-Mar. Crib $8. Pet accepted. TV; cable (premium). Restaurant nearby. Game room. Pool. Business services. Sundries. Gift shop. Cr cds: A, D, DS, MC, V.

⊡ ⇥ ⇌ ⊠ SC

★ **HAMPTON INN.** *201 Bypass Rd (23185). Phone 757/220-0880; fax 757/229-7175. www.hamptoninn.com.* 122 rooms, 4 story. Mid-June-early Sept: S, D $89-$109; lower rates rest of year, higher rates: July 4, Labor Day. Crib free. Complimentary continental breakfast. Check-out 11 am. TV; cable (premium). Sauna. Game room. Indoor pool, whirlpool. Meeting room. Business services. Cr cds: A, C, D, DS, MC, V.

⊡ ⇌ ⊠

★ ★ **HOLIDAY INN.** *814 Capitol Landing Rd (23185). Phone 757/229-0200; toll-free 800/465-4329; fax 757/220-1642. www.holidayinn.com.* 139 rooms, 3 story. Apr-Oct: S, D $89-$109; each additional $6; under 18 free; weekend rates; golf plan; lower rates rest of year. Crib free. TV; cable (premium). Indoor pool; whirlpool, poolside service. Restaurant 7 am-10 pm. Room service. Bar 5-11 pm. Check-out noon. Coin laundry. Meeting rooms. Business services available. Bellstaff. Gift shop. Exercise equipment; sauna. Game room. Refrigerators, microwaves available. Cr cds: A, D, DS, JCB, MC, V.

[D] [≈] [⇡] [≋] [SC]

★ **HOWARD JOHNSON.** *7135 Pocahontas Trail (23185). Phone 757/229-6900; toll-free 800/841-9100; fax 757/220-3211. www.hojohst.com.* 100 rooms, 4 story. Mid-June-Labor Day (2-day minimum weekends): S, D $89-$140; suites $120-$150; under 18 free; lower rates rest of year. Crib free. TV; cable (premium). Pool; wading pool, poolside service. Restaurant adjacent 7 am-2 pm. Check-out noon. Coin laundry. Meeting rooms. Business services available. Valet service. Sundries. Health club privileges. Game rooms. Cr cds: A, C, D, DS, JCB, MC, V.

[D] [≈] [≋] [SC]

★ **LA QUINTA INN.** *119 Bypass Rd (23185). Phone 757/253-1663; toll-free 800/283-1663; fax 757/220-9117. www.laquinta.com.* 131 rooms, 2 story. Mid-June-Labor Day: S, D $72-$94; each additional $6; under 19 free; lower rates rest of year. Crib free. Complimentary continental breakfast. Check-out 11 am. TV; cable (premium). In-room modem link. Pool. Meeting rooms. Business services. Cr cds: A, C, D, DS, MC, V.

[D] [≈] [≋]

★ ★ **QUALITY INN.** *901 Capitol Landing Rd (23185). Phone 757/229-4444; toll-free 800/638-7949; fax 757/220-9314. www.qualityinn.com.* 94 rooms, 1-2 story. May-Oct: S, D $59-$89; suites $89-$109; lower rates rest of year. Crib free. TV; cable (premium). Pool; wading pool. Restaurant 7 am-10 pm. Check-out 11 am. Coin laundry. Bellstaff. Putting green. Refrigerators, microwaves available. On 7 1/2 wooded acres with small fishing lake. Cr cds: A, C, D, DS, ER, JCB, MC, V.

[D] [⚓] [≈] [≋] [SC]

★ **QUARTERPATH INN.** *620 York St (23185). Phone 757/220-0960; toll-free 800/446-9222; fax 757/220-1531. www.quarterpathinn.com.* 130 rooms, 2 story. Pet accepted, some restrictions. Check-out noon, check-in 2 pm. TV; cable (premium). Outdoor pool. Cr cds: A, C, DS, MC, V. **$**

[D] [🐾] [≈] [≋] [SC]

★ ★ **RADISSON FORT MAGRUDER HOTEL & CONFERENCE CENTER.** *6945 Pocahontas Trail (23185). Phone 757/220-2250; toll-free 800/582-1010; fax 757/220-3215.* Situated on a historic battlefield, this property caters to both the business and leisure traveler. 303 rooms, 4 story. Apr-Oct: S $79-$129; D $99-$148; each additional $10; suites $145-$250; under 18 free; lower rates rest of year. Crib free. Check-out 11 am. TV; cable (premium). Balconies; many private patios. Refrigerators; some in-room whirlpools. Coin laundry. Restaurant 6:30 am-10 pm. Bar 11:30-1 am. Room service. Exercise equipment, sauna. Game room. Two pools, one indoor; wading pool, whirlpool. Golf privileges, greens fee $65-$115. Lighted tennis. Bicycles. Business center. Convention center/facilities. Concierge. Gift shop. Cr cds: A, C, D, DS, ER, JCB, MC, V.

[D] [🏋] [🏃] [≈] [⇡] [≋] [SC] [🚶]

★ ★ **RAMADA INN.** *725 Bypass Rd (23185). Phone 757/220-1776; toll-free 800/465-4329; fax 757/220-3124. www.ramada.com.* 202 rooms, 2 story. Mid-June-late Aug: S, D $89-$129; each additional $6; suites $129-$150; under 18 free; lower rates rest of year. Crib free. TV; cable (premium). Pool; wading pool, poolside service. Playground. Supervised children's activities (Memorial Day-Labor Day), ages 4-12. Restaurant 7 am-2 pm, 5-10 pm. Room service. Bar from 4 pm; Sat, Sun from 1 pm. Check-out 11 am. Coin laundry. Meeting rooms. Business services available. Bellstaff. Valet service. Concierge (in season). Sundries. Lighted tennis. Game room. Lawn games. Picnic tables. Cr cds: A, C, D, DS, JCB, MC, V.

[D] [🏃] [≈] [≋] [SC]

Hotels

★ ★ ★ **COLONIAL HOUSES - HISTORIC LODGING.** *302-B Francis St (23185). Phone 757/565-8440; fax 757/565-8444.* These 18th-century historic buildings are very secluded, located on the 173 acres of Colonial Williamsburg. Guests can choose from a small house or a larger one with with up to 16 rooms, each furnished with period reproductions. All are within walking distance of shops, museums, interpreters, and horse-drawn carriages. 77 rooms, 2 story. Complimentary continental breakfast. Check-out 11 am, check-in 4 pm. TV; cable (premium). In-room modem link. Business center. Some houses are more than 200 years old; furnished in the period. Totally nonsmoking. Cr cds: A, D, DS, MC, V. **$$**

[D] [≋] [🚶]

★ ★ ★ **MARRIOTT'S MANOR CLUB AT FORD'S COLONY.** *101 St. Andrews Dr (23188). Phone 757/258-1120; toll-free 800/845-5279; fax 757/258-5705. www.marriott.com.* Just minutes away from historic

Williamsburg, this 2,500-acre Colonial-style property, offers the ultimate in vacation luxuries. 135 kitchen suites, 3 story. Memorial Day-Labor Day: kitchen suites $264/day, $1,418/week; family rates; lower rates rest of year. Crib free. Check-out 10 am. TV; cable (premium), VCR (movies). In-room modem link. Balconies. Refrigerators, microwaves, fireplaces, in-room whirlpools. Restaurant 11:30 am-9:30 pm. Exercise equipment, massage. Two pools, one indoor; whirlpools. 45-hole golf, greens fee $50-$100, pro, putting green, driving range. Lighted tennis. Meeting rooms. Business services. Concierge. Sundries. Gift shop. Cr cds: A, C, D, DS, MC, V.

★ ★ ★ **MARRIOTT WILLIAMSBURG.** *50 Kingsmill Rd (23185). Phone 757/220-2500; toll-free 800/288-2662; fax 757/221-0653. www.marriott.com.* This hotel is close to Busch Gardens as well as Colonial Williamsburg, Jamestown and Yorktown sites, and shopping and outlet centers. 295 rooms, 6 story. Check-out noon, check-in 4 pm. TV; cable (premium). In-room modem link. Restaurant. Bar. Room service. Children's activity center. Sauna. Game room. Indoor, outdoor pool; whirlpool. Outdoor tennis. Business center. Concierge. Cr cds: A, C, D, DS, ER, JCB, MC, V. **$**

★ ★ ★ **WILLIAMSBURG HOSPITALITY HOUSE.** *415 Richmond Rd (23185). Phone 757/229-4020; toll-free 800/522-2063; fax 757/229-9557. www.williamsburghosphouse.com.* Enjoy a walk through the brick courtyard or relax by the roaring fire in the lobby and share conversation with other visitors among 18th-century furnishings. 297 rooms, 4 story. Mid-Mar-Dec: S, D $123-$153; each additional $10; suites $250-$500; under 18 free; weekend rates; golf plan; lower rates rest of year. Crib free. TV; cable (premium). Heated pool; poolside service. Restaurant 6:30 am-11 pm. Bar 11:30-1 am. Check-out noon. Meeting rooms. Business services available. In-room modem link. Concierge. Gift shop. Indoor parking. Health club privileges. Cr cds: A, C, D, DS, MC, V.

★ ★ ★ ★ **WILLIAMSBURG INN.** *136 E Francis St (23187). Phone 757/220-7978; fax 757/220-7096.* Pedigreed patriots make the Williamsburg Inn their home away from home while exploring the rich history of colonial America. The inn rolls out the red carpet for its guests, offering fine accommodations, gourmet dining, and unsurpassed levels of service. Furnished in English Regency style, the guest rooms have just the right amount of sophistication to appeal to adults while keeping children comfortable and satisfied. Blessed with a central location in the heart of this re-created 18th-century village, the inn is within a leisurely stroll of the blacksmith's shop, the candlemaker, and the cobbler. After reliving history, guests reap the rewards of the inn's plentiful activities and play a round of golf, dive into the spring-fed pool, rally on the clay tennis courts, head to the fitness center to keep in shape, or spoil themselves at the spa or gourmet restaurant. 110 rooms, 2 story. Pet accepted. Complimentary breakfast. Check-out 11 am, check-in 4 pm. TV; cable (premium), VCR available. In-room modem link. Fireplaces. Room service 24 hours. Restaurant. Bar; entertainment. Supervised children's activities (July 4-Labor Day), ages 4-12. Babysitting services available. Sauna, steam room, massage. Indoor, outdoor pool; children's pool, whirlpool. Golf; greens fee $95. Outdoor tennis. Lawn games, Bicycle rentals. Card room. Airport transportation. Business center. Concierge. Cr cds: A, C, D, DS, MC, V. **$$$**

★ ★ **WILLIAMSBURG LODGE.** *310 S England St (23185). Phone 757/229-1000; toll-free 800/447-8679; fax 757/220-7799. www.history.org.* A lobby with native Virginia cypress paneling and flagstone floors greets guests to this year-round inn. Folk art decorates the guest rooms and public areas and most overlook the gardens and lawns. 264 rooms, 3 story. Complimentary continental breakfast. Check-out 11 am, check-in 4 pm. TV; VCR available. In-room modem link. Fireplaces. Restaurant. Bar. Supervised children's activities center (Memorial Day-Labor Day), ages 4-12, babysitting services available. In-house fitness room, spa, sauna. Indoor, outdoor pools; children's pool, whirlpool. Golf on premise. Outdoor tennis. Lawn games, bicycles. Lounge, verandas. At edge of Colonial Williamsburg historic district. Cr cds: A, D, DS, MC, V. **$$**

★ ★ ★ **WOODLANDS HOTEL AND SUITES.** *105 Visitor Center Dr (23185). Phone 757/220-7960; toll-free 800/447-8679; fax 757/565-8942. www.colonialwilliamsburg.org.* Woodland tones are found in the rooms in these guest quarters located on the grounds of the visitor center and surrounded by pine trees. 300 rooms. Complimentary continental breakfast. Check-out 11 am, check-in 4 pm. TV. Restaurant. Supervised children's activities (mid-June-Aug), ages 5-12. Health club privileges. Outdoor pool, children's pool. Lawn games. Cr cds: A, D, DS, MC, V. **$**

Resorts

★ ★ ★ **KINGSMILL RESORT.** *1010 Kingsmill Rd (23185). Phone 757/253-1703; toll-free 800/832-5665; fax*

757/253-3993. www.kingsmill.com. Colonial Williamsburg may only be 3 miles down the road, but the Kingsmill Resort is decidedly 21st century. This playground for adults attracts golfers, tennis players, and those seeking rest and relaxation to its 2,900 manicured acres along the James River. Three 18-hole golf courses and a nine-hole par-three course challenge and charm players, while the Golf Academy provides clinics and individual instruction. Tennis players take their pick from fast-drying clay, Deco-Turf, and hydro courts at the state-of-the-art facility, while other racquet sports and a fitness center are discovered at the Sports Club. The spa rejuvenates and restores with its wide variety of treatments. After a day filled with activities, hearty appetites are always satisfied at the resort's six restaurants and lounges. 412 rooms, 2 story. Complimentary continental breakfast. Check-out 11 am, check-in 4-6 pm. TV; cable (premium), VCR available. In-room modem link. Fireplaces. Restaurant. Bar; entertainment. Room service. Supervised children's activities (Memorial Day-Labor Day), ages 5-12. Baby-sitting services available. In-house fitness room, spa, massage, sauna. Beach. Indoor, outdoor pools; children's pool, whirlpool. Golf on premise, greens fee. Outdoor tennis, lighted courts. Marina privileges. Paddle boats. Racquetball courts. Concierge. Cr cds: A, C, D, DS, JCB, MC, V. **$$$**

🄳 ⚅ 🛏 ⛷ ⌖ 🏃 🎿 SC

B&B/Small Inns

★ ★ **COLONIAL CAPITAL BED AND BREAK-FAST.** *501 Richmond Rd (23185). Phone 757/229-0233; toll-free 800/776-0570; fax 757/253-7667. www.ccbb.com.* 5 rooms, 3 story. No elevator. Mid-Mar-Dec: S $85-$110; D $105-$135; each additional $20; suite $150; package plans; lower rates rest of year. Children over 8 years only. Complimentary full breakfast. Restaurant adjacent 6:30 am-10 pm. Check-out 11 am, check-in 2 pm. Built in 1926; antiques. Totally nonsmoking. Cr cds: A, DS, MC, V.

🖼

★ ★ **COLONIAL GARDENS INN.** *1109 Jamestown Rd (23185). Phone 757/220-8087; toll-free 800/886-9715; fax 757/253-1495. www.ontheline.com/cgbb.* 4 rooms, 2 share bath, 2 suites, 2 story. S, D $105-$115; each additional $25; suites $130; weekends, holidays (2-3-day minimum). TV; cable (premium), VCR (movies). Complimentary full breakfast; afternoon refreshments. Restaurant nearby. Check-out 11 am, check-in 4-6 pm. In-room modem link. Luggage handling. Built 1960; Southern design. Antiques. Totally nonsmoking. Cr cds: A, MC, V.

🖼 SC

★ ★ ★ **EDGEWOOD BED AND BREAKFAST.** *4800 John Tyler Memorial Hwy, Charles City, (23030). Phone 804/829-2962; fax 804/829-2962.* This Gothic home built in 1870 houses a collection of country primitives. It is famous for its ghost which has been experienced by generations of occupants. The property includes a grist-mill that ground corn for both the Union and Confederate armies. 8 rooms, 3 with shower only, 3 story. S, D $120-$198. Children over 12 years only. TV; VCR. Pool. Complimentary full breakfast. Restaurant nearby. Check-out 11:30 am, check-in 3 pm. Microwaves available. Once part of the Berkeley Plantation; has served as church, post office, and nursing home. Cr cds: A, MC, V.

🖼

★ ★ **LEGACY OF WILLIAMSBURG BED AND BREAKFAST.** *930 Jamestown Rd (23185). Phone 757/220-0524; toll-free 800/962-4722; fax 757/220-2211. www.legacyofwilliamsburgbb.com.* 4 rooms, 3 suites, 2 story. Mar-Dec: S, D $95; suites $140. Adults only. TV in sitting room; cable, VCR (free movies). Complimentary full breakfast. Restaurant nearby. Check-out 10:30 am, check-in by 5 pm. Business services available. Recreation room. Billiards. Some balconies. Built in 18th-century style; period antiques, furnishings; library. Large rear deck overlooks small ravine. Totally nonsmoking. Cr cds: A, MC, V.

🖼

★ ★ ★ **LIBERTY ROSE BED AND BREAKFAST.** *1022 Jamestown Rd (23185). Phone 757/253-1260; toll-free 800/545-1825. www.libertyrose.com.* This restored house is decorated in a Victorian-style with European antiques and is located just 1 mile from Colonial Williamsburg's historic village. 4 rooms, 2 story. S, D $135-$205; each additional $50. Children over 12 years only. TV; VCR (free movies). Complimentary full breakfast; afternoon refreshments. Restaurant nearby. Check-out 11 am, check-in 3 pm. Picnic tables. Built 1920; many antiques. Wooded grounds. Totally nonsmoking. Cr cds: A, MC, V.

🖼

★ ★ **NORTH BEND PLANTATION BED AND BREAKFAST.** *12200 Weyanoke Rd, Charles City (23030). Phone 804/829-5176. www.northbendplantation.com.* 4 rooms, 2 story. S $105-$140; D $115-$140; each additional $40. TV. Pool. Complimentary full breakfast. Restaurant nearby. Check-out 11 am, check-in 3 pm. Fireplaces. Greek Revival house (1819); antiques. Cr cds: MC, V.

★ ★ **PINEY GROVE.** *16920 Southall Plantation Ln, Charles City, (23030). Phone 804/829-2480; fax 804/829-6888. www.pineygrove.com.* 4 rooms, 1 suite, 2 story. No room phones. S, D $125-$150; suite $160; holidays (2-day minimum). TV available in some rooms; cable, VCR available (movies) in common room. Complimentary full breakfast. Check-out noon, check-in 4 pm. Luggage handling. Pool. Lawn games. Refrigerators. 2 historic farmhouses (circa 1800). Totally nonsmoking. Cr cds: A, MC, V.

★ **WAR HILL INN BED AND BREAKFAST.** *4560 Longhill Rd (23188). Phone 757/565-0248; toll-free 800/743-0248; fax 757/565-4550. www.ngetaway.com/va/ warhill.* 5 rooms, 2 suites. No room phones. S, D $75-$165; each additional $15; suites $105-$135. Crib free. TV; cable. Playground. Complimentary full breakfast. Restaurant nearby. Check-out 11 am, check-in 4 pm. On working farm; built 1969 in colonial style. Totally nonsmoking. Cr cds: MC, V.

★ ★ ★ **WILLIAMSBURG SAMPLER BED AND BREAKFAST.** *922 Jamestown Rd (23185). Phone 757/ 253-0398; toll-free 800/722-1169; fax 757/253-2669. www. williamsburgsampler.com.* This 18th-century, plantation-style colonial home is located in the City of Williamsburg's Architectural Corridor Protection District. 4 rooms, 3 story. Room phones available. S, D $100-$150. TV; cable (premium). Complimentary full breakfast. Restaurant nearby. Check-out 11 am, check-in 1 pm. Business services available. Picnic tables. Plantation-style house; fireplaces, antiques, colonial-style furnishings; gardens. Near William and Mary College; walking distance to historic area. Totally nonsmoking. Cr cds: MC, V.

Restaurants

★ ★ **ABERDEEN BARN.** *1601 Richmond Rd (23185). Phone 757/229-6661; fax 757/227-4440. www.aberdeen-barn.com.* Closed Thanksgiving, Dec 25; also 1st 2 weeks in Jan. Dinner. Bar. Children's menu. Cr cds: A, MC, V. **$$**

★ ★ **BERRET'S SEAFOOD RESTAURANT AND TAPHOUSE GRILL.** *199 S Boundary St (23185). Phone 757/253-1847; fax 757/220-0415. www.berrets.com.* Regional American, seafood menu. Closed Jan 1, Dec 25; also Mon in Jan and Feb. Lunch, dinner. Bar. Children's menu. Casual attire. Outdoor seating. Cr cds: A, DS, MC, V. **$$**

★ ★ **COACH HOUSE TAVERN.** *12604 Harrison Landing Rd, Charles City (23030). Phone 804/829-6003; fax 804/829-6907.* Seafood menu. Hours: 11 am-4 pm; Fri-Sat 6-9 pm; Sun brunch 11 am-4 pm. Closed Dec 25. Lunch $3.95-$14.95. Dinner $24-$35. Sun brunch $3.95-$14.95. Bar. Children's menu. Reservations required on Fri, Sat. Cr cds: A, DS, MC, V.

★ ★ ★ **THE DINING ROOM AT FORD'S COLONY.** *240 Ford's Colony Dr (23188). Phone 757/ 258-4107; fax 757/258-4168. www.fordscolony.com.* Rich, imaginative American and European dishes are served by an impeccable waitstaff in a quiet, elegant dining room. American, seafood menu. Hours: 6-9:30 pm; Sun brunch 11:30 am-2:30 pm. Closed Sun, Mon; also early Jan. Dinner $52. Sun brunch $18.95. Bar. Children's menu. Jacket required. Cr cds: A, MC, V.

★ **GAZEBO HOUSE OF PANCAKES.** *409 Bypass Rd (23185). Phone 757/220-0883.* Breakfast $3.75-$7.75, lunch $2.50-$8.50. Children's menu. Cr cds: A, DS, MC, V.

★ ★ **GIUSEPPE'S.** *5601 Richmond Rd (23188). Phone 757/565-1977; fax 757/564-0853. www.giuseppes.com.* Italian menu. Closed Sun; major holidays. Lunch, dinner. Bar. Children's menu. Outdoor seating. Cr cds: A, D, DS, MC, V. **$**

★ ★ **INDIAN FIELDS TAVERN.** *9220 John Tyler Memorial Hwy, Charles City (23030). Phone 804/829-5004; fax 804/829-5411. www.indianfields.com.* Hours: 11 am-3:30 pm, 5-9 pm; Fri, Sat to 10 pm. Sun brunch to 3:30 pm. Closed Dec 24, 25; also Mon in Jan. Reservations accepted. Bar. Lunch $5.95-$14.95, dinner $17.95-$27.95. Sun brunch $7-$16.95. Children's menu. Specialties: crab cakes Harrison, bourbon chocolate pecan pie, bread pudding. Parking. Screened porch dining area. Turn-of-the-century farmhouse on working farm. Cr cds: A, DS, MC, V.

★ ★ **JEFFERSON INN.** *1453 Richmond Rd (23185). Phone 757/229-2296; fax 757/258-2533.* Hours: 4-11 pm. Closed Thanksgiving, Dec 24, 25. Reservations accepted. Italian, continental menu. Dinner $8.95-$21.95. Children's menu. Specializes in steak, fresh seafood, Southern favorites. Family-owned. Cr cds: A, C, D, ER, JCB, MC, V.

★ ★ **KING'S ARMS TAVERN.** *416 E Duke of Glouchester St (23185). Phone 757/229-2141; fax 757/565-8806. www.colonialwilliamsburg.com.* Hours: 11:30 am-2:30 pm, 5-8:45 pm. Dinner $24-$50. Bar. Garden bar service. Children's menu. Restored 18th-century tavern; Colonial décor. Reservations required dinner. Garden dining. Own apple cider. Colonial balladeers. Cr cds: A, D, DS, MC, V.

★ ★ ★ **KITCHEN AT POWHATAN.** *3601 Ironbound Rd (23188). Phone 757/220-0741; fax 757/253-0987. www.kitchenatpowhatan.com.* An 18th-century plantation kitchen is the setting for this cozy, intimate restaurant. The simple menu features contemporary American dishes inspired by fresh local ingredients. Hours: 5:30-10 pm. Closed Mon. Reservations accepted. Bar. Dinner $15-$28. Prix fixe: dinner $40. Specializes in game, seafood, regional cuisine. Parking. In 1737 structure on grounds of Powhatan Plantation. Cr cds: A, D, DS, MC, V.

★ ★ **KYOTO JAPANESE STEAK AND SEAFOOD HOUSE.** *1621 Richmond Rd (23185). Phone 757/220-8888; fax 804/220-3611. www.kyoto2.com.* Japanese, seafood menu. Dinner. Bar. Children's menu. Outdoor seating. Fish pond. Karaoke. Cr cds: A, D, DS, MC, V. **$**
D SC

★ ★ **LE YACA.** *1915 Pocahontas Trail #C10 (23185). Phone 757/220-3616; fax 757/259-0138.* Southern French menu. Closed Sun. Lunch, dinner. Bar. Cr cds: A, DS, MC, V. **$**
D

★ **OLD CHICKAHOMINY HOUSE.** *1211 Jamestown Rd (23185). Phone 757/229-4689; fax 757/253-2276. www.visitwilliamsburg.com.* Closed Thanksgiving, Dec 25; also 2 weeks mid-Jan. Breakfast $.95-$7.75, lunch $2-$6.98. 18th-century stagecoach stop atmosphere. Totally nonsmoking. Cr cds: MC, V.

★ ★ **PEKING.** *122 Waller Mill Rd (23185). Phone 757/229-2288. www.peking-va.com.* Chinese menu. Closed Thanksgiving. Buffet, lunch, dinner, brunch. Bar. Reservations required weekends. Cr cds: A, DS, MC, V. **$**
D

★ ★ **PRIME RIB HOUSE.** *1433 Richmond Rd (23185). Phone 757/229-6823. www.primeribhouse.com.* Southwestern menu. Dinner. Bar. Children's menu. Cr cds: A, D, DS, MC, V. **$$**
D

★ ★ ★ **REGENCY DINING ROOM.** *136 E Francis St (23185). Phone 757/229-2141; fax 757/220-7096. www.colonialwilliamsburg.com.* Set in the charming Williamsburg Inn (see also), the Regency Dining Room offers diners a graceful place to relax and enjoy a leisurely dinner of well executed and beautifully presented contemporary regional Southern fare. The menu runs the gamut from modern dishes like tomato-rosemary ravioli with smoked duck and oxtail rillettes to tried-and-true classics like Chateaubriand and the signature Williamsburg Inn crab cake. Diners with two left feet may want to brush up on their waltzing before dinner, as live music and dancing are served up on Friday and Saturday nights. American menu. Breakfast, lunch, dinner. Bar. Children's menu. Jacket required. Outdoor seating. Cr cds: A, D, DS, MC, V. **$$$**
D

★ ★ **SEASONS CAFE.** *110 S Henry (23185). Phone 757/259-0018; fax 757/259-0513. www.seasonsofwilliamsburg.com.* International menu. Closed Dec 25. Lunch, dinner, brunch. Bar. Children's menu. Casual attire. Cr cds: A, D, DS, MC, V. **$$**
D

★ **THAT SEAFOOD PLACE.** *1647 Richmond Rd (23185). Phone 757/220-3011; fax 757/220-5661.* Hours: 11:30 am-2:30 pm, 4:30-9 pm; Fri, Sat 4:30-10 pm; Sun noon-9 pm; summer hours vary. Closed Dec 25. Reservations accepted. Bar. Lunch $4.95-$6.95, dinner $8.25-$18.50. Children's menu. Specialties: shrimp sampler, sauteed shrimp and scallops. Salad bar. Parking. Outdoor seating. Nautical décor. Cr cds: A, MC, V.
D

★ ★ ★ **THE TRELLIS.** *403 Duke of Gloucester St (23185). Phone 757/229-8610; fax 757/221-0450. www.thetrellis.com.* American menu. Lunch, dinner, brunch. Bar. Entertainment. Casual attire. Outdoor seating. Cr cds: A, MC, V. **$$**
D

★ ★ **WHALING COMPANY.** *494 McLaw Cir (23185). Phone 757/229-0275. www.whalingcompany.com.* Steak menu. Dinner. Bar. Children's menu. Cr cds: A, D, DS, MC, V. **$$**
D

★ ★ **YORKSHIRE STEAK AND SEAFOOD HOUSE.** *700 York St (23185). Phone 757/229-9790; fax 757/229-7685. www.yorkshire-wmbg.com.* Hours: 4-10 pm; summer to 10:30 pm. Closed Dec 25. Reservations accepted. Bar. Dinner $10.95-$22.95. Children's menu. Specialties: shish kebab, prime rib. Parking. In colonial-style building. Totally nonsmoking. Cr cds: A.
D SC

Winchester (D-9)

See also Front Royal

Settled 1732 **Pop** 23,585 **Elev** 720 ft **Area code** 540

Information Winchester-Frederick County Visitor Center, 1360 S Pleasant Valley Rd, 22601; 540/662-4135 or 800/662-1360

This is the oldest colonial city west of the Blue Ridge, a Civil War prize that changed hands 72 times (once, 13 times in a day). Sometimes called the "apple capital of the world," it is located at the northern approach to the Shenandoah Valley.

George Washington, a red-haired 16-year-old, blithely headed for Winchester and his first surveying job in 1748, and began a decade of apprenticeship for the awesome military and political responsibilities he would later assume as a national leader. During the French and Indian Wars, Colonel Washington made the city his defense headquarters while he built Fort Loudoun in Winchester. Washington was elected to his first political office as a representative from Frederick County to the House of Burgesses.

At the intersection of travel routes, both east-west and north-south, Winchester grew and prospered. By the time of the Civil War it was a major transportation and supply center, strategically located to control both Union approaches to Washington and Confederate supply lines through the Shenandoah Valley. More than 100 minor engagements and six battles took place in the vicinity. General Stonewall Jackson had his headquarters here during the winter of 1861-1862. From his headquarters in Winchester, Union General Philip Sheridan started his famous ride to rally his troops at Cedar Creek, 11 miles away, and turn a Confederate victory into a Union rout.

Approximately 3.5 million bushels of apples are harvested annually in Frederick County and are one of Winchester's economic mainstays today. The world's largest apple cold storage plant and one of the world's largest apple processing plants are here.

What to See and Do

Abram's Delight and Log Cabin. *1340 S Pleasant Valley Ave. Phone 540/662-6519 or 540/662-6550.* (1754) Oldest house in city, restored, furnished in 18th-century style; boxwood garden; log cabin, basement kitchen. (Apr-Oct, daily; rest of year, by appointment, weather permitting) Inquire about combination ticket. **$$**

First Presbyterian Church of Winchester. *116 S Loudoun St. Phone 540/662-3824.* (1788) Building has been used as a church, a stable by Union troops in Civil War, a public school, and an armory; restored in 1941. (Daily)

Handley Library and Archives. *100 W Piccadilly St. Phone 540/662-9041.* Completed in 1913, public library was designed in Beaux Arts style. Rotunda is crowned on the outside with a copper-covered dome and on the inside by a dome of stained glass. Interesting interior features include wrought-iron staircases and glass floors. Historical archives are housed on lower level (nonresident fee). (Mon-Sat; closed holidays)

Stonewall Jackson's Headquarters. *415 N Braddock St. Phone 540/667-3242 or 540/662-6550.* Jackson's headquarters Novmber 1861-March 1862; now a museum housing Jackson memorabilia and other Confederate items of the war years. (Apr-Oct, daily; rest of year, by appointment, weather permitting) Inquire about combination ticket. **$$**

Washington's Office-Museum. *Jct Cork and Braddock sts. Phone 540/662-4412 or 540/662-6550.* Building used by George Washington in 1755-1756 during construction of Fort Loudoun. Housed in this museum are French and Indian, Revolutionary, and Civil War relics. (Apr-Oct, daily; rest of year, by appointment, weather permitting) **$**

Special Events

Apple Harvest Arts & Crafts. *Jim Barnett Park.* Pie contests, apple-butter making, music, arts and crafts. Third weekend in Sept.

Historic Garden Tour. *1340 S Pleasant Valley Rd. Phone 540/662-6550.* Open house and gardens in historic Winchester. Mid-Apr.

Shenandoah Apple Blossom Festival. *135 N Cameron St. Phone 540/662-3863.* Apple Blossom Queen, parades, arts and crafts, band contests, music, food, and attractions. Late-Apr-early May.

Motels/Motor Lodges

★ ★ **BEST WESTERN LEE-JACKSON.** *711 Millwood Ave (22601). Phone 540/662-4154; toll-free 800/528-1234; fax 540/662-2618. www.bestwestern.com.* 140 rooms, 2 story. Apr-Oct: S $52; D $57; each additional $5; suites $65-$70; kitchen units $35 (14-day minimum); under 13 free; lower rates rest of year. Crib available. Pet accepted. TV; cable (premium). Pool. Restaurant 6 am-10 pm. Room service. Bar 5-10:30 pm. Check-out noon. Coin laundry. Meeting rooms. Business services available. Valet service. Free airport transportation. Health club privileges. Some refrigerators, microwaves. Picnic tables, grills. Cr cds: A, C, D, DS, MC, V.

⊡ 🔾 ⩥ ⩥ SC

★ **COMFORT INN.** *167 Town Run Ln, Stephens City (22655). Phone 540/869-6500; toll-free 800/228-5150; fax 540/869-2558. www.comfortinn.com.* 58 rooms, 2 story. S $43-$70; D $49-$80; each additional $6; under 18 free. Crib free. TV; cable (premium), VCR available (movies). Pool. Complimentary continental breakfast. Restaurant adjacent 11 am-9 pm. Check-out noon. Business services available. In-room modem link. Sundries. Refrigerators, microwaves available. Cr cds: A, C, D, DS, ER, JCB, MC, V.

⊡ ⇌ ⊠ **SC**

★ **ECONO LODGE.** *1593 Martinsburg Pike (22603). Phone 540/662-4700; fax 540/665-1762; res 800/553-2666.* 50 rooms, 2 story. S $46.95; D $50.95; each additional $5; under 19 free. Crib free. Complimentary continental breakfast. Check-out 11 am. TV; cable (premium). In-room modem link. Restaurant nearby. Business services. Cr cds: A, C, D, DS, JCB, MC, V.

⊡ ⊠

★ **HAMPTON INN.** *1655 Apple Blossom Dr (22601). Phone 540/667-8011; fax 540/667-8033. www.hamptoninn. com.* 103 rooms, 4 story. S, D $60-$67; under 18 free. Crib free. Complimentary continental breakfast. Check-out noon. TV; cable (premium). In-room modem link. Valet services. Restaurant nearby. Health club privileges. Pool. Meeting rooms. Business services. Cr cds: A, C, D, DS, JCB, MC, V.

⊡ ⇌ ⊠

★ ★ **HOLIDAY INN.** *1017 Millwood Pike (22602). Phone 540/667-3300; fax 540/722-2730. www.holiday-inn.com.* 175 rooms, 2 story. S, D $49-$79; each additional $6; under 18 free. Crib free. TV; cable. Pool. Restaurant 6:30 am-10 pm. Room service. Bar 5:30 pm-midnight. Check-out noon. Meeting rooms. Business services available. In-room modem link. Bellstaff. Valet service. Sundries. Tennis. Health club privileges. Some refrigerators, microwaves. Balconies. Cr cds: A, C, D, DS, JCB, MC, V.

⊡ ⚓ ✈ ⇌ ⊠ ⊠

★ **SHONEY'S INN.** *1347 Berryville Ave (22601). Phone 540/665-1700; fax 540/665-3037.* 98 rooms, 4 with shower only, 3 story. May-Oct: S $53; D $58-$61; each additional $5; under 18 free; lower rates rest of year. Crib free. TV; cable (premium). Indoor pool; whirlpool. Restaurant 6 am-11 pm; Fri, Sat to 1 am. Check-out noon. Meeting room. Business services available. Sundries. Valet service. Exercise equipment; sauna. Some in-room whirlpools, refrigerators, microwaves. Cr cds: A, C, D, DS, MC, V.

⊡ ⇌ ⊠ ⊠

★ **TRAVELODGE.** *160 Front Royal Pike (22602). Phone 540/665-0685; toll-free 800/578-7878; fax 540/665-0689. www.travelodge.com.* 149 rooms, 3 story. S $46-$63; D $52-$69; each additional $5; suites $125; under 17 free. Crib free. Pet accepted; $5. TV; cable (premium), VCR available (movies). Heated pool. Complimentary continental breakfast. Restaurant nearby. Check-out 11 am. Coin laundry. Business services available. In-room modem link. Health club privileges. Refrigerators, microwaves available. Cr cds: A, C, D, DS, ER, JCB, MC, V.

⊡ 🐾 ⇌ ⊠ **SC**

B&B/Small Inns

★ ★ ★ **ASHBY INN.** *692 Federal St, Paris (20130). Phone 540/592-3900; fax 540/592-3781. www.ashbyinn. com.* This restored 1829 inn is charming and elegant. Guests should certainly make a point to dine in the restaurant which features seasonal fare. 9 rooms, 3 story. Room phones available. S, D $130-$200; each additional $20; suite $220. Children over 10 years only. Complimentary full breakfast. Check-out noon, check-in 3 pm. TV in some rooms. Restaurant (See ASHBY INN). Lawn games. Business services. Totally nonsmoking. Converted residence (1829) and one-room schoolhouse; stone fireplace; antique furnishings. Cr cds: MC, V.

⊠

★ ★ ★ **THE INN AT VAUCLUSE SPRING.** *231 Vaucluse Spring Ln, Stephens City (22655). Phone 540/869-0200; toll-free 800/869-0525; fax 540/869-9546.* Located on 100 acres of land, this inn is spread over four buildings: the Manor House, Chumley Homeplace, Gallery, and Millhouse Studio. Visitors will enjoy the nearby wineries and scenic location. 10 rooms, 2 story. No room phones, Children over 10 years only. Complimentary full breakfast. Check-out 11 am, check-in 3-5 pm. Fireplaces. Pool. Cross-country ski on site. Business center. Built in 1785; Federal-style décor. On 100 acres. Cr cds: MC, V. **$$**

⊡ ⚐ ⇌ ⊠ 🎿

★ ★ ★ **L'AUBERGE PROVENÇAL FRENCH COUNTRY INN.** *Rte 340 S, Boyce (22663). Phone 540/837-1375; toll-free 800/638-1702; fax 540/837-2004. www.laubergeprovencale.com.* This French-style inn, decorated with Victorian and European antiques, is located in the heart of Virginia hunt country. 14 rooms, 2 story. Children over 10 years only. Complimentary full breakfast. Check-out 11 am, check-in 3 pm. Restaurant. Room service. Health club privileges. 36-hole golf privileges. Free airport transportation. Originally a sheep farm (1753) owned by Lord Fairfax. French country décor. Cr cds: A, C, D, MC, V. **$$**

🎿 ⊠

Restaurants

★ ★ ★ **ASHBY INN.** *692 Federal St, Paris (20130).* *Phone 540/592-3900; fax 540/592-3781. www.ashbyinn.com.* Seasonal provisions inspire the simple, hearty menu that rivals those of trendy city restaurants. Look for garden fresh tomatoes in the summer and wild game in the fall. Relax in a very warm, very country atmosphere. Menu changes daily. Closed Mon, Tues; Jan 1, July 4, Dec 25. Dinner, Sun brunch. Reservations required. Outdoor seating. Plank flooring dates back to original inn (1829). Cr cds: MC, V. **$$**

D

★ ★ ★ **L'AUBERGE PROVENÇAL.** *Rte 340 S, Boyce (22620). Phone 540/837-1375. www.laubergeprovencale .com.* This country inn has earned a reputation for fine cuisine served with detailed, personal attention. Innkeeper/chef Alain Borel, from Avignon, and his wife Celeste provide an authentic, garden-inspired menu. French Provençal menu. Closed Mon, Tues; July 4, Dec 25. Dinner. Bar. Outdoor seating. Totally nonsmoking. Cr cds: A, D, DS, MC, V. **$$$**

Wise (H-3)

See also Big Stone Gap, Breaks Interstate Park

Pop 3,255 **Elev** 2,454 ft **Area code** 540 **Zip** 24293

What to See and Do

Recreation Areas. *Coeburn Rd. Phone 540/328-2931.* In George Washington and Jefferson National Forest (see HARRISONBURG). **High Knob,** 4 miles S on US 23 to Norton, then 3 miles S via VA 619, 1 1/2 miles E on FS Road 238. Camping, swimming, picnicking. Parking fee. **Bark Camp,** [E]4 miles S on US 23 to Norton, then 6 miles E on US 58 A to Tacoma, then 4 miles S off VA 706, 3 miles S on VA 822. Camping, boating, fishing, picnicking. Parking fee. **Cave Springs,** 7 miles W of Big Stone Gap on US 58 A, then 1 mile N on VA 622, then 3 miles W on VA 621. Camping (fee). Swimming. Parking fee. **North Fork of Pound Lake,** US 23 to Pound, then W on VA 671. Camping (fee), picnicking, swimming, boat ramp, hiking. Clinch Ranger District office is in Wise.

Woodstock (D-9)

See also Basye, Front Royal, Luray, New Market

Founded 1761 **Pop** 3,952 **Elev** 780 ft **Area code** 540 **Zip** 22664

Information Chamber of Commerce, 143 N Main St, PO Box 605; 540/459-2542

Web www.woodstockva.com/chamber

A German immigrant, Jacob Mller, received a land grant from Lord Fairfax and came here in 1752 with his wife and six children. A few years later he set aside 1,200 acres for a town, first called Müllerstadt, later Woodstock. In a small log church here, John Peter Gabriel Mühlenberg, in January 1776, preached his famous sermon based on Ecclesiastes 3:1-8: "There is a time to every purpose . . . a time to war and a time to peace," at the end of which he flung back his vestments to reveal the uniform of a Continental colonel and began to enroll his parishioners in the army that was to overthrow British rule.

The *Shenandoah Valley-Herald,* a weekly newspaper established in 1817, is still published here.

What to See and Do

Shenandoah County Court House. *Main St (1792).* Oldest courthouse still in use west of the Blue Ridge Mountains; interior restored to original design. (Mon-Fri)

Shenandoah Vineyards. *3659 S Ox Rd (22824). From I-81 exit 279 at Edinburg, W on VA 675, make first right on VA 686, go 1 1/2 miles to winery. Phone 540/984-8699.* Valley's first winery. Premium wines; hand-picked and processed in the European style. Picnic area. Tours, free tastings available. (Daily; closed Jan 1, Thanksgiving, Dec 25) **FREE**

Woodstock Tower. *4 miles E on Mill Rd, crest of Massanutten Mountain.* Panoramic view of seven horseshoe bends of the Shenandoah River.

Special Events

Shenandoah County Fair. *300 Fairgrounds Rd (22664). Phone 540/459-3867.* One of the oldest county fairs in the state. Harness racing last four days. Late Aug-early Sept.

Shenandoah Valley Music Festival. *102 N Main St. Phone 540/459-3396.* Symphony pops, classical, folk, jazz, country, and big band concerts. Pavilion and lawn seating. Outdoor pavilion on grounds of historic Orkney Springs Hotel in Orkney Springs. Contact Festival, PO Box 12. Four weekends, mid-July-Labor Day weekend.

Motels/Motor Lodges

★ **BUDGET HOST INN.** *1290 S Main St (22664). Phone 540/459-4086; fax 540/459-4043. www.budgethost. com.* 43 rooms, 1-2 story. S $30; D $37-$40; each additional $5; under 6 free; weekly rates. Crib $5. Pet accepted, some restrictions. Check-out 11 am. TV; cable. Coin laundry. Restaurant 6:30 am-9 pm; Sun from 7 am. Pool. Downhill ski 20 miles. Picnic tables. Business services. Cr cds: A, DS, MC, V.

D

★ **RAMADA INN.** *1130 Motel Dr (22664). Phone 540/459-5000; toll-free 800/272-6232; fax 540/459-8219. www.ramada.com.* 124 rooms, 3 story. May-Oct: S $62; D $70; each additional $8; under 18 free; lower rates rest of year. Crib free. TV; cable (premium). Heated pool. Restaurant 7 am-1:30 pm, 5-9 pm. Room service. Bar 5 pm-midnight. Check-out noon. Meeting rooms Business services available. Valet service. Sundries. Some refrigerators. Cr cds: A, C, D, DS, JCB, MC, V.

D ⊠ ⊠ SC

B&B/Small Inn

★ ★ ★ **INN AT NARROW PASSAGE.** *Rte 11; 30 Chapman Landing Rd (22664). Phone 540/459-8000; toll-free 800/459-8002; fax 540/459-8001. www. innatnarrowpassage.com.* This restored colonial wagon stop along the Old Valley Pike is located on the Shenandoah River. The guest rooms are decorated with Early American reproductions and antiques are available. Views of both the river and the Massanutten Mountains are enjoyed. 12 rooms, 2 with bath, 2 story. Room phones available. S, D $95-$145; each additional $10. TV. Complimentary full breakfast. Check-out 11 am, check-in 2 pm. Meeting rooms. Business services available. Lawn games. On river; canoeing. Historic inn (1740), used as headquarters by General Stonewall Jackson during Civil War. Totally nonsmoking. Cr cds: DS, MC, V.

D ⛷ ⊠

Restaurant

★ ★ **SPRING HOUSE TAVERN.** *325 S Main St (US 11) (22664). Phone 540/459-4755. www.jesara.com.* Lunch, dinner. Bar. Children's menu. Reservations not accepted. Five dining rooms include a log lounge. Cr cds: A, D, DS, MC, V. **$$**

D

Wytheville (H-5)

Founded 1792 **Pop** 7,804 **Elev** 2,284 ft **Area code** 540 **Zip** 24382

Information Wytheville-Wythe-Bland Chamber of Commerce, 150 E Monroe St, PO Box 563; 540/223-3365

Web chamber.wytheville.com

With lead mines and the only salt mine in the South nearby, Wytheville was a Union target during the Civil War. One story states a detachment of Union cavalry attempted to take the town in July 1863, only to be thwarted by Molly Tynes, who rode 40 miles over the mountains from Rocky Dell to tell the countryside that the Yankees were coming. The alerted home guard turned them away. A transportation center today, Wytheville is a vacationland nestled

between the Blue Ridge and Allegheny mountains. Rural Retreat Lake is nearby. Wythe Ranger District office for the George Washington and Jefferson national forests (see HARRISONBURG) is located here.

What to See and Do

Big Walker Lookout. *US 52 N. On Big Walker Mountain Scenic Byway. Phone 276/228-4401.* A 120-foot observation tower at 3,405-feet elevation; swinging bridge. Gift shop; snack bar. (Apr-late May, Thurs-Sun; Memorial Day-Oct, Tues-Sun) **$$**

Shot Tower Historical Park. *176 Orphanage Dr (24360). At Jackson's Ferry, 6 miles E on I-81, then 7 miles S on US 52; or I-77 S, Poplar Camp exit. Phone 276/699-6778 (New River Trail State Park).* (1807) On bluff overlooking New River. One of three shot towers still standing in US; fortresslike stone shaft has 2 1/2 foot thick walls rising 75 feet above ground and boring 75 feet below to a water tank. Molten lead was poured through sheet iron colanders from the tower top; during the 150-foot descent it became globular before hitting the water. Pellets were then sorted by rolling them down an incline; well-formed shot rolled into a receptacle; faulty ones zig-zagged off and were remelted. Visitor center, programs; hiking trails, picnicking. (Memorial Day-Labor Day, daily) Standard fees. **$**

Wytheville State Fish Hatchery. *1260 Red Hollow Rd (05301). 12 miles SE on US 52 to VA 629. Phone 276/637-3212 or 804/525-FISH.* Approximately 150,000 pounds of rainbow trout produced annually. Five-tank aquarium; displays. Self-guided tours. (Daily) **FREE**

Special Event

Chautauqua Festival. Held over a nine-day period. Includes parade, educational events, performing arts, art shows, children's activities, music, food, entertainment. Third week in June.

Motels/Motor Lodges

★ **BEST WESTERN WYTHEVILLE INN.** *355 Nye Rd (24382). Phone 540/228-7300; fax 540/228-4223. www.bestwestern.com.* 100 rooms, 2 story. Apr-Oct: S $45-$60; D $50-$66; each additional $6; under 18 free; higher rates special events; lower rates rest of year. Pet accepted. Complimentary continental breakfast. Check-out noon. TV; cable (premium). Pool. Cr cds: A, C, D, DS, MC, V.

D 🐾 ⊠ ⊠ SC

★ **COMFORT INN.** *315 Holston Rd (24382). Phone 540/228-4488; fax 540/228-4092.* 80 rooms, 2 story. S $58; D $68; each additional $5; under 18 free. Crib free. TV; cable (premium). Pool. Complimentary continental breakfast. Restaurant nearby. Check-out 11 am. Business services available. Cr cds: A, C, D, DS, JCB, MC, V.

D ⊠ ⊠

★ **DAYS INN.** *150 Malin Dr (24382). Phone 540/228-5500; toll-free 800/329-7466; fax 540/228-6301. www.daysinn.com.* 118 rooms, 1-3 story. Apr-Oct: S, D $48-$58; each additional $5; under 17 free; higher rates: holidays, Bristol auto races; lower rates rest of year. Crib free. TV; cable (premium). Restaurant adjacent 6 am-midnight. Check-out noon. Business services available. Microwaves available. View of mountains. Cr cds: A, C, D, DS, JCB, MC, V.

D ≥ SC

★ **ECONO LODGE.** *1160 E Main St (24382). Phone 540/228-5517; toll-free 800/228-5050; fax 540/228-5517. www.econolodge.com.* 72 rooms, 2 story. Apr-Oct: S $35.95-$55.95; D $38.99-$58.99; each additional $5; under 18 free; higher rates special events; lower rates rest of year. Crib free. TV; cable. Restaurant adjacent 11 am-9:30 pm. Check-out 11 am. Business services available. Cr cds: A, C, D, DS, JCB, MC, V.

D ≥ SC

★ ★ **HOLIDAY INN.** *1800 E Main St (24382). Phone 540/228-5483; toll-free 800/465-4329; fax 540/228-5417. www.holiday-inn.com.* 199 rooms, 1-4 story. Mar-Oct: S $49-$70; D $54-$70; each additional $5; suites $104-$150; under 18 free; weekly rates; higher rates auto races; lower rates rest of year. Crib free. Pet accepted. TV; cable (premium). Pool; wading pool. Restaurant 6 am-2 pm, 5-9 pm. Room service. Bar. Check-out 11 am. Meeting rooms. Business services available. Cr cds: A, C, D, DS, JCB, MC, V.

D 🐾 ≥ SC

★ **RAMADA INN.** *955 Peppers Ferry Rd (24382). Phone 540/228-6000; toll-free 800/272-6232; fax 540/228-6009. www.ramada.com.* 154 rooms, 2 story. S $64-$85; D $69-$85; each additional $5; under 18 free. Crib free. Pet accepted. TV; cable (premium). Pool. Restaurant 6:30 am-9 pm. Room service. Bar 5-11 pm; Sun 6 pm-midnight. Check-out noon. Coin laundry. Meeting rooms. Business services available. Cr cds: A, C, D, DS, ER, JCB, MC, V.

D 🐾 ≥ SC

★ **SHENANDOAH INN.** *140 Lithia Rd (24382). Phone 540/228-3188; fax 540/228-6458.* 100 rooms, 1-2 story. S $35-$45; D $43-$60; each additional $6; under 16 free; weekly, weekend, holiday rates; higher rates some special events. Crib free. Pet accepted; $5. TV; cable. Restaurant nearby. Check-out 11 am. Balconies. Cr cds: A, C, D, DS, MC, V.

D 🐾 ≥ SC

Restaurant

★ **LOG HOUSE.** *520 E Main St (24382). Phone 540/228-4139.* Closed Sun; Dec 25. Lunch, dinner. Children's menu. Colonial motif; built 1776. Outdoor seating. Cr cds: A, D, MC, V. **$**

D

Yorktown (H-12)

See also Colonial Parkway, Gloucester, Jamestown (Colonial National Historical Park), Newport News, Williamsburg

Founded 1691 **Pop** 203 **Elev** 54 ft

Information Colonial National Historical Park, PO Box 210, 23690; 757/898-3400

Web www.nps.gov/colo

Free land offered in 1630 to those adventurous enough "to seate and inhabit" the 50-foot bluffs on the south side of the York River "formerly known by ye Indyan name of Chiskiacke" brought about the beginning of settlement. When the Assembly authorized a port, started in 1691, the town slowly expanded and in the following years became a busy shipping center, with prosperity reaching a peak about 1750. From then on the port declined along with the Tidewater Virginia tobacco trade.

Yorktown's moment in history came in 1781. British commander Cornwallis, after raiding up and down Virginia with minimal resistance from the Marquis de Lafayette, was sent here to establish a naval base in which supplies and reinforcements could be shipped to him. The Comte de Grasse's French fleet effectively blockaded the British, however, by controlling the mouth of the Chesapeake Bay. At the Battle of the Capes on September 5, 1781, a British fleet sent to investigate the French presence was defeated by the French. Cornwallis found himself bottled up in Yorktown by combined American and French forces under Washington, which arrived on September 28.

Shelling began October 9. The siege of Yorktown ended on October 17 with Cornwallis requesting terms of capitulation. On October 19, Cornwallis' troops marched out with flags and arms cased, their bands playing. Then they laid down their arms, bringing the last major battle of the Revolutionary War to a close.

Yorktown Battlefield, part of Colonial National Historical Park, surrounds the village. Though Yorktown itself is still an active community, many surviving and reconstructed colonial structures supply an 18th-century atmosphere.

What to See and Do

Grace Episcopal Church. *111 Church St. Phone 757/898-3261.* (1697) Walls of local marl (a mixture of clay, sand, and limestone); damaged in 1781, gutted by fire in 1814. A 1649 communion service is still in use. (Daily)

⭐ **Yorktown Battlefield in Colonial National Historic Park.** *From Williamsburg, take the Colonial Parkway 13 miles E to Yorktown. Phone 757/898-2410.* Surrounds and includes part of town. Remains of 1781 British fortifications, modified and strengthened by Confederate forces in Civil War. Reconstructed American and French lines lie beyond. Roads lead to headquarters, encampment areas of Americans, French. Admission fee includes access to Visitor Center, battlefield tour, Moore House, and Nelson House. Golden Access, Age, and Eagle passports honored (see MAKING THE MOST OF YOUR TRIP). (Daily; closed Dec 25) **$** Stop first at

Moore House. *Located along battlefield tour road. Phone 757/898-3400.* In this 18th-century house the "Articles of Capitulation" were drafted. These were signed by General Washington in the captured British Redoubt #10 on October 19. (Mid-June-mid-Aug, daily; spring and fall, weekends)

Nelson House. *Nelson and Main sts.* Original restored mansion built by "Scotch Tom" Nelson in the early 1700s. Home of his grandson, Thomas Nelson, Jr., a signer of the Declaration of Independence. Impressive example of Georgian architecture. (Apr-Oct, daily)

Self-guided battlefield tour. Markers, displays aid in visualizing siege. Highlights include headquarters sites of Lafayette, von Steuben, Rochambeau, Washington; American Battery #2; Grand French Battery; a key point is Surrender Field where British forces laid down their arms.

Visitor Center. *Colonial Parkway and Yorktown Visitor Center (23692). E side of town, at end of Colonial Pkwy. Phone 757/898-3400.* Information; special exhibits, General Washington's field tents. (Daily; closed Dec 25)

Yorktown National Civil War Cemetery. 2,183 interments (1,436 unknown).

Yorktown Victory Monument. *E end of Main St.* Elaborately ornamented 95-foot granite column memorializes American-French alliance in Revolutionary War. **$$**

Yorktown Victory Center. *31 Rte S Jamestown Rd. 1/2 mile W on VA 238. Phone 757/253-4838 or 888/593-4682.* Museum of the Revolutionary War chronicles the struggle for independence from the beginnings of colonial unrest to the formation of the new nation. Exhibit galleries, living history Continental Army encampment, and late-18th-century farm. (Daily; closed Jan 1, Dec 25) Combination ticket with Jamestown Settlement (see JAMESTOWN COLONIAL NATIONAL HISTORICAL PARK) available. **$$$$**

Special Event

Yorktown Day. Observance of America's Revolutionary War victory at Yorktown in 1781. Oct 19.

Motel/Motor Lodge

★ ★ **DUKE OF YORK MOTOR HOTEL.** *508 Water St (23690). Phone 757/898-3232; fax 757/898-5922.* 57 rooms, 2-3 story story. Check-out noon, check-in 2 pm. TV. Restaurant. Beach. Outdoor pool. Cr cds: A, C, D, DS, MC, V. **$**
🛏️ 🖼️

Restaurant

★ ★ **RIVER'S INN RESTAURANT & CRAB DECK.** *8109 Yacht Haven Dr, Gloucester Point (23062). Phone 804/642-9942; toll-free 888/780-CRAB; fax 804/642-9945. www.riversinnrestaurant.com.* Seafood menu. Closed Dec 25; also Mon-Tues Oct-Mar. Lunch, dinner. Bar. Children's menu. Casual attire. Outdoor seating. Cr cds: A, MC, V. **$$**
Ⓓ

District of Columbia

Designed by Major Pierre Charles L'Enfant in about 1791, Washington was the first American city planned for a specific purpose. It is a beautiful city, with wide, tree-lined streets laid out according to a design that is breathtaking in its scope and imagination. For its purpose the broad plan still works well even though L'Enfant could not have foreseen the automobile or the fact that the United States would come to have a population of more than 250 million people. Nevertheless, L'Enfant's concept was ambitious, allowing for vast growth. Washington, named for the first US president, has been the nation's capital since 1800. The city's business is centered around government and tourism; there is little heavy industry.

The District of Columbia and Washington are one and the same. Originally the District was a 10-mile-square crossing the Potomac River into Virginia, but the Virginia portion (31 square miles) was turned back to the state in 1846. Residences of workers spill into Virginia and Maryland; so do government offices. In 1800, there were 130 federal employees; at the end of the Civil War there were 7,000; now there are well over half a million. Although the city was a prime Confederate target in the Civil War, it was barely damaged. The assassination of Abraham Lincoln, however, struck a blow to the nation and drove home to Americans the fact that Washington was not merely a center of government. What happened here affected everyone.

This is a cosmopolitan city. Perhaps no city on earth has a populace with so many different origins. Representatives from all nations and men and women from every state work here—and vote in their home states by absentee ballot. It is a dignified, distinguished capital. Many who visit the city go first to the House of Representatives or Senate office buildings and chat with their representatives, who receive constituent visitors when they can. At these offices visitors obtain tickets to the Senate and House galleries. From the top of the Washington Monument there is a magnificent view of the capital. The Lincoln and Jefferson memorials cannot fail to capture the imagination.

Population: 572,059
Area: 63 square miles
Elevation: 1-410 feet
Peak: Tenleytown
Entered Union: Founded in 1790
Flower: American Beauty Rose
Bird: Wood Thrush
Time Zone: Eastern
Website: www.washington.org
Fun Facts:
1. The Bureau of Engraving and Printing (BEP), located in Washington, DC, is responsible for designing and printing paper currency for the United States.
2. During World War II, to protect the city from possible enemy invasion, anti-aircraft guns where placed on top of several government office buildings. One of those guns accidentally went off and the projectile hit the roof of the Lincoln Monument.

When to Go/Climate

DC winters are relatively mild, while summers are hot and humid. The city is alive with color in spring and fall—cherry blossoms bloom in April and May and vibrant fall foliage begins around September.

AVERAGE HIGH/LOW TEMPERATURES (°F)

Washington National Airport

Jan 47/27	**May** 76/57	**Sept** 80/63
Feb 46/29	**June** 85/67	**Oct** 69/50
Mar 57/38	**July** 89/71	**Nov** 58/41
Apr 67/46	**Aug** 87/70	**Dec** 47/32

Additional Visitor Information

Washington DC Convention and Visitors Association, 1212 New York Ave NW, Suite 600, Washington, DC 20005, has brochures and schedules of events; phone 202/789-7000 (Mon-Fri, 9 am-5 pm).

By writing to your representative or senator ahead of time, tickets can be obtained for two Congressional Tours: a guided White House tour that differs slightly from the normal tour and begins at 8:15, 8:30, or 8:45 am (Tues-Sat; specific times are assigned); or passes to the House and Senate visitors' galleries to watch Congressional sessions in progress. Without this ticket, the chambers can only be viewed when Congress is not in session.

Write to your senator at the United States Senate, Washington, DC 20510. Address your representative at the United States House of Representatives, Washington, DC 20515. All tickets are free, but in peak season, which starts in spring, White House tickets may be limited. In the letter, include the dates you will be in Washington, first- and second-choice dates for the tours, and the number of people in your party. Also include your home phone number, should your representative's or senator's aide need to contact you. You can also get tickets, if available, directly from the office of your senator or representative after you arrive in Washington.

The National Park Service maintains information kiosks at several key points in the city as well as a White House Visitor Center at 1450 Pennsylvania Ave NW, which distributes free tickets to tour the White House.

For additional attractions and accommodations, see ARLINGTON COUNTY (RONALD REAGAN WASHINGTON-NATIONAL AIRPORT AREA) and DULLES INTERNATIONAL AIRPORT AREA in Virginia. Also see BALTIMORE/WASHINGTON INTERNATIONAL AIRPORT AREA in Maryland.

The following suburbs and towns in the Washington, DC, area are included in this book. For information on any one of them, see the individual alphabetical listing. In Virginia: Alexandria, Arlington County (Ronald Reagan Washington-National Airport Area), Fairfax, Falls Church, McLean, Springfield, Tyson's Corner.

In Maryland: Bethesda, Bowie, College Park, Laurel, Rockville, Silver Spring.

Transportation

Car Rental Agencies See IMPORTANT TOLL-FREE NUMBERS.

Public Transportation The Metrorail system is the least expensive means of getting around the capital. Metro (as it is called) provides a coordinated transportation system between buses and rail. The rapid rail system links major commercial districts and neighborhoods from the Capitol to the Pentagon and from the National Zoo to the National Airport and beyond. Trains operate every 6-12 minutes on the average: Monday-Friday, 5:30 am-midnight; Saturday and Sunday from 8 am. Phone 202/637-7000.

Rail Passenger Service Amtrak 800/872-7245.

Driving in Washington

Since the city is divided into four quarters, or quadrants, emanating from the Capitol, driving may be confusing for the first-time visitor. The quadrants are northeast (NE), northwest (NW), southeast (SE), and southwest (SW). All Washington addresses have these designations listed after the street name. It is advisable to obtain a city map before attempting to drive through the city, expecially during rush hours.

Safety belts are mandatory for all persons in the front seat of a vehicle. All children under 3 years must be in approved safety seats anywhere in the vehicle. Children 3-16 years must be properly restrained in either safety belts or child safety seats anywhere in the vehicle. For further information phone 202/939-8018.

Washington (C-6)

Settled 1790 **Pop** 572,059 **Elev** 1-410 feet **Area code** 202

Web www.washington.org

What to See and Do

2:K:9. *2009 8th St NW. Phone 202/667-7750.* Flash helps you get in the door here (no jeans or athletic wear, please); pulsating hip hop, house, and techno beats will keep you dancing until all hours. Dazzling lighting effects and a powerful sound system make the enormous dance floor rock. Exhausted? Take a breather at the swank 42-foot bar or just hang back and watch the dancers in cages—always inspiring. The place draws a glam, multiethnic crowd of under-30s. **$$$**

African American Civil War Memorial. *1200 U St NW. Phone 202/667-2667.* Sculpture pays tribute to the more than 200,000 African American soldiers who fought in the Civil War. **FREE**

American Red Cross. *1730 E St NW. Phone 202/737-8300.* National headquarters includes three buildings bounded by 17th, 18th, D, and E sts NW. The 17th St building includes marble busts Faith, Hope, and Charity by sculptor Hiram Powers and three original Tiffany stained-glass windows. (Daily 8:30 am-4 pm, closed most federal holidays) **FREE**

Anacostia Museum, Smithsonian Institution. *1901 Fort Place SE. Phone 202/357-2700.* An exhibition and research center for black heritage in the historic Anacostia section of southeast Washington. Changing exhibits. (Daily; closed Dec 25) **FREE**

Anderson House Museum. *2118 Massachusetts Ave NW. Phone 202/785-2040.* Museum of the Revolutionary War and national headquarters of the Society of the Cincinnati has portraits by early American artists; 18th-century paintings; 17th-century tapestries; decorative arts of Europe and Asia; displays of books, medals, swords, silver, glass, and china. (Tues-Sat afternoons; closed holidays). **FREE**

Arthur M. Sackler Gallery. *1200 Jefferson Dr SW. Phone 202/357-2700.* Changing exhibitions of Asian art, both Near- and Far-Eastern, from major national and international collections. Permanent collection includes Chinese and South and Southeast Asian art objects presented by Arthur Sackler. Between the Freer Gallery and the Arts and Industries Building is the Enid A. Haupt Garden, four acres that compose the "roof" of the Sackler Gallery, the International Gallery, an underground Smithsonian research and education complex, and 1050 Independence Ave SW. **FREE**

Art Museum of the Americas, OAS. *201 18th St NW. Phone 202/458-6016.* Dedicated to Latin American and Caribbean contemporary art; paintings, graphics, sculpture. (Tues-Sun; closed holidays) **FREE**

Arts and Industries Building. *900 Jefferson Dr SW.* The south hall contains the Experimental Gallery, an exhibit space dedicated to innovative and creative exhibits from museums in the Smithsonian and from around the world. Discovery Theater (fee) hosts performances for children. **FREE**

B'nai B'rith Klutznick Museum. *B'nai B'rith International Center, 1640 Rhode Island Ave NW. Phone 202/857-6583.* Permanent exhibition of Jewish ceremonial and folk art. Changing exhibits. (Mon-Fri, Sun; closed holidays, Jewish holidays) **FREE**

Basilica of the National Shrine of the Immaculate Conception. *400 Michigan Ave NE. Phone 202/526-8300.* Largest Roman Catholic church in US and one of the largest in the world. Byzantine and Romanesque architecture; extensive and elaborate collection of mosaics and artwork. (Daily) Carillon concerts (Sun afternoons); organ recitals (June-Aug, Sun evenings). Guided tours (daily). **FREE**

Black History Recreation Trail. *1100 Ohio Dr SW. Phone 202/619-7222.* Trail through Washington neighborhoods highlights important sites in African American history.

Blair House. *1651 Pennsylvania Ave NW.* (1824) Guest house for heads of government and state who are visiting the US as guests of the president. Not open to public.

Blues Alley. *1073 Wisconsin Ave NW. Phone 202/337-4141.* For nearly 40 years, serious jazz lovers have flocked to this intimate club to hear such noted artists as Dizzy Gillespie, Sarah Vaughan, and Maynard Ferguson, along with a host of outstanding but lesser known musicians. Nightly shows run the gamut from vocal and instrumental sounds to solo performers to larger ensembles. Housed in an 18th-century brick carriage house in Georgetown, the club has a sophisticated ambience and a Creole-themed dinner menu to match.

Bureau of Engraving and Printing. *14th and C sts SW, S of Mall; enter on 14th St. Phone 202/874-3019.* Watch millions of dollars being made—printed, that is—on the tour of this site, which takes visitors through many of the steps involved in producing currency. You'll see large, blank sheets of paper transformed, as if by magic, into wallet-size bills and learn about the latest high-tech steps the Bureau has taken to thwart counterfeiting. You can buy uncut sheets of bills in different ominations, as well as shredded cash, at the BEP store. Guided tours 9 am-2 pm. (Closed weekends, federal holidays, and Dec 24-Jan 3) **FREE**

Capital Children's Museum. *800 3rd St NE (20002). Phone 202/675-4120.* Make delicious tortillas and hot chocolate in "Mexico," slide down a fire pole in "Cityscapes," or design a cartoon character in "Chuck Jones: An Animated Life"—learning and playing feel pretty much the same at this lively, hands-on museum. Young problem-solvers will enjoy the challenge of the 20 puzzling tasks of "Brain Teasers," while their younger siblings can take on "Teasers for Tots." The charming old building that houses the museum is a former convent. (Daily; closed Mon during school year except holidays) **$$**

⭐ **The Capitol.** *Capitol Hill (20002). Between Constitution and Independence aves, at Pennsylvania Ave, east end of the National Mall. Phone 202/225-6827.* With its graceful dome making it one of the most famous American landmarks, the Capitol has been the seat of the legislative branch of the US government for more than 200 years. Visitors can take guided tours of several sections, including the beautifully restored Old Supreme Court Chamber and Old Senate Chamber. The breathtaking Rotunda, a ceremonial space beneath the soaring dome, is a gallery for paintings and sculptures of historic significance. Below it is the Crypt, built for the remains of George Washington (who asked to be buried at Mount Vernon instead), now used for exhibits. Don't miss the National Statuary Hall, where statues of prominent citizens have been donated by all 50 states, and the ornate Brumidi Corridors, named for the Italian artist who designed their murals and many other decorative elements in the Capitol. A state-of-the-art visitor center, currently under construction, is scheduled to open in 2005. (Mon-Sat; closed Jan 1, Thanksgiving, Dec 25). Tickets for tours are available at the Capitol Guide Service kiosk near the intersection of First St SW and Independence Ave. **FREE**

Capitol City Brewing Company. *2 Massachusetts Ave NE. Phone 202/842-2337.* Shiny copper vats and a large oval copper bar are the centerpieces of this huge—and hugely popular—brew pub situated in the beautifully restored 1911 Postal Square Building. Hill staffers and tourists crowd in for made-on-the-premises ales, lagers, and pilsners that go down well with warm pretzels and mustard or with whole meals. This is one of four Capitol City pubs in the area, and the only one swathed in neoclassical marble. (Daily)

Catholic University of America. *620 Michigan Ave NE. Phone 202/319-5000.* (1887) 5,510 students. Open to all faiths. Performances at Hartke Theatre (year-round).

Chesapeake & Ohio Canal Boat Rides. *Departs 1057 Thomas Jefferson St NW, between 30th and 31st sts. Phone 202/653-5190.* Narrated round-trip canal tours (1 hour) by park rangers in period clothing aboard mule-drawn boats. Ticket office adjacent. (Apr-Nov, Wed-Sun) **$$**

Chesapeake & Ohio Canal Towpath. *1057 Thomas Jefferson St NW (Georgetown Visitor Center) (20007). Phone 202/653-5190 or 301/739-4200.* Biking (or simply strolling) along the fascinating Chesapeake & Ohio Canal towpath is a great way to immerse yourself in both history and nature. The canal, which runs 184.5 miles between Georgetown and Cumberland, MD, was completed in 1850. The mostly level path takes you past locks, lockhouses, aqueducts, and other intriguing original structures from the route's commercial heyday. Expect spectacular scenery and all manner of wildlife along the way, including deer, fox, and woodpeckers. Fee (**$**) per cyclist at Great Falls. Towpath (daily). Georgetown Visitor Center (Sat, Sun).

Chinatown. *G and H sts, between 6th and 8th sts NW.* Recognizable by the Chinatown Friendship Archway at 7th and H sts. Archway is decorated in Chinese architectural styles of Qing and Ming dynasties and is topped with nearly 300 painted dragons.

Christian Heurich Mansion. *800 Mt Vernon Place NW, City Museum. Phone 202/785-2068.* (1892) Four-story, 31-room neo-Renaissance/late Victorian mansion has elaborate furnishings and garden; houses the Historical Society of Washington, DC, and the society's Library of Washington History; changing exhibits. House tours (Wed-Sat; closed holidays). Library (Wed, Fri, Sat; closed holidays). **$**

Clara Barton National Historic Site. *5801 Oxford Rd, 8 miles NW in Glen Echo, MD. Phone 301/492-6245.* Thirty-six-room house (1891) of unusual architecture was both the national headquarters of the Red Cross and the home of Clara Barton for the last 15 years of her life. Contents include many items belonging to the founder of the American Red Cross. Period costumes worn during some special programs. Guided tours only. (Daily; closed holidays) **FREE**

Congress. *Capitol Hill (20002).* Tickets to the House and Senate visitors' galleries can be obtained from the office of your representative or senator. Foreign visitors can obtain passes to the Senate Gallery from the appointment desk, first floor, Senate Wing; and to the House of Representatives Gallery from the check stand, third floor, House wing (identification required).

Constitution Gardens. *Along Constitution Ave between 18th and 22nd sts NW. (20011) Phone 202/426-6841.* This 50-acre park, with a man-made lake, is also the site of the Signers of the Declaration of Independence Memorial. **FREE**

Corcoran Gallery of Art. *500 17th St NW (20006). 17th St between New York Ave and E St NW. Phone 202/639-1700.* The city's oldest art museum—and its largest non-federal one—is also one of its liveliest. Known for its strong collection of 19th-century American art (don't miss John Singer Sargent's luminous "Oyster Gatherers of Cancale") and its support for local artists, the museum also shows important European pieces and eye-opening contemporary works, including photography, performance art, and new media. A glamorous, Frank Gehry-designed addition to the landmark Beaux Arts building is in the works. (Wed-Mon; closed Jan 1, Thanksgiving, Dec 25) Free admission Mon, Thurs after 5 pm. **$**

DC United (MLS). *RFK Memorial Stadium. 2400 E Capitol St. Phone 202/547-9077.*

DAR Headquarters. *1776 D St NW. Phone 202/879-3241.* Includes Memorial Continental Hall (1904) and Constitution Hall (1920); DAR Museum Gallery, located in administration building, has 33 state period rooms; outstanding genealogical research library (fee for non-members). Guided tours (Mon-Sat). **FREE**

Department of Commerce Building. *Pennsylvania Ave, between 14th and 15th sts NW. (20230). Phone 202/482-4883.* (1932)

Department of Energy. *Pennsylvania Ave between 12th and 13th sts NW.* Includes the **Interstate Commerce Commission** *(1934), Constitution Ave between 12th and 13th sts NW;* **Customs Department,** *Constitution Ave between 13th and 14th sts NW;* and the **District Building,** *Pennsylvania Ave between 13th and 14th sts NW,* Washington's ornate 1908 city hall.

Department of Justice Building. (1934) *Pennsylvania Ave between 9th and 10th sts NW. (20003).* (Not open to the public)

Department of State Building. *2201 C St NW (20520). Phone 202/647-3241.* The State Department's diplomatic reception rooms, furnished with 18th-century American furniture and decorative art, are used by Secretary of State and cabinet members for formal entertaining. Tours (Mon-Fri; closed federal holidays and special events; 3-4 weeks advance reservations; children over 12 years preferred). **FREE**

Department of the Interior. *1849 C St NW and 19th sts NW. Phone 202/208-3100.* (1938) Within is museum including exhibits and dioramas depicting history and activities of the department and its various bureaus. Photo ID required. (Mon-Fri; closed holidays) Reference library open to public. **FREE**

Department of the Treasury. *1500 Pennsylvania Ave NW, E of White House. Phone 202/622-0896.* According to legend, this Greek Revival building, one of the oldest (1836-1869) in the city, was built in the middle of Pennsylvania Ave because Andrew Jackson, tired of endless wrangling over the location, walked out of the White House, planted his cane in the mud, and said, "Here." The building has been extensively restored. **FREE**

Dumbarton Oaks. *1703 32nd St NW; garden entrance at 31st and R sts. Phone 202/339-6401.* (1800) Famous gardens (16 acres) are both formal and Romantic in design.

Mansion has antiques and European art, including El Greco's *The Visitation;* galleries of Byzantine art; library of rare books on gardening and horticulture. Museum of pre-Columbian artifacts housed in structure by Philip Johnson. Garden (daily; closed holidays); house and museum (Tues-Sun afternoons; closed holidays). **$$**

Dupont-Kalorama Museum Walk. A joining of forces of seven museums to create an awareness of the area. Information and brochures are available at any of the museums concerned.

Eastern Market. *225 7th St SE. Phone 202/546-2698.* Meat, fish, and produce sold. Also crafts and farmers market on weekends. (Tues-Sun)

Eighteenth Street Lounge. *1212 18th St NW. Phone 202/466-3922.* Lovers of modern dance music and techno all over the world know about ESL, the music label; DC residents and visitors flock to the lounge itself, a cooler-than-cool, atmospheric three-story space where the music, often spun by the DJ duo Thievery Corporation (one member is an owner), never stops. Relax by a fireplace or hang out on the patio, depending on the weather. A strict door policy weeds out wearers of athletic garb and the attitudinally impaired. (Tues-Sat) **$$$$**

Emancipation Statue. *Lincoln Park. E Capitol St NE between 11th and 13th sts NE.* Bronze work of Thomas Ball paid for by voluntary subscriptions from emancipated slaves, depicting Lincoln presenting Emancipation Proclamation to black man, was dedicated Apr 14, 1876, the 11th anniversary of Lincoln's assassination, with Fredrick Douglass in attendance. Also here is

> **Mary McLeod Bethune Memorial.** *East Capitol St, SE (20003).* Honors the noted educator and advisor to President Lincoln and founder of the National Council of Negro Women.

Embassy Row. *Massachusetts Ave and 23rd St NW (20036).* This neighborhood, within the city's northwest quadrant, is centered around Sheridan Circle. Dozens of foreign legations can be found in the area and north along Massachusetts Ave.

Explorers Hall. *1145 17th St NW (20036). 17th and M sts NW. Phone 202-857-7588 (recording).* National Geographic Society headquarters. Several traveling exhibits, call for information. (Daily; closed Dec 25) **FREE**

FBI Headquarters. *J. Edgar Hoover Building, 935 Pennsylvania Ave NW, between 9th and 10th sts NW; tour entrance on 9th St NW. Phone 202/324-3447.* Tours of historical exhibits, includes FBI laboratory; very large firearm collection; demonstration of firearms. (Mon-Fri; closed holidays) **FREE**

Federal Reserve Building. *C St between 20th and 21st sts NW. (20002). Phone 202/452-3149.* (1937) Primarily an office building but noteworthy for its architecture; rotating art exhibits; film (20 minutes). **FREE**

Federal Trade Commission Building. *Pennsylvania Ave NW, between 6th and 7th sts. Phone 202/326-2222. (1938)* (Mon-Fri; closed holidays) **FREE**

Federal Triangle. *Pennsylvania Ave and 13th St NW (20004).* The Triangle consists of a group of government buildings, nine of which were built for $78 million in the 1930s in modern classic design. The "crown jewel" of the triangle is the Ronald Reagan International Trade Center, located on Pennsylvania Ave at 13th St NW.

Folger Shakespeare Library. *201 E Capitol St SE. Phone 202/544-4600. (1932)* Houses the finest collection of Shakespeare materials in the world, including the 1623 First Folio edition and large holdings of rare books and manuscripts of the English and continental Renaissance. The Great Hall offers year-round exhibits from the Folger's extensive collection. The Elizabethan Theatre, which was designed to resemble an innyard theater of Shakespeare's day, is the site of the Folger Shakespeare Library's series of museum and performing arts programs, which include literary readings, drama, lectures, and education and family programs. Self-guided tours. Guided tours (11 am). (Mon-Sat; closed federal holidays) **FREE**

Fondo del Sol. *2112 R St NW. Phone 202/483-2777.* Dedicated to presenting, promoting, and preserving cultures of the Americas, the museum presents exhibitions of contemporary artists and crafters; holds special events; hosts traveling exhibits for museums and other institutions. (Tues-Sat afternoons; closed holidays) **$$**

★ **Ford's Theatre.** *511 10th St NW (20004). Phone 202/426-6924 (visitor information); 202/347-4833 (box office).* Seeing a play in this historic old theater, famous as the site of Abraham Lincoln's assassination, is deeply moving. A museum in the basement exhibits the clothes the president was wearing that night, as well as John Wilkes Booth's derringer; upstairs, the presidential box has been restored to its 1865 condition. Ford's became a working theater again in 1968; recent productions have included the play *Inherit the Wind* and a one-man show about George Gershwin. Self-guided tours (daily; closed Dec 25).

Fort Dupont Park. *Randle Cir and Minnesota Ave SE. (20019). Phone 202/426-7723 or 202/426-7745.* Picnicking, hiking, and bicycling in hilly terrain; cultural arts performances in summer (see SPECIAL EVENTS). Also films, slides, and activities including natural science; environmental education programs; nature discovery room; Junior Ranger program; programs for senior citizens and disabled persons; garden workshops and programmed activities by reservations. Nearby is

Fort Dupont Sports Complex. *3779 Ely Pl SE (20019). E on Pennsylvania Ave SE; N on Minnesota Ave; E on Ely Pl. Phone 202-584-5007 (ice rink). Phone 202/584-5007 (ice rink).* Skating, ice hockey (fee); tennis courts, basketball courts, ball fields (daily; free), jogging. **FREE**

Fort Stevens Park. *13th and Rittenhouse St NW (20019). Phone 202/895-6000.* General Jubal Early and his Confederate troops tried to invade Washington at this point on July 11-12, 1864. President Lincoln risked his life at the fort during the fighting. (Daily) **FREE**

Fort Washington National Park. *4 miles S on MD 210, 3 1/2 miles at 13551 Fort Washington Rd in Fort Washington, MD. Phone 301/763-4600.* Earliest defense of the city (1809), the original fort was destroyed in 1814; reconstructed by 1824. View of the Potomac River; picnicking; history exhibits. (Daily) **$$**

Franciscan Monastery. *1400 Quincy St NE. Phone 202/526-6800.* Within the church and grounds is the "Holy Land of America"; replicas of sacred Holy Land shrines including the Manger at Bethlehem, Garden of Gethsemane, and Holy Sepulchre. Also Grotto at Lourdes and Roman catacombs. Guided tours by the friars (daily). **DONATION**

★ **Franklin Delano Roosevelt Memorial.** *West Basin Dr (20003). West Potomac Park near the Lincoln Memorial. Phone 202/426-6841.* This newer memorial, dedicated in 1997, features a series of sculptures depicting the 32nd US President Franklin Roosevelt and his wife, Eleanor. Four outdoor rooms represent each of FDR's four presidential terms, which began in the Great Depression and ended at the close of World War II. Visitors can feel his presence in broadcasts of his "fireside chats" throughout the exhibits. (Daily 24 hours; interpretive ranger staff on site 8 am-11:45 pm; closed Dec 25) **FREE**

Frederick Douglass National Historic Site, "Cedar Hill". *1411 W St SE. Phone 202/426-5961 or 800/967-2283 (tour reservations).* This 21-room house on 9 acres is where Douglass, a former slave who became Minister to Haiti and a leading black spokesman, lived from 1877 until his death in 1895; visitor center with film, memorabilia. (Daily; closed Jan 1, Thanksgiving, Dec 25) **FREE**

Freer Gallery. *1200 Jefferson Dr SW (20560). Jefferson Dr at 12th St SW. Phone 202/357-2700.* Asian art with objects dating from Neolithic period to the early 20th century. Also works by late 19th- and early 20th-century American artists, including a major collection of James McNeill Whistler's work, highlighted by the famous Peacock Room. Next to the Freer is the Smithsonian Institution Building, or "the Castle." **FREE**

Fresh Farm Market. *20th St NW between Massachusetts Ave and Q St NW.* Phone 202/331-7300. Looking for the slenderest stalks of asparagus? Herbs that really taste like herbs? How about a bright bouquet of tulips? You'll find those delights and many others, including in-season fruits, mushrooms, artisanal cheeses, and organic offerings, at this weekly market, which brings together more than 25 local farmers with customers who prefer to skip the middleman. Vendors here sell only goods grown or produced on their land; every dollar spent goes directly to them. (Apr-Dec, Sun)

General Services Administration Building. *18th and E sts NW.* (1917) Was originally Department of Interior.

Georgetown. Georgetown, a neighborhood within the city's northwest quadrant, is actually older than Washington. In Colonial days it was a busy commercial center along the Potomac. Today Georgetown is an area of fine 18th- and 19th-century residences and fashionable shops and restaurants; the commercial center radiates from the intersection of Pennsylvania Ave and M St, NW of the White House.

Georgetown Flea Market. *Wisconsin Ave NW (20007). Just north of S St.* Phone 202/296-4989. This friendly neighborhood flea market has been giving local collectors of antique furniture, jewelry, books, rugs, toys, linens, and other vintage treasures a reason to get out of the house on Sundays since 1973. It's also known as a place to spot celebrities (actress Diane Keaton has been a frequent patron). About 70 dealers set up booths year-round; come early for the biggest selection or late for the best bargains, but feel free to dicker anytime. (Sun)

Georgetown University. *Main entrance 37th and O sts NW.* Phone 202/687-0100. (1789) 12,000 students. Oldest Catholic college in US, a Jesuit school. Campus tours (Mon-Sat, by reservation).

George Washington University. *2033 K St NW (20006).* Phone 202/994-1000. (1821) 20,000 students. Theater; art exhibits in Dimock Gallery (Mon-Fri; closed holidays) and University Library.

Glow. *714 6th St NW.* Phone 202/271-1171. Mix eye-popping special effects—heavy, high-tech lighting with a state-of-the-art sound system, add some of the city's hippest DJs and hundreds of gotta-dance clubgoers, and you've got—on Saturday nights, anyway—the party to end all parties. A once-a-week club within a club, Glow fills gigantic Club Insomnia with the hottest trance, techno, British, and Latin sounds, working the young, sexily dressed crowd (no boots or athletic wear) into a froth of sensory overload. (Sat) **$$$$**

Government Printing Office. *710 N Capitol St NW (20403). On N Capitol St, between G and H sts.* Phone 202/512-0132. Four buildings with 35 acres of floor space where most of the material issued by US Government, including production and distribution of the Congressional Record, Federal Register, and US passports, is printed. (No public tours; for information on the agency, call 202/512-1991.) Office includes the Main Government Bookstore, 710 N Capitol St NW. Nearly 20,000 publications available (Mon-Fri; closed holidays).

Gray Line bus tours. *50 Massachusetts Ave NE.* Phone 301/386-8300 or 800/862-1400. Tours of city and area attractions depart from terminal in Union Station. Contact 5500 Tuxedo Rd, Tuxedo, MD 20781.

Great Falls of the Potomac. (See CHESAPEAKE AND OHIO CANAL NATIONAL HISTORICAL PARK in Maryland)

Harness racing. *Rosecroft Raceway. 6336 Rosecroft Dr, 8 miles SE in Oxon Hill, MD.* Phone 301/567-4000. (Daily, races Thurs-Sat) **$$**

Hirshhorn Museum and Sculpture Garden. *Independence Ave and 7th St SW (20560).* Phone 202/357-2700 or 202/633-8043 (TTY). The cool modernity of the paintings and sculptures here—and of the curvy building itself—are a delicious respite for history-sated visitors. Inside is some of the most interesting art produced in the last 100 years: everything from Constantin Brancusi's egglike "Sleeping Muse I" to Nam June Paik's "Video Flag" made with 70 video monitors. Outdoors, the greenery of the plaza and sculpture garden make this an inviting spot for a National Mall rendezvous. (Daily; closed Dec 25) **DONATION**

House Office Buildings. *Along Independence Ave, south side of Capitol grounds at Independence and New Jersey aves.* Pedestrian tunnel connects two of the oldest House office buildings with the Capitol.

Howard University. *Main campus: 2400 6th St NW between W and Harvard sts NW. West Campus: 2900 Van Ness St NW. Three other campuses in area.* Phone 202/806-6100. (1867) 12,000 students. Main campus has Gallery of Fine Art, with permanent Alain Locke African Collection; changing exhibits (Sept-July, Mon-Fri).

HR-57. *1610 14th St NW (20009).* Phone 202/667-3700. This ultra-friendly, bare-bones spot is the performance arm of the Center for the Preservation of Jazz and Blues, a not-for-profit cultural center that named its club after a 1987 House Resolution designating jazz as "a rare and valuable national American treasure." Musical integrity—and the ability to appreciate a great jam—are everything here; expect to hear well-known and lesser-known artists at the top of their game, and a crowd that eats it up. (Wed-Sat) **$$**

The Improv. *1140 Connecticut Ave NW.* Phone 202/296-7008. The crowd is youngish and the comedy free-flowing here, where almost anything is good for a laugh, especially the local industry: politics. Onstage talent includes established stars as well as hilariously original newcomers you may have caught on Comedy Central or elsewhere on TV. Open mic nights enable wannabe comics to step into the limelight and compete for prizes. Appetizers, sandwiches, beer, and wine are available. (Daily) **$$$$**

International Spy Museum. *800 F Street NW (20004). Phone 202/393-7798 or 866/779-6873.* Learn more about people who keep secrets for a living at this private museum that opened in 2002. It sheds light on the world of international espionage with artifacts that run the gamut from invisible ink and high-tech eavesdropping devices to a through-the-wall camera and a KGB lipstick pistol. Find out how codes were made and broken throughout history, how successful disguises are created, and what real-life James Bonds think of the high-stakes "game" of spying. (Daily; closed Jan 1, Thanksgiving, Dec 25). **$$$$**

Islamic Center. *2551 Massachusetts Ave NW. Phone 202/332-8343.* Leading mosque in the US has landscaped courtyard, intricate interior mosaics. (Daily; no tours during Fri prayer service)

Iwo Jima Statue. *Meade St (22211). Across Theodore Roosevelt Bridge on Arlington Blvd.* (See ARLINGTON COUNTY in Virginia)

John F. Kennedy Center for the Performing Arts. *2700 F St NW (20566). New Hampshire Ave at F St. NW. Phone 202/467-4600, 202/416-8340 (tours) or 800/444-1324.* The glittering home of the National Symphony Orchestra and Washington Opera hosts an impressive array of internationally known artists in dance, theater, and music. It opened in 1971 as a memorial to John F. Kennedy; a large bronze bust of the former president graces the Grand Foyer. The sleekly designed complex houses a number of dazzling performance spaces and reception areas, as well as paintings, sculptures, and other artwork presented by foreign governments. (Daily) **FREE**

Judiciary Square. *D, E, and F sts, between 4th and 5th sts NW.* Two square blocks of judiciary buildings, including five federal and district courts, the US District Court (1820), and US Court of Appeals (1910). At D St halfway between 4th and 5th sts is the first completed statue of Abraham Lincoln (1868).

Kenilworth Aquatic Gardens. *Anacostia Ave and Douglas St NE (20019). Phone 202/426-6905.* Water lilies, lotuses, and other water plants bloom from mid-May until the frost. Gardens (daily). Guided walks (Memorial Day-Labor Day, Sat, Sun, and holidays, also by appointment; closed Jan 1, Thanksgiving, Dec 25). **FREE**

Korean War Memorial. *French Dr SW (20242). Adjacent to the Lincoln Memorial. Phone 202/426-6841.* This massive sculpture honors the Americans who served in the Korean conflict, showing 19 soldiers dressed and armed for battle heading toward the American flag, their symbolic goal. The adjacent wall features etched photographs that pay tribute to military support personnel. (Daily 8 am-11:45 pm; closed Dec 25) **FREE**

Labor Department. *Francis H. Perkins Building, 200 Constitution Ave NW. Phone 202/219-6992 (library).* Lobby contains the Labor Hall of Fame, an exhibit depicting labor in US; library on second floor is open to public. (Mon-Fri; closed holidays) **FREE**

Lafayette Square. *Pennsylvania Ave NW (20004). Phone 202/673-7647.* Statue of Andrew Jackson on horseback in the center was first equestrian figure in Washington (1853). One of the park benches was known as Bernard Baruch's office in 1930s and is dedicated to him. On square is

> **Decatur House Museum.** *748 Jackson Pl NW. Phone 202/842-0920. (1818)* Federal town house built for naval hero Commodore Stephen Decatur by Benjamin H. Latrobe, second architect of the Capitol. After Decatur's death in 1820, the house was occupied by a succession of American and foreign statespeople and was a center of political and social life in the city. The ground floor family rooms reflect Decatur's Federal-period lifestyle. Operated by National Trust for Historic Preservation. (Tues-Sun; closed Jan 1, Thanksgiving, Dec 25) **FREE**

Library of Congress. *10 1st St SE. Phone 202/707-6400 (reading room schedule, calendar of events) or 202/707-8000 (information on exhibitions and free guided tours).* (1800) Treasures include a Gutenberg Bible, the first great book printed with movable metal type; the Giant Bible of Mainz, a 500-year-old illuminated manuscript. Collection includes books, manuscripts, newspapers, maps, recordings, prints, photographs, posters, and more than 30 million books and pamphlets in 60 languages. In the elaborate Jefferson Building is the Great Hall, decorated with murals, mosaics, and marble carvings; exhibition halls. In the Madison Building, a 22-minute audiovisual presentation, America's Library, provides a good introduction to the library and its facilities. (Mon-Sat; closed federal holidays) **FREE**

⭐ **Lincoln Memorial.** *23rd St NW at Daniel French and Henry Beacon Dr. (20242). Phone 202/426-6841.* Dedicated in 1922, Daniel Chester French's Abraham Lincoln looks across a reflecting pool to the Washington Monument and the Capitol. Lincoln's Gettysburg Address and Second Inaugural Address are inscribed on the walls of the templelike structure, which is particularly impressive at night. The 36 columns represent the 36 states in the Union in existence at the time of Lincoln's death. (Daily 8 am-11:45 pm; closed Dec 25) **FREE**

Lincoln Museum. *511 10th St NW (20004). Phone 202/ 347-4833.* Exhibits and displays focus on Lincoln's life and assassination. (Daily; closed Dec 25) **FREE**

Lulu's Club Mardi Gras. *1217 22nd St NW. Phone 202/861- 5858.* This freewheeling spot is all about raucous music, dancing, and checking out members of the opposite sex. Beer is the beverage of choice; food is served until 10 pm. Salsa lessons draw regular crowds, but Lulu's is also known for special events such as "Shred Your Ex, Meet Your Next," where patrons are invited—in a spirit of communal catharsis—to run photos of formerly significant others through a shredder. (Daily) **$$**

Martin Luther King, Jr. Memorial Library. *901 G St NW.* (1972) Main branch of DC public library was designed by architect Mies van der Rohe. Martin Luther King mural. Books, periodicals, photographs, films, videocassettes, recordings, microfilms, Washingtoniana, and the *Washington Star* collection. Library for the visually impaired; librarian for the hearing impaired; black studies division; AP wire service machine; community information service. Underground parking. (Mon-Sat, also Sun afternoons; closed holidays) **FREE**

MCI Center. *601 F St NW (20004). Phone 202/628-3200.* This 20,000-seat, state-of-the-art arena, home to the NBA's Washington Wizards, the WNBA's Washington Mystics, the NHL's Washington Capitals, and the Georgetown Hoyas, is also a popular venue for concerts and other events, from Liza Minnelli to the Harlem Globetrotters. Even when nothing is scheduled, you can check out Nick and Stef's Steakhouse (open for dinner every day, lunch Monday through Friday), the F Street Sports Bar, or Modell's Sporting Goods for logo-heavy, team-themed athletic wear. (Mon-Sat; closed major holidays; days and fees for events vary)

MCI National Sports Gallery. *601 F St NW (20004). Phone 202/661-5133.* This 25,000-square-foot museum commemorates and showcases the best of American sports history. Includes sports memorabilia collections; participatory and technology-driven exhibits with basketball, football, hockey, and baseball themes. Rotating exhibits feature special-interest sports. Home of the American Sportscasters Association Hall of Fame and Museum, honoring the memorable voices that brought great sports moments. **$$$**

Meridian International Center. *1630 Crescent Pl NW. Phone 202/939-5568.* Housed in two historic mansions designed by John Russell Pope; hosts international exhibits, concerts, lectures, and symposia promoting international understanding. Period furnishings, Mortlake tapestry; gardens with linden grove. (Wed-Sun afternoons; closed holidays) **FREE**

⭐ **Mount Vernon.** *18 miles S via George Washington Memorial Pkwy. Phone 703/780-2000.* (See MOUNT VERNON in Virginia) Touring Mount Vernon, George Washington's home for more than 45 years, gives visitors a fascinating glimpse of the world of landed gentry in 18th-century America, as well as the personal vision of the first US president. Washington designed sections of the beautifully landscaped "pleasure grounds" himself, incorporating woods, meadows, and serpentine walkways into the plan. He also added the red-roofed mansion's cupola, weather vane, and 2-story piazza, from which guests may enjoy an awe-inspiring view of the Potomac River. Exploring the working areas of the estate, including the wash house, stable, and kitchen, gives visitors an idea of how Mount Vernon operated: an audio tour describes the lives of some of the more than 300 slaves who lived and worked there. The house has been restored to its 1799 appearance, the year Washington died. He is buried on the estate with his wife, Martha. (Daily) **$$$$**

National Academy of Sciences. *2101 Constitution Ave NW, between 21st and 22nd sts NW. Phone 202/334- 2000.* (1924) Established in 1863 to stimulate research and communication among scientists and to advise the federal government in science and technology. A famous 21-foot bronze statue of Albert Einstein by Robert Berks is on the front lawn. Art exhibits, concerts. (Schedule varies) **FREE**

⭐ **National Air and Space Museum.** *600 Independence Ave SW (20202). Independence Ave, between 7th and 4th sts SW. Phone 202/357-1387.* This popular museum thrills those who have lived through the age of space exploration, as well as those whose memories go back further. View the Wright brothers' 1903 *Kitty Hawk Flyer*, Charles Lindbergh's *Spirit of St. Louis*, and the command module *Columbia*, which carried the first men to walk on the moon. World War II buffs will want to see not only American fighter planes but also the British Supermarine Spitfire, the Japanese Mitsubishi Zero, and the German Messerschmitt. In the Apollo to the Moon exhibit, you'll see lunar rocks, spacesuits, and John Glenn's squeeze-tube beef stew, among other artifacts. An IMAX theater enables you to view—on a huge, 5-story-high screen—Earth as seen from the space shuttle. And don't miss the high-tech shows at the Albert Einstein Planetarium, which combine ideas about the size and origins of the universe with eye-popping images taken from the Hubble Space Telescope and Mars Global Surveyor. (Daily; closed Dec 25) **FREE**

National Aquarium. *1700 K St NW (20006). Phone 202/ 482-2826.* The nation's oldest public aquarium was established in 1873. It now exhibits more than 1,700 specimens representing approximately 260 species, both freshwater and saltwater. Touch tank; theater. Shark feeding (Mon, Wed, Sat); piranha feeding (Tues, Thurs, Sun). (Daily; closed Dec 25) **$$**

National Archives. *700 Pennsylvania Ave NW (20408); exhibition entrance on Constitution Ave.* Phone 202/501-5205 or 202/501-5000 (recording). (1934) Original copies of the Declaration of Independence, Bill of Rights, Constitution; a 1297 version of the Magna Carta and other historic documents, maps, and photographs. Guided tours by appointment only. Archives also available to public for genealogical and historical research (Mon-Sat; closed federal holidays). (Daily; closed Dec 25) **FREE**

National Building Museum. *Housed in Old Pension Building, 401 F St NW.* Phone 202/272-2448. Deals with architecture, design, engineering, and construction. Permanent exhibits including drawings, blueprints, models, photographs, artifacts; architectural evolution of Washington's buildings and monuments. The museum's enormous Great Hall is supported by eight of the world's largest Corinthian columns. Guided tours (afternoons: weekdays, one tour; weekends, two tours). Museum (Mon-Sat; also Sun afternoons). **FREE**

National Colonial Farm. *I-95 exit 3 A, then 10 miles S on MD 210, right on Bryan Point Rd, 3 miles in Accokeek, MD.* Phone 301/283-2113. Approximately 150 acres in Piscataway National Park. A "living history" farm of mid-18th century; crops, herb garden, livestock, methods of the period are used; replicated farm buildings. (Tues-Sun; closed Jan 1, Thanksgiving, Dec 25) **$**

National Gallery of Art. *600 Constitution Ave NW (20002).* Phone 202/737-4215. The West Building (1941), designed by John Russell Pope, contains Western European and American art spanning periods between the 13th and 20th centuries: highlights include the only Leonardo da Vinci painting in the western hemisphere, *Ginevra de' Benci;* a comprehensive collection of Italian paintings and sculpture; major French Impressionists; numerous Rembrandts and examples of the Dutch school; masterpieces from the Mellon, Widener, Kress, Dale, and Rosenwald collections; special exhibitions. The East Building (1978), designed by architect I. M. Pei, houses the gallery's growing collection of 20th-century art, including Picasso's *Family of Saltimbanques* and Jackson Pollock's *Lavender Mist.* (Daily; closed Jan 1, Dec 25) **FREE**

National Museum of African Art. *950 Independence Ave SW (20560).* Phone 202/357-4600; 202/357-4814. With everything from masks to musical instruments, sacred objects to simple wooden headrests, the diverse cultures of Africa past and present are on view at this small but fascinating museum. Permanent exhibits display ceramics, textiles, household tools, and the visual arts of the sub-Sahara. Traveling shows cover even more ground; recent ones have featured colonial-era photography and Ethiopian religious icons. A full schedule of films, musical presentations, lectures, and children's events keeps things lively. (Daily; closed Dec 25) **FREE**

⭐ **National Museum of American History.** *Constitution Ave, between 12th and 14th sts NW.* Phone 202/357-2700 or 202/357-1729 (TTY). More than 17 million artifacts cover aspects of American cultural heritage large and small, public and private. Want to see Julia Child's gleaming black six-burner stove? Check out the cheerfully comfortable kitchen from the famous chef's longtime home in Cambridge, Massachusetts, reassembled here in 2001. Or watch textile conservators take painstaking steps to restore the fragile Star-Spangled Banner, the actual flag that inspired Francis Scott Key in 1814 to write the poem that became America's national anthem. The museum's endlessly fascinating collections include everything from the lap desk at which Thomas Jefferson drafted the Declaration of Independence to Henry Ford's 1913 Model-T, from first ladies' inaugural gowns to Dorothy's ruby slippers from *The Wizard of Oz.* Children will especially enjoy the Hands On History Room, where they can harness a life-size model of a mule or tap out a telegraph message in Morse code. (Daily; closed Dec 25) **FREE**

National Museum of Health and Medicine. *Walter Reed Army Medical Center, Building #54, 6825 16th St NW (20306).* Phone 202/782-2200. One of the most important medical collections in America. Interprets the link between history and technology; AIDS education exhibit; an interactive exhibit on human anatomy and lifestyle choices; collection of microscopes, medical teaching aids, tools, and instruments (1862-1965) and famous historical icons exhibits. (Daily; closed Dec 25) **FREE**

National Museum of Natural History. *10th St and Constitution Ave NW (20560).* Phone 202/357-2700. Gems (including the Hope Diamond), minerals; botanical, zoological, and geological materials; live insect "zoo"; Dinosaur Hall, Discovery Room with hands-on activities for children; living coral reef; cultures of Africa, Asia, the Pacific, and the Americas are explored; Western civilization is traced to its roots. Cafeteria. Special exhibition hall. **FREE**

National Museum of Women in the Arts. *1250 New York Ave NW.* Phone 202/783-5000. Focus on women's contributions to the arts. More than 1,200 works by women artists from the Renaissance to the present. Paintings, drawings, sculpture, pottery, prints. Library, research center by appointment. Performances. Guided tours (by appointment). (Daily; closed Jan 1, Thanksgiving, Dec 25) **DONATION**

National Portrait Gallery. *8th and F sts NW.* Phone 202/357-2700. Portraits and statues of people who have made significant contributions to the history, development, and culture of the US. (Daily; closed Dec 25)

National Presbyterian Church and Center. *4101 Nebraska Ave NW. Phone 202/537-0800.* Chapel of the President contains memorabilia of past US presidents; faceted glass windows depict history of man and church. Self-guided tours (daily; no tours holidays). Guided tours (Sun following service).

National Theatre. *1321 Pennsylvania Ave NW (20004). Phone 202/628-6161 (information) or 800/447-7400 (tickets).* Sarah Bernhardt, Laurence Olivier, and the Barrymores are just some of the theatrical luminaries who have performed at this historic playhouse, which is said to be haunted by the ghost of a murdered actor. These days, you'll see touring productions of such shows as *The Tale of the Allergist's Wife* and *42nd Street.* On Mondays, there are films in summer and performances drawing on local talent the rest of the year. Saturday mornings feature children's shows. Tours (Mon-Fri) by reservation 202/783-6854. Fees vary with performance.

Navy Yard. *901 M St SE (20374). Phone 202/433-4882.* Along the Anacostia River at a location chosen by George Washington, the yard was founded in 1799 and was nearly destroyed during the War of 1812. Outside the yard at 636 G St SE is the John Phillip Sousa house, where the "March King" wrote many of his famous compositions; the house is private. One block E is

Marine Barracks. *Entrance to Navy Yard is at end of 9th St at M St SE. Inside is G St between 8th and 9th sts SE. Phone 202/433-6060.* Parade ground, more than two centuries old, is surrounded by handsome and historic structures including the Commandant's House facing G St, which is said to be the oldest continuously occupied public building in the city. Spectacular parade is open to public Tues and Fri evenings in summer (see SPECIAL EVENTS).

Marine Corps Museum. *901 M St SE. Building 58 in Navy Yard. Phone 202/433-3840.* Weapons, uniforms, maps, flags, and other artifacts describe the history of the US Marine Corps. Housed in restored 19th-century structure; also used as marine barracks from 1941-1975. (Mon, Wed-Fri; Sat, Sun by appointment only; closed Jan 1, Dec 25) **FREE**

Navy Museum. *Building 76, Washington Navy Yard, 805 Kidder Breese SE. Phone 202/433-6897 or 202/433-4882.* History of US Navy from the Revolutionary War to the space age. Dioramas depict achievements of early naval heroes; displays development of naval weapons; fully rigged foremast fighting top and gun deck from frigate *Constitution* on display; WWII guns that can be trained and elevated; submarine room has operating periscopes. Approximately 5,000 objects on display including paintings, ship models, flags, uniforms, naval decorations, and the bathyscaphe *Trieste.* Two-acre outdoor park displays 19th- and 20th-century guns, cannon, other naval artifacts; US Navy destroyer *Barry* located on the waterfront. (Daily; closed holidays. Tours Mon-Fri.) **FREE**

New York Avenue Presbyterian Church. *1313 New York Ave, at H St NW. Phone 202/393-3700.* The church where Lincoln worshiped; rebuilt 1950-1951, with Lincoln's pew. Dr. Peter Marshall was pastor 1937-1949. Mementos on display include first draft of Emancipation Proclamation. (Daily, services Sun morning; closed holidays)

The Octagon. *1799 New York Ave NW, at 18th and E sts NW. Phone 202/638-3105 or 202/638-3221.* (1799-1801) Federal townhouse built for Colonel John Tayloe III, based on designs by Dr. William Thornton. Served as temporary quarters for President and Mrs. James Madison after the White House burned in the War of 1812; also the site of the ratification of the Treaty of Ghent. Restored with period furnishings (1800-1828). Changing exhibits on architecture and allied arts. (Tues-Sun; closed holidays) **$$**

Old Executive Office Building. *17th St and Pennsylvania Ave NW (20501). Phone 202/395-5895.* (1875) Second Empire/Victorian architecture. Built as War Office; was also home to State Department; now offices for president's staff. Guided tours by appointment (Sat morning only). **FREE**

Old Senate Chamber. *First and Constitution Av NE (20001). North of rotunda. Phone 202/225-6827.* Original Senate chamber has been restored to its 1850s appearance.

Old Stone House. *3051 M St NW. Phone 202/426-6851 (also TTY service).* (1765) Believed to be the oldest pre-Revolutionary building in Washington. Constructed on parcel No. 3 of the original tract of land that was then Georgetown, the house was used as both a residence and a place of business; five rooms are furnished with household items that reflect a middle-class residence of the late 18th century. The grounds are lush with fruit trees and seasonal blooms. (Wed-Sun; closed holidays) **FREE**

Organization of American States (OAS). *201 18th St NW (20006). Phone 202/458-3000.* Headquarters of OAS, set up to maintain international peace and security and to promote integral development in the Americas. Tropical patio, Hall of Heroes and Flags, Hall of the Americas, Aztec Garden, Council Chamber. (Mon-Fri; closed holidays) **FREE**

Oxon Hill Farm. *6411 Oxon Hill Rd (20745). Entrance from Oxon Hill Rd, 300 yds W of junction MD 210 and I-95 in Oxon Hill, MD. Phone 301/839-1177.* Living history farm (circa 1898-1914) located on working farm with livestock; participatory activities. Represents life from early 1800s to present. (Daily; closed Jan 1, Thanksgiving, Dec 25) **FREE**

Pavilion at the Old Post Office. *1100 Pennsylvania Ave NW. Phone 202/289-4224.* (1899) Romanesque structure which for years was headquarters of the US Postal Service has been remodeled into a marketplace with 100 shops and restaurants, and daily entertainment. In the 315-foot tower are replicas of the bells of Westminster Abbey, a Bicentennial gift from Great Britain; the tower, which is the second-highest point in DC, offers spectacular views from an open-air observation deck (free). Above the Pavilion shops are headquarters for the National Endowment for the Arts. (Daily; closed Jan 1, Thanksgiving, Dec 25) **FREE**

Petersen House. *516 10th St NW.* The house where President Lincoln was taken after the shooting at Ford's Theatre; he died here the following morning. The house has been restored to its appearance at that time. (Daily; closed Dec 25) **FREE**

Phillips Collection. *1600 21st St NW. Phone 202/387-2151 or 202/387-0961.* First museum of modern art in the nation. Founded in 1918, the museum continues to emphasize the work of emerging as well as established international artists. Permanent collection of 19th- and 20th-century Impressionist, Post-Impressionist, and modern painting and sculpture. (Tues-Sun; closed holidays) Introductory tours (Wed and Sat). Concerts (Sept-May, Sun). Weekday admission by donation. **$$$**

Polly Esther's. *605 12th St NW. Phone 202/737-1970.* Sometimes familiarity breeds fun! If your idea of the good old days is the '70s, '80s, or '90s, you'll love it here, where dancing to a retro beat is all the rage and the Hustle is more than a memory. Period kitsch adds to the ambience; the moderately priced drink list includes potions made with Tang. Part of a New York-based chain, this Polly Esther's is especially popular for bachelorette parties. (Thurs-Sat) **$$**

Potomac Park (East and West). *NW and SE of the Jefferson Memorial. Phone 202/619-7222 (park information).* On the banks of the Potomac River, park recreational activities include fishing, pedalboating; golf, tennis, picnicking. Washington's famous cherry trees can be found around the Tidal Basin. Hundreds of Yoshino and Akebono cherry trees, a gift from Japan in 1912, come into full bloom in a celebration of spring (see SPECIAL EVENTS), an unforgettable floral display (late-Mar-early-Apr). West Potomac park is the site of the Franklin Delano Roosevelt Memorial (see).

⭐ **President Kennedy's Gravesite.** *South Gate, Arlington National Cemetery.* (See ARLINGTON COUNTY in Virginia)

Renwick Gallery at the American Art Museum. *Pennsylvania Ave at 17th St NW (20006). Phone 202/275-1500.* The Patent Office Building, home of the American Art Museum, is closed for renovations until 2006, but the museum's Renwick Gallery, housed in an elegant Second Empire-style building, remains open, and its exhibitions of American crafts and decorative arts are knockouts. The permanent collection features superb, one-of-a-kind pieces in clay, fiber, glass, metal, and wood. Make sure to see the sculptural furniture by Sam Maloof and the playful "Game Fish" by Larry Fuente. (Daily; closed Dec 25) **FREE**

Rock Creek Park. *3542 Williamsburg Ln NW (20015). From downtown DC, take the Rock Creek and Potomac Pkwy north to Beach Dr. Exit onto Beach Dr north, take it to Broad Branch Rd, make a left and then a right onto Glover Rd, and follow the signs to the Nature Center. Phone 202/895-6070.* Leave urban commotion behind by going for a brisk hike in Rock Creek Park. Just 5 miles from the White House are dozens of miles of clearly marked, well-maintained, easy and moderately hard hiking trails through the park's 1,754 acres of meadows and woodlands. There's also a gentle walk along Beach Drive that takes you through dramatic Rock Creek Gorge; on weekends and holidays, cars are prohibited, making it even more peaceful. (Daily) Also here are

Art Barn. *2401 Tilden St and Beach Dr NW. Phone 202/244-2482.* Historic carriage house (1831). Art exhibitions. (Thurs-Sun afternoons) **FREE**

Carter Barron Amphitheater. *4850 Colorado Ave NW (20001). Phone 202/426-6837 (tickets) or 202/426-0486 (concert line).* This 4,200-seat outdoor theater in wooded area is setting for summer performances of symphonic, folk, pop, and jazz music (see SPECIAL EVENTS) and Shakespearean theater. Some fees.

National Zoo. *Main entrance at 3000 block of Connecticut Ave NW; other entrances at Beach Dr (Rock Creek Pkwy) and the junction of Adams Mill Rd and Harvard St. Phone 202/673-4800.* A branch of the Smithsonian Institution, the National Zoo features 5,000 animals of 500 species. Come when the zoo first opens or after 2 pm if you want to see giant pandas Tian Tian and Mei Xiang without waiting in long lines. The pair, on ten-year loan from China, are this lovely and interesting zoological park's most famous residents, but the other animals, from butterflies to American bison, have charms of their own and shouldn't be missed. The zoo is set amid the urban greenery of Rock Creek Park. (Daily from 10 am; closed Dec 25) **FREE**

Nature Center. *5200 Glover Rd NW. Phone 202/865-6070.* Planetarium, films, exhibits, nature demonstrations. (Wed-Sun; closed holidays) **FREE**

Theodore Roosevelt Memorial. *18050 W Basin Dr SW (20024). N end of Theodore Roosevelt Island, accessible only by footbridge from George Washington Memorial Pkwy, northbound lane, in Arlington, VA.* The island is an 88-acre wilderness preserve; the 17-foot statue of Roosevelt was designed by Paul Manship. (Daily; closed Dec 25) **FREE**

Senate Office Buildings. *114 Constitution Ave NE (20002).* Linked by private subway to the Capitol.

Sewall-Belmont House. *144 Constitution Ave NE. Phone 202/546-1210.* (1680, 1800) The Sewall-Belmont House is a monument to Alice Paul, the author of the Equal Rights Amendment. From this house she spearheaded the fight for the passage of the amendment. Now a national landmark, the house contains portraits and sculptures of women from the beginning of the suffrage movement; extensive collection of artifacts of the suffrage and equal rights movements; historic headquarters of the National Woman's Party. (Tues-Fri, also Sat afternoons; closed Jan 1, Thanksgiving, Dec 25) **FREE**

Shops at Georgetown Park. *3222 M St NW (20007). Phone 202/298-5577.* This stylish urban mall has four levels of upscale shops and restaurants to explore, and is especially strong in apparel. Look for Ann Taylor, Abercrombie & Fitch, J. Crew, Talbots, and other nationally popular brands. If your energy flags, you'll find fresh-baked pretzels and cookies to munch on, as well as Godiva chocolates. An accommodating Concierge Center on Level One offers gift wrapping, stroller and wheelchair loan, postal services, parking validation, photocopying, faxing, and other amenities. (Daily)

Shops at National Place. *1331 Pennsylvania Ave NW; enter at 13th and F sts. Phone 202/662-1200.* Trilevel marketplace—at, above, and below street grade—featuring more than 100 specialty shops and restaurants. (Daily)

Shops at Union Station. *50 Massachusetts Ave NE (20002). Phone 202/289-1908.* This is shopping in some of the most elegant surroundings imaginable—architect Daniel Burnham's extraordinary 1907 Union Station, restored to its former glory and reopened in 1988. The white granite Beaux Arts masterpiece is still a functioning train station and is now home to more than 130 upscale restaurants and shops, many of them catering to the special needs of travelers. But many locals patronize the shops too (including President Bill Clinton, who regularly bought holiday presents here). (Daily)

Six Flags America. *From Washington, take I-495/I-95 to exit 15A and go 5 miles (follow signs). From Baltimore, take I-695 to I-97 S, Rte 3/301 S to Rte 214 W, and go 3 miles (follow signs). Phone 301/249-1500.* This colorful theme park offers thrills both gentle and extreme, with everything from an old-fashioned carousel to classic, 50-mph wooden roller coasters and the high-tech Batwing, which gives riders the feeling of free-flight. Smaller kids will love Looney Tunes MovieTown, where Bugs Bunny and his cartoon pals roam free. Too hot to ride? Cool down with Paradise Island Water Park's splash-happy waterslides, wave pool, inner-tube ride, and interactive water tree house. (Daily June-Aug; limited schedule in Apr, May, Sept, and Oct) **$$$$**

⭐ **Smithsonian Institution.** *1442 Q St NW (20009). Phone 202/357-2700 (general information and schedule).* The majority of Smithsonian museums are located on the National Mall. Smithsonian headquarters are in the Smithsonian Institution Building, the "Castle" (1855), located at 1000 Jefferson Dr SW, on the Mall. The headquarters contain administrative offices, Smithson's crypt, and the Smithsonian Information Center, which has information on all Smithsonian museums. Many visitors begin their day here. (All buildings open daily; closed Dec 25; Anacostia Museum and National Zoo hours vary) **FREE**

St. John's Church Georgetown Parish. *3240 O St NW. Phone 202/338-1796.* Oldest Episcopal congregation in Georgetown, established 1796; original design of church by William Thornton, architect of the Capitol. Many presidents since Madison have worshiped here. Francis Scott Key was a founding member. Tours (by appointment).

Supreme Court of the United States. *1st St NE at Maryland Ave, E of the Capitol. Phone 202/479-3211.* Designed by Cass Gilbert in Neo-Classical style. Court is in session Oct-Apr (Mon-Wed, at two-week intervals from the first Mon in Oct) and on the first workday of each week in May and June; court sessions are open to the public (10 am and 1 pm), on a first-come basis; lectures are offered in the courtroom (Mon-Fri except when court is in session; 20-minute lectures hourly on 1/2 hour); on the ground floor are exhibits and a film (23 minutes), cafeteria, snack bar, and gift shop (Mon-Fri; closed holidays). **FREE**

Textile Museum. *2320 S St NW. Phone 202/667-0441.* Founded in 1925 with the collection of George Hewitt Myers, the museum features changing exhibits of non-Western textiles, Oriental rugs, and other handmade textile art. Guided tours (Sept-May, Wed, Sat, Sun; by appointment). (Daily) **DONATION**

Theaters. *Phone 202/547-1122.* **Shakespeare Theatre, Lansburgh Theater,** *450 7th St NW, phone 202/547-1122.* **The National,** *1321 Pennsylvania Ave NW, phone 202/628-6161.* **Arena Stage,** *1101 6th at Maine Ave SW, phone 202/488-3300.* **The Warner,** *13th and E sts NW, phone 202/783-4000.* Also see John F. Kennedy Center.

⭐ **Thomas Jefferson Memorial.** *East Basin Dr SW (20003). S edge of Tidal Basin. Phone 202/426-6841.* This memorial, dedicated in 1943, honors the third President of the United States and the author of both the Declaration of Independence and the Bill of Rights. The white marble dome surrounded by columns, representing the classic style that Jefferson introduced to the US, is a memorable Washington landmark and is quite beautiful especially when lit up at night. In the basement, you'll find a museum and the plaster statue from which the 19-foot bronze one in the center of the monument was created. (Daily 8 am-midnight; closed Dec 25) **FREE**

Tourmobile Sightseeing. *1000 Ohio Dr SW. Phone 202/554-5100.* Narrated shuttle tours to 18 historic sites on the National Mall and in Arlington National Cemetery. Unlimited reboarding throughout day (daily; no tours Dec 25). Additional tours separately or in combinations: Arlington National Cemetery; Mount Vernon (seasonal) and Frederick Douglass Home (seasonal). **$$$$**

Tudor Place. *1644 31st St NW. Phone 202/965-0400.* (1805) Twelve-room Federal-style mansion was designed by Dr. William Thornton, architect of Capitol, for Martha Custis Peter, granddaughter of Martha Washington. The Peter family lived in the house for 180 years. All furnishings and *objets d'art* are original. More than 5 acres of gardens (Mon-Sat). Guided tours (Tues-Sat, by reservation; closed holidays). **$$$**

Union Station. *50 Massachusetts Ave NE (20002). Phone 703/371-9441.* Restored Beaux Arts train station designed by Daniel Burnham and completed in 1907 features lavish interior spaces under a 96-foot-high, coffered, gold-leafed ceiling. Located within the original station and train shed are 130 shops, restaurants, and a movie theater complex. Original spaces, such as the presidential suite, have been turned into restaurants without extensive alteration. Also located within the station are the Amtrak depot and Gray Line and Tourmobile Sightseeing operators (see SIGHTSEEING TOURS). (Daily) **FREE**

US Botanic Gardens. *100 Maryland Ave SW, at base of Capitol Hill. Phone 202/225-8333.* The Botanic Garden, one of the oldest in the country, was established by Congress in 1820 for public education and exhibition. It features plants collected by the famous Wilkes Expedition of the South Seas. Conservatory has tropical, subtropical, and desert plants; seasonal displays. Exterior gardens are planted for seasonal blooming; also here is Bartholdi Fountain, designed by the sculptor of the Statue of Liberty. (Daily) **FREE**

★ **US Holocaust Memorial Museum.** *100 Raoul Wallenberg Plaza SW (20024). Entrances at Raoul Wallenberg Plz (15th St SW) and at 14th St SW. Phone 202/488-0400 or 202/488-0406 (TTY).* Opened in 1993, this privately funded museum is noteworthy for its effective presentation of information, images, and artifacts in an architectural setting that enhances visitors' understanding of the Holocaust. Temporary exhibits cover everything from the diary of Anne Frank to the role of Oskar Schindler in saving the lives of hundreds of Jews. At the heart of the museum is its self-guided Permanent Exhibition, which includes powerful photos; film footage; eyewitness testimonies; clothing, suitcases, children's drawings, and other victims' belongings; and reconstructions of concentration camp buildings. Especially stirring is the Hall of Faces, a narrow, 3-story-high space crammed with framed photographs of the Jewish residents of a single Lithuanian town, more than 3,000 of whom were murdered in September 1941. Visitors are welcome to reflect privately on their experience in the quiet, skylighted Hall of Remembrance and to light memorial candles in the niches of its walls. (Daily; closed Yom Kippur, Dec 25). Timed daily-use passes are necessary for visiting the museum's permanent exhibition and can be obtained each day at the museum starting at 10 am or in advance by calling 800/400-9373. **FREE**

US National Arboretum. *3501 New York Ave NE. Phone 202/245-2726.* Floral displays spring, summer, fall, and winter on 446 acres; Japanese garden, National Bonsai and Penjing Museum (daily); National Herb Garden, major collections of azaleas (15,000), wildflowers, ferns, magnolias, crabapples, cherries, dogwoods; aquatic plantings; dwarf conifers (world's largest evergreen collection). (Daily; closed Dec 25) Under 16 years admitted only with adult. **FREE**

US Navy Memorial. *701 Pennsylvania Ave NW (20004). Phone 202/737-2300.* Dedicated to those who have served in the Navy in war and in peacetime. A 100-foot diameter granite world map dominates the Plaza, where the *Lone Sailor,* a 7-foot bronze sculpture, stands and the US Navy Band stages performances (Memorial Day-Labor Day, Tues evenings). Visitor Center features electronic kiosks with interactive video displays on naval history; also Navy Memorial Log Room and US Presidents Room. (Tues-Sat) **FREE** Also here is

At Sea. *Arleigh and Roberta Burke Theater.* Underwritten by ExxonMobil, this award-winning high-resolution 70mm film conveys the experience of being at sea aboard a US Navy aircraft carrier. The 241-seat theater employs a 2-story, 52-foot-wide screen and 6-track digital audio to surround the audience with the sights and sounds of carrier operations. Showings (Mon-Sat, four times daily; Sun, two times).

★ **Vietnam Veterans Memorial.** *900 Ohio Dr SW (20242). Phone 202/426-6841.* Designed by Maya Ying Lin and funded by private citizens' contributions, this memorial's polished black granite walls are inscribed with the names of the 58,175 US servicemen who died in or remain missing from the Vietnam War (a large directory helps visitors locate specific names). Deliberately apolitical, the memorial aims to foster reconciliation and healing given the divisiveness the war caused in American society. Also on site are the Three Servicemen Statue and Flagpole and the Vietnam Women's Memorial. (Daily 8 am-11:45 pm; closed Dec 25) **FREE**

Voice of America. *330 Independence Ave SW between 3rd and 4th sts SW; enter on C St. Phone 202/619-3919.* Live radio broadcasts to foreign countries; 45-minute guided tours (Mon-Fri, reservations required; closed holidays). **FREE**

Washington Capitals (NHL). *MCI Center, 601 F St NW. Phone 202/661-5050.*

Washington Dolls' House & Toy Museum. *5236 44th St NW. Phone 202/244-0024.* Splendid collection of antique doll houses, dolls, toys, and games; museum shop. (Tues-Sun; closed Jan 1, Thanksgiving, Dec 25) **$$**

Washington Harbour. *3000 K St NW (20007).* Dining and shopping complex that features lavish fountains, life-size statuary, and a boardwalk with a view of the Potomac River.

⭐ **Washington Monument.** *15th St SW (20242). Parking lot on north side, off Constitution Ave. Phone 202/426-6841 or 202/426-6839.* This obelisk, the tallest masonry structure in the world at 555 feet, was dedicated in 1885 to the memory of the first US president, George Washington. Before its dedication, it had been under construction for almost 40 years, a lack of funds and the Civil War both getting in the way of its completion. You can see where construction resumed after a 28-year delay about a quarter of the way up the monument, where two different shades of marble meet. Views of the majestic structure can be enjoyed anytime, but to enter, you must have a ticket. You can try your luck at getting one of the free tickets distributed at the kiosk at 15th and Madison starting at 8 am for same-day tours, or you can reserve tickets ahead of time by calling 800/967-2283. There is an elevator to the observation room at the 500-foot level. To take the 898 steps up or down, arrangements must be made in advance. (Daily 9 am-4:45 pm; closed Dec 25) **FREE**

Washington Mystics (WNBA). *MCI Center, 601 F St NW. Phone 202/661-5050.*

⭐ **Washington National Cathedral.** *3000 Wisconsin Ave NW (20016). Phone 202/537-6207 (tours) or 202/537-6200 (recording).* This inspiring edifice, 83 years in the making, was completed in 1990, its $65 million cost covered by private donations. It was built largely of Indiana limestone using traditional methods, with flying buttresses rather than steel providing support. Graced with intricate carvings inside and out, it has a 30-story central tower and 215 stained glass windows, including one that contains a piece of lunar rock presented by the astronauts of Apollo XI. Bring binoculars if you want to see, close up, the more than 100 gargoyles, which depict not just dragons but also a child with his hand in a cookie jar and Star Wars villain Darth Vader. Worshippers of all faiths are welcome at services held daily. There are also frequent musical events, including recitals given on the magnificent pipe organ most Sundays at 5 pm. Famous Americans interred at the cathedral include Woodrow Wilson and Helen Keller. **DONATION**

Washington Redskins (NFL). *FedEx Field, 1 Redskins Rd. Landover, MD. Phone 301/276-6050.*

Washington Walks. *Phone 202/484-1565.* Guided tours sponsored by Washington Walks are a great way to see the city up close. The group (along with Children's Concierge) runs two tours that kids will especially like: for Goodnight Mr. Lincoln, children can show up in pajamas at the Lincoln Memorial for stories, games, and music about Honest Abe. The White House Un-Tour offers role-playing (you might be asked to impersonate the president who loved bowling) and fun facts about the executive mansion. (Apr-Oct, days vary; rest of year by appointment) **$$**

Washington Wizards (NBA). *MCI Center, 601 F St NW. Phone 202/661-5050.*

West Front. *Phone 202/225-6827.* Along the Capitol's west front are terraces, gardens, and lawns designed by Frederick Law Olmstead, who also planned New York City's Central Park. Halfway down the hill are the Peace Monument (on the north) and the Garfield Monument (on the south). At the foot of Capitol Hill is Union Square with a reflecting pool and Grant Monument.

⭐ **The White House.** *1600 Pennsylvania Ave NW. Phone 202/456-7041 (recording).* (1800) Constructed under the supervision of George Washington, the house has been lived in by every president since John Adams. It was burned by the British during the War of 1812 and reconstructed under the guidance of James Monroe (1817-1825). The West Wing, which includes the Oval Office, was built during Theodore Roosevelt's administration (1901-1909); before its construction, executive offices shared the second floor with the president's private quarters. The interior of the White House was gutted and rebuilt, using modern construction techniques, during the Truman administration; President Truman and family resided at Blair House for four years during the reconstruction. The Library and the Vermeil Room (on the Ground Floor), the East Room, Green, Blue, and Red Rooms, and the State Dining Room (on State Floor) are accessible to certain groups for educational tours. Tickets must be obtained through the particular state's Congressman or Senator. (Closed Jan 1, Dec 25, and presidential functions) **FREE**

Woodrow Wilson House. *2340 S St NW. Phone 202/387-4062.* (1915) Red brick Georgian Revival townhouse to which President Wilson retired after leaving office; family furnishings and gifts-of-state. A National Trust for Historic Preservation property. (Tues-Sun; closed Jan 1, Thanksgiving, Dec 25) **$$**

Yellow House. *1430 33rd St NW (20007).* (1733) One of Georgetown's oldest homes (a private residence), typical of the area's mansions.

Special Events

Cherry Blossom Festival. *Tidal Basin, West Potomac Park, East Potomac Park, Washington Monument grounds. Phone 202/547-1500.* Nothing says spring more spectacularly than the sight of thousands of cherry trees in full bloom around the Jefferson Memorial. About 150 trees remain from the original 1912 gift of 3,000 from the city of Tokyo, but thousands of others have been planted in parks along the Tidal Basin, and for two weeks each year their lush pink and white blooms transform the cityscape. The festival celebrates this annual event with activities that appeal to visitors of all ages. Don't miss the Smithsonian's Kite Festival on the National Mall, the rousing parade, or Sakura Matsuri, a day-long Japanese street festival. Visitors can enjoy drummers, traditional dancers, and musical performances; demonstrations of flower arranging, calligraphy, and martial arts; a Taste of Japan food fair (who says that sushi isn't street food?); and the bustling Ginza Arcade, with shops selling everything from origami paper to antique kimonos. Late Mar-early Apr.

Concerts. *Independence and 15th St NW (20008). Phone 202/619-7222.* **Sylvan Theater,** Washington Monument grounds, June-Aug, days vary, phone 202/619-7222. **US Capitol,** west terrace, June-late Aug, Mon-Wed, Fri, Sun, phone 202/619-7222. **National Gallery of Art,** west garden court, Oct-June, Sun eves; first-come basis, phone 202/842-6941. **Phillips Collection,** at Dupont-Kalorama Museum, Sept-May, Sun, phone 202/387-2151.

Easter Egg Roll. *White House Lawn. 1600 Pennsylvania Ave NW (20500). Phone 202/456-2200.* First introduced to Washington by Dolley Madison. Mon after Easter.

Evening Parade. *US Marine Barracks, I St between 8th and 9th sts SE. Phone 202/433-6060.* Spectacular parade with Marine Band, US Marine Drum and Bugle Corps, Color Guard, Silent Drill Team, and marching companies. Written request for reservations suggested at least three weeks in advance. Tues and Fri evenings, early-May-late Aug.

Festival of American Folklife. *The National Mall. Constitution Ave (20004). Phone 202/357-2700.* Festival of folklife traditions from America and abroad. Sponsored by the Smithsonian Institution and National Park Service. Late June-early July.

Fort Dupont Summer Theatre. *Fort Dupont Park. Phone 202/426-7723.* Musicals, concerts, plays, dancing. Fri evenings, late June-late Aug.

Georgetown Garden Tour. *3224 N St NW (20007). Phone 202/333-6896.* Fourteen or more different gardens open to the public. Proceeds go to Georgetown Children's House; incl "Evermay" garden, which features grand expanses, fountains, and sculptures. Self-guided tours. Second Sat in May.

Georgetown House Tour. *3240 O St NW (20007). Phone 202/338-1796.* Held since 1927, participants view 12 well-known and less well-known houses in Georgetown. St. John's Episcopal Church members serve as hosts and guides, and serve tea in the Parish Hall in the afternoon. Late Apr.

Goodwill Industries Embassy Tour. *220 S Dakota Ave NE (20018). Phone 202/636-4225.* The only time six to eight embassies are open to the public; visitors can view artifacts and design peculiar to each government's legation. Complimentary refreshments and illustrated tour booklet. Walking tour with shuttle bus between embassies. Tickets limited. No children under age 10. Second Sat in May.

July 4th Fireworks on the Mall. *National Mall (20001). Phone 202/426-6841.* You have to like a city that holds its fireworks show on the Fourth of July and not on the 3rd or whenever it's convenient. This display is extra-spectacular because the bombs burst in air over the monuments on the National Mall—a truly stirring sight. One of the best viewing spots is the Capitol, where the National Symphony Orchestra gives a rousing concert before the fireworks begin. Arrive early (the crowds get quite large) and picnic while you wait. July 4. **FREE**

Memorial Day Ceremony. *Memorial Dr (22111). Phone 703/685-2851.* Arlington National Cemetery (See ARLINGTON COUNTY in Virginia). Wreaths placed at the Tomb of the Unknown Soldier. The National Symphony Orchestra gives a free concert later in the evening on the lawn of the Capitol.

Musical programs. *In Carter Barron Amphitheater, Rock Creek Park. 5000 Glover Rd NW. Phone 202/619-7222.* Mid-June-Aug.

Pageant of Peace. *15th and E sts NW (20319). Ellipse, south of White House. Phone 202/619-7222.* Seasonal music, caroling; giant Christmas tree near the White House is lit by the president. Dec.

Taste of DC. *Pennsylvania Ave NW, between 7th and 14th sts. Phone 202/789-7002.* Enjoy sample-size portions of scrumptious fare from local restaurants at the biggest, liveliest food and music festival on the East Coast. In an area as culturally diverse as DC, the vendors represent many of the world's great cuisines, including Indian, Jamaican, Italian, and Thai. Enjoy music and other live entertainment as you munch on your jerk chicken and vegetable samosas, and make sure to save room for Key lime pie or a good, old-fashioned funnel cake. Columbus Day weekend.

Washington National Cathedral Open House. *3000 Wisconsin Ave NW (20016). Phone 202/537-6200.* Special tours, entertainment, food; demonstrations of cathedral arts. Only day of the year when central tower is open to the public. Sat nearest Sept 29.

Wolf Trap Farm Park for the Performing Arts. *In Vienna, VA, 14 miles NW via Washington Memorial Pkwy, VA 123, US 7, then S on Towlston Rd (Trap Rd), (VA 676), then follow signs. Phone 703/255-1900.* (See FAIRFAX in Virginia) Late May-Sept (Filene Center) and mid-Oct-mid-May (The Barns).

Motels/Motor Lodges

★ ★ **CHANNEL INN HOTEL.** *650 Water St SW (20024). Phone 202/554-2400; toll-free 800/368-5668; fax 202/863-1164. www.channelinn.com.* 100 rooms, 3 story. S, D $115-$145; each additional $10; suites $200; under 13 free; weekend rates. Crib free. TV; cable (premium). Pool; lifeguard. Restaurant 7 am-11 pm; Sun to 9 pm. Bar 11:30-1 am; Fri, Sat to 2 am; Sun to 10 pm; entertainment. Check-out noon. Meeting rooms. In-room modem link. Bellhops. Garage parking. Health club privileges. Balconies. Near piers. Cr cds: A, C, D, DS, JCB, MC, V.

D ➛ SC

★ **WINDSOR PARK HOTEL.** *2116 Kalorama Rd NW (20008). Phone 202/483-7700; toll-free 800/247-3064; fax 202/332-4547. www.windsorparkhotel.com.* 43 rooms, 6 suites, 5 story. S $98-$110; D $108-$122; each additional $10; suites $125-$155; under 16 free; weekend rates (2-day minimum). TV; cable (premium). Complimentary continental breakfast. Restaurant nearby. Check-out noon. Business services available. Refrigerators. Cr cds: A, C, D, DS, MC, V.

➛ SC

Hotels

★ ★ ★ **CAPITAL HILTON.** *1001 16th St NW (20036). Phone 202/393-1000; toll-free 800/774-1500; fax 202/639-5784.* 544 rooms, 15 story. Check-out noon, check-in 3 pm. TV; cable (premium). Internet access. Restaurant. Bar. Room service. In-house fitness room, massage, steam room. Business center. Cr cds: A, C, D, DS, ER, JCB, MC, V. **$**

D 🛠 ➛ 🏋

★ ★ **CENTER CITY HOTEL.** *1201 13th St NW (20005). Phone 202/682-5300; toll-free 800/458-2817; fax 202/371-9624. www.centercityhotel.com.* 100 rooms, 8 story. Apr-Sept: S $85-$115; D $95-$125; each additional $10; under 16 free; weekend rates; lower rates rest of year. Complimentary continental breakfast. Check-out 11 am. TV; cable (premium). Laundry services. Restaurant. Parking. Cr cds: A, C, D, DS, MC, V.

D ➛ SC

★ ★ **CHURCHILL HOTEL.** *1914 Connecticut Ave NW (20009). Phone 202/797-2000; fax 202/462-0944. www.thechurchillhotel.com.* Near Embassy Row and Dupont Circle, this property has a pleasant, French style. 144 rooms, 9 story. D $159-$259. TV; cable (premium). In-room modem link. Restaurant 6:30 am-10:30 pm. Bar noon-11:30 pm; Fri, Sat to 1 am. Room service. Health club privileges. Exercise equipment. Valet $21. Concierge. Refurbished apartment building; built in 1904. Cr cds: A, C, D, JCB, MC, V.

🛠 ➛ SC

★ ★ **COURTYARD BY MARRIOTT.** *1900 Connecticut Ave NW (20009). Phone 202/332-9300; fax 202/328-7039. www.courtyard.com.* 147 rooms, 9 story. S $89-$200; D $89-$200; each additional $15; under 18 free; weekend rates (2-day minimum). Crib free. Garage parking, valet $15. TV; cable (premium), VCR available. Pool; lifeguard. Complimentary coffee in rooms. Restaurant 6:30-10:30 am, 5-10 pm. Bar 5-11 pm. Check-out noon. Coin laundry. Meeting rooms. Business services available. In-room modem link. Exercise equipment. Health club privileges. Cr cds: A, C, D, DS, JCB, MC, V.

D ➛ 🛠 ➛

★ ★ **CROWNE PLAZA.** *1001 14th St NW (20005). Phone 202/682-0111; fax 202/682-9525. www.crowneplaza washington.com.* 318 rooms, 17 suites, 14 story. S, D $159-$229; suites $400. Crib available. Valet parking available. TV; cable. Complimentary coffee in rooms, newspaper. Restaurant 6:30 am-11 pm. Bar. Check-out noon, check-in 3 pm. Conference center, meeting rooms. Business center. Bellhops. Concierge service. Dry cleaning. Gift shop. Exercise privileges. Cr cds: A, D, DS, MC, V.

D 🛠 ➛ ➛ 🏋

★ ★ ★ ★ **FOUR SEASONS HOTEL.** *2800 Pennsylvania Ave NW (20007). Phone 202/342-0444; fax 202/944-2076. www.fshr.com.* This Four Seasons Hotel is nestled within Washington's lovely and historic Georgetown neighborhood. Just outside the hotel's doors are enticing shops, energetic nightlife, and delectable dining. The warm and inviting atmosphere of the Four Seasons is instantly recognizable in the gracious lobby, where bountiful floral displays and Oriental rugs set a refined, residential tone. The guest accommodations are some of the most spacious in the city and are magnificently appointed with polished formal furnishings, beautiful fabrics, and exquisite attention to detail. The views of Rock Creek Park (see) and the C & O Canal further enhance the relaxing mood. Popular fitness classes are offered in the extremely well-equipped fitness center, complete with a lap pool, while the seven spa treatment rooms provide a restful alternative for personal well-being. Consistently delicious meals are available at Seasons (see), or you can retreat to the cozy Garden Lounge for afternoon tea or cocktails. Not only is the food memorable, but the politically charged crowd is unparalleled! *Secret Inspector's Notes:* No time to finish your e-mails before lunch? No problem! When dining at Seasons for lunch, guests are greeted not only with gracious charm but also with the offer of wireless connectivity from an available laptop. 260 rooms, 6 story. S $350-$365; D $350-$395; each additional $30; suites $750-$4,000; under 18 free; weekend rates. Pet accepted. Check-out noon. TV; cable (premium), VCR available (movies). In-room modem link. Restaurant 7-2 am. Bar from 11 am. Room service 24 hours. Exercise room, steam room. Spa. Indoor pool. Valet parking $25. Business center. Concierge. Afternoon tea. Cr cds: A, C, D, ER, JCB, MC, V.

★ ★ **GEORGETOWN INN.** *1310 Wisconsin Ave NW (20007). Phone 202/333-8900; toll-free 800/368-5922; fax 202/333-8308. www.georgetowninn.com.* 98 rooms, 10 suites, 6 story. Check-out noon, check-in 3 pm. TV; cable (premium), VCR available. In-room modem link. Restaurant. Bar. Babysitting services available. In-house fitness room. Valet parking. Cr cds: A, C, D, DS, MC, V. **$$**

★ **THE GOVERNORS HOUSE HOTEL.** *1615 Rhode Island Ave NW (20036). Phone 202/296-2100; toll-free 800/821-4367; fax 202/463-6614. www.governorshouse wdc.com.* 149 units, 24 kitchen units, 9 story. Mar-June, Sept-Oct: S $125-$195; D $140-$210; each additional $20; suites $175-$225; kitchen units $145-$155; under 16 free; weekend, monthly rates. Crib free. Check-out noon. TV; cable (premium). In-room modem link. Microwaves available. Restaurant 7 am-midnight. Bar from 11:30 am. Health club privileges. Exercise room. Pool; lifeguard. Valet parking $19. Meeting rooms, business services. On original site of governor of Pennsylvania's house. Cr cds: A, C, D, DS, JCB, MC, V.

★ ★ ★ **GRAND HYATT WASHINGTON.** *1000 H St NW (20001). Phone 202/582-1234; fax 202/634-4781. www.grandwashington.hyatt.com.* A convenient downtown location, situated close to the MCI Center, the US Capitol and other federal agencies, makes this property a popular choice for travelers. 888 rooms, 36 suites, 12 story. Check-out noon, check-in 3 pm. TV; cable (premium). In-room modem link. Laundry services. Restaurant. Bar; entertainment. Room service 24 hours. Babysitting services available. In-house fitness room, health club privileges, massage, sauna, steam room. Indoor pool, whirlpool. Valet parking. Business center. 3-story cascading waterfall. Cr cds: A, C, D, DS, ER, JCB, MC, V. **$$**

★ ★ ★ ★ **THE HAY-ADAMS HOTEL.** *16th and H sts NW (20006). Phone 202/638-6600; toll-free 800/424-5054; fax 202/638-2716. www.hayadams.com.* The Hay-Adams seems to radiate the power of the nation's capital. Set on Lafayette Square across from the White House, the hotel has been welcoming notables since the 1920s. Reading like a Who's Who of American history, the Hay-Adams' guest list is truly fascinating. If only these walls could talk! Originally designed as the private residences of two influential men, the hotel retains the majestic style

of its former incarnation. The guest rooms are a happy marriage of historic preservation and 21st-century conveniences; intricately carved plaster ceilings and ornamental fireplaces reside alongside high-speed Internet access and multiline telephones. Windows frame views of the White House, St. John's Church, and Lafayette Square, further convincing visitors that they are in the center of Washington's universe. All-day dining is available at Lafayette (see), while the Off the Record bar is a popular watering hole for politicians and hotel guests. 145 rooms, 8 story. Pet accepted, some restrictions. Check-out noon, check-in 3 pm. TV; cable (premium). In-room modem link. Fireplaces. Room service 24 hours. Restaurant. Bar. Babysitting services available. Parking. Concierge. Cr cds: A, C, D, DS, JCB, MC, V. **$$$$**

★ ★ ★ **HENLEY PARK HOTEL.** *926 Massachusetts NW (20001). Phone 202/638-5200; toll-free 800/222-8474; fax 202/414-0513. www.henleypark.com.* This intimate, historic property is within walking distance of the Washington Convention Center and convenient to various DC attractions. All rooms have a charming, European style. 96 rooms, 8 story. Mar-May, Oct-Nov: S $165-$235; D $185-$255; each additional $20; suites $295-$375; under 16 free; weekend rates; lower rates rest of year. Crib free. Valet parking $16. TV; cable (premium). Restaurant 7-10:30 am, 11:30 am-2 pm, 6-10 pm. Room service 24 hours. Bar 11-12:30 am; entertainment. Check-out noon. Meeting rooms. Business services available. In-room modem link. Health club privileges. Bathroom phones, refrigerators, minibars. Wet bar in suites. Tudor detailing; 1918 structure. Cr cds: A, C, D, DS, MC, V.

★ ★ ★ **HILTON WASHINGTON EMBASSY ROW.** *2015 Massachusetts Ave NW (20036). Phone 202/265-1600; fax 202/328-7526.* This Europeon-style boutique hotel is located on the "Avenue of the Embassies," just half a block from Dupont Circle and the metro system. 193 rooms, 9 story. S, D $130-$200; each additional $20; under 17 free; family, weekend, weekly, holiday rates; higher rates special events. Crib free. Complimentary coffee in rooms. Check-out noon. TV; cable (premium). In-room modem link. Many bathroom phones; some refrigerators, microwaves. Free guest laundry. Restaurant 6:30 am-10 pm. Bar 11:30-1 am; entertainment. Room service 24 hours. Exercise equipment. Pool; poolside service, lifeguard. Valet parking $15. Meeting rooms, business center. Concierge. Cr cds: A, C, D, DS, MC, V.

★ ★ **HOLIDAY INN.** *550 C St SW (20024). Phone 202/479-4000; toll-free 800/465-4329; fax 202/479-4353. www.holiday-inn.com.* 516 rooms, 13 suites; 9 story. S, D $179; suites $219-$299; under 18 free; weekend rates. Crib free. Check-out noon. TV; cable (premium). In-room modem link. Microwaves available. Coffee in rooms. Coin laundry. Restaurant 6:30 am-10 pm. Bar 11-1 am. Health club privileges. Exercise equipment. Pool; lifeguard. Garage $16. Business services, convention facilities. Cr cds: A, C, D, DS, JCB, MC, V.

[D] [⛱] [🚶] [⛵] [SC]

★ ★ **HOLIDAY INN.** *2101 Wisconsin Ave NW (20007). Phone 202/338-4600; toll-free 800/465-4329; fax 202/338-4458. www.holiday-inn.com.* 296 rooms, 4 suites, 7 story. S $110-$140; D $120-$149; each additional $10; suites $175; under 18 free. Crib free. Parking in/out $10. TV; cable (premium). Pool; lifeguard. Restaurant 6:30 am-2 pm; 5-10 pm. Bar 4-11 pm. Check-out noon. Coin laundry. Meeting rooms. Business services available. In-room modem link. Gift shop. Exercise equipment. Refrigerators available. Cr cds: A, C, D, DS, JCB, MC, V.

[D] [⛱] [🚶] [⛵] [SC]

★ ★ **HOLIDAY INN.** *415 New Jersey Ave NW (20001). Phone 202/638-1616; toll-free 800/638-1116; fax 202/638-0707. www.holiday-inn.com.* 343 rooms, 10 suites, 10 story. Feb-May, Sept-Nov: S, D $99-$249; each additional $10; suites $198-$475; under 18 free; weekend rates; lower rates rest of year. Crib free. Check-out noon. TV; cable (premium). In-room modem link. Refrigerators, microwaves available. Restaurant 6:30 am-midnight. Bar 11-2 am. Exercise equipment. Pool, poolside service, lifeguard. Covered parking. 10,000 square-feet of meeting space. Business services. Sundries. Cr cds: A, C, D, DS, JCB, MC, V.

[D] [⛱] [🚶] [⛵] [SC]

★ ★ ★ **HOTEL GEORGE.** *15 E St NW (20001). Phone 202/347-4200; toll-free 800/576-8331; fax 202/347-4213. www.hotelgeorge.com.* If you need to be downtown but are tired of the traditional options, the neo-classical atmosphere of this business and leisure-friendly hotel is just what you need. The guest rooms are individually designed, with a comfortable, but elegant, residential feel. 139 rooms, 5 suites, 8 story. Feb-June, Sep-Dec: S, D $295; each additional $25; suites $750-$875; lower rates rest of year. Crib available, fee. Complimentary coffee in rooms, newspaper. Check-out noon, check-in 3 pm. TV; cable (premium), VCR, CD available. Dry cleaning. Restaurant 7 am-10:30 pm. Bar. Exercise privileges, sauna, steam room. Valet parking $15-$24 per day. Meeting rooms, business services. Concierge. Cr cds: A, D, DS, MC, V.

[D] [🚶] [⛵]

★ ★ **HOTEL HARRINGTON.** *436 11th St NW (20004). Phone 202/628-8140; toll-free 800/424-8532; fax 202/347-3924. www.hotel-harrington.com.* 260 rooms, 29 suites, 11 story. Mar-Oct: S $89; D $99-$109; each additional $5; suites $115; under 16 free; package plans;

lower rates rest of year. Pet accepted, some restrictions. Check-out noon. TV; cable (premium). Laundry services. Restaurant. Bar. Cr cds: A, D, DS, JCB, MC, V.

[D] [🐾] [⛵] [SC]

★ ★ **HOTEL WASHINGTON.** *515 15th and Pennsylvania Ave NW (20004). Phone 202/638-5900; toll-free 800/424-9540; fax 202/638-1595. www.hotelwashington.com.* 344 rooms, 11 story. Pet accepted, some restrictions. Check-out 1 pm, check-in 3 pm. TV; cable (premium). In-room modem link. Restaurant. Bar. In-house fitness room, exercise equipment, sauna. Business center. One of the oldest continuously operated hotels in the city. Original Jardin d'Armide tapestry (1854). Cr cds: A, C, D, DS, JCB, MC, V. **$$**

[D] [🐾] [🚶] [⛵] [SC] [🏃]

★ ★ ★ **THE JEFFERSON.** *1200 16th St NW (20036). Phone 202/347-2200; toll-free 800/235-6397; fax 202/331-7982. www.loweshotels.com.* Just four blocks from the White House, this Beaux Arts hotel, dating to 1923, is a masterpiece of quiet luxury. The antique-filled public rooms recall the elegance of the past, and the museum-quality collection of artwork and original documents signed by Thomas Jefferson is astounding. The guest rooms are a stylish blend of old and new. The seamless, attentive service is outstanding and satisfies every need. A fitness center is available, as are privileges at the University Club, with its Olympic-size pool. The restaurant feels like old Washington with its faux tortoiseshell walls and leather chairs, yet its New American cuisine is all the rage. 100 rooms, 32 suites; 8 story. Jan-June, Sept-Nov: S $270-$310; D $285-$325; each additional $25; suites $450-$1,200; under 12 free; weekend rates; lower rates rest of year. Check-out 1 pm. TV; cable (premium), VCR (movies). In-room modem link. Restaurant 6:30 am-10:30 pm. Bar 11-1 am. Room service 24 hours. Health club privileges. Pool privileges. Garage, valet parking $25. Concierge. Afternoon tea 3-5 pm. Opened in 1923; individually decorated rooms have four-poster beds. Cr cds: A, C, D, DS, JCB, MC, V.

[D] [🐾] [⛱] [⛵]

★ ★ **JURYS NORMANDY INN.** *2118 Wyoming Ave NW (20008). Phone 202/483-1350; fax 202/387-8241. www.jurysdoyle.com.* 75 rooms, 6 story. S $103-$133; D $113-$143; each additional $10; under 12 free. Crib free. Complimentary coffee in rooms. Check-out noon. TV; cable (premium). In-room modem link. Refrigerators. Coin laundry. Restaurant nearby. Health club privileges. Garage $13-$20. In residential neighborhood. Cr cds: A, C, D, DS, MC, V.

[D] [⛵]

★ ★ ★ **J. W. MARRIOTT HOTEL.** *1331 Pennsylvania Ave NW (20004). Phone 202/393-2000; toll-free 800/228-9290; fax 202/626-6991. www.marriotthotels.com/wasjw.* Located in the heart of Washington, this elegant hotel offers guests superb service and a relaxing stay. Centrally located to theaters, shops, and some wonderful sightseeing, this hotel has something for everyone. 772 rooms, 12 story. D $199-$349. Check-out noon. TV; cable (premium). In-room modem link. Restaurant 7 am-11 pm. Room service 24 hours. Exercise room, sauna. Massage. Indoor pool, whirlpool. Valet parking $25. Business center. Concierge. Luxury level. Cr cds: A, C, D, DS, ER, JCB, MC, V.

D ⌨ ⛲ 🏃 SC 🏃

★ ★ ★ **THE LATHAM HOTEL.** *3000 M St NW (20007). Phone 202/726-5000; toll-free 800/368-5922; fax 202/337-4250. www.lathamhotel.com.* The quaintness of Georgetown sits just steps away from this European-style boutique hotel, given its prime location on the city's main street. Simply walk outside its front doors and you'll find good shopping and tasty food. For the latter, however, you may not even want to leave the Latham. Michel Richard, a high-profile local chef with an international reputation, owns and operates the onsite Citronelle restaurant (see), where diners savor award-winning French and American cuisine. The well-appointed guest rooms come with marble showers, high-speed Internet access, and more. In summer, cool off in the rooftop swimming pool, the only outdoor hotel pool in Georgetown. 143 rooms, 10 story. Check-out 11 am, check-in 3 pm. TV. In-room modem link. Restaurant. Outdoor pool. Valet parking $20. Concierge. Overlooks historic Chesapeake and Ohio Canal. Cr cds: A, C, D, DS, MC, V. **$$**

D ⛲ 🏃 SC

★ ★ ★ **LOEWS L'ENFANT PLAZA HOTEL.** *480 L'Enfant Plaza SW (20024). Phone 202/484-1000; fax 202/646-4456. www.loewshotels.com.* Sitting just blocks from the DC Mall, this hotel cannot be beat for its central location. 370 rooms on floors 11-15. S, D $189-$279; each additional $20; suites $370-$1,200; under 18 free; weekend rates. Crib free. Pet accepted. Valet parking $22. TV; cable (premium), VCR (movies available). Pool; poolside service, lifeguard. Restaurant 6:30 am-midnight. Bar from 11:30 am. Check-out 1 pm. Convention facilities. Business center. In-room modem link. Concierge. Underground shopping arcade with Metro subway stop. Gift shop. Extensive exercise room. Refrigerators, minibars; microwaves available. Many balconies. Cr cds: A, C, D, DS, JCB, MC, V.

D ⌨ ⛲ 🏃 ⛲ 🏃

★ ★ ★ **MARRIOTT WARDMAN PARK HOTEL.** *2660 Woodley Rd NW (20008). Phone 202/328-2000; fax 202/234-0015. www.marriott.com.* Located in a prestigious area of the capital, this hotel is just minutes from the National Zoo. It is ideal for business or leisure travelers. 1,350 rooms, 125 suites, 10 story. Mar-June: S, D $149-$209; each additional $30; suites $250-$2,200; under 18 free; lower rates rest of year. Crib free. Pet accepted. Complimentary coffee in rooms. Check-out noon. TV; cable (premium), VCR available. Balconies. Some refrigerators. Restaurant 6:30 am-11 pm. Bar 11-2 am. Exercise equipment, sauna. Heated pool. Valet parking $23; garage $19. Business center. Convention facilities. Concierge. Gift shop. Cr cds: A, C, D, DS, ER, JCB, MC, V.

D ⌨ ⛲ 🏃 ⛲ 🏃

★ ★ ★ **MARRIOTT WASHINGTON.** *1221 22nd St NW (20037). Phone 202/872-1500; toll-free 800/228-9290; fax 202/872-1424. www.marriott.com/waswe.* Located in the West End, just on the edge of Georgetown, this hotel offers the facilities, amenities, and services that business travelers have come to expect, as well as comfort and convenience for leisure travelers, minutes from DC attractions. 416 rooms, 9 story. Check-out noon, check-in 4 pm. TV; cable (premium). In-room modem link. Restaurant. Bar. In-house fitness room, sauna. Pool, poolside service, lifeguard. Business center. Concierge. Luxury level. Cr cds: A, C, D, DS, MC, V. **$$**

D ⛲ 🏃 ⛲ 🏃

★ ★ **MARRIOTT WASHINGTON METRO CENTER.** *775 12th St NW (20005). Phone 202/737-2200; fax 202/347-5886. www.marriotthotels.com.* Located in the heart of downtown, business travelers will appreciate the location, facilities and amenities of this hotel. 345 rooms, 15 story. Check-out noon, check-in 4 pm. TV; cable (premium). In-room modem link. Restaurant. Bar. Room service to midnight. Babysitting services available. In-house fitness room, sauna. Indoor pool, whirlpool. Valet parking fee. Business center. Concierge, luxury level. Cr cds: A, C, D, DS, ER, JCB, MC, V. **$$**

D ⛲ 🏃 ⛲ 🏃

★ ★ **THE MELROSE HOTEL.** *2430 Pennsylvania Ave NW (20037). Phone 202/955-6400; toll-free 800/MELROSE; fax 202/775-8489. www.melrosehotel.com.* 240 rooms, 37 suites, 8 story. S $179-$219; D $199-$229; each additional $20; suites $285-$850; under 17 free; monthly rates; weekend plans. Crib free. Valet garage parking $16. TV; cable, VCR available. Complimentary coffee in rooms. Restaurant 6:30 am-11 pm. Room service 24 hours. Bar 11-1 am. Check-out noon. Meeting rooms. Business services available. In-room modem link. Concierge. Exercise equipment. Bathroom phones; microwaves available. Classic English furnishings, art. Cr cds: A, C, D, DS, JCB, MC, V.

D 🏃 ⛲ SC

★ ★ ★ **MONARCH HOTEL.** *2401 M St NW (20037). Phone 202/429-2400; toll-free 877/222-2266; fax 202/457-5010. www.monarchdc.com.* This recently renovated property is within walking distance of Georgetown and minutes from many national attractions. 415 rooms, 10 story. S, D $235-$330; each additional $30; suites $1,100-$3,000; under 18 free; weekend, summer rates. Crib free. Pet accepted, some restrictions. Check-out 1 pm. TV; cable (premium), CD player. In-room modem link. Some balconies. Bathroom phones, refrigerators, minibars. Restaurant 6:30 am-11 pm. Bar 4 pm-midnight; entertainment. Room service 24 hours. Exercise room; sauna, steam room. Indoor pool; whirlpool. Squash, racquetball courts. Covered parking; valet $23. Business center. Convention facilities. Concierge. Gift shop. Cr cds: A, C, D, DS, JCB, MC, V.

D ⛵ 🛏 ⛷ SC 🏃

★ ★ ★ **OMNI SHOREHAM HOTEL.** *2500 Calvert St NW (20008). Phone 202/234-0700; toll-free 800/843-6664; fax 202/265-7972. www.omnihotels.com.* A retreat in the middle of the city, this hotel is located on 11 acres in Rock Creek Park, offering guests picturesque views. 836 rooms, 34 suites, 8 story. S, D $109-$259; each additional $30; suites $400-$1,600; under 18 free; weekend, holiday rates. Crib free. Pet accepted, some restrictions. Check-out noon. TV; cable (premium), VCR available. Microwaves available in suites. Restaurant 6:30 am-11 pm. Bar 11-2 am; entertainment. Exercise equipment, sauna. Pool; wading pool, poolside service, lifeguard. Valet parking $26; self park $22; garage $14. Meeting rooms. Business center. Cr cds: A, C, D, DS, JCB, MC, V.

D ⛵ 🛏 ⛷ SC 🏃

★ ★ **ONE WASHINGTON CIRCLE HOTEL.** *1 Washington Cir NW (20037). Phone 202/872-1680; toll-free 800/424-9671; fax 202/887-4989. www.onewashcirclehotel.com.* 151 kitchen suites, 9 story. S, D $125-$275; each additional $15; under 18 free; weekend rates. Garage $16. TV; cable (premium), VCR available. Pool. Coffee in rooms. Restaurant 7 am-11:30 pm; Fri, Sat to midnight. Bar; entertainment. Check-out noon. Meeting rooms. Business services available. In-room modem link. Concierge. Exercise equipment. Some bathroom phones; microwaves available. Balconies. Elegant furnishings; landscaped grounds. Cr cds: A, C, D, DS, MC, V.

🛏 ⛷ SC

★ ★ ★ ★ **PARK HYATT WASHINGTON.** *1201 24th St NW (20037). Phone 202/789-1234; fax 202/457-8823. www.hyatt.com.* The awe-inspiring monuments and world-class museums of Washington, DC are within easy reach of the Park Hyatt. Located in the city's West End, the hotel is several blocks from Georgetown and downtown. The Park Hyatt maintains a handsome style throughout the hotel, from the gleaming lobby with its palette of gold and cream to the guest rooms and suites, which include the latest technology while maintaining a cozy ambience. Rivaling a small museum, the hotel boasts an impressive art collection: Picasso, Leger, Matisse, and Miro adorn the walls of the public and private spaces. Melrose (see) is recognized for its distinguished cuisine, served in the formal dining room or outside on the terrace during warmer months. The health club is comprehensive, including the latest exercise equipment, indoor pool, whirlpool, and sauna. 223 rooms, 10 story. Check-out noon, check-in 3 pm. TV; cable (premium), VCR available. Room service 24 hours. Restaurant. Bar. In-house fitness room, spa, steam room, sauna, massage. Indoor pool; whirlpool, poolside service. Valet parking. Cr cds: A, C, D, DS, MC, V. **$$$**

D ⛵ 🛏 ⛷

★ ★ **PHOENIX PARK HOTEL.** *520 N Capitol St NW (20001). Phone 202/638-6900; toll-free 800/824-5419; fax 202/393-3236. www.phoenixparkhotel.com.* 148 rooms, 9 story. S $179-$219; D $199-$239; each additional $20; suites $350-$750; under 16 free; weekend plans. Crib free. Valet parking $21. TV; cable (premium). Coffee in rooms. Restaurant 7-2 am. Bar from 11 am; Fri, Sat to 3 am; entertainment. Check-out 1 pm. Meeting rooms. Business center. In-room modem link. Exercise equipment. Minibars; some refrigerators. Near Capitol; traditional European décor. Cr cds: A, C, D, DS, MC, V.

D 🛏 ⛷ SC 🏃

★ ★ ★ **RENAISSANCE MAYFLOWER HOTEL.** *1127 Connecticut Ave NW (20036). Phone 202/347-3000; toll-free 800/HOTELS-1; fax 202/466-9082. www.renaissancehotels.com.* If you like to get comfortable in stately old hotels, you'll want to book a room at this high-rise property in the heart of the city's business district. Built in 1925 for Calvin Coolidge's inauguration, this hotel played host to the likes of Franklin Delano Roosevelt and J. Edgar Hoover. You'll find popular shops and restaurants just outside its front doors; the White House is only four blocks away. Be ready for the eye-pleasing view when you check in: all the gilded trim, crystal chandeliers, and Oriental rugs in the block-long lobby will awe you. The guest rooms themselves are quite homey, so you'll likely feel right at home in yours. For business travelers, each room has a desk with work lamp, a two-line phone with a dataport, and a speakerphone. For groups, the Mayflower offers state-of-the-art meeting facilities. 660 rooms, 186 suites, 10 story. Pet accepted. Check-out noon, check-in 3 pm. TV; cable (premium). In-room modem link. Restaurant. Bar; entertainment. Room service 24 hours. Babysitting services available. In-house fitness room, health club privileges. Valet parking $23. Business center. Concierge. Foreign currency exchange. Cr cds: A, C, D, DS, JCB, MC, V. **$$$**

D ⛵ 🛏 ⛷ 🏃

★ ★ ★ ★ **THE RITZ-CARLTON, WASHINGTON DC.** *1150 22nd St NW (20037). Phone 202/835-0500; fax 202/974-5519. www.ritzcarlton.com.* A convenient West End location, stylish accommodations, and superior service make The Ritz-Carlton, Washington, DC a favorite of sophisticated travelers. The supremely knowledgeable staff truly pampers its guests. The Ritz-Carlton's attention to detail is marvelous, and it continues to exceed expectations with innovative amenities. On-call technology butlers assist with computer woes, while the Luggageless Travel program is offered to frequent guests, inviting them to leave behind items for their next visit. Traditional European décor defines the 300 rooms and suites, and Club Level accommodations are treated to five food and beverage presentations daily. Perhaps most impressive is the Sports Club/LA access granted to all guests of The Ritz-Carlton. Adjacent to the hotel, this massive 100,000-square-foot complex is a veritable nirvana for fitness buffs with cutting-edge fitness programming, multiple athletic courts, and a pool. The complex also includes Splash, one of Washington's leading day spas. 300 rooms, 15 story. Pet accepted. Check-out noon, check-in 3 pm. TV; cable (premium). In-room modem link. Restaurant. Bar. Babysitting services available. In-house fitness room, exercise room, spa. Indoor pool, whirlpool. Business center. Concierge. Cr cds: A, C, D, DS, ER, JCB, MC, V. **$$$**

★ ★ ★ **THE RITZ-CARLTON GEORGETOWN.** 3100 South St NW (20007). Phone 202/835-0500; toll-free 800/241-3333; fax 202/974-5519. www.ritzcarlton.com. Embassy delegations often stay at this elegant, intimate hotel that blends contemporary décor with a historical setting. It's located on the banks of the Potomac River in Washington Harbour, an entertainment/residential/office complex located on land that was once the site of the original village of George Towne. Many of its executive suites and deluxe rooms offer gorgeous river views, and each comes with all the extra creature comforts you'd expect from a Ritz-Carlton, including feather duvets, goose-down pillows, and oversized marble baths. But don't spend all your time in your cushy room. Sip one of the fire-red martinis served in the Degrees Bar and Lounge, and then dine in Fahrenheit, which dishes out American/Italian cuisine. Soothe yourself with a facial or a full-body massage at the Boutique Spa, or tone those muscles at the fully equipped fitness center. 86 rooms. Pet accepted. Check-out noon, check-in 3 pm. TV; cable (premium). Restaurant. Bar. Babysitting services available. In-house fitness room, spa. Cr cds: A, C, D, DS, ER, JCB, MC, V. **$$$$**

★ ★ ★ ★ **THE ST. REGIS, WASHINGTON.** 923 16th and K sts NW (20006). Phone 202/638-2626; toll-free 800/562-5661; fax 202/638-4231. www.sheraton.com. The St. Regis is a treasure in the nation's capital. Since 1926, the St. Regis has been a preferred residence of discerning travelers visiting Washington. Just a stone's throw from the White House, the hotel enjoys a prime city location with nearly all of Washington's attractions nearby. Stepping into this esteemed hotel offers an enchanting glimpse of a grander time. Its gilded lobby of coffered ceilings and sparkling chandeliers is a work of art. Reflecting its Italian Renaissance roots, the 193 rooms and suites recall the splendor of European palaces with silk-covered walls and antique furnishings. English-style butlers attend to the individual needs of each guest. Formal afternoon tea is served to the gentle strains of a harp, and dining at the Library Restaurant completes this sublimely elegant experience. 193 rooms, 8 story. Pet accepted, some restrictions; fee. Check-out 1 pm, check-in 3 pm. TV; cable (premium), VCR available. In-room modem link. Room service 24 hours. Restaurant. Bar. Concierge. Babysitting services available. In-house fitness room, health club privileges. Valet parking. Cr cds: A, C, D, DS, ER, JCB, MC, V. **$$$**

★ ★ **SUMMERFIELD SUITES EMBASSY SQUARE.** 2000 North St NW (20036). Phone 202/659-9000; toll-free 800/424-2999; fax 202/429-9546. www.staydc.com. This hotel is located just a mile from the White House and near more than 40 restaurants and shops. 278 suites, 10 story. Mar-mid-June, mid-Sept-mid-Nov: S $139-$250; D $159-$279; each additional $20; under 18 free; weekly, weekend rates; lower rates rest of year. Crib free. Garage $15. TV; cable (premium). Pool; lifeguard. Complimentary continental breakfast. Check-out noon. Coin laundry. Meeting rooms. Business services available. In-room modem link. Exercise equipment. Microwaves. Some balconies. Cr cds: A, C, D, DS, MC, V.

★ ★ ★ **SWISSOTEL WASHINGTON - THE WATERGATE.** 2650 Virginia Ave NW (20037). Phone 202/965-2300; toll-free 800/424-2736; fax 202/337-7915. www.swissotel.com. Neighboring the Kennedy Center along the Potomac River, this luxury hotel is walking distance to the mall and historic Georgetown. Views from the expansive guest rooms make any extended stay a pleasure. 232 rooms, 13 story. S, D $225-$255; each additional $25; suites $245-$385; under 18 free; weekend, holiday rates. Crib free. Pet accepted, some restrictions. Valet parking $25. TV; cable (premium), VCR available (movies). Indoor pool; whirlpool, lifeguard. Restaurant (see AQUARELLE). Room service 24 hours. Bar 11:30-1 am; pianist. Check-out noon. Meeting rooms. Business center. In-room modem link. Concierge. Shopping arcade. Barber, beauty shop. Exercise room; sauna, steam room. Massage. Bathroom phones, minibars; microwaves available. Many balconies. Kennedy Center adjacent. Overlooks Potomac River. Cr cds: A, C, D, DS, JCB, MC, V.

★★ **TOPAZ HOTEL.** *1733 North St NW (20036). Phone 202/393-3000; toll-free 800/424-2950; fax 202/785-9581. www.topazhotel.com.* 99 kitchen units, 10 story. S $140-$195; D $160-$215; each additional $20; under 12 free; weekend plans. Crib free. Garage $13. TV; cable (premium), VCR available. Complimentary continental breakfast, coffee in rooms. Restaurant 7 am-2:30 pm, 5-10 pm; weekend hours vary. Bar 5-10 pm. Check-out noon. Meeting rooms. Business services available. In-room modem link. Health club privileges. Refrigerators, microwaves. On the site of the "Little White House" where Theodore Roosevelt lived during his vice-presidency and first weeks of his presidency. Cr cds: A, C, D, DS, JCB, MC, V.

★★★ **WASHINGTON COURT HOTEL.** *525 New Jersey Ave NW (20001). Phone 202/628-2100; toll-free 800/321-3010; fax 202/879-7918. www.washingtoncourthotel.com.* The elegant 4-story lobby sets the stage at this luxury business hotel, two blocks from the Capitol Building. 264 rooms, 15 story. S, D $195-$275; each additional $25; suites $250-$1,500; under 16 free; weekend rates. Crib free. Pet accepted, some restrictions. Valet parking $24. TV; cable (premium), VCR available. Restaurant 6:30 am-11 pm. Bar; pianist. Check-out noon. Meeting rooms. Business services available. In-room modem link. Concierge. Exercise equipment. Gift shop. Bathroom phones. Large atrium lobby. Cr cds: A, C, D, DS, MC, V.

★★★ **THE WESTIN EMBASSY ROW.** *2100 Massachusetts Ave NW (20008). Phone 202/293-2100; toll-free 800/434-9990; fax 202/293-0641. www.westin.com.* Since 1927 this Embassy Row property has welcomed guests with turn-of-the-century style. All 206 rooms and suites are decorated with Federal and Empire furnishings, including rich fabrics and antique reproductions, and boast beautiful views of Washington Cathedral and historic Georgetown. Join the distinguished political and social crowd at the Jockey Club for innovative American cuisine. 206 rooms, 8 story. S, D $185-$500; suites $400-$3,000; under 18 free; weekend rates. Crib free. Valet parking $23. TV; cable (premium), VCR available. Restaurant 6:30 am-10:30 pm. Bar 3 pm-1 am; entertainment. Check-out noon. Meeting rooms. Business center. In-room modem link. Concierge. Tennis privileges. Golf privileges. Exercise equipment; sauna. Massage. Health club privileges. Bathroom phones, minibars. Cr cds: A, C, D, DS, JCB, V.

★★★ **THE WESTIN GRAND.** *2350 M St NW (20037). Phone 202/429-0100; toll-free 888/627-8406; fax 202/429-9759. www.westin.com.* Not as glitzy as many of the other top DC properties, the Westin offers attentive service and a more private, low key environment than some of the others. The rooms are comfortable and stylish with ultracomfortable beds and sizeable bathrooms. 263 rooms, 4 story. D $249-$325. Check-out noon. TV; cable (premium), VCR available. In-room modem link. Restaurant 6:30 am-10:30 pm. Bar. Room service 24 hours. Exercise equipment. Heated pool, poolside service. Covered valet parking $20/day. Business center. Concierge. Luxury level. Cr cds: A, C, D, DS, JCB, MC, V.

★★★ **WILLARD INTER-CONTINENTAL WASHINGTON.** *1401 Pennsylvania Ave NW (20004). Phone 202/628-9100; toll-free 800/327-0200; fax 202/637-7326. www.washington.interconti.com.* The Willard Inter-Continental is steeped in history. Only two blocks from the White House, this legendary Beaux Arts hotel has been at the center of Washington's political scene since 1850. The Willard's lobby has always served as a drawing room to the world; it is here that Lincoln held fireside staff meetings, Grant escaped the rigors of the White House to enjoy brandy and cigars, and the term "lobbyist" was coined. Henry Clay shared the secret of the mint julep in the Round Robin Bar, while the Willard Room's continental cuisine (see WILLARD ROOM) makes history today. This landmark's guest rooms and suites are a traditional blend of Edwardian and Victorian styles furnished in deep jewel tones. The Jenny Lind suite is perfect for honeymooners with its mansard roof and canopy bed, while the Oval suite, inspired by the office of the same name, makes guests feel like masters of the universe. 341 rooms, 12 story. Pet accepted, some restrictions. Check-out noon, check-in 3 pm. TV; cable (premium), VCR available. In-room modem link. Room service 24 hours. Restaurant. Bar. Babysitting services available. In-house fitness room. Valet parking, covered parking. Business center. Concierge. Cr cds: A, C, D, DS, ER, JCB, MC, V. **$$$$**

★★ **WYNDHAM CITY CENTER HOTEL.** *1143 New Hampshire Ave NW (20037). Phone 202/775-0800; toll-free 800/544-5064; fax 202/331-9491. www.wyndham.com.* 352 rooms, 16 suites, 9 story. Mar-May, Aug-Oct: S $199-$220; D $219-$245; each additional $15; suites $250-$600; under 18 free; lower rates rest of year. Crib free. Parking $22. TV; cable (premium). Coffee in rooms. Restaurant 6 am-10 pm. Bar noon-1 am; entertainment Mon-Fri. Check-out noon. Meeting rooms. Business center. In-room modem link. Concierge. Gift shop. Exercise equipment. Health club privileges. Some refrigerators. Luxury level. Cr cds: A, C, D, DS, JCB, MC, V.

All Suites

★ ★ **EMBASSY SUITES.** *1250 22nd St NW (20037). Phone 202/857-3388; toll-free 800/362-2779; fax 202/293-3173. www.embassysuites.com.* This downtown hotel is conveniently located near all attractions and the business district. 318 suites, 9 story. S $159-$369; D $179-$389; each additional $20; 2-bedroom suites $600-$900; under 16 free; weekend rates. Crib free. TV; cable (premium). Indoor pool; whirlpool, lifeguard. Complimentary full breakfast, coffee in rooms. Restaurant 11 am-11 pm. Bar. Check-out noon. Meeting rooms. Business center. In-room modem link. Concierge. Exercise equipment; sauna. Game room. Refrigerators, microwaves, wet bars. Cr cds: A, C, D, DS, JCB, MC, V.

D ⊷ 🖈 ⊠ SC 🏃

★ ★ **RIVER INN.** *924 25th St NW (20037). Phone 202/337-7600; toll-free 800/424-2741; fax 202/337-6520. www.theriverinn.com.* 126 kitchen suites. S, D $99-$219; each additional $15; under 18 free; weekend rates; higher rates Apr-May, Sept-Oct. Crib free. Pet accepted, some restrictions; $100. Parking $20. TV; cable (premium). Restaurant 7-10 am, 11:30 am-2 pm, 5-10 pm; Sat 8-10 am, 11 am-2 pm, 5:30-11:30 pm; Sun 8-10 am, 11 am-2 pm, 5-10 pm. Bar. Check-out noon. Meeting room. Business services available. In-room modem link. Health club privileges. Microwaves. Cr cds: A, C, D, MC, V.

D ⊷ ⊠ SC

★ **WASHINGTON SUITES GEORGETOWN.** *2500 Pennsylvania Ave NW (20037). Phone 202/333-8060; toll-free 877/736-2500; fax 202/338-3818. www.washington suiteshotel.com.* 123 kitchen suites, 10 story. S, D $109-$269; each additional $20; under 18 free. Crib free. Pet accepted; $15/day. Garage $23. TV; cable (premium). Coffee in rooms. Restaurant adjacent 11 am-midnight. Check-out noon. Business services available. In-room modem link. Health club privileges. Microwaves. Cr cds: A, C, D, DS, MC, V.

⊷ ⊠ SC

B&B/Small Inns

★ **KALORAMA GUEST HOUSE.** *1854 Mintwood Pl NW (20009). Phone 202/667-6369; fax 202/319-1262. www.washingtonpost.com/yp/kgh.* 30 rooms, some share bath. 3 story. S $55-$95; D $60-$100; each additional $5; suites $95-$135; weekly rates. Complimentary continental breakfast. Check-out 11 am, check-in noon. TV in common room. Limited parking available. Business services. Created from four Victorian town houses (1890s); rooms individually decorated. Totally nonsmoking. Cr cds: A, D, DS, MC, V.

⊠ SC

★ **KALORAMA GUEST HOUSE.** *2700 Cathedral Ave NW (20008). Phone 202/328-0860; fax 202/328-8730.* 19 rooms, 7 share baths. 2 suites, 4 story. No room phones. Mar-mid-June, Sept-Nov: S $45-$95; D $55-$105; each additional $5; weekly rates; lower rates rest of year. Children over 5 years only. Complimentary continental breakfast. Check-out 11 am, check-in noon. TV in sitting room. Free laundry facilities. Restaurant nearby. Limited off-street parking. Two early 20th-century townhouses (1910). Cr cds: A, C, D, DS, MC, V.

⊠

★ ★ ★ **MORRISON CLARK HOTEL.** *1015 L St NW (20001). Phone 202/898-1200; toll-free 800/332-7898; fax 202/289-8576. www.morrisonclark.com.* This small, elegant hotel has historic charm, architecture, furnishings, and paintings. The guest rooms are all renovated with the most up-to-date amenities. Guests will enjoy a visit to the capital that will take them back to the time when the nation was first born. 54 units, 14 suites, 4 story. Mar-June, Sept-Nov: S $155-$240; D $175-$260; each additional $20; suites $180-$240; under 12 free; weekend rates; lower rates rest of year. Crib free. Complimentary continental breakfast. Check-out noon, check-in 3 pm. TV; cable (premium), VCR available. In-room modem link. Minibars; microwaves available. Valet services. Dining room (see MORRISON-CLARK). Room service. Health club privileges. Exercise equipment. Underground parking. Business services. Restored Victorian mansion (1864); period furnishings. Cr cds: A, C, D, DS, MC, V.

🖈 ⊠ SC

★ **TAFT BRIDGE INN.** *2007 Wyoming Ave NW (20009). Phone 202/387-2007; fax 202/387-5019. www.taftbridgeinn.com.* 12 rooms, 7 share bath, 3 with shower only, 3 story. Mar-June, Sept-Nov: S $59-$135; D $84-$150; each additional $15; weekly, holiday rates; lower rates rest of year. TV in some rooms; cable, VCR available. Complimentary full breakfast. Restaurant nearby. Check-out 11 am, check-in 2 pm. In-room modem link. Valet service. Guest laundry. Some balconies. Georgian-style house built in 1905; eclectic antique, art collection. Totally nonsmoking. Cr cds: MC, V.

⊠

★ **WINDSOR INN.** *1842 16th St NW (20009). Phone 202/667-0300; toll-free 800/423-9111; fax 202/667-4503.* 45 rooms, 9 suites, 3 story. No elevator. S $79-$110; D $89-$139; suites $105-$175; under 14 free; weekend rates. Crib free. Complimentary continental breakfast. Check-out noon, check-in 2 pm. TV; cable (premium). Refrigerator in suites. Restaurant nearby. Health club privileges. Business services. Originally a boarding house (1922). Cr cds: A, C, D, MC, V.

⊠ SC

Restaurants

★ ★ ★ **1789.** *1226 36th St NW (20007). Phone 202/965-1789; fax 202/337-1541. www.1789restaurant.com.* This quietly elegant establishment, located just on the edge of Georgetown University's campus, is a top destination for students with visiting relatives. The service is extraordinary. Specializes in seafood, rack of lamb. Hours: 6-10 pm; Fri, Sat to 11 pm. Closed Dec 25. Dinner $18-$38, prix fixe: pre-theater dinner $25. Bar. In restored mansion; 5 dining rooms on 3 levels. Jacket required. Reservations accepted. Valet parking. Cr cds: A, C, D, DS, MC, V.

★ ★ ★ **701 RESTAURANT.** *701 Pennsylvania Ave NW (20004). Phone 202/393-0701; fax 202/393-0242.* Overlooking the Navy Memorial fountains, this restaurant features a varied menu as well as a caviar bar. The roomy tables, comfortable chairs, and live piano music provide a nice atmosphere for guests. Continental menu. Closed holidays. Lunch, dinner. Bar. Reservations accepted. Outdoor seating. Cr cds: A, DS, MC, V. **$$$**

Ⓓ

★ ★ **ADITI.** *3299 M St NW (20007). Phone 202/625-6825.* Indian, seafood, vegetarian menu. Closed Thanksgiving. Lunch, dinner. Bar. Cr cds: A, D, DS, MC, V. **$**

★ **AFTERWORDS.** *1517 Connecticut Ave NW (20036). Phone 202/387-1462; fax 202/232-6777. www.kramers.com.* Closed Thanksgiving, Dec 25. Breakfast, lunch, dinner, brunch. Bar. Entertainment Wed-Sat. Outdoor dining. In 2-story greenhouse and terrace behind Kramer Books bookshop. Cr cds: A, D, MC, V. **$**

Ⓓ

★ ★ **ANNA MARIA'S.** *1737 Connecticut Ave NW (20009). Phone 202/667-1444; fax 202/667-2699.* Italian menu. Specialties: homemade pasta, veal. Hours: 11-1 am; Fri to 3 am; Sat 5 pm-3 am; Sun 5 pm-1 am. Closed holidays. Lunch $7.95-$10.95, dinner $12.95-$19.95. Bar. Reservations accepted. Atrium room; fireplace. Cr cds: A, D, DS, MC, V.

★ ★ ★ **AQUARELLE.** *2650 Virginia Ave NW (20037). Phone 202/298-4455; fax 202/298-4483.* Continental menu. Breakfast, lunch, dinner, Sun brunch. Bar. Valet parking available. Cr cds: A, D, DS, MC, V. **$$**

Ⓓ

★ **AUSTIN GRILL.** *2404 Wisconsin Ave NW (20007). Phone 202/337-8080. www.austingrill.com.* Tex-Mex menu. Southwestern décor. Hours: 11:30 am-11 pm; Mon to 10:30 pm; Fri, Sat to midnight; Sun 11 am-10:30 pm. Closed Thanksgiving, Dec 25. Lunch $4.95-$14.95. Dinner $4.95-$14.95. Sun brunch $4.95-$6.95. Bar. Cr cds: A, D, DS, MC, V.

★ ★ **BACCHUS.** *1827 Jefferson Pl NW (20036). Phone 202/785-0734. www.bacchusdc.net.* Lebanese menu. Closed Sun; holidays. Lunch, dinner. Valet parking (dinner). Cr cds: A, MC, V. **$$**

✑

★ ★ **BEDUCI.** *2100 P St NW (20037). Phone 202/223-3824; fax 202/296-1143. www.beduci.com.* Mediterranean menu. Closed late Aug; holidays. Lunch, dinner. Bar. Three dining areas. Cr cds: A, D, DS, MC, V. **$$$**

★ **BILLY MARTIN'S TAVERN.** *1264 Wisconsin Ave NW (20007). Phone 202/333-7370; fax 202/333-6089. www.billymartinstavern.com.* Seafood, steak menu. Closed Dec 25. Breakfast, lunch, dinner; Sat, Sun brunch. Bar. Established 1933. Reservations accepted. Outdoor dining. Cr cds: A, D, DS, MC, V. **$**

★ ★ ★ **BISTRO BIS.** *15 E Street NW (20001). Phone 202/661-2700; fax 202/661-2747. www.bistrobis.com.* The long zinc bar is the only concession to the bistro theme at this sleek, downtown spot. The food is classic French bistro, with well-executed items. As unstuffy as DC gets; a fun night out. Closed Dec 25. Lunch, dinner, brunch. Entertainment. Children's menu. Cr cds: A, D, DS, MC, V. **$$**

Ⓓ ✑

★ ★ **BISTRO FRANCAIS.** *3128 M St NW (20007). Phone 202/338-3830; fax 202/338-1421.* Country French menu. Specializes in rotisserie chicken, fresh seafood. Hours: 11-3 am; Fri, Sat to 4 am; early-bird dinner 5-7 pm, 10:30 pm-1 am; Sat, Sun brunch 11 am-4 pm. Closed Dec 24, 25. Lunch $6.95-$14.95, Sat, Sun brunch $18.95. Reservations accepted. Cr cds: A, D, MC, V.

Ⓓ

★ ★ **BISTROT LEPIC.** *1736 Wisconsin Ave NW (20007). Phone 202/333-0111; fax 202/333-2209. www.bistrotlepic.net.* French menu. Closed Mon; holidays. Lunch, dinner. Storefront restaurant. Cr cds: A, D, DS, MC, V. **$$$**

★ ★ ★ **BOMBAY CLUB.** *815 Connecticut Ave NW (20006). Phone 202/659-3727; fax 202/659-5012.* This restaurant maintains its position as one of the most respected Indian restaurants in the area. The menu is divided into sections including house, vegetarian, Goan, Moghlai and Northwest Frontier specialties. Indian menu. Lunch, dinner $7-$18.50. Hours: 11:30 am-2:30 pm, 6-10:30 pm; Sat 6-11 pm; Sun 5:30-9 pm; Sun brunch 11:30 am-2:30 pm. Closed Dec 25, Jan 1. Sun brunch $16.50. Bar 11:30 am-3 pm, 5-11 pm. Reservations accepted. Valet parking (dinner). Outdoor dining. Cr cds: A, DS, MC, V.

Ⓓ

★ ★ **BOMBAY PALACE.** *2020 K St NW (20006). Phone 202/331-4200; fax 202/331-1505. www.bombay-palace. com.* Northern Indian menu. Indian décor and original art; 350-gallon fish tank. Lunch, dinner. Bar. Reservations accepted. Totally nonsmoking. Cr cds: A, DS, MC, V. **$$**
D ⊠

★ **THE BREAD LINE.** *1751 Pennsylvania Ave NW (20006). Phone 202/822-8900; fax 202/822-8256.* Closed Sat, Sun. Breakfast, lunch. Outdoor seating. Food inspired by international street foods. Cr cds: A, MC, V. **$**
D

★ **BUA.** *1635 P St NW (20036). Phone 202/265-0828. www.buathai.com.* Thai menu. Closed Thanksgiving, Dec 25. Lunch, dinner. Bar. Outdoor seating. Cr cds: A, C, D, DS, MC, V. **$**
D

★ **BURMA.** *740 6th St NW (20001). Phone 202/638-1280.* Burmese menu. Closed holidays. Lunch, dinner. Cr cds: A, C, D, DS, MC, V. **$**

★ ★ **BUSARA.** *2340 Wisconsin Ave NW (20007). Phone 202/337-2340; fax 202/333-1364. www.busara.us.* Thai menu. Closed holidays. Lunch, dinner. Bar. Reservations required Fri, Sat. Outdoor seating. Cr cds: A, D, DS, MC, V. **$**
D

★ **C.F. FOLKS.** *1225 19th St NW (20036). Phone 202/293-0162; fax 202/457-9078.* Old-fashioned lunch counter. Closed Sat, Sun; holidays. Outdoor seating. Cash only. Cr cds: A, D, DS, MC, V. **$**
D

★ ★ ★ **CAFE15.** *806 15th St NW (200005). Phone 202/737-8800; fax 202/730-8500.* French menu. Breakfast, lunch, dinner. Bar. Casual attire. Outdoor seating. **$$$**
D

★ ★ **CAFE ATLANTICO.** *405 8th St NW (20004). Phone 202/393-0812; fax 202/393-0555. www.cafeatlanticodc .com.* Latin American menu. Menu changes bi-weekly. Closed holidays. Lunch, dinner, brunch. Bar. Valet parking. Outdoor seating. Cr cds: A, D, DS, MC, V. **$$$**
D

★ ★ **CAFE MILANO.** *3251 Prospect St NW (20007). Phone 202/333-6183; fax 202/333-6594. www.cafemilano.net.* Italian menu. Closed Thanksgiving, Dec 25. Lunch, dinner. Bar. Outdoor seating. Large tie/scarf collection hanging on walls. Cr cds: A, C, D, DS, MC, V. **$$**
D

★ **CAFE MOZART.** *1331 H St NW (20005). Phone 202/347-5732; fax 202/347-4958. www.cafemozartgermandeli. com.* Austrian, German menu. Closed Jan 1, Thanksgiving, Dec 25. Breakfast, lunch, dinner. Bar. Entertainment Thurs-Sat. Children's menu. German deli on premises. Cr cds: A, C, D, DS, MC, V. **$$**
D

★ ★ ★ **THE CAPITAL GRILLE.** *601 Pennsylvania Ave NW (20004). Phone 202/737-6200; fax 202/637-8821. www.thecapitalgrille.com.* Specializes in steak. Hours: 11:30 am-3 pm, 5-10 pm; Fri, Sat 5-11 pm; Sun from 2 pm. Closed Thanksgiving, Dec 25. Dinner $17.95-$32.95. Bar. Reservations accepted. Free valet parking (dinner). Totally nonsmoking. Cr cds: A, D, DS, MC, V.
D ⊠

★ ★ **CASHION'S EAT PLACE.** *1819 Columbia Rd NW (20009). Phone 202/797-1819; fax 202/797-0048. www.cashionseatplace.com.* Specialties: lamb, duck, seafood. Closed Mon; holidays. Dinner, brunch. Bar. Valet parking. Outdoor seating. Cr cds: MC, V. **$$**
D

★ ★ ★ **CHRISTOPHER MARKS.** *1301 Pennsylvania Ave NW (20004). Phone 202/628-5939; fax 202/737-0072. www.opentable.com.* You'll feel like a power player upon stepping into this clubby restaurant. The menu is a bit predictable but all of the choices are well executed and served by a professional staff. Specializes in New England seafood pie, walnut-crusted salmon. Hours: 11:30 am-11 pm; Sat 4-11 pm; Mon to 10 pm. Closed Sun. Reservations accepted. Wine, beer. Lunch $7.50-$18; dinner $12-$28. Children's menu. Entertainment. Cr cds: A, C, D, MC, V.
D ⊠

★ ★ ★ ★ **CITRONELLE.** *3000 M St NW (20007). Phone 202/625-2150; fax 202/339-6326. www.citronelledc.com.* Citronelle's chef-owner Michel Richard is one talented guy. Not only has he created a restaurant that has stood the test of time (he's had it for more than ten years), but he has also managed to keep the menu vibrant, exciting, and just on the safe side of daring. Like his food, the restaurant is stylish and elegant. Filled with fresh flowers and lit with a creamy, golden glow, the room has a chic vibe and an open kitchen for a bird's-eye view of the chefs, dressed in white and hard at work. This is a terrific spot for most any occasion so long as fine dining is the order of business. Ingredients are the stars here; the chef manages to wow diners by highlighting the simple flavors of each dish's main component. Global accents—herbs, spices, fruits, nuts, and vegetables—come into play to draw out flavors, to spotlight sweetness or acidity, and to maintain balance on the palate. Richard is a poetic culinarian. Nabbing a seat at one of his coveted tables is like winning the lottery. French menu. Closed major holidays. Breakfast, lunch, dinner. Bar. Children's menu. Jacket required. Outdoor seating. Cr cds: A, D, DS, MC, V. **$$$**

D

★ ★ **CLYDE'S OF GEORGETOWN.** *3236 M St NW (20007). Phone 202/333-9180. www.clydes.com/ restaurants/cl-georgetown.html.* One of the oldest saloons in Washington, this is the original Clyde's (now one of a dozen establishments owned by the Clyde's Group). Its cozily crowded main bar draws a loyal following with its nice selection of draft beers. The brass-and-wood dining room features ambitious menu choices well beyond the burgers and chili for which the place is famous. Its afternoon appetizer offerings were the inspiration for the 1976 pop hit "Afternoon Delight." Seafood menu. Hours: 11:30-2 am; Fri to 3 am; Sat 10-3 am; Sun from 9 am. Closed Dec 25. Dinner $9.95-$14.95. Sunday brunch. Bars. Children's menu. Atrium dining. Cr cds: A, D, DS, MC, V.

D

★ ★ ★ **DC COAST.** *1401 K St NW (20005). Phone 202/ 216-5988; fax 202/371-2221. www.dccoast.com.* Specialties: Chinese-style smoked lobster, mushroom-crusted halibut. Closed Sun; holidays. Lunch, dinner. Cr cds: A, C, D, DS, MC, V. **$$$**

D

★ ★ **DISTRICT CHOPHOUSE.** *509 7th St NW (20004). Phone 202/347-3434; fax 202/347-3388. www. districtchophouse.com.* Closed Thanksgiving, Dec 25. Lunch, dinner. Bar. Brewery. Children's menu. Cr cds: A, MC, V. **$$**

D

★ ★ **FILOMENA.** *1063 Wisconsin Ave NW (20007). Phone 202/338-8800; fax 202/338-8806. www.filomena.com.* Italian menu. Closed Jan 1, Thanksgiving, Dec 25. Lunch, dinner, brunch. Bar. Cr cds: A, D, MC, V. **$$$**

★ **FRAN O'BRIEN'S STADIUM STEAK HOUSE.** *1001 16th St NW (20036). Phone 202/783-2599; fax 202/ 783-3444. www.fobss.com.* Closed holidays. Lunch, dinner. Bar. Children's menu. Cr cds: A, D, DS, MC, V. **$$**

D

★ ★ **GABRIEL.** *2121 P St NW (20037). Phone 202/ 956-6690; fax 202/956-6641. www.washingtonpost.com/ yp/gabriel.* Latin American, Spanish menu. Closed Dec 25. Breakfast, dinner, brunch. Bar. Cr cds: A, D, DS, MC, V. **$$**

D

★ ★ ★ **GALILEO.** *1110 21st St NW (20036). Phone 202/293-7191; fax 202/331-9364. www.robertodonna.com.* This is the flagship enterprise of Roberto Donna, the celebrity chef whose reputation in the area is legendary (he is also behind Il Radicchio, I Matti, and many others). In keeping with the cutting-edge trends, there's even a much-sought-after kitchen table. Northern Italian menu. Closed holidays. Lunch, dinner. Bar. Outdoor seating. Cr cds: A, D, DS, MC, V. **$$**

D

★ **GARRETT'S.** *3003 M St NW (20007). Phone 202/333-1033; fax 202/333-8055. www.garrettsdc.com.* Specializes in steak, pasta, seafood. Lunch, dinner. Bar. 1794 landmark building; originally house of MD governor T. S. Lee. Cr cds: A, D, DS, MC, V. **$**

★ ★ ★ **GEORGIA BROWN'S.** *950 15th St NW (20005). Phone 202/393-4499; fax 202/393-7134. www.gbrowns.com.* At this McPherson Square spot, one of Washington's favorite restaurants for several years running, diners will have trouble choosing from among the many creative, modern dishes. The dining room is the definition of "casual elegance." South Carolina Low Country menu. Specialties: head-on Carolina shrimp and grits with spicy sausage, frogmore stew, Southern fried chicken. Hours: 11:30 am-10:30 pm; Fri to 11:30 pm; Sat 5:30-11:30 pm; Sun 11:30 am-2:30 pm (brunch), 5:30-10:30 pm. Closed Dec 25. Lunch, dinner $6.95-$22.95. Bar. Jazz, blues Sun afternoons. Reservations accepted. Valet parking (dinner). View of McPherson Sqare. Cr cds: A, D, DS, MC, V.

D

★ ★ ★ **GERARD'S PLACE.** *915 15th St NW (20005). Phone 202/737-4445; fax 202/737-5555.* Gerard's Place is an intimate little hideaway for people who love the art of dining. Elegant and civilized, it is perfect for romance, special occasions, or dinner with close friends. The menu is a product of meticulous attention to detail. Fresh ingredients are at work here, as are classic French technique and a healthy dose of creativity. Aromatic herbs like sage, mint, basil, lavender, sorrel, and lemon thyme often play supporting roles. Meals are served on mismatched china plates—a nice touch that adds a sweet sense of home to this precious place. The kitchen offers a five-course tasting menu as well as a tempting à la carte menu. The wine list is lengthy and features mostly French bottles, with a more modest American selection. Desserts are all made to order and must be selected at the beginning of the meal, or at least 25 minutes before you'd like to dig in. These desserts are worth the wait, so don't miss out. French menu. Hours: 11:30 am-2:30 pm, 5:30-10 pm; Fri to 10:30 pm; Sat 5:30-10:30 pm. Closed Sun; holidays. Dinner $16.50-$32.50; prix fixe $78. Outdoor dining. Cr cds: A, D, MC, V.

D

★ ★ ★ **THE GRILL AT RITZ-CARLTON.** *1150 22nd St NW (20037). Phone 202/835-0500; fax 202/835-1588. www.ritzcarlton.com.* American menu. Hours: 6:30-10 am, 11 am-2:30 pm, 6 pm-midnight. Breakfast $12.95-$15.95, lunch $15.95-$20.05, dinner $19.95-$32.95. Reservations accepted. Cr cds: A, C, D, DS, ER, JCB, MC, V.

★ **GRILL FROM IPANEMA.** *1858 Columbia Rd NW (20009). Phone 202/986-0757; fax 202/265-4229. www.thegrillfromipanema.com.* Brazilian menu. Closed major holidays. Dinner, brunch. Bar. Cr cds: A, D, DS, MC, V. **$$**

Ⓓ

★ **GUAPO'S.** *4515 Wisconsin Ave NW (20016). Phone 202/686-3588; fax 202/686-5490. www.guaposrestaurant. com.* Latin American, Mexican menu. Specialties: fajitas. Hours: 11:30 am-11:30 pm; Fri, Sat to midnight. Lunch $6.95-$7.95, dinner $12. Bar. Reservations accepted. Outdoor dining. Colorful dining rooms; Mexican decor. Cr cds: A, D, MC, V.

Ⓓ

★ **GUARDS.** *2915 M St NW (20007). Phone 202/965-2350; fax 202/342-6112.* Continental, seafood menu. Lunch, dinner, Sun brunch. Bar. Cr cds: A, D, DS, MC, V. **$$**

★ **HAAD THAI.** *1100 New York Ave NW (20005). Phone 202/682-1111; fax 202/682-0824. www.haadthai.com.* Thai menu. Specialties: pad Thai, pla yang, surf 'n turf. Hours: 11:30 am-2:30 pm, 5-10:30 pm; Sun from noon pm. Closed holidays. Lunch $5.95-$8.50, dinner $8.95-$15.95. Bar. Reservations accepted. Tropical atmosphere. Cr cds: A, MC, V.

Ⓓ

★ ★ **HOGATE'S.** *800 Water St SW (20024). Phone 202/484-6300; fax 202/484-3840. www.arabian-nights.com.* Specialties: mariner's platter, wood-grilled fish. Closed Dec 25. Lunch, dinner, brunch. Bar. Brunch entertainment. Children's menu. Outdoor seating. Cr cds: A, D, DS, MC, V. **$$$**

Ⓓ

★ ★ **HUNAN CHINATOWN.** *624 H St NW (20001). Phone 202/783-5858; fax 202/393-1375. www.marriott worldcenter.com.* Hunan, Szechwan menu. Lunch, dinner. Modern, bilevel dining room. Cr cds: A, D, DS, MC, V. **$$**

★ **J. PAUL'S.** *3218 M St NW (20007). Phone 202/333-3450; fax 202/342-6721. www.j-pauls.com.* Lunch, dinner $8.50-$21.95. Hours: 11:30 am-11:30 pm; Fri, Sat 1 am; Sun brunch to 4 pm. Sun brunch $7.95-$12.95. Bar to 1:30 am. Children's menu. Cr cds: A, D, DS, MC, V.

Ⓓ

★ ★ **JALEO.** *480 7th St NW (20004). Phone 202/628-7949; fax 202/628-7952.* Spanish menu. Hours: 11:30 am-11:30 pm; Sun, Mon to 10 pm; Fri, Sat to midnight. Closed Thanksgiving, Dec 24, 25. Bar. Lunch $15, dinner $25. Specializes in hot and cold tapas, Spanish-style fish. Sevillanas dancers Wed nights. Valet parking $8. Murals of flamenco dancers. Cr cds: A, D, DS, MC, V.

Ⓓ

★ ★ ★ **THE JEFFERSON.** *16th and M sts (20036). Phone 202/833-6206; fax 202/331-7982. www.thejeffersondc.com.* Here, diners seeking an intimate, secluded restaurant will find professional and very discreet service, perfect for those seeking anonymity in this high-profile town. The chef demonstrates a high degree of culinary talent and sensibility with the freshest seasonal ingredients. Natural American cuisine. Breakfast, lunch, dinner, brunch. Bar. Valet parking. Cr cds: A, D, DS, MC, V. **$$**

Ⓓ

★ ★ ★ ★ **KINKEAD'S.** *2000 Pennsylvania Ave NW (20006). Phone 202/296-7700; fax 202/296-7688. www.kinkead.com.* Senators, journalists, models, financiers, and media moguls rub elbows at chef-owner Bob Kinkead's stunning spot for jazzy, distinctive, and fun-to-eat global fare. The deep cherry wood-paneled dining room has an intimate, clubby feel to it, with warm, low lighting, vintage wrought-iron staircases, tufted chocolate leather seating, and elegant table settings. As for what to eat, diners here have a tough choice to make. The palatial raw bar is a great place to start. But then again, the menu, which changes daily and draws influences from Spain, France, Italy, Morocco, and Asia, offers a terrific selection of appetizers, soups, salads, chops, and seafood, not to mention incredibly creative side dishes. It is not possible to order a disappointment. To complement the menu, you'll find one of the most user-friendly wine lists in the capital. The list is color coded from light to dark according to nose, weight, body, and flavor. Kinkead's hosts live jazz in the evenings and is a perfect choice for a lively meal with family, friends, or colleagues. Hours: 11:30 am-2:30 pm, 5:30-9:30 pm; Fri, Sat to 10 pm. Closed major holidays. Dinner $24-$32. Bar to midnight. Jazz pianist. Free valet parking (dinner). Cr cds: A, D, DS, MC, V.

Ⓓ

★ ★ **KRUPIN'S.** *4620 Wisconsin Ave NW (20016). Phone 202/686-1989; fax 202/686-3566.* Specialties: smoked fish, meatloaf. Closed Dec 25. Breakfast, lunch, dinner. Children's menu. Totally nonsmoking. Cr cds: A, MC, V. **$$**

Ⓓ ⊠

★ ★ **LA CHAUMIERE.** *2813 M St NW (20007). Phone 202/338-1784; fax 202/965-4597. www.washingtonpost/yp/ lachaumiere.* Country French menu. Specialties: seafood, veal, game. Hours: 11:30 am-2:30 pm, 5:30-10:30 pm; Sat from 5:30 pm. Closed Sun; holidays. Lunch $13-$18, dinner $14-$28. Family-owned. Reservations accepted. Intimate room with beamed ceiling, open-hearth fireplace. Cr cds: A, MC, V.

Ⓓ

★ ★ **LA COLLINE.** *400 N Capitol St NW (20001). Phone 202/737-0400; fax 202/737-3026.* French menu. Specialties: seasonal foods, fowl, seafood. Hours: 7-10 am, 11:30 am-3 pm, 6-10 pm; Sat from 6 pm. Closed Sun; holidays. Breakfast $3.50-$8.75, lunch $9-$17, dinner $15-$22. Prix fixe: dinner $22-$27. Bar. Reservations accepted. Outdoor dining. Across from Union Station. Cr cds: A, D, DS, MC, V.

Ⓓ

★★**LA FOURCHETTE.** *2429 18th St NW (20009). Phone 202/332-3077.* French menu. Closed holidays. Lunch, dinner, brunch. Former townhouse; painted murals on walls. Outdoor seating. Cr cds: A, D, MC, V. **$$**

★ ★ **LAURIOL PLAZA.** *1835 18th St NW (20009). Phone 202/387-0035; fax 202/362-5649. www.lauriol plazarestaurant.com.* Latin American menu. Lunch, dinner, brunch. Bar. Outdoor seating. Cr cds: A, DS, MC, V. **$$**

Ⓓ

★ ★ **LAVANDOU.** *3321 Connecticut Ave NW (20008). Phone 202/966-3002; fax 202/966-0982. www.lavandou restaurant.net.* Southern French menu. Hours: 11:30 am-10 pm; Fri, Sat to 11 pm. Closed holidays. Lunch $8.95-$14.95, dinner $15.95. Reservations accepted, required on weekends. Cr cds: A, D, MC, V.

Ⓓ

★ ★ **LEBANESE TAVERNA.** *2641 Connecticut Ave NW (20008). Phone 202/265-8681; fax 202/483-3007. www.lebanesetaverna.com.* Lebanese menu. Closed major holidays. Lunch, dinner. Bar. Cr cds: A, D, DS, MC, V. **$$**

Ⓓ

★ **LES HALLES.** *1201 Pennsylvania Ave NW (20004). Phone 202/347-6848; fax 202/347-6911. www.leshalles.net.* American, French menu. Lunch, dinner, brunch. Bar. Children's menu. Outdoor seating. Three-level dining area. Cr cds: A, D, DS, MC, V. **$$**

Ⓓ Ⓢ︎Ⓒ︎

★ ★ **LUIGINO.** *1100 New York Ave NW (20005). Phone 202/371-0595; fax 202/371-6482. www.luigino.com.* Nothern Italian menu. Closed holidays. Lunch, dinner. Bar. Children's menu. Outdoor seating. Cr cds: A, D, DS, MC, V. **$$**

Ⓓ

★ ★ ★ **MAKOTO RESTAURANT.** *4822 MacArthur Blvd NW (20007). Phone 202/298-6866; fax 202/625-6602.* Looking for the best Japanese food in town? Come here but be forewarned that reservations at this 25-seat restaurant are limited. For the uninitiated, we recommend the eight to ten course prix fixe meal. No matter what you select, you are guaranteed impeccable service of the freshest ingredients presented in an artful creation. Closed Mon. Lunch, dinner. Reservations required. Cr cds: MC, V. **$$$**

▧

★ **MARKET INN.** *200 E St SW (20024). Phone 202/554-2100; fax 202/863-1052. www.marketinndc.com.* Hours: 11 am-11 pm; Fri to midnight; Sat 4:30 pm-midnight; major holidays from 5 pm. Closed Thanksgiving, Dec 25. Lunch $10-$20, dinner $14.95-$22.95, Sunday brunch $19.95. Bar. Entertainment. Children's menu. Reservations accepted. Outdoor dining. English pub ambience. Cr cds: A, D, DS, MC, V.

Ⓓ

★ ★ ★ **MELROSE.** *1201 24th St NW (20037). Phone 202/955-3899; fax 202/408-6118.* Finding a hotel restaurant that feels like a dining experience and not just an obligatory feeding ground for the hotel's guests can be a tough task. The Melrose Restaurant, located in the Park Hyatt (see PARK HYATT WASHINGTON), is far from a standard hotel feeder. It is fairly formal in its décor, with cushioned neutral-toned seating, cream-colored walls, high ceilings, lots of windows, and lots of sunlight. The room is lovely, but in a battle between décor and food, the food wins hands down. The kitchen sees food as an inspiration for energy and creativity, and this contemporary menu is filled with dishes that are alive with flavor and ingenuity. It is clear that the chefs behind closed doors are not afraid to play with products from around the world. The menu shows a special fondness for Asian ingredients, but nods are also made to Spanish, Italian, and regional American styles of cooking. Contemporary American menu. Dinner, Sun brunch. Piano. Children's menu. Valet parking. Outdoor seating. Cr cds: A, D, DS, MC, V. **$$$**

Ⓓ

★ ★ ★ **MENDOCINO GRILL AND WINE BAR.** *2917 M St NW (20007). Phone 202/333-2912; fax 202/ 625-7888.* The excellent, all American wine list is the most impressive feature of this wine bar-cum-restaurant. The food is designed to complement the wine and the menu is comprised of creative choices that all sound tempting. The décor is upscale 1960s modern (think Brady Bunch wine bar) but it somehow manages to work. Lunch, dinner. Entertainment. Cr cds: A, D, DS, MC, V. **$$$**

Ⓓ

★ ★ **MESKEREM.** *2434 18th St NW (20009). Phone 202/462-4100; fax 202/362-5812. www.meskeremonline. com.* Ethiopian menu. Closed Thanksgiving, Dec 25. Lunch, dinner. Bar. Cr cds: A, MC, V. **$**

D

★ ★ **MONOCLE.** *107 D St NE (20002). Phone 202/546-4488; fax 202/546-7235.* Specialties: seafood, aged beef. Hours: 11:30 am-midnight. Closed Sat, Sun; holidays. A la carte entrées: lunch $13-$17, dinner $16-$25. Bar. Family-owned. Children's menu. Located in 1865 Jenkens Hill building; fireplace. Reservations accepted. Valet parking. Close to Capitol; frequented by members of Congress and other politicians. Cr cds: A, D, MC, V.

★ ★ **MORRISON-CLARK.** *1015 L St NW (20001). Phone 202/289-8580; fax 202/289-8576. www.morrison clark.com.* American style cuisine with Caribbean twist. Closed holidays. Lunch, dinner, brunch. Bar. Outdoor seating. Cr cds: A, D, DS, MC, V. **$$**

D

★ ★ ★ **MORTON'S OF CHICAGO.** *3251 Prospect St NW (20007). Phone 202/342-6258; fax 202/338-8033. www.mortons.com.* This Georgetown location is one of three in the DC area. Specialties: steak, lobster. Hours: 5:30-11 pm. Closed holidays. Dinner $20-$34. Bar. Reservations accepted. Valet parking. Cr cds: A, D, MC, V.

D

★ **MR. SMITH'S.** *3104 M St NW (20007). Phone 202/333-3104. www.mrsmiths.com.* Hours: 11:30-2 am; Fri, Sat to 3 am; Sat, Sun brunch 11 am-4:30 pm. Bar. Lunch, dinner $4.95-$14.95. Sat, Sun brunch $4.50-$8. Specializes in seafood, pasta, hamburgers. Pianist 9 pm-1 am. Old tavern atmosphere. Outdoor dining. Family-owned. Cr cds: A, MC, V.

★ **MR. YUNG'S.** *740 6th St NW (20001). Phone 202/628-1098; fax 202/628-1128.* Chinese, Cantonese menu. Hours: 11 am-10:30 pm. Lunch $5.95-$7.95, dinner $6.50-$25.95. Service bar. Enclosed outdoor dining. Cr cds: A, D, MC, V.

D

★ **MURPHY'S OF DC.** *2609 24th St NW (20008). Phone 202/462-7171; fax 202/462-7901. www.murphysofdc .com.* American, Irish menu. Lunch, dinner. Children's menu. Outdoor seating. Cr cds: A, D, MC, V. **$**

★ ★ **NATHAN'S.** *3150 M St NW (20007). Phone 202/338-2000; fax 202/333-2509.* American, northern Italian menu. Dinner, brunch. Bar. Cr cds: A, D, DS, MC, V. **$$**

★ ★ **NEW HEIGHTS.** *2317 Calvert St NW (20008). Phone 202/234-4110; fax 202/234-0789. www.newheights restaurant.com.* New American cuisine. Menu changes seasonally. Closed holidays. Dinner, brunch. Bar. Outdoor seating. Cr cds: A, D, DS, MC, V. **$$$**

★ ★ ★ **OBELISK.** *2029 P St NW (20036). Phone 202/872-1180.* Italian menu. Seasonal dishes. Menu changes daily. Hours: 6-10 pm. Closed Sun, Mon; holidays. Dinner $58. Totally nonsmoking. Cr cds: D, MC, V.

🚭

★ ★ **OCCIDENTAL GRILL.** *1475 Pennsylvania Ave NW (20004). Phone 202/783-1475; fax 202/783-1478. www.occidentaldc.com.* Regional American menu. Hours: 11:30 am-10:30 pm; Fri, Sat to 11 pm. Closed Thanksgiving, Dec 25. Lunch $10-$20. Bar. Reservations accepted. Cr cds: A, D, MC, V.

D

★ ★ **OLD EBBITT GRILL.** *675 15th St NW (20005). Phone 202/347-4800; fax 202/347-6136. www.ebbitt.com.* Proximity to the White House, monuments, and museums makes this famous watering hole a draw for the power-hungry as well as the merely hungry. Known for big breakfasts in the early hours and oysters and burgers later, Old Ebbitt also serves seasonal specialties such as corn on the cob and berry cobbler. Its Beaux Arts façade and glamorous marble, brass, and mahogany interior allow tourists to feel like high-placed political insiders. Seafood menu. Breakfast, lunch, dinner, brunch. Bar. In Vaudeville theater built in early 1900s. Victorian décor, gaslights; atrium dining. Valet parking (dinner, Sun brunch). Cr cds: A, D, DS, MC, V. **$$**

D

★ ★ **OLD EUROPE.** *2434 Wisconsin Ave NW (20007). Phone 202/333-7600; fax 202/625-0553. www.old-europe. com.* German menu. Closed July 4, Dec 24. Lunch, dinner. Children's menu. Cr cds: A, D, MC, V. **$$**

D SC

★ ★ **OVAL ROOM.** *800 Connecticut Ave NW (20006). Phone 202/463-8700; fax 202/785-9863. www. ovalroom.com.* New American cuisine. Menu changes seasonally. Hours: 11:30 am-3:00 pm, 5:30-10 pm; Fri, Sat to 10:30 pm. Closed Sun; July 4th, Dec 25. Dinner $16.95-$25.50. Bar. Reservations accepted. Valet parking after 5:30 pm. Outdoor dining. Cr cds: A, D, MC, V.

D

★ ★ ★ **PALM.** *1225 19th St NW (20036). Phone 202/293-9091; fax 202/775-1468. www.thepalm.com.* Specializes in steak, lobster. Closed holidays. Lunch, dinner. Bar. Valet parking (dinner). Cr cds: A, D, DS, MC, V. **$$$**

D

★ ★ **PAOLO'S.** *1303 Wisconsin Ave NW (20007). Phone 202/333-7353; fax 202/342-2846. www.capitalrestaurants. com.* California menu. Lunch, dinner, brunch. Bar.

Outdoor seating. Wood burning pizza oven. Cr cds: A, D, DS, MC, V. **$$**

🖼️

★ ★ **PESCE.** *2016 P St NW (20036). Phone 202/466-3474; fax 202/466-8302. www.pescebistro.com.* Seafood menu. Closed Jan 1, Memorial Day, Labor Day, Dec 25. Lunch, dinner. Valet parking Mon-Sat. Cr cds: A, D, DS, MC, V. **$$**

🖼️

★ **PIZZERIA PARADISO.** *2029 P St NW (20036). Phone 202/223-1245; fax 202/223-5699.* Italian menu. Hours: 11 am-11:30 pm; Fri, Sat to midnight; Sun noon-10 pm. Closed holidays. Lunch and dinner $10-$15. Totally nonsmoking. Cr cds: D, DS, MC, V.

🖼️

★ ★ ★ **PRIME RIB.** *2020 K St NW (20006). Phone 202/466-8811; fax 202/466-2010. www.theprimerib.com.* This K Street spot remains one of the best steakhouses inside the Beltway. Specialties: roast prime rib, Chesapeake seafood, aged thick-cut steak. Hours: 11:30 am-3 pm, 5-11 pm; Fri, Sat to 11:30 pm. Closed Sun; holidays. A la carte entrées: dinner $30. Lunch $18. Bar. Pianist. Jacket and tie required. Reservations accepted. Free valet parking (dinner). Art Deco decor; 1920s lithographs. 1940s New York supper club atmosphere. Cr cds: A, D, MC, V.

🖼️

★ **RAKU.** *1900 Q St NW (20009). Phone 202/265-7258; fax 202/265-5488. www.raku/dc.com.* Pan-Asian menu. Closed Thanksgiving, Dec 25. Lunch, dinner. Bar. Casual teahouse décor with varied Asian accents. Outdoor seating. Cr cds: A, MC, V. **$**

🖼️

★ ★ ★ **RED SAGE.** *605 14th St NW (20005). Phone 202/638-4444; fax 202/628-8430. www.redsage.com.* American, continental menu. Closed major holidays. Lunch, dinner. Bar. Children's menu. Casual attire. Outdoor seating. Cr cds: A, D, DS, MC, V. **$$**

🖼️

★ ★ ★ **RESTAURANT NORA.** *2132 Florida Ave NW (20008). Phone 202/462-5143; fax 202/234-6232. www.noras.com.* Organic seasonal ingredients, many purchased from local family farms, are the stars of this intimate, former 19th-century grocery store turned organic American eatery. Chef-owner Nora Pouillon is a pioneer in the organic movement; Restaurant Nora was the first certified organic restaurant in the country (95% of all products used are organic). And it's not only the purity of the edible ingredients that is attended to—all the water used at Nora is filtered three times on premises, including the water that washes your dishes and is used for cooking. While Nora's focuses on healthful cooking,

this is not flavorless spa cuisine. Pouillon coaxes intense flavors from nature's superstar ingredients, creating stylish, delicious meals that integrate accents from places far and near—from the American South to Spain, and from Latin America to Asia and India. (If you're looking for a soy burger on spelt bread, this is not the place.) The mouthwatering and imaginative menu changes daily and includes a selection of starters, main-course salads, and entrées, as well as two tasting menus. The rustic dining room is decorated with dried flowers and museum-quality antique Mennonite and Amish quilts. Soothing amber lighting warms the room, and Nora's wonderful food warms the tummy. Continental menu. Closed Sun; holidays; last week Aug, 1st week Sept. Dinner. Bar. Atrium dining. Totally nonsmoking. Cr cds: A, MC, V. **$$**

🖼️

★ ★ **SAIGON GOURMET.** *2635 Connecticut Ave NW (20008). Phone 202/265-1360; fax 202/265-2092.* Vietnamese menu. Hours: 11 am-3 pm, 5-10:30 pm. Closed Thanksgiving. Reservations accepted. Service bar. Lunch $5.95-$7.95, dinner $8.95-$13.95. Specialties: Saigon noodles, roasted quail, caramel chicken. Valet parking. Patio dining overlooking upper Connecticut Ave. Cr cds: A, D, DS, MC, V.

🖼️

★ **SAIGONNAIS.** *2307 18th St NW (20009). Phone 202/232-5300. www.dcnet.com/saigonnais.* Vietnamese menu. Closed Jan 1, Thanksgiving, Dec 25. Lunch, dinner. Outdoor seating. Cr cds: A, MC, V. **$**

★ ★ ★ **SAM AND HARRY'S.** *1200 19th St NW (20036). Phone 202/296-4333; fax 202/785-1070. www.samandharrys.com.* Specialties: prime aged beef, Maine lobster. Hours: 11:30 am-2:30 pm, 5:30-10:30 pm; Sat from 5:30 pm. Closed Sun; holidays. Dinner $20-$34. Bar. Reservations accepted. Valet parking (dinner). Cr cds: A, D, DS, MC, V.

🖼️

★ ★ **SEA CATCH.** *1054 31st St NW (20007). Phone 202/337-8855; fax 202/337-7159. www.seacatchrestaurant.com.* Seafood menu. Closed Sun. Lunch, dinner. Bar. Valet parking. Outdoor dining on deck overlooking historic Chesapeake and Ohio Canal. Cr cds: A, C, D, DS, MC, V. **$$**

🖼️

★ ★ ★ **SEASONS.** *2800 Pennsylvania Ave NW (20007). Phone 202/342-0444; fax 202/944-2076. www.fourseasons.com.* Enclosed in glass and tastefully decorated with deep armchairs, dark wood, fresh flowers, and a good dose of style, Seasons is the elegant flagship restaurant of the Four Seasons Hotel (see). The sophisticated American menu offers simple, elegant fare that makes this an ideal locale for a business meal. The kitchen is not

trying to win awards for wild, far-out food. The dishes here will all be familiar, but even the most familiar foods can surprise you when they're prepared with the best ingredients, passion, and skill. To complement the classic menu, you can chose from old-world or North American wines, or an extensive selection of wines by the glass. For an afternoon delight, stop by the Garden Terrace for tea service with all the trimmings—scones with clotted cream, cucumber and watercress sandwiches with the crusts cut off, petit fours, chocolate-dipped strawberries, and assorted butter cookies. Hours: 6:30-11 am, noon-2:30 pm, 6:30-10:30 pm; Sun brunch 10 am-2:30 pm. Dinner $25-$40. Sun brunch. Bar 11-2 am. Piano. Children's menu. Valet parking. Cr cds: A, D, DS, MC, V.
D

★ ★ **SEQUOIA.** *3000 K St NW (20007). Phone 202/ 944-4200; fax 202/944-4210. www.arkrestaurants.com.* American menu. Lunch, dinner, brunch. Bar. Outdoor seating. Cr cds: A, D, DS, MC, V. **$$**
D

★ **SUSHI-KO.** *2309 Wisconsin Ave NW (20007). Phone 202/333-4187; fax 202/333-7594. www.sushiko.us.* Japanese menu. Closed July 4, Thanksgiving, Dec 25. Lunch, dinner. Casual attire. Cr cds: A, MC, V. **$$$**
D

★ ★ ★ **TABERNA DEL ALABARDERO.** *1776 I St NW (20006). Phone 202/429-2200; fax 202/775-3713. www.americascuisine.com/dc/taberna.html.* The joyousness of this restaurant (a favorite of DC celebs for birthdays) is only matched by the highly skilled staff of servers. Basque, Spanish menu. Specialties: beef, fish, paella. Own baking. Hours: 11:30 am-2:30 pm, 6-10:30 pm; Fri to 11 pm; Sat 6-11 pm. Closed Sun; holidays. Tapas bar. Lunch $14-$20, dinner $16-$28. Complete meals: lunch $17.50, dinner $35. Bar. Jacket. Reservations accepted. Garage parking (dinner). Outdoor dining. Ornate, 19th-century Spanish décor. Flamenco dancers Mar, Oct. Cr cds: A, D, DS, MC, V.
D

★ ★ ★ **TEATRO GOLDONI.** *1909 K St (20036). Phone 202/955-9494; fax 202/955-9584. www.teatrogoldoni.com.* This restaurant serves innovative, complex Venetian dishes. Italian menu. Hours: 11:30 am-3 pm, 5:30-10 pm; Fri 11:30 am-2 pm, 5-10:30 pm; Sat 5-10:30 pm. Closed Sun, holidays. Lunch $20-$30, dinner $45-$60. Bar. Reservations accepted. Valet parking. Cr cds: A, C, D, DS, MC, V.
D

★ **THAI KINGDOM.** *2021 K St NW (20006). Phone 202/835-1700; fax 202/466-4147.* Thai menu. Closed holidays. Lunch, dinner. Bar. Cr cds: A, D, DS, MC, V. **$$**
D

★ **THE TOMBS.** *1226 36th St NW (20007). Phone 202/ 337-6668; fax 202/337-1541. www.clydes.com.* Did someone say "Rah"? Since 1962, this classic sports-themed bar and grill has been dear to the hearts of Georgetown University students, faculty, and alums—raucously dear to them when GU teams have a home game or are playing on TV. Vintage sporting prints and rowing paraphernalia contribute to the ambience. You'll find burgers, pizza, and other bar standards on the menu, as well as desserts (and a good wine list) from the restaurant upstairs, 1789. Closed Thanksgiving, Dec 24, 25. Lunch, dinner, brunch. Bar. Cr cds: A, D, DS, MC, V. **$**

★ ★ **TONY AND JOE'S SEAFOOD PLACE.** *3000 K St NW (20007). Phone 202/944-4545; fax 202/944-4587. www.tonyandjoes.com.* Closed Dec 25. Lunch, dinner, brunch. Bar. Entertainment Tues-Sat. Outdoor seating. Cr cds: A, D, DS, MC, V. **$$**
D

★ ★ **TONY CHENG'S MONGOLIAN BARBECUE.** *619 H St NW (20001). Phone 202/842-8669; fax 202/842-3669.* Mongolian barbecue menu. Lunch, dinner. Reservations accepted. Food bar encircles Mongolian grill. Cr cds: A, MC, V. **$$**
D

★ ★ **TWO QUAIL.** *320 Massachusetts Ave NE (20002). Phone 202/543-8030; fax 202/543-8035.* New American menu. Closed Dec 25. Lunch, dinner. Cr cds: A, D, DS, MC, V. **$$**

★ ★ ★ **VIDALIA.** *1990 M St NW (20036). Phone 202/ 659-1990; fax 202/223-8572. www.vidaliadc.com.* Chef-owner Jeffrey Buben, taking his lead from the South as well as the Chesapeake Bay, transforms regional cuisine into a delectable art. Specialties: sautéed shrimp with creamed grits, pan-roasted sweetbreads. Hours: 11:30 am-2:30 pm, 5:30-10 pm; Fri to 10:30 pm; Sat 5:30-10:30 pm; Sun 5-9:30 pm. Closed Sun; Dec 25, Jan 1. Lunch $12.50-$21.50, dinner $20-$30. Bar. Reservations accepted. Cr cds: A, D, DS, MC, V.
D

★ ★ ★ **WILLARD ROOM.** *1401 Pennsylvania Ave NW (20004). Phone 202/637-7440; fax 202/637-7326. www.washington.interconti.com.* Located in the Inter-Continental Hotel (see WILLARD INTER-CONTINENTAL WASHINGTON), The Willard Room may look familiar to you if you've seen the Steven Spielberg film *Minority Report*—a scene was filmed in the restaurant. But you needn't be Tom Cruise on a mission to enjoy a meal at this sophisticated Victorian-style dining room. An eclectic American menu that changes with the seasons is offered at lunch and dinner. Spa selections are popular choices for those on a waistline-preservation plan; these dishes are marked with an asterisk to indicate that they are lower in fat, cholesterol, and sodium. Those who have no interest in anything labeled "Spa," unless it means a massage, will be fine with the menu's other choices— innovative takes on fish, shellfish, game, lamb, beef, and poultry prepared with a French flair. In addition to dessert, the restaurant offers an after-dinner cheese course for those who are extremely anti-spa. The Willard Room also houses a wonderful selection of wines from France and Italy, as well as new-world bottles from Australia and North America. Another perk is the classic cocktail list that adds to the old-world charm of dining here. *Secret Inspector's Notes:* This restaurant has been (and continues to be) a hotbed of politicos. You'll feel as if coalitions are being formed around you as you glance from table to table. American menu. Closed Sun. Breakfast, lunch, dinner. Bar. Piano. Jacket required. Reservations required. Valet parking available. Cr cds: A, C, D, DS, ER, JCB, MC, V. **$$$**

D

★ **ZED'S ETHIOPIAN CUISINE.** *1201 28th NW St. (20007). Phone 202/333-4710; fax 202/333-1085. www.zeds.net.* Ethiopian menu. Closed Thanksgiving, Dec 25. Lunch, dinner. Silverware provided at customer's request, communal dining from trays. Cr cds: A, D, DS, MC, V. **$**

West Virginia

The wild, rugged topography that made settlement of this area difficult in the early days has today made West Virginia a paradise for outdoor enthusiasts. The state's ski industry has taken advantage of the highest total altitude of any state east of the Mississippi River by opening several Alpine and Nordic ski areas. Outfitters offer excellent whitewater rafting on the state's many turbulent rivers. Rock climbing, caving, and hiking are popular in the Monongahela National Forest, and West Virginia also boasts an impressive state park system, as well as extensive hunting and fishing areas.

The nickname "Mountain State" gives only a hint of West Virginia's scenic beauty, which is unsurpassed in the East. West Virginia is also a land of proud traditions, with many festivals held throughout the year as tributes to the state's rich heritage. These events include celebrations honoring the state's sternwheel riverboat legacy, its spectacular autumn foliage, and even its strawberries, apples, and black walnuts.

Population: 1,808,344

Area: 24,078 square miles

Elevation: 240-4,863 feet

Peak: Spruce Knob (Pendleton County)

Entered Union: June 20, 1863 (35th state)

Capital: Charleston

Motto: Mountaineers are always free

Nickname: Mountain State

Flower: Rhododendron

Bird: Cardinal

Tree: Sugar Maple

Fair: August in Lewisburg

Time Zone: Eastern

Website: www.state.wv.us

Fun Facts:
1. Nearly 75 percent of West Virginia is covered by forests.
2. West Virginia was the first state to have sales tax. It became effective July 1, 1921.

The occupation of West Virginia began with the Mound Builders, a prehistoric Ohio Valley culture that left behind at least 300 conical earth mounds that challenge the imagination. Many have been worn away by erosion, but excavations in some have revealed elaborately adorned human skeletons and artifacts of amazing beauty and utility.

Pioneers who ventured into western Virginia in the 18th century found fine vistas and forests, curative springs, and beautiful rivers. George Washington and his family frequented the soothing mineral waters of Berkeley Springs (see), and White Sulphur Springs (see) later became a popular resort among the colonists. But much of this area was still considered "the wild West" in those days, and life here was not easy.

The Commonwealth of Virginia largely ignored its western citizens—only one governor was elected from the western counties before 1860. When the counties formed their own state during the Civil War, it was the result of many years of strained relations with the parent state. The move had been debated over the years and the war finally provided the opportunity

the counties needed to break away from Virginia. Although many sentiments in the new state remained pro-South, West Virginia's interests were best served by staying with the Union.

The first land battle of the Civil War took place in the western counties (see PHILIPPI) soon after Fort Sumter was fired upon in April 1861. Through the rest of 1861 and into 1862, Union forces under Generals George McClellan and William S. Rosecrans chased the Confederates back toward rebel Virginia. Succeeding battles were fought farther and farther south until major Confederate resistance became impossible. For the rest of the war, Confederate Army activity in the state was limited to destructive lightning raids designed to wreck railroad lines and damage Union supply sources.

The war left West Virginia a new state, but like other war-ravaged areas, it had suffered heavy losses of life and property. The recovery took many years. West Virginians eventually rebuilt their state; new industry was developed, railroads were built, and resources like coal, oil, and natural gas brought relative prosperity.

Calendar Highlights

MAY

Webster Springs Woodchopping Festival *(Webster Springs)*. Southeastern World Woodchopping Championships; state championship turkey calling contest, draft horse pull, horse show, fireman's rodeo; arts and crafts, music, parades, concessions.

Vandalia Gathering *(Charleston)*. Phone 304/344-5075. A festival of traditional arts; craft demonstrations, clogging, gospel music, fiddling, banjo picking, special exhibits.

JUNE

Mountain Heritage Arts and Crafts Festival *(Harpers Ferry)*. Phone 304/725-2055 or 800/624-0577. More than 190 craftspeople and artisans demonstrate quilting, wool spinning, pottery throwing, vegetable dyeing, and other crafts; concerts. Also in Sept.

JULY

Jamboree in the Hills *(Wheeling)*. Phone 800/828-3097. A four-day country music festival featuring more than 30 hours of music; top country stars. Camping is available.

AUGUST

State Fair *(Lewisburg)*. Phone 304/645-1090. Fairgrounds. Exhibitors from a number of other states; horse shows, harness racing.

SEPTEMBER

Sternwheel Regatta Festival *(Charleston)*. Phone 304/348-6419. Sternwheel and towboat races, parades, contests, hot air balloon race, fireworks; nationally known entertainers nightly; arts and crafts.

Stonewall Jackson Heritage Arts and Crafts Jubilee *(Weston)*. Phone 304/269-1863. Jackson's Mill State 4-H Conference Center. Mountain crafts, music, dance, and food.

OCTOBER

Mountain State Forest Festival *(Elkins)*. Phone 304/636-1824. Some events on campus of Davis & Elkins College. Queen Silvia is crowned; carnival, parades, entertainment, tilting at rings on horseback, sawing and woodchopping contests, marksmanship tests, State Championship Fiddle and Banjo Contest, juried craft fair and art exhibit.

Bridge Day *(Fayetteville)*. Contact Fayetteville Chamber of Commerce, 304/465-5617. New River Gorge Bridge. Bridge is opened to pedestrians; parachutists test their skills by jumping off the bridge and floating to the bottom of the gorge.

West Virginia continues to be an important source of bituminous coal and a major producer of building stone, timber, glass, and chemicals. The state is also the home of such technological wonders as the National Radio Astronomy Observatory (see MARLINTON), where scientists study the universe via radio telescopes, and the New River Gorge Bridge (see GAULEY BRIDGE), the world's longest steel span bridge.

When to Go/Climate

West Virginia summers are hot and humid, although temperatures in elevated areas rarely top 90°F. Snowfall can range from 10-15 ft in some areas.

AVERAGE HIGH/LOW TEMPERATURES (°F)

Charleston

Jan 41/23	May 76/52	Sept 79/57
Feb 45/26	June 83/60	Oct 68/44
Mar 57/35	July 86/64	Nov 57/36
Apr 67/43	Aug 84/63	Dec 46/28

Elkins

Jan 38/16	May 71/44	Sept 74/50
Feb 41/18	June 78/52	Oct 64/37
Mar 52/27	July 80/57	Nov 53/30
Apr 62/35	Aug 79/56	Dec 43/21

Parks and Recreation

Water-related activities, hiking, riding, various other sports, picnicking and visitor centers, as well as camping, are available in many of these areas. There is a small fee for swimming and game court use. Campgrounds with picnic facilities are available in 22 state parks and forests; all have drinking water and sanitary facilities; some have showers, coin laundries, utility hookups; 2-week limit; $6-$14/night for 6 persons or less, $1 each additional person. Camping season runs from mid-April-October in all parks except Canaan Valley and Pipestem resorts, which are open year-round. Campground reservations may be made at Babcock, Beech Fork, Blackwater Falls, Bluestone, Canaan Valley Resort, Cedar Creek, Chief Logan, Holly River, North Bend, Pipestem Resort, Stonewall Jackson Lake, Tomlinson Run, Twin Falls Resort, Tygart Lake, and Watoga state parks and at Greenbrier and Kanawha state forests. There is a $5 handling fee; reservations must be made 7-14 days in advance. Camping at all other state parks is on a first-come, first-served basis. Pets on leash only. Many cabins and lodges are available for seasonal or year-round use; seven-day minimum from the second Monday in June-Labor Day. Most parks are open daily, 8 am-sunset. For information and reservations contact individual parks or phone 800/225-5982 (except AK and HI).

FISHING AND HUNTING
In addition to a million acres of prime federal hunting and fishing land, West Virginia has 48 wildlife management areas. Nonresident statewide fishing license $30; 3-day license $5. Nonresident (except KY, OH, PA) hunting, basic license $100; archery deer, muzzleloader deer, and turkey stamps $30; six-day, small-game license $20. Nonresident migratory waterfowl stamp $5. A conservation stamp is required in addition to all regular hunting and fishing licenses (nonresident $5). For further information, contact the Division of Natural Resources, Wildlife Resources Section, State Capitol Complex, Building 3, Charleston 25305. Phone 304/558-2771.

Driving Information
Children under 9 must be in an approved passenger restraint anywhere in vehicle; ages 3-8 may use a regulation safety belt; children under 3 years must use an approved safety seat. For more information, phone 304/746-2121.

INTERSTATE HIGHWAY SYSTEM
The following alphabetical listing of West Virginia towns in this book shows that these cities are within 10 miles of the indicated interstate highways. Check a highway map for the nearest exit.

Highway Number	Cities/Towns within ten miles
Interstate 64	Beckley, Charleston, Huntington, Lewisburg, Nitro, White Sulphur Springs
Interstate 70	Wheeling
Interstate 77	Charleston, Parkersburg, Princeton, Ripley
Interstate 79	Charleston, Clarksburg, Fairmont, Morgantown, Sutton
Interstate 81	Martinsburg

Additional Visitor Information
Travel materials, including information on accommodations, skiing, caving, rock climbing, whitewater rafting, and other activities, are available from the West Virginia Division of Tourism, State Capitol Complex, 2101 Washington St E, Charleston 25305. Phone 800/225-5982. The Information & Education Section, Department of Natural Resources, State Capitol, Charleston 25305, publishes a monthly magazine, *Wonderful West Virginia*.

Information on hiking along the completed portion of the Allegheny Trail, including a hiking guide (fee), is available from the West Virginia Scenic Trails Association, 633 West Virginia Ave, Morgantown 26505. The trail runs north-south from the Pennsylvania state line near Coopers Rock State Forest to Peters Mountain, SE of Lindside, at the Virginia state line.

There are several welcome centers in West Virginia; visitors who stop by will find information and brochures most helpful in planning stops at points of interest. Locations are as follows: on I-64, westbound near White Sulphur Springs and eastbound near Huntington; on I-81, southbound by the West Virginia/Maryland border and northbound near the West Virginia/Virginia border; on I-79, southbound north of Morgantown; on I-77, southbound near Mineral Wells; on I-70, westbound near the West Virginia/Pennsylvania border. The West Virginia Information Center is located at Harpers Ferry. All centers are open (daily; closed Jan 1, Thanksgiving, Dec 25). Personnel at any of these locations will also assist visitors in making lodging reservations. In addition, information may be obtained at the Capitol Guides Desk in the rotunda of the State Capitol at Charleston (Memorial Day-Labor Day, Mon-Sat, also Sun afternoons).

SPRUCE KNOB/MONONGAHELA HIGH COUNTRY

In the big cities of the Mid-Atlantic, it is sometimes hard to believe that there is a vast and rugged mountain wilderness just to the west. You can find plenty of this unspoiled nature in West Virginia, where soaring mountain ridges stretch into the distance and countless splashing streams beckon. This one-day, 150-mile loop out of the pretty college town of Elkins takes you through some of the Mid-Atlantic's most scenic mountain terrain. The route crisscrosses 100,000-acre Spruce Knob-Seneca Rocks National Recreation Area in the Monongahela National Forest. From Elkins, take US 250 south through the national forest to Thornwood. Mile after mile, the road climbs and dips alongside splashing streams. At Thornwood, head north on State Route 28 toward Riverton. Two miles south of Riverton, turn west (left) onto Forest Service Road 112 and follow the signs to Spruce Knob, about 15 miles. At an altitude of 4,861 feet, Spruce Knob is the state's loftiest mountain peak–although peak isn't really an apt description. The summit is a broad, oddly flat plateau scattered with piles of age-smoothed rocks. A thin forest of red spruce, stunted by the strong and nearly constant westerly winds, struggles for a foothold. This is one of the most remote and rugged areas of the Mid-Atlantic that can be reached in a passenger sedan. A rock-lined trail leads to the Observation Tower, a three-story stone structure that boosts sightseers above the trees for a majestic 360-degree panorama. Return to Route 28 and continue north to Seneca Rocks, a slender 900-foot-high forested ridge favored by rock climbers. You can watch them from the Discovery Center or take the easier 1 1/2-mile trail to the summit. Pause for snacks or lunch at Harper's Old Country Store. To continue, head west on Route 55 to Harmon and pick up Route 32 north to Davis. The road passes alongside 6,000-acre Canaan Valley Resort State Park, where you can stop to hike, bicycle, or go for a swim in the outdoor pool. A year-round resort, the park operates a downhill skiing complex. In summer, the chairlift will carry you to the top for grand views. About 15 miles long and 3 miles wild, the valley is situated at an altitude of 3,200 feet, which all but guarantees moderate summer temperatures. Just to the north, the town of Davis has become a major center for mountain biking, mostly on abandoned US Forest Service roads. Outfitters offer rentals and maps. On the edge of Davis, turn left into Blackwater Falls State Park, a rumpled expanse of woodland ridges and valleys cut by the impressively deep canyon of the Blackwater River. Motorists approach the park's 55-room lodge on a long, winding road that carries them deeper and deeper into the forest. Suddenly a clearing appears, revealing the lodge clinging to the precipitous edge of the canyon. The river races far below, the thunder of crashing whitewater clearly audible. Visitors can view the 65-foot plunge of Blackwater Falls from the canyon rim just upriver from the lodge or descend 214 steps to its base. In summer, the beach at little Pendleton Lake makes a refreshing rest stop. Continue north 2 miles to Thomas, an old mining town built in a double tier on a mountainside, and then return to Elkins on US 219 south. **(Approximately 150 miles)**

CANYON COUNTRY-AROUND NEW RIVER GORGE

The New River, a twisted strand of tumbling water, has cut a deep and narrow gorge for more than 50 miles through the rugged mountains of southeastern West Virginia. Rafting enthusiasts consider the New to be one of the best whitewater rivers in the nation. It's also very pretty to look at while standing on a cliff's edge high above. This two-day, 300-mile scenic drive out of Charleston, which circles the gorge, provides plenty of scenic viewing opportunities. At the same time, the tour offers a look at the state's coal-mining heritage. At the turn of the century King Coal ruled the gorge, and at one time two dozen coal-mining towns prospered on the banks of the New. Now, much of the gorge is protected as the New River Gorge National River. From Charleston, head east on US 60, following the old Midland Trail up the Kanawha River. In the first few miles, the highway winds past industrial plants, which are interesting to see in their ugly strangeness. The mountain scenery begins in about 30 miles at Gauley

Bridge, where the New flows into the Kanawha. Here, as the New begins to display whitewater turbulence, the road climbs steeply and you spot the first of many waterfalls spilling from overhead. One of finest gorge views is just ahead at Hawk's Nest State Park, which has a 31-room lodge at cliff's edge. A steep hiking trail down to the river provides a chance to stretch your legs. About 25 minutes on, detour south on US 19 to Canyon Rim Visitor Center, which provides information about the park and the region. You also get a good look at the New River Gorge Bridge, one of the highest bridges in the country. Linking the north and south rims of the gorge, it has become famous for its once-a year parachute jumps in October. Dozens of parachutists leap from its concrete safety barriers and float 876 feet to the river sandbar below. A stairway takes you partway down the cliff for more river and bridge views. Continue east on US 60 to State Route 41, where you again detour south (right) to Babcock State Park to see its old stone gristmill and to try its hiking trails. Back on US 60, head east to Route 20 south to Hinton, a picturesque riverfront town. A river-level road leads to views of Sandstone Falls on the New. You can stay in Hinton or continue south on Route 20 to Pipestem Resort State Park, a 4,000-acre preserve with a 113-room lodge and an 18-hole golf course. From Pipestem, double back on Route 20 to Route 3 west to US 19 north to Beckley. Here you can ride a coal car deep into the Beckley Exhibition Coal Mine. From Beckley, take Route 61 north to Glen Jean and then head east on Route 25 to Thurmond, a former riverside mining boom town. The still-active train tracks run down the main street next to the sidewalk. An Amtrak station doubles as a railroad museum. Return to Route 61 north to I-64/I-77 and back to Charleston. **(Approximately 300 miles)**

Aurora (D-7)

See also Davis, Grafton

Settled 1787 **Pop** 150 **Elev** 2,641 ft **Area code** 304
Zip 26705

Located at the summit of Cheat Mountain, Aurora offers visitors clean air and high altitude.

What to See and Do

Cathedral State Park. *1 mile E on US 50. Phone 304/735-3771.* Hiking trails through 132 acres of deep, virgin hemlock forest; cross-country skiing, picnicking. Standard hours.

Beckley (G-5)

See also Gauley Bridge, Hinton

Founded 1838 **Pop** 17,254 **Elev** 2,416 ft **Area code** 304

Information Southern West Virginia Convention & Visitors Bureau, PO Box 1799, 25802; 304/252-2244 or 800/VISIT-WV

Web www.visitwv.org

The "smokeless coal capital of the world" is a center for more than 200 small mining and farming towns. Beckley is situated on a high plateau surrounded by fertile valleys. During the Civil War the village was held at various times by both armies; Union troops shelled it in 1863. Coal was found here in 1774 but was not mined until 1890. Smokeless coal became the standard bunker fuel during World War I, and the demand continued for years thereafter. Beckley now serves as a commercial, medical, and tourist center.

What to See and Do

Babcock State Park. *13 miles NE via US 19 to WV 41, near Landisburg. Phone 304/438-3003 or 800/CALL-WVA.* More than 4,100 acres of rugged mountain scenery with trout stream and waterfalls, views of New River Canyon, rhododendrons (May-July); restored operating gristmill. Swimming pool, lake and stream fishing, boating (rowboat, paddleboat rentals); hiking trails, horseback riding, game courts (equipment rentals), cross-country skiing, camping (electrical hookups), 26 cabins (rentals, spring and fall). Nature and recreation programs (summer). Standard hours, fees. (Mid-Apr-Oct)

Beckley Exhibition Coal Mine. *513 Ewart Ave (25801). 1 1/2 miles SE off I-77, exit 44 on Ewart Ave in New River Park. Phone 304/256-1747.* Riding tours in coal cars through 1,500 feet of underground passageways, constant 56°F temperature; museum, coal company house, superintendent of coal mines' house, church, campground. (Apr-Oct, daily) **$$$$**

Grandview Unit of New River Gorge National River. *4700 Grandview Rd (25813). 5 miles SE on US 19, then 5 miles NE via Airport, Glen Hedrick and Grandview rds. Contact the Superintendent, PO Box 246, Glen Jean 25846. Phone 304/763-3715 or 304/465-0508.* Nearly 900 wooded acres at the northern end of the New River Gorge National River area (see HINTON); offers spectacular overlooks of New River Gorge and Horseshoe Bend; rhododendron gardens. Hiking trails, game courts (some fees), cross-country skiing, picnicking, playgrounds, concession. Outdoor dramas (June-Labor Day, Tues-Sun).

Lake Stephens. *350 Lake Stephens Rd. W of town. Phone 304/934-5323.* A 303-acre lake with swimming, fishing, boating; trailer camping (hookups).

Plum Orchard Lake Wildlife Management Area. *11 miles N on I-77 to Pax exit, then E on Rural Rte 23. Phone 304/469-9905.* More than 3,200 acres with rabbit, grouse, squirrel hunting. Also a 202-acre lake with more than 6 miles of shoreline; boating; fishing for bass, channel catfish, crappie, and bluegill; picnicking, playground, camping.

Twin Falls Resort State Park. *25 miles SW via WV 16 and WV 54, then W on WV 97, near Maben. Phone 304/294-4000.* Approximately 4,000 acres with restored pioneer house and farm. Swimming pool; hiking trails, 18-hole golf course, clubhouse, tennis, game courts, picnicking, playground, restaurant, lodge, camping, 14 cabins (equipment rentals). Recreation center, programs. Standard hours, fees. (Daily)

Whitewater rafting. *New River Park. Phone 304/252-2244 or 800/VISIT-WV.* Many outfitters offer guided trips on the New and Gauley rivers. For a list of outfitters, contact the Southern West Virginia Convention & Visitors Bureau, PO Box 1799, 25802.

WinterPlace Ski Resort. *17 miles S via I-77, exit 28 (Ghent/Flat Top), follow signs. Phone 304/787-3221; 800/607-SNOW.* On southern West Virginia's highest peak. Two quad, three triple, two double chairlifts; two surface lifts; ski school, rentals; snowmaking; snow-tubing; cafeteria, lounge; restaurants; entertainment; children's program; sporting goods shops. Night skiing. Twenty-seven runs; longest run 1 1/4 mile; vertical drop 603 feet. Snowboard park. (Dec-late Mar, daily) **$$$$**

Youth Museum of Southern West Virginia. *Ewart Ave, in New River Park. Phone 304/252-3730.* Hands-on exhibits, planetarium, log house. (May-Labor Day, daily; rest of year, Tues-Sat) **$$**

Special Events

Appalachian Festival. *245 N Kanewha St (25801). Phone 304/252-7328.* Tamarack. Exhibitions and demonstrations of native crafts; entertainment, food. Aug.

Theatre West Virginia. *4700 Grandview Rd (25813). Cliffside Amphitheatre at Grandview Park, W on I-64, exit 129B, follow signs. Contact PO Box 1205, 25802; phone 304/256-6800 or 800/666-9142.* Outdoor musical dramas. Mid-June-mid-Aug.

Motels/Motor Lodges

★ **COMFORT INN.** *1909 Harper Rd (25801). Phone 304/255-2161; toll-free 800/888-2598; fax 304/255-2161. www.comfortinn.com.* 130 rooms, 3 story. Under 19 free. Pet accepted. Complimentary continental breakfast. Check-out noon, check-in 2 pm. TV; cable (premium). In-room modem link. Exercise equipment. Downhill ski 15 miles. Cr cds: A, C, D, DS, JCB, MC, V.

D ⬛ ⬛ ⬛ SC $

★ **HAMPTON INN.** *110 Harper Park Dr (25801). Phone 304/252-2121; toll-free 800/426-7866; fax 304/255-6238. www.hamptoninn.com.* 108 rooms, 5 story. Under 18 free. Complimentary continental breakfast. Check-out noon, check-in 2 pm. TV; cable (premium). In-room modem link. Exercise equipment. Pool. Downhill ski 15 miles. Cr cds: A, C, D, DS, MC, V.

D ⬛ ⬛ ⬛ SC $

★ ★ **HOLIDAY INN.** *1924 Harper Rd (25801). Phone 304/255-1511; toll-free 800/465-4329; fax 304/256-0526. www.holiday-inn.com.* 104 rooms, 3 story. No elevator. Under 19 free. Check-out 1 pm, check-in 3 pm. TV; cable (premium). In-room modem link. Restaurant 6 am-2 pm, 5-10 pm. Bar 3 pm-3 am; Sun to 1 am. Room service. Exercise equipment. Heated pool. Downhill ski 15 miles. Cr cds: A, C, D, DS, JCB, MC, V.

D ⬛ ⬛ ⬛ SC $

Berkeley Springs (C-9)

See also Martinsburg

Founded 1776 **Pop** 735 **Elev** 612 ft **Area code** 304 **Zip** 25411

Information Berkeley Springs-Morgan County Chamber of Commerce, 127 Fairfax St; 304/258-3738 or 800/447-8797

Web www.berkeleysprings.com

Popularized by George Washington, who surveyed the area for Lord Fairfax in 1748, Berkeley Springs is the oldest spa in the nation. Fairfax later granted the land around the springs to Virginia. The town is officially named Bath,

for the famous watering place in England, but the post office is Berkeley Springs. The waters, which are piped throughout the town, are fresh and slightly sweet, without the medicinal flavor of most mineral springs. Washington and his family returned again and again. The popularity of the resort reached its peak after the Revolutionary War, becoming something of a summer capital for Washingtonians in the 1830s. But like all resort towns, Berkeley Springs declined as newer, more fashionable spas came into vogue. The Civil War completely destroyed the town's economy. Today, the town is again visited for its healthful waters, spas, and charming downtown.

What to See and Do

Berkeley Springs State Park. *121 S Washington St (25411). Center of town. Phone 304/258-2711 or 304/258-5860.* Famous resort with health baths of all types (fees); five warm springs. Main bathhouse (daily; closed holidays). Roman bathhouse with second-floor museum (Memorial Day-mid-Oct, daily). Swimming pool (Memorial Day-Labor Day, daily; fee).

Cacapon Resort State Park. *10 miles S off US 522. Phone 304/258-1022.* More than 6,100 acres with swimming, sand beach, fishing, boating (rowboat and paddleboat rentals); hiking and bridle trails, horseback riding, 18-hole golf course, tennis, game courts, cross-country skiing, picnicking, playground, concession, restaurant, lodge. No camping; 30 cabins. Nature, recreation programs. Nature center. Standard hours, fees.

Sleepy Creek Wildlife Management Area *1910 Sleepy Creek Rd (25427). 15 miles SE, E of US 522. Phone 304/754-3855.* Approximately 23,000 acres of rugged forest offer wild turkey, deer, grouse, and squirrel hunting; boating and bass fishing on 205-acre lake; primitive camping (fee). Also 70 miles of hiking trails crossing two mountains, several valleys.

View from Prospect Peak. *On WV 9, near town.* Potomac River winds through what the National Geographic Society has called one of the nation's outstanding vistas.

Special Event

Apple Butter Festival. *304 Fairfax St (25411). Phone 800/447-8797.* Crafts demonstrations, music, contests. Columbus Day weekend.

Motel/Motor Lodge

★ **SUPER 8.** *118 Limestone Rd, Hancock (21750). Phone 301/678-6101; fax 301/678-5376. www.super8.com.* 50 rooms, 2 story. Under 18 free. Pet accepted. Complimentary continental breakfast. Check-out noon, check-in 3 pm. TV; cable (premium). In-room modem link. Cr cds: A, C, D, DS, MC, V.

D ⬛ SC $

George Washington's Spa and Berkeley Springs

Tucked in a narrow, rock-shadowed valley along the Cacapon River, the little mountain community of Berkeley Springs has transformed itself into "Spa Town USA." A total of five separate spas employ more than 40 message therapists—three times the number of practicing lawyers, town officials claim. The clustering of so many spas in the town is relatively new, but Berkeley Springs has a long heritage as a spa destination. Well before white settlers arrived, Native Americans sought out the warm, 74.3-degree mineral springs. Still bubbling forth from the base of Warm Springs Ridge at 2,000 gallons per minute, the water was believed to have curative powers. George Washington, who first visited the springs in 1748 as a 16-year-old surveyor, returned nearly a dozen times in later years seeking health benefits. In 1776, he and prominent friends and family established the Town of Bath, intent on making it a popular spa, and the first bath houses were built. Because of this, Berkeley Springs claims to be "the country's first spa." You can explore the town's spa heritage in a 30-minute, half-mile stroll in Berkeley Springs State Park, which doubles as the community's town square. One of America's most curious public parklands, the seven-acre Berkeley Springs State Park operates year-round as a very affordable government-run spa. Begin a loop around the park at the large public swimming pool, fed by spring waters. Heading clockwise, take a peek inside the Main Bath House, where you can enjoy a private hot-tub soak and Swedish-style message. Continue on to a stone-lined natural pool of flowing spring water, dubbed George Washington's Bath Tub in his honor. Move on to the Gentlemen's Spring House, where you are welcome to draw jugs of the famed drinking water for free. Conclude this plunge into historic bathing with a look into the Roman Bath House, where you can indulge in a private hot-tub soak without an accompanying message.

Resorts

★ ★ **CACAPON STATE PARK.** *818 Cacapon Dr (25411). Phone 304/258-1022; fax 304/258-5323. www.cacaponresort.com.* 48 rooms, 31 kitchen cabins, 3 story. Check-out noon, check-in 3 pm. TV. In-room modem link. Dining room 7 am-9 pm; winter 8 am-7 pm. Game room. Golf, greens fee $25-$30. Tennis. Near lake; boat rentals, sandy beach. Hiking trails. Cr cds: A, D, DS, MC, V. **$$$$**

★ ★ **COOLFONT RESORT.** *3621 Cold Run Valley Rd (25411). Phone 304/258-4500; toll-free 800/888-8768; fax 304/258-5499. www.coolfont.com.* 19 rooms, 35 cabins, 3 story. D $174-$268; each additional $84-$94 package plans; fitness plan. Check-out 11 am, check-in 4 pm. In-room modem link. Dining room 8 am-2 pm, 5:30-8:30 pm; Fri, Sat to 9:30 pm; Sun 8 am-3 pm, 5:30-8 pm. Bar, entertainment Sat. Supervised children's activities (June-Aug; weekends only rest of year), ages 5-12. Exercise room, massage, sauna. Boats. Heated indoor pool, whirlpool. Tennis. Cross-country ski on site. Lawn games. Fishing. Hiking. Sleighing. Cr cds: A, D, DS, MC, V.

B&B/Small Inns

★ ★ **COUNTRY INN.** *207 S Washington St (25411). Phone 304/258-2210; toll-free 800/822-6630; fax 304/258-3986. www.countryinnwv.com.* This colonial-style inn enjoys the healthful waters of the area and provides access for guests to mineral baths and spa. 70 rooms, 3 story, 13 rooms share bath. D $39-$165; each additional $15. Check-out noon, check-in 3 pm. TV; cable (premium), VCR available (movies). Dining room 7-11 am, 11:30 am-2 pm, 5-9 pm; Fri, Sat to 10 pm. Entertainment Sat, Sun. Massage. Cr cds: A, C, D, DS, MC, V.

★ ★ ★ **HIGHLAWN INN.** *304 Market St (25411). Phone 304/258-5700; toll-free 888/290-4163. www.highlawninn.com.* This Victorian-style manor, built in the late 1890s, has authentic furnishings and ornate fireplaces. The mineral bath waters of the area are an added feature. 12 rooms, 2-3 story. No room phones. D $145-$195. Children over 14 years only. Complimentary breakfast. Check-out noon, check-in 2 pm. TV; cable (premium). Cr cds: MC, V.

Bethany

See also Weirton, Wheeling

Pop 985 **Elev** 932 ft **Area code** 304 **Zip** 26032

What to See and Do

Bethany College. *1 Main St.* (1840) 800 students. Founded by Alexander Campbell, the leading influence in the 19th-century religious movement that gave rise to the Disciples of Christ, Churches of Christ, and Christian churches. Historic buildings on the 300-acre campus include Old Main, styled after the University of Glasgow in Scotland; Pendleton Heights, a 19th-century house used as the college president's residence; Old Bethany Meeting House (1852), Delta Tau Delta Founder's House (1854), and the

Campbell Mansion. *Phone 304/829-7285 or 304/829-7000.* A 24-room house where Campbell lived; antique furnishings. On property is hexagonal brick study, one-room schoolhouse, and smokehouse. The Campbell family cemetery, "God's Acre," is across from the mansion. (Apr-Oct, Tues-Sun; rest of year, by appointment) **$$**

Bluefield (G-5)

See also Princeton

Founded 1889 **Pop** 11,451 **Elev** 2,611 ft **Area code** 304 **Zip** 24701

Information Convention & Visitors Bureau, 500 Bland St, PO Box 4099; 304/325-8438 or 800/221-3206

Web www.bluestonecvb.com

Named for the bluish chicory covering the nearby hills, Bluefield owes its existence to the Pocahontas Coal Field. The town came to life in the 1880s when the railroad came through to transport coal. This commercial and industrial center of southern West Virginia is known as nature's "air-conditioned city" because of its altitude—one-half mile above sea level. Bluefield has a sister city by the same name in Virginia, directly across the state line.

What to See and Do

Eastern Regional Coal Archives. *In Craft Memorial Library, 600 Commerce St. Phone 304/325-3943.* Center highlights the history of West Virginia coal fields; exhibits, photographs, mining implements; films, research material. (Mon-Fri afternoons; closed holidays) **FREE**

Panther State Forest. *50 miles NW off US 52 near Panther. Phone 304/938-2252.* More than 7,800 acres of rugged hills. Swimming pool (Memorial Day-Labor Day), fishing; hunting, hiking trails, picnicking, playground, concession, camping. Standard hours, fees.

Pinnacle Rock State Park. *P.O. Box 1 (24715). 7 miles NW on US 52. Phone 304/248-8565.* Approximately 250-acre park contains a 15-acre lake and interesting sandstone formations, which resemble a giant cockscomb. Hiking, picnicking. Standard hours, fees.

Motels/Motor Lodges

★ **ECONO LODGE.** *3400 Cumberland Rd (24701). Phone 304/327-8171; fax 304/324-4259. www.econolodge.com.* 47 rooms, 2 story. Pet accepted; $10. Complimentary continental breakfast. Coffee in lobby. Check-out 11 am. Check-in 3 pm. TV; cable (premium). In-room modem link. Cr cds: A, C, D, DS, JCB, MC, V. $

[D] [🐾] [⊠] [SC] $

★ ★ **HOLIDAY INN.** *3350 Big Laurel Hwy (24701). Phone 304/325-6170; toll-free 800/465-4329; fax 304/323-2451. www.holiday-inn.com.* 122 rooms, 2 story. D $73-$90; each additional $10; under 18 free. Pet accepted. Check-out noon, check-in 2 pm. TV; cable (premium), VCR available. In-room modem link. Restaurant 6 am-2 pm, 5 pm-10 pm. Room service. Exercise equipment, sauna. Cr cds: A, C, D, DS, ER, JCB, MC, V.

[D] [🐾] [⊠] [⊠] [SC]

★ **RAMADA INN.** *3175 E Cumberland Rd (24701). Phone 304/325-5421; toll-free 888/613-9080; fax 304/325-6045. www.ramada.com.* 98 rooms, 2 story. D $63-$90; each additional $5; under 18 free; ski plans. Pet accepted. Check-out noon, check-in 2 pm. TV; cable (premium), VCR available. In-room modem link. Restaurant 6 am-10 pm. Bar 5 pm-1 am, entertainment Fri, Sat. Room service 24 hours. Exercise equipment, sauna. Game room. Heated indoor pool, children's pool, whirlpool. Cr cds: A, C, D, DS, JCB, MC, V.

[D] [🐾] [⊠] [🏋] [⊠]

Restaurant

★ **MAYFLOWER I.** *105 Hockman Pike (24605). Phone 540/322-4578.* Seafood menu. Hours: 4-9:30 pm; Sat 2-9 pm; Sun 11:30 am-8 pm. Closed Mon; most major holidays. Dinner $6.30-$18. Children's menu. Casual atmosphere with nautical décor. Cr cds: MC, V.

[D] [SC]

Buckhannon (D-6)

See also Elkins, Philippi, Weston

Settled 1770 **Pop** 5,725 **Elev** 1,433 ft **Area code** 304 **Zip** 26201

Information Buckhannon-Upshur Chamber of Commerce, 16 S Kanawha St, PO Box 442; 304/472-1722

What to See and Do

Audra State Park. *8 miles N on US 119, then 6 miles E on WV 11. Phone 304/457-1162.* Approximately 360 acres offer swimming in a natural mountain stream surrounded by tall timber; bathhouse. Hiking trails, picnicking, playground, concession, tent and trailer camping. Standard hours, fees.

Holly River State Park. *32 miles S of Buckhannon on WV 20. Phone 304/493-6353.* More than 8,100 acres and the second largest state park in the state. Camping, cabins, picnicking, hiking. Standard fees.

West Virginia State Wildlife Center. *12 miles S on WV 4, 20. Phone 304/924-6211.* Fenced-in habitats of approximately 50 species of birds and animals native to West Virginia, including deer, elk, buffalo, timber wolf, mountain lion, and black bear. Loop walkway (1 1/4 miles). Trout pond; picnicking, concession. (May-Oct, daily; Apr and Nov, weekends and holidays only; Dec-Mar, days vary) **$**

West Virginia Wesleyan College. *College Ave and Meade St. Phone 304/473-8000.* (1890) 1,600 students. An 80-acre campus featuring Georgian architecture. Wesley Chapel, the largest place of worship in the state, contains a Casavant organ with 1,474 pipes.

Special Event

West Virginia Strawberry Festival. *Phone 304/472-9036.* Parades, dances, exhibits, air show, arts and crafts, other activities. Usually the week before Memorial Day.

Motel/Motor Lodge

★ **BICENTENNIAL MOTEL.** *90 E Main St (26201). Phone 304/472-5000; fax 304/472-9159.* 45 rooms, 2 story. Pet accepted; $10. Check-out 11 am, check-in 2 pm. TV; cable (premium). In-room modem link. Bar. Room service. Outdoor pool. Cr cds: A, D, DS, MC, V. $

D ⊃ ⌤ ⊠ SC

Charleston (E-4)

See also Nitro

Settled 1794 **Pop** 53,421 **Elev** 601 ft **Area code** 304

Information Convention & Visitors Bureau, Charleston Civic Center, 200 Civic Center Dr, 25301; 304/344-5075 or 800/733-5469

Web www.charlestonwv.com

Charleston, the state capital, is the trading hub for the Great Kanawha Valley, where deposits of coal, oil, natural gas, and brine have greatly contributed to this region's national importance as a production center for chemicals and glass. Two institutions of higher learning, West Virginia State College and the University of Charleston, are located in the metropolitan area. Charleston is also the northern terminus of the spectacular West Virginia Turnpike.

Daniel Boone lived around Charleston until 1795. During his residence he was appointed a lieutenant colonel in the county militia in 1789 and was elected to the Virginia assembly the same year. The area became important as a center of salt production in 1824, when steam engines were used to operate brine pumps. After Charleston became the capital of West Virginia in 1885, following a dispute with Wheeling, the town came into its own. During World War I, an increased demand for plate and bottle glass, as well as for high explosives, made Charleston and the nearby town of Nitro (see) boom.

What to See and Do

Coonskin Park. *2000 Coonskin Dr (25311). 3/4 mile N off WV 114. Phone 304/341-8000.* Recreation area includes swimming, fishing for bass and catfish, pedal boating; hiking trails, 18-hole golf, miniature golf, tennis. Picnicking, playground, concession. (Daily; closed Dec 25; some activities seasonal) Fees for activities.

Cultural Center. *1900 E Kanawha Blvd (25305). Next to the state capitol, on Greenbrier St. Phone 304/558-0220.* The Center houses the Division of Culture and History and Library Commission; archives library (Mon-Sat); state museum; special events, changing exhibits. (Daily; closed holidays) **FREE** Also here is

Mountain Stage. *1900 Kanawha Blvd E (25305). Phone 304/342-5757.* Live public radio show heard on stations nationwide; features jazz, folk, blues, and rock. Visitors may watch show; afternoon performances (Sun). **$$$**

Elk River Scenic Drive. Beautiful drive along the Elk River from Charleston northeast to Sutton (approximately 60 miles). Begins just north of town; take US 119 NE to Clendenin, then WV 4 NE to US 19 in Sutton.

Kanawha State Forest. *Loudendale Rd. 7 miles S off US 119. Phone 304/558-3500.* Approximately 9,300 acres with swimming pool, bathhouse (Memorial Day-Labor Day); hunting, hiking, interpretive trail for the disabled, horseback riding, cross-country skiing, picnicking, playground, concession, camping. Standard hours, fees.

State Capitol. *1900 E Kanawha Blvd (25305). On river between Greenbrier St and California Ave. Phone 304/558-4839 or 800/225-5982.* (1932) One of America's most beautiful state capitols, the building was designed by Cass Gilbert in Italian Renaissance style. Within the gold-leaf dome, which rises 300 feet above the street, hangs a 10,080-piece, hand-cut imported chandelier weighing more than two tons. Guided tours available. (Mon-Fri, Sat afternoons) **FREE** Across the grounds is the

Governor's Mansion. *1716 Kanawha Blvd E. Phone 304/558-3809.* (1925) Beautiful Georgian structure of red Harvard brick with white Corinthian columns. Tours (Thurs and Fri; also by appointment). **FREE**

Sunrise Museum. *746 Myrtle Rd, across South Side Bridge. Phone 304/344-8035.* On 16 acres of wooded grounds with gardens and trails, this art and science museum is housed in two historic mansions built by William MacCorkle, ninth governor of West Virginia. Guided tours by appointment. (Wed-Sun; closed holidays) **$$**

Art Museum. *746 Myrtle Rd. Phone 800/344-8035.* American paintings, graphics and sculpture from 19th through 20th centuries; rotating exhibits; films and lectures. **$$**

Science Museum. *746 Myrtle Rd. Phone 800/344-8035.* Exhibits in natural sciences and technology; planetarium, programs, lectures. Interactive exhibits, demonstrations. **$$**

West Virginia State College. *8 miles W via I-64 exit 50, in Institute. Phone 304/766-3000.* (1891) 4,635 students. On campus are Davis Fine Arts Building with periodic exhibits (Mon-Sat; closed holidays); Asian art collection in library (daily; closed holidays); and East Hall (1895), formerly president's residence. Tours.

Whitewater rafting. *90 MacCorkle Ave SW (25303). Phone toll-free 800/225-5982.* Many outfitters offer guided rafting, canoeing, and fishing trips on the New and Gauley rivers. For a list of outfitters contact the West Virginia Division of Tourism, Research, and Development, 90 MacCorkle Ave SW, South Charleston, WV 25303.

Special Events

Sternwheel Regatta Festival. *Phone 304/348-6419.* Sternwheeler and towboat races, parades, contests, hot-air balloon race, fireworks; nationally known entertainers nightly; arts and crafts. Late Aug-early Sept.

Vandalia Gathering. *1900 Kanawha Blvd E (25305). Phone 304/558-0220.* A festival of traditional arts; craft demonstrations, clogging, gospel music, fiddling, banjo picking, special exhibits. Memorial Day weekend.

Motels/Motor Lodges

★ **DAYS INN.** *6400 SE MacCorkle Ave (25304). Phone 304/925-1010; toll-free 800/304-3809; fax 304/925-1364. www.daysinn.com.* 147 rooms, 2-3 story. D $55-$95; each additional $5; under 12 free. Pet accepted, some restrictions. Complimentary continental breakfast.

Check-out 11 am, check-in 3 pm. TV; cable (premium). In-room modem link. Exercise equipment. Pool. Cr cds: A, C, D, DS, JCB, MC, V.

D ⊞ ⇌ ⋏ ⊠

★ **HAMPTON INN.** *1 Preferred Pl (25309). Phone 304/746-4646; fax 304/746-4665. www.hamptoninn.com.* 104 rooms, 6 story. D $78-$135; each additional $5; under 18 free. Complimentary continental breakfast. Check-out noon, check-in 2 pm. TV; cable (premium). In-room modem link. Restaurant 10-1 am. Exercise equipment. Heated indoor pool, whirlpool. Free airport transportation. Business center. Cr cds: A, C, D, DS, JCB, MC, V.

D ⇌ ⋏ ⊠ SC ⋏

★ **HAMPTON INN.** *1 Virginia St W (25302). Phone 304/343-9300; fax 304/342-9393. www.hamptoninn.com.* 110 rooms, 5 story. D $81-$94; each additional $5; under 18 free; higher rates during basketball tournament. Complimentary continental breakfast. Check-out noon, check-in 2 pm. TV; cable (premium). Exercise room. Whirlpool. Free airport transportation. Cr cds: A, C, D, DS, MC, V.

D ⇌ ⋏ ⊠ SC

★★ **HOLIDAY INN.** *600 Kanawha Blvd E (25301). Phone 304/344-4092; toll-free 800/465-4329; fax 304/345-4847. www.holiday-inn.com.* 258 rooms, 11 story. D $69-$109; each additional $6; under 18 free. Check-out noon, check-in 3 pm. TV; cable (premium). In-room modem link. Restaurant 6:30 am-2 pm; dining room 5-10 pm. Bar 4 pm-2 am; closed Sun. Exercise equipment. Free airport transportation. Some rooms with river view. Cr cds: A, C, D, DS, JCB, MC, V.

D ⇌ ⋏ ⊠ SC

★ **HOLIDAY INN EXPRESS.** *100 Civic Center Dr (25301). Phone 304/345-0600; fax 304/343-1322. www.charleston-holidayinn.com.* 196 rooms, 6 story. D $81-$91; under 18 free. Pet accepted, some restrictions. Complimentary continental breakfast. Check-out noon, check-in 2 pm. TV; VCR available. In-room modem link. Exercise equipment. Free airport transportation. Cr cds: A, C, D, DS, JCB, MC, V.

D ⊠ SC

★ **KANAWHA CITY MOTOR LODGE.** *3103 MacCorkle Ave SE (25304). Phone 304/344-2461; fax 304/345-1419.* 50 rooms, 2 story. D $44-$61; each additional $5; under 18 free. Check-out noon, check-in 1 pm. TV; cable (premium). Cr cds: A, C, D, DS, MC, V.

D ⊠ SC

★ **RED ROOF INN.** *6305 MacCorkle Ave SE, Kanawha City. Phone 304/925-6953; toll-free 800/843-7663; fax 304/925-8111. www.redroof.com.* 108 rooms, 2 story. D

$38-$70; each additional $5; under 18 free. Pet accepted. Check-out noon, check-in 2 pm. TV; cable (premium). Restaurant 6 am-10:30 pm. Cr cds: A, C, D, DS, MC, V.

D ↩ ⊠ SC

Hotel

★ ★ ★ MARRIOTT CHARLESTON TOWN CEN-TER. *200 Lee St E (25301). Phone 304/345-6500; toll-free 800/228-9290; fax 304/353-3722. www.marriott.com.* This hotel, which is conveniently located in the heart of downtown Charleston, offers a complete collection of services and amenities. There are many recreational activities, restaurants, and shops in the immediate area. 358 rooms, 15 story. D $59-$129; under 18 free. Check-out noon, check-in 4 pm. TV; cable (premium), VCR available. In-room modem link. Restaurant 6:30 am-11 pm; Sun 7 am-10 pm; dining room 5:30-11 pm. Bar 11-1 am. Room service. Exercise equipment, sauna. Heated indoor pool, whirlpool, poolside service. Free airport transportation. Business center. Luxury level. Cr cds: A, C, D, DS, MC, V.

D ⊶ 🕇 ⊠ SC 🏃

Restaurants

★ ★ BLOSSOM DELI. *904 Quarrier St (25301). Phone 304/345-2233; fax 304/345-4412.* Don't be fooled by the name. Although it operates as a New York-style deli during the day, at night it is transformed into a romantic French-style bistro. And if longevity is a criteria for success, they first opened their doors in 1930 as a deli/soda fountain and, according to locals, it just keeps on getting better. Continental menu. Hours: 8 am-9 pm; Mon to 3 pm; Fri to 10 pm; Sat 10 am-3 pm, 5-10 pm. Closed Sun; holidays. Dinner $14-$21. Soda fountain, dairy bar. Totally nonsmoking. Cr cds: A, D, DS, MC, V.

D ⊠

★ ★ CHEF DAN'S. *222 Leon Sullivan Blvd (25301). Phone 304/344-2433; fax 304/344-2446.* American, Italian menu. Hours: 11 am-9 pm; Fri to 10 pm; Sat 4-10 pm. Closed Sun; major holidays. Dinner $11-$17. Bar. Children's menu. Cr cds: A, D, DS, MC, V.

D SC

★ ★ JOE FAZIO'S SPAGHETTI HOUSE. *1008 Bullitt St (25301). Phone 304/344-3071.* Just five minutes from downtown, this restaurant has the feeling of Little Italy at its finest. Choose from one of four dining rooms where big portions of food are served in a casual, no-frills atmosphere. Italian menu. Hours: 5-10 pm. Closed Mon; Jan 1, Easter, Dec 24, 25. Dinner $11-$22. Children's menu. Cr cds: A, D, MC, V.

D SC

★ ★ ★ LAURY'S. *350 MacCorkle Ave SE (25314). Phone 304/343-0055.* Located downtown near the Kanawha River in the old C&O Railroad Depot, this continental restaurant has welcomed diners since 1979. The dining room is an elegant, charming space. American, continental menu. Hours: 11 am-2 pm, 5-11 pm; Sat 5-10 pm. Closed Sun; major holidays. Dinner $14-$37. Bar. entertainment Fri, Sat. Near the Kanawha River. Cr cds: A, C, D, DS, MC, V.

D SC

Charles Town (D-10)

See also Harpers Ferry, Martinsburg, Shepherdstown; also see Winchester, VA

Founded 1786 **Pop** 2,907 **Elev** 530 ft **Area code** 304 **Zip** 25414

Information Jefferson County Chamber of Commerce, 201 Frontage Rd, PO Box 426; 304/725-2055

Web www.jeffersoncounty.com/chamber

Charles Town is serene, aristocratic, and full of tradition, with orderly, tree-shaded streets and 18th-century houses. It was named for George Washington's youngest brother, Charles, who laid out the town and named most of the streets after members of his family. Charles Washington's family lived here for many years. Charles Town is also famed as the place where John Brown was jailed, tried, and hanged in 1859 after his antislavery raid on Harpers Ferry.

What to See and Do

Charles Town Races and Gaming. *Flowing Springs Rd. Route 340 N. 1 mile. E on US 340. Phone 304/725-7001 or 800/795-7001.* Thoroughbred racing; clubhouse, video machines, dining room. (Daily; closed holidays) **FREE**

Jefferson County Courthouse. *100 E Washington (25414). Corner of N George and E Washington sts. Phone 304/728-3240.* (1836) This red brick, Georgian colonial structure was the scene of John Brown's trial, one of three treason trials held in the US before WWII. The courthouse was shelled during the Civil War but was later rebuilt; the original courtroom survived both the shelling and fires and is open to the public. In 1922, leaders of the miners' armed march on Logan City were tried here; one, Walter Allen, was convicted and sentenced to ten years. (Mon-Fri; closed holidays) **FREE**

Jefferson County Museum. *200 E Washington (25414). N Samuel and E Washington sts. Phone 304/725-8628.* Houses John Brown memorabilia, old guns, Civil War artifacts. (Apr-Nov, Mon-Sat) **DONATION**

Site of John Brown Gallows. *S Samuel and Hunter sts.* Marked by a pyramid of three stones supposedly taken from Brown's cell in Charles Town jail. At the execution, 1,500 troops were massed around the scaffold. Some were commanded by Major Thomas "Stonewall" Jackson; among them was John Wilkes Booth, Virginia militiaman.

Tours of Charles Town. *Phone 304/728-7713.* Historical walking tours; candlelit tours of Jefferson County Courthouse (evenings); carriage rides. All tours by appointment. **FREE**

Zion Episcopal Church. *300 E Congress St (25414). E Congress between S Mildred and S Church sts. Phone 304/725-5312.* (1852) Buried in the cemetery around the church are about 75 members of the Washington family, as well as many Revolutionary War and Confederate soldiers. (Interior, by appointment)

Special Events

Founders Day-Washington Heritage. *Phone 800/733-5469.* Exhibits, performances, tours. First weekend in May.

Jefferson County Fair. *Phone 304/728-7415.* Livestock show, entertainment, amusement rides, exhibits. Late Aug.

Motels/Motor Lodges

★ **TOWNE HOUSE MOTOR LODGE.** *549 E Washington St (25414). Phone 304/725-8441; toll-free 800/227-2339; fax 304/725-5484.* 114 rooms, 2 story. D $35-$60; each additional $5. Check-out 11 am, check-out 3 pm. TV; cable (premium). Restaurant 7 am-8 pm; Fri, Sat to 9 pm. Pool. Cr cds: A, C, D, DS, MC, V.

[D] [≋] [⬚]

★ **TURF MOTEL.** *608 E Washington St (25414). Phone 304/725-2081; toll-free 800/422-8873; fax 304/728-7605.* 47 rooms, 2 story. D $42-$160; each additional $2-$5. Pet accepted. Check-out 11:30 am, check-in 2 pm. TV; cable (premium). In-room modem link. Restaurant 6:30 am-9 pm; Fri, Sat to 10 pm. Bar 10-2 am. Room service. Pool. Cr cds: A, C, D, DS, MC, V.

[D] [🐾] [≋] [⬚] [SC]

Chesapeake and Ohio Canal National Historic Park

(See Maryland)

Clarksburg (D-6)

See also Fairmont, Grafton, Weston

Settled 1773 **Pop** 16,743 **Elev** 1,007 ft **Area code** 304 **Zip** 26301

Information Greater Bridgeport Conference & Visitors Center, 164 W Main St, Bridgeport 26330; 304/842-7272 or 800/368-4324

Web www.bridgeport-clarksburg.com

In the heart of the West Virginia hills, Clarksburg is the trading center for an area of grading lands, coal mines, and oil and gas fields. The Criminal Justice Information Services Division of the FBI is located here. During the Civil War it was an important supply base for Union troops. The famous Civil War General "Stonewall" Jackson was born in Clarksburg in 1824. His statue stands before the courthouse.

What to See and Do

North Bend Rail Trail. *121 N Court St. I-79, exit 119 to US 50. Phone 304/643-2500 or 800/899-6278.* Seventy-one miles of scenic countryside trails featuring 13 tunnels, numerous bridges, and several historic sites. Bike, hike, or horseback ride trail from nearby Wilsonburg to North Bend State Park (see PARKERSBURG). **FREE**

Salem International University. *223 W Main St (26426). 12 miles W in Salem. Phone 304/782-5011 or 304/782-5378.* (1888) 750 students. On campus is the Jennings Randolph Center (by appointment; fee), which houses papers and memorabilia of the former senator. Also here is

Fort New Salem. *Phone 304/782-5245.* Collection of 20 log houses from throughout the state were relocated to campus; pioneer history is re-created through crafts and folklore. Special events throughout the year (fee); summer concerts (July, Sat evenings). (Memorial Day weekend-Oct, Wed-Sun; Apr-mid-May, Mon-Fri) **$$**

Stealey-Goff-Vance House. *123 W Main St. Phone 304/842-3073 or 304/624-6512.* (1807) House restored by Harrison County Historical Society as a museum with period rooms, antique furniture, tools, and Native American artifacts. (May-Sept, Fri, limited hours) **$**

Watters Smith Memorial State Park. *Rural Rte 1, Duck Creek Rd. 8 miles S on US 19, then SE on unnumbered road. Phone 304/745-3081.* More than 500 acres on Duck Creek with visitor center/museum and 19th-century pioneer homestead. Swimming pool (seasonal); hiking, game courts, picnicking, playground, concession. Recreation building. Standard hours, fees.

Special Event

West Virginia Italian Heritage Festival. *309 Clark St (26301). Phone 304/622-7314.* Italian arts, music, contests, entertainment. Labor Day weekend.

Motels/Motor Lodges

★★HOLIDAY INN. *100 Lodgeville Rd, Bridgeport (26330). Phone 304/842-5411; fax 304/842-7258. www. holiday-inn.com.* 159 rooms, 2 story. S, D $79-$110; under 19 free. Private club 5 pm-10 pm; closed Sat, Sun. Pet accepted. Check-out noon. TV; cable (premium). In-room modem link. Restaurant 6 am-11 am, 5-10 pm; Sat, Sun 7 am-11 am, 5-10 pm. Room service. Pool. Airport transportation. Cr cds: A, C, D, DS, JCB, MC, V.

★ RAMADA. *250 Emily Dr (26301). Phone 304/623-2600; fax 304/622-5240. www.ramada.com.* 112 rooms, 2 story. S, D $49.95-$54.95; each additional $5; under 18 free. Complimentary continental breakfast. Check-out noon. TV; cable (premium). In-room modem link. Restaurant adjacent 11 am-10 pm. Cr cds: A, C, D, DS, MC, V.

★ SLEEP INN. *115 Tolley Dr, Bridgeport (26330). Phone 304/842-1919; fax 304/842-9524. www.sleepinn.com.* 73 rooms, 2 story. S $59; D $69; under 18 free. Pet accepted. Complimentary continental breakfast. Check-out 11 am. TV; cable (premium), VCR available. Restaurant nearby. Cr cds: A, C, D, DS, JCB, MC, V.

Restaurant

★★MINARD'S SPAGHETTI INN. *813 E Pike St (26301). Phone 304/623-1711.* Italian menu. Closed major holidays. Lunch, dinner. Bar. Children's menu. Casual attire. Cr cds: A, D, DS, MC, V. $

Davis (D-7)

See also Aurora, Elkins

Settled 1883 **Pop** 624 **Elev** 3,099 ft **Area code** 304
Zip 26260

Information West Virginia Mountain Highlands, PO Box 1456, Elkins 26241; 304/636-8400

Davis, the highest town in the state, was founded by Henry Gassaway Davis, US senator from 1871-1883. Senator Davis established the first night train in America (1848). He and his son-in-law, Senator Stephen B. Elkins, became wealthy from coal, lumber, and railroading.

What to See and Do

Blackwater Falls State Park. *County Rte 29. 2 miles W off WV 32. Phone 304/259-5216.* This 1,688-acre park includes a deep river gorge with 66-foot falls of dark, amber-colored water. Swimming in lake (fee), bath houses (Memorial Day-Labor Day), fishing, boating (rowboat, paddleboat rentals); nature trails, horseback riding; cross-country ski trails, center (rentals, school); sledding, picnicking, playground, concession, lodge, cabins, tent and trailer campground. Nature, recreation programs and tours. Paved falls viewing area for the disabled. Standard hours, fees.

Canaan Valley Resort State Park. *9 miles S on WV 32. Phone 304/866-4121 or toll-free 800/622-4121.* Approximately 6,000 acres include a valley 3,200 feet above sea level, which is surrounded by spectacular mountain peaks. Swimming pool, bathhouse, fishing, boating; hiking trails, 18-hole golf course, tennis courts, ice rink, playground, lodge, cabins, camping (dump station). Nature, recreation programs. Standard hours, fees. Ski area has quad, two triple chairlifts, Pomalift; patrol, school, SKIwee program, rentals; snowmaking; restaurant, cafeteria; lodging, nursery; night skiing (Fri-Sun). Twenty-two trails, 34 slopes; vertical drop 850 feet. (Dec-Mar, daily) 18 miles of cross-country trails. Chairlift rides (early May-Oct, daily). Special programs for the disabled. **$$$$**

Timberline Four Seasons Resort. *8 miles S off WV 32. Phone 304/866-4801; 800/SNOWING.* Triple, two double chairlifts; patrol, school, SKIwee program, rentals; snowmaking; restaurant, bar; nursery; lodging, night skiing and special events. Thirty-five slopes and trails; longest run 2 miles, vertical drop 1,000 feet. (Dec-Apr, daily) Cross-country skiing. Chairlift rides (July-Oct, Sat and Sun, also Mon holidays). **$$$$**

White Grass Touring Center. *9 miles S on WV 32 to Freeland Rd; 1/2 mile N of Canaan Valley Resort State Park. Phone 304/866-4114.* Thirty-six miles of cross-country trails, some machine-groomed; patrol, school, rentals; snowfarming; restaurant; telemark slopes, guided tours. (Late Nov-Mar, daily) **$$$**

Whitewater rafting. *Phone toll-free 800/225-5982.* Many outfitters offer guided trips on the Cheat River. For a list of outfitters contact the West Virginia Division of Tourism, Research, and Development, 90 MacCorkle Ave SW, South Charleston, WV 25303

Special Event

Tucker County Alpine Winter Festival. *William Ave and Fourth St (26260). Phone 304/866-4121.* Governor's Cup ski races. First weekend in Mar.

Motel/Motor Lodge

★ ★ **ALPINE LODGE.** *Williams Ave (26260). Phone 304/259-5245; fax 304/259-5168.* 46 rooms, 1-2 story. S, D $59-$80; each additional $2. Check-out 11 am. TV; cable (premium). In-room modem link. Restaurant 6 am-9 pm. Indoor pool. Downhill ski 10 miles; cross-country ski 2 miles. Cr cds: A, C, D, DS, MC, V.

D ⌨ 🏊 🔧

Resorts

★★**BLACKWATER LODGE.** *County Rte 29 (26260). Phone 304/259-5216; fax 304/259-5881.* 54 rooms in lodge, 26 kitchen cabins, 1-2 story. S, D $68-$78; each additional $6; cabins for 2-8, $90-$150, $450-$900/week. Lodge: Check-out noon, check-in 3 pm. Cabins: Check-out 10 am, check-in 4 pm. TV in lodge; cable (premium). In-room modem link. Dining room 7 am-9 pm. Supervised children's activities, ages 6-12. Exercise equipment. Game room. Whirlpool. Tennis. Downhill ski 10 miles, cross-country ski on site. Lawn games. All state park facilities available. Cr cds: A, D, DS, MC, V.

D ⌨ 🔧 🏊 🎿 🔧

★ ★ ★ **CANAAN VALLEY RESORT AND CONFERENCE CENTER.** *HC 70 Box 330 (26260). Phone 304/866-4121; toll-free 800/622-4121; fax 304/866-2172. www.canaanresort.com.* Whether you visit in the winter or summer, this resort holds wonderful surprises for the young at heart. 256 rooms, 2 story. June-mid-Oct, late-Dec-mid-Mar: S, D $89-$99; each additional $7; suites $120; 2-4 bedroom cabins $690-$1,140/week; family rates; package plans; lower lodge rates rest of year. Check-out 11 am, check-in 4 pm. TV; cable (premium). In-room modem link. Fireplace in cabins. Dining room 7 am-11 pm, noon-2 pm, 5-9 pm. Entertainment, movies. Supervised child's activities (winter, summer), ages 6-12. Exercise room, sauna. Game room. Two pools, one indoor, whirlpool. Greens fee $24-$33. Lighted tennis. Downhill/cross-country ski on site. Lawn games. Bicycles. Fishing privileges. Naturalist program. Deposit required. Camping sites available. Cr cds: A, D, DS, MC, V.

D ⛹ ⌨ 🎿 🎿 🏊 🔧 🔧 SC

Elkins (D-7)

See also Buckhannon, Davis, Philippi

Founded 1890 **Pop** 7,032 **Elev** 1,830 ft **Area code** 304 **Zip** 26241

Information West Virginia Mountain Highlands, PO Box 1456; 304/636-8400

Elkins was named for US Senator Stephen B. Elkins, an aggressive politician and powerful industrial magnate who was Secretary of War under Benjamin Harrison (1888-1892). This town is in a coal and timber region and is also a railroad terminus and trade center. Some of the finest scenery in the state can be seen in and around Elkins.

What to See and Do

Bowden National Fish Hatchery. *10 miles E on Old US 33. Phone 304/637-0238.* Produces brook, brown, and rainbow trout for stocking in state and national forest streams; also striped bass for Chesapeake Bay restoration project. Hatchery (daily). Visitor center (Memorial Day-mid-Oct, daily). **FREE**

Monogahela National Forest. (see)

The Old Mill. *25 miles E via US 33 to WV 32 N, in Harman. Phone 304/227-4466.* (1877) A gristmill powered by water turbines rather than a waterwheel. It was also used for planing wood and for producing white flour. Today it still uses water power to grind corn, wheat, rye, and buckwheat. Observation hive has live bees. West Virginia crafts shop includes rug weaving. (Memorial Day-Labor Day, Mon-Sat) **DONATION**

Special Events

Augusta Festival. *(26241). On campus of Davis & Elkins College, 100 Sycamore St. Phone 304/637-1209.* Celebration of traditional folk life and arts, featuring local and national performers, dances, juried craft fair, storytelling sessions, children's activities, and homemade foods. Mid-Aug.

Mountain State Forest Festival. *101 Lough St (26241). Phone 304/636-1824.* Some events on campus of Davis & Elkins College. Queen Silvia is crowned; carnival, parades, entertainment, tilting at rings on horseback, sawing and woodchopping contests, marksmanship tests, State Championship Fiddle and Banjo Contest; juried craft fair and art exhibit. Late Sept-early Oct.

Seneca Rocks

Serious rock climbers rate West Virginia's massive Seneca Rocks as one of the top East Coast destinations for their sport. More than 375 major mapped climbing routes ascend the sheer, slender rocks that thrust 900 feet above the tumbling North Fork River. On any nice day you're apt to see a half-dozen or more climbers laboriously pulling themselves, hand over hand, slowly up the wall. It might take them hours to get to the top; you can enjoy the same view from the summit as they get, but without the effort. A 1 1/2-mile foot trail—rated only moderately difficult—zigzags to the top. Heavily traveled and well-marked, it is a non-climber's introduction to West Virginia's panoramic vistas. A notable West Virginia landmark, the dramatic rock formation is worth a visit simply as a scenic attraction. From the edge of the river, which tumbles in a fury of white water, a thickly forested ridge forms an imposing pedestal for the rocks. From this base, the twin towers seem to leap into the sky.

They form a rough, craggy wall with a knife's-edge point barely 15 feet wide. Begin your ascent near the foot of the rocks at Seneca Rocks Discovery Center, a beautiful structure of stone and glass. Inside, exhibits detail the natural history of the rocks; outside, the deck is positioned for great views of the climbers. The hiker's trail to the top begins just across the river from the Discovery Center. It climbs steadily through shady woods. Sturdy benches are placed along the way if you need to rest. At several especially steep points, stone steps seem to stretch endlessly above, but that's only your imagination. From the summit overlooks, the view of the river-traced valley below is a generous reward for your pains. Give yourself an hour to reach the top, 30 minutes to enjoy your lofty perch and another 30 minutes for the much easier descent. Afterward, cross the road (State Route 55) for refreshments in the village of Seneca Rocks at Harper's Old Country Store, which looks much as it must have on its opening day in 1902.

Motels/Motor Lodges

★ **ECONO LODGE.** *40 Cherry St (26241). Phone 304/636-5311; toll-free 800/446-6900; fax 304/636-5311. www.econolodge.com.* 72 rooms, 1-2 story. S $42-$47; D $44-$92; each additional $5; suites $54-$69; kitchen units $56-$70; under 18 free; package plans; higher rates during Forest Festival. Pet accepted; $50. Complimentary continental breakfast. Check-out 11 am. TV; cable (premium). In-room modem link. Indoor pool. Cr cds: A, C, D, DS, MC, V.

Ⓓ ⛖ ⊠ Ⓢ Ⓒ

★★ **ELKINS MOTOR LODGE.** *Harrison Ave (26241). Phone 304/636-1400; fax 304/636-6318.* 55 rooms, 1-2 story. S, D $41-$50; each additional $3; suites $75. Pet accepted; $5. Check-out noon. TV; cable (premium). In-room modem link. Restaurant 5-10 pm; Sun to 8 pm. Room service. Free airport transportation. Cr cds: A, D, DS, MC, V.

Ⓓ ⊠

★ **FOUR SEASONS MOTEL.** *1091 Harrison Ave (26241). Phone 304/636-1990; toll-free 800/367-7130; fax 304/636-6475. www.elkinsfourseasons.com.* 18 rooms, 1-2 story. S, D $38-$48; each $3; under 12 free; weekly rates. Suite $56. Check-out 11 am. TV; cable (premium). Restaurant nearby. Cr cds: A, D, DS, MC, V.

⊠ Ⓢ Ⓒ

★ **SUPER 8.** *350 Beverly Pike; Rte 219 S (26241). Phone 304/636-6500; fax 304/636-6500. www.super8.com.* 44 rooms, 2 story. S, D $48-$60; each additional $6; under 12 free; higher rates: Forest Festival, graduation, ski week. Pet accepted. Complimentary continental breakfast. Check-out 11 am. TV; cable (premium). In-room modem link. Restaurant opposite 7 am-10 pm. Cr cds: A, C, D, DS, MC, V.

Ⓓ ⊠ Ⓢ Ⓒ

B&B/Small Inns

★ **THE POST HOUSE BED AND BREAKFAST.** *306 Robert E. Lee Ave (26241). Phone 304/636-1792.* 5 rooms, 2 share bath, 2 story. S $64; D $65; each additional $10. Closed Nov-June. Complimentary continental breakfast. Check-out 11 am, check-in 2 pm. TV; cable (premium). Restaurant nearby. Massage. Built in 1936. Totally nonsmoking.

⊠

★★★ **THE WARFIELD HOUSE.** *318 Buffalo St (26241). Phone 304/636-4555; toll-free 888/636-4555. www.warfieldhousebandb.com.* The nearby attractions include Blackwater Falls State Park, Spruce Knob-Seneca Rocks Recreation Area, and the Cass Scenic Railroad. 5 rooms, 2 story. No room phones. Apr-Nov: S, D $79-$89; each additional $10; package plans. Children over 12 years only. Complimentary continental breakfast. Check-out 11 am, check-in 6 pm. TV; cable (premium) in common room. Street parking. Built in 1901; Colonial Revival style. Totally nonsmoking. Cr cds: MC, V.

⊠ SC

Restaurant

★ ★ **CHEAT RIVER INN.** *US 33E (26241). Phone 304/636-6265; fax 304/636-4495. www.cheatriverlodge.com.* Hours: 4-10 pm. Closed Mon, major holidays. Dinner $14-$26. Bar. Children's menu. Reservations accepted. Outdoor dining. Mounted fish on display. Cr cds: D, DS, MC, V.

D

Fairmont (C-7)

See also Clarksburg, Morgantown

Settled 1793 **Pop** 19,097 **Elev** 883 ft **Zip** 26554

Information Convention & Visitors Bureau of Marion County, 110 Adams St, PO Box 58, 26555-0058; 304/368-1123 or 800/834-7365

Web www.marioncvb.com

Fairmont was a Union supply depot plundered by Confederate cavalry in April 1863. General William Ezra Jones's division swept through town, took 260 prisoners, destroyed the $500,000 bridge across the Monongahela River, and raided the governor's residence. After the war, resources in the region were developed and coal became the mainstay. Today Fairmont manufactures aluminum, mine machinery, and other products.

What to See and Do

Fairmont State College. *1201 Locust Ave (26554). Phone 304/367-4000.* (1867) 7,000 students. On campus is a one-room schoolhouse with original desks, books, and other artifacts related to early era of education (Apr-Oct, schedule varies).

Marion County Museum. *211 Adams St. (26554) Adjacent to courthouse. Phone 304/367-5398.* Displays of B & O china, five furnished rooms covering 1776-1920s; doll, train, and toy collection. (Mon-Sat; closed holidays) **FREE**

Prickett's Fort State Park. *I-79, exit 139, then 2 miles W. Phone 800/CALL-WVA or 304/363-3030 (museum).* Approximately 200 acres with reconstructed 18th-century log fort, colonial trade and lifestyle demonstrations by costumed interpreters, outdoor historical drama (July, Wed-Sat). Boating (ramps); picnicking. Visitor center. Fort and museum (mid-Apr-Oct, daily). Museum (fee).

Special Event

Three Rivers Festival. *Palatine Park. Phone 304/363-2625.* Entertainment, parade, Civil War reenactment, carnival games. Third weekend in May.

Motels/Motor Lodges

★ **COMFORT INN AND SUITES.** *1185 Airport Rd (26554). Phone 304/367-1370; toll-free 800/228-5150; fax 304/367-1806. www.comfortinn.com.* 100 rooms, 18 suites, 2 story. S, D $59-$79; suites $95; under 18 free; higher rates special events. Complimentary continental breakfast. Check-out noon. TV; cable (premium). In-room modem link. Restaurant nearby. Exercise equipment. Pool. Cr cds: A, C, D, DS, JCB, MC, V.

D ⟷ 🎿 ⊠ SC

★ ★ **HOLIDAY INN.** *930 E Grafton (26554). Phone 304/366-5500; toll-free 800/465-4329; fax 304/363-3975. www.holiday-inn.com.* 106 rooms, 2 story. S, D $69-$99; under 18 free; higher rates: WVU football games, graduation. Pet accepted. Check-out noon. TV; cable (premium). In-room modem link. Restaurant 6 am-2 pm, 5-10 pm. Bar, room service. Pool. Cr cds: A, C, D, DS, JCB, MC, V.

D 🐾 ⟷ ⊠ SC

★ **RED ROOF INN.** *50 Middletown Rd (26554). Phone 304/366-6800; toll-free 800/733-7663; fax 304/366-6812. www.redroof.com.* 108 rooms, 2 story. S, D $39.95-$65.99; each additional $3; under 18 free. Pet accepted. Check-out noon. TV. Restaurant nearby. Cr cds: A, C, D, DS, MC, V.

D 🐾 ⊠ SC

Restaurant

★ ★ **MURIALE'S.** *1742 Fairmont Ave South Fairmont (26554). Phone 304/363-3190; fax 304/363-0828.* Italian menu. Closed Dec 25. Lunch, dinner. Bar. Children's menu. Casual attire. Outdoor seating. Cr cds: A, C, D, DS, MC, V. **$**

D SC

Franklin (E-8)

See also Petersburg; also see Harrisonburg, VA

Settled 1794 **Pop** 797 **Elev** 1,731 ft **Area code** 304 **Zip** 26807

Information West Virginia Mountain Highlands, PO Box 1456, Elkins 26241; 304/636-8400

What to See and Do

Seneca Caverns. *Approximately 15 miles NW on US 33 to Riverton, then 3 miles E. Phone 304/567-2691; toll-free*

800/239-7647. Caves contain magnificent stalagmites and stalactites; were used as a refuge by the Seneca people. (Daily) **$$$**

Special Event

Treasure Mountain Festival. *Phone 304/249-5422.* Square dancing, clogging; parade, gospel and mountain music, drama; rifle demonstration, cross-cut sawing contest; children's contests, games; trail rides craft exhibits, country food. Third weekend in Sept.

Gauley Bridge (F-5)

See also Beckley, Charleston, Summersville

Pop 738 **Elev** 680 ft **Area code** 304 **Zip** 25085

Information Upper Kanawha Valley Chamber of Commerce, PO Box 831, Montgomery 25136; 304/442-5756

This town at the junction of the New and Gauley rivers was the key to the Kanawha Valley during the Civil War. In November 1861 Union General W. S. Rosecrans defeated Confederate General John B. Floyd, a victory that assured Union control of western Virginia. Stone piers of the old bridge, which was destroyed by retreating Confederates in 1861, can be seen near the present bridge.

What to See and Do

Contentment Museum Complex. *7 miles E on US 60, 1 mile E of Hawk's Nest State Park. Phone 304/658-5695 or 304/465-0165.* (Circa 1830) Former residence of Confederate Colonel George W. Imboden contains original woodwork, period furniture, toy collection. Adjacent Fayette County Historical Society Museum features displays of Native American relics, local artifacts, Civil War items; restored one-room schoolhouse. (June-Aug, Mon-Sat; rest of year, by appointment) **$$**

Hawk's Nest State Park. *6 miles E on US 60. Phone 304/658-5212 or 304/658-5196.* Approximately 280 acres on Gauley Mountain, with fine views of New River Gorge from rocks 585 feet above the river. A 600-foot aerial tramway carries passengers to canyon floor. Swimming pool, fishing; hiking trails, tennis, picnic area, playground, concession, restaurant, lodge. Log museum with early West Virginia artifacts (May-Nov, daily; free). Standard hours, fees.

New River Gorge Bridge. *13 miles SE on US 60, then 6 miles SW on US 19, near Fayetteville. Phone 304/574-2115.* A masterpiece of engineering, this four-lane, single arch steel-span bridge rises 876 feet above the New River Gorge National River (see HINTON), making it the second-highest bridge in the US, and at 3,030 feet, the longest bridge of its type in the world. Just north of the bridge on US 19 is the Canyon Rim Visitors Center (daily; closed Dec 25), providing two overlooks of the bridge and river, a 70-foot descending boardwalk, slide presentation, exhibits, and ranger-guided walks (May-Oct).

★ **Whitewater rafting.** *Phone 800/225-5982; or the Fayette County Chamber of Commerce, 310 Oyler Ave, Oak Hill 25901; phone 800/927-0263.* Many outfitters offer guided trips on the New and Gauley rivers. For a list of outfitters, contact the West Virginia Division of Tourism, Research, and Development, 90 MacCorkle Ave SW, South Charleston 25303.

Special Event

Bridge Day. *New River Gorge Bridge. Phone 304-442-5756.* Bridge is opened to pedestrians; parachutists test their skills by jumping off the bridge and floating to the bottom of the gorge. Third Sat in Oct.

Motel/Motor Lodge

★ ★ **HAWKS NEST STATE PARK LODGE.** *Rte 60, Ansted (25812). Phone 304/658-5212; toll-free 800/225-5982; fax 304/658-4549.* 32 rooms, 4 story. D $70-$82; each additional $6; under 13 free; Check-out noon, check-in 3 pm. TV; cable (premium). In-room modem link. Dining room 7 am-9 pm; Dec-Feb to 8 pm. Pool. Tennis. 1,100-foot vertical tramway to marina. Cr cds: A, D, DS, MC, V.

⊡ ⊱ ⊶ ⊠ ⓢⓒ

B&B/Small Inn

★ ★ **GLEN FERRIS INN.** *US 60, Glen Ferris (25090). Phone 304/632-1111; fax 304/632-0113.* 16 rooms, 3 story. D $60-$75. Check-out 11 am, check-in 4 pm. TV; cable (premium). Dining room 6 am-9 pm; Sun from 7 am. Renovated 1840s inn, originally Federal style in design; built by the grandson of one of the signers of the Declaration of Indepedence. Totally nonsmoking. Cr cds: A, DS, MC, V.

⊡ ⊾ ⊠

Grafton (C-7)

See also Clarksburg, Fairmont, Morgantown, Philippi

Founded 1856 **Pop** 5,489 **Elev** 1,004 ft **Area code** 304 **Zip** 26354

Information Grafton-Taylor County Convention and Visitors Bureau, 214 W Main St, Room 205; 304/265-3938

Mother's Day started in Grafton in 1908 when Anna Jarvis observed the anniversary of her mother's death during a religious service. The idea caught on nationally, and in 1914 President Woodrow Wilson issued a proclamation urging nationwide observance. The International Shrine to Motherhood in the original Mother's Day church is located at 11 East Main St.

During the Civil War Grafton was an important railroad center; 4,000 Union troops camped here before the Battle of Philippi in 1861. General McClellan also had his headquarters in the town. The first land soldier killed in the war, T. Bailey Brown, fell at Grafton. He is buried in the Grafton National Cemetery.

What to See and Do

Tygart Lake State Park. *2 miles S off US 119, 250. Phone 304/265-3383.* This scenic 2,100-acre park contains one of the largest concrete dams east of the Mississippi (1,900 feet by 209 feet). Swimming, waterskiing, fishing, boating (ramp, rentals, marina); hiking, game courts, picnic area, playground, concession, lodge, tent and trailer camping, ten cabins. Nature and recreation programs, dam tours (summer; phone 304/265-1760). Standard hours, fees.

Special Event

Taylor County Fair. *Fairgrounds, US 50. Phone 304/265-4155.* Horse racing, livestock shows, auctions, carnival, crafts. Last week of July.

Motels/Motor Lodges

★ **CRISLIP MOTOR LODGE.** *300 Moritz Ave (26354). Phone 304/265-2100; fax 304/265-2017.* 40 rooms, 2 story. S, D $46-$50; each additional $5; suites $37-$46. Pet accepted; $5/day. Check-out 11 am. TV; cable (premium). In-room modem link. Restaurant nearby. Pool. Cr cds: A, D, DS, MC, V.

[D] [icons]

★ ★ **TYGART LAKE STATE PARK LODGE.** *Rte 1 (26354). Phone 304/265-6144; fax 304/265-6147. www.tygartlake.com.* 20 rooms, 1 story. May-Oct: S, D $65-$77; each additional $6; cabins $456-$510/week; under 13 free; golf plans; lower rates Nov, Dec. Closed Jan-Apr. Check-out noon. TV; cable (premium). In-room modem link. Restaurant 8 am-8 pm. Free supervised child's activities (Memorial Day-Labor Day). Lawn games. Cr cds: A, D, DS, MC, V.

[D] [icon]

Harpers Ferry (C-10)

See also Charles Town, Martinsburg, Shepherdstown

Settled 1732 **Pop** 307 **Elev** 247 ft **Area code** 304 **Zip** 25425

Information Jefferson County Chamber of Commerce, 201 Frontage Rd, PO Box 426, Charles Town 25414; 304/725-2055

Web www.jeffersoncounty.com/chamber

Scene of abolitionist John Brown's raid in 1859, Harpers Ferry is at the junction of the Shenandoah and Potomac rivers, where West Virginia, Virginia, and Maryland meet. A US armory and rifle factory made this an important town in early Virginia; John Brown had this in mind when he began his insurrection. He and 16 other men seized the armory and arsenal the night of October 16 and took refuge in the engine house of the armory when attacked by local militia. On the morning of the 18th, the engine house was stormed, and Brown was captured by 90 marines from Washington under Brevet Colonel Robert E. Lee and Lt J. E. B. Stuart. Ten of Brown's men were killed, including two of his sons. He was hanged in nearby Charles Town (see) for treason, murder, and inciting slaves to rebellion.

When war broke out, Harpers Ferry was a strategic objective for the Confederacy, which considered it the key to Washington. "Stonewall" Jackson captured 12,693 Union prisoners here before the Battle of Antietam in 1862. The town changed hands many times in the war, during which many buildings were damaged. In 1944 Congress authorized a national monument here, setting aside 1,500 acres for that purpose. In 1963 the same area was designated a National Historical Park, now occupying more than 2,200 acres.

What to See and Do

⭐ **Harpers Ferry National Historical Park.** *Shenandoah and High sts (25425). Phone 304/535-6298.* Here the old town has been restored to its 19th-century appearance; exhibits and interpretive presentations explore the park's relation to the water-power industry, the Civil War, John Brown, and Storer College, a school established for freed slaves after the war. A Visitor Center is located just off US 340. Visitors should park there; a bus will take them to Lower Town. Contact the Visitor Center, PO Box 65. **$$**

Information Center. *S side of Shenandoah St near High St (25425). Phone 304/535-6029.* Restored Federalist house built in 1859 by US government as residence for the master armorer of the US Armory. During the Civil War it was used as headquarters by various commanding officers. Also on this street is the site of the US Armory that John Brown attempted to seize; it was destroyed during the Civil War. Farther down Shenandoah St and right under the trestle is

The Point. Three states, West Virginia, Virginia, and Maryland, and two rivers, the Shenandoah and Potomac, meet at the Blue Ridge Mtns. Back under the trestle is

John Brown's Fort. *On Arsenal Sq.* Where John Brown made his last stand; rebuilt and moved near original site. Across the street is

John Brown Museum. *Arsenal Square and High St.* Contains an exhibit and film on John Brown and a ten-minute slide presentation on the history of the park. Exiting the museum to the right is High St, which has two Civil War museums and two black history museums. Up the stone steps from High St is

Harper House. Three-story stone house built between 1775-1782 by the founder of the town; both George Washington and Thomas Jefferson were entertained as overnight guests. Restored and furnished with period pieces. Behind this house is

Camp Hill. Four restored, private houses built 1832-1850. Continue up the hill to

Ruins of St. John's Episcopal Church. Used as a guardhouse and hospital during the Civil War. Approximately 100 yards farther is

Jefferson's Rock. From here Thomas Jefferson, in 1783, pronounced the view "one of the most stupendous scenes in nature." Farther along, above the cemetery, is

Lockwood House. (1848) Greek Revival house used as headquarters, barracks, and stable during Civil War; later used as a classroom building by Storer College (1867), which was founded to educate freed men after the war.

Other buildings. Open to the public during the summer are the dry goods store, provost, office, and blacksmith shop.

John Brown Wax Museum. *168 High St. Phone 304/535-6342 or 304/535-2792.* Sound and animation depict Brown's exploits, including the raid on Harpers Ferry. **$$**

Whitewater rafting. *Phone toll-free 800/225-5982.* Many outfitters offer guided trips on the Shenandoah and Potomac rivers. For a list of outfitters, contact the West Virginia Division of Tourism, Research, and Development, 90 MacCorkle Ave SW, South Charleston 25303.

Special Events

Election Day 1860. *Phone 304/535-6298.* More than 100 people in 19th-century attire reenact the 1860 presidential election. Second Sat in Oct.

Mountain Heritage Arts and Crafts Festival. *102 Frontage Rd (25414). Phone 304/725-2055.* More than 190 craftspeople and artisans demonstrate quilting, wool spinning, pottery throwing, vegetable dyeing, and other crafts; concerts. Second full weekend in June and last full weekend in Sept.

Old Tyme Christmas. *Phone 304/535-2627.* Caroling, musical programs, children's programs, taffy pull, candlelight walk. First two weekends of Dec.

Motel/Motor Lodge

★**COMFORT INN.** *Rte 340 and Union St (25425). Phone 304/535-6391; toll-free 800/535-9909; fax 304/535-6395. www.comfortinn.com.* 50 rooms, 2 story. D $69-$100; each additional $6; under 18 free. Complimentary continental breakfast. Check-out 11 am, check-in 3 pm. TV; cable (premium), VCR available (movies). In-room modem link. Health club privileges. Cr cds: A, D, DS, MC, V.
⊡ ⊠ SC

Hillsboro (F-7)

See also Marlinton

Settled 1765 **Pop** 243 **Elev** 2,303 ft **Area code** 304 **Zip** 24946

Information West Virginia Mountain Highlands, PO Box 1456, Elkins 26241; 304/636-8400

Civil War troops marched through Hillsboro and Confederates camped in town before the decisive Battle of Droop Mountain. Novelist Pearl S. Buck was born in her grandparents' house while her parents, missionaries on leave from China, were visiting.

What to See and Do

Beartown State Park. *1 1/2 miles S off US 219. Phone 304/653-4254.* Approximately 110 acres of dense forest with unique rock formations created by erosion; a boardwalk with interpretive signs winds through the park. Standard hours.

Droop Mountain Battlefield State Park. *5 miles S on US 219. Phone 304/653-4254.* Encompasses approximately 285 acres on site where on Nov 6, 1863, Union forces under General William W. Averell defeated Confederates under General John Echols, destroying the last major rebel resistance in the state. Park features graves, breastworks, and monuments. Hiking, picnic areas, playground. Museum. Battle reenactments (second week of Oct, every even year). Standard hours.

⭐ **Pearl S. Buck Birthplace Museum.** *(Stulting House) 1/2 mile N on US 219. Phone 304/653-4430.* Birthplace of Pulitzer and Nobel Prize-winning novelist, restored to its 1892 appearance; original and period furniture; memorabilia. Sydenstricker House, home of Buck's father and his ancestors, was moved 40 miles from its original site and restored here. Guided tours. (May-Nov, Mon-Sat) **$$**

Watoga State Park. *Rte 39 and Beaver's Creek Rd (24954). 1 miles N on US 219, then SE. Phone 304/799-4087.* More than 10,100 acres make this West Virginia's largest state park. Watoga, derived from the Cherokee term watauga, means "river of islands." It aptly describes the Greenbrier River, which forms several miles of the park's boundary. Swimming pool, bathhouses, fishing, boating on 11-acre Watoga Lake (rentals); hiking and bridle trails, horseback riding, tennis, game courts, cross-country skiing, picnicking, playground, concession, restaurant (seasonal), tent and trailer camping, 33 cabins. Brooks Memorial Arboretum; nature, recreation programs (summer). Standard hours, fees.

Calvin Price State Forest. *Rte 39 and Beaver's Creek Rd (24954). Phone 304/799-4087.* This vast, undeveloped forest has more than 9,400 acres for fishing; deer and small-game hunting, hiking, and primitive camping (fee).

Hinton (G-5)

See also Beckley

Founded 1873 **Pop** 2,880 **Elev** 1,382 ft **Area code** 304 **Zip** 25951

Information Summers County Chamber of Commerce, 200 Ballangee St; 304/466-5332

Hinton, a railroad town on the banks of the New River, is the seat of Summers County, where the Bluestone and Greenbrier rivers join the scenic and protected New River.

What to See and Do

Bluestone State Park. *5 miles S on WV 20. Phone 304/466-2805.* More than 2,100 acres on Bluestone Lake, which was created by the Bluestone Dam. Swimming pool (Memorial Day-Labor Day), wading pool, bathhouses, waterskiing, fishing, boating (ramps, marina nearby; canoe, rowboat, and motorboat rentals); hiking trails, game courts, picnicking, playground, tent and trailer

camping (dump station), 25 cabins. Nature, recreation programs (summer). Gift shop. Standard hours, fees.

New River Gorge National River. *Phone 304/465-0508.* One of the oldest rivers on the continent, the New River rushes northward through a deep canyon with spectacular scenery. The 52-mile section from Hinton to Fayetteville is popular among outdoor enthusiasts, especially whitewater rafters and hikers. The Hinton Visitor Center is located along the river at WV 3 Bypass (Memorial Day-Labor Day, daily); phone 304/466-0417. A year-round visitor center is located on US 19 near the New River Gorge Bridge (see GAULEY BRIDGE). For further information and a list of whitewater outfitters, contact Superintendent, PO Box 246, Glen Jean 25846.

Pipestem Resort State Park. *12 miles SW on WV 20. Phone 304/466-1800.* More than 4,000 acres with 3,600-foot aerial tramway to Bluestone River complex. Swimming, bathhouses, fishing, canoeing, paddleboating; hiking trails, horseback riding, 9- and 18-hole golf courses, miniature golf, tennis, archery, lighted game courts, cross-country skiing, sledding, playground, two lodges, four restaurants, tent and trailer camping (dump station), 25 cabins. Visitor center; nature, recreation programs. Aerial tramway, arboretum, observation tower. Amphitheater; dances. Standard hours, fees.

Resort

★★★ **MOUNTAIN CREEK LODGE.** *Pipestem State Park, Pipestem (25979). Phone 304/466-1800; toll-free 800/922-5582; fax 304/466-5679.* 174 rooms, 7 story. D $75-$165; each additional $6; under 13 free. Check-out noon, check-in 4 pm. TV; cable (premium), VCR available (movies $4). In-room modem link. Restaurant. Bar (seasonal). Entertainment in summer. Exercise equipment, sauna. Two pools, one indoor, children's pool, poolside service. Lighted tennis. Cross-country ski on site. Lawn games. Sleighing, tobogganing. Mountain Creek Lodge (open May-Oct) is located at foot of Bluestone Canyon; it is accessible only by aerial tram. The resort is state-owned and operated; all state park facilities are available to guests. Cr cds: A, DS, MC, V.

⬚ 🛗 ⛽ 🍽 🎿 🛥 🛶 SC

B&B/Small Inn

★ **PENCE SPRINGS HOTEL.** *Rte 3, Pence Springs (24962). Phone 304/445-2606; toll-free 800/826-1829; fax 304/445-2204.* 17 rooms, 2 story. D $84.50-$94.50; under 3 free. Complimentary full breakfast. Check-out 11 am, check-in 1 pm. Dining room 8-10 am, 5-9 pm; weekend hours vary. Bar 5 pm-midnight. Lawn games. Cr cds: A, C, D, DS, MC, V.

⬚ ⛽ 🛶 SC

Restaurants

★ ★ **BLUESTONE DINING ROOM.** *Pipestem Resort, Pipestem (25979). Phone 304/466-1800.* Hours: 7 am-2 pm, 5:30-9 pm. Wine, beer. Breakfast $3.95-$7.95, lunch $5.95-$7.95, dinner $9.95-$15.95. Buffet: breakfast $5.50, lunch $6.95, dinner $10-$20. Children's menu. Specializes in seafood, steak, country dishes. Outdoor dining. View of gorge and mountains. Cr cds: D, MC, V.

D

★ **KIRK'S.** *HC 76 Box 3 (25951). Phone 304/466-4600.* American menu; hamburgers, hot dogs. Closed Thanksgiving, Dec 25. Breakfast, lunch, dinner. On New River near Bluestone Resort Park; patio overlooks river. Casual attire. Outdoor seating. **$**

D

★★**MOUNTAIN CREEK.** *Pipestem Resort, Pipestem (25979). Phone 304/466-1800.* American menu. Hours: 7 am-2 pm, 5:30-9 pm; Tues, Thurs 7-11 am, 5:30-9 pm; Sat to 10 pm. Closed Nov-May. Reservations accepted (dinner). French, Bar. Breakfast $2.25-$4.50, lunch $4.95, dinner $14.95-$27. Children's menu. Specialties: roasted pork filet, rack of lamb, prime rib of beef, seafood. Own pastries. Park in Pipestem Resort State Park. Dining room at 1,000-foot-deep gorge; accessible by tram only. Totally nonsmoking. Cr cds: D, MC, V.

D ⬙

★ ★ **OAK SUPPER CLUB.** *Just N of Pipestem State Park entrance, Pipestem (25979). Phone 304/466-4800; fax 304/466-4800.* Specializes in pork, duckling, fresh mountain trout. Hours: 5:30-9 pm. Closed Thanksgiving, Dec 25; also Jan-Mar. Dinner $10.95-$24.95. Bar. Children's menu. Reservations accepted. Cr cds: MC, V.

D

Huntington (E-3)

Founded 1871 **Pop** 51,475 **Elev** 564 ft **Area code** 304

Information Cabell-Huntington Convention & Visitors Bureau, PO Box 347, 25708; 304/525-7333 or 800/635-6329

Web www.wvvisit.org

The millionaire president of the Chesapeake & Ohio Railroad, Collis P. Huntington, founded this city and named it for himself. Originally a rail and river terminus, commerce and industry have made it the second-largest city in the state. Thoroughly planned and meticulously laid out, Huntington is protected from the Ohio River by an 11-mile floodwall equipped with 17 pumping stations and 45 gates. Glass, railroad products, and metals are important city industries.

What to See and Do

Beech Fork State Park. *5601 Longbranch Rd (25504). Approximately 15 miles SE via WV 10, then 7 miles W on Hughes Branch Rd, near Bowen. Phone 304/528-5794.* Nearly 4,000 acres on 720-acre Beech Fork Lake. Fishing, boating (ramp, marina); hiking trails, physical fitness trail, tennis, game courts, picnicking, camping. Store. Visitor center; nature, recreation programs (summer). Meeting rooms. Standard hours, fees.

Blenko Glass Company, Inc. *Fairground Rd. 16 miles E via US 60, in Milton; I-64 exit 28. Phone 304/743-9081.* Famous glass factory; makers of Country Music Award, presidential gifts, and original supplier to Colonial Williamsburg. Visitor center (daily; closed holidays) has stained glass from nine leading studios; observation gallery for viewing hand-blown glassmaking and blown stained glass. (Mon-Fri; closed holidays; also first two weeks of July, Dec 25-Jan 1) Museum of Historical Glass; Garden of Glass beside a 3-acre lake. **FREE**

Camden Park. *US 60 E. Phone 304/429-4231.* Amusement park with 27 rides, games, concession; boat and train rides, log flume, miniature golf, roller rink, picnicking. (Mid-Apr-Memorial Day, Sat, Sun; Memorial Day-Labor Day, Tues-Sun) Rides individually priced; also unlimited ride plan. **$$$**

East Lynn Wildlife Management Area. *Mcclintic Rd. 15 miles SE via WV 152 and WV 37, near East Lynn. Phone 304/675-0871.* Almost 23,000 acres used primarily by sportsmen; trails, primitive camping (fee).

Heritage Village. *210 11th St (25701). 11th St and Veterans Memorial Blvd. Phone 304/696-5954.* Restored Victorian B & O Railroad yard surrounding brick courtyard. Restaurant in original passenger station (1887), restored Pullman car, shops in renovated freight and box cars, warehouses. (Mon-Sat) **FREE**

Huntington Museum of Art. *2033 McCoy Rd; I-64, exit 8. Phone 304/529-2701.* Museum with American and European paintings, prints, and sculpture; Herman P. Dean Firearms Collection; Georgian silver; Asian prayer rugs; pre-Columbian art; Appalachian folk art; Ohio Valley historical and contemporary glass. Complex includes exhibition galleries, library, studio workshops, amphitheater, auditorium, sculpture garden, observatory, art gallery for young people, nature trails. (Tues-Sat, also Sun afternoons; closed holidays) **FREE**

Motels/Motor Lodges

★ **DAYS INN.** *5196 US Rte 60 E (25705). Phone 304/733-4477; toll-free 800/694-8999; fax 304/733-4493. www.daysinn.com.* 153 rooms, 2 story. S, D $55-$85; each additional $5; under 16 free. Complimentary continental breakfast. Check-out noon. TV; cable (premium). In-room modem link. Restaurant nearby. Indoor pool. Cr cds: A, C, D, DS, JCB, MC, V.

D ⊷ ⩙ SC

★ ★ **RADISSON HOTEL.** *1001 3rd Ave (25701). Phone 304/525-1001; toll-free 800/333-3333; fax 304/525-1048. www.radisson.com.* This high-rise hotel is located downtown, just one block from Riverfront Park. 210 rooms, 11 story. S, D $79-$119; each additional $10; suites $300-$475; under 18 free; weekend rates. Check-out noon. TV; cable (premium), VCR available. In-room modem link. Restaurant 6:30 am-11 pm; Fri, Sat to midnight. Bar 4 pm-midnight. Room service. Exercise equipment, sauna. Valet parking. Airport transportation. Business center. On Ohio River. Cr cds: A, C, D, DS, ER, JCB, MC, V.

D ⊷ 🏋 ⩙ SC 🚶

★ **RED ROOF INN.** *5190 US Rte 60E (25705). Phone 304/733-3737; toll-free 800/733-7663; fax 304/733-3786. www.redroof.com.* 108 rooms, 2 story. S, D $40-$70; each additional $5; under 18 free. Pet accepted. Check-out noon. TV. In-room modem link. Cr cds: A, C, D, DS, MC, V.

D 🐾 ⩙ SC

★ ★ **STONE LODGE.** *5600 Rte 60 E (25705). Phone 304/736-3451; fax 304/736-3451.* 120 rooms, 3 story. S, D $49-$65; each additional $5; under 18 free. Complimentary continental breakfast. Check-out noon. TV; cable (premium). Restaurant 4-10 pm. Pool. Cr cds: A, C, D, DS, MC, V.

D ⊷ ⩙ SC

Restaurants

★ ★ **HERITAGE STATION.** *11th St and Veterans Memorial Blvd (25701). Phone 304/523-6373; fax 304/523-6399.* American menu. Closed Sun; Thanksgiving, Dec 25. Lunch, dinner. Bar. Children's menu. Former railroad station built in 1887; memorabilia, antiques. Casual attire. Outdoor seating. Cr cds: A, C, D, DS, MC, V. **$$**

D

★ ★ **REBELS & REDCOATS TAVERN.** *412 W 7th Ave (25701). Phone 304/523-8829; fax 304/697-8676.* This family-owned restaurant offers a varied menu and has been in business for 35 years. The casual, colonial dining room has a pleasant red and green décor with rustic finishes and a fireplace. American menu. Closed Sun, Mon; major holidays; also the week of July 4. Lunch, dinner. Bar. Children's menu. Casual attire. Cr cds: A, DS, MC, V. **$$**

D

Lewisburg (G-6)

See also White Sulphur Springs

Founded 1782 **Pop** 3,624 **Elev** 2,099 ft **Area code** 304 **Zip** 24901

Information Greenbrier County Convention and Visitors Center, 105 Church St; 304/645-1000 or 800/833-2068

Web www.greenbrierwv.com

At the junction of two important Native American trails, the Seneca (now US 219) and the Kanawha (now US 60), Lewisburg was the site of colonial forts as well as a Civil War battle. The town's 236-acre historic district has more than 60 buildings from the 18th and 19th centuries in a variety of architectural styles.

What to See and Do

Lost World Caverns. *1 mile N on Fairview Rd. Phone 304/645-6677.* Scenic trail over subterranean rock mountain; prehistoric ocean floor; stalagmites, stalactites; flow stone, ribbons, hex stones. Self-guided tours (daily; closed holidays). **$$$**

North House Museum. *301 W Washington St. Phone 304/645-3398.* Colonial and 19th-century objects and artifacts. (Mon-Sat) **$$**

Old Stone Presbyterian Church. *200 Church St. Phone 304/645-2676.* Original log church (1783) was replaced by present native limestone structure (1796). (Daily) **FREE**

Organ Cave. *417 Masters Rd, Ronceverte (24970). Phone 304/645-7600.* One of the longest caves in the US. Forty-five miles of mapped passageways. (Daily)

Special Event

State Fair. *Fairgrounds, 2 miles S on US 219. Phone 304/645-1090.* Exhibitors from a number of other states; horse shows, harness racing. Mid-Aug.

Motels/Motor Lodges

★ ★ **BRIER INN.** *540 N Jefferson St (24901). Phone 304/645-7722; fax 304/645-7865. www.brierinn.com.* 164 rooms, 2 story. D $54-$59; each additional $5; under 12 free. Pet accepted, some restrictions; fee. Check-out 11 am, check-in 2 pm. TV; cable; VCR available (movies). In-room modem link. Restaurant 11 am-10 pm; Fri, Sat to 11 pm. Bar 10-2 am; entertainment Fri. Room service. Exercise room. Pool. Cr cds: A, D, DS, MC, V.

D 🐾 ⊷ 🏋 🚶 ✈ ⩙

★ **BUDGET HOST INN.** *204 N Jefferson St (24901). Phone 304/645-3055; toll-free 800/283-4678; fax 304/645-3033.* 68 rooms, 1-3 story. D $55-$120; each additional $5; under 18 free. Pet accepted; fee. Check-out 11 am, check-in 2 pm. TV; cable. Restaurant 6 am-10 pm. Room service. Pool, whirlpool. Airport transportation. Cr cds: A, C, D, DS, MC, V.

D ⬛ ⬛ ⬛ SC

★ **DAYS INN.** *635 N Jefferson St (24901). Phone 304/645-2345; toll-free 800/325-2525; fax 304/645-5501. www.daysinn.com.* 26 rooms. D $50-$85; each additional $6. Pet accepted, some restrictions; fee. Check-out 11 am, check-in 1 pm. TV; cable (premium). Health club privileges. Airport transportation. Cr cds: A, D, DS, JCB, MC, V.

⬛ ⬛ SC

B&B/Small Inns

★ ★ ★ **GENERAL LEWIS INN.** *301 E Washington St (24901). Phone 304/645-2600; toll-free 800/628-4454; fax 304/645-2601. www.generallewisinn.com.* Operating as a guest house since 1928, this bed-and-breakfast was built in the early 1800s. It is surrounded by flower gardens and lawns with a lily pond. Every room is furnished with antiques and crafts made by early settlers. 27 rooms, 2 story. D $89-$120; each additional $12; package plans. Check-out 11 am, check-in 3 pm. TV; cable. Dining room 7 am-9 pm. Bar 11 am-9 pm. Room service. Health club privileges. Totally nonsmoking. Cr cds: A, DS, MC, V.

D ⬛

Marlinton (F-7)

See also Hillsboro

Settled 1749 **Pop** 1,204 **Elev** 2,130 ft **Area code** 304
Zip 24954

Information West Virginia Mountain Highlands, PO Box 145, Elkins 26241; 304/636-8400

Marlinton is the seat of Pocahontas County, an area known for its wide variety of outdoor recreational opportunities. A Ranger District office of the Monongahela National Forest (see) is located in the town.

What to See and Do

Cass Scenic Railroad State Park. *5 miles E on WV 39, then 19 miles N on WV 28 to WV 66 in Cass. Phone 304/456-4300.* Steam train makes 8-mile round-trip (90 minutes) up the mountain to Whittaker (daily) and 22-mile round-trip (4 1/2 hours) to top of Bald Knob (Tues-Sun); picnic stopover; dinner trains (some Sat starting in June; call for reservations). On the 1,089-acre property are two museums, a country store, and 14 renovated logging camp houses now serving as tourist cottages. Picnicking, camping. Standard hours, fees. **$$$$**

Cranberry Mountain Visitor Center-Monongahela National Forest. *WV 150 and WV 39/55 (26261). Approximately 7 miles NW of Mill Point via US 219 and WV 39. Phone 304/653-4826 or 304/846-2695 (off-season).* Exhibits, videos, and publications on conservation and forest management. (Apr-Nov, daily) **FREE**

Cranberry Glades. *WV Hwy 150 and WV Hwy 39-55 (26261). Phone 304/653-4826.* A USDA Forest Service botanical area. Approximately 750 acres featuring open bog fringed by forest and alder thicket. Boardwalk with interpretive signs. Guided tours leave from visitor center (June-Labor Day, wkends). Glades (year-round, weather permitting). **FREE**

Elk River Touring Center. *16 miles N on US 219, follow signs, near Slatyfork. Phone 304/572-3771.* Features 34 miles of cross-country trails in the Monongahela National Forest (see); rentals; restaurant; lodging. Night skiing. Also guided mountain bike tours, cave tours in season. **$$$$**

Greenbrier River Trail. *WV 39 and Beaver's Creek Rd (24954). Phone 304/799-4087.* Part of the state park system, this 76-mile trail runs along the Greenbrier River from the town of Cass, on the north, through Marlinton to North Caldwell, on the south; passes through small towns, over 35 bridges, and through two tunnels. Originally the trail was part of the Chesapeake & Ohio Railroad. Activities include backpacking, bicycling, and cross-country skiing; trail also provides access for fishing and canoeing. No developed sites.

National Radio Astronomy Observatory. *5 miles SE on WV 39, then 21 miles N on WV 28, 92 in Green Bank. Phone 304/456-2209.* Study of the universe by radio telescopes. Slide show, exhibits, and one-hour bus tour of site. (Mid-June-Labor Day weekend, daily; Memorial Day weekend-mid-June and after Labor Day-Oct, Sat and Sun) **FREE**

Pocahontas County Historical Museum. *810 2nd Ave. On US 219 S, at WV 39. Phone 304/799-4973.* Displays on history of the county from its beginnings to present. Extensive photo collection. (Early June-Labor Day, daily) **$**

Seneca State Forest. *5 miles E via WV 39, then 10 miles NE on WV 28. Phone 304/799-6213.* Approximately 12,000 acres with fishing and boating on a 4-acre lake; hunting, hiking trails, picnicking, playground, camping, eight rustic cabins. Standard hours, fees.

Snowshoe Mountain Resort. *1 Snowshoe Dr. 26 miles N on US 219, near Slatyfork. Phone 304/572-4636 (ski report).* Four quad, seven triple chairlifts; two handle tows; patrol, school, rentals; snowmaking; restaurants, lodging, nursery, health club, four pools. Fifty-six slopes and trails; longest run 6,200 feet; vertical drop 1,500 feet. Night skiing. (Mid-Nov-mid-Apr, daily) Summer activities include horseback riding, fishing, and hiking. **$$$$**

Special Event

Pioneer Days. *900 9th St (24954). Phone 304/799-4315.* Craft exhibits and demonstrations; horse-pulling contests, frog and turtle races; bluegrass and mountain music shows; 4x4 truck pulling; parade; antique car show. Early-mid-July.

Martinsburg (C-10)

See also Berkeley Springs, Charles Town, Harpers Ferry, Shepherdstown; also see Hagerstown, MD.

Settled 1732 **Pop** 14,972 **Elev** 457 ft **Area code** 304 **Zip** 25401

Information Martinsburg-Berkeley County Chamber of Commerce, 198 Viking Way; 304/267-4841 or 800/332-9007

Web www.berkeleycounty.org

Martinsburg is located in the center of an apple- and peach-producing region in the state's eastern panhandle. Because of its strategic location at the entrance to the Shenandoah Valley, the town was the site of several battles during the Civil War. The famous Confederate spy Belle Boyd was a resident. Officially chartered in 1778, Martinsburg is recognized for the preservation of its many 18th- and 19th-century houses and mercantile and industrial buildings.

What to See and Do

General Adam Stephen House. *309 E John St. Phone 304/267-4434.* (1789) Restored residence of Revolutionary War soldier and surgeon Adam Stephen, founder of Martinsburg. Period furnishings; restored smokehouse and log building. (May-Oct, Sat and Sun, limited hours; also by appointment) **FREE** Adjacent is

Triple-Brick Building. *Phone 304/267-4434.* Completed in three sections just after the Civil War, the structure was used to house railroad employees. A museum of local history is located on the top two floors. (May-Oct, Sat and Sun, limited hours; also by appointment) **FREE**

Special Event

Mountain State Apple Harvest Festival. *Phone 304/263-2500.* Parade, celebrity breakfast, contests, entertainment, Apple Queen coronation, square dancing, grand ball, arts and crafts show. Third weekend in Oct.

Motels/Motor Lodges

★ **COMFORT INN.** *1872 Edwin Miller Blvd (25401). Phone 304/263-6200; toll-free 800/228-5150; fax 304/267-0995. www.comfortinn.com.* 109 rooms, 11 suites, 5 story. Apr-Oct: S, D $49-$125; each additional $10; suites $98; under 18 free; weekend, holidays rates; lower rates rest of year. Complimentary continental breakfast. Check-out noon. TV; cable (premium). In-room modem link. Restaurant adjacent 11 am-10 pm. Exercise equipment. Game room. Pool. Cr cds: A, C, D, DS, JCB, MC, V.

⊡ ⇌ ⊼ ⊠ SC

★ **COMFORT INN.** *Rte 9 E Short Rd (25401). Phone 304/263-8888; toll-free 800/228-5050; fax 304/263-1540. www.comfortinn.com.* 76 rooms, 3 story. May-Oct: S, D $68-$90; each additional $5; under 18 free; lower rates rest of year. Complimentary continental breakfast. Check-out 11 am. TV; cable (premium), VCR available. In-room modem link. Restaurant nearby. Exercise equipment. Pool. Golf privileges. Cr cds: A, C, D, DS, JCB, MC, V.

⊡ ⊀⎮ ⇌ ⊼ ⊠ SC

★ ★ **HOLIDAY INN.** *301 Foxcroft Ave (25401). Phone 304/267-5500; toll-free 800/465-4329; fax 304/264-9157. www.holiday-inn.com.* 120 rooms, 5 story. Apr-Oct: S, D $59-$89; under 17 free; lower rates rest of year. Pet accepted, some restrictions. Check-out noon. TV; cable (premium). In-room modem link. Restaurant 6:30 am-10 pm; Sun 7 am-9 pm. Bar 4 pm-1 am. Room service. Exercise room, sauna. Two pools, one indoor; whirlpool, poolside service. Lighted tennis. Lawn games. Cr cds: A, C, D, DS, JCB, MC, V.

⊡ ⬤ ⍢ ⇌ ⊼ ⊠ SC

★ **KNIGHTS INN.** *1997 Edwin Miller Blvd (25401). Phone 304/267-2211; toll-free 800/843-5644; fax 304/267-9606. www.knightsinn.com.* 59 rooms, 1-story. Apr-Dec: S, D $46-$57; each additional $5; kitchens, $46.95-$55; under 17 free; lower rates rest of year. Pet accepted; $5/day. Check-out 11 am. TV; cable (premium), VCR available. In-room modem link. Restaurant adjacent 6 am-11 pm. Cr cds: A, C, D, DS, JCB, MC, V.

⊡ ⬤ ⊠ SC

★ **SUPER 8.** *2048 Edwin Miller Blvd (25401). Phone 304/263-0801; toll-free 800/800-8000; fax 304/263-0801. www.super8.com.* 43 rooms, 3 story. June-Sept: S, D $45-

$55; each additional $6; under 16 free; weekly, weekend rates; higher rates during special events; lower rates rest of year. Pet accepted. Check-out 11 am. TV; cable (premium). In-room modem link. Restaurant adjacent 6 am-11 pm. Cr cds: A, C, D, DS, JCB, MC, V.

D ◼ ◼ SC

Resort

★ ★ ★ **WOODS RESORT & CONFERENCE CENTER.** *Mountain Lake Rd, Hedgesville (25427). Phone 304/754-7977; toll-free 800/248-2222; fax 304/754-8146. www.thewoodsresort.com.* This resort is adjoined to the 23,000-acre Sleepy Creek Wilderness. 62 rooms, 14 kitchen cabins, 1-2 story. MAP: D $78.50-$98.50/person; EP: S, D $89-$109; each additional $11; kitchen cabins $138; under 5 free; weekends (2-night minimum). Check-out noon, check-in 4 pm. TV; cable (premium), VCR available. In-room modem link. Some fireplaces. Whirlpools in lodge rooms. Dining room 7 am-3 pm, 5-9 pm; Fri 5-10 pm; Sat 3-10 pm; Sun 3-9 pm. Bar noon-midnight; entertainment Sat. Supervised child's activities (June-Aug), ages 6-12. Exercise room, massage, sauna. Four pools, one indoor, wading pools, whirlpool. 36-hole golf privileges, greens fee $18-$50. Indoor/outdoor lighted tennis. Lawn games. Fishing, horseback riding. Cr cds: A, C, D, DS, MC, V.

D ◼ ◼ ◼ ◼ ◼ ◼ ◼

Monongahela National Forest (F-6)

Entrance is E of Elkins on US 33. Contact Supervisor, US Department of Agriculture Building, 200 Sycamore St, Elkins. Phone 304/636-1800.

This 901,000-acre forest, in the heart of the Alleghenies, has some of the loftiest mountains in the East. Spruce Knob (4,862 ft) is the highest point in the state. Headwaters of the Ohio and Potomac rivers are here. The forest is a meeting ground of northern and southern plant life, with stands of red spruce and northern hardwoods joining with oak, hickory, and other southern hardwoods. There are also many interesting secondary and tertiary plants and wildflowers. Several recreation areas, including five wilderness areas, Spruce Knob/Seneca Rocks National Recreation Area near Petersburg (see), and Blue Bend and Lake Sherwood recreation areas near White Sulphur Springs (see), are all located within the forest. Swimming, fishing, boating; hunting, hiking, rock climbing, caving,

picnicking, camping (fee). Fees charged at the more developed recreation sites. Part of the Greenbrier River Trail (see MARLINTON) runs through the southern section of the forest. Forest headquarters in Elkins (see); Cranberry Mountain Visitor Center near Marlinton (see); and Seneca Rocks Visitor Center in Seneca Rocks (see PETERSBURG).

Moorefield (D-8)

See also Petersburg

Settled 1777 **Pop** 2,375 **Elev** 821 ft **Area code** 304 **Zip** 26836

Information West Virginia Mountain Highlands, PO Box 1456, Elkins 26241; 304/636-8400

What to See and Do

Lost River State Park. *18 miles E on WV 55 to Baker, then 13 miles S on WV 259, near Mathias. Phone 304/897-5372 or 800/CALL-WVA.* More than 3,700 acres where Lee's White Sulphur Springs was once a famous resort; an original cabin still stands; museum. Swimming pool, wading pool (Memorial Day-Labor Day); hiking trails, horseback riding, tennis, game courts, picnicking, playground, restaurant, 24 cabins. Recreation building; nature programs (summer); scenic overlooks. Standard hours, fees.

Special Event

Hardy County Heritage Weekend. *Main St and Winchester (26836). Phone 304/538-6560.* Tours of antebellum houses, medieval jousting, crafts, traditional events. Last full weekend in Sept.

Morgantown (C-7)

See also Fairmont

Settled 1776 **Pop** 26,809 **Elev** 892 ft **Area code** 304 **Zip** 26505

Information Greater Morgantown Convention & Visitors Bureau, 709 Beechurst Ave; 304/292-5081 or 800/458-7373

Web www.mgtn.com

Morgantown is both an educational and industrial center. West Virginia University was founded here in 1867, the Morgantown Female Collegiate Institute in 1839. Known internationally for its glass, Morgantown is home to a number of glass plants which produce wares ranging from lamp parts to decorative paper weights and crystal tableware. The town is also home to a number of research laboratories maintained by the federal government.

What to See and Do

Coopers Rock State Forest. *10 miles E on I-68. Phone 304/594-1561.* More than 12,700 acres. Trout fishing; hunting, hiking trails to historical sites; Henry Clay iron furnace (1834-1836). Cross-country ski trails, picnicking, playground, concession, tent and trailer camping. Standard hours, fees.

Chestnut Ridge Regional Park. *Sand Springs Rd. Phone 304/594-1773.* Swimming beach, fishing; tent and trailer camping (hookups, dump station), rustic cabins, lodge (fees), hiking, picnicking, cross-country ski trails (Dec-Feb). Nature center. Park (daily).

West Virginia University. (1867) 22,712 students. University has 15 colleges. Tours (Mon-Sat; for reservations phone 304/293-3489). The Visitors Center in the Communications Building on Patterson Dr has touch-screen monitors and video presentations about the university and upcoming special events (phone 304/293-6692 for 24-hour event information). Of special interest on the downtown campus are Stewart Hall and the university's original buildings, located on Woodburn Cir. In the Evansdale area of Morgantown are the Creative Arts Center, the 75-acre Core Arboretum, the 63,500-seat Coliseum, and the

Cook-Hayman Pharmacy Museum. *1 Medical Dr (26505). Health Sciences Center North, room 1136. Phone 304/293-5101.* Re-creates pharmacy of yesteryear with old patent medicines. (Mon-Fri; weekends by request; closed holidays) **DONATION**

Personal Rapid Transit System (PRT). *88 Beechhurst Ave (26506). Phone 304/293-5011.* A pioneering transit system, the PRT is the world's first totally automated system. Operating without conductors or ticket takers, computer-directed cars travel between university campuses and downtown Morgantown. (Mon-Sat; may not operate holidays and university breaks) **$**

Whitewater rafting. *Phone toll-free 800/458-7373.* Many outfitters offer guided trips on the Cheat and Tygart rivers. For a list of outfitters contact the Greater Morgantown Convention and Visitors Bureau, 709 Beechurst Ave.

Special Events

Mason-Dixon Festival. *Morgantown Riverfront Park. Phone 304/599-1104.* River parade, boat races, arts and crafts, concessions. Mid-Sept.

Mountaineer Balloon Festival. *Morgantown Municipal Airport. 100 Hart Field Rd (26505). Phone 304/296-8356.* Hot air balloon races, carnival, music, food. Mid-Oct.

Motels/Motor Lodges

★ **COMFORT INN.** *225 Comfort Inn Dr (26508).* Phone 304/296-9364; toll-free 800/228-5150; fax 304/296-0469. www.comfortinn.com. 80 rooms, 2 story. S, D $59-$139; each additional $5; suites $80-$115; kitchen units $45-$95; under 18 free; higher rates: football weekends, graduation. Pet accepted. Complimentary continental breakfast. Check-out noon. TV; cable (premium), VCR available. In-room modem link. Restaurant adjacent 11 am-10 pm; Fri, Sat to 2 pm; Sun noon-9 pm. Exercise equipment. Pool, whirlpool. Cr cds: A, C, D, DS, JCB, MC, V.

⧉ 🛏 🏋 🏊 SC

★ **ECONO LODGE.** *3506 Monongahela Blvd (26505).* Phone 304/599-8181; fax 304/599-8181; toll-free 800/446-6900; www.econolodge.com. 71 rooms, 2 story. S, D $66; higher rates: football weekends, graduation. Pet accepted. Complimentary continental breakfast. Check-out 11 am. TV; cable (premium). In-room modem link. Restaurant adjacent 6 am-midnight. Cr cds: A, C, D, DS, JCB, MC, V.

⧉ 🛏 🏊

★ **ECONO LODGE.** *15 Commerce Dr, Westover (26507).* Phone 304/296-8774; toll-free 800/446-6900; fax 304/296-8774. www.econolodge.com. 81 rooms, 2 story. S, D $58; each additional $5; under 18 free. Check-out noon. TV; cable (premium). Restaurant nearby. Cr cds: A, C, D, DS, JCB, MC, V.

⧉ 🏊 SC

★ **HAMPTON INN.** *1053 Van Voorhis Rd (26505).* Phone 304/599-1200; fax 304/598-7331. www.hamptoninn.com. 108 rooms, 5 story. S, D $68-$104; suites $140; under 18 free; higher rates during special events. Complimentary continental breakfast. Check-out noon. TV; cable (premium), VCR available. In-room modem link. Restaurant adjacent. Cr cds: A, C, D, DS, JCB, MC, V.

⧉ 🏊

★ ★ **HOLIDAY INN.** *1400 Saratoga Ave (26505).* Phone 304/599-1680; toll-free 800/465-4329; fax 304/598-0989. www.holiday-inn.com. 147 rooms, 2-4 story. S, D $69-$85; under 18 free; higher rates: graduation, athletic events. Pet accepted, $10. Check-out noon. TV; cable (premium). In-room modem link. Restaurant 6-11 am, 5-10 pm. Bar 4 pm-2 am. Pool. Cr cds: A, C, D, DS, JCB, MC, V.

⧉ 🛏 🏊 🏊 SC

★ **RAMADA INN.** *US Rte 119 N, I-68 and I-79 (26506).* Phone 304/296-3431; toll-free 800/834-9766; fax 304/296-8841. www.ramada.com. 151 rooms, 4 story. S, D $75-$185; each additional $5; suites, studio rooms $100-$220; under 18 free; higher rates: special events, football games, Dec 31, Memorial Day weekend, graduation. Pet accepted; $75. Complimentary continental breakfast. Check-out noon. TV; cable (premium). In-room modem link. Restaurant 6 am-10 pm. Bar 11 am-1 am, Sat to 2 am. Entertainment Wed, Fri, Sat. Exercise equipment. Heated pool. Free airport transportation. Cr cds: A, C, D, DS, JCB, MC, V.

D 🕊 ⛱ 🏋 ⛝ SC

Hotel

★ ★ **HISTORIC CLARION HOTEL MORGAN.** *127 High St (26505). Phone 304/292-8200; fax 888/241-7944. www.clarionhotelmorgan.com.* 76 rooms, 5 story. S, D $95-$130; under 12 free; monthly rates; higher rates: football season, graduation. Complimentary continental breakfast. Check-out 11 am. TV; cable (premium). In-room modem link. Exercise equipment. Historic brick hotel (1925). Cr cds: A, C, D, DS, JCB, MC, V.

D 🏋 ⛝

Resort

★ ★ ★ **LAKEVIEW SCANTICON GOLF RESORT, SPA & CONFERENCE CENTER.** *1 Lakeview Dr (26508). Phone 304/594-1111; toll-free 800/624-8300; fax 304/594-9472. www.lakeviewresort.com.* Even the most stressed-out guest will find true relaxation at this resort. 187 rooms, 1-3 story. Apr-Nov: S, D $79-$199; each additional $10; suites $250-$450; under 18 free; summer, winter rates; golf plans; lower rates rest of year. Check-out 2 pm, check-in 4 pm. TV; cable (premium). In-room modem link. Dining rooms 6:30 am-10 pm. Bar 11-1 am; Sun from 1 pm; entertainment Mon-Sat. Supervised children's activities, ages 4-15. Exercise room, massage, sauna. Four pools, two indoor; whirlpool, poolside service. Greens fee $39-$79. Indoor tennis. Free airport transportation. Business center. On 400 acres. Cr cds: A, C, D, DS, MC, V.

D 🎿 🏌 ⛱ 🏋 ⛝ SC 🏃

B&B/Small Inn

★ **FIELDCREST MANOR BED AND BREAK-FAST.** *1440 Stewartstown Rd (26505). Phone 304/599-2686; toll-free 866/599-2686; fax 304/599-3796. www.fieldcrestmanor.com.* 5 rooms, 2 story. S $75; D $90; under 10 free; package plans; weekends, holidays (2-day minimum). Complimentary full breakfast. Check-out 11 am, check-in 3 pm. TV; cable (premium). In-room modem link. Built in 1900; hillside location. Totally non-smoking. Cr cds: A, MC, V.

⛝

Restaurants

★ ★ **BACK BAY.** *1869 Mileground (26505). Phone 304/296-3027; fax 304/296-2624. www.backbaywv.com.* Seafood menu. Closed major holidays. Lunch, dinner. Bar. Children's menu. Casual attire. Outdoor seating. Cr cds: A, D, DS, MC, V. **$$**

D

★ **GARFIELD'S.** *9801 Mall Rd (26501). Phone 304/983-6811.* Southwestern, steak menu. Lunch, dinner. Bar. Children's menu. Casual attire. **$**

D

★ **PUGLIONI'S.** *1137 Van Voorhis Rd (26505). Phone 304/599-7521.* Italian menu. Closed major holidays. Lunch, dinner. Bar. Children's menu. Casual attire. Cr cds: A, D, DS, MC, V. **$$**

D

Nitro (E-4)

See also Charleston

Founded 1918 **Pop** 6,824 **Elev** 604 ft **Area code** 304 **Zip** 25143

Information Putnam County Chamber of Commerce, 5664 WV Rte 34, PO Box 553, Teays 25569; 304/757-6510

Web www.putnamcounty.org

Nitro experienced explosive growth around a huge smoke-less powder plant during World War I, when the town's population reached 35,000 overnight and some 3,400 buildings were erected. When the war ended the demand for smokeless powder fizzled and the town dried up; factory buildings were scrapped and whole houses were shipped down the river. Now a western suburb of Charleston, Nitro produces chemicals.

What to See and Do

Tri-State Greyhound Park. *1 Greyhound Dr (25313). E via I-64 exit 47A to Goff Mountain Rd, then to Greyhound Dr in Cross Lanes. Phone 304/776-1000.* Indoor grandstand, clubhouse, concessions. (Mon-Sat evenings; matinees Sat, Sun, and holidays) Must be 18 to wager.

Waves of Fun. *2 Valley Park Rd (25526). W via I-64 exit 39, then 3 miles S on WV 34, at Valley Park in Hurricane. Phone 304/562-0518.* Water park featuring three water slides, wave pool, swimming areas, bathhouse, tube rentals (fee), lockers, concessions; miniature golf. (Memorial Day-June, weekends; early June-Labor Day, daily) **$$$**

Motels/Motor Lodges

★ **COMFORT INN.** *102 Racer Dr, Cross Lanes (25313). Phone 304/776-8070; fax 304/776-6460. www.comfortinn.com.* 113 rooms, 2 story. S $62-$75; D $70-$75; each additional $5; under 18 free. Suite $125. Complimentary continental breakfast. Check-out noon. TV; cable (premium). Restaurant adjacent 7 am-midnight. Bar 4 pm-12 am; Fri, Sat to 2 am. Exercise room. Pool, whirlpool. Cr cds: A, C, D, DS, JCB, MC, V.

⬚ ⬚ ⬚ ⬚ SC

★ **ECONO LODGE.** *4115 1st Ave (25143). Phone 304/755-8341; toll-free 800/780-7234; fax 304/755-2933. www.econolodge.com.* 42 rooms, 2-3 story. No elevator. S, D $56-$66; under 12 free. Check-out 11 am. TV; cable (premium). Restaurant adjacent open 24 hours. Cr cds: A, C, D, DS, ER, JCB, MC, V.

⬚ ⬚

★ **SUPER 8.** *419 Hurricane Creek Rd, Hurricane (25526). Phone 304/562-3346; toll-free 1-800/726-7016; fax 304/562-7408. www.super8.com.* 146 rooms, 2 story. Apr-Sept: S, D $40-$56; each additional $5; under 16 free; weekly rates; higher rates during special events; lower rates rest of year. Pet accepted, some restrictions; $10. Complimentary continental breakfast. Check-out noon. TV; cable (premium). In-room modem link. Restaurant adjacent 7 am-10 pm. Game room. Pool. Cr cds: A, C, D, DS, MC, V.

⬚ ⬚ ⬚ ⬚ SC

Parkersburg (D-4)

Settled 1785 **Pop** 33,099 **Elev** 616 ft **Area code** 304 **Zip** 26101

Information Parkersburg/Wood Co Convention & Visitor's Bureau, 350 7th St; 304/428-1130 or 800/752-4982

Web www.parkersburgcvb.org

In 1770 George Washington came to this area to inspect lands awarded to him by Virginia for his military services. After the Revolutionary War, Blennerhassett Island, in the Ohio River west of Parkersburg, was the scene of the alleged Burr-Blennerhassett plot. Harman Blennerhassett, a wealthy Irishman, built a lavish mansion on this island. After killing Alexander Hamilton in a duel, Aaron Burr came to the island, allegedly with the idea of seizing the Southwest and setting up an empire; Blennerhassett may have agreed to join him. On December 10, 1806, the plot was uncovered. Both men were acquitted of treason but ruined financially in the process. The Blennerhassett mansion burned in 1811 but was later rebuilt.

Today Parkersburg is the center for many industries, including glass, chemicals, petrochemicals, and ferrous and other metals. Fishing is popular in the area, especially below the Belleville and Willow Island locks and dams on the Ohio River.

What to See and Do

Actors Guild Playhouse. *724 Market St (26101). 8th and Market sts. Phone 304/485-1300.* Musical, comedic, and dramatic performances. (Fri-Sun) **$$$**

Blennerhassett Island Historical State Park. *137 Juliana St (26101). 2 miles S in Ohio River. Phone 304/420-4800.* A 500-acre island accessible only by sternwheeler. There are self-guided walking tours of the island; horse-drawn wagon rides; tours of the Blennerhassett mansion. Bicycle rentals, picnicking, concession. (May-Labor Day, Tues-Sun, also holidays; Sept-Oct, Thurs-Sun) Tickets available for boat ride at Blennerhassett Museum. **$$**

Blennerhassett Museum. *2nd and Juliana sts. Phone 304/420-4840.* Features archaeological and other exhibits relating to history of Blennerhassett Island and Parkersburg area; includes artifacts dating back 12,000 years. Theater with video presentation. (May-Oct, Tues-Sun; rest of year, Sat and Sun; closed Jan 1, Thanksgiving, Dec 25) **$**

City Park. *Park Ave and 23rd St. Phone 304/424-8572.* A 55-acre wooded area with the Cooper Log Cabin Museum, which dates from 1804. Swimming pool, fishing, paddle boats; miniature golf, tennis, shelters and picnic facilities.

Middleton Doll Company. *2 miles W via US 50, at 1301 Washington Blvd in Belpre, OH. Phone 740/423-1481.* Tour of vinyl and porcelain doll factory (20 minutes). Factory store (Mon-Sat; closed holidays). **FREE**

Mountwood Park. *12 miles E via US 50 to Volcano Rd. Phone 304/679-3611.* Wooded area with fishing, boating (no gasoline motors); hiking, mountain biking, nature trails; picnic area. **FREE**

North Bend State Park. *22 miles E on US 50, then 7 miles SE on WV 31, near Cairo. Phone 304/643-2931 or 800/CALL-WVA.* Approximately 1,400 acres in the wide valley of the North Fork of the Hughes River; scenic overlooks of famous horseshoe bend. Swimming pool, bathhouse, fishing; miniature golf, tennis, game courts; hiking, bicycle, and bridle trail; 71-mile North Bend Rail Trail (see Clarksburg). Picnicking, playground, concession, restaurant, lodge, tent and trailer camping (dump station), eight cabins. Nature, recreation programs. Nature trail for disabled. Standard hours, fees.

Parkersburg Art Center. *725 Market St. Phone 304/485-3859.* Changing exhibits. (Tues-Sun; closed holidays) **$**

Rubles Sternwheelers Riverboat Cruises. *Depart from Point Park, 2nd and Ann sts. Phone 740/423-7268.* To Blennerhassett Island. (May-early Sept, Tues-Sun; early Sept-Oct, Thurs-Sun) **$$$**

Special Events

Parkersburg Homecoming. *2nd and Avery (26101). Point Park, just off WV 68 at foot of 2nd St. Phone 304/422-3588.* Riverfront celebration features entertainment, parade, sternwheeler races, waterskiing show, miniature car races, fireworks. Third weekend in Aug.

West Virginia Honey Festival. *Phone 304/428-1130.* 4-H Grounds. Honey-related exhibits, baking, food, arts and crafts. Mid-Sept.

Motels/Motor Lodges

★ ★ **HOLIDAY INN.** *Rte 50 & I-77 (26104). Phone 304/485-6200; fax 304/485-6261. www.holiday-inn.com.* 149 rooms, 2 story. S, D $55-$97; under 18 free; weekend packages. Check-out noon. TV. cable (premium). In-room modem link. Restaurant 6 am-9 pm; Sat from 7 am; Sun 7 am-2 pm, 5-8 pm. Bar 11 am-midnight. Exercise equipment, sauna. Game room. Heated indoor pool, whirlpool. Cr cds: A, D, DS, MC, V.

[D] [⌘] [✈] [≈] [SC]

★ ★ **NORTH BEND STATE PARK LODGE.** *RR 1 Box 221, Cairo (26337). Phone 304/643-2931; toll-free 800/225-5982; fax 304/643-2970. www.northbendsp.com.* 29 rooms, 8 cabins, 2 story. Memorial Day weekend-Labor Day: S, D $51-$67; each additional $6; 2-3 bedroom cabins $528-$666/wk; under 12 free; lower rates rest of year. Check-out noon (lodge), 10 am (cabins). TV. Restaurant 7 am-8 pm. Room service. Free supervised children's activities (June-Aug). Tennis. On river. View of mountains. State owned, operated. Cr cds: A, D, DS, MC, V.

[D] [✄] [≈] [SC]

★ **RED ROOF INN.** *3714 E 7th St (26104). Phone 304/485-1741; toll-free 800/733-7663; fax 304/485-1746. www.redroof.com.* 106 rooms, 2 story. S, D $40-$52; each additional $5; under 18 free. Pet accepted. Check-out noon. TV; cable (premium). In-room modem link. Exercise equipment. Cr cds: A, C, D, DS, MC, V.

[D] [⌘] [≈] [SC]

Hotel

★ ★ **BLENNERHASSETT HOTEL.** *320 Market St (26101). Phone 304/422-3131; toll-free 800/262-2536; fax 304/485-0267. www.blennerhassett.com.* This landmark hotel was built before the turn of the century in the "gaslight era" and was fully restored in 1986. The Victorian style of the hotel is evident in the rich crown mouldings, authentic English doors, brass and leaded-glass chandeliers, and antiques. 108 rooms, 5 story. S, D $95-$115; each additional $6; suites $145-$165; under 18 free. Pet accepted; $10. Check-out noon. TV; cable (premium), VCR available. In-room modem link. Restaurant 6 am-10 pm. Bar 11-1 am. Room service. Valet parking. Free airport transportation. Cr cds: A, C, D, DS, MC, V.

[D] [⌘] [✉] [≈]

B&B/Small Inn

★ ★ ★ **WILLIAMS' HOUSE BED AND BREAKFAST.** *5406 Grand Central Ave (26105). Phone 304/295-7212; fax 304/295-5550.* At this romantic getaway near the Ohio state line, hosts Barbara and Bob Williams run a bed-and-breakfast out of their country home. Barbara even makes a full breakfast that usually includes hot biscuits, grits, and the like. 5 rooms, 3 story. No elevator. S $65; D $74; suite $89; weekend May-Nov (2-night minimum); each additional $10. Complimentary full breakfast. Check-out 11:30 am, check-in 3 pm. TV; cable (premium), VCR available (movies). Exercise equipment. Pool. Lawn games. Airport transportation. Built in 1920. Some room phones. Totally nonsmoking. Cr cds: MC, V.

[≈] [✈] [≈]

Restaurant

★ **MOUNTAINEER FAMILY RESTAURANT.** *4006 E 7th St (26101). Phone 304/422-0101.* American menu. Closed Dec 25. Breakfast, lunch, dinner, 24-hour service. Children's menu. Casual attire. Cr cds: D, DS, MC, V. $

[D] [SC]

Petersburg (D-8)

See also Franklin, Moorefield

Settled 1745 **Pop** 2,423 **Elev** 937 ft **Area code** 304 **Zip** 26847

Information West Virginia Mountain Highlands, 1200 Harrison Ave, Lower Level, Suite A, Elkins 26241; 304/636-8400

A Ranger District office of the Monongahela National Forest (see) is located in Petersburg.

What to See and Do

Monongahela National Forest. (see) *USDA Forest Service, H659, PO Box 240. Phone 304/257-4488.* Recreation area is popular for canoeing, hiking, and other outdoor sports. Camping (fee). **FREE**

Smoke Hole Caverns. *8 miles S on WV 28 and 55. Phone 304/257-4442; toll-free 800/828-8478.* Caverns were used centuries ago by the Seneca both for shelter and the smoking of meat. During the Civil War they were used by troops on both sides for storing ammunition. Later, they hid "moonshiners," illegal distillers of corn whiskey. It is claimed the caverns contain the longest ribbon stalactite and the second-highest cave room in the world. Guided tours. Large gift shop with wildlife exhibits; concessions. Tours. (Daily; closed Thanksgiving, Dec 25) **$$**

Motels/Motor Lodges

★ ★ **HERMITAGE MOTOR INN.** *203 Virginia Ave (26847). Phone 304/257-1711; toll-free 800/437-6482; fax 304/257-4330.* 38 rooms, 2 story. S $47; D $55; each additional $6; under 12 free. Complimentary continental breakfast. Check-out noon. TV; cable (premium). In-room modem link. Restaurant 11 am-9 pm; Sat 4-9 pm; Sun 11 am-3 pm. Pool. Craft shop, bookstore in 1840s inn. Cr cds: A, C, D, DS, MC, V.

D ⊒ ⊠ SC

★ **SMOKE HOLE HOTEL & LOG CABINS.** *WV 28 S; HC 59 Box 39, Seneca Rocks (26884). Phone 304/257-4442; toll-free 800/828-8478; fax 304/257-2745. www.smokehole.com.* 10 rooms, 3 suites, 1 story. S, D $49-$79; each additional $10; kitchen cottages $94-$189; weekends (2-day minimum); holidays (3-day minimum); family, weekly rates. Check-out 11 am. TV; cable (premium). In-room modem link. Pool. Lawn games. Adjacent to Smoke Hole Caverns. Cr cds: A, D, DS, MC, V.

D ⊾ ⊬ ⊒ ⊠

Philippi (D-7)

See also Buckhannon, Clarksburg, Grafton

Settled 1780 **Pop** 2,870 **Elev** 1,307 ft **Area code** 304 **Zip** 26416

Information Barbour County Chamber of Commerce, PO Box 5000; 304/457-1958

The first land battle of the Civil War, a running rout of the Confederates known locally as the Philippi Races, was fought here on June 3, 1861. A historical marker on the campus of Alderson-Broaddus College marks the site. The Union attacked to protect the Baltimore & Ohio Railroad, whose main line between Washington and the West ran near the town.

What to See and Do

Barbour County Historical Society Museum. *146 N Main St. Phone 304/457-4846.* This B & O Railroad station

(1911), used until 1956, is now restored as a museum; also local arts and crafts. (May-Oct, daily; rest of year, by appointment)

Covered bridge. *200 N Main St (26416). Phone 304/645-7195.* Spanning the Tygart River since 1852; restored in recent years; believed to be the only two-lane bridge of its type still in daily use on a federal highway (US 250).

Special Events

Barbour County Fair. *Fairgrounds, 5 miles SE on US 250 between Phillipi and Belington (26416). Phone 304/823-1328 or 304/457-3254.* Horse and antique car shows, quilt and livestock exhibits, carnival rides, nightly entertainment, parade, and more. Week before Labor Day.

Blue & Gray Reunion. *Phone 304/457-4265.* Commemorates the first land battle of the Civil War; reenactment, parade, crafts. First weekend in June.

Motel/Motor Lodge

★ **PHILIPPI LODGING.** *US 250 S RT 4 Box 155 (26416). Phone 304/457-5888; fax 304/457-5888.* 39 rooms, 2 story. S, D $50-$80; each additional $6; under 12 free. Pet accepted. Check-out 11 am. TV; cable (premium). In-room modem link. Restaurant adjacent 6 am-9 pm. Cr cds: A, C, D, DS, MC, V.

D ⊠

Point Pleasant (D-3)

See also Ripley

Settled 1774 **Pop** 4,637 **Elev** 569 ft **Area code** 304 **Zip** 25550

Information Mason County Area Chamber of Commerce, 305 Main St; 304/675-1050

On October 10, 1774, British-incited Shawnees under Chief Cornstalk fought a battle here against 1,100 frontiersmen. The colonists won and broke the Native American power in the Ohio Valley. Historians later argued that this, rather than the battle at Lexington, Massachusetts, was the first battle of the Revolutionary War. In 1908 the US Senate rewrote history by recognizing this claim.

What to See and Do

Krodel Park and Lake. *WV 2 and WV 62 (25550). 1 mile SE via WV 62/2. Phone 304/675-1068 (seasonal).* A 44-acre park with a replica of Fort Randolph (circa 1775). Fishing (license required), paddle boats (fee); miniature golf (fee); playground, camping (Apr-Nov; fee). **FREE**

McClintic Wildlife Management Area. *McClintic Rd. 7 miles NE off WV 62.* Phone 304/675-0871. Approximately 2,800 acres with primitive camping (fee). Also fishing and hunting (licenses required).

Point Pleasant Battle Monument State Park. *1 Main St, in Tu-Endie-Wei Park (Native American for "where two rivers meet").* Phone 304/675-0869. An 84-foot granite shaft was erected here in 1909, after the US Senate agreed to a claim made by historians that the first battle of the Revolutionary War was fought here. Park also contains a marker where Joseph Celeron de Bienville buried a leaden plate in 1749, claiming the land for France, and the graves of Chief Cornstalk and "Mad Anne" Bailey, noted pioneer scout. **FREE** Also here is

Mansion House. *#1 Main St (25550).* Phone 304/675-0869. (1796) Oldest log building in Kanawha Valley, restored as a museum. (May-Oct, daily) **FREE**

West Virginia State Farm Museum. *4 miles N via WV 62, adjacent to county fairgrounds.* Phone 304/675-5737. Contains more than 30 farm buildings depicting early rural life, including a log church, one-room schoolhouse, kitchen, scale house, and four-unit building. Barn contains mount of one of the largest horses in the world; also animals. (Apr-Nov, Tues-Sun) **FREE**

Special Event

Mason County Fair. *County Fairgrounds.* Phone 304/675-5463. Livestock show, arts and crafts, contests, Nashville entertainers. Mid-Aug.

Motel/Motor Lodge

★ ★ **LOWE HOTEL.** *401 Main St (25550).* Phone 304/675-2260. 42 rooms, 4 story. S $48; D $69; suites $109. Check-out noon. TV; cable (premium), VCR available. Restaurant nearby. Cr cds: A, C, D, DS, MC, V.

Princeton (G-5)

See also Bluefield

Settled 1826 **Pop** 6,347 **Elev** 2,446 ft **Area code** 304 **Zip** 24740

Information Princeton-Mercer County Chamber of Commerce, 910 Oakvale Rd; 304/487-1502

Web www.pmcc.com

Princeton is the southern terminus of the spectacular 88-mile West Virginia Turnpike and a trade center for an agricultural, industrial, and coal mining area.

What to See and Do

Camp Creek State Park. *13 miles N on I-77, exit 20, then 2 miles NW, at Camp Creek.* Phone 304/425-9481. Approximately 500 acres. Fishing; hiking trails, game courts, biking, horseback riding, picnicking, playgrounds, camping. Standard hours, fees.

Motels/Motor Lodges

★ **COMFORT INN.** *Ambrose Ln and US 460 W (24740).* Phone 304/487-6101; toll-free 800/228-5150; fax 304/425-7002. www.comfortinn.com. 52 rooms, 2 story. S, D $65-$85; each additional $6; under 18 free. Complimentary continental breakfast. Check-out noon. TV; cable (premium). In-room modem link. Restaurant nearby. Downhill ski 20 miles. Cr cds: A, C, D, DS, JCB, MC, V.

★ **DAYS INN.** *347 Meadowfield Ln (24740).* Phone 304/425-8100; toll-free 800/329-7466; fax 304/487-1734. www.daysinn.com. 122 rooms, 2 story. D $63-$78. Pet accepted; $6. Complimentary continental breakfast. Check-out 11 am. TV; cable (premium). In-room modem link. Restaurant adjacent 6 am-10 pm. Heated indoor pool, whirlpool. Downhill ski 15 miles. Cr cds: A, D, DS, ER, JCB, MC, V.

Ripley (D-4)

See also Point Pleasant

Settled 1768 **Pop** 3,263 **Elev** 616 ft **Area code** 304 **Zip** 25271

What to See and Do

Washington's Lands Museum and Park. *6 miles N via I-77 exit 146 to Ravenswood, then 2 1/2 miles S on WV 68.* Phone 304/372-5343. Housed in converted river lock building and restored Sayre Log House; exhibits trace the pioneer and river history of the area. Park, on the Ohio River, has picnicking and boat launching facilities. Museum (Memorial Day-Labor Day, Sat-Sun afternoons). **DONATION**

Special Events

Mountain State Art & Craft Fair. *Cedar Lakes Conference Center.* Phone 304/372-7860 or 304/372-7866. Features traditional crafts, art, folk music, and foods. Early July.

West Virginia Black Walnut Festival. *273 E Main St (25276).* 25 miles E on US 33/119 in Spencer. Phone 304/927-1780. Parade, carnival, band festival, car show, contests, livestock show, arts and crafts. Mid-Oct.

Motels/Motor Lodges

★★ **BEST WESTERN MCCOYS INN AND CONFERENCE CENTER.** *701Main St (25271). Phone 304/372-9122; toll-free 800/288-9122; fax 304/372-4400. www.bestwestern.com.* 149 rooms, 2 story. S, D $59-$79; suites $149; under 12 free. Restaurant 11 am-10 pm; closed Sun. Complimentary continental breakfast. Check-out 11 am. TV; cable (premium). In-room modem link. Fireplaces. Restaurant 11 am-10 pm; closed Sun. Room service. Exercise equipment, massage, steam room. Pool. Cr cds: A, C, D, DS, MC, V.

D ⬛ 🐾 ➿ ➘ SC

★ **HOLIDAY INN EXPRESS.** *1 Hospitality Dr (25271). Phone 304/372-5000; toll-free 800/465-4329; fax 304/372-5600. www.holiday-inn.com.* 67 rooms, 2 story. S, D $55-$79; suites $109-$120; under 18 free; higher rates during the Mountain State Arts and Crafts Fair. Complimentary continental breakfast. Check-out 11 am. TV; cable (premium). In-room modem link. Restaurant adjacent 6:30 am-11 pm. Exercise equipment. Cr cds: A, C, D, DS, MC, V.

D ➘

Shepherdstown (C-10)

See also Charlestown, Harpers Ferry, Martinsburg; also see Frederick, Hagerstown, MD

Settled circa 1730 **Pop** 803 **Elev** 406 ft **Area code** 304 **Zip** 25443

Information Jefferson County Chamber of Commerce, 201 Frontage Rd, PO Box 426, Charles Town 25414; 304/725-2055

Web www.jeffersoncounty.com/chamber

In 1787 Shepherdstown was the site of the first successful public launching of a steamboat. However, James Rumsey, inventor of the craft, died before he could exploit his success. Rival claims by John Fitch, and Robert Fulton's commercial success with the *Clermont* 20 years later, have clouded Rumsey's achievement.

The state's first newspaper was published here in 1790, and Shepherdstown almost became the national capital. (George Washington considered it as a possible site, according to letters in the Library of Congress.) Shepherdstown is also the location of one of the early gristmills, which is believed to have been constructed around 1739 and finally ceased production in 1939. This is the oldest continuously settled town in the state.

What to See and Do

Historic Shepherdstown Museum. *129 E German St. In the old Entler Hotel (1786), German and Princess sts. Phone 304/876-0910.* Artifacts dating to the 1700s, including many items concerning the founding of the town. Guided tours (by appointment). (Apr-Oct, daily) **FREE** Also available here are

> **Guided walking tours.** *Phone 304/876-0910.* Historic sites in Shepherdstown. **$$**

B&B/Small Inns

★★★ **BAVARIAN INN & LODGE.** *Rte 34 (25443). Phone 304/876-2551; fax 304/876-9355. www.bavarianinnwv.com.* This inn is decorated with Federal period reproductions and provides European-style hospitality. Four-poster mahogany beds, brass chandeliers, and bathrooms with imported marble grace each room. 73 rooms, 2 in main building, 3-4 story. S, D $105-$272; each additional $10; suites $210-$275; under 12 free; package plans; golf plan. Check-out noon, check-in 3 pm. TV; cable (premium), VCR available. In-room modem link. Fireplaces. Dining room, bar 5 pm-midnight; Sun from 1 pm. Exercise equipment. Pool, poolside service. Tennis on premises. Totally nonsmoking. Cr cds: A, C, D, DS, MC, V.

D ⬛ ➿ 🎾 ➘

★★★ **THOMAS SHEPHERD INN.** *300 W German St (25443). Phone 304/876-3715; toll-free 888/889-8952; fax 304/876-3313. www.thomasshepherdinn.com.* This cozy inn was built in 1868 in the Federal style of architecture. The guest rooms have been lovingly restored, boasting the original floors, and have Oriental rugs, wardrobes, and a variety of corner cupboards. 6 rooms, 2 story. S, D $85-$101 weekdays (2-day minimum); weekends $125-$135. Children over 8 years only. Complimentary full breakfast. Check-out 11 am, check-in 2-6 pm. TV; VCR in sitting room (movies). In-room modem link. Fireplaces. Restaurant nearby. Golf privileges. On land originally owned by the town founder, Thomas Shepherd. Totally nonsmoking. Cr cds: A, DS, MC, V.

⬛ ➿ ➘ SC

Restaurants

★★★ **BAVARIAN INN AND LODGE.** *Rte 34 (25443). Phone 304/876-2551. www.bavarianinnwv.com.* Few places serve traditional German fare that's so authentic. Stone fireplaces and dark woods create a rustic yet elegant ambience. German menu. Hours: 7:30-10:30 am, 11:30 am-2:30 pm, 5-10 pm; Sat from 4 pm; Sun noon-9 pm. Breakfast $4.50-$9.75, lunch $5.50-$17.50, dinner $15-$30. Bar 5 pm-midnight; Sun from 1 pm. Entertainment. Children's menu. Reservations accepted. Fireplaces. Cr cds: A, D, DS, MC, V.

D

★ **OLD PHARMACY CAFE & SODA FOUNTAIN.** *138 E German St (25443). Phone 304/876-2085; fax 304/ 876-4376.* Hours: 11 am-9 pm; Fri, Sat to 10 pm. Closed Thanksgiving, Dec 25, Jan 1. Lunch $5.95-$8.95, dinner $15-$18. Bar. Entertainment Thurs-Sat evenings. Children's menu. In former pharmacy (1911); many original pieces, including a marble soda fountain. Reservations accepted. Cr cds: D, DS, MC, V.

D

★ ★ ★ **YELLOW BRICK BANK & LITTLE INN.** *201 German at Princess St (25443). Phone 304/876-2208; fax 304/876-2208.* Housed in a 19th-century bank building in a rural town near the upper Potomac, this surprisingly inventive restaurant serves creative cuisine in an airy, high-ceilinged dining room. Hours: 11:30 am-10 pm; Sun brunch 11 am-4 pm. Closed Thanksgiving, Dec 25. Lunch $5-$14, dinner $15-$25. Sun brunch $5-$14. Bar. Entertainment Fri, Sat. Reservations accepted. Overnight stays available. Cr cds: D, MC, V.

D

Summersville (F-5)

See also Gauley Bridge

Settled 1824 **Pop** 3,294 **Elev** 1,894 ft **Area code** 304 **Zip** 26651

Information Chamber of Commerce, 411 Old Main Dr, PO Box 567; 304/872-1588

Twenty-year-old Nancy Hart led a surprise Confederate attack on Summersville in July 1861, captured a Union force, and burned the town. She was captured but her jail guard succumbed to her charms. The guard was then disarmed and killed by the young woman. She escaped to Lee's lines. After the war she returned to Summersville.

What to See and Do

Carnifex Ferry Battlefield State Park. *12 miles W on WV 39, then SE on WV 129, near Kesslers Cross Lanes. Phone 304/872-0825.* Here on Sept 10, 1861, 7,000 Union troops under General William S. Rosecrans fought and defeated a lesser number of Confederates under General John B. Floyd. The 156-acre park includes Patteson House

Museum (Memorial Day-weekend after Labor Day, Sat, Sun, holidays), which displays Civil War relics. Hiking trails, picnicking, game courts, playgrounds, concession. Civil War reenactment (weekend after Labor Day). Park (May-early Sept, daily). **FREE**

Gauley River National Recreation Area. *Phone 304/465-0508.* Designated a federally protected area in Oct 1988, the 25-mile stretch of the Gauley from the Summersville Dam west to just above the town of Swiss is famous for whitewater rafting. There are no developed sites. Large tracts of land along the river are privately owned. For further information and a list of whitewater outfitters, contact Superintendent, New River Gorge National River, PO Box 246, Glen Jean 25846.

Summersville Lake. *5 miles S on US 19. Phone 304/872-3459.* A 2,700-acre lake. Swimming, waterskiing, fishing, boating; hiking, picnicking. Battle Run Campground is 3 miles W on WV 129 (fee). (May-Oct, daily) Fee for some activities.

Special Events

Nicholas County Fair. *616 Church St (26651). Phone 304/ 872-1454. 3 miles N at Nicholas County Memorial Park.* Midway; flower show; agricultural and crafts exhibits. July.

Nicholas County Potato Festival. *411 Old Main Dr (26651). Phone 304/872-3722.* Citywide. Includes parades, entertainment, volleyball tournament, arts and crafts show, bed races. First full week in Sept.

Motels/Motor Lodges

★ ★ **BEST WESTERN SUMMERSVILLE LAKE MOTOR LODGE.** *1203 S Broad St (26651). Phone 304/872-6900; toll-free 800/214-9551; fax 304/872-6908. www.bestwestern.com.* 57 rooms, 3 story. April-Oct: S, D $50-$83; each additional $5; under 12 free; lower rates rest of year. Pet accepted, some restrictions; $5. Complimentary continental breakfast. Check-out 11 am. TV; cable (premium), VCR available. In-room modem link. Restaurant 11 am-10 pm. Bar. Cr cds: A, C, D, DS, JCB, MC, V.

D 🐾 🕭 🖾

★ **COMFORT INN.** *903 Industrial Dr N (26651). Phone 304/872-6500; toll-free 800/872-1752; fax 304/872-3090. www.comfortinn.com.* 99 rooms, 2 story. June-Oct: S, D $69-$90; each additional $5-$7; suites $90-$125; under 18 free; lower rates rest of year. Pet accepted, some restrictions; $5. Complimentary continental breakfast. Check-out 11 am. TV; cable (premium), VCR available (movies). In-room modem link. Restaurant nearby. Exercise equipment, sauna. Children's pool. Cr cds: A, C, D, DS, JCB, MC, V.

D 🐾 ⛱ 🏃 🏊 SC

★ **SLEEP INN.** *701 Professional Park Dr (26651). Phone 304/872-4500; toll-free 800/872-1751; fax 304/872-0288. www.sleepinn.com.* 97 rooms, 2 story. June-Oct: S, D $50-$66; each additional $5; under 18 free; higher rates special events; lower rates rest of year. Pet accepted, some restrictions; $5. Complimentary continental breakfast. Check-out 11 am. TV; cable (premium), VCR available (movies). In-room modem link. Restaurant adjacent 11 am-10 pm. Lawn games. Cr cds: A, C, D, DS, JCB, MC, V.

D 🐾 ⛱ 🏊

Sutton (E-6)

Settled 1826 **Pop** 1,011 **Elev** 840 ft **Area code** 304 **Zip** 26601

What to See and Do

Sutton Lake. *S Stonewall St. Phone 304/765-2816 or 304/765-2705 (recording).* Dam is 1 mile E. Swimming in designated areas, boat launch (fee); camping (May-Dec; some electric hookups; fees) at Gerald R. Freeman Campground, 16 miles E on WV 15; and at Mill Creek-Bakers Run Area, 16 miles SE on WV 17.

Motel/Motor Lodge

★ ★ **DAYS INN.** *2000 Sutton Ln (26601). Phone 304/765-5055; toll-free 800/329-7466; fax 304/765-2067. www.flatwoodsusa.com.* 203 rooms, 5 story. Mar-Nov: S $75; D $90; each additional $5; suites $135-$160; under 13 free; lower rates rest of year. Check-out 11 am. TV; cable (premium). In-room modem link. Restaurant 5-10 pm; Sun 6-10 am. Bar 5 pm-midnight. Exercise equipment, sauna. Heated indoor pool. Cr cds: A, D, DS, MC, V.

D ⛱ 🏃 🏊

Webster Springs (E-6)

Settled 1860 **Pop** 990 **Elev** 1,509 ft **Area code** 304 **Zip** 26288

Information Mayor's Office, 146 McGraw Ave; 304/847-5411

Once a resort famed for its medicinal "lick," or spring, the town is now a trading center and meeting place for sportsmen.

What to See and Do

Holly River State Park. *20 miles N on WV 20 to Hacker Valley, then 1 mile E. Phone 304/493-6353.* More than 8,000 acres of heavy forest with excellent trout fishing in Laurel Fork. Swimming pool, bathhouse; hiking trails to waterfalls and Potato Knob, tennis, game courts, picnicking, playground, restaurant (seasonal), camping (dump station), nine cabins. Nature, recreation programs (summer). Standard hours, fees.

Kumbrabow State Forest. *25 miles NE on WV 15, then 5 miles N, near Monterville. Phone 304/335-2219.* More than 9,400 acres of wild, rugged country with trout fishing; deer, turkey, and grouse hunting; hiking trails, cross-country skiing, picnicking, playground, tent and trailer camping, five rustic cabins. Standard hours, fees.

Special Events

Webster County Fair. *11 miles S on WV 20 to 4-H Camp Caesar. Phone 304/226-3888.* Rides, agricultural exhibits, entertainers, horse show. Labor Day week.

Webster Springs Woodchopping Festival. *Phone 304/847-7666.* Southeastern World Woodchopping Championships; state championship turkey calling contest, draft horse pull, horse show, fireman's rodeo; arts and crafts, music, parades, concessions. Memorial Day weekend.

Weirton (A-6)

See also Pittsburgh, Wheeling

Founded 1910 **Pop** 20,411 **Elev** 760 ft **Area code** 304 **Zip** 26062

Information Chamber of Commerce, 3200 Maine St; 304/748-7212

Weirton has been a steel producing town since its founding in 1910 by Ernest T. Weir, who also founded the Weirton Steel Company. In 1984 Weirton Steel became the largest employee-owned steel company in the world. Modern plants produce tin plate and hot-rolled, cold-rolled, and galvanized steels for containers, automobiles, appliances, and other products.

What to See and Do

Mountaineer Racetrack & Resort. *12 miles N on WV 2. Phone 304/387-2400.* Thoroughbred racing on 1-mile track; three restaurants. (Mon, Thurs-Sun)

Tomlinson Run State Park. *15 miles N off WV 8. Phone 304/564-3651.* Approximately 1,400 acres. Swimming pool, bathhouse, fishing, boating on 27-acre lake (rowboat and paddleboat rentals); hiking trails, miniature golf, tennis, picnicking, playground, tent and trailer camping (dump station). Nature, recreation programs (summer). Standard hours, fees.

Weirton Steel Corp and Half Moon Industrial Park. *400 Three Springs Dr (26062). Phone 304/748-7212.* Tours of Alpo and others. Contact Chamber of Commerce for details.

Weston (D-6)

See also Buckhannon, Clarksburg

Settled 1784 **Pop** 4,317 **Elev** 1,009 ft **Area code** 304 **Zip** 26452

Information Lewis County Convention & Visitors Bureau, 345 Center St, PO Box 379; 304/269-7328

Surveyed originally by "Stonewall" Jackson's grandfather, Weston today is a center for coal, oil, and gas production, as well as the manufacture of glass products. The Weston State Hospital, completed in 1880 and said to be the largest hand-cut stone building in the nation, is located in town.

What to See and Do

Cedar Creek State Park. *31 miles SW off US 33/119, near Glenville. Phone 304/462-8517.* More than 2,400 acres. Swimming pool, bathhouse, fishing, boating (rentals); hiking trails, miniature golf, tennis, game courts, picnicking, playground, concession, tent and trailer camping (dump station). Park office in restored log cabin. Standard hours, fees.

Jackson's Mill State 4-H Conference Center. *Jacksons Mill Rd. 4 miles N off US 19. Phone 304/269-5100.* First camp of its kind in US; 43 buildings, gardens, swimming pool, amphitheater, interfaith chapel. Picnicking. Also here is

Jackson's Mill Historic Area. *Phone 304/269-5100.* Includes Blaker's Mill, an operating water-powered gristmill; blacksmith shop; McWharten cabin (circa 1700s); Mary Conrad's cabin (circa 1800s); and Jackson's Mill Museum, where "Stonewall" Jackson lived and worked as a boy. Museum represents grist and saw milling agriculture and home arts of the area as practiced 100 years ago. (Memorial Day-Labor Day, Tues-Sun; May and after Labor Day-mid-Oct, weekends only) **$$**

Stonewall Jackson Lake and Dam. *Rte 33 W. Just S off I-79 exit 96, follow signs to dam. Phone 304/269-4588 or 304/269-0523.* Approximately 2,500-acre lake with over 82 miles of shoreline created by impounding the waters of the West Fork River. Swimming, scuba diving, waterskiing, fishing, boating (ramps, rentals, marinas); picnicking, camping. Visitor center.

Stonewall Jackson Lake State Park. *Rte 33 W. 11 miles S on US 19. Phone 304/269-0523.* Approximately 3,000 acres. Fishing, boating (launch, marina); nature and fitness trails, picnicking, playground, camping (hookups). Visitor center. Standard hours, fees.

Special Events

Horse show. *Rt 88 and National Rd (26003). Trefz Farm, 3 miles E on US 33. Phone 304/269-3257.* Saddle, walking, harness, pony, western, and Arabian riding. Usually July.

Stonewall Jackson Heritage Arts & Crafts Jubilee. *Jackson's Mill State 4-H Conference Center. Phone 304/269-1863.* Mountain crafts, music, dance, and food. Labor Day weekend.

Motel/Motor Lodge

★ ★ **COMFORT INN.** *Rte 33 E and I-79 (26452). Phone 304/269-7000; toll-free 800/228-5150; fax 304/269-7011. www.comfortinn.com.* 62 rooms, 2 story. S, D $49-$89; under 18 free. Pet accepted; $10. Complimentary continental breakfast. Check-out noon. TV; cable (premium). In-room modem link. Restaurant 6 am-9 pm. Bar 5-9 pm. Cr cds: A, C, D, DS, MC, V.

D ⌨ ☖ ⤢ SC

Wheeling (B-6)

Settled 1769 **Pop** 31,419 **Elev** 678 ft **Area code** 304 **Zip** 26003

Information Convention & Visitors Bureau, 1401 Main St; 304/233-7709 or 800/828-3079

Web www.wheelingcvb.com

Wheeling stands on the site of Fort Henry, built in 1774 by Colonel Ebenezer Zane and his two brothers, who named the fort for Virginia's Governor Patrick Henry. In 1782 the fort was the scene of the final battle of the Revolutionary War, a battle in which the valiant young pioneer Betty Zane was a heroine. The fort had withstood several Native American and British sieges during the war. However, during the last siege (after the war was officially ended), the defenders of the fort ran out of powder. Betty Zane, sister of the colonel, volunteered to run through the gunfire to the outlying Zane cabin for more. With the powder gathered in her apron, she made the 150-yard trek back to the fort and saved the garrison. Zane Grey, a descendant of the Zanes, wrote a novel about Betty and her exploit.

Today Wheeling is home to many industries, including producers of steel, iron, tin, chemical products, pottery, glass, paper, tobacco, plastics, and coal.

What to See and Do

The Artisan Center. *Heritage Sq, 1400 Main St. Phone 304/ 233-4555.* Restored 1860s Victorian warehouse houses River City Ale Works, West Virginia's largest brew pub. "Made in Wheeling" crafts and exhibits; artisan demonstrations. (Daily) **FREE**

Grave Creek Mound State Park. *801 Jefferson Ave (26041). 9 miles S via WV 2, in Moundsville. Phone 304/843-1410.* Features the nation's largest prehistoric Adena burial mound—79 feet high, 900 feet around, 50 feet across the top. Some excavating was done in 1838; exhibits in Delf Norona Museum & Cultural Center (daily; fee).

Jamboree, USA. *Capitol Music Hall, 1015 Main St. Phone 304/234-0050 or 800/624-5456.* Live country music shows presented by WWVA Radio since 1933. (Sat) **$$$$**

Kruger Street Toy & Train Museum. *144 Kruger St. Phone 304/242-8133.* Collection of antique toys, games, and playthings. (Daily; Jan-Apr) **$$$**

Oglebay Resort Park. *3 miles NE of I-70, on WV 88. Phone 304/243-4000 or 800/624-6988.* (See SPECIAL EVENTS). A 1,650-acre municipal park. Indoor and outdoor swimming pools, fishing, paddle boating on 3-acre Schenk Lake; three 18-hole golf courses, miniature golf, tennis courts, picnicking, restaurant, snack shop, cabins, lodge. Train ride; 65-acre Good Children's Zoo (fee) with animals in natural habitat. Benedum Natural Science Theater; garden center; arboretum with 4 miles of walking paths; greenhouses; observatory. Fee for most activities.

> **Mansion Museum.** *Phone 304/242-7272.* Period rooms, exhibits trace history from 1835-present. (Daily) **$$**

Site of Fort Henry. *Main St, near 11th St. Phone 304/233-7709.* Bronze plaque marks the location of the fort that Betty Zane saved.

West Virginia Independence Hall-Custom House. *1528 Market St (26003). Phone 304/238-1300.* (1859) Site of the meeting at which Virginia's secession from the Union was declared unlawful and the independent state of West Virginia was created. The building, used as a post office, custom office, and federal court until 1912, has been restored. It now houses exhibits and events relating to the state's cultural heritage, including an interpretive film and rooms with period furniture. (Mar-Dec, daily; rest of year, Mon-Sat; closed state holidays) **FREE**

Wheeling Park. *1801 National Rd (26003). 5 miles E on US 40. Phone 304/242-3770.* Approximately 400 acres. Swimming pool, water slide, boating on Good Lake; golf, miniature golf, indoor/outdoor tennis, ice skating (rentals), picnicking, playground, refreshment area with video screen and lighted dance floor. Aviary. Fees for activities. (Daily; some facilities seasonal)

Special Events

City of Lights. *Oglebay Resort Park. Route 88 North (26003). Phone 304/243-4000.* A 350-acre lighting display featuring lighted buildings, holiday themes with more than 500,000 lights, including 28-foot candy canes and giant swans on Schenk Lake. Winter Fantasy in Good Zoo. Nov-Jan.

Jamboree in the Hills. *1015 Main St (26003). 15 miles W off I-70 exit 208 or 213, in St. Clairsville, OH. Phone 800/624-5456.* A four-day country music festival featuring more than 30 hours of music; top country stars. Camping available. Third weekend in July.

Oglebayfest. *Route 88 North (26003). Oglebay Resort Park. Phone 304/243-4000.* Country fair, artists' market, fireworks, parade, ethnic foods, contests, square and round dancing, entertainment. First weekend in Oct.

Motels/Motor Lodges

★★ **BEST WESTERN INN.** *949 Main St (26003). Phone 304/233-8500; toll-free 800/780-7234; fax 304/233-8500. www.bestwestern.com.* 82 rooms, 4 story. S, D $56-$88; each additional $8; suites $136; under 12 free; higher rates weekends, special events. Weekend $68-$99-$140. Pet accepted; $10. Complimentary continental breakfast. Check-out 11 am. TV; cable (premium). In-room modem link. Restaurant 11 am-10 pm; Sat, Sun from 7 am. Bar 11-2 am. Exercise equipment, sauna. Cr cds: A, C, D, DS, MC, V.

D 🐾 🏋 ⊠ **SC**

★ **DAYS INN.** *I-70 and Dallas Pike, exit 11, Tridelphia (26059). Phone 304/547-0610; toll-free 800/329-7466; fax 304/547-9029. www.daysinn.com.* 106 rooms, 2 story. S, D $54-$70; each additional $6; under 18 free. Bar 5 pm-1 am, closed Sun. Pet accepted. Complimentary continental breakfast. Check-out noon. TV; cable (premium). VCR available. In-room modem link. Pool. Bar 5 pm-1 am, closed Sun. Cr cds: A, C, D, DS, JCB, MC, V.

D 🐾 ⊠ ⊠

★ **HAMPTON INN.** *795 National Rd (26003). Phone 304/233-0440; toll-free 800/426-7866; fax 304/233-2198. www.hamptoninn.com.* 104 rooms, 5 story. S, D $79-$94, under 18 free; weekends (2-day minimum). Weekend $84-$99. Complimentary continental breakfast. Check-out noon. TV; cable (premium), VCR available. In-room modem link. Restaurant adjacent 6:30 am-11 pm. Bar. Room service. Exercise equipment. Cr cds: A, C, D, DS, MC, V.

D 🏋 ⊠ **SC**

Resort

★ ★ ★ OGLEBAY CONFERENCE CENTER.
Oglebay Park (26003). Phone 304/243-4000; toll-free 800/624-6988; fax 304/243-4070. www.oglebay-resort.com. This 1,650-acre resort features beautiful gardens and fine accommodations. 261 rooms, 2 story. S, D $99-$200; suites $190-$490; kitchen cottages $625-$1,350/week; golf plans. Pet accepted. Check-out 11 am, check-in 3 pm. TV; cable (premium), VCR available (movies). In-room modem link. Fireplaces. Dining room 6:30-10:30 am, noon-2 pm, 5-9 pm. Snack bar. Supervised children's activities (June-Aug), ages 6-14. Exercise equipment. Massage. Game room. Two pools, one indoor; wading pool, whirlpool, poolside service. Greens fee. Lighted tennis courts. Downhill ski 1/2 mile. Lawn games. Paddleboats. Fishing. Valet parking available. Airport transportation. Business center. Children's zoo. Lounge noon-midnight. Mansion museum, garden center. Stables. Rustic setting in Oglebay Park. Cr cds: A, C, D, DS, MC, V.

Restaurant

★ ★ ★ ERNIE'S ESQUIRE.
1055 E Bethlehem Blvd I 470 Exit 2 (26003). Phone 304/242-2800; fax 304/242-2809. A local landmark for nearly 50 years, this fine dining restaurant serves a wide variety of options to suit any palate. Continental menu. Hours: 11 am-midnight; Fri to 1 am; Sat to 2 am; Sun to 10:30 pm; Sun brunch noon to 2 pm. Closed Dec 25. Lunch $3.75-$8.95, dinner $11-$29, Sun brunch $8.95. Bar. Entertainment Fri, Sat. Children's menu. Reservations accepted. Valet parking. Cr cds: A, D, DS, MC, V.

White Sulphur Springs (G-6)

See also Lewisburg; also see Covington, VA

Settled 1750 **Pop** 2,315 **Elev** 1,923 ft **Area code** 304 **Zip** 24986

Information Chamber of Commerce, PO Box 11, 24986; 304/536-2500

Web www.wsswv.com

In the 18th century, White Sulphur Springs became a fashionable destination for rich and famous colonists, who came for the "curative" powers of the mineral waters. It has, for the most part, remained a popular resort ever since. A number of US presidents summered in the town in the days before air conditioning made Washington habitable in hot weather. The John Tylers spent their honeymoon at the famous "Old White" Hotel. In 1913 the Old White Hotel gave way to the present Greenbrier Hotel, where President Wilson honeymooned with the second Mrs. Wilson. During World War II the hotel served as an internment camp for German and Japanese diplomats and, later, as a hospital.

The first golf course in America was laid out near the town in 1884, but the first game was delayed when golf clubs, imported from Scotland, were held for three weeks by customs men who were suspicious of a game played with "such elongated blackjacks or implements of murder."

What to See and Do

Fishing, swimming, boating, camping, hiking. *Phone 304/536-2144.* In Monongahela National Forest (see): Blue Bend Recreation Area, 6 miles N on WV 92, then 4 miles W on WV 16/21; Lake Sherwood Recreation Area, 23 miles N via WV 92, then 11 miles NE on WV 14.

Greenbrier State Forest. *3 miles W on US 60, then 1 1/2 miles S on Harts Run Rd. Phone 304/536-1944.* More than 5,100 acres. Swimming pool (Memorial Day-Labor Day), bass fishing in Greenbrier River; hunting, hiking trails, picnicking, playground, tent and trailer camping, 12 cabins. Nature, recreation programs (summer). Standard hours, fees.

Memorial Park. *Greenbrier Ave.* Swimming pool (Memorial Day-Labor Day; fee); tennis courts, ball fields, track, horseshoe pits, playground. (Daily)

National Fish Hatchery. *400 E Main St, on US 60. Phone 304/536-1361.* Rainbow trout in raceways and ponds. Visitor center has display pool, aquariums, and exhibits. (Memorial Day-Labor Day, daily) **FREE**

Special Event

Dandelion Festival. *Phone 304/536-2323.* Entertainment, exhibits; arts and crafts. Memorial Day weekend.

Motel/Motor Lodge

★ OLD WHITE MOTEL.
865 E Main St (24986). Phone 304/536-2441; toll-free 800/867-2441; fax 304/536-1836. www.oldwhitemotel.com. 26 rooms. D $37-$55; each additional $3; under 12 free. Pet accepted, some restrictions. Check-out 11 am, check-in 11 am. TV; cable (premium). Pool. Cr cds: A, C, D, DS, MC, V.

Resort

★ ★ ★ ★ THE GREENBRIER.
300 W Main St (US 60) (24986). Phone 304/536-1110; toll-free 800/624-6070; fax 304/536-7874. www.greenbrier.com. Resting on a

2,500-acre estate in the picturesque Allegheny Mountains of West Virginia, The Greenbrier is one of America's oldest and finest resorts. Fiercely proud of its 200-year history, this all-encompassing resort continues to appeal to active-minded visitors seeking a respite from the everyday. This resort is the embodiment of a sportsman's paradise, with more than 50 activities on its sprawling grounds. In addition to three championship golf courses, the highly acclaimed Sam Snead Golf Academy, tennis courts, and fitness and spa facilities, guests are invited to partake in unique adventures like falconry, trap and skeet shooting at the Gun Club, and the Land Rover Driving School. The fascinating tour of the federal government's Cold War bunker constructed under the resort is particularly notable. Comprised of rooms, suites, estate houses, and guest houses, the accommodations reflect the resort's aristocratic tradition, while seven restaurants satisfy all appetites. 803 rooms, 6 story. Service charge of $21/person/day. Check-out noon, check-in 4 pm. TV; VCR available. In-room modem link. Fireplaces. Room service 24 hours. Restaurant, bar, entertainment. Children's activity center, babysitting services available. In-house fitness room, spa, sauna, steam room. Indoor pool, outdoor pool, children's pool, whirlpool. Golf; greens fee $135. Outdoor tennis, lighted courts, indoor tennis. Lawn games. Bicycling. Ice skating. Canoeing; rafting (seasonal). Stables, English saddles. Horse-drawn sleighing and carriage rides. Trap and skeet shooting. Hunt club and game preserve. British regulation croquet court. Airport transportation. Business center. Cr cds: A, D, DS, MC, V. **$$$$**

⊡ 🏌 🎋 🏊 🚶 ⛷ 🎿

Restaurants

★ ★ ★ **THE GREENBRIER MAIN DINING ROOM.** *300 W Main St (24986). Phone 304/536-1110; fax 304/536-7854. www.greenbrier.com.* Capitol Hill elite and local celebrities alike get a dose of gracious Southern hospitality at this legendary resort. American, continental menu. Hours: 7:30-10 am, 6:30-9 pm. Dinner $80-$90. Chamber music at dinner. Children's menu. Jacket required. Reservations required. Valet parking available. Private club 5 pm-1 am. Cr cds: A, D, MC, V.

⊡

★ ★ ★ ★ **THE TAVERN ROOM.** *300 W Main St (24986). Phone 304/536-1110; toll-free 800/624-6070; fax 304/536-7854. www.greenbrier.com.* Located in the majestic Greenbrier Resort at White Sulphur Springs, The Tavern Room is a cozy, intimate restaurant with exposed brick walls, high wine cellar-styled archways, dark wood accents, glowing hurricane lamps, and deep garnet-colored walls that lend richness and rusticity to the warm dining room. Magnificent floral arrangements and pretty tabletops dressed up with petite vases of fresh flowers add a burst of natural color to the space. The contemporary French menu is elegant and refined but approachable and simple, offering a variety of classically prepared fish, beef, lamb, and poultry (most purchased from regional farmers), as well as traditional French indulgences like caviar and foie gras. Attentive service and soothing live piano music add to the luxury and serenity of dining at The Tavern Room. American menu. Closed Wed, Sun; early May-Oct. Dinner. Bar. Piano. Jacket required. Reservations required. Valet parking available. Cr cds: A, D, MC, V. **$$$$**

⊡

Williamson

Founded 1892 **Pop** 3,414 **Elev** 665 ft **Area code** 304 **Zip** 25661

Information Tug Valley Chamber of Commerce, 45 E 2nd Ave, PO Box 376; 304/235-5240

Web www.tugvalleychamberofcommerce.com

The center of the "billion-dollar coal field," Williamson is truly a coal town; the walls of the local Chamber of Commerce building, at the west corner of Courthouse Square, are made of coal. The surrounding Tug River Valley was the scene of the bitter Hatfield-McCoy mountaineer family feud.

What to See and Do

Cabwaylingo State Forest. *38 miles N off US 52, WV 152 near Wilsondale. Phone 304/385-4255.* Approximately 8,100 acres. Swimming pool (Memorial Day-Labor Day), fishing; hunting, hiking trails, game courts, picnicking, playground, concession, tent and trailer camping (dump station), 13 cabins. Standard hours, fees.

Matewan. *Mate St Bldg 9. 12 miles SW via WV 49. Phone 304/426-4239.* This tiny hamlet was the site of the famous feud between the West Virginia Hatfields and the Kentucky McCoys. On Election Day, Aug 7, 1882, three McCoy sons stabbed and shot Ellison Hatfield. Devil Anse Hatfield avenged his brother by executing the three McCoys. Soon Kentucky bounty hunters made raids into West Virginia to capture the Hatfields, who retaliated in 1888 by attacking a McCoy homestead. By 1890 the killings had ended but the feud continued to be sensationalized. In 1920, Matewan was the scene of a shootout between union organizers and coal company operators that left ten dead, including the mayor.

Special Event

King Coal Festival. *28 Oak St (25661). Phone 304/235-5560.* Entertainment, exhibits; theatrical presentation; country music, square dancing. Mid-Sept.

Index

Establishment names are listed in alphabetical order followed by their classificiaton and then city and state. The classification symbols are: [S] for Special Events, [W] for What to See and Do, [AS] for All Suites, [BB] for B&Bs/Small Inns, [CAS] for Casinos, [CC] for Cottage Colonies, [CON] for Villas/Condos, [CONF] for Conference Centers, [EX] for Extended Stays, [HOT] for Hotels, [MOT] for Motels/Motor Lodges, [RAN] for Guest Ranches, [RST] for Resorts, and [RES] for Restaurants.

YORKTOWNE HOTEL [HOT]
York, PA, 293
YORKTOWN NATIONAL CIVIL
WAR CEMETERY [W] *Yorktown,
VA, 426*
YORKTOWN VICTORY CENTER
[W] *Yorktown, VA, 426*
YORKTOWN VICTORY
MONUMENT [W] *Yorktown,
VA, 426*
YOUTH MUSEUM OF SOUTHERN
WEST VIRGINIA [W] *Beckley,
WV, 465*

ZANZIBAR BLUE [RES] *Philadelphia,
PA, 255*
ZANZIBAR BLUE [RES] *Wilmington,
DE, 21*
ZED'S ETHIOPIAN CUISINE [RES]
Washington, DC, 459
ZESTY'S [RES] *Philadelphia, PA, 255*
ZION EPISCOPAL CHURCH [W]
Charles Town, WV, 472
ZION LUTHERAN CHURCH [W]
Manheim, PA, 223
ZOCALO [RES] *Philadelphia, PA, 255*
ZOOAMERICA [W] *Hershey, PA, 204*
ZWAANENDAEL HERITAGE
GARDEN TOUR [S] *Lewes, DE, 2*
ZWAANENDAEL INN [HOT]
Lewes, DE, 9
ZWAANENDAEL MUSEUM [W]
Lewes, DE, 8, 9

Notes

Notes

Notes

Notes

Notes

Notes

Notes